www.wadsworth.com

wadsworth.com is the World Wide Web site for Wadsworth and is your direct source to dozens of online resources.

At *wadsworth.com* you can find out about supplements, demonstration software, and student resources. You can also send email to many of our authors and preview new publications and exciting new technologies.

wadsworth.com
Changing the way the world learns®

Psychology
Themes and Variations
Briefer Version

5th EDITION

Wayne Weiten
Santa Clara University

With Critical Thinking Applications
By Diane F. Halpern, California State University, San Bernardino

WADSWORTH
THOMSON LEARNING

Australia • Canada • Mexico • Singapore • Spain • United Kingdom • United States

WADSWORTH
THOMSON LEARNING

*T. J.,
this one's
for you.*

Psychology Publisher: Edith Beard Brady
Developmental Editor: Sherry Symington
Assistant Editor: Julie Dillemuth
Editorial Assistant: Maritess A. Tse
Marketing Manager: Joanne Terhaar
Marketing Assistant: Justine Ferguson
Technology Project Manager: Leslie Krongold
Project Manager, Editorial Production: Lisa Weber
Print/Media Buyer: Karen Hunt
Permissions Editor: Robert Kauser
Production Service: Tom Dorsaneo

Text Designer: Gladys Rosa-Mendoza, rosa+wesley
Permissions and Photo Researcher: Linda L. Rill
Copy Editor: Jackie Estrada
Illustrators: John Odam, Kim Fraley, Jeff Gruenwald,
C. H. Wooley
Cover Designer: Stephen Rapley
Cover Image: *Untitled* (screenprint) by Victor Vasarely
(1908–97); Private Collection/Bridgeman Art Library; © 2001
Artists Rights Society (ARS), New York/ADAGP, Paris
Cover Printer: Phoenix Color Corporation
Compositor: rosa+wesley
Printer: R. R. Donnelley & Sons, Roanoke

Wadsworth/Thomson Learning
10 Davis Drive
Belmont, CA 94002-3098
USA

For more information about our products, contact us:
Thomson Learning Academic Resource Center
1-800-423-0563
http://www.wadsworth.com

International Headquarters
Thomson Learning
International Division
290 Harbor Drive, 2nd Floor
Stamford, CT 06902-7477
USA

UK/Europe/Middle East/South Africa
Thomson Learning
Berkshire House
168-173 High Holborn
London WC1V 7AA
United Kingdom

Asia
Thomson Learning
60 Albert Street, #15-01
Albert Complex
Singapore 189969

Canada
Nelson Thomson Learning
1120 Birchmount Road
Toronto, Ontario M1K 5G4
Canada

Library of Congress Cataloging-in-Publication Data

Weiten, Wayne,
   Psychology: themes and variations : briefer version (5th ed.) / Wayne Weiten.
     p. cm.
   Includes bibliographical references and index.
   ISBN 0-534-59400-X (alk. paper)—ISBN 0-534-59310-0 (pbk. : alk. paper)
   1. Psychology. I. Weiten, Wayne, 1950- Psychology (5th ed.). II. Title.

BF121.W38 2001
150—dc21
                                  2001022236

Psychology is an exciting, dynamic discipline that has grown by leaps and bounds in recent decades. This progress has been reflected in the field's introductory texts, which have grown longer and longer. However, the length of the introductory psychology course generally has not changed. Hence, an increasing number of professors are reporting that they find it difficult to cover the wealth of material found in the typical introductory text. With this reality in mind, I decided to write a briefer version of *Psychology: Themes and Variations* to help meet the needs of those teachers who would like a challenging, but concise, introductory text.

If I had to sum up in a single sentence what I hope will distinguish this text, the sentence would be this: I have set out to create a *paradox* instead of a *compromise*.

Let me elaborate. An introductory psychology text must satisfy two disparate audiences: professors and students. Because of the tension between the divergent needs and preferences of these audiences, textbook authors usually indicate that they have attempted to strike a compromise between being theoretical versus practical, comprehensive versus comprehensible, research oriented versus applied, rigorous versus accessible, and so forth. However, I believe that many of these dichotomies are false. As Kurt Lewin once remarked, "What could be more practical than a good theory?" Similarly, is rigorous really the opposite of accessible? Not in my dictionary. I maintain that many of the antagonistic goals that we strive for in our textbooks only *seem* incompatible, and that we may not need to make compromises as often as we assume.

In my estimation, a good introductory textbook is a paradox in that it integrates characteristics and goals that appear contradictory. With this in mind, I have endeavored to write a text that is paradoxical in three ways. First, in surveying psychology's broad range of content, I have tried to show that our interests are characterized by diversity *and* unity. Second, I have emphasized both research *and* application and how they work in harmony. Finally, I have aspired to write a book that is challenging to think about *and* easy to learn from. Let's take a closer look at these goals.

Goals

1. *To show both the unity and the diversity of psychology's subject matter.* Students entering an introductory

psychology course often are unaware of the immense diversity of subjects studied by psychologists. I find this diversity to be part of psychology's charm, and throughout the book I highlight the enormous range of questions and issues addressed by psychology. Of course, our diversity proves disconcerting for some students who see little continuity between such disparate areas of research as physiology, motivation, cognition, and abnormal behavior. Indeed, in this era of specialization, even some psychologists express concern about the fragmentation of the field.

However, I believe that there is considerable overlap among the subfields of psychology and that we should emphasize their common core by accenting the connections and similarities among them. Consequently, I portray psychology as an integrated whole rather than as a mosaic of loosely related parts. A principal goal of this text, then, is to highlight the unity in psychology's intellectual heritage (the themes), as well as the diversity of psychology's interests and uses (the variations).

2. *To illuminate the process of research and its intimate link to application.* For me, a research-oriented book is not one that bulges with summaries of many studies but one that enhances students' appreciation of the logic and excitement of empirical inquiry. I want students to appreciate the strengths of the empirical approach and to see scientific psychology as a creative effort to solve intriguing behavioral puzzles. For this reason, the text emphasizes not only *what* we know (and don't know) but *how* we attempt to find out. It examines methods in some detail and encourages students to adopt the skeptical attitude of a scientist and to think critically about claims regarding behavior.

Learning the virtues of research should not mean that students cannot also satisfy their desire for concrete, personally useful information about the challenges of everyday life. Most researchers believe that psychology has a great deal to offer those outside the field and that psychologists should share the practical implications of their work. In this text, practical insights are carefully qualified and closely tied to data, so that students can see the interdependence of research and application. I find that students come to appreciate the science of psychology more when they see that worthwhile practical applications are derived from careful research and sound theory.

3. *To make the text challenging to think about and easy to learn from.* Perhaps most of all, I have sought to create a book of ideas rather than a compendium of studies. I consistently emphasize concepts and theories over facts, and I focus on major issues and tough questions that cut across the subfields of psychology (for example, the extent to which behavior is governed by nature, nurture, and their interaction), as opposed to parochial debates (such as the merits of averaging versus adding in impression formation). Challenging students to think also means urging them to confront the complexity and ambiguity of our knowledge. Hence, the text doesn't skirt gray areas, unresolved questions, and theoretical controversies. Instead, readers are encouraged to contemplate open-ended questions, to examine their assumptions about behavior, and to apply psychological concepts to their own lives. My goal is not simply to describe psychology but to stimulate students' intellectual growth.

However, students can grapple with "the big issues and tough questions" only if they first master the basic concepts and principles of psychology—ideally, with as little struggle as possible. In my writing, I never let myself forget that a textbook is a tool for teaching. Accordingly, I and my publisher have taken great care to ensure that the book's content, organization, writing, illustrations, and pedagogical aids work in harmony to facilitate instruction and learning.

Admittedly, these goals are ambitious. If you're skeptical, you have every right to be. Let me explain how I have tried to realize the objectives I have outlined.

Special Features

This text has a variety of unusual features, each contributing in its own way to the book's paradoxical nature. These special features include unifying themes, Personal Application sections, Critical Thinking Application sections, a didactic illustration program, WebLinks and other Internet-related features, an integrated running glossary, Concept Checks, and Practice Tests.

Unifying Themes

Chapter 1 introduces seven key ideas that serve as unifying themes throughout the text. The themes serve several purposes. First, they provide threads of continuity across chapters that help students see the connections among different areas of research in psychology. Second, as the themes evolve over the course of the book, they provide a forum for a

relatively sophisticated discussion of enduring issues in psychology, thus helping to make this a "book of ideas." Third, the themes focus a spotlight on a number of basic insights about psychology and its subject matter that should leave lasting impressions on your students. In selecting the themes, the question I asked myself (and other professors) was, "What do I really want students to remember five years from now?" The resulting themes are grouped into two sets.

THEMES RELATED TO PSYCHOLOGY AS A FIELD OF STUDY

Theme 1: Psychology is empirical. This theme is used to enhance the student's appreciation of psychology's scientific nature and to demonstrate the advantages of empiricism over uncritical common sense and speculation. I also use this theme to encourage the reader to adopt a scientist's skeptical attitude and to engage in more critical thinking about information of all kinds.

Theme 2: Psychology is theoretically diverse. Students are often confused by psychology's theoretical pluralism and view it as a weakness. I don't downplay or apologize for our field's theoretical diversity, because I honestly believe that it is one of our greatest strengths. Throughout the book, I provide concrete examples of how clashing theories have stimulated productive research, how converging on a question from several perspectives can yield increased understanding, and how competing theories are sometimes reconciled in the end.

Theme 3: Psychology evolves in a sociohistorical context. This theme emphasizes that psychology is embedded in the ebb and flow of everyday life. The text shows how the spirit of the times has often shaped psychology's evolution and how progress in psychology leaves its mark on our society.

THEMES RELATED TO PSYCHOLOGY'S SUBJECT MATTER

Theme 4: Behavior is determined by multiple causes. Throughout the book, I emphasize, and repeatedly illustrate, that behavioral processes are complex and that multifactorial causation is the rule. This theme is used to discourage simplistic, single-cause thinking and to encourage more critical reasoning.

Theme 5: Our behavior is shaped by our cultural heritage. This theme is intended to enhance students' appreciation of how cultural factors moderate psychological processes and how the viewpoint of one's own culture can distort one's interpretation of the behavior of people from other cultures. The discussions that elaborate on this theme do not simply celebrate diversity. They strike a careful balance—that accurately reflects the research in this area—highlighting both cultural variations and similarities in behavior.

Theme 6: Heredity and environment jointly influence behavior. Repeatedly discussing this theme permits me to explore the nature versus nurture issue in all its complexity. Over a series of chapters, students gradually learn how biology shapes behavior, how experience shapes behavior, and how scientists estimate the relative importance of each. Along the way, students will gain an in-depth appreciation of what we mean when we say that heredity and environment interact.

Theme 7: Our experience of the world is highly subjective. All of us tend to forget the extent to which we view the world through our own personal lens. This theme is used to explain the principles that underlie the subjectivity of human experience, to clarify

Unifying Themes Highlighted In Each Chapter

Chapter	1 Empiricism	2 Theoretical Diversity	3 Sociohistorical Context	4 Multifactorial Causation	5 Cultural Heritage	6 Heredity and Environment	7 Subjectivity of Experience
1. The Evolution of Psychology	●	●	●	●	●	●	●
2. The Research Enterprise in Psychology	●						●
3. The Biological Bases of Behavior	●			●		●	
4. Sensation and Perception		●			●		●
5. Variations in Consciousness		●	●		●		●
6. Learning Through Conditioning			●			●	
7. Human Memory		●		●			●
8. Language and Thought	●				●	●	●
9. Intelligence and Psychological Testing			●		●	●	
10. Motivation and Emotion		●	●	●	●	●	
11. Development Across the Life Span		●	●	●	●	●	
12. Personality: Theory, Research, and Assessment			●		●		
13. Stress, Coping, and Health				●			●
14. Psychological Disorders			●	●	●	●	
15. Treatment of Psychological Disorders		●			●	●	
16. Social Behavior	●				●		●

its implications, and to repeatedly remind the readers that their view of the world is not the only legitimate view.

After all seven themes have been introduced in Chapter 1, different sets of themes are discussed in each chapter, as they are relevant to the subject matter. The connections between a chapter's content and the unifying themes are highlighted in a standard section near the end of the chapter, in which I reflect on the "lessons to be learned" from the chapter. The discussions of the unifying themes are largely confined to these sections, titled "Putting It in Perspective." No effort was made to force every chapter to illustrate a certain number of themes. The themes were allowed to emerge naturally, and I found that two to five surfaced in any given chapter. The accompanying chart shows which themes are highlighted in each chapter.

Personal Applications

To reinforce the pragmatic implications of theory and research stressed throughout the text, each chapter includes a Personal Application section that highlights the practical side of psychology. Each Personal Application devotes three to six *pages* of text (rather than the usual box) to a single issue that should be of special interest to many of your students. Although most of the Personal Application sections have a "how to" character, they continue to review studies and summarize data in much the same way as the main body of each chapter. Thus, they portray research and application not as incompatible polarities but as two sides of the same coin. Many of the Personal Applications—such as those on finding and reading journal articles, understanding art and illusion, and improving stress management—provide topical coverage unusual for an introductory text.

Critical Thinking Applications

A great deal of unusual coverage can also be found in the new Critical Thinking Applications that now follow the Personal Applications. Conceived by Diane Halpern (California State University, San Bernardino), a leading authority on critical thinking, these applications are based on the assumption that critical thinking skills can be taught. They do not simply review research critically, as is typically the case in other introductory texts. Instead, they introduce and model a host of critical thinking skills, such as looking for contradictory evidence or alternative explanations; recognizing anecdotal evidence, circular reasoning, hindsight bias, reifica-

tion, weak analogies, and false dichotomies; evaluating arguments systematically, and working with cumulative and conjunctive probabilities.

The specific skills discussed in the Critical Thinking Applications are listed in the accompanying table, where they are organized into five categories using a taxonomy developed by Halpern (1994). In each chapter, some of these skills are applied to topics and issues related to the chapter's content. For instance, in the chapter that covers drug abuse (chapter 5), the concept of alcoholism is used to highlight the immense power of definitions and to illustrate how circular reasoning can seem so seductive. Skills that are particularly important may surface in more than one chapter, so students see them applied in a variety of contexts. For example, in Chapter 7 students learn how hindsight bias can contaminate memory and in Chapter 12 they see how hindsight can distort analyses of personality. Repeated practice across chapters should help students to spontaneously recognize the relevance of specific critical thinking skills when they encounter certain types of information. The skills approach taken to critical thinking and the content it has spawned are unprecedented for an introductory psychology text.

A Didactic Illustration Program

When I first outlined my plans for this text, I indicated that I wanted every aspect of the illustration program to have a genuine didactic purpose and that I wanted to be deeply involved in its development. In retrospect, I had no idea what I was getting myself into, but it has been a rewarding learning experience. In any event, I have been intimately involved in planning every detail of the illustration program. I have endeavored to create a program of figures, diagrams, photos, and tables that work hand in hand with the prose to strengthen and clarify the main points in the text.

The most obvious results of our didactic approach to illustration are the four summary spreads that combine tabular information, photos, diagrams, and sketches to provide exciting overviews of key ideas in the areas of learning, personality theory, psychopathology, and psychotherapy. But I hope you will also notice the subtleties of the illustration program. For instance, diagrams of important concepts (conditioning, synaptic transmission, EEGs, experimental design, and so forth) are often repeated in several chapters (with variations) to highlight connections among research areas and to enhance students' mastery of key ideas. Numerous easy-to-understand graphs of

Taxonomy of Skills Covered in the Critical Thinking Applications

Verbal Reasoning Skills

Understanding the way definitions shape how people think about issues	Chapter 5
Identifying the source of definitions	Chapter 5
Avoiding the nominal fallacy in working with definitions and labels	Chapter 5
Understanding the way language can influence thought	Chapter 8
Recognizing semantic slanting	Chapter 8
Recognizing name calling and anticipatory name calling	Chapter 8
Recognizing and avoiding reification	Chapter 9

Argument/Persuasion Analysis Skills

Understanding the elements of an argument	Chapter 10
Recognizing and avoiding common fallacies, such as irrelevant reasons, circular reasoning, slippery slope reasoning, weak analogies, and false dichotomies	Chapters 10 and 11
Evaluating arguments systematically	Chapter 10
Recognizing and avoiding appeals to ignorance	Chapter 9
Understanding how Pavlovian conditioning can be used to manipulate emotions	Chapter 6
Developing the ability to detect conditioning procedures used in the media	Chapter 6
Recognizing social influence strategies	Chapter 16
Judging the credibility of an information source	Chapter 16

Skills in Thinking as Hypothesis Testing

Looking for alternative explanations for findings and events	Chapters 1, 9, and 11
Looking for contradictory evidence	Chapters 1, 3, and 9
Recognizing the limitations of anecdotal evidence	Chapters 2 and 15
Understanding the need to seek disconfirming evidence	Chapter 7
Understanding the limitations of correlational evidence	Chapters 11 and 13
Understanding the limitations of statistical significance	Chapter 13
Recognizing situations in which placebo effects might occur	Chapter 15

Skills in Working with Likelihood and Uncertainty

Utilizing base rates in making predictions and evaluating probabilities	Chapter 13
Understanding cumulative probabilities	Chapter 14
Understanding conjunctive probabilities	Chapter 14
Understanding the limitations of the representativeness heuristic	Chapter 14
Understanding the limitations of the availability heuristic	Chapter 14
Recognizing situations in which regression toward the mean may occur	Chapter 15
Understanding the limits of extrapolation	Chapter 3

Decision-Making and Problem-Solving Skills

Using evidence-based decision making	Chapter 2
Recognizing the bias in hindsight analysis	Chapters 7 and 12
Seeking information to reduce uncertainty	Chapter 13
Making risk-benefit assessments	Chapter 13
Generating and evaluating alternative courses of action	Chapter 13
Recognizing overconfidence in human cognition	Chapter 7
Understanding the limitations and fallibility of human memory	Chapter 7
Understanding how contrast effects can influence judgments and decisions	Chapter 4
Recognizing when extreme comparitors are being used	Chapter 4

research results underscore psychology's foundation in research, and photos and diagrams often bolster each other (for example, see the treatment of classical conditioning in Chapter 6). Color is used carefully as an organizational device, and visual schematics help simplify hard-to-visualize concepts (see, for instance, the figure explaining reaction range for intelligence in Chapter 9). All of these efforts have gone toward the service of one master: the desire to make this an inviting book that is easy to learn from.

Internet-Related Features

The Internet is rapidly altering the landscape of modern life, and students clearly need help dealing with the information explosion in cyberspace. To assist them, this edition has two features. First, I recruited Web expert Vincent Hevern (Le Moyne College), the Internet editor for the Society for the Teaching of Psychology, to write a concise preface that explains the essentials of the Internet to the uninitiated. This preface, which follows the student preface, briefly explains URLs, domain names, hyperlinks, search engines, and so forth. Second, I also asked Professor Hevern to evaluate hundreds of psychology-related sites on the Web and come up with some recommended sites that appear to provide reasonably accurate, balanced, and empirically sound information. Short descriptions of these recommended Web sites (called Web Links) are dispersed throughout the chapters, adjacent to related topical coverage. Because URLs change frequently, we have placed the URLs for our Web Links in an Appendix (C) in the back of the book. Insofar as students are interested in visiting these sites, we recommend that they do so through the *Psychology: Themes & Variations* home page at the Wadsworth Psychology Study Center Web site (http://psychology.wadsworth. com). Links to all the recommended Web sites are maintained there, and the Wadsworth Webmaster periodically updates the URLs.

Integrated Running Glossary

An introductory text should place great emphasis on acquainting students with psychology's technical language—not for the sake of jargon, but because a great many of our key terms are also our cornerstone concepts (for example, *independent variable, reliability, and cognitive dissonance*). This text handles terminology with a running glossary embedded in the prose itself. The terms are set off in boldface italics, and the definitions follow in boldface roman type. This approach retains the two advantages of a conventional running glossary:

vocabulary items are made salient, and their definitions are readily accessible. However, it does so without interrupting the flow of discourse, while eliminating redundancy between text matter and marginal entries.

Concept Checks

To help students assess their mastery of important ideas, Concept Checks are sprinkled throughout the book. In keeping with my goal of making this a book of ideas, the Concept Checks challenge students to apply ideas instead of testing rote memory. For example, in Chapter 6 the reader is asked to analyze realistic examples of conditioning and identify conditioned stimuli and responses, reinforcers, and schedules of reinforcement. Many of the Concept Checks require the reader to put together ideas introduced in different sections of the chapter. For instance, in Chapter 4 students are asked to identify parallels between vision and hearing. Some of the Concept Checks are quite challenging, but students find them engaging, and they report that the answers (available in Appendix A in the back of the book) are often illuminating.

Practice Tests

Each chapter ends with a 15-item multiple-choice Practice Test that should give students a realistic assessment of their mastery of that chapter and valuable practice taking the type of test that many of them will face in the classroom (if the instructor uses the Test Bank). This new feature grew out of some research that I conducted on students' use of textbook pedagogical devices (see Weiten, Guadagno, & Beck, 1996). This research indicated that students pay scant attention to some standard pedagogical devices. When I grilled my students to gain a better undertstanding of this finding, it quickly became apparent that students are very pragmatic about pedagogy. Essentially, their refrain was "We want study aids that will help us pass the next test." With this mandate in mind, I devised the Practice Tests. They should be useful, as I took all the items from the Test Bank for previous editions.

In addition to the special features just described, the text includes a variety of more conventional, "tried and true" features as well. The back of the book contains a standard *alphabetical glossary.* Opening *outlines* preview each chapter, and a thorough *review* of *key ideas* appears at the end of each chapter, along with lists of *key terms* and *key people* (important theorists and researchers). I make frequent use of *italics for emphasis,* and I depend on *frequent headings* to maximize organizational clarity. The preface for students describes these pedagogical devices in more detail.

Content

The text is divided into 16 chapters, which follow a traditional ordering. The chapters are not grouped into sections or parts, primarily because such groupings can limit your options if you want to reorganize the order of topics. The chapters are written in a way that facilitates organizational flexibility, as I always assumed that some chapters might be omitted or presented in a different order.

The topical coverage in the text is relatively conventional, but there are some subtle departures from the norm. For instance, Chapter 1 presents a relatively "meaty" discussion of the evolution of ideas in psychology. This coverage of history lays the foundation for many of the crucial ideas emphasized in subsequent chapters. The historical perspective is also my way of reaching out to the students who find that psychology just isn't what they expected it to be. If we want students to contemplate the mysteries of behavior, we must begin by clearing up the biggest mysteries of them all: "Where did these rats, statistics, synapses, and genes come from; what could they possibly have in common; and why doesn't this course bear any resemblance to what I anticipated?" I use history as a vehicle to explain how psychology evolved into its modern form and why misconceptions about its nature are so common.

I also devote an entire chapter (Chapter 2) to the scientific enterprise—not just the mechanics of research methods but the logic behind them. I believe that an appreciation of the nature of empirical evidence can contribute greatly to improving students' critical thinking skills. Ten years from now, many of the "facts" reported in this book will have changed, but an understanding of the methods of science will remain invaluable. An introductory psychology course, by itself, isn't going to make a student think like a scientist, but I can't think of a better place to start the process.

As its title indicates, this book is a condensed version of my introductory text, *Psychology: Themes and Variations*. I have reduced the length of the book from 325,000 words to 248,000 words, which is very close to the average length for brief introductory psychology texts (Griggs, Jackson, & Napolitano, 1994). How was this reduction in size accomplished? It required a great many difficult decisions, but fortunately, I had excellent advice from a team of professors who served as consultants. About one-third of the reduction came from deleting entire topics, such as psychophysics, mental retardation, blocking in classical conditioning, and so forth. However, the bulk of the reduction was achieved by compressing and simplifying coverage throughout the book. I carefully scrutinized the parent book sentence by sentence and forced myself to justify the existence of every study, every example, every citation, every phrase. The result is a thoroughly *rewritten* text, rather than one that was *reassembled* through "cut and paste" techniques.

Changes in the Fifth Edition

A good textbook must evolve with the field of inquiry it covers. Although the professors and students who used the first four editions of this book did not clamor for alterations, there are some changes. The most significant change is the addition of the Critical Thinking Applications. Although this text has always emphasized thinking critically about research and psychological issues, this is the first time it contains a formal component dedicated to enhancing students' critical thinking skills. Other changes include the following.

First, I have greatly increased my coverage of evolutionary psychology, which I have come to regard as a major new theoretical perspective in the field. In recent years, evolutionary psychologists have published a great deal of thought-provoking research on an increasingly broad range of topics. I don't always agree with their conclusions, but I could make the same comment about all the major theoretical perspectives in psychology. In any event, Chapter 3 has a major new section on evolutionary psychology that constitutes about one-quarter of the chapter. This section introduces basic evolutionary concepts and—using animal examples—shows how species' behavioral characteristics, like their physical characteristics, can be shaped by evolutionary processes. The coverage in Chapter 3 sets the stage for the evolutionary analyses that follow in subsequent chapters in roughly 30 different places. A detailed summary of the coverage of evolutionary psychology throughout the book can be found on page xvi (accompanied by similar lists of the integrated coverage of cultural factors and gender issues).

Second, you will find a fresh, new design and an abundance of new graphics in this edition. Overall, there are 72 entirely new or dramatically revised figures and tables.

Third, the book has been thoroughly updated to reflect recent advances in the field. One of the exciting things about psychology is that it is not a stagnant discipline. It continues to move forward at what seems a faster and faster pace. This progress has necessitated a host of specific content changes that you'll find sprinkled throughout the chapters. Of the roughly 2600 references cited in the text, over 1000 are new to this edition.

Psyk.trek: A Multimedia Introduction to Psychology

Psyk.trek is a multimedia supplement that will provide students with new opportunities for active learning and reach out to "visual learners" with greatly increased efficacy. *Psyk.trek* is intended to give students a second pathway to learning much of the content of introductory psychology. Although it does not cover all of the content of the introductory course, I think you will see that a great many key concepts and principles can be explicated *more effectively* in an interactive audio-visual medium than in a textbook.

The revised *Psyk.trek—General Version* consists of four components. The main component is a set of 59 *Interactive Learning Modules* that present the core content of psychology in a whole new way. These tutorials include thousands of graphics, hundred of photos, hundreds of animations, approximately four hours of narration, 36 carefully selected videos, and about 150 uniquely visual concept checks and quizzes. The *Simulations* allow students to explore complex psychological phenomena in depth. They are highly interactive, experiential demonstrations that will enhance students' appreciation of research methods. A *Multimedia Glossary* allows students to look up over 800 psychological terms, access hundreds of pronunciations of obscure words, and pull up hundreds of related diagrams, photos, and videos. The *Video Selector* allows students to directly access the 36 video segments that are otherwise embedded in the Interactive Learning Modules.

The key strength of *Psyk.trek* is its ability to give students new opportunities for active learning outside of the classroom. For example, students can run themselves through re-creations of classic experiments to see the complexities of data collection in action. Or they can play with visual illusions on screen in ways that will make them doubt their own eyes. Or they can stack color filters on screen to demonstrate the nature of subtractive color mixing. *Psyk.trek* is intended to supplement and complement *Psychology: Themes & Variations*.

For instance, after reading about operant conditioning in the text, a student could work through three interactive tutorials on operant principles, watch three videos, (including historic footage of B. F. Skinner shaping a rat), and then try to shape Morphy, the virtual rat, in one of the simulations.

Other Supplementary Materials

The teaching/learning package that has been developed to supplement *Psychology: Themes and Variations* also includes many other useful tools. The development of all its parts was carefully coordinated so that they are mutually supported.

Concept Charts for Study and Review

To help your students organize and assimilate the main ideas contained in the text, I have created an entirely new supplement—a booklet of Concept Charts. This booklet contains a two-page Concept Chart for each chapter. Each Concept Chart provides a detailed visual map of the key ideas found in the main body of that chapter. These color-coded, hierarchically-organized charts create snapshots of the chapters that should allow your students to quickly see the relationships among ideas and sections.

Study Guide (by Richard Stalling and Ronald Wasden)

For your students, there is an exceptionally thorough *Study Guide* available to help them master the information in the text. It was written by two of my former professors, Richard Stalling and Ronald Wasden of Bradley University. They have over 30 years of experience as a team writing study guides for introductory psychology texts, and their experience is readily apparent in the high-quality materials that they have developed.

The review of key ideas for each chapter is made up of an engaging mixture of matching exercises, fill-in-the-blank items, free-response questions, and programmed learning. Each review is organized around learning objectives that I wrote. The *Study Guide* is closely coordinated with the *Test Bank*, as the same learning objectives guided the construction of the questions in the *Test Bank*. The *Study Guide* also includes a review of key terms, a review of key people, and a self-test for each chapter in the text.

Instructor's Resource Manual (coordinated by Randolph Smith)

A talented roster of professors have contributed to the *Instructor's Resource Manual (IRM)* in their respective areas of expertise. The *IRM* was developed under the guidance of Randolph Smith, the editor of the journal *Teaching of Psychology*. It contains a diverse array of materials designed to facilitate efforts to teach the introductory course and includes the following sections.

- The *Instructor's Manual,* by Randolph Smith (Ouachita Baptist University), contains a wealth of detailed suggestions for lecture topics, class demonstrations, exercises, discussion questions, and suggested readings, organized around the content of each chapter in the text. It also highlights the connections between the text coverage and *Psyk.trek* content and features an expanded collection of masters for class handouts.
- *Strategies for Effective Teaching,* by Joseph Lowman (University of North Carolina), discusses practical issues such as what to put in a course syllabus, how to handle the first class meeting, how to cope with large classes, and how to train and organize teaching assistants.
- *Films and Videos for Introductory Psychology,* by Russ Watson (College of DuPage), provides a comprehensive, up-to-date critical overview of educational films relevant to the introductory course.
- *The Use of Computers in Teaching Introductory Psychology,* by Susan J. Shapiro and Michael Shapiro (Indiana University-East), offers a thorough listing of computer materials germane to the introductory course and analyzes their strengths and weaknesses.
- *Integrating Writing into Introductory Psychology,* by Jane Jegerski (Elmhurst College), examines the writing-across-the-curriculum movement and provides suggestions and materials for specific writing assignments chapter by chapter.
- *Crossing Borders/Contrasting Behaviors: Using Cross-Cultural Comparisons to Enrich the Introductory Psychology Course,* by Bill Hill and Michael Reiner (Kennesaw State College), discusses the movement toward "internationalizing" the curriculum and provides suggestions for lectures, exercises, and assignments that can add a cross-cultural flavor to the introductory course.
- *Using the Internet to Teach Introductory Psychology,* by Michael R. Snyder (University of Alberta), discusses how to work Internet assignments into the introductory course and provides a guide to many psychology-related sites on the World Wide Web.

Test Bank (by S. A. Hensch)

Shirley Hensch (University of Wisconsin, Marshfield/Wood County) has done an excellent job revising all the test questions for this edition of the book. The questions are closely tied to the chapter learning objectives and to the lists of key terms and key people found in both the text and the *Study Guide.* The items are categorized as (a) factual, (b) conceptual/applied, (c) integrative, or (d) critical thinking questions. This edition's revision of the test bank was guided by an extensive item analysis of the questions in the fourth edition test bank. The test bank also includes a separate section that contains about 700 multiple-choice questions based on the content of *Psyk.trek's* Interactive Learning Modules.

Computerized Test Items

Electronic versions of the *Test Bank* are available for a variety of computer configurations. The *ExamView* software is user-friendly and allows teachers to insert their own questions and to customize those provided.

Transparencies (by Susan Shapiro)

A collection of *text-specific transparencies* has been created to enhance visual presentations in the classroom. The development of the transparencies was supervised by Susan Shapiro (Indiana University-East), who has great expertise in the use of visual media in the classroom. Suzie has done a terrific job making the transparencies clear, readable, pedagogically sound, and technically accurate. A second set of transparencies from other Wadsworth psychology texts is also available.

Challenging Your Preconceptions: Thinking Critically About Psychology, Second Edition (by Randolph Smith)

This brief paperback book is a wonderful introduction to critical thinking as it applies to psychological issues. Written by Randolph Smith (Ouachita Baptist University), this book helps students apply their critical thinking skills to a variety of topics, including hypnosis, advertising, misleading statistics, IQ testing, gender differences, and memory bias. Each chapter ends with critical thinking challenges that give students opportunities to practice their critical thinking skills.

Culture and Modern Life (by David Matsumoto)

If you emphasize cultural diversity in your course, this is an ideal supplementary book. Written by David Matsumoto (San Francisco State University), a leading authority on cross-cultural psychology, this brief paperback will help students appreciate how cultural factors affect psychological processes. It includes chapters on self, social behavior, gender, work, and abnormal psychology.

Wadsworth Psychology Study Center on the World Wide Web

Students using *Psychology: Themes & Variations* can use the Wadsworth Psychology Study Center on the Web (http://psychology.wadsworth.com/product/ 0534593100s). Through the Study Center, they can access updates on hot topics, demonstrations, tutorials, quizzes on the chapters in the text, and links to additional psychology web sites.

PsychLink 2002

This lecture tool makes it easy to assemble, edit, publish, and present custom lectures for your introductory psychology course, using Microsoft *Power Point*. *PsychLink 2002* lets you bring together text-specific lecture outlines, art, video, and animations from this CD-ROM, the Web, and your own material.

Webtutor Advantage 2.0

For students, *WebTutor 2.0 Advantage* offers real-time access to a full array of study tools, including flashcards (with audio), practice quizzes, online tutorials, Web links, and access to definitions (including audio pronunciations). *WebTutor 2.0 Advantage* also offers video clips and images from the *Psyk.trek* CD-ROM.

WebTutor Advantage Plus

WebTutor Advantage Plus includes all the features of *WebTutor 2.0 Advantage* plus the complete text and Microsoft *Power Point* slides.

Acknowledgments

Creating an introductory psychology text is a complicated challenge, and a small army of people have contributed to the evolution of this book. Foremost among them are the psychology editors I have worked with at Brooks/Cole and Wadsworth—Claire Verduin, C. Deborah Laughton, Phil Curson, Eileen Murphy, and Edith Beard Brady—and the developmental editors for this book, John Bergez and Sherry Symington. They have helped me immeasurably, and each has become a treasured friend along the way. I am especially indebted to Claire, who educated me in the intricacies of textbook publishing, and to John, who has left an enduring imprint on my writing.

The challenge of meeting a difficult schedule in producing this book was undertaken by a talented team of people coordinated by Tom Dorsaneo and Susan Mitz, who both did a superb job pulling it all together. Credit for the revised design goes to Gladys Rosa-Mendoza, who was very creative in building on the previous design developed by John Odam. Linda Rill handled permissions and photo research with enthusiasm and extraordinary efficiency, and Jackie Estrada did an outstanding job once again in copy editing the manuscript.

A host of psychologists deserve thanks for the contributions they made to this book. I am grateful to Diane Halpern for her work on the Critical Thinking Applications; to Vinny Hevern for contributing the Web Links and Internet essay; to Rick Stalling and Ron Wasden for their work on the *Study Guide;* to Shirley Hensch for her work on the *Test Bank;* to Randy Smith, Joseph Lowman, Russ Watson, Jane Jegerski, Bill Hill, Michael Reiner, Susan Shapiro, Michael Shapiro, and Michael Snyder for their contributions to the *Instructor's Resource Package;* to Susan Shapiro for her work on the transparencies; to Randy Smith and David Matsumoto for contributing ancillary books; to Jim Calhoun for providing the item analysis data for the test items; to Harry Upshaw, Larry Wrightsman, Shari Diamond, Rick Stalling, and Claire Etaugh for their help and guidance over the years; and to the chapter consultants listed on page xviii and the reviewers listed on page xix, who provided insightful and constructive critiques of various portions of the manuscript.

Many other people have also contributed to this project, and I am grateful to all of them for their efforts. Bill Roberts, Craig Barth, Nancy Sjoberg, John Odam, Marjorie Sanders, Fiorella Ljunggren, Vernon Boes and Jim Brace-Thompson helped with varied aspects of previous editions. Susan Badger, Sean Wakely, Joanne Terhaar, Tanya Nigh, Lisa Weber, Stephen Rapley, Joy Westberg, Robyn Roth, Sherry Symington, and Margaret Parks made valuable contributions to the current edition. At the College of DuPage, where I taught until 1991, all of my colleagues in psychology provided support and information at one time or another, but I am especially indebted to Barb Lemme and Don Green. I also want to thank my colleagues at Santa Clara University (especially Tracey Kahan, Tom Plante, and Jerry Burger), who have been a fertile source of new ideas, and my students who helped complete the reference entries (Rebecca Andrews, Theresa Carroll, Jennifer Kortes, and Carrie Littlefield).

I am also deeply indebted to the diverse array of people who contributed to the development of the *Psyk.trek* CD-ROM. At Thomson Learning, Eileen Murphy, Chris Evers, Marlene Thom, and May Clark worked above and beyond the call of duty. At Luminair Multimedia, George Elder, Kent Johnson, Laddie Odom, John Fuller, and Jocelyn Turpin worked with maniacal intensity to deliver *Psyk.trek* on time. Crucial contributions were also made by Alan Lanning, Roger Harnish, Linda Noble, Linda Rill, and Jackie Estrada.

My greatest debt is to my wife, Beth Traylor, who has been a steady source of emotional sustenance while enduring the grueling rigors of her medical career, and to my son T. J., for making Dad laugh all the time.

Wayne Weiten

Integrated Coverage of Evolutionary Psychology

Emergence of evolutionary psychology as a major theory, pp. 13–140

Evolutionary basis of sex differences in spatial skills, pp. 13, 26–27

Overview of Darwin's original theory and key concepts, pp. 4, 82–83

Further refinements to evolutionary theory, including inclusive fitness, pp. 83–84

Evolutionary bases of selected animal behaviors, pp. 84–85

Parental investment theory and animal mating systems, pp. 85–86

Evolutionary significance of color vision, p. 103

Evolutionary basis of cortical "face detectors," p. 103

Evolution and sex differences in taste sensitivity, p. 121

Evolutionary roots of consciousness, p. 137

Evolutionary bases of sleep, p. 144

Evolution and animal foraging patterns, pp. 182–183

Evolutionary significance of conditioned taste aversion, p. 187

Evolution and species-specific learning propensities, pp. 187–188

Language in evolutionary context, p. 241

Evolutionary analysis of error and bias in decision making, pp. 253–254.

Evolution and mate selection in animals, p. 300

Implications of parental investment theory for human sexual behavior, pp. 300–301.

Evolution and sex differences in sexual activity, p. 301

Evolutionary basis of mating priorities, pp. 301–302

Evolution and sex differences in reactions to infidelity, pp. 302–303

Evolutionary theories of emotion, p. 315

Evolutionary perspective on innate cognitive abilities, p. 340

Evolutionary significance of varied attachment patterns, p. 334

Evolutionary approach to explaining gender differences in human abilities, p. 353

Evolutionary basis of Big-five personality traits, pp. 380–381

Problem of hindsight in evolutionary analyses of personality, p. 391

Evolutionary psychologists' approach to defining the critieria of abnormality, pp. 427–428

Evolution, preparedness, and phobias, p. 432

Evolutionary explanations of bias in person perception, pp. 494–495

Evolutionary analyses of how aspects of physical appearance influence reproductive fitness, p. 502

Evolutionary basis of mate-attraction tactics, pp. 502–503

Evolutionary basis of sex differences in the perception of sexual interest and relationship commitment, p. 503

Integrated Coverage of Cultural Factors

Increased interest in cultural diversity, pp. 12–13

Introduction of theme: Behavior is shaped by cultural heritage, pp. 19–20

Cultural variations in the pace of life, pp. 42–43

Culture and depth perception, pp. 112–113

Cultural variations in susceptibility to illusions, pp. 114–115

Cultural variations in taste preferences, p. 121

Cultural variations in pain tolerance, p. 123

Culture and patterns of sleeping, pp. 142, 144

Cultural variations in the significance of dreams, pp. 147–148

Cultural similarities in the pace of language development, p. 240

Effects of bilingualism, pp. 238–239

Factors influencing second language acquisition, p. 239

Linguistic relativity hypothesis, pp. 241–242

Cultural variations in cognitive style, pp. 248–249

IQ testing in non-Western cultures, p. 274

Cultural and ethnic differences in IQ scores, pp. 278–280

Cultual bias in IQ testing, pp. 280–281

Culture and food preferences, pp. 296–297

Cross-cultural similarity of mating preferences, p. 302

Cultural similarities in expressive aspects of emotions, p. 312

Cultural variations in categories of emotions, display rules, p. 312

Culture and motor development, pp. 330–331

Culture and patterns of attachment, p. 333–334

Cross-cultural validity of Piaget's theory, p. 339

Cross-cultural validity of Kohlberg's theory, p. 342

Culture and modal personality, p. 381

Cross-cultural validity of the Big Five trait model, p. 381

Culture and independent versus interdependent views of self, pp. 381, 384

Culture, self-enhancement, and self-criticism, p. 384

Culture and the concept of normality, p. 427

Relativistic versus pancultural view of psychological disorders, pp. 447, 450

Culture-bound disorders, p. 450

Cultural variations in existence of eating disorders, p. 452

Contribution of Western cultural values to eating disorders, pp. 452–453

Western cultural roots of psychotherapy, p. 477

Barriers to the use of therapy by ethnic minorities, p. 477

Culture, collectivism, and individualism, p. 498

Culture and attributional bias, p. 498

Cultural variations in romantic relationships, p. 502

Cultural variations in conformity and obedience, p. 511

Culture and social loafing, p. 513

Ethnic stereotypes and modern racism, p. 517

Contribution of attribution bias to ethnic stereotypes, pp. 518–519

Learning of ethnic stereotypes, p. 519

Outgroup homogeneity and ethnic stereotypes, p. 519

Integrated Coverage of Issues Related to Gender

Chapter Consultants

Chapter 1
Charles L. Brewer
Furman University
C. James Goodwin
Wheeling Jesuit University
David Hothersall
Ohio State University
E. R. Hilgard
Stanford University

Chapter 2
Larry Christensen
Texas A & M University
Francis Durso
University of Oklahoma
Donald H. McBurney
University of Pittsburgh
Wendy Schweigert
Bradley University

Chapter 3
Nelson Freedman
Queen's University at Kingston
Michael W. Levine
University of Illinois at Chicago
James M. Murphy
Indiana University–Purdue University Indianapolis
Paul Wellman
Texas A & M University

Chapter 4
Nelson Freedman
Queen's University at Kingston
Kevin Jordan
San Jose State University
Michael W. Levine
University of Illinois at Chicago
John Pittenger
University of Arkansas, Little Rock
Lawrence Ward
University of British Columbia

Chapter 5
Frank Etscorn
New Mexico Institute of Mining and Technology
Tracey L. Kahan
Santa Clara University
Charles F. Levinthal
Hofstra University
Wilse Webb
University of Florida

Chapter 6
A. Charles Catania
University of Maryland
Michael Domjan
University of Texas, Austin
William C. Gordon
University of New Mexico
Barry Schwartz
Swarthmore College

Chapter 7
Tracey L. Kahan
Santa Clara University
Ian Neath
Purdue University
Tom Pusateri
Loras College
Stephen K. Reed
San Diego State University
Patricia Tenpenny
Loyola University, Chicago

Chapter 8
John Best
Eastern Illinois University
David Carroll
University of Wisconsin-Superior
Tom Pusateri
Loras College
Stephen K. Reed
San Diego State University

Chapter 9
Charles Davidshofer
Colorado State University
Shalynn Ford
Teikyo Marycrest University
Timothy Rogers
University of Calgary
Dennis Saccuzzo
San Diego State University

Chapter 10
Robert Franken
University of Calgary
Russell G. Geen
University of Missouri
Douglas Mook
University of Virginia
D. Louis Wood
University of Arkansas, Little Rock

Chapter 11
Ruth L. Ault
Davidson College
John C. Cavanaugh
University of Delaware
Claire Etaugh
Bradley University
Barbara Hansen Lemme
College of DuPage

Chapter 12
Susan Cloninger
Russel Sage College
Caroline Collins
University of Victoria
Christopher F. Monte
Manhattanville College

Chapter 13
Robin M. DiMatteo
University of California, Riverside
Jess Feist
McNeese State University
Chris Kleinke
University of Alaska

Chapter 14
David A. F. Haaga
American University
Richard Halgin
University of Massachusetts, Amherst
Chris L. Kleinke
University of Alaska, Anchorage
Elliot A. Weiner
Pacific University

Chapter 15
Gerald Corey
California State University, Fullerton
Herbert Goldenberg
California State University, Los Angeles
Jane S. Halonen
Alverno College
Thomas G. Plante
Santa Clara University

Chapter 16
Jerry M. Burger
Santa Clara University
Stephen L. Franzoi
Marquette University
Donelson R. Forsyth
Virginia Commonwealth University

Reviewers for the Briefer Version

Bart Bare
Caldwell Community College

Mitchell Berman
University of Southern Mississippi

Charles B. Blose
MacMurray College

Frederick Bonato
Saint Peter's College

Edward Brady
Belleville Area College

James F. Calhoun
University of Georgia

Monica Chakravertti
Mary Washington College

Thomas Collins
Mankato State University

Luis Cordon
Eastern Connecticut State University

Joan Doolittle
Anne Arundel Community College

Kimberly Duff
Cerritos College

Christina Frederick
Southern Utah University

Barry Fritz
Quinnipiac College

Linda Gibbons
Westark College

Richard Griggs
University of Florida

Jane Halonen
James Madison University

Patricia Hinton
Cumberland College

Stephen Hoyer
Pittsburgh State University

Nancy Jackson
Johnson & Wales University

Cindy Kamilar
Pikes Peak Community College

Margaret Karolyi
The University of Akron

Gary Levy
University of Wyoming

Laura Madson
New Mexico State University

Kathleen Malley-Morrison
Boston University

Deborah R. McDonald
New Mexico State University

Le'Ann Milinder
New England College

Jack J. Mino
Holyoke Community College

Joel Morogovsky
Brookdale Community College

Dirk W. Mosig
University of Nebraska at Kearney

David R. Murphy
Waubonsee College

Edward I. Pollack
West Chester University of Pennsylvania

Rose Preciado
Mount San Antonio College

Elizabeth A. Rider
Elizabethtown College

Alysia Ritter
Murray State University

Jayne Rose
Augustana College

Heide Sedwick
Mount Aloysius College

George Shardlow
City College of San Francisco

Randolph A. Smith
Ouachita Baptist University

Thomas Smith
Vincennes University

James L. Spencer
West Virginia State College

Iva Trottier
Concordia College

Travis Tubre
University of Southern Mississippi

Jim Turcott
Kalamazoo Valley Community College

Mary Ann Valentino
Reedley College

Doris C. Vaughn
Alabama State University

Randall Wight
Ouachita Baptist University

Brief Contents

The Evolution of Psychology 1

© Bill Ross/CORBIS

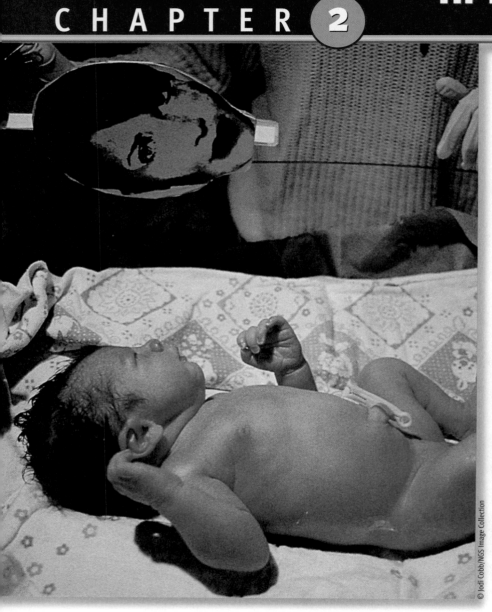

© Jodi Cobb/NGS Image Collection

The Biological Bases of Behavior 58

CHAPTER 3

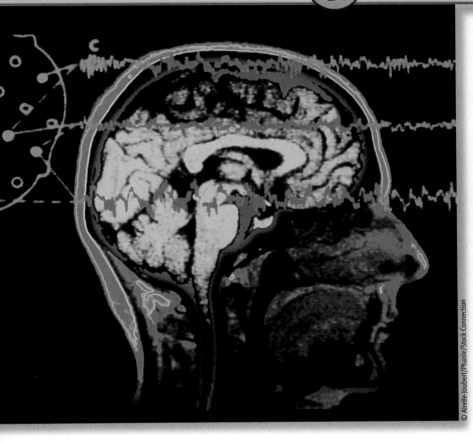

© Airelle-Joubert/Phanie/Stock Connection

CHAPTER 4

Sensation and Perception 94

© Eastcott-Momatiuk/The Image Works

CHAPTER 5

Variations in Consciousness 134

© Mitchell Funk

© Carl Vanderschuit/Index Stock Imagery

© Goavec Pierre-Yves/The Image Bank

© William Whitehurst 1997/The Stock Market

© Hal Lee Miller Photography

Intelligence and Psychological Testing 262

CHAPTER 9

CHAPTER 10

Motivation and Emotion 292

© Kwame Zikomo / Superstock

Stone/Ed Honowitz

Personality: Theory, Research, and Assessment 360

Stone/Marty Loken

CHAPTER 13

Stress, Coping, and Health 394

© 2001 Corbis

© by Diana Ong/Superstock

Treatment of Psychological Disorders 458

CHAPTER 15

© Michael Agliolo/International Stock

Social Behavior 490

© Lisette Le Bon/Superstock

To the Student

Welcome to your introductory psychology textbook. In most college courses, students spend more time with their textbooks than with their professors, so it helps if students *like* their textbooks. Making textbooks likable, however, is a tricky proposition. By its very nature, a textbook must introduce students to many complicated concepts, ideas, and theories. If it doesn't, it isn't much of a textbook, and instructors won't choose to use it. Nevertheless, in writing this book I've tried to make it as likable as possible without compromising the academic content that your instructor demands. I've especially tried to keep in mind your need for a clear, well-organized presentation that makes the important material stand out and yet is interesting to read. Above all else, I hope you find this book challenging to think about and easy to learn from.

Before you plunge into your first chapter, let me introduce you to the book's key features. Becoming familiar with how the book works will help you to get more out of it.

Key Features

You're about to embark on a journey into a new domain of ideas. Your text includes some important features that are intended to highlight certain aspects of psychology's landscape.

Unifying Themes

To help you make sense of a complex and diverse field of study, I introduce seven themes in Chapter 1 that reappear in a number of variations as we move from chapter to chapter. These unifying themes are meant to provoke thought about important issues and to highlight the connections between chapters. They are discussed at the end of each chapter in a section called "Putting It in Perspective."

Personal Applications

Toward the end of each chapter you'll find a Personal Application section that shows how psychology is relevant to everyday life. Some of these sections provide concrete, practical advice that could be helpful to you in your educational endeavors, such as those on improving academic performance, improving everyday memory, and achieving self-control. So, you may want to jump ahead and read some of these Personal Applications early.

Critical Thinking Applications

Each Personal Application is always followed by a two-page Critical Thinking Application that teaches and models basic critical thinking skills. I think you will find that these sections are refreshing and interesting. Like the Personal Applications, they are part of the text's basic content and should be read unless you are told otherwise by your instructor. Although the "facts" of psychology will gradually change after you take this course (thanks to scientific progress), the critical thinking skills modeled in these sections should prove valuable for many years to come.

Web Links and Internet Essay

To help make this book a rich resource guide, we have included dozens of Web Links, which are recommended Web sites that can provide you with additional information on many topics. The recommended sites were selected by Professor Vincent Hevern, who sought out resources that are interesting and that provide accurate, empirically sound information. The WebLinks are dispersed throughout the chapters, adjacent to related topical coverage. Because Web addresses change frequently, we have placed the URLs for our WebLinks in Appendix C in the back of the book. If you are interested in visiting these sites, we recommend that you do so through the *Psychology: Themes & Variations* home page at the Wadsworth Psychology Study Center Web site (http://psychology. wadsworth.com). Links to all the recommended Web sites are maintained there and the Wadsworth Webmaster periodically updates the URLs. By the way, if you are not particularly sophisticated about the Internet, I strongly suggest that you read Professor Hevern's essay on Internet basics, which follows this preface.

Learning Aids

This text contains a great deal of information. A number of learning aids have been incorporated into the book to help you digest it all.

An *outline* at the beginning of each chapter provides you with an overview of the topics covered in that chapter. Think of the outlines as road maps, and bear in mind that it's easier to reach a destination if you know where you're going.

Headings serve as road signs in your journey through each chapter. Four levels of headings are used to make it easy to see the organization of each chapter.

Italics (without boldface) are used liberally throughout the text to emphasize crucial points.

Key terms are identified with ***italicized boldface*** type to alert you that these are important vocabulary items that are part of psychology's technical language. The key terms are also listed at the end of the chapter.

An *integrated running glossary* provides an on-the-spot definition of each key term as it's introduced in the text. These formal definitions are printed in **boldface** type. Becoming familiar with psychology's terminology is an essential part of learning about the field. The integrated running glossary should make this learning process easier.

Concept Checks are sprinkled throughout the chapters to let you test your mastery of important ideas. Generally, they ask you to integrate or organize a number of key ideas, or to apply ideas to real-world situations. Although they're meant to be engaging and fun, they do check conceptual *understanding,* and some are challenging. But if you get stuck, don't worry; the answers (and explanations, where they're needed) are in the back of the book in Appendix A.

Illustrations in the text are important elements in your complete learning package. Some illustrations provide enlightening diagrams of complicated concepts; others furnish examples that help flesh out ideas or provide concise overviews of research results. Careful attention to the tables and figures in the book will help you understand the material discussed in the text.

A *Chapter Review* at the end of each chapter provides a summary of the chapter's *Key Ideas,* a list of *Key Terms,* and a list of *Key People* (important theorists and researchers). It's wise to read over these review materials to make sure you've digested the information in the chapter.

Each chapter ends with a 15-item *Practice Test* that should give you a realistic assessment of your mastery of that chapter and valuable practice in taking multiple-choice tests.

An *alphabetical glossary* is provided in the back of the book. Most key terms are formally defined in the integrated running glossary only when they are first introduced. So if you run into a technical term a second time and can't remember its meaning, it may be easier to look it up in the alphabetical glos-sary than to try to find the definition where the term was originally introduced.

A Few Footnotes

Psychology textbooks customarily identify the studies, theoretical treatises, books, and articles that information comes from. These *citations* occur (1) when names are followed by a date in parentheses, as in "Smith (1988) found that . . ." or (2) when names and dates are provided together within parentheses, as in "In one study (Smith, Miller, & Jones, 1997), the researchers attempted to . . . ." All of the cited publications are listed by author in the alphabetized *References* section in the back of the book. The citations and references are a necessary part of a book's scholarly and scientific foundation. Practically speaking, however, you'll probably want to glide right over them as you read. You definitely don't need to memorize the names and dates. The only names you may need to know are the handful listed under Key People in each Chapter Review (unless your instructor mentions a personal favorite that you should know).

Concept Charts for Study and Review

Your text should be accompanied by a booklet of Concept Charts that are designed to help you organize and master the main ideas contained in each chapter. Each Concept Chart provides a detailed visual map of the key ideas found in the main body of that chapter. Seeing how it all fits together should help you to better understand each chapter. You can use these charts to preview chapters, to double-check your mastery of chapters, and to memorize the crucial ideas in chapters.

Psyk.trek: A Multimedia Introduction to Psychology

Psyk.trek is a multimedia CD-ROM developed to accompany this textbook. It is an enormously powerful learning tool that can enhance your understanding of many complex processes and theories, provide you with an alternative way to assimilate many crucial concepts, and add a little more fun to your journey through introductory psychology. *Psyk.trek* has been designed to supplement and complement your textbook. I strongly encourage you to use it. The CD icons that you will see in many of the headings in the upcoming chapters refer to the content of *Psyk.trek*. An icon indicates that the textbook topic referred to in the heading is covered in the Interactive Learning Modules or Simulations found on *Psyk.trek*. The relevant simulations (Sim1, Sim2, and so forth) and the relevant Interactive Learning Modules (1a, 1b, 1c, and so forth) are listed to the right of the icons.

A Word About the Study Guide

A *Study Guide* is available to accompany this text. It was written by two of my former professors, who introduced me to psychology years ago. They have done a great job of organizing review materials to help you master the information in the book. I suggest that you seriously consider using it to help you study.

A Final Word

I'm pleased to be a part of your first journey into the world of psychology, and I sincerely hope that you'll find the book as thought provoking and as easy to learn from as I've tried to make it. If you have any comments or advice on the book, please write to me in care of the publisher (Wadsworth Publishing Company, 10 Davis Drive, Belmont, CA 94002). You can be sure I'll pay careful attention to your feedback. Finally, let me wish you good luck. I hope you enjoy your course and learn a great deal.

Wayne Weiten

What Should Introductory Psychology Students Know About the Internet?

by Vincent W. Hevern, Le Moyne College

After dinner one night Wayne Weiten, the author of this textbook, challenged me: Using no more than three pages, could I tell introductory psychology students the most important things they need to know about the Internet? Wait a minute, I thought, that's tough! I've been using the Internet intensively for more than four years in teaching and research with undergraduates, so I know there's an awful lot to talk about. But, after a couple of days I decided to accept his challenge. So, I'm going to share with you here what I believe to be the really important stuff about the Internet ("the Net")—information that should make your life as a student easier and, in the end, help you to learn even more about the fascinating world of psychology.

General Comments About the Internet

We now know that something of a fundamental change in the way people exchange ideas and information took place around the time many of you were beginning junior high or high school. For over 20 years, the Internet had been the tool of a relatively small group of lab scientists communicating mostly with each other. Suddenly, in the mid-1990s, the Net began to expand rapidly beyond the research laboratory. It first reached tens and then hundreds of millions of people as vast numbers of computers, large and small, were interconnected to form what is often called *cyberspace.* In the 21st century, learning to navigate the Internet will become as crucial as learning to read or to write—most of us will probably use the Net in some form at work or at home for the rest of our lives.

So, what are some basic notions necessary to understanding the Internet and how it works? Let me propose briefly eight crucial ideas.

1. *The goal of the Internet is communication—the rapid exchange of information—between people separated from each other.* Electronic mail (e-mail) and the World Wide Web (WWW, or just "the Web") are currently the two most important ways of communicating in cyberspace, even though the Net also uses other formats to do so.

2. *Every piece of information on the Net—every Web page, every graphic, every movie or sound, every e-mail box—has a unique, short, and structured address called a URL (or uniform resource locator).* Take, for example, the URL for the online Psychology Conference Calendar maintained by the publisher of this book:

http://psychology.wadsworth.com/conference/index.html

This example shows all three elements of a URL: (a) To the left of the double forward slashes (//) is the *protocol* that tells the Net *how* to transfer the information. Here it is *http:* which means "use hypertext transfer protocol"—the most frequent protocol on the Net (b) To the right of the double slashes up to the first forward slash (/) is the *domain name* that indicates *which computer* on the Net to get the information from. Here the name of the computer is "psychology.wadsworth.com." (c) Finally, everything after the first forward slash is called the *pathway,* which indicates where the information is located within that particular computer. Here the pathway consists of the location "conference/index.html."

3. *The foundation of the Web rests on hypertext links ("hyperlinks"), which are contained within documents (or "Web pages") displayed online.* A hyperlink is a highlighted word, phrase, or graphic image within an onscreen document that refers to some other document or Web page elsewhere. Part of every hyperlink on a computer screen includes the URL for the document that is hidden from view but stored within the computer displaying the document. Users can easily move from one document to another because of hypertext links and their URLs.

4. *The last element of the domain name (the "domain" itself) indicates what type of organization sponsors the link.* Four important domains are *.com* (commercial businesses), *.edu* (colleges and universities), *.gov* (governmental agencies), and *.org* (nonprofit organizations).

5. *The Internet is too large for any one individual to know all the important resources that can be found there.* Users, even experienced ones, often need help to find what they're looking for. In the chapters ahead, you will find many recommended Web sites that I have carefully selected based on their quality and their suitability for undergraduates. In making these selections, I emphasized quality over quantity and strived to send you to excellent gateway sites that are rich in links to related sites. I hope these suggested Web Links help you begin to explore the field of psychology on the Internet.

6. *URLs are relatively unstable.* Many Web sites are moved or changed each year, and new computer systems are installed to replace older ones. Thus, links or URLs that are good one day may be useless the next. That is why we have relegated the URLs for our recommended Web sites to Appendix C found in the back of this book. If you want to check out a recommended Web site, we suggest that you do so through the *Psychology: Themes and Variations* home page at the Wadsworth Psychology Study Center Web site (http://psychology.wadsworth. com). Links to all of the recommended Web sites will be maintained there, and the Wadsworth Webmaster will periodically update the URLs.

7. *The Web is a worldwide democracy on which anyone can post materials. Hence, the quality of information found online varies tremendously.* Some material is first-rate, up-to-date, and backed up by good research and professional judgment. But a great deal of information online is junk—based on poor or invalid research and filled with many errors. Frankly, some sites are downright wacky, and others are run by hucksters and hatemongers. Thus, users need to learn to tell the difference between reputable and disreputable Web resources.

8. *Knowledge has a monetary value.* Although the Internet started out as a noncommerical enterprise where almost everything was free, things have changed swiftly. Owners of knowledge (the holders of commercial "copyrights") usually expect to be paid for sharing what they own over the Net. Thus, many commercial businesses, such as the publishers of academic journals or books, either do not make journal articles available on line for free or expect users to pay some type of fee for accessing their materials. Cognizant of this problem, the publisher of this text has entered into an agreement with a major online resource for magazine and journal articles and other types of information called *InfoTrac.* Your text may have come bundled with a four-month subscription to *InfoTrac,* which provides easy access to full-text versions of thousands of periodicals. If you received an *InfoTrac* subscription with this book, it would be wise to take advantage of this valuable resource.

Suggestions for Action

In light of these ideas, how might you approach the Internet? What should you do to make the most of your time online? Let's review some general suggestions for exploring the Internet.

1. *Learn to navigate the Net before you get an assignment requiring you to do so.* If you've never used the Net before, start now to get a feel for it. Consider doing what lots of students do: Ask a friend who knows the Net to work with you directly so you can quickly get personal experience in cyberspace. What if you "hate" computers or they make you uncomfortable? Recent research has shown that students' fears of using computers tend to diminish once they get some practical experience in the course of a single semester.

2. *Learn how the software browser on your computer works.* The two most popular Web browser programs, Netscape Navigator and Microsoft Internet Explorer, are filled with many simple tricks and helpful shortcuts. Ask your friends or the computer consultants at school. Learning the tricks makes Net-based research much easier. (Hint: Find out what happens when you hold down the righthand mouse button on a PC or the whole button on a Mac once you have the cursor on top of a hyperlink.)

3. *Get to know the different types of online help to find resources on the Web.* These aids currently fall into three general categories: (a) General guides or directories such as Yahoo! (www.yahoo.com) are similar to the Yellow Pages for telephones. You ask the online guide to show you what's listed in its directory under a category heading you supply. (b) *Search engines* such as AltaVista (www.altavista. com) or Hotbot (www.hotbot.com), and *metasearch engines* such as Metacrawler (www. metacrawler. com) are huge databases that generally collect the names and URLs of millions of pages on the Net along with many lines of text from these pages. They can be searched by keywords or phrases and provide ranked listings of Web pages that contain the search target words or phrases. (c) *Expert Subject Guides* such as Russ Dewey's *Psych Web* (www.psychwww.com) or Jeffrey Browndyke's *Neuropsychology Central* (www.neuropsychologycentral.com) provide links to online resources in more narrow or specific fields. Volunteer specialists who claim to be experts on the topic of the guide select the links.

4. *Check very carefully everything you type online because even the slightest error in spelling a URL or an e-mail address will cause a failure to retrieve the Web page or to deliver the e-mail message.* Remember that computers are stupid and will do exactly and only what you tell them to do. They don't read minds, so you have to very precise.

Using the Internet in Psychology

Here are five specific suggestions to help students of psychology when using the Net.

1. *Plan what to look for before going online.* Too many psychology students jump right to the Web when they're given a research task, before giving careful thought to what they're looking for. They easily get frustrated because the Web doesn't seem to have anything about the topic. It would be better (a) to think about the subject you are researching and what specifically you want to learn about that topic, (b) to recall what you already know that relates to the topic, especially psychological concepts and vocabulary words associated with the topic, and (c) to devise a strategy for getting the information you desire. Consult your school's reference library staff or your teachers for suggestions.

2. *Do not rely on the Internet as your principal or only source of data or references in a research project* (especially if you want a good grade). The Net may be easy to use, but your teachers will expect you to cite journal articles, books, and other printed sources more than you cite Internet materials in research. Developing your library skills is essential.

3. *As noted before, don't expect to find many full-text journal articles or other copyrighted commercial materials online for free.* Consult your school's reference librarians about online access to such materials. You are more likely to uncover government reports, specialized technical materials from non-profit organizations, current news and opinion, and general sorts of information rather than findings of specific research studies (although, if the findings were recently in the news, you may find some news reports describing the research).

4. *Learn to recognize the characteristics of a good online resource site.* Good sites have Webmasters or editors personally identified by name and affiliation. Such persons may be professionals or staff members at a reputable institution such as a hospital or university. These sites tend to provide a broad set of resources, are balanced and reasonably objective in their content, and avoid sensational or one-sided viewpoints. Reputable sites tend not to promote specific products or services for money—or, if they do, they acknowledge that there are other resources that browsers may consider.

5. *If you contact anyone online for help, be courteous.* Introduce yourself as you would if you were standing in a faculty member's office. Give your name, your school, and a full statement of what help you are asking for and what you've tried to do that hasn't worked. Don't demand that someone help you. Be sure you've done adequate research on your own before contacting an expert on the Web. And don't be surprised if your request for help is turned down by a Webmaster or editor. Frankly, he or she has already done a lot of volunteer work by editing the site online.

I hope some of these ideas and suggestions help. The Internet offers an awesome array of learning resources related to psychology. Welcome to an exciting new world of discovery.

CHAPTER 1

© Bill Ross/CORBIS

The Evolution of Psychology

© Bill Ross/CORBIS

What is psychology? Your initial answer to this question is likely to bear little resemblance to the picture of psychology that will emerge as you work your way through this book. I know that when I ambled into my introductory psychology course years ago, I had no idea what psychology involved. I was a prelaw/political science major fulfilling a general education requirement with what I thought would be my one and only psychology course. I encountered two things I didn't expect. The first was to learn

that psychology is about a great many things besides abnormal behavior and ways to win friends and influence people. I was surprised to discover that psychology is also about how we are able to perceive color, how hunger is actually regulated by the brain, whether chimpanzees can use language to communicate, and a multitude of other topics I'd never thought to wonder about. The second thing I didn't expect was that I would be so completely seduced by the subject. Before long I changed majors and embarked on a career in psychology—a decision I never regretted.

Why has psychology continued to fascinate me? One reason is that *psychology is practical*. It offers a vast store of information about issues that concern everyone. These issues range from broad social questions, such as how to reduce the incidence of mental illness, to highly personal questions, such as how to improve your self-control. In a sense, psychology is about you and me. It's about life in our modern world. The practical side of psychology will be apparent throughout this text, especially in the end-of-chapter Personal Applications. These Applications focus on everyday problems, such as

improving memory, enhancing performance in school, and dealing with sleep difficulties.

Another element of psychology's appeal for me is that it represents a *way of thinking*. We are all exposed to claims about psychological issues. For instance, we hear assertions that men and women have different abilities or that violence on television has a harmful effect on children. As a science, psychology demands that researchers ask precise questions about such issues and that they test their ideas through systematic observation. Psychology's commitment to testing ideas encourages a healthy brand of critical thinking. In the long run, this means that psychology provides a way of building knowledge that is relatively accurate and dependable.

Of course, psychological research cannot discover an answer for every interesting question about the mind and behavior. You won't find the meaning of life or the secret of happiness in this text. But you *will* find an approach to investigating questions that has proven very fruitful. The more you learn about psychology as a way of thinking, the better equipped you will be to evaluate the psychological assertions you encounter in daily life.

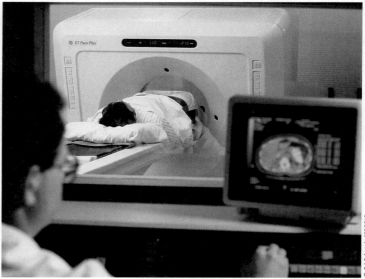

Susumu Takahaski/Reuters/Archive Photos

© Ed Eckstein/CORBIS

Modern psychology ranges widely in its investigations, looking at divergent topics such as work, sleep, and brain function. As you progress through this book, you will see that the range and diversity of psychology's subject matter are enormous.

There is still another reason for my fascination with psychology. As you proceed through this text, you will find that psychologists study an enormous diversity of subjects, from acrophobia (fear of heights) to zoophobia (fear of animals), from problem solving in apes to the symbolic language of dreams. Psychologists look at all the seasons of human life, from development in the womb to the emotional stages that people go through in the process of dying. Psychologists study observable behaviors such as eating, fighting, and mating. But they also dig beneath the surface to investigate how hormones affect emotions and how the brain registers pain. They probe the behavior of any number of species, from humans to house cats, from monkeys to moths. This rich diversity is, for me, perhaps psychology's most appealing aspect.

Mental illness, rats running in mazes, the physiology of hunger, the mysteries of love, creativity, and prejudice—what ties all these subjects together in a single discipline? How did psychology come to be such a diverse field of study? Why is it so different from what most people expect? If psychology is a social science, why do psychologists study subjects such as brain chemistry and the physiological basis of vision? To answer these questions, we begin our introduction to psychology by retracing its development. By seeing how psychology grew and changed, you will discover why it has the shape it does today.

After our journey into psychology's past, we will examine a formal definition of psychology. We'll also look at psychology as it is today—a sprawling, multifaceted science and profession. To help keep psychology's diversity in perspective, the chapter concludes with a discussion of seven unifying themes that will serve as connecting threads in the chapters to come. Finally, in the chapter's Personal Application, we'll return to psychology's practical side, as we review research that gives insights on how to be an effective student, and in the Critical Thinking Application we'll discuss how critical thinking skills can be enhanced.

From Speculation to Science: How Psychology Developed

Psychology's story is one of people groping toward a better understanding of themselves. As psychology has evolved, its focus, methods, and explanatory models have changed. Let's look at how psychology has developed from philosophical speculations about the mind into a modern behavioral science.

The term *psychology* comes from two Greek words, *psyche,* meaning the soul, and *logos,* referring to the study of a subject. These two Greek roots were first put together to define a topic of study in the 16th century, when *psyche* was used to refer to the soul, spirit, or mind, as distinguished from the body (Boring, 1966). Not until the early 18th century did the term *psychology* gain more than rare usage among scholars. By that time it had acquired its literal meaning, "the study of the mind."

Of course, people have always wondered about the mysteries of the mind. To take just one example, in ancient Greece the philosopher Aristotle engaged in intriguing conjecture about thinking, intelligence, motives, and emotions in his work *Peri Psyches (About the Soul)*. Philosophical speculation about psychological issues is as old as the human race. But it was only a little over a hundred years ago that psychology emerged as a scientific discipline.

A New Science is Born

Psychology's intellectual parents were the disciplines of *philosophy* and *physiology*. By the 1870s a small number of scholars in both fields were actively exploring questions about the mind. How are bodily sensations turned into a mental awareness of the outside world? Are our perceptions of the world accurate reflections of reality? How do mind and body interact? The philosophers and physiologists who were interested in the mind viewed such questions as fascinating issues *within* their respective fields. It was a German professor, Wilhelm Wundt (1832–1920), who eventually changed this view. Wundt mounted a campaign to make psychology an independent discipline rather than a stepchild of philosophy or physiology.

The time and place were right for Wundt's appeal. German universities were in a healthy period of expansion, so resources were available for new disciplines. Furthermore, the intellectual climate favored the scientific approach that Wundt advocated. Hence, his proposals were well received by the academic community. In 1879 Wundt succeeded in establishing the first formal laboratory for research in psychology at the University of Leipzig. In deference to this landmark event, historians have christened 1879 as psychology's "date of birth." Soon afterward, in 1881, Wundt established the first journal devoted to publishing research on psychology. All in all, Wundt's campaign was so successful that today he is widely characterized as the founder of psychology.

Wundt's conception of psychology dominated the field for two decades and was influential for several more. Borrowing from his training in physiology, Wundt (1874) declared that the new psychology should be a science modeled after fields such as physics and chemistry. What was the subject matter of the new science? According to Wundt, it was *consciousness*—the awareness of immediate experience. *Thus, psychology became the scientific study of conscious experience.* This orientation kept psychology focused squarely on the mind. But it demanded that the methods used to investigate the mind be as scientific as those of chemists or physicists.

Wundt was a tireless, dedicated scholar who generated an estimated 54,000 pages of books and articles in his career (Bringmann & Balk, 1992). His hard work and provocative ideas soon attracted attention. Many outstanding young scholars came to Leipzig to study under Wundt and do research on vision, hearing, touch, taste, attention, and emotion. Many of his students then fanned out across Germany and America, establishing laboratories that formed the basis for the new, independent science of psychology.

Indeed, it was in North America that Wundt's new science grew by leaps and bounds. Between 1883 and 1893, some 24 new psychological research laboratories sprang up in the United States and Canada, at the schools shown in Figure 1.1 on the next page (Garvey, 1929). Many of the laboratories were started by Wundt's students, or by his students' students.

Exactly why Americans took to psychology so quickly is hard to say. Perhaps it was because America's relatively young universities were more open to new disciplines than were the older, more tradition-bound universities elsewhere in the world. In any case, although psychology was born in Germany, it blossomed into adolescence in America. Like many adolescents, however, the young science was about to enter a period of turbulence and turmoil.

The Battle of the "Schools" Begins: Structuralism Versus Functionalism

When you read about how psychology became a science, you might have imagined that psychologists became a unified group of scholars who busily added new discoveries to an uncontested store of "facts." In reality, no science works that way. Competing schools of thought exist in most scientific disciplines. Sometimes the disagreements among these schools are sharp. Such diversity in thought is natural and often stimulates enlightening debate. In psychology, the first two major schools of thought, *structuralism* and *functionalism,* were entangled in the first great intellectual battle in the field.

Structuralism emerged through the leadership of Edward Titchener, an Englishman who emigrated to the United States in 1892 and taught for decades at Cornell University. Although Titchener earned his degree in Wundt's Leipzig laboratory and expressed great admiration for Wundt's work, he brought his own version of Wundt's psychology to America (Hilgard, 1987; Thorne & Henley, 1997).

Physiology informs us about those life phenomena that we perceive by our external senses. In psychology, the person looks upon himself as from within and tries to explain the interrelations of those processes that this internal observation discloses.
WILHELM WUNDT
1832–1920

Web Link 1.1

HistPsyc: History of Psychology Headlines Index
More than 300 years of psychology's history and prehistory—1650 to 1959—are detailed in the form of newspaper headlines and short articles at David Likely's (University of New Brunswick) valuable site.

Note: The URLs for the recommended web sites can be found in an appendix in the back of the book, and links to the sites can be found on the web site for this text : (http://psychology.wadsworth.com/product/0534593100S).

Figure 1.1

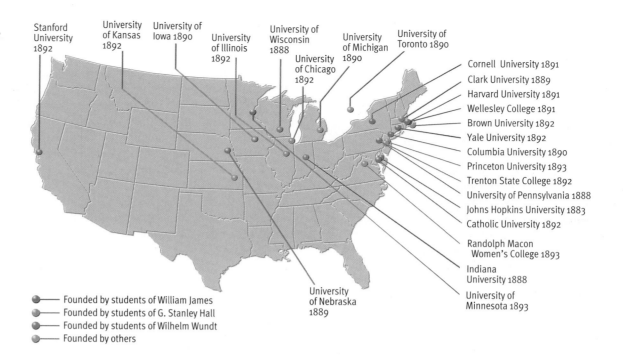

Early research laboratories in North America. This map highlights the location and year of founding for the first 24 psychological research labs established in North American colleges and universities. As the color coding shows, a great many of these labs were founded by the students of Wilhelm Wundt, William James, and G. Stanley Hall, who established the first research lab in America at Johns Hopkins University in 1883. (Based on Garvey, 1929; Hilgard, 1987)

Stanford University 1892
University of Kansas 1892
University of Iowa 1890
University of Illinois 1892
University of Wisconsin 1888
University of Chicago 1892
University of Michigan 1890
University of Toronto 1890

Cornell University 1891
Clark University 1889
Harvard University 1891
Wellesley College 1891
Brown University 1892
Yale University 1892
Columbia University 1890
Princeton University 1893
Trenton State College 1892
University of Pennsylvania 1888
Johns Hopkins University 1883
Catholic University 1892
Randolph Macon Women's College 1893
Indiana University 1888
University of Minnesota 1893

University of Nebraska 1889

Founded by students of William James
Founded by students of G. Stanley Hall
Founded by students of Wilhelm Wundt
Founded by others

"*It is just this free water of consciousness that psychologists resolutely overlook.*"
WILLIAM JAMES
1842–1910

Structuralism **was based on the notion that the task of psychology is to analyze consciousness into its basic elements and investigate how these elements are related.** Just as physicists were studying how matter is made up of basic particles, the structuralists wanted to identify and examine the fundamental components of conscious experience, such as sensations, feelings, and images.

Although the structuralists explored many questions, most of their work concerned sensation and perception in vision, hearing, and touch. To examine the contents of consciousness, the structuralists depended on the method of **introspection, or the careful, systematic self-observation of one's own conscious experience.** As practiced by the structuralists, introspection required training to make the *subject*—the person being studied—more objective and more aware. Once trained, participants were typically exposed to auditory tones, optical illusions, and visual stimuli such as pieces of fruit and were asked to analyze what they experienced.

The functionalists took a different view of psychology's task. *Functionalism* **was based on the belief that psychology should investigate the function or purpose of consciousness, rather than its structure.** The chief architect of functionalism was William James (1842–1910), a brilliant American scholar (and brother of novelist Henry James). James's formal training was in medicine. However, he was too sickly to pursue a medical practice (he couldn't imagine standing all day long),

so he joined the faculty of Harvard University to pursue a less arduous career (Ross, 1991). Medicine's loss proved to be a boon for psychology, as James quickly became an intellectual giant in the field. James's landmark book, *Principles of Psychology* (1890), became standard reading for generations of psychologists and is perhaps the most influential text in the history of psychology (Weiten & Wight, 1992).

James's thinking illustrates how psychology, like any field, is deeply embedded in a network of cultural and intellectual influences. James had been impressed with Charles Darwin's (1859, 1871) theory of *natural selection*. According to the principle of *natural selection,* **heritable characteristics that provide a survival or reproductive advantage are more likely than alternative characteristics to be passed on to subsequent generations and thus come to be "selected" over time.** This cornerstone notion of Darwin's evolutionary theory suggested that the typical characteristics of a species must serve some purpose. Applying this idea to humans, James (1890) noted that consciousness obviously is an important characteristic of our species. Hence, he contended that psychology should investigate the *functions* rather than the *structure* of consciousness.

James also argued that the structuralists' approach missed the real nature of conscious experience. Consciousness, he argued, consists of a continuous *flow* of thoughts. In analyzing consciousness into its "elements," the structuralists were looking at static points in that flow. James wanted to understand the flow itself, which he called the "stream of consciousness."

Whereas structuralists naturally gravitated to the laboratory, functionalists were more interested in how people adapt their behavior to the demands of the real world around them. This practical slant led them to introduce new subjects into psychology. Instead of focusing on sensation and perception, functionalists such as G. Stanley Hall, James McKeen Cattell, and John Dewey began to investigate mental testing, patterns of development in children, the effectiveness of educational practices, and behavioral differences between the sexes. These new topics may have played a role in attracting the first women into the field of psychology (see Figure 1.2).

The impassioned advocates of structuralism and functionalism saw themselves as fighting for high stakes: the definition and future direction of the new science of psychology. Their war of ideas continued energetically for many years. Who won? Most historians give the edge to functionalism. Although the structuralists can be credited with strengthening psychology's commitment to laboratory research, Leahey (1991) notes, "structuralism depended on one man, Titchener, and when he unexpectedly died in 1927 the school collapsed" (p. 61). In contrast, functionalism left a more enduring imprint on psychology. Indeed, Buxton (1985) has remarked that "nowadays no one is called a functionalist in psychology, and yet almost every psychologist is one" (p. 138). Although functionalism faded as a school of thought, its practical orientation fostered the development of two descendants that have dominated modern psychology: applied psychology and behaviorism.

Web Link 1.2

Mind and Body: René Descartes to William James
Designed originally to celebrate psychology's first century as an independent discipline, this online exhibition traces three historical themes: the mind–body problem posed in the 17th century by philosopher René Descartes, the rise of experimental psychology, and the beginnings of psychology in America.

Figure 1.2

Women pioneers in the history of psychology.
Women have long made major contributions to the development of psychology (Russo & Denmark, 1987), and today roughly one-third of all psychologists are female. As in other fields, however, women have often been overlooked in histories of psychology (Furumoto & Scarborough, 1986). The three psychologists profiled here demonstrate that women have been making significant contributions to psychology almost from its beginning—despite formidable barriers to pursuing their academic careers. (All photos: Archives of the History of American Psychology, University of Akron, Akron, Ohio)

Mary Whiton Calkins (1863–1930)	Margaret Floy Washburn (1871–1939)	Leta Stetter Hollingworth (1886–1939)

Mary Calkins, who studied under William James, founded one of the first dozen psychology laboratories in America at Wellesley College in 1891, invented a widely used technique for studying memory, and became the first woman to serve as president of the American Psychological Association in 1905. Ironically, however, she never received her Ph.D. in psychology. Because she was a woman, Harvard University only reluctantly allowed her to take graduate classes as a "guest student." When she completed the requirements for her Ph.D., Harvard would only offer her a doctorate from its undergraduate sister school, Radcliffe. Calkins felt that this decision perpetuated unequal treatment of the sexes, so she refused the Radcliffe degree.

Margaret Washburn was the first woman to receive a Ph.D. in psychology. She wrote an influential book, *The Animal Mind* (1908), which served as an impetus to the the subsequent emergence of behaviorism and was standard reading for several generations of psychologists. In 1921 she became the second woman to serve as president of the American Psychological Association. Washburn studied under James McKeen Cattell at Columbia University, but like Mary Calkins, she was only permitted to take graduate classes unofficially, as a "hearer." Hence, she transferred to Cornell University, which was more hospitable toward women, and completed her doctorate in 1894. Like Calkins, Washburn spent most of her career at a college for women (Vassar).

Leta Hollingworth did pioneering work on adolescent development, mental retardation, and gifted children. Indeed, she was the first person to use the term *gifted* to refer to youngsters who scored exceptionally high on intelligence tests. Hollingworth (1914, 1916) also played a major role in debunking popular theories of her era that purported to explain why women were "inferior" to men. For instance, she conducted a study refuting the myth that phases of the menstrual cycle are reliably associated with performance decrements in women. Her careful collection of objective data on gender differences forced other scientists to subject popular, untested beliefs about the sexes to skeptical, empirical inquiry.

Watson Alters Psychology's Course as Behaviorism Makes Its Debut

The debate between structuralism and functionalism was only the prelude to other fundamental controversies in psychology. In the early 1900s, another major school of thought appeared that dramatically altered the course of psychology. Founded by John B. Watson (1878–1958), **behaviorism is a theoretical orientation based on the premise that scientific psychology should study only observable behavior.** It is important to understand what a radical change this definition represents. Watson (1913, 1919) was proposing that psychologists *abandon the study of consciousness altogether* and focus exclusively on behaviors that they could observe directly. In essence, he was redefining what scientific psychology should be about.

Why did Watson argue for such a fundamental shift in direction? Because to him, the power of the scientific method rested on the idea of *verifiability*. In principle, scientific claims can always be verified (or disproved) by anyone who is able and willing to make the required observations. However, this power depends on studying things that can be observed objectively. Otherwise, the advantage of using the scientific approach—replacing vague speculation and personal opinion with reliable, exact knowledge—is lost. For Watson, mental processes were not a proper subject for scientific study because they are ultimately private events. After all, no one can see or touch another's thoughts. Consequently, if psychology was to be a science, it would have to give up consciousness as its subject matter and become instead the *science of behavior*.

Behavior refers to any overt (observable) response or activity by an organism. Watson asserted that psychologists could study anything that people do or say—shopping, playing chess, eating, complimenting a friend—but they could *not* study scientifically the thoughts, wishes, and feelings that might accompany these behaviors.

Watson's radical reorientation of psychology did not end with his redefinition of its subject matter. He also took an extreme position on one of psychology's oldest and most fundamental questions: the issue of *nature versus nurture*. This age-old debate is concerned with whether behavior is determined mainly by genetic inheritance ("nature") or by environment and experience ("nurture"). To oversimplify, the question is this: Is a great concert pianist or a master criminal born, or made?

"The time seems to have come when psychology must discard all references to consciousness."
JOHN B. WATSON
1878–1958

Watson argued that each is made, not born. He discounted the importance of heredity, maintaining that behavior is governed entirely by the environment. Indeed, he boldly claimed:

Give me a dozen healthy infants, well-formed, and my own special world to bring them up in and I'll guarantee to take any one at random and train him to become any type of specialist I might select—doctor, lawyer, artist, merchant-chief, and yes, even beggar-man and thief, regardless of his talents, penchants, tendencies, abilities, vocations and race of his ancestors. I am going beyond my facts and I admit it, but so have the advocates of the contrary and they have been doing it for many thousands of years. (1924, p. 82)

For obvious reasons, Watson's tongue-in-cheek challenge was never put to a test. Although this widely cited quote overstated and oversimplified Watson's views on the nature-nurture issue (Todd & Morris, 1992), his writings contributed to the environmental slant that became associated with behaviorism (Horowitz, 1992).

Although it met resistance and skepticism in some quarters, Watson's behavioral point of view gradually took hold (Samelson, 1981, 1994). Actually, psychology had already been edging away from the study of consciousness toward the study of behavior for two decades before Watson's influential campaign (Leahey, 1992). Among other things, this gradual transition to the study of behavior contributed to the rise of animal research in psychology. Having deleted consciousness from their scope of concern, behaviorists no longer needed to study human subjects who could report on their mental processes. Many psychologists thought that animals would make better research subjects anyway. One key reason was that experimental research is often more productive if experimenters can exert considerable *control* over their subjects. Otherwise, too many complicating factors enter into the picture and contaminate the experiment. Obviously, a researcher can exert much more control over a laboratory rat or pigeon than over a human subject, who arrives at a lab with years of uncontrolled experience and who will probably insist on going home at night. Thus, the discipline that had begun its life a few decades earlier as the study of the mind now found itself heavily involved in the study of simple responses made by laboratory animals.

Ironically, although Watson's views shaped the evolution of psychology for many decades, he ended up watching the field's progress from the sidelines. Because of a heavily publicized divorce scandal in 1920, Watson was forced to resign from Johns Hopkins University (Buckley, 1994). Bitterly disappointed, he left academia at the age of 42, never to return. Psychology's loss proved to be the business world's gain, as Watson went on to become an innovative, successful advertising executive (Brewer, 1991; Coon, 1994).

Watson was extremely influential, but his ideas did not go unchallenged. In Germany opposition came from an emerging school of thought called *Gestalt psychology*. The Gestalt theorists, who were primarily concerned with perception (we'll discuss their ideas in Chapter 4), argued that psychology should continue to study conscious experience rather than overt behavior. Another alternative conception of psychology emerged from Austria, where an obscure physician named Sigmund Freud had been contemplating the mysteries of unconscious mental processes. We'll look at Freud's ideas next.

Freud Brings the Unconscious into the Picture

1a, 10a

Long before he turned his attention to psychology, Sigmund Freud (1856–1939) dreamed of achieving fame by making an important discovery. His determination was such that in medical school he dissected 400 male eels to prove for the first time that they had testes. His work with eels did not make him famous, but his subsequent work with people did. Indeed, his theories made him one of the most influential—and controversial—intellectual figures of modern times.

Freud's (1900, 1933) approach to psychology grew out of his efforts to treat mental disorders. In his medical practice, Freud treated people troubled by psychological problems such as irrational fears, obsessions, and anxieties with an innovative procedure he called *psychoanalysis* (described in detail in Chapter 15). Decades of experience probing into his patients' lives provided much of the inspiration for Freud's theory. He also gathered material by looking inward and examining his own anxieties, conflicts, and desires.

His work with patients and his own self-exploration persuaded Freud of the existence of what he called the *unconscious*. According to Freud, **the** *unconscious* **contains thoughts, memories, and desires that are well below the surface of conscious awareness but that nonetheless exert great influence on behavior.** Freud based his concept of the unconscious on a variety of observations. For instance, he noticed that seemingly

meaningless slips of the tongue (such as "I decided to take a summer school curse") often appeared to reveal a person's true feelings. He also noted that his patients' dreams often seemed to express important feelings that they were unaware of. Knitting these and other observations together, Freud eventually concluded that psychological disturbances are largely caused by personal conflicts existing at an unconscious level. More generally, his *psychoanalytic theory* **attempts to explain personality, motivation, and mental disorders by focusing on unconscious determinants of behavior.**

Freud's concept of the unconscious was not entirely new (Rieber, 1998). However, it was a major departure from the prevailing belief that people are fully aware of the forces governing their behavior. In arguing that behavior is governed by unconscious forces, Freud made the disconcerting suggestion that people are not masters of their own minds. Other aspects of Freud's theory also stirred up debate. For instance, he proposed that behavior is greatly influenced by how people cope with their sexual urges. At a time when people were far less comfortable discussing sexual issues than they are today, even scientists were offended and scandalized by Freud's emphasis on sex. Small wonder, then, that Freud was soon engulfed in controversy.

In part because of their controversial nature, Freud's ideas gained influence only very slowly. By 1920 psychoanalytic theory was widely known around the world, but it continued to meet with considerable resistance in psychology. Why? The main reason was that it conflicted with the spirit of

The unconscious is the true psychical reality; in its innermost nature it is as much unknown to us as the reality of the external world.
SIGMUND FREUD
1856–1939

A portrait taken at the famous Clark University psychology conference, September 1909. Pictured are Freud, G. Stanley Hall, and four of Freud's students and associates. Seated, left to right: Freud, Hall, and Carl Jung; standing: Abraham Brill, Ernest Jones, and Sandor Ferenczi.

the times in psychology. Many psychologists were becoming uncomfortable with their earlier focus on conscious experience and were turning to the less murky subject of observable behavior. If they felt that conscious experience was inaccessible to scientific observation, you can imagine how they felt about trying to study unconscious experience. Most psychologists contemptuously viewed psychoanalytic theory as unscientific speculation that would eventually fade away (Hornstein, 1992).

They turned out to be wrong. Psychoanalytic ideas steadily gained acceptance in the culture at large, influencing thought in medicine, the arts, and literature (Rieber, 1998). Then, in the 1930s and 1940s, more and more psychologists found themselves becoming interested in areas Freud had studied: personality, motivation, and abnormal behavior. As they turned to these topics, many of them saw merit in some of Freud's notions (Rosenzweig, 1985). Although psychoanalytic theory continued to generate heated debate, it survived to become an influential theoretical perspective. Today, many psychoanalytic concepts have filtered into the mainstream of psychology (Hillner, 1984; Westen, 1998).

Skinner Questions Free Will as Behaviorism Flourishes

While psychoanalytic thought was slowly gaining a foothold within psychology, the behaviorists were temporarily softening their stance on the acceptability of studying internal mental events. However, this movement toward the consideration of internal states was dramatically reversed in the 1950s by the work of B. F. Skinner (1904–1990), one of the most influential of all American psychologists. In

"I submit that what we call the behavior of the human organism is no more free than its digestion"
B. F. SKINNER
1904–1990

response to the softening in the behaviorist position, Skinner (1953) championed a return to Watson's strict stimulus-response approach. Skinner did not deny the existence of internal mental events. However, he insisted that they could not be studied scientifically. Moreover, he maintained, there was no need to study them. According to Skinner, if the stimulus of food is followed by the response of eating, we can fully describe what is happening without making any guesses about whether the animal is experiencing hunger. Like Watson, Skinner also emphasized how environmental factors mold behavior. Although he repeatedly acknowledged that an organism's behavior is influenced by its biological endowment, he argued that psychology could understand and predict behavior adequately without resorting to physiological explanations (Delprato & Midgley, 1992).

The fundamental principle of behavior documented by Skinner is deceptively simple: *Organisms tend to repeat responses that lead to positive outcomes, and they tend not to repeat responses that lead to neutral or negative outcomes.* Despite its simplicity, this principle turns out to be quite powerful. Working primarily with laboratory rats and pigeons, Skinner showed that he could exert remarkable control over the behavior of animals by manipulating the outcomes of their responses. He was even able to train animals to perform unnatural behaviors. For example, he once trained some pigeons to play Ping-Pong! Skinner's followers eventually showed that the principles uncovered in their animal research could be applied to complex human behaviors as well. Behavioral principles are now widely used in factories, schools, prisons, mental hospitals, and a variety of other settings.

Skinner's ideas had repercussions that went far beyond the debate among psychologists about what they should study. Skinner spelled out the full implications of his findings in his book *Beyond Freedom and Dignity* (1971). There he asserted that all behavior is fully governed by external stimuli. In other words, your behavior is determined in predictable ways by lawful principles, just as the flight of an arrow is governed by the laws of physics. Thus, if you believe that your actions are the result of conscious decisions, you're wrong. According to Skinner, we are all controlled by our environment, not by ourselves. In short, Skinner arrived at the conclusion that *free will is an illusion.*

As you can readily imagine, such a disconcerting view of human nature was not universally acclaimed. Like Freud, Skinner was the target of harsh criticism. Despite the controversy, however,

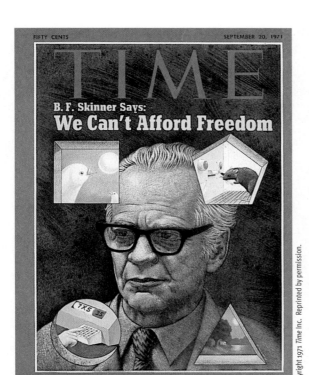

B. F. Skinner created considerable controversy when he asserted that free will is an illusion.

behaviorism flourished as the dominant school of thought in psychology during the 1950s and 1960s (Gilgen, 1982). And when 93 psychology department chairpersons were surveyed in 1990 about the field's most important contributors (Estes, Coston, & Fournet, 1990), Skinner was ranked at the top of the list (see Figure 1.3).

The Humanists Revolt 1a, 10C

By the 1950s behaviorism and psychoanalytic theory had become the most influential schools of thought in psychology. However, many psychologists found these theoretical orientations unappealing. The principal charge hurled at both schools was that they were "dehumanizing." Psychoanalytic theory was attacked for its belief that behavior is dominated by primitive, sexual urges. Behaviorism was criticized for its preoccupation with the study of simple animal behavior. Both theories were criticized because they suggested that people are not masters of their own destinies. Above all, many people argued, both schools of thought failed to recognize the unique qualities of *human* behavior.

Beginning in the 1950s, the diverse opposition to behaviorism and psychoanalytic theory blended into a loose alliance that eventually became a new school of thought called "humanism" (Bühler &

Allen, 1972). In psychology, ***humanism* is a theoretical orientation that emphasizes the unique qualities of humans, especially their freedom and their potential for personal growth.** Some of the key differences between the humanistic, psychoanalytic, and behavioral viewpoints are summarized in Table 1.1 on the next page, which compares six contemporary theoretical perspectives in psychology.

Humanists take an *optimistic* view of human nature. They maintain that people are not pawns of either their animal heritage or environmental circumstances. Furthermore, they say, because humans are fundamentally different from other animals, research on animals has little relevance to the understanding of human behavior. The most prominent architects of the humanistic movement have been Carl Rogers (1902–1987) and Abraham Maslow (1908–1970). Rogers (1951) argued that human behavior is governed primarily by each individual's sense of self, or "self-concept"—which animals presumably lack. Both he and Maslow (1954) maintained that to fully understand people's behavior, psychologists must take into account the fundamental human drive toward personal growth. They asserted that people have a basic need to continue to evolve as human beings and to fulfill their potentials.

Fragmentation and dissension have reduced the influence of humanism in recent decades, although some advocates are predicting a renaissance for the

Figure 1.3

Important figures in the history of psychology. In a 1990 survey, 93 chairpersons of psychology departments ranked psychology's most important contributors (Estes, Coston, & Fournet, 1990). As you can see, B. F. Skinner edged out Sigmund Freud for the top ranking. Although these ratings of scholarly eminence are open to considerable debate, the data should give you some idea of the relative impact of various figures discussed in this chapter. : (Adapted from "Historians' and Chairpersons' Judgements of Eminence Among Psychologists," by J. H. Korn, R. Davis & S. F. Davis, 1991, *American Psychologist, 46* (7), 789-792, [with data from "Rankings of the Most Notable Psychologists by Department Chairpersons," by R. E. Estes, M. L. Coston & G. P. Fournet, 1990, unpublished manuscript, and adapted by permission.] Copyright © 1991 by the American Psychological Association.)

Rank	Individual	Rank Points
1	B. F. Skinner	508
2	Sigmund Freud	459
3	William James	372
4	Jean Piaget	237
5	G. Stanley Hall	216
6	Wilhelm Wundt	203
7	Carl Rogers	192
8	John B. Watson	188
9	Ivan Pavlov	152
10	E. L. Thorndike	124

It seems to me that at bottom each person is asking, "Who am I, really? How can I get in touch with this real self, underlying all my surface behavior? How can I become myself?"
CARL ROGERS
1902–1987

Web Link 1.3

History and Philosophy of Psychology Web Resources
Christopher Green of York University in Canada has assembled a wide range of Web-based materials relating to psychology's theoretical and historical past, including a collection of sites focused on specific individuals. Web pages devoted to key figures mentioned in this chapter (such as Mary Whiton Calkins, William James, B. F. Skinner, and Margaret Floy Washburn) can be accessed here.

Perspective and Its Influential Period	Principal Contributors	Subject Matter	Basic Premise
Behavioral (1913–present)	John B. Watson Ivan Pavlov B. F. Skinner	Effects of environment on the overt behavior of humans and animals	Only observable events (stimulus-response relations) can be studied scientifically.
Psychoanalytic (1900–present)	Sigmund Freud Carl Jung Alfred Adler	Unconscious determinants of behavior	Unconscious motives and experiences in early childhood govern personality and mental disorders.
Humanistic (1950s–present)	Carl Rogers Abraham Maslow	Unique aspects of human experience	Humans are free, rational beings with the potential for personal growth, and they are fundamentally different from animals.
Cognitive (1950s–present)	Jean Piaget Noam Chomsky Herbert Simon	Thoughts; mental processes	Human behavior cannot be fully understood without examining how people acquire, store, and process information.
Biological (1950s–present)	James Olds Roger Sperry David Hubel Torsten Wiesel	Physiological bases of behavior in humans and animals	An organism's functioning can be explained in terms of the bodily structures and biochemical processes that underlie behavior.
Evolutionary (1980s–present)	David Buss Martin Daly Margo Wilson Leda Cosmides John Tooby	Evolutionary bases of behavior in humans and animals	Behavior patterns have evolved to solve adaptive problems; natural selection favors behaviors that enhance reproductive success.

humanistic movement (Taylor, 1999). To date, the humanists' greatest contribution to psychology has probably been their innovative treatments for psychological problems and disorders. More generally, the humanists have argued eloquently for a different picture of human nature than those implied by psychoanalysis and behaviorism (Wertz, 1998).

Psychology Comes of Age as a Profession

1a

The 1950s also saw psychology come of age as a profession. As you know, psychology is not all pure science. It has a highly practical side. Many psychologists provide a variety of professional services to the public. Their work falls within the domain of *applied psychology,* **the branch of psychology concerned with everyday, practical problems.**

This branch of psychology, which is so prominent today, was actually slow to develop. Although the first psychological clinic was established as early as 1896, few psychologists were concerned with applications of their science until World War I (1914–1918). The war created a huge demand for mental testing of military personnel so that recruits could be assigned to jobs according to their abilities. The war thus brought many psychologists into the applied arena for the first time and established mental testing as a routine professional activity conducted by psychologists.

After World War I, psychology continued to grow as a profession, but only very slowly. The principal professional arm of psychology was *clinical psychology.* As practiced today, **clinical psychology is the branch of psychology concerned with the diagnosis and treatment of psychological problems and disorders.** In its early days, however, the emphasis was almost exclusively on psychological testing, and few psychologists were involved in clinical work. As late as 1937 only about one in five psychologists reported an interest in clinical psychology (Goldenberg, 1983).

That picture was about to change with dramatic swiftness. Once again the impetus was a world war. During World War II (1939–1945), many academic psychologists were pressed into service as clinicians. They were needed to screen military recruits and to treat soldiers suffering from trauma. Many of these psychologists (often to their surprise) found the clinical work to be challenging and rewarding, and a substantial portion continued to do clinical work after the war. More significantly, some 40,000 American veterans, many with severe psychological scars, returned to seek postwar

Understanding the Implications of Major Theories: Freud, Skinner, and Rogers

Check your understanding of the implications of some of the major theories reviewed in this chapter by indicating who is likely to have made each of the statements quoted below. Choose from the following: (a) Sigmund Freud, (b) B. F. Skinner, and (c) Carl Rogers. You'll find the answers in Appendix A in the back of the book.

B. **1.** "In the traditional view, a person is free. . . . He can therefore be held responsible for what he does and justly punished if he offends. That view, together with its associated practices, must be reexamined when a scientific analysis reveals unsuspected controlling relations between behavior and environment."

A. **2.** "He that has eyes to see and ears to hear may convince himself that no mortal can keep a secret. If the lips are silent, he chatters with his fingertips; betrayal oozes out of him at every pore. And thus the task of making conscious the most hidden recesses of the mind is one which it is quite possible to accomplish."

C. **3.** "I do not have a Pollyanna view of human nature. . . . Yet one of the most refreshing and invigorating parts of my experience is to work with [my clients] and to discover the strongly positive directional tendencies which exist in them, as in all of us, at the deepest levels."

treatment in Veterans Administration (VA) hospitals. With the demand for clinicians far greater than the supply, the VA stepped in to finance many new training programs in clinical psychology. These programs, emphasizing training in the treatment of psychological disorders as well as in psychological testing, proved attractive. Within a few years, about half of the new Ph.D.'s in psychology were specializing in clinical psychology (Goldenberg, 1983). Thus, during the 1950s the prewar orphan of applied/professional psychology rapidly matured into a robust, powerful adult.

Since the 1950s, the professionalization of psychology has continued at a steady pace. In fact, the trend has spread into additional areas of psychology. Today the broad umbrella of applied psychology covers a variety of professional specialties, including school psychology, industrial and organizational psychology, and counseling psychology. Whereas psychologists were once almost exclusively research scientists, roughly two-thirds of today's psychologists devote some of their time to providing professional services.

Psychology Returns to Its Roots: Renewed Interest in Cognition and Physiology

While applied psychology has blossomed in recent years, scientific research has continued to progress. Ironically, two of the latest trends in research hark back a century to psychology's beginning, when psychologists were principally interested in consciousness and physiology. Today psychologists are showing renewed interest in consciousness (now called "cognition") and the physiological bases of behavior.

Cognition **refers to the mental processes involved in acquiring knowledge.** In other words, cognition involves thinking or conscious experience. For many decades, the dominance of behaviorism discouraged investigation of "unobservable" mental processes, and most psychologists showed little interest in cognition. During the 1950s and 1960s, however, this situation slowly began to change. Major progress in the study of cognitive development (Piaget, 1954), memory (Miller, 1956), language (Chomsky, 1957), and problem solving (Newell, Shaw, & Simon, 1958) sparked a surge of interest in cognitive psychology.

Cognitive theorists argue that psychology must study internal mental events to fully understand human behavior (Gardner, 1985; Neisser, 1967). Advocates of the *cognitive perspective* point out that our manipulations of mental images surely influence how we behave. Consequently, focusing exclusively on overt behavior yields an incomplete picture of why we behave as we do. Equally important, psychologists investigating decision making, reasoning, and problem solving have shown that methods *can* be devised to study cognitive processes scientifically. Although the methods are different from those used in psychology's early days, recent research on the inner workings of the mind has put the *psyche* back in contemporary psychology. In fact, many observers maintain that the cognitive perspective has become the dominant perspective in contemporary psychology—and there are some interesting data to support this assertion, which can be seen in Figure 1.4 on the next page (Robins, Gosling, & Craik, 1999).

The 1950s and 1960s also saw many discoveries that highlighted the interrelations among mind, body, and behavior. For example, psychologists

Figure 1.4

The relative prominence of three major schools of thought in psychology. To estimate the relative influence of various theoretical orientations in recent decades, Robins, Gosling, and Craik (1999) analyzed the subject matter of four prestigious, general, flagship publications in psychology, measuring the percentage of articles relevant to each school of thought. Obviously, their approach is just one of many ways one might gauge the prominence of various theoretical orientations. Nonetheless, the data are thought provoking. Their findings suggest that the cognitive perspective surpassed the behavioral perspective in influence sometime around 1970. As you can see, the psychoanalytic perspective has always had a modest impact on the mainstream of psychology. (Adapted from "An Empirical Analysis of Trends in Psychology," by R. W. Robins, S. D. Gosling, & K. H. Craik, 1999, *American Psychologist, 54* (2), 117-128. Copyright © 1999 by the American Psychological Association. Reprinted by permission of the author.)

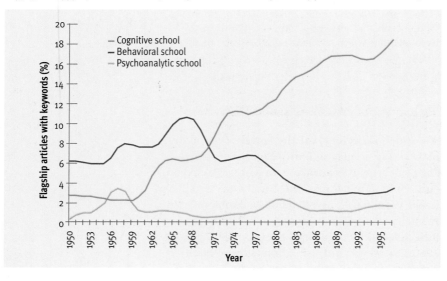

demonstrated that electrical stimulation of the brain could evoke emotional responses such as pleasure and rage in animals (Olds, 1956). Other work, which eventually earned a Nobel prize for Roger Sperry (in 1981), showed that the right and left halves of the brain are specialized to handle different types of mental tasks (Gazzaniga, Bogen, & Sperry, 1965). The 1960s also brought the publication of David Hubel and Torsten Wiesel's (1962, 1963) Nobel-prize–winning work on how visual signals are processed in the brain. These and many other findings stimulated an increase in research on the biological bases of behavior. Advocates of the *biological perspective* maintain that much of human and animal behavior can be explained in terms of the bodily structures and biochemical processes that allow organisms to behave. As you know, in the 19th century the young science of psychology had a heavy physiological emphasis. Thus, the recent interest in the biological bases of behavior represents another return to psychology's heritage.

Although adherents of the cognitive and biological perspectives haven't done as much organized campaigning for their viewpoint as proponents of the older, traditional schools of thought, these newer perspectives have become important theoretical orientations in modern psychology. They are increasingly influential viewpoints regarding what psychology should study and how. The cognitive and biological perspectives are compared to other contemporary theoretical perspectives in Table 1.1.

Psychology Broadens Its Horizons: Increased Interest in Cultural Diversity

Throughout psychology's history, most researchers have worked under the assumption that they were seeking to identify general principles of behavior that would be applicable to all of humanity. In reality, however, psychology has largely been a Western (North American and European) enterprise with a remarkably provincial slant (Gergen et al. 1996). The vast preponderance of research has been conducted in the United States by middle- and upper-class white psychologists who have used mostly middle- and upper-class white males as subjects (Hall, 1997; Segall et al., 1990). Traditionally, Western psychologists have paid scant attention to how well their theories and research might apply to non-Western cultures, to ethnic minorities in Western societies, or even to women as opposed to men.

However, in recent years Western psychologists have begun to recognize that their neglect of cultural variables has diminished the value of their work, and they are devoting increased attention to culture as a determinant of behavior. What brought about this shift? The new interest in culture appears mainly attributable to two recent trends: (1) advances in communication, travel, and international trade have "shrunk" the world and increased global interdependence, bringing more and more Americans and Europeans into contact with people from non-Western cultures, and (2) the ethnic makeup of the Western world has become an increasingly diverse multicultural mosaic (Brislin, 1993; Hermans & Kempen, 1998; Mays et al., 1996).

These trends have prompted more and more Western psychologists to broaden their horizons and incorporate cultural factors into their theories and research (Miller, 1999; Shweder & Sullivan, 1993). These psychologists are striving to study previously underrepresented groups of subjects to test the generality of earlier findings and to catalog both the differences and similarities among cultural groups. They are working to increase knowledge of how culture is transmitted through socialization practices and how culture colors one's view of the world. They are seeking to learn how people cope with cultural change and to find ways to reduce misunderstandings and conflicts in intercultural interactions. In addition, they are trying to enhance understanding of how cultural groups are affected by prejudice, discrimination, and racism. In all these efforts, they are striving to understand the unique experiences of culturally diverse people *from the point of view of those people.* These efforts to ask new questions, study new groups, and apply new perspectives promise to enrich the discipline of psychology as it moves into the 21st century (Betancourt & Lopez, 1993; Fowers & Richardson, 1996).

Psychology Adapts: The Emergence of Evolutionary Psychology

The most recent major development in psychology has been the emergence of *evolutionary psychology,* a new theoretical perspective that is likely to be influential in the years to come. Led most prominently by David Buss (1995, 1996, 1999), evolutionary psychologists assert that the patterns of behavior seen in a species are products of evolution in the same way that anatomical characteristics are. **Evolutionary psychology examines behavioral processes in terms of their adaptive value for members of a species over the course of many generations.** The basic premise of evolutionary psychology is that natural selection favors behaviors that enhance organisms' reproductive success—that is, passing on genes to the next generation. Thus, if a species is highly aggressive, evolutionary psychologists argue that it's because aggressiveness conveys a survival or reproductive advantage for members of that species, so genes that promote aggressiveness are more likely to be passed on to the next generation. Although evolutionary psychologists have a natural interest in animal behavior, they have not been bashful about analyzing the evolutionary bases of human behavior. As La Cerra and Kurzban (1995) put it, "The human mind was sculpted by natural selection, and it is this evolved organ that constitutes the subject matter of psychology" (p. 63).

Consider, for instance, evolutionary psychologists' analysis of differences between males and females in visual-spatial ability. On the average, males tend to perform slightly better than females on visual-spatial tasks involving mental rotation of images, map reading, and maze learning (see Chapter 11). Silverman and Eals (1992) assert that these aspects of spatial ability would have facilitated skill at *hunting,* a chore largely assigned to men over the course of human evolutionary history. In contrast, women have generally had responsibility for *gathering* food rather than hunting it. Hence,

Silverman and Eals hypothesized that females ought to be superior to males on spatial skills that would have facilitated gathering, such as memory for locations, which is exactly what they found in a series of four studies. Thus, evolutionary psychologists explain gender differences in spatial ability—and many other aspects of human behavior—in terms of how such abilities evolved to meet the adaptive pressures faced by our ancestors.

Looking at behavioral patterns in terms of their evolutionary significance is not an entirely new idea (Graziano, 1995). As noted earlier, William James and other functionalists were influenced by Darwin's concept of natural selection over a century ago. Until recently, however, applications of evolutionary concepts to *psychological* processes were piecemeal, half-hearted, and not particularly well received. The 1960s and 1970s brought major breakthroughs in the field of evolutionary *biology* (Hamilton, 1964; Trivers, 1971, 1972; Williams, 1966), but these advances had little immediate impact in psychology. The situation began to change in the middle to late 1980s. A growing cadre of evolutionary psychologists—led by David Buss (1985, 1988, 1989), Martin Daly and Margo Wilson (1985, 1988), and Leda Cosmides and John Tooby (Cosmides & Tooby, 1989; Tooby & Cosmides, 1989)—published widely cited studies on a broad range of topics, including mating preferences, jealousy, aggression, sexual behavior, language, decision making, personality, and development. In 1989–1990, Buss, Daly, Wilson, Cosmides, and Tooby gathered at the Center for Advanced Study in the Behavioral Sciences in Palo Alto, California to sketch out an ambitious research agenda for evolutionary psychology (Buss, 1999). By the mid-1990s, it became clear that psychology was witnessing the birth of its first major, new theoretical perspective since the cognitive revolution in the 1950s and 1960s.

As with all prominent theoretical perspectives in psychology, evolutionary theory has its critics (Caporael & Brewer, 1995; Gould, 1993). Among other things, they argue that evolutionary theory is untestable and that evolutionary explanations are *post hoc* accounts for obvious behavioral phenomena. However, evolutionary psychologists have articulated persuasive rebuttals to these and other criticisms, and the evolutionary perspective is rapidly gaining acceptance (Kenrick, 1995). Advocates of the evolutionary approach have heralded it as an "immense advance over traditional perspectives" (Masters, 1995, p. 65), a "revolutionary scientific paradigm" (Buss, 1995, p. 85), and a "renaissance in the sciences of mind" (La Cerra & Kurzban, 1995, p. 62).

These proclamations will probably prove to be overly enthusiastic, as is often the case when a new school of thought strives to establish its identity. Nonetheless, evolutionary psychology undeniably provides a thought-provoking, innovative perspective that is rapidly gaining influence and promises to shake things up in the future.

Our review of psychology's past has shown how the field has evolved. We have seen psychology develop from philosophical speculation into a rigorous science committed to research. We have seen how a highly visible professional arm involved in mental health services emerged from this science. We have seen how psychology's focus on physiology is rooted in its 19th-century origins. We have seen how and why psychologists began conducting research on lower animals. We have seen how psychology has evolved from the study of mind and body to the study of behavior. And we have seen how the investigation of mind and body has been welcomed back into the mainstream of modern psychology. We have seen how different theoretical schools have defined the scope and mission of psychology in different ways. We have seen how psychology's interests have expanded and become increasingly diverse. Above all else, we have seen that psychology is a growing, evolving intellectual enterprise.

Psychology's history is already rich, but its story has barely begun. The century or so that has elapsed since Wilhelm Wundt put psychology on a scientific footing is only an eyeblink of time in human history. What has been discovered during those years, and what remains unknown, is the subject of the rest of this book.

Psychology Today: Vigorous and Diversified

We began this chapter with an informal description of what psychology is about. Now that you have a feel for how psychology has developed, you can better appreciate a definition that does justice to the field's modern diversity: *Psychology* **is the science that studies behavior and the physiological and cognitive processes that underlie behavior, and it is the profession that applies the accumulated knowledge of this science to practical problems.**

Contemporary psychology is a thriving science and profession. Its growth has been remarkable. One simple index of this growth is the dramatic rise in membership in the American Psychological Association (APA), a national organization devoted to the advancement of psychology. The APA was founded in 1892 with just 26 members. Today, the APA has over 80,000 members. Moreover, as Figure 1.5 shows, APA membership has increased eightfold since 1950. In the United States, psychology now accounts for about 10% of all doctoral degrees awarded in the sciences and humanities. The comparable figure in 1945 was only 4% (Howard et al., 1986). Of course, psychology is an international enterprise. Today, over 1100 technical journals from all over the world publish research articles on psychology. Thus, by any standard of measurement—the number of people involved, the number of degrees granted, the number of studies conducted, the number of journals published—psychology is a healthy, growing field.

Psychology's vigorous presence in modern society is also demonstrated by the great variety of settings in which psychologists work. The distribution of psychologists employed in various categories of settings can be seen in Figure 1.6. Psychologists were once found almost exclusively in the halls of academia. However, today only about one-fourth of

Web Link 1.5

Psychology: Careers for the 21st Century
This online guide from the American Psychological Association describes what psychologists actually do and how students can prepare themselves to become psychology's next generation. The personal stories of 15 psychologists demonstrate the many career paths available.

Figure 1.5

Membership in the American Psychological Association, 1900–1999. The steep rise in the number of psychologists in the APA since 1950 testifies to psychology's remarkable growth as a science and a profession. If student affiliates are also counted, the APA has over 150,000 members. (Adapted from data from the American Psychological Association by permission.)

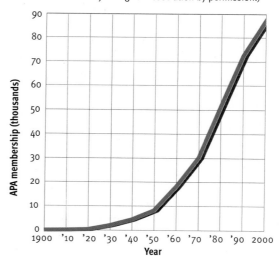

American psychologists work in colleges and universities. The remaining three-fourths work in hospitals, clinics, police departments, research institutes, government agencies, business and industry, schools, nursing homes, counseling centers, and private practice.

Clearly, contemporary psychology is a multifaceted field, a fact that is especially apparent when we consider the many areas of specialization within psychology today. Let's look at the current areas of specialization in both the science and the profession of psychology.

Research Areas in Psychology

Although most psychologists receive broad training that provides them with knowledge about many areas of psychology, they usually specialize when it comes to doing research. Such specialization is necessary because the subject matter of psychology has become so vast over the years. Today it is virtually impossible for anyone to stay abreast of the new research in all specialties. Specialization is also necessary because specific skills and training are required to do research in some areas.

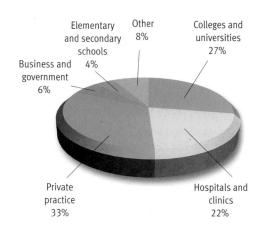

Figure 1.6

Employment of psychologists by setting. The work settings in which psychologists are employed have become quite diverse. Survey data on the primary employment setting of APA members indicate that one-third are in private practice (compared to 12% in 1976) and only 27% work in colleges and universities (compared to 47% in 1976). (Data based on 1997 APA Directory Survey)

Web Link 1.6

Marky Lloyd's Career Page
For those who think they might want to find a job or career in psychology or a related field, Marky Lloyd of Georgia Southern University has put together a fine set of resources to help in both planning and making choices.

The seven major research areas in modern psychology are (1) developmental psychology, (2) social psychology, (3) experimental psychology, (4) physiological psychology, (5) cognitive psychology, (6) personality, and (7) psychometrics. Figure 1.7 describes these areas briefly and shows the percentage of research psychologists who identify each area as their primary interest (American Psychological Association, 1997). As you can see, social psychology and developmental psychology have become especially popular areas of specialization.

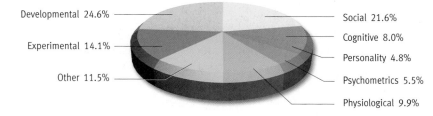

Area	Focus of research
Developmental psychology	Looks at human development across the life span. Developmental psychology once focused primarily on child development but today devotes a great deal of research to adolescence, adulthood, and old age.
Social psychology	Focuses on interpersonal behavior and the role of social forces in governing behavior. Typical topics include attitude formation, attitude change, prejudice, conformity, attraction, aggression, intimate relationships, and behavior in groups.
Experimental psychology	Encompasses the traditional core of topics that psychology focused on heavily in its first half-century as a science: sensation, perception, learning, conditioning, motivation, and emotion. The name experimental psychology is somewhat misleading, as this is not the only area in which experiments are done. Psychologists working in all the areas listed here conduct experiments.
Physiological psychology	Examines the influence of genetic factors on behavior and the role of the brain, nervous system, endocrine system, and bodily chemicals in the regulation of behavior.
Cognitive psychology	Focuses on "higher" mental processes, such as memory, reasoning, information processing, language, problem solving, decision making, and creativity.
Personality	Is interested in describing and understanding individuals' consistency in behavior, which represents their personality. This area of interest is also concerned with the factors that shape personality and with personality assessment.
Psychometrics	Is concerned with the measurement of behavior and capacities, usually through the development of psychological tests. Psychometrics is involved with the design of tests to assess personality, intelligence, and a wide range of abilities. It is also concerned with the development of new techniques for statistical analysis.

Figure 1.7

Major research areas in contemporary psychology. Most research psychologists specialize in one of the seven broad areas described here. The figures in the pie chart reflect the percentage of research psychologists belonging to the APA who identify each area as their primary interest. (Data based on 1997 APA Directory Survey)

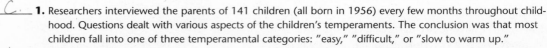

Understanding the Major Research Areas in Contemporary Psychology

Check your understanding of the various research areas in psychology reviewed in this chapter by indicating which type of psychologist would be most likely to perform each of the investigations described below. Choose from the following: (a) physiological psychology, (b) cognitive psychology, (c) developmental psychology, (d) psychometrics, and (e) personality. You'll find the answers in Appendix A at the back of the book.

_C._ **1.** Researchers interviewed the parents of 141 children (all born in 1956) every few months throughout child-hood. Questions dealt with various aspects of the children's temperaments. The conclusion was that most children fall into one of three temperamental categories: "easy," "difficult," or "slow to warm up."

_A_ **2.** It was discovered that rats will work extremely hard (pressing a lever, for instance) to earn small amounts of electrical stimulation directed to specific areas of their brains. Research indicates that the human brain may also contain similar "pleasure centers."

_E._ **3.** The Sensation Seeking Scale (SSS) was developed to measure individual differences in the extent to which people prefer high or low levels of sensory stimulation. People such as skydivers tend to score high on the SSS, while someone whose idea of a good time is settling down with a good book would tend to score low.

Web Link 1.7

A Student's Guide to Careers in the Helping Professions
Prepared by Melissa J. Himeline of the University of North Carolina at Asheville, this online guide provides detailed career information for 15 of the most important helping professions that psychology majors often consider entering.

Professional Specialties in Psychology

Within applied psychology there are four clearly identified areas of specialization: (1) clinical psychology, (2) counseling psychology, (3) educational and school psychology, and (4) industrial and organizational psychology. Descriptions of these specialties can be found in Figure 1.8, along with the percentage of professional psychologists specializing in each area (American Psychological Association, 1997). As the figure indicates, clinical

psychology is currently the most widely practiced professional specialty.

The data in Figures 1.7 and 1.8 are based on psychologists' reports of their single, principal area of specialization. However, many psychologists work on both research and application. Some academic psychologists work as consultants, therapists, and counselors on a part-time basis. Similarly, some applied psychologists conduct basic research on issues related to their specialty. For example, many clinical psychologists are involved in research on the nature and causes of abnormal behavior.

Clinical 67.5%
Other 3.2%
Industrial/organizational 5.5%
Counseling 15.0%
Educational/school 8.8%

Figure 1.8

Principal professional specialties in contemporary psychology. Most psychologists who deliver professional services to the public specialize in one of the four areas described here. The figures in the pie chart reflect the percentage of applied psychologists belonging to the APA who identify each area as their chief specialty. (Data based on 1997 APA Directory Survey)

Specialty	Focus of professional practice
Clinical psychology	Clinical psychologists are concerned with the evaluation, diagnosis, and treatment of individuals with psychological disorders, as well as treatment of less severe behavioral and emotional problems. Principal activities include interviewing clients, psychological testing, and providing group or individual psychotherapy .
Counseling psychology	Counseling psychology overlaps with clinical psychology in that specialists in both areas engage in similar activities—interviewing, testing, and providing therapy. However, counseling psychologists usually work with a somewhat different clientele, providing assistance to people struggling with everyday problems of moderate severity. Thus, they often specialize in family, marital, or career counseling.
Educational and school psychology	Educational psychologists work to improve curriculum design, achievement testing, teacher training, and other aspects of the educational process. School psychologists usually work in elementary or secondary schools, where they test and counsel children having difficulties in school and aid parents and teachers in solving school-related problems.
Industrial and organizational psychology	Psychologists in this area perform a wide variety of tasks in the world of business and industry. These tasks include running human resources departments, working to improve staff morale and attitudes, striving to increase job satisfaction and productivity, examining organizational structures and procedures, and making recommendations for improvements.

The enormous breadth and diversity of psychology make it a challenging subject for the beginning student. In the pages ahead you will be introduced to many areas of research and a multitude of new ideas, concepts, and principles. Fortunately, all ideas are not created equal. Some are far more important than others. In this section, I will highlight seven fundamental themes that will reappear in a number of variations as we move from one area of psychology to another in this text. You have already met some of these key ideas in our review of psychology's past and present. Now we will isolate them and highlight their significance. In the remainder of the book these ideas serve as organizing themes to provide threads of continuity across chapters and to help you see the connections among the various areas of research in psychology.

In studying psychology, you are learning about both behavior and the scientific discipline that investigates it. Accordingly, our seven themes come in two sets. The first set consists of statements highlighting crucial aspects of psychology as a way of thinking and as a field of study. The second set consists of broad generalizations about psychology's subject matter: behavior and the cognitive and physiological processes that underlie it.

Themes Related to Psychology as a Field of Study

Looking at psychology as a field of study, we see three crucial ideas: (1) psychology is empirical; (2) psychology is theoretically diverse; and (3) psychology evolves in a sociohistorical context. Let's look at each of these ideas in more detail.

Theme 1: Psychology Is Empirical

Everyone tries to understand behavior. Most of us have developed our own personal answers to such questions as why some people are hard workers, why some are overweight, and why others stay in demeaning relationships. If all of us are amateur psychologists, what makes scientific psychology different? The critical difference is that psychology is *empirical*.

What do we mean by empirical? **Empiricism is the premise that knowledge should be acquired through observation.** This premise is crucial to the scientific method that psychology embraced in the late 19th century. To say that psychology is empirical means that its conclusions are based on direct observation rather than on reasoning, speculation, traditional beliefs, or common sense. Psychologists are not content with having ideas that sound plausible. They conduct research to test their ideas. Is intelligence higher on the average in some social classes than in others? Are men more aggressive than women? Psychologists find a way to make direct, objective, and precise observations to answer such questions.

The empirical approach requires a certain attitude—a healthy brand of skepticism. Empiricism is a tough taskmaster. It demands data and documentation. Psychologists' commitment to empiricism means that they must learn to think critically about generalizations concerning behavior. If someone

CONCEPT CHECK 1.4

Understanding the Principal Professional Specialties in Contemporary Psychology

Check your understanding of the four major professional specialties in psychology reviewed in this chapter by indicating which type of psychologist would be most likely to deal with each of the situations described below. Choose from the following: (a) clinical psychology, (b) counseling psychology, (c) educational and school psychology, and (d) industrial and organizational psychology. You'll find the answers in Appendix A at the back of the book.

_D._ **1.** Many American companies are concerned that their employees seem to be less productive in their jobs and to have less positive feelings about their work than do workers in other countries.

_C._ **2.** In recent years much concern has been expressed about whether American children are being adequately equipped with the tools they need for individual and collective success in our rapidly changing world. One result of this concern is an increase in the amount of achievement testing required of children.

_A._ **3.** The often-bizarre condition of multiple personality disorder was once thought to be rare, but some clinicians and researchers increasingly believe that the disorder is much more common than previously suspected.

_B._ **4.** The number of occupations available is growing, yet many students feel that they could use more assistance with their vocational decisions.

asserts that people tend to get depressed around Christmas, a psychologist is likely to ask, "How many people get depressed? In what population? In comparison to what baseline rate of depression? How is depression defined and measured?" Their skeptical attitude means that psychologists are trained to ask, "Where's the evidence? How do you know?" If psychology's empirical orientation rubs off on you (and I hope it does), you will be asking similar questions by the time you finish this book.

Theme 2: Psychology Is Theoretically Diverse

Although psychology is based on observation, a string of unrelated observations would not be terribly enlightening. Psychologists do not set out to just collect isolated facts; they seek to explain and understand what they observe. To achieve these goals they must construct theories. **A *theory* is a system of interrelated ideas used to explain a set of observations.** In other words, a theory links apparently unrelated observations and tries to explain them. As an example, consider Sigmund Freud's observations about slips of the tongue, dreams, and psychological disturbances. On the surface, these observations appear unrelated. By devising the concept of the *unconscious,* Freud created a theory that links and explains these seemingly unrelated aspects of behavior.

Our review of psychology's past should have made one thing abundantly clear: psychology is marked by theoretical diversity. Why do we have so many competing points of view? One reason is that no single theory can adequately explain everything that is known about behavior. Sometimes different theories focus on different aspects of behavior—that is, different collections of observations. Sometimes there is simply more than one way to look at something. Is the glass half empty or half full? Obviously, it is both. To take an example from another science, physicists wrestled for years with the nature of light. Is it a wave, or is it a particle? In the end, it proved useful to think of light sometimes as a wave and sometimes as a particle. Similarly, if a business executive lashes out at her employees with stinging criticism, is she releasing pent-up aggressive urges (a psychoanalytic view)? Is she making a habitual response to the stimulus of incompetent work (a behavioral view)? Or is she scheming to motivate her employees with "mind games" (a cognitive view)? In some cases, all three of these explanations might have some validity. In short, it is an oversimplification to expect that one view has to be right while all others are wrong. Life is rarely that simple.

Students are often troubled by psychology's many conflicting theories, which they view as a weakness. *However, contemporary psychologists increasingly recognize that theoretical diversity is a strength rather than a weakness* (Hilgard, 1987). As we proceed through this text, you will see how clashing theories have stimulated productive research and how several theoretical perspectives often provide a more complete understanding of behavior than could be achieved by any one perspective alone.

Theme 3: Psychology Evolves in a Sociohistorical Context

Science is often seen as an "ivory tower" undertaking, isolated from the ebb and flow of everyday life. In reality, however, psychology and other sciences do not exist in a cultural vacuum. Dense interconnections exist between what happens in psychology and what happens in society at large (Altman, 1990; Danziger, 1990). Trends, issues, and values in society influence psychology's evolution. Similarly, progress in psychology affects trends, issues, and values in society. To put it briefly, psychology develops in a *sociohistorical* (social and historical) context.

Our review of psychology's past is filled with examples of how social trends have left their imprint on psychology. For example, Sigmund Freud's groundbreaking ideas emerged out of a specific sociohistorical context. Cultural values in Freud's era encouraged the suppression of sexuality. Hence, people tended to feel guilty about their sexual urges to a much greater extent than is common today. This situation clearly contributed to Freud's emphasis on unconscious sexual conflicts. As another example, consider how World War II sparked the rapid growth of psychology as a profession.

If we reverse our viewpoint, we can see that psychology has in turn left its mark on society. Consider, for instance, the pervasive role of mental testing in modern society. Your own career success may depend in part on how well you weave your way through a complex maze of intelligence and achievement tests made possible (to the regret of some) by research in psychology. As another example of psychology's impact on society, consider the influence that various theorists have had on parenting styles. Trends in child-rearing practices have been shaped by the ideas of John B. Watson, Sigmund Freud, B. F. Skinner, and Carl Rogers—not to mention a host of additional psychologists yet to be discussed. In short, society and psychology influence each other in complex ways. In the chapters to come, we will frequently have occasion to notice this dynamic relationship.

© Bob Daemmrich/Stock Boston

Social trends and values have shaped the evolution of psychology and progress in psychology has left its mark on everyday life in our society. For example, standardized psychological tests are pervasive in our educational system where they exert great influence over students lives.

Themes Related to Psychology's Subject Matter

Looking at psychology's subject matter, we see four additional crucial ideas: (4) behavior is determined by multiple causes; (5) our behavior is shaped by our cultural heritage; (6) heredity and environment jointly influence behavior; and (7) our experience of the world is highly subjective.

Theme 4: Behavior Is Determined by Multiple Causes

As psychology has matured, it has provided more and more information about the forces that govern behavior. This growing knowledge has led to a deeper appreciation of a simple but important fact: Behavior is exceedingly complex and most aspects of behavior are determined by multiple causes.

Although the complexity of behavior may seem self-evident, people usually think in terms of single causes. Thus, they offer explanations such as "Andrea flunked out of school because she is lazy." Or they assert that "teenage pregnancies are increasing because of all the sex in the media." Single-cause explanations are sometimes accurate insofar as they go, but they usually are incomplete. In general, psychologists find that behavior is governed by a complex network of interacting factors, an idea referred to as the *multifactorial causation of behavior.*

As a simple illustration, consider the multiple factors that might influence your performance in your introductory psychology course. Relevant personal factors might include your overall intelligence, your reading ability, your memory skills, your motivation, and your study skills. In addition, your grade could be affected by numerous situational factors, including whether you like your psychology professor, whether you like your assigned text, whether the class meets at a good time for you, whether your work schedule is light or heavy, and whether you're having any personal problems. As you proceed through this book, you will learn that complexity of causation is the rule rather than the exception. If we expect to understand behavior, we usually have to take into account multiple determinants.

Theme 5: Our Behavior Is Shaped by Our Cultural Heritage

Among the multiple determinants of human behavior, cultural factors are particularly prominent. Just as psychology evolves in a sociohistorical context, so, too, do individuals. Our cultural backgrounds exert considerable influence over our behavior. What is *culture?* It's the human-made part of our environment. More specifically, *culture* **refers to the widely shared customs, beliefs, values, norms, institutions, and other products of a community that are transmitted socially across generations.** Culture is a very broad construct, encompassing everything from a society's legal system to its assumptions about family roles, from its dietary habits to its political ideals, from its technology to its attitudes about time, from its modes of dress to its spiritual beliefs, and from its art and music to its unspoken rules about sexual liaisons. We tend to think of culture as belonging to entire societies or broad ethnic groups within societies—which it does—but the concept can also be applied to small groups (a tiny Aboriginal tribe in Australia, for example) and to nonethnic groups (gay/homosexual culture, for instance).

Much of one's cultural heritage is invisible (Brislin, 1993). Assumptions, ideals, attitudes, beliefs, and unspoken rules exist in people's minds and may not be readily apparent to outsiders. Moreover, because our cultural background is widely shared, we feel little need to discuss it with others, and we often take it for granted. For example, you probably don't spend much time thinking about the importance of living in rectangular rooms, trying to minimize body odor, limiting yourself to one spouse at a time, or using credit cards to obtain material goods and services. Although we generally fail to appreciate its influence, our cultural heritage has a pervasive impact on our thoughts, feelings, and behavior.

Let's look at a couple examples of this influence. In North America, when people are invited to dinner in someone's home they generally show their appreciation of their host's cooking efforts by eating all of the food they are served. In India, this behavior would be insulting to the host, as guests are expected to leave some food on their plates. The leftover food acknowledges the generosity of the host, implying that he or she provided so much food the guest could not eat it all (Moghaddam, Taylor, & Wright, 1993). Cultures also vary in their emphasis on punctuality. In North America, we expect people to show up for meetings on time; if someone is more than 10 to 15 minutes late, we begin to get upset. We generally strive to be on time, and many of us are quite proud of our precise and dependable punctuality. However, in many Asian and Latin American countries, social obligations that arise at the last minute are given just as much priority as scheduled commitments. Hence, people often show up for important meetings an hour or two late with little remorse, and they may be quite puzzled by the consternation of their Western visitors (Brislin, 1993). These examples may seem trivial, but culture can also influence crucial matters, such as educational success, physical health, and a host of other things, as you will see throughout this book.

In discussing the importance of culture, Segall and his colleagues (1990) go so far as to assert that "it is rare (perhaps even impossible) for any human being ever to behave without responding to some aspect of culture" (p. 5). Although the influence of culture is everywhere, generalizations about cultural groups must always be tempered by the realization that great diversity exists within any society or ethnic group. Researchers may be able to pinpoint genuinely useful insights about Ethiopian, Korean American, or Ukrainian culture, for example, but it would be foolish to assume that all Ethiopians, Korean Americans, or Ukrainians exhibit identical behavior. It is also important to realize that *both differences and similarities in behavior occur across cultures*. As we will see repeatedly, psychological processes are characterized by both cultural variance and invariance. Caveats aside, if we hope to achieve a sound understanding of human behavior, we need to consider cultural determinants.

Theme 6: Heredity and Environment Jointly Influence Behavior

Are we who we are—athletic or artistic, quick-tempered or calm, shy or outgoing, energetic or laid back—because of our genetic inheritance or because of our upbringing? This question about the importance of nature versus nurture, or heredity versus environment, has been asked in one form or another since ancient times. Historically, the nature versus nurture question was framed as an all-or-none proposition. In other words, theorists argued that personal traits and abilities are governed entirely by heredity or entirely by environment. John B. Watson, for instance, asserted that personality and ability depend almost exclusively on an individual's environment. In contrast, Sir Francis Galton, a pioneer in mental testing, maintained that personality and ability depend almost entirely on genetic inheritance (see Chapter 9).

Today, most psychologists agree that heredity and environment are both important. A century of research has shown that genetics and experience jointly influence individuals' intelligence, temperament, personality, and susceptibility to many psychological disorders (Plomin & Rende, 1991; Rose, 1995). If we ask whether people are born or made, psychology's answer is "Both." This response does not mean that nature versus nurture is a dead issue. Lively debate about the *relative influence* of genetics and experience continues unabated. Furthermore, psychologists are actively seeking to understand the complex ways in which genetic inheritance and experience interact to mold behavior.

Theme 7: Our Experience of the World Is Highly Subjective

People's experience of the world is highly subjective. Even elementary perception—for example, of sights and sounds—is not a passive process. We actively process incoming stimulation, selectively focusing on some aspects of that stimulation while ignoring others. Moreover, we impose organization on the stimuli that we pay attention to. These tendencies combine to make perception personalized and subjective.

The subjectivity of perception was demonstrated nicely in a study by Hastorf and Cantril (1954). They showed students at Princeton and Dartmouth universities a film of a football game between the two schools. The students were told to watch for rules infractions. Both groups saw the same film, but the Princeton students "saw" the Dartmouth players engage in twice as many infractions as the Dartmouth students "saw." The investigators concluded that the game "actually was many different games and that each version of the events that transpired was just as 'real' to a particular person as other versions were to other people" (Hastorf & Cantril, 1954). This study showed how people sometimes see what they *want* to see. Other studies have demonstrated that people also tend to see what they *expect* to see (Kelley, 1950). Thus, it is clear that motives and expectations color our experiences.

Human subjectivity is precisely what the scientific method is designed to counteract. In using the scientific approach, psychologists strive to make their observations as objective as possible. In some respects, overcoming subjectivity is what science is all about. Left to their own subjective experience, people might still believe that the earth is flat and that the sun revolves around it. Thus, psychologists are committed to the scientific approach because they believe it is the most reliable route to accurate knowledge.

Now that you have been introduced to the text's organizing themes, let's turn to an example of how psychological research can be applied to the challenges of everyday life. In our first Personal Application, we'll focus on a subject that should be highly relevant to you: how to be a successful student. In the Critical Thinking Application that follows it, we discuss the nature and importance of critical thinking skills.

CONCEPT CHECK 1.5

Understanding the Seven Key Themes

Check your understanding of the seven key themes introduced in the chapter by matching the vignettes with the themes they exemplify. You'll find the answers in Appendix A.

Themes
1. Psychology is empirical.
2. Psychology is theoretically diverse.
3. Psychology evolves in a sociohistorical context.
4. Behavior is determined by multiple causes.
5. Our behavior is shaped by our cultural heritage.
6. Heredity and environment jointly influence behavior.
7. People's experience of the world is highly subjective.

Vignettes
_2_ **a.** Several or more theoretical models of emotion have contributed to our overall understanding of the dynamics of emotion.
_6_ **b.** According to the stress-vulnerability model, some people are at greater risk for developing certain psychological disorders for genetic reasons. Whether these people actually develop the disorders depends on how much stress they experience in their work, their families, or other areas of their lives.
_4_ **c.** Physical health and illness seem to be influenced by a complex constellation of psychological, biological, and social system variables.
_7_ **d.** One of the difficulties in investigating the effects of drugs on consciousness is that individuals tend to have different experiences with a given drug because of their different expectations.

PERSONAL APPLICATION

Improving Academic Performance

Answer the following "true" or "false."

F 1 If you have a professor who delivers chaotic, hard-to-follow lectures, there is little point in attending class.

F 2 Cramming the night before an exam is an efficient method of study.

F 3 In taking lecture notes, you should try to be a "human tape recorder" (that is, write down everything your professor says).

F 4 You should never change your answers to multiple-choice questions, because your first hunch is your best hunch.

All of the above statements are false. If you answered them all correctly, you may have already acquired the kinds of skills and habits that facilitate academic success. If so, however, you are not typical. Today, many students enter college with poor study skills and habits, and it's not entirely their fault. Our educational system generally provides minimal instruction on good study techniques. In this first Application, I will try to remedy this situation to some extent by reviewing some insights that psychology offers on how to improve academic performance. We will discuss how to promote better study habits, how to enhance reading efforts, how to get more out of lectures, and how to improve test-taking strategies. You may also want to jump ahead and read the Personal Application for Chapter 7, which focuses on how to improve everyday memory.

Developing Sound Study Habits

Effective study is crucial to success in college. Although you may run into a few classmates who boast about getting good grades without studying, you can be sure that if they perform well on exams, they do study. Students who claim otherwise simply want to be viewed as extremely bright rather than as studious.

Learning can be immensely gratifying, but studying usually involves hard work. The first step toward effective study habits is to face up to this reality. You don't have to feel guilty if you don't look forward to studying. Most students don't. Once you accept the premise that studying doesn't come naturally, it should be apparent that you need to set up an organized program to promote adequate study. According to Siebert (1995), such a program should include the following considerations:

1. *Set up a schedule for studying.* If you wait until the urge to study strikes you, you may still be waiting when the exam rolls around. Thus, it is important to allocate definite times to studying. Review your various time obligations (work, chores, and so on) and figure out in advance when you can study. When allotting certain times to studying, keep in mind that you need to be wide awake and alert. Be realistic about how long you can study at one time before you wear down from fatigue. Allow time for study breaks; they can revive sagging concentration.

It's important to write down your study schedule. A written schedule serves as a reminder and increases your commitment to following it. You should begin by setting up a general schedule for the quarter or semester, like the one in Figure 1.9. Then, at the beginning of each week, plan the specific assignments that you intend to

Weekly Activity Schedule

	Monday	Tuesday	Wednesday	Thursday	Friday	Saturday	Sunday
8 A.M.						Work	
9 A.M.	History	Study	History	Study	History	Work	
10 A.M.	Psychology	French	Psychology	French	Psychology	Work	
11 A.M.	Study	French	Study	French	Study	Work	
NOON	Math	Study	Math	Study	Math	Work	Study
1 P.M.							Study
2 P.M.	Study	English	Study	English	Study		Study
3 P.M.	Study	English	Study	English	Study		Study
4 P.M.							
5 P.M.							
6 P.M.	Work	Study	Study	Work			Study
7 P.M.	Work	Study	Study	Work			Study
8 P.M.	Work	Study	Study	Work			Study
9 P.M.	Work	Study	Study	Work			Study
10 P.M.	Work			Work			

Figure 1.9

One student's general activity schedule for a semester. Each week the student fills in the specific assignments to work on during each study period. A formal schedule increases the likelihood of engaging in an adequate amount of study.

work on during each study session. This approach to scheduling should help you avoid cramming for exams at the last minute. Cramming is an ineffective study strategy for most students (Underwood, 1961; Zechmeister & Nyberg, 1982). It will strain your memorization capabilities, can tax your energy level, and may stoke the fires of test anxiety.

In planning your weekly schedule, try to avoid the tendency to put off working on major tasks such as term papers and reports. Time-management experts, such as Alan Lakein (1996), point out that many of us tend to tackle simple, routine tasks first, saving larger tasks for later when we supposedly will have more time. This common tendency leads many of us to repeatedly delay working on major assignments until it's too late to do a good job. You can avoid this trap by breaking major assignments down into smaller component tasks that can be scheduled individually.

2. *Find a place to study where you can concentrate.* Where you study is also important. The key is to find a place where distractions are likely to be minimal. Most people cannot study effectively while the TV or stereo is on or while other people are talking. Don't depend on willpower to carry you through such distractions. It's much easier to plan ahead and avoid the distractions altogether. In fact, you would be wise to set up one or two specific places used solely for study (Hettich, 1998).

3. *Reward your studying.* One reason that it is so difficult to be motivated to study regularly is that the payoffs often lie in the distant future. The ultimate reward, a degree, may be years away. Even more short-term rewards, such as an A in the course, may be weeks or months away. To combat this problem, it helps to give yourself immediate, tangible rewards for studying, such as a snack, TV show, or phone call to a friend. Thus, you should set realistic study goals for yourself and then reward yourself when you meet them. The systematic manipulation of rewards involves harnessing the principles of behavior modification described by B. F. Skinner and other behavioral psychologists. These principles are covered in the Chapter 6 Personal Application.

Improving Your Reading

Much of your study time is spent reading and absorbing information. These efforts must be active. Many students deceive themselves into thinking that they are studying by running a marker through a few sentences here and there in their book. If they do so without thoughtful selectivity, they are simply turning a textbook into a coloring book.

You can use a number of methods to actively attack your reading assignments. One of the more worthwhile strategies is Robinson's (1970) SQ3R method. *SQ3R* **is a study system designed to promote** **effective reading by means of five steps: survey, question, read, recite, and review.** Its name is an acronym for the five steps in the procedure.

Step 1: Survey. Before you plunge into the reading itself, glance over the topic headings in the chapter. Try to get a general overview of the material. If you know where the chapter is going, you can better appreciate and organize the information you are about to read.

Step 2: Question. Once you have an overview of your reading assignment, you should proceed through it one section at a time. Take a look at the heading of the first section and convert it into a question. Doing so is usually quite simple. If the heading is "Prenatal Risk Factors," your question should be "What are sources of risk during prenatal development?" If the heading is "Stereotyping," your question should be "What is stereotyping?" Asking these questions gets you actively involved in your reading and helps you identify the main ideas.

Step 3: Read. Only now, in the third step, are you ready to sink your teeth into the reading. Read only the specific section that you have decided to tackle. Read it with an eye toward answering the question you have just formulated. If necessary, reread the section until you can answer that question. Decide whether the segment addresses any other important questions and answer them as well.

Step 4: Recite. Now that you can answer the key question for the section, recite the answer out loud to yourself in your own words. Don't move on to the next section until you understand the main ideas of the current section. You may want to write down these ideas for review later. When you have fully digested the first section, you may go on to the next. Repeat steps 2 through 4 with the next section. Once you have mastered the crucial points there, you can go on again. Keep repeating steps 2 through 4, section by section, until you finish the chapter.

Some locations, such as the one shown here, are far less conducive to successful studying than others. Most people cannot study very effectively when lots of people are nearby engaging in more enjoyable activities.

© Chuck Pelley/Stock, Boston

Step 5: Review. When you have read the entire chapter, refresh your memory by going back over the key points. Repeat your questions and try to answer them without consulting your book or notes. This review should fortify your retention of the main ideas. It should also help you see how the main ideas are related.

The SQ3R method should probably be applied to many texts on a paragraph-by-paragraph basis. Obviously, this approach will require you to formulate some questions without the benefit of topic headings. If you don't have enough headings, you can simply reverse steps 2 and 3. Read the paragraph first and then formulate a question that addresses the basic idea of the paragraph. Then work at answering the question in your own words. The point is that you can be flexible in your use of the SQ3R technique. *What makes SQ3R effective is that it breaks a reading assignment into manageable parts and requires understanding before you move on.* Any method that accomplishes these goals should enhance your reading.

Getting More Out of Lectures

Although lectures are sometimes boring and tedious, it is a simple fact that poor class attendance is associated with poor grades. For example, in one study (see Figure 1.10), Lindgren (1969) found that absences from class were much more common among "unsuccessful" students (grade average C– or below) than among "successful" students (grade average B or above). Even when you have an instructor who delivers hard-to-follow lectures, it is still important to go to class. If nothing else, you can get a feel for how the instructor thinks, which can help you anticipate the content of exams and respond in the manner expected by your professor.

Fortunately, most lectures are reasonably coherent. Books on study skills (Longman & Atkinson, 1996; Sotiriou, 1996) offer a number of suggestions on how to take good lecture notes, some of which are summarized here:

Figure 1.10

Attendance and grades. When Lindgren (1969) compared the class attendance of successful students (B average or above) and unsuccessful students (C– average or below), he found a clear association between poor attendance and poor grades. (Adapted from *The Psychology of College Success: A Dynamic Approach* by H.C. Lindgren, 1969. John Wiley & Sons. Copyright © 1969 by Henry Clay Lindgren. Adapted by permission of H.C. Lindgren.)

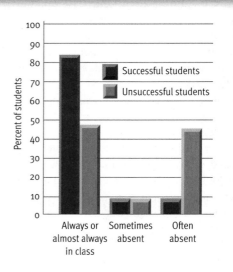

- Extracting information from lectures requires active listening. Focus full attention on the speaker. Try to anticipate what's coming and search for deeper meanings.
- When course material is especially complex, it is a good idea to prepare for the lecture by reading ahead on the scheduled subject in your text. Then you have less brand-new information to digest.
- You are not supposed to be a human tape recorder. Insofar as possible, try to write down the lecturer's thoughts in your own words. Doing so forces you to organize the ideas in a way that makes sense to you. In taking notes, pay attention to clues about what is most important. These clues may range from subtle hints, such as an instructor repeating a point, to not-so-subtle hints, such as an instructor saying "You'll run into this again."
- Asking questions during lectures can be helpful. Doing so keeps you actively involved in the lecture and allows you to clarify points that you may have misunderstood. Many students are more bashful about asking questions than they should be. They don't realize that most professors welcome questions.

Improving Test-Taking Strategies

Let's face it—some students are better than others at taking tests. **Testwiseness is the ability to use the characteristics and format of a cognitive test to maximize one's score.** Students clearly vary in testwiseness, and such variations are reflected in performance on exams (Geiger, 1997; Rogers & Yang, 1996). Testwiseness is *not* a substitute for knowledge of the subject matter. However, skill in taking tests can help you show what you know when it is critical to do so.

A number of myths exist about the best way to take tests. For instance, it is widely believed that students shouldn't go back and change their answers to multiple-choice questions. Benjamin, Cavell, and Shallenberger (1984) found this to be the dominant belief among college *faculty* as well as students (see Figure 1.11). However, the old adage that "your first hunch is your best hunch on tests" has been shown to be wrong. Empirical studies clearly and consistently indicate that, over the long run, changing answers pays off. Benjamin and his colleagues reviewed 20 studies on this issue; their findings are presented in

Figure 1.12. As you can see, answer changes that go from a wrong answer to a right answer outnumber changes that go from a right answer to a wrong one by a sizable margin. The popular belief that answer changing is harmful is probably attributable to painful memories of right-to-wrong changes. In any case, you can see how it pays to be familiar with sound test-taking strategies.

General Tips

The principles of testwiseness were first described by Millman, Bishop, and Ebel (1965). Let's look at some of their general ideas.

- If efficient time use appears crucial, set up a mental schedule for progressing through the test. Make a mental note to check whether you're one-third finished when a third of your time is gone.
- Don't waste time pondering difficult-to-answer questions excessively. If you have no idea at all, just guess and go on. If you need to devote a good deal of time to the question, skip it and mark it so you can return to it later if time permits.
- Adopt the appropriate level of sophistication for the test. Don't read things into questions. Sometimes students make things more complex than they were intended to be. Often, simple-looking questions are just what they appear to be.
- If you complete all of the questions and still have some time remaining, review the test. Make sure that you have recorded your answers correctly. If you were unsure of some answers, go back and reconsider them.

Tips for Multiple-Choice Exams

Sound test-taking strategies are especially important with multiple-choice (and true-false) questions. These types of questions often include clues that may help you converge on the correct answer (Mentzer, 1982; Weiten, 1984). You may be able to improve your performance on such tests by considering the following points:

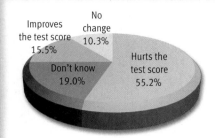

Figure 1.11

Beliefs about the effects of answer changing on tests. Benjamin et al. (1984) asked 58 college faculty whether changing answers on tests is a good idea. Like most students, the majority of the faculty felt that answer changing usually hurts a student's test score, even though the evidence contradicts this belief (see Figure 1.12). (Figures 1.11 and 1.12, adapted from L. T. Benjamin, Jr., et al. © 1994 Lawrence Erlbaum Associates, Inc.)

Figure 1.12

Actual effects of changing answers on multiple-choice tests. When the data from all the relevant studies are combined, they indicate that answer changing on tests generally does not reduce students' test scores (Benjamin et al., 1984). As you can see, wrong-to-right changes outnumber right-to-wrong changes by almost three to one. It is interesting to note the contrast between beliefs about answer changing (see Figure 1.11) and the actual results of this practice, as determined by empirical research.

- As you read the stem of each multiple-choice question, *anticipate* the answer if you can, before looking at the options. If the answer you anticipated is among the options, it is likely to be the correct one.
- Always read each question completely. Continue reading even if you find your anticipated answer among the options. There may be a more complete option farther down the list.
- Learn how to quickly eliminate options that are highly implausible. Many questions have only two plausible options, accompanied by "throwaway" options for filler. You should work at spotting these implausible options so that you can quickly discard them and narrow your choices.
- Be alert to the fact that information relevant to one question is sometimes given away in another test item.
- On items that have "all of the above" as an option, if you know that just two of the options are correct, you should choose "all of the above." If you are confident that one of the options is

incorrect, you should eliminate this option and "all of the above" and choose from the remaining options.
- Options that represent broad, sweeping generalizations tend to be incorrect. You should be vigilant for words such as *always, never, necessarily, only, must, completely, totally,* and so forth that create these improbable assertions.
- In contrast, options that represent carefully qualified statements tend to be correct. Words such as *often, sometimes, perhaps, may,* and *generally* tend to show up in these well-qualified statements.

In summary, sound study skills and habits are crucial to academic success. Intelligence alone won't do the job (although it certainly helps). Good academic skills do not develop overnight. They are acquired gradually, so be patient with yourself. Fortunately, tasks such as reading textbooks, writing papers, and taking tests get easier with practice. Ultimately, I think you'll find that the rewards—knowledge, a sense of accomplishment, and progress toward a degree—are worth the effort.

CRITICAL THINKING APPLICATION

Developing Critical Thinking Skills: An Introduction

If you ask any group of professors, parents, employers, or politicians, "What is the most important outcome of an education?" the most popular answer is likely to be "the development of the ability to think critically." **Critical thinking is the use of cognitive skills and strategies that increase the probability of a desirable outcome.** Such outcomes would include good career choices, effective decisions in the workplace, wise investments, and so forth. In the long run, critical thinkers should have more desirable outcomes than people who are not skilled in critical thinking (Halpern, 1996, 1998). Critical thinking is purposeful, reasoned, goal-directed thinking that involves solving problems, formulating inferences, working with probabilities, and making carefully thought-out decisions. Here are some of the skills exhibited by critical thinkers:

- They understand and use the principles of scientific investigation (How can the effectiveness of punishment as a disciplinary procedure be determined?).
- They apply the rules of formal and informal logic. (If most people disapprove of sex sites on the World Wide Web, then why are these sites so popular?)
- They think effectively in terms of probabilities. (What is the likelihood of being able to predict who will commit a violent crime?)
- They carefully evaluate the quality of information. (Can I trust the claims made by this politician?)
- They analyze arguments for the soundness of the conclusions. (Does the rise in drug use mean a stricter drug policy is needed?).

The topic of thinking has a long history in psychology, dating back to Wilhelm Wundt in the 19th century. Modern cognitive psychologists have found that a useful model of critical thinking has at least two components: It consists of knowledge of the skills of critical thinking—the *cognitive component*—as well as the attitude or disposition of a critical thinker—the *emotional or affective component*. Both are needed for effective critical thinking.

The Skills of Critical Thinking

Instruction in critical thinking is based on two assumptions: (1) a set of skills or strategies exists that students can learn to recognize and apply in appropriate contexts, and (2) if the skills are applied appropriately, students will become more effective thinkers. Critical thinking skills that would be useful in any context might include understanding how reasons and evidence support or refute conclusions; distinguishing among facts, opinions, and reasoned judgments; using principles of likelihood and uncertainty when thinking about probabilistic events; generating multiple solutions to problems and working systematically toward a desired goal; and understanding how causation is determined. This list provides some typical examples of what is meant by the term *critical thinking skills*. Because these skills are useful in a wide variety of contexts, they are sometimes called *transcontextual skills*.

The Attitude of a Critical Thinker

It is of little use to know the skills of critical thinking if you are unwilling to exert the hard mental work to use them or if you have a sloppy or careless attitude toward thinking. A critical thinker is willing to plan, flexible in thinking, persistent, able to admit mistakes and make corrections, and mindful of the thinking process. The use of the word *critical* represents the notion of a critique or evaluation of thinking processes and outcomes. It is not meant to be negative (as in a "critical person") but rather is intended to convey that critical thinkers are vigilant about their thinking.

The Need to Teach Critical Thinking

Decades of research on instruction in critical thinking have shown that the skills and attitudes of critical thinking need to be deliberately and consciously taught because they often do not develop by themselves with standard instruction in a content area (Nisbett, 1993). For this reason, each chapter in this text ends with a "Critical Thinking Application." The material presented in each of these Critical Thinking Applications relates to the chapter topics, but the focus is on how to think about a particular issue, line of research, or controversy. Because the emphasis is on the thinking process, you may be asked to consider conflicting interpretations of data, judge the credibility of information sources, or generate your own testable hypotheses. The specific critical thinking skills highlighted in each Application are summarized in a table so that they are easily identified. Some of the skills will show up in multiple chapters because the goal is to help you spontaneously select the appropriate critical thinking skills when you encounter new information. Repeated practice with selected skills across chapters should help you develop this ability.

An Example

As explained in the main body of the chapter, *evolutionary psychology* is emerging as an influential school of thought. As one example of evolutionary theorizing in psychology, we looked at evolutionary analyses of gender differences in spatial abilities. To show you how critical thinking skills can be applied to psychological issues, let's reexamine the evolutionary explanation of sex differences in spatial talents, expand on it slightly, and then use some critical thinking strategies to evaluate this explanation.

Evolutionary psychologists explain gender differences in spatial abilities in terms of how these abilities presumably evolved to meet the adaptive pressures faced by our ancient ancestors (Silverman & Eals, 1992). These theorists focus on how natural selection would have favored certain skills that would have been adaptive in hunting and gathering societies since most of the human race's time on earth has been spent in such societal arrangements. Specifically, they assert that the typical division of labor between the sexes in hunting and gathering societies created different adaptive pressures for males and females. For example, it is believed that in such societies adult males often traveled long distances to hunt, while the women and children stayed closer to home to gather food. This was an efficient division of labor because women spent much of their adult lives pregnant, nursing, or caring for the young and, therefore, could not travel long distances. Building on these assumptions, evolutionary theorists assert that males tend to perform somewhat better than females on visual-spatial tasks involving mental rotation of images (see Figure 1.13), mental reconstruction of figures, map reading, and maze learning because these skills would have fostered success in the hunting tasks traditionally handled by males (by helping them to traverse long distances, aim projectiles at prey, and so forth). In contrast, the theorists argue that females exhibit a slight superiority on tasks measuring memory for locations because this talent would have fostered success in the foraging and gathering tasks traditionally handled by females (Silverman & Phillips, 1998).

How can you critically evaluate these claims? If your first thought was that you need more information, then good for you, because you are already showing an aptitude for critical thinking. Some additional information about gender differences in cognitive abilities is presented in Chapter 11 of this text. You also need to develop the habit of asking good questions, such as,

"Are there alternative explanations for these results?" "Are there contradictory data?" Let's briefly consider each of these questions.

Are there alternative explanations for gender differences in spatial skills? Well, there certainly are other explanations for males' superiority on most spatial tasks. For example, one could attribute this finding to the sex-typed activities that males are encouraged to engage in more than females, such as playing with building blocks, Lego sets, Lincoln Logs, and various types of construction sets, as well as a host of spatially oriented video games. These sex-typed activities appear to provide boys with more practice than girls on most types of spatial tasks (Baenninger & Newcombe, 1995), and experience with spatial activities appears to enhance spatial skills (Smail, 1983; Subrahmanyam & Greenfield, 1996). If we can explain sex differences in spatial abilities in terms of disparities in the everyday activities of males and females, then we may have no need to appeal to natural selection.

Are there data that run counter to the evolutionary explanation for modern sex differences in spatial skills? Again, the answer is yes. Some scholars who have studied hunting and gathering societies suggest that women often traveled long distances to gather food and that women were often involved in hunting (Adler, 1993). In addition, women wove baskets and clothing and worked on other tasks that required spatial thinking (Halpern, 1997). Moreover—think about it—men on long hunting trips obviously needed to develop a good memory for locations or they might never have returned home. So, there is room for some argument about exactly what kinds of adaptive pressures our ancient ancestors faced.

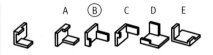

Figure 1.13

An example of a spatial task involving mental rotation. Spatial reasoning tasks can be divided into a variety of subtypes. Studies indicate that males perform slightly better than females on most, but not all, spatial tasks. The tasks on which males are superior often involve mentally rotating objects, such as in the problem shown here. In this problem, the person has to figure out which object on the right (A Through E) could be a rotation of the object at the left. (From Form AA, 1962, *Identical Blocks*, by R. E. Stafford and H. Gullikson.)

A B C D E

"B" is the correct answer.

Thus, you can see how considering alternative explanations and contradictory evidence weakens the evolutionary explanation of gender differences in spatial abilities. The questions we raised about alternative explanations and contradictory data are two generic critical thinking questions that can be asked in a wide variety of contexts. The answers to these questions do *not* prove that evolutionary psychologists are wrong in their explanation of sex differences in visual-spatial skills, but they do *weaken* the evolutionary explanation. In thinking critically about psychological issues, you will see that it makes more sense to talk about the *relative strength of an argument,* as opposed to whether an argument is right or wrong, because we will be dealing with complex issues that rarely lend themselves to being correct or incorrect.

Table 1.2   Critical Thinking Skills Discussed in This Application

Skill	Description
Looking for alternative explanations for findings and events	In evaluating explanations, the critical thinker explores whether other explanations could also account for the findings or events under scrutiny.
Looking for contradictory evidence	In evaluating the evidence presented on an issue, the critical thinker attempts to look for contradictory evidence that may have been left out of the debate.

REVIEW

Key Ideas

From Speculation to Science: How Psychology Developed

● Psychology's intellectual parents were 19th-century philosophy and physiology, which shared an interest in the mysteries of the mind. Psychology was born as an independent discipline when Wilhelm Wundt established the first psychological research laboratory in 1879 at Leipzig, Germany. He argued that psychology should be the scientific study of consciousness. The new discipline grew rapidly in North America in the late 19th century.

● The structuralists believed that psychology should use introspection to analyze consciousness into its basic elements. Functionalists, such as William James, believed that psychology should focus on the purpose and adaptive functions of consciousness. Functionalism left a more enduring imprint on psychology.

● Behaviorists, led by John B. Watson, argued that psychology should study only observable behavior. Thus, they campaigned to redefine psychology as the science of behavior. Emphasizing the importance of the environment over heredity, they often used laboratory animals as research subjects.

● Sigmund Freud's psychoanalytic theory emphasized the unconscious determinants of behavior and the importance of sexuality. Freud's controversial ideas were met with resistance in academic psychology. However, as more psychologists developed an interest in personality, motivation, and abnormal behavior, psychoanalytic concepts were incorporated into mainstream psychology.

● Behaviorism continued as a powerful force in psychology, boosted greatly by B. F. Skinner's research. Like Watson before him, Skinner asserted that psychology should study only observable behavior, and he generated controversy by arguing that free will is an illusion.

● Finding both behaviorism and psychoanalysis unsatisfactory, advocates of humanism, such as Carl Rogers and Abraham Maslow, became influential in the 1950s. Humanism emphasizes the unique qualities of human behavior and humans' freedom and potential for personal growth.

● Stimulated by the demands of World War II, clinical psychology grew rapidly in the 1950s. Thus, psychology became a profession as well as a science. This movement toward professionalization eventually spread to other areas in psychology. During the 1950s and 1960s advances in the study of cognitive processes and the physiological bases of behavior led to renewed interest in cognition and physiology.

● In the 1980s, Western psychologists, who had previously been rather provincial, developed a greater interest in how cultural factors influence thoughts, feelings, and behavior. This trend was sparked in large part by growing global interdependence and by increased cultural diversity in Western societies.

● The 1990s witnessed the emergence of a new theoretical perspective called evolutionary psychology. The central premise of this new school of thought is that patterns of behavior are the product of evolutionary forces, just as anatomical characteristics are shaped by natural selection.

Psychology Today: Vigorous and Diversified

● Contemporary psychology is a diversified science and profession that has grown rapidly in recent decades. Major areas of research in modern psychology include developmental psychology, social psychology, experimental psychology, physiological psychology, cognitive psychology, personality, and psychometrics. Applied psychology encompasses four professional specialties: clinical psychology, counseling psychology, educational and school psychology, and industrial and organizational psychology.

Putting It in Perspective: Seven Key Themes

● As we examine psychology in all its many variations, we will emphasize seven key ideas as unifying themes. Looking at psychology as a field of study, our three key themes are (1) psychology is empirical, (2) psychology is theoretically diverse, and (3) psychology evolves in a sociohistorical context.

● Looking at psychology's subject matter, the remaining four themes are (4) behavior is determined by multiple causes, (5) behavior is shaped by cultural heritage, (6) heredity and environment jointly influence behavior, and (7) people's experience of the world is highly subjective.

Personal Application ● Improving Academic Performance

● To foster sound study habits, you should devise a written study schedule and reward yourself for following it. You should also try to find one or two specific places for studying that are relatively free of distractions.

● You should use active reading techniques to select the most important ideas from the material you read. SQ3R, one approach to active reading, breaks a reading assignment into manageable segments and requires that you understand each segment before you move on.

● Good note taking can help you get more out of lectures. It's important to use active listening techniques and to record lecturers' ideas in your own words. It also helps if you read ahead to prepare for lectures and ask questions as needed.

● Being an effective student also requires sound test-taking skills. In general, it's a good idea to devise a schedule for progressing through an exam, to adopt the appropriate level of sophistication, to avoid wasting time on troublesome questions, and to review your answers whenever time permits.

Critical Thinking Application ● Developing Critical Thinking Skills: An Introduction

● Critical thinking refers to the use of cognitive skills and strategies that increase the probability of a desirable outcome. Critical thinking is purposeful, reasoned thinking. A critical thinker is flexible, persistent, able to admit mistakes, and mindful of the thinking process.

● Evolutionary psychologists have attributed contemporary sex differences in spatial abilities to the sex-based division of labor in hunting and gathering societies. However, there are alternative explanations for these differences that focus on the sex-typed activities that modern males and females engage in. There also are contradictory data regarding the adaptive pressures faced by females and males in hunting and gathering societies.

Key Terms

Applied psychology
Behavior
Behaviorism
Clinical psychology
Cognition
Critical thinking
Culture
Empiricism
Evolutionary
  psychology
Functionalism
Humanism
Introspection
Natural selection
Psychoanalytic theory
Psychology
SQ3R
Structuralism
Testwiseness
Theory
Unconscious

Key People

Sigmund Freud
William James
Carl Rogers
B. F. Skinner
John B. Watson
Wilhelm Wundt

PRACTICE TEST

1. For which of the following is Wilhelm Wundt primarily known?
- A. The establishment of the first formal laboratory for research in psychology
- B. The distinction between mind and body as two separate entities
- C. The discovery of how signals are conducted along nerves in the body
- D. The development of the first formal program for training in psychotherapy

2. Leta Hollingworth is noted for:
- A. Being the first woman to receive a Ph.D. in psychology.
- B. Being the first woman president of the American Psychological Association.
- C. Founding one of the early psychology laboratories in America.
- D. Collecting objective data on gender differences in behavior.

3. Which of the following approaches might William James criticize for examining a movie frame by frame instead of seeing the motion in the motion picture?
- A. Structuralism
- B. Functionalism
- C. Dualism
- D. Humanism

4. Fred, a tennis coach, insists that he can make any reasonably healthy individual into an internationally competitive tennis player. Fred is echoing the thoughts of:
- A. Sigmund Freud.
- B. John B. Watson.
- C. Abraham Maslow.
- D. William James.

5. Which of the following approaches might suggest that forgetting to pick his mother up at the airport was Henry's unconscious way of saying that he did not welcome her visit?
- A. Psychoanalytic
- B. Behavioral
- C. Humanistic
- D. Cognitive

6. Which of the following is a statement with which Skinner's followers would agree?
- A. The whole is greater than the sum of its parts.
- B. The goal of behavior is self-actualization.
- C. Nature is more influential than nurture.
- D. Free will is an illusion.

7. Which of the following approaches has the most optimistic view of human nature?
- A. Humanism
- B. Behaviorism
- C. Psychoanalysis
- D. Structuralism

8. Which of the following historical events created a demand for clinicians that was far greater than the supply?
- A. World War I
- B. The Depression
- C. World War II
- D. The Korean War

9. _____ psychology examines behavioral processes in terms of their adaptive value for a species over the course of many generations.
- A. Clinical
- B. Cognitive
- C. Evolutionary
- D. Physiological

10. The study of the endocrine system and genetic mechanisms would most likely be undertaken by a:
- A. Clinical psychologist.
- B. Physiological psychologist.
- C. Social psychologist.
- D. Educational psychologist.

11. The fact that psychologists do not all agree about the nature and development of personality demonstrates:
- A. That there are many ways of looking at the same phenomenon.
- B. The fundamental inability of psychologists to work together in developing a single theory.
- C. The failure of psychologists to communicate with one another.
- D. The possibility that personality may simply be incomprehensible.

12. A multifactorial causation approach to behavior suggests that:
- A. Most behaviors can be explained best by single-cause explanations.
- B. Most behavior is governed by a complex network of interrelated factors.
- C. Data need to be analyzed by the statistical technique called factor analysis in order for the data to make sense.
- D. Explanations of behavior tend to build up from the simple to the complex in a hierarchical manner.

13. Psychology's answer to the question of whether we are "born" or "made" tends to be:
- A. We are "born."
- B. We are "made."
- C. We are both "born" and "made."
- D. Neither.

14. The reason the SQ3R method is effective is that:
- A. It breaks a reading assignment down into manageable segments and requires understanding before you move on.
- B. With this method, you only have to skim the reading assignment to pick out the main points.
- C. It allows you to memorize and recite great quantities of material even if you don't fully understand it.
- D. It requires you to read and reread your text over and over.

15. Critical thinking skills:
- A. are abstract abilities that cannot be identified.
- B. usually develop spontaneously through normal content instruction.
- C. usually develop spontaneously without any instruction.
- D. need to be deliberately taught because they often do not develop by themselves with standard content instruction.

Answers

1	A	page 3	**6**	D	page 8	**11**	A	page 18
2	D	page 5	**7**	A	page 9	**12**	B	page 19
3	A	pages 4–5	**8**	C	pages 10–11	**13**	C	page 20
4	B	page 6	**9**	C	page 13	**14**	A	page 24
5	A	page 7	**10**	B	page 15	**15**	D	page 26

INFOTRAC COLLEGE EDITION

Go to the Wadsworth Psychology Study Center for quiz questions, research updates, interactive exercises, and suggested readings in INFOTRAC related to this chapter: http://psychology.wadsworth.com/product/0534593100s

CHAPTER 2

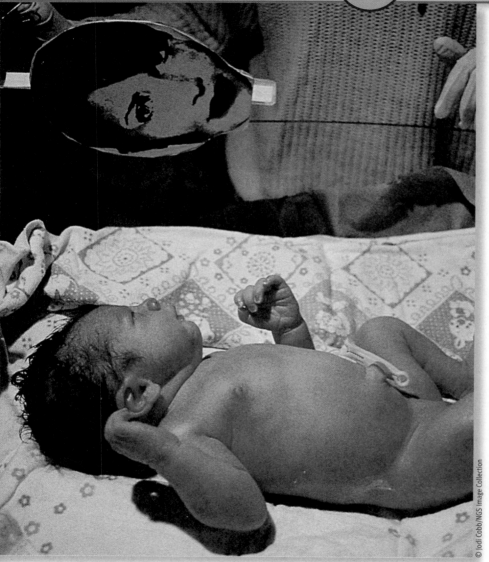

© Jodi Cobb/NGS Image Collection

The Research Enterprise in Psychology

© Jodi Cobb/NGS Image Collection

● Can chronic inhibition of emotions increase people's vulnerability to physical disease? ● How does anxiety affect people's desire to be with others? ● Does misery love company? ● Are there substantial differences between cultures when it comes to the pace of everyday life? ● What are the psychological characteristics of people who receive the death penalty? ● How common is it for college men to force women into sexual acts against their will?

Questions, questions, questions—everyone has questions about behavior. The most basic question is: How should these questions be investigated? As noted in Chapter 1, psychology is empirical. Psychologists rely on formal, systematic observations to address their questions about behavior. This methodology is what makes psychology a scientific endeavor.

The scientific enterprise is an exercise in creative problem solving. Scientists have to figure out how to make observations that will shed light on the puzzles they want to solve. To make these observations, psychologists use a variety of research methods because different questions call for different strategies of study. In this chapter, you will see how researchers have used such methods as experiments, case studies, surveys, and naturalistic observation to investigate the questions listed at the beginning of this chapter. Psychology's methods are worth a close look for at least two reasons. First, a better appreciation of the empirical approach will enhance your understanding of the research-based information you will be reading about in the remainder of this book. Second, familiarity with the logic of the empirical approach should improve your ability to think critically about research. This skepticism is important because you hear about research findings nearly every day. The news media constantly report on studies that yield conclusions about how you should raise your children, improve your health, and enhance your interpersonal relationships. Learning how to evaluate these reports with more sophistication can help you use such information wisely.

In this chapter, we will examine the scientific approach to the study of behavior and then look at the specific research methods that psychologists use most frequently. After you learn how research is done, we'll review some common flaws in doing research. Finally, we will take a look at ethical issues in behavioral research. In the Personal Application, you'll learn how to find and read journal articles that report on research. In the chapter's Critical Thinking Application, we'll take a critical look at the nature and validity of anecdotal evidence.

Looking for Laws: The Scientific Approach to Behavior

Whether the object of study is gravitational forces or people's behavior under stress, *the scientific approach assumes that events are governed by some lawful order.* As scientists, psychologists assume that behavior is governed by discernible laws or principles, just as the movement of the earth around the sun is governed by the laws of gravity. The behavior of living creatures may not seem as lawful and predictable as the "behavior" of planets. However, the scientific enterprise is based on the belief that there are consistencies or laws that can be uncovered. Fortunately, the plausibility of applying this fundamental assumption to psychology has been supported by the discovery of a great many such consistencies in behavior, some of which provide the subject matter for this text.

Goals of the Scientific Enterprise

Psychologists and other scientists share three sets of interrelated goals: measurement and description, understanding and prediction, and application and control.

1. *Measurement and description.* Science's commitment to observation requires that an investigator figure out a way to measure the phenomenon under study. For example, a psychologist could not investigate whether men are more or less sociable than women without first developing some means of measuring sociability. Thus, the first goal of psychology is to develop measurement techniques that make it possible to describe behavior clearly and precisely.

2. *Understanding and prediction.* A higher-level goal of science is understanding. Scientists believe that they understand events when they can explain the reasons for their occurrence. To evaluate their understanding, scientists make and test predictions called hypotheses. **A *hypothesis* is a tentative statement about the relationship between two or more variables. *Variables* are any measurable conditions, events, characteristics, or behaviors that are controlled or observed in a study.** If we predicted that putting people under time pressure would lower the accuracy of their time perception, the variables in our study would be time pressure and accuracy of time perception.

3. *Application and control.* Ultimately, most scientists hope that the information they gather will be of some practical value in helping to solve everyday problems. Once people understand a phenomenon, they often can exert more control over it. Today, the profession of psychology attempts to apply research findings to practical problems in schools, businesses, factories, and mental hospitals. For example, a school psychologist might use findings about the causes of math anxiety to devise a program to help students control their math phobias.

How do theories help scientists to achieve their goals? As noted in Chapter 1, psychologists do not set out to just collect isolated facts about relationships between variables. To build toward a better understanding of behavior, they construct theories. **A *theory* is a system of interrelated ideas used to explain a set of observations.** For example, using a handful of concepts, such as natural selection and reproductive fitness, evolutionary theory (Buss, 1995, 1996) purports to explain a diverse array of known facts about mating preferences, jealousy, aggression, sexual behavior, and so forth (see Chapter 1). Thus, by integrating apparently unrelated facts and principles into a coherent whole, theories permit psychologists to make the leap from the *description* of behavior to the *understanding* of behavior. Moreover, the enhanced understanding afforded by theories guides future research by generating new predictions and suggesting new lines of inquiry.

A scientific theory must be testable, as the cornerstone of science is its commitment to putting ideas to an empirical test. Most theories are too complex to be tested all at once. For example, it would be impossible to devise a single study that could test all the many facets of evolutionary theory. Rather, in a typical study, investigators test one or two specific hypotheses derived from a theory. If their findings support the hypotheses, confidence in the theory that the hypotheses were derived from grows. If their findings fail to support the hypotheses, confidence in the theory diminishes, and the theory may be revised or discarded (see Figure 2.1). Thus, theory construction is a gradual, iterative process that is always subject to revision.

Steps in a Scientific Investigation

Curiosity about a question provides the point of departure for any kind of investigation, scientific or otherwise. Scientific investigations, however, are *systematic.* They follow an orderly pattern, which is outlined in Figure 2.2 on page 34. Let's look at how this standard series of steps was followed in a

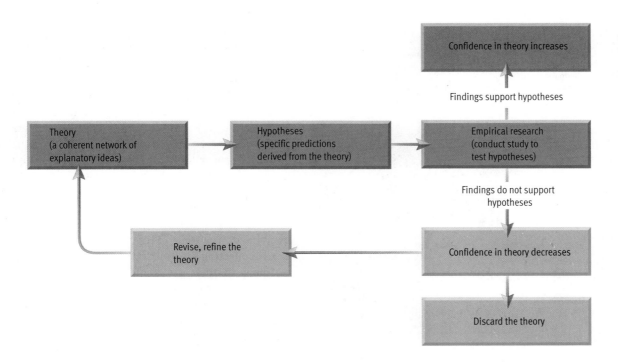

Figure 2.1

Theory construction. A good theory will generate a host of testable hypotheses. In a typical study, only one or a few of these hypotheses can be evaluated. If the evidence supports the hypotheses, confidence in the theory they were derived from generally grows. If the hypotheses are not supported, confidence in the theory decreases and revisions to the theory may be made to accommodate the new findings. If the hypotheses generated by a theory consistently fail to garner empirical support, the theory may be discarded altogether. Thus, theory construction and testing is a gradual process.

study of psychological inhibition and physical health by Steve Cole, Margaret Kemeny, Shelley Taylor, and Barbara Visscher (1996) of UCLA. Cole and his colleagues wanted to investigate whether the psychological inhibition required by gay men who conceal their homosexual identity might lead to increased vulnerability to certain kinds of physical illness.

Step 1: Formulate a Testable Hypothesis

The first step in a scientific investigation is to translate a theory or an intuitive idea into a testable hypothesis. Cole et al. (1996) noted that over the years a variety of theorists had speculated that frequent inhibition of emotions might create chronic physiological arousal that could lead to an increased incidence of physical illness. However, scientific evidence on this issue was sparse and inconsistent, in part because the concept of psychological inhibition had proven difficult to measure. Cole and his colleagues decided to approach the question in a new way. They reasoned that many gay individuals who are not "out of the closet" inhibit the public expression of their homosexuality to avoid stigmatization, discrimination, and even physical assault. They hypothesized that the vigilant inhibition of one's true feelings required by this strategy might have ramifications for gay individuals' health. Normally, hypotheses are expressed as predictions. They spell out how changes in one variable will be related to changes in another variable. Thus, Cole and colleagues

predicted that the degree to which men concealed their gay identity would be associated with the amount of physical illness they experienced.

To be testable, scientific hypotheses must be formulated precisely, and the variables under study must be clearly defined. Researchers achieve these clear formulations by providing operational definitions of the relevant variables. **An *operational definition* describes the actions or operations that will be used to measure or control a variable.** Operational definitions—which may be quite different from concepts' dictionary definitions—establish precisely what is meant by each variable in the context of a study.

To illustrate, let's examine the operational definitions used by Cole and his colleagues. They measured concealment of homosexual identity by having gay participants rate themselves as *definitely in the closet, in the closet most of the time, half in and half out, out of the closet most of the time,* or *completely out of the closet.* The extent of participants' physical illness was measured by having them come in for a medical examination and interview every six months for five years. The medical exams focused on five specific diseases: cancer, pneumonia, bronchitis, sinusitis, and tuberculosis.

Step 2: Select the Research Method and Design the Study

The second step in a scientific investigation is to figure out how to put the hypothesis to an empirical test. The research method chosen depends to a

Web Link 2.1

PubMed
Few commercial databases of journal articles or abstracts in the health sciences are available online for no charge. Fortunately, the National Library of Medicine has opened the 9 million items of MEDLINE's abstracts and references to anyone wanting to do research within the scientific literature of medical journals, including some important psychology publications.

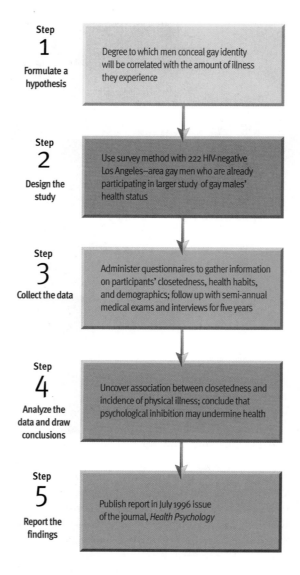

Figure 2.2

Flowchart of steps in a scientific investigation.
As illustrated in the study by Cole and his colleagues (1996), a scientific investigation consists of a sequence of carefully planned steps, beginning with the formulation of a testable hypothesis and ending with the publication of the study, if its results are worthy of examination by other researchers.

Step 1
Formulate a hypothesis

Degree to which men conceal gay identity will be correlated with the amount of illness they experience

Step 2
Design the study

Use survey method with 222 HIV-negative Los Angeles–area gay men who are already participating in larger study of gay males' health status

Step 3
Collect the data

Administer questionnaires to gather information on participants' closetedness, health habits, and demographics; follow up with semi-annual medical exams and interviews for five years

Step 4
Analyze the data and draw conclusions

Uncover association between closetedness and incidence of physical illness; conclude that psychological inhibition may undermine health

Step 5
Report the findings

Publish report in July 1996 issue of the journal, *Health Psychology*

large degree on the nature of the question under study. The various methods—experiments, case studies, surveys, naturalistic observation, and so forth—each have advantages and disadvantages. The researcher has to ponder the pros and cons and then select the strategy that appears to be the most appropriate and practical. In this case, Cole and colleagues decided that their question called for *survey* research, which involves administering questionnaires and interviews to a large number of people.

Once researchers have chosen a general method, they must make detailed plans for executing their study. Thus, Cole and associates had to decide when they would conduct their survey, how many people they needed to survey, and where they would get their participants. ***Participants* or *subjects* are the persons or animals whose behavior is systematically observed in a study.** For their

study, the Cole research team chose to use 222 HIV-negative gay and bisexual men recruited from the Los Angeles–area gay community who had previously volunteered to participate in a larger study of gay males' health status. Although their hypothesis relating psychological inhibition to health ought to apply to both gay men and women, the researchers chose to focus on men because of the convenient availability of a local sample of gay men whose health status was already under study.

Step 3: Collect the Data

The third step in the research enterprise is to collect the data. Thus, Cole and his colleagues spent about a year collecting information on participants' concealment of their gay identity and other demographic and health-related variables (such as age, education, exercise habits, and alcohol consumption). Data on subjects' health were collected every six months for an additional five years. Researchers use a variety of ***data collection techniques*, which are procedures for making empirical observations and measurements.** Commonly used techniques include direct observation, questionnaires, interviews, psychological tests, physiological recordings, and examination of archival records (see Table 2.1). The data collection techniques used in a study depend largely on what is being investigated. For example, questionnaires are well suited for studying attitudes, psychological tests for studying personality, and physiological recordings for studying brain function.

Step 4: Analyze the Data and Draw Conclusions

The observations made in a study are usually converted into numbers, which constitute the raw data of the study. Researchers use *statistics* to analyze their data and to decide whether their hypotheses have been supported. Thus, statistics play an essential role in the scientific enterprise. Based on their statistical analyses, Cole et al. (1996) concluded that their data supported their hypothesis. As predicted, they found an association between the degree to which participants concealed their homosexual identity and the incidence of physical illness (see Figure 2.3). Although the data supported the notion that psychological inhibition may be detrimental to one's health, the researchers were appropriately cautious about drawing far-reaching conclusions. Acknowledging that many variables were left uncontrolled in their correlational research, they noted that it would be premature to infer that coming out of the closet would result in improved health for gay men.

Table **2.1**   Key Data Collection Techniques in Psychology

Technique	Description
Direct observation	Observers are trained to watch and record behavior as objectively and precisely as possible. They may use some instrumentation, such as a stopwatch or video recorder.
Questionnaire	Subjects are administered a series of written questions designed to obtain information about attitudes, opinions, and specific aspects of their behavior.
Interview	A face-to-face dialogue is conducted to obtain information about specific aspects of a subject's behavior.
Psychological test	Subjects are administered a standardized measure to obtain a sample of their behavior. Tests are usually used to assess mental abilities or personality traits.
Physiological recording	An instrument is used to monitor and record a specific physiological process in a subject. Examples include measures of blood pressure, heart rate, muscle tension, and brain activity.
Examination of archival records	The researcher analyzes existing institutional records (the archives), such as census, economic, medical, legal, educational, and business records.

Step 5: Report the Findings

Scientific progress can be achieved only if researchers share their findings with one another and with the general public. Therefore, the final step in a scientific investigation is to write up a concise summary of the study and its findings. Typically, researchers prepare a report that is delivered at a scientific meeting and submitted to a journal for publication. **A *journal* is a periodical that publishes technical and scholarly material, usually in a narrowly defined area of inquiry.** The study by Cole and his colleagues (1996) was accepted for publication in a journal called *Health Psychology*.

Figure **2.3**

Results of the Cole et al. (1996) study. In their sample of gay and bisexual men, Cole et al. (1996) found that the more the men concealed their homosexual identity, the more likely they were to experience various diseases. The data shown here are for the combined incidence of sinusitis, bronchitis, pneumonia, and tuberculosis. A similar association was observed between closetedness and an elevated risk for skin cancer. (Data from "Elevated Physical Health Risk Among Gay Men Who Conceal Their Homosexual Identity," by S. W. Cole, M. E. Taylor, B. R. Visscher, 1996, *Health Psychology, 15,* 243–251.)

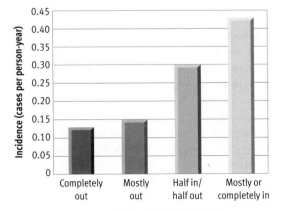

The process of publishing scientific studies allows other experts to evaluate and critique new research findings. Sometimes this process of critical evaluation discloses flaws in a study. If the flaws are serious enough, the results may be discounted or discarded. This evaluation process is a major strength of the scientific approach because it gradually weeds out erroneous findings.

Advantages of the Scientific Approach

Science is certainly not the only method that can be used to draw conclusions about behavior. We all use logic, casual observation, and good old-fashioned common sense. Because the scientific method requires painstaking effort, it seems reasonable to ask what advantages make it worth the trouble.

Basically, the scientific approach offers two major advantages. The first is its clarity and precision. Commonsense notions about behavior tend to be vague and ambiguous. Consider the old adage "Spare the rod and spoil the child." What exactly does this generalization about child rearing amount to? How severely should children be punished if parents are not to "spare the rod"? How do we assess whether a child qualifies as "spoiled"? A fundamental problem is that such statements have different meanings, depending on the person. In contrast, the scientific approach requires that people specify *exactly* what they are talking about when they formulate hypotheses. This clarity and precision enhance communication about important ideas.

The second and perhaps greatest advantage offered by the scientific approach is its relative intolerance of error. Scientists are trained to be skeptical. They subject their ideas to empirical tests.

Web Link 2.2

PsycINFO Direct
PsycINFO is an online database that provides summaries of professional literature related to psychology. Maintained by the American Psychological Association, it is the best means for tracking down psychological research on specific topics (see the Personal Application for this chapter). It contains over 1.5 million abstracts dating back to 1887. PsycINFO Direct is a version of the database that can be accessed by the general public (for a fee, of course).

Web Link 2.3

Links to Psychological Journals
Relatively few journals actually post their articles online for free. But, this searchable index to the online sites of more than 1600 psychology journals may lead you to recent tables of contents or abstracts or even identify research resources on more unusual topics in psychology.

They also scrutinize one another's findings with a critical eye. They demand objective data and thorough documentation before they accept ideas. When the findings of two studies conflict, the scientist tries to figure out why, usually by conducting additional research. In contrast, commonsense analyses involve little effort to verify ideas or detect errors.

All this is not to say that science has an exclusive copyright on truth. However, the scientific approach does tend to yield more accurate and dependable information than casual analyses and armchair speculation do. Knowledge of scientific data can thus provide a useful benchmark against which to judge claims and information from other kinds of sources.

Now that we have had an overview of how the scientific enterprise works, we can focus on how specific research methods are used. **Research methods consist of differing approaches to the observation, measurement, manipulation, and control of variables in empirical studies.** In other words, they are general strategies for conducting studies. No single research method is ideal for all purposes and situations. Much of the ingenuity in research involves selecting and tailoring the method to the question at hand. The next two sections of this chapter discuss the two basic types of methods used in psychology: *experimental research methods* and *descriptive/correlational research methods*.

Looking for Causes: Experimental Research

Does misery love company? This question intrigued social psychologist Stanley Schachter. When people feel anxious, he wondered, do they want to be left alone, or do they prefer to have others around? Schachter's review of relevant theories suggested that in times of anxiety people would want others around to help them sort out their feelings. Thus, his hypothesis was that increases in anxiety would cause increases in the desire to be with others, which psychologists call the *need for affiliation*. To test this hypothesis, Schachter (1959) designed a clever experiment.

The *experiment* **is a research method in which the investigator manipulates a variable under carefully controlled conditions and observes whether any changes occur in a second variable as a result.** The experiment is a relatively powerful procedure that allows researchers to detect cause-and-effect relationships. Psychologists depend on this method more than any other. To see how an experiment is designed, let's use Schachter's study as an example.

Independent and Dependent Variables

 SIM1, 1b

The purpose of an experiment is to find out whether changes in one variable (let's call it *X*) cause changes in another variable (let's call it *Y*). To put it more concisely, we want to find out *how X affects Y*. In this formulation, we refer to *X* as the *independent variable* and to *Y* as the *dependent variable*.

An *independent variable* **is a condition or event that an experimenter varies in order to see its impact on another variable.** The independent variable is the variable that the experimenter controls or manipulates. It is hypothesized to have some effect on the dependent variable, and the experiment is conducted to verify this effect. **The *dependent variable* is the variable that is thought to be affected by manipulation of the independent variable.** In psychology studies, the dependent variable is usually a measurement of some aspect of the subjects' behavior. The independent variable is called *independent* because it is *free* to be varied by the experimenter. The dependent variable is called *dependent* because it is thought to *depend* (at least in part) on manipulations of the independent variable.

In Schachter's experiment, *the independent variable was the participants' anxiety level*. He manipulated anxiety level in a clever way. Subjects assembled in his laboratory were told by a "Dr. Zilstein" that they would be participating in a study on the physiological effects of electric shock. They were further informed that during the experiment they would receive a series of electric shocks while their pulse and blood pressure were being monitored. Half of the participants were warned that the shocks would be very painful. They made up the *high-anxiety* group. The other half of the participants (the *low-anxiety* group) were told that the shocks would be mild and painless. In reality, there was no plan to shock anyone at any time. These orientation procedures were simply intended to evoke different levels of anxiety. After the orientation, the experimenter indicated that there would be a delay while he prepared the shock apparatus for use. The subjects were asked whether they would prefer to wait alone or in the company of others. *The subjects' desire to affiliate with others was the dependent variable.*

Experimental and Control Groups

 SIM1, 1b

In an experiment the investigator typically assembles two groups of subjects who are treated differently with regard to the independent variable. These two groups are referred to as the *experimental group* and the *control group*. **The *experimental group* consists of the subjects who receive some special treatment in regard to the independent variable. The *control group* consists of similar subjects who do not receive the special treatment given to the experimental group.**

In the Schachter study, the participants in the high-anxiety condition constituted the experimental group. They received a special treatment designed to create an unusually high level of anxiety. The participants in the low-anxiety condition constituted the control group. They were not exposed to the special anxiety-arousing procedure.

It is crucial that the experimental and control groups in a study be very similar, except for the different treatment that they receive in regard to the independent variable. This stipulation brings us to the logic that underlies the experimental method. If the two groups are alike in all respects *except for the variation created by the manipulation of the independent variable*, then any differences between the two groups on the dependent variable *must be due to the manipulation of the independent variable*. In this way researchers isolate the effect of the independent variable on the dependent variable. Schachter, for example, isolated the impact of anxiety on the need for affiliation. As predicted, he found that increased anxiety led to increased affiliation. As Figure 2.4 indicates, the percentage of subjects in the high-anxiety group who wanted to wait with others was nearly twice that of the low-anxiety group.

Extraneous Variables

 SIM1, 1b

As we have seen, the logic of the experimental method rests on the assumption that the experimental and control groups are alike except for their treatment in regard to the independent variable. Any other differences between the two groups can cloud the situation and make it difficult to draw conclusions about how the independent variable affects the dependent variable.

In practical terms, of course, it is impossible to ensure that two groups of subjects are exactly alike in *every* respect. The experimental and control groups only have to be alike on dimensions that are relevant

Recognizing Independent and Dependent Variables

Check your understanding of the experimental method by identifying the independent variable (IV) and dependent variable (DV) in the following investigations. Note that one study has two IVs and another has two DVs. You'll find the answers in Appendix A in the back of the book.

1. A researcher is interested in how heart rate and blood pressure are affected by viewing a violent film sequence as opposed to a nonviolent film sequence.
   IV _____
   DV _____

2. An organizational psychologist develops a new training program to improve clerks' courtesy to customers in a large chain of retail stores. She conducts an experiment to see whether the training program leads to a reduction in the number of customer complaints.
   IV _____
   DV _____

3. A researcher wants to find out how stimulus complexity and stimulus contrast (light/dark variation) affect infants' attention to stimuli. He manipulates stimulus complexity and stimulus contrast and measures how long infants stare at various stimuli.
   IV _____
   DV _____

4. A social psychologist investigates the impact of group size on subjects' conformity in response to group pressure.
   IV _____
   DV _____

to the dependent variable. Thus, Schachter did not need to worry about whether his two groups were similar in hair color, height, or interest in ballet. Obviously, these variables weren't likely to influence the dependent variable of affiliation behavior.

Instead, experimenters concentrate on making sure that the experimental and control groups are alike on a limited number of variables that could have a bearing on the results of the study. These variables are called extraneous, secondary, or nuisance

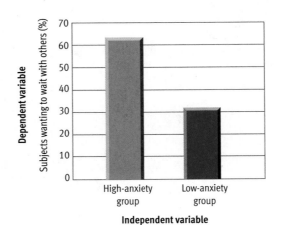

Figure 2.4

Results of Schachter's (1959) study of affiliation. The percentage of people wanting to wait with others was higher in the high-anxiety (experimental) group than in the low-anxiety (control) group, consistent with Schachter's hypothesis that anxiety would increase the desire for affiliation. The graphic portrayal of these results allows us to see at a glance the effects of the experimental manipulation on the dependent variable.

variables. *Extraneous variables* **are any variables other than the independent variable that seem likely to influence the dependent variable in a specific study.**

In Schachter's study, one extraneous variable would have been the participants' tendency to be sociable. Why? Because subjects' sociability could affect their desire to be with others (the dependent variable). If the subjects in one group had happened to be more sociable (on the average) than those in the other group, the variables of anxiety and sociability would have been confounded. **A** *confounding of variables* **occurs when two variables are linked in a way that makes it difficult to sort out their specific effects.** When an extraneous variable is confounded with an independent variable, a researcher cannot tell which is having what effect on the dependent variable.

Unanticipated confoundings of variables have wrecked innumerable experiments. That is why so much care, planning, and forethought must go into designing an experiment. A key quality that separates a talented experimenter from a mediocre one is the ability to foresee troublesome extraneous variables and control them to avoid confoundings.

Experimenters use a variety of safeguards to control for extraneous variables. For instance, subjects are usually assigned to the experimental and control groups randomly. *Random assignment* **of subjects occurs when all subjects have an equal chance of being assigned to any group or condition in the study.** When experimenters distribute subjects into groups through some random procedure, they can be reasonably confident that the groups will be similar in most ways.

To summarize the essentials of experimental design, Figure 2.5 provides an overview of the elements in an experiment, using Schachter's study as an example.

Variations in Designing Experiments SIM1, 1b

We have discussed the experiment in only its simplest format, with just one independent variable and one dependent variable. Actually, many variations are possible in conducting experiments. *Sometimes it is advantageous to use only one group of subjects who serve as their own control group.* The effects of the independent variable are evaluated by exposing this single group to two different conditions: an experimental condition and a control condition. For example, imagine that you wanted to study the effects of loud music on typing performance. You could have a group of participants work on a typing task while loud music was played (experimental condition) and in the absence of music (control condition). This approach would ensure that the participants in the experimental and control conditions would be alike on any extraneous variables involving their personal characteristics, such as motivation or typing skill. After all, the same people would be studied in both conditions.

Figure 2.5

The basic elements of an experiment. As illustrated by the Schachter (1959) study, the logic of experimental design rests on treating the experimental and control groups exactly alike (to control for extraneous variables) except for the manipulation of the independent variable. In this way, the experimenter attempts to isolate the effects of the independent variable on the dependent variable.

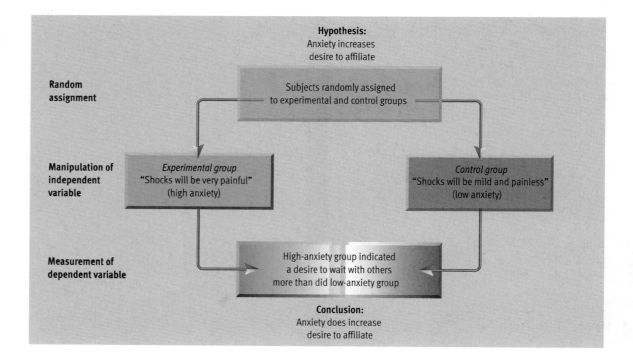

It is also possible to manipulate more than one independent variable or measure more than one dependent variable in a single experiment. For example, in another study of typing performance, you could vary both room temperature and the presence of distracting music as independent variables (see Figure 2.6), while measuring two aspects of typing performance (speed and accuracy) as dependent variables.

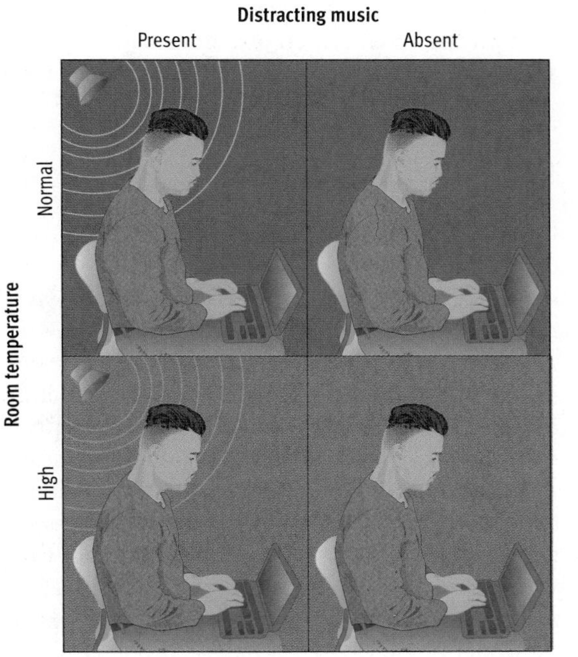

Advantages and Disadvantages of Experimental Research

The experiment is a powerful research method. Its principal advantage is that it permits conclusions about cause-and-effect relationships between variables. Researchers are able to draw these conclusions about causation because the precise control allows them to isolate the relationship between the independent variable and the dependent variable, while neutralizing the effects of extraneous variables. No other research method can duplicate this strength of the experiment. This advantage is why psychologists usually prefer to use the experimental method whenever possible.

For all its power, however, the experiment has limitations. One problem is that experiments are often artificial. Because experiments require great control over proceedings, researchers must often construct simple, contrived situations to test their hypotheses experimentally. For example, to investigate decision making in juries, psychologists have conducted many experiments in which participants read a brief summary of a trial and then record their individual "verdicts" of innocence or guilt. However, critics have pointed out that having a subject read a short case summary and make an individual decision is terribly artificial in comparison to the complexities of real trials (Weiten & Diamond, 1979). When experiments are highly artificial, doubts arise

Distracting music
Present · Absent

Room temperature: Normal · High

Figure 2.6

Manipulation of two independent variables in an experiment. As this example shows, when two independent variables are manipulated in a single experiment, the researcher has to compare four groups of subjects (or conditions) instead of the usual two. The main advantage of this procedure is that it allows an experimenter to see whether two variables interact.

about the applicability of findings to everyday behavior outside the experimental laboratory.

Another disadvantage is that the experimental method can't be used to explore some research questions. Psychologists are frequently interested in the effects of factors that cannot be manipulated as independent variables because of ethical concerns or practical realities. For example, you might want to know whether being brought up in an urban as opposed to a rural area affects people's values. An experiment would require you to assign similar families to live in urban and rural areas, which obviously is impossible to do. To explore this question, you would have to use descriptive/correlational research methods, which we turn to next.

Looking for Links: Descriptive/Correlational Research

As we just saw, in some situations psychologists cannot exert experimental control over the variables they want to study. The research of Cole et al. (1996) on the relationship between psychological inhibition and vulnerability to illness provides another example of this problem. Obviously, Cole and his colleagues could not manipulate the degree to which their gay participants were in or out of the closet.

In such situations, investigators must rely on *descriptive/correlational research methods.* What

distinguishes these methods is that the researcher cannot manipulate the variables under study. This lack of control means that these methods cannot be used to demonstrate a cause-and-effect relationship between variables. *Descriptive/correlational methods permit investigators to see only whether there is a link or association between the variables of interest.* Such an association is called a *correlation,* and the results of descriptive research are often summarized with a statistic called the *correlation coefficient.* In this section, we'll take a close look at the concept of correlation and then examine three specific approaches to descriptive research: naturalistic observation, case studies, and surveys.

The Concept of Correlation

In descriptive research, investigators often want to determine whether there is a correlation between two variables. **A *correlation* exists when two variables are related to each other.** A correlation may be either positive or negative, depending on the nature of the association between the variables measured. A *positive* correlation indicates that two variables covary in the *same* direction. This means that high scores on variable *X* are associated with high scores on variable *Y* and that low scores on variable *X* are associated with low scores on variable *Y*. For example, there is a positive correlation between high school grade point average (GPA) and subsequent college GPA. That is, people who do well in high school tend to do well in college, and those who perform poorly in high school tend to perform poorly in college (see Figure 2.7).

In contrast, a *negative* correlation indicates that two variables covary in the *opposite* direction. This means that people who score high on variable *X* tend to score low on variable *Y*, whereas those who score low on *X* tend to score high on *Y*. For example, in most college courses, there is a negative correlation between how frequently students are absent and how well they perform on exams. Students who have a high number of absences tend to get low exam scores, while students who have a low number of absences tend to earn higher exam scores (see Figure 2.7).

Strength of the Correlation

The strength of an association between two variables can be measured with a statistic called the correlation coefficient. **The *correlation coefficient* is a numerical index of the degree of relationship between two variables.** This coefficient can vary between 0 and +1.00 (if the correlation is positive) or between 0 and –1.00 (if the correlation is negative). A coefficient near zero indicates no relationship between the variables. That is, high or low scores on variable *X* show no consistent relationship to high or low scores on variable *Y*. A coefficient of +1.00 or –1.00 indicates a perfect, one-to-one correspondence between the two variables. Most correlations fall between these extremes.

The closer the correlation is to either –1.00 or +1.00, the stronger the relationship (see Figure 2.8). Thus, a correlation of .90 represents a stronger tendency for variables to be associated than a correlation of .40. Likewise, a correlation of –.75 represents a stronger relationship than a correlation of –.45. Keep in mind that the *strength* of a correlation depends only on the size of the coefficient. The positive or negative sign simply indicates the direction of the relationship. Therefore, a correlation of –.60 reflects a stronger relationship than a correlation of +.30.

Correlation and Prediction

You may recall that one of the key goals of scientific research is accurate *prediction*. There is a close link between the magnitude of a correlation and the power it gives scientists to make predictions. *As a correlation increases in strength (gets closer to either –1.00 or +1.00), the ability to predict one variable based on knowledge of the other variable increases.*

Web Link 2.4

HyperStat Online
For psychology researchers who find they've temporarily misplaced their statistics textbook, here's one written in hypertext by David M. Lane of Rice University and always available online for free. He also includes many links to excellent resources involving statistics, the analysis of experimental data, and even some statistical humor.

Figure 2.7

Positive and negative correlation. Notice that the terms positive and negative refer to the direction of the relationship between two variables, not to its strength. Variables are positively correlated if they tend to increase and decrease together and are negatively correlated if one tends to increase when the other decreases.

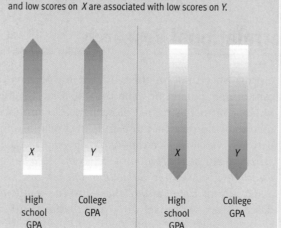

Positive correlation

High scores on *X* are associated with high scores on *Y*, and low scores on *X* are associated with low scores on *Y*.

X   Y   X   Y

High school GPA   College GPA   High school GPA   College GPA

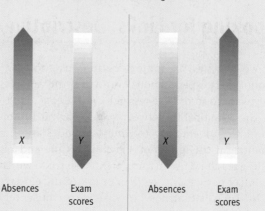

Negative correlation

High scores on *X* are associated with low scores on *Y*, and low scores on *X* are associated with high scores on *Y*.

X   Y   X   Y

Absences   Exam scores   Absences   Exam scores

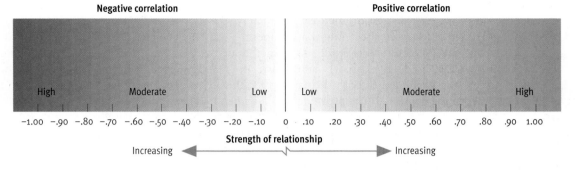

Negative correlation   **Positive correlation**

High   Moderate   Low   Low   Moderate   High

−1.00 −.90 −.80 −.70 −.60 −.50 −.40 −.30 −.20 −.10   0   .10 .20 .30 .40 .50 .60 .70 .80 .90 1.00

Strength of relationship

Increasing ← → Increasing

Figure 2.8

Interpreting correlation coefficients. The magnitude of a correlation coefficient indicates the strength of the relationship between two variables. The sign (plus or minus) indicates the direction of the relationship. If a correlation coefficient is shown with no sign, you can assume that it is a positive correlation. The closer the coefficient is to +1.00 or −1.00, the stronger the relationship between the variables.

To illustrate, consider how college admissions tests (such as the SAT or ACT) are used to predict college performance. When students' admissions test scores and college GPA are correlated, researchers generally find moderate positive correlations in the .40s and .50s (Gregory, 1996). Because of this relationship, college admissions committees can predict with modest accuracy how well prospective students will do in college. Admittedly, the predictive power of these admissions tests is far from perfect. But it's substantial enough to justify the use of the tests as one factor in making admissions decisions. However, if this correlation were much higher, say .90, admissions tests could predict with superb accuracy how students would perform. In contrast, if this correlation were much lower, say .20, the tests' prediction of college performance would be so poor that considering the test scores in admissions decisions would be unreasonable.

Correlation and Causation

Although a high correlation allows us to predict one variable on the basis of another, it does not tell us whether a cause-effect relationship exists between the two variables. The problem is that variables can be highly correlated even though they are not causally related.

When we find that variables X and Y are correlated, we can safely conclude only that X and Y are related. We do not know *how* X and Y are related. We do not know whether X causes Y or Y causes X, or whether both are caused by a third variable. For example, survey studies have found a positive correlation between smoking and the risk of experiencing a major depressive disorder (Breslau, Kilbey, & Andreski, 1991, 1993). Although it's clear that there is an association between smoking and depression, it's hard to tell what's causing what. The investigators acknowledge that they don't

CONCEPT CHECK 2.2

Understanding Correlation

Check your understanding of correlation by interpreting the meaning of the correlation in item 1 and by guessing the direction (positive or negative) of the correlations in item 2. You'll find the answers in Appendix A.

1. Researchers have found a substantial positive correlation between youngsters' self-esteem and their academic achievement (measured by grades in school). Check any acceptable conclusions based on this correlation.

_____ **a.** Low grades cause low self-esteem.

_____ **b.** There is an association between self-esteem and academic achievement.

_____ **c.** High self-esteem causes high academic achievement.

_____ **d.** High ability causes both high self-esteem and high academic achievement.

_____ **e.** Youngsters who score low in self-esteem tend to get low grades, and those who score high in self-esteem tend to get high grades.

2. Indicate whether you would expect the following correlations to be positive or negative.

_____ **a.** The correlation between age and visual acuity (among adults).

_____ **b.** The correlation between years of education and income.

_____ **c.** The correlation between shyness and the number of friends one has.

know whether smoking makes people more vulnerable to depression or whether depression increases the tendency to smoke. Moreover, they note that they can't rule out the possibility that both are caused by a third variable (Z). Perhaps anxiety and neuroticism increase the likelihood of both taking up smoking and becoming depressed. The plausible causal relationships in this case are diagrammed in Figure 2.9, which illustrates the "third variable problem" in interpreting correlations. This is a common problem in research, and you'll see this type of diagram again when we discuss other correlations. Thus, it is important to remember that *correlation is not equivalent to causation.*

Naturalistic Observation

Does the pace of everyday life vary substantially from one culture to the next? Do people operate at a different speed in say, Germany, as opposed to Canada or Brazil? Are factors such as economic vitality and climate related to differences in the pace of life? These are the kinds of questions that intrigued Robert V. Levine and Ara Norenzayan (1999), who compared the pace of life in 31 countries around the world. Perhaps they could have devised an experiment to examine this question, but they wanted to focus on the pace of life in the real world rather than in the laboratory.

To study the pace of life, Levine and Norenzayan (1999) had to come up with concrete ways to measure it—their operational definition of the concept. The measure they chose depended on *naturalistic observation.* **In *naturalistic observation* a researcher engages in careful observation of behavior without intervening directly with the subjects.** In this instance, the researchers observed (1) the average walking speed in downtown locations, (2) the accuracy of public clocks, and (3) the speed with which postal clerks completed a simple request. Their collection of data on walking speed illustrates the careful planning required to execute naturalistic observation effectively. In the main downtown area

of each city, they had to find two flat, unobstructed, uncrowded 60-foot walkways where they could unobtrusively time pedestrians during normal business hours. Only adult pedestrians walking alone and not window shopping were timed. In most cities, the observations continued until 35 men and 35 women had been timed.

Levine and Norenzayan conducted their naturalistic observations in 31 countries, typically using the largest city in each country as the locale for their research. Their findings, based on all three measures, are summarized in Table 2.2, which ranks the pace of life in the countries studied. Their data suggest that the pace of life is fastest in the countries of Western Europe and in Japan. Using archival data, they also conducted correlational analyses to see whether variations in the pace of life were associated with factors such as climate, economic vitality, or population size. Among other things, they found that the pace of life was faster in colder climates and in countries that were more economically productive.

This type of research is called *naturalistic* because behavior is allowed to unfold naturally (without interference) in its natural environment—that is, the setting in which it would normally occur. The major strength of naturalistic observation is that it allows researchers to study behavior under conditions that are less artificial than in experiments. A major problem with this method is that researchers often have trouble making their observations unobtrusively so they don't affect their subjects' behavior.

Case Studies

Are death-row inmates the shrewd, coldly calculating individuals that many people believe them to be? A research team at New York University wanted to investigate the psychological characteristics of people given the death penalty (Lewis et al., 1986). Until this study, no one had done research either confirming or refuting the popular image of criminals sentenced to die.

Figure 2.9

Three possible causal relations between correlated variables. If variables *X* and *Y* are correlated, does *X* cause *Y*, does *Y* cause *X*, or does some hidden third variable, *Z*, account for the changes in both *X* and *Y*? As the relationship between smoking and depression illustrates, a correlation alone does not provide the answer. We will encounter this problem of interpreting the meaning of correlations frequently in this text.

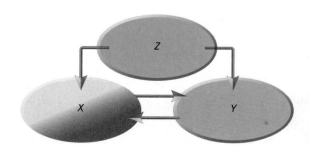

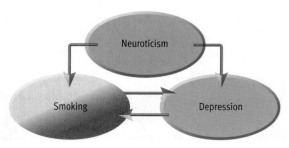

Table 2.2	Levine and Norenzayan's (1999) Ranking of the Pace of Life in 31 Cultures

Rank	Country	Rank	Country	Rank	Country
1	Switzerland	11	France	21	Greece
2	Ireland	12	Poland	22	Kenya
3	Germany	13	Costa Rica	23	China
4	Japan	14	Taiwan	24	Bulgaria
5	Italy	15	Singapore	25	Romania
6	England	16	United States	26	Jordan
7	Sweden	17	Canada	27	Syria
8	Austria	18	S. Korea	28	El Slavador
9	Netherlands	19	Hungary	29	Brazil
10	Hong Kong	20	Czech Republic	30	Indonesia
				31	Mexico

(Adapted from "The Pace of Life in 31 Countries" by R. V. Levine and A. Norenzayan, 1999, *Journal of Cross-Cultural Psychology, 30* (2), 178–205. Copyright © 1999 by Sage Publications, Inc. Reprinted by permission.)

The research team decided that their question called for a case study approach. **A *case study* is an in-depth investigation of an individual subject.** The researchers compiled case studies for 15 condemned individuals whose execution dates were close at hand. The findings were surprising. All 15 inmates had histories of severe head injuries. Twelve of them showed signs of brain damage, and most were well below average in intelligence. The investigators concluded that their data showed an unexpected correlation between neurological impairment and ending up on death row. Their findings suggest that our legal system doles out its harshest penalty to individuals who are anything but shrewd.

A variety of data collection techniques can be used in case studies. Typical techniques include interviews with and direct observation of the subject, examination of records, and psychological testing. Clinical psychologists, who diagnose and treat psychological problems, routinely do case studies of their clients. When clinicians assemble a case study, they are *not* conducting empirical research. Case study *research* takes place only when investigators analyze a collection of case studies, looking for threads of consistency that permit general conclusions.

Case studies are particularly well suited for investigating some issues, such as the causes of psychological disorders. The main problem with case studies is that they are highly subjective. Information from several sources must be knit together in an impressionistic way. In this process, researchers may focus selectively on information that fits with their expectations, which usually reflect their theoretical

slant. Thus, it is relatively easy for investigators to see what they expect to see in case study research.

Surveys

How common is it for college men to force women into sexual acts against their will? Karen Rapaport and Barry Burkhart (1984) set out to answer this question by conducting a survey. **In a *survey* researchers use questionnaires or interviews to gather information about specific aspects of participants' behavior.**

Naturalistic observation can be complex and challenging, as the study by Levine and Norenzayan (1999) illustrates. One of their measures of the pace of life in 31 cultures involved estimating people's walking speed in downtown locations. To reduce the influence of confounding factors, they had to find sidewalks that were unobstructed, uncrowded, not dominated by window shoppers, and so forth. Moreover, they had to find reasonably comparable locations in 31 very different types of cities.

© Peter Turnley/CORBIS

In their study, Rapaport and Burkhart defined coercive sexual behavior as any sexual act with a woman that is engaged in "against her will." They administered a questionnaire to 201 college men. It inquired whether the participants had ever engaged in any of 11 coercive sexual acts, such as placing a hand on a woman's breast or removing her underclothing, against her will. As you can see in Table 2.3, the survey revealed that a substantial proportion of the men had engaged in sexually coercive acts.

Surveys are often used to obtain information on aspects of behavior that are difficult to observe directly (such as sexual behavior). Surveys also make it relatively easy to collect data on attitudes and opinions from large samples of subjects. The major problem with surveys is that they depend on self-report data. As we'll discuss later, intentional deception and wishful thinking can distort participants' verbal reports about their behavior.

Advantages and Disadvantages of Descriptive/Correlational Research

Descriptive/correlational research methods have advantages and disadvantages, which are compared to the strengths and weaknesses of experimental research in Figure 2.10. As a whole, the foremost advantage of these methods is that they give researchers a way to explore questions that they could not examine with experimental procedures. For example, after-the-fact analyses would be the only ethical way to investigate the possible link between poor maternal nutrition and birth defects in humans. In a similar vein, if researchers hope to learn how urban and rural upbringing relate to people's values, they have to depend on descriptive methods, since they can't control where subjects grow up. Thus, *descriptive research broadens the scope of phenomena that psychologists are able to study.*

Unfortunately, descriptive methods have one significant disadvantage: Investigators cannot control events to isolate cause and effect. *Consequently, descriptive/correlational research cannot demonstrate conclusively that correlated variables are causally related.* As an example, consider the cross-cultural investigation of the pace of life that we discussed earlier. Although Levine and Norenzayan (1996) found an association between colder climates and a faster pace of life, their data do not permit us to conclude that a cold climate causes a culture to move at a faster pace. Too many factors were left uncontrolled in the study. For example, we do not know how similar the cold and warm cities were. Climate could covary with some other factors, such as modernization or economic vitality, that might have led to the observed differences in the pace of life.

Table 2.3   College Men's Responses to Items on Coercive Sexuality Scale (%)

Coercive Act Engaged in "Against Her Will"	Never	Once or Twice	Several Times	Often
Held a woman's hand	57	34	7	1
Kissed a woman	47	41	10	2
Placed hand on a woman's knee	39	43	15	3
Placed hand on a woman's breast	39	37	18	5
Placed hand on a woman's thigh or crotch	42	40	16	2
Unfastened a woman's outer clothing	51	34	13	2
Removed or disarranged a woman's outer clothing	58	31	9	2
Removed or disarranged a woman's underclothing	68	27	3	2
Removed own underclothing	78	18	3	2
Touched a woman's genital area	63	30	6	1
Had intercourse with a woman	85	13	2	0

NOTE: Some rows do not total 100% because of rounding.

(Adapted from "Personality and Attitudinal Characteristics of Sexually Coercive College Males," by D. Rapaport and B. R. Burkhart, 1984. *Journal of Abnormal Psychology, 93, (2)*, 216–221. Copyright © 1984 by the American Psychological Association. Adapted by permission of the author.)

Research method		Description	Example	Advantages	Disadvantages
Experiment 		Manipulation of an independent variable under carefully controlled conditions to see whether any changes occur in a dependent variable	Youngsters are randomly assigned to watch a violent or nonviolent film, and their aggression is measured in a laboratory situation	Precise control over variables; ability to draw conclusions about cause-and-effect relationships	Contrived situations often artificial; ethical concerns and practical realities preclude experiments on many important questions
Naturalistic observation 		Careful, usually prolonged observation of behavior without direct intervention	Youngsters' spontaneous acts of aggression during recreational activities are observed unobtrusively and recorded	Minimizes artificiality; can be good place to start when little is known about phenomena under study	Often difficult to remain unobtrusive; can't explain why certain patterns of behavior were observed
Case studies 		In-depth investigation of a single participant using direct interview, direct observation, and other data collection techniques	Detailed case histories are worked up for youngsters referred to counseling because of excessive aggressive behavior	Well-suited for study of certain phenomena; can provide compelling illustrations to support a theory	Subjectivity makes it easy to see what one expects to see based on one's theoretical slant; clinical samples often unrepresentative
Surveys 		Use of questionnaires or interviews to gather information about specific aspects of participants' behavior	Youngsters are given questionnaire that describes hypothetical scenarios and are asked about the likelihood of aggressive behavior	Can gather data on difficult-to-observe aspects of behavior; relatively easy to collect data from large samples	Sef-report data often unreliable, due to intentional deception, social desirability bias, response sets, memory lapses, and wishful thinking

Figure 2.10

Comparison of major research methods. This chart pulls together a great deal of information on key research methods in psychology and gives a simple example of how each method might be applied in research on aggression. As you can see, the various research methods each have their strengths and weaknesses.

CONCEPT **CHECK 2.3**

Matching Research Methods to Questions

Check your understanding of the uses and strengths of various research methods by figuring out which method would be optimal for investigating the following questions about behavioral processes. Choose from the following methods: (a) experiment, (b) naturalistic observation, (c) case study, and (d) survey. Indicate your choice (by letter) next to each question. You'll find the answers in Appendix A in the back of the book.

_____ **1.** Are people's attitudes about nuclear disarmament related to their social class or education?

_____ **2.** Do people who suffer from anxiety disorders share similar early childhood experiences?

_____ **3.** Do troops of baboons display territoriality—that is, do they mark off an area as their own and defend it from intrusion.

_____ **4.** Can the presence of food-related cues (delicious-looking desserts in advertisements, for example) cause an increase in the amount of food that people eat?

Scientific research is a more reliable source of information than casual observation or popular belief. However, it would be wrong to conclude that all published research is free of errors. Scientists are fallible human beings, and flawed studies do make their way into the body of scientific literature.

That is one of the reasons that scientists often try to replicate studies. *Replication* is the repetition of a study to see whether the earlier results are duplicated. The replication process helps science identify and purge erroneous findings. Of course, the replication process sometimes leads to contradictory results. You'll see some examples in the upcoming chapters. Fortunately, one of the strengths of the empirical approach is that scientists work to reconcile or explain conflicting results. In fact, scientific advances often emerge out of efforts to explain contradictory findings.

Like all sources of information, scientific studies need to be examined with a critical eye. This section describes a number of common methodological problems that often spoil studies. Being aware of these pitfalls will make you more skilled in evaluating research.

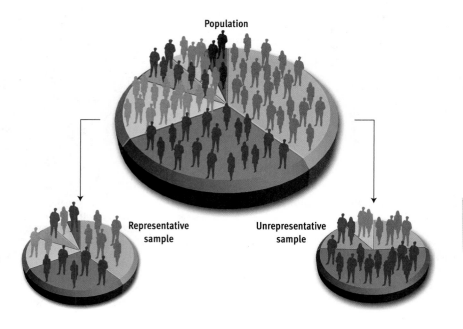

Population

Representative sample

Unrepresentative sample

Figure 2.11

The relationship between the population and the sample. The process of drawing inferences about a population based on a sample only works if the sample is reasonably representative of the population. A sample is representative if its demographic makeup is similar to that of the population, as shown on the left. If some groups in the population are overrepresented or underrepresented in the sample, as shown on the right, inferences about the population may be skewed or inaccurate.

Sampling Bias

A *sample* is the collection of subjects selected for observation in an empirical study. In contrast, **the *population* is the much larger collection of animals or people (from which the sample is drawn) that researchers want to generalize about.** For example, when political pollsters attempt to predict elections, all of the voters in a jurisdiction represent the population, and the voters who are actually surveyed constitute the sample. If researchers were interested in the ability of 6-year-old children to form concepts, those 6-year-olds actually studied would be the sample, and all similar 6-year-old children (perhaps those in modern, Western cultures) would be the population.

The strategy of observing a limited sample in order to generalize about a much larger population rests on the assumption that the sample is reasonably *representative* of the population. A sample is representative if its composition is similar to the composition of the population (see Figure 2.11). ***Sampling bias* exists when a sample is not representative of the population from which it was drawn.** When a sample is not representative, generalizations about the population may be inaccurate. For instance, if a political pollster were to survey only people in posh shopping areas frequented by the wealthy, the pollster's generalizations about the voting public as a whole would be off the mark.

Limits on available time and money often prevent researchers from obtaining as representative a sample as they would like. In general, when you have doubts about the results of a study, the first thing to examine is the composition of the sample.

Placebo Effects

In pharmacology, a *placebo* is a substance that resembles a drug but has no actual pharmacological effect. In studies that assess the effectiveness of medications, placebos are given to some participants to control for the effects of a treacherous extraneous variable: subjects' expectations. Placebos are used because researchers know that participants' expectations can influence their feelings, reactions, and behavior. Thus, *placebo effects* occur when subjects' expectations lead them to experience some change even though they receive empty, fake, or ineffectual treatment. In medicine, placebo effects are legendary. Many physicians tell of patients being "cured" by prescriptions of sugar pills. Similarly, psychologists have found that participants' expectations can be powerful determinants of their perceptions and behavior when they are under the microscope in an empirical study.

In describing placebo effects, I cannot help but recall a friend from my college days who would gulp one drink and start behaving in a drunken fashion before the alcohol could possibly have taken effect. In fact, this sort of placebo effect has been observed in a number of laboratory experiments on the effects of alcohol (Wilson, 1982). In these studies, some subjects are led to believe that they are drinking alcoholic beverages when in reality the drinks only seem to contain alcohol. Many of the subjects act intoxicated, even though they haven't really consumed any alcohol.

Researchers should guard against placebo effects whenever participants are likely to have expectations that a treatment will affect them in a certain way. The possible role of placebo effects can be assessed by including a fake version of the experimental treatment (a placebo condition) in a study.

Distortions in Self-Report Data

Research psychologists often work with *self-report data,* made up of participants' verbal accounts of their behavior. This is the case whenever questionnaires, interviews, or personality inventories are used to measure variables. Self-report methods can be quite useful, taking advantage of the fact that people have a unique opportunity to observe themselves full-time. However, self-reports can be plagued by several kinds of distortion.

One of the most problematic of these distortions is **the *social desirability bias,* which is a tendency to give socially approved answers to questions about oneself.** Subjects who are influenced by this bias work overtime trying to create a favorable impression (DeMaio, 1984). For example, many survey respondents will report that they voted in an election or gave to a charity when in fact it is possible to determine that they did not (Granberg & Holmberg, 1991).

Other problems can also produce distortions in self-report data (Krosnick, 1999; Schuman & Kalton, 1985). Respondents misunderstand questionnaire items surprisingly often, and the way questions are worded can shape participants' responses (Schwarz, 1999). Memory errors can undermine the accuracy of verbal reports. In responding to certain kinds of scales, some people tend to agree with nearly all of the statements, while others tend to disagree with nearly everything (Krosnick & Fabrigar, 1998). Obviously, distortions like these can produce inaccurate results. Although researchers have devised ways to neutralize these problems, we should be especially cautious in drawing conclusions from self-report data.

Experimenter Bias

As scientists, psychologists try to conduct their studies in an objective, unbiased way so that their own views will not influence the results. However, objectivity is a *goal* that scientists strive for, not an accomplished fact that can be taken for granted (MacCoun, 1998). In reality, most researchers have an emotional investment in the outcome of their research. Often they are testing hypotheses that they have developed themselves and that they would like to see supported by the data. It is understandable, then, that *experimenter bias* is a possible source of error in research.

***Experimenter bias* occurs when a researcher's expectations or preferences about the outcome of a study influence the results obtained.** Experimenter bias can slip through to influence studies in many subtle ways. One problem is that researchers, like others, sometimes *see what they want to see.* For instance, when experimenters make apparently honest mistakes in recording subjects' responses, the mistakes tend to be heavily slanted in favor of supporting the hypothesis (O'Leary, Kent, & Kanowitz, 1975).

Research by Robert Rosenthal (1976) suggests that experimenter bias may lead researchers to unintentionally influence the behavior of their subjects. In one study, Rosenthal and Fode (1963) recruited undergraduate psychology students to serve as the "experimenters." The students were told that they would be collecting data for a study of how participants rated the success of people portrayed in photographs. In a pilot study, photos were selected that generated (on the average) neutral ratings on a scale extending from –10 (extreme failure) to +10 (extreme success). Rosenthal and Fode then manipulated the expectations of their experimenters. Half of them were told that they would probably obtain average ratings of –5. The other half were led to expect average ratings of +5. The experimenters were forbidden from conversing with their subjects except for reading some standardized instructions. Even though the photographs were exactly the same for both groups, the experimenters who *expected* positive ratings *obtained* significantly higher ratings than those who expected negative ones.

Courtesy of Robert Rosenthal

"Quite unconsciously, a psychologist interacts in subtle ways with the people he is studying so that he may get the response he expects to get."
ROBERT ROSENTHAL

Detecting Flaws in Research

Check your understanding of how to conduct sound research by looking for methodological flaws in the following studies. You'll find the answers in Appendix A.

Study 1. A researcher announces that he will be conducting an experiment to investigate the detrimental effects of sensory deprivation on perceptual-motor coordination. The first 40 students who sign up for the study are assigned to the experimental group, and the next 40 who sign up serve in the control group. The researcher supervises all aspects of the study's execution. Experimental subjects spend two hours in a sensory deprivation chamber, where sensory stimulation is minimal. Control subjects spend two hours in a waiting room that contains magazines and a TV. All subjects then perform ten 1-minute trials on a pursuit-rotor task that requires them to try to keep a stylus on a tiny rotating target. The dependent variable is their average score on the pursuit-rotor task.

Study 2. A researcher wants to know whether there is a relationship between age and racial prejudice. She designs a survey in which respondents are asked to rate their prejudice against six different ethnic groups. She distributes the survey to over 500 people of various ages who are approached at a shopping mall in a low-income, inner-city neighborhood.

Check the flaws that are apparent in each study.

Methodological flaw	Study 1	Study 2
Sampling bias	____	____
Placebo effects	____	____
Distortions in self-report	____	____
Confounding of variables	____	____
Experimenter bias	____	____

How could the experimenters have swayed the participants' ratings? According to Rosenthal, the experimenters may have unintentionally influenced their subjects by sending subtle nonverbal signals as the experiment progressed. Without realizing it, they may have smiled, nodded, or sent other positive cues when participants made ratings that were in line with the experimenters' expectations. Thus, experimenter bias may influence both researchers' observations and their subjects' behavior (Rosenthal, 1994).

The problems associated with experimenter bias can be neutralized by using a double-blind procedure. **The *double-blind procedure* is a research strategy in which neither subjects nor experimenters know which subjects are in the experimental or control groups.** It's not particularly unusual for subjects to be "blind" about their treatment condition. However, the double-blind procedure keeps the experimenter in the dark as well. Of course, a member of the research team who isn't directly involved with subjects keeps track of who is in which group.

Looking at Ethics: Do the Ends Justify the Means?

Web Link 2.5

The Troubling Legacy of the Tuskegee Syphilis Study
The enduring damage of unethical scientific and medical research—here seen in the infamous 1932–1972 Tuskegee Syphilis Study among 399 poor African American men in Alabama—is detailed in several government reports and a rare presidential apology to its victims.

Think back to Stanley Schachter's (1959) study on anxiety and affiliation. Imagine how you would have felt if you had been one of the subjects in Schachter's high-anxiety group. You show up at a research laboratory, expecting to participate in a harmless experiment. The room you are sent to is full of unusual electronic equipment. An official-looking man in a lab coat announces that this equipment will be used to give you a series of painful electric shocks. His statement that the shocks will leave "no permanent tissue damage" is hardly reassuring. Surely, you think, there must be a mistake. All of a sudden, your venture into research has turned into a nightmare! Your stomach knots up in anxiety. The researcher explains that there will be a delay while he prepares his apparatus. He asks you to fill out a short questionnaire about whether you would prefer to wait alone or with others. Still reeling in dismay at the prospect of being shocked, you fill out the questionnaire. He takes it and then announces that you won't be shocked after all—it was all a hoax! Feelings of relief wash over you, but they're mixed with feelings of anger. You feel as though the experimenter has just made a fool out of you, and you're embarrassed and resentful.

Should researchers be allowed to play with your feelings in this way? Should they be permitted to deceive participants in such a manner? Is this the cost that must be paid to advance scientific knowledge? As these questions indicate, the research enterprise sometimes presents scientists with difficult ethical dilemmas. *These dilemmas reflect concern about the possibility for inflicting harm on subjects.* In psychological research, the major ethical dilemmas center on the use of deception and the use of animals.

The Question of Deception

Elaborate deception, such as that seen in Schachter's study, has been fairly common in psychological research since the 1960s, especially in the area of social psychology (Christensen, 1988; Epley & Huff, 1998). Over the years, psychologists have faked fights, thefts, muggings, faintings, epileptic seizures, rapes, and automobile breakdowns to explore a host of issues. Researchers have led subjects to believe that they (the subjects) were hurting others with electrical shocks, had homosexual tendencies, and were overhearing negative comments about themselves. Why have psychologists used so much deception in their research? Because of the methodological problems discussed in the last section. Subjects are often misled to avoid problems such as placebo effects and distortions in self-report data.

Critics argue against the use of deception on several grounds (Baumrind, 1985; Kelman, 1982; Ortmann & Hertwig, 1997). First, they assert that deception is only a nice word for lying, which they see as inherently immoral. Second, they argue that by deceiving unsuspecting participants, psychologists may undermine many individuals' trust in others. Third, they point out that many deceptive studies produce distress for participants who were not forewarned about that possibility. Specifically, participants may experience great stress during a study or be made to feel foolish when the true nature of a study is explained.

Those who defend the use of deception in research maintain that many important issues could not be investigated if experimenters were not permitted to mislead subjects (Aronson, Brewer, & Carlsmith, 1985). They argue that most research deceptions involve "white lies" that are not likely to harm participants. A review of the relevant research by Larry Christensen (1988) suggests that deception studies are *not* harmful to participants. Indeed, most subjects who participate in experiments involving deception report that they enjoyed the experience and that they didn't mind being misled. Moreover, Sharpe, Adair, and Roese (1992) found no support for the notion that deceptive research undermines subjects' trust in others. Curiously, the weight of the evidence suggests that researchers are more concerned about the negative effects of deception on participants than the participants themselves are (Fisher & Fyrberg, 1994; Korn, 1987). Finally, researchers who defend deception argue that the benefits—advances in knowledge that often improve human welfare—are worth the costs.

The Question of Animal Research

Psychology's other major ethics controversy concerns the use of animals in research. Psychologists use animals as research subjects for several reasons. Sometimes they simply want to know more about the behavior of a specific type of animal. In other instances, they want to identify general laws of behavior that apply to both humans and animals. Finally, in some cases psychologists use animals because they can expose them to treatments that clearly would be unacceptable with human subjects. For example, most of the research on the relationship between deficient maternal nutrition during pregnancy and the incidence of birth defects has been done with animals.

It's this third reason for using animals that has generated most of the controversy. Some people maintain that it is wrong to subject animals to harm or pain for research purposes. Essentially, they argue that animals are entitled to the same rights as humans (Regan, 1989). They accuse researchers of violating these rights by subjecting animals to unnecessary cruelty in many "trivial" studies (Hollands, 1989). They also argue that most animal studies are a waste of time because the results may not even apply to humans (Millstone, 1989; Ulrich, 1991). Some of the more militant animal rights activists have broken into laboratories, destroyed scientists' equipment and research records, and stolen experimental animals (Johnson, 1990).

In spite of the great furor, only 7%–8% of all psychological studies involve animals (mostly rodents and birds). Relatively few of these studies require subjecting the animals to painful or harmful manipulations (American Psychological Association, 1984). Psychologists who defend animal research, such as Neal Miller, point to the advances achieved through such work, including advances in the treatment of mental disorders, neuromuscular disorders, strokes, brain injuries, visual defects, headaches, memory impairments, high blood pressure, and problems with pain (Domjan & Purdy, 1995; Greenough, 1991; Miller, 1985).

The manner in which animals can ethically be used for research is a highly charged controversy. Psychologists are becoming increasingly sensitive to this issue. Although animals continue to be used in research, psychologists are taking greater pains to justify their use in relation to the potential benefits of the research. They are also striving to ensure that laboratory animals receive humane care.

The ethics issues that we have discussed in this section have led the APA to develop a set of ethical standards for researchers (American Psychological Association, 1992). Although most psychological studies are fairly benign, these ethical principles are intended to ensure that both human and animal subjects are treated with dignity. Some of the key guidelines in these ethical principles are summarized in Figure 2.12 on the next page.

Web Link 2.6

Animal Welfare Information Center
This site, maintained by the U.S. Department of Agriculture, is an excellent starting point for information relating to all aspects of how animals are (and should be) cared for in research, laboratory, and other settings.

Yale University

"*Who are the cruel and inhumane ones, the behavioral scientists whose research on animals led to the cures of the anorexic girl and the vomiting child, or those leaders of the radical animal activists who are making an exciting career of trying to stop all such research and are misinforming people by repeatedly asserting that it is without any value?*"
NEAL MILLER

Figure 2.12

Ethics in research. Key ethical principles in psychological research, as set forth by the American Psychological Association (1992), are summarized here. These principles are meant to ensure the welfare of both human and animal subjects.

A P A   E t h i c a l   G u i d e l i n e s   f o r   R e s e a r c h

1 A subject's participation in research should be voluntary and based on informed consent. Subjects should never be coerced into participating in research. They should be informed in advance about any aspects of the study that might be expected to influence their willingness to cooperate. Furthermore, they should be permitted to withdraw from a study at any time if they so desire.

2 Participants should not be exposed to harmful or dangerous research procedures. This guideline is intended to protect subjects from psychological as well as physical harm. Thus, even stressful procedures that might cause emotional discomfort are largely prohibited. However, procedures that carry a modest risk of moderate mental discomfort may be acceptable.

3 If an investigation requires some deception of participants (about matters that do not involve risks), the researcher is required to explain and correct any misunderstandings as soon as possible. The deception must be disclosed to subjects in "debriefing" sessions as soon as it is practical to do so without compromising the goals of the study.

4 Participants' rights to privacy should never be violated. Information about a subject that might be acquired during a study must be treated as highly confidential and should never be made available to others without the consent of the participant.

5 Harmful or painful procedures imposed upon animals must be thoroughly justified in terms of the knowledge to be gained from the study. Furthermore, laboratory animals are entitled to decent living conditions that are spelled out in detailed rules that relate to their housing, cleaning, feeding, and so forth.

6 Prior to conducting studies, approval should be obtained from host institutions and their research review committees. Research results should be reported fully and accurately, and raw data should be promptly shared with other professionals who seek to verify substantive claims. Retractions should be made if significant errors are found in a study subsequent to its publication.

Putting It in Perspective

Two of our seven unifying themes have emerged strongly in this chapter. First, the entire chapter is a testimonial to the idea that psychology is empirical. Second, the discussion of methodological flaws in research provides numerous examples of how people's experience of the world can be highly subjective. Let's examine each of these points in more detail.

As explained in Chapter 1, the empirical approach entails testing ideas, basing conclusions on systematic observation, and relying on a healthy brand of skepticism. All of those features of the empirical approach have been apparent in this chapter. As you have seen, psychologists test their ideas by formulating clear hypotheses that involve predictions about relations between variables. They then use a variety of research methods to collect data, so they can see whether their predictions are supported. The data collection methods are designed to make researchers' observations systematic and precise. The entire venture is saturated with skepticism. In planning and executing their research, scientists are constantly on the lookout for methodological flaws. They publish their findings so that other experts can subject their methods and conclusions to critical scrutiny. Collectively, these procedures represent the essence of the empirical approach.

The subjectivity of personal experience became apparent in the discussion of methodological problems, especially placebo effects and experimenter bias. When research participants report beneficial effects from a fake treatment (the placebo), it's because they expected to see these effects. The studies showing that many subjects start feeling intoxicated just because they think that they have consumed alcohol are striking demonstrations of the enormous power of people's expectations. As pointed out in Chapter 1, psychologists and other scientists are not immune to the effects of subjective experience. Although they are trained to be objective, even scientists may see what they expect to see or what they want to see. This is one reason that the empirical approach emphasizes precise measurement and a skeptical attitude. The highly subjective nature of experience is exactly what the empirical approach attempts to neutralize.

The publication of empirical studies allows us to apply our skepticism to the research enterprise. However, you cannot critically analyze studies unless you know where and how to find them. In the upcoming Personal Application, we will discuss where studies are published, how to find studies on specific topics, and how to read research reports. In the subsequent Critical Thinking Application, we'll analyze the shortcomings of anecdotal evidence, which should help you appreciate the value of empirical evidence.

PERSONAL APPLICATION

Finding and Reading Journal Articles

Answer the following "yes" or "no."

_____ **1** I have read about scientific studies in newspapers and magazines and sometimes wondered, "How did they come to those conclusions?"

_____ **2** When I go to the library, I often have difficulty figuring out how to find information based on research.

_____ **3** I have tried to read scientific reports and found them to be too technical and difficult to understand.

If you responded "yes" to any of the above statements, you have struggled with the information explosion in the sciences. We live in a research-oriented society. The number of studies conducted in most sciences is growing at a dizzying pace. This expansion has been particularly spectacular in psychology. Moreover, psychological research increasingly commands attention from the popular press because it is often relevant to people's personal concerns.

This Personal Application is intended to help you cope with the information explosion in psychology. It assumes that there may come a time when you need to examine original psychological research. Perhaps it will be in your role as a student (working on a term paper, for instance), in another role (parent, teacher, nurse, administrator), or merely out of curiosity. In any case, this Application explains the nature of technical journals and discusses how to find and read articles in them. You can learn more about how to use library resources in psychology from an excellent little book titled *Library Use: A Handbook for Psychology* (Reed & Baxter, 1992).

The Nature of Technical Journals

As you will recall from earlier in the chapter, a journal is a periodical that publishes technical and scholarly material, usually in a narrowly defined area of inquiry. Scholars in most fields—whether economics, chemistry, education, or psychology—publish the bulk of their work in these journals. Journal articles represent the core of intellectual activity in any academic discipline.

In general, journal articles are written for other professionals in the field. Hence, authors assume that their readers are other interested economists or chemists or psychologists. Because journal articles are written in the special language unique to a particular discipline, they are often difficult for nonprofessionals to understand. You will be learning a great deal of psychology's special language in this course, which will improve your ability to understand articles in psychology journals.

In psychology, most journal articles are reports that describe original empirical studies. These reports permit researchers to disseminate their findings to the scientific community. Another common type of article is the review article. *Review articles* summarize and reconcile the findings of a large number of studies on a specific issue. Some psychology journals also publish comments or critiques of previously published research, book reviews, theoretical treatises, and descriptions of methodological innovations.

Finding Journal Articles

Reports of psychological research are commonly mentioned in newspapers and popular magazines. These summaries can be helpful to readers, but they often embrace the most sensational conclusions that might be drawn from the research. They also tend to include many oversimplifications and factual errors. Hence, if a study mentioned in the press is of interest to you, you may want to track down the original article to ensure that you get accurate information.

Most discussions of research in the popular press do not mention where you can find the original technical article. However, there is a way to find out. A computerized database called PsycINFO makes it possible to locate journal articles by specific researchers or scholarly work on specific topics. This huge, online database, which is updated constantly, contains brief summaries, or *abstracts*, of journal articles, books, and chapters in edited books, reporting, reviewing, or theorizing about psychological research. Over 1600 journals are scanned regularly in order to select items for inclusion. The abstracts are concise—about 75 to 175 words. They briefly describe the hypotheses, methods, results, and conclusions of the studies. Each abstract should allow you to determine whether an article is relevant to your interests. If it is, you should be able to find the article in your library (or to order it) because a complete bibliographic reference is provided.

Craig McClain

Although news accounts of research rarely mention where a study was published, they often mention the name of the researcher. If you have this information, the easiest way to find a specific article is to search PsycINFO for materials published by that researcher. For example, let's say you read a news report that summarizes an interesting study on whether alcohol hangovers affect managerial effectiveness in the business world that was published by Siegfried Streufert in the mid-1990s. To track down the original article, you would search for journal articles authored by Streufert. Given that you know the approximate year of publication, you could select the PsycINFO option to narrow your search to materials published between 1990 and 1996. If you conducted this search, you would turn up the list of eight articles shown in Figure 2.13. The sixth item in the list appears to be the article you are interested in. Figure 2.14 shows what you would see if you clicked to obtain the Abstract and Citation for this article. As you can see, the abstract shows that the original report was published in the October 1995 issue of *Alcoholism: Clinical and Experimental Research.* Armed with this information, you could obtain the article easily.

You can also search PsycINFO for research literature on particular topics, such as achievement motivation, aggressive behavior, alcoholism, appetite disorders, or artistic ability. These computerized literature searches can be much more powerful, precise, and thorough than traditional, manual searches in a library. PsycINFO can sift through a half-million articles in a matter of seconds to identify *all* the articles on a subject, such as alcoholism. Obviously, there is no way you can match this efficiency stumbling around in the stacks at your library. Moreover, the computer allows you to pair up topics to swiftly narrow your search to exactly those issues that interest you. For example, Figure 2.15 shows a PsycINFO search that identified all the articles on marijuana *and* memory. If you were preparing a term paper on whether marijuana affects memory, this precision would be invaluable.

The PsycINFO database can be accessed online at many libraries or via the Internet (see Web Link 2.2 on p. 35 for a description of PsycINFO Direct). The database is also available at some libraries that have the information stored on CD-ROM discs. This version of the database is updated monthly. The summaries contained in PsycINFO can also be found in a monthly print journal called *Psychological Abstracts,* but fewer and fewer libraries are subscribing to this traditional publication because it cannot match the swift and efficient search capabilities of PsycINFO.

Reading Journal Articles

Once you find the journal articles you want to examine, you need to know how to decipher them. You can process the information in such articles more efficiently if you understand how they are organized. Depending on your needs and purpose, you may want to simply skim through some of the sections. Journal articles follow a fairly standard organization, which includes the following sections and features.

Figure 2.13

Searching PsycINFO. If you searched PsycINFO for journal articles authored by Siegfried Streufert during the period of 1990–1996, the database would return the eight titles shown here. For each article, you can click to see its abstract or its full PsycINFO record (the abstract plus subject descriptors and other details). In some cases (depending on the version of PsycINFO that your library has ordered), you can even click to see the full text of some articles (those articles that appeared in journals published by APA since 1988). (This material is reprinted with permission of the American Psychological Association, publisher of PsycINFO Database, Copyright © 1887–2001 APA, and may not be reproduced without prior permission.)

found 8 documents, (8 returned).
for Your Query : *(streufert, siegfried):Author*

1. **Effects of alcohol intoxication on risk taking, strategy, and error rate in visuomotor performance.**
   By Streufert, Siegfried; Pogash, Rosanne M.; Roache, John D.; Gingrich, Dennis; et al
   Journal of Applied Psychology. 1992 Aug Vol 77(4) 515-524
   Abstract and Citation | Full PsycINFO Record | Full Text of Article

2. **Age and management team performance.**
   By Streufert, Siegfried; Pogash, Rosanne; Piasecki, Mary; Post, Gerald M.
   Psychology & Aging. 1990 Dec Vol 5(4) 551-559
   Abstract and Citation | Full PsycINFO Record | Full Text of Article

3. **Authoring of complex learning environments: Design considerations for dynamic simulations.**
   By Breuer, Klaus; Streufert, Siegfried
   Journal of Structural Learning. 1996 Nov Vol 12(4) 315-321
   Abstract and Citation | Full PsycINFO Record

4. **Effects of alprazolam on complex human functioning.**
   By Streufert, Siegfried; Satish, Usha; Pogash, Rosanne; Gingrich, Dennis; et al
   Journal of Applied Social Psychology. 1996 Nov Vol 26(21) 1912-1930
   Abstract and Citation | Full PsycINFO Record

5. **Effects of caffeine deprivation on complex human functioning.**
   By Streufert, Siegfried; Pogash, Rosanne; Miller, Jill; Gingrich, Dennis; et al
   Psychopharmacology. 1995 Apr Vol 118(4) 377-384
   Abstract and Citation | Full PsycINFO Record

6. **Alcohol hangover and managerial effectiveness.**
   By Streufert, Siegfried; Pogash, Rosanne; Braig, Daniela; Gingrich, Dennis; et al
   Alcoholism: Clinical & Experimental Research. 1995 Oct Vol 19(5) 1141-1146
   Abstract and Citation | Full PsycINFO Record

7. **Alcohol and management performance.**
   By Streufert, Siegfried; Pogash, Rosanne; Roache, John; Severs, Walter; et al
   Journal of Studies on Alcohol. 1994 Mar Vol 55(2) 230-238
   Abstract and Citation | Full PsycINFO Record

8. **Alcohol and complex functioning.**
   By Streufert, Siegfried; Pogash, Rosanne M.; Gingrich, Dennis; Kantner, Anne; et al
   Journal of Applied Social Psychology. 1993 Jun Vol 23(11) 847-866
   Abstract and Citation | Full PsycINFO Record

Figure 2.14

Example of a PsycINFO abstract. This information is what you would see if you clicked to see the abstract of item 6 in the list shown in Figure 2.13. It is a typical abstract from the online PsycINFO database. Each abstract in PsycINFO provides a summary of a specific journal article, book, or chapter in an edited book, and complete bibliographical information. (This material is reprinted with permission of the American Psychological Association, publisher of PsycINFO Database, Copyright © 1887–2001 APA, and may not be reproduced without permission.)

Your source for psychological abstracts

TITLE	Alcohol hangover and managerial effectiveness.
ABSTRACT	21 male managers who normally drank moderate amounts of alcohol participated in a placebo-controlled, double-blind, crossover experiment to determine whether alcohol-induced hangovers would influence managerial/professional task performance characteristics. Ss consumed either placebo or alcoholic drinks to attain a breath alcohol level of 0.10 during the evening before participation in Strategic Management Simulations. By the following morning, breath alcohol levels were measured at 0.00. Questionnaire responses indicated considerable hangover discomfort. Responses to semantic differential evaluative scales suggested that Ss evaluated their own managerial performance in the simulation setting as impaired. However, multiple measures of decision-making performance obtained in the simulation task did not show any deterioration of functioning. (PsycINFO Database Record © 2000 APA, all rights reserved)
AUTHOR	*Streufert, Siegfried;* Pogash, Rosanne; Braig, Daniela; Gingrich, Dennis; et al
AFFILIATION	Pennsylvania State U, Coll of Medicine, Dept of Behavioral Science, Hershey, USA
SOURCE	Alcoholism: Clinical & Experimental Research. 1995 Oct Vol 19(5) 1141-1146

Abstract

Most journals print a concise summary at the beginning of each article. This abstract allows readers scanning the journal to quickly decide whether articles are relevant to their interests.

Introduction

The introduction presents an overview of the problem studied in the research. It mentions relevant theories and quickly reviews previous research that bears on the problem, usually citing shortcomings in previous research that necessitate the current study. This review of the state of knowledge on the topic usually progresses to a specific and precise statement regarding the hypotheses under investigation.

Method

The next section provides a thorough description of the research methods used in the study. Information is provided on the subjects used, the procedures followed, and the data collection techniques employed. This description is made detailed enough to permit another researcher to attempt to replicate the study.

Results

The data obtained in the study are reported in the results section. This section often creates problems for novice readers because it includes complex statistical analyses, figures, tables, and graphs. This section does not include any inferences based on the data, as such conclusions are supposed to follow in the next section. Instead, it simply contains a concise summary of the raw data and the statistical analyses.

Discussion

In the discussion section you will find the conclusions drawn by the author(s). In contrast to the results section, which is a straightforward summary of empirical observations, the discussion section allows for interpretation and evaluation of the data. Implications for theory and factual knowledge in the discipline are discussed. Conclusions are usually qualified carefully, and any limitations in the study may be acknowledged. This section may also include suggestions for future research on the issue.

References

At the end of each article is a list of bibliographic references for any studies cited. This list permits the reader to examine firsthand other relevant studies mentioned in the article. The references list is often a rich source of leads about other articles that are germane to the topic that you are looking into.

Figure 2.15

Using PsycINFO to locate journal articles.
A computerized literature search can be a highly efficient way to locate relevant research. In this example, the first command (FIND MARIJUANA) asks PsycINFO to find all the entries on marijuana in the database. The computer labels the 1178 articles it finds Set 1 (S1). The second command searches for all the articles on memory; the 37,155 such articles make up Set 2 (S2). To identify those articles that deal with both marijuana and memory, the third command searches S1 and S2 to find any articles that are listed in both sets (as depicted by the overlap in the circles). The resulting Set 3 (S3) consists of 53 articles on marijuana and memory. The fourth command directs the computer to scan these 53 articles and find any that are on short-term memory (it finds ten such articles). The last command asks the computer to narrow these articles to reasonably recent ones published after 1986 (PY = publication year). As you can see, only three articles meet this criterion. At any step along the way, the computer can print out the abstracts of the articles in a set.

The Perils of Anecdotal Evidence: "I Have a Friend Who . . ."

Here's a tough problem. Suppose you are the judge in a family law court. As you look over the cases that will come before you today, you see that one divorcing couple have managed to settle almost all of the important decisions with minimal conflict—such as who gets the house, who gets the car and the dog, and who pays which bills. However, there is one crucial issue left: Each parent wants custody of the children, and because they could not reach an agreement on their own, the case is now in your court. You will need the wisdom of the legendary King Solomon for this decision. How can you determine what is in the best interests of the children?

Child custody decisions have major consequences for all of the parties involved. As you review the case records, you see that both parents are loving and competent, so there are no obvious reasons for selecting one parent over the other as the primary caretaker. In considering various alternatives, you mull over the possibility of awarding *joint custody,* an arrangement in which the children spend half their time with each parent, instead of the more usual arrangement where one parent has primary custody and the other has visitation rights. Joint custody seems to have some obvious benefits, but you are not sure how well these arrangements actually work. Will the children feel more attached to both parents if the parents share custody equally? Or will the children feel hassled by always moving around, perhaps spending half the week at one parent's home and half at the other parent's home? Can parents who are already feuding over child custody issues make these complicated arrangements work? Or is joint custody just too disruptive to everyone's life? You really don't know the answer to any of these vexing questions.

One of the lawyers involved in the case knows that you are thinking about the possibility of joint custody. She also understands that you want more information about how well joint custody tends to work before you render a decision. To help you make up your mind, she tells you about a divorced couple who have had a joint custody arrangement for many years and offers to have them appear in court to describe their experiences "firsthand." They and their children can answer any questions you might have about the pros and cons of joint custody. They should be in the best position to know how well joint custody works because they are living it. Sounds like a reasonable plan. What do you think?

Hopefully, you said, "No, No, No!" What's wrong with asking someone who's been there how well joint custody works? The crux of the problem is that the evidence a single family brings to the question of joint custody is *anecdotal evidence,* which consists of personal stories about specific incidents and experiences. Anecdotal evidence can be very seductive. For example, one study found that psychology majors' choices of future courses to enroll in were influenced more by a couple of students' brief anecdotes than by extensive statistics on many other students' ratings of the courses from the previous term (Borgida & Nisbett, 1977). Anecdotes readily sway people because they often are concrete, vivid, and memorable. Indeed, people tend to be influenced by anecdotal information even when they are explicitly forewarned that the information is *not* representative (Hammill, Wilson, & Nisbett, 1980). Many politicians are keenly aware of the power of anecdotes and they frequently rely on a single vivid story rather than solid data to sway voters' views. However, anecdotal evidence is fundamentally flawed.

People in politics understand the enormous power of a compelling anecdote. For example, former President Ronald Reagan had a marvelous ability to use anecdotes to make his points. Actress Shirley MacLaine's widely read stories of past lives also illustrate how anecdotes can spark interest. However, as the text explains, anecdotal evidence is flawed in many ways.

© Wally McNamee/CORBIS

© Douglas Kirkland/CORBIS

What, exactly, is wrong with anecdotal evidence? Let's use some of the concepts introduced in the main body of the chapter to analyze the shortcomings of anecdotal evidence. First, in the language of research designs, the anecdotal experiences of one family resemble a single *case study*. The story they tell about their experiences with joint custody may be quite interesting, but their experiences—good or bad—cannot be used to generalize to other couples. Why not? Because they are only one family, and they may be unusual in some way that affects how well they manage joint custody. To draw general conclusions based on the case study approach, you need a systematic series of case studies, so you can look for threads of consistency. A single family is a sample size of one, which surely is not large enough to derive broad principles that would apply to other families.

Second, anecdotal evidence is similar to *self-report data,* which can be distorted for a variety of reasons, such as people's tendency to give socially approved information about themselves (the *social desirability bias*). When researchers use tests and surveys to gather self-report data, they can take steps to reduce or assess the impact of distortions in their data, but there are no comparable safeguards with anecdotal evidence. Thus, the family that appears in your courtroom may be eager to make a good impression and unknowingly slant their story accordingly.

Anecdotes are often inaccurate and riddled with embellishments. We will see in Chapter 7 that memories of personal experiences are far more malleable and far less reliable than widely assumed (Roediger, Wheeler, & Rajaram, 1993). And, although it would not be an issue in this case, in other situations *anecdotal evidence often consists of stories that people have heard about others' experiences.* Hearsay evidence is not accepted in courtrooms for good reason. As stories are passed on from one person to another, they often become increasingly distorted and inaccurate.

Can you think of any other reasons for being wary of anecdotal evidence? After reading the chapter, perhaps you thought about the possibility of *sampling bias.* Do you think that the lawyer will pick a couple at random from all those who have been awarded joint custody? It seems highly unlikely. If she wants you to award joint custody, she will find a couple for whom this arrangement worked very well; and if she wants you to award sole custody to her client, she will find a couple whose inability to make joint custody work had dire consequences for their children. One reason people love to work with anecdotal evidence is that it is so readily manipulated; they can usually find an anecdote or two to support their position, whether or not these anecdotes are representative of most people's experiences.

If the testimony of one family cannot be used in making this critical custody decision, what sort of evidence should you be looking for? One goal of effective critical thinking is to make decisions based on solid evidence. This process is called *evidence-based decision making.* In this case, you would need to consider the overall experiences of a large sample of families who have tried joint custody arrangements. In general, across many different families, did the children in joint custody develop well? Was there a disproportionately high rate of emotional problems or other signs of stress for the children or the parents? Was the percentage of families who returned to court at a later date to change their joint custody arrangements higher than for other types of custody arrangements? You can probably think of additional information that you would want to collect regarding the outcomes of various custody arrangements.

In examining research reports, many people recognize the need to evaluate the evidence by looking for the types of flaws described in the main body of the chapter (sampling bias, experimenter bias, and so forth). Curiously, though, many of the same people then fail to apply the same principles of good evidence to their personal decisions in everyday life. The tendency to rely on the anecdotal experiences of a small number of people is sometimes called the *"I have a friend who" syndrome,* because no matter what the topic is, it seems that someone will provide a personal story about a friend as evidence for his or her particular point of view. In short, when you hear people support their assertions with personal stories, a little skepticism is in order.

Table 2.4   Critical Thinking Skills Discussed in This Application

Skill	Description
Recognizing the limitations of anecdotal evidence	The critical thinker is wary of anecdotal evidence, which consists of personal stories used to support one's assertions. Anecdotal evidence tends to be unrepresentative, inaccurate, and unreliable.
Using evidence-based decision making	The critical thinker understands the need to seek sound evidence to guide decisions in everyday life.

REVIEW

Key Ideas

Looking for Laws: The Scientific Approach to Behavior

● The scientific approach assumes that there are laws of behavior that can be discovered through empirical research. The goals of the science of psychology include (1) the measurement and description of behavior, (2) the understanding and prediction of behavior, and (3) the application of this knowledge to the task of controlling behavior. By integrating apparently unrelated facts into a coherent whole, theories permit psychologists to make the leap from the description of behavior to understanding behavior.

● A scientific investigation follows a systematic pattern that includes five steps: (1) formulate a testable hypothesis, (2) select the research method and design the study, (3) collect the data, (4) analyze the data and draw conclusions, and (5) report the findings. The two major advantages of the scientific approach are its clarity in communication and its relative intolerance of error.

Looking for Causes: Experimental Research

● Experimental research involves the manipulation of an independent variable to ascertain its effect on a dependent variable. This research is usually done by comparing experimental and control groups, which must be alike in regard to important extraneous variables. Any differences between the groups in the dependent variable are presumably due to the manipulation of the independent variable.

● Experimental designs may vary. Sometimes an experimental group serves as its own control group. And many experiments have more than one independent variable or more than one dependent variable.

● An experiment is a powerful research method that permits conclusions about cause-and-effect relationships between variables. However, the experimental method is often not usable for a specific problem, and many experiments tend to be artificial.

Looking for Links: Descriptive/Correlational Research

● When psychologists are unable to manipulate the variables they want to study, they use descriptive/correlational research methods that seek to discover correlations between variables. Key descriptive methods include naturalistic observation, case studies, and surveys.

● Correlations may be either positive (the variables covary in the same direction) or negative (the variables covary in the opposite direction). The closer a correlation is to either +1.00 or –1.00, the stronger the association is. Higher correlations yield greater predictability. However, a high correlation is no assurance of causation.

● Descriptive/correlational research methods allow psychologists to explore issues that might not be open to experimental investigation. They are also less artificial than experiments. However, these research methods cannot demonstrate cause-effect relationships.

Looking for Flaws: Evaluating Research

● Scientists often try to replicate research findings to double-check their validity. Although this process leads to some contradictory findings, science works toward reconciling and explaining inconsistent results.

● Sampling bias occurs when a sample is not representative of the population of interest. Placebo effects occur when subjects' expectations cause them to change in response to a fake treatment. Distortions in self-reports are a source of concern whenever questionnaires and personality inventories are used to collect data. Experimenter bias occurs when researchers' expectations and desires sway their observations.

Looking at Ethics: Do the Ends Justify the Means?

● Research sometimes raises complex ethical issues. In psychology, the key questions concern the use of deception with human subjects and the use of harmful or painful manipulations with animal subjects. The APA has formulated ethical principles to serve as guidelines for researchers.

Putting It in Perspective

● Two of the book's unifying themes are apparent in this chapter's discussion of the research enterprise in psychology: psychology is empirical, and people's experience of the world can be highly subjective.

Personal Application ● Finding and Reading Journal Articles

● Journals publish technical and scholarly material. Usually they are written for other professionals in a narrow area of inquiry.

● PsycINFO is an online database that summarizes and indexes scholarly literature related to psychology. It contains brief summaries of journal articles, books, and chapters in edited books. You can search PsycINFO for publications by specific authors or for materials on specific topics.

● Journal articles are easier to understand if one is familiar with the standard format. Most articles include six elements: abstract, introduction, method, results, discussion, and references.

Critical Thinking Application ● The Perils of Anecdotal Evidence: "I Have a Friend Who . . ."

● Anecdotal evidence consists of personal stories about specific incidents and experiences. Anecdotes often influence people because they tend to be concrete, vivid, and memorable.

● However, anecdotal evidence is usually based on the equivalent of a single case study, which is not an adequate sample, and there are no safeguards to reduce the distortions often found in self-report data. Many anecdotes are inaccurate, second-hand reports of others' experiences. Effective critical thinking depends on evidence-based decision making.

Key Terms

Anecdotal evidence
Case study
Confounding of variables
Control group
Correlation
Correlation coefficient
Data collection techniques
Dependent variable
Double-blind procedure
Experiment
Experimental group
Experimenter bias
Extraneous variables
Hypothesis
Independent variable
Journal
Naturalistic observation
Operational definition
Participants
Placebo effects
Population
Random assignment
Replication
Research methods
Sample
Sampling bias
Social desirability bias
Subjects
Survey
Theory
Variables

Key People

Neal Miller
Robert Rosenthal
Stanley Schachter

PRACTICE TEST

1. Theories permit researchers to move from:
   A. understanding to application.
   B. concept to description.
   C. application to control.
   D. description to understanding.

2. Researchers must describe the actions that will be taken to measure or control each variable in their studies. In other words, they must:
   A. provide operational definitions of their variables.
   B. decide whether their studies will be experimental or correlational.
   C. use statistics to summarize their findings.
   D. decide how many subjects should participate in their studies.

3. A researcher found that clients who were randomly assigned to same-sex groups participated more in group therapy sessions than clients who were randomly assigned to coed groups. In this experiment, the independent variable was:
   A. the amount of participation in the group therapy sessions.
   B. whether or not the group was coed.
   C. the clients' attitudes toward group therapy.
   D. how much the clients' mental health improved.

4. A researcher wants to see whether a protein-enriched diet will enhance the maze-running performance of rats. One group of rats is fed the high-protein diet for the duration of the study; the other group continues to receive ordinary rat chow. In this experiment, the diet fed to the two groups of rats is the _____ variable.
   A. correlated
   B. control
   C. dependent
   D. independent

5. In a study of the effect of a new teaching technique on students' achievement test scores, an important extraneous variable would be the students':
   A. hair color.
   B. athletic skills.
   C. IQ scores.
   D. sociability.

6. Whenever you have a cold, you rest in bed, take aspirin, and drink plenty of fluids. You can't determine which remedy is most effective because of which of the following problems?
   A. Sampling bias
   B. Distorted self-report data
   C. Confounding of variables
   D. Experimenter bias

7. A psychologist monitors a group of nursery school children during the school day, recording each instance of altruistic behavior as it occurs, without any intervention. The psychologist is using:
   A. the experimental method.
   B. naturalistic observation.
   C. case studies.
   D. the survey method.

8. Among the advantages of descriptive/correlational research is (are):
   A. it can often be used in circumstances in which an experiment would be unethical.
   B. it permits researchers to examine subjects' behavior in natural, real-world circumstances.
   C. it can demonstrate conclusively that two variables are causally related.
   D. both a and b.

9. Which of the following correlation coefficients would indicate the strongest relationship between two variables?
   A. .58   C. −.97
   B. .19   D. −.05

10. As interest rates increase, house sales decline, indicating a(n) _____ between the two variables.
    A. direct correlation
    B. negative correlation
    C. positive correlation
    D. indirect correlation

11. Sampling bias exists when:
    A. the sample is representative of the population.
    B. the sample is not representative of the population.
    C. two variables are confounded.
    D. the effect of the independent variable can't be isolated.

12. The problem of experimenter bias can be avoided by:
    A. not informing subjects of the hypothesis of the experiment.
    B. telling the subjects that there are no "right" or "wrong" answers.
    C. using a research strategy in which neither subjects nor experimenter know which subjects are in the experimental and control groups.
    D. having the experimenter use only nonverbal signals when communicating with the subjects.

13. Critics of deception in research have assumed that deceptive studies are harmful to subjects. The empirical data on this issue suggests that:
    A. many deceptive studies do produce significant distress for subjects who were not forewarned about the possibility of deception.
    B. most participants in deceptive studies report that they enjoyed the experience and didn't mind being misled.
    C. deceptive research seriously undermines subjects' trust in others.
    D. Both a and c.

14. Which of the following would not be included in the results section of a journal article?
    A. Descriptive statistics summarizing the data
    B. Statistical analysis of the data
    C. Graphs and/or tables presenting the data pictorially
    D. Interpretation, evaluation, and implications of the data

15. Anecdotal evidence
    A. is often concrete, vivid, and memorable.
    B. tends to influence people.
    C. is fundamentally flawed and unreliable.
    D. is all of the above.

Answers

1	D	page 32	6	C	page 38	11	B page 46
2	A	page 33	7	B	page 42	12	C page 48
3	B	page 36	8	D	page 44	13	B page 49
4	D	page 36	9	C	pages 40–41	14	D page 53
5	C	pages 37–38	10	B	page 40	15	D pages 54–55

INFOTRAC
COLLEGE EDITION

Go to the Wadsworth Psychology Study Center for quiz questions, research updates, interactive exercises, and suggested readings in INFOTRAC related to this chapter:
http://psychology.wadsworth.com/product/0534593100s

CHAPTER 3

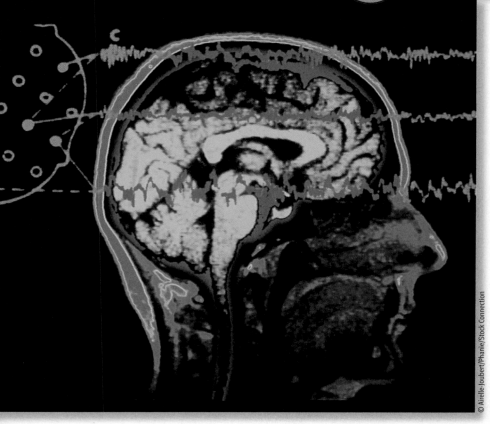

© Airelle-Joubert/Phanie/Stock Connection

The Biological Bases of Behavior

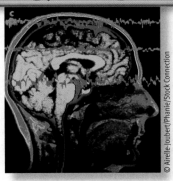

If you have ever visited an aquarium, you may have encountered one of nature's more captivating animals: the octopus. Although this jellylike mass of arms and head appears to be a relatively simple creature, it is capable of a number of interesting behaviors. The octopus has highly developed eyes that enable it to respond to stimuli in the darkness of the ocean. When threatened, it can release an inky cloud to befuddle enemies while it makes good its escape by a kind of rocket propulsion. If that doesn't work, it can camouflage itself by changing color and texture to blend into its surroundings. Furthermore, the

animal is surprisingly intelligent. In captivity, an octopus can learn, for example, to twist the lid off a jar with one of its tentacles to get at a treat that is inside.

Despite its talents, there are many things an octopus cannot do. An octopus cannot study psychology, plan a weekend, dream about its future, or discover the Pythagorean theorem. Yet the biological processes that underlie these uniquely human behaviors are much the same as the biological processes that enable an octopus to escape from a predator or forage for food. Indeed, some of science's most important insights about how the nervous system works came from studies of a relative of the octopus, the squid.

Organisms as diverse as humans and squid share many biological processes. However, their unique behavioral capacities depend on the differences in their physiological makeup. You and I have a larger repertoire of behaviors than the octopus because we

come equipped with a more complex brain and nervous system. The activity of the human brain is so complex that no computer has ever come close to duplicating it. Your nervous system contains as many cells busily integrating and relaying information as there are stars in our galaxy. Whether you are scratching your nose or composing an essay, the activity of those cells underlies what you do. It is little wonder, then, that many psychologists have dedicated themselves to exploring the biological bases of behavior.

How do mood-altering drugs work? Are the two halves of the brain specialized to perform different functions? What happens inside the body when you feel a strong emotion? Are some mental illnesses the result of chemical imbalances in the brain? To what extent is intelligence determined by biological inheritance? These questions only begin to suggest the countless ways in which biology is fundamental to the study of behavior.

Communication in the Nervous System

Imagine that you are watching a scary movie. As the tension mounts, your palms sweat and your heart beats faster. You begin shoveling popcorn into your mouth, carelessly spilling some in your lap. If someone were to ask you what you are doing at this moment, you would probably say, "Nothing—just watching the movie." Yet some highly complex processes are occurring without your thinking about them. A stimulus (the light from the screen) is striking your eye. Almost instantaneously, your brain is interpreting the light stimulus, and signals are flashing to other parts of your body, leading to a flurry of activity. Your sweat glands are releasing perspiration, your heartbeat is quickening, and muscular movements are enabling your hand to find the popcorn and, more or less successfully, lift it to your mouth.

Even in this simple example, you can see that behavior depends on rapid information processing. Information travels almost instantaneously from your eye to your brain, from your brain to the muscles of your arm and hand, and from your palms back to your brain. In essence, your nervous system is a complex communication network in which signals are constantly being received, integrated, and transmitted. The nervous system handles information, just as the circulatory system handles blood. In this section, we take a close look at communication in the nervous system.

Nervous Tissue: The Basic Hardware

Your nervous system is living tissue composed of cells. The cells in the nervous system fall into two major categories: *glia* and *neurons*. *Glia* are cells found throughout the nervous system that provide structural support and insulation for neurons. Glia (literally "glue") hold the nervous system together and help maintain the chemical environment of the neurons. **Neurons are individual cells in the nervous system that receive, integrate, and transmit information.** They are the basic links that permit communication within the nervous system. The vast majority of them communicate only with other neurons. However, a small minority receive signals from outside the nervous system (from sensory organs) or carry messages from the nervous system to the muscles that move the body.

A highly simplified drawing of a few "typical" neurons is shown in Figure 3.1. Actually, neurons come in such a tremendous variety of types and shapes that no single drawing can adequately represent them. Trying to draw the "typical" neuron is like trying to draw the "typical" tree. In spite of this diversity, the drawing in Figure 3.1 highlights some common features of neurons.

The *soma*, or cell body, contains the cell nucleus and much of the chemical machinery common to most cells (*soma* is Greek for "body"). The rest of the neuron is devoted exclusively to handling information. The neuron at the left in Figure 3.1 has a number of branched, feelerlike structures called *dendritic trees* (*dendrite* is a Greek word for "tree"). Each individual branch is a *dendrite*. **Dendrites are the parts of a neuron that are specialized to receive information.** Most neurons receive information from many other cells—sometimes thousands of others—and so have extensive dendritic trees.

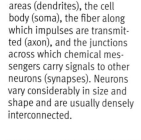

Figure 3.1

Structure of the neuron. Neurons are the communication links of the nervous system. This diagram highlights the key parts of a neuron, including specialized receptor areas (dendrites), the cell body (soma), the fiber along which impulses are transmitted (axon), and the junctions across which chemical messengers carry signals to other neurons (synapses). Neurons vary considerably in size and shape and are usually densely interconnected.

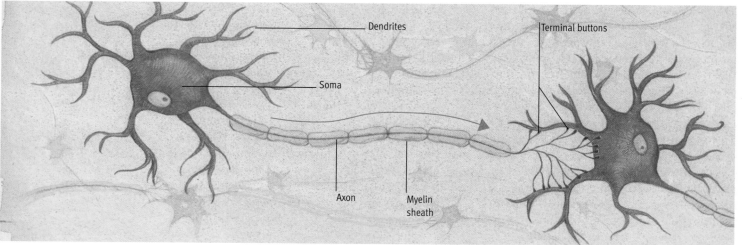

Dendrites

Terminal buttons

Soma

Axon

Myelin sheath

From the many dendrites, information flows into the cell body and then travels away from the soma along the *axon* (from the Greek for "axle"). **The *axon* is a long, thin fiber that transmits signals away from the soma to other neurons or to muscles or glands.** Axons may be quite long (sometimes several feet), and they may branch off to communicate with a number of other cells.

In humans, many axons are wrapped in cells with a high concentration of a white, fatty substance called myelin. The *myelin sheath* is insulating material, derived from glial cells, that encases some axons. The myelin sheath speeds up the transmission of signals that move along axons. If an axon's myelin sheath deteriorates, its signals may not be transmitted effectively. The loss of muscle control seen with the disease *multiple sclerosis* is due to a degeneration of myelin sheaths (Adams & Victor, 1993).

The axon ends in a cluster of **terminal buttons, which are small knobs that secrete chemicals called neurotransmitters.** These chemicals serve as messengers that may activate neighboring neurons. The points at which neurons interconnect are called *synapses*. **A *synapse* is a junction where information is transmitted from one neuron to another** (*synapse* is from the Greek for "junction").

To summarize, information is received at the dendrites, is passed through the soma and along the axon, and is transmitted to the dendrites of other cells at meeting points called synapses. Unfortunately, this nice, simple picture has more exceptions than the U.S. Tax Code. For example, some neurons do not have an axon, while others have multiple axons. Also, although neurons typically synapse on the dendrites of other cells, they may also synapse on a soma or an axon. Despite these and other complexities, however, the fundamental function of neurons is clear: they are the nervous system's input-output devices that receive, integrate, and transmit informational signals.

The Neural Impulse: Using Energy to Send Information

What happens when a neuron is stimulated? What is the nature of the signal—the *neural impulse*—that moves through the neuron? These were the questions that Alan Hodgkin and Andrew Huxley set out to answer in their groundbreaking experiments with axons removed from squid. Why did they choose to work with squid axons? Because the squid has a pair of "giant" axons that are about a hundred times larger than those in humans (which still makes them only about as thick as a human hair).

Their large size permitted Hodgkin and Huxley to insert fine wires called *microelectrodes* into them. By using the microelectrodes to record the electrical activity in individual neurons, Hodgkin and Huxley unraveled the mystery of the neural impulse.

The Neuron at Rest: A Tiny Battery

Hodgkin and Huxley (1952) learned that the neural impulse is a complex electrochemical reaction. Both inside and outside the neuron are fluids containing electrically charged atoms and molecules called *ions*. Positively charged sodium and potassium ions and negatively charged chloride ions flow back and forth across the cell membrane, but they do not cross at the same rate. The difference in flow rates leads to a slightly higher concentration of negatively charged ions inside the cell. The resulting voltage means that the neuron at rest is a tiny battery, a store of potential energy. **The *resting potential* of a neuron is its stable, negative charge when the cell is inactive.** As shown in Figure 3.2(a) on the next page, this charge is about –70 millivolts, roughly one-twentieth of the voltage of a flashlight battery.

The Action Potential

As long as the voltage of a neuron remains constant, the cell is quiet, and no messages are being sent. When the neuron is stimulated, channels in its cell membrane open, briefly allowing positively charged sodium ions to rush in. For an instant, the neuron's charge is less negative, or even positive, creating an action potential (Koester, 1991). **An *action potential* is a very brief shift in a neuron's electrical charge that travels along an axon.** The firing of an action potential is reflected in the voltage spike shown in Figure 3.2(b). Like a spark traveling along a trail of gunpowder, the voltage change races down the axon.

After the firing of an action potential, the channels in the cell membrane that opened to let in sodium close up. Some time is needed before they are ready to open again, and until that time the neuron cannot fire. **The *absolute refractory period* is the minimum length of time after an action potential during which another action potential cannot begin.** This "down time" isn't very long, only 1 or 2 milliseconds (msec).

The All-or-None Law

The neural impulse is an all-or-none proposition, like firing a gun. You can't half-fire a gun. The same is true of the neuron's firing of action potentials. Either the neuron fires or it doesn't, and its action potentials are all the same size. That is, weaker stimuli do not produce smaller action potentials.

Web Link 3.1

Neuropsychology Central
This content-rich site, maintained by Jeffrey Browndyke of Louisiana State University, is dedicated to all aspects of human neuropsychology from the perspectives of the experimental research laboratory as well as the applied clinical setting of the hospital and professional office.

Figure **3.2**

The neural impulse. The electrochemical properties of the neuron allow it to transmit signals. The electric charge of a neuron can be measured with a pair of electrodes connected to a device called an oscilloscope, as Hodgkin and Huxley showed with a squid axon. Because of its exceptionally thick axons, the squid has frequently been used by scientists studying the neural impulse. (a) At rest, the neuron is like a tiny wet battery with a resting potential of about −70 millivolts. (b) When a neuron is stimulated, a brief jump in its electric potential occurs, resulting in a spike on the oscilloscope recording of the neuron's electrical activity. This change in voltage, called an action potential, travels along the axon like a spark traveling along a trail of gunpowder.

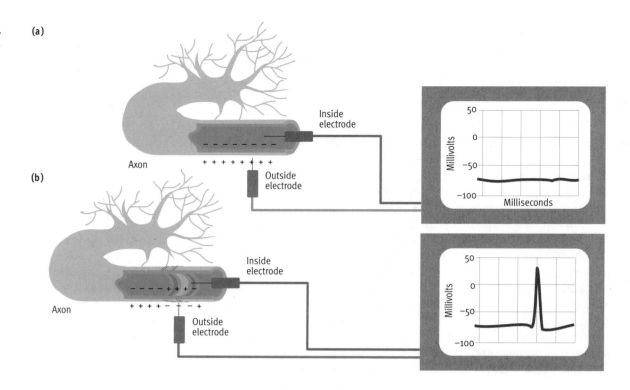

Web Link 3.2

Molecular Neurobiology: A Gallery of Animations
Site editor and physician Neil Busis brings together a set of QuickTime animations demonstrating activities at the molecular level of the synapse, such as the fusion of synaptic vesicles with the presynaptic membrane.

Even though the action potential is an all-or-nothing event, neurons *can* convey information about the strength of a stimulus. They do so by varying the *rate* at which they fire action potentials. In general, a stronger stimulus will cause a cell to fire a more rapid volley of neural impulses than a weaker stimulus will.

Various neurons transmit neural impulses at different speeds. For example, thicker axons transmit neural impulses more rapidly than thinner ones do. Although neural impulses do not travel as fast as electricity along a wire, they *are* very fast, moving at up to 100 meters per second, which is equivalent to more than 200 miles per hour. The entire complicated process of neural transmission takes only a few thousandths of a second. In the time it has taken you to read this description of the neural impulse, billions of such impulses have been transmitted in your nervous system!

The Synapse: Where Neurons Meet

In the nervous system, the neural impulse functions as a signal. For that signal to have any meaning for the system as a whole, it must be transmitted from the neuron to other cells. As noted earlier, this transmission takes place at special junctions called *synapses,* which depend on *chemical* messengers.

Sending Signals: Chemicals as Couriers

A "typical" synapse is shown in Figure 3.3. The first thing that you should notice is that the two neurons don't actually touch. They are separated by the ***synaptic cleft,* a microscopic gap between the terminal button of one neuron and the cell membrane of another neuron.** Signals have to jump this gap to permit neurons to communicate. In this situation, the neuron that sends a signal across the gap is called the *presynaptic neuron,* and the neuron that receives the signal is called the *postsynaptic neuron.*

How do messages travel across the gaps between neurons? The arrival of an action potential at an axon's terminal buttons triggers the release of ***neurotransmitters*—chemicals that transmit information from one neuron to another.** Within the buttons, most of these chemicals are stored in small sacs, called *synaptic vesicles.* The neurotransmitters are released when a vesicle fuses with the membrane of the presynaptic cell and its contents spill into the synaptic cleft. After their release, neurotransmitters diffuse across the synaptic cleft to the membrane of the receiving cell. There they may bind with special molecules in the postsynaptic cell membrane at various *receptor sites.* These sites are specifically "tuned" to recognize and respond to some neurotransmitters but not to others.

Receiving Signals: Postsynaptic Potentials

When a neurotransmitter and a receptor molecule combine, reactions in the cell membrane cause a *postsynaptic potential (PSP)*, **a voltage change at a receptor site on a postsynaptic cell membrane.** Postsynaptic potentials do *not* follow the all-or-none law as action potentials do. Instead, postsynaptic potentials are *graded*. That is, they vary in size and they increase or decrease the *probability* of a neural impulse in the receiving cell in proportion to the amount of voltage change.

Two types of messages can be sent from cell to cell: excitatory and inhibitory. An *excitatory PSP* is a positive voltage shift that increases the likelihood that the postsynaptic neuron will fire action potentials. An *inhibitory PSP* is a negative voltage shift that decreases the likelihood that the postsynaptic neuron will fire action potentials. The direction of the voltage shift, and thus the nature of the PSP (excitatory or inhibitory), depends on which receptor sites are activated in the postsynaptic neuron (Kandel & Schwartz, 1991).

The excitatory or inhibitory effects produced at a synapse last only a fraction of a second. Then neurotransmitters drift away from receptor sites or are inactivated by enzymes that metabolize (convert) them into inactive forms. Most are reabsorbed into the presynaptic neuron through **reuptake, a process in which neurotransmitters are sponged up from the synaptic cleft by the presynaptic membrane.** Reuptake allows synapses to recycle their materials. Reuptake and the other key processes in synaptic transmission are summarized in Figure 3.4 on the next page.

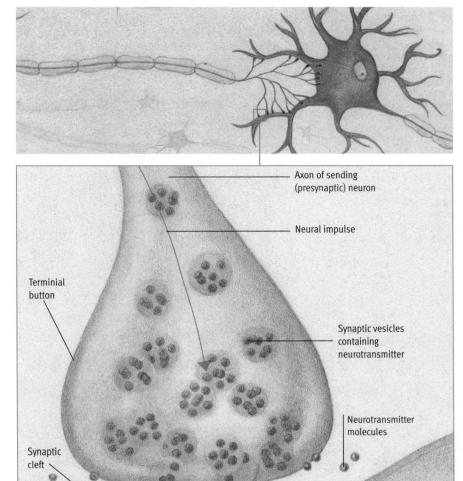

Axon of sending (presynaptic) neuron

Neural impulse

Terminial button

Synaptic vesicles containing neurotransmitter

Neurotransmitter molecules

Synaptic cleft

Cell membrane of receiving (postsynaptic) neuron

Receptor sites

Transmitter fits receptor site, binds to cell membrane, producing postsynaptic potential

Transmitter does not fit at receptor site, cannot bind to cell membrane

Figure 3.3

The synapse. When a neural impulse reaches an axon's terminal buttons, it triggers the release of chemical messengers called neurotransmitters. The neurotransmitter molecules diffuse across the synaptic cleft and bind to receptor sites on the postsynaptic neuron. A specific neurotransmitter can bind only to receptor sites that its molecular structure will fit into, much like a key must fit a lock.

CONCEPT CHECK 3.1

Understanding Nervous System Hardware Using Metaphors

A useful way to learn about the structures and functions of parts of the nervous system is through metaphors. Check your understanding of the basic components of the nervous system by matching the metaphorical descriptions below with the correct terms in the following list: (a) glia, (b) neuron, (c) soma, (d) dendrite, (e) axon, (f) myelin, (g) terminal button, (h) synapse. You'll find the answers in Appendix A.

_____ **1.** Like a tree. Also, each branch is a telephone wire that carries incoming messages to you.

_____ **2.** Like the insulation that covers electrical wires.

_____ **3.** Like a silicon chip in a computer that receives and transmits information between input and output devices as well as between other chips.

_____ **4.** Like an electrical cable that carries information.

_____ **5.** Like the maintenance personnel who keep things clean and in working order so the operations of the enterprise can proceed.

_____ **6.** Like the nozzle at the end of a hose, from which water is squirted.

_____ **7.** Like a railroad junction, where two trains may meet.

Figure **3.4**

Overview of synaptic transmission. The main elements in synaptic transmission are summarized here, superimposed on a blowup of the synapse seen in Figure 3.3. The five key processes involved in communication at synapses are (1) synthesis, (2) release, (3) binding, (4) inactivation, and (5) reuptake of neurotransmitters. As you'll see in this chapter and the remainder of the book, the effects of many phenomena—such as stress, drug use, and some diseases—can be explained in terms of how they alter one or more of these processes (usually at synapses releasing a specific neurotransmitter).

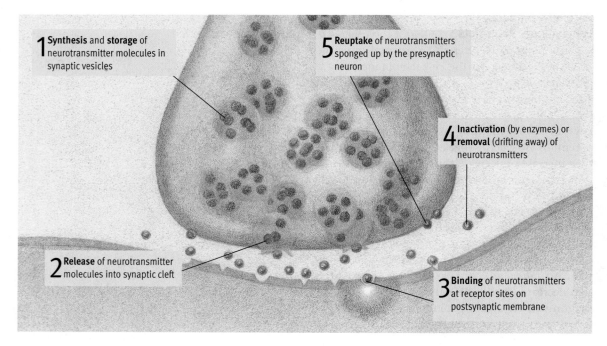

1 **Synthesis** and **storage** of neurotransmitter molecules in synaptic vesicles

5 **Reuptake** of neurotransmitters sponged up by the presynaptic neuron

4 **Inactivation** (by enzymes) or **removal** (drifting away) of neurotransmitters

2 **Release** of neurotransmitter molecules into synaptic cleft

3 **Binding** of neurotransmitters at receptor sites on postsynaptic membrane

Integrating Signals: A Balancing Act

Most neurons are interlinked in complex, dense networks. In fact, a neuron may receive a symphony of signals from *thousands* of other neurons. The same neuron may pass its messages along to thousands of neurons as well. Thus, a neuron must do a great deal more than simply relay messages it receives. It must *integrate* signals arriving at many synapses before it "decides" whether to fire a neural impulse. If enough excitatory PSPs occur in a neuron, the electrical currents can add up, causing the cell's voltage to reach the threshold at which an action potential will be fired. However, if many inhibitory PSPs also occur, they will tend to cancel the effects of excitatory PSPs. Thus, the state of the neuron is a weighted balance between excitatory and inhibitory influences.

Neurotransmitters and Behavior

As we have seen, the nervous system relies on chemical couriers to communicate information between neurons. These *neurotransmitters* are fundamental to behavior, playing a key role in everything from muscle movements to moods and mental health.

You might guess that the nervous system would require only two neurotransmitters—one for excitatory potentials and one for inhibitory potentials. However, 15 to 20 chemical substances appear to qualify as neurotransmitters. In addition, scientists suspect that a number of other substances *may*

function as transmitters, and new candidates are still being discovered.

Specific neurotransmitters work at specific kinds of synapses. You may recall that transmitters deliver their messages by binding to receptor sites on the postsynaptic membrane. However, a transmitter cannot bind to just any site. The binding process operates much like a lock and key, as was shown in Figure 3.3. Just as a key has to fit a lock to work, a transmitter has to fit into a receptor site for binding to occur. Hence, specific transmitters can deliver signals only at certain locations on cell membranes.

Why are there many different neurotransmitters, each of which works only at certain synapses? This variety and specificity reduces crosstalk between densely packed neurons, making the nervous system's communication more precise. Let's briefly review some of the most interesting findings about how neurotransmitters regulate behavior, which are summarized in Table 3.1.

Acetylcholine

The discovery that cells communicate by releasing chemicals was first made in connection with the transmitter *acetylcholine* (ACh). ACh has been found throughout the nervous system. It is the only transmitter between motor neurons and voluntary muscles. Every move you make—walking, talking, breathing—depends on ACh released to your muscles by motor neurons (Kandel & Schwartz, 1991). ACh also appears to contribute to attention, arousal, and perhaps memory.

The activity of ACh (and other neurotransmitters) may be influenced by other chemicals in the brain. Although synaptic receptor sites are sensitive to specific neurotransmitters, sometimes they can be "fooled" by other chemical substances. For example, if you smoke tobacco, some of your ACh synapses will be stimulated by the nicotine that arrives in your brain. At these synapses, the nicotine acts like ACh itself. It binds to receptor sites for ACh, causing postsynaptic potentials (PSPs). In technical language, nicotine is an ACh agonist. **An *agonist* is a chemical that mimics the action of a neurotransmitter.**

Not all chemicals that fool synaptic receptors are agonists. Some chemicals bind to receptors but fail to produce a PSP (the key slides into the lock, but it doesn't work). In effect, they temporarily *block* the action of the natural transmitter by occupying its receptor sites, rendering them unusable. Thus, they act as antagonists. **An *antagonist* is a chemical that opposes the action of a neurotransmitter.** For example, the drug *curare* is an ACh antagonist. It blocks action at the same ACh synapses that are fooled by nicotine. As a result, muscles are unable to move. Some South American natives use a form of curare on arrows. If they wound an animal, the curare blocks the synapses from nerve to muscle, paralyzing the animal.

Monoamines

The *monoamines* include three neurotransmitters: dopamine, norepinephrine, and serotonin. Neurons using these transmitters regulate many aspects of everyday behavior. Dopamine (DA), for example, is used by neurons that control voluntary movements. The degeneration of such neurons apparently causes *Parkinsonism,* a disease marked by tremors, muscular rigidity, and reduced control over voluntary movements (Coté & Crutcher, 1991).

Although other neurotransmitters are also involved, serotonin-releasing neurons appear to play a prominent role in the regulation of sleep and wakefulness (Vodelholzer et al., 1998) and eating behavior (Blundell & Halford, 1998). There also is considerable evidence that neural circuits using serotonin modulate aggressive behavior in animals (Bernhardt, 1997) and some preliminary evidence relating serotonin activity to aggression and impulsive behavior in humans (Bond & Cleare, 1997; Spoont, 1992).

Abnormal levels of monoamines in the brain have been related to the development of certain psychological disorders. For example, people who suffer from depression appear to have lowered levels of activation at norepinephrine (NE) and serotonin synapses. Although a host of other biochemical

Table 3.1 **Common Neurotransmitters and Some of Their Functions**

Neurotransmitter	Functions and Characteristics
Acetylcholine (ACh)	Activates motor neurons controlling skeletal muscles Contributes to the regulation of attention, arousal, and memory Some ACh receptors stimulated by nicotine
Dopamine (DA)	Contributes to control of voluntary movement, pleasurable emotions Decreased levels associated with Parkinson's disease Overactivity at DA synapses associated with schizophrenia Cocaine and amphetamines elevate activity at DA synapses
Norepinephrine (NE)	Contributes to modulation of mood and arousal Cocaine and amphetamines elevate activity at NE synapses
Serotonin	Involved in regulation of sleep and wakefulness, eating, aggression Abnormal levels may contribute to depression and obsessive-compulsive disorder Prozac and similar antidepressant drugs affect serotonin circuits
Endorphins	Resemble opiate drugs in structure and effects Contribute to pain relief and perhaps to some pleasurable emotions "Runner's high" may be associated with high endorphin levels

changes may also contribute to depression, abnormalities at NE and serotonin synapses appear to play a central role, as most antidepressant drugs exert their main effects at these synapses (Charney et al., 1995; Nathan et al., 1995).

In a similar fashion, abnormalities in activity at dopamine synapses have been implicated in the development of *schizophrenia*. This severe mental illness is marked by irrational thought, hallucinations, poor contact with reality, and deterioration of routine adaptive behavior. Afflicting roughly 1% of the population, schizophrenia requires hospitalization more often than any other psychological disorder (see Chapter 14). Studies suggest, albeit with many complications, that overactivity at DA synapses is the neurochemical basis for schizophrenia. Why? Primarily because the therapeutic drugs that tame schizophrenic symptoms are known to be DA antagonists that reduce the neurotransmitter's activity (Marder & Van Putten, 1995).

Temporary alterations at monoamine synapses also appear to account for the powerful effects of some widely abused drugs, including amphetamines and cocaine. Amphetamines and cocaine seem to exert most of their effects by increasing the release of dopamine and norepinephrine from presynaptic neurons and by slowing the reuptake of DA and NE (Gold & Miller, 1997; King & Ellinwood, 1997). These actions leave an overabundance of DA and NE in synaptic clefts, thus causing a storm of increased activity at these synapses.

Endorphins

In 1970, after a horseback-riding accident, Candace Pert, a graduate student in neuroscience, lay in a

Web Link 3.3

Neurosciences on the Internet
Neil Busis has gathered together what appears to be the largest collection of neuroscience links currently on the web, along with a search engine to help the user.

© 1991 Analisa Kraft

"*When human beings engage in various activities, it seems that neurojuices are released that are associated with either pain or pleasure. And the endorphins are very pleasurable.*"
CANDACE PERT

"Brain research of the past decade, especially the study of neurotransmitters, has proceeded at a furious pace, achieving progress equal in scope to all the accomplishments of the preceding fifty years—and the pace of discovery continues to accelerate."
SOLOMON SNYDER

hospital bed receiving frequent shots of *morphine,* a painkilling drug derived from the opium plant. This experience left her with a driving curiosity about how morphine works. A few years later, she and Solomon Snyder rocked the scientific world by showing that *morphine exerts its effects by binding to specialized receptors in the brain* (Pert & Snyder, 1973).

This discovery raised a perplexing question: Why would the brain be equipped with receptors for morphine, a powerful, addictive opiate drug not normally found in the body? It occurred to Pert and others that the nervous system must have its own, endogenous (internally produced) morphine-like substances. Investigators dubbed these as-yet undiscovered substances "endorphins" (endogenous morphines). A search for the body's natural opiate ensued. In short order, a number of endogenous, opiatelike substances were identified (Hughes et al., 1975). Subsequent studies revealed that endorphins and their receptors are widely distributed in the human body and that they clearly contribute to the modulation of pain, as well as a variety of other phenomena (E. Simon, 1992). The term **endorphins** refers to the entire family of internally produced chemicals that resemble opiates in structure and effects.

The discovery of endorphins has led to new theories and findings on the neurochemical bases of pain and pleasure. In addition to their painkilling effects, opiate drugs such as morphine and heroin produce highly pleasurable feelings of euphoria. This euphoric effect explains why heroin is so widely abused. Researchers suspect that the body's natural endorphins may also be capable of producing feelings of pleasure. This capacity might explain why joggers sometimes experience a "runner's high." The pain caused by a long run may trigger the release of endorphins, which neutralize some of the pain and create a feeling of exhilaration (Harte, Eifert, & Smith, 1995).

In this section we have highlighted just a few of the more interesting connections between neurotransmitters and behavior. These highlights barely begin to convey the rich complexity of biochemical processes in the nervous system. Most aspects of behavior are probably regulated by several types of transmitters. To further complicate matters, researchers are finding fascinating *interactions* between various neurotransmitter systems, such as serotonin and dopamine circuits (G. S. Smith et al., 1997). Although scientists have learned a great deal about neurotransmitters and behavior, much still remains to be discovered.

CONCEPT **CHECK 3.2**

Linking Brain Chemistry to Behavior

Check your understanding of relations between brain chemistry and behavior by indicating which neurotransmitters or other biological chemicals have been linked to the phenomena listed below. Choose your answers from the following list: (a) acetylcholine, (b) norepinephrine, (c) dopamine, (d) serotonin, (e) endorphins. Indicate your choice (by letter) in the spaces on the left. You'll find the answers in Appendix A.

_____ **1.** A transmitter involved in the regulation of sleep, eating, and aggression.
_____ **2.** The two monoamines that have been linked to depression.
_____ **3.** Chemicals that resemble opiate drugs in structure and that are involved in feelings of pain and pleasure.
_____ **4.** A neurotransmitter for which abnormal levels have been implicated in schizophrenia.
_____ **5.** The only neurotransmitter between motor neurons and voluntary muscles.

Organization of the Nervous System

Clearly, communication in the nervous system is fundamental to behavior. So far we have looked at how individual cells communicate with one another. In this section, we examine the organization of the nervous system as a whole.

Experts believe that there are *85 to 180 billion* neurons in the human brain (Kolb & Whishaw, 1990; Williams & Herrup, 1988). Obviously, this is

only an *estimate.* If you counted them nonstop at the rate of one per second, you'd be counting for about 6000 years! The multitudes of neurons in your nervous system have to work together to keep information flowing effectively. To do so, they are organized into teams. The various teams have specialized functions and duties that depend primarily on their location. To see how the nervous system is

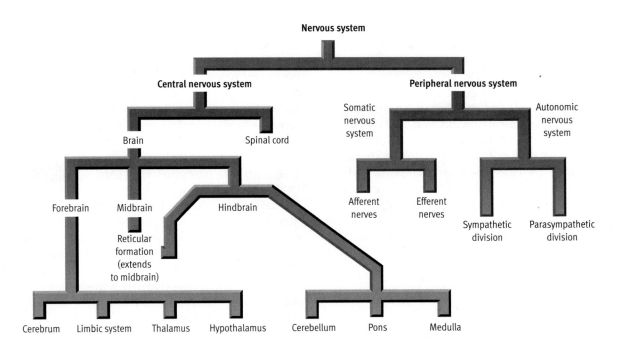

Nervous system

Central nervous system

Brain — Spinal cord

Forebrain — Midbrain — Hindbrain

Reticular formation (extends to midbrain)

Cerebrum — Limbic system — Thalamus — Hypothalamus — Cerebellum — Pons — Medulla

Peripheral nervous system

Somatic nervous system — Autonomic nervous system

Afferent nerves — Efferent nerves

Sympathetic division — Parasympathetic division

Figure 3.5

Organization of the human nervous system. The central nervous system is composed mostly of the brain, which is traditionally divided into three regions: the hindbrain, the midbrain, and the forebrain. The reticular formation runs through both the midbrain and hindbrain on its way up and down the brainstem. These and other parts of the brain are discussed in detail later in the chapter. The peripheral nervous system is made up of the somatic nervous system, which controls voluntary muscles and sensory receptors, and the autonomic nervous system, which controls smooth muscles, blood vessels, and glands.

organized, we will perform a series of "cuts" that will divide it into parts. In many instances, the parts will be divided once again. Figure 3.5 presents an organizational chart that shows the relationships of all the parts of the nervous system.

The Peripheral Nervous System 2a, 8c

The first and most important cut separates the *central nervous system* (the brain and spinal cord) from the *peripheral nervous system* (see Figure 3.6). **The peripheral nervous system is made up of all those nerves that lie outside the brain and spinal cord.** *Nerves* are bundles of neuron fibers (axons) that are routed together in the peripheral nervous system. This portion of the nervous system is just what it sounds like, the part that extends to the periphery (the outside) of the body. The peripheral nervous system can be subdivided into the somatic nervous system and the autonomic nervous system.

The Somatic Nervous System 2a

The *somatic nervous system* is made up of nerves that connect to voluntary skeletal muscles and to sensory receptors. These nerves are the cables that carry information from receptors in the skin, muscles, and joints to the central nervous system and that carry commands from the central nervous system to the muscles. These functions require two kinds of nerve fibers. *Afferent nerve fibers* are axons that carry information inward to the central

nervous system from the periphery of the body. *Efferent nerve fibers* are axons that carry information outward from the central nervous system to the periphery of the body. Each body nerve contains many axons of each type. Thus, somatic nerves are "two-way streets" with incoming (afferent) and outgoing (efferent) lanes. The somatic nervous system lets you feel the world and move around in it.

The Autonomic Nervous System 2a, 8c

The *autonomic nervous system (ANS)* is made up of nerves that connect to the heart, blood vessels, smooth muscles, and glands. As its name hints, the autonomic system is a separate (autonomous) system, although it is ultimately controlled by the central nervous system. The autonomic nervous system controls automatic, involuntary, visceral functions that people don't normally think about, such as heart rate, digestion, and perspiration.

The autonomic nervous system mediates much of the physiological arousal that occurs when people experience emotions. For example, imagine that you are walking home alone one night when a seedy-looking character falls in behind you and begins to follow you. If you feel threatened, your heart rate and breathing will speed up. Your blood pressure may surge, you may get goose bumps, and your palms may begin to sweat. These difficult-to-control reactions are aspects of autonomic arousal. Walter Cannon (1932), one of the first psychologists to study this reaction, called it the *fight-or-flight response.*

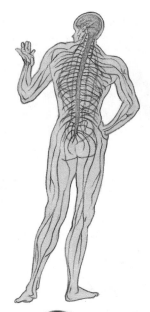

Figure 3.6

The central and peripheral nervous systems. The human nervous system is divided into the *central nervous system,* which consists of the brain and the spinal cord, and the *peripheral nervous system,* which consists of the remaining nerves that fan out throughout the body. The peripheral nervous system is divided into the somatic nervous system, shown in green, and the autonomic nervous system, shown in red.

Cannon carefully monitored this response in animals. He concluded that organisms generally respond to threat by preparing physically for attacking (fight) or fleeing (flight) the enemy.

The autonomic nervous system can be subdivided into two branches: the sympathetic division and the parasympathetic division (see Figure 3.7). The *sympathetic division* is the branch of the autonomic nervous system that mobilizes the body's resources for emergencies. It creates the fight-or-flight response. Activation of the sympathetic division slows digestive processes and drains blood from the periphery, lessening bleeding in the case of an injury. Key sympathetic nerves send signals to the adrenal glands, triggering the release of hormones that ready the body for exertion. In contrast, the *parasympathetic division* is the branch of the autonomic nervous system that generally conserves bodily resources. It activates processes that allow the body to save and store energy. For example, actions by parasympathetic nerves slow heart rate, reduce blood pressure, and promote digestion.

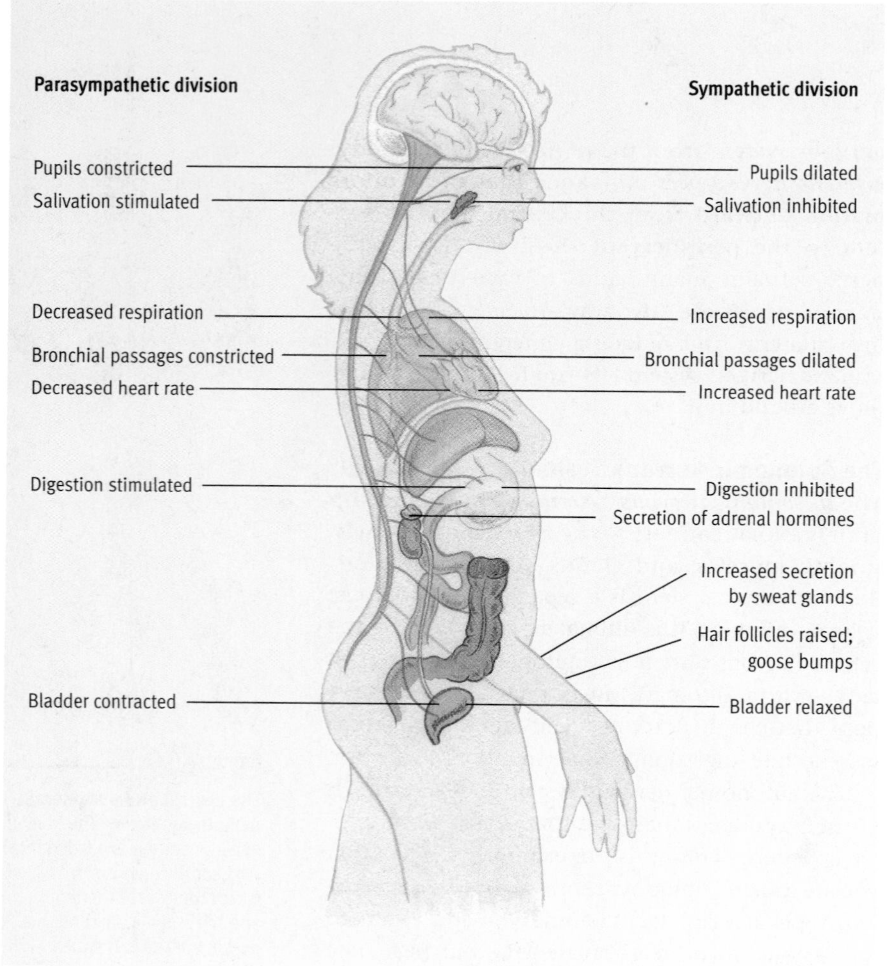

The Central Nervous System

The central nervous system is the portion of the nervous system that lies within the skull and spinal column. Thus, **the *central nervous system (CNS)* consists of the brain and the spinal cord.** The CNS is bathed in its own special nutritive "soup," called *cerebrospinal fluid* (CSF). This fluid nourishes the brain and provides a protective cushion for it. Although derived from the blood, the CSF is carefully filtered. To enter the CSF, substances in the blood have to cross the *blood-brain barrier,* a semipermeable membranelike mechanism that stops some chemicals from passing between the bloodstream and the brain. This barrier prevents some drugs from entering the CSF and affecting the brain.

The Spinal Cord

The *spinal cord* connects the brain to the rest of the body through the peripheral nervous system. Although the spinal cord looks like a cable from which the somatic nerves branch, it is part of the central nervous system. The spinal cord runs from the base of the brain to just below the level of the waist. It houses bundles of axons that carry the brain's commands to peripheral nerves and that relay sensations from the periphery of the body to the brain. Many forms of paralysis result from spinal cord damage, a fact that underscores the critical role it plays in transmitting signals from the brain to the neurons that move the body's muscles.

The Brain

The crowning glory of the central nervous system is, of course, the *brain.* Anatomically, the *brain* is the part of the central nervous system that fills the upper portion of the skull. Although it weighs only about three pounds and could be held in one hand, the brain contains billions of interacting cells that integrate information from inside and outside the body, coordinate the body's actions, and enable us to talk, think, remember, plan, create, and dream. Because of its central importance for behavior, the brain is the subject of the next two sections of the chapter.

Parasympathetic division

Pupils constricted
Salivation stimulated

Decreased respiration
Bronchial passages constricted
Decreased heart rate

Digestion stimulated

Bladder contracted

Sympathetic division

Pupils dilated
Salivation inhibited

Increased respiration
Bronchial passages dilated
Increased heart rate

Digestion inhibited
Secretion of adrenal hormones

Increased secretion by sweat glands

Hair follicles raised; goose bumps

Bladder relaxed

Figure 3.7

The autonomic nervous system (ANS). The ANS is composed of the nerves that connect to the heart, blood vessels, smooth muscles, and glands. The ANS is divided into the *sympathetic division,* which mobilizes bodily resources in times of need, and the *parasympathetic division,* which conserves bodily resources. Some of the key functions controlled by each division of the ANS are summarized in the diagram.

Scientists who want to find out how parts of the brain are related to behavior are faced with a formidable task, because mapping out brain *function* requires a working brain. These scientists use a variety of specialized techniques to investigate brain-behavior relations. For instance, researchers sometimes observe what happens when specific brain structures in animals are purposely destroyed through a process called *lesioning*. This procedure involves inserting an electrode into a brain structure and passing a high-frequency electric current through it to burn the tissue and disable the structure. Another valuable technique is *electrical stimulation of the brain (ESB)*, which involves sending a weak electric current into a brain structure to stimulate (activate) it. As in lesioning, the current is delivered through an implanted electrode, but the current is different. This sort of electrical stimulation does not exactly duplicate normal electrical

signals in the brain. However, it is usually a close enough approximation to activate the brain structures in which the electrodes are lodged. Obviously, these invasive procedures are largely limited to animal research, although ESB is occasionally used on humans in the context of brain surgery required for medical purposes.

Fortunately, in recent years, the invention of new brain-imaging devices has led to dramatic advances in scientists' ability to look inside the human brain. The *CT (computerized tomography) scan* is a computer-enhanced X ray of brain structure. Multiple X rays are shot from many angles, and the computer combines the readings to create a vivid image of a horizontal slice of the brain (see Figure 3.8). The more recently developed *MRI (magnetic resonance imaging) scan* uses magnetic fields, radio waves, and computerized enhancement to map out brain structure and brain function. MRI scans provide much better

Figure 3.8

CT technology. CT scans are widely used in research to examine aspects of brain structure. They provide computer-enhanced X rays of horizontal slices of the brain.

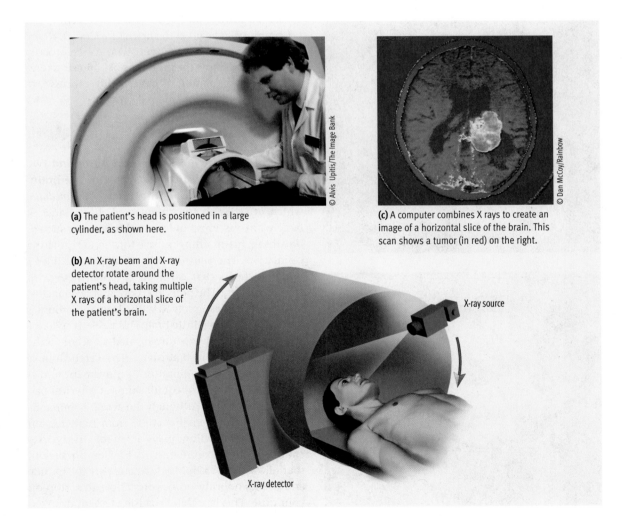

(a) The patient's head is positioned in a large cylinder, as shown here.

(c) A computer combines X rays to create an image of a horizontal slice of the brain. This scan shows a tumor (in red) on the right.

(b) An X-ray beam and X-ray detector rotate around the patient's head, taking multiple X rays of a horizontal slice of the patient's brain.

X-ray source

X-ray detector

images of brain structure than CT scans (Bohning et al., 1998), producing three-dimensional pictures of the brain that have remarkably high resolution (see Figure 3.9). Using CT and MRI scans, researchers have found abnormalities in brain structure among people suffering from specific types of mental illness, especially schizophrenia (Andreasen, 1988; G. N. Smith et al., 1997; see Chapter 14).

In research on how brain and behavior are related, *PET (positron emission tomography) scans* are proving especially valuable (Nahas et al., 1998). PET scans use radioactive markers to map chemical activity in the brain over time. Thus, a PET scan can provide a color-coded map indicating which areas of the brain become active and which neurotransmitters are used when subjects clench their fist, sing, or contemplate the mysteries of the universe (see Figure 3.10). In this way, neuroscientists are using PET scans to better pinpoint the brain areas that handle various types of mental activities (Craik et al., 1999; Raichle, 1994). PET scans are also being used to investigate which areas of the brain become active when people experience specific emotions, such as happiness or sadness (George et al., 1995). Research with PET scans has given neuroscientists a new appreciation of the complexity and interdependence of brain organization. The opportunity to look at ongoing brain function has revealed that even simple, routine mental operations depend on coordinated activation of several or more areas in the brain (Posner & Raichle, 1994).

Now that we have discussed a few approaches to brain research, let's look at what scientists have discovered about the functions of different parts of the brain. The brain can be divided into three major regions: the hindbrain, the midbrain, and the forebrain. The principal structures found in each of these regions are listed in the organizational chart of the nervous system in Figure 3.5. You can see where these regions are located in the brain by looking at Figure 3.11. They can be found easily in relation to the *brainstem*. The brainstem looks like its name—it appears to be a stem from which the rest of the brain "flowers," like a head of cauliflower. At its lower end the stem is contiguous with the spinal cord. At its higher end it lies deep within the brain. We'll begin at the brain's lower end, where the spinal cord joins the brainstem. As we proceed upward, notice how the functions of brain structures go from the regulation of basic bodily processes to the control of "higher" mental processes.

The Hindbrain 2d

The *hindbrain* includes the cerebellum and two structures found in the lower part of the brainstem: the medulla and the pons. The *medulla*, which attaches to the spinal cord, has charge of largely unconscious but essential functions, such as breathing, maintaining muscle tone, and regulating circulation. The *pons* (literally "bridge") includes a bridge of fibers that connects the brainstem with the cerebellum. The pons also contains several clusters of cell bodies involved with sleep and arousal.

The *cerebellum* ("little brain") is a relatively large and deeply folded structure located adjacent to the back surface of the brainstem. The cerebellum is involved in the coordination of movement and is critical to the sense of equilibrium, or physical balance (Ghez, 1991). Although the actual commands for muscular movements come from higher brain centers, the cerebellum plays a key role in the execution of these commands. It is your cerebellum that allows you to hold your hand out to the side and then smoothly bring your finger to a stop on your nose. This is a useful roadside test for drunken

Figure 3.9

MRI scans. MRI scans can be used to produce remarkably high-resolution pictures of brain structure. A vertical view of the left side of a brain is shown here.

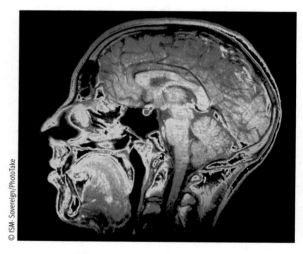

© ISM- Sovereign/PhotoTake

Figure 3.10

PET scans. PET scans are used to map brain activity. They provide color-coded maps that show areas of high activity in the brain over time. The PET scan shown here pinpointed two areas of high activity (indicated by the red and green colors) when a subject worked on a verbal short-term memory task.

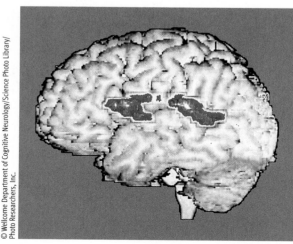

© Wellcome Department of Cognitive Neurology/Science Photo Library/ Photo Researchers, Inc.

Figure 3.11

Structures and areas in the human brain. (Top left) This photo of a human brain shows many of the structures discussed in this chapter. (Top right) The brain is divided into three major areas: the hindbrain, midbrain, and forebrain. These subdivisions actually make more sense for animal brains than for human brains. In humans, the forebrain has become so large, it makes the other two divisions look trivial. However, the hindbrain and midbrain aren't trivial; they control such vital functions as breathing, waking, remembering, and maintaining balance. (Bottom) This cross section of the brain highlights key structures and some of their principal functions. As you read about the functions of a brain structure, such as the corpus callosum, you may find it helpful to visualize it.

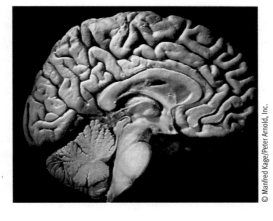

© Manfred Kage/Peter Arnold, Inc.

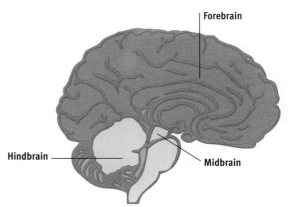

Forebrain

Hindbrain

Midbrain

Cerebrum
Responsible for sensing, thinking, learning, emotion, consciousness, and voluntary movement

Corpus callosum
Bridge of fibers passing information between the two cerebral hemispheres

Amygdala
Part of limbic system involved in emotion and aggression

Thalamus
Relay center for cortex; handles incoming and outgoing signals

Hypothalamus
Responsible for regulating basic biological needs: hunger, thirst, temperature control

Cerebellum
Structure that coordinates fine muscle movement, balance

Pituitary gland
"Master" gland that regulates other endocrine glands

Brainstem

Hippocampus
Part of limbic system involved in learning and memory

Spinal cord
Responsible for transmitting information between brain and rest of body; handles simple reflexes

Reticular formation
Group of fibers that carry stimulation related to sleep and arousal through brainstem

Medulla
Responsible for regulating largely unconscious functions such as breathing and circulation

Pons
Involved in sleep and arousal

driving because the cerebellum is one of the structures first depressed by alcohol. Damage to the cerebellum disrupts fine motor skills, such as those involved in writing, dancing, or playing tennis.

The Midbrain

The *midbrain* is the segment of the brainstem that lies between the hindbrain and the forebrain. The midbrain is concerned with certain sensory processes, such as locating where things are in space. For instance, when a sound triggers a reflexive turning of the head, an area in the midbrain is at work (Middlebrooks & Knudsen, 1984). An important system of dopamine-releasing neurons that projects into various higher brain centers originates in the midbrain. Among other things, this dopamine system is involved in the performance of voluntary movements. The decline in dopamine synthesis that causes Parkinsonism is due to degeneration of a structure located in the midbrain (Braak et al., 1995).

Running through both the hindbrain and the midbrain is the *reticular formation.* Lying at the central core of the brainstem, the reticular formation contributes to the modulation of muscle reflexes, breathing, and pain perception (Role & Kelly, 1991). It is best known, however, for its role in the regulation of sleep and wakefulness. Activity in the ascending fibers of the reticular formation contributes to arousal (Coenen, 1998).

The Forebrain

The *forebrain* is the largest and most complex region of the brain, encompassing a variety of structures, including the thalamus, hypothalamus, limbic system, and cerebrum. This list is not exhaustive, and some of these structures have their own subdivisions, as you can see in the organizational chart of the nervous system (Figure 3.5). The thalamus, hypothalamus, and limbic system form the core of the forebrain. All three structures are located near the top of the brainstem. Above them is the *cerebrum*—the seat of complex thought. The wrinkled surface of the cerebrum is the *cerebral cortex*—the outer layer of the brain, the part that looks like a cauliflower.

The Thalamus: A Way Station

The *thalamus* is a structure in the forebrain through which all sensory information (except smell) must pass to get to the cerebral cortex. This way station is made up of a number of clusters of cell bodies, or somas. Each cluster is concerned with relaying sensory information to a particular part of the cortex. However, it would be a mistake to characterize the thalamus as nothing more than a passive relay station. The thalamus also appears to play an active role in integrating information from various senses.

The Hypothalamus: A Regulator of Biological Needs

The *hypothalamus* is a structure found near the base of the forebrain that is involved in the regulation of basic biological needs. The hypothalamus lies beneath the thalamus (*hypo* means "under," making the hypothalamus the area under the thalamus). Although no larger than a kidney bean, the hypothalamus contains various clusters of cells that have many key functions. One such function is to control the autonomic nervous system.

The hypothalamus plays a major role in the regulation of basic biological drives related to survival, including the so-called "four F's": fighting, fleeing, feeding, and mating. For example, when researchers lesion the lateral areas (the sides) of the hypothalamus, animals lose interest in eating. The animals must be fed intravenously or they starve, even in the presence of abundant food. In contrast, when electrical stimulation (ESB) is used to *activate* the lateral hypothalamus, animals eat constantly and gain weight rapidly (Grossman et al., 1978; Keesey & Powley, 1975). Does this mean that the lateral hypothalamus is the "hunger center" in the brain? Not necessarily. The regulation of hunger turns out to be complex and multifaceted, as you'll see in Chapter 10. Nonetheless, the hypothalamus clearly contributes to the control of hunger and other basic biological processes, including thirst, sex drive, and temperature regulation (Kupfermann, 1991).

The Limbic System: The Seat of Emotion

The *limbic system* is a loosely connected network of structures located roughly along the border between the cerebral cortex and deeper subcortical areas (hence the term *limbic,* which means "edge"). First described by Paul MacLean (1954), the limbic system is not a well-defined anatomical system with clear boundaries. Indeed, scientists disagree about which structures should be included in the limbic system. Broadly defined, the limbic system includes parts of the thalamus and hypothalamus, the *hippocampus,* the *amygdala,* the *septum,* and other structures that are shown in Figure 3.12.

The hippocampus clearly plays a role in memory processes, although the exact nature of that role is the subject of debate. Similarly, there is ample evidence linking the limbic system to the experience of emotion, but the exact mechanisms of control are not yet well understood (Mega et al., 1997; Paradiso et al., 1997). Recent evidence suggests that the *amygdala* may play a central role in the learning of fear responses (Mori et al., 1999; Phillips & LeDoux, 1992).

The limbic system also appears to contain emotion-tinged "pleasure centers." This intriguing possibility first surfaced, quite by chance, in brain stimulation research with rats. James Olds and Peter Milner (1954) accidentally discovered that a rat would press a lever repeatedly to send brief bursts of electrical stimulation to a specific spot in its brain where an electrode was implanted (see Figure 3.13). They thought that they had inserted the electrode in the rat's reticular formation. However, they learned later that the electrode had been bent during implantation and ended up elsewhere (probably in the hypothalamus). Much to their surprise, the rat kept coming back for more self-stimulation in this area. Subsequent studies showed that rats and monkeys would press a lever *thousands of times* per hour to stimulate certain brain sites. Although the experimenters obviously couldn't ask the animals about it, they *inferred* that the animals were experiencing some sort of pleasure.

Where are the pleasure centers located in the brain? Many self-stimulation sites have been found in the limbic system (Olds & Fobe, 1981).

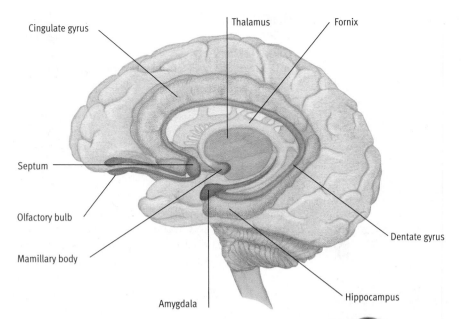

The heaviest concentration appears to be where the *medial forebrain bundle* (a bundle of axons) passes through the hypothalamus. The medial forebrain bundle is rich in dopamine-releasing neurons. The rewarding effects of ESB at self-stimulation sites may be largely mediated by the activation of these dopamine circuits (Nakajima & Patterson, 1997). The rewarding, pleasurable effects of opiate and stimulant drugs (cocaine and amphetamines) may also depend on excitation of this dopamine system (Gratton, 1996; Wise, 1995).

Figure 3.12

The limbic system.
The limbic system is a network of interconnected structures that play a role in emotion, motivation, memory, and many other aspects of behavior. These structures fall mostly along the border between the cortex and deeper, subcortical areas.

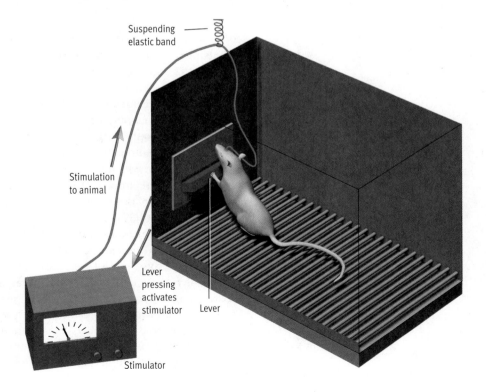

Figure 3.13

Electrical stimulation of the brain (ESB) in the rat.
Olds and Milner (1954) were using an apparatus like that depicted here when they discovered self-stimulation centers, or "pleasure centers," in the brain of a rat. In this setup, the rat's lever pressing earns brief electrical stimulation that is sent to a specific spot in the rat's brain where an electrode has been implanted.

The Cerebrum: The Seat of Complex Thought

 2f

The *cerebrum* is the largest and most complex part of the human brain. It includes the brain areas that are responsible for our most complex mental activities, including learning, remembering, thinking, and consciousness itself. **The *cerebral cortex* is the convoluted outer layer of the cerebrum.** The cortex is folded and bent, so that its large surface area—about 1.5 square feet—can be packed into the limited volume of the skull (Hubel & Wiesel, 1979).

The cerebrum is divided into two halves called hemispheres. Hence, **the *cerebral hemispheres* are the right and left halves of the cerebrum** (see Figure 3.14). The hemispheres are separated in the center of the brain by a longitudinal fissure that runs from the front to the back. This fissure descends to a thick band of fibers called the *corpus callosum* (also shown in Figure 3.14). **The *corpus callosum* is the structure that connects the two cerebral hemispheres.** We'll discuss the functional specialization of the cerebral hemispheres in the next section of this chapter.

Each cerebral hemisphere is divided into four parts called *lobes*. To some extent, each of these lobes is dedicated to specific purposes. The location of these lobes can be seen in Figure 3.15.

The *occipital lobe*, at the back of the head, includes the cortical area where most visual signals are sent and visual processing is begun. This area is called the *primary visual cortex*. We will discuss how it is organized in Chapter 4.

The *parietal lobe* is forward of the occipital lobe. It includes the area that registers the sense of touch, called the *primary somatosensory cortex*. Various sections of this area receive signals from different regions of the body. When ESB is delivered in these parietal lobe areas, people report physical sensations—as if someone actually touched them on the arm or cheek, for example. The parietal lobe is also involved in integrating visual input and in monitoring the body's position in space.

The *temporal lobe* (meaning "near the temples") lies below the parietal lobe. Near its top, the temporal lobe contains an area devoted to auditory processing, the *primary auditory cortex*. As we will see momentarily, damage to an area in the temporal lobe on the left side of the brain can impair the ability to comprehend speech and language.

Continuing forward, we find the *frontal lobe,* the largest lobe in the human brain. It contains the principal areas that control the movement of muscles, the *primary motor cortex*. ESB applied in these areas can cause actual muscle contractions. The amount of motor cortex allocated to the control of a body part depends not on the part's size but on the diversity and precision of its movements. Thus, more of the cortex is given to parts we have fine control over, such as the fingers, lips, and tongue. Less of the cortex is devoted to larger parts that make crude movements, such as the thighs and shoulders.

The portion of the frontal lobe to the front of the motor cortex, which is called the *prefrontal cortex* (see Figure 3.15), is something of a mystery. This area is disproportionately large in humans, accounting for about 28% of the human cerebral cortex (Shimamura, 1996). In light of this fact, it was once assumed to house the highest, most abstract intellectual functions, but this view was eventually dismissed as an oversimplification. Still, recent studies suggest that the prefrontal cortex *does* contribute to an impressive variety of higher-order functions, such as memory for temporal sequences (Kesner, 1998); working memory, which is a temporary buffer that processes current information (Goldman-Rakic, 1993, 1998); and reasoning about relations between objects and events (Waltz et al., 1999). Its contribution to working memory and relational reasoning have led some theorists to suggest that the prefrontal cortex houses some sort of "executive control system," which is thought to monitor, organize, and direct thought processes (Kimberg, D'Esposito, & Farah, 1998; Shimamura, 1995). Consistent with this hypothesis, people who suffer damage in the prefrontal cortex often show deficits in planning, paying attention, and getting organized (Fuster, 1996).

Figure 3.14

The cerebral hemispheres and the corpus callosum.
In this drawing the cerebral hemispheres have been "pulled apart" to reveal the corpus callosum. This band of fibers is the communication bridge between the right and left halves of the human brain.

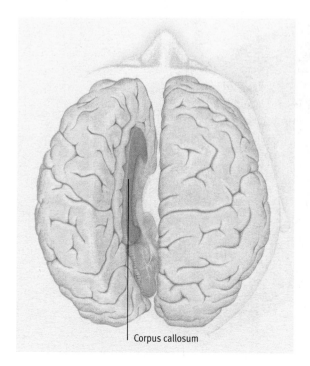

Corpus callosum

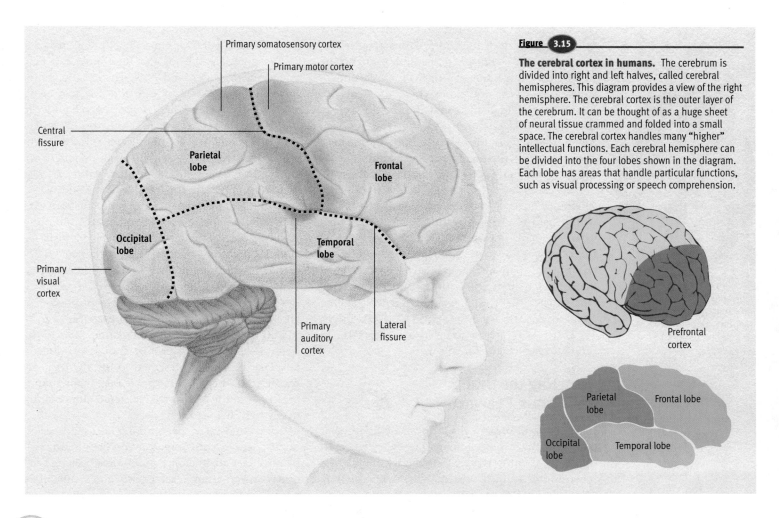

Primary somatosensory cortex

Primary motor cortex

Central fissure

Parietal lobe

Frontal lobe

Occipital lobe

Temporal lobe

Primary visual cortex

Primary auditory cortex

Lateral fissure

Figure 3.15

The cerebral cortex in humans. The cerebrum is divided into right and left halves, called cerebral hemispheres. This diagram provides a view of the right hemisphere. The cerebral cortex is the outer layer of the cerebrum. It can be thought of as a huge sheet of neural tissue crammed and folded into a small space. The cerebral cortex handles many "higher" intellectual functions. Each cerebral hemisphere can be divided into the four lobes shown in the diagram. Each lobe has areas that handle particular functions, such as visual processing or speech comprehension.

Prefrontal cortex

Parietal lobe

Frontal lobe

Occipital lobe

Temporal lobe

Right Brain/Left Brain: Cerebral Specialization

As noted a moment ago, the cerebrum—the seat of complex thought—is divided into two separate hemispheres (see Figure 3.14). Recent decades have seen an exciting flurry of research on the specialized abilities of the right and left cerebral hemispheres. Some theorists have gone so far as to suggest that people really have two brains in one!

Hints of this hemispheric specialization have been available for many years, from cases in which one side of a person's brain has been damaged. The left hemisphere was implicated in the control of language as early as 1861, by Paul Broca, a French surgeon. Broca was treating a patient who had been unable to speak for 30 years. After the patient died, Broca showed that the probable cause of his speech deficit was a localized lesion on the left side of the frontal lobe. Since then, many similar cases have shown that this area of the brain—known as *Broca's area*—plays an important role in the production of speech (see Figure 3.16). Another major language center—*Wernicke's area*—was identified in the temporal lobe of the left hemisphere in 1874. Damage in Wernicke's area (Figure 3.16) usually leads to problems with the *comprehension* of language.

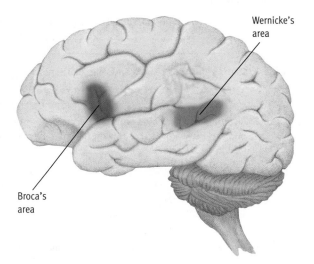

Wernicke's area

Broca's area

Figure 3.16

Language processing in the brain. This view of the left hemisphere highlights the location of two centers for language processing in the brain: *Broca's area*, which is involved in speech production, and *Wernicke's area*, which is involved in language comprehension.

"Both the left and right hemispheres of the brain have been found to have their own specialized forms of intellect."
ROGER SPERRY

Courtesy of Roger Sperry

Evidence that the left hemisphere usually processes language led scientists to characterize it as the "dominant" hemisphere. Because thoughts are usually coded in terms of language, the left hemisphere was given the lion's share of credit for handling the "higher" mental processes, such as reasoning, remembering, planning, and problem solving. Meanwhile, the right hemisphere came to be viewed as the "nondominant," or "dumb," hemisphere, lacking any special functions or abilities.

This characterization of the left and right hemispheres as major and minor partners in the brain's work began to change in the 1960s. It all started with landmark research by Roger Sperry, Michael Gazzaniga, and their colleagues who studied "split-brain" patients: individuals whose cerebral hemispheres had been surgically disconnected (Gazzaniga, 1970; Gazzaniga, Bogen, & Sperry, 1965; Levy, Trevarthen, & Sperry, 1972; Sperry, 1982). In 1981 Sperry received a Nobel prize in physiology/medicine for this work.

Bisecting the Brain: Split-Brain Research

 SIM2, 2f

In *split-brain surgery* the bundle of fibers that connects the cerebral hemispheres (the corpus callosum) is cut to reduce the severity of epileptic seizures. It is a radical procedure that is chosen only in exceptional cases that have not responded to other forms of treatment. But the surgery provides

scientists with an unusual opportunity to study people who have had their brain literally split in two.

To appreciate the logic of split-brain research, you need to understand how sensory and motor information is routed to and from the two hemispheres. *Each hemisphere's primary connections are to the opposite side of the body.* Thus, the left hemisphere controls, and communicates with, the right hand, right arm, right leg, right eyebrow, and so on. In contrast, the right hemisphere controls, and communicates with, the left side of the body.

Vision and hearing are more complex. Both eyes deliver information to both hemispheres, but input is still separated. Stimuli in the right half of the visual field are registered by receptors on the left side of each eye, which send signals to the left hemisphere. Stimuli in the left half of the *visual field* are transmitted by both eyes to the right hemisphere (see Figure 3.17). Auditory inputs to each ear also go to both hemispheres. However, connections to the opposite hemisphere are stronger or more immediate. That is, sounds presented to the right ear are registered in the left hemisphere first, while sounds presented to the left ear are registered more quickly in the right hemisphere.

For the most part, people don't notice this asymmetric, "crisscrossed" organization because the two hemispheres are in close communication with each other. Information received by one hemisphere is readily shared with the other via the corpus callosum. However, when the two hemispheres are

CONCEPT CHECK 3.3

Relating Disorders to the Nervous System

Imagine that you are working as a neuropsychologist at a clinic. You are involved in the diagnosis of the cases described below. You are asked to identify the probable cause(s) of the disorders in terms of nervous system malfunctions. Based on the information in this chapter, indicate the probable location of any brain damage or the probable disturbance of neurotransmitter activity. The answers can be found in the back of the book in Appendix A.

Case 1. Miriam is exhibiting language deficits. In particular, she does not seem to comprehend the meaning of words.

_____

_____

Case 2. Camille displays tremors and muscular rigidity and is diagnosed as having Parkinsonism.

_____

_____

Case 3. Ricardo, a 28-year-old computer executive, has gradually seen his strength and motor coordination deteriorate badly. He is diagnosed as having multiple sclerosis.

_____

_____

Case 4. Wendy is highly irrational, has poor contact with reality, and reports hallucinations. She is given a diagnosis of schizophrenic disorder.

_____

_____

surgically disconnected, the functional specialization of the brain becomes apparent.

In their classic study of split-brain patients, Gazzaniga, Bogen, and Sperry (1965) presented visual stimuli such as pictures, symbols, and words in a single visual field (the left or the right), so that the stimuli would be sent to only one hemisphere. The stimuli were projected onto a screen in front of the subjects, who stared at a fixation point (a spot) in the center of the screen. The images were flashed to the right or the left of the fixation point for only a split second. Thus, the subjects did not have a chance to move their eyes, and the stimuli were glimpsed in only one visual field.

When pictures were flashed in the right visual field and thus sent to the left hemisphere, the split-brain subjects were able to name and describe the objects depicted (such as a cup or spoon). However, the subjects were *not* able to name and describe the same objects when they were flashed in the left visual field and sent to the right hemisphere. In a similar fashion, an object placed out of view in the right hand (communicating with the left hemisphere) could be named. However, the same object placed in the left hand (right hemisphere) could not be. These findings supported the notion that language is housed in the left hemisphere.

Although the split-brain subjects' right hemisphere was not able to speak up for itself, further tests revealed that it was processing the information presented. If subjects were given an opportunity to *point out a picture* of an object they had held in their left hand, they were able to do so. They were also able to point out pictures that had been flashed to the left visual field. Furthermore, the right hemisphere (left hand) turned out to be *superior* to the left hemisphere (right hand) in assembling little puzzles and copying drawings, even though the subjects were right-handed. These findings provided the first compelling demonstration that the right hemisphere has its own special talents. Subsequent studies of additional split-brain patients showed the right hemisphere to be better than the left on a variety of visual-spatial tasks, including discriminating colors, arranging blocks, and recognizing faces.

Hemispheric Specialization in the Intact Brain SIM2, 2f

The problem with the split-brain operation, of course, is that it creates an abnormal situation. The vast majority of us remain "neurologically intact." Moreover, the surgery is done only with people who suffer from prolonged, severe cases of epilepsy.

Figure 3.17

Visual input in the split brain. If a subject stares at a fixation point, the point divides the subject's visual field into right and left halves. Input from the right visual field strikes the left side of each eye and is transmitted to the left hemisphere. Input from the left visual field strikes the right side of each eye and is transmitted to the right hemisphere. Normally, the hemispheres share the information from the two halves of the visual field, but in split-brain patients, the corpus callosum is severed, and the two hemispheres cannot communicate. Hence, the experimenter can present a visual stimulus to just one hemisphere at a time.

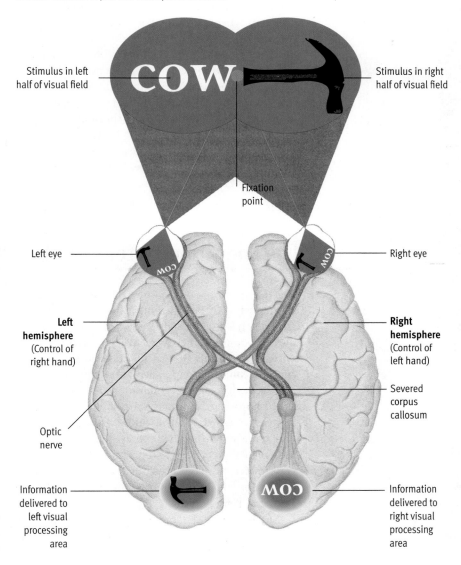

These people may have had somewhat atypical brain organization even before the operation. Thus, theorists couldn't help wondering whether it was safe to generalize broadly from the split-brain studies. For this reason, researchers developed methods that allowed them to study cerebral specialization in the intact brain.

One method involves looking at left-right imbalances in visual or auditory processing, called *perceptual asymmetries.* As we have seen, it is possible to present visual stimuli to just one visual field at a time. In normal individuals, the input sent to one hemisphere is quickly shared with the other. However, subtle differences in the "abilities" of the two hemispheres can be detected by precisely measuring how long it takes subjects to recognize different types of stimuli. For instance, when verbal stimuli are presented to the right visual field (and thus sent to the *left hemisphere* first), they are identified more quickly and more accurately than when they are presented to the left visual field (and sent to the right hemisphere first). The faster reactions in the left hemisphere presumably occur because it can recognize verbal stimuli on its own, while the right hemisphere has to take extra time to "consult" the left hemisphere. In contrast, the *right hemisphere* is faster than the left on *visual-spatial*

tasks, such as locating a dot or recognizing a face (Bradshaw, 1989; Bryden, 1982).

Researchers have used a variety of other approaches to explore hemispheric specialization in normal people. For the most part, their findings have converged nicely with the results of the split-brain studies (Reuter-Lorenz & Miller, 1998). Overall, the findings suggest that the two hemispheres are specialized, with each handling certain types of cognitive tasks better than the other (Springer & Deutsch, 1998). *The left hemisphere usually is better on tasks involving verbal processing, such as language, speech, reading, and writing. The right hemisphere exhibits superiority on many tasks involving nonverbal processing, such as most spatial, musical, and visual recognition tasks.* Obviously, cerebral lateralization is a burgeoning area of research that has broad implications, which we will discuss further in the Personal Application. For now, however, let's leave the brain and turn our attention to the endocrine system.

The Endocrine System: Another Way to Communicate

The major way the brain communicates with the rest of the body is through the nervous system. However, the body has a second communication system that is also important to behavior. **The *endocrine system* consists of glands that secrete chemicals into the bloodstream that help control bodily functioning.** The messengers in this communication network are called hormones. ***Hormones* are the chemical substances released by the endocrine glands.** The endocrine system tends to be involved in the long-term regulation of basic bodily processes, as its action can't match the high speed of neural transmission. The major endocrine glands and their functions are shown in Figure 3.18.

Much of the endocrine system is controlled by the nervous system through the *hypothalamus.* This structure at the base of the forebrain has intimate connections with the pea-sized *pituitary gland,* to which it is adjacent. **The *pituitary gland* releases a great variety of hormones that fan out within the body, stimulating actions in the other endocrine glands.** In this sense, the pituitary is the "master gland" of the endocrine system, although the hypothalamus is the real power behind the throne.

The intermeshing of the nervous system and the endocrine system can be seen in the fight-or-flight response described earlier. In times of stress, the

hypothalamus sends signals along two pathways—through the autonomic nervous system and through the pituitary gland—to the adrenal glands (Sapolsky, 1992). In response, the adrenal glands secrete hormones that radiate throughout the body, preparing it to cope with an emergency.

Hormones also play important roles in modulating human physiological development. For example, among the more interesting hormones released by the pituitary are the *gonadotropins,* which affect the *gonads,* or sexual glands. Prior to birth, these hormones direct the formation of the external sexual organs in the developing fetus (Breedlove, 1992). Thus, your sexual identity as a male or female was shaped during prenatal development by the actions of hormones. At puberty, increased levels of sexual hormones are responsible for the emergence of secondary sexual characteristics, such as male facial hair and female breasts (Chumlea, 1982). The actions of other hormones are responsible for the spurt in physical growth that occurs around puberty.

These developmental effects of hormones illustrate how genetic programming has a hand in behavior. Obviously, the hormonal actions that launched your adolescent growth spurt and sparked your interest in sexuality were preprogrammed over a decade earlier by your genetic inheritance, which brings us to the role of heredity in shaping behavior.

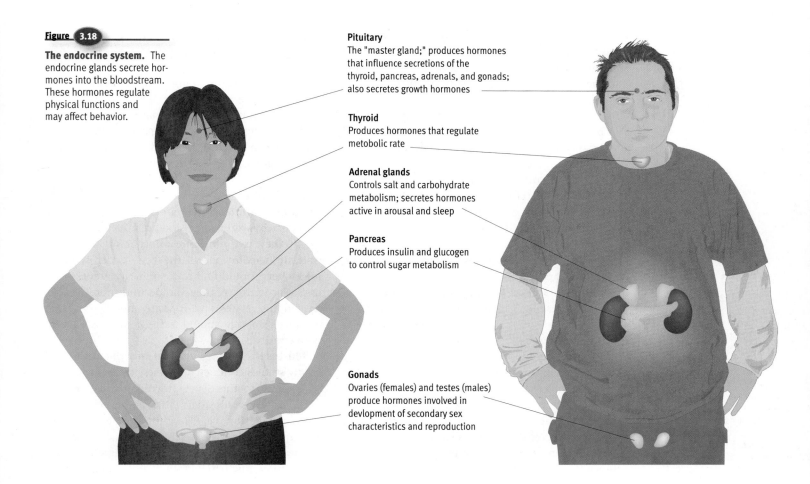

Figure 3.18

The endocrine system. The endocrine glands secrete hormones into the bloodstream. These hormones regulate physical functions and may affect behavior.

Pituitary
The "master gland;" produces hormones that influence secretions of the thyroid, pancreas, adrenals, and gonads; also secretes growth hormones

Thyroid
Produces hormones that regulate metobolic rate

Adrenal glands
Controls salt and carbohydrate metabolism; secretes hormones active in arousal and sleep

Pancreas
Produces insulin and glucogen to control sugar metabolism

Gonads
Ovaries (females) and testes (males) produce hormones involved in devlopment of secondary sex characteristics and reproduction

Heredity and Behavior: Is It All in the Genes?

Most people realize that physical characteristics such as height, hair color, blood type, and eye color are largely shaped by heredity. But what about psychological characteristics, such as intelligence, moodiness, impulsiveness, and shyness? To what extent are people's behavioral qualities molded by their genes? As we saw in Chapter 1, questions about the relative importance of heredity versus environment are very old ones in psychology. The nature versus nurture debate will continue to surface in many of the upcoming chapters. To help you appreciate the complexities of this debate, we will outline some basic principles of genetics and describe the methods that investigators use to assess the effects of heredity.

Basic Principles of Genetics

Every cell in your body contains enduring messages from your mother and father. These messages are found on the *chromosomes* that lie within the nucleus of each cell. *Chromosomes* **are threadlike strands of DNA (deoxyribonucleic acid) molecules that carry genetic information.** With the exception of sex cells (sperm and eggs), every cell in humans contains 46 chromosomes. These chromosomes operate in 23 pairs, with one chromosome of each pair coming from each parent. Each chromosome, in turn, contains thousands of biochemical messengers called genes. *Genes* **are DNA segments that serve as the key functional units in hereditary transmission.**

If all offspring are formed by a union of the parents' sex cells, why aren't family members identical clones? The reason is that a single pair of parents can produce an extraordinary variety of combinations of chromosomes. Each parent's 23 chromosome pairs can be scrambled in over 8 million (2^{23}) different ways, yielding roughly 70 trillion possible configurations when sperm and egg unite. Thus, genetic transmission is a complicated process, and everything is a matter of probability. Except for identical twins, each person ends up with a unique genetic blueprint.

Although different combinations of genes explain why family members aren't all alike, the overlap among these combinations explains why family members do tend to resemble one another. Members of a family share more of the same genes than nonmembers. Ultimately, each person shares half of her or his genes with each parent. On the average, full siblings (except identical twins) also share half their genes. More distant relatives share smaller proportions of genes. Figure 3.19 shows the amount of genetic overlap for various kinship relations. The proportion of shared genes ranges from 100% for identical twins down to a mean of 6.25% for second cousins.

Like chromosomes, genes operate in pairs, with one gene of each pair coming from each parent. In the simplest scenario, a single pair of genes determines a trait. However, most human characteristics appear to be *polygenic traits,* **or characteristics that are influenced by more than one pair of genes.** For example, three to five gene pairs are thought to interactively determine skin color. Complex physical abilities, such as motor coordination, may be influenced by tangled interactions among a great many pairs of genes. Most psychological characteristics that appear to be affected by heredity seem to involve complex polygenic inheritance (Plomin, 1990).

Figure 3.19

Genetic overlap in relatives. Research on the genetic bases of behavior takes advantage of the different degrees of genetic overlap between various types of relatives. If heredity influences a trait, then relatives who share more genes should be more similar with regard to that trait than are more distant relatives, who share fewer genes. Comparisons involving various degrees of biological relationships will come up frequently in later chapters.

Relationship	Degree of relatedness		
Identical twins		100%	
Fraternal twins Brother or sister Parent or child	First-degree relatives	50%	
Grandparent or grandchild Uncle, aunt, nephew, or niece Half-bother or half-sister	Second-degree relatives	25%	
First cousin	Third-degree relatives	12.5%	
Second cousin	Fourth-degree relatives	6.25%	
Unrelated		0%	

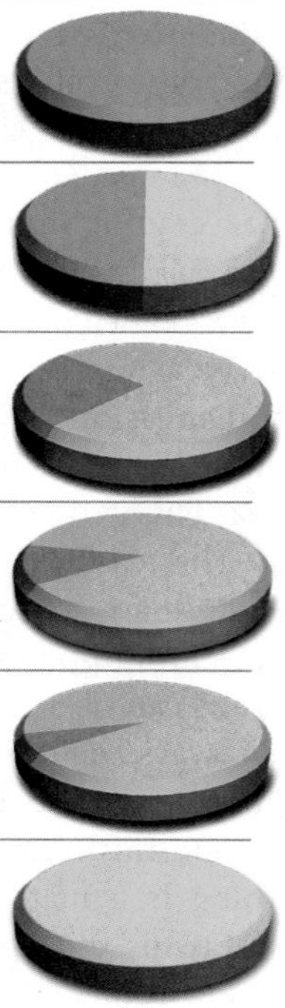

Detecting Hereditary Influence: Research Methods

How do scientists disentangle the effects of genetics and experience to determine how heredity affects human behavior? Researchers have designed special types of studies to assess the impact of heredity. The three most important methods are family studies, twin studies, and adoption studies.

Family Studies

In *family studies* **researchers assess hereditary influence by examining blood relatives to see how much they resemble one another on a specific trait.** If heredity affects the trait under scrutiny, researchers should find trait similarity among relatives. Furthermore, they should find more similarity among relatives who share more genes. For instance, siblings should exhibit more similarity than cousins.

Illustrative of this method are the numerous family studies conducted to assess the contribution of heredity to the development of schizophrenic disorders. These disorders strike approximately 1% of the population, yet 9% of the siblings of schizophrenic patients exhibit schizophrenia themselves (Gottesman, 1991). Thus, these first-degree relatives of schizophrenic patients show a risk for the disorder that is nine times higher than normal. This risk is greater than that observed for second-degree relatives, such as nieces and nephews (4%), which is greater than that found for third-degree relatives, such as first cousins (2%), and so on. This pattern of results is consistent with the hypothesis that genetic inheritance influences the development of schizophrenic disorders (Gottesman, 1993).

Family studies can indicate whether a trait runs in families. However, this correlation does not provide conclusive evidence that the trait is influenced by heredity. Why not? Because family members generally share not only genes but also similar environments. Furthermore, closer relatives are more likely to live together than more distant relatives. Thus, genetic similarity and environmental similarity both tend to be greater for closer relatives. Either of these confounded variables could be responsible when greater trait similarity is found in closer relatives. Family studies can offer useful insights about the possible impact of heredity, but they cannot provide definitive evidence.

Twin Studies

Twin studies can yield better evidence about the possible role of genetic factors. **In *twin studies*** researchers assess hereditary influence by comparing the resemblance of identical twins and fraternal twins with respect to a trait. *Identical (monozygotic) twins* emerge when a single fertilized egg splits for unknown reasons. Thus, they have exactly the same genetic blueprint; their genetic overlap is 100%. *Fraternal (dizygotic) twins* result when two separate eggs are fertilized simultaneously. Fraternal twins are no more alike in genetic makeup than any two siblings born to a pair of parents at different times. Their genetic overlap averages 50%.

Fraternal twins provide a useful comparison to identical twins because in both cases the twins usually grow up in the same home, at the same time, exposed to the same configuration of relatives, neighbors, peers, teachers, events, and so forth. Thus, both kinds of twins normally develop under equally similar environmental conditions. However, identical twins share more genetic kinship than fraternal twins. Consequently, if sets of identical twins tend to exhibit more similarity on a trait than sets of fraternal twins do, it is reasonable to infer that this greater similarity is probably due to heredity.

Twin studies have been conducted to assess the impact of heredity on a variety of traits; some representative results are summarized in Figure 3.20. The higher correlations found for identical twins indicate that they tend to be more similar to each other than fraternal twins on measures of general intelligence (McGue et al., 1993) and measures of specific personality traits, such as extraversion (Loehlin, 1992). These results support the notion that these traits are influenced to some degree by genetic makeup.

Adoption Studies

Adoption studies assess hereditary influence by examining the resemblance between adopted children and both their biological and their adoptive parents. If adopted children resemble their biological parents on a trait, even though they were not raised by them, genetic factors probably influence that trait. In contrast, if adopted children resemble their adoptive parents, even though they inherited no genes from them, environmental factors probably influence the trait.

In recent years, adoption studies have contributed to science's understanding of how genetics and the environment influence intelligence. The research shows modest similarity between adopted children and their biological parents, as indicated by an average correlation of .24 (McGue et al., 1993).

Interestingly, adopted children resemble their adoptive parents just as much (also an average correlation of .24). These findings suggest that both heredity and environment have an influence on intelligence.

The Interplay of Heredity and Environment

We began this section by asking, is it all in the genes? When it comes to behavioral traits, the answer clearly is no. According to Robert Plomin (1993), perhaps the leading behavioral genetics researcher in the last decade, what scientists find again and again is that heredity and experience jointly influence most aspects of behavior. Moreover, their effects are interactive—they play off each other (Rutter, 1997).

For example, consider what researchers have learned about the development of schizophrenic disorders. Although the evidence indicates that genetic factors influence the development of schizophrenia, it does not appear that anyone directly inherits the disorder itself. Rather, what people appear to inherit is a certain degree of *vulnerability* to the disorder (Zubin, 1986). Whether this vulnerability is ever converted into an actual disorder depends on each person's experiences in life. Thus, as Richard Rose (1995) puts it in a major review of behavioral genetics research, "We inherit dispositions, not destinies."

The Pennsylvania State University Center for Development and Health Genetics

"*The transformation of the social and behavioral sciences from environmentalism to biological determinism is happening so fast that I find I more often have to say, 'Yes, genetic influences are substantial, but environmental influences are important, too.***"**
ROBERT PLOMIN

Figure 3.20

Twin studies of intelligence and personality. Identical twins tend to be more similar than fraternal twins (as reflected in higher correlations) with regard to general mental ability and specific personality traits, such as extraversion. These findings suggest that intelligence and personality are influenced by heredity. (Intelligence data from "Behavioral Genetics of Cognitive Ability: A Life-Span Perspective," by M. McGue, T.J. Bouchard, W.G. Iacono & D.T. Lykken, 1993. In R. Plomin & G.E. McClearn Eds., *Nature, Nurture and Psychology.* American Psychological Association. Extraversion data based on *Genes and Environment in Personality Development,* by J. C. Loehlin, 1992, Sage Publications.)

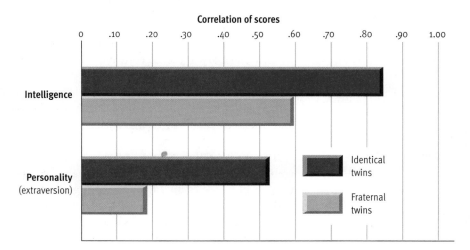

Recognizing Hereditary Influence

Check your understanding of the methods scientists use to explore hereditary influences on specific behavioral traits by filling in the blanks in the descriptive statements below. The answers can be found in the back of the book in Appendix A.

1. The findings from family studies indicate that heredity may influence a trait if _____ show more trait similarity than _____ .
2. The findings from twin studies suggest that heredity influences a trait if _____ show more trait similarity than _____ .
3. The findings from adoption studies suggest that heredity influences a trait if children adopted at a young age share more trait similarity with their _____ than their _____ .
4. The findings from family studies, twin studies, and adoption studies suggest that heredity does not influence a trait when _____ is not related to _____ .

The Evolutionary Bases of Behavior

Bettmann/CORBIS

"Can we doubt (remembering that many more individuals are born than can possibly survive) that individuals having any advantage, however slight, over others, would have the best chance of surviving and procreating their kind?... This preservation of favourable variations and the rejection of injurious variations, I call Natural Selection."
CHARLES DARWIN

To round out our look at the biological bases of behavior, we need to discuss how evolutionary forces have shaped many aspects of human and animal behavior. As you may recall from Chapter 1, *evolutionary psychology* is a major new theoretical perspective in the field that analyzes behavioral processes in terms of their adaptive significance. In this section, we will outline some basic principles of evolutionary theory and relate them to animal behavior. These ideas will create a foundation for forthcoming chapters, where we'll see how these principles can enhance our understanding of many aspects of human behavior.

Darwin's Insights

Charles Darwin, the legendary British naturalist, was *not* the first person to describe the process of evolution. Well before Darwin's time, other biologists who had studied the earth's fossil record noted that various species appeared to have undergone gradual changes over the course of a great many generations. What Darwin (1859) contributed in his landmark book, *On the Origin of the Species,* was a creative, new explanation for *how and why* evolutionary changes unfold over time. He identified *natural selection* as the mechanism that orchestrates the process of evolution.

The mystery that Darwin set out to solve was complicated. He wanted to explain how the characteristics of a species might change over generations and why these changes tended to be surprisingly adaptive. In other words, he wanted to shed light on why organisms tend to have characteristics that

serve them well in the context of their environments. How did giraffes acquire their long necks that allow them to reach high into acacia trees to secure their main source of food? How did woodpeckers develop their sharp, chisel-shaped beaks that permit them to probe trees for insects so effectively? Darwin's explanation for the seemingly purposive nature of evolution centered on four crucial insights.

First, he noted that organisms vary in endless ways, such as size, speed, strength, aspects of appearance, visual abilities, hearing capacities, digestive processes, cell structure, and so forth. Second, he noted that some of these characteristics are heritable—that is, they are passed down from one generation to the next. Although genes and chromosomes had not yet been discovered, the concept of heredity was well established. Third, borrowing from the work of Thomas Malthus, he noted that organisms tend to produce offspring at a pace that outstrips the local availability of food supplies, living space, and other crucial resources. As a population increases and resources dwindle, the competition for precious resources intensifies. Thus, it occurred to Darwin—and this was his grand insight—that variations in hereditary traits might affect organisms' ability to obtain the resources necessary for survival and reproduction. Fourth, building on this insight, Darwin argued that if a specific heritable trait contributes to an organism's survival or reproductive success, organisms with that trait should produce more offspring than those without the trait (or those with less of the trait), and the prevalence of that trait should gradually increase over generations—resulting in evolutionary change.

Although evolution is widely characterized as a matter of "survival of the fittest," Darwin recognized from the beginning that survival is important only insofar as it relates to reproductive success. Indeed, in evolutionary theory, **fitness refers to the reproductive success (number of descendants) of an individual organism relative to the average reproductive success in the population.** *Variations in reproductive success are what really fuels evolutionary change.* But survival is crucial because organisms typically need to mature and thrive before they can reproduce. So, Darwin theorized that there ought to be two ways in which traits might contribute to evolution: by providing either a survival advantage or a reproductive advantage. For example, a turtle's shell has great protective value that provides a survival advantage. In contrast, a firefly's emission of light is a courtship overture that provides a reproductive advantage.

To summarize, the principle of **natural selection posits that heritable characteristics that provide a survival or reproductive advantage are more likely than alternative characteristics to be passed on to subsequent generations and thus they come to be "selected" over time.** Please note, the process of natural selection works on *populations* rather than *individual organisms*. Evolution occurs when the gene pool in a population changes gradually as a result of selection pressures. Although there are occasional exceptions (Gould & Eldredge, 1977), this process tends to be extremely gradual— it generally takes thousands to millions of generations for one trait to be selected over another.

Darwin's theory was highly controversial for at least two reasons: (a) it suggested that the awe-inspiring diversity of life is the result of an unplanned, natural process rather than divine creation, and (b) it implied that humans are not unique and that they share a common ancestry with other species. Nonetheless, Darwin's theory eventually gained considerable acceptance because it provided a compelling explanation for how the characteristics of various species gradually changed over many generations and for the functional, adaptive direction of these changes.

Subsequent Refinements to Evolutionary Theory

Although Darwin's evolutionary theory quickly acquired many articulate advocates, it also remained controversial for decades. Eventually, advances in the understanding of heredity were sufficient to permit Theodore Dobzhansky (1937) to write a fairly comprehensive account of the evolutionary process in genetic terms. Dobzhansky's synthesis of Darwin's ideas and modern genetics was enormously influential, and by the 1950s the core tenets of evolutionary theory enjoyed widespread acceptance among scientists.

Contemporary models of evolution recognize that natural selection operates on the gene pool of a population. *Adaptations* are the key product of this process. **An *adaptation* is an inherited characteristic that increased in a population (through natural selection) because it helped solve a problem of survival or reproduction during the time it emerged.** Because of the gradual, incremental nature of evolution, adaptations sometimes linger in a population even though they no longer provide a survival or reproductive advantage. For example, humans show a taste preference for fatty substances that was adaptive in an era of hunting and gathering, when dietary fat was a scarce source of important

The fight-or-flight response discussed earlier in the chapter (see pages 67–68), is an example of a behavior that provides a survival advantage. Although traits that convey a survival advantage can contribute to evolution, it is variations in reproductive fitness that ultimately fuel evolutionary change.

John Dominis, *Life Magazine* © Time Inc.

calories. However, in our modern world, where dietary fat is typically available in abundance, this taste preference leads many people to consume too much fat, resulting in obesity, heart disease, and other health problems. Thus, the preference for fatty foods has become a liability for human survival (although its impact on reproductive success is more difficult to gauge). As you will see, evolutionary psychologists have found that many aspects of human nature reflect the adaptive demands faced by our ancient ancestors rather than contemporary demands. Of course, as natural selection continues to work, these formerly adaptive traits should gradually be eliminated, but the process is extremely slow.

In recent decades, theorists have broadened Darwin's original concept of reproductive fitness to better explain a variety of phenomena. For example, traditional evolutionary theory had difficulty explaining self-sacrifice. If organisms try to maximize their reproductive success, why does a blackbird risk death to signal the approach of a hawk to others in the flock? And why would a tribesman risk life and limb to race into a burning hut to save young children? In 1964, W. D. Hamilton proposed the theory of *inclusive fitness* to explain the paradox of self-sacrifice. According to Hamilton, an organism may contribute to passing on its genes by sacrificing itself to save others that share the same genes. Helping behavior that evolves as members of a species protect their own offspring, for example, can be extended to other, more distantly related members of the species. Thus, **inclusive fitness is the sum of an individual's own reproductive success plus the effects the organism has on the reproductive success of related others.** The concept of inclusive fitness suggests that the probability of self-sacrifice decreases as the degree of relatedness between a helper and potential recipients declines, a prediction that has been supported in studies of organisms as diverse as ground squirrels (Sherman, 1981) and humans (Burnstein, Crandall, & Kitayama, 1994).

Behaviors as Adaptive Traits

Scholarly analyses of evolution have focused primarily on the evolution of *physical characteristics* in the animal kingdom, but from the very beginning, Darwin recognized that natural selection was applicable to *behavioral traits* as well. Modern evolutionary psychology is based on the well-documented assumption that a species' typical patterns of behavior often reflect evolutionary solutions to adaptive problems.

Consider, for instance, the eating behavior of rats, who show remarkable caution when they encounter new foods. Rats are versatile animals that are found in an enormous range of habitats and can live off quite a variety of foods, but this diet variety can present risks, as they need to be wary of consuming toxic substances. When rats encounter unfamiliar foods, they consume only small amounts and won't eat two new foods together. If the consumption of a new food is followed by illness, they avoid that food in the future (Logue, 1991). These precautions allow rats to learn what makes them sick while reducing the likelihood of consuming a lethal amount of something poisonous. These patterns of eating behavior are highly adaptive solutions to the food selection problems faced by rats.

Let's look at some additional examples of how evolution has shaped organisms' behavior. Avoiding predators is a nearly universal problem for organisms. Because of natural selection, many species, such as the grasshopper shown in the photo on this page, have developed physical characteristics that allow them to blend in with their environments, making detection by predators more difficult. Many organisms also engage in elaborate *behavioral maneuvers* to hide themselves. For example, the pictured grasshopper has dug itself a small trench in which to hide and has used its midlegs to pull pebbles over its back (Alcock, 1998). This clever hiding behavior is just as much a product of evolution as the grasshopper's remarkable camouflage.

Many behavioral adaptations are designed to improve organisms' chances of reproductive success. Consider, for instance, the wide variety of species in which females actively choose which male to mate with. In many such species, females demand material goods and services from males in return for copulation opportunities. For example, in one type of moth, males have to spend hours extracting sodium from mud puddles, which they then transfer to prospective mates, who use it to supply their larvae with an important nutritional element (Smedley & Eisner, 1996). In the black-tipped hangingfly, females insist on a nuptial gift of food before they mate. They reject suitors bringing unpalatable food and tie the length of subsequent copulation to the size of the nuptial gift (Thornhill, 1976).

The adaptive value of trading sex for material goods that can aid the survival of an organism and its offspring is obvious, but the evolutionary significance of other mating strategies is more perplexing. In some species characterized by female choice, the choices hinge on males' appearance and courtship behavior. Females usually prefer males

The behavior that helps the grasshopper hide from predators is a product of evolution, just like the physical characteristics that help it to blend in with its surroundings.

sporting larger or more brightly colored ornaments, or those capable of more extreme acoustical displays. For example, female house finches are swayed by redder feathers, whereas female wild turkeys are enticed by larger beak ornaments (see Table 3.2 for additional examples). What do females gain by selecting males with redder feathers, larger beaks, and other arbitrary characteristics? It appears that favored attributes generally seem to be indicators of males' relatively good genes, sound health, low parasite load, or superior ability to provide future services, such as protection or food gathering, all of which may serve to make their offspring more viable (Alcock, 1998). For example, the quality of peacocks' plumage appears to be an indicator of their parasite load (Hamilton & Zuk, 1982). So, even mating preferences for seemingly nonadaptive aspects of appearance may often have adaptive significance.

Parental Investment and Mating Systems

Given that variations in reproductive success are what really fuels evolutionary change, theorists have been particularly interested in understanding the evolutionary bases of various organisms' mating systems. In the 1970s, Robert Trivers (1972) contributed influential extensions of evolutionary theory that shed new light on patterns of mating. According to Trivers, a species' courtship and mating strategies depend primarily on sex differences in parental investment.

Parental investment **refers to what each sex has to invest—in terms of time, energy, survival risk, and forgone opportunities—to produce and nurture offspring.** For example, the efforts required to guard eggs, build nests, or nourish offspring represent parental investments. In most species, there are striking disparities between males and females in their parental investment, and these discrepancies shape mating strategies. *In general, the sex that makes the smaller investment will compete for mating opportunities with the sex that makes the larger investment, and the sex with the larger investment will tend to be more discriminating in selecting its partners.*

In most mammalian species, males have to invest little beyond the act of copulation, so their reproductive potential is maximized by mating with as many females as possible. Hence, males compete with each other for mating opportunities. In contrast, females typically have to invest weeks or months of effort to carry and nourish offspring, thereby limiting the number of offspring they can produce in a breeding season, regardless of how many males they mate with. Hence, females have no incentive for mating with many males. In mammalian species, females typically can optimize their reproductive potential by being discriminating in mate selection—choosing mates that can provide them with better quality genes or material resources that can be invested in offspring. *Thus, the typical result when parental investment is high for females and low for males is* **polygyny, a mating system in which each male seeks to mate with multiple females, whereas each female mates with only one male.** Polygyny comes in many forms and is the most common mating system in nature (Siiter, 1999).

In polygynous mating systems, natural selection favors males who compete aggressively with rivals for copulation opportunities. Thus, the males of many species engage in ferocious battles, biting, kicking, head butting, and locking horns with each other. Elephant seals, for example, hurl their huge bodies (often 1700 pounds) at each other in bitter battles to see who will control a harem of up to 50 females (see Figure 3.21 on the next page). Females mate with the winners of these battles because the winners presumably have "better genes" that will provide their mutual offspring with greater strength and other adaptive traits. In this situation, natural selection obviously favors animals of larger size. Hence, in species where males fight for the right to control multiple females, the males often evolve to be much larger than the females (Alexander et al., 1979).

Although polygyny is the most common mating system, other arrangements are seen when male and female parental investment is roughly equal and when parental investment is high for males and low for females. The key point is that sex differences in parental investment appear to be a major factor shaping organisms' mating systems and that these systems reflect the adaptive demands that specific organisms must face to maximize their reproductive fitness.

Table 3.2 Female Mate Choices Based on Differences in Males' Morphological and Behavioral Attributes

Species	Favored Attribute
Scorpionfly	More symmetrical wings
Barn swallow	More symmetrical and larger tail ornaments
Wild turkey	Larger beak ornaments
House finch	Redder feathers
Satin bowerbird	Bowers with more ornaments
Cichlid fish	Taller display "bower"
Field cricket	Longer calling bouts
Woodhouse's toad	More frequent calls

(Adapted from *Animal Behavior* by John Alcock, 1998, p. 463. Copyright © 1998 John Alcock. Reprinted by permission of Sinauer Associates and the author.)

Figure **3.21**

Social dominance and reproductive fitness in elephant seals. These data, based on observation of a group of southern elephant seals, show that dominant males get far more copulation opportunities than less dominant males (McCann, 1981). Thus, in male elephant seals, aggressive behavior that leads to higher dominance enhances reproductive fitness. A strong association between dominance and reproductive fitness is seen in many, but not all species that have dominance hierarchies. (From "Aggression and Sexual Activity of Male Southern Elephant Seals, *Mirounga leonina*," by T. S. McCann, 1981, *Journal of Zoology, 195*, 295-310.)

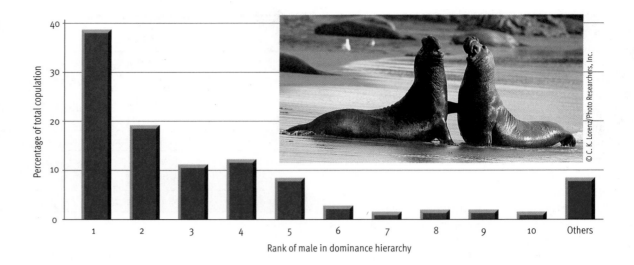

Putting It in Perspective

Three of our seven themes stood out in this chapter: (1) heredity and environment jointly influence behavior, (2) behavior is determined by multiple causes, and (3) psychology is empirical. Let's look at each of these points.

In Chapter 1, when it was first emphasized that heredity and environment jointly shape behavior, you may have been a little perplexed about how your genes could be responsible for your sarcastic wit or your interest in art. In fact, there are no genes for behavior per se. Experts do not expect to find genes for sarcasm or artistic interest, for example. Insofar as your hereditary endowment plays a role in your behavior, it does so *indirectly*, by molding the physiological machine that you work with. Thus, your genes influence your physiological makeup, which in turn influences your personality, temperament, intelligence, interests, and other traits. Bear in mind, however, that genetic factors do not operate in a vacuum. Genes exert their effects in an environmental context. The impact of genetic makeup depends on environment, and the impact of environment depends on genetic makeup.

It was evident throughout the chapter that behavior is determined by multiple causes, but this theme was particularly apparent in the discussions of schizophrenia. At different points in the chapter we saw that schizophrenia may be a function of (1) abnormalities in neurotransmitter activity (especially dopamine), (2) structural abnormalities

in the brain identified with CT and MRI scans, and (3) genetic vulnerability to the illness. These findings do not contradict one another. Rather, they demonstrate that a complex array of biological factors are involved in the development of schizophrenia. In Chapter 14, we'll see that a host of environmental factors also play a role in the multifactorial causation of schizophrenia.

The empirical nature of psychology was apparent in the numerous discussions of the specialized research methods used to study the physiological bases of behavior. As you know, the empirical approach depends on precise observation. Throughout this chapter, you've seen how investigators have come up with innovative methods to observe and measure elusive phenomena such as neural impulses, brain function, cerebral specialization, and the impact of heredity on behavior. The point is that empirical methods are the lifeblood of the scientific enterprise. When researchers figure out how to better observe something, their findings usually facilitate major advances in our scientific knowledge. That is why the new brain-imaging techniques hold exciting promise for neuroscientists.

The importance of empiricism will also be apparent in the upcoming Personal Application and in the Critical Thinking Application that follows. In both applications you'll see the importance of learning to distinguish between scientific findings and conjecture based on those findings.

PERSONAL APPLICATION

Evaluating the Concept of "Two Minds in One"

Answer the following "true" or "false."

_____ 1 Each half of the brain has its own special mode of thinking.

_____ 2 Some people are left-brained while others are right-brained.

_____ 3 Our schools should devote more effort to teaching the overlooked right side of the brain.

Do we have two minds in one that think differently? Do some of us depend on one side of the brain more than the other? Is the right side of the brain neglected? These questions are too complex to resolve with a simple "true" or "false," but in this Application we'll take a closer look at the issues involved in these proposed extensions of the findings on cerebral specialization. You'll learn that some of these ideas are plausible, but in many cases the hype has outstripped the evidence.

Cerebral Specialization and Cognitive Processes

SIM2, 2f

Using a variety of methods, scientists have compiled mountains of data on the specialized abilities of the right and left hemispheres. These findings have led to extensive theorizing about how the right and left brains might be related to cognitive processes. Some of the more intriguing ideas include the following:

1. *The two hemispheres are specialized to process different types of cognitive tasks* (Corballis, 1991; Ornstein, 1977). Research findings have been widely interpreted as showing that the left hemisphere handles verbal tasks, including language, speech, writing, math, and logic, while the right hemisphere handles nonverbal tasks, including spatial problems, music, art, fantasy, and creativity. These conclusions have attracted a great deal of public interest and media attention. For example, Figure 3.22

shows a *Newsweek* artist's depiction of how the brain supposedly divides its work.

2. *The two hemispheres have different modes of thinking* (Banich & Heller, 1998, Joseph, 1992). According to this notion, the documented differences between the hemispheres in dealing with verbal and nonverbal materials are due to more basic differences in how the hemispheres process information. This theory holds that the reason the left hemisphere handles verbal material well is that it is analytic, abstract, rational, logical, and linear. In contrast, the right hemisphere is thought to be better equipped to handle spatial and musical material because it is synthetic, concrete, nonrational, intuitive, and holistic. These proposed hemispheric differences in cognitive style are summarized in Figure 3.23 on the next page.

3. *People vary in their reliance on one hemisphere as opposed to the other* (Bakan, 1971; Zenhausen, 1978). Allegedly, some people

are "left-brained." Their greater dependence on their left hemisphere supposedly makes them analytic, rational, and logical. Other people are "right-brained." Their greater use of their right hemisphere supposedly makes them intuitive, holistic, and irrational. Being right-brained or left-brained is thought to explain many personal characteristics, such as whether an individual likes to read, is good with maps, or enjoys music. This notion of "brainedness" has even been used to explain occupational choice. Supposedly, right-brained people are more likely to become artists or musicians, while left-brained people are more likely to become writers or scientists.

4. *Schools should place more emphasis on teaching the right side of the brain* (Blakeslee, 1980; Kitchens, 1991). Some educational experts have argued that American schools overemphasize logical, analytical left-hemisphere thinking (required by English,

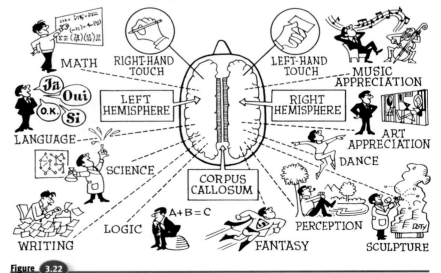

Figure 3.22

Popular conceptions of hemispheric specialization. As this *Newsweek* diagram illustrates, depictions of hemispheric specialization in the popular press have often been oversimplified. (© Roy Doty)

Author Alice Walker and architect I. M. Pei exemplify two types of thinking widely associated with the left brain and the right brain, respectively. Did the talents of each really arise from a different cerebral hemisphere? The empirical evidence is ambiguous at best.

Left Hemisphere's Modes of Thinking	Right Hemisphere's Modes of Thinking
Verbal: Using words to name, describe, define	**Nonverbal:** Showing an awareness of things but minimal connection with words
Analytic: Figuring things out step by step and part by part	**Synthetic:** Putting things together to form wholes
Symbolic: Using a symbol to stand for something	**Analogic:** Seeing likenesses between things; understanding metaphoric relationships
Abstract: Taking out a small bit of information and using it to represent a whole thing	**Concrete:** Relating to things as they are at the present moment
Temporal: Keeping track of time; sequencing one thing after another, doing first things first, second things second, and so forth	**Nontemporal:** Being without a sense of time
Rational: Drawing conclusions based on reason and facts	**Nonrational:** Not requiring a basis of reason or facts; willing to suspend judgment
Digital: Using numbers as in counting	**Spatial:** Seeing where things are in relation to other things and how parts go together to form a whole
Logical: Drawing conclusions based on logic; one thing following another in logical order—for example, developing a mathematical theorem or a well-stated argument	**Intuitive:** Making leaps of insight, often based on incomplete patterns, hunches
Linear: Thinking in terms of linked ideas, one thought directly following another, often leading to a convergent conclusion	**Holistic:** Seeing whole things all at once; perceiving overall patterns and structures, which often leads to divergent conclusions

Figure 3.23

Proposed differences between the left and right hemispheres in cognitive style. It is popular to suggest that the two hemispheres exhibit different modes of thinking. This summary, adapted from Edwards (1989), shows that theorists have tried to relate many polarities in cognitive style to the right and left brains. However, as the text explains, there is relatively little direct evidence to support these proposed dichotomies. (Reprinted by permission of Jeremy P. Tarcher, Inc., a division of Penguin Putnam Publishing Group from *Drawing on the Right Side of the Brain* by Betty Edwards. Copyright © 1989 Betty Edwards.)

math, and science) while shortchanging intuitive, holistic right-hemisphere thinking (required by art and music). These educators have concluded that modern schools turn out an excess of left-brained graduates. They advocate curriculum reform to strengthen the right side of the brain in their students.

Complexities and Qualifications

The ideas just outlined are intriguing and have clearly captured the imagination of the general public. However, the research on cerebral specialization is complex, and these ideas have to be qualified very carefully (Efron, 1990; Springer & Deutsch, 1998). Let's examine each point.

1. There *is* ample evidence that the right and left hemispheres are specialized to handle different types of cognitive tasks, *but only to a degree* (Brown & Kosslyn, 1993). Doreen Kimura (1973) compared the abilities of the right and left hemispheres to quickly recognize letters, words, faces, and melodies in a series of perceptual asymmetry studies. She found that the superiority of one hemisphere over the other on specific types of tasks was usually quite modest (see Figure 3.24). In a neurologically intact person, the hemispheres don't work alone (Hellige, 1993). Most tasks probably engage both hemispheres, albeit to different degrees (Beeman & Chiarello, 1998).

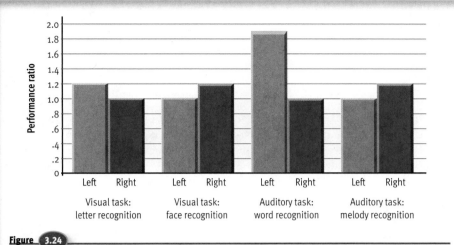

Figure 3.24

Relative superiority of one brain hemisphere over the other in studies of perceptual asymmetry.
The performance ratios show the degree to which one hemisphere was "superior" to the other on each
type of task in one study of normal subjects. For example, the right hemisphere was 20% better than
the left hemisphere in quickly recognizing melodic patterns (ratio 1.2 to 1). Most differences in the
performance of the two hemispheres are quite small. (Data from "The Asymmetry of the Human Brain,"
by D. Kimura, 1973, *Scientific American, 228,* 70-78.)

Furthermore, people differ in their patterns of cerebral specialization (Springer & Deutsch, 1998). Some people display little specialization—that is, their hemispheres seem to have equal abilities on various types of tasks. Others even reverse the usual specialization, so that verbal processing might be housed in the right hemisphere. These unusual patterns are especially common among left-handed people (Rasmussen & Milner, 1977). These variations are not well understood yet. However, they clearly indicate that the special abilities of the cerebral hemispheres are not set in concrete.

2. Little direct evidence has been found to support the notion that each hemisphere has its own mode of thinking, or cognitive style (Bradshaw, 1989). This notion is plausible

and there *is* some supportive evidence, but the evidence is inconsistent and more research is needed (Gordon, 1990; Reuter-Lorenz & Miller, 1998). One key problem with this idea is that aspects of cognitive style have proven difficult to define and measure (Brownell & Gardner, 1981). For instance, there is debate about the meaning of analytic versus synthetic thinking, or linear versus holistic thinking.

3. The evidence on the assertion that some people are left-brained while others are right-brained is inconclusive at best (Hellige, 1990). This notion has some plausibility—if it means only that some people consistently display more activation of one hemisphere than the other. However, the practical significance of any such

"preferences" remains to be determined. At present, researchers do not have convincing data linking brainedness to musical ability, occupational choice, or the like (Springer & Deutsch, 1998).

4. The idea that schools should be reformed to better exercise the right side of the brain borders on nonsense. In neurologically intact people it is impossible to teach just one hemisphere at a time, and there is no evidence that it is beneficial to "exercise" a hemisphere of the brain (Levy, 1985). There are many sound arguments for reforming American schools to encourage more holistic, intuitive thinking, but these arguments have nothing to do with cerebral specialization.

In summary, the theories linking cerebral specialization to cognitive processes are highly speculative. There's nothing wrong with theoretical speculation. Unfortunately, the tentative, conjectural nature of these ideas about hemispheric specialization has gotten lost in the popular magazine descriptions of research on right and left brains (Coren, 1992). Commenting on this popularization, Hooper and Teresi (1986) note: "A widespread cult of the right brain ensued, and the duplex house that Sperry built grew into the K mart of brain science. Today our hairdresser lectures us about the Two Hemispheres of the Brain" (p. 223). Cerebral specialization is an important and intriguing area of research. However, it is unrealistic to expect that the hemispheric divisions in the brain will provide a biological explanation for every dichotomy or polarity in modes of thinking.

CRITICAL THINKING APPLICATION

Building Better Brains: The Perils of Extrapolation

Summarizing the implications of recent research in neuroscience, science writer Ronald Kotulak (1996) concluded, "The first three years of a child's life are critically important to brain development" (pp. ix–x). Echoing this sentiment, the president of a U.S. educational commission asserted that "research in brain development suggests it is time to rethink many educational policies" (Bruer, 1999, p. 16). Based on recent findings in neuroscience, many states launched expensive programs and initiatives in the 1990s intended to foster better neural development in infants. For example, Georgia Governor Zell Miller sought funding to distribute classical music tapes to the state's infants, saying, "No one doubts that listening to music, especially at a very early age, affects the spatial-temporal reasoning that underlies math, engineering, and chess" (Bruer, 1999, p. 62). Well-intended educational groups and even some Hollywood celebrities have argued for the creation of schools for infants on the grounds that because the first three years of life are especially critical to brain development, enriched educational experiences during infancy will lead to smarter adults.

What are these practical, new discoveries about the brain that will permit parents and educators to optimize infants' brain development? Well, we will discuss the pertinent research momentarily, but it is not as new or as practical as suggested in many quarters. Unfortunately, as we saw in our discussion of research on hemispheric specialization, the hype in the media has greatly outstripped the realities of what scientists have learned in the laboratory.

The 1990s were recognized by the United States Congress as "The Decade of the Brain." The focus on the brain led many child-care advocates and educational reformers to use research in neuroscience as the rationale for the programs and policies they sought to promote. The people advocating these ideas

have good intentions, and many of their proposals appear to have merit, but the neuroscience rationale has been stretched to the breaking point. The result? An enlightening case study in the perils of overextrapolation.

The Key Findings on Neural Development

The education and child-care reformers who have used brain science as the basis for their campaigns have primarily cited two key findings: the discovery of critical periods in neural development and the demonstration that rats raised in "enriched environments" have more synapses than rats raised in "impoverished environments." Let's look at each of these findings.

A *critical period* is a limited time span in the development of an organism when it is optimal for certain capacities to emerge because the organism is especially responsive to certain experiences. The seminal research on critical periods in neural development was conducted by David Hubel and Torsten Wiesel (1963, 1965) in the 1960s. They showed that if an eye of a newborn kitten is sutured shut early in its development (typically the first four to six weeks), the kitten will become permanently blind in that eye, but if the eye is covered for the same amount of time at later ages (after four months) blindness does not result. Such studies show that certain types of visual input are necessary during a critical period of development or neural pathways between the eye and brain will not form properly. Basically, what happens is that the inactive synapses from the closed eye are displaced by the active synapses from the open eye. Critical periods have been found for other aspects of neural development and in other species, but a great deal remains to be learned. Based on this type of research, some educational and child-care reformers have argued that the

first three years of life are a critical period for human neural development.

The pioneering work on environment and brain development was begun in the 1960s by Mark Rosenzweig and his colleagues (1961, 1962). They raised some rats in an impoverished environment, (housed individually in small, barren cages) and other rats in an enriched environment (housed in groups of 10 to 12 in larger cages, with a variety of objects available for exploration), as shown in Figure 3.25. They found that the rats raised in the enriched environment performed better on problem-solving tasks than the impoverished rats and had slightly heavier brains and a thicker cerebral cortex in some areas of the brain. Subsequent research by William Greenough demonstrated that enriched environments resulted in heavier and thicker cortical areas by virtue of producing denser dendritic branching, more synaptic contacts, and richer neural networks (Greenough, 1975; Greenough & Volkmar, 1973). Based on this type of research, some child-care reformers have argued that human infants need to be brought up in enriched environments during the critical period before age 3, to promote synapse formation and to optimize the development of their emerging neural circuits.

The findings on critical periods and the effects of enriched environments were genuine breakthroughs in neuroscience, but they certainly aren't *new* findings, as suggested by various political action groups. Moreover, one can raise many doubts about whether this research can serve as a meaningful guide for decisions about parenting practices, day-care programs, educational policies, and welfare reform.

The Risks of Overextrapolation

Extrapolation occurs when an effect is estimated by extending beyond some known values or conditions. Extrapolation is a

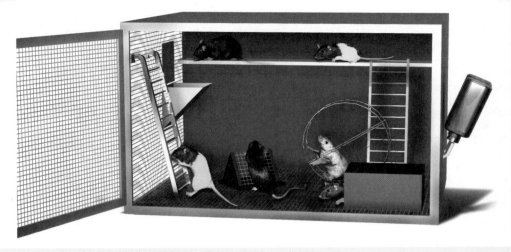

Figure 3.25

Enriched environments in the study of rats' neural development. In the studies by Rosenzweig and colleagues (1961, 1962), rats raised in an impoverished environment were housed alone in small cages, whereas rats raised in enriched environments were housed in groups and were given playthings that were changed daily. Although the enriched conditions provided more stimulating environments than what laboratory rats normally experience, they may not be any more stimulating than rats' natural habitats. Thus, the "enriched" condition may reveal more about the importance of normal stimulation than about the benefits of extra stimulation (Gopnik, Meltzoff, & Kuhl, 1999).

normal process, but some extrapolations are conservative, plausible projections drawn from directly relevant data, whereas others are wild leaps of speculation based on loosely related data. The extrapolations made regarding the educational implications of critical periods and environmental effects on synapse formation are highly conjectural *overextrapolations*. The studies that highlighted the possible importance of early experience in animals have all used extreme conditions to make their comparisons, such as depriving an animal of all visual input or raising it in stark isolation. In light of the findings, it seems plausible to speculate that children probably need normal stimulation to experience normal brain development. However, great difficulty arises when these findings are extended to conclude that adding *more* stimulation to a normal environment will be beneficial to brain development (Shatz, 1992).

The ease with which people fall into the trap of overextrapolating has been particularly apparent in recent recommendations that infants listen to classical music to enhance their brain development. These recommendations have been derived from two studies that showed that college students' performance on spatial reasoning tasks was enhanced slightly for about 10–15 minutes after listening to a brief Mozart recording (Rauscher, Shaw, & Ky, 1993, 1995). This peculiar finding, dubbed the "Mozart effect," has proven difficult to replicate (Steele, Bass, & Crook, 1999), but the pertinent point here

is that there was no research on how classical music affects *infants,* no research relating classical music to *brain development,* and no research on anyone showing *lasting effects.* Nonetheless, many people (including the Governor of Georgia) were quick to extrapolate the shaky findings on the Mozart effect to infants' brain development.

As discussed in Chapter 1, thinking critically about issues often involves asking questions such as: What is missing from this debate? Is there any contradictory evidence? In this case, there is some contradictory evidence that is worthy of consideration. The basis for advocating infant educational programs is the belief that brain development is more rapid and malleable during the hypothesized critical period of birth to age 3 than at later ages. However, Greenough's work on synaptic formation and other lines of research suggest that the brain remains malleable throughout life, responding to stimulation into old age (Innocenti, 1994). Thus, advocates for the aged could just as readily argue for new educational initiatives for the

elderly to help them maximize their intellectual potential. Another problem is the implicit assumption that greater synaptic density is associated with greater intelligence. There is quite a bit of evidence that infant animals and humans begin life with an overabundance of synaptic connections and that learning involves selective pruning of inactive synapses, which gradually give way to heavily used neural pathways (Huttenlocher, 1979; Rakic, Bourgeois, & Goldman-Rakic, 1994). Thus, in the realm of synapses, more may *not* be better.

In conclusion, there may be many valid reasons for increasing educational programs for infants, but research in neuroscience does not appear to provide a clear rationale for much in the way of specific infant care policies. One problem in evaluating these proposals is that few people want to argue against high-quality child care or education. But modern societies need to allocate their limited resources to the programs that appear most likely to have beneficial effects, so even intuitively appealing ideas need to be subjected to critical scrutiny.

Table 3.3   Critical Thinking Skills Discussed in This Application

Skill	Description
Understanding the limits of extrapolation	The critical thinker appreciates that extrapolations are based on certain assumptions, vary in plausibility, and ultimately involve speculation.
Looking for contradictory evidence	In evaluating the evidence presented on an issue, the critical thinker attempts to look for contradictory evidence that may have been left out of the debate.

REVIEW

Key Ideas

Communication in the Nervous System

● Cells in the nervous system receive, integrate, and transmit information. Neurons are the basic communication links. They normally transmit a neural impulse (a change in electrical charge, called an action potential) along an axon to a synapse with another neuron.

● Action potentials trigger the release of chemicals called neurotransmitters that diffuse across a synapse to communicate with other neurons. There are a variety of neurotransmitters that bind at specific receptor sites according to a lock-and-key model.

Organization of the Nervous System

● The nervous system can be divided into two main subdivisions, the central nervous system and the peripheral nervous system. The central nervous system consists of the brain and spinal cord. The brain plays a crucial role in virtually all aspects of behavior.

● The peripheral nervous system consists of the nerves that lie outside the brain and spinal cord. It can be subdivided into the somatic nervous system, which connects to muscles and sensory receptors, and the autonomic nervous system, which connects to blood vessels, smooth muscles, and glands.

The Brain and Behavior

● Neuroscientists use a variety of invasive and noninvasive techniques to study the living brain. These methods include lesioning, electrical stimulation, CT scans, MRI scans, and PET scans. The brain has three major regions: the hindbrain, midbrain, and forebrain. Structures in the hindbrain and midbrain handle essential functions such as breathing, circulation, and coordination of movement.

● The forebrain includes many structures that handle higher functions. The thalamus is primarily a relay station. The hypothalamus is involved in the regulation of basic biological drives such as hunger and sex. The limbic system is a network of loosely connected structures involved in emotion, motivation, and memory.

● The cerebrum is the brain area implicated in most complex mental activities. The cortex is the cerebrum's convoluted outer layer, which is subdivided into four areas. These areas and their primary known functions are the occipital lobe (vision), the parietal lobe (touch), the temporal lobe (hearing), and the frontal lobe (movement of the body).

Right Brain/Left Brain: Cerebral Specialization

● The cerebrum is divided into right and left hemispheres connected by the corpus callosum. Studies have revealed that the right and left halves of the brain each have unique talents, with the right hemisphere being specialized to handle visual-spatial functions, whereas the left hemisphere handles verbal processing.

The Endocrine System: Another Way to Communicate

● The endocrine system consists of the glands that secrete hormones, which are chemicals involved in the regulation of basic bodily processes. The control centers for the endocrine system are the hypothalamus and the pituitary gland.

Heredity and Behavior: Is It All in the Genes?

● The basic units of genetic transmission are genes housed on chromosomes. Most behavioral qualities appear to involve polygenic inheritance. Researchers assess hereditary influence through family studies, twin studies, and adoption studies. These studies indicate that most behavioral traits are influenced by a complex interaction between heredity and environment.

The Evolutionary Bases of Behavior

● Darwin argued that if a heritable trait contributes to an organism's survival or reproductive success, organisms with that trait should produce more offspring than those without the trait and that the prevalence of the trait should gradually increase over generations—thanks to natural selection.

● Adaptations sometimes linger in a population even though they no longer provide a survival or reproductive advantage. Hamilton proposed the theory of inclusive fitness to explain the paradox of self-sacrifice. According to Trivers, a species' courtship and mating strategies depend primarily on sex differences in parental investment.

Putting It in Perspective

● Three of the book's unifying themes stand out in this chapter. First, we saw how heredity interacts with experience to govern behavior. Second, the discussions of biological factors underlying schizophrenia highlighted the multifactorial causation of behavior. Third, we saw how innovations in research methods often lead to advances in knowledge, underscoring the empirical nature of psychology.

Personal Application ● Thinking Critically About the Concept of "Two Minds in One"

● The cerebral hemispheres are specialized for handling different cognitive tasks, but only to a degree, and people vary in their patterns of specialization. Evidence on whether people vary in braineness and whether the two hemispheres vary in cognitive style is inconclusive. There is no evidence that exercising a hemisphere of the brain is useful.

Critical Thinking Application ● Building Better Brains: The Perils of Extrapolation

● Although some education and child-care reformers have used neuroscience as the basis for their campaigns, research has not demonstrated that birth to 3 is a critical period for human neural development or that specific enrichment programs can enhance brain development. These assertions are highly conjectural overextrapolations from existing data.

Key Terms

Absolute refractory period
Action potential
Adaptation
Adoption studies
Afferent nerve fibers
Agonist
Antagonist
Autonomic nervous system (ANS)
Axon
Central nervous system (CNS)
Cerebral cortex
Cerebral hemispheres
Chromosomes
Corpus callosum
Critical period
Dendrites
Efferent nerve fibers
Endocrine system
Endorphins
Family studies
Fitness
Forebrain
Genes
Hindbrain
Hormones
Hypothalamus
Inclusive fitness
Limbic system
Midbrain
Natural selection
Neurons
Neurotransmitters
Parental investment
Peripheral nervous system
Pituitary gland
Polygenic traits
Polygyny
Postsynaptic potential (PSP)
Resting potential
Reuptake
Soma
Somatic nervous system
Split-brain surgery
Synapse
Synaptic cleft
Terminal buttons
Thalamus
Twin studies

Key People

Alan Hodgkin and Andrew Huxley
James Olds and Peter Milner
Candace Pert and Solomon Snyder
Robert Plomin
Roger Sperry and Michael Gazzaniga

PRACTICE TEST

1. A neural impulse is initiated when a neuron's charge momentarily becomes less negative, or even positive. This event is called:
   A. an action potential.
   B. a resting potential.
   C. impulse facilitation.
   D. neuromodulation.

2. Neurons convey information about the strength of stimuli by varying:
   A. the size of their action potentials.
   B. the speed of their action potentials.
   C. the rate at which they fire action potentials.
   D. all of the above.

3. Alterations in activity at dopamine synapses have been implicated in the development of:
   A. anxiety.
   B. schizophrenia.
   C. Alzheimer's disease.
   D. nicotine addiction.

4. Jim has just barely avoided a head-on collision on a narrow road. With heart pounding, hands shaking, and body perspiring, Jim recognizes that these are signs of the body's fight-or-flight response, which is controlled by the:
   A. empathetic division of the peripheral nervous system.
   B. parasympathetic division of the autonomic nervous system.
   C. somatic division of the peripheral nervous system.
   D. sympathetic division of the autonomic nervous system.

5. The hindbrain consists of the:
   A. endocrine system and the limbic system.
   B. reticular formation.
   C. thalamus, the hypothalamus, and the cerebrum.
   D. cerebellum, the medulla, and the pons.

6. The thalamus can be characterized as:
   A. a regulatory mechanism.
   B. the consciousness switch of the brain.
   C. a relay system.
   D. a bridge between the two cerebral hemispheres.

7. The _____ lobe is to hearing as the occipital lobe is to vision.
   A. frontal
   B. temporal
   C. parietal
   D. cerebellar

8. The scientist who won a Nobel prize for his work with split-brain patients is:
   A. Walter Cannon.
   B. Paul Broca.
   C. Roger Sperry.
   D. James Olds.

9. Sounds presented to the right ear are registered:
   A. only in the right hemisphere.
   B. only in the left hemisphere.
   C. more quickly in the right hemisphere.
   D. more quickly in the left hemisphere.

10. In people whose corpus callosums have not been severed, verbal stimuli are identified more quickly and more accurately:
    A. when sent to the right hemisphere first.
    B. when sent to the left hemisphere first.
    C. when presented to the left visual field.
    D. when presented auditorally rather than visually.

11. Hormones are to the endocrine system as _____ are to the nervous system.
    A. nerves
    B. synapses
    C. neurotransmitters
    D. action potentials

12. Adopted children's similarity to their biological parents is generally attributed to _____; adopted children's similarity to their adoptive parents is generally attributed to _____.
    A. heredity; the environment
    B. the environment; heredity
    C. the environment; the environment
    D. heredity; heredity

13. Which of the following statements represents the most logical resolution of the nature-nurture controversy?
    A. Environment is most important, at least for those individuals who have a normal genotype.
    B. Heredity and environment interact to affect an individual's development.
    C. Heredity is most important, but a high-quality environment can make up for genetic defects.
    D. The environment is like a rubber band that stretches to meet the needs of an individual's genotype.

14. In evolutionary theory, *fitness* refers to:
    A. the ability to survive.
    B. the ability to adapt to environmental demands.
    C. reproductive success.
    D. the physical skills necessary for survival.

15. For which of the following assertions is the empirical evidence strongest?
    A. The two cerebral hemispheres are specialized to handle different types of cognitive tasks.
    B. Schools should be reformed to better educate the right hemisphere.
    C. Each hemisphere has its own cognitive style.
    D. Some people are right-brained, while others are left-brained.

Answers

1	A	page 61	6	C	page 72	11	C	page 78
2	C	page 62	7	B	pages 74–75	12	A	page 81
3	B	page 65	8	C	page 00	13	B	page 81
4	D	pages 67–68	9	D	page 00	14	C	page 83
5	D	page 70	10	B	page 00	15	A	pages 88–89

INFOTRAC
COLLEGE EDITION

Go to the Wadsworth Psychology Study Center for quiz questions, research updates, interactive exercises, and suggested readings in INFOTRAC related to this chapter:
http://psychology.wadsworth.com/product/0534593100s

CHAPTER 4

© Eastcott-Momatiuk/The Image Works

Sensation and Perception

Take a look at the adjacent photo. What do you see? You probably answered, "a rose" or "a flower." But is that what you really see? No, this isn't a trick question. Let's examine the odd case of "Dr. P." It shows that there's more to seeing than meets the eye.

Dr. P was an intelligent and distinguished music professor who began to exhibit some worrisome behaviors that seemed to be related to his vision. Sometimes he failed to recognize familiar students by sight, though he knew them instantly by the sound of their voices. Sometimes he acted as if he saw faces in inanimate objects, cordially

greeting fire hydrants and parking meters as if they were children. On one occasion, reaching for what he thought was his hat, he took hold of his wife's head and tried to put it on! Except for these kinds of visual mistakes, Dr. P was a normal, talented man.

Ultimately Dr. P was referred to Oliver Sacks, a neurologist, for an examination. During one visit, Sacks handed Dr. P a fresh red rose to see whether he would recognize it. Dr. P took the rose as if he were being given a model of a geometric solid rather than a flower. "About six inches in length," Dr. P observed, "a convoluted red form with a linear green attachment."

"Yes," Sacks persisted, "and what do you think it is, Dr. P?"

"Not easy to say," the patient replied. "It lacks the simple symmetry of the Platonic solids . . ."

"Smell it," the neurologist suggested. Dr. P looked perplexed, as if being asked to smell symmetry, but he complied and brought the flower to his nose. Suddenly, his confusion cleared up. "Beautiful. An early rose. What a heavenly smell" (Sacks, 1987, pp. 13–14).

What accounted for Dr. P's strange inability to recognize faces and familiar objects by sight? There was nothing wrong with his eyes. He could readily spot a pin on the floor. If you're thinking that he *must* have had something wrong with his vision, look again at the photo of the rose. What you see *is* "a convoluted red form with a linear green attachment." It doesn't occur to you to describe it that way only because, without thinking about it, you instantly perceive that combination of form and color as a flower. This is precisely what Dr. P was unable to do. He could see perfectly well, but he was losing the ability to assemble what he saw into a meaningful picture of the world. Technically, he suffered from a condition called *visual agnosia,* an inability to recognize objects through sight. As Sacks (1987) put it, "Visually, he was lost in a world of lifeless abstractions" (p. 15).

As Dr. P's case illustrates, without effective processing of sensory input, our familiar world can become a chaos of bewildering sensations. To acknowledge the need to both take in and process sensory information, psychologists distinguish between sensation

Figure 4.1

The distinction between sensation and perception. Sensation involves the stimulation of sensory organs, whereas perception involves the processing and interpretation of sensory input. As this illustration shows, the two processes merge at the point where sensory receptors convert physical energy into neural impulses.

and perception. *Sensation* **is the stimulation of sense organs.** *Perception* **is the selection, organization, and interpretation of sensory input.** Sensation involves the absorption of energy, such as light or sound waves, by sensory organs, such as the eyes and ears. Perception involves organizing and translating sensory input into something meaningful (see Figure 4.1). For example, when you look at the photo of the rose, your eyes are sensing the light reflected from the page, including areas of low reflectance where ink has been deposited in an irregular shape. What you *perceive,* however, is a picture of a rose.

The distinction between sensation and perception stands out in Dr. P's case of visual agnosia. His eyes were doing their job of registering sensory input and transmitting signals to the brain. However, damage in his brain interfered with his ability to put these signals together into organized wholes. Thus, Dr. P's process of visual *sensation* was intact, but his process of visual *perception* was severely impaired.

Dr. P's case is unusual, of course. Normally, the processes of sensation and perception are difficult to separate because people automatically start organizing incoming sensory stimulation the moment it arrives. The distinction between sensation and perception has been useful in organizing theory and research, but in actual operation the two processes merge.

We'll begin our discussion of sensation and perception with a long look at vision and then take a briefer look at the other senses. As we examine each of the sensory systems, we'll see repeatedly that people's experience of the world depends on both the physical stimuli they encounter (sensation) and their active processing of stimulus inputs (perception). The chapter's Personal Application explores how principles of visual perception come into play in art and illusion. The Critical Thinking Application discusses how perceptual contrasts can be manipulated in persuasive efforts.

Light waves

Sound waves

Sensation

Perception

Sensory organs absorb energy from physical stimuli in the environment.

Sensory receptors detect stimulus energies and convert them into neural impulses, which are sent to the brain.

The brain organizes this input and translates it into something meaningful.

Our Sense of Sight: The Visual System

"Seeing is believing." Good ideas are "bright," and a good explanation is "illuminating." This section is an "overview." Do you see the point? As these common expressions show, humans are visual animals. People rely heavily on their sense of sight, and they virtually equate it with what is trustworthy (seeing is believing). Although it is taken for granted, you'll see (there it is again) that the human visual system is amazingly complex. Furthermore, as in all sensory domains, what people "sense" and what they "perceive" may be quite different.

The Stimulus: Light

For people to see, there must be light. *Light* is a form of electromagnetic radiation that travels as a wave, moving, naturally enough, at the speed of light. As

Figure 4.2(a) shows, light waves vary in *amplitude* (height) and in *wavelength* (the distance between peaks). Amplitude affects mainly the perception of brightness, while wavelength affects mainly the perception of color. The lights humans normally see are mixtures of different wavelengths. Hence, light can also vary in its *purity* (how varied the mix is). Purity influences perception of the saturation or richness of colors. Saturation is difficult to describe, but if you glance ahead to Figure 4.10, you'll find it clearly illustrated. Of course, most objects do not emit light, they reflect it (the sun, lamps, and fireflies being some exceptions).

What most people call light includes only the wavelengths that humans can see. But as Figure 4.2(c) shows, the visible spectrum is only a slim portion of the total range of wavelengths. Vision is

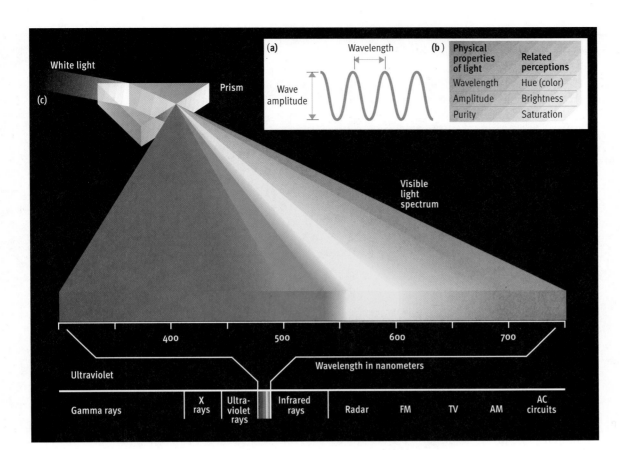

Figure 4.2

Light, the physical stimulus for vision. **(a)** Light waves vary in amplitude and wavelength. **(b)** Within the spectrum of visible light, amplitude (corresponding to physical intensity) affects mainly the experience of brightness. Wavelength affects mainly the experience of color, and purity is the key determinant of saturation. **(c)** If white light (such as sunlight) passes through a prism, the prism separates the light into its component wavelengths, creating a rainbow of colors. However, visible light is only the narrow band of wavelengths to which human eyes happen to be sensitive.

a filter that permits people to sense only a fraction of the real world. Other animals have different capabilities and so live in a quite different visual world. For example, many insects can see shorter wavelengths than humans can see, in the *ultraviolet* spectrum, whereas many fish and reptiles can see longer wavelengths, in the *infrared* spectrum.

Although the sense of sight depends on light waves, for people to see, incoming visual input must be converted into neural impulses that are sent to the brain. Let's investigate how this transformation is accomplished.

The Eye: A Living Optical Instrument

The eyes serve two main purposes: they channel light to the neural tissue that receives it, called the *retina,* and they house that tissue. The structure of the eye is shown in Figure 4.3 on the next page. Each eye is a living optical instrument that creates an image of the visual world on the light-sensitive retina lining its inside back surface.

Light enters the eye through a transparent "window" at the front, the *cornea.* The cornea and the crystalline *lens,* located behind it, form an upside-down image of objects on the retina. It might seem disturbing that the image is upside down, but the arrangement works. It doesn't matter how the image sits on the retina, as long as the brain knows the rule for relating positions on the retina to the corresponding positions in the world. **The *lens* is the transparent eye structure that focuses the light rays falling on the retina.** The lens is made up of relatively soft tissue, capable of adjustments that facilitate a process called accommodation. *Accommodation* occurs when the curvature of the lens adjusts to alter visual focus. When you focus on a close object, the lens of your eye gets fatter (rounder) in order to give you a clear image. When you focus on distant objects, the lens flattens out to give you a better image of them.

A number of common visual deficiencies are caused by focusing problems or defects in the lens (Guyton, 1991). For example, **in *nearsightedness,* close objects are seen clearly but distant objects appear blurry** because the focus of light from distant objects falls a little short of the retina (see Figure 4.4 on page 99). This focusing problem occurs when the cornea or lens bends light too much, or when the eyeball is too long. **In *farsightedness,* distant objects are seen clearly but close objects appear**

Figure 4.3

The human eye and retina. Light passes through the cornea, pupil, and lens and falls on the light-sensitive surface of the retina, where images of objects are reflected upside down. The closeup shows the several layers of cells in the retina. The cells closest to the back of the eye (the rods and cones) are the receptor cells that actually detect light. The intervening layers of cells receive signals from the rods and cones and form circuits that begin the process of analyzing incoming information before it is sent to the brain. These cells feed into many optic fibers, all of which head toward the "hole" in the retina where the optic nerve leaves the eye—the point known as the optic disk (which corresponds to the blind spot).

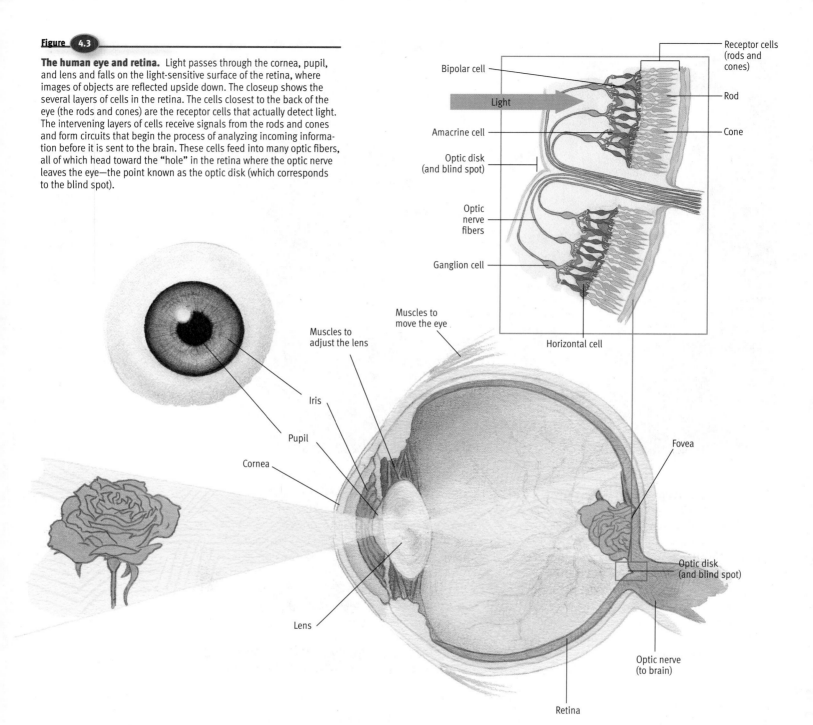

Web Link 4.1

Vision Science: An Internet Resource for Research in Human and Animal Vision
There are many online sites devoted to the sense of sight and visual processes. Vision Science provides a convenient guide to the best of these sites, especially for online demonstrations and tutorials.

blurry because the focus of light from close objects falls behind the retina (again, see Figure 4.4). This focusing problem typically occurs when the eyeball is too short. A *cataract* is a lens that is clouded. This defect occurs mainly in older age groups, affecting three out of four people over the age of 65.

The eye also makes adjustments to alter the amount of light reaching the retina. The *iris* is the colored ring of muscle surrounding the *pupil*, or black center of the eye. **The *pupil* is the opening in the center of the iris that helps regulate the amount of light passing into the rear chamber of the eye.** When the pupil constricts, it lets less light into the eye, but it sharpens the image falling on the retina. When the pupil dilates (opens), it lets more light in, but the image is less sharp. In bright light, the pupils constrict to take advantage of the sharpened image. But in dim light, the pupils dilate. Image sharpness is sacrificed to allow more light to fall on the retina so that more remains visible.

The Retina: The Brain's Envoy in the Eye

The *retina* is the *paper-thin sheet of* neural tissue lining the inside back surface of the eye; it absorbs light, processes images, and sends visual information to the brain. You may be surprised to learn that the retina *processes* images. But it's a piece of the central nervous system that happens to be located in the eyeball. Much as the spinal cord is a complicated extension of the brain, the retina is the brain's envoy in the eye. Although the retina is only a paper-thin sheet of neural tissue, it contains a complex network of specialized cells arranged in layers, as shown in Figure 4.3.

The axons that run from the retina to the brain converge at a single spot where they exit the eye. At that point, all the fibers dive through a hole in the retina called the *optic disk*. Since the optic disk is a *hole* in the retina, you cannot see the part of an image that falls on it. It is therefore known as the *blind* spot. You may not be aware that you have a blind spot in each eye, since each normally compensates for the blind spot of the other.

Visual Receptors: Rods and Cones

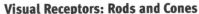

The retina contains millions of receptor cells that are sensitive to light. Surprisingly, these receptors are located in the innermost layer of the retina. Hence, light must pass through several layers of cells before it gets to the receptors that actually detect it. Only about 10% of the light arriving at the cornea reaches these receptors (Leibovic, 1990). The retina contains two types of receptors, *rods* and *cones*. Their names are based on their shapes, as rods are elongated and cones are stubbier. Rods outnumber cones by a huge margin, about 125 million to 6.4 million (Pugh, 1988).

Cones are specialized visual receptors that play a key role in daylight vision and color vision. The cones handle most of our daytime vision, because bright lights dazzle the rods. The special sensitivities of cones also allow them to play a major role in the perception of color. However, cones do not respond well to dim light, which is why you don't see color very well in low illumination. Nonetheless, cones provide better *visual acuity*—that is, sharpness and precise detail—than rods. Cones are concentrated most heavily in the center of the retina and quickly fall off in density toward its periphery. **The** *fovea* **is a tiny spot in the center of the retina that contains only cones; visual acuity is greatest at this spot.** When you want to see something sharply, you usually move your eyes to center the object in the fovea.

Rods are specialized visual receptors that play a key role in night vision and peripheral vision. Rods handle night vision because they are more sensitive than cones to dim light. They handle the lion's share of peripheral vision because they greatly outnumber cones in the periphery of the retina. The density of the rods is greatest just outside the fovea and gradually decreases toward the periphery of the retina. Because of the distribution of rods, when you want to see a faintly illuminated object in the dark, it's best to look slightly above or below the place it should be. Averting your gaze this way moves the image from the cone-filled fovea, which requires more light, to the rod-dominated area just outside the fovea, which requires less light. This trick of averted vision is well known to astronomers, who use it to study dim objects viewed through the eyepiece of a telescope.

Dark and Light Adaptation

You've probably noticed that when you enter a dark theater on a bright day, you stumble about almost blindly. But within minutes you can make your way about quite well in the dim light. This adjustment is called *dark adaptation*—the process in which the eyes become more sensitive to light in low illumination. Figure 4.5 on the next page maps out the course of this process. It shows how, as time passes, you require less and less light to see. Dark

Nearsightedness

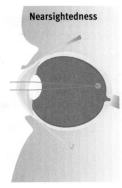

Farsightedness

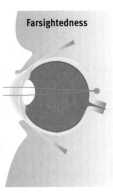

Craig McClain

Figure 4.4

Nearsightedness and farsightedness. The photos on the right simulate how a scene might look to near-sighted and farsighted people. Nearsightedness occurs because light from distant objects focuses in front of the retina. Farsightedness is due to the opposite situation—light from close objects focuses behind the retina.

Understanding Sensory Processes in the Retina

Check your understanding of sensory receptors in the retina by completing the following exercises. Consult Appendix A for the answers.

The receptors for vision are rods and cones in the retina. These two types of receptors have many important differences, which are compared systematically in the chart below. Fill in the missing information to finish the chart.

Dimension	Rods	Cones
1. Physical shape	*Elongated*	*Stubby*
2. Number in the retina	*125 million*	*6.4 million*
3. Area of the retina in which they are dominant receptor	*Periphery*	*Fovea-center*
4. Critical to color vision	*No*	*Yes*
5. Critical to peripheral vision	*Yes*	*No*
6. Sensitivity to dim light	*Strong*	*Weak*
7. Speed of dark adaptation	*Slow*	*Rapid*

adaptation is virtually complete in about 30 minutes, with considerable progress occurring in the first 10 minutes. The curve in Figure 4.5 that charts this progress consists of two segments because cones adapt more rapidly than rods (Walraven et al., 1990).

When you emerge from a dark theater on a sunny day, you need to squint to ward off the overwhelming brightness, and the reverse of dark adaptation occurs. **Light adaptation is the process whereby the eyes become less sensitive to light in high illumination.** As with dark adaptation, light adaptation improves your visual acuity under the prevailing circumstances.

Information Processing in the Retina **3b**

In processing visual input, the retina transforms a pattern of light falling onto it into a very different representation of the visual scene. Light striking the retina's receptors (rods and cones) triggers neural signals that pass into the intricate network of cells in the retina. Signals move from receptors to bipolar cells to ganglion cells (see the inset in Figure 4.3), which in turn send impulses along the *optic nerve—a collection of axons that connect the eye with the brain.* These axons, which depart the eye through the optic disk, carry visual information, encoded as a stream of neural impulses, to the brain.

A great deal of complex information processing goes on in the retina itself before visual signals are sent to the brain. Ultimately, the information from over 130 million rods and cones converges to travel along "only" 1 million axons in the optic nerve (Slaughter, 1990). This means that the bipolar and ganglion cells in the intermediate layers of the retina integrate and compress signals from many receptors. The collection of rod and cone receptors that funnel signals to a particular visual cell in the retina (or ultimately in the brain) make up that cell's *receptive field*. Thus, **the receptive field of a visual cell is the retinal area that, when stimulated, affects the firing of that cell.**

Receptive fields in the retina come in a variety of shapes and sizes. Particularly common are circular fields with a center-surround arrangement (Tessier-Lavigne, 1991). In these receptive fields, light falling in the center has the opposite effect of light falling in the surrounding area (see Figure 4.6). For example, the rate of firing of a visual cell might be *increased* by light in the center of its receptive field and *decreased* by light in the *surrounding area*. Other visual cells may work in just the opposite way. Either way, when receptive fields are stimulated, retinal cells send signals both toward the brain and *laterally* (sideways) toward nearby visual cells. These lateral signals, carried by the horizontal and amacrine cells (see the inset in Figure 4.3), allow visual cells in the retina to have interactive effects on each other.

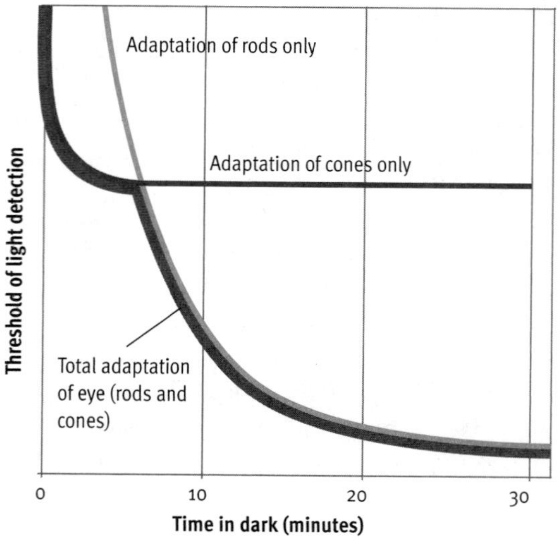

Figure 4.5

The process of dark adaptation. Visual sensitivity improves markedly during the first 5 to 10 minutes after entering a dark room, as the eye's bright-light receptors (the cones) rapidly adapt to low light levels. Further improvement comes from the rods, which are slower to adapt but are capable of far greater visual sensitivity in low levels of light.

Adaptation of rods only

Adaptation of cones only

Threshold of light detection

Total adaptation of eye (rods and cones)

Time in dark (minutes)

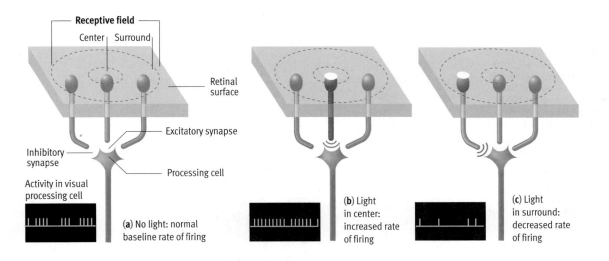

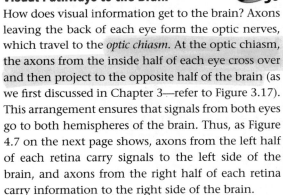

(a) No light: normal baseline rate of firing

(b) Light in center: increased rate of firing

(c) Light in surround: decreased rate of firing

Figure 4.6

Receptive fields in the retina. Visual cells' receptive fields in the retina are often circular with a center-surround arrangement, so that light striking the center of the field produces the opposite result of light striking the surround. In the receptive field depicted here, light in the center produces increased firing in the visual cell, whereas light in the surround produces decreased firing; the arrangement in other receptive fields may be just the opposite.

Vision and the Brain

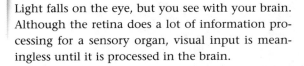 3C

Light falls on the eye, but you see with your brain. Although the retina does a lot of information processing for a sensory organ, visual input is meaningless until it is processed in the brain.

Visual Pathways to the Brain

3C

How does visual information get to the brain? Axons leaving the back of each eye form the optic nerves, which travel to the *optic chiasm*. At the optic chiasm, the axons from the inside half of each eye cross over and then project to the opposite half of the brain (as we first discussed in Chapter 3—refer to Figure 3.17). This arrangement ensures that signals from both eyes go to both hemispheres of the brain. Thus, as Figure 4.7 on the next page shows, axons from the left half of each retina carry signals to the left side of the brain, and axons from the right half of each retina carry information to the right side of the brain.

After reaching the optic chiasm, the optic nerve fibers diverge along two pathways. The main pathway projects into the thalamus, where visual signals are processed and then distributed to areas in the occipital lobe that make up the *primary visual cortex*. After the initial cortical processing of visual input takes place here, signals are typically shuttled through the secondary visual cortex and on to the temporal and parietal lobes for additional processing. The second visual pathway leaving the optic chiasm branches off to an area in the midbrain (the *superior colliculus*) before traveling through the thalamus and on to the occipital lobe. However, the second pathway projects into different areas of the thalamus and the occipital lobe than the main visual pathway does. The principal function of the second pathway appears to be the coordination of visual input with other sensory input (Stein & Meredith, 1993).

The main visual pathway is subdivided into two more specialized pathways called the *magnocellular* and *parvocellular* channels (based on the types of ganglion cells they originate in). These channels engage in **parallel processing, which involves simultaneously extracting different kinds of information from the same input.** The two visual channels have sometimes been characterized as the *what and where pathways*, with the parvocellular channel processing the details of *what* objects are out there and the magnocellular channel processing *where* the objects are (Ungerleider & Haxby, 1994; Wandell, 1995). Thus, the parvocellular channel handles the perception of color, form, and texture, while the magnocellular pathway processes information regarding motion and depth (Shapley, 1995).

Information Processing in the Visual Cortex

 3C

Visual input ultimately arrives in the primary visual cortex located in the occipital lobe. How these cortical cells respond to light once posed a perplexing problem. Researchers investigating the question placed microelectrodes in the visual cortex of animals to record action potentials from individual cells. They would flash spots of light in the retinal receptive fields that the cells were thought to monitor, but the cells rarely responded.

According to David Hubel and Torsten Wiesel (1962, 1963), they discovered the solution to this mystery quite by accident. One of the projector slides they used to present a spot to a cat had a crack in it. The spot elicited no response, but when they removed the slide, the crack moved through the cell's receptive field, and the cell fired like crazy in response to the moving dark line. It turns out that cortical cells don't really respond much to little spots—they are much more sensitive to lines,

© Ira Wyman/CORBIS-Sygma

❝One can now begin to grasp the significance of the great number of cells in the visual cortex. Each cell seems to have its own specific duties.❞
DAVID HUBEL

Handwritten margin notes:

Optic Chiasm
Optic Nerve
     /   \
Thalamus   Midbrain
1. Magnocellular
   "where" objects are
2. Parvocellular
   "what" objects

Margin annotations: MAIN / SECONDARY

Figure 4.7

Visual pathways to the brain. (a) Input from the right half of the visual field strikes the left side of each retina and is transmitted to the left hemisphere (shown in red). Input from the left half of the visual field strikes the right side of each retina and is transmitted to the right hemisphere (shown in green). The nerve fibers from each eye meet at the optic chiasm, where fibers from the inside half of each retina cross over to the opposite side of the brain. After reaching the optic chiasm, the major visual pathway projects through the lateral geniculate nucleus in the thalamus and onto the primary visual cortex (shown with solid lines). A second pathway detours through the superior colliculus and then projects through another area of the thalamus and onto slightly different areas of the primary visual cortex (shown with dotted lines). **(b)** This inset shows a vertical view of how the optic pathways project through the thalamus and onto the visual cortex in the back of the brain [the two pathways mapped out in diagram **(a)** are virtually indistinguishable from this angle].

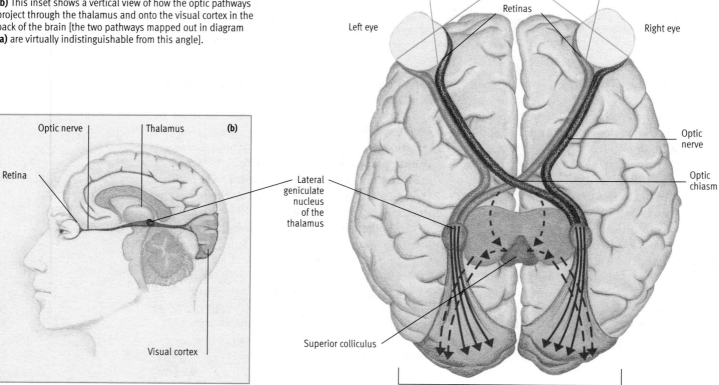

edges, and other more complicated stimuli. Armed with new slides, Hubel and Wiesel embarked on years of painstaking study of the visual cortex. Their work eventually earned them a Nobel prize in 1981.

Hubel and Wiesel (1962, 1979) identified three major types of visual cells in the cortex, which they called simple cells, complex cells, and hypercomplex cells. *Simple cells* are quite specific about which stimuli will make them fire. A simple cell responds best to a line of the correct width, oriented at the correct angle, and located in the correct position in its receptive field (see Figure 4.8). *Complex cells* also care about width and orientation, but they respond to any position in their receptive fields. Some complex cells are most responsive if a line sweeps across their receptive field—but only if it's moving in the

"right" direction. *Hypercomplex* cells are cells that are particularly fussy about the length of a stimulus line.

The key point of all this is that the cells in the visual cortex seem to be highly specialized. They have been characterized as *feature detectors*, **neurons that respond selectively to very specific features of more complex stimuli.** Ultimately, most visual stimuli could be represented by combinations of lines such as those registered by these feature detectors. Some theorists believe that feature detectors are registering the basic building blocks of visual perception and that the brain somehow assembles the blocks into a coherent picture of complex stimuli (Maguire, Weisstein, & Klymenko, 1990).

After visual input is processed in the primary visual cortex, it is often routed to other cortical areas

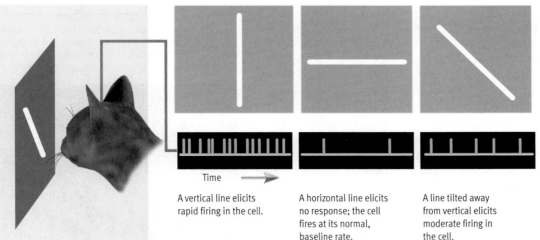

Figure 4.8

Hubel and Wiesel's procedure for studying the activity of neurons in the visual cortex. As the cat is shown various stimuli, a microelectrode records the firing of a neuron in the cat's visual cortex. The figure shows the electrical responses of a simple cell apparently "programmed" to respond to lines oriented vertically.

Time ⟶

A vertical line elicits rapid firing in the cell.

A horizontal line elicits no response; the cell fires at its normal, baseline rate.

A line tilted away from vertical elicits moderate firing in the cell.

for additional processing. For example, much of the information in the magnocellular channel (the *where* pathway) is sent on to the secondary visual cortex and then the parietal lobes (see Figure 4.9). Much of the input in the parvocellular channel (the *what* pathway) is shuttled through the secondary visual cortex and onward to the temporal lobes (see Figure 4.9). As signals move further along in the visual processing system, neurons become even more specialized or fussy about what turns them on and the stimuli that activate them become more and more complex. For example, researchers have identified cells in the temporal lobe (along the what pathway) of monkeys and humans that respond best to pictures of faces (Rolls, 1992; Rolls & Tovee, 1995). This incredible specificity has led researchers to joke that they may eventually find a cell that only recognizes one's grandmother (Cowey, 1994). The discovery of neurons that respond to facial stimuli raises an obvious question: Why does the cortex have face detectors? Theorists are far from sure, but one line of thinking is that the ability to quickly recognize faces—such as those of friends or foes—probably has had adaptive significance over the course of evolution (Desimone, 1991). Thus, natural selection *may* have wired the brains of some species to quickly respond to faces.

Viewing the World in Color

So far, we've considered only how the visual system deals with light and dark. Let's journey now into the world of color. Of course, you can see perfectly well without seeing in color. Many animals get by with little or no color vision, and no one seemed to suffer back when all photographs, movies, and TV shows were in black and white. However, color adds not only spectacle but information to perceptions

of the world. The ability to identify objects against a complex background is enhanced by the addition of color. Quickly identifying objects probably has had adaptive value in terms of finding food and detecting predators. Indeed, some theorists have suggested that color vision evolved in humans and monkeys because it improved their ability to find fruit in the forest (Mollon, 1989). Although the purpose of color vision remains elusive, scientists have learned a great deal about the mechanisms underlying the perception of color.

The Stimulus for Color

As noted earlier, the lights people see are mixtures of different wavelengths. Perceived color is primarily a function of the dominant wavelength in these mixtures. In the visible spectrum, lights with the longest wavelengths appear red, whereas those with the shortest appear violet. Notice the word *appear.* Color is a psychological interpretation. It's not a physical property of light itself.

Although wavelength wields the greatest influence, perception of color depends on complex blends

Figure 4.9

Visual pathways from the primary visual cortex. Cortical processing of visual input is begun in the primary visual cortex. From there, signals are shuttled through the secondary visual cortex and onward to a variety of other areas in the cortex along a number of pathways. Two prominent pathways are highlighted here. The magnocellular, or "where pathway," which processes information about motion and depth, moves on to areas of the parietal lobe. The parvocellular, or "what pathway," which processes information about color, form, and texture, moves on to areas of the temporal lobe.

Magnocellular "Where pathway"

Secondary visual cortex

Primary visual cortex

Parvocellular "What pathway"

of all three properties of light. Wavelength is most closely related to hue, amplitude to brightness, and purity to saturation. These three dimensions of color are illustrated in the *color solid* shown in Figure 4.10.

As a color solid demonstrates systematically, people can perceive many different colors. Indeed, experts estimate that humans can discriminate between roughly a million colors (Boynton, 1990). Most of these diverse variations are the result of mixing a few basic colors. There are two kinds of color mixture: subtractive and additive. *Subtractive color mixing works* by removing some wavelengths of light, leaving less light than was originally there. You probably became familiar with subtractive mixing as a child when you mixed yellow and blue paints to make green. Paints yield subtractive mixing because pigments *absorb* most wavelengths, selectively reflecting back specific wavelengths that give rise to particular colors (see Figure 4.11). Subtractive color mixing can also be demonstrated by stacking color filters. If you look through a sandwich of yellow and blue cellophane filters, they will block out certain wavelengths. The middle wavelengths that are left will look green.

Additive color mixing works by superimposing lights, putting more light in the mixture than exists in any one light by itself. If you shine red, green, and blue spotlights on a white surface, you'll have an additive mixture. As Figure 4.12 shows, additive and subtractive mixtures of the same colors produce different results.

White light actually includes the entire visible spectrum, as you can demonstrate by allowing white light to pass through a prism (consult Figure 4.2 once again). Accordingly, when all wavelengths are mixed

Figure 4.10

The color solid. The color solid shows how color varies along three perceptual dimensions: brightness (increasing from the bottom to the top of the solid), hue (changing around the solid's perimeter), and saturation (increasing toward the periphery of the solid).

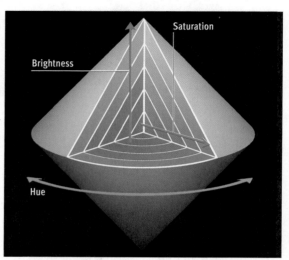

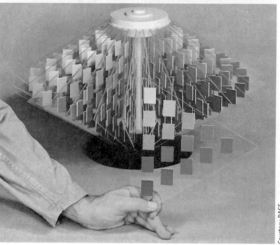

Figure 4.11

Subtractive color mixing. Paints selectively reflect specific wavelengths that give rise to particular colors, as you can see here for blue and yellow, which both also reflect back a little green. When we mix blue and yellow paint, the mixture absorbs all the colors that blue and yellow absorbed individually. The mixture is subtractive because more wavelengths are removed by both than by each paint alone. The yellow paint in the mixture absorbs the wavelengths associated with blue and the blue paint in the mixture absorbs the wavelengths associated with yellow. The only wavelengths left to be reflected back are some of those associated with green, so the mixture is seen as green.

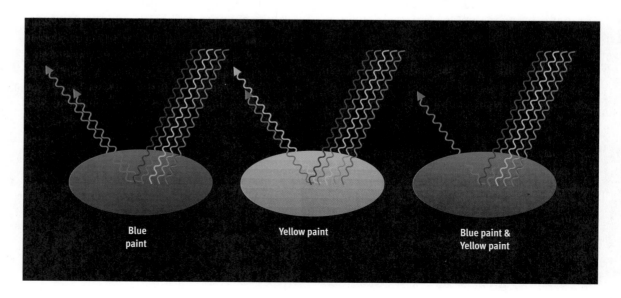

Blue paint   Yellow paint   Blue paint & Yellow paint

Lights   Paints

Figure 4.12

Additive color mixing.
Lights mix additively because all the wavelengths contained in each light reach the eye. If red, blue, and green lights are projected onto a white screen, they produce the colors shown on the left, with white at the intersection of all three lights. If paints of the same three colors were combined in the same way, the subtractive mixture would produce the colors shown on the right, with black at the intersection of all three colors.

additively, they yield natural white light. Human processes of color perception parallel additive color mixing much more closely than subtractive mixing, as you'll see in the following discussion of theories of color vision.

Trichromatic Theory of Color Vision

The trichromatic theory of color vision (*tri* for "three," *chroma* for "color") was first stated by Thomas Young and modified later by Hermann von Helmholtz (1852). The *trichromatic theory holds that the human eye has three types of receptors with differing sensitivities to different light wavelengths.* Helmholtz believed that the eye contains specialized receptors sensitive to the wavelengths associated with red, green, or blue. According to this model, people can see all the colors of the rainbow because the eye does its own "color mixing" by varying the ratio of neural activity among these three types of receptors.

The impetus for the trichromatic theory was the demonstration that a light of any color can be matched by the additive mixture of three *primary colors.* (Any three colors that are appropriately spaced out in the visible spectrum can serve as primary colors, although red, green, and blue are usually used.) Does it sound implausible that three colors should be adequate for creating all other colors? If so, consider that this phenomenon is exactly what happens on your color TV screen. Additive mixtures of red, green, and blue fool you into seeing all the colors of a natural scene.

Most of the known facts about color blindness also meshed well with trichromatic theory. *Color blindness encompasses a variety of deficiencies in the ability to distinguish among colors.* Color blindness occurs much more frequently in males than in females. Actually, the term color *blindness* is somewhat misleading, as complete blindness to differences in colors is quite rare. Most people who are color blind are *dichromats;* that is, they make do

with only two color channels. There are three types of dichromats, and each type is insensitive to a different color (red, green, or blue, although the latter is rare) (Gouras, 1991). The three deficiencies seen among dichromats support the notion that there are three channels for color vision, as proposed by trichromatic theory.

Opponent Process Theory of Color Vision

Although trichromatic theory explained some facets of color vision well, it ran aground in other areas. Consider complementary afterimages, for instance. *Complementary colors are pairs of colors that produce gray tones when mixed together.* The various pairs of complementary colors can be arranged in a *color circle,* such as the one in Figure 4.13. If you stare at a strong color and then look at a white background, you'll see an *afterimage—a visual image that persists after a stimulus is removed.* The color of the afterimage will be the *complement* of the color you originally stared at. Trichromatic theory cannot account for the appearance of complementary afterimages.

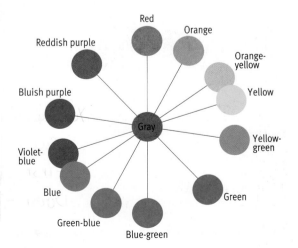

Figure 4.13

Complementary colors.
Colors opposite each other on this color circle are complements, or "opposites." Additively, mixing complementary colors produces gray. Opponent process principles help explain this effect as well as the other peculiarities of complementary colors noted in the text.

Figure 4.14

Three types of cones. Research has identified three types of cones that show varied sensitivity to different wavelengths of light. As the graph shows, these three types of cones correspond only roughly to the red, green, and blue receptors predicted by trichromatic theory, so it is more accurate to refer to them as cones sensitive to short, medium, and long wavelengths. (Based on data from "Human Color Vision and Color Blindness," by G. Wald and P.K. Brown, 1965, *Symposium Cold Spring Harbor Laboratory of Quantitative Biology, 30*, 345-359, p. 351. Copyright © 1965. Reprinted by permission of the author.)

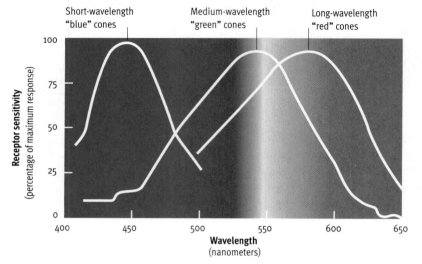

Here's another peculiarity to consider. If you ask people to describe colors but restrict them to using three names, they run into difficulty. For example, using only red, green, and blue, they simply don't feel comfortable describing yellow as "reddish green." However, if you let them have just one more name, they usually choose yellow. Then they can describe any color quite well (Abramov & Gordon, 1994; Boynton & Gordon, 1965). If colors are reduced to three channels, why are four color names required to describe the full range of possible colors?

In an effort to answer questions such as these, Ewald Hering proposed the *opponent process theory* of color vision in 1878. *The opponent process theory*

holds *that color perception depends on receptors that make antagonistic responses to three pairs of colors.* The three pairs of opponent colors posited by Hering were red versus green, yellow versus blue, and black versus white. The antagonistic processes in this theory provide plausible explanations for complementary afterimages and the need for four names (red, green, blue, and yellow) to describe colors. Opponent process theory also explains some aspects of color blindness. For instance, it can explain why dichromats typically find it hard to distinguish either green from red or yellow from blue.

Reconciling Theories of Color Vision

Advocates of trichromatic theory and opponent process theory argued about the relative merits of their models for almost a century. Most researchers assumed that one theory must be wrong and the other must be right. In recent decades, however, it has become clear that it takes *both theories to explain color vision.* Eventually a physiological basis for both theories was found. Research that earned George Wald a Nobel prize demonstrated that *the eye has three types of cones,* with each type being most sensitive to a different band of wavelengths, as shown in Figure 4.14 (Bowmaker & Dartnall, 1980; Wald, 1964). The three types of cones represent the three different color receptors predicted by trichromatic theory.

Researchers also discovered a biological basis for opponent processes. They found cells in the retina, the thalamus, and the visual cortex *that respond in opposite ways to red versus green and blue versus yellow* (DeValois & Jacobs, 1984; Zrenner et al., 1990). For example, some ganglion cells in the retina are excited by green and inhibited by red. Other ganglion cells in the retina work in just the opposite way, as predicted by opponent process theory.

CONCEPT **CHECK 4.2**

Comparing Theories of Color Vision

Check your understanding of the differences between the trichromatic and opponent process theories of color vision by filling in the blanks below. The answers are in Appendix A.

	Trichromatic theory	Opponent process theory
1. Theory proposed by:	Young, Helmholtz	Hering
2. Can/can't account for complementary afterimages	Can't	Can
3. Explains first/later stage of color processing	First	Later
4. Does/doesn't account for need for four terms to describe colors	Doesn't	Does

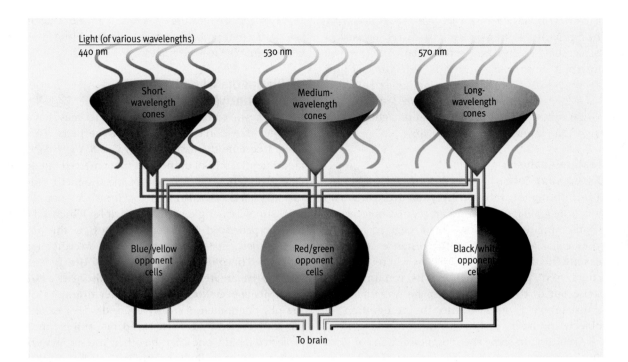

Light (of various wavelengths)

440 nm

530 nm

570 nm

Short-wavelength cones

Medium-wavelength cones

Long-wavelength cones

Blue/yellow opponent cells

Red/green opponent cells

Black/white opponent cells

To brain

Figure 4.15

Explaining color perception. Contemporary theories of color vision include aspects of both the trichromatic and opponent process theories. As predicted by trichromatic theory, there are three types of receptors for color—cones sensitive to short, medium, and long wavelengths. However, these cones are organized into receptive fields that excite or inhibit the firing of higher-level visual cells in the retina, thalamus, and cortex. As predicted by opponent process theory, these cells respond in antagonistic ways to blue versus yellow, red versus green, and black versus white when lights of these colors stimulate their receptive fields.

In summary, the perception of color appears to involve sequential stages of information processing (Hurvich, 1981). The receptors that do the first stage of processing (the cones) seem to follow the principles outlined in trichromatic theory. In later stages of processing, cells in the retina and the brain seem to follow the principles outlined in opponent process theory (see Figure 4.15). As you can see, vigorous theoretical debate about color vision produced a solution that went beyond the contributions of either theory alone.

Perceiving Forms, Patterns, and Objects

 3c, 3e

The drawing in Figure 4.16 is a poster for a circus act involving a trained seal. What do you see?

No doubt you see a seal balancing a ball on its nose and a trainer holding a fish and a whip. But suppose you had been told that the drawing is actually a poster for a costume ball. Would you have perceived it differently?

If you focus on the idea of a costume ball (stay with it a minute if you still see the seal and trainer), you will probably see a costumed man and woman in Figure 4.16. She's handing him a hat, and he has a sword in his right hand. This tricky little sketch was made ambiguous quite intentionally. It's a *reversible figure,* **a drawing that is compatible with two different interpretations that can shift back and forth.**

Figure 4.16

A poster for a trained seal act. Or is it? The picture is an ambiguous figure, which can be interpreted as either of two scenes.

The point of this demonstration is simply this: *The same visual input can result in radically different perceptions.* There is no one-to-one correspondence between sensory input and what you perceive. *This is a principal reason that people's experience of the world is subjective.* Perception involves much more than passively receiving signals from the ouside world. It involves the *interpretation* of sensory input. perception

In this case, your interpretations result in two different "realities" because your *expectations* have been manipulated. Information given to you about the drawing has created **a *perceptual set*—a readiness to perceive a stimulus in a particular way.** A perceptual set creates a certain slant in how you interpret sensory input. An understanding of how people perceive forms, patterns, and objects requires knowledge of how people *organize and interpret* visual input. Several influential approaches to this question emphasize *feature analysis*.

Feature Analysis: Assembling Forms

The information received by your eyes would do you little good if you couldn't recognize objects and forms, ranging from words on a page to mice in your cellar and friends in the distance. This was exactly the fate that befell Dr. P. As you recall, Dr. P could "see" perfectly well. Yet he couldn't make sense out of the world because he was unable to translate what he saw into the recognition of objects and faces.

According to some theories, perceptions of form and pattern entail *feature analysis* (Lindsay & Norman, 1977; Maguire et al., 1990). **Feature analysis is the process of detecting specific elements in visual input and assembling them into a more complex form.** In other words, you start with the components of a form, such as lines, edges, and corners, and build them into perceptions of squares, triangles, stop signs, bicycles, ice cream cones, and telephones. An application of this model of form perception is diagrammed in Figure 4.17. It shows how, in theory, people might recognize the letter T by registering and assembling the configuration of features that make up this letter. The plausibility of this model was bolstered greatly when Hubel and Wiesel showed that cells in the visual cortex operate as

highly specialized feature detectors. It appears that at least some (but probably not all) aspects of form perception involve feature analysis.

Looking at the Whole Picture: Gestalt Principles

Sometimes a whole, as we perceive it, may have qualities that don't exist in any of the parts. This insight became the basic tenet of *Gestalt psychology,* an influential school of thought that emerged out of Germany during the first half of the twentieth century. (*Gestalt* is a German word for "form" or "shape.")

A simple example of this principle, which you have experienced innumerable times, is the *phi phenomenon,* first described by Max Wertheimer in 1912. **The *phi phenomenon* is the illusion of movement created by presenting visual stimuli in rapid succession.** You encounter examples of the phi phenomenon nearly every day. For example, movies and TV consist of separate still pictures projected rapidly one after the other. You *see* smooth motion, but in reality the "moving" objects merely take slightly different positions in successive frames. Viewed as a whole, a movie has a property (motion) that isn't evident in any of its parts (the individual frames).

The Gestalt psychologists formulated a series of principles that describe how the visual system organizes a scene into discrete forms. Let's examine some of these principles.

Figure and Ground Take a look at Figure 4.18. Do you see the figure as two silhouetted faces against a white background, or as a white vase against a black background? This reversible figure illustrates the Gestalt principle of figure and ground. Dividing

"The fundamental 'formula' of Gestalt theory might be expressed in this way: There are wholes, the behaviour of which is not determined by that of their individual elements."
MAX WERTHEIMER

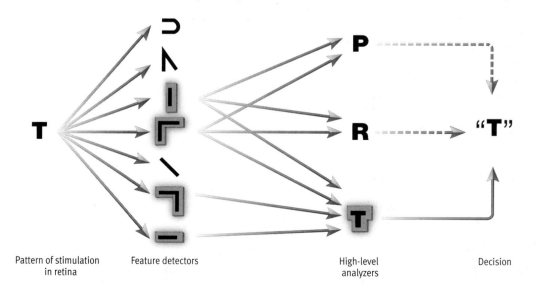

Figure 4.17

Feature analysis in form perception. One vigorously debated theory of form perception is that the brain has cells that respond to specific aspects or features of stimuli, such as lines and angles. Neurons functioning as higher-level analyzers then respond to input from these "feature detectors." The more input each analyzer receives, the more active it becomes. Finally, other neurons weigh signals from these analyzers and make a "decision" about the stimulus. In this way perception of a form is arrived at by assembling elements from the bottom up.

Pattern of stimulation in retina   Feature detectors   High-level analyzers   Decision

visual displays into figure and ground is a fundamental way in which people organize visual perceptions (Baylis & Driver, 1995). The figure is the thing being looked at, and the ground is the background against which it stands. The figure seems to have substance and appears to stand out in front of the ground. More often than not, your visual field may contain many figures sharing a background. The following Gestalt principles relate to how these elements are grouped into higher-order figures.

Proximity Things that are near one another seem to belong together. The black dots in Figure 4.19(a) could be grouped into vertical columns or horizontal rows. However, people tend to perceive rows because of the effect of proximity (the dots are closer together horizontally).

Closure People often group elements to create a sense of *closure,* or completeness. Thus, you may "complete" figures that actually have gaps in them. This principle is demonstrated in Figure 4.19(b).

Similarity People also tend to group stimuli that are similar. This principle is apparent in Figure 4.19(c), where elements of similar darkness are grouped into the number two.

Simplicity The Gestaltists' most general principle was the law of *Pragnanz,* which translates from German as "good form." The idea is that people

tend to group elements that combine to form a good figure. This principle is somewhat vague in that it's often difficult to spell out what makes a figure "good" (Biederman, Hilton, & Hummel, 1991). Some theorists maintain that goodness is largely a matter of simplicity, asserting that people tend to organize forms in the simplest way possible (see Figure 4.19(d).

Continuity The principle of continuity reflects people's tendency to follow in whatever direction they've been led. Thus, people tend to connect points that result in straight or gently curved lines that create "smooth" paths, as shown in Figure 4.19(e).

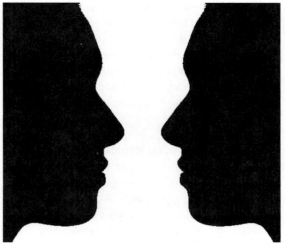

Figure 4.18

The principle of figure and ground. Whether you see two faces or a vase depends on which part of this drawing you see as figure and which as background. Although this reversible drawing allows you to switch back and forth between two ways of organizing your perception, you can't perceive the drawing both ways at once.

Figure 4.19

Gestalt principles of perceptual organization. Gestalt principles help explain how people subjectively organize perception. **(a) Proximity:** These dots might well be organized in vertical columns rather than horizontal rows, but because of proximity (the dots are closer together horizontally), they tend to be perceived in rows. **(b) Closure:** Even though the figures are incomplete, you fill in the blanks and see a circle and a dog. **(c) Similarity:** Because of similarity of color, you see dots organized into the number 2 instead of a random array. If you did not group similar elements, you wouldn't see the number 2 here. **(d) Simplicity:** You could view this as a complicated 11-sided figure, but given the preference for simplicity, you are more likely to see it as a rectangle and a triangle. **(e) Continuity:** You tend to group these dots in a way that produces a smooth path rather than an abrupt shift in direction.

(a) Proximity
Elements that are close to one another tend to be grouped together.

(b) Closure
Viewers tend to supply missing elements to close or complete a familiar figure.

(c) Similarity
Elements that are similar tend to be grouped together.

(d) Simplicity
Viewers tend to organize elements in the simplest way possible.

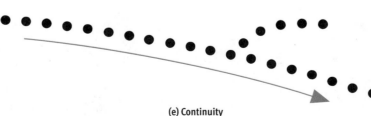

(e) Continuity
Viewers tend to see elements in ways that produce smooth continuation.

Although Gestalt psychology is no longer an active theoretical orientation in modern psychology, its influence is still felt in the study of perception (Banks & Krajicek, 1991). The Gestalt psychologists raised many important questions that still occupy researchers, and they left a legacy of many useful insights about form perception that have stood the test of time.

Formulating Perceptual Hypotheses

The Gestalt principles provide some indications of how people organize visual input. However, scientists are still one step away from understanding how these organized perceptions result in a representation of the real world. Understanding the problem requires distinguishing between two kinds of stimuli: distal and proximal (Hochberg, 1988). *Distal stimuli* **are stimuli that lie in the distance (that is, in the world outside the body).** In vision, these are the objects that you're looking at. They are "distant" in that your eyes don't touch them. What your eyes do "touch" are the images formed by patterns of light falling on your retinas. These images are *proximal stimuli,* **the stimulus energies that impinge directly on sensory receptors.** The distinction is important, because there are great differences between the objects you perceive and the stimulus energies that represent them.

In visual perception, the proximal stimuli are distorted, two-dimensional versions of their actual, three-dimensional counterparts. For example, consider the distal stimulus of a square such as the one in Figure 4.20. If the square is lying on a desk in front of you, it is actually projecting a trapezoid (the proximal stimulus) on your retinas, because the top of the square is farther from your eyes than the bottom. Obviously, the trapezoid is a distorted representation of the square. If what people have to work with is so distorted a picture, how do they get an accurate view of the world out there?

One explanation is that people bridge the gap between distal and proximal stimuli by constantly making and testing *hypotheses* about what's out there in the real world (Gregory, 1973). Thus, **a *perceptual hypothesis* is an inference about which distal stimuli could be responsible for the proximal stimuli sensed.** In effect, people make educated guesses about what form could be responsible for a pattern of sensory stimulation. The square in Figure 4.20 may project a trapezoidal image on your retinas, but your perceptual system "guesses" correctly that it's a square—and that's what you see.

Let's look at another ambiguous drawing to further demonstrate the process of making a perceptual hypothesis. Figure 4.21 is a famous reversible figure, first published as a cartoon in a humor magazine. Perhaps you see a drawing of a young woman looking back over her right shoulder. Alternatively, you might see an old woman with her chin down on her chest. The ambiguity exists because there isn't enough information to force your perceptual system to accept only one of these hypotheses.

If you can see only one of the women, you may be wondering where the other is. To guide you, Figure 4.22 shows unambiguous drawings of the young woman on the left and of the old woman on the right. Now you should be able to find either woman in Figure 4.21. You just needed some guidance as to how to make the other perceptual hypothesis. Incidentally, studies show that people who are led to *expect* the young woman or the old woman tend to see the one they expect (Leeper, 1935). This is another example of how perceptual sets influence what people see.

Psychologists have used a variety of reversible figures to study how people formulate perceptual hypotheses. Another example can be seen in Figure 4.23, which shows the *Necker cube.* The shaded surface can appear as either the front or the rear of the transparent cube. If you look at the cube for a while, your perception will alternate between these possibilities. Later, in the Personal Application on art and illusion, you'll see how M. C. Escher used the Necker cube to create a fascinating piece of art.

Figure **4.20**

Distal and proximal stimuli. Proximal stimuli are often distorted, shifting representations of distal stimuli in the real world. If you look directly down at a small, square piece of paper on a desk **(a)**, the distal stimulus (the paper) and the proximal stimulus (the image projected on your retina) will both be square. But as you move the paper away on the desktop **(b)** and **(c)**, the square distal stimulus projects an increasingly trapezoidal image on your retina, making the proximal stimulus more and more distorted. Nevertheless, you continue to perceive a square.

(a)

Retinal image

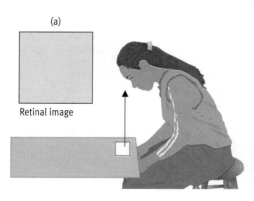

(b)

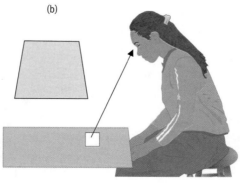

(c)

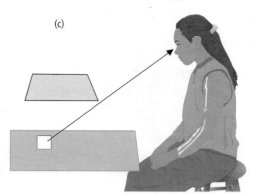

Figure 4.21

A famous reversible figure. What do you see?

Figure 4.22

Unambiguous drawings of the young and old woman. These versions of the reversible figure in Figure 4.21 have been redrawn slightly to make the young woman more apparent on the left and the old woman more apparent on the right.

The *context* in which something appears often guides our perceptual hypotheses. To illustrate, take a look at Figure 4.24. What do you see? You probably saw the words "THE CAT." But look again; the middle characters in both words are identical. You identified an "H" in the first word and an "A" in the second because of the surrounding letters, which shaped your expectations. The power of expectations explains why typographical errors like those in this sentence often pass unoberved (Lachman, 1996).

Perceiving Depth or Distance

More often than not, forms and figures are objects in space. Spatial considerations add a third dimension to visual perception. *Depth perception* involves interpretation of visual cues that indicate how near or far away objects are. To make judgments of distance, people rely on quite a variety of clues, which can be classified into two types: binocular cues and monocular cues (Hochberg, 1988).

Binocular Cues

Because the eyes are set apart, each eye has a slightly different view of the world. *Binocular depth cues* are clues about distance based on the differing views of the two eyes. "Stereo" viewers like the Viewmaster toy you may have had as a child make use of this principle by presenting slightly different flat images of the same scene to each eye. The brain then supplies the "depth," and you perceive a three-dimensional scene.

The principal binocular depth cue is *retinal disparity,* which refers to the fact that objects within 25 feet project images to slightly different

Figure 4.23

The Necker cube. The tinted surface can become either the front or the back of the cube.

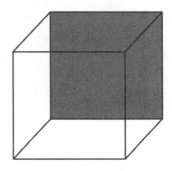

Figure 4.24

Context effects. The context in which a stimulus is seen can affect your perceptual hypotheses.

THE OAT

locations on the right and left retinas, so the right and left eyes see slightly different views of the object. The closer an object gets, the greater the disparity between the images seen by each eye. Thus, retinal disparity increases as objects come closer, providing information about distance.

Monocular Cues

Monocular depth cues are clues about distance based on the image in either eye alone. There are two kinds of monocular cues to depth. One kind is the result of active use of the eye in viewing the world. For example, as an object comes closer, you may sense the accommodation (the change in the curvature of the lens) that must occur for the eye to adjust its focus.

The other kind of monocular cues are *pictorial depth cues*—cues about distance that can be given in a flat picture. There are many pictorial cues to depth, which is why paintings and photographs can seem so realistic that you feel you can climb

Linear perspective Parallel lines that run away from the viewer seem to get closer together.

Texture gradient A texture is coarser for near areas and finer for more distant ones.

Interposition The shapes of near objects overlap or mask those of more distant ones.

Relative size If separate objects are expected to be of the same size, the larger ones are seen as closer.

Height in plane Near objects are low in the visual field; more distant ones are higher up.

Light and shadow Patterns of light and dark suggest shadows that can create an impression of three-dimensional forms.

Figure 4.25

Six pictorial cues to depth. In most visual experiences, several depth cues are present at once. The world rarely looks "flat," even through only one eye. Try looking at the light and shadow picture upside down. The change in shadowing reverses what you see.

Figure 4.26

Testing understanding of pictorial depth cues. In his cross-cultural research, Hudson (1960) asked subjects to indicate whether the hunter is trying to spear the antelope or the elephant. He found cultural disparities in subjects' ability to make effective use of the pictorial depth cues, which place the elephant in the distance and make it an unlikely target.

(Adapted by permission from an illustration by Ilil Arbel on page 83 of "Pictorial Perception and Culture," by Jan B. Deregowski in *Scientific American, 227* (5) November 1972. Copyright © 1972 by Scientific American, Inc. All rights reserved.)

right into them. Six prominent pictorial depth cues are described and illustrated in Figure 4.25. *Linear perspective* is a depth cue reflecting the fact that lines converge in the distance. Because details are too small to see when they are far away, *texture gradients* can provide information about depth. If an object comes between you and another object, it must be closer to you, a cue called *interposition*. *Relative size* is a cue because closer objects appear larger. *Height in plane* reflects the fact that distant objects appear higher in a picture. Finally, the familiar effects of shadowing make *light* and *shadow* useful in judging distance.

There appear to be some cultural differences in the ability to take advantage of pictorial depth cues in two-dimensional drawings. These differences were first investigated by Hudson (1960, 1967), who presented pictures like the one in Figure 4.26 to various cultural groups in South Africa. Hudson's approach was based on the assumption that subjects who indicate that the hunter is trying to spear the elephant instead of the antelope don't understand the depth cues (interposition, relative size, height in plane) in the picture, which place the elephant in the distance. Hudson found that subjects from a rural South African tribe (the Bantu), which had little exposure at that time to pictures and photos, frequently misinterpreted the depth cues in his pictures. Similar difficulties with depth cues in pictures have been documented for other cultural groups that have little experience with two-dimensional

Recognizing Pictorial Depth Cues

Painters routinely attempt to create the perception of depth on a flat canvas by using pictorial depth cues. Figure 4.25 describes and illustrates six pictorial depth cues, most of which are apparent in Vincent van Gogh's colorful piece, titled *Corridor in the Asylum* (1889). Check your understanding of depth perception by trying to spot the depth cues in the painting.

In the list below, check off the depth cues used by van Gogh. The answers can be found in Appendix A. You can learn more about how artists use the principles of visual perception in the Personal Application at the end of this chapter.

✓ **1.** Interposition *Arches in front cut off corridor*
✓ **2.** Height in plane *Back is higher than front*
✓ **3.** Texture gradient *closer portions have detail*
✓ **4.** Relative size *Arches in distant are smaller*
✓ **5.** Light and shadow *Light shining in contrasts*
✓ **6.** Linear perspective *Lines converge in distance*

(van Gogh, Vincent, *Corridor in the Asylum* (1889), gouche and water-color, 24-3/8 x 18-1/2 inches [61.5 x 47.cm.]. Metropolitan Museum of Art. Bequest of Abby Aldrich Rockefeller, 1948 [48.190.2]. Photograph © 1998 The Metropolitan Museum of Art.)

representations of three-dimensional space (Berry et al., 1992). Based on this evidence, Deregowski (1989) concludes that the application of pictorial depth cues to pictures is partly an acquired skill that depends on experience.

Perceptual Constancies in Vision

When a person approaches you from the distance, his or her image on your retinas gradually changes in size. Do you perceive that the person is growing right before your eyes? Of course not. Your perceptual system constantly makes allowances for this variation in visual input. The task of the perceptual system is to provide an accurate rendition of distal stimuli based on distorted, everchanging proximal stimuli. In doing so, it relies in part on perceptual constancies. A *perceptual constancy* is a tendency to experience a stable perception in the face of continually changing sensory input. Among other things, people tend to view objects as having a stable size, shape, brightness, hue (color), and location in space. Perceptual constancies such as these help impose some order on the surrounding world.

The Power of Misleading Cues: Optical Illusions

3, 3g

In general, perceptual constancies, depth cues, and principles of visual organization (such as the Gestalt laws) help people perceive the world accurately. Sometimes, however, perceptions are based on inap-

propriate assumptions, and *optical illusions* can result. An *optical illusion* involves an apparently inexplicable discrepancy between the appearance of a visual stimulus and its physical reality.

One famous optical illusion is the *Müller-Lyer illusion,* shown in Figure 4.27. The two vertical lines in this figure are equally long, but they certainly don't look that way. Why not? Several mechanisms probably play a role (Day, 1965; Gregory, 1978). The figure on the left looks like the outside of a building, thrust toward the viewer, while the one on the right looks like an inside corner, thrust away (see Figure 4.28). The vertical line in the left figure therefore seems closer. If two lines cast equally long retinal images but one seems closer, the closer one is assumed to be shorter. Thus, the Müller-Lyer illusion may be due largely to a combination of size constancy processes and misperception of depth.

Figure 4.27

The Müller-Lyer illusion. Go ahead, measure them: the two vertical lines are of equal length.

Figure 4.28

Explaining the Müller-Lyer illusion. The figure on the left seems to be closer, since it looks like an outside corner, thrust toward you. Given retinal images of the same length, you assume that the "closer" line is shorter.

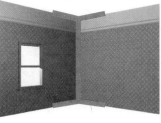

Web Link 4.3

IllusionWorks

IllusionWorks bills itself as "the most comprehensive collection of optical and sensory illusions on the World Wide Web." At both "introductory" and "advanced" levels of explanation, this is an excellent resource for experiencing some of the strangest and most thought-provoking illusions ever created.

Web Link 4.4

The Moon Illusion Explained

Don McCready, professor emeritus at the University of Wisconsin, addresses the age-old puzzle of why the moon appears much larger at the horizon than overhead. He uses a helpful collection of illustrations in a comprehensive review of alternative theories.

The *Ponzo illusion,* which is shown in Figure 4.29, appears to result from the same factors (Coren & Girgus, 1978). The upper and lower horizontal lines are the same length, but the upper one appears longer. This probably occurs because the converging lines convey linear perspective, a key depth cue suggesting that the upper line lies farther in the distance. Figure 4.30 is a drawing by Stanford University psychologist Roger Shepard (1990) that creates a similar illusion. The second monster appears much larger than the first, even though they are really identical in size. This variation on the Ponzo illusion and the other geometric illusions shown in Figure 4.29 demonstrate that visual stimuli can be highly deceptive.

Impossible figures create another form of illusion. **Impossible figures are objects that can be represented in two-dimensional pictures but cannot exist in three-dimensional space.** These figures may look fine at first glance, but a closer look reveals that they are geometrically inconsistent or impossible. Three classic impossible figures are shown in Figure 4.31 and a newer impossible figure drawn by Roger Shepard (1990) can be seen in Figure 4.32. Notice that you perceive specific features of the figure as acceptable but are baffled as they are built into a whole. Your perceptual hypothesis about one portion of the figure turns out to be inconsistent with your hypothesis about another portion.

Obviously, impossible figures involve a conspiracy of cues intended to deceive the viewer. Many visual illusions, however, occur quite naturally and are part of everyday life. A well-known example is the *moon illusion.* The full moon appears to be much smaller when overhead than when looming over the horizon. As with many of the other illusions we have discussed, the moon illusion appears to result mainly from size constancy effects coupled with the misperception of distance (Coren & Aks, 1990; Kaufman & Rock, 1962).

Cross-cultural studies have uncovered some interesting differences among cultural groups in their propensity to see certain illusions. For example, Segall, Campbell, and Herskovits (1966) found that people from Western cultures are more susceptible to the Müller-Lyer illusion than people from some non-Western cultures. The most plausible explanation is that in the West, we live in a "carpentered world" dominated by straight lines, right angles, and rectangular rooms, buildings, and furniture. Thus, our experience prepares us to readily view the Müller-Lyer figures as inside and outside corners of buildings—inferences that help foster the illusion (Segall et al., 1990).

Figure 4.29

Four geometric illusions.
Ponzo: The horizontal lines are the same length.
Poggendorff: The two diagonal segments lie on the same straight line. **Upside-down T:** The vertical and horizontal lines are the same length.
Zollner: The long diagonals are all parallel (try covering up some of the short diagonal lines if you don't believe it).

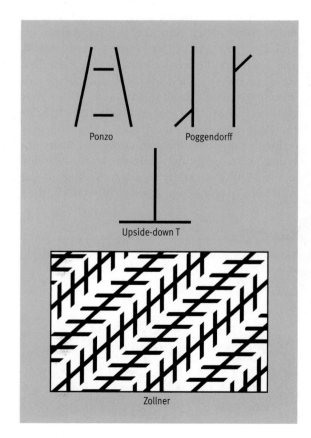

Figure 4.30

A monster of an illusion. The principles underlying the Ponzo illusion also explain the striking illusion seen here, in which two identical monsters appear to be quite different in size. (From *Mind Sights,* by Shepard. Copyright © 1990 by Roger N. Shepard. Used by permission of W. H. Freeman and Company.)

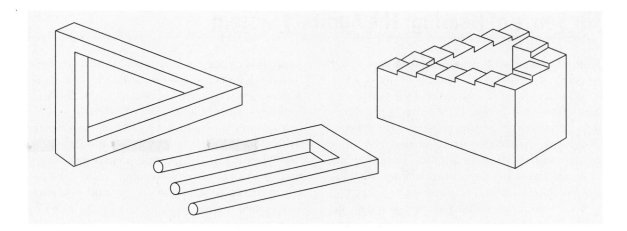

Figure 4.31

Three impossible figures.
The figures are impossible, yet they clearly exist—on the page. What makes them impossible is that they appear to be three-dimensional representations yet are drawn in a way that frustrates mental attempts to "assemble" their features into possible objects. It's difficult to see the drawings simply as lines lying in a plane—even though this perceptual hypothesis is the only one that resolves the contradiction.

What do optical illusions reveal about visual perception? They drive home the point that people go through life formulating perceptual hypotheses about what lies out there in the real world. The fact that these are only hypotheses becomes especially striking when the hypotheses are wrong, as they are with illusions. Optical illusions also show how context factors such as depth cues shape perceptual hypotheses. Finally, like ambiguous figures, illusions clearly demonstrate that human perceptions are not simple reflections of objective reality. Once again, we see that perception of the world is subjective.

These insights do not apply to visual perception only. We will encounter these lessons again as we examine other sensory systems, such as hearing, which we turn to next.

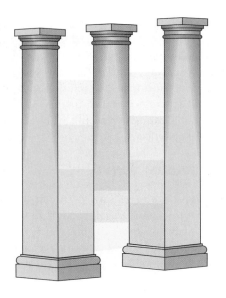

Figure 4.32

Another impossible figure.
This impossible figure, drawn by Shepard (1990), seems even more perplexing than the classic impossible figure that it is based on (the tuning fork seen in Figure 4.31). (From *Mind Sights* by Shepard. Copyright © 1990 by Roger N. Shepard. Used by permission of W. H. Freeman and Company.)

Unlike people in Western nations, the Zulus live in a culture where straight lines and right angles are scarce, if not entirely absent. Thus, they are not affected by such phenomena as the Müller-Lyer illusion nearly as much as people raised in environments that abound with rectangular structures.

© Peter Menzel/Stock, Boston

Stop reading for a moment, close your eyes, and listen carefully. What do you hear?

Chances are, you'll discover that you're immersed in sounds: street noises, a dog barking, the hum of a fluorescent lamp, perhaps some background music you put on a while ago but forgot about. As this little demonstration shows, physical stimuli producing sound are present almost constantly, but you're not necessarily aware of these sounds.

Like vision, the auditory (hearing) system provides input about the world "out there," but not until incoming information is processed by the brain. A distal stimulus—a screech of tires, someone laughing, the hum of the refrigerator—produces a proximal stimulus in the form of sound waves reaching the ears. The perceptual system must somehow transform this stimulation into the psychological experience of hearing. We'll begin our discussion of hearing by looking at the stimulus for auditory experience: sound.

The Stimulus: Sound

Sound waves are vibrations of molecules, which means that they must travel through some physical medium, such as air. They move at a fraction of the speed of light. Sound waves are usually generated by vibrating objects, such as a guitar string, a loudspeaker cone, or your vocal cords. However, sound waves can also be generated by forcing air past a chamber (as in a pipe organ), or by suddenly releasing a burst of air (as when you clap).

Like light waves, sound waves are characterized by their *amplitude*, their *wavelength*, and their *purity* (see Figure 4.33). The physical properties of amplitude, wavelength, and purity affect mainly the perceived (psychological) qualities of loudness, pitch, and timbre, respectively. However, the physical properties of sound interact in complex ways to produce perceptions of these sound qualities (Hirsh & Watson, 1996).

Human Hearing Capacities

Wavelengths of sound are described in terms of their *frequency*, which is measured in cycles per second, or *hertz* (Hz). For the most part, higher frequencies are perceived as having higher pitch. That is, if you strike the key for high C on a piano, it will produce higher-frequency sound waves than the key for low C. Although the perception of pitch depends mainly on frequency, the amplitude of the sound waves also influences it.

Just as the visible spectrum is only a portion of the total spectrum of light, so, too, what people can hear is only a portion of the available range of

Figure 4.33

Sound, the physical stimulus for hearing. (a) Like light, sound travels in waves—in this case, waves of air pressure. A smooth curve would represent a pure tone, such as that produced by a tuning fork. Most sounds, however, are complex. For example, the wave shown here is for middle C played on a piano. The sound wave for the same note played on a violin would have the same wavelength (or frequency) as this one, but the "wrinkles" in the wave would be different, corresponding to the differences in timbre between the two sounds. **(b)** The table shows the main relations between objective aspects of sound and subjective perceptions.

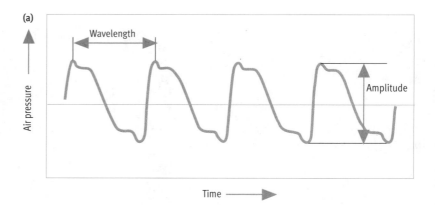

(a)

Physical properties of sound	Related perceptions
Wave amplitude	Loudness
Wavelength or frequency	Pitch
Wave purity or mixture	Timbre

(b)

sounds. Humans can hear sounds ranging in frequency from a low of 20 Hz up to a high of about 20,000 Hz. Sounds at either end of this range are harder to hear, and sensitivity to high-frequency tones declines as adults grow older. Other organisms have different capabilities. Low-frequency sounds under 10 Hz are audible to homing pigeons, for example. At the other extreme, bats and porpoises can hear frequencies well above 20,000 Hz.

In general, the greater the amplitude of sound waves, the louder the sound perceived. Whereas frequency is measured in hertz, amplitude is measured in *decibels* (dB). The relationship between decibels (which measure a physical property of sound) and loudness (a psychological quality) is complex. A rough rule of thumb is that perceived loudness doubles about every 10 decibels (Stevens, 1955). To make this less abstract, Figure 4.34 shows approximate decibel levels for a wide range of common sounds. Very loud sounds can jeopardize the quality of your hearing. Even brief exposure to sounds over 120 decibels can be painful and may cause damage to your auditory system (Henry, 1984). As shown in Figure 4.34, the weakest sound a person can hear

depends on its frequency. The human ear is most sensitive to sounds at frequencies near 2000 Hz. Thus, loudness ultimately depends on an interaction between amplitude and frequency.

People are also sensitive to variations in the purity of sounds. The purest sound is one that has only a single frequency of vibration, such as that produced by a tuning fork. Most everyday sounds are complex mixtures of many frequencies. The purity or complexity of a sound influences how *timbre* is perceived. To understand timbre, think of a note with precisely the same loudness and pitch played on a French horn and then on a violin. The difference you perceive in the sounds is a difference in timbre.

Sensory Processing in the Ear 3h

Like your eyes, your ears channel energy to the neural tissue that receives it. Figure 4.35 on the next page shows that the human ear can be divided into three sections: the external ear, the middle ear, and the inner ear. Sound is conducted differently in each section. The external ear depends on the *vibration of*

Figure 4.34

Sound pressure and auditory experience. Sound pressure, measured in decibels, interacts with frequency to produce different auditory effects. For example, the threshold for human hearing is a function of both decibel level and frequency. Human hearing is keenest for sounds at a frequency of about 2000 Hz; at other frequencies, higher decibel levels are needed to produce sounds people can detect (lower curve in graph). On the other hand, the human threshold for pain is almost purely a function of decibel level (upper curve). Some common sounds corresponding to various decibel levels are listed to the right, together with the amount of time at which exposure to higher levels becomes dangerous. (Table 5-3, adapted from *Introduction to Psychology*, Ninth Edition, by Rita L. Atkinson, Richard C. Atkinson, Edward F. Smith, and Ernest R. Hilgard, Copyright © 1987 by Harcourt Inc., reprinted by permission of the publisher.)

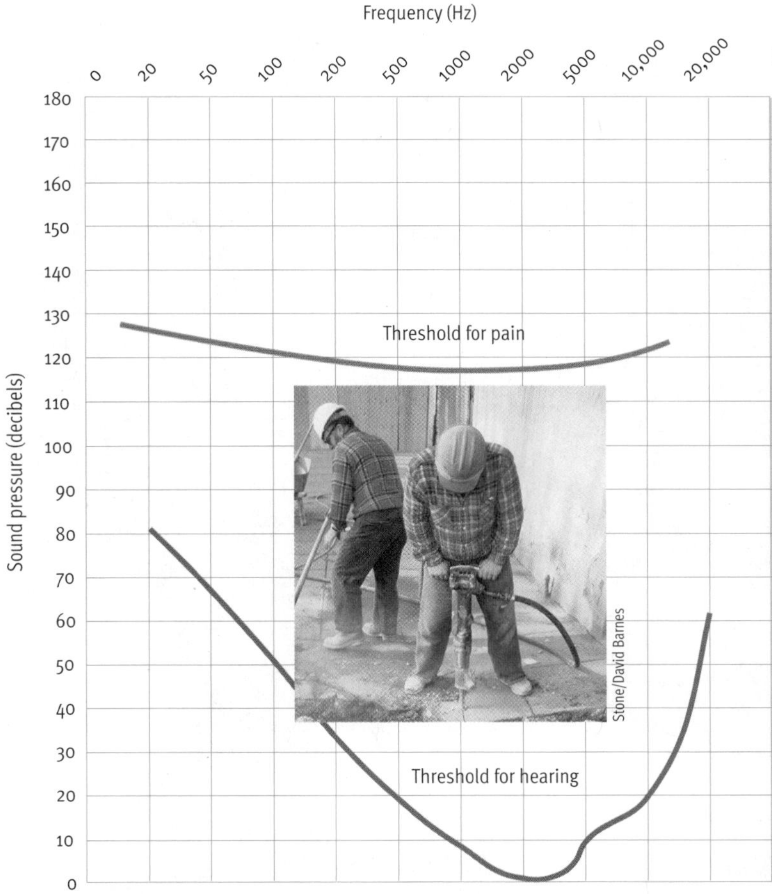

Frequency (Hz)

Sound pressure (decibels)

Threshold for pain

Threshold for hearing

Stone/David Barnes

Decibel level	Example	Dangerous time exposure
170	• Rocket launching pad	Hearing loss inevitable
140	• Shotgun blast, jet plane	Any exposure is dangerous
120	• Rock concert in front of speakers, sandblasting, thunderclap	Immediate danger
100	• Chainsaw, boiler shop, pneumatic drill	2 hours
90	• Truck traffic, noisy home appliances, shop tools, lawnmower	Less than 8 hours
80	• Subway , heavy city traffic, alarm clock at 2 feet, factory noise	More than 8 hours
70	• Busy traffic, noisy restaurant (constant exposure)	Critical level begins
60	• Air conditioner at 20 feet, conversation, sewing machine	
50	• Light traffic at a distance, refrigerator, gentle breeze	
40	• Quiet office, living room, bedroom away from traffic	
30	• Quiet library, soft whisper	
0	• Lowest sound audible to human ear	

air molecules. The middle ear depends on the *vibration of movable bones.* And the inner ear depends on *waves in a fluid,* which are finally converted into a stream of neural signals sent to the brain (Kiang & Peake, 1988).

The *external ear* consists mainly of the *pinna,* a sound-collecting cone. When you cup your hand behind your ear to try to hear better, you are augmenting that cone. Many animals have large external ears that they can aim directly toward a sound source. However, humans can adjust their aim only crudely, by turning their heads. Sound waves collected by the pinna are funneled along the auditory canal toward the *eardrum,* a taut membrane that vibrates in response.

In the *middle ear,* the vibrations of the eardrum are transmitted inward by a mechanical chain made up of the three tiniest bones in your body (the hammer, anvil, and stirrup), known collectively as the *ossicles.* The ossicles form a three-stage lever system that converts relatively large movements with little force into smaller motions with greater force. The ossicles serve to amplify tiny changes in air pressure.

The *inner ear* consists largely of **the *cochlea,* a fluid-filled, coiled tunnel that contains the receptors for hearing.** The term *cochlea* comes from the Greek word for a spiral-shelled snail, which this chamber resembles (see Figure 4.35). Sound enters the cochlea through the *oval window,* which is vibrated by the ossicles. The ear's neural tissue, analogous to the retina in the eye, lies within the cochlea. This tissue sits on the basilar membrane that divides the cochlea into upper and lower chambers. **The *basilar membrane,* which runs the length of the spiraled cochlea, holds the auditory receptors, called hair cells.** Waves in the fluid of the inner ear stimulate the hair cells. Like the rods and cones in the eye, the hair cells convert this physical stimulation into neural impulses that are sent to the brain (Dallos, 1981). These signals are routed through the thalamus to the auditory cortex, which is located mostly in the temporal lobes of the brain.

Figure 4.35

The human ear. Converting sound pressure to information processed by the nervous system involves a complex relay of stimuli: Waves of air pressure create vibrations in the eardrum, which in turn cause oscillations in the tiny bones in the inner ear (the hammer, anvil, and stirrup). As they are relayed from one bone to the next, the oscillations are magnified and then transformed into pressure waves moving through a liquid medium in the cochlea. These waves cause the basilar membrane to oscillate, stimulating the hair cells that are the actual auditory receptors (see Figure 4.36).

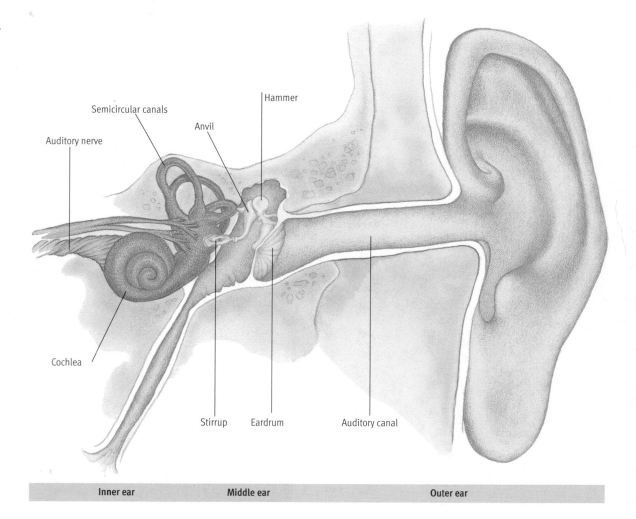

Semicircular canals
Anvil
Hammer
Auditory nerve
Stirrup
Eardrum
Auditory canal
Cochlea

Inner ear   Middle ear   Outer ear

Auditory Perception: Theories of Hearing

Theories of hearing need to account for how sound waves are physiologically translated into perceptions of pitch, loudness, and timbre. To date, most of the theorizing about hearing has focused on the perception of pitch, which is reasonably well understood. Researchers' understanding of loudness and timbre perception is primitive by comparison. Hence, we'll limit our coverage to theories of pitch perception.

Place Theory

There have been two influential theories of pitch perception: *place theory* and *frequency theory.* You'll be able to follow the development of these theories more easily if you can imagine the spiraled cochlea unraveled, so that the basilar membrane becomes a long, thin sheet, lined with about 25,000 individual hair cells (see Figure 4.36). Long ago, Hermann von Helmholtz (1863) proposed that specific sound frequencies vibrate specific portions of the basilar membrane, producing distinct pitches, just as plucking specific strings on a harp produces sounds of varied pitch. *Thus, place theory holds that perception of pitch corresponds to the vibration of different portions, or places, along the basilar membrane.* Place theory assumes that hair cells at various locations respond independently and that different sets of hair cells are vibrated by different sound frequencies. The brain then detects the frequency of a tone according to which area along the basilar membrane is most active.

Frequency Theory

Other theorists in the 19th century proposed an alternative theory of pitch perception, called frequency theory (Rutherford, 1886). *Frequency theory holds that perception of pitch corresponds to the rate, or frequency, at which the entire basilar membrane vibrates.* This theory views the basilar membrane as more like a drumhead than a harp. According to frequency theory, the whole membrane vibrates in unison in response to sounds. However, a particular

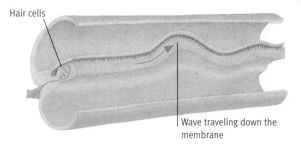

Hair cells

Wave traveling down the membrane

Figure 4.36

The basilar membrane.
The figure shows the cochlea unwound and cut open to reveal the basilar membrane, which is covered with thousands of hair cells (the auditory receptors). Pressure waves in the fluid filling the cochlea cause oscillations to travel in waves down the basilar membrane, stimulating the hair cells to fire. Although the entire membrane vibrates, as predicted by frequency theory, the point along the membrane where the wave peaks depends on the frequency of the sound stimulus, as suggested by place theory.

sound frequency, say 3000 Hz, causes the basilar membrane to vibrate at a corresponding rate of 3000 times per second. The brain detects the frequency of a tone by the rate at which the auditory nerve fibers fire.

Reconciling Place and Frequency Theories

The competition between these two theories is reminiscent of the dispute between the trichromatic and opponent process theories of color vision. Like that argument, the debate between place and frequency theories generated roughly a century of research. Although both theories proved to have some flaws, *both turned out to be valid in part.*

Helmholtz's place theory was basically on the mark except for one detail. The hair cells along the basilar membrane are not independent. They vibrate together, as suggested by frequency theory. The actual pattern of vibration, described in Nobel prize–winning research by Georg von Békésy (1947), is a traveling wave that moves along the basilar membrane. Place theory is correct, however, in that the wave peaks at a particular place, depending on the frequency of the sound wave.

Although the original theories had to be revised, the current thinking is that pitch perception depends on both place and frequency coding of vibrations along the basilar membrane (Goldstein, 1996). Sounds under 1000 Hz appear to be translated into pitch through frequency coding. For sounds between 1000 and 5000 Hz, pitch perception seems to depend on a combination of frequency and place coding. Sounds over 5000 Hz seem to be handled through place coding only. Again we find that theories that were pitted against each other for decades are complementary rather than contradictory.

Our Chemical Senses: Taste and Smell

Psychologists have devoted most of their attention to the visual and auditory systems. Although less is known about the chemical senses, taste and smell also play a critical role in people's experience of the world. Let's take a brief look at what psychologists have learned about the *gustatory system*—the sensory system for taste—and its close cousin, *the olfactory system*—the sensory system for smell.

Comparing Vision and Hearing

Check your understanding of both vision and audition by comparing key aspects of sensation and perception in these senses. The dimensions of comparison are listed in the first column below. The second column lists the answers for the sense of vision. Fill in the answers for the sense of hearing in the third column. The answers can be found in Appendix A in the back of the book.

Dimension	Vision	Hearing
1. Stimulus	Light waves	Sound waves
2. Elements of stimulus and related perceptions	Wavelength/hue Amplitude/brightness Purity/saturation	Frequency/pitch/amplitude/loudness/purity/timbre
3. Receptors	Rods and cones	Hair cells
4. Location of receptors	Retina	Basilar membrane
5. Main location of processing in brain	Occipital lobe, visual cortex	Temporal lobe, auditory cortex

Taste: The Gustatory System

True wine lovers go through an elaborate series of steps when they are served a good bottle of wine. Typically, they begin by drinking a little water to clean their palate. Then they sniff the cork from the wine bottle, swirl a small amount of the wine around in a glass, and sniff the odor emerging from the glass. Finally, they take a sip of the wine, rolling it around in their mouth for a short time before swallowing it. At last they are ready to confer their approval or disapproval. Is all this activity really a meaningful way to put the wine to a sensitive test? Or is it just a harmless ritual passed on through tradition? You'll find out in this section.

The physical stimuli for the sense of taste are chemical substances that are soluble (dissolvable in water). The gustatory receptors are clusters of taste cells found in the *taste buds* that line the trenches around tiny bumps on the tongue. When these cells absorb chemicals dissolved in saliva, neural impulses are triggered that are routed through the thalamus to the cortex. Interestingly, taste cells have a short life, spanning only about ten days, and they are constantly being replaced (Pfaffmann, 1978). New cells are born at the edge of the taste bud and migrate inward to die at the center.

It's generally (but not universally) agreed that there are four *primary tastes:* sweet, sour, bitter, and salty (Bartoshuk, 1988). Sensitivity to these tastes is distributed somewhat unevenly across the tongue. However, Linda Bartoshuk (1993b), a leading authority on taste research, emphasizes that these variations in sensitivity are quite small and very complicated (see Figure 4.37). Although most taste cells respond to more than one of the primary tastes, they typically respond best to one. Perceptions of taste quality appear to depend on complex patterns of neural activity initiated by taste receptors (Castelloci, 1986; Pfaffmann, 1974).

Although some basic aspects of taste perception may be innate, taste preferences are largely learned and heavily influenced by social processes (Rozin, 1990). Most parents are aware of this reality and intentionally try—with varied success—to mold their

Figure 4.37

The tongue and taste. Taste buds are clustered around tiny bumps on the tongue called papillae. There are three types of papillae, which are distributed as shown here. The taste buds found in each type of papillae show slightly different sensitivities to the four basic tastes, as mapped out in the graph at the top. Thus, sensitivity to the primary tastes varies across the tongue, but these variations are small, and all four primary tastes can be detected wherever there are taste receptors. (Adapted from "Genetic and Pathological Taste Variation: What Can We Learn from Animal Models and Human Disease?," by L. M. Bartoshuk, 1993. In D. Chadwick, J. Marsh & J. Goode [Eds.], *The Molecular Basis of Smell and Taste Transduction*, pp. 251–267. John Wiley & Sons, Inc.)

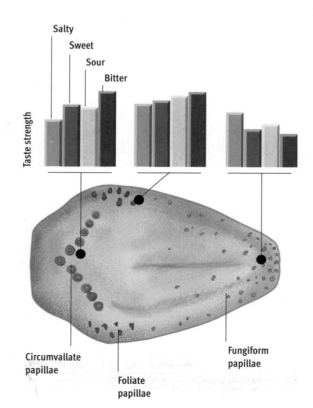

Salty
Sweet
Sour
Bitter

Taste strength

Circumvallate papillae
Foliate papillae
Fungiform papillae

children's taste preferences early in life (Casey & Rozin, 1989). This extensive social influence contributes greatly to the striking ethnic and cultural disparities found in taste preferences (Kittler & Sucher, 1989). Foods that are a source of disgust in Western cultures—such as worms, fish eyes, and blood—may be delicacies in other cultures. Indeed, Rozin (1990) asserts that feces may be the only universal source of taste-related disgust in humans. To a large degree, variations in taste preferences depend on what one has been exposed to (Capaldi & VandenBos, 1991). Exposure to various foods varies along ethnic lines because different cultures have different traditions in food preparation, different agricultural resources, different climates to work with, and so forth.

People vary considerably in their sensitivity to certain tastes. These differences depend in part on the density of taste buds on the tongue, which appears to be a matter of genetic inheritance (Bartoshuk, 1993a). People characterized as *supertasters* tend to have about four times as many taste buds per square centimeter as people at the other end of the spectrum, who are called *nontasters* (Miller & Reedy, 1990). Women are more likely to be supertasters than men are (Bartoshuk, Duffy, & Miler, 1994). Supertasters and nontasters respond similarly to many foods, but supertasters are much more sensitive to certain sweet and bitter substances. For example, supertasters react far more strongly to the chemical (capsaicin) in hot peppers (Tepper & Nurse, 1997). Some psychologists *speculate* that the gender gap in this trait may have evolutionary significance. Over the course of evolution, women have generally been more involved in feeding children than men. Increased reactivity to sweet and bitter tastes would have been adaptive in that it would have made women more sensitive to the relatively scarce high-caloric foods (which often taste sweet) needed for survival and to the toxic substances (which often taste bitter) that hunters and gatherers needed to avoid.

When you eat, you are constantly mixing food and saliva and moving it about in your mouth, so the stimulus is constantly changing. However, if you place a flavored substance in a single spot on your tongue, the taste will fade until it vanishes (Krakauer & Dallenbach, 1937). This fading effect is an example of *sensory adaptation—a gradual decline in sensitivity to prolonged stimulation.* Sensory adaptation is not unique to taste. This phenomenon occurs in other senses as well. In the taste system, sensory adaptation can leave aftereffects (Bartoshuk, 1968). For example, adaptation to a sour solution makes water taste sweet, whereas adaptation to a sweet solution makes water taste bitter.

So far, we've been discussing taste, but what we are really interested in is the *perception of flavor.* You probably won't be surprised to learn that odor contributes greatly to flavor (Bartoshuk, 1991). The ability to identify flavors declines noticeably when odor cues are absent (Mozell et al., 1969). Although taste and smell are distinct sensory systems, they interact extensively. You might have noticed this interaction when you ate a favorite meal while enduring a severe head cold. The food probably tasted bland, because your stuffy nose impaired your sense of smell—and taste.

Now that we've explored the dynamics of taste, we can return to our question about the value of the wine-tasting ritual. This elaborate ritual is indeed an authentic way to put wine to a sensitive test. The aftereffects associated with sensory adaptation make it wise to clean one's palate before tasting the wine. Sniffing the cork, and the wine in the glass, is important because odor is a major determinant of flavor. Swirling the wine in the glass helps release the wine's odor inside the glass. Rolling the wine around in your mouth is especially critical because it distributes the wine over the full diversity of taste cells. It also forces the wine's odor up into the nasal passages. Thus, each action in this age-old ritual makes a meaningful contribution to the tasting.

Smell: The Olfactory System

In many ways, the sense of smell is much like the sense of taste. The physical stimuli are chemical substances—volatile ones that can evaporate and be carried in the air. These chemical stimuli are dissolved in fluid—specifically, the mucus in the nose. The receptors for smell are *olfactory cilia,* hairlike structures located in the upper portion of the nasal passages (Getchell & Getchell, 1991) (see Figure 4.38 on the next page). They resemble taste cells in that they have a short life and are constantly being replaced (Farbman, 1992). The olfactory receptors have axons that synapse directly with cells in the olfactory bulb at the base of the brain. This arrangement is unique. *Smell is the only sensory system that is not routed through the thalamus before it projects onto the cortex.*

Odors cannot be classified as neatly as tastes, since efforts to identify primary odors have proven unsatisfactory (Doty, 1991). If primary odors exist, there must be a fairly large number of them. Most olfactory receptors respond to a wide range of odors (Sicard & Holley, 1984). Hence, the perception of

Courtesy of the Yale School of Medicine

"*Good and bad are so intimately associated with taste and smell that we have special words for the experiences (e.g., repugnant, foul). The immediacy of the pleasure makes it seem absolute and thus inborn. This turns out to be true for taste but not for smell.*"
LINDA BARTOSHUK

Web Link 4.5

Seeing, Hearing, and Smelling the World
Hosted by the Howard Hughes Medical Institute, this site provides a graphically attractive review of what scientific research has discovered about human sensory systems, with suggestions about where research will be moving in the future.

Figure 4.38

The olfactory system. Odor molecules travel through the nasal passages and stimulate olfactory cilia. An enlargement of these hairlike olfactory receptors is shown in the inset. The olfactory nerve transmits neural impulses through the olfactory bulb to the brain.

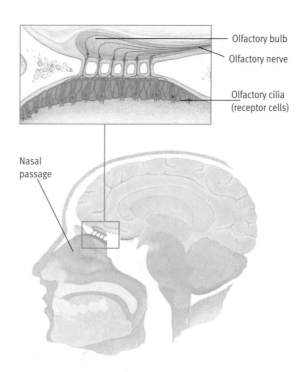

Olfactory bulb

Olfactory nerve

Olfactory cilia (receptor cells)

Nasal passage

various odors probably depends on a great many types of receptors that are uniquely responsive to specific chemical structures (Bartoshuk & Beauchamp, 1994). Like the other senses, the sense of smell shows sensory adaptation. The perceived strength of an odor usually fades to less than half its original strength within about 4 minutes (Cain, 1988). For example, let's say you walk into your kitchen and find that the garbage has started to smell. If you stay in the kitchen without removing the garbage, the stench will soon start to fade.

Humans can distinguish among about 10,000 odors (Axel, 1995). However, when people are asked to identify the sources of specific odors (such as smoke or soap), their performance is rather mediocre (Engen, 1987). For some unknown reason, people have a hard time attaching names to odors (Richardson & Zucco, 1989). Gender differences have been found in the ability to identify odors, with females tending to be somewhat more accurate than males on odor recognition tasks (de Wijk, Schab, & Cain, 1995).

Our Other Senses

Figure 4.39

Receptive field for touch. A receptive field for touch is an area on the skin surface that, when stimulated, affects the firing of a cell that responds to pressure on the skin. Shown here is a center-surround receptive field for a cell in the thalamus of a monkey.

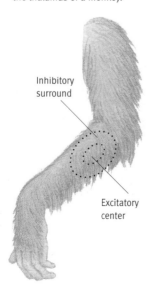

Inhibitory surround

Excitatory center

We have discussed the dynamics of sensation and perception in four sensory domains: vision, hearing, taste, and smell. Since it is widely known that humans have five senses, all that remains is touch. Right? Wrong! In addition to touch, people have still other sensory systems, including the kinesthetic system (which monitors positions of the body in space) and the vestibular system (sense of balance). Let's take a brief look at these three sensory systems.

Touch: Sensory Systems in the Skin

The physical stimuli for touch consist of mechanical, thermal, and chemical energy that impinges on the skin. These stimuli can produce perceptions of tactile stimulation (the pressure of touch against the skin), warmth, cold, and pain. The human skin is saturated with at least six types of sensory receptors (Gardner, 1975). To some degree, these different types of receptors are specialized for different functions, such as the registration of pressure, heat, cold, and so forth. However, these distinctions are not as clear as researchers had originally thought (Sinclair, 1981).

If you've been to a mosquito-infested picnic lately, you'll appreciate the need to quickly know where tactile stimulation is coming from. The sense of touch is set up to meet this need for tactile localization with admirable precision and efficiency. Cells in the nervous system that respond to touch are sensitive to specific patches of skin. These skin patches, which vary considerably in size, are the functional equivalents of *receptive fields* in vision. Like visual receptive fields, they often involve a center-surround arrangement, as shown in Figure 4.39 (Kandel & Jessell, 1991). If a stimulus is applied continuously to a specific spot on the skin, the perception of pressure gradually fades. Thus, *sensory adaptation* occurs in the perception of touch as it does in other sensory systems.

The nerve fibers that carry incoming information about tactile stimulation are routed through the spinal cord to the brainstem. The tactile pathway then projects through the thalamus and onto the *somatosensory cortex* in the brain's parietal lobes. The entire body is sensitive to touch. However, in humans the bulk of the somatosensory cortex is devoted to processing signals coming from the fingers, lips, and tongue. Some cells in the somatosensory cortex function like the *feature detectors* discovered in vision (Cholewiak & Collins, 1991). They respond to specific features of touch, such as a movement across the skin in a particular direction.

The receptors for pain are mostly free nerve endings in the skin. As unpleasant as pain is, the sensation of pain is crucial to survival. Pain is a marvelous warning system. It tells people when they should stop shoveling snow, or it lets them know that they have a pinched nerve that requires treatment. However, *chronic* pain is a frustrating, demoralizing affliction that affects over 50 million people in American society, at a cost of more than $70 billion annually (Turk, 1994). Thus, there are pressing practical reasons for psychologists' keen interest in the perception of pain.

Pain messages are transmitted to the brain via two pathways that pass through different areas in the thalamus (Willis, 1985). One is a *fast pathway* that registers localized pain and relays it to the cortex in a fraction of a second. This is the system that hits you with sharp pain when you first cut your finger. The second system uses a *slow pathway*, routed through the limbic system, that lags a second or two behind the fast system. This pathway (which also carries information about temperature) conveys the less localized, longer-lasting aching or burning pain that comes after the initial injury (see Figure 4.40).

As with other perceptions, pain is not an automatic result of certain types of stimulation. The perception of pain can be influenced greatly by expectations, personality, mood, and other factors involving higher mental processes (Rollman, 1992). The psychological element in pain perception becomes clear when something distracts your attention from pain and the hurting temporarily disappears.

Cultural variations in the experience of pain provide further evidence for the subjective quality of pain. Melzack and Wall (1982) have described a number of anecdotal examples of remarkable pain tolerance in non-Western cultures. Moreover, systematic empirical comparisons have found ethnic and cultural differences in the experience of chronic pain (Bates, Edwards, & Anderson, 1993) and the pain associated with childbirth (Jordan, 1983). According to Melzack and Wall (1982), culture doesn't affect the process of pain perception so much as the willingness to tolerate certain types of pain, a conclusion echoed by Zatzick and Dimsdale (1990).

As you can see, then, tissue damage that sends pain impulses on their way to the brain doesn't necessarily result in the experience of pain. Cognitive and emotional processes that unfold in higher brain centers can sometimes block pain signals coming from peripheral receptors.

How are incoming pain signals blocked? In an influential effort to answer this question, Ronald

Melzack and Patrick Wall (1965) devised the gate-control theory of pain. *Gate-control theory holds that incoming pain sensations must pass through a "gate" in the spinal cord that can be closed, thus blocking ascending pain signals.* The gate in this model is not an anatomical structure but a pattern of neural activity that inhibits incoming pain signals. Melzack and Wall suggested that this imaginary gate can be closed by signals from peripheral receptors or by signals from the brain. They theorized that the latter mechanism can help explain how factors such as attention and expectations can shut off pain signals. As a whole, research suggests that the concept of a gating mechanism for pain has merit (Craig & Rollman, 1999). However, relatively little support has been found for the neural circuitry originally hypothesized by Melzack and Wall. Other neural mechanisms, discovered after gate-control theory was proposed, appear to be responsible for blocking the perception of pain.

One of these discoveries was the identification of endorphins. As discussed in Chapter 3, *endorphins are the body's own natural morphinelike pain-killers, which are widely distributed in the central*

Figure 4.40

The two pathways for pain signals. Pain signals are sent from receptors to the brain along the two pathways depicted here. The fast pathway, shown in red, and the slow pathway, shown in black, depend on different types of nerve fibers and are routed through different parts of the thalamus. The gate control mechanism posited by Melzack and Wall (1965) apparently depends on descending signals originating in an area of the midbrain (the pathway shown in green).

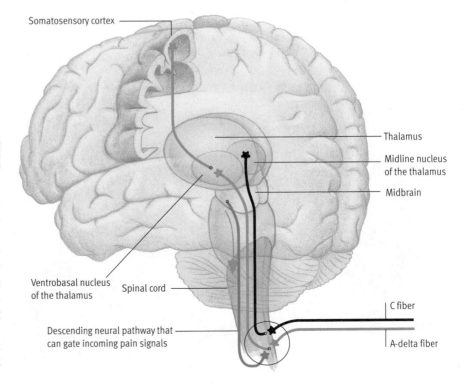

Somatosensory cortex

Thalamus

Midline nucleus of the thalamus

Midbrain

Ventrobasal nucleus of the thalamus   Spinal cord

C fiber

A-delta fiber

Descending neural pathway that can gate incoming pain signals

Comparing Taste, Smell, and Touch

Check your understanding of taste, smell, and touch by comparing these sensory systems on the dimensions listed in the first column below. A few answers are supplied; see whether you can fill in the rest. The answers can be found in Appendix A.

Dimension	Taste	Smell	Touch
1. Stimulus	Soluble chemicals saliva	Volatile chemicals in air	Mechanical, thermal, & chemical energy due to external contact
2. Receptors	Clusters of taste cells	Olfactory cilia	Many (at least 6) types
3. Location of receptors	Taste buds on tongue	Upper areas of nasal passages	Skin
4. Basic elements of perception	Sweet, sour, salty, bitter	No satisfactory classification scheme	Pressure, hot, cold, pain

nervous system. The other discovery involved the identification of a descending neural pathway that mediates the suppression of pain (Basbaum & Fields, 1984). This pathway appears to originate in an area of the midbrain (see Figure 4.40). Neural activity in this pathway is probably initiated by endorphins. The circuits in this pathway synapse in the spinal cord, where they inhibit the activity of neurons that would normally transmit incoming pain impulses to the brain. The painkilling effects of morphine appear to be at least partly attributable to activity in this descending pathway, as cutting the fibers in this pathway reduces the analgesic effects of morphine (Jessell & Kelly, 1991). In contrast, activation of this pathway by electrical stimulation of the brain can produce an analgesic effect. Clearly, this pathway plays a central role in gating incoming pain signals. The impact of cognitive and emotional factors on pain may be mediated by signals sent down this pathway from higher brain centers.

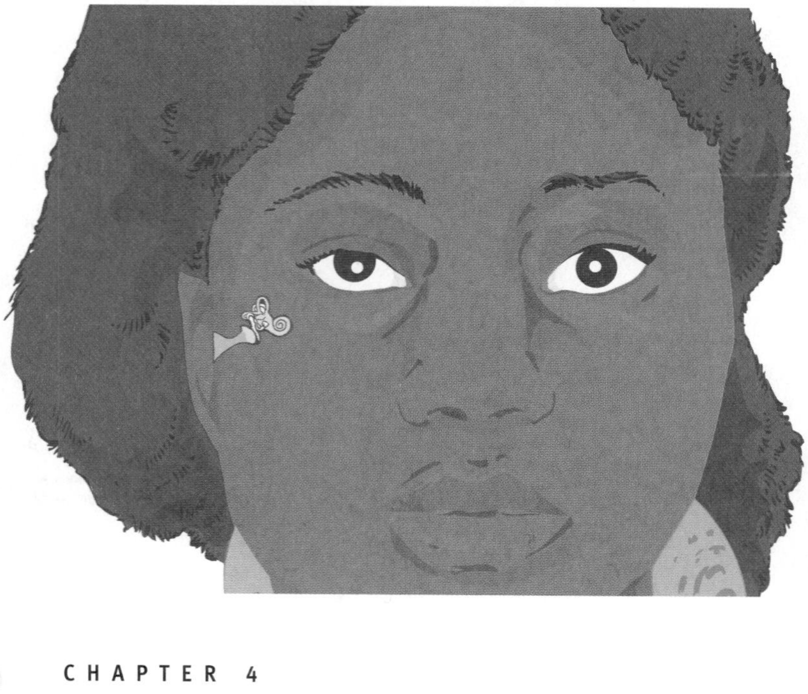

Figure **4.41**

The vestibular system.
The semicircular canals in the inner ear (which are shown disproportionately large here) are the sensory organ for balance and head movement. Fluid movements in these canals stimulate neural impulses that travel along the vestibular nerve to the brain.

The Kinesthetic System

The *kinesthetic system* monitors the positions of the various parts of the body. To some extent, you know where your limbs are because you commanded the muscles that put them there. Nonetheless, the kinesthetic system allows you to double-check these locations. Where are the receptors for your kinesthetic sense? Some reside in the joints, indicating how much they are bending. Others reside within the muscles, registering their tautness, or extension. Most kinesthetic stimulation is transmitted to the brain along the same pathway as tactile stimulation. However, the two types of information are kept separate (Vierck, 1978).

The Vestibular System

When you're jolting along in a bus, the world outside the bus window doesn't seem to jump about as your head bounces up and down. Yet a movie taken with a camera fastened to the bus would show a bouncing world. How are you and the camera different? Unlike the camera, you are equipped with a *vestibular system,* **which responds to gravity and keeps you informed of your body's location in space.** The vestibular system provides the sense of balance, or equilibrium, compensating for changes in the body's position (Parker, 1980).

The vestibular system shares space in the inner ear with the auditory system. The *semicircular canals* make up the largest part of the vestibular system (see Figure 4.41). They look like three inner tubes joined at the base. Any rotational motion of the head is uniquely represented by a combination of fluid flows in the semicircular canals (Kelly, 1991). These shifts in fluid are detected by hair cells similar to those found along the basilar membrane in the cochlea. Your perceptual system integrates the vestibular input about your body's position with information from other senses. After all, you can see where you are and you know where you've instructed your muscles to take you.

This integration of sensory input raises a point that merits emphasis as we close our tour of the human sensory systems. Although we have discussed the various sensory domains separately, it's important to remember that all the senses send sig-nals to the same brain, where the information is pooled. Sensory integration is the norm in perceptual experience. For example, when you sit beside a campfire, you *see* it blazing, you *hear* it crackling, you *smell* it burning, and you feel the *touch* of its warmth. If you cook something over it, you may even *taste* it. Thus, perception involves building a unified model of the world out of integrated input from all the senses.

Putting It in Perspective

In this chapter, three of our unifying themes stood out in sharp relief: (1) psychology is theoretically diverse, (2) people's experience of the world is highly subjective, and (3) our behavior is shaped by our cultural heritage. Let's discuss the value of theoretical diversity first.

Contradictory theories about behavior can be disconcerting and frustrating for theorists, researchers, teachers, and students alike. Yet this chapter provides two dramatic demonstrations of how theoretical diversity can lead to progress in the long run. For decades, the trichromatic and opponent process theories of color vision and the place and frequency theories of pitch perception were viewed as fundamentally incompatible. These competing theories generated and guided the research that now provides a fairly solid understanding of how people perceive color and pitch. As you know, in each case the evidence eventually revealed that the opposing theories were not really incompatible. Both were needed to fully explain the sensory processes that each sought to explain individually. If it hadn't been for these theoretical debates, our current understanding of color vision and pitch perception might be far more primitive.

This chapter should also have enhanced your appreciation of why human experience of the world is highly subjective. As ambiguous figures and optical illusions clearly show, there is no one-to-one correspondence between sensory input and perceived experience of the world. Perception is an active process in which people organize and interpret the information received by the senses. Small wonder, then, that people often perceive the same event in very different ways. Thus, individuals' experience of the world is subjective because the process of perception is inherently subjective.

Finally, this chapter provided numerous examples of how cultural factors can shape behavior—in an area of research where one might expect to find little cultural influence. Most people are not surprised to learn that there are cultural differences in attitudes, values, social behavior, and development. But perception is widely viewed as a basic, universal process that should be invariant across cultures. In most respects it is, as the similarities among cultural groups in perception far outweigh the differences. Nonetheless, we saw cultural variations in depth perception, susceptibility to illusions, taste preferences, and pain tolerance. Thus, even a fundamental, heavily physiological process such as perception can be modified to some degree by one's cultural background.

The following Personal Application highlights the subjectivity of perception once again. It focuses on how painters have learned to use the principles of visual perception to achieve a variety of artistic goals.

PERSONAL APPLICATION

Appreciating Art and Illusion

Answer the following multiple-choice question:

Artistic works such as paintings

_____ 1 render an accurate picture of reality

_____ 2 create an illusion of reality

_____ 3 provide an interpretation of reality

_____ 4 make us think about the nature of reality

_____ 5 all of the above

The answer to this question is (5), "all of the above." Historically, artists have had many and varied purposes, including each of those listed in the question. To realize their goals, artists have had to use a number of principles of perception—sometimes quite deliberately, and sometimes not. Let's use the example of painting to explore the role of perceptual principles in art and illusion.

The goal of most early painters was to produce a believable picture of reality. This goal immediately created a problem familiar to most of us who have attemped to draw realistic pictures: the real world is three-dimensional, but a canvas or a sheet of paper is flat. Paradoxically, then, painters who set out to re-create reality had to do so by creating an *illusion* of three-dimensional reality.

Prior to the Renaissance, these efforts to create a convincing illusion of reality were awkward by modern standards. Why? Because artists did not understand how to use depth cues. This fact is apparent in Figure 4.42, a religious scene painted around 1300. The painting clearly lacks a sense of depth. The people seem paper-thin. They have no real position in space.

Although earlier artists made *some* use of depth cues, Renaissance artists manipulated the full range of pictorial depth cues and really harnessed the crucial cue of linear perspective (Solso, 1994). Figure 4.43 dramatizes the resulting transition in art. This scene, painted by Italian Renaissance artists Gentile and Giovanni Bellini, seems much more realistic and lifelike than the painting in Figure 4.42 because it uses a number of pictorial depth cues. Notice how the buildings on the sides converge to make use of linear perspective. Additionally, distant objects are smaller than nearby ones, an application of relative size. This painting also uses height in plane, as well as interposition. By taking advantage of pictorial depth cues, an artist can enhance a painting's illusion of reality.

In the centuries since the Renaissance, painters have adopted a number of viewpoints about the portrayal of reality. For instance, the French Impressionists of the 19th century did not want to re-create the photographic "reality" of a scene. They set out to interpret a viewer's fleeting perception or impression of reality. To accomplish this end, they worked with color in unprecedented ways.

Figure 4.42

Master of the Arrest of Christ (detail, central part) by S. Francesco, Assisi, Italy (circa 1300). Notice how the absence of depth cues makes the painting seem flat and unrealistic. (Scala/Art Resource, New York)

Figure 4.43

A painting by the Italian Renaissance artists Gentile and Giovanni Bellini (circa 1480). In this painting a number of depth cues—including linear perspective, relative size, height in plane, light and shadow, and interposition—enhance the illusion of three-dimensional reality. (Scala/Art Resource, New York)

Consider, for instance, the work of Georges Seurat, a French artist who used a technique called pointillism. Seurat carefully studied what scientists knew about the composition of color in the 1880s, then applied this knowledge in a calculated, laboratory-like manner. Indeed, critics in his era dubbed him the "little chemist." Seurat constructed his paintings out of tiny dots of pure, intense colors. He used additive color mixing, a departure from the norm in painting, which usually depends on subtractive mixing of pigments. A famous result of Seurat's "scientific" approach to painting was *Sunday Afternoon on the Island of La Grande Jatte* (see Figure 4.44). As the work of Seurat illustrates, modernist painters were moving away from attempts to re-create the world as it is literally seen.

If 19th-century painters liberated color, their successors at the turn of the 20th century liberated form. This was particularly true of the Cubists. Cubism was begun in 1909 by Pablo Picasso, a Spanish artist who went on to experiment with other styles in his prolific career. The Cubists didn't try to portray reality so much as to reassemble it. They attempted to reduce everything to combinations of geometric forms (lines, circles, triangles, rectangles, and such) laid out in a flat space, lacking depth. In a sense,

they applied the theory of feature analysis to canvas, as they built their figures out of simple features.

The resulting paintings were decidedly unrealistic, but the painters would leave realistic fragments that provided clues about the subject. Picasso liked to challenge his viewers to decipher the subject of his paintings. Take a look at the painting in Figure 4.45 and see whether you can figure out what Picasso was portraying.

The work in Figure 4.45 is titled *Violin and Grapes*. Note how Gestalt principles of perceptual organization are at work to create these forms. Proximity and similarity serve to bring the grapes together in the bottom right corner. Closure accounts for your being able to see the essence of the violin.

The Surrealists toyed with reality in a different way. Influenced by Sigmund Freud's writings on the unconscious, the Surrealists explored the world of dreams and fantasy.

Figure 4.45

***Violin and Grapes* by Pablo Picasso (1912).** This painting makes use of the Gestalt principles of perceptual organization. (Pablo Picasso, *Violin and Grapes, Céret and Sorgues,* spring-early fall 1912, oil on canvas, 20 x 24 inches, 50.6 x 61 cm, collection, © The Museum of Modern Art, New York, Mrs. David M. Levy Bequest. © 2001 Estate of Pablo Picasso / Artists Rights Society (ARS), New York.)

Specific elements in their paintings are often depicted realistically, but the strange juxtaposition of elements yields a disconcerting irrationality reminiscent of dreams. A prominent example of this style is Salvador Dali's *Slave Market with the Disappearing Bust of Voltaire*, shown in Figure 4.46. Notice the reversible figure near the center of the painting. The "bust of Voltaire" is made up of human figures in the distance, standing in front of an arch. Dali often used reversible figures to enhance the ambiguity of his bizarre visions.

Perhaps no one has been more creative in manipulating perceptual ambiguity than M. C. Escher, a modern Dutch artist. Escher closely followed the work of the Gestalt psychologists, and he readily acknowledged his debt to psychology as a source of inspiration (Teuber, 1974). *Waterfall*, a 1961 lithograph by Escher, is an impossible figure that appears to defy the law of gravity (see Figure 4.47). The puzzling problem here is that a level channel of water terminates in a waterfall that "falls" into the same channel two levels "below." This drawing is made up of two of the impossible triangles shown earlier, in Figure 4.31. In case you need help seeing them, the waterfall itself forms one side of each triangle.

The Necker cube, a reversible figure mentioned earlier, was the inspiration for Escher's 1958 lithograph *Belvedere*, shown in Figure 4.48. You have to look carefully to realize that this is another impossible figure. Note that the top story runs at a right angle from the first story. Note also how the pillars are twisted around. The pillars that start on one side of the building end up supporting the second story on the other side! Escher's debt to the Necker cube is manifested in several places. Notice, for instance, the drawing of a Necker cube on the floor next to the seated boy (on the lower left).

Like Escher, Hungarian artist Victor Vasarely, who pioneered Kinetic Art, challenged viewers to think about the process of perception. His paintings are based on optical illusions, as squares seem to advance and recede, or spheres seem to inflate and deflate. For example, note how Vasareley used the depth cues of texture gradient and linear perspective to convey the look of great depth in his painting *Tukoer-Ter-Ur*, shown in Figure 4.49.

While Escher and Vasarely challenged viewers to think about perception, Belgian artist René Magritte challenged people to think about the conventions of painting. Many of his works depict paintings on an easel, with the "real" scene continuing unbroken at the edges. The painting in Figure 4.50 is such a picture within a picture. Ultimately, Magritte's painting blurs the line between the real world and the illusory world created by the artist, suggesting that there is no line—that everything is an illusion. In this way, Magritte "framed" the ageless, unanswerable question: What is reality?

Figure 4.46

Salvador Dali's *Slave Market with the Disappearing Bust of Voltaire* (1940). This painting playfully includes a reversible figure (two nuns form the bust of Voltaire, a philosopher known for his stringent criticisms of the Catholic church). (Salvador Dali, *The Slave Market with the Disappearing Bust of Voltaire*, 1940, oil on canvas, 18-1/4 x 25-3/8 inches. Collection of The Salvador Dali Museum, St. Petersburg, Fl. Copyright © 2001 The Salvador Dali Museum, Inc. © 2001 Kingdom of Spain, Gala-Salvador Dali Foundation/Artists Rights Society (ARS), New York.)

Figure 4.47

Escher's lithograph *Waterfall* (1961). Escher's use of depth cues and impossible triangles deceives the brain into seeing water flow uphill. (M.C. Escher's *Waterfall* © Gordon Art BV-Baarn-Holland. All rights reserved.)

Figure 4.48

Escher's *Belvedere* (1958). This lithograph depicts an impossible figure inspired by the Necker cube. The cube appears in the architecture of the building, in the model held by the boy on the bench, and in the drawing lying at his feet. (M.C. Escher's *Belvedere* © Gordon Art BV-Baarn-Holland. All rights reserved.)

Figure 4.50

René Magritte's *Les Promenades d'Euclide* (1955). Notice how the pair of nearly identical triangles each looks quite different in different contexts. (Magritte, Rene, *Les Promenades d'Euclide*, The Minneapolis Institute of Arts, The William Hood Dunwoody Fund. Copyright © 2001 C. Herscovic, Brussels/Artists Rights Society (ARS) New York.)

Figure 4.49

Victor Vasarely's *Tukor-Ter-Ur* (1989). Vasarely manipulates texture gradients and linear perspective to create an illusion of depth. (Vasarely, Victor. *Tukoer-Ter-Ur*, 1989 Private Collection, Monaco. Erich Lessing/Art Resource, NY. Copyright © 2001 Artists Rights Society (ARS), New York/ADAGP, Paris).

Recognizing Contrast Effects: It's All Relative

You're sitting at home one night, when the phone rings. It's Simone, an acquaintance from school who needs help with a recreational program for youngsters that she runs for the local park district. She tries to persuade you to volunteer four hours of your time every Friday night throughout the school year to supervise the volleyball program. The thought of giving up your Friday nights and adding this sizable obligation to your already busy schedule makes you cringe with horror. You politely explain to Simone that you can't possibly afford to give up that much time and you won't be able to help her. She accepts your rebuff graciously, but the next night she calls again. This time she wants to know whether you would be willing to supervise volleyball every third Friday. You still feel like it's a big obligation that you really don't want to take on, but the new request seems much more reasonable than the original one. So, with a sigh of resignation, you agree to Simone's request.

What's wrong with this picture? Well, there's nothing wrong with volunteering your time for a good cause, but you just succumbed to a social influence strategy called the *door-in-the face technique*. The *door-in-the-face technique* involves making a large request that is likely to be turned down as a way to increase the chances that people will agree to a smaller request later (see Figure 4.51). The name for this strategy is derived from the expectation that the initial request will be quickly rejected (hence, the door is slammed in the salesperson's face). Although they may not be familiar with the strategy's name, many people use this manipulative tactic. For example, a husband who wants to coax his frugal wife into agreeing to buy a $25,000 sports car might begin by proposing that they purchase a $44,000 sports car. By the time the wife talks her husband out of the $44,000 car, the $25,000 price tag may look quite reasonable to her—which is what the husband wanted all along.

Research has demonstrated that the door-in-the-face technique is a highly effective persuasive strategy (Cialdini, 1993). One of the reasons it works so well is that it depends on a simple and pervasive perceptual principle: in the domain of perceptual experience, *everything is relative*. This relativity means that people are easily swayed by *contrast effects*. For example, lighting a match or a small candle in a dark room will produce a burst of light that seems quite bright, but if you light the same match or candle in a well-lit room, you may not even detect the additional illumination. The relativity of perception is apparent in the painting by Josef Albers shown in Figure 4.52. The two Xs are exactly the same color, but the X in the top half looks yellow, whereas the X in the bottom half looks brown. These varied perceptions occur because of contrast effects—the two X's are contrasted against different background colors.

The same principles of relativity and contrast that operate when people make judgments about the intensity or color of visual stimuli also affect the way they make judgments in a wide variety of domains. For example, a 6'3" basketball player, who is really quite tall, can look downright small when surrounded by teammates who are all over 6'8". And a salary of $30,000 per year for your first full-time job may seem like a princely sum, until a close friend gets an offer of $55,000 a year. The assertion that everything is relative raises the issue of *relative to what*? *Comparitors* are people, objects, events, and other standards that

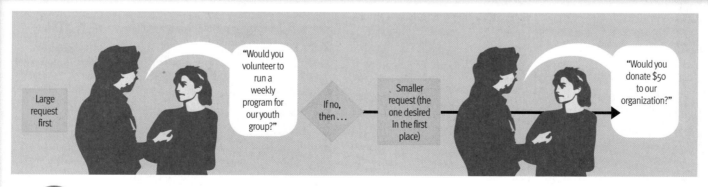

Figure 4.51

The door-in-the-face technique. The door-in-the-face technique is a frequently used compliance strategy in which you begin with a large request and work down to the smaller request you are really after. The technique depends in part on contrast effects.

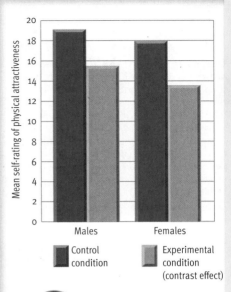

Figure 4.52

Contrast effects in visual perception.
This composition by Joseph Albers shows how one color can be perceived differently when contrasted against different backgrounds. The top X looks yellow and the bottom X looks brown, but they're really the same color. (From Alber, Joseph, *Interaction of Color*. Reprinted by permission of the publisher, Yale University Press.)

Figure 4.53

Contrast effects in judgments of physical attractiveness. Participants rated their own physical attractiveness under two conditions. In the experimental condition, the ratings occurred after subjects were exposed to a series of photos depicting very attractive models. The resulting contrast effects led to lower self-ratings in this condition. (Data based on Thornton & Moore, 1993)

are used as a baseline for comparison in making judgments. It is fairly easy to manipulate many types of judgments by selecting *extreme* comparitors that may be unrepresentative.

The influence of extreme comparitors was demonstrated in a couple of interesting studies of judgments of physical attractiveness. In one study, undergraduate males were asked to rate the attractiveness of an average-looking female (who was described as a potential date for another male in the dorm) presented in a photo either just before or just after the participants watched a TV show dominated by strikingly beautiful women (Kenrick & Gutierres, 1980). The female was viewed as less attractive when the ratings were obtained just after the men had seen gorgeous women cavorting on TV as opposed to when they hadn't. In another investigation by Thornton and Moore (1993), both male and female participants rated *themselves* as less attractive after being exposed to many pictures of extremely attractive models (see Figure 4.53). Thus, contrast effects can influence important social judgments that are likely to affect how people feel about themselves and others.

Anyone who understands how easily judgments can be manipulated by a careful choice of comparitors could influence your thinking. For example, a politician who is caught in some illegal or immoral act could sway public opinion by bringing to mind (perhaps subtly) the fact that many other politicians have committed acts that were much worse. When considered against a backdrop of more extreme comparitors, the politician's transgression will probably seem less offensive. A defense attorney could use a similar strategy in an attempt to obtain a lighter sentence for a client by comparing the client's offense to much more serious crimes. And a realtor who wants to sell you an expensive house that will require huge mortage payments will be quick to mention other homeowners who have taken on even larger mortgages.

In summary, critical thinking is facilitated by conscious awareness of the way comparitors can influence and perhaps distort a wide range of judgments. In particular, it pays to be vigilant about the possibility that others may manipulate contrast effects in their persuasive efforts. One way to reduce the influence of contrast effects is to consciously consider comparitors that are both worse and better than the event you are judging, as a way of balancing the effects of the two extremes.

Table 4.1   **Critical Thinking Skills Discussed in This Application**

Skill	Description
Understanding how contrast effects can influence judgments and decisions	The critical thinker appreciates how striking contrasts can be manipulated to influence many types of judgments.
Recognizing when extreme comparitors are being used	The critical thinker is on the lookout for extreme comparitors that distort judgments.

REVIEW

Key Ideas

Our Sense of Sight: The Visual System

⦿ Light varies in terms of wavelength, amplitude, and purity. Light enters the eye through the cornea and pupil and is focused on the retina by the lens. Rods and cones are the visual receptors found in the retina. Cones play a key role in daylight vision and color perception, while rods are critical to night vision and peripheral vision. Dark adaptation and light adaptation both involve changes in the retina's sensitivity to light.

⦿ The retina transforms light into neural impulses that are sent to the brain via the optic nerve. Receptive fields are areas in the retina that affect the firing of visual cells. They vary in shape and size, but center-surround arrangements are common.

⦿ Two visual pathways to the brain send signals through the thalamus to different areas of the primary visual cortex. The main pathway, which is routed through the LGN in the thalamus, is subdivided into the what and where pathways, which engage in parallel processing. The visual cortex contains cells that appear to function as feature detectors.

⦿ Perceptions of color (hue) are primarily a function of light wavelength, while amplitude affects brightness and purity affects saturation. Perceptions of colors depend on processes that resemble additive color mixing. The accumulated evidence suggests that both the trichromatic and opponent process theories of color perception are partly correct.

⦿ According to feature analysis theories, people detect specific elements in stimuli and build them into recognizable forms. Gestalt psychology emphasized that the whole may be greater than the sum of its parts (features). Other approaches to form perception emphasize that people develop perceptual hypotheses about the distal stimuli that could be responsible for the proximal stimuli that are sensed.

⦿ Depth perception depends primarily on monocular cues such as linear perspective, texture gradient, interposition, relative size, height in plane, and light and shadow. Binocular cues such as retinal disparity can also contribute to depth perception. Cultures may vary in their use of pictorial depth cues.

⦿ Perceptual constancies in vision help viewers deal with the ever-shifting nature of proximal stimuli. Optical illusions demonstrate that perceptual hypotheses can be inaccurate and that perceptions are not simple reflections of objective reality. Researchers have found some interesting cultural variations in the susceptibility to certain illusions.

Our Sense of Hearing: The Auditory System

⦿ Sound varies in terms of wavelength (frequency), amplitude, and purity. These properties affect mainly perceptions of pitch, loudness, and timbre, respectively.

⦿ Sound is transmitted through the external ear via air conduction to the middle ear. In the inner ear, fluid conduction vibrates hair cells along the basilar membrane in the cochlea. These hair cells are the receptors for hearing. Modern evidence suggests that the place and frequency theories of pitch perception are complementary rather than incompatible.

Our Chemical Senses: Taste and Smell

⦿ The taste buds are sensitive to four basic tastes: sweet, sour, bitter, and salty. Sensitivity to these tastes is distributed somewhat unevenly across the tongue, but the variations in sensitivity are quite small. Taste preferences are shaped by experience and culture. Supertasters are more sensitive to bitter and sweet tastes than others.

⦿ Like taste, smell is a chemical sense. Chemical stimuli activate olfactory receptors lining the nasal passages. Most of these receptors respond to more than one odor.

Our Other Senses

⦿ Sensory receptors in the skin respond to pressure, temperature, and pain. Pain signals are sent to the brain along two pathways that are characterized as fast and slow. The perception of pain is highly subjective. Gate-control theory holds that incoming pain signals can be blocked in the spinal cord. Endorphins and a descending neural pathway appear responsible for the suppression of pain.

⦿ The kinesthetic system monitors the position of various body parts. The sense of balance depends primarily on activity in the vestibular system.

Putting It in Perspective

⦿ This chapter underscored three of our unifying themes: the value of theoretical diversity, the subjective nature of experience, and the importance of one's cultural heritage.

Personal Application • Appreciating Art and Illusion

⦿ The principles of visual perception are often applied to artistic endeavors. Painters routinely use pictorial depth cues to make their scenes more lifelike. Color mixing, feature analysis, Gestalt principles, reversible figures, and impossible figures have also been used in influential paintings.

Critical Thinking Application • Recognizing Contrast Effects: It's All Relative

⦿ The study of perception often highlights the relativity of experience. This relativity can be manipulated by carefully arranging for contrast effects. Critical thinking is enhanced by an awareness of how comparitors can distort many types of judgments.

Key Terms

Additive color mixing
Afterimage
Basilar membrane
Binocular depth cues
Cochlea
Color blindness
Comparitors
Complementary colors
Cones
Dark adaptation
Depth perception
Distal stimuli
Door-in-the-face
  technique
Farsightedness
Feature analysis
Feature detectors
Fovea
Gustatory system
Impossible figures
Kinesthetic sense
Lens
Light adaptation
Monocular depth cues
Nearsightedness
Olfactory system
Optical illusion
Parallel processing
Perception

Perceptual constancy
Perceptual hypothesis
Perceptual set
Phi phenomenon
Pictorial depth cues
Proximal stimuli
Pupil
Receptive field of a
  visual cell
Retina
Retinal disparity
Reversible figure
Rods
Sensation
Sensory adaptation
Subtractive color
  mixing
Vestibular system

Key People

Linda Bartoshuk
Hermann von
  Helmholtz
David Hubel and
  Torsten Wiesel
Ronald Melzack and
  Patrick Wall
Max Wertheimer

PRACTICE TEST

1. The term used to refer to the stimulation of the sense organs is:
   A. sensation.
   B. perception.
   C. transduction.
   D. adaptation.

2. Our perception of the brightness of a color is affected mainly by:
   A. the wavelength of light waves.
   B. the amplitude of light waves.
   C. the purity of light waves.
   D. the saturation of light waves.

3. The structure that controls the amount of light passing into the rear chamber of the eye is the:
   A. lens.
   B. pupil.
   C. ciliary muscle.
   D. vitreous humor.

4. In farsightedness:
   A. close objects are seen clearly but distant objects appear blurry.
   B. the focus of light from close objects falls behind the retina.
   C. the focus of light from distant objects falls a little short of the retina.
   D. a and b.
   E. a and c.

5. The collection of rod and cone receptors that funnel signals to a particular visual cell in the retina make up that cell's:
   A. blind spot.
   B. optic disk.
   C. opponent process field.
   D. receptive field.

6. The primary visual cortex is located in the:
   A. occipital lobe.
   B. temporal lobe.
   C. parietal lobe.
   D. frontal lobe.

7. Which theory would predict that the American flag would have a green, black, and yellow afterimage?
   A. subtractive color mixing
   B. opponent process theory
   C. additive color mixing
   D. trichromatic theory

8. A readiness to perceive a stimulus in a particular way is referred to as (a):
   A. Gestalt.
   B. feature analysis.
   C. perceptual set.
   D. congruence.

9. In a painting, train tracks may look as if they go off into the distance because the artist draws the tracks as converging lines, a monocular cue to depth known as:
   A. interposition.
   B. texture gradient.
   C. relative size.
   D. linear perspective.

10. The fact that cultural groups with little exposure to carpentered buildings are less susceptible to the Müller-Lyer illusion suggests that:
    A. not all cultures test perceptual hypotheses.
    B. people in technologically advanced cultures are more gullible.
    C. optical illusions can be experienced only by cultures that have been exposed to the concept of optical illusions.
    D. perceptual inferences can be shaped by experience.

11. Perception of pitch can best be explained by:
    A. place theory.
    B. frequency theory.
    C. both place theory and frequency theory.
    D. neither theory.

12. In what way(s) is the sense of taste like the sense of smell?
    A. There are four primary stimulus groups for both senses.
    B. Both systems are routed through the thalamus on the way to the cortex.
    C. The physical stimuli for both senses are chemical substances dissolved in fluid.
    D. All of the above.
    E. None of the above.

13. The fact that theories originally seen as being incompatible, such as the trichromatic and opponent process theories of color vision, are now seen as both being necessary to explain sensory processes illustrates:
    A. that psychology evolves in a sociohistorical context.
    B. the subjectivity of experience.
    C. the value of psychology's theoretical diversity.
    D. the nature-nurture controversy.

14. Which school of painting applied the theory of feature analysis to canvas by building figures out of simple features?
    A. Pointillism
    B. Impressionism
    C. Surrealism
    D. Cubism

15. In the study by Kenrick and Gutierres (1980), exposing male subjects to a TV show dominated by extremely beautiful women:
    A. had no effect on their ratings of the attractiveness of a prospective date.
    B. increased their ratings of the attractiveness of a prospective date.
    C. decreased their ratings of the attractiveness of a prospective date.
    D. decreased their ratings of their own attractiveness.

Answers

1	A	page 96	6	A	pages 101–103	11	C	page 119
2	B	pages 96–97	7	B	page 105	12	C	page 121
3	B	page 98	8	C	page 108	13	C	page 125
4	B	pages 97–99	9	D	page 112	14	D	page 127
5	D	pages 100–101	10	D	page 114	15	C	page 131

INFOTRAC COLLEGE EDITION

Go to the Wadsworth Psychology Study Center for quiz questions, research updates, interactive exercises, and suggested readings in INFOTRAC related to this chapter: http://psychology.wadsworth.com/product/0534593100s

CHAPTER 5

© Mitchell Funk

Variations in Consciousness

© Mitchell Funk

A young woman sat alone in a room. Attached to her scalp were recording electrodes from an electroencephalograph (EEG)—a machine that monitors the electrical activity of the brain. Connected to the EEG was another device that increased the sound of a tone when the EEG registered a particular pattern of brain waves. As long as the brain-wave pattern persisted, the tone filled the room. When the woman's EEG pattern changed, the room fell silent. As the woman sat quietly, the tone gradually began to sound more frequently. What was happening here?

The young woman was a subject in one of a series of experiments conducted by Joe Kamiya, a researcher who set out to see whether people could learn to control the electrical activity in their brains by altering their mental states (Kamiya, 1969; Nowlis & Kamiya, 1970). The tone provided the subjects with *biofeedback*—information about internal bodily changes that would normally be imperceptible. In the experiment described here, the tone sounded whenever the young woman produced a specific pattern of brain waves called *alpha waves*. Kamiya found that when people are provided with EEG biofeedback, the vast majority can learn to alter their brain-wave activity to some extent.

In the course of this research, Kamiya also made some other interesting observations. Although subjects could increase alpha activity, they had difficulty explaining *how* they did it. When pressed, subjects would offer explanations, but the explanations tended to be tentative and vague. Their responses were equally hazy when Kamiya asked them to describe *what it felt like* when they were producing alpha-wave activity. They mostly agreed that the alpha state was quite pleasant, but beyond that they had great difficulty describing it. When questioned, one subject replied, "You keep asking me to describe this darned alpha state. I can't do it. It has a certain feel about it, sure, but really, it's best left undescribed" (Kamiya, 1969, p. 515).

The difficulty Kamiya's subjects experienced when asked to describe their mental state during alpha activity is hardly unique. Researchers find that people also have difficulty describing the states of consciousness associated with hypnosis, meditation, and drug use. Even everyday mental states can defy description. Can you provide a lucid description of exactly how you feel when you daydream? Ironically, the very thing people are most intimately acquainted with—their conscious experience—eludes their best efforts to describe it (Schooler & Fiore, 1997). The problem may be that consciousness is the ultimate in subjective experience. Your consciousness can be directly experienced by only one person—you.

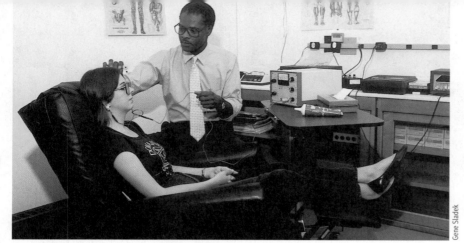

In biofeedback research, subjects may be hooked up to equipment that monitors their brain waves via electrodes attached to the scalp.

Our review will begin with a few general points about the nature of consciousness. After that, much of the chapter will be a "bedtime story," as we take a long look at sleep and dreams. We'll continue our tour of variations in consciousness by examining hypnosis, meditation, and the effects of mind-altering drugs. The Personal Application will address a number of practical questions about sleep and dreams. Finally, the Critical Thinking Application looks at the concept of alcoholism to highlight the power of definitions.

On the Nature of Consciousness

What is consciousness? *Consciousness* **is the awareness of internal and external stimuli.** Your consciousness includes (1) your awareness of external events ("The professor just asked me a difficult question about medieval history"), (2) your awareness of your internal sensations ("My heart is racing and I'm beginning to sweat"), (3) your awareness of your *self* as the unique being having these experiences ("Why me?"), and (4) your awareness of your thoughts about these experiences ("I'm going to make a fool of myself!"). To put it more concisely, consciousness is personal awareness.

The contents of your consciousness are continually changing. Rarely does consciousness come to a standstill. It moves, it flows, it fluctuates, it wanders (Wegner, 1997). Recognizing this situation, William James (1902) christened this continuous flow the *stream of consciousness*. If you could tape-record your thoughts, you would find an endless flow of ideas that zigzag all over the place. As you will soon learn, even when you sleep your consciousness moves through a series of transitions. To be constantly shifting and changing seems to be part of the essential nature of consciousness.

Variations in Levels of Awareness

While William James emphasized the stream of consciousness, Sigmund Freud (1900) wanted to examine what went on beneath the surface of this stream. As explained in Chapter 1, Freud argued that people's feelings and behavior are influenced by *unconscious* needs, wishes, and conflicts that lie below the surface of conscious awareness. According to Freud, the stream of consciousness has depth.

Conscious and unconscious processes are different *levels of awareness*. Thus, Freud was one of the first theorists to recognize that consciousness is not an all-or-none phenomenon.

Since Freud's time, research has shown that people continue to maintain some awareness during sleep and even when they are put under anesthesia for surgery. How do we know? Because some stimuli can still penetrate awareness. For example, people under surgical anesthesia occasionally hear comments made during their surgery, which they later repeat to their surprised surgeons (Bennett, 1993). Research also indicates that while asleep some people remain aware of external events to some degree (Badia, 1990; Evans, 1990). For example, in laboratory studies, subjects who are clearly asleep (based on monitoring of physiological indicators) have responded to faint tones by pressing a palm-mounted button (Ogilvie & Wilkinson, 1988). People can also discriminate among stimuli while asleep. A good example is the new parent who can sleep through a loud thunderstorm or a buzzing alarm clock but who immediately hears the muffled sound of the baby crying down the hall. The parent's selective sensitivity to sounds means that some mental processing must be going on even during sleep.

Indeed, some theorists have recently argued that mental processes during sleep are more similar to waking thought processes than is widely assumed (Kahan & LaBerge, 1994; Moffitt, 1995). For example, when Kahan and LaBerge (1996) had subjects write detailed descriptions of dreaming and waking experiences, they found similar levels of focused attention, public self-consciousness, emotion, and self-reflection (among other things) in the participants' dreaming and waking thoughts. Based on these findings, they argue that mental processes in dreams are surprisingly sophisticated and that dreaming and waking cognition are not fundamentally different.

The Evolutionary Roots of Consciousness

Why do humans experience consciousness? Like other aspects of human nature, consciousness must have evolved because it helped our ancient ancestors survive and reproduce (Ornstein & Dewan, 1991). That said, there is plenty of debate about exactly how consciousness proved adaptive. One line of thinking is that consciousness allowed our ancestors to think through courses of action and their consequences—and choose the best course—without actually executing ill-advised actions (by trial and error) that may have led to disastrous consequences (Plotkin, 1998). In other words, a little forethought and planning may have proved valuable in efforts to obtain food, avoid predators, and find mates. Although this analysis seems plausible, theorists have put forth a host of alternative explanations that focus on other adaptive benefits of personal awareness, and relatively little empirical evidence is available to judge the merits of any of these explanations. Hence, the evolutionary bases of consciousness remain elusive.

Consciousness and Brain Activity

Variations in consciousness are intimately related to changes in electrical activity in the brain. Investigators have been exploring this relationship ever since Hans Berger (1929) invented the EEG (the machine Kamiya used in his research on biofeedback). **The *electroencephalograph (EEG)* is a device that monitors the electrical activity of the brain over time by means of recording electrodes attached to the surface of the scalp.** The EEG records and amplifies electrical activity in the outer layer of the brain, the cortex.

Ultimately, the EEG summarizes the rhythm of cortical activity in the brain in terms of line tracings called *brain waves*. These brain-wave tracings vary in *amplitude* (height) and *frequency* (cycles per second, abbreviated cps). You can see what brain waves look like if you glance ahead to Figure 5.4. Human brain-wave activity is usually divided into four principal bands based on the frequency of the

Table 5.1	EEG Patterns Associated with States of Consciousness	
EEG Pattern	**Frequency (cps)**	**Typical States of Consciousness**
Beta (β)	13–24	Normal waking thought, alert problem solving
Alpha (α)	8–12	Deep relaxation, blank mind, meditation
Theta (θ)	4–7	Light sleep
Delta (Δ)	less than 4	Deep sleep

brain waves. These bands, named after letters in the Greek alphabet, are *beta* (13–24 cps), *alpha* (8–12 cps), *theta* (4–7 cps), and *delta* (under 4 cps).

Different patterns of EEG activity are associated with different states of consciousness, as is summarized in Table 5.1. For instance, when you are alertly engaged in problem solving, beta waves tend to dominate. When you are relaxed and resting, alpha waves increase. When you slip into deep, dreamless sleep, delta waves become more prevalent. Although these correlations are far from perfect, changes in brain activity are closely related to variations in consciousness (Wallace & Fisher, 1999).

As is often the case with correlations, researchers are faced with a chicken-or-egg puzzle when it comes to the relationship between mental states and the brain's electrical activity. If you become drowsy while you are reading this passage, your brain-wave activity will probably change. But are these changes causing your drowsiness, or is your drowsiness causing the changes in brain-wave activity? Or are the drowsiness and the shifts in brain-wave activity both caused by a *third* factor—perhaps signals coming from a subcortical area in the brain? (See Figure 5.1.) Frankly, no one knows. All that is known for sure is that variations in consciousness are correlated with variations in brain activity.

Measures of brain-wave activity have provided investigators with a method for mapping out the mysterious state of consciousness called sleep. As we will see in the next two sections of the chapter, this state turns out to be far more complex and varied than you might expect.

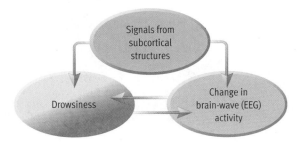

Figure 5.1

The correlation between mental states and electrical activity in the brain. Correlations alone do not establish causation. For example, there is a correlation between the occurrence of drowsiness and a particular pattern of brain-wave activity. But does drowsiness cause a change in brain waves, or do changes in brain waves cause drowsiness? Or does some third variable account for the changes in both?

Biological Rhythms and Sleep

Variations in consciousness are shaped in part by biological rhythms. Rhythms pervade the world around us. The daily alternation of light and darkness, the annual pattern of the seasons, and the phases of the moon all reflect this rhythmic quality of repeating cycles. Humans and many other animals display biological rhythms that are tied to these planetary rhythms (Schwartz, 1996). **Biological rhythms are periodic fluctuations in physiological functioning.** The existence of these rhythms means that organisms have internal "biological clocks" that somehow monitor the passage of time.

The Role of Circadian Rhythms

Circadian rhythms **are the 24-hour biological cycles found in humans and many other species.** In humans, circadian rhythms are particularly influential in the regulation of sleep (Moore, 1990). However, daily cycles also produce rhythmic variations in blood pressure, urine production, hormonal secretions, and other physical functions, some of which are highlighted in Figure 5.2 (Kryger, Roth, & Carskadon, 1994). For instance, body temperature varies rhythmically in a daily cycle, usually peaking in the afternoon and reaching its low point in the depths of the night.

Research indicates that people generally fall asleep as their body temperature begins to drop and awaken as it begins to ascend once again (McGinty, 1993). Investigators have concluded that circadian rhythms can leave individuals physiologically primed to fall asleep most easily at a particular time of day (Richardson, 1993). This optimal time varies from person to person, depending on their schedules, but each individual may have an "ideal" time for going to bed. This ideal bedtime may also promote better quality sleep during the night (Akerstedt et al., 1997), which is interesting in light of evidence that sleep *quality* may be more strongly correlated with health and well-being than the sheer quantity of sleep (Pilcher, Ginter, & Sadowsky, 1997).

Based on animal studies, researchers have a pretty good idea of how the day-night cycle resets human biological clocks. When exposed to light, some receptors in the retina send direct inputs to a small structure in the hypothalamus called the *suprachiasmatic nucleus* (SCN) (Schwartz, 1996). The SCN sends signals to the nearby *pineal gland,* whose secretion of the hormone *melatonin* plays a key role in adjusting biological clocks (Moore, 1995). Circadian rhythms in humans actually appear to be regulated by *several* internal clocks, but the central

Figure 5.2

Examples of circadian rhythms. These graphs show how alertness, core body temperature, and the secretion of growth hormone typically fluctuate in a 24-hour rhythm. Note how alertness tends to diminish with declining body temperature. (Adapted from *Wide Awake at 3:00 AM*, by Coleman. Copyright © 1986 by Richard M. Coleman. Used with permission of W. H. Freeman and Company.)

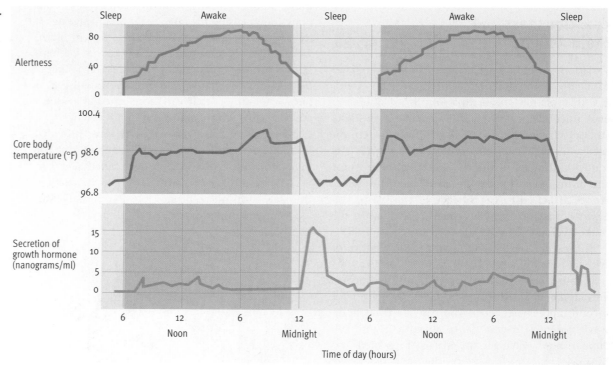

pacemaker clearly is located in the SCN (Harrington, Rusak, & Mistlberger, 1994).

Ignoring Circadian Rhythms

What happens when you ignore your biological clock and go to sleep at an unusual time? Typically, the quality of your sleep suffers. Getting out of sync with your circadian rhythms also causes *jet lag*. When you fly across several time zones, your biological clock keeps time as usual, even though official clock time changes. You then go to sleep at the "wrong" time and are likely to experience difficulty falling asleep and poor quality sleep (Moline, 1993). This inferior sleep, which can continue to occur for several days, can make you feel fatigued, sluggish, and irritable.

People differ in how quickly they can reset their biological clocks to compensate for jet lag, but a rough rule of thumb is that the readjustment process takes about a day for each time zone crossed (Colquhoun, 1984; Moline, 1993). In addition, the speed of readjustment depends on the direction traveled (see Figure 5.3). Generally, it's easier to fly westward and lengthen your day (a phase-delay shift) than it is to fly eastward and shorten it (a phase-advance shift).

Of course, you don't have to hop on a jet to get out of sync with your biological clock. Just going to bed a couple hours later than usual can affect how you sleep (Czeisler, Moore-Ede, & Coleman, 1980). Rotating work shifts that force many nurses, firefighters, and other workers to keep changing their sleep schedule play havoc with biological rhythms. Shift rotation tends to be even harder to adjust to than jet lag (Monk, 1994). Studies show that workers get less total sleep and poorer quality sleep when they go on rotating shifts (Torsvall et al., 1989). Shift rotation can also have a negative impact on employees' productivity and accident-proneness at work, the quality of their social relations at home, and their physical and mental health (Costa, 1996; Regestein & Monk, 1991).

Melatonin and Circadian Rhythms

As scientists have come to appreciate the importance of circadian rhythms, they have begun to look for new ways to help people harness their daily rhythms. A promising line of research has focused on giving people small doses of the pineal gland hormone melatonin, which appears to regulate the human biological clock. The evidence from a number of studies suggests that melatonin can reduce the effects of jet lag, but the findings are not entirely consistent, and more research is needed (Arendt, 1994; Spitzer et al., 1999). Exploratory studies also suggest that melatonin may be effective as a mild sedative that can be useful in the treatment of some forms of insomnia and some other sleep disorders (Haimov & Lavie, 1996; Zhdanova et al., 1995).

Although these results are encouraging, some words of caution are also in order. In the United States, melatonin is classified as a dietary supplement. Unlike in Canada, Great Britain, and many other countries, it is not a regulated drug. It is sold in health food stores, where it is often touted as a miracle preparation that slows the aging process, enhances sex, and fights cancer and AIDS! There is little or no scientific evidence to support any of these unlikely claims (Arendt, 1996; Bonn, 1996). If people were merely wasting their money, there wouldn't be much cause for concern, but medical experts are worried that health food stores are encouraging people to take excessive doses of what is really an untested drug. The doses used in research on melatonin's sleep-related effects have usually been less than 0.5 milligram; health food stores sell doses ranging up to 5 milligrams—10 times higher than the dose needed to reset one's biological clock (Murphy, 1996). A variety of ill effects have been reported from these preparations, which can raise melatonin levels in the blood to 3,000 times higher than normal (Bonn, 1996; Hearn, 1995).

Web Link 5.1

NSF Center for Biological Timing
The role of biological rhythms in the functioning of living organisms has become an important focus of both medical and psychological research. This center's online tutorial about biological timing, or "chronobiology," is a broad and well-illustrated introduction to this field.

Figure 5.3

Circadian rhythms and jet lag. Jet lag can be assessed in a variety of ways. In a study of people flying between Detroit and London, which requires a 5-hour time shift, Nicholson et al. (1986) looked at the time it took travelers to fall asleep the night before their trip and the next five nights after their flight. As you can see, subjects who flew eastward had increased difficulty falling asleep, whereas subjects who flew westward showed no evidence of jet lag on this measure. The data are consistent with other findings that air travelers generally adjust more slowly after flying east (which shortens their day) than after flying west (which lengthens it). (Data from "Sleep After Transmeridian Flights," by A. N. Nicholson, P.A. Pascoe, M. B. Spencer, B.M. Stone, T. Roehis & T. Roth, 1986, *Lancet*, *2*, 1201-08.)

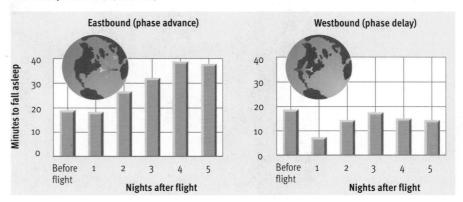

The Sleep and Waking Cycle

Sleep is a variation in consciousness that is familiar to everyone. If you live to be 75, you'll probably spend somewhere between 18 and 25 years lost in sleep. Although it is a familiar state of consciousness, sleep is widely misunderstood. People consider sleep to be a uniform state of physical and mental inactivity, during which the brain is "turned off." In reality, sleepers pass through several states of consciousness and experience quite a bit of physical and mental activity.

The advances in our understanding of sleep have been the result of hard work by researchers who have spent countless nighttime hours watching other people sleep. This work is done in sleep laboratories, where volunteer subjects come to spend the night. Sleep labs have one or more "bedrooms" in which the subjects retire, usually after being hooked up to a variety of physiological recording devices. In addition to an EEG, these devices typically include an *electromyograph (EMG),* **which records muscular activity and tension; an** *electrooculograph* *(EOG),* **which records eye movements; and an** *electrocardiograph (EKG),* **which records the contractions of the heart** (Carskadon & Rechtschaffen, 1994). Other instruments monitor breathing, pulse rate, and body temperature. The researchers observe the sleeping subject through a window (or with a video camera) from an adjacent room, where they also monitor their elaborate physiological recording equipment. It takes most people a night to adapt to the strange bedroom and the recording devices and to return to their normal mode of sleeping (Carskadon & Dement, 1994).

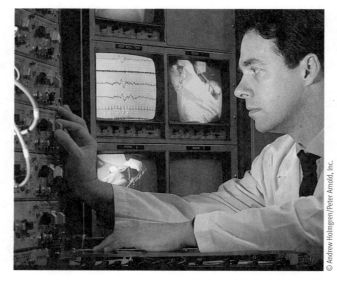

Researchers in a sleep laboratory can observe subjects while using elaborate equipment to record physiological changes during sleep. This kind of research has disclosed that sleep is a complex series of physical and mental states.

© Andrew Holmgren/Peter Arnold, Inc.

Cycling Through the Stages of Sleep

Not only does sleep occur in a context of daily rhythms, but subtler rhythms are evident within the experience of sleep itself. During sleep, people cycle through a series of five distinct stages. Let's take a look at what researchers have learned about the many types of changes that occur during these sleep stages (Anch et al., 1988; Carskadon & Dement, 1994).

Stages 1–4

Although it may only take a few minutes, the onset of sleep is gradual and there is no obvious transition point between wakefulness and sleep (Rechtschaffen, 1994). When you first fall asleep, your sleep tends to be relatively light and you can be awakened easily. Stage 1 is a brief transitional stage that usually lasts only a few (1–7) minutes. Your breathing and heart rate slow as your muscle tension and body temperature decline. The alpha waves that probably dominated your EEG activity just before you fell asleep give way to lower-frequency EEG activity in which theta waves are prominent (see Figure 5.4).

As you descend through stages 2, 3, and 4 of the sleep cycle, your respiration rate, heart rate, muscle tension, and body temperature continue to decline. During stage 2, brief bursts of higher-frequency brain waves, called *sleep spindles,* appear against a background of mixed EEG activity (see Figure 5.4 once again). Gradually, your brain waves become higher in amplitude and slower in frequency, as you move into a deeper form of sleep, called slow-wave sleep. *Slow-wave* **sleep consists of sleep stages 3 and 4, during which low-frequency delta waves become prominent in EEG recordings.** Typically you reach slow-wave sleep in less than an hour and stay there for roughly a half-hour. Then the sleep cycle reverses itself and you gradually move upward through lighter stages of sleep. That's when things start to get interesting.

REM Sleep

When you reach what should be stage 1 once again, you usually go into the *fifth* stage of sleep, which is most widely known as *REM sleep.* REM is an abbreviation for *rapid eye movements,* which are prominent during this stage of sleep. In a sleep lab, researchers use an electrooculograph to monitor these lateral movements that occur beneath the sleeping person's closed eyelids. However, they can be seen with the naked eye if you closely watch someone in the REM stage of sleep (little ripples move back and forth across his or her closed eyelids).

REM sleep was discovered accidentally in the 1950s in Nathaniel Kleitman's lab at the University of Chicago (Aserinsky & Kleitman, 1953; Dement, 1994). Kleitman and his colleagues found that the REM stage is a deep stage of sleep in the conventional sense that it is relatively hard to awaken a person from it. The REM stage is also marked by irregular breathing and pulse rate. Muscle tone is extremely relaxed—so much so that bodily movements are minimal and the sleeper is virtually paralyzed. Although REM is a deep stage of sleep, EEG activity is dominated by high-frequency beta waves that resemble those observed when people are alert and awake (consult Figure 5.4 again). This pairing of deep sleep with "wide awake" brain waves is a paradox that continues to leave scientists perplexed.

This paradox is probably related to the association between REM sleep and dreaming. Soon after the discovery of REM sleep, researchers learned that *this is the stage of sleep during which most dreaming occurs.* How do we know that? When researchers systematically awaken subjects to ask them whether they have been dreaming, most dream reports come from awakenings during the REM stage. William Dement (1978), who coined the term REM sleep, compiled the results of eight early studies of this sort, involving nearly 1500 awakenings of subjects. REM awakenings produced dream recall 78% of the time. Awakenings from other stages were accompanied by dream recall only 14% of the time. Although some dreaming occurs in other stages, dreaming is most frequent, vivid, and memorable during REM sleep.

To summarize, **REM sleep is a deep stage of sleep marked by rapid eye movements, high-frequency brain waves, and dreaming.** It is such a special stage of sleep that the other four stages are often characterized simply as "non-REM sleep." **Non-REM (NREM) sleep consists of sleep stages 1 through 4, which are marked by an absence of rapid eye movements, relatively little dreaming, and varied EEG activity.**

Repeating the Cycle

During the course of a night, people usually repeat the sleep cycle about four times. As the night wears on, the cycle changes gradually. The first REM period is relatively short, lasting only a few minutes. Subsequent REM periods get progressively longer, peaking at around 40–60 minutes in length. Additionally, NREM intervals tend to get

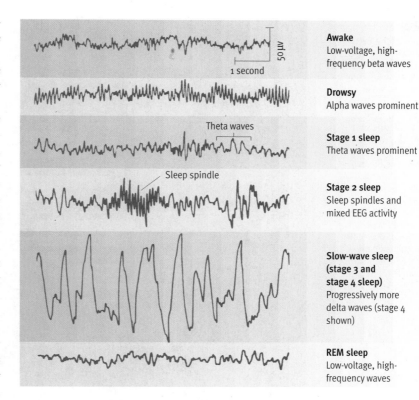

Awake
Low-voltage, high-frequency beta waves

1 second

Drowsy
Alpha waves prominent

Theta waves

Stage 1 sleep
Theta waves prominent

Sleep spindle

Stage 2 sleep
Sleep spindles and mixed EEG activity

Slow-wave sleep (stage 3 and stage 4 sleep)
Progressively more delta waves (stage 4 shown)

REM sleep
Low-voltage, high-frequency waves

shorter, and descents into NREM stages usually become more shallow. These trends can be seen in Figure 5.5 on the next page, which provides an overview of a typical night's sleep cycle.

These trends mean that most slow-wave sleep occurs early in the sleep cycle, gradually giving way to alternating periods of REM sleep and stage 2 sleep. Most dreaming occurs during the later part of a night's sleep. Summing across the entire sleep cycle, young adults typically spend about 60% of their sleep time in light sleep (stages 1 and 2), 20% in slow-wave sleep (stages 3 and 4), and 20% in REM sleep (Mendelson, 1987). Individuals have their unique variations from the typical pattern of sleep, but a person's sleep pattern tends to be moderately consistent from night to night.

Age, Culture, and Sleep

Now that we have described the basic architecture of sleep, let's take a look at a couple of factors that contribute to variations in patterns of sleeping: age and culture.

Age Trends

Age alters the sleep cycle. What we have described so far is the typical pattern for young to middle-aged adults. Children, however, display different patterns (Bliwise, 1994; Roffwarg, Muzio, & Dement,

Figure 5.4

EEG patterns in sleep and wakefulness. Characteristic brain waves vary depending on one's state of consciousness. Generally, as people move from an awake state through deeper stages of sleep, their brain waves decrease in frequency (cycles per second) and increase in amplitude (height). However, brain waves during REM sleep resemble "wide-awake" brain waves. (Figure from "Current Concepts: The Sleep Disorders," by P. Hauri, 1982, The Upjohn Company, Kalamazoo, Michigan. Reprinted by permission.)

Figure 5.5

An overview of the cycle of sleep. The white line charts how a typical person moves through the various stages of sleep during the course of a night. This diagram also shows how dreams and rapid eye movements coincide with REM sleep, whereas posture changes occur in between REM periods (because the body is nearly paralyzed during REM sleep). Notice how the person cycles into REM four times, as descents into NREM sleep get shallower and REM periods get longer. Thus, slow-wave sleep is prominent early in the night, while REM and stage 2 sleep dominate the second half of a night's sleep.

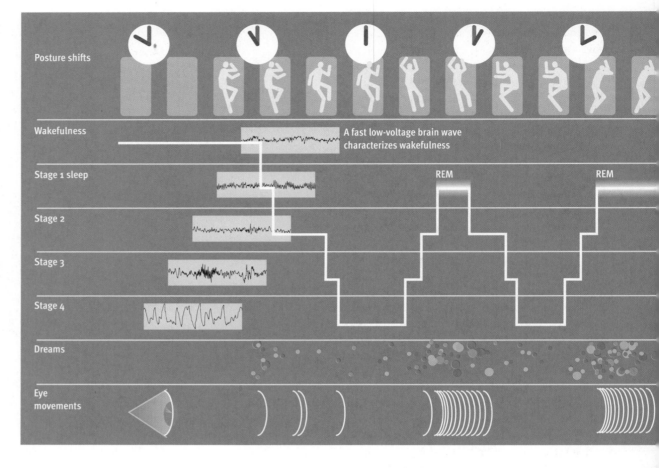

Posture shifts

Wakefulness — A fast low-voltage brain wave characterizes wakefulness

Stage 1 sleep — REM — REM

Stage 2

Stage 3

Stage 4

Dreams

Eye movements

1966). Newborns will sleep six to eight times in a 24-hour period, often exceeding a total of 16 hours of sleep (see Figure 5.6). Fortunately for parents, during the first several months much of this sleep begins to get consolidated into one particularly long night-time sleep period (Webb, 1992a). Interestingly, infants spend much more of their sleep time than adults do in the REM stage. In the first few months, REM accounts for about 50% of babies' sleep, as compared to 20% of adults' sleep. During the remainder of the first year, the REM portion of infants' sleep declines to roughly 30%. The REM portion of sleep continues to decrease gradually until it levels off at about 20% during adolescence (see Figure 5.6).

During adulthood, gradual, age-related changes in sleep continue. The proportion of slow-wave sleep declines and the percentage of time spent in stage 1 increases (Bliwise, 1994; Ehlers & Kupfer, 1989). These shifts toward lighter sleep *may* contribute to the increased frequency of nighttime awakenings seen among the elderly. As Figure 5.6 shows, the average amount of total sleep time also declines with advancing age. However, these averages mask important variability, as total sleep

increases with age in a substantial portion of older people (Webb, 1992a).

Cultural Variations

Although age clearly affects the nature and structure of sleep itself, the psychological and physiological experience of sleep does not appear to vary systematically across cultures. Cultural disparities in sleep are limited to more peripheral matters, such as sleeping arrangements and napping customs. For example, cultural differences occur in *co-sleeping*, the practice of children and parents sleeping together (McKenna, 1993). In modern Western societies, co-sleeping is actively discouraged. As part of their effort to foster self-reliance, American parents teach their children to sleep alone. In contrast, co-sleeping is more widely accepted in Japanese culture, which emphasizes interdependence and group harmony (Latz, Wolf, & Lozoff, 1999). Around the world as a whole, co-sleeping is the norm rather than the exception. Strong pressure against co-sleeping appears to be largely an urban, Western phenomenon.

Napping practices also vary along cultural lines. For example, the Temiars of Indonesia depend

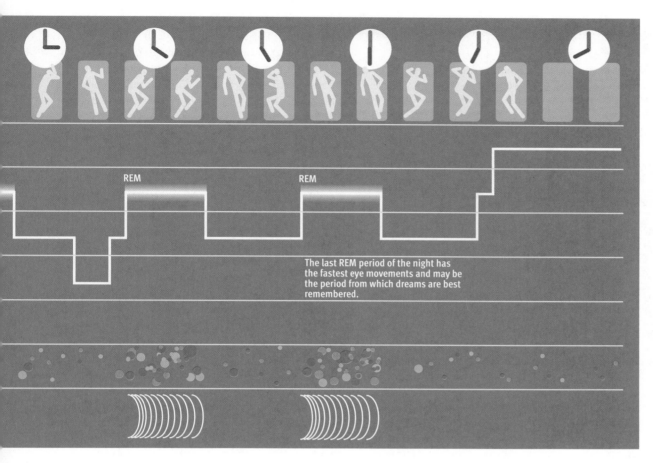

REM

REM

The last REM period of the night has the fastest eye movements and may be the period from which dreams are best remembered.

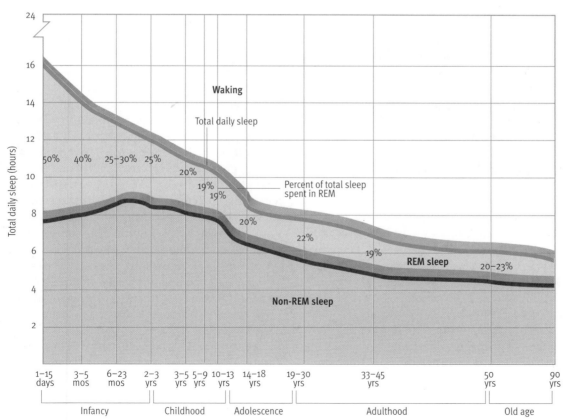

Figure 5.6

Changes in sleep patterns over the life span. Both the total amount of sleep per night and the portion of REM sleep change with age. Sleep patterns change most dramatically during infancy, with total sleep time and amount of REM sleep declining sharply in the first two years of life. After a noticeable drop in the average amount of sleep in adolescence, sleep patterns remain relatively stable, although total sleep and slow-wave sleep continue to decline gradually with age. (Figure adapted from an updated revision of a figure in "Ontogenetic Development of Human Sleep Dream Cycle," by H.P. Roffwarg, J.N. Muzio, and W.C. Dement, 1966. *Science, 152,* 604-609. Copyright © 1966 by the American Association for the Advancement of Science. Adapted and revised by permission of the author.)

Comparing REM and NREM Sleep

A table here could have provided you with a systematic comparison of REM sleep and NREM sleep, but that would have deprived you of the opportunity to check your understanding of these sleep phases by creating your own table. Try to fill in each of the blanks below with a word or phrase highlighting the differences between REM and NREM sleep with regard to the various characteristics specified. As usual, you can find the answers at the back of the book in Appendix A.

Characteristic	REM sleep	NREM sleep
1. Type of EEG activity	_____	_____
2. Eye movements	_____	_____
3. Dreaming	_____	_____
4. Depth (difficulty in awakening)	_____	_____
5. Percentage of total sleep (in adults)	_____	_____
6. Increases or decreases (as percentage of sleep) during childhood	_____	_____
7. Timing in sleep cycle (dominates early or late)	_____	_____

heavily on daytime naps because their nighttime routines (fishing, cooking, watching over the fire) limit their nocturnal sleep to about 4 to 6 hours per night (Stampi, 1989). In many societies, shops close and activities are curtailed in the afternoon to permit people to enjoy a 1- to 2-hour midday nap. These "siesta cultures" are found mostly in tropical regions of the world (Webb & Dinges, 1989). There, this practice is adaptive in that it allows people to avoid working during the hottest part of the day. As a rule, the siesta tradition is not found in industrialized societies, where it conflicts with the emphasis on productivity and the philosophy that "time is money."

The Evolutionary Bases of Sleep

What is the evolutionary significance of sleep? The fact that sleep is seen in a highly diverse array of organisms and that it appears to have evolved independently in birds and mammals suggests that sleep has considerable adaptive value (Zepelin, 1993). But theorists disagree about *how* exactly sleep is adaptive. One hypothesis is that sleep evolved to conserve organisms' energy. According to this notion, sleep evolved millions of years ago in service of warmbloodedness, which requires the maintenance of a constant, high body temperature by metabolic means. An alternative hypothesis is that the immobilization associated with sleep is adaptive because it reduces exposure to predators and other sources of danger. A third hypothesis is that sleep is adaptive because it helps animals restore energy and other bodily resources depleted by waking activities. Overall, the evidence seems strongest for the energy conservation hypothesis (Zepelin, 1993), but there is room for extensive debate about the evolutionary bases of sleep.

Doing Without: Sleep Deprivation

Scientific research on sleep deprivation presents something of a paradox. On the one hand, research suggests that sleep deprivation is not as detrimental as most people subjectively feel it to be. On the other hand, evidence suggests that sleep deprivation may be a major social problem, undermining efficiency at work and contributing to countless accidents.

Complete Deprivation

What happens when people go completely without sleep for a period of days? As you might expect, complete deprivation of sleep has negative effects on participants' mood and their performance on both cognitive and perceptual-motor tasks (Pilcher & Huffcutt, 1996). However, these negative effects tend to be modest, and many researchers have been impressed by how *well* sleep-deprived subjects can perform if they are motivated to do so (Anch et al., 1988). The effects of complete sleep deprivation would probably be more severe except that most people have a hard time going very long without sleep. Most experience great difficulty getting beyond a third or fourth sleepless day.

Partial Deprivation

Partial sleep deprivation, or *sleep restriction,* occurs when people make do with substantially less sleep than normal over a period of time. Partial deprivation occurs far more often in everyday life than complete sleep deprivation. Indeed, many sleep experts believe that much of American society chronically suffers from partial sleep deprivation. It appears that more and more people are trying to squeeze additional waking hours out of their days as they attempt to juggle conflicting work, family, household, and school responsibilities, leading William Dement to comment that "Most Americans no longer know what it feels like to be fully alert" (Toufexis, 1990, p. 79).

How serious are the effects of partial sleep deprivation? A great deal of recent research suggests that the effects of partial sleep deprivation are not as benign as widely believed. Studies indicate that sleep restriction can impair individuals' attention, reaction time, motor coordination, and decision making (Dinges, 1995; Pilcher & Huffcutt, 1996). Evidence suggests that sleep deprivation contributes to a large proportion of transportation accidents and mishaps in the workplace (Dement, 1997; Mitler, 1993). Studies also suggest that nighttime workers in many industries frequently fall asleep on the job. For example, in one study of train engineers, 59% admitted to having dozed off while on duty (Akerstedt, 1988). Obviously, if a person is running a punch press, driving a bus, or working as an air traffic controller, a momentary lapse in attention could be very, very costly. In recent years, a number of major ecological disasters, such as the nuclear accidents at Three Mile Island and Chernobyl and the running aground of the Exxon *Valdez,* have been blamed in part on lapses in judgment and attention resulting from sleep deprivation (Mitler, Dinges, & Dement, 1994). Experts have *estimated* that accidents attributable to drowsiness induced by sleep deprivation cost the U.S. economy over $56 billion annually, lead to the loss of over 52 million work days each year, and result in over 24,000 deaths per year (Coren, 1996).

Selective Deprivation

The unique quality of REM sleep led researchers to look into the effects of a special type of partial sleep deprivation—*selective deprivation.* In a number of laboratory studies, subjects were awakened over a period of nights whenever they began to go into the REM stage. These subjects usually got a decent amount of sleep in NREM stages, but they were selectively deprived of REM sleep.

What are the effects of REM deprivation? The evidence indicates that it has little impact on daytime functioning and task performance (Pearlman, 1982). However, REM deprivation *does* have some interesting effects on subjects' patterns of sleeping (Ellman et al., 1991). As the nights go by in REM-deprivation studies, it becomes necessary to awaken the subjects more and more often to deprive them of their REM sleep, because they spontaneously shift into REM more and more frequently. Whereas most subjects normally go into REM about four times a night, REM-deprived subjects start slipping into REM every time the researchers turn around. In one study, researchers had to awaken a subject 64 times by the third night of REM deprivation (Borbely, 1986). Furthermore, when a REM-deprivation experiment comes to an end and subjects are allowed to sleep without interruption, they experience a "rebound effect." That is, they spend extra time in REM periods for one to three nights to make up for their REM deprivation.

A large number of automobile accidents occur because drivers get drowsy or fall asleep at the wheel. Although the effects of sleep deprivation seem innocuous, sleep loss can be deadly.

Similar results have been observed when subjects have been selectively deprived of slow-wave sleep (Klerman, 1993). What do theorists make of these spontaneous pursuits of REM and slow-wave sleep? They conclude that people must have specific *needs* for REM and slow-wave sleep—and rather strong needs, at that.

Problems in the Night: Insomnia

People are plagued by a variety of sleep problems, but insomnia is far and away the most common sleep disorder. **Insomnia refers to chronic problems in getting adequate sleep.** It occurs in three basic patterns: (1) difficulty in falling asleep initially, (2) difficulty in remaining asleep, and (3) persistent early-morning awakening. Insomnia may sound like a minor problem to those who haven't struggled with it, but it is a very unpleasant malady, which is associated with daytime fatigue, impaired functioning, reduced productivity, and increased health problems (Simon & VonKorff, 1997).

Prevalence

Nearly everyone suffers occasional sleep difficulties because of stress, disruptions of biological rhythms, or other temporary circumstances. Fortunately, these problems clear up spontaneously for most people. However, about 15% of adults report severe or frequent insomnia, and another 15% complain of mild or occasional insomnia (Bootzin et al., 1993). The prevalence of insomnia increases noticeably during old age (Neubauer, 1999).

Causes

Insomnia has many causes (Roehrs, Zorick, & Roth, 1994; Wooten, 1994). In some cases, excessive anxiety and tension prevent relaxation and keep people awake. Insomnia is frequently a side effect of emotional problems, such as depression, or

"Sleep deprivation is a major epidemic in our society. . . . Americans spend so much time and energy chasing the American dream, that they don't have much time left for actual dreaming."
WILLIAM DEMENT

Figure 5.7

The vicious circle of dependence on sleeping pills.
Because of the body's ability to develop tolerance to drugs, using sedatives routinely to "cure" insomnia can lead to a vicious circle of escalating dependency as larger and larger doses of the sedative are needed to produce the same effect.

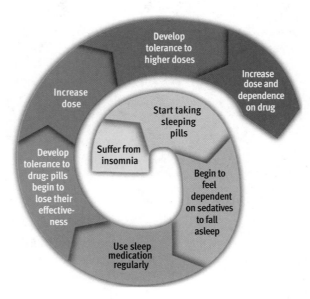

of significant stress, such as pressures at work. Understandably, health problems such as back pain, ulcers, and asthma can lead to insomnia. The use of certain drugs, especially stimulants such as cocaine and amphetamines, may also lead to problems in sleeping.

Treatment

The most common approach to the treatment of insomnia is the prescription of sedative drugs (sleeping pills). Sedatives are fairly effective in helping people fall asleep more quickly, and they reduce nighttime awakenings and increase total sleep (Mendelson, 1990). Nonetheless, these drugs are probably used to combat insomnia *too* frequently. Sleep experts are virtually unanimous in maintaining that in the past physicians prescribed sleeping pills far too readily. As a result of this criticism, prescriptions for sleeping pills declined significantly during the 1970s and 1980s (Ray & Ksir, 1990). In spite of this trend, about 5%–15% of adults still use sleep medication with some regularity (Partinen, 1994).

Sedatives are a poor long-range solution for insomnia for a number of reasons (Mendelson, 1993). For example, there is the danger of overdose, and some people become dependent on sedatives in order to fall asleep. Sedatives also have carryover effects that can make people drowsy and sluggish the next day. Moreover, with continued use sedatives gradually become less effective, so people need to increase their dose to more dangerous levels, creating a vicious circle of escalating dependency (see Figure 5.7). Ironically, sedatives also interfere with the normal cycle of sleep. Although they promote sleep, they reduce the proportion of time spent in REM and slow-wave sleep (Nishino, Mignot, & Dement, 1995). Furthermore, if medication is stopped abruptly, many people experience even worse insomnia than before their treatment was begun—a condition called *rebound insomnia* (Roehrs et al., 1992).

Sedatives do have a place in the treatment of insomnia, but they need to be used cautiously and conservatively. They should be used primarily for short-term treatment of sleep problems. Fortunately, a new generation of sleeping pills that are eliminated from the body "ultrarapidly" may reduce some of the problems that have been associated with sedatives. In this chapter's Personal Application, we'll discuss some alternative strategies for grappling with insomnia.

The World of Dreams

For the most part, dreams are not taken very seriously in Western societies. Paradoxically, though, Robert Van de Castle (1994) points out that dreams have sometimes changed the world. For example, Van de Castle describes how René Descartes's philosophy of dualism, Frederick Banting's discovery of insulin, Elias Howe's refinement of the sewing machine, Mohandas Gandhi's strategy of nonviolent protest, and Lyndon Johnson's withdrawal from the 1968 presidential race were all inspired by dreams. He also explains how Mary Shelley's *Frankenstein* and Robert Louis Stevenson's *The Strange Case of Dr. Jekyll and Mr. Hyde* emerged out of their dream experiences. In his wide-ranging discussion, Van de Castle also relates how the Surrealist painter Salvador Dali characterized his work as "dream photographs," and how legendary filmmakers Ingmar Bergman, Orson Welles, and Federico Fellini all drew on their dreams in making their films. Thus, Van de Castle concludes that "dreams have had a dramatic influence on almost every important aspect of our culture and history" (p. 10).

The Nature and Contents of Dreams

What exactly is a dream? This question is more complex and controversial than you might guess. The conventional view is that dreams are mental experiences during REM sleep that have a storylike quality, include vivid visual imagery, are often bizarre, and are regarded as perceptually real by the dreamer (Antrobus, 1993). However, theorists have begun to question virtually every aspect of this characterization. Decades of research on the contents of dreams have shown that dreams are not as bizarre as widely assumed (Cartwright, 1994). In recent years, there has been renewed interest in the fact that dreams are not the exclusive property of REM sleep. Moreover, studies that have focused on dream reports from non-REM stages of sleep have found that these dreams appear to be less vivid and storylike than REM dreams (Pivik, 1994). And work on reflective awareness in dreams suggests that dreamers realize they are dreaming more often than previously thought (Kahan & LaBerge, 1994). Thus, the concept of dreaming is undergoing some revision in scientific circles.

What do people dream about? Overall, dreams are not as exciting as advertised. Perhaps dreams are seen as exotic because people are more likely to remember their more bizarre nighttime dramas. After analyzing the contents of more than 10,000 dreams, Calvin Hall (1966) concluded that most dreams are relatively mundane. They tend to unfold in familiar settings with a cast of characters dominated by family, friends, and colleagues, with a sprinkling of strangers. Researchers have found that certain themes are more common than others in dreams. For example, people dream quite a bit about sex, aggression, and misfortune. According to Hall, dreams tend to center on classic sources of internal conflict, such as the conflict between taking chances and playing it safe. Hall was struck by how little people dream about public affairs and current events. Typically, dreams are very self-centered; people dream mostly about themselves.

Though dreams seem to belong in a world of their own, what people dream about is affected by what is going on in their lives (Kramer, 1994). If you're struggling with financial problems, worried about an upcoming exam, or sexually attracted to a classmate, these themes may very well show up in your dreams. Freud noticed long ago that the contents of waking life tend to spill into dreams. He labeled this spillover the *day residue*. The connection between a person's real world and his or her dream world probably explains why thematic continuity can be found among successive dreams occurring in different REM periods on a given night (Cipolli et al., 1987).

On occasion, the contents of dreams can also be affected by external stimuli experienced while one is dreaming (Arkin & Antrobus, 1991). For example, William Dement sprayed water on one hand of sleeping subjects while they were in the REM stage (Dement & Wolpert, 1958). Subjects who weren't awakened by the water were awakened by the experimenter a short time later and asked what they had been dreaming about. Dement found that 42% of the subjects had incorporated the water into their dreams. They said that they had dreamt that they were in rainfalls, floods, baths, swimming pools, and the like. Some people report that they occasionally experience the same phenomenon at home when the sound of their alarm clock fails to awaken them. The alarm is incorporated into their dream as a loud engine or a siren, for instance.

Culture and Dreams

Striking cross-cultural variations occur in beliefs about the nature of dreams and the importance attributed to them. In modern Western society, we typically make a distinction between the "real" world we experience while awake and the "imaginary" world we experience while dreaming. Some people realize that events in the real world can affect their dreams, but few believe that events in their dreams hold any significance for their waking life. Although a small minority of individuals take their dreams seriously, in Western cultures dreams are largely written off as insignificant, meaningless meanderings of the unconscious (Tart, 1988).

In many non-Western cultures, however, dreams are viewed as important sources of information about oneself, about the future, or about the spiritual world (Kracke, 1991). Although no culture confuses dreams with waking reality, many view events in dreams as another type of reality that may be just as

Dreaming is the focal point of traditional Aboriginal existence as it is in many other cultures.

© Christine Caborne/CORBIS

important as, or perhaps even more important than, events experienced while awake. In some instances, people are even held responsible for their dream actions. Among the New Guinea Arapesh, for example, an erotic dream about someone may be viewed as the equivalent of an adulterous act. In many cultures, dreams are seen as a window into the spiritual world, permitting communication with ancestors or supernatural beings (Bourguignon, 1972). People in some cultures believe that dreams provide information about the future—good or bad omens about upcoming battles, hunts, births, and so forth (Tedlock, 1992).

The tendency to remember one's dreams varies across cultures. In modern Western societies where little significance is attributed to dreams, dream recall tends to be mediocre. Many people remember their dreams only infrequently. In contrast, dream recall tends to be much better in cultures that take dreams seriously (Kracke, 1992).

In regard to dream content, both similarities and differences occur across cultures in the types of dreams that people report (Hunt, 1989). Some basic dream themes appear to be nearly universal (dreams of falling, being pursued, having sex). However, the contents of dreams vary some from one culture to another because people in different societies deal with different worlds while awake. For example, a 1950 study of the Siriono, a hunting-and-gathering people of the Amazon who were almost always hungry and spent most of their time in a grim search for food, found that *half* of the reported dreams focused on hunting, gathering, and eating food (D'Andrade, 1961). Shared systems for interpreting the contents of dreams also vary from one society to another. Table 5.2 lists a number of

common dream interpretations among the Toraja of Indonesia (Hollan, 1989). Although some of these interpretations (example: standing on mountaintop = becoming a leader) might be common in other societies, some clearly are peculiar to Toraja society (example: buffalo in the rice fields = rats will eat the rice harvest).

Theories of Dreaming

Many theories have been proposed to explain the purposes of dreaming. Sigmund Freud (1900), who analyzed clients' dreams in therapy, believed that the principal purpose of dreams is *wish fulfillment.* He thought that people fulfill ungratified needs from waking hours through wishful thinking in dreams. For example, someone who is sexually frustrated would tend to have highly erotic dreams, while an unsuccessful person would dream about great accomplishments.

Other theorists, such as Rosalind Cartwright, have proposed that dreams provide an opportunity to work through everyday problems (Cartwright, 1977; Cartwright & Lamberg, 1992). According to her cognitive, *problem-solving view,* there is considerable continuity between waking and sleeping thought. Proponents of this view believe that dreams allow people to engage in creative thinking about problems because dreams are not restrained by logic or realism.

J. Allan Hobson and Robert McCarley have argued that dreams are simply the by-product of bursts of activity emanating from subcortical areas in the brain (Hobson, 1988; Hobson & McCarley, 1977; McCarley, 1994). Their *activation-synthesis* model proposes that dreams are side effects of the

[Dreams are] the royal road to the unconscious.
SIGMUND FREUD

National Library of Medicine

One function of dreams may be to restore our sense of competence. . . . It is also probable that in times of stress, dreams have more work to do in resolving our problems and are thus more salient and memorable.
ROSALIND CARTWRIGHT

Rush Presbyterian St. Luke's Medical Center

Table 5.2   Examples of Common Dream Interpretations Among the Toraja of Indonesia

"Good" Dreams	Interpretation	"Bad" Dreams	Interpretation
Receive gold	Good rice harvest	Buffalo in the rice fields	Rats will eat rice harvest
Carry pig or buffalo meat	Good rice harvest		
Act "crazy"	Receive wealth	Naked	Get sick
Objects are thrown at dreamer	Rain will fall	Enter a burial cave	Die
Stand on mountaintop	Become a leader	Carried off by an ancestor	Die
Steal objects	Receive those objects/ become wealthy	Objects are stolen/lost/ carried away	Lose those objects
Swim in ocean or river	Receive wealth	House burns or is destroyed	Lose wealth/ become poor
Jump over or cross water	Become wise/clever		
Gored by a buffalo	Buy a buffalo		

(Adapted from "The Personal Use of Dream Beliefs in the Toraja Highlands," by D. Hollan, 1989, *Ethos,* 17, 166-186. Copyright © 1989 by the American Anthropological Association. Reproduced by permission of the American Anthropological Association from *Ethos* 17:2, June 1989. Not for further reproduction.)

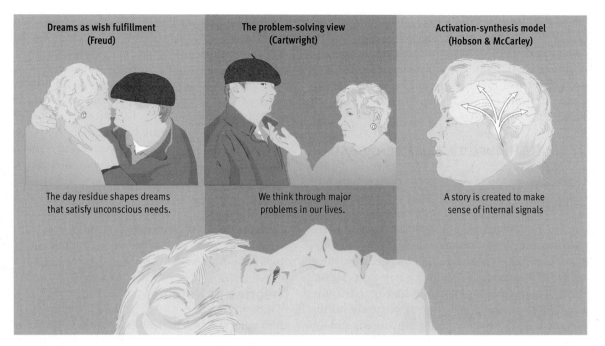

Figure 5.8

Three theories of dreaming.
Dreams can be explained in a variety of ways. Freud stressed the wish-fulfilling function of dreams. Cartwright emphasizes the problem-solving function of dreams. Hobson and McCarley assert that dreams are merely a by-product of periodic neural activation.

Dreams as wish fulfillment (Freud)

The day residue shapes dreams that satisfy unconscious needs.

The problem-solving view (Cartwright)

We think through major problems in our lives.

Activation-synthesis model (Hobson & McCarley)

A story is created to make sense of internal signals

neural activation that produces "wide awake" brain waves during REM sleep. According to this model, neurons firing periodically in lower brain centers send random signals to the cortex (the seat of complex thought). The cortex supposedly constructs a dream to make sense out of these signals. In contrast to the theories of Freud and Cartwright, this theory obviously downplays the role of emotional factors as determinants of dreams.

These theories, which are summarized in Figure 5.8, are only three of a host of ideas about the functions of dreams. All of these theories are based more on conjecture than research. In part, this is because the private, subjective nature of dreams makes it difficult to put the theories to an empirical test. Thus, the purpose of dreaming remains a mystery.

We'll encounter more unsolved mysteries in the next two sections of this chapter as we discuss hypnosis and meditation. Whereas sleep and dreams are familiar to everyone, most people have little familiarity with hypnosis and meditation, which both involve deliberate efforts to temporarily alter consciousness.

Hypnosis: Altered Consciousness or Role Playing?

Hypnosis has a long and checkered history. It all began with a flamboyant 18th-century Austrian by the name of Franz Anton Mesmer. Working in Paris, Mesmer claimed to cure people of illnesses through an elaborate routine involving a "laying on of hands." Mesmer had some complicated theories about how he had harnessed "animal magnetism." However, we know today that he had simply stumbled onto the power of suggestion. Eventually he was dismissed as a charlatan and run out of town by the local authorities. Although officially discredited, Mesmer inspired followers—practitioners of "mesmerism"—who continued to ply their trade. To this day, our language preserves the memory of Franz Mesmer: When we are under the spell of an event or a story, we are "mesmerized."

Eventually, a Scottish physician, James Braid, became interested in the trancelike state that could be induced by the mesmerists. It was Braid who popularized the term *hypnotism* in 1843, borrowing it from the Greek word for sleep. Braid thought that hypnotism could be used to produce anesthesia for surgeries. However, just as hypnosis was catching on as a general anesthetic, more powerful and reliable chemical anesthetics were discovered, and interest in hypnotism dwindled.

Since then, hypnotism has led a curious dual existence. On the one hand, it has been the subject of numerous scientific studies. Furthermore, it has enjoyed considerable use as a clinical tool by physicians, dentists, and psychologists for over a century (Gibson & Heap, 1991). On the other hand, an

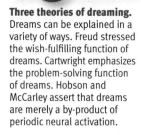

Web Link 5.4

States of Consciousness
PsychWeb, Russ Dewey's (Georgia Southern University) superb resource page, hosts this fine collection of scientifically grounded guides to three topics that too often provoke nonsensical claims: hypnosis, out-of-body experiences, and dreaming.

assortment of entertainers and quacks have continued in the less respectable tradition of mesmerism, using hypnotism for parlor tricks and chicanery. It is little wonder, then, that most people don't know what to make of the whole subject. In this section, we'll work on clearing up some of the confusion surrounding hypnosis.

Hypnotic Induction and Phenomena

Hypnosis is a systematic procedure that typically produces a heightened state of suggestibility. It may also lead to passive relaxation, narrowed attention, and enhanced fantasy. If only in popular films, virtually everyone has seen a *hypnotic induction* enacted with a swinging pendulum. Actually, there are many techniques for inducing hypnosis (Meyer, 1992). Usually, the hypnotist will suggest to the subject that he or she is relaxing. Repetitively, softly, subjects are told that they are getting tired, drowsy, or sleepy. Often, the hypnotist vividly describes bodily sensations that should be occurring. Subjects are told that their arms are going limp, that their feet are getting warm, that their eyelids are getting heavy. Gradually, most subjects succumb and become hypnotized.

People differ in how well they respond to hypnotic induction. Not everyone can be hypnotized. About 10% of the population doesn't respond well at all, while at the other end of the continuum, about 10% of people are exceptionally good hypnotic subjects (Hilgard, 1965). Among people who are susceptible to hypnosis, many interesting effects can be produced. Some of the more prominent hypnotic phenomena include:

1. *Anesthesia.* Under the influence of hypnosis, some subjects can withstand treatments that would normally cause considerable pain (Finer, 1980). As a result, some physicians and dentists have used hypnosis as a substitute for anesthetic drugs. Although drugs are more reliable, hypnosis is a surprisingly effective anesthetic for some people (Patterson, Adcock, & Bombardier, 1997).

2. *Sensory distortions and hallucinations.* Hypnotized subjects may be led to experience auditory or visual hallucinations. They may hear sounds or see things that are not there, or fail to hear or see stimuli that are present (Spiegel et al., 1985). Subjects may also have their sensations distorted so that something sweet tastes sour or an unpleasant odor smells fragrant.

3. *Disinhibition.* Hypnosis can sometimes reduce inhibitions that would normally prevent subjects from acting in ways that they would see as immoral or unacceptable. In experiments, hypnotized subjects have been induced to throw what they believed to be nitric acid into the face of a research assistant. Similarly, stage hypnotists are sometimes successful in getting people to disrobe in public. This disinhibition effect may occur simply because hypnotized people feel that they cannot be held responsible for their actions while they are hypnotized.

4. *Posthypnotic suggestions and amnesia.* Suggestions made during hypnosis may influence a subject's later behavior (Barnier & McConkey, 1998). The most common posthypnotic suggestion is the creation of posthypnotic amnesia. That is, subjects are told that they will remember nothing that happened while they were hypnotized. Such subjects usually claim to remember nothing, as ordered.

Theories of Hypnosis

Although a number of theories have been developed to explain hypnosis, it is still not well understood. Most theories attribute hypnotic effects either to dramatic role playing or to a special, altered state of consciousness (a trance).

Hypnosis as Role Playing

Hypnotized subjects may feel as though they are in an altered state, but their patterns of EEG activity cannot be distinguished from their EEG patterns in normal waking states (Dixon & Laurence, 1992; Orne & Dinges, 1989). The failure to find any special physiological changes associated with hypnosis has led theorists such as Theodore Barber (1979) and Nicholas Spanos (1986; Spanos & Coe, 1992) to conclude that hypnosis produces a normal state of consciousness in which suggestible people act out the role of a hypnotized subject and behave as they think hypnotized people are supposed to. According to this notion, it is subjects' role expectations that produce hypnotic effects, rather than a special trancelike state of consciousness.

Two other lines of evidence support the role-playing view. First, many of the seemingly amazing effects of hypnosis have been duplicated by nonhypnotized subjects or have been shown to be exaggerated (Kirsch, 1997). For example, much has been made of the fact that hypnotized subjects can be used as "human planks" (see the photo on page 151), but it turns out that nonhypnotized subjects can easily match this and other hypnotic feats (Barber, 1986). This finding suggests that no special state of consciousness is required to explain hypnotic feats.

The second line of evidence involves demonstrations that hypnotized subjects are often acting out

Biomedical Research Foundation

"Thousands of books, movies and professional articles have woven the concept of 'hypnotic trance' into the common knowledge. And yet there is almost no scientific support for it."
THEODORE BARBER

a role. For example, Martin Orne (1951) regressed hypnotized subjects back to their sixth birthday and asked them to describe it. They responded with detailed descriptions that appeared to represent great feats of hypnosis-enhanced memory. However, instead of accepting this information at face value, Orne compared it with information that he had obtained from the subjects' parents. It turned out that many of the subjects' memories were inaccurate and invented! Many other studies have also found that age-regressed subjects' recall of the distant past tends to be more fanciful than factual (Nash, 1987). Thus, the role-playing explanation of hypnosis suggests that situational factors lead suggestible subjects to act out a certain role in a highly cooperative manner.

Hypnosis as an Altered State of Consciousness

Despite the doubts raised by role-playing explanations, many prominent theorists still maintain that hypnotic effects are attributable to a special, altered state of consciousness (Beahrs, 1983; Fromm, 1979, 1992; Hilgard, 1986). These theorists argue that it is doubtful that role playing can explain all hypnotic phenomena. For instance, they assert that even the most cooperative subjects are unlikely to endure surgery without a drug anesthetic just to please their physician and live up to their expected role.

Of late, the most influential explanation of hypnosis as an altered state of awareness has been offered by Ernest Hilgard (1986, 1992). According to Hilgard, hypnosis creates a *dissociation* in consciousness. **Dissociation is a splitting off of mental processes into two separate, simultaneous streams of awareness.** In other words, Hilgard theorizes that hypnosis splits consciousness into two streams. One stream is in communication with the hypnotist and the external world, while the other is a difficult-to-detect "hidden observer." Hilgard believes that many

Some feats performed under hypnosis can be performed equally well by nonhypnotized subjects. Here the "Amazing Kreskin" demonstrates that proper positioning is the only requirement for the famous human plank feat.

hypnotic effects are a product of this divided consciousness. For instance, he suggests that a hypnotized subject might appear unresponsive to pain because the pain isn't registered in the portion of consciousness that communicates with other people.

One appealing aspect of Hilgard's theory is that *divided consciousness* is a common, normal experience. For example, people will often drive a car a great distance, responding to traffic signals and other cars, with no recollection of having consciously done so. In such cases, consciousness is clearly divided between driving and the person's thoughts about other matters. Interestingly, this common experience has long been known as *highway hypnosis*. In this condition, there even is an "amnesia" for the component of consciousness that drove the car, similar to posthypnotic amnesia. In summary, Hilgard presents hypnosis as a plausible variation in consciousness that has continuity with everyday experience.

The debate about whether hypnosis involves an altered or a normal state of consciousness appears likely to continue for the foreseeable future (Kihlstrom, 1998a; Kirsch & Lynn, 1998). As you will see momentarily, a similar debate has dominated the scientific discussion of meditation.

"Many psychologists argue that the hypnotic trance is a mirage. It would be unfortunate if this skeptical view were to gain such popularity that the benefits of hypnosis are denied to the numbers of those who could be helped."
ERNEST HILGARD

Meditation: Pure Consciousness or Relaxation?

Recent years have seen growing interest in the ancient discipline of meditation. **Meditation refers to a family of practices that train attention to heighten awareness and bring mental processes under greater voluntary control.** In North America, the most widely practiced approaches to meditation are those associated with yoga, Zen, and transcendental meditation (TM). All three are rooted in Eastern religions (Hinduism, Buddhism, and Taoism). However, meditation has been practiced throughout history as an element of all religious

and spiritual traditions, including Judaism and Christianity. Moreover, the practice of meditation can be largely divorced from religious beliefs. In fact, most Americans who meditate have only vague ideas regarding its religious significance. Of interest to psychology is the fact that meditation involves a deliberate effort to alter consciousness.

Most meditative techniques are deceptively simple. For example, in TM a person is supposed to sit in a comfortable position with eyes closed and silently focus attention on a *mantra*. A mantra is a specially assigned Sanskrit word that is personalized for each meditator. This exercise in mental self-discipline is to be practiced twice daily for about 20 minutes. The technique has been described as "diving from the active surface of the mind to its quiet depths" (Bloomfield & Kory, 1976, p. 49). Most proponents of TM believe that it involves an altered state of "pure consciousness." Many skeptics counter that meditation is simply an effective relaxation technique. Let's look at the evidence.

What happens when an experienced meditator goes into the meditative state? An intriguing finding in many studies is that alpha waves and theta waves become more prominent in EEG recordings (Fenwick, 1987). Most studies also find that subjects' heart rate, respiration rate, oxygen consumption, and carbon dioxide elimination decline (see Figure 5.9). Many researchers have also observed increases in

skin resistance and decreases in blood lactate—physiological indicators associated with relaxation (Davidson, 1976; Dillbeck & Orme-Johnson, 1987; Woolfolk, 1975). Taken together, these changes suggest that meditation leads to a potentially beneficial physiological state characterized by suppression of bodily arousal.

However, some researchers argue that many systematic relaxation training procedures can produce similar results (Shapiro, 1984). Hence, there is debate about whether the physiological changes associated with meditation are unique to it (Holmes, 1987).

The evidence on the long-term effects of meditation is also controversial. Some studies have found that meditation can improve mood, lessen fatigue, and reduce anxiety and drug abuse (Carrington, 1987; Eppley, Abrams, & Shear, 1989; Gelderloos et al., 1991). Studies also suggest that meditation is associated with improved physical health (Orme-Johnson, 1987), superior mental health (Alexander, Rainforth, & Gelderloos, 1991), and even increased longevity among the elderly (Alexander et al., 1989). Research also indicates that meditation may have value in reducing the effects of stress (Anderson et al., 1999; Winzelberg & Luskin, 1999). Some psychologists argue that at least some of these effects may be just as attainable through systematic relaxation or other mental focusing procedures (Shapiro, 1984; Smith, 1975). Critics also wonder whether placebo effects, sampling bias, and other methodological problems may contribute to some of the reported benefits of meditation (Shapiro, 1987).

In summary, it seems safe to conclude that meditation is a potentially worthwhile relaxation strategy. And it's possible that meditation involves more than mere relaxation, as TM advocates insist. At present, however, there is little evidence that meditation produces a unique state of "pure consciousness."

Figure 5.9

The suppression of physiological arousal during transcendental meditation. The physiological changes shown in the graph are evidence of physical relaxation during the meditative state. However, such changes can also be produced by systematic relaxation procedures. (Redrawn from illustration on p. 86 by Lorelle A. Raboni of *Scientific American*, *226*, 85-90, Feb. 1972. From "The Physiology of Meditation," by R. K. Wallace and H. Benson. Copyright © 1972 by Scientific American, Inc.)

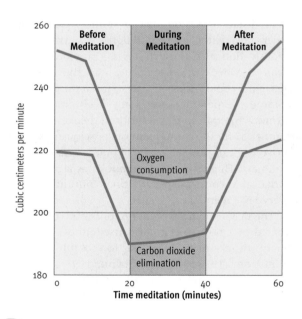

Altering Consciousness with Drugs

Like hypnosis and meditation, drugs are commonly used in deliberate efforts to alter consciousness. In this section, we focus on the use of drugs for nonmedical purposes, commonly referred to as "drug abuse" or "recreational drug use." Drug abuse reaches into every corner of American society. Recreational drug use involves personal, moral, political, and legal issues that are not matters for science to resolve. However, the more knowledgeable you are about drugs, the more informed your decisions and opinions about them will be. Accordingly, this section describes the types of drugs that are most

commonly used for recreational purposes and summarizes their effects on consciousness, behavior, and health.

Principal Abused Drugs and Their Effects

The drugs that people use recreationally are termed *psychoactive*. **Psychoactive drugs are chemical substances that modify mental, emotional, or behavioral functioning.** Not all psychoactive drugs produce effects that lead to recreational use.

Generally, people prefer drugs that elevate their mood or produce other pleasurable alterations in consciousness.

The principal types of recreational drugs are described in Table 5.3. The table lists representative drugs in each of six categories. It also summarizes how the drugs are taken, their medical uses, their effects on consciousness, and their common side effects (based on Julien, 1998; Levinthal, 1999; Lowinson et al., 1997). The six categories of psychoactive drugs that we will focus on are narcotics, sedatives, stimulants, hallucinogens, cannabis, and alcohol.

Narcotics, **or** ***opiates,*** **are drugs derived from opium that are capable of relieving pain.** The main drugs in this category are heroin and morphine, although less potent opiates such as codeine, Demerol, and methadone are also abused. In sufficient dosages these drugs can produce an overwhelming sense of euphoria or well-being. This euphoric effect has a relaxing, "Who cares?" quality that makes the high an attractive escape from reality.

CONCEPT CHECK 5.2

Relating EEG Activity to Variations in Consciousness

Early in the chapter we emphasized the intimate relationship between brain activity and variations in consciousness. Check your understanding of this relationship by indicating the kind of EEG activity (alpha, beta, theta, or delta) that would probably be dominant in each of the following situations. The answers are in Appendix A.

_____ **1.** You are playing a video game.
_____ **2.** You are deep in meditation.
_____ **3.** You have just fallen asleep.
_____ **4.** You are sleepwalking across the lawn.
_____ **5.** You are a novice typist, practicing your typing.

Sedatives **are sleep-inducing drugs that tend to decrease central nervous system activation and behavioral activity.** Over the years, the most widely abused sedatives have been the *barbiturates,* which are compounds derived from barbituric acid. People abusing sedatives, or "downers," generally consume larger doses than are prescribed for medical purposes. The desired effect is a euphoria similar to that

Table 5.3 Psychoactive Drugs: Methods of Ingestion, Medical Uses, and Effects

Drugs	Methods of Ingestion	Principal Medical Uses	Desired Effects	Short-Term Side Effects
Narcotics (opiates) Morphine Heroin	Injected, smoked, oral	Pain relief	Euphoria, relaxation, anxiety reduction, pain relief	Lethargy, drowsiness, nausea, impaired coordination, impaired mental functioning, constipation
Sedatives Barbiturates (e.g., Seconal) Nonbarbiturates (e.g., Quaalude)	Oral, injected	Sleeping pill, anticonvulsant	Euphoria, relaxation, anxiety reduction, reduced inhibitions	Lethargy, drowsiness, severely impaired coordination, impaired mental functioning, emotional swings, dejection
Stimulants Amphetamines Cocaine	Oral, sniffed, injected, freebased, smoked	Treatment of hyperactivity and narcolepsy, local anesthetic (cocaine only)	Elation, excitement, increased alertness, increased energy, reduced fatigue	Increased blood pressure and heart rate, increased talkativeness, restlessness, irritability, insomnia, reduced appetite, increased sweating and urination, anxiety, paranoia, increased aggressiveness, panic
Hallucinogens LSD Mescaline Psilocybin	Oral	None	Increased sensory awareness, euphoria, altered perceptions, hallucinations, insightful experiences	Dilated pupils, nausea, emotional swings, paranoia, jumbled thought processes, impaired judgment, anxiety, panic reaction
Cannabis Marijuana Hashish THC	Smoked, oral	Treatment of glaucoma; other uses under study	Mild euphoria, relaxation, altered perceptions, enhanced awareness	Bloodshot eyes, dry mouth, reduced short-term memory, sluggish motor coordination, sluggish mental functioning, anxiety
Alcohol	Drinking	None	Mild euphoria, relaxation, anxiety reduction, reduced inhibitions	Severely impaired coordination, impaired mental functioning, increased urination, emotional swings, depression, quarrelsomeness, hangover

produced by drinking large amounts of alcohol. Feelings of tension or dejection are replaced by a relaxed, pleasant state of intoxication, accompanied by loosened inhibitions.

Stimulants **are drugs that tend to increase central nervous system activation and behavioral activity.** Stimulants range from mild, widely available drugs, such as caffeine and nicotine, to stronger, carefully regulated ones, such as cocaine. We will focus on cocaine and amphetamines. Cocaine is a natural substance that comes from the coca shrub. In contrast, amphetamines ("speed") are synthesized in a pharmaceutical laboratory. Cocaine and amphetamines have fairly similar effects, except that cocaine produces a briefer high. Stimulants produce a euphoria very different from that created by narcotics or sedatives. They produce a buoyant, elated, energetic, "I can conquer the world!" feeling accompanied by increased alertness. In recent years, cocaine and amphetamines have become available in much more potent (and dangerous) forms than before. "Freebasing" is a chemical treatment used to extract nearly pure cocaine from ordinary street cocaine. "Crack" is the most widely distributed by-product of this process, consisting of chips of pure cocaine that are usually smoked. Amphetamines are increasingly sold as a crystalline powder, called "crank," that may be snorted or injected intravenously. Drug dealers are also marketing a smokable form of methamphetamine called "ice."

Hallucinogens **are a diverse group of drugs that have powerful effects on mental and emotional functioning, marked most prominently by distortions in sensory and perceptual experience.** The principal hallucinogens are LSD, mescaline, and psilocybin. These drugs have similar effects, although they vary in potency. Hallucinogens produce euphoria, increased sensory awareness, and a distorted sense of time. In some users, they lead to profound, dreamlike, "mystical" feelings that are difficult to describe. The latter effect is why they have been used in religious ceremonies for centuries in some cultures. Unfortunately, at the other end of the emotional spectrum hallucinogens can also produce nightmarish feelings of anxiety and paranoia, commonly called a "bad trip."

Cannabis **is the hemp plant from which marijuana, hashish, and THC are derived.** Marijuana is a mixture of dried leaves, flowers, stems, and seeds taken from the plant. Hashish comes from the plant's resin. Smoking is the usual route of ingestion for both marijuana and hashish. THC, the active chemical ingredient in cannabis, can be synthesized for research purposes (for example, to give to animals, who can't very well smoke marijuana). When smoked, cannabis has an immediate impact that may last several hours. The desired effects of the drug are a mild, relaxed euphoria and enhanced sensory awareness.

Alcohol **encompasses a variety of beverages containing ethyl alcohol,** such as beers, wines, and distilled spirits. The concentration of ethyl alcohol varies from about 4% in most beers up to 40% in 80-proof liquor, and occasionally more in higher-proof liquors. When people drink heavily, the central effect is a relaxed euphoria that temporarily boosts self-esteem, as problems seem to melt away and inhibitions diminish. Alcohol is the most widely used recreational drug in our society. Because alcohol is legal, many people use it casually without even thinking of it as a drug.

Heavy drinking is particularly prevalent on college campuses, according to a large-scale survey by researchers at the Harvard School of Public Health (Wechsler et al., 1994). Unfortunately the survey also indicated that drinking contributes to many social problems in college life. With their inhibitions released, some drinkers become argumentative and prone to aggression. In the Harvard survey of over 17,000 undergraduates, 34% of the students from "heavy drinking" schools reported that they had been insulted or humiliated by a drunken student, 20% had experienced serious arguments, and 13% had been pushed or assaulted (Wechsler et al.,

Web Link 5.5

Web of Addictions
From the earliest days of the World Wide Web, this page at The Well has been regularly recognized as a primary source for accurate and responsible information about alcohol and other drugs.

Figure **5.10**

Detecting a drinking problem. Experts estimate that as many as 19 million people in the United States may have a drinking problem (Winick, 1992). However, facing the reality that one has a problem with alcohol is always difficult. This list of the chief warning signs associated with problem drinking is intended to facilitate this process. (Figure 5.15 from *Health and Wellness*, Third Edition, by Edlin and Golanty, p. 294. Copyright © 1992, Jones & Bartlett Publishers, Inc. Reprinted with permission.)

Warning Signs of Problem Drinking or Alcoholism

1. Gulping drinks.

2. Drinking to modify uncomfortable feelings.

3. Personality or behavioral changes after drinking.

4. Getting drunk frequently.

5. Experiencing "blackouts"—not being able to remember what happened while drinking.

6. Frequent accidents or illness as a result of drinking.

7. Priming—preparing yourself with alcohol before a social gathering at which alcohol is going to be served.

8. Not wanting to talk about the negative consequences of drinking (avoidance).

9. Preoccupation with alcohol.

10. Focusing social situations around alcohol.

11. Sneaking drinks or clandestine drinking.

1994). Worse yet, alcohol appears to contribute to about 90% of student rapes and 95% of violent crime on campus. Moreover, alcohol can contribute to reckless sexual behavior. In the Harvard survey, 41% of the binge drinkers reported that they had unplanned sex due to drinking, and 22% indicated that their drinking had led to unprotected sex. And, as you might expect, heavier drinking is associated with poorer academic performance among college students (Gliksman et al., 1997; Lall & Schandler, 1991). Some warning signs associated with problem drinking are summarized in Figure 5.10.

Factors Influencing Drug Effects

The drug effects summarized in Table 5.3 are the *typical* ones. Drug effects can vary from person to person and even for the same person in different situations. The impact of any drug depends in part on the user's age, mood, motivation, personality, previous experience with the drug, body weight, and physiology. The dose and potency of a drug, the method of administration, and the setting in which a drug is taken also are likely to influence its effects (Leavitt, 1995). Our theme of *multifactorial causation* clearly applies to the effects of drugs.

So, too, does our theme emphasizing the *subjectivity of experience*. Expectations are potentially powerful factors that can influence the user's perceptions of a drug's effects. You may recall from our discussion of placebo effects in Chapter 2 that some people who are misled to *think* that they are drinking alcohol show signs of intoxication (Wilson, 1982). If people expect a drug to make them feel giddy, serene, or profound, their expectation may contribute to the feelings they experience.

A drug's effects can also change as the person's body develops a *tolerance* to the chemical. **Tolerance refers to a progressive decrease in a person's responsiveness to a drug as a result of continued use.** Tolerance usually leads people to consume larger and larger doses of a drug to attain the effects they desire. Most drugs produce tolerance, but some do so more rapidly than others. For example, tolerance to alcohol usually builds slowly, while tolerance to heroin increases much more quickly. Table 5.4 indicates whether various categories of drugs tend to produce tolerance rapidly or gradually.

Mechanisms of Drug Action

Most drugs have effects that reverberate throughout the body. However, psychoactive drugs work primarily by altering neurotransmitter activity in the brain. As we discussed in Chapter 3, *neurotransmitters* are chemicals that transmit information between neurons at junctions called synapses.

The actions of amphetamines illustrate how drugs have selective, multiple effects on neurotransmitter activity. Amphetamines exert their effects on two of the monoamine neurotransmitters: norepinephrine (NE) and dopamine (DA). Indeed, the name amphet-*amines* reflects the kinship between these drugs and the monoa*mines*. Amphetamines appear to have two key effects at DA and NE synapses (Cooper, Bloom, & Roth, 1996; Snyder, 1996), which are summarized in Figure 5.11 on the next page. First, they increase the release of dopamine and norepinephrine by

Table 5.4   Psychoactive Drugs: Tolerance, Dependence, Potential for Fatal Overdose, and Health Risks

Drugs	Tolerance	Risk of Physical Dependence	Risk of Psychological Dependence	Fatal Overdose Potential	Health Risks
Narcotics (opiates)	Rapid	High	High	High	Infectious diseases, accidents, immune suppression
Sedatives	Rapid	High	High	High	Accidents
Stimulants	Rapid	Moderate	High	Moderate to high	Sleep problems, malnutrition, nasal damage, hypertension, respiratory disease, stroke, liver disease, heart attack
Hallucinogens	Gradual	None	Very low	Very low	Accidents
Cannabis	Gradual	None	Low to moderate	Very low	Accidents, lung cancer, respiratory disease, pulmonary disease
Alcohol	Gradual	Moderate	Moderate	Low to high	Accidents, liver disease, malnutrition, brain damage, neurological disorders, heart disease, stroke, hypertension, ulcers, cancer, birth defects

Figure **5.11**

Amphetamines and neurotransmitters. Like other drugs, amphetamines alter neurotransmitter activity. Depicted here are two ways in which amphetamines appear to increase dopamine (DA) and norepinephrine (NE) activity.

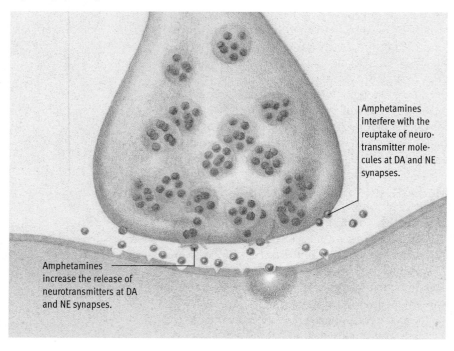

Amphetamines interfere with the reuptake of neurotransmitter molecules at DA and NE synapses.

Amphetamines increase the release of neurotransmitters at DA and NE synapses.

Figure **5.12**

The "reward pathway" in the brain. The mesolimbic dopamine pathway is highlighted in this diagram. Recreational drugs affect a variety of neurotransmitter systems, but theorists believe that heightened dopamine activity in this pathway is responsible for the reinforcing effects of most abused drugs. The mesolimbic dopamine pathway probably does not mediate all forms of reward, but it does appear to play a central role in drug-induced pleasure. (Adapted from "Drug Abuse and Addiction as Biomedical Problems," by A. I. Leshner, *Hospital Practice*, April, 2-4, 1997.)

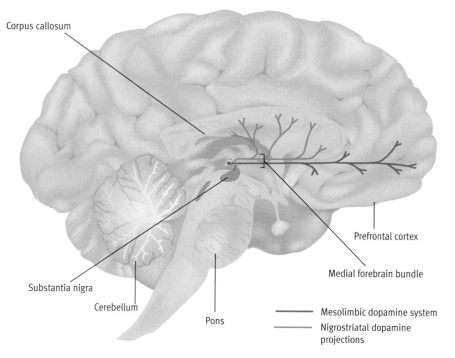

Corpus callosum

Prefrontal cortex

Medial forebrain bundle

Substantia nigra

Cerebellum

Pons

Mesolimbic dopamine system

Nigrostriatal dopamine projections

presynaptic neurons. Second, they interfere with the reuptake of DA and NE from synaptic clefts. These actions serve to increase the levels of dopamine and norepinephrine at the affected synapses. Cocaine shares some of these actions, which is why cocaine and amphetamines produce similar stimulant effects.

Sedatives and alcohol appear to exert many of their key effects at synapses releasing a neurotransmitter called GABA (Brady, Myrick, & Malcolm, 1999). The convergence of alcohol and sedatives on the same synapses probably explains why these drugs are *synergistic* when taken at the same time. That is, their combined effect is greater than the sum of their individual effects. Synergistic effects explain why mixing alcohol and sedatives is so dangerous. The combination of these drugs has caused many fatal overdoses by depressing CNS activity excessively.

The discovery of endorphins and special receptor sites in the brain for opiate drugs has led to new insights about the actions of narcotic drugs, although much remains to be learned (see Chapter 3). These drugs apparently bind to specific subtypes of opiate receptors, and their actions at these receptor sites indirectly elevate dopamine activity (Koob & Bloom, 1988; Stine & Kosten, 1999). Neuroscientists' understanding of how LSD works remains relatively primitive, but altered activity at certain types of serotonin receptors may be critical (Pechnick & Ungerleider, 1997). Scientists have recently found receptors in the brain for THC, the active chemical ingredient in marijuana (Stephens, 1999). They have also found an internally produced chemical, christened *anandamide* (from a Sanskrit word for "internal bliss"), that activates these receptors (Wiley, 1999). The discovery of this endogenous cannabinoid promises to gradually shed new light on how marijuana produces its effects.

Although specific drugs exert their initial effects in the brain on a wide variety of neurotransmitter systems, many theorists believe that virtually all abused drugs eventually increase activity in a particular neural pathway, called the *mesolimbic dopamine pathway*. This neural circuit, which runs from the midbrain, through part of the limbic system, and on to the prefrontal cortex (see Figure 5.12), has been characterized as a "reward pathway." Increased dopamine release along this pathway is thought to be the principal source of the reinforcing effects of most abused drugs (Gardner, 1997; Koob, 1997; Self, 1997). Whether changes in this neural circuit also play a role in the *addictive* properties of abused drugs (the craving experienced by users) remains to be seen (Volkow, 1997).

Drug Dependence

People can become either physically or psychologically dependent on a drug. Physical dependence is a common problem with narcotics, sedatives, and alcohol and is an occasional problem with stimulants. *Physical dependence* **exists when a person must continue to take a drug to avoid withdrawal illness.** The symptoms of withdrawal illness depend on the specific drug. Withdrawal from heroin, barbiturates, and alcohol can produce fever, chills, tremors, convulsions, vomiting, cramps, diarrhea, and severe aches and pains. Withdrawal from stimulants leads to a more subtle syndrome, marked by fatigue, apathy, irritability, depression, and disorientation.

Psychological dependence **exists when a person must continue to take a drug to satisfy intense mental and emotional craving.** Psychological dependence is more subtle than physical dependence, but the need it creates can be powerful. Cocaine, for instance, can produce an overwhelming psychological need for continued use. Psychological dependence is possible with all recreational drugs, although it seems rare for hallucinogens.

Both types of dependence are established gradually with repeated use of a drug. Drugs vary in their potential for creating either physical or psychological dependence. Table 5.4 provides estimates of the risk of each kind of dependence for the six categories of recreational drugs covered in our discussion.

Drugs and Physical Health

Recreational drug use can affect physical health in a variety of ways. The three principal risks are overdose, tissue damage (direct effects), and health-impairing behavior that results from drug use (indirect effects).

Overdose

Any drug can be fatal if a person takes enough of it, but some drugs are much more dangerous than others. Table 5.4 shows estimates of the risk of accidentally consuming a *lethal* overdose of each listed drug. Drugs that are CNS depressants—sedatives, narcotics, and alcohol—carry the greatest risk of overdose. It's important to remember that these drugs are synergistic with each other, so many overdoses involve lethal *combinations* of CNS depressants. What happens when a person overdoses on these drugs? The respiratory system usually grinds to a halt, producing coma, brain damage, and death within a brief period.

Fatal overdoses with CNS stimulants usually involve a heart attack, stroke, or cortical seizure. Deaths due to overdoses of stimulant drugs used to be relatively infrequent (Kalant & Kalant, 1979). However, cocaine overdoses have increased sharply as more people have experimented with more potent forms of cocaine, such as crack (Gold, 1997).

Direct Physical Effects

In some cases, drugs cause tissue damage directly. For example, snorting cocaine can damage nasal membranes. Cocaine can also alter cardiovascular functioning in ways that increase the risk of heart attack and stroke, and crack smoking is associated with a host of respiratory problems (Kerfoot, Sakoulas, & Hyman, 1996; Weaver & Schnoll, 1999). Long-term, excessive alcohol consumption is associated with an elevated risk for a wide range of serious health problems, including liver damage, ulcers, hypertension, stroke, heart disease, neurological disorders, and some types of cancer (Goodwin & Gabrielli, 1997; Moak & Anton, 1999). The health risks of marijuana have generated considerable debate in recent years. Many reported dangers appear to have been exaggerated in the popular press, but the evidence does suggest that heavy use of marijuana increases the chances for respiratory and pulmonary diseases, including lung cancer (Grinspoon & Bakalar, 1997; Stephens, 1999).

Indirect Behavioral Effects

The negative effects of drugs on physical health are often indirect results of the drugs' impact on behavior. For instance, people using stimulants often do not eat or sleep properly. Sedatives increase the

Web Link 5.6

National Institute of Alcohol Abuse and Alcoholism
Among the many research sources here are the entire collection of the bulletin *Alcohol Alert*, issued since 1988 on specific topics related to alcoholism, and *ETOH* Database, a searchable repository of more than 1000,000 records on alcoholism and alcohol abuse.

CONCEPT CHECK 5.3

Recognizing the Unique Characteristics of Commonly Abused Drugs

From our discussion of the principal abused drugs, it is clear that considerable overlap exists among the categories of drugs in terms of their methods of ingestion, medical uses, desired effects, and short-term side effects. Each type of drug, however, has at least one or two characteristics that make it different from the other types. Check your understanding of the unique characteristics of each type of drug by indicating which of them has the characteristics listed below. Choose from the following: (a) narcotics, (b) sedatives, (c) stimulants, (d) hallucinogens, (e) cannabis, and (f) alcohol. You'll find the answers in Appendix A.

_____ **1.** Increases alertness and energy, reduces fatigue.
_____ **2.** No recognized medical use. May lead to insightful or "mystical" experiences.
_____ **3.** Used as a "sleeping pill" because it reduces CNS activity.
_____ **4.** Contributes to 40% of all traffic fatalities.
_____ **5.** Derived from opium. Used for pain relief.
_____ **6.** Most likely health risk is respiratory and pulmonary disease.

risk of accidental injuries because they severely impair motor coordination. People who abuse downers often trip down stairs, fall off stools, and suffer other mishaps. Many drugs impair driving ability, increasing the risk of automobile accidents. Alcohol, for instance, may contribute to roughly 40% of all automobile fatalities (Liu et al., 1997). Intravenous drug users risk contracting infectious diseases that can be spread by unsterilized needles, including AIDS.

The major health risks (other than overdose) of various recreational drugs are listed in the sixth column of Table 5.4. As you can see, alcohol appears to have the most diverse negative effects on physical health. The irony, of course, is that alcohol is the only recreational drug listed that is legal.

Putting It in Perspective

This chapter highlights four of our unifying themes. First, we can see how psychology evolves in a sociohistorical context. Research on consciousness dwindled to almost nothing after John B. Watson (1913, 1919) and others redefined psychology as the science of behavior. However, in the 1960s, people began to turn inward, showing a new interest in altering consciousness through drug use, meditation, hypnosis, and biofeedback. Psychologists responded to these social trends by beginning to study variations in consciousness in earnest. This shift shows how social forces can have an impact on psychology's evolution.

A second theme that predominates in this chapter is the idea that people's experience of the world is highly subjective. We encountered this theme at the start of the chapter when we discussed the difficulty that people have describing their states of consciousness. The subjective nature of consciousness was apparent elsewhere in the chapter, as well. For instance, we found that the alterations of consciousness produced by drugs depend significantly on personal expectations.

Third, we saw once again how culture molds some aspects of behavior. Although the basic physiological process of sleep appears largely invariant from one society to another, culture influences certain aspects of sleep habits and has a dramatic impact on whether people remember their dreams and how they interpret and feel about their dreams. If not for space constraints, we might also have discussed cross-cultural differences in patterns of recreational drug use, which vary considerably from one society to the next.

Finally, the chapter illustrates psychology's theoretical diversity. We discussed conflicting theories about dreams, hypnosis, meditation, and the evolutionary bases of sleep and consciousness. For the most part, we did not see these opposing theories converging toward reconciliation, as we did in the previous chapter. However, it's important to emphasize that rival theories do not always merge neatly into tidy models of behavior. While it's always nice to resolve a theoretical debate, the debate itself can advance knowledge by stimulating and guiding empirical research.

Indeed, our upcoming Personal Application demonstrates that theoretical debates need not be resolved in order to advance knowledge. Many theoretical controversies and enduring mysteries remain in the study of sleep and dreams. Nonetheless, researchers have accumulated a great deal of practical information on these topics, which we'll discuss in the next few pages.

PERSONAL APPLICATION

Addressing Practical Questions About Sleep and Dreams

Indicate whether the following statements are "true" or "false."

_____ 1 Naps rarely have a refreshing effect.

_____ 2 Some people never dream.

_____ 3 When people cannot recall their dreams, it's because they are trying to repress them.

These assertions were all drawn from the Sleep and Dreams Information Questionnaire (Palladino & Carducci, 1984), which measures practical knowledge about sleep and dreams. Are they true or false? You'll see in this Application.

Common Questions About Sleep

How much sleep do people need? The average amount of daily sleep for young adults is 7.5 hours. However, people vary considerably in how long they sleep. Based on a synthesis of data from many studies, Webb (1992b) estimates that sleep time is distributed as shown in Figure 5.13. As the diagram shows, sleep needs vary from person to person. That said, many sleep experts believe that most people would function more effectively if they increased their amount of sleep (Maas, 1998).

Can short naps be refreshing? Some naps are beneficial and some are not. The effectiveness of napping varies from person to person. Also, the benefits of any specific nap depend on the time of day and the amount of sleep one has had recently (Dinges, 1993). In general, naps are not a very efficient way to sleep because you're often just getting into the deeper stages of sleep when your nap time is up. Napping can also disrupt nighttime sleep (Dinges, 1989). Nonetheless, most naps enhance subsequent alertness and reduce sleepiness (Gillberg et al., 1996; Hayashi, Watanabe, & Hori, 1999). Many highly productive people, including Thomas Edison, Winston

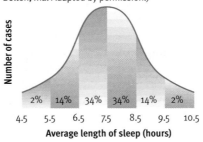

Figure 5.13

Variation in sleep needs. Based on data from a variety of sources, Webb (1992b) estimates that average sleep length among young adults is distributed normally, as shown here. Although most young adults sleep an average of 6.5 to 8.5 hours per night, some people need less and some people need more sleep. (Adapted from *Sleep, the Gentle Tyrant*, 2nd Ed. by Wilse B. Webb, 1992. Copyright © 1992 by Anker Publishing Co., Bolton, Ma. Adapted by permission.)

Churchill, and John F. Kennedy, have made effective use of naps. In conclusion, naps can be refreshing for many people, so the first statement opening this Application is false.

Is there such a thing as sleep learning? Yes, but it won't get you through college. Studies show that cognitive responding to external stimuli can occur during the lighter stages (1 and 2) of sleep (Ogilvie, Wilkinson, & Allison, 1989). This and other lines of evidence suggest that sleep learning is a legitimate possibility (Eich, 1990). However, studies indicate that people have minimal ability to assimilate information of any complexity into long-term memory while asleep (Badia, 1990). It would be nice if people could learn Spanish by listening to an audiotape while they slept. But the evidence indicates that trying to do so is pointless.

Can people learn to awaken without an alarm clock? Some people who have consistent sleep habits find themselves awakening on their own just before their alarm clock goes off. This phenomenon is fairly common and presumably reflects the influence of circadian rhythms. A smaller number of people claim that they can reliably awaken

themselves at predetermined, nonhabitual times. However, when some of these people have been tested carefully in sleep laboratories, their performance has been inconsistent (Zepelin, 1993). Thus, people who claim that they have an adjustable internal alarm clock are probably exaggerating its reliability.

What is the significance of snoring? Snoring is a common phenomenon that is seen in about 20% of adults (Lugaresi et al., 1994). Snoring increases after age 35, occurs in men more than women, and is more frequent among people who are overweight (Kryger, 1993; Stoohs et al., 1998). Many factors, including obesity, colds, allergies, smoking, and some drugs, can contribute to snoring, mainly by forcing people to breathe through their mouths while sleeping. Some people who snore loudly disrupt their own sleep as well as that of their bed partners. It can be difficult to prevent snoring in some people, whereas other people can reduce their snoring by simply losing weight or sleeping on their side instead of their back (Lugaresi et al., 1994). Snoring may seem like a trivial problem, but it is associated with sleep apnea (frequent gasping for air) and cardiovascular disease, and it may have more medical significance than most people realize (Dement & Vaughn, 1999).

What can be done to avoid sleep problems? There are many ways to improve your chances of getting satisfactory sleep (see Figure 5.14 on the next page). Most of them involve developing sensible daytime habits that won't interfere with sleep (Catalano, 1990; Dement & Vaughn, 1999; Maas, 1998; Zarcone, 1994). For example, if you've been having trouble sleeping at night, it's wise to avoid daytime naps, so you're tired when bedtime arrives. Some people find that daytime exercise helps them fall asleep more readily at bedtime (King et al., 1997).

It's wise to minimize consumption of stimulants such as caffeine or nicotine. Because coffee and cigarettes aren't prescription drugs,

Figure 5.14

Suggestions for better sleep. In his book *Power Sleep*, James Maas (1998) offers the following advice for people concerned about enhancing their sleep. Maas argues convincingly that good daytime habits can make all the difference in the world to the quality of one's sleep. (Adapted from *Power Sleep* by James B. Maas, PhD. Copyright © 1998 by James B. Mass, Ph. D. Reprinted by permission of Villard Books, a division of Random House, Inc.)

1. Reduce stress as much as possible
2. Exercise to stay fit.
3. Keep mentally stimulated during the day.
4. Eat a proper diet.
5. Stop smoking.
6. Reduce caffeine intake.
7. Avoid alcohol near bedtime.
8. Take a warm bath before bed.
9. Maintain a relaxing atmosphere in the bedroom.
10. Establish a bedtime ritual.
11. Have pleasurable sexual activity.
12. Clear your mind at bedtime.
13. Try some bedtime relaxation techniques.
14. Avoid trying too hard to get to sleep.
15. Learn to value sleep.

People typically get very upset when they have difficulty falling asleep. Unfortunately, the emotional distress tends to make it even harder for people to get to sleep.

© Topham/The Image Works

people don't appreciate how much the stimulants they contain can heighten physical arousal. Many foods (such as chocolate) and beverages (such as cola drinks) contain more caffeine than people realize. Also, bear in mind that ill-advised eating habits can interfere with sleep. Try to avoid going to bed hungry, uncomfortably stuffed, or soon after eating foods that disagree with you. It's also a good idea to try to establish a reasonably regular bedtime. This habit will allow you to take advantage of your circadian rhythm, so you'll be trying to fall asleep when your body is primed to cooperate.

What can be done about insomnia? First, don't panic if you run into a little trouble sleeping. An overreaction to sleep problems can begin a vicious circle of escalating problems, like that depicted in Figure 5.15. If you jump to the conclusion that you are becoming an insomniac, you may approach sleep with anxiety that will aggravate the problem. The harder you work at falling asleep, the less success you're likely to have. As noted earlier, temporary sleep problems are common and generally clear up on their own.

One sleep expert, Dianne Hales (1987), lists 101 suggestions for combating insomnia in her book *How to Sleep Like a Baby*. Many involve "boring yourself to sleep" by playing alphabet games, reciting poems, or listening to your clock. Another recommended strategy is to engage in some not-so-engaging activity. For instance, you might try reading your dullest textbook. It could turn out to be a superb sedative.

It's often a good idea to simply launch yourself into a pleasant daydream. This normal presleep process can take your mind off your difficulties. Whatever you think about, try to avoid ruminating about the current stresses and problems in your life. Research has shown that the tendency to ruminate is one of the key factors contributing to insomnia (Kales et al., 1984), as the data in Figure 5.16 show. Anything that relaxes you—whether it's music, meditation, prayer, a warm bath, or a systematic relaxation procedure—can aid you in falling asleep.

Common Questions About Dreams

Does everyone dream? Yes. Some people just don't *remember* any of their dreams. However, when these people are brought into a sleep lab and awakened from REM sleep, they report having been dreaming — much to their surprise (Hall & Nordby, 1972). Thus, statement 2 at the start of this Application is false.

Why don't some people remember their dreams? The evaporation of dreams appears to be quite normal. Given the lowered level of awareness during sleep, it's understandable that memory of dreams is mediocre. Dream recall is best when people are awakened during or soon after a dream (Goodenough, 1991). Most of the time, people who *do* recall dreams upon waking are remembering either *their* last dream from their final REM period or a dream that awakened them earlier in the night. Hobson's (1989) educated guess is that people probably forget 95%–99% of their dreams. This forgetting is natural and is not due to repression (statement 3 is also false). People who never remember their dreams probably have a sleep pattern that puts too

Figure 5.15

The vicious circle of anxiety and sleep difficulty. Anxiety about sleep difficulties leads to poorer sleep, which increases anxiety further, which in turn leads to even greater difficulties in sleeping.

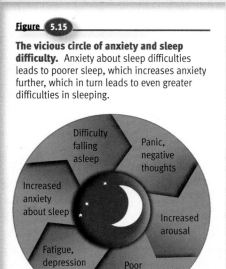

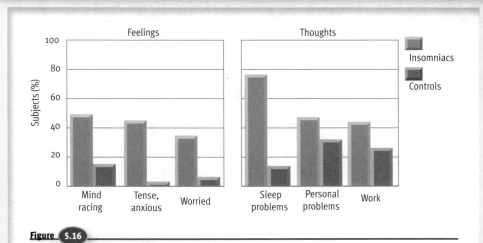

Figure 5.16

Thoughts and emotions associated with insomnia. This graph depicts the percentage of insomniacs and control subjects reporting various presleep feelings and thoughts. Insomniacs' tendency to ruminate about their problems contributes to their sleep difficulties. (Based on data from *Evaluation and Treatment of Insomnia*, by A. Kales and J.D. Kales, p. 95, 1984. Copyright © 1984 by Oxford University Press. Reprinted by permission.)

much time between their last REM/dream period and awakening, so even their last dream is forgotten.

Can people improve their recall of dreams? Yes. Most people don't have any significant reason to work at recalling their dreams, so they just let them float away. However, many people have found that they can remember more dreams if they merely place that goal uppermost in their minds as they go to sleep (Goodenough, 1991). Dream recall is also aided by making a point of trying to remember dreams upon first awakening, before opening one's eyes or getting out of bed.

Do dreams require interpretation? Yes, but interpretation may not be as difficult as generally assumed. People have long believed that dreams are symbolic and that it is necessary to interpret the symbols to understand the meaning of dreams. Freud, for instance, made a distinction between the *manifest content* and the *latent content* of a dream. **The *manifest content* consists of the plot of a dream at a surface level. The *latent content* refers to the hidden or disguised meaning of the events in the plot.** Thus, a Freudian therapist might equate such dream events as walking into a tunnel, mounting a horse, or riding a roller coaster with sexual intercourse. Freudian theorists assert that dream interpretation is a complicated task requiring considerable knowledge of symbolism.

However, many dream theorists argue that symbolism in dreams is less deceptive and mysterious than Freud thought (Faraday, 1974; Foulkes, 1985; Hall, 1979). Calvin Hall makes the point that dreams require some interpretation simply because they are more visual than verbal. That is, pictures need to be translated into ideas. According to Hall, dream symbolism is highly personal and the dreamer may be the person best equipped to decipher a dream. Unfortunately, you'll never know whether you're "correct," because there is no definitive way to judge the validity of different dream interpretations.

Could a shocking dream be fatal? According to folklore, if you fall from a height in a dream, you'd better wake up on the plunge downward, because if you hit the bottom the shock to your system will be so great that you will actually die in your sleep. Think about this one for a moment. *If* it were a genuine problem, who would have reported it? You can be sure that no one has ever testified to experiencing a fatal dream. This myth presumably exists because many people do awaken during the downward plunge, thinking they've averted a close call. A study by Barrett (1988–1989) suggests that dreams of one's own death are relatively infrequent. However, people do have such dreams—and live to tell about them.

Is Alcoholism a Disease?
The Power of Definitions

Alcoholism is a major problem in most, perhaps all, societies. As we saw in the main body of the chapter, alcohol is a dangerous drug. Alcoholism destroys countless lives, tears families apart, and is associated with an elevated risk for a host of physical maladies (Goodwin & Gabrielli, 1997). With roughly 19 million problem drinkers in the United States (Winick, 1992), it seems likely that alcoholism has touched the lives of a majority of Americans.

In almost every discussion about alcoholism someone will ask, "Is alcoholism a disease?" If alcoholism is a disease, it is a strange one, because the alcoholic is the most direct cause of his or her own sickness. If alcoholism is *not* a disease, then what else might it be? Over the course of history, alcoholism has been categorized under many labels, from a personal weakness to a crime, a sin, a mental disorder, and a physical illness (Meyer, 1996). Each of these definitions carries important personal, social, political, and economic implications.

Consider, for instance, the consequences of characterizing alcoholism as a disease. If that is the case, then alcoholics should be treated like diabetics, heart patients, or victims of other physical illnesses. That is, they should be viewed with sympathy and should be given appropriate medical and therapeutic interventions to foster recovery from their illness. These treatments should be covered by medical insurance and delivered by health care professionals. Just as important, if alcoholism is defined as a disease, it should lose much of its stigma. After all, we don't blame people with diabetes or heart disease for their illnesses. Yes, alcoholics admittedly contribute to their own disease (by drinking too much), but so do many victims of diabetes and heart disease (by eating the wrong foods and failing to control their weight). And, as is the case with many physical illnesses, one can inherit a genetic vulnerability to alcoholism

(Anthenelli & Schuckit, 1997), so it is difficult to argue that alcoholism is caused solely by one's behavior.

Alternatively, if alcoholism is defined as a personal failure or a moral weakness, alcoholics are less likely to be viewed with sympathy and compassion. They might be admonished to quit drinking, put in prison, or punished in some other way. These responses to their alcoholism would be administered primarily by the legal system rather than the health care system, as medical interventions are not designed to remedy moral failings. Obviously, the interventions that would be available would not be covered by health insurance, which would have enormous financial repercussions (for both health care providers and alcoholics).

The key point here is that definitions lie at the center of many complex debates, and they can have profound and far-reaching implications. People tend to think of definitions as insignificant, arbitrary, abstruse sets of words found buried in the obscurity of thick dictionaries compiled by ivory tower intellectuals. Well, much of this characterization may be accurate, but definitions are not insignificant. They are vested with enormous power to shape how people think about important issues. And an endless array of issues boil down to matters of definition. For example, the next time you hear people arguing over whether a particular movie is pornographic, whether the death penalty is cruel and unusual punishment, or whether spanking is child abuse, you'll find it helps to focus the debate on clarifying the definitions of the crucial concepts.

The Power to Make Definitions

So, how can we resolve the debate about whether alcoholism is a disease? Scientists generally try to resolve their debates by conducting research to achieve a better understanding of the phenomena under scrutiny.

You may have noticed already that the assertion "We need more research on this issue . . ." is a frequent refrain in this text. Is more research the answer in this case? For once, the answer is "no." There is no conclusive way to determine whether alcoholism is a disease. It is not as though there is a "right" answer to this question that we can discover through more and better research.

The question of whether alcoholism is a disease is a *matter of definition:* Does alcoholism fit the currently accepted definition of what constitutes a disease? If you consult medical texts or dictionaries, you will find that *disease is typically defined as an impairment in the normal functioning of an organism that alters its vital functions.* Given that alcoholism clearly impairs people's normal functioning and disrupts a variety of vital functions (see Figure 5.17), it seems reasonable to characterize it as a disease, and this has been the dominant view in the United States since the middle of the 20th century (Maltzman, 1994; Meyer, 1996). Still, many critics express vigorous doubts about the wisdom of defining alcoholism as a disease (Peele, 1989). They often raise a question that comes up frequently in arguments about definitions: Who should have the power to make the definition? In this case, the power lies in the hands of the medical community, which seems sensible, given that disease is a medical concept. But some critics argue that the medical community has a strong bias in favor of defining conditions as diseases because this creates new markets and fuels economic growth for the health industry (Nikelly, 1994). Thus, debate about whether alcoholism is a disease seems likely to continue for the indefinite future.

To summarize, definitions generally do not emerge out of research. They are typically crafted by experts or authorities in a specific field who try to reach a consensus about how to best define a particular concept. Thus, in analyzing the validity of a definition, you need to look not only at the definition itself but at where it came from. Who decided what the definition should be? Does the source of the definition seem legitimate and appropriate? Did the authorities who formulated the definition have any biases that should be considered?

Definitions, Labels, and Circular Reasoning

There is one additional point about definitions that is worth discussing. Perhaps because definitions are imbued with so much power, people have an interesting tendency to incorrectly use them as *explanations* for the phenomena they describe. This logical error, which equates *naming* something with *explaining* it, is sometime called the *nominal fallacy*. Names and labels that are used as explanations often sound quite reasonable at first. *But definitions do not really have any explanatory value; they simply specify what certain terms mean.* Consider an example. Let's say your friend, Frank, has a severe drinking problem. You are sitting around with some other friends discussing why Frank drinks so much. Rest assured, at least one of these friends will assert that "Frank drinks too much because he is an alcoholic." This is *circular reasoning,* which is just as useless as explaining that Frank is an alcoholic because he drinks too much. It tells us nothing about *why* Frank has a drinking problem. The diagnostic labels that are used in the classification of mental disorders—labels such as schizophrenia, depression, autism, and obsessive-compulsive disorder (see Chapter 14)—also seem to invite this type of circular reasoning. For example, people often say things like "That person is delusional because she is schizophrenic," or "He is afraid of small, enclosed places because he is claustrophobic." These statements may sound plausible, but they are no more logical or insightful than saying "She is a redhead because she has red hair." The logical fallacy of mistaking a label for an explanation will get us as far in our understanding as a cat gets in chasing its own tail.

Figure 5.17

Physiological malfunctions associated with alcoholism. This chart amply demonstrates that alcoholism is associated with a diverse array of physiological maladies. In and of itself, however, this information does not settle the argument about whether alcoholism should be regarded as a disease. It all depends on one's definition of what constitutes a disease. (From *Health and Wellness,* Third edition by Edlin and Golanty, 1992, p. 286. Copyright © 1992 by Jones & Bartlett Publishers, Inc. Reprinted by permission.)

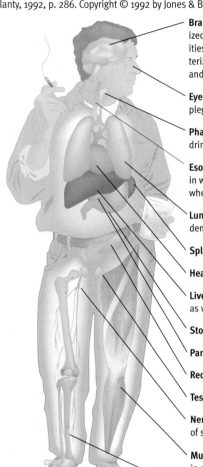

Brain Wernicke's syndrome, an acute condition characterized by ataxia, mental confusion, and ocular abnormalities; Korsakoff's syndrome, a psychotic condition characterized by impairment of memory and learning, apathy, and degeneration of the white brain matter

Eyes Tobacco-alcohol blindness; Wernicke's ophthalmoplegia, a reversible paralysis of the muscles of the eye

Pharynx Cancer of the pharynx increases tenfold for drinkers who smoke

Esophagus Esophagael varices, an irreversible condition in which the person can die by drowning in his own blood when the varices open

Lungs Lowered resistance thought to lead to greater incidence of tuberculosis, pneumonia, and emphysema

Spleen Hypersplenism

Heart Alcoholic cardiomyopathy, a heart condition

Liver Acute enlargement of liver, which is reversible, as well as irreversible alcoholic's liver (cirrhosis)

Stomach Gastritis and ulcers

Pancreas Acute and chronic pancreatitis

Rectum Hemorrhoids

Testes Atrophy of the testes

Nerves Polyneuritis, a condition characterized by loss of sensation

Muscles Alcoholic myopathy, a condition resulting in painful muscle contractions

Blood and bone marrow Coagulation defects and anemia

Table 5.5   Critical Thinking Skills Discussed in This Application

Skill	Description
Understanding the way definitions shape how people think about issues	The critical thinker appreciates the enormous power of definitions and the need to clarify definitions in efforts to resolve disagreements.
Identifying the source of definitions	The critical thinker recognizes the need to determine who has the power to make specific definitions and to evaluate their credibility.
Avoiding the nominal fallacy in working with definitions and labels	The critical thinker understands that labels do not have explanatory value.

REVIEW

Key Ideas

On the Nature of Consciousness
● Consciousness is the continually changing stream of mental activity. Some theorists believe that mental processes during sleep are more similar to waking thought processes than widely assumed. Consciousness clearly is adaptive, but the question of exactly why it evolved is open to debate. Variations in consciousness are related to brain activity, as measured by the EEG.

Biological Rhythms and Sleep
● Sleep is influenced by biological rhythms, especially 24-hour circadian rhythms. Exposure to light may reset biological clocks by affecting the activity of the suprachiasmatic nucleus and the pineal gland, which secretes melatonin.

● Being out of sync with circadian rhythms is one reason for jet lag and for the unpleasant nature of rotating shift work. Melatonin may have value in efforts to alleviate the effects of jet lag and rotating shift work, but there is little or no evidence for the other alleged benefits of this hormone.

The Sleep and Waking Cycle
● When you fall asleep, you evolve through a series of stages in cycles of approximately 90 minutes. During the REM stage you experience rapid eye movements, a brain wave that is characteristic of waking thought, and the bulk of your dreaming. The sleep cycle tends to be repeated about four times in a night, as REM sleep gradually becomes more predominant and NREM sleep dwindles.

● The REM portion of sleep declines during childhood, leveling off at around 20% during adolescence. During adulthood, slow-wave sleep declines. Culture appears to have little impact on the architecture of sleep, but it does influence sleeping arrangements and napping patterns. Hypotheses about the evolutionary bases of sleep focus on energy conservation, reduced exposure to predators, and restoration of depleted resources.

● The only consistent effect of sleep deprivation is sleepiness. However, increased sleepiness can contribute to work accidents and other mishaps. Insomnia involves three distinct patterns of sleep difficulty. Insomnia has a variety of causes. Sleeping pills generally are a poor solution for insomnia.

The World of Dreams
● Research on dream content indicates that dreams are not as exotic as widely believed. The content of one's dreams may be affected by events in one's life, as well as by external stimuli that are experienced during the dream.

● Dramatic variations occur across cultures in beliefs about the nature of dreams and their importance, dream recall, dream content, and dream interpretation. Theories of dreaming remain largely untested, and scientists do not really know why people dream.

Hypnosis: Altered Consciousness or Role Playing?
● People vary in their susceptibility to hypnosis. Among other things, hypnosis can produce anesthesia, sensory distortions, disinhibition, and posthypnotic amnesia. Theories of hypnosis view it either as an altered state of consciousness or as a normal state in which subjects assume a hypnotic role.

Meditation: Pure Consciousness or Relaxation?
● Evidence suggests that meditation can be beneficial. However, some experts suggest that the observed benefits are not unique to meditation and are a product of any effective relaxation procedure.

Altering Consciousness with Drugs
● The principal categories of abused drugs are narcotics, sedatives, stimulants, hallucinogens, cannabis, and alcohol. Although it's possible to describe the typical effects of various drugs, the actual effect on any individual depends on a host of factors, including subjective expectations and tolerance to the drug.

● Psychoactive drugs exert their main effects in the brain, where they alter neurotransmitter activity. The mesolimbic dopamine pathway may mediate the reinforcing effects of most abused drugs. Drugs vary in their potential for psychological and physical dependence. Recreational drug use can prove harmful to health by producing an overdose, by causing tissue damage, or by increasing health-impairing behavior.

Putting It in Perspective
● Four of our unifying themes were highlighted in this chapter. First, we saw how psychology's study of consciousness reflects concurrent social trends, showing that psychology evolves in a sociohistorical context. Second, we saw how states of consciousness are highly subjective. Third, we saw how culture molds some aspects of sleep and dreaming. Fourth, we saw extensive theoretical diversity that continues to generate vigorous debate about many issues in this area.

Personal Application • Addressing Practical Questions About Sleep and Dreams
● Sleep needs vary, and the value of short naps depends on many factors. Learning can occur during sleep, but it has little practical value. People can do many things to avoid or reduce sleep problems. People troubled by transient insomnia should avoid panic, pursue effective relaxation, and try distracting themselves.

● Everyone dreams, but some people cannot remember their dreams, probably because of the nature of their sleep cycle. Most theorists believe that dreams require some interpretation, but this may not be as complicated as once assumed.

Critical Thinking Application • Is Alcoholism a Disease? The Power of Definitions
● Like many questions, the issue of whether alcoholism should be regarded as a disease is a matter of definition. In evaluating the validity of a definition, one should look not only at the definition but also at where it came from. People have a tendency to use definitions as explanations for the phenomena they describe, but doing so involves circular reasoning.

Key Terms

Alcohol
Biological rhythms
Cannabis
Circadian rhythms
Consciousness
Dissociation
Electrocardiograph (EKG)
Electroencephalograph (EEG)
Electromyograph (EMG)
Electrooculograph (EOG)
Hallucinogens
Hypnosis
Insomnia
Latent content
Manifest content
Meditation
Narcotics

Non-REM (NREM) sleep
Opiates
Physical dependence
Psychoactive drugs
Psychological dependence
REM sleep
Sedatives
Slow-wave sleep
Stimulants
Tolerance

Key People

William Dement
Sigmund Freud
Calvin Hall
Ernest Hilgard
J. Alan Hobson

PRACTICE TEST

1. An EEG would indicate primarily _____ activity while you take this test.
   A. alpha
   B. beta
   C. delta
   D. theta

2. Readjusting your biological clock would be most difficult under which of the following circumstances?
   A. Flying west from Los Angeles to Hawaii
   B. Flying north from Miami to New York
   C. Flying east from Hawaii to Los Angeles
   D. Flying south from New York to Miami

3. As the sleep cycle evolves through the night, people tend to:
   A. spend more time in REM sleep and less time in NREM sleep.
   B. spend more time in NREM sleep and less time in REM sleep.
   C. spend a more or less equal amount of time in REM sleep and NREM sleep.
   D. spend more time in stage 4 sleep and less time in REM sleep.

4. Newborn infants spend about _____% of their sleep time in REM and adults spend about _____% of their sleep time in REM.
   A. 20; 50
   B. 50; 20
   C. 20; 20
   D. 50; 50

5. After being selectively deprived of REM sleep, people typically experience:
   A. hypochondriasis.
   B. Non-REM dysfunction.
   C. emotional breakdowns.
   D. a REM rebound effect.

6. Which of the following is not true of sleeping pills?
   A. Sleeping pills are an excellent long-range solution for all types of insomnia.
   B. There is some danger of overdose.
   C. Sleeping pills reduce the proportion of time spent in REM sleep.
   D. Sleeping pills gradually become less effective with continued use.

7. Which of the following is not true of cultural influences on dream experiences?
   A. The ability to recall dreams is fairly consistent across cultures.
   B. In some cultures, people are held responsible for their dream actions.
   C. In many cultures, dreams are seen as a window into the spiritual world.
   D. People in some cultures believe that dreams provide information about the future.

8. The activation-synthesis theory of dreaming contends that:
   A. dreams are simply the by-product of bursts of activity in the brain.
   B. dreams provide an outlet for energy invested in socially undesirable impulses.
   C. dreams represent the brain's attempt to process information taken in during waking hours.
   D. dreams are an attempt to restore a neurotransmitter balance within the brain.

9. A common driving experience is "highway hypnosis," in which one's consciousness seems to be divided between the driving itself and one's conscious train of thought. This phenomenon has been cited to support the idea that hypnosis is:
   A. an exercise in role playing.
   B. a dissociated state of consciousness.
   C. a goal-directed fantasy.
   D. not an altered state of consciousness.

10. Stimulant is to depressant as:
    A. cocaine is to sedative.
    B. mescaline is to crack cocaine.
    C. caffeine is to amphetamine.
    D. alcohol is to barbiturate.

11. Amphetamines work by increasing activity at _____ synapses in a variety of ways.
    A. GABA and glycine
    B. serotonin and dopamine
    C. acetylcholine
    D. norepinephrine and dopamine

12. Which of the following drugs would be most likely to result in a fatal overdose?
    A. LSD
    B. Mescaline
    C. Marijuana
    D. Barbiturates

13. Which of the following is a true statement about naps?
    A. Daytime naps invariably lead to insomnia.
    B. Daytime naps are invariably refreshing and an efficient way to rest.
    C. Daytime naps are not very efficient ways to sleep, but their effects are variable.
    D. Taking many naps during the day can substitute for a full night's sleep.

14. Peter rarely remembers his dreams. What can we say about Peter?
    A. Peter must be psychologically repressed.
    B. Peter obviously does not dream very much.
    C. Peter's dreams are probably not very memorable.
    D. Peter dreams, but he simply does not remember his dreams.

15. Definitions
    A. generally emerge out of research.
    B. often have great explanatory value.
    C. generally exert little influence over how people think.
    D. are usually constructed by experts or authorities in a specific field.

Answers

1	B	page 137	6	A	page 146	11	D	page 156
2	C	page 139	7	A	pages 147–148	12	D	pages 156–157
3	A	pages 141–143	8	A	pages 146–149	13	C	page 159
4	B	pages 142–143	9	B	pages 151–152	14	D	pages 160–161
5	D	page 145	10	A	pages 153–154	15	D	pages 162–163

INFOTRAC COLLEGE EDITION

Go to the Wadsworth Psychology Study Center for quiz questions, research updates, interactive exercises, and suggested readings in INFOTRAC related to this chapter:
http://psychology.wadsworth.com/product/0534593100s

CHAPTER 6

© Carl Vanderschuit/Index Stock Imagery

Learning

© Carl Vanderschuit/Index Stock Imagery

● You're sitting in the waiting room of your dentist's office. You cringe when you hear the whirring of a dental drill coming from the next room. ● A four-year-old boy pinches his hand in one of his toys and curses loudly. His mother looks up in dismay and says to his father, "Where did he pick up that kind of language?" ● A seal waddles across the stage, bows ceremoniously, and "doffs his cap" by flipping it into the air and catching it in his mouth. The spectators at the aquatic show clap appreciatively as the

trainer tosses the seal a fish as a reward. ● The crowd hushes as an Olympic diver prepares to execute her dive. In a burst of motion she propels herself into the air and glides smoothly through a dazzling corkscrew somersault.

What do all of these scenarios have in common? At first glance, very little. They are a diverse collection of events, some trivial, some impressive. However, they do share one common thread: *they all involve learning*. This may surprise you. When most people think of learning, they envision students reading textbooks or novices working to acquire a specific skill, such as riding a bicycle or skiing. Although these activities do involve learning, they represent only the tip of the iceberg in psychologists' eyes.

Learning refers to a relatively durable change in behavior or knowledge that is due to experience. This broad definition means that learning is one of the most fundamental concepts in all of psychology. Learning includes the acquisition of knowledge and skills, but it also shapes personal habits such as nailbiting, personality traits such as shyness, emotional responses such as a fear of storms, and personal preferences, such as a taste for tacos or a distaste for formal clothes. Most of your behavior is

the result of learning. If it were possible to strip away your learned responses, little behavior would be left. You would not be able to read this book, find your way home, or cook yourself a hamburger. You would be about as complex and exciting as a turnip.

Although you and I depend on learning, it is *not* an exclusively human process. Most organisms are capable of learning. Even the lowly flatworm can acquire a learned response. As this chapter unfolds, you may be surprised to see that much of the research on learning has been conducted using lower animals as subjects.

In this chapter, we will focus most of our attention on a specific kind of learning: conditioning. *Conditioning* involves learning associations between events that occur in an organism's environment. In investigating conditioning, psychologists study learning at a very fundamental level. This strategy has paid off with fruitful insights that have laid the foundation for the study of more complex forms of learning, including learning by means of observation. In our chapter Personal Application, you'll see how you can harness the principles of conditioning to improve your self-control. The Critical Thinking Application shows how conditioning procedures can be used to manipulate emotions.

Classical Conditioning

Do you go weak in the knees at the thought of standing on the roof of a tall building? Does your heart race when you imagine encountering a harmless garter snake? If so, you can understand, at least to some degree, what it's like to have a phobia. *Phobias are irrational fears of specific objects or situations.* Mild phobias are commonplace (Eaton, Dryman, & Weissman, 1991). Over the years, students in my classes have described their phobic responses to a diverse array of stimuli, including bridges, elevators, tunnels, heights, dogs, cats, bugs, snakes, professors, doctors, strangers, thunderstorms, and germs. If you have a phobia, you may have wondered how you managed to acquire such a foolish fear. Chances are, it was through classical conditioning (Ayres, 1998). *Classical conditioning is a type of learning in which a stimulus acquires the capacity to evoke a response that was originally evoked by another stimulus.* The process was first described in 1903 by Ivan Pavlov, and it is sometimes called *Pavlovian conditioning* in tribute to him.

Pavlov's Demonstration: "Psychic Reflexes"

Pavlov was a prominent Russian physiologist who did Nobel prize–winning research on digestion. Something of a "classic" himself, he was an absent-minded but brilliant professor obsessed with his research. Legend has it that Pavlov once reprimanded an assistant who arrived late for an experiment because of trying to avoid street fighting in the midst of the Russian Revolution. The assistant defended his tardiness, saying, "But Professor, there's a revolution going on with shooting in the streets!" Pavlov supposedly replied, "What the hell difference does a revolution make when you've work to do in the laboratory? Next time there's a revolution, get up earlier!" Apparently, dodging bullets wasn't an adequate excuse for delaying the march of scientific progress (Fancher, 1979; Gantt, 1975).

Pavlov was studying the role of saliva in the digestive processes of dogs when he stumbled onto what he called "psychic reflexes" (Pavlov, 1906). Like many great discoveries, Pavlov's was partly accidental, although he had the insight to recognize its significance. His subjects were dogs restrained in harnesses in an experimental chamber (see Figure 6.1). Their saliva was collected by means of a surgically implanted tube in the salivary gland. Pavlov would present meat powder to a dog and then collect the resulting saliva. As his research progressed, he noticed that dogs accustomed to the procedure would start salivating *before* the meat powder was presented. For instance, they would salivate in response to a clicking sound made by the device that was used to present the meat powder.

Intrigued by this unexpected finding, Pavlov decided to investigate further. To clarify what was happening, he paired the presentation of the meat powder with various stimuli that would stand out in the laboratory situation. For instance, he used a simple, auditory stimulus—the presentation of a tone. After the tone and the meat powder had been presented together a number of times, the tone was presented alone. What happened? The dogs responded by salivating to the sound of the tone alone.

"*Next time there's a revolution, get up earlier!*"
IVAN PAVLOV

Sovfoto/Eastfoto

Figure 6.1

Classical conditioning apparatus. An experimental arrangement similar to the one depicted here (taken from Yerkes & Morgulis, 1909) has typically been used in demonstrations of classical conditioning, although Pavlov's original setup (see inset) was quite a bit simpler. The dog is restrained in a harness. A tone is used as the conditioned stimulus (CS), and the presentation of meat powder is used as the unconditioned stimulus (UCS). The tube inserted into the dog's salivary gland allows precise measurement of its salivation response. (Inset) The less elaborate setup that Pavlov originally used to collect saliva on each trial is shown here. (Adapted from "The Method of Pavlov in Animal Psychology," by R. M. Yerkes and S. Morgulis, 1909, *Psychological Bulletin, 6,* 257–273. American Psychological Association.)

What was so significant about a dog salivating when a tone was sounded? The key is that the tone had started out as a *neutral* stimulus. That is, it did not originally produce the response of salivation. However, Pavlov managed to change that by pairing the tone with a stimulus (meat powder) that *did* produce the salivation response. Through this process, the tone acquired the capacity to trigger the response of salivation. What Pavlov had demonstrated was how stimulus-response associations—the basic building blocks of learning—are formed by events in an organism's environment. Based on this insight, he built a broad theory of learning that attempted to explain aspects of emotion, temperament, neuroses, and language (Windholz, 1997).

Terminology and Procedures 5a

There is a special vocabulary associated with classical conditioning. It often looks intimidating to the uninitiated, but it's really not all that mysterious. The bond Pavlov noted between the meat powder and salivation was a natural, unlearned association. It did not have to be created through conditioning. It is therefore called an *unconditioned* association. In unconditioned bonds, **the *unconditioned stimulus* (UCS) is a stimulus that evokes an unconditioned response without previous conditioning. The *unconditioned response (UCR)* is an unlearned reaction to an unconditioned stimulus that occurs without previous conditioning.**

In contrast, the link between the tone and salivation was established through conditioning. It is therefore called a *conditioned* association. In conditioned bonds, **the *conditioned stimulus (CS)* is a previously neutral stimulus that has, through conditioning, acquired the capacity to evoke a conditioned response. The *conditioned response (CR)* is a learned reaction to a conditioned stimulus that occurs because of previous conditioning.**

To avoid possible confusion, it is worth noting that the unconditioned response and conditioned response are virtually the same behavior, although there may be subtle differences between them. In Pavlov's initial demonstration, the unconditioned response and conditioned response were both salivation. When evoked by the UCS (meat powder), salivation was an unconditioned response. When evoked by the CS (the tone), salivation was a conditioned response. The procedures involved in classical conditioning are outlined in Figure 6.2.

Pavlov's "psychic reflex" came to be called the *conditioned reflex*. Classically conditioned responses have traditionally been characterized as reflexes

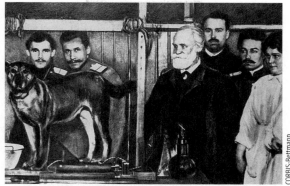

Surrounded by his research staff, the great Russian physiologist Ivan Pavlov (center, white beard) demonstrates his famous classical conditioning experiment with dogs.

CORBIS-Bettmann

Figure 6.2

The sequence of events in classical conditioning. As we encounter examples of classical conditioning throughout the book, we will see many diagrams like the one in the fourth panel, which summarizes the process.

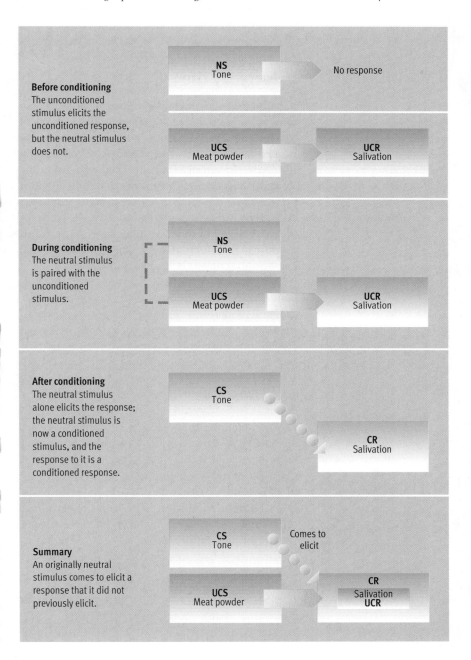

and said to be *elicited* (drawn forth) because most of them are relatively automatic or involuntary. However, research in recent decades has demonstrated that classical conditioning is involved in a wider range of human and animal behavior than previously appreciated, including some types of nonreflexive responding (Allan, 1998; Turkkan, 1989). Finally, a *trial* in classical conditioning consists of any presentation of a stimulus or pair of stimuli. Psychologists are interested in how many trials are required to establish a particular conditioned bond. The number needed to form an association varies considerably. Although classical conditioning generally proceeds gradually, it can occur quite rapidly, sometimes in just one pairing of the conditioned stimulus and unconditioned stimulus.

Classical Conditioning in Everyday Life

In laboratory experiments on classical conditioning, researchers have generally worked with extremely simple responses. Besides salivation, frequently studied favorites include eyelid closure, knee jerks, the flexing of various limbs, and fear responses. The study of such simple responses has proven both practical and productive. However, these responses do not even begin to convey the rich diversity of everyday behavior that is regulated by classical conditioning. Let's look at some examples of classical conditioning drawn from everyday life.

Conditioned Fear and Anxiety

Classical conditioning often plays a key role in shaping emotional responses such as fear and anxiety. Phobias are a good example of such responses. Case studies of patients suffering from phobias suggest that many irrational fears can be traced back to experiences that involve classical conditioning (Ayres, 1998; McAllister & McAllister, 1995). It is easy to imagine how such conditioning can occur outside of the laboratory. For example, a student of mine was troubled by a bridge phobia so severe that she couldn't drive on interstate highways because of all the viaducts that had to be crossed. She was able to pinpoint the source of her phobia as something that had happened during her childhood. Whenever her family drove to visit her grandmother, they had to cross a little-used, rickety, dilapidated bridge out in the countryside. Her father, in a misguided attempt at humor, made a major production out of these crossings. He would stop short of the bridge and carry on about the enormous danger. Obviously, he thought the bridge

was safe or he wouldn't have driven across it. However, the naive young girl was terrified by her father's scare tactics. Hence, the bridge became a conditioned stimulus eliciting great fear (see Figure 6.3). Unfortunately, the fear spilled over to all bridges. Forty years later she was still carrying the burden of this phobia. Although a number of processes besides conditioning can contribute to the development of phobias (Marks, 1987), it's clear that classical conditioning is responsible for a great many irrational fears.

Everyday anxiety responses that are less severe than phobias may also be products of classical conditioning. For instance, if you cringe when you hear the sound of a dentist's drill, this response is due to classical conditioning. In this case, the pain you have experienced from dental drilling is the UCS. This pain has been paired with the sound of the drill, which became a CS eliciting your cringe.

Other Conditioned Responses

Classical conditioning is not limited to producing unpleasant emotions such as fear and anxiety. Many pleasant emotional responses are also acquired through classical conditioning. Consider the following example, described by a 53-year-old woman who wrote a letter to newspaper columnist Bob Greene about the news that a company was bringing back a discontinued product—Beemans gum. She wrote:

That was the year (1949) I met Charlie. I guess first love is always the same. . . . Charlie and I went out a lot. He chewed Beemans gum and he smoked. . . . We would go to all the passion pits—the drive-in movies and the places to park. We did a lot of necking, but we always stopped at a certain point. Charlie wanted to get married when we got out of high school . . . [but] Charlie and I drifted apart. We both ended up getting married to different people.

Figure 6.3

Classical conditioning of a fear response. Many emotional responses that would otherwise be puzzling can be explained by classical conditioning. In the case of one young woman's bridge phobia, the fear originally elicited by her father's scare tactics has become a conditioned response to the stimulus of bridges.

Web Link 6.1

Behaviour Analysis
A multitude of annotated links, all focusing on learning through conditioning, have been gathered together at the excellent Psychology Centre site at Athabasca University (Alberta, Canada).

And the funny thing is . . . for years the combined smell of cigarette smoke and Beemans gum made my knees weak. Those two smells were Charlie to me. When I would smell the Beemans and the cigarette smoke, I could feel the butterflies dancing all over my stomach.

The writer clearly had a unique and long-lasting emotional response to the smell of Beemans gum and cigarettes. The credit for this *pleasant* response goes to classical conditioning (see Figure 6.4).

Classical conditioning affects not only overt behaviors but *physiological processes* as well. For example, studies have shown that the functioning of the immune system can be influenced by conditioning. Robert Ader and Nicholas Cohen (1981, 1984, 1993) have shown that classical conditioning procedures can lead to *immunosuppression*—a decrease in the production of antibodies. In a typical study, animals are injected with a drug (the UCS) that *chemically* causes immunosuppression while they are simultaneously given an unusual-tasting liquid to drink (the CS). Days later, after the chemical immunosuppression has ended, some of the animals are reexposed to the CS by giving them the unusual-tasting solution. Measurements of antibody production indicate that animals exposed to the CS show a reduced immune response (see Figure 6.5).

Studies have also demonstrated that classical conditioning can modulate *sexual arousal.* For example, research has shown that quail can be conditioned to become sexually aroused by a neutral, nonsexual stimulus—such as a red light—that has been paired with opportunities to copulate (Domjan, 1992, 1994). Conditioned stimuli can even elicit increased sperm release in male quail (Domjan, Blesbois, & Williams, 1998). Psychologists have long suspected that stimuli routinely paired with sex, such as seductive nightgowns, mood music, lit candles, and the like, probably become conditioned stimuli that elicit arousal, but this hypothesis is difficult to investigate with human subjects. Classical conditioning may also underlie the development of *fetishes* for inanimate objects. If quail can be conditioned to find a red light arousing, it seems likely that humans may be conditioned to be aroused by objects such as shoes, boots, leather, and undergarments.

Basic Processes in Classical Conditioning

Classical conditioning is often portrayed as a mechanical process that inevitably leads to a certain result. This view reflects the fact that most conditioned responses are reflexive and difficult to

Craig McClain

Figure 6.4

Classical conditioning and romance. Pleasant emotional responses can be acquired through classical conditioning, as illustrated by one woman's unusual conditioned response to the aroma of Beemans gum and cigarette smoke.

control. Pavlov's dogs would have been hard pressed to withhold their salivation. Similarly, most people with phobias have great difficulty suppressing their fear. However, this vision of classical conditioning as an "irresistible force" is misleading because it fails to consider the many factors involved in classical conditioning (Kehoe & Macrae, 1998). In this section, we'll look at basic processes in classical conditioning to expand on the rich complexity of this form of learning.

Acquisition: Forming New Responses

We have already discussed *acquisition* without attaching a formal name to the process. **Acquisition is the formation of a new conditioned response tendency.** Pavlov theorized that the acquisition of a conditioned response depends on stimulus *contiguity,* which literally means "touching." **Stimulus contiguity is a temporal (time) association between two events.** Thus, Pavlov thought that the key to classical conditioning is the *pairing* of stimuli in time. Do the two stimuli have to occur simultaneously to produce conditioning? No, but some CS-UCS timing arrangements work better than others (Miller & Barnet, 1993). Conditioning is most likely to occur when the CS begins about a half-second before the UCS and stops at the same time as the UCS (Heth & Rescorla, 1973; Kamin, 1965).

Stimulus contiguity is important, but learning theorists now realize that contiguity alone doesn't automatically produce conditioning. People are

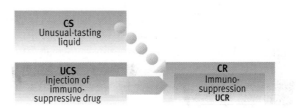

Figure 6.5

Classical conditioning of immunosuppression. When a neutral stimulus is paired with a drug that chemically causes immunosuppression, it can become a CS that elicits immunosuppression on its own. Thus, even the immune response can be influenced by classical conditioning.

Identifying Elements in Classical Conditioning

Check your understanding of classical conditioning by trying to identify the unconditioned stimulus (UCS), unconditioned response (UCR), conditioned stimulus (CS), and conditioned response (CR) in each of the examples below. Fill in the diagram accompanying each example. You'll find the answers in Appendix A.

1. Sam is 3 years old. One night his parents build a roaring fire in the family room fireplace. The fire spits out a large ember that hits Sam in the arm, giving him a nasty burn that hurts a great deal for several hours. A week later, when Sam's parents light another fire in the fireplace, Sam becomes upset and fearful, crying and running from the room.

2. Melanie is driving to work on a rainy highway when she notices that the brake lights of all the cars just ahead of her have come on. She hits her brakes but watches in horror as her car glides into a four-car pileup. She's badly shaken up in the accident. A month later she's driving in the rain again and notices that she tenses up every time she sees brake lights come on ahead of her.

3. At the age of 24, Tyrone has recently developed an allergy to cats. When he's in the same room with a cat for more than 30 minutes, he starts wheezing. After a few such allergic reactions, he starts wheezing as soon as he sees a cat in a room.

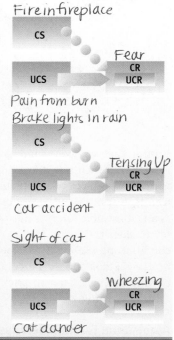

bombarded daily by countless stimuli that could be perceived as being paired, yet only some of these pairings produce classical conditioning. Consider the woman who developed a conditioned emotional reaction to the smell of Beemans gum and cigarettes. Certainly, there were other stimuli that shared contiguity with her boyfriend, Charlie. He smoked, so ashtrays were probably present, but she doesn't get weak in the knees at the sight of an ashtray.

If conditioning does not occur to all the stimuli present in a situation, what determines its occurrence? Evidence suggests that *stimuli that are novel or especially intense have more potential to become CS's than routine stimuli,* probably because they are more likely to stand out among other stimuli (Hearst, 1988).

Extinction: Weakening Conditioned Responses

Fortunately, a newly formed stimulus-response bond does not necessarily last indefinitely. If it did, learning would be inflexible, and organisms would have difficulty adapting to new situations. Instead, the right circumstances produce **extinction, the gradual weakening and disappearance of a conditioned response tendency.**

What leads to extinction in classical conditioning? The consistent presentation of the conditioned stimulus *alone,* without the unconditioned stimulus. For example, when Pavlov consistently presented *only* the tone to a previously conditioned dog, the tone gradually lost its capacity to elicit the response of salivation. Such a sequence of events is depicted in the left portion of Figure 6.6, which graphs the amount of salivation by a dog over a series of conditioning trials. Note how the salivation response declines during extinction.

For an example of extinction from outside the laboratory, let's assume that you cringe at the sound of a dentist's drill, which has been paired with pain in the past. You take a job as a dental assistant and you start hearing the drill (the CS) day in and day out without experiencing any pain (the UCS). Your cringing response will gradually diminish and extinguish altogether.

How long does it take to extinguish a conditioned response? That depends on many factors, but particularly the strength of the conditioned bond when extinction begins. Some conditioned responses extinguish quickly, while others are difficult to weaken.

Spontaneous Recovery: Resurrecting Responses

Some conditioned responses display the ultimate in tenacity by "reappearing from the dead" after being extinguished. Learning theorists use the term *spontaneous recovery* to describe such a resurrection from the graveyard of conditioned associations. **Spontaneous recovery is the reappearance of an extinguished response after a period of nonexposure to the conditioned stimulus.**

Pavlov (1927) observed this phenomenon in some of his pioneering studies. He fully extinguished a dog's CR of salivation to a tone and then returned the dog to its home cage for a "rest interval" (a period of nonexposure to the CS). On a subsequent day, when the dog was brought back to the experimental chamber for retesting, the tone was sounded and the salivation response reappeared. Although it had returned, the rejuvenated response was weak. There was less salivation than when the response was at its peak strength. If Pavlov consistently presented the CS by itself again, the response reextinguished quickly. However, in some of the dogs the response made still another spontaneous recovery (typically even weaker than the first) after they had spent another period in their cages (consult Figure 6.6 once again).

The theoretical meaning of spontaneous recovery is complex and the subject of some debate. However,

Figure 6.6

Acquisition, extinction, and spontaneous recovery. During acquisition, the strength of the dog's conditioned response (measured by the amount of salivation) increases rapidly and then levels off near its maximum. During extinction, the CR declines erratically until it's extinguished. After a "rest" period in which the dog is not exposed to the CS, a spontaneous recovery occurs, and the CS once again elicits a (weakened) CR. Repeated presentations of the CS alone reextinguish the CR, but after another "rest" interval, a weaker spontaneous recovery occurs.

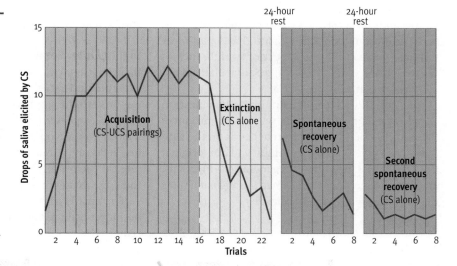

its practical meaning is quite simple. Even if you manage to rid yourself of an unwanted conditioned response (such as cringing when you hear a dental drill), there is an excellent chance that it may make a surprise reappearance later.

Stimulus Generalization and the Case of Little Albert

 5b

After conditioning has occurred, organisms often show a tendency to respond not only to the exact CS used but also to other, similar stimuli. For example, Pavlov's dogs might have salivated in response to a different tone, or you might cringe at the sound of a jeweler's as well as a dentist's drill. These are examples of stimulus generalization. **_Stimulus generalization occurs when an organism that has learned a response to a specific stimulus responds in the same way to new stimuli that are similar to the original stimulus._**

Generalization is adaptive given that organisms rarely encounter the exact same stimulus more than once (Thomas, 1992). Stimulus generalization is also commonplace. We have already discussed a real-life example: the woman who acquired a bridge phobia during her childhood because her father scared her whenever they went over a particular old bridge. The original CS for her fear was that specific bridge, but her fear was ultimately *generalized* to all bridges.

John B. Watson, the founder of behaviorism (see Chapter 1), conducted an influential early study of generalization. Watson and a colleague, Rosalie Rayner, examined the generalization of conditioned fear in an 11-month-old boy, known in the annals of psychology as "Little Albert." Like many babies, Albert was initially unafraid of a live white rat. Then Watson and Rayner (1920) paired the presentation of the rat with a loud, startling sound (made

by striking a steel bar with a hammer). Albert *did* show fear in response to the loud noise. After seven pairings of the rat and the gong, the rat was established as a CS eliciting a fear response (see Figure 6.7).

Figure 6.7

The conditioning of Little Albert. The diagram shows how Little Albert's fear response to a white rat was established. Albert's fear response to other white, furry objects illustrates generalization. In the photo, made from a 1919 film, Rosalie Rayner and John Watson are shown with little Albert before he was conditioned to fear the rat.

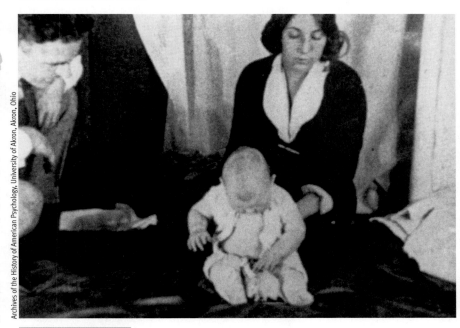

"Surely this proof of the conditioned origin of a fear response puts us on natural science grounds in our study of emotional behavior."
JOHN B. WATSON

Five days later, Watson and Rayner exposed the youngster to other stimuli that resembled the rat in being white and furry. They found that Albert's fear response generalized to a variety of stimuli, including a rabbit, a dog, a fur coat, a Santa Claus mask, and Watson's hair.

Like conditioning itself, stimulus generalization does not occur in just any set of circumstances (Balsam, 1988). Generalization depends on the similarity between the new stimulus and the original CS. The basic law governing generalization is this: *The more similar new stimuli are to the original CS, the greater the likelihood of generalization.*

Stimulus Discrimination

Stimulus discrimination is just the opposite of stimulus generalization. ***Stimulus discrimination* occurs when an organism that has learned a response to a specific stimulus does not respond in the same way to new stimuli that are similar to the original stimulus.** Like generalization, discrimination is adaptive in that an animal's survival may hinge on its being able to distinguish friend from foe, or edible from poisonous food (Thomas, 1992). Organisms can gradually learn to discriminate between the original CS and similar stimuli if they have adequate experience with both. For instance, let's say your dog runs around, excitedly wagging its tail, whenever it hears your car pull up in the driveway. Initially it will probably respond to *all* cars that pull into the driveway (stimulus generalization). However, if there is anything distinctive about the sound of your car, your dog may gradually respond with excitement only to your car and not to other cars (stimulus discrimination).

The development of stimulus discrimination usually requires that the original CS (your car) continues to be paired with the UCS (your arrival), while similar stimuli (the other cars) are not paired with the UCS. As with generalization, a basic law governs discrimination: *The less similar new stimuli are to the original CS, the greater the likelihood (and ease) of discrimination.* Conversely, if a new stimulus is quite similar to the original CS, discrimination will be relatively difficult to learn.

Higher-Order Conditioning

Imagine that you were to conduct the following experiment. First, you condition a dog to salivate in response to the sound of a tone by pairing the tone with meat powder. Once the tone is firmly established as a CS, you pair the tone with a new stimulus, let's say a red light, for 15 trials. You then present the red light alone, without the tone. Will the dog salivate in response to the red light?

The answer is "yes." Even though the red light has never been paired with the meat powder, it will acquire the capacity to elicit salivation by virtue of being paired with the tone (see Figure 6.8). This is a demonstration of ***higher-order conditioning,* in which a conditioned stimulus functions as if it were an unconditioned stimulus.** Higher-order conditioning shows that classical conditioning does not depend on the presence of a genuine, natural UCS. An already established CS will do just fine. In higher-order conditioning, new conditioned responses are built on the foundation of already established conditioned responses.

Many human conditioned responses are the product of higher-order conditioning (Rescorla, 1980). For instance, if your heart leaps into your throat when you spot a police car while driving—even if you're driving at the speed limit—this reflexive anxiety response is due to higher-order conditioning. The stimulus of a police car shouldn't elicit anxiety unless it has previously been paired with an anxiety-arousing event, such as getting a traffic ticket. However, a traffic ticket is not an unconditioned stimulus for anxiety. People aren't born fearing traffic tickets. A traffic ticket is a conditioned stimulus that elicits anxiety in certain people because of their previous learning. Thus, conditioning can occur when neutral stimuli are paired with previously established CSs. The phenomenon of higher-order conditioning greatly extends the reach of classical conditioning.

Figure 6.8

Higher-order conditioning. Higher-order conditioning involves a two-phase process. In the first phase, a neutral stimulus (such as a tone) is paired with an unconditioned stimulus (such as meat powder) until it becomes a conditioned stimulus that elicits the response originally evoked by the UCS (such as salivation). In the second phase, another neutral stimulus (such as a red light) is paired with the previously established CS, so that it also acquires the capacity to elicit the response originally evoked by the UCS.

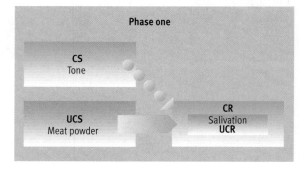

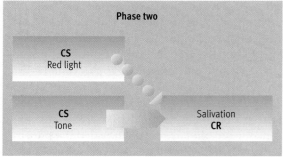

Recognizing Basic Processes in Classical Conditioning

Check your understanding of basic processes in classical conditioning by reading each of the following vignettes and identifying the process at work. Choose from the following: (a) acquisition, (b) extinction, (c) spontaneous recovery, (d) stimulus generalization, (e) stimulus discrimination, (f) higher-order conditioning. The answers can be found in Appendix A.

_D._ **1.** Lucy has flunked algebra twice. Now whenever she sees any kind of math book, she begins to get that same old sick feeling in the pit of her stomach.

_A._ **2.** Little Suzy is experiencing her first thunderstorm. A bolt of lightning flashes across the sky, but this doesn't bother her; she thinks it's pretty. A second later, however, she just about jumps out of her skin when a tremendous crash of thunder shakes the room.

_F._ **3.** Alonzo has gotten A's on all of his quizzes in history, so he likes Professor Olden quite a bit. But he's not too crazy about Professor Datum, because he's received nothing but C's and D's in his research methods class.

_E._ **4.** Glenda tried sushi for the first time when she visited her cousin in San Francisco, and she loved it. Back home in Kansas City she eagerly searched until she found a restaurant that served sushi, but the fish wasn't fresh, so she didn't like it much. On a visit to St. Louis she tried again, but she was disappointed once more. Glenda no longer gets excited by the prospect of eating sushi, unless it's San Francisco sushi, which still makes her mouth water.

_C._ **5.** On his first day at work at the Joy Ice Cream Shop, Arnold helped himself and overdid it. He got sick and swore he'd never eat ice cream again. True to his word, he stayed off the stuff for the rest of the summer, though he continued working at the shop. For a while it was hard, because the sight and smell of the ice cream made him feel nauseous, but eventually those feelings faded. The following summer Arnold decided to visit his old employer, but as soon as he walked in the door, he felt so sick he had to turn around and leave immediately.

_B._ **6.** Little Carlos used to get excited whenever Grandpa would come to visit, because Grandpa always brought Carlos some neat new toy. As Grandpa got older, however, he became forgetful. He no longer brings toys when he visits. Now Grandpa's visits don't excite Carlos as much.

Operant Conditioning

Even Pavlov recognized that classical conditioning is not the only form of conditioning. Classical conditioning best explains reflexive responding that is largely controlled by stimuli that *precede* the response. However, humans and other animals make a great many responses that don't fit this description. Consider the response that you are engaging in right now: studying. It is definitely not a reflex (life might be easier if it were). The stimuli that govern it (exams and grades) do not precede it. Instead, your studying is mainly influenced by stimulus events that *follow* the response—specifically, its *consequences*.

In the 1930s, this kind of learning was christened *operant conditioning* by B. F. Skinner (1938, 1953, 1969). The term was derived from his belief that in this type of responding, an organism "operates" on the environment instead of simply reacting to stimuli. Learning occurs because responses come to be influenced by the consequences that follow them. Thus, **operant conditioning is a form of learning in which voluntary responses come to be controlled by their consequences.** Learning theorists originally distinguished between classical and operant conditioning on the grounds that the former regulated reflexive, involuntary responses, whereas the latter governed voluntary responses. This distinction holds up much of the time, but it is not absolute. Research in recent decades has shown that classical conditioning sometimes contributes to the regulation of voluntary behavior, that operant conditioning can influence involuntary, visceral responses, and that the two types of conditioning jointly and interactively govern some aspects of behavior (Allan, 1998; Turkkan, 1989).

Skinner's Demonstration: It's All a Matter of Consequences 5c

Like Pavlov, Skinner conducted some deceptively simple research that became enormously influential (Lattal, 1992). The fundamental principle of operant conditioning is uncommonly elementary. *Skinner*

Courtesy of B. F. Skinner

"Operant conditioning shapes behavior as a sculptor shapes a lump of clay."
B. F. SKINNER

demonstrated that organisms tend to repeat those responses that are followed by favorable consequences. This fundamental principle is embodied in Skinner's concept of reinforcement. **Reinforcement occurs when an event following a response increases an organism's tendency to make that response.** In other words, a response is strengthened because it leads to rewarding consequences (see Figure 6.9).

The principle of reinforcement may be simple, but it is immensely powerful. Skinner and his followers have shown that much of our everyday behavior is regulated by reinforcement. For example, you study hard because good grades are likely to follow as a result. You go to work because this behavior leads to your receiving paychecks. Perhaps you work extra hard because promotions and raises tend to follow such behavior. You tell jokes, and your friends laugh—so you tell some more. The principle of reinforcement clearly governs complex aspects of human behavior. Paradoxically, though, this principle emerged out of Skinner's research on the behavior of rats and pigeons in exceptionally simple situations. Let's look at that research.

Terminology and Procedures 5c

Like Pavlov, Skinner created a prototype experimental procedure that has been repeated (with variations) thousands of times. In this procedure, an animal, typically a rat or a pigeon, is placed in an *operant chamber* that has come to be better known as a "Skinner box." A **Skinner box** is a small enclosure in which an animal can make a specific response that is systematically recorded while the consequences of the response are controlled. In the boxes designed for rats, the main response made available is pressing a small lever mounted on

one side wall (see Figure 6.10). In the boxes made for pigeons, the designated response is pecking a small disk mounted on a side wall.

Operant responses such as lever pressing and disk pecking are said to be *emitted* rather than *elicited*. **To emit means to send forth.** This word was chosen because operant conditioning governs mainly *voluntary* responses. In contrast, classical conditioning governs mainly *involuntary,* reflexive responses.

The Skinner box permits the experimenter to control the reinforcement contingencies that are in effect for the animal. **Reinforcement contingencies are the circumstances or rules that determine whether responses lead to the presentation of reinforcers.** Typically, the experimenter manipulates whether positive consequences occur when the animal makes the designated response. The main positive consequence is usually delivery of a small bit of food into a food cup mounted in the chamber. Because the animals are deprived of food for a while prior to the experimental session, their hunger virtually ensures that the food serves as a reinforcer.

The key dependent variable in most research on operant conditioning is the subjects' *response rate* over time. An animal's rate of lever pressing or disk pecking in the Skinner box is monitored continuously by a device known as a cumulative recorder (see Figure 6.10). **The *cumulative recorder* creates a graphic record of responding and reinforcement in a Skinner box as a function of time.** The recorder works by means of a roll of paper that moves at a steady rate underneath a movable pen. When there is no responding, the pen stays still and draws a straight horizontal line, reflecting the passage of time. Whenever the designated response occurs, however, the pen moves upward a notch. The pen's movements produce a graphic summary of the animal's responding over time. The pen also makes slash marks to record the delivery of each reinforcer.

The results of operant-conditioning studies are usually portrayed in graphs. In these graphs, the horizontal axis is used to mark the passage of time, while the vertical axis is used to plot the accumulation of responses, as shown in Figure 6.11. In interpreting these graphs, the key consideration is the *slope* of the line that represents the record of responding. *A rapid response rate produces a steep slope, whereas a slow response rate produces a shallow slope.* Because the response record is cumulative, the line never goes down. It can only go up as more responses are made or flatten out if the response rate slows to zero. The magnifications in Figure 6.11 show how slope and response rate are related.

Figure 6.9

Reinforcement in operant conditioning. According to Skinner, reinforcement occurs when a response is followed by rewarding consequences and the organism's tendency to make the response increases. The two examples diagrammed here illustrate the basic premise of operant conditioning—that voluntary behavior is controlled by its consequences. These examples involve positive reinforcement (for a comparison of positive and negative reinforcement, see Figure 6.15).

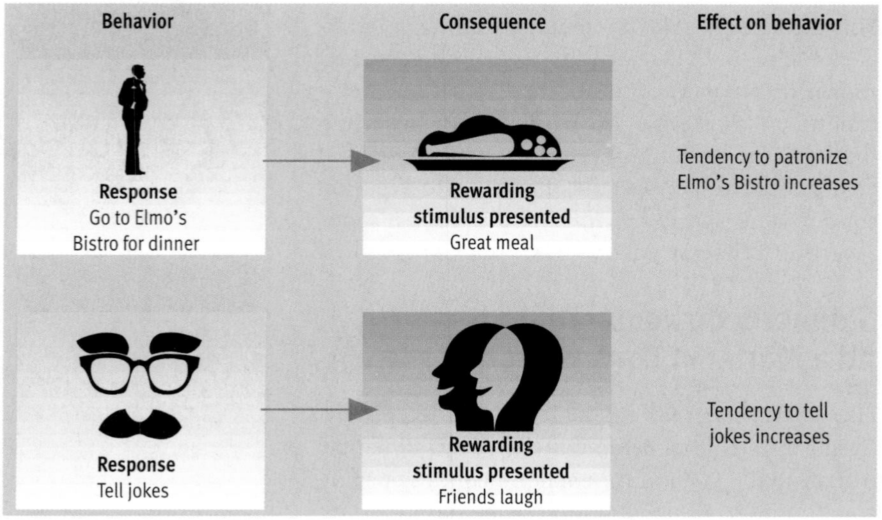

Behavior	Consequence	Effect on behavior
Response Go to Elmo's Bistro for dinner	**Rewarding stimulus presented** Great meal	Tendency to patronize Elmo's Bistro increases
Response Tell jokes	**Rewarding stimulus presented** Friends laugh	Tendency to tell jokes increases

Figure 6.10

Skinner box and cumulative recorder. **(a)** This diagram highlights some of the key features of a Skinner box. In this apparatus designed for rats, the response under study is lever pressing. Food pellets, which may serve as reinforcers, are delivered into the food cup on the right. The speaker and light permit manipulations of visual and auditory stimuli, and the electric grid gives the experimenter control over aversive consequences (shock) in the box. **(b)** A cumulative recorder connected to the box keeps a continuous record of responses and reinforcements. Each lever press moves the pen up a step, and each reinforcement is marked with a slash. **(c)** This photo shows the real thing—a rat being conditioned in a Skinner box. Note the food dispenser on the left, which was omitted from the top diagram.

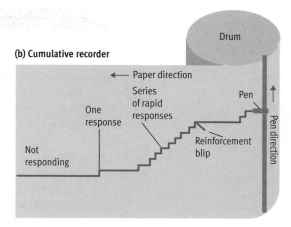
(b) Cumulative recorder

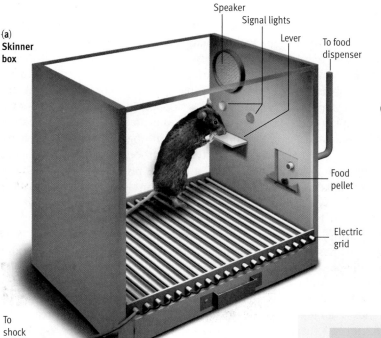
(a) Skinner box

Speaker
Signal lights
Lever
To food dispenser
Food pellet
Electric grid
To shock generator

Basic Processes in Operant Conditioning

 SIM4, 5C

Although the principle of reinforcement is strikingly simple, many other processes involved in operant conditioning make this form of learning just as complex as classical conditioning. In fact, some of the same processes are involved in both types of conditioning. In this section, we'll discuss how the processes of acquisition, extinction, generalization, and discrimination occur in operant conditioning.

Acquisition and Shaping

 SIM4, 5C

As in classical conditioning, *acquisition* in operant conditioning is the formation of a new response tendency. However, the procedures used to establish a tendency to emit a voluntary operant response are different from those used to create a reflexive conditioned response. Operant responses are typically established through a gradual process

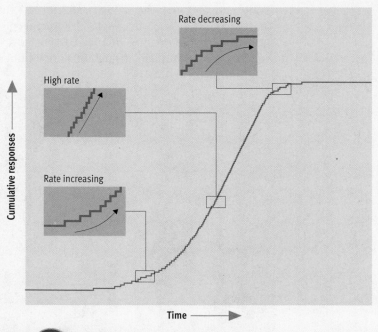

Figure 6.11

A graphic portrayal of operant responding. The results of operant conditioning are often summarized in a graph of cumulative responses over time. The insets magnify small segments of the curve to show how an increasing response rate yields a progressively steeper slope (bottom); a high, steady response rate yields a steep, stable slope (middle); and a decreasing response rate yields a progressively flatter slope (top).

called *shaping: the reinforcement of closer and closer approximations of a desired response.*

Shaping is necessary when an organism does not, on its own, emit the desired response. For example, when a rat is first placed in a Skinner box, it may not press the lever at all. In this case an experimenter begins shaping by releasing food pellets whenever the rat moves toward the lever. As this response becomes more frequent, the experimenter starts requiring a closer approximation of the desired response, possibly releasing food only when the rat actually touches the lever. As reinforcement increases the rat's tendency to touch the lever, the rat will spontaneously press the lever on occasion, finally providing the experimenter with an opportunity to reinforce the designated response. These reinforcements will gradually increase the rate of lever pressing.

Shaping molds many aspects of both human and animal behavior. For instance, it is the key to training animals to perform impressive tricks. When you go to a zoo, circus, or marine park and see bears riding bicycles, monkeys playing the piano, and whales leaping through hoops, you are witnessing the results of shaping. To demonstrate the power of shaping techniques, Skinner once trained some pigeons so that they appeared to play Ping-Pong! They would run about on opposite ends of a Ping-Pong table and peck the ball back and forth. Keller and Marian Breland, a couple of psychologists influenced by Skinner, went into the business of training animals for advertising and entertainment purposes. One of their better known feats was shaping "Priscilla, the Fastidious Pig," to turn on a radio, eat at a kitchen table, put dirty clothes in a hamper, run a vacuum, and then "go shopping" with a shopping cart (see photo). Of course, Priscilla picked the sponsor's product off the shelf in her shopping expedition (Breland & Breland, 1961).

Extinction

SIM4, 5C

In operant conditioning, *extinction* refers to the gradual weakening and disappearance of a response tendency because the response is no longer followed by reinforcement. Extinction begins in operant conditioning whenever previously available reinforcement is stopped. In laboratory studies with rats, this usually means that the experimenter stops delivering food when the rat presses the lever. When the extinction process is begun, a brief surge often occurs in the rat's responding, followed by a gradual decline in response rate until it approaches zero. The same effects are generally seen in the extinction of human behavior.

A key issue in operant conditioning is how much *resistance to extinction* an organism will display when reinforcement is halted. *Resistance to extinction occurs when an organism continues to make a response after delivery of the reinforcer for it has been terminated.* The greater the resistance to extinction, the longer the responding will continue. Thus, if a researcher stops giving reinforcement for lever pressing and the response tapers off very slowly, the response shows high

Shaping—an operant technique in which an organism is rewarded for closer and closer approximations of the desired response—is used in teaching both animals and humans. It is the main means of training animals to perform unnatural tricks. Breland and Breland's (1961) famous subject, "Priscilla, the Fastidious Pig," is shown on the left.

Courtesy of Animal Behavior Enterprises, Inc.

© Gerald Davis/Colorific!

resistance to extinction. However, if the response tapers off quickly, it shows relatively little resistance to extinction.

Resistance to extinction may sound like a matter of purely theoretical interest, but actually it's quite practical. People often want to strengthen a response in such a way that it will be relatively resistant to extinction. For instance, most parents want to see their child's studying response survive even if the child hits a rocky stretch when studying doesn't lead to reinforcement (good grades). In a similar fashion, a casino wants to see patrons continue to gamble, even if they encounter a lengthy losing streak.

Stimulus Control: Generalization and Discrimination

Operant responding is ultimately controlled by its consequences, as organisms learn response-outcome (R-O) associations (Colwill, 1993). However, stimuli that *precede* a response can also influence operant behavior. When a response is consistently followed by a reinforcer in the presence of a particular stimulus, that stimulus comes to serve as a "signal" indicating that the response is likely to lead to a reinforcer. Once an organism learns the signal, it tends to respond accordingly (Honig & Alsop, 1992). For example, a pigeon's disk pecking may be reinforced only when a small light behind the disk is lit. When the light is out, pecking does not lead to the reward. Pigeons quickly learn to peck the disk only when it is lit. The light that signals the availability of reinforcement is called a discriminative stimulus. *Discriminative stimuli are cues that influence operant behavior by indicating the probable consequences (reinforcement or non-reinforcement) of a response.*

Discriminative stimuli play a key role in the regulation of operant behavior. For example, birds learn that hunting for worms is likely to be reinforced after a rain. Children learn to ask for sweets when their parents are in a good mood. Drivers learn to slow down when the highway is wet. Human social behavior is also regulated extensively by discriminative stimuli. Consider the behavior of asking someone out for a date. Many people emit this response cautiously, only after receiving many signals—such as eye contact, smiles, and encouraging conversational exchanges (the discriminative stimuli)—that a favorable answer (reinforcement) is fairly likely.

Reactions to a discriminative stimulus are governed by the processes of *stimulus generalization* and *stimulus discrimination,* just like reactions to a CS in classical conditioning. For instance, envision a cat that gets excited whenever it hears the sound of a can opener because that sound has become a discriminative stimulus signaling a good chance of its getting fed. If the cat also responded to the sound of a new kitchen appliance (say a blender), this response would represent *generalization*—responding to a new stimulus as if it were the original. *Discrimination* would occur if the cat learned to respond only to the can opener and not to the blender.

As you have learned in this section, the processes of acquisition, extinction, generalization, and discrimination in operant conditioning parallel these same processes in classical conditioning. Table 6.1 compares these processes in the two kinds of conditioning.

Reinforcement: Consequences That Strengthen Responses

Although it is convenient to equate reinforcement with reward and the experience of pleasure, strict behaviorists object to this practice. Why? Because the experience of pleasure is an unobservable event that takes place within an organism. As explained in Chapter 1, most behaviorists believe that scientific assertions must be limited to what can be observed.

In keeping with this orientation, Skinner said that reinforcement occurs whenever an outcome strengthens a response, as measured by an increase in the rate of responding. This definition avoids the issue of what the organism is feeling and focuses on observable events. Thus, the central process in reinforcement is the *strengthening of a response tendency.*

Web Link 6.3

Animal Behavior and Welfare Sites
Marina Haynes of the Philadelphia Zoo has brought together an incredible number of links for animal-related issues. The "Animal Behavior" subpage leads to many resources that apply learning principles to the training and living situation of pets and other animals.

Table 6.1   Comparison of Basic Processes in Classical and Operant Conditioning

Process and Definition	Description in Classical Conditioning	Description in Operant Conditioning
Acquisition: The initial stage of learning	CS and UCS are paired, gradually resulting in CR.	Responding gradually increases because of reinforcement, possibly through shaping.
Extinction: The gradual weakening and disappearance of a conditioned response tendency	CS is presented alone until it no longer elicits CR.	Responding gradually slows and stops after reinforcement is terminated.
Stimulus generalization: An organism's responding to stimuli other than the original stimulus used in conditioning	CR is elicited by new stimulus that resembles original CS.	Responding increases in the presence of new stimulus that resembles original discriminative stimulus.
Stimulus discrimination: An organism's lack of response to stimuli that are similar to the original stimulus used in conditioning	CR is not elicited by new stimulus that resembles original CS.	Responding does not increase in the presence of new stimulus that resembles original discriminative stimulus.

Thus, reinforcement is defined *after the fact,* in terms of its *effect* on behavior. Something that is clearly reinforcing for an organism at one time may not function as a reinforcer later (Catania, 1992). Food will reinforce lever pressing by a rat only if the rat is hungry. Similarly, something that serves as a reinforcer for one person may not function as a reinforcer for another person. For example, parental approval is a potent reinforcer for most children, but not all.

Operant theorists make a distinction between unlearned, or primary, reinforcers as opposed to conditioned, or secondary, reinforcers. *Primary reinforcers* **are events that are inherently reinforcing because they satisfy biological needs.** A given species has a limited number of primary reinforcers because they are closely tied to physiological needs. In humans, primary reinforcers include food, water, warmth, sex, and perhaps affection expressed through hugging and close bodily contact. *Secondary,* **or** *conditioned, reinforcers* **are events that acquire reinforcing qualities by being associated with primary reinforcers.** The events that function as secondary reinforcers vary among members of a species because they depend on learning. Examples of common secondary reinforcers in humans include money, good grades, attention, flattery, praise, and applause. Most of the material things that people work hard to earn are secondary reinforcers. For example, people learn to find stylish clothes, sports cars, fine jewelry, elegant china, and state-of-the-art stereos reinforcing.

Intermittent Reinforcement: Effects of Basic Schedules 5d

Organisms make innumerable responses that do *not* lead to favorable consequences. It would be nice if people were reinforced every time they took an exam, watched a movie, hit a golf shot, asked for a date, or made a sales call. However, in the real world most responses are reinforced only some of the time. How does this situation affect the potency of reinforcers? To find out, operant psychologists have devoted an enormous amount of attention to how *schedules of reinforcement* influence operant behavior (Ferster & Skinner, 1957; Skinner, 1938, 1953).

A *schedule of reinforcement* **is a specific pattern of presentation of reinforcers over time.** The simplest pattern is continuous reinforcement. *Continuous reinforcement* **occurs when every instance of a designated response is reinforced.** In the laboratory, experimenters often use continuous reinforcement to shape and establish a new response before moving on to more realistic schedules involving intermittent, or partial, reinforcement. *Intermittent reinforcement* **occurs when a designated response is reinforced only some of the time.**

Which do you suppose leads to longer-lasting effects—being reinforced every time you emit a response, or being reinforced only some of the time? Studies show that, given an equal number of reinforcements, *intermittent* reinforcement makes a response more resistant to extinction than continuous reinforcement does (Falls, 1998; Schwartz & Robbins, 1995). In other words, organisms continue responding longer after removal of reinforcers when a response has been reinforced only *some* of the time.

In fact, intermittent schedules of reinforcement that provide only sporadic delivery of reinforcers can yield great resistance to extinction. This explains why behaviors that are reinforced only occasionally can be very durable. Consider a child who persists in throwing temper tantrums on a regular basis. The parents may be proud of the fact that they give in to these temper tantrums (thus reinforcing them) only about one in seven times. They believe that they are working toward eliminating the tantrums, and they may be mystified when the tantrums persist. Parents in this situation usually fail to realize that they are providing steady intermittent reinforcement for the tantrums. This schedule of reinforcement will make the temper tantrums relatively difficult to eliminate.

Reinforcement schedules come in many varieties, but four particular types of intermittent schedules have attracted the most interest. These schedules are described here along with examples drawn from the laboratory and everyday life (see Figure 6.12 for additional examples).

Ratio schedules require the organism to make the designated response a certain number of times to gain each reinforcer. **In a** *fixed-ratio (FR) schedule,* **the reinforcer is given after a fixed number of nonreinforced responses.** *Examples:* (1) A rat is reinforced for every tenth lever press. (2) A salesperson receives a bonus for every fourth set of golf clubs sold. **In a** *variable-ratio (VR) schedule,* **the reinforcer is given after a variable number of nonreinforced responses.** The number of nonreinforced responses varies around a predetermined average. *Examples:* (1) A rat is reinforced for every tenth lever press on the average. The exact number of responses required for reinforcement varies from one time to the next. (2) A slot machine in a casino pays off once every six tries on the average. The number of nonwinning responses between payoffs varies greatly from one time to the next.

Interval schedules require a time period to pass between the presentation of reinforcers. **In a *fixed-interval (FI)* schedule, the reinforcer is given for the first response that occurs after a fixed time interval has elapsed.** *Examples:* (1) A rat is reinforced for the first lever press after a 2-minute interval has elapsed and then must wait 2 minutes before receiving the next reinforcement. (2) Students can earn grades (let's assume the grades are reinforcing) by taking exams every three weeks. **In a *variable-interval (VI) schedule,* the reinforcer is given for the first response after a variable time interval has elapsed.** The interval length varies around a predetermined average. *Examples:* (1) A rat is reinforced for the first lever press after a 1-minute interval has elapsed, but the following intervals are 3 minutes, 2 minutes, 4 minutes, and so on—with an average length of 2 minutes. (2) A person repeatedly dials a busy phone number (getting through is the reinforcer).

More than 40 years of research has yielded an enormous volume of data on how these schedules of reinforcement are related to patterns of responding (Williams, 1988; Zeiler, 1977). Some of the more prominent findings are summarized in Figure 6.13, which depicts typical response patterns generated by each schedule. For example, with fixed-interval schedules, a pause in responding usually occurs after each reinforcer is delivered, and then responding gradually increases to a rapid rate at the end of the interval. This pattern of behavior yields a "scalloped" response curve. In general, ratio schedules tend to produce more rapid responding than interval schedules. Why? Because faster responding leads to quicker reinforcement when a ratio schedule is in effect. Variable schedules tend to generate steadier response rates and greater resistance to extinction than their fixed counterparts.

Most of the research on reinforcement schedules was conducted on rats and pigeons in Skinner boxes. However, psychologists have found that humans react to schedules of reinforcement in much the same way as lower animals (de Villiers, 1977; Perone, Galizio, & Baron, 1988). For example, when animals are placed on ratio schedules, shifting to a higher ratio (that is, requiring more responses per reinforcement) tends to generate faster responding. Managers who run factories that pay on a piecework basis (a fixed-ratio schedule) have seen the same reaction in humans.

There are many other parallels between animals' and humans' reactions to schedules of reinforcement. For instance, in rats and pigeons variable-ratio schedules yield steady responding and great

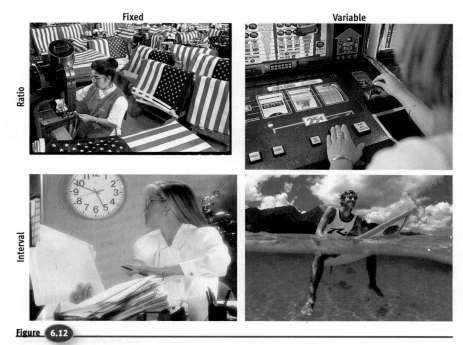

Figure 6.12

Reinforcement schedules in everyday life. Complex human behaviors are regulated by schedules of reinforcement. Piecework in factories is reinforced on a fixed-ratio schedule. Playing a slot machine is based on variable-ratio reinforcement. Watching the clock at work is rewarded on a fixed-interval basis (the arrival of quitting time is the reinforcer). Surfers waiting for a big wave are rewarded on a variable-interval basis. (Top left, © Julian Cotton/International Stock; top right, © David Falconer/Folio, Inc.; bottom left, © David Woods/The Stock Market; bottom right, © Rick Doyle/Uniphoto)

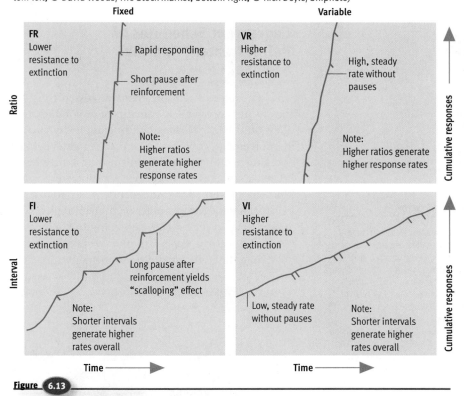

Figure 6.13

Schedules of reinforcement and patterns of response. Each type of reinforcement schedule tends to generate a characteristic pattern of responding. In general, ratio schedules tend to produce more rapid responding than interval schedules (note the steep slopes of the FR and VR curves). In comparison to fixed schedules, variable schedules tend to yield steadier responding (note the smoother lines for the VR and VI schedules on the right) and greater resistance to extinction.

Recognizing Schedules of Reinforcement

Check your understanding of schedules of reinforcement in operant conditioning by indicating the type of schedule that would be in effect in each of the examples below. In the spaces on the left, fill in CR for continuous reinforcement, FR for fixed-ratio, VR for variable-ratio, FI for fixed-interval, and VI for variable-interval. The answers can be found in Appendix A.

_FR_ **1.** Sarah is paid on a commission basis for selling computer systems. She gets a bonus for every third sale.

_VI_ **2.** Juan's parents let him earn some pocket money by doing yard work _approximately_ once a week.

_VR_ **3.** Martha is fly-fishing. Think of each time that she casts her line as the response that may be rewarded.

_CR_ **4.** Jamal, who is in the fourth grade, gets a gold star from his teacher for every book he reads.

_FI_ **5.** Skip, a professional baseball player, signs an agreement that his salary increases will be renegotiated every third year.

---

resistance to extinction. Similar effects are routinely observed among people who gamble. Most gambling is reinforced according to variable-ratio schedules, which tend to produce rapid, steady responding and great resistance to extinction—exactly what casino operators want.

Concurrent Schedules of Reinforcement and the Study of Choice

The schedules of reinforcement discussed thus far clearly are powerful determinants of responding, but they only begin to suggest the complexity of the reinforcement contingencies that regulate behavior. Humans and other organisms constantly have to make choices between two or more responses that are governed by independent schedules of reinforcement. For example, on a given night, you might have to choose between going to a movie or attending a party. Each response has the potential to yield a different type of reinforcement and each

Figure 6.14

An example of concurrent schedules of reinforcement. In this example of a study of pigeons responding to concurrent schedules of reinforcement, pecking disk A is reinforced according to a VI-60 seconds schedule, whereas responding to disk B is reinforced according to a FR-10 schedule. Experimental arrangements such as these allow operant psychologists to study complex choice behavior under controlled laboratory conditions. (Adapted from _Principles of Learning and Behavior_, 4th edition, by M. Domjan, © 1998.)

Schedule A
VI 60 sec

Schedule B
FR 10

Disk A   Disk B

has its own history of intermittent reinforcement. Similarly, animals foraging for their next meal must choose between different behaviors that have been reinforced according to different schedules.

To gain insight into how organisms make choices among operant responses, researchers have studied _concurrent schedules of reinforcement,_ which consist of two or more reinforcement schedules that operate simultaneously and independently, each for a different response. In the simplest experiments, animals are placed in Skinner boxes that allow for two responses that are reinforced according to independent schedules. For example, a pigeon might be able to peck either of two disks, one of which is reinforced on a variable interval schedule and the other on a fixed ratio schedule (see Figure 6.14). How will the pigeon distribute its responses in this complicated situation? Even simple organisms turn out to be remarkably savvy. The pigeon's proportion of responding to each disk will correspond closely to the relative amount of overall reinforcement each disk can yield (Nevin, 1998; Shettleworth, 1998). This phenomenon is called the _matching law,_ **which states that under concurrent schedules of reinforcement, organisms' relative rate of responding to each alternative tends to match each alternative's relative rate of reinforcement.** Moreover, if the _magnitude_ or _quality_ of reinforcement earned by each alternative is manipulated, organisms will adjust their responding to match up well with these factors as well (Gibbon & Fairhurst, 1994). Of course, animals don't match their responding to the realities of reinforcement perfectly, but they come surprisingly close (B.A. Williams, 1994).

Although there is healthy debate about the details, most explanations of matching assume that organisms are working to maximize their overall reinforcement (Nevin, 1998). This conclusion may seem far-fetched, but the maximizing found in the laboratory may simply reflect behavioral adaptations seen in the real world. Scientists studying the foraging behavior of many species in their natural environments have been impressed by how optimized animals' patterns of food seeking are (Krebs & McCleery, 1984; Parker & Smith, 1990). According to _optimal foraging theory,_ **the food-seeking behaviors of many animals maximize the nutrition gained in relation to the energy expended to locate, secure, and consume various foods.** For example, in choosing whether to pursue several small prey that are easy to catch or one large prey that will take more effort to subdue, or in choosing whether to continue foraging in a depleting patch

of food or move on to another patch, animals tend to make sound choices that approximate optimal responding. Exactly *how* animals achieve these impressive results is not well understood. Obviously, they are not capable of making complex calculations about future costs, benefits, and probabilities. Rather, it appears that they follow some simple rules of thumb that yield surprisingly good results. These response tendencies appear to be learned the same way other operant responses are learned—through the principles of reinforcement (Shettleworth, 1998). However, theorists suspect that evolution also contributes to optimal foraging. Animals are probably preprogrammed by evolution to attend to, remember, and be guided by crucial features of the environment that allow them to readily learn effective foraging behaviors based on their reinforcement history.

Positive Reinforcement Versus Negative Reinforcement 5e, 5f

According to Skinner, reinforcement can take two forms, which he called *positive reinforcement* and *negative reinforcement* (see Figure 6.15). ***Positive reinforcement* occurs when a response is strengthened because it is followed by the presentation of a rewarding stimulus.** Thus far, for purposes of simplicity, our examples of reinforcement have involved positive reinforcement. Good grades, tasty meals, paychecks, scholarships, promotions, nice clothes, nifty cars, attention, and flattery are all positive reinforcers.

In contrast, ***negative reinforcement* occurs when a response is strengthened because it is followed by the removal of an aversive (unpleasant) stimulus.** Don't let the word "negative" confuse you.

Research on the foraging strategies of animals has revealed that they tend to make surprisingly good choices. This discovery led to the formulation of optimal foraging theory.

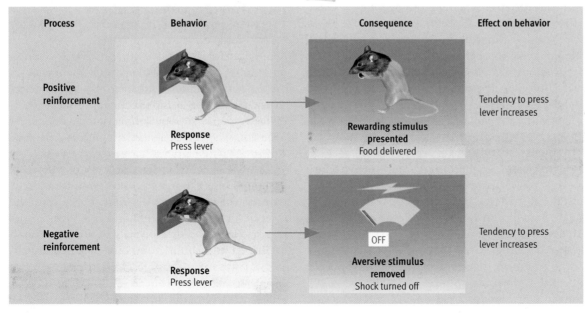

Figure 6.15

Positive reinforcement versus negative reinforcement. In positive reinforcement, a response leads to the presentation of a rewarding stimulus. In negative reinforcement, a response leads to the removal of an aversive stimulus. Both types of reinforcement involve favorable consequences and both have the same effect on behavior: the organism's tendency to emit the reinforced response is strengthened.

Process	Behavior	Consequence	Effect on behavior
Positive reinforcement	Response Press lever	Rewarding stimulus presented Food delivered	Tendency to press lever increases
Negative reinforcement	Response Press lever	OFF Aversive stimulus removed Shock turned off	Tendency to press lever increases

Negative reinforcement *is* reinforcement. Like all reinforcement it involves a favorable outcome that *strengthens* a response tendency. However, this strengthening takes place because a response leads to the *removal of an aversive stimulus* rather than the arrival of a pleasant stimulus (see Figure 6.15).

In laboratory studies, negative reinforcement is usually accomplished as follows: While a rat is in a Skinner box, a moderate electric shock is delivered to the animal through the floor of the box. When the rat presses the lever, the shock is turned off for a period of time. Thus, lever pressing leads to removal of an aversive stimulus (shock). Although this sequence of events is different from those for positive reinforcement, it reliably strengthens the rat's lever-pressing response.

Everyday human behavior is regulated extensively by negative reinforcement. Consider a handful of examples. You rush home in the winter to get out of the cold. You clean house to get rid of a mess. You give in to your child's begging to halt the whining. You give in to a roommate or spouse to bring an unpleasant argument to an end.

Negative reinforcement plays a key role in both escape learning and avoidance learning. **In *escape learning*, an organism acquires a response that decreases or ends some aversive stimulation.** Psychologists often study escape learning in the laboratory with dogs or rats that are conditioned in a *shuttle box*. The shuttle box has two compartments connected by a doorway, which can be opened and closed by the experimenter, as depicted in Figure 6.16(a). In a typical study, an animal is placed in one compartment and the shock in the floor of that chamber is turned on, with the doorway open. The animal learns to escape the shock by running to the other compartment. This escape response leads to the removal of an aversive stimulus (shock), so it is strengthened through negative reinforcement. If you were to leave a party where you were getting picked on by peers, you would be engaging in an escape response.

Escape learning often leads to avoidance learning. **In *avoidance learning* an organism acquires a response that prevents some aversive stimulation from occurring.** In shuttle box studies of avoidance learning, the experimenter simply gives the animal a signal that shock is forthcoming. The typical signal is a light that goes on a few seconds prior to the shock. At first the dog or rat runs only when shocked (escape learning). Gradually, however, the animal learns to run to the safe compartment as soon as the light comes on, showing avoidance learning. Similarly, if you were to quit going to parties because

of your concern about being picked on by peers, you would be demonstrating avoidance learning.

Avoidance learning presents an interesting example of how classical conditioning and operant conditioning can work together to regulate behavior (Levis, 1989; Mowrer, 1947). In avoidance learning, the warning light that goes on before the shock becomes a CS (through classical conditioning) eliciting reflexive, conditioned fear in the animal. However, the response of fleeing to the other side of the box is operant behavior. This response is strengthened through negative reinforcement *because it reduces the animal's conditioned fear* (see Figure 6.16b).

The principles of avoidance learning shed some light on why phobias are so resistant to extinction (Levis, 1989). For example, suppose you have a phobia of elevators. Chances are, you acquired your phobia through classical conditioning. At some point in your past, elevators became paired with a frightening event. Now whenever you need to use an elevator, you experience conditioned fear. If your phobia is severe, you probably take the stairs instead. Taking the stairs is an avoidance response that should lead to consistent negative reinforcement by relieving your conditioned fear. Thus, it's hard to get rid of phobias for two reasons. First, responses that allow you to avoid a phobic stimulus earn negative reinforcement each time they are made—so avoidance behavior is strengthened and continues. Second, these avoidance responses prevent any opportunity to extinguish the phobic conditioned response because you're never exposed to the conditioned stimulus (in this case, riding in an elevator).

Punishment: Consequences That Weaken Responses

Reinforcement is defined in terms of its consequences. It *strengthens* an organism's tendency to make a certain response. Are there also consequences that *weaken* an organism's tendency to make a particular response? Yes. In Skinner's model of operant behavior, such consequences are called *punishment*.

***Punishment* occurs when an event following a response weakens the tendency to make that response.** In a Skinner box, the administration of punishment is very simple. When a rat presses the lever or a pigeon pecks the disk, it receives a brief shock. This procedure usually leads to a rapid decline in the animal's response rate (Dinsmoor, 1998). Punishment typically involves presentation of an aversive stimulus (for instance, spanking a child). However, punishment may also involve the

ex.

ex.

removal of a rewarding stimulus (for instance, taking away a child's TV-watching privileges).

The concept of punishment in operant conditioning is confusing to many students, on two counts. First, they often confuse it with negative reinforcement, which is entirely different. Negative reinforcement involves the *removal* of an aversive stimulus, thereby *strengthening* a response. Punishment, on the other hand, involves the *presentation* of an aversive stimulus, thereby *weakening* a response. Thus, punishment and negative reinforcement are *opposite procedures* that yield *opposite effects* on behavior (see Figure 6.17).

The second source of confusion involves the tendency to equate punishment with *disciplinary procedures* used by parents, teachers, and other authority figures. In the operant model, punishment occurs any time undesirable consequences weaken a response tendency. Defined in this way, the concept of punishment goes far beyond things like parents spanking children and teachers handing out detentions. For example, if you wear a new outfit and your schoolmates make fun of it, your behavior will have been punished and your tendency to emit this response (wear the same clothing) will probably decline. Similarly, if you go to a restaurant and have a horrible meal, your response will have been punished, and your tendency to go to that restaurant will probably decline.

Although punishment in operant conditioning encompasses far more than disciplinary acts, it *is*

(a)

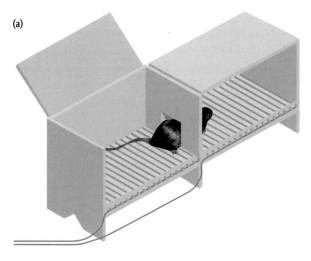

(b) **1. Classical conditioning**

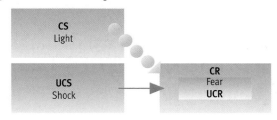

2. Operant conditioning
(negative reinforcement)

Figure 6.16

Escape and avoidance learning. (a) Escape and avoidance learning are often studied with a shuttle box like that shown here. Warning signals, shock, and the animal's ability to flee from one compartment to another can be controlled by the experimenter. (b) Avoidance behavior involves both classical and operant conditioning. Avoidance *begins* because classical conditioning creates a conditioned fear that is elicited by the warning signal (panel 1). Avoidance *continues* because it is maintained by operant conditioning (panel 2). Specifically, the avoidance response is strengthened through negative reinforcement, because it leads to removal of the conditioned fear.

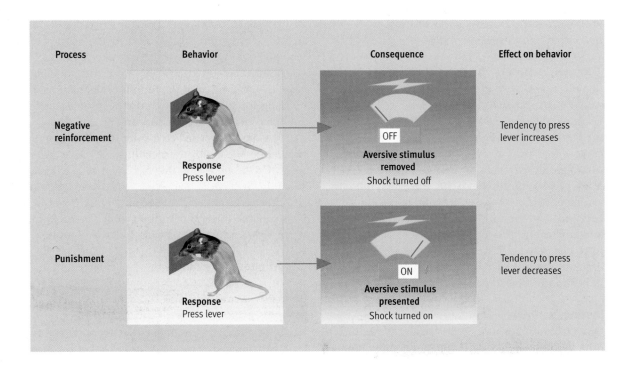

Figure 6.17

Comparison of negative reinforcement and punishment. Although punishment can occur when a response leads to the removal of a rewarding stimulus, it more typically involves the presentation of an aversive stimulus. Students often confuse punishment with negative reinforcement because they associate both with aversive stimuli. However, as this diagram shows, punishment and negative reinforcement represent opposite processes that have opposite effects on behavior.

Recognizing Outcomes in Operant Conditioning

Check your understanding of the various types of consequences that can occur in operant conditioning by indicating whether the examples below involve positive reinforcement (PR), negative reinforcement (NR), punishment (P), or extinction (E). The answers can be found in Appendix A.

_P_ **1.** Antonio gets a speeding ticket.

_PR_ **2.** Diane's supervisor compliments her on her hard work.

_P_ **3.** Leon goes to the health club for a rare workout and pushes himself so hard that his entire body aches and he throws up.

_NR_ **4.** Audrey lets her dog out so she won't have to listen to its whimpering.

_NR_ **5.** Richard shoots up heroin to ward off tremors and chills associated with heroin withdrawal.

_E_ **6.** Sharma constantly complains about minor aches and pains to obtain sympathy from colleagues at work. Three co-workers who share an office with her decide to ignore her complaints instead of responding with sympathy.

used frequently for disciplinary purposes. In light of this fact, it is worth looking at the implications of operant research for the use of punishment as a disciplinary measure. One key problem with punishment is that even when it is effective in weakening a response, it can have unintended side effects (Newsom, Favell, & Rincover, 1983; Van Houten, 1983). For example, punishment often triggers *strong emotional responses,* including fear, anxiety, anger, and resentment. Strong emotions can temporarily disrupt normal functioning and generate hostility toward the source of the punishment, such as a parent or teacher. Moreover, studies show that *physical* punishment often leads to an increase in *aggressive behavior.* Children who are subjected to a lot of physical punishment tend to become more aggressive than the average youngster (Parke & Slaby, 1983). You'll see why shortly, when we discuss observational learning.

Changing Directions in the Study of Conditioning

Negative Reinforcement - in a way is like an excuse to get out of something that an individual does not want to deal with

As you learned in Chapter 1, science is constantly evolving and changing in response to new research and new thinking. Such change certainly has occurred in the study of conditioning (Domjan, 1998). In this section, we will examine two major changes in thinking about conditioning that have emerged in recent decades. First, we'll consider the growing recognition that an organism's biological heritage can limit or channel conditioning. Second, we'll discuss the increased appreciation of the role of cognitive processes in conditioning.

Recognizing Biological Constraints on Conditioning

Learning theorists have traditionally assumed that the fundamental laws of conditioning have great generality—that they apply to a wide range of species. Although no one ever suggested that hamsters could learn physics, until the 1960s most psychologists assumed that associations could be conditioned between any stimulus an organism could register and any response it could make. However, findings in recent decades have demonstrated that there are limits to the generality of conditioning principles—limits imposed by an organism's biological heritage.

Instinctive Drift

One biological constraint on learning is instinctive drift. *Instinctive drift* occurs when an animal's innate

response tendencies interfere with conditioning processes. Instinctive drift was first described by the Brelands, the operant psychologists who went into the business of training animals for commercial purposes (Breland & Breland, 1966). They have described many amusing examples of their "failures" to control behavior through conditioning. For instance, they once were training some raccoons to deposit coins in a piggy bank. They were successful in shaping the raccoons to pick up a coin and put it into a small box, using food as the reinforcer. However, when they gave the raccoons a couple of coins, an unexpected problem arose: the raccoons wouldn't give the coins up! In spite of the reinforcers available for depositing the coins, they would sit and rub the coins together like so many little misers.

What had happened to disrupt the conditioning program? Apparently, associating the coins with food had brought out the raccoons' innate food-washing behavior. Raccoons often rub things together to clean them. The Brelands report that they have run into this sort of instinct-related interference on many occasions with a wide variety of species.

Conditioned Taste Aversion

Research on *conditioned taste aversion* also demonstrates that an organism's biological heritage can channel conditioning in certain directions. A number of years ago a prominent psychologist, Martin Seligman, dined out with his wife and enjoyed a steak

Web Link 6.4

Journal of the Experimental Analysis of Behavior and *Journal of Applied Behavioral Analysis*

Two important journals devoted to behavioral analysis share a site at the University of Rochester's Environmental Health Sciences Center. Among the site's many resources are a searchable abstract database for both journals and an archive of audio and video clips demonstrating selected learning principles.

Trying to teach something/ new, but organism/ individual does what used to doing.

with sauce béarnaise. About six hours afterward, he developed a wicked case of stomach flu and endured severe nausea. Subsequently, when he ordered sauce béarnaise, he was chagrined to discover that its aroma alone nearly made him throw up.

Seligman's experience was not unique. Many people have developed aversions to foods when eating them has been followed by nausea from illness, alcohol intoxication, or food poisoning. However, Seligman was puzzled by his problem (Seligman & Hager, 1972). On the one hand, it appeared to be the straightforward result of classical conditioning. A neutral stimulus (the sauce) had been paired with an unconditioned stimulus (the flu), which caused an unconditioned response (the nausea). Hence, the sauce béarnaise became a conditioned stimulus eliciting nausea (see Figure 6.18).

On the other hand, Seligman recognized that his aversion to béarnaise sauce violated certain basic principles of conditioning. First, the lengthy delay of six hours between the CS (the sauce) and the UCS (the flu) should have prevented conditioning from occurring. In laboratory studies, a delay of more than *30 seconds* between the CS and UCS makes it difficult to establish a conditioned response, yet this conditioning occurred in just one pairing. Second, why was it that only the béarnaise sauce became a CS eliciting nausea? Why not other stimuli that were present in the restaurant? Shouldn't plates, knives, tablecloths, or his wife, for example, also trigger Seligman's nausea?

The riddle of Seligman's aversion to sauce béarnaise was solved by John Garcia (1989) and his colleagues. They conducted a series of studies on conditioned taste aversion (Garcia & Koelling, 1966; Garcia, Clarke, & Hankins, 1973; Garcia & Rusiniak, 1980). In these studies, they manipulated the kinds of stimuli preceding the onset of nausea and other noxious experiences in rats, using radiation to artificially induce the nausea. They found that when taste cues were followed by nausea, rats quickly acquired conditioned taste aversions. However, when taste cues were followed by other types of noxious stimuli (such as shock), rats did not develop conditioned taste aversions. Furthermore, visual and auditory stimuli followed by nausea also failed to produce conditioned aversions.

In short, Garcia and his co-workers found that taste aversions were conditioned *only* through the pairing of taste stimuli and stimuli inducing nausea. When taste stimuli or nausea-inducing stimuli were paired with other types of stimuli—rather than each other—minimal conditioning occurred. In contrast, the taste-nausea connection was made

so readily that conditioned taste aversions could develop in spite of remarkably long CS-UCS delays. These findings contradicted the long-held belief that associations could be created between virtually any stimulus and any response. Garcia found that it was almost impossible to create certain associations, whereas taste-nausea associations (and odor-nausea associations) were almost impossible to prevent.

What is the theoretical significance of this unique readiness to make connections between taste and nausea? Garcia argues that it is a by-product of the evolutionary history of mammals. Animals that consume poisonous foods and survive must learn not to repeat their mistakes. Natural selection will favor organisms that quickly learn what *not* to eat. Thus, evolution may have programmed some organisms to learn certain types of associations more easily than others.

An Evolutionary Perspective on Learning

The research on instinctive drift and conditioned taste aversion suggest that there are species-specific biological constraints on conditioning. So, what is the current thinking on the idea that the laws of learning are *universal* across various species? The emerging consensus seems to be that the basic mechanisms of learning are *similar* across species but that these mechanisms have sometimes been modified in the course of evolution as species have adapted to the specialized demands of their environments (Shettleworth, 1998). According to this view, learning is a very general process because the neural substrates of learning and the basic problems confronted by various organisms are much the same across species. For example, it is probably adaptive for virtually any organism to develop the ability to recognize stimuli that signal important events.

However, given that learning can contribute to reproductive success in myriad ways, it makes sense that learning has evolved along different paths in different species (Hollis, 1997; Sherry, 1992). Most animals must learn what is edible and what isn't, how to spot predators quickly, how to attract a mate, and so forth. Any heritable change in learning that makes an organism's performance of these tasks more effective should increase the organism's reproductive success, and hence be favored by

Courtesy of John Garcia

"Taste aversions do not fit comfortably within the present framework of classical or instrumental conditioning: These aversions selectively seek flavors to the exclusion of other stimuli. Interstimulus intervals are a thousandfold too long."
JOHN GARCIA

Figure 6.18

Conditioned taste aversion. Taste aversions can be established through classical conditioning. However, as the text explains, taste aversions can be acquired in ways that seem to violate basic principles of classical conditioning.

natural selection. Thus, differences in the adaptive challenges faced by various species have probably led to some species-specific learning tendencies, which explain how an organism's biological heritage can channel conditioning in certain directions.

Recognizing Cognitive Processes in Conditioning

Pavlov, Skinner, and their followers traditionally viewed conditioning as a mechanical process in which stimulus-response associations are stamped in by experience. Learning theorists asserted that if a flatworm can be conditioned, then conditioning can't depend on higher mental processes. Although this viewpoint did not go entirely unchallenged (for example, Tolman, 1922, 1932), mainstream theories of conditioning did not allocate a major role to cognitive processes. In recent decades, however, research findings have led theorists to shift toward more cognitive explanations of conditioning.

Signal Relations

The cognitive element in classical conditioning is especially prominent in research conducted by Robert Rescorla (1978, 1980; Rescorla & Wagner, 1972). Rescorla asserts that environmental stimuli serve as signals and that some stimuli are better, or more dependable, signals than others. Hence, he has manipulated *signal relations* in classical conditioning—that is, CS-UCS relations that influence whether a CS is a good signal. A "good" signal is one that allows accurate prediction of the UCS.

In essence, Rescorla manipulates the *predictive value* of a conditioned stimulus. How does he do so? He varies the proportion of trials in which the CS and UCS are paired. Consider the following example. A tone and shock are paired 20 times for one group of rats. Otherwise, these rats are never shocked. For these rats the CS (tone) and UCS (shock) are paired in 100% of the experimental trials. Another group of rats also receives 20 pairings of the tone and shock. However, this group is also exposed to the shock on 20 other trials when the tone does not precede it. For this group, the CS and UCS are paired in only 50% of the trials. Thus, the two groups of rats have had an equal number of CS-UCS pairings, but the CS is a better signal or predictor of shock for the 100% CS-UCS group than for the 50% CS-UCS group.

What did Rescorla find when he tested the two groups of rats for conditioned fear? He found that the CS elicits a much stronger response in the 100% CS-UCS group than in the 50% CS-UCS group. Given that the two groups have received an equal number of CS-UCS pairings, this difference must be due to the greater predictive power of the CS for the 100% group. Numerous studies of signal relations have shown that the predictive value of a CS is an influential factor governing classical conditioning (Rescorla, 1978). These studies of signal relations suggest that classical conditioning may involve information processing rather than reflexive responding.

Response-Outcome Relations and Reinforcement

Studies of response-outcome relations and reinforcement also highlight the role of cognitive

Pavlovian conditioning is a sophisticated and sensible mechanism by which organisms represent the world. . . . I encourage students to think of animals as behaving like little statisticians. . . . They really are very finely attuned to small changes in the likelihood of events.
ROBERT RESCORLA

University of Pennsylvania

CONCEPT **CHECK 6.5**

Distinguishing Between Classical Conditioning and Operant Conditioning

Check your understanding of the usual differences between classical conditioning and operant conditioning by indicating the type of conditioning process involved in each of the following examples. In the space on the left, place a C if the example involves classical conditioning, an O if it involves operant conditioning, or a B if it involves both. The answers can be found in Appendix A.

_C_ **1.** Whenever Midori takes her dog out for a walk, she wears the same old blue windbreaker. Eventually, she notices that her dog becomes excited whenever she puts on this windbreaker.

_O_ **2.** The Wailing Creatures are a successful rock band with three hit albums to their credit. They begin their U.S. tour featuring many new, unreleased songs, all of which draw silence from their concert fans. The same fans cheer wildly when the Wailing Creatures play any of their old hits. Gradually, the band reduces the number of new songs it plays and starts playing more of the old standbys.

_C_ **3.** When Cindy and Mel first fell in love, they listened constantly to the Wailing Creatures' hit song "Transatlantic Obsession." Although several years have passed, whenever they hear this song, they experience a warm, romantic feeling.

_B_ **4.** For nearly 20 years Ralph has worked as a machinist in the same factory. His new foreman is never satisfied with his work and criticizes him constantly. After a few weeks of heavy criticism, Ralph experiences anxiety whenever he arrives at work. He starts calling in sick more and more frequently to evade this anxiety.

processes in conditioning. Imagine that on the night before an important exam you study very hard while repeatedly playing a Smash Mouth album. The next morning you earn an A on your exam. Does this result strengthen your tendency to play Smash Mouth albums before exams? Probably not. Chances are, you will recognize the logical relation between the response of studying hard and the reinforcement of a good grade, and only the response of studying will be strengthened (Killeen, 1981).

Thus, reinforcement is *not* automatic when favorable consequences follow a response. People actively reason out the relations between responses and the outcomes that follow. When a response is followed by a desirable outcome, the response is more likely to be strengthened if the person thinks that the response *caused* the outcome. You might guess that only humans would engage in this causal reasoning. However, evidence suggests that under the right circumstances even pigeons can learn to recognize causal relations between responses and outcomes (Killeen, 1981).

In sum, modern, reformulated models of conditioning view it as a matter of detecting the *contingencies* among environmental events (Matute & Miller, 1998). According to these theories, organisms actively try to figure out what leads to what (the contingencies) in the world around them. Stimuli are viewed as signals that help organisms minimize their aversive experiences and maximize their pleasant experiences.

The new, cognitively oriented theories of conditioning are quite a departure from older theories that depicted conditioning as a mindless, mechanical process. We can also see this new emphasis on cognitive processes in our next subject, observational learning.

Observational Learning

Can classical and operant conditioning account for all of our learning? Absolutely not. Consider how people learn a fairly basic skill such as driving a car. They do not hop naively into an automobile and start emitting random responses until one leads to favorable consequences. On the contrary, most people learning to drive know exactly where to place the key and how to get started. How are these responses acquired? Through *observation*. Most new drivers have years of experience observing others drive and they put those observations to work. Learning through observation accounts for a great deal of learning in both animals and humans.

Observational learning occurs when an organism's responding is influenced by the observation of others, who are called models. This process has been investigated extensively by Albert Bandura (1977, 1986). Bandura does not see observational learning as entirely separate from classical and operant conditioning. Instead, he asserts that it greatly extends the reach of these conditioning processes. Whereas previous conditioning theorists emphasized the organism's direct experience, Bandura has demonstrated that both classical and operant conditioning can take place vicariously through observational learning.

Essentially, observational learning involves being conditioned indirectly by virtue of observing another's conditioning (see Figure 6.19). To illustrate, suppose you observe a friend behaving assertively with a car salesperson. You see your friend's assertive behavior reinforced by the exceptionally good buy she gets on the car. Your own tendency to behave assertively with salespeople might well be strengthened as a result. Notice that the reinforcement is experienced by your friend, not you. The good buy should strengthen your friend's tendency to bargain assertively, but your tendency to do so may also be strengthened indirectly.

Figure 6.19

Observational learning.
In observational learning, an observer attends to and stores a mental representation of a model's behavior (*example:* assertive bargaining) and its consequences (*example:* a good buy on a car). If the observer sees the modeled response lead to a favorable outcome, the observer's tendency to emit the modeled response will be strengthened.

Courtesy of Albert Bandura

"*Most human behavior is learned by observation through modeling.*"
ALBERT BANDURA

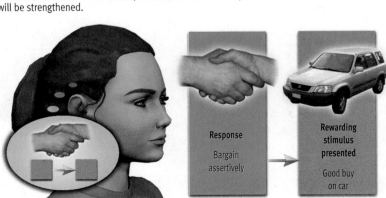

Response

Bargain assertively

Rewarding stimulus presented

Good buy on car

Three Types of Learning

Type of learning	Procedure	Diagram	Result

Classical conditioning

Ivan Pavlov

A neutral stimulus (for example, a tone) is paired with an unconditioned stimulus (such as food) that elicits an unconditioned response (salivation).

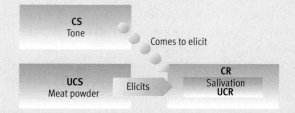

CS
Tone

Comes to elicit

UCS
Meat powder

Elicits

CR
Salivation
UCR

The neutral stimulus becomes a conditioned stimulus that elicits the conditioned response (for example, a tone triggers salivation).

Operant conditioning

B. F. Skinner

In a stimulus situation, a response is followed by favorable consequences (reinforcement) or unfavorable consequences (punishment).

Response
Press lever

Followed by

Rewarding or aversive stimulus presented or removed
Food delivery or shock

If reinforced, the response is strengthened (emitted more frequently); if punished, the response is weakened (emitted less frequently).

Observational learning

Albert Bandura

An observer attends to a model's behavior (for example, aggressive bargaining) and its consequences (for example, a good buy on a car).

Response
Bargain assertively

Rewarding stimulus presented
Good buy on car

The observer stores a mental representation of the modeled response; the observer's tendency to emit the response may be strengthened or weakened, depending on the consequences observed.

Typical kinds of responses	**Examples in animals**	**Examples in humans**

Mostly (but not always) involuntary reflexes and visceral responses

Dogs learn to salivate to the sound of a tone that has been paired with meat powder.

CORBIS-Bettmann

Little Albert learns to fear a white rat and other white, furry objects through classical conditioning

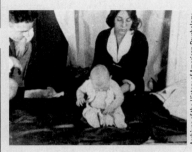

Archives of the History of American Psychology, University of Akron, Akron, Ohio

Mostly (but not always) voluntary, spontaneous responses

Trained animals perform remarkable feats because they have been reinforced for gradually learning closer and closer approximations of responses they do not normally emit.

© Gerald Davis/Colorific!

Casino patrons tend to exhibit high, steady rates of gambling, as most games of chance involve complex variable-ratio schedules of reinforcement.

© David Falconer/Folio, Inc.

A young boy performs a response that he has acquired through observational learning.

Mostly voluntary responses, often consisting of novel and complex sequences

An English titmouse learns to break into milk bottles by observing the thievery of other titmice.

© J. Markham/Bruce Coleman, Inc.

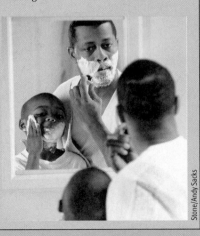

Stone/Andy Sacks

Bandura's theory of observational learning has shed light on many important aspects of behavior. For example, it explains why physical punishment tends to increase aggressive behavior in children, even when it is intended to do just the opposite. Parents who depend on physical punishment often punish a child for hitting other children—by spanking the child. The parents may sincerely intend to reduce the child's aggressive behavior, but they are unwittingly serving as *models* of such behavior. Although they may tell the child that "hitting people won't accomplish anything," they are in the midst of hitting the child in order to accomplish something. Because parents usually accomplish their immediate goal of stopping the child's hitting, the child witnesses the reinforcement of aggressive

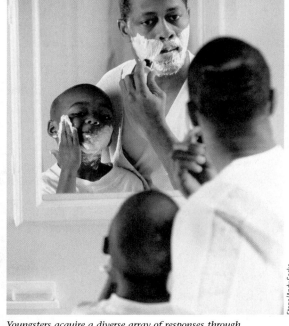

Youngsters acquire a diverse array of responses through observational learning.

behavior. In this situation, actions speak louder than words—because of observational learning.

Clearly, observational learning plays an important role in regulating behavior. It represents a third major type of learning that builds on the first two types—classical conditioning and operant conditioning. These three basic types of learning are summarized and compared in a pictorial table on pages 190–191.

Observational learning is seen in animals as well as humans. For instance, the English titmouse has learned how to open cardboard caps on milk bottles to swipe milk and cream from its human neighbors. This clever learned behavior has been passed down from one generation of titmouse to the next through observational learning.

Putting It in Perspective

Two of our unifying themes stand out in this chapter: (1) nature and nurture interactively govern behavior, and (2) dense interconnections exist between psychology and events in the world at large. Let's examine each of these points in more detail.

In regard to nature versus nurture, research on learning has clearly and repeatedly demonstrated the enormous power of the environment and experience in shaping behavior. Indeed, many learning theorists once believed that *all* aspects of behavior could be explained in terms of environmental determinants. In recent decades, however, evidence on instinctive drift and conditioned taste aversion has shown that there are biological constraints on conditioning. Thus, even in explanations of learning—an area once dominated by nurture theories—we see again that heredity and environment jointly influence behavior.

The history of research on conditioning also shows how progress in psychology can seep into every corner of society. For example, Skinner's ideas on the power of positive reinforcement have influenced patterns of discipline in our society. Research on operant conditioning has also affected management styles in the business world, leading to an increased emphasis on positive reinforcement. The fact that the principles of conditioning are routinely applied in homes, businesses, schools, and factories clearly shows that psychology is not an ivory tower endeavor.

In the upcoming Personal Application, you will see how you can apply the principles of conditioning to improve your self-control, as we discuss the technology of behavior modification.

PERSONAL APPLICATION

Achieving Self-Control Through Behavior Modification

Answer the following "yes" or "no."

___ 1 Do you have a hard time passing up food, even when you're not hungry?

___ 2 Do you wish you studied more often?

___ 3 Would you like to cut down on your smoking or drinking?

___ 4 Do you experience diffculty in getting yourself to exercise regularly?

If you answered "yes" to any of these questions, you have struggled with the challenge of self-control. This Application discusses how you can use the principles and techniques of behavior modification to improve your self-control. *Behavior modification is a systematic approach to changing behavior through the application of the principles of conditioning.* Advocates of behavior modification assume that behavior is mainly a product of learning, conditioning, and environmental control. They further assume that *what is learned can be unlearned.* Thus, they set out to "recondition" people to produce more desirable and effective patterns of behavior.

The technology of behavior modification has been applied with great success in schools, businesses, hospitals, factories, child-care facilities, prisons, and mental health centers (Kazdin, 1982; O'Donohue, 1998; Rachman, 1992). Moreover, behavior modification techniques have proven particularly valuable in efforts to improve self-control. Our discussion will borrow liberally from an excellent book on self-modification by David Watson and Roland Tharp (1997). We will discuss five steps in the process of self-modification, which are outlined in Figure 6.20.

Specifying Your Target Behavior

The first step in a self-modification program is to specify the target behavior(s) that you want to change. Behavior modification can only be applied to a clearly defined, overt response, yet many people have difficulty pinpointing the behavior they hope to alter. They tend to describe their problems in terms of unobservable personality *traits* rather than overt *behaviors*. For example, asked what behavior he would like to change, a man might say, "I'm too irritable." That may be true, but it is of little help in designing a self-modification program. To use a behavioral approach, vague statements about traits need to be translated into precise descriptions of specific target behaviors.

To identify target responses, you need to ponder past behavior or closely observe future behavior and list specific *examples* of responses that lead to the trait description. For instance, the man who regards himself as "too irritable" might identify two overly frequent responses, such as arguing with his wife and snapping at his children. These are specific behaviors for which he could design a self-modification program.

Gathering Baseline Data

The second step in behavior modification is to gather baseline data. You need to systematically observe your target behavior for a period of time (usually a week or two) before you work out the details of your program. In gathering your baseline data, you need to monitor three things.

First, you need to determine the initial response level of your target behavior. After all, you can't tell whether your program is working effectively unless you have a baseline for comparison. In most cases, you would simply keep track of how often the target response occurs in a certain time interval. Thus, you might count the daily frequency of snapping at your children, smoking cigarettes, or biting your fingernails. *It is crucial to gather accurate data.* You should keep permanent written records, and it is usually best to portray these records graphically (see Figure 6.21 on the next page).

Second, you need to monitor the antecedents of your target behavior. *Antecedents are events that typically precede the target response.* Often these events play a major

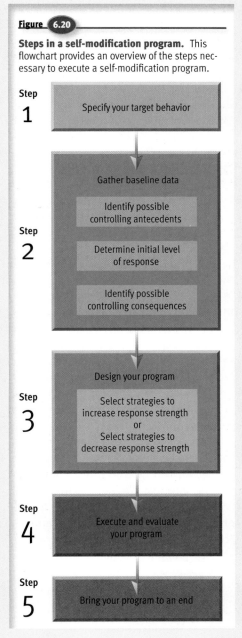

Figure 6.20

Steps in a self-modification program. This flowchart provides an overview of the steps necessary to execute a self-modification program.

Step 1 — Specify your target behavior

Step 2 — Gather baseline data
- Identify possible controlling antecedents
- Determine initial level of response
- Identify possible controlling consequences

Step 3 — Design your program
- Select strategies to increase response strength
  or
  Select strategies to decrease response strength

Step 4 — Execute and evaluate your program

Step 5 — Bring your program to an end

role in evoking your target behavior. For example, if your target is overeating, you might discover that the bulk of your overeating occurs late in the evening while you watch TV. If you can pinpoint this kind of antecedent-response connection, you may be able to design your program to circumvent or break the link.

Third, you need to monitor the typical consequences of your target behavior. Try to identify the reinforcers that are maintaining an undesirable target behavior or the unfavorable outcomes that are suppressing a desirable target behavior. In trying to identify reinforcers, remember that avoidance behavior is usually maintained by negative reinforcement. That is, the payoff for avoidance is usually the removal of something aversive, such as anxiety or a threat to self-esteem. You should also take into account the fact that a response may not be reinforced every time, as most behavior is maintained by intermittent reinforcement.

Designing Your Program

Once you have selected a target behavior and gathered adequate baseline data, it is time to plan your intervention program. Generally speaking, your program will be designed either to increase or to decrease the frequency of a target response.

Increasing Response Strength
Efforts to increase the frequency of a target response depend largely on the use of positive reinforcement. In other words, you reward yourself for behaving properly. Although the basic strategy is quite simple, doing it skillfully involves a number of considerations.

Selecting a Reinforcer To use positive reinforcement, you need to find a reward that will be effective for you. Reinforcement is subjective. What is reinforcing for one person may not be reinforcing for another. Figure 6.22 lists questions you can ask yourself to help you determine your personal reinforcers.

You don't have to come up with spectacular new reinforcers that you've never experienced before. *You can use reinforcers that you*

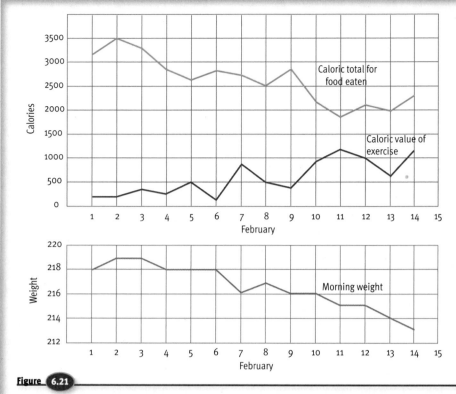

Figure 6.21

Example of record keeping in a self-modification program for losing weight. Graphic records are ideal for tracking progress in behavior modification efforts.

are already getting. However, you have to restructure the contingencies so that you get them only if you behave appropriately. For example, if you normally buy two compact discs per week, you might make these purchases contingent on studying a certain number of hours during the week.

Arranging the Contingencies Once you have chosen your reinforcer, you have to set up reinforcement contingencies. These contingencies will describe the exact behavioral goals that must be met and the reinforcement that may then be awarded. For example, in a program to increase exercise, you might make spending $40 on clothes (the reinforcer) contingent on having jogged 15 miles during the week (the target behavior).

Try to set behavioral goals that are both challenging and realistic. You want your goals to be challenging so that they lead to improvement in your behavior. However, setting unrealistically high goals—a common mistake in self-modification—often leads to unnecessary discouragement.

You also need to be concerned about doling out too much reinforcement. If reinforcement is too easy to get, you may become *satiated,* and the reinforcer may lose its motivational power. For example, if you were to reward yourself with virtually all the compact discs you wanted, this reinforcer would lose its incentive value.

One way to avoid the satiation problem is to put yourself on a token economy. A *token economy* is a system for doling out symbolic reinforcers that are exchanged later for a variety of genuine reinforcers. Thus, you might develop a point system for exercise behavior, accumulating points that can be spent on compact discs, movies, restaurant meals, and so forth (see Figure 6.23).

Decreasing Response Strength
Let's turn now to the challenge of reducing the frequency of an undesirable response. You can go about this task in a number of ways. Your principal options include reinforcement, control of antecedents, and punishment.

Figure 6.22

Selecting a reinforcer. Finding a good reinforcer to use in a behavior modification program can require a lot of thought. The questions listed here can help people identify their personal reinforcers. (Adapted from Watson and Tharp, 1997.)

1. What will be the rewards of achieving your goal?
2. What kind of praise do you like to receive, from yourself and others?
3. What kinds of things do you like to have?
4. What are your major interests?
5. What are your hobbies?
6. What people do you like to be with?
7. What do you like to do with those people?
8. What do you do for fun?
9. What do you do to relax?
10. What do you do to get away from it all?
11. What makes you feel good?
12. What would be a nice present to receive?
13. What kinds of things are important to you?
14. What would you buy if you had an extra $20? $50? $100?
15. On what do you spend your money each week?
16. What behaviors do you perform every day? (Don't overlook the obvious or commonplace.)
17. Are there any behaviors you usually perform instead of the target behavior?
18. What would you hate to lose?
19. Of the things you do every day, which would you hate to give up?
20. What are your favorite daydreams and fantasies?
21. What are the most relaxing scenes you can imagine?

Reinforcement Reinforcers can be used in an indirect way to decrease the frequency of a response. This may sound paradoxical, since you have learned that reinforcement strengthens a response. The trick lies in how you define the target behavior. For example, in the case of overeating you might define your target behavior as eating more than 1600 calories a day (an excess response that you want to decrease) or eating less than 1600 calories a day (a deficit response that you want to increase). You can choose the latter definition and reinforce yourself whenever you eat less than 1600 calories in a day. Thus, you can reinforce yourself for not emitting a response, or for emitting it less, and thereby decrease a response through reinforcement.

Control of Antecedents A worthwhile strategy for decreasing the occurrence of an undesirable response may be to identify its antecedents and avoid exposure to them. This strategy is especially useful when you are trying to decrease the frequency of a consummatory response, such as smoking or eating. In the case of overeating, for instance, the easiest way to resist temptation is to avoid having to face it. Thus, you might stay away from enticing restaurants, minimize time spent in your kitchen, shop for groceries just after eating (when willpower is higher), and avoid purchasing favorite foods.

Punishment The strategy of decreasing unwanted behavior by punishing yourself for that behavior is an obvious option that people tend to overuse. The biggest problem with punishment in a self-modification effort is that it is difficult to follow through and punish yourself. Nonetheless, there may be situations in which your manipulations of reinforcers need to be bolstered by the threat of punishment.

If you're going to use punishment, keep two guidelines in mind. First, do not use punishment alone. Use it in conjunction with positive reinforcement. If you set up a program in which you can earn only negative consequences, you probably won't stick to it. Second, use a relatively mild punishment so that you will actually be able to administer it to yourself.

Executing and Evaluating Your Program

Once you have designed your program, the next step is to put it to work by enforcing the contingencies that you have carefully planned. During this period, you need to continue to accurately record the frequency of your target behavior so you can evaluate your progress. The success of your program depends on your not "cheating." The most common form of cheating is to reward yourself when you have not actually earned it.

You can do two things to increase the likelihood that you will comply with your program. One is to make up a *behavioral contract—a written agreement outlining a promise to adhere to the contingencies of a behavior modification program.* The formality of signing such a contract in front of friends or family seems to make many people take their program more seriously. You can further reduce the likelihood of cheating by having someone other than yourself dole out the reinforcers and punishments.

Behavior modification programs often require some fine-tuning. So don't be surprised if you need to make a few adjustments. Several flaws are especially common in designing self-modification programs. Among those that you should look out for are (1) depending on a weak reinforcer, (2) permitting lengthy delays between appropriate behavior and delivery of reinforcers, and (3) trying to do too much too quickly by setting unrealistic goals. Often, a small revision or two can turn a failing program around and make it a success.

Ending Your Program

Generally, when you design your program you should spell out the conditions under which you will bring it to an end. This involves setting terminal goals such as reaching a certain weight, studying with a certain regularity, or going without cigarettes for a certain length of time. Often, it is a good idea to phase out your program by planning a gradual reduction in the frequency or potency of your reinforcement for appropriate behavior.

Figure 6.23

Example of a token economy. This token economy was set up to strengthen three types of exercise behavior. The person can exchange tokens for four types of reinforcers.

Response earning tokens

Response	Amount	Number of tokens
Jogging	1/2 mile	4
Jogging	1 mile	8
Jogging	2 miles	16
Tennis	1 hour	4
Tennis	2 hours	8
Sit-ups	25	1
Sit-ups	50	2

Redemption value of tokens

Reinforcer	Tokens required
Purchase one compact disc of your choice	30
Go to movie	50
Go to nice restaurant	100
Take special weekend trip	500

CRITICAL THINKING APPLICATION

Manipulating Emotions: Pavlov and Persuasion

With all due respect to the great Ivan Pavlov, when we focus on his demonstration that dogs can be trained to slobber in response to a tone, it is easy to lose sight of the importance of classical conditioning. At first glance, most people do not see a relationship between Pavlov's slobbering dogs and anything that they are even remotely interested in. However, in the main body of the chapter, we saw that classical conditioning actually contributes to the regulation of many important aspects of behavior, including fears, phobias, and other emotional reactions; immune function and other physiological processes; food preferences; and even sexual arousal. In this Application you will learn that classical conditioning is routinely used to manipulate emotions in persuasive efforts. If you watch TV, you have been subjected to Pavlovian techniques! An understanding of these techniques can help you recognize when your emotions are being manipulated by advertisers, politicians, and the media.

Perhaps the most interesting aspect of classically conditioned emotional responses is that people often are unaware of the origin of these responses, or even that they feel the way they do. Obviously, if a cockroach can be conditioned, the process does not depend on conscious awareness. The fact that conditioning can take place without awareness makes it a highly attractive tool for people who seek to shape others' attitudes. The key to the process is simply to manipulate the automatic, subconscious associations that people make in response to various stimuli. Let's look at how this manipulation is done in advertising, business negotiations, and the world of politics.

Classical Conditioning in Advertising

The art of manipulating people's associations has been perfected by the advertising industry. Advertisers consistently endeavor to pair the products they are peddling with stimuli that seem likely to elicit positive emotional responses (see Figure 6.24). An extensive variety of stimuli are used for this purpose. Products are paired with well-liked celebrity spokespersons; depictions of warm, loving families; beautiful pastoral scenery; cute, cuddly pets; enchanting, rosy-cheeked children; upbeat, pleasant music; opulent surroundings that reek of wealth; and, above all else, extremely attractive models—especially, glamorous, alluring women. Advertisers also like to pair their products with exciting events, such as the NBA Finals, and cherished symbols, such as flags and the Olympic rings insignia.

Advertisers mostly seek to associate their products with stimuli that evoke pleasurable feelings of a general sort, but in some cases they try to create more specific associations. For example, cigarette brands sold mainly to men are frequently paired with tough-looking guys in rugged settings to create an association between the cigarettes and masculinity. In contrast, cigarette brands that are mainly marketed to women are paired with images that evoke feelings of femininity. In a similar vein, manufacturers of designer jeans typically seek to forge associations between their products and things that are young, urban, and hip. Advertisers marketing expensive automobiles or platinum credit cards pair their products with symbols of affluence, luxury, and privilege, such as mansions, butlers, and dazzling jewelry.

Classical Conditioning in Business Negotiations

In the world of business interactions, two standard practices are designed to get customers to make an association between one's business and pleasureable feelings. The first is to take customers out to dinner at fine restaurants. The provision of delicious food and fine wine in a luxurious

Figure 6.24

Classical conditioning in advertising. Many advertisers attempt to make their products conditioned stimuli that elicit pleasant emotional responses. The most common strategy is to present a product in association with an attractive or likable person or with enjoyable surroundings.

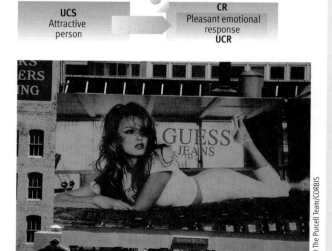

CS
Products
(e.g., clothes)

UCS
Attractive
person

CR
Pleasant emotional
response
UCR

© The Purcell Team/CORBIS

environment is a powerful unconditioned stimulus that reliably elicits pleasant feelings that are likely to be associated with one's host. The second practice is the strategy of entertaining customers at major events, such as concerts and football games. Over the last decade, America's sports arenas have largely been rebuilt with vastly more "luxury skyboxes" to accommodate this business tactic. It reaches its zenith every year at the Super Bowl, where most of the seats go to the guests of Fortune 500 corporations. This practice pairs the host with both pleasant feelings and the excitement of a big event.

It is worth noting that these strategies take advantage of other processes besides classical conditioning. They also make use of the *reciprocity norm*—the social rule that one should pay back in kind what one receives from others (Cialdini, 1993). Thus, wining and dining clients creates a sense of obligation that they should reciprocate their hosts' generosity—presumably in their business dealings.

Classical Conditioning in the World of Politics

Like advertisers, candidates running for election need to influence the attitudes of many people quickly, subtly, and effectively—and they depend on classical conditioning to help them do so. For example, have you noticed how politicians show up at an endless variety of pleasant public events (such as the opening of a new mall) that often have nothing to do with their public service? When a sports team wins some sort of championship, local politicians are drawn like flies to the subsequent celebrations. They want to pair themselves with these positive events, so that they are associated with pleasant emotions.

Election campaign ads use the same techniques as commercial ads. Candidates are paired with popular celebrities, wholesome families, pleasant music, and symbols of patriotism. Cognizant of the power of classical conditioning, politicians also exercise great care to ensure that they are not paired with people or events that might trigger negative feelings. For example, in 1999, when the U.S. government finally turned control of the Panama Canal over to Panama, President Clinton and Vice-President Gore chose to not attend the ceremonies because this event was viewed negatively in some quarters.

The ultimate political perversion of the the principles of classical conditioning probably occurred in Nazi Germany. The Nazis used many propaganda techniques to create prejudice toward Jews and members of other targeted groups (such as Gypsies). One such stategy was the repeated pairing of disgusting, repulsive images with stereotypical pictures of Jews. For example, the Nazis would show alternating pictures of rats or roaches crawling over filthy garbage and stereotypical Jewish faces, so that the two images would become associated in the minds of the viewers. Thus, the German population was conditioned to have negative emotional reactions to Jews and to associate them with vermin subject to extermination. The Nazis reasoned that if people would not hesitate to exterminate rats and roaches, then why not human beings associated with these vermin?

Becoming More Aware of Classical Conditioning Processes

How effective are the efforts to manipulate people's emotions through Pavlovian conditioning? It's hard to say. In the real world, these strategies are always used in combination with other persuasive tactics, which creates multiple confounds that make it difficult to assess the impact of the Pavlovian techniques. Laboratory research can eliminate these confounds, but surprisingly little research on these strategies has been published, and virtually all of it has dealt with advertising. The advertising studies suggest that classical conditioning can be effective and leave enduring imprints on consumers' attitudes (Grossman & Till, 1998; Stuart, Shimp, & Engle, 1987), but a great deal of additional research is needed. Given the monumental sums that advertisers spend using these techniques, it seems reasonable to speculate that individual companies have data on their specific practices to demonstrate their efficacy, but these data are not made available to the public.

What can you do to reduce the extent to which your emotions are manipulated through Pavlovian procedures? Well, you could turn off your radio and TV, close up your magazines, stop your newspaper, disconnect your modem, and withdraw into a media-shielded shell, but that hardly seems realistic for most people. Rather, the best defense is to make a conscious effort to become more aware of the pervasive attempts to condition your emotions and attitudes. Some research on persuasion suggests that *to be forewarned is to be forearmed* (Pfau et al., 1990). In other words, if you know how media sources try to manipulate you, you should be more resistant to their strategies.

Table 6.2	Critical Thinking Skills Discussed in This Application
Skill	**Description**
Understanding how Pavlovian conditioning can be used to manipulate emotions	The critical thinker understands how stimuli can be paired together to create automatic associations that people may not be aware of.
Developing the ability to detect conditioning procedures used in the media	The critical thinker can recognize Pavlovian conditioning tactics in commercial and political advertisements.

REVIEW

Key Ideas

Classical Conditioning
• Classical conditioning explains how a neutral stimulus can acquire the capacity to elicit a response originally evoked by another stimulus. This kind of conditioning was originally described by Ivan Pavlov, who conditioned dogs to salivate when a tone was presented. Many kinds of everyday responses are regulated through classical conditioning, including phobias, anxiety responses, pleasant emotional responses, and physiological responses.

• Stimulus contiguity plays a key role in the acquisition of new conditioned responses. A conditioned response may be weakened and extinguished entirely when the CS is no longer paired with the UCS. In some cases, spontaneous recovery occurs, and an extinguished response reappears after a period of nonexposure to the CS.

• Conditioning may generalize to additional stimuli that are similar to the original CS. The opposite of generalization is discrimination, which involves not responding to stimuli that resemble the original CS. Higher-order conditioning occurs when a CS functions as if it were a UCS, to establish new conditioning.

Operant Conditioning
• Operant conditioning, which was pioneered by B. F. Skinner, involves largely voluntary responses that are governed by their consequences. The key dependent variable in operant conditioning is the rate of response over time. New operant responses can be shaped by gradually reinforcing closer and closer approximations of the desired response.

• In operant conditioning, when reinforcement is terminated, the response rate usually declines and extinction may occur. Operant responses are regulated by discriminative stimuli that are cues for the likelihood of obtaining reinforcers.

• The central process in reinforcement is the strengthening of a response. Primary reinforcers are unlearned. In contrast, secondary reinforcers acquire their reinforcing quality through conditioning.

• Schedules of reinforcement influence patterns of operant responding. Intermittent schedules produce greater resistance to extinction than similar continuous schedules. Ratio schedules tend to yield higher rates of response than interval schedules. Shorter intervals and higher ratios are associated with faster responding.

• Concurrent schedules of reinforcement permit researchers to study how organisms make choices among operant responses. The matching law suggests that organisms strive to maximize their reinforcement. Optimal foraging theory asserts that animals' food seeking behaviors optimize the nutrition gained in relation to the effort expended.

• Responses can be strengthened through either the presentation of positive reinforcers or the removal of negative reinforcers. Negative reinforcement regulates escape and avoidance learning. Punishment involves unfavorable consequences that lead to a decline in response strength. Some of the side effects associated with punishment include negative emotional responses and increased aggressive behavior.

Changing Directions in the Study of Conditioning
• Recent decades have brought profound changes in our understanding of conditioning. The findings on instinctive drift and conditioned taste aversion have led to the recognition that there are biological constraints on conditioning. Evolutionary psychologists argue that learning processes vary somewhat across species because learning mechansims have sometimes been modified in the course of evolution.

• Studies have also demonstrated that cognitive processes play a larger role in conditioning than originally believed. Modern theories hold that conditioning is a matter of detecting the contingencies that govern events.

Observational Learning
• In observational learning, an organism is conditioned by watching a model's conditioning. Both classical and operant conditioning can occur through observational learning. Modeling appears to explain why physical punishment increases youngsters' aggressiveness.

Putting It in Perspective
• Two of our key themes were especially apparent in our coverage of learning and conditioning. One theme involves the interaction of heredity and the environment in governing behavior. The other involves the way progress in psychology affects society at large.

Personal Application • Achieving Self-Control Through Behavior Modification
• The first step in self-modification is to specify the overt target behavior to be increased or decreased. The second step involves gathering baseline data about the initial rate of the target response and identifying any typical antecedents and consequences associated with the behavior.

• The third step is to design a program. If you are trying to increase the strength of a response, you'll depend on positive reinforcement. A number of strategies can be used to decrease the strength of a response, including reinforcement, control of antecedents, and punishment. The fourth step involves executing and evaluating your program. The final step is to determine how and when you will phase out your program.

Critical Thinking Application • Manipulating Emotions: Pavlov and Persuasion
• Advertisers routinely pair their products with stimuli that seem likely to elicit positive emotional responses or other specific feelings. The practice of taking customers out to dinner or to major events also takes advantage of Pavlovian conditioning. Politicians also work to pair themselves with positive events. The best defense is to become more aware of efforts to manipulate your emotions.

Key Terms

Acquisition
Antecedents
Avoidance learning
Behavior modification
Behavioral contract
Classical conditioning
Concurrent schedules of reinforcement
Conditioned reinforcers
Conditioned response (CR)
Conditioned stimulus (CS)
Continuous reinforcement
Cumulative recorder
Discriminative stimuli
Elicit
Emit
Escape learning
Extinction
Fixed-interval (FI) schedule
Fixed-ratio (FR) schedule
Higher-order conditioning
Intermittent reinforcement
Learning
Matching law
Negative reinforcement
Observational learning
Operant conditioning
Optimal foraging theory
Pavlovian conditioning
Positive reinforcement
Primary reinforcers
Punishment
Reinforcement
Reinforcement contingencies
Resistance to extinction
Schedule of reinforcement
Secondary reinforcers
Shaping
Skinner box
Spontaneous recovery
Stimulus contiguity
Stimulus discrimination
Stimulus generalization
Token economy
Trial
Unconditioned response (UCR)
Unconditioned stimulus (UCS)
Variable-interval (VI) schedule
Variable-ratio (VR) schedule

Key People

Albert Bandura
Ivan Pavlov
Robert Rescorla
B. F. Skinner
John B. Watson

PRACTICE TEST

1. After repeated pairings of a tone with meat powder, Pavlov found that a dog will salivate when the tone is presented. Salivation to the tone is a(n):
   A. unconditioned stimulus.
   B. unconditioned response.
   C. conditioned stimulus.
   D. conditioned response.

2. Sam's wife always wears the same black nightgown whenever she is "in the mood" for sexual relations. Sam becomes sexually aroused as soon as he sees his wife in the nightgown. For Sam, the nightgown is a(n):
   A. unconditioned stimulus.
   B. unconditioned response.
   C. conditioned stimulus.
   D. conditioned response.

3. Watson and Rayner (1920) conditioned "Little Albert" to fear white rats by banging a hammer on a steel bar as he played with a white rat. Later, it was discovered that Albert feared not only white rats but white stuffed toys and Santa's beard as well. Albert's fear of these other objects can be attributed to:
   A. shaping.
   B. stimulus generalization.
   C. stimulus discrimination.
   D. an overactive imagination.

4. The phenomenon of higher-order conditioning shows that:
   A. only a genuine, natural UCS can be used to establish a CR.
   B. auditory stimuli are easier to condition than visual stimuli.
   C. visual stimuli are easier to condition than auditory stimuli.
   D. an already established CS can be used in the place of a natural UCS.

5. Which of the following statements is (are) true?
   A. Classical conditioning regulates reflexive, involuntary responses exclusively.
   B. Operant conditioning regulates voluntary responses exclusively.
   C. The distinction between the two types of conditioning is not absolute, with both types jointly and interactively governing some aspects of behavior.
   D. a and b.

6. In a Skinner box, the dependent variable is:
   A. the force with which the lever is pressed or the disk is pecked.
   B. the schedule of reinforcement used.
   C. the rate of responding.
   D. the speed of the cumulative recorder.

7. A primary reinforcer has _____ reinforcing properties; a secondary reinforcer has _____ reinforcing properties.
   A. biological; acquired
   B. conditioned; unconditioned
   C. weak; potent
   D. immediate; delayed

8. The steady, rapid responding of a person playing a slot machine is an example of the pattern of responding typically generated on a _____ schedule.
   A. fixed-ratio
   B. variable-ratio
   C. fixed-interval
   D. variable-interval

9. Positive reinforcement _____ the rate of responding; negative reinforcement _____ the rate of responding.
   A. increases; decreases
   B. decreases; increases
   C. increases; increases
   D. decreases; decreases

10. Analyses of avoidance learning suggest that many phobias are acquired through _____ conditioning and maintained through _____ conditioning.
    A. classical; operant
    B. operant; classical
    C. classical; classical
    D. operant; operant

11. The studies by Garcia and his colleagues demonstrate that rats very easily learn to associate a taste CS with a(n) _____ UCS.
    A. shock
    B. visual
    C. auditory
    D. nausea-inducing

12. According to Rescorla, the strength of a conditioned response depends on:
    A. the number of trials in which the CS and UCS are paired.
    B. the number of trials in which the CS is presented alone.
    C. the percentage of trials in which the CS and UCS are paired.
    D. the schedule of reinforcement employed.

13. The evolutionary perspective on learning suggests that:
    A. only mammals respond to operant conditioning.
    B. species-specific learning tendencies are a myth.
    C. differences in the adaptive challenges faced by various species have led to some species-specific learning tendencies.
    D. only mammals respond to classical conditioning.

14. Albert Bandura:
    A. was the first to describe species-specific learning tendencies.
    B. was the founder of behaviorism.
    C. pioneered the study of classical conditioning.
    D. pioneered the study of observational learning.

15. In designing a self-modification program, control of antecedents should be used:
    A. by people who are in poor physical condition.
    B. only when your usual reinforcers are unavailable.
    C. when you want to decrease the frequency of a response.
    D. when you are initially not capable of making the target response.

Answers

1	D	pages 169–171	6	C	page 176	11	D	page 187
2	C	pages 169–171	7	A	page 180	12	C	page 188
3	B	pages 173–174	8	B	pages 180–181	13	C	pages 187–188
4	D	page 174	9	C	pages 183–184	14	D	page 189
5	C	page 175	10	A	page 184	15	C	page 195

INFOTRAC COLLEGE EDITION

Go to the Wadsworth Psychology Study Center for quiz questions, research updates, interactive exercises, and suggested readings in INFOTRAC related to this chapter:
http://psychology.wadsworth.com/product/0534593100s

CHAPTER 7

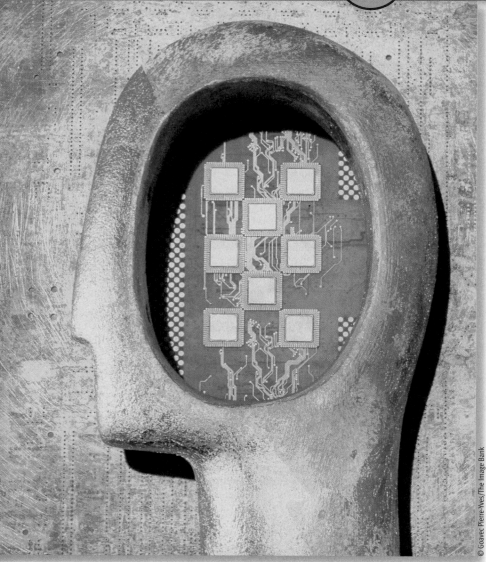

© Goavec Pierre-Yves/The Image Bank

Human Memory

© Goavec Pierre-Yves/The Image Bank

If you live in the United States, you've undoubtedly handled thousands upon thousands of American pennies. Surely, then, you remember what a penny looks like—or do you? Take a look at Figure 7.1. Which drawing corresponds to a real penny?

Did you have a hard time selecting the real one? If so, you're not alone. Nickerson and Adams (1979) found that most people can't recognize the real penny in this collection of drawings. And their surprising finding was not a fluke. Undergraduates in England showed even worse memory for British coins (Jones, 1990).

How can that be? Why do most of us have so poor a memory for an object we see every day?

Let's try another exercise. A definition of a word follows. It's not a particularly common word, but there's a good chance that you're familiar with it. Try to think of the word.

Definition: Favoritism shown or patronage granted by persons in high office to relatives or close friends.

If you can't think of the word, perhaps you can remember what letter of the alphabet it begins with, or what it sounds like. If so, you're experiencing the *tip-of-the-tongue phenomenon,* in which forgotten information feels like it's just out of reach. In this case, the word you may be reaching for is *nepotism.*

You've probably endured the tip-of-the-tongue phenomenon while taking exams. You blank out on a term that you're sure you know. You may feel as if you're on the verge of remembering the term, but you can't quite come up with it. Later, perhaps while you're driving home, the term suddenly comes to you. "Of course," you may say to yourself,

"how could I forget that?" That's an interesting question. Clearly, the term was stored in your memory.

As these examples suggest, memory involves more than taking in information and storing it in some mental compartment. In fact, psychologists probing the workings of memory have had to grapple with three enduring questions: (1) How does information get *into* memory? (2) How is information

Figure 7.1

A simple memory test. Nickerson and Adams (1979) presented these 15 versions of an object most people have seen hundreds or thousands of times and asked, **"Which one is correct?"** (From "Long-Term Memory for a Common Object," by R. S. Nickerson and M.J. Adams, 1979, *Cognitive Psychology, 11,* 287–307. Copyright © 1979 by Academic Press, Inc. Reprinted by permission.)

Figure **7.2**

Three key processes in memory. Memory depends on three sequential processes: encoding, storage, and retrieval. Some theorists have drawn an analogy between these processes and elements of information processing by computers as depicted here. The analogies for encoding and retrieval work pretty well, but the storage analogy is somewhat misleading. When information is stored on a hard drive, it remains unchanged indefinitely and you can retrieve an exact copy. As you will learn in this chapter, human memory storage is a much more dynamic process. Our memories change over time and are rough reconstructions rather than exact copies of past events.

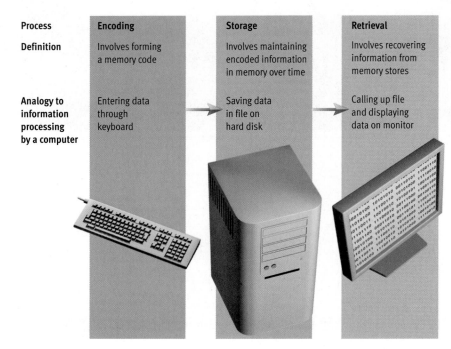

Process	Encoding	Storage	Retrieval
Definition	Involves forming a memory code	Involves maintaining encoded information in memory over time	Involves recovering information from memory stores
Analogy to information processing by a computer	Entering data through keyboard	Saving data in file on hard disk	Calling up file and displaying data on monitor

maintained in memory? (3) How is information *pulled back out* of memory? These three questions correspond to the three key processes involved in memory (see Figure 7.2 above): *encoding* (getting information in), *storage* (maintaining it), and *retrieval* (getting it out).

Encoding involves forming a memory code. For example, when you form a memory code for a word, you might emphasize how it looks, how it sounds, or what it means. Encoding usually requires attention, which is why you may not be able to recall exactly what a penny looks like—most people don't pay much attention to the appearance of a penny. As you'll see throughout this chapter, memory is largely an active process. For the most part, you're unlikely to remember something unless you make a conscious effort to do so. **Storage involves maintaining encoded information in memory over time.** Psychologists have focused much of their memory research on trying to identify just what factors help or hinder memory storage. But, as

the tip-of-the-tongue phenomenon shows, information storage isn't enough to guarantee that you'll remember something. You need to be able to get information out of storage. **Retrieval involves recovering information from memory stores.** Research issues concerned with retrieval include the study of how people search memory and why some retrieval strategies are more effective than others.

Most of this chapter is devoted to an examination of memory encoding, storage, and retrieval. As you'll see, these basic processes help explain the ultimate puzzle in the study of memory: why people forget. After our discussion of forgetting, we will take a brief look at the physiological bases of memory. Finally, we will discuss the theoretical controversy about whether there are separate memory systems for different types of information. The chapter's Personal Application provides some practical advice on how to improve your memory. The Critical Thinking Application discusses some reasons that memory is less reliable than people assume it to be.

Encoding: Getting Information into Memory

Have you ever been embarrassed because you couldn't remember someone's name? Perhaps you realized only 30 seconds after meeting someone that you had already "forgotten" his or her name. More often than not, this familiar kind of forgetting is due to a failure to form a memory code for the name. When you're introduced to people, you're often busy sizing them up and thinking

about what you're going to say. With your attention diverted in this way, names go in one ear and out the other. You don't remember them because they are never encoded for storage into memory.

This problem illustrates that encoding is an important process in memory. In this section, we discuss the role of attention in encoding, types of encoding, and ways to enrich the encoding process.

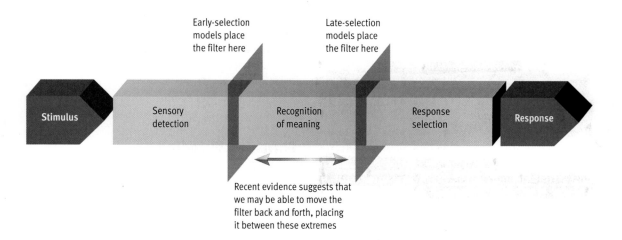

Figure 7.3

Models of selective attention. Early-selection models propose that input is filtered before meaning is processed. Late-selection models hold that filtering occurs after the processing of meaning. There is evidence to support early, late, and intermediate selection, suggesting that the location of the attentional filter may not be fixed.

Early-selection models place the filter here

Late-selection models place the filter here

Recent evidence suggests that we may be able to move the filter back and forth, placing it between these extremes

The Role of Attention

Although there are some fascinating exceptions, you generally need to pay attention to information if you intend to remember it (Craik et al., 1996; Mulligan, 1998). For example, if you sit through a class lecture but pay little attention to it, you're unlikely to remember much of what the professor had to say.

Attention involves focusing awareness on a narrowed range of stimuli or events. Psychologists routinely refer to "selective attention," but the words are really redundant. Attention *is* selection of input. If you pause to devote a little attention to the matter, you'll realize that selective attention is critical to everyday functioning. If your attention were distributed equally among all stimulus inputs, life would be utter chaos. If you weren't able to filter out most of the potential stimulation around you, you wouldn't be able to read a book, converse with a friend, or even carry on a coherent train of thought.

Attention is usually likened to a *filter* that screens out most potential stimuli while allowing a select few to pass through into conscious awareness. However, a great deal of debate has been devoted to *where* the filter is located in the information-processing system. The key issue in this debate is whether stimuli are screened out early, during sensory input, or late, after the brain has processed the meaning or significance of the input. Hence, models of attention are often characterized as *early-selection* or *late-selection* theories (see Figure 7.3).

Which view is supported by the weight of evidence—early selection or late selection? There is ample evidence for *both* as well as for intermediate selection (Cowan, 1988; Johnston & Dark, 1986). These findings have led some theorists to conclude that the location of the attention filter may be flexible rather than fixed (Johnston & Heinz, 1978; Shiffrin, 1988).

Levels of Processing

SIM5, 6a

Attention is critical to the encoding of memories, but not all attention is created equal. You can attend to things in different ways, focusing on different aspects of the stimulus input. According to some theorists, these qualitative differences in *how* people attend to information are the main factors influencing how much they remember. For example, Fergus Craik and Robert Lockhart (1972) argue that different rates of forgetting occur because some methods of encoding create more durable memory codes than others.

Craik and Lockhart propose that incoming information can be processed at different levels. For instance, they maintain that in dealing with verbal information, people engage in three progressively deeper levels of processing: structural, phonemic, and semantic encoding (see Figure 7.4). *Structural encoding* is relatively shallow processing that emphasizes the physical structure of the stimulus. For example, if words are flashed on a screen, structural

Figure 7.4

Levels-of-processing theory. According to Craik and Lockhart (1972), structural, phonemic, and semantic encoding—which can be elicited by questions such as those shown on the right—involve progressively deeper levels of processing, which should result in more durable memories.

Level of processing	Type of encoding	Example of questions used to elicit appropriate encoding
Shallow processing	*Structural encoding:* emphasizes the physical structure of the stimulus	Is the word written in capital letters?
Intermediate processing	*Phonemic encoding:* emphasizes what a word sounds like	Does the word rhyme with weight?
Deep processing	*Semantic encoding:* emphasizes the meaning of verbal input	Would the word fit in the sentence: "He met a _____ on the street"?

Depth of processing

encoding registers such things as how they were printed (capital, lowercase, and so on) or the length of the words (how many letters). Further analysis may result in *phonemic encoding,* which emphasizes what a word sounds like. Phonemic encoding involves naming or saying (perhaps silently) the words. Finally, *semantic encoding* emphasizes the meaning of verbal input. Semantic encoding involves thinking about the objects and actions the words represent. ***Levels-of-processing theory** pro-poses that deeper levels of processing result in longer-lasting memory codes.*

In one experimental test of levels-of-processing theory, Craik and Tulving (1975) compared the durability of structural, phonemic, and semantic encoding. They directed subjects' attention to particular aspects of briefly presented stimulus words by asking them questions about various characteristics of the words (examples are in Figure 7.4). The questions were designed to engage the participants in different levels of processing. The key hypothesis was that retention of the stimulus words would increase as subjects moved from structural to phonemic to semantic encoding. After responding to 60 words, the participants received an unexpected test of their memory for the words. As predicted, the subjects' recall was low after structural encoding, notably better after phonemic encoding, and highest after semantic encoding.

The hypothesis that deeper processing leads to enhanced memory has been replicated in many studies (Koriat & Melkman, 1987; Lockhart & Craik, 1990). Nonetheless, the levels-of-processing model is not without its weaknesses. Critics ask, what exactly is a "level" of processing? And how do we determine whether one level is deeper than another? Craik and Lockhart had hoped that the

time required for processing would prove to be a good indicator of depth. However, they found that it's possible to design a task in which structural encoding takes longer than deeper, semantic encoding. Thus, processing time has not proven to be a reliable index of processing depth, and the levels in levels-of-processing theory remain vaguely defined.

Enriching Encoding

Structural, phonemic, and semantic encoding do not exhaust your options when it comes to forming memory codes. There are other dimensions to encoding, dimensions that can enrich the encoding process and thereby improve memory.

Elaboration *can be created by examples*

Semantic encoding can often be enhanced through a process called elaboration. ***Elaboration** is linking a stimulus to other information at the time of encoding.* For example, let's say you read that phobias are often caused by classical conditioning, and you apply this idea to your own fear of spiders. In doing so, you are engaging in elaboration. The additional associations created by elaboration usually help people remember information. Differences in elaboration can help explain why different approaches to semantic processing result in varied amounts of retention (Craik & Tulving, 1975; Willoughby, Motz, & Wood, 1997).

Elaboration often consists of thinking of examples that illustrate an idea. The value of examples was demonstrated in a study in which participants read 32 paragraphs of information about a fictitious African country (Palmere et al., 1983). Each paragraph communicated one main idea, which was followed by no example, 1 example, 2 examples, or 3 examples. The effect of examples on memory was dramatic. As you can see in Figure 7.5, additional examples led to better memory. In this study, the examples were provided to the students, but self-generated examples created through elaboration would probably be even more valuable in enhancing memory.

Visual Imagery

Imagery—the creation of visual images to represent the words to be remembered—can also be used to enrich encoding. Of course, some words are easier to create images for than others. If you were asked to remember the word *juggler,* you could readily form an image of someone juggling balls. However, if you were asked to remember the word *truth,* you would probably have more difficulty forming

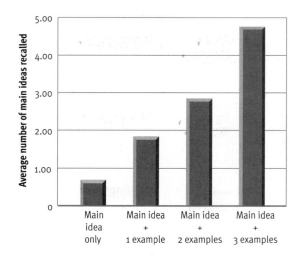

Figure 7.5

Effects of examples on retention of ideas. Palmere et al. (1983) manipulated the number of examples provided to illustrate the main idea of various paragraphs. As the number of examples increased from none to three, so did subjects' retention of the main ideas. (Data from Palmere et al., 1983)

a suitable image. The difference is that *juggler* refers to a concrete object whereas *truth* refers to an abstract concept. Allan Paivio (1969) points out that it is easier to form images of concrete objects than of abstract concepts. He believes that this ease of image formation affects memory. For example, in one study he found that subjects given pairs of words to remember showed better recall for high-imagery than low-imagery pairings (see Figure 7.6), demonstrating that visual imagery enriches encoding (Paivio, Smythe, & Yuille, 1968).

According to Paivio (1986), imagery facilitates memory because it provides a second kind of memory code, and two codes are better than one. His *dual-coding theory* holds that memory is enhanced by forming both semantic and visual codes, since either can lead to recall. Although some aspects of his theory have been questioned, it's clear that the use of mental imagery can enhance memory in many situations (Marschark, 1992; McCauley, Eskes, & Moscovitch, 1996). The value of visual imagery demonstrates once again that encoding plays a critical role in memory. But encoding is only one of the three key processes in memory. We turn next to the process of storage, which for many people is virtually synonymous with memory.

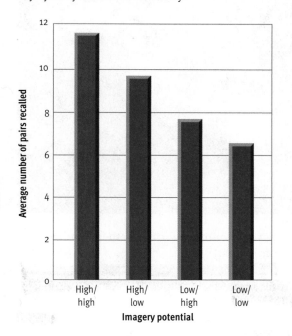

Figure 7.6

The effect of visual imagery on retention. Paivio, Smythe, and Yuille (1968) asked subjects to learn a list of 16 pairs of words. They manipulated whether the words were concrete, high-imagery words or abstract, low-imagery words. In terms of imagery potential, the list contained four types of pairings: high-high (*juggler-dress*), high-low (*letter-effort*), low-high (*duty-hotel*), and low-low (*quality-necessity*). The impact of imagery was quite evident. The best recall was of high-high pairings, and the worst recall was of low-low pairings. (Data from Paivio, Smythe, & Yuille, 1968)

Storage: Maintaining Information in Memory

In their efforts to understand memory storage, theorists have historically related it to the technologies of their age (Roediger, 1980). One of the earliest models used to explain memory storage was the wax tablet. Both Aristotle and Plato compared memory to a block of wax that differed in size and hardness for various individuals. Remembering, according to this analogy, was like stamping an impression into the wax. As long as the image remained in the wax, the memory would remain intact.

Modern theories of memory reflect the technological advances of the 20th century. For example, many theories formulated at the dawn of the computer age drew an analogy between information storage by computers and information storage in human memory (Atkinson & Shiffrin, 1968, 1971; Broadbent, 1958; Waugh & Norman, 1965). The main contribution of these *information-processing theories* was to subdivide memory into three separate memory stores (Estes, 1999; Pashler & Carrier, 1996). The names for these stores and their exact characteristics varied some from one theory to the next. For purposes of simplicity, we'll organize our discussion around the model devised by Atkinson and Shiffrin, which proved to be the most influential of the information-processing theories. According to their model, incoming information passes through two temporary storage buffers—the sensory store and short-term store—before it is transferred into a long-term store (see Figure 7.7 on the next page). Like the wax tablet before it, the information-processing model of memory is a metaphor; the three memory stores are not viewed as anatomical structures in the brain, but rather as functionally distinct types of memory.

Sensory Memory

The *sensory memory* preserves information in its original sensory form for a brief time, usually only a fraction of a second. Sensory memory allows the sensation of a visual pattern, sound, or touch to linger for a brief moment after the sensory stimulation is over. In the case of vision, people really perceive an *afterimage* rather than the actual stimulus. You can demonstrate the existence of afterimages for yourself by rapidly moving a light in circles in the dark. If you move the light fast enough, you should see a complete circle even though the light source is only a single point (see the photo on the next page). The sensory memory preserves the sensory image long enough for you to

Because the image of the flashlight persists briefly in sensory memory, when the flashlight is moved fast enough, the blending of afterimages causes people to see a continuous stream of light instead of a succession of individual points.

perceive a continuous circle rather than separate points of light.

The brief preservation of sensations in sensory memory gives you additional time to try to recognize stimuli. However, you'd better take advantage of sensory storage immediately, because it doesn't last long. In a classic experiment, George Sperling (1960) demonstrated that the memory trace in the visual sensory store decays in about one-quarter of a second. Memory traces in the auditory sensory store also appear to last approximately 1/4 of a second (Massaro & Loftus, 1996).

Short-Term Memory

Short-term memory (STM) is a limited-capacity store that can maintain unrehearsed information for up to about 20 seconds. In contrast, information stored in long-term memory may last weeks, months, or years. Actually, you can maintain

information in your short-term store for longer than 20 seconds. How? Primarily, by engaging in *rehearsal—the process of repetitively verbalizing or thinking about information.* You surely have used the rehearsal process on many occasions. For instance, when you obtain a phone number from the information operator, you probably recite it over and over until you can dial the number. Rehearsal keeps recycling the information through your short-term memory. In theory, this recycling could go on indefinitely, but in reality something eventually distracts you and breaks the rehearsal loop.

People's dependence on recitation to maintain information in short-term memory is apparent from the kinds of mistakes they tend to make when their efforts break down. For example, suppose that you were asked to remember a list of random letters such as

QPLHSX

presented briefly on a screen. Mistakes on this task usually involve *acoustic confusions*, in which the incorrect answers *sound* like the correct answers (Conrad, 1964; Hanson, 1990). For instance, you might mistakenly convert P to E because they sound alike. Notice, you are far less likely to convert P to R because they *look* alike. Even when information is presented visually, people tend to make acoustic mistakes, because they largely depend on phonemic encoding in short-term memory.

Durability of Storage

Without rehearsal, information in short-term memory is lost in less than 20 seconds (Wickens, 1999). This rapid loss was demonstrated in a study by Peterson and Peterson (1959). They measured how long undergraduates could remember three consonants if they couldn't rehearse them. To prevent

© Jeffry W. Myers/Stock, Boston

Figure 7.7

The Atkinson and Shiffrin (1971) model of memory storage. Atkinson and Shiffrin proposed that memory is made up of three information stores. *Sensory memory* can hold a large amount of information just long enough for a small portion of it to be selected for longer storage. *Short-term memory* has a limited capacity, and unless aided by rehearsal, its storage duration is brief. *Long-term memory* can store an apparently unlimited amount of information for indeterminate periods.

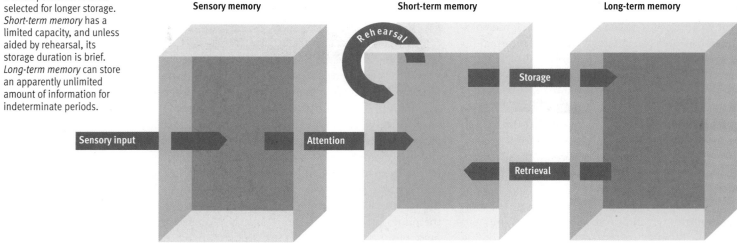

rehearsal, the Petersons required the students to count backward by threes from the time the consonants were presented until they saw a light that signaled the recall test (see Figure 7.8). Their results showed that participants' recall accuracy was pretty dismal after only 15 seconds. Other approaches to the issue have suggested that the typical duration of STM storage may even be shorter (Baddely, 1986). Theorists originally believed that the loss of information from short-term memory was due purely to time-related *decay* of memory traces, but follow-up research showed that *interference* from competing material also contributes (Cowan et al., 1997; Nairne, Neath, & Serra, 1997).

Capacity of Storage

Short-term memory is also limited in the number of items it can hold. The small capacity of STM was pointed out by George Miller (1956) in a famous paper titled "The Magical Number Seven, Plus or Minus Two: Some Limits on Our Capacity for Processing Information." Miller noticed that people could recall only about seven items on tasks that required them to remember unfamiliar material. The common thread in these tasks, Miller argued, was that they required the use of STM.

When short-term memory is filled to capacity, the insertion of new information often *displaces* some of the information currently in STM. For example, if you're memorizing a ten-item list of basic chemical

elements, the eighth, ninth, and tenth items in the list will begin to "bump out" earlier items. Similarly, if you're reciting the phone number of a pizza parlor you're about to call when someone asks, "How much is this pizza going to cost?" your retrieval of the cost information into STM may knock part of the phone number out of STM. The limited capacity of STM constrains people's ability to perform tasks in which they need to mentally juggle various pieces of information (Baddeley & Hitch, 1974).

You can increase the capacity of your short-term memory by combining stimuli into larger, possibly higher-order, units called *chunks* (Simon, 1974). A *chunk* is a group of familiar stimuli stored as a single unit. You can demonstrate the effect of chunking by asking someone to recall a sequence of 12 letters grouped in the following way:

FB - ITW - AC - IAIB - M

As you read the letters aloud, pause at the hyphens. Your subject will probably attempt to remember each letter separately because there are no obvious groups or chunks. But a string of 12 letters is too long for STM, so errors are likely. Now present the same string of letters to another person, but place the pauses in the following locations:

FBI - TWA - CIA - IBM

The letters now form four familiar chunks that should occupy only four slots in short-term memory, resulting in successful recall (Bower & Springston, 1970).

Web Link 7.1

The Magical Number Seven Plus or Minus Two.
In 1956, Princeton psychology professor George A. Miller published one of the most famous papers in the history of psychology: "The Magical Number Seven Plus or Minus Two: Some Limits on Our Capacity for Processing Information." At this site you'll find a copy of the original text with tables for you to see why this is such an important research milestone in psychology.

Courtesy of George Miller

"*The Magical Number Seven, Plus or Minus Two.*"
GEORGE MILLER

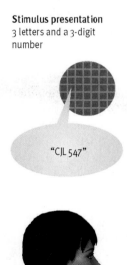

Warning
Green signal light: trial about to begin

Stimulus presentation
3 letters and a 3-digit number

"CJL 547"

Retention interval
Subject counts backward by threes for intervals of 3 to 18 seconds

547...
544...
541...
538...
535...

Recall signal and report
Red signal light: recall letters

"CJL ?"

Time (seconds)

Figure 7.8

Peterson and Peterson's (1959) study of short-term memory. After a warning light was flashed, the subjects were given three consonants to remember. The researchers prevented rehearsals by giving the subjects a three-digit number at the same time and telling them to count backward by three from that number until given the signal to recall the letters. By varying the amount of time between stimulus presentation and recall, Peterson and Peterson were able to measure the rate of decay in short-term memory.

To successfully chunk the letters I B M, a subject must first recognize these letters as a familiar unit. This familiarity has to be stored somewhere in long-term memory. Hence, in this case information was transferred from long-term into short-term memory. This is not unusual. People routinely draw information out of their long-term memory banks to evaluate and understand information that they are working with in short-term memory.

Short-Term Memory as "Working Memory" 6b

Twenty years of research eventually uncovered a number of problems with the original model of short-term memory (Nairne, 1996; Neath, 1998). Among other things, studies showed that short-term memory is *not* limited to phonemic encoding and that decay and displacement are *not* the only processes responsible for the loss of information from STM. These and other findings suggest that short-term memory involves more than a simple rehearsal buffer, as originally envisioned. To make sense of such findings, Alan Baddeley (1989, 1992) has proposed a more complex model of short-term memory that characterizes it as "working memory."

According to Baddeley, working memory consists of three components (see Figure 7.9). The first is the *rehearsal loop* that represented all of STM in the original model. This component is at work when you use recitation to temporarily hold on to a phone number. The second component in working memory is a *visuospatial sketchpad* that permits people to temporarily hold and manipulate visual images. This component is at work when you try to mentally rearrange the furniture in your bedroom. The third component is an *executive control system*. It handles the limited amount of information that people can juggle at one time as they engage in reasoning and decision making. This component is at work when you mentally weigh all the pros and cons before deciding whether to buy a particular car.

The two key characteristics that originally defined short-term memory—small capacity and short storage duration—are still present in the concept of working memory. However, Baddeley's model accounts for evidence that STM handles a greater variety of functions and depends on more complicated processes than previously thought.

Long-Term Memory 6b

Long-term memory (LTM) is an unlimited capacity store that can hold information over lengthy periods of time. Unlike sensory and short-term memory, which decay rapidly, LTM can store information indefinitely. Long-term memories are durable. Some information may remain in LTM across an entire lifetime.

One point of view is that all information stored in long-term memory is stored there *permanently.* According to this view, forgetting occurs only because people sometimes cannot *retrieve* needed information from LTM. To draw an analogy, imagine that memories are stored in LTM like marbles in a barrel. According to this view, none of the marbles ever leak out. When you forget, you just aren't able to dig out the right marble, but it's there—somewhere. An alternative point of view assumes that some memories stored in LTM do vanish forever. According to this view, the barrel is leaky and some of the marbles roll out, never to return.

The existence of *flashbulb memories* provides some support for the notion that LTM storage may be permanent. **Flashbulb memories, which are unusually vivid and detailed recollections of momentous events,** provide striking examples of seemingly permanent storage (Brown & Kulik, 1977). Many American adults, for instance, can remember exactly where they were, what they were doing, and how they felt when they learned that President John F. Kennedy had been shot. You may have a similar recollection related to the 1997 death of Princess Diana.

Evidence consistent with the notion of permanent memory storage also comes from reports of exceptional recall through hypnosis. Hypnotized subjects who have been regressed back to early childhood have described in remarkable detail events that they thought they had forgotten (Spiegel & Spiegel, 1985). These hypnosis-aided recoveries of lost memories suggest that normal forgetfulness is just a matter of poor retrieval.

Figure 7.9

Short-term memory as working memory. This diagram depicts the revised model of the short-term store proposed by Alan Baddeley (1986), who views STM as a mental scratch pad or temporary workspace. According to Baddeley, working memory includes three components: a phonological rehearsal loop, a visuospatial sketch pad, and an executive control system.

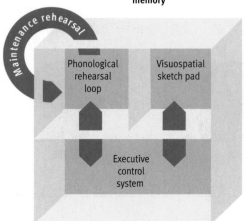

Working (short-term) memory

Maintenance rehearsal

Phonological rehearsal loop

Visuospatial sketch pad

Executive control system

Do these lines of evidence demonstrate that LTM storage is permanent? No, there are problems with both lines of evidence just discussed. Although flashbulb memories are remarkably durable, studies suggest that they are neither as accurate nor as special as once believed (Neisser & Harsch, 1992). Like other memories, they become less detailed and complete with time (McCloskey, 1992; Weaver, 1993). Similarly, when hypnosis-aided recollections of age-regressed subjects have been double-checked, they have often turned out to be inaccurate (DuBreuil, Garry, & Loftus, 1998; Lynn et al., 1997). That is, hypnotized subjects often make things up and distort recollections to be consistent with their current beliefs. Thus, although psychologists can't absolutely rule out the possibility, there is no convincing evidence that LTM storage is permanent (Payne & Blackwell, 1998; Schacter, 1996).

Flashbulb memories are unusually vivid and detailed recollections of momentous events. For example, many people can remember exactly where they were and how they felt when they learned that Princess Diana had died in an automobile crash.

Are Short-Term Memory and Long-Term Memory Really Separate?

The partitioning of memory into the sensory, short-term, and long-term stores has dominated thinking about memory for many decades, but over the years some theorists have expressed doubts about whether there really are separate memory stores. A handful of theorists have questioned the concept of sensory memory on the grounds that it may be nothing more than perceptual processes at work, rather than memory. A larger number of theorists have questioned the concept of short-term memory on the grounds that it really isn't all that different from long-term memory (Crowder, 1993; Healy & McNamara, 1996). The view of short-term memory and long-term memory as independent systems was originally based, in part, on the belief that they depended on different types of encoding and were subject to different mechanisms of forgetting. STM was thought to depend on *phonemic* encoding (based on sound), whereas LTM encoding was thought to be largely *semantic* (based on meaning). Information

loss from STM was believed to be mostly due to time-related *decay*, whereas *interference* was viewed as the principal mechanism of LTM forgetting. However, decades of research have undermined both of these distinctions, as both semantic encoding and interference effects have been found in research on short-term memory (Meiser & Klauer, 1999; Walker & Hulme, 1999).

How do theorists who doubt the existence of separate memory stores view the structure of memory? Their views vary, but generally they see short-term memory as a tiny and constantly changing portion of long-term memory that happens to be in a heightened state of activation (Nairne, 1996). In other words, they believe that there is a single, unitary, "generic" memory store that is governed by one set of rules and processes (Crowder & Neath, 1991). Thus, when you recite an unfamiliar phone number to keep it available for a brief time, the number goes into a single, huge, generic memory store, but your recitation temporarily keeps it in an elevated state of activation, which you subjectively experience as short-term memory. The outcome of the debate about whether there are separate memory stores is difficult to predict. At present, the multiple stores viewpoint remains dominant, but alternative approaches are becoming increasingly influential.

CONCEPT **CHECK 7.1**

Comparing the Memory Stores

Check your understanding of the three memory stores by filling in the blanks in the table below. The answers can be found in the back of the book in Appendix A.

Feature	Sensory memory	Short-term memory	Long-term memory
Main encoding format	*copy of input*	Largely phonemic	*largely semantic*
Storage capacity	*limited*	Small-chunks	No Known limit
Storage duration	about ¼ sec.	*up to 20 seconds*	Mins. to years

How Is Knowledge Represented and Organized in Memory?

Over the years memory researchers have wrestled endlessly with another major question relating to memory storage: How is knowledge represented and organized in memory? In other words, what forms do our mental representations of information take? Most theorists seem to agree that our mental representations probably take a variety of forms, depending on the nature of the material that needs to be tucked away in memory. For example, memories of visual scenes, of how to perform actions (such as typing or hitting a backhand stroke in tennis), and of factual information (such as definitions or dates in history) are probably represented and organized in very different ways. Most of the theorizing to date has focused on how factual knowledge may be represented in memory. In this section, we'll look at a small sample of the organizational structures that have been proposed for semantic information.

Schemas

Imagine that you've just visited Professor Smith's office, which is shown in the photo below. Take a brief look at the photo and then cover it up. Now pretend that you want to describe Professor Smith's office to a friend. Write down what you saw in the office (the picture).

Professor Smith's office is shown in this photo. Follow the instructions in the text to learn how Brewer and Treyens (1981) used it in a study of memory.

Courtesy of W. F. Brewer

After you finish, compare your description with the picture. Chances are, your description will include elements—filing cabinets, for instance—that were *not* in the office. This common phenomenon demonstrates how *schemas* can influence memory.

A *schema* is an organized cluster of knowledge about a particular object or sequence of events. For example, college students have schemas for what professors' offices are like. People are more likely to remember things that are consistent with their schemas than things that are not. This principle was quite apparent when Brewer and Treyens (1981) tested the recall of 30 participants who had briefly visited the office shown in the photo. Most participants recalled the desks and chairs, but few recalled the wine bottle or the picnic basket. Indeed, the tendency to recall things that are consistent with a schema can lead to memory errors. For instance, nine subjects in the Brewer and Treyens study falsely recalled that the office contained books. Perhaps you made the same mistake. Information stored in memory is often organized around schemas. Thus, recall of an object or event will be influenced by both the actual details observed and the person's schemas for these objects and events.

Semantic Networks

Much of people's knowledge seems to be organized into semantic networks (Collins & Loftus, 1975). A *semantic network* consists of nodes representing concepts, joined together by pathways that link related concepts. Figure 7.10 shows a small semantic network. The ovals are the nodes, and the words inside the ovals are the interlinked concepts. The lines connecting the nodes are the pathways. A more detailed figure would label the pathways to show how the concepts are related to one another. However, in this instance the relations should be fairly clear. For example, *fire engine* is linked to *red* because of its color, to *vehicle* because it's a vehicle, and to *house* because fires often occur in houses. The length of each pathway represents the degree of association between two concepts. Shorter pathways imply stronger associations.

Semantic networks have proven useful in explaining why thinking about one word (such as *butter*) can make a closely related word (such as *bread*) easier to remember (Meyer & Schvaneveldt, 1976). According to Collins and Loftus (1975), when people think about a word, their thoughts naturally go to related words. These theorists call this process spreading activation within a semantic network. They assume that activation spreads out along the pathways of the semantic network surrounding the word. They also

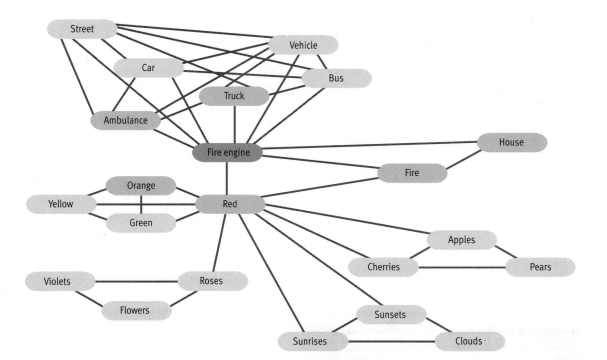

Figure 7.10

A semantic network. Much of the organization of long-term memory depends on networks of associations among concepts. In this highly simplified depiction of a fragment of a semantic network, the shorter the line linking any two concepts, the stronger the association between them. The coloration of the concept boxes represents activation of the concepts. This is how the network might look just after a person hears the words *fire engine*. (Adapted from "A Spreading Activation Theory of Semantic Processing," by A.M. Collins and E.F. Loftus, 1975, *Psychological Review, 82,* 407–428. Copyright © 1975 by the American Psychological Association. Adapted by permission.)

theorize that the strength of this activation decreases as it travels outward, much as ripples decrease in size as they radiate outward from a rock tossed into a pond. Consider again the semantic network shown in Figure 7.10. If subjects see the word *red,* words that are closely linked to it (such as *orange*) should be easier to recall than words that have longer links (such as *sunrises*).

Connectionist Networks

Connectionist models of memory take their inspiration from how neural networks appear to handle information. As we noted in our discussion of visual pathways in Chapter 4, the human brain appears to depend extensively on *parallel distributed processing*—that is, simultaneous processing of the same information that is spread across networks of neurons. Based on this insight and basic findings about how neurons operate, **connectionist, or *parallel distributed processing (PDP), models* assume that cognitive processes depend on patterns of activation in highly interconnected computational networks that resemble neural networks** (McClelland & Rumelhart, 1985; Smolensky, 1995). A PDP system consists of a large network of interconnected computing units, or *nodes,* that operate much like neurons. These nodes may be inactive or they may send either excitatory or inhibitory signals to other units. Like an individual neuron, a specific node's level of activation reflects the weighted balance of excitatory and inhibitory inputs from many

other units. Given this framework, *PDP models assert that specific memories correspond to particular patterns of activation in these networks* (McClelland, 1992). Connectionist networks bear some superficial resemblance to semantic networks, but there is a crucial difference. In semantic networks, specific nodes represent specific concepts or pieces of knowledge. In connectionist networks, a piece of knowledge is represented by a particular *pattern* of activation across an entire network. Thus, the information lies in the strengths of the *connections,* which is why the parallel distributed processing approach is called "connectionism."

Connectionist models are much more general in scope than the other organizational structures that we have just discussed. Schemas and semantic networks are largely limited to explaining how factual information might be represented in memory. In contrast, other forms of knowledge, such as memory for visual images or motor skills, could be explained with connectionist networks. Another strength of connectionist models is that they provide a highly plausible account for how mental structures may be derived from neural structures. In other words, they make sense in light of what research has revealed about neurophysiology.

In summary, memory storage is a complex matter, involving several memory stores and a variety of organizational devices. Let's now turn to the process of memory retrieval.

Entering information into long-term memory is a worthy goal, but an insufficient one if you can't get the information back out again when you need it. Fortunately, recall often occurs without much effort. But occasionally a planned search of LTM is necessary. For instance, imagine that you were asked to recall the names of all 50 states in the United States. You would probably conduct your memory search systematically, recalling states in alphabetical order or by geographical location. Although this example is rather simple, retrieval is a complex process, as you'll see in this section.

Using Cues to Aid Retrieval

At the beginning of this chapter we discussed the *tip-of-the-tongue phenomenon*—**the temporary inability to remember something you know, accompanied by a feeling that it's just out of reach.** The tip-of-the-tongue phenomenon is a common experience that occurs to the average person about once a week (A. Brown, 1991). It clearly represents a failure in retrieval. Fortunately, memories can often be jogged with *retrieval cues*—stimuli that help gain access to memories. This was apparent when Roger Brown and David McNeill (1966) studied the tip-of-the-tongue phenomenon. They gave participants definitions of obscure words and asked them to think of the words. Our example at the beginning of the chapter (the definition for *nepotism*) was taken from their study. Brown and McNeill found that subjects groping for obscure words were correct in guessing the first letter of the missing word 57% of the time. This figure far exceeds chance and shows that partial recollections are often headed in the right direction.

Reinstating the Context of an Event

Let's test your memory: What did you have for breakfast two days ago? If you can't immediately answer, you might begin by imagining yourself sitting at the breakfast table (or wherever you usually have breakfast). Trying to recall an event by putting yourself back in the context in which it occurred involves working with context cues to aid retrieval.

Context cues often facilitate the retrieval of information (Smith, 1988). Most people have experienced the effects of context cues on many occasions. For instance, when people return after a number of years to a place where they used to live, they typically are

flooded with long-forgotten memories. Or consider how often you have gone from one room to another to get something (scissors, perhaps), only to discover that you can't remember what you were after. However, when you return to the first room (the original context), you suddenly recall what it was ("Of course, the scissors!"). These examples illustrate the potentially powerful effects of context cues on memory. The technique of reinstating the context of an event has been used effectively in legal investigations to enhance eyewitness recall (Chandler & Fisher, 1996). The eyewitness may be encouraged to retrieve information about a crime by replaying the sequence of events.

Reconstructing Memories

When you retrieve information from long-term memory, you're not able to pull up a "mental videotape" that provides an exact replay of the past. To some extent, your memories are sketchy *reconstructions* of the past that may be distorted and may include details that did not actually occur (Roediger, Wheeler, & Rajaram, 1993).

Research by Elizabeth Loftus (1979, 1992) and others on the *misinformation effect* has shown that reconstructive distortions show up frequently in eyewitness testimony. **The *misinformation effect* occurs when participants' recall of an event they witnessed is altered by introducing misleading postevent information.** For example, in one study Loftus and Palmer (1974) showed participants a videotape of an automobile accident. Participants were then "grilled" as if they were providing eyewitness testimony, and biasing information was introduced. Some subjects were asked, "How fast were the cars going when they *hit* each other?" Other subjects were asked, "How fast were the cars going when they *smashed into* each other?" A week later, participants' recall of the accident was tested and they were asked whether they remembered seeing any broken glass in the accident (there was none). Subjects who had earlier been asked about the cars *smashing into* each other were more likely to "recall" broken glass. Why would they add this detail to their reconstructions of the accident? Probably because broken glass is consistent with their schemas for cars *smashing* together (see Figure 7.11). Although postevent misinformation does not inevitably introduce errors into recollections of events, the misinformation effect has been replicated in

University of Washington News and Information Office

"One reason most of us, as jurors, place so much faith in eyewitness testimony is that we are unaware of how many factors influence its accuracy."
ELIZABETH LOFTUS

numerous studies by Loftus and other researchers (Ayers & Reder, 1998; Lindsay, 1993).

The misinformation effect appears to be due, *in part,* to the unreliability of **source monitoring—the process of making attributions about the origins of memories.** Marcia Johnson and her colleagues maintain that source monitoring is a crucial facet of memory retrieval that contributes to many of the mistakes that people make in reconstructing their experiences (Johnson, 1996; Johnson, Hashtroudi, & Lindsay, 1993; Lindsay & Johnson, 1991). According to Johnson, memories are not tagged with labels that specify their sources. Hence, when people pull up specific memory records, they have to make decisions *at the time of retrieval* about where the memories came from (example: "Did I read that in the *New York Times* or *Rolling Stone?*"). Much of the time, these decisions are so easy and automatic, people make them without being consciously aware of the source-monitoring process. In other instances, however, they may consciously struggle to pinpoint the source of a memory. **A *source-monitoring error* occurs when a memory derived from one source is misattributed to another source.** For example, you might attribute something that your roommate said to your psychology professor, or something you heard on *Oprah* to your psychology textbook. Inaccurate memories that reflect source-monitoring errors may seem quite compelling, and people often feel quite confident about their authenticity even though the recollections really are inaccurate (Lampinen, Neuschatz, & Payne, 1999).

Figure 7.11

The effect of leading questions on eyewitness recall. Subjects who were asked leading questions in which cars were described as *hitting* or *smashing* each other were prone to recall the same accident differently one week later, demonstrating the reconstructive nature of memory. (Based on "Reconstruction of Automobile Destruction: An Example of Interaction Between Language and Memory," by E. F. Loftus and J.C. Palmer, 1974, *Journal of Verbal Learning and Verbal Behavior, 13,* 585–589. Academic Press, Inc. Adapted by permission of the author.)

Leading question asked during witness testimony	Possible schemas activated	Response of subjects asked one week later, "Did you see any broken glass?" (There was none.)
"About how fast were the cars going when they hit each other?"		"Yes"—14%
"About how fast were the cars going when they smashed into each other?"		"Yes"—32%

Source-monitoring errors appear to be commonplace and may shed light on many interesting memory phenomena. For instance, in studies of eyewitness suggestibility, some subjects have gone so far as to insist that they "remember" seeing something that was only verbally suggested to them. Most theories have a hard time explaining how people can have memories of events that they never actually saw or experienced, but this paradox doesn't seem all that perplexing when it is explained as a source-monitoring error.

Forgetting: When Memory Lapses

Why do people forget information—even information they would like very much to remember? Many theorists believe that there isn't one simple answer to this perplexing question. They point to the complex, multifaceted nature of memory and assert that forgetting can be caused by deficiencies in encoding, storage, retrieval, or some combination of these processes.

How Quickly We Forget: Ebbinghaus's Forgetting Curve

The first person to conduct scientific studies of forgetting was Hermann Ebbinghaus. He published a series of insightful memory studies way back in 1885. Ebbinghaus studied only one subject—himself. To give himself lots of new material to memorize, he invented ***nonsense syllables*—consonant-vowel-consonant arrangements that do not correspond to words** (such as BAF, XOF, VIR, and MEQ). He wanted to work with meaningless materials that would be uncontaminated by his previous learning.

Ebbinghaus was a remarkably dedicated researcher. For instance, in one study he went through over 14,000 practice repetitions, as he tirelessly memorized 420 lists of nonsense syllables (Slamecka, 1985). He tested his memory of these lists after various time intervals had elapsed. Figure 7.12 on the next page shows what he found. This diagram, called a ***forgetting curve,* graphs retention and forgetting over time.** Ebbinghaus's forgetting curve shows a precipitous drop in retention during the first few hours after the nonsense syllables were memorized. He forgot more than 60% of the syllables in less than 9 hours! Thus, he concluded that most forgetting occurs very rapidly after learning something.

Welcome Institute for the History of Medicine, London

"*Left to itself every mental content gradually loses its capacity for being revived. . . . Facts crammed at examination time soon vanish.*"
HERMANN EBBINGHAUS

Figure 7.12

Ebbinghaus's forgetting curve for nonsense syllables. From his experiments on himself, Ebbinghaus concluded that forgetting is extremely rapid immediately after the original learning and then levels off. However, subsequent research has suggested that this forgetting curve is unusually steep. (Data from Ebbinghaus, 1885)

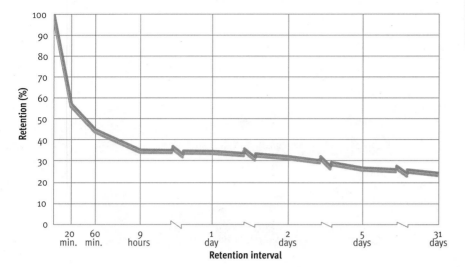

That's a depressing conclusion. What is the point of memorizing information if you're going to forget it all right away? Fortunately, subsequent research showed that Ebbinghaus's forgetting curve was unusually steep (Postman, 1985). Forgetting usually isn't as swift or as extensive as Ebbinghaus thought. One problem was that he was working with such meaningless material. When participants memorize more meaningful material, such as prose or poetry, forgetting curves aren't nearly as steep. Studies of how well people recall their high school classmates suggest that forgetting curves for autobiographical information are even shallower (Bahrick, Bahrick, & Wittlinger, 1975). Also, different methods of measuring forgetting yield varied estimates of how quickly people forget. This variation underscores

the importance of the methods used to measure forgetting, the matter we turn to next.

Measures of Forgetting SIM5

To study forgetting empirically, psychologists need to be able to measure it precisely. Measures of forgetting inevitably measure retention as well. **Retention refers to the proportion of material retained (remembered).** In studies of forgetting, the results may be reported in terms of the amount forgotten or the amount retained. In these studies, the *retention interval* is the length of time between the presentation of materials to be remembered and the measurement of forgetting. Psychologists use three methods to measure forgetting: recall, recognition, and relearning (Lockhart, 1992).

Who is the current U.S. secretary of state? What movie won the Academy Award for best picture last year? These questions involve recall measures of forgetting. **A *recall* measure of retention requires participants to reproduce information on their own without any cues.** If you were to take a recall test on a list of 25 words you had memorized, you would simply be told to write down on a blank sheet of paper as many of the words as you could remember.

In contrast, in a recognition test you might be shown a list of 100 words and asked to choose the 25 words that you had memorized. **A *recognition* measure of retention requires participants to select previously learned information from an array of options.** Subjects not only have cues to work with, they have the answers right in front of them. In educational testing, multiple-choice, true-false, and matching questions are recognition measures; essay questions and fill-in-the-blanks questions are recall measures.

If you're like most students, you probably prefer multiple-choice tests over essay tests. This preference is understandable, because evidence shows that recognition measures (such as multiple-choice tests) tend to yield higher scores than recall measures (such as essay tests) of memory for the same information. This was demonstrated many years ago in a study by Luh (1922), who measured subjects' retention of nonsense syllables with both a recognition test and a recall test. As Figure 7.13 shows, participants' performance on the recognition measure was far superior to their performance on the recall measure. There are two ways of looking at this disparity between recall and recognition tests. One view is that recognition tests are especially *sensitive* measures of retention. The other

Figure 7.13

Recognition versus recall in the measurement of retention. Luh (1922) had subjects memorize lists of nonsense syllables and then measured their retention with either a recognition test or a recall test at various intervals up to two days. As you can see, the forgetting curve for the recall test was quite steep, whereas the recognition test yielded much higher estimates of subjects' retention.

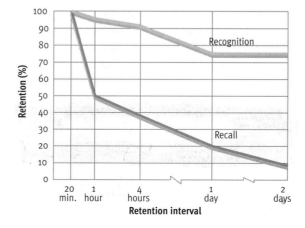

view is that recognition tests are excessively easy measures of retention.

Actually, there is no guarantee that a recognition test will be easier than a recall test. Although this tends to be the case, the difficulty of a recognition test can vary greatly, depending on the number, similarity, and plausibility of the options provided as possible answers. To illustrate, see whether you know the answer to the following multiple-choice question:

The capital of Washington is:
a. Seattle   *c. Tacoma*
b. Spokane   *d. Olympia*

Most students who aren't from Washington find this a fairly difficult question. The answer is Olympia. Now take a look at the next question:

The capital of Washington is:
a. London   *c. Tokyo*
b. New York   *d. Olympia*

Virtually anyone can answer this question because the incorrect options are readily dismissed. Although this illustration is a bit extreme, it shows that two recognition measures of the same information can be dramatically different in difficulty.

The third method of measuring forgetting is relearning. A *relearning* measure of retention requires a participant to memorize information a second time to determine how much time or effort is saved by having learned it before. To use this method, a researcher measures how much time (or how many practice trials) a person needs to memorize something. At a later date, the participant is asked to relearn the information. The researcher measures how much more quickly the material is memorized the second time. Participants' *savings scores* provide an estimate of their retention. For example, if it takes you 20 minutes to memorize a list the first time and only 5 minutes to memorize it a week later, you've saved 15 minutes. Your savings score of 75% ($^{15}/_{20} = ¾ = 75\%$) suggests that you have retained 75% and forgotten the remaining 25% of the information. Relearning measures can detect retention that is overlooked by recognition tests (Nelson, 1978).

Why We Forget

Measuring forgetting is only the first step in the long journey toward explaining why forgetting occurs. In this section, we explore the possible causes of forgetting, looking at factors that may affect encoding, storage, and retrieval processes.

Ineffective Encoding

A great deal of forgetting may only *appear* to be forgetting. The information in question may never have been inserted into memory in the first place. Since you can't really forget something you never learned, this phenomenon is sometimes called *pseudoforgetting*. We opened the chapter with an example of pseudoforgetting. People usually assume that they know what a penny looks like, but most have actually failed to encode this information. Pseudoforgetting is usually due to *lack of attention*.

Even when memory codes are formed for new information, subsequent forgetting may be due to *ineffective* encoding. The research on levels of processing shows that some approaches to encoding lead to more forgetting than others (Craik & Tulving, 1975). For example, if you're distracted while you read your textbooks, you may be doing little more than saying the words to yourself. This is *phonemic encoding,* which is inferior to *semantic encoding* for retention of verbal material. When you can't remember the information that you've read, your forgetting may be due to ineffective encoding.

Decay

Instead of focusing on encoding, decay theory attributes forgetting to the impermanence of memory storage. **Decay theory** proposes that forgetting occurs because memory traces fade with time. The implicit assumption is that decay occurs in the physiological mechanisms responsible for memories. According to decay theory, the mere passage of time produces forgetting. This notion meshes nicely with commonsense views of forgetting.

As we saw earlier, decay *does* appear to contribute to the loss of information from the sensory and short-term memory stores. However, the critical task for theories of forgetting is to explain the loss of information from long-term memory. Researchers have *not* been able to demonstrate that decay causes LTM forgetting (Slamecka, 1992).

If decay theory is correct, the principal cause of forgetting should be the passage of time. In studies of long-term memory, however, researchers have repeatedly found that time passage is not as influential as what happens during the time interval. Research has shown that forgetting depends not on the amount of time that has passed since learning but on the amount, complexity, and type of information that subjects have had to assimilate *during* the retention interval. The negative impact of competing information on retention is called *interference.*

Web Link 7.2

Mind Tools—Memory Techniques and Mnemonics
The Mind Tools site details practical techniques to help people improve their cognitive efficiency in many areas. The subpage dedicated to memory functioning offers an excellent collection of suggestions for ways to enhance memory.

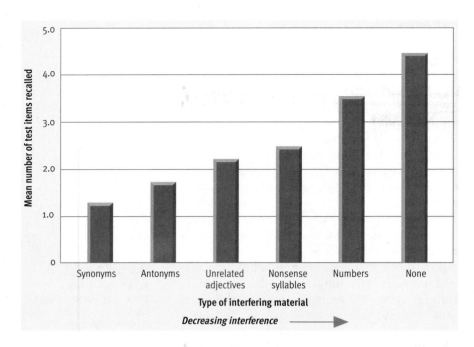

Type of interfering material

Decreasing interference ⟶

exactly what McGeoch and McDonald (1931) found in an influential study (see Figure 7.14). They had participants memorize test material that consisted of a list of two-syllable adjectives. They varied the similarity of intervening learning by having subjects then memorize one of five lists. In order of decreasing similarity to the test material, they were synonyms of the test words, antonyms of the test words, unrelated adjectives, nonsense syllables, and numbers. Later, subjects' recall of the test material was measured. Figure 7.14 shows that as the similarity of the intervening material decreased, the amount of forgetting also decreased—because of reduced interference.

There are two kinds of interference: *retroactive* interference and *proactive* interference (see Figure 7.15). ***Retroactive interference*** **occurs when new information impairs the retention of previously learned information.** Retroactive interference occurs between the original learning and the retest on that learning, during the retention interval. For example, the interference manipulated by McGeoch and McDonald (1931) was retroactive interference. In contrast, ***proactive interference*** **occurs when previously learned information interferes with the retention of new information.** Proactive interference is rooted in learning that comes before exposure to the test material. The evidence indicates that both types of interference can have powerful effects on how much you forget. They may exert their effects by disrupting *retrieval* (Tulving & Psotka, 1971), which we turn to next.

Retrieval Failure

People often remember things that they were unable to recall at an earlier time. This may be obvious only

Figure 7.14

Effects of interference. According to interference theory, more interference from competing information should produce more forgetting. McGeoch and McDonald (1931) controlled the amount of interference with a learning task by varying the similarity of an intervening task. The results were consistent with interference theory. The amount of interference is greatest at the left of the graph, as is the amount of forgetting. As interference decreases (moving to the right on the graph), retention improves.

Interference

Interference theory **proposes that people forget information because of competition from other material.** Although demonstrations of decay in long-term memory have remained elusive, hundreds of studies have shown that interference influences forgetting (Anderson & Neely, 1996; Bjork, 1992). In many of these studies, researchers have controlled interference by varying the similarity between the original material given to subjects (the test material) and the material studied in the intervening period. Interference is assumed to be greatest when intervening material is most similar to the test material. Decreasing the similarity should reduce interference and cause less forgetting. This is

Figure 7.15

Retroactive and proactive interference. Retroactive interference occurs when learning produces a "backward" effect, reducing recall of previously learned material. Proactive interference occurs when learning produces a "forward" effect, reducing recall of subsequently learned material.

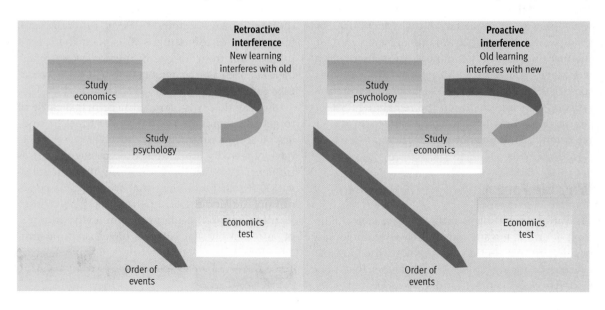

during struggles with the tip-of-the-tongue phenomenon, but it happens frequently. In fact, a great deal of forgetting may be due to breakdowns in the process of retrieval.

Why does an effort to retrieve something fail on one occasion and succeed on another? That's a tough question. One theory is that retrieval failures may be more likely when there is a mismatch between retrieval cues and the encoding of the information you're searching for. According to Tulving and Thomson (1973), a good retrieval cue is consistent with the original encoding of the information to be recalled. If the sound of a word—its phonemic quality—was emphasized during encoding, an effective retrieval cue should emphasize the sound of the word. If the meaning of the word was emphasized during encoding, semantic cues should be best. A general statement of the principle at work here was formulated by Tulving and Thomson (1973). The *encoding specificity principle* states that the value of a retrieval cue depends on how well it corresponds to the memory code. This principle provides one explanation for the inconsistent success of retrieval efforts.

Motivated Forgetting

Many years ago, Sigmund Freud (1901) came up with an entirely different explanation for retrieval failures. As we noted in Chapter 1, Freud asserted that people often keep embarrassing, unpleasant, or painful memories buried in their unconscious. For example, a person who was deeply wounded by perceived slights at a childhood birthday party might suppress all recollection of that party. In his therapeutic work with patients, Freud recovered many such buried memories. He theorized that the memories were there all along, but their retrieval was blocked by unconscious avoidance tendencies.

The tendency to forget things one doesn't want to think about is called *motivated forgetting*, or to use Freud's terminology, *repression*. In Freudian theory, *repression* refers to keeping distressing thoughts and feelings buried in the unconscious (see Chapter 12). Psychologists have not been able to unambiguously demonstrate the operation of repression in controlled laboratory experiments (Holmes, 1990). Nonetheless, a number of experiments suggest that people don't remember anxiety-laden material as readily as emotionally neutral material, just as Freud proposed (Guenther, 1988; Reisner, 1998). Thus, when you forget unpleasant things such as a dental appointment, a promise to help a friend move, or a term paper deadline, motivated forgetting may be at work.

CONCEPT **CHECK 7.2**

Figuring Out Forgetting

Check your understanding of why people forget by identifying the probable causes of forgetting in each of the following scenarios. Choose from (a) motivated forgetting (repression), (b) decay, (c) ineffective encoding, (d) proactive interference, (e) retroactive interference, or (f) retrieval failure. You will find the answers in Appendix A.

C **1.** Ellen can't recall the reasons for the Webster-Ashburton Treaty because she was daydreaming when it was discussed in history class. *lack of attention*

F/A **2.** Rufus hates his job at Taco Heaven and is always forgetting when he is scheduled to work.

D **3.** Ray's new assistant in the shipping department is named John Cocker. Ray keeps calling him Joe, mixing him up with the rock singer Joe Cocker.

E. **4.** Tania studied history on Sunday morning and sociology on Sunday evening. It's Monday, and she's struggling with her history test because she keeps mixing up prominent historians with influential sociologists.

The Repressed Memories Controversy

Although the concept of repression has been around for a century, interest in this phenomenon has surged in recent years, thanks to a spate of prominent reports involving the return of long-lost memories of sexual abuse and other traumas during childhood. The media have been flooded with reports of adults accusing their parents, teachers, and neighbors of horrific child abuse decades earlier, based on previously repressed memories of these travesties. For the most part, these parents, teachers, and neighbors have denied the allegations. Many of the accused have seemed genuinely baffled by the charges, which have torn some previously happy families apart (Loftus & Ketcham, 1994; Wylie, 1998). In an effort to make sense of the charges, some accused parents have argued that their children's recollections are false memories created inadvertently by well-intentioned therapists through the power of suggestion.

What do psychologists and psychiatrists have to say about the authenticity of repressed memories? They are sharply divided on the issue. Many psychologists and psychiatrists, especially clinicians involved in the treatment of psychological disorders, largely accept recovered memories of abuse at face value (Banyard & Williams, 1999; Briere & Conte, 1993; Herman, 1994; Terr, 1994; Whitfield, 1995). They assert that sexual abuse in childhood is far more widespread than most people realize. For example, a recent, large-scale survey (MacMillan et al., 1997), using a random sample of 9953 residents of Ontario, found that 12.8% of the

Figure 7.16

Estimates of the prevalence of childhood physical and sexual abuse. MacMillan and her colleagues (1997) questioned a random sample of almost 10,000 adults living in Ontario, Canada about whether they were abused during childhood. As you can see, males were more likely to experience physical abuse and females were more likely to have suffered from sexual abuse. Moreover, the data support the assertion that millions of people have been victimized by childhood sexual abuse. (Based on data from "Prevalence of Child Physical and Sexual Abuse in the Community," by H. L. MacMillan, J. E. Fleming, N. Trocme, M. H. Boyle, M. Wong, Y. A. Racine, W. R. Beardslee, & D. R. Offord, 1997, *JAMA, 278* (2), 131-135.)

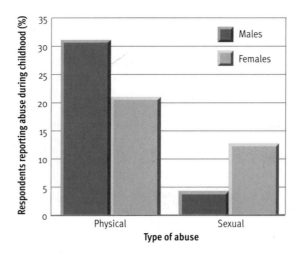

Figure 7.17

A case of recovered memories recanted. Revelations of repressed memories of sexual abuse are viewed with skepticism in some quarters. One reason is that some people who have recovered previously repressed recollections of child abuse have subsequently realized that their "memories" were the product of suggestion, as in this case history. (From "Lies of the Mind" *Time*, 11/29/93. Copyright © 1993 Time Inc. Reprinted by permission.)

females and 4.3% of the males reported that they had been victims of sexual abuse during childhood (see Figure 7.16). They further assert that it is common for people to bury traumatic incidents of sexual abuse in their unconscious. For instance, in a recent study of psychiatric patients hospitalized for posttraumatic or dissociative disorders (see Chapter 14), one-third of those who reported childhood sexual abuse said that they experienced complete amnesia for the abuse at some point in their lives (Chu et al., 1999).

In contrast, many other psychologists, especially memory researchers, have expressed skepticism about the recent upsurge of recovered memories of abuse (Kihlstrom, 1998b; Lindsay & Poole, 1995; Loftus, 1998; Lynn & Nash, 1994). They are skeptical about retrospective self-reports of amnesia—such as those seen in the Chu et al. (1999) study—because self-assessments of personal memory are often distorted and because it is difficult to distinguish between a period when a memory was not *accessed* versus a period when a memory was not *available* due to repression (Belli et al., 1998; Schooler, 1999).

A Case History of Recovered Memories Recanted

Suffering from a prolonged bout of depression and desperate for help, Melody Gavigan, 39, a computer specialist from Long Beach, California, checked herself into a local psychiatric hospital. As Gavigan recalls the experience, her problems were just beginning. During five weeks of treatment there, a family and marriage counselor repeatedly suggested that her depression stemmed from incest during her childhood. While at first Gavigan had no recollection of any abuse, the therapist kept prodding. "I was so distressed and needed help so desperately, I latched on to what he was offering me," she says. "I accepted his answers."

When asked for details, she wrote page after page of what she believed were emerging repressed memories. She told about running into the yard after being raped in the bathroom. She incorporated into another lurid rape scene an actual girlhood incident, in which she had dislocated a shoulder. She went on to recall being molested by her father when she was only a year old—as her diapers were being changed—and sodomized by him at five. Following what she says was the therapist's advice, Gavigan confronted her father with her accusations, severed her relationship with him, moved away, and formed an incest survivors' group.

But she remained uneasy. Signing up for a college psychology course, she examined her newfound memories more carefully and concluded that they were false. Now Gavigan has begged her father's forgiveness and filed a lawsuit against the psychiatric hospital for the pain that she and her family suffered.

The skeptics do *not* argue that people are lying about their previously repressed memories. Rather, they maintain that some suggestible people wrestling with emotional problems have been convinced by persuasive therapists that their emotional problems must be the result of abuse that occurred years before. Critics blame a minority of therapists who presumably have good intentions but who operate under the dubious assumption that most or even all psychological problems are attributable to childhood sexual abuse (Lindsay & Read, 1994; Spanos, 1994). Using hypnosis, dream interpretation, and leading questions, they supposedly prod and probe patients until they inadvertently create the memories of abuse that they are searching for.

Psychologists who doubt the authenticity of repressed memories support their analysis by pointing to discredited cases of recovered memories. For example, with the help of a church counselor, one woman recovered memories of how her minister father had repeatedly raped her, got her pregnant, and then aborted the pregnancy with a coat-hanger, but subsequent evidence revealed that the woman was still a virgin and that her father had had a vasectomy years before (Loftus, 1997; Testa, 1996). The skeptics also point to published case histories that clearly involved suggestive questioning and to cases in which patients have recanted recovered memories of sexual abuse (see Figure 7.17) after realizing that these memories were implanted by their therapists (Goldstein & Farmer, 1993; Loftus, 1994).

Those who question the accuracy of repressed memories also point to findings on the misinformation effect, research on source-monitoring errors, and a host of other studies that demonstrate the relative ease of creating "memories" of events that never happened. For example, working with college students, Ira Hyman and his colleagues have managed to implant recollections of fairly substantial events (such as spilling a punch bowl at a wedding, being in a grocery store when the fire sprinkler system went off, being hospitalized for an earache) in about 25% of their subjects, just by asking them to elaborate on events supposedly reported by their parents (Hyman, Husband, & Billings, 1995; Hyman & Kleinnecht, 1999).

Of course, psychologists who believe in recovered memories have mounted rebuttals to the arguments raised by the skeptics. For example, Kluft (1999) argues that a recantation of a recovered memory of abuse does not prove that the memory was false. Gleaves (1994) points out that individuals with a history of sexual abuse often vacillate between denying and accepting that the abuse occurred. Harvey (1999) argues that laboratory demonstrations showing that it is easy to create false memories have involved trivial memory distortions that are a far cry from the vivid, emotionally wrenching recollections of sexual abuse that have generated the recovered memories controversy. Moreover, even if one accepts the assertion that therapists *can* create false memories of abuse in their patients, some critics have noted that there is virtually no direct evidence on how often this occurs and no empirical basis for the claim that there has been an *epidemic* of such cases (Berliner & Briere, 1999; Calof, 1998; Pope & Brown, 1996).

Although both sides seem genuinely concerned about the welfare of the people involved, the debate about recovered memories of sexual abuse has grown increasingly bitter and emotionally charged (Lindsay, 1998; Pope, 1996). So, what can we conclude about the recovered memories controversy? It seems pretty clear that therapists can unknowingly create false memories in their patients and that a significant portion of recovered memories of abuse are the product of suggestion. But it also seems likely that some cases of recovered memories are authentic. At this point, we don't have adequate data to estimate what proportion of recovered memories of abuse fall in each category (Brown, Scheflin, & Hammond, 1998). Thus, the matter needs to be addressed with great caution. On the one hand, people should be extremely careful about accepting recovered memories of abuse in the absence of convincing corroboration. On the other hand, recovered memories of abuse cannot be summarily dismissed and it would be tragic if the repressed memories controversy made people overly skeptical about the all-too-real problem of childhood sexual abuse.

The repressed memories controversy deserves one last comment regarding its impact on memory research and scientific conceptions of memory. The controversy has helped to inspire a great deal of research that has increased our understanding of just how fragile, fallible, malleable, and subjective human memory is. Indeed, the implicit dichotomy underlying the repressed memories debate—that some memories are true, whereas others are false—is misleading and oversimplified. Research demonstrates that all our memories are imperfect reconstructions of the past that are subject to many types of distortion.

Tom Rutherford (shown here with his wife, Joyce) received a $1 million settlement in a suit against a church therapist and a Springfield, Missouri, church in a false memory case. The Rutherfords' daughter, Beth, had "recalled" under the church counselor's guidance, childhood memories of having been raped repeatedly by her minister father, gotten pregnant, and undergone a painful coat-hanger abortion. Her father lost his job and was ostracized. After he later revealed he'd had a vasectomy when Beth was age 4, and a physical exam revealed that at age 23 she was still a virgin, the memories were shown to be false.

Web Link 7.3

False Memory Syndrome Foundation (FMSF) Online
This site marshals evidence that "recovered memories" of childhood abuse are often false, therapist-induced, and grounded in shoddy and non-objective scientific claims. Dealing with perhaps the most bitterly contested topic in current psychology, the FMSF has elicited fierce opposition, as the material presented in Web Link 7.4 demonstrates.

Web Link 7.4

False Memory Syndrome Facts
Social worker and psychotherapist Linda Chapman editor of the online *Wounded Healer Journal*, has brought together scientific and clinical evidence that "false memory syndrome" is a misleading label and that older individuals may well recover repressed memories of abuse in childhood.

In Search of the Memory Trace: The Physiology of Memory

For decades, neuroscientists have ventured forth in search of the physiological basis for memory. On several occasions scientists have been excited by new leads, only to be led down blind alleys. For example, in the 1960s James McConnell rocked the world of science when he reported that he had chemically transferred a specific memory from one flatworm to another. McConnell (1962) created a conditioned reflex (contraction in response to light) in flatworms and then transferred RNA (a basic molecular constituent of all living cells) from trained worms to untrained worms. The untrained worms showed evidence of "remembering" the conditioned reflex.

McConnell boldly speculated that in the future, chemists might be able to formulate pills containing the information for Physics 201 or History 101! Unfortunately, the RNA transfer studies proved difficult to replicate (Rilling, 1996). Today, 40 years after McConnell's "breakthrough," we are still a long way from breaking the chemical code for memory.

Investigators continue to explore a variety of leads about the physiological bases for memory. In light of past failures, these lines of research should probably be viewed with guarded optimism. Nonetheless, in this section we'll look at some of the more promising research.

Figure **7.18**

Retrograde versus antero-grade amnesia. In retrograde amnesia, memory for events that occurred prior to the onset of amnesia is lost. In anterograde amnesia, memory for events that occur subsequent to the onset of amnesia suffers.

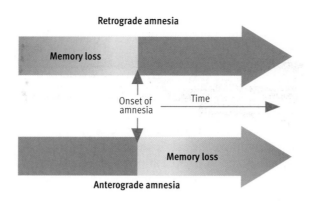

Retrograde amnesia

Memory loss

Onset of amnesia | Time

Memory loss

Anterograde amnesia

The Anatomy of Memory 6c

Cases of amnesia (extensive memory loss) due to head injury are a useful source of clues about the anatomical bases of memory. There are two basic types of amnesia: retrograde and anterograde (see Figure 7.18). **In *retrograde amnesia* a person loses memories for events that occurred prior to the injury.** For example, a 25-year-old gymnast who sustains a head trauma might find 3 years, 7 years, or perhaps her entire lifetime erased. **In *anterograde amnesia* a person loses memories for events that occur after the injury.** For instance, after her accident, the injured gymnast might suffer impaired ability to remember people she meets, where she has parked her car, and so on.

Figure **7.19**

The anatomy of memory. All of the brain structures identified here have been implicated in efforts to discover the anatomical structures involved in memory. Although researchers have made some exciting discoveries, the physiological bases of memory are extremely complex and are not yet well understood.

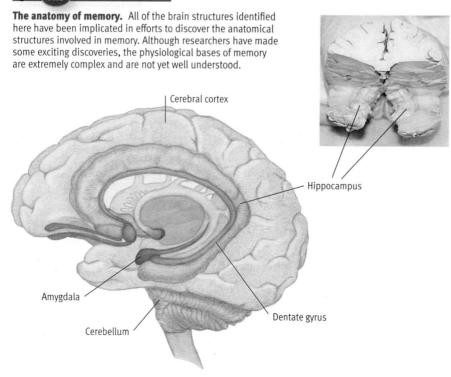

Cerebral cortex

Hippocampus

Amygdala

Dentate gyrus

Cerebellum

Because victims' current memory functioning is impaired, cases of anterograde amnesia have been especially rich sources of information about the brain and memory. One well-known case, that of a man referred to as H. M., has been followed since 1953 (Corkin, 1984; Scoville & Milner, 1957). H. M. had surgery to relieve debilitating epileptic seizures. Unfortunately, the surgery inadvertently wiped out most of his ability to form long-term memories. H. M.'s short-term memory is fine, but he has no recollection of anything that has happened since 1953 (other than about the most recent 20 seconds of his life). He doesn't recognize the doctors treating him, he can't remember routes to and from places, and he doesn't know his age. He can't remember what he did yesterday, let alone what he has done for the last 50 years. He doesn't even recognize a current photo of himself, as aging has changed his appearance considerably.

H.M.'s memory losses were originally attributed to the removal of his *hippocampus* (see Figure 7.19), although theorists now understand that other nearby structures that were removed also contributed to H.M.'s dramatic memory deficits (Delis & Lucas, 1996). Based on decades of additional research, scientists now believe that the entire *hippocampal region* (including the hippocampus, dentate gyrus, subiculum, and entorhinal cortex), as well as the adjacent *parahippocampal region* are critical for many types of long-term memory (Gluck & Myers, 1997). Consistent with this conclusion, it is interesting to note that the hippocampal region is one of the first areas of the brain to sustain significant damage in the course of Alzheimer's disease, which produces severe memory impairment in many people, typically after age 65 (Ashford, Mattson, & Kumar, 1998).

Do these findings mean that memories are stored in the hippocampal region and adjacent areas? Probably not. Many theorists believe that the hippocampal region plays a key role in the *consolidation* of memories (Alvarez & Squire, 1994; Gluck & Myers, 1997). **Consolidation is a hypothetical process involving the gradual conversion of information into durable memory codes stored in long-term memory.** According to this view, memories are consolidated in the hippocampal region and then stored in various areas of the cortex. Which areas? Memories are probably stored in the same cortical areas that were originally involved in processing the sensory input that led to the memories (Gabrielli, 1998; Squire, Knowlton, & Musen, 1993). For instance, memories of visual information may be stored in areas of the visual cortex.

Theorists who have been influenced by parallel distributed processing (PDP) models of memory have come up with a slightly different take on the hippocampal region's contribution to memory. They suggest that the hippocampal area functions to bind together the individual elements of a specific memory, which are stored in widely distributed areas of the cortex (Cohen et al., 1999; Nadel & Jacobs, 1998). For example, your memory of attending a baseball game might include a variety of elements—such as when and where it occurred, the final score, certain key plays, the location of your seat, who went with you, and the weather—that are stored in dispersed brain modules. The hippocampal complex may provide a mechanism for bringing these disaggregated elements of a memory together by activating certain ensembles of neurons. In other words, the hippocampal area may play a key role in organizing neural networks that represent specific memories. This analysis is not entirely incompatible with the notion that the hippocampal region handles the consolidation of long-term memories.

The Neural Circuitry and Biochemistry of Memory

Richard F. Thompson (1989, 1992) and his colleagues have shown that specific memories may depend on *localized neural circuits* in the brain. In other words, memories may create unique, reusable pathways in the brain along which signals flow. Thompson has traced the pathway that accounts for a rabbit's memory of a conditioned eyeblink response. The key link in this circuit is a microscopic spot in the *cerebellum,* a structure in the hindbrain (see Figure 7.19). When this spot is destroyed, the conditioned stimulus no longer elicits the eyeblink response, even though the unconditioned stimulus still does (Steinmetz, 1998). This finding does *not* mean that the cerebellum is the key to all memory. Thompson theorizes that other memories probably create entirely different pathways in other areas of the brain. The key implication of Thompson's work is that it may be possible to map out specific neural circuits that correspond to specific memories.

Various other lines of research have implicated biochemical processes in the operation of memory. Among other things, studies have related memory functioning to (1) alterations in neurotransmitter secretions at specific synaptic sites (Kennedy, Hawkins, & Kandel, 1992), (2) hormonal fluctuations that can facilitate or impair memory (McGaugh, 1992, 1995), and (3) protein synthesis in the brain that may be necessary for the formation of memories (Rose, 1992; Rosenzweig, 1996).

In summary, a host of anatomical structures, neural circuits, and biochemical processes have been implicated as playing a role in memory. Does all this sound confusing? It should, because it is. The bottom line is that neuroscientists are still assembling the pieces of the puzzle that will explain the physiological basis of memory. Although they have identified many of the puzzle pieces, they're not sure how the pieces fit together. Their difficulty is probably due to the complex, multifaceted nature of memory. Looking for the physiological basis for memory is only slightly less daunting than looking for the physiological basis for thought itself.

Web Link 7.5

Alzheimer Page
The Alzheimer Disease Research Center at Washington University has fashioned a companion site to ALZHEIMER, a Usenet discussion group for clinicians, researchers, and the various publics affected by this memory-destroying disease. A broad, annotated set of links as well as a search facility for the massive archives of the discussion group itself invite further exploration of all facets of this illness.

Are There Multiple Memory Systems?

Some theorists believe that evidence on the physiology of memory is confusing because investigators are unwittingly probing into several distinct memory systems that have different physiological bases. A number of research findings inspired this view, foremost among them the discovery of *implicit memory.* Let's look at this perplexing phenomenon.

Implicit Versus Explicit Memory

As we noted earlier, patients with anterograde amnesia often appear to have virtually no ability to form long-term memories. If they're shown a list of words and subsequently given a test of retention, their performance is miserable. However, different findings emerge when "sneaky" techniques are used to measure their memory indirectly. For instance, they might be asked to work on a word recognition task in which they are shown fragments of words (example: _ss_ss__ for assassin) and are asked to complete the fragments with the first appropriate word that comes to mind. The series of word fragments includes ones that correspond to words on a list they saw earlier. In this situation, the amnesiac subjects respond with words that were on the list just as frequently as normal subjects who also saw the initial list (Schacter, Chiu, & Ochsner, 1993). Thus, the amnesiacs *do* remember words from the list. However, when asked, they don't even remember having been shown the first list!

The demonstration of long-term retention in amnesiacs who previously appeared to have no long-term memory shocked experts when it was first reported by Warrington and Weiskrantz (1970). However, this surprising finding has been replicated in many subsequent studies. This phenomenon has come to be known as implicit memory. *Implicit memory* **is apparent when retention is exhibited on a task that does not require intentional remembering.** Implicit memory is contrasted with *explicit memory,* **which involves intentional recollection of previous experiences.**

Is implicit memory peculiar to people suffering from amnesia? No. When normal subjects are exposed to material and their retention of it is measured indirectly, they, too, show implicit memory (Schachter, 1987, 1989). To draw a parallel with everyday life, implicit memory is simply incidental, unintentional remembering (Mandler, 1989). People frequently remember things that they didn't deliberately store in memory. For example, you might recall the color of a jacket that your professor wore yesterday. Likewise, people remember things without deliberate retrieval efforts. For instance, you might be telling someone about a restaurant, which somehow reminds you of an unrelated story about a mutual friend.

Research has uncovered many interesting differences between implicit and explicit memory (Roediger, 1990; Tulving & Schachter, 1990). Explicit memory is conscious, is accessed directly, and can be best assessed with recall or recognition measures of retention. Implicit memory is unconscious, must be accessed indirectly, and can be best assessed with variations on relearning (savings) measures of retention. Implicit memory is largely unaffected by amnesia, age, the administration of certain drugs (such as alcohol), the length of the retention interval, and manipulations of interference. In contrast, explicit memory is affected very much by all these factors.

Some theorists think these differences are found because implicit and explicit memory rely on *different cognitive processes* in encoding and retrieval (Graf & Gallie, 1992; Roediger, 1990). However, many other theorists argue that the differences exist because implicit and explicit memory are handled by *independent memory systems* (Schachter, 1992, 1994; Squire, 1994). These independent systems are referred to as declarative and procedural memory.

Declarative Versus Procedural Memory 6c

Many theorists have suggested that people have separate memory systems for different kinds of information (see Figure 7.20). The most basic division of memory into distinct systems contrasts declarative memory with procedural memory (Winograd, 1975). **The** *declarative memory system* **handles factual information.** It contains recollections of words, definitions, names, dates, faces, events, concepts, and ideas. **The** *procedural memory system* **houses**

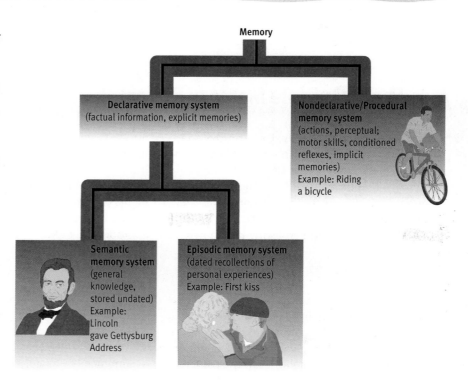

Figure 7.20

Theories of independent memory systems. There is some evidence that different types of information are stored in separate memory systems, which may have distinct physiological bases. The diagram shown here, which blends the ideas of several theorists, is an adaptation of Larry Squire's (1987) scheme. Note that implicit and explicit memory are not memory systems. They are observed behavioral phenomena that appear to be handled by different hypothetical memory systems (the procedural and declarative memory systems), which cannot be observed directly.

Memory

Declarative memory system
(factual information, explicit memories)

Nondeclarative/Procedural memory system
(actions, perceptual; motor skills, conditioned reflexes, implicit memories)
Example: Riding a bicycle

Semantic memory system
(general knowledge, stored undated)
Example: Lincoln gave Gettysburg Address

Episodic memory system
(dated recollections of personal experiences)
Example: First kiss

memory for actions, skills, and operations. It contains memories of how to execute such actions as riding a bike, typing, and tying one's shoes. To illustrate the distinction, if you know the rules of tennis (the number of games in a set, scoring, and such), this factual information is stored in declarative memory. If you remember how to hit a serve and swing through a backhand, these perceptual-motor skills are stored in procedural memory.

Some theorists believe that an association exists between implicit memory and the procedural memory system (Squire et al., 1993). Why? Because memory for skills is largely unconscious. People execute perceptual-motor tasks such as playing the piano or swimming with little conscious awareness of what they're doing. In fact, performance on such tasks often deteriorates if people think too much about what they're doing. Another parallel with implicit memory is that the memory for skills (such as typing and bike riding) doesn't decline much over long retention intervals. Thus, the procedural memory system may handle implicit remembering, while the declarative memory system handles explicit remembering.

Although much remains to be learned, researchers have made some progress toward identifying the neural bases of declarative versus nondeclarative memory. Declarative memory appears to be handled by the hippocampal complex and the far-flung areas of the cortex with which it communicates (Eichenbaum, 1997). It has proven more difficult to pinpoint the neural bases of nondeclarative memory because it consists of more of a hodge-podge of memory functions, but structures such as the cerebellum, amygdala, and basal ganglia appear to contribute (Delis & Lucas, 1996).

The recollections that allow these musicians to play their instruments are thought to be stored in the procedural memory system, which houses memories for actions and perceptual-motor skills.

Semantic Versus Episodic Memory

Endel Tulving (1986, 1993) has further subdivided declarative memory into semantic and episodic memory (see Figure 7.20). Both contain factual information, but episodic memory contains *personal facts* and semantic memory contains *general facts*. **The *episodic memory system* is made up of chronological, or temporally dated, recollections of personal experiences.** Episodic memory is a record of things you've done, seen, and heard. It includes information about *when* you did these things, saw them, or heard them. It contains recollections about being in a ninth-grade play, visiting the Grand Canyon, attending a Depeche Mode concert, or going to a movie last weekend.

Courtesy of Endel Tulving

❝Memory systems constitute the major subdivisions of the overall organization of the memory complex. . . . An operating component of a system consists of a neural substrate and its behavioral or cognitive correlates.❞
ENDEL TULVING

CONCEPT **CHECK 7.3**

Recognizing Various Types of Memory

Check your understanding of the various types of memory discussed in this chapter by matching the definitions below with the following: (a) declarative memory, (b) episodic memory, (c) explicit memory, (d) implicit memory, (e) long-term memory, (f) procedural memory, (g) semantic memory, (h) sensory memory, (i) short-term memory. The answers can be found in Appendix A.

A **1.** Memory for factual information.

E **2.** An unlimited capacity store that can hold information over lengthy periods of time.

H **3.** The preservation of information in its original sensory form for a brief time, usually only a fraction of a second.

D **4.** Type of memory apparent when retention is exhibited on a task that does not require intentional remembering.

B **5.** The repository of memories for actions, skills, and operations.

E **6.** General knowledge that is not tied to the time when the information was learned.

G **7.** A limited-capacity store that can maintain unrehearsed information for about 20 seconds.

The *semantic memory system* contains general knowledge that is not tied to the time when the information was learned. Semantic memory contains information such as Christmas is December 25th, dogs have four legs, and Phoenix is located in Arizona. You probably don't remember when you learned these facts. Information like this is usually stored undated. The distinction between episodic and semantic memory can be better appreciated by drawing an analogy to books: Episodic memory is like an autobiography, while semantic memory is like an encyclopedia.

The memory deficits seen in some cases of amnesia suggest that episodic and semantic memory are separate systems. For instance, some amnesiacs forget most personal facts, while their recall of general facts is largely unaffected (Wood, Ebert, & Kinsbourne, 1982). However, debate continues about whether episodic and semantic memory have distinct neural bases (Barba et al., 1998; Wiggs, Weisberg, & Martin, 1999).

Putting It in Perspective

One of our integrative themes—the idea that people's experience of the world is subjective—stood head and shoulders above the rest in this chapter. Let's briefly review how the study of memory has illuminated this idea.

First, our discussion of attention as inherently selective should have shed light on why people's experience of the world is subjective. To a great degree, what you see in the world around you depends on where you focus your attention. This is one of the main reasons why two people can be exposed to the "same" events and walk away with entirely different perceptions.

Second, the reconstructive nature of memory should further explain people's tendency to view the world with a subjective slant. When you observe an event, you don't store an exact copy of the event in your memory. Instead, you store a rough, "bare bones" approximation of the event that may be reshaped as time goes by. With the passage of time, people tend to put more and more of a personal, subjective imprint on memories.

Another theme also surfaced in this chapter. The multifaceted nature of memory demonstrates once again that behavior is governed by multiple causes. For instance, your memory of a specific event may be influenced by the following factors:

- The amount of attention you devote to the event.
- The level at which you process the incoming information.
- Whether you enrich your encoding with some form of elaboration.
- How you organize the information.
- How you search through your memory store.
- The extent to which you use schemas to reconstruct the event.
- The amount of interference you experience.

Given the multifaceted nature of memory, it should come as no surprise that there are many ways to improve memory. We discuss a variety of strategies in our Personal Application.

PERSONAL APPLICATION

Improving Everyday Memory

Answer the following "true" or "false."

_____ **1** Memory strategies were recently invented by psychologists.

_____ **2** Overlearning of information leads to poor retention.

_____ **3** Outlining what you read is not likely to affect retention.

_____ **4** Massing practice in one long study session is better than distributing practice across several shorter sessions.

Mnemonic devices **are strategies for enhancing memory.** They have a long and honorable history. In fact, one of the mnemonic devices covered in this Application—the method of loci—was described in Greece as early as 86–82 B.C. (Yates, 1966). Actually, mnemonic devices were even more crucial in ancient times than they are today. In ancient Greece and Rome, for instance, paper and pencils were not readily available for people to write down things they needed to remember, so they had to depend heavily on mnemonic devices.

Are mnemonic devices the key to improving one's everyday memory? No. Mnemonic devices clearly can be helpful in some situations (Wilding & Valentine, 1996), but they are not a panacea. They can be hard to use and hard to apply to many everyday situations. Most books and training programs designed to improve memory probably overemphasize mnemonic techniques (Searleman & Herrmann, 1994). Although less exotic strategies such as increasing rehearsal, engaging in deeper processing, and organizing material are more crucial to everyday memory, we will discuss some popular mnemonics as we proceed through this Application. Along the way, you'll learn that all of our opening true-false statements are false.

Engage in Adequate Rehearsal

Practice makes perfect, or so you've heard. In reality, practice is not likely to guarantee perfection, but it usually leads to improved retention. Studies show that retention improves with increased rehearsal (Greene, 1992a). This improvement presumably occurs because rehearsal helps to transfer information into long-term memory. It even pays to overlearn material (Driskell, Willis, & Copper, 1992). *Overlearning refers to continued rehearsal of material after you first appear to have mastered it.* In one study, after subjects had mastered a list of nouns (they recited the list without error), Krueger (1929) required them to continue rehearsing for 50% or 100% more trials. Measuring retention at intervals up to 28 days, Krueger found that greater overlearning was related to better recall of the list. The practical implication of this finding is simple: You should not quit rehearsing material as soon as you appear to have mastered it.

One other point related to rehearsal is also worth mentioning. If you are memorizing some type of list, be aware of the serial-position effect, which is often observed when subjects are tested on their memory of lists (Healy, 1992). **The *serial-position effect* occurs when subjects show better recall for items at the beginning and end of a list than for items in the middle** (see Figure 7.21). The reasons for the serial-position effect are complex and need not concern us, but its pragmatic implications are clear: If you need to learn a list, allocate extra practice trials to items in the middle of the list and check your memorization of those items very carefully.

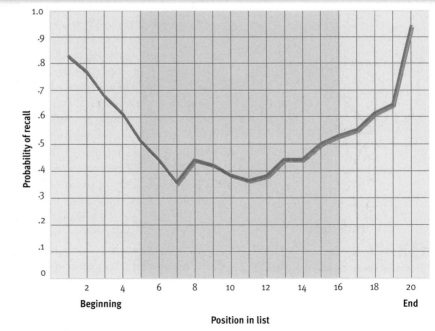

Figure 7.21

The serial-position effect. After hearing a list of items to remember, people reliably recall more of the items from the beginning and the end of the list than from the middle, producing the characteristic U-shaped curve shown here. (Adapted from "Analysis of Rehearsal Processes in Free Recall," by D. Rundus, 1971, *Journal of Experimental Psychology, 89,* 63–77. Copyright © 1971 by the American Psychological Association. Adapted by permission of the author.)

Schedule Distributed Practice and Minimize Interference

Let's assume that you need to study 9 hours for an exam. Should you "cram" all your studying into one 9-hour period (massed practice)? Or is it better to distribute your study among, say, three 3-hour periods on successive days (distributed practice)? The evidence indicates that retention tends to be greater after distributed practice than after massed practice (Glenberg, 1992; Payne & Wenger, 1996). This advantage is especially apparent if the intervals between practice periods are fairly long, such as 24 hours (Zechmeister & Nyberg, 1982). For instance, Underwood (1970) studied children (ages 9 to 14) who practiced a list of words four times, either in one long session or in four separate sessions. He found that distributed practice led to better recall than a similar amount of massed practice (see Figure 7.22). The superiority of distributed practice suggests that cramming is an ill-advised approach to studying for exams (Dempster, 1996).

Because interference is a major cause of forgetting, you'll probably want to think about how you can minimize it. This issue is especially important for students, because memorizing information for one course can interfere with the retention of information for another course. It may help to allocate study for specific courses to separate days. Thorndyke and Hayes-Roth (1979) found that similar material produced less interference when it was learned on different days. Thus, the day before an exam in a course, you should study for that course only—if possible. If demands in other courses make that plan impossible, you should study the test material last.

Engage in Deep Processing and Organize Information

Research on levels of processing suggests that how *often* you go over material is less critical than the *depth* of processing that you engage in (Craik & Tulving, 1975). Thus, if you expect to remember what you read, you have to wrestle fully with its meaning. Many students could probably benefit if they spent less time on rote repetition and devoted more effort to actually paying attention to and analyzing the meaning of their reading assignments. In particular, it is useful to make material *personally* meaningful. When you read your textbooks, try to relate information to your own life and experience. For example, when you read about classical conditioning, try to think of your own responses that are attributable to classical conditioning.

It is also important to understand that retention tends to be greater when information is well organized. The value of organization has been apparent in studies of people who exhibit remarkable memory capability. For example, Ericsson and Polson (1988) have studied a waiter, known as J. C., who can remember up to 20 complicated dinner orders without taking notes. They found that J. C. organized information by dinner element (salad dressings, vegetables, and so on), whereas other people memorized dinner requests in the order in which the requests were presented. J. C. also used acronyms to remember orders within a dinner element. For instance, he used the word *boot* to remember salad dressing orders

for blue cheese, oil and vinegar, oil and vinegar, and thousand island.

Gordon Bower (1970) has shown that hierarchical organization is particularly helpful when it is applicable. Thus, it may be a good idea to *outline* reading assignments for school, since outlining forces you to organize material hierarchically. Consistent with this reasoning, there is some empirical evidence that outlining material from textbooks can enhance retention of the material (McDaniel, Waddill, & Shakesby, 1996).

Enrich Encoding with Verbal Mnemonics

Although it's often helpful to make information personally meaningful, it's not always easy to do so. For instance, when you study chemistry you may have a hard time relating to polymers at a personal level. Thus, many mnemonic devices—such as acrostics, acronyms, and narrative methods—are designed to make abstract material more meaningful.

Acrostics and Acronyms

Acrostics are phrases (or poems) in which the first letter of each word (or line) functions as a cue to help you recall information to be remembered. For instance, you may remember the order of musical notes with the saying "Every good boy does fine" (or "deserves favor"). A slight variation on acrostics is the *acronym*—a word formed out of the first letters of a series of words. Students memorizing the order of colors in the light spectrum often store the name "Roy G. Biv" to remember red, orange, yellow, green, blue, indigo, and violet. Notice that this acronym takes advantage of the principle of chunking.

Narrative Methods

Another useful way to remember a list of words is to create a story that includes the words in the appropriate order. The narrative both increases the meaningfulness of the words and links them in a specific order. Examples of this technique can be seen in Figure 7.23. Bower and Clark (1969) found that this procedure greatly enhanced subjects' recall of lists of unrelated words.

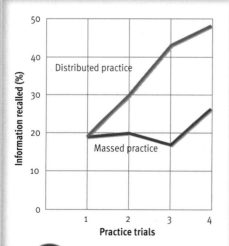

Figure 7.22

Effects of massed versus distributed practice on retention. Children in this study showed better recall of information when practice sessions were distributed over time. (Adapted from "A Breakdown of the Total-Time Law in Free-Recall Learning," by B. J. Underwood, 1970, *Journal of Verbal Learning and Verbal Behavior, 9,* 573–580. Copyright © 1970 by Academic Press, Inc. Adapted by permission of the publisher and author.)

Rhymes

Another verbal mnemonic that people often rely on is rhyming. You've probably repeated, "I before E except after C . . ." thousands of times. Perhaps you also remember the number of days in each month with the old standby, "Thirty days hath September . . ." Rhyming something to remember it is an old and useful trick.

Word list: Bird, Costume, Mailbox, Head, River, Nurse, Theater, Wax, Eyelid, Furnace

Story: A man dressed in a *Bird Costume* and wearing a *Mailbox* on his *Head* was seen leaping into the *River*. A *Nurse* ran out of a nearby *Theater* and applied *Wax* to his *Eyelids*, but her efforts were in vain. He died and was tossed into the *Furnace*.

Word list: Rustler, Penthouse, Mountain, Sloth, Tavern, Fuzz, Gland, Antler, Pencil, Vitamin

Story: A *Rustler* lived in a *Penthouse* on top of a *Mountain*. His specialty was the three-toed *Sloth*. He would take his captive animals to a *Tavern* where he would remove *Fuzz* from their *Glands*. Unfortunately, all this exposure to sloth fuzz caused him to grow *Antlers*. So he gave up his profession and went to work in a *Pencil* factory. As a precaution he also took a lot of *Vitamin* E.

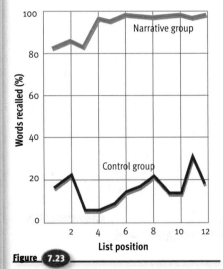

Figure 7.23

Narrative methods of remembering. Bower and Clark (1969) presented subjects with 12 lists of words. Subjects in the "narrative group" were asked to recall the words by constructing a story out of them (like the stories shown here). Subjects in the control group were given no special instructions. Recoding the material in story form dramatically improved recall, as the graph clearly shows. (Adapted from "Narrative Stories as Mediators of Serial Learning," by G.H. Bower and M.C. Clark, 1969, *Psychonomic Science, 14,* 181–182. Copyright © 1969 by the Psychonomic Society. Adapted by permisson of the Psychonomic Society.)

Enrich Encoding with Visual Imagery

Memory can be enhanced by the use of visual imagery. As you may recall, Allan Paivio (1986) believes that visual images create a second memory code and that two codes are better than one. Many popular mnemonic devices depend on visual imagery, including the link method and the method of loci.

Link Method

The *link method* involves forming a mental image of items to be remembered in a way that links them together. For instance, suppose that you need to remember some items to pick up at the drugstore: a news magazine, shaving cream, film, and pens. To remember these items, you might visualize a public figure on the magazine cover shaving with a pen while being photographed. The more bizarre you make your image, the more helpful it is likely to be (McDaniel & Einstein, 1986).

Figure 7.24

The method of loci. In this example from Bower (1970), a person about to go shopping pairs items to remember with familiar places (*loci*) arranged in a natural sequence: (1) hot dogs/driveway; (2) cat food/garage interior; (3) tomatoes/front door; (4) bananas/coat closet shelf; (5) whiskey/kitchen sink. The shopper then uses imagery to associate the items on the shopping list with the loci, as shown in the drawing: (1) giant *hot dog* rolls down a *driveway;* (2) a cat noisily devours *cat food* in the garage; (3) ripe *tomatoes* are splattered on the *front door;* (4) bunches of *bananas* are hung from the *closet shelf;* (5) the contents of a bottle of *whiskey* gurgle down the *kitchen sink.* As the last panel shows, the shopper recalls the items by mentally touring the loci associated with them. (From "Analysis of a Mnemonic Device," by G.H. Bower, 1970, *American Scientist, 58,* Sept–Oct., 496–499. Copyright © 1970 by Scientific Research Society. Reprinted by permission.)

Method of Loci

The *method of loci* involves taking an imaginary walk along a familiar path where images of items to be remembered are associated with certain locations. The first step is to commit to memory a series of loci, or places along a path. Usually these loci are specific locations in your home or neighborhood. Then envision each thing you want to remember in one of these locations. Try to form distinctive, vivid images. When you need to remember the items, imagine yourself walking along the path. The various loci on your path should serve as cues for the retrieval of the images that you formed (see Figure 7.24). Evidence suggests that the method of loci can be effective in increasing retention (Cornoldi & De Beni, 1996). Moreover, this method ensures that items are remembered in their *correct order* because the order is determined by the sequence of locations along the pathway.

Understanding the Fallibility of Eyewitness Accounts

A number of years ago, the Wilmington, Delaware, area was plagued by a series of armed robberies committed by a perpetrator who was dubbed the "gentleman bandit" by the press because he was an unusually polite and well-groomed thief. The local media published a sketch of the gentleman bandit and eventually an alert resident turned in a suspect who resembled the sketch. Much to everyone's surprise, the accused thief was a Catholic priest named Father Bernard Pagano—who vigorously denied the charges. Unfortunately for Father Pagano, his denials and alibis were unconvincing and he was charged with the crimes. At the trial, *seven* eyewitnesses confidently identified Father Pagano as the gentleman bandit. The prosecution was well on its way to a conviction when there was a stunning turn of events—another man, Ronald Clouser, confessed to the police that he was the gentleman bandit. The authorities dropped the charges against Father Pagano and the relieved priest was able to return to his normal existence (Rodgers, 1982).

This bizarre tale of mistaken identity—which sounds like it was lifted from a movie script—raises some interesting questions about memory. How could seven people "remember" seeing Father Pagnano commit armed robberies that he had nothing to do with? How could they mistake him for Ronald Clouser, when the two really didn't look very similar (see the photos below)? How could they be so confident when they were so wrong? Perhaps you're thinking that this is just one case and it must be unrepresentative (which would be sound critical thinking). Well, yes, it is a rather extreme example of eyewitness fallibility, but researchers have compiled mountains of evidence that eyewitness testimony is not nearly as reliable or as accurate as widely assumed (Cutler & Penrod, 1995; Loftus, 1993). This finding is ironic in that people are most confident about their assertions when they can say "I saw it with my own eyes." Television news shows like to use the title "Eyewitness News" to create the impression that they chronicle events with great clarity and accuracy. And our legal system accords special status to eyewitness testimony because it is considered much more dependable than hearsay or circumstantial evidence.

So, why are eyewitness accounts surprisingly inaccurate? Well, a host of factors and processes contribute to this inaccuracy. Let's briefly review some of the relevant processes that were introduced in the main body of the chapter; then we'll focus on two common errors in thinking that also contribute.

Can you think of any memory phenomena described in the chapter that seem likely to undermine eyewitness accuracy? You could point to the fact that *memory is a reconstructive process,* and eyewitness recall is likely to be distorted by the schemas that people have for various events. A second consideration is that *witnesses sometimes make source-monitoring errors* and get confused about where they saw a face. For example, one rape victim mixed up her assailant with a guest on a TV show that she was watching when she was attacked. Fortunately, the falsely accused suspect had an airtight alibi, as he could demonstrate that he was on live television when the rape occurred (Schacter, 1996). Perhaps the most pervasive factor is the misinformation effect (Loftus, 1993). *Witnesses' recall of events is routinely distorted by information introduced after the event* by police officers, attorneys, news reports, and so forth. In addition to these factors, eyewitness inaccuracy is fueled by the *hindsight bias* and *overconfidence effects.*

The Contribution of Hindsight Bias

The *hindsight bias* is the tendency to mold our interpretation of the past to fit how events actually turned out. When you know the outcome of an event, this knowledge slants your recall of how the event unfolded and what your thinking was at the time. With the luxury of hindsight, there is a curious tendency to say, "I knew it all along" when explaining events

Although he doesn't look that much like the real "gentleman bandit," who is shown on the left, seven eyewitnesses identified Father Pagnano (right) as the gentleman bandit, showing just how unreliable eyewitness accounts can be.

CORBIS/Bettmann—UPI

CORBIS/Bettmann—UPI

Although courts give special credence to eyewitness testimony, scientific evidence indicates that eyewitness accounts are less reliable than widely assumed.

that objectively would have been difficult to foresee. With regard to eyewitnesses, their recollections may often be distorted by knowing that a particular person has been arrested and accused of the crime in question. For example, Wells and Bradfield (1998) had simulated eyewitnesses select a perpetrator from a photo lineup. Their confidence in their identifications tended to be quite modest, which made sense given that the actual perpetrator was not even in the lineup. But when some subjects were told, "Good, you identified the actual suspect," they became highly confident about their identifications, which obviously were incorrect. In another study, participants read identical scenarios about a couple's first date that either had no ending or ended in a rape (described in one additional sentence). The subjects who received the rape ending reconstructed the story to be more consistent with their stereotypes of how rapes occur (Carli, 1999).

The Contribution of Overconfidence

Another flaw in thinking that contributes to inaccuracy in eyewitness accounts is people's tendency to be overconfident about the reliability of their memory. When tested for their memory of general information, people tend to overestimate their accuracy (Lichtenstein, Fischhoff, & Phillips, 1982). In studies of eyewitness recall, participants also tend to be overconfident about their recollections. Although jurors tend to be more convinced by eyewitnesses who appear confident, the evidence indicates that there is

only a modest correlation between eyewitness confidence and eyewitness accuracy (Bornstein & Zickafoose, 1999).

Strategies to Reduce Overconfidence

Can you learn to make better judgments of the accuracy of your recall of everyday events? Yes, with effort you can get better at making accurate estimates of how likely you are to be correct in the recall of some fact or event. One reason that people tend to be overconfident is that if they can't think of any reasons they might be wrong, they assume they must be right. Thus, overconfidence is fueled by yet another common error in thinking—*the failure to seek disconfirming evidence*. Even veteran scientists fall prey to this weakness, as most people don't seriously consider why they might be wrong about something (Mynatt, Doherty, & Tweney, 1978).

Thus, to make more accurate assessments of what you know and don't know, it helps to engage in a deliberate process of considering why you might be wrong. Here is an example. Based on your reading of Chapter 1, write down the schools of thought associated with the following major theorists: William James, John B. Watson, and Carl Rogers. After you provide your answers, rate your confidence that the information you just provided is correct. Now, write three reasons that your answers might be wrong and three reasons that they

might be correct. Most people will balk at this exercise, arguing that they cannot think of any reasons they might be wrong, but after some resistance, they can come up with several. Such reasons might include "I was half asleep when I read that part of the chapter" or "I might be confusing Watson and James." Reasons for thinking you're right could include "I distinctly recall discussing this with my friend" or "I really worked on those names in Chapter 1." After listing reasons that you might be right and might be wrong, rate your confidence in your accuracy once again. Guess what? Most people are less confident after going through such an exercise than they were before (depending, of course, on the nature of the topic).

The new confidence ratings tend to be more realistic than the original ratings (Koriat, Lichtenstein, & Fischhoff, 1980). Why? Because this exercise forces you to think more deeply about your answers and to search your memory for related information. Most people stop searching their memory as soon as they generate an answer they believe to be correct. Thus, the process of considering reasons you might be wrong about something—a process that people rarely engage in—is a useful critical thinking skill that can reduce overconfidence effects. Better assessment of what you know and don't know can be an important determinant of the quality of the decisions you make and the way you solve problems and reason from evidence.

Table 7.1	Critical Thinking Skills Discussed in This Application
Skill	**Description**
Understanding the limitations and fallibility of human memory	The critical thinker appreciates that memory is reconstructive and that even eyewitness accounts may be distorted or inaccurate.
Recognizing the bias in hindsight analysis	The critical thinker understands that knowing the outcome of events biases recall and interpretation of the events.
Recognizing overconfidence in human cognition	The critical thinker understands that people are frequently overconfident about the accuracy of their projections for the future and their recollections of the past.
Understanding the need to seek disconfirming evidence	The critical thinker understands the value of thinking about how or why one might be wrong about something.

REVIEW

Key Ideas

Encoding: Getting Information into Memory

● The multifaceted process of memory begins with encoding. Attention, which facilitates encoding, is inherently selective and has been compared to a filter.

● According to levels-of-processing theory, deeper processing results in better recall of information. Structural, phonemic, and semantic encoding represent progressively deeper and more effective levels of processing.

● Elaboration enriches encoding by linking a stimulus to other information. Visual imagery may work in much the same way, creating two memory codes rather than just one.

Storage: Maintaining Information in Memory

● Information-processing theories of memory assert that people have three kinds of memory stores: a sensory memory, a short-term memory, and a long-term memory.

● Short-term memory has a limited capacity (capable of holding about seven chunks of information) and can maintain unrehearsed information for about 20 seconds. Short-term memory is working memory, and it appears to involve more than a simple rehearsal loop.

● Long-term memory is an unlimited capacity store that may hold information indefinitely. Phenomena such as flashbulb memories and reports of exceptional recall through hypnosis suggest that LTM storage may be permanent, but the evidence is not convincing.

● Information in LTM can be organized in a variety of ways. A schema is an organized cluster of knowledge about a particular object or sequence of events. Semantic networks consist of concepts joined together by pathways. PDP models of memory assert that specific memories correspond to particular patterns of activation in connectionist networks.

Retrieval: Getting Information Out of Memory

● Recall is often guided by partial information. Reinstating the context of an event can facilitate recall. Memory is highly reconstructive and information learned after an event can alter our memory of it.

● Source monitoring is the process of making attributions about the origins of memories. Source-monitoring errors may explain why people sometimes "recall" something that was only suggested to them.

Forgetting: When Memory Lapses

● Ebbinghaus's early studies of nonsense syllables suggested that we forget very rapidly.

Subsequent research showed that Ebbinghaus's forgetting curve was exceptionally steep. Forgetting can be measured by asking people to recall, recognize, or relearn information.

● Some forgetting, including pseudoforgetting, is due to ineffective encoding of information. Decay theory proposes that forgetting occurs spontaneously with the passage of time. It has proven difficult to show that decay occurs in long-term memory.

● Interference theory proposes that people forget information because of competition from other material. Evidence that either prior (proactive interference) or subsequent (retroactive interference) material can cause forgetting supports interference theory.

● Forgetting is often due to retrieval failure, which may sometimes involve repression. Recent years have seen a surge of reports of repressed memories of sexual abuse in childhood. The authenticity of these recovered memories is the subject of controversy because empirical studies have demonstrated that it is not all that difficult to create inaccurate memories.

In Search of the Memory Trace: The Physiology of Memory

● The study of amnesia and other research has implicated the hippocampal region as a key player in memory processes, but its exact role remains the subject of debate.

● Thompson's research suggests that memory traces may consist of localized neural circuits. Other lines of research indicate that biochemical processes may contribute to the formation of memories.

Are There Multiple Memory Systems?

● Differences between implicit and explicit memory suggest that people may have several separate memory systems. Declarative memory is memory for facts, while procedural memory is memory for actions and skills. Declarative memory can be subdivided into episodic memory (for personal facts) and semantic memory (for general facts).

Putting It in Perspective

● Our discussion of attention and memory enhances our understanding of why our experience of the world is highly subjective. Work in this area also shows that behavior is governed by multiple factors.

Personal Application ● Improving Everyday Memory

● Rehearsal, even when it involves overlearning, facilitates retention, although one should be wary of the serial position effect. Distributed practice tends to be more efficient than massed practice. It is wise to plan study sessions so as to minimize interference. Deep processing

during rehearsal and good organization enhance recall.

● Meaningfulness can be enhanced through the use of verbal mnemonics such as acrostics, acronyms, and narrative methods. The link method and the method of loci are mnemonic devices that depend on the value of visual imagery.

Critical Thinking Application ● Understanding the Fallibility of Eyewitness Accounts

● Research indicates that eyewitness memory is not nearly as reliable or accurate as widely believed. Two common errors in thinking that contribute to this phenomenon are hindsight bias and overconfidence effects. The process of considering why you might be wrong can reduce overconfidence about the accuracy of your memories.

Key Terms

Anterograde amnesia
Attention
Chunk
Connectionist models
Consolidation
Decay theory
Declarative memory system
Dual-coding theory
Elaboration
Encoding
Encoding specificity principle
Episodic memory system
Explicit memory
Flashbulb memories
Forgetting curve
Hindsight bias
Implicit memory
Interference theory
Levels-of-processing theory
Link method
Long-term memory (LTM)
Method of loci
Misinformation effect
Mnemonic devices
Nonsense syllables
Overlearning
Parallel distributed processing (PDP) models
Proactive interference
Procedural memory system
Recall
Recognition
Rehearsal
Relearning
Repression
Retention
Retrieval
Retroactive interference
Retrograde amnesia
Schema
Semantic memory system
Semantic network
Sensory memory
Serial-position effect
Short-term memory (STM)
Source monitoring
Source-monitoring error
Storage
Tip-of-the-tongue phenomenon

Key People

Richard Atkinson and Richard Shiffrin
Fergus Craik and Robert Lockhart
Hermann Ebbinghaus
Elizabeth Loftus
George Miller
Endel Tulving

PRACTICE TEST

1. Getting information into memory is called _____; getting information out of memory is called _____.
   A. storage; retrieval
   B. encoding; storage
   C. encoding; retrieval
   D. storage; encoding

2. The word *big* is flashed on a screen. A mental picture of the word *big* represents a _____ code; the definition "large in size" represents a _____ code; "sounds like pig" represents a _____ code.
   A. structural; phonemic; semantic
   B. phonemic; semantic; structural
   C. structural; semantic; phonemic
   D. phonemic; structural; semantic

3. The capacity of short-term memory is:
   A. about 50,000 words.
   B. unlimited.
   C. about 25 stimuli.
   D. about 7 "chunks" of information.

4. Which statement best represents current evidence on the durability of long-term storage?
   A. All forgetting involves breakdowns in retrieval.
   B. LTM is like a barrel of marbles in which none of the marbles ever leak out.
   C. There is no convincing evidence that all one's memories are stored away permanently.
   D. All long-term memories gradually decay at a constant rate.

5. An organized cluster of knowledge about a particular object or sequence of events is called a:
   A. semantic network.
   B. conceptual hierarchy.
   C. schema.
   D. retrieval cue.

6. The tip-of-the-tongue phenomenon:
   A. is a temporary inability to remember something you know, accompanied by a feeling that it's just out of reach.
   B. is clearly due to a failure in retrieval.
   C. reflects a permanent loss of information from LTM.
   D. is both a and b.

7. Loftus's work on eyewitness testimony has clearly demonstrated that:
   A. Memory errors are surprisingly infrequent.
   B. Memory errors are mainly due to repression.
   C. Information given after an event can alter a person's memory of the event.
   D. Information given after an event cannot alter a person's memory of the event.

8. If decay theory is correct:
   A. information can never be permanently lost from long-term memory.
   B. forgetting is simply a case of retrieval failure.
   C. the principal cause of forgetting should be the passage of time.
   D. all of the above.

9. Pseudoforgetting is information loss due to ineffective:
   A. encoding.
   B. storage.
   C. retrieval.
   D. all of the above.

10. Many amnesiacs demonstrate _____ memory, even though their _____ memory is extremely impaired.
    A. declarative; procedural
    B. conscious; unconscious
    C. implicit; explicit
    D. semantic; episodic

11. Your memory of how to brush your teeth is contained in your _____ memory.
    A. declarative
    B. procedural
    C. structural
    D. episodic

12. Your knowledge that birds fly, that the sun rises in the east, and that 2 + 2 = 4 is contained in your _____ memory.
    A. structural
    B. procedural
    C. implicit
    D. semantic

13. Dorothy memorized her shopping list. When she got to the store, however, she found she had forgotten many of the items from the middle of the list. This is an example of:
    A. inappropriate encoding.
    B. retrograde amnesia.
    C. proactive interference.
    D. the serial-position effect.

14. The method of loci involves:
    A. taking an imaginary walk along a familiar path where you have associated images of items you want to remember with certain locations.
    B. forming a mental image of items to be remembered in a way that links them together.
    C. creating a phrase in which the first letter of each word functions as a cue to help you recall more abstract words that begin with the same letter.
    D. creating a story that includes each of the words to be remembered in the appropriate order.

15. The tendency to mold our interpretation of the past to fit how events actually turned out is called:
    A. the overconfidence effect.
    B. selective amnesia.
    C. retroactive interference.
    D. the hindsight bias.

Answers

1	C	page 202	6	D	page 212	11	B	pages 222–223
2	C	pages 203–204	7	C	pages 212–213	12	D	pages 223–224
3	D	page 207	8	C	page 215	13	D	page 225
4	C	pages 208–209	9	A	page 215	14	A	page 227
5	C	page 210	10	C	pages 221–222	15	D	pages 228–229

CHAPTER 8

© William Whitehurst 1997/The Stock Market

Language and Thought

© William Whitehurst 1997/The Stock Market

*"*M*r. Watson—Mr. Sherlock Holmes," said Stamford, introducing us. "How are you?" he said, cordially, gripping my hand with a strength for which I should hardly have given him credit. "You have been in Afghanistan, I perceive."*

"How on earth did you know that?" I asked, in astonishment.

(From A Study in Scarlet *by Arthur Conan Doyle)*

If you've ever read any Sherlock Holmes stories, you know that the great detective continually astonished his stalwart companion, Dr. Watson, with his extraordinary deductions.

Obviously, Holmes could not arrive at his conclusions without a chain of reasoning. Yet to him even an elaborate reasoning process was a simple, everyday act. Consider his feat of knowing at once, upon first meeting Watson, that the doctor had been in Afghanistan. When asked, Holmes explained his reasoning as follows:

"I knew you came from Afghanistan. From long habit the train of thought ran so swiftly through my mind that I arrived at the conclusion without being conscious of the intermediate steps. There were such steps, however. The train of reasoning ran: 'Here is a gentleman of a medical type, but with the air of a military man. Clearly an army doctor, then. He has just come from the tropics, for his face is dark, and that is not the natural tint of his skin, for his wrists are fair. He has undergone hardship and sickness, as his haggard face says clearly. His left arm has been injured. He holds it in a stiff and unnatural manner. Where in the tropics could an English army doctor have seen much hardship and got his arm wounded? Clearly in Afghanistan.' The whole train of thought did not occupy a second."

Admittedly, Sherlock Holmes's deductive feats are fictional. But even to read about them appreciatively—let alone imagine them, as Sir Arthur Conan Doyle did—is a remarkably complex mental act. Our everyday thought processes seem ordinary to us only because we take them for granted, just as Holmes saw nothing extraordinary in what to him was a simple deduction.

Carnegie-Mellon University

"You couldn't use a word like mind *in a psychology journal—you'd get your mouth washed out with soap."*
HERBERT SIMON

In reality, everyone is a Sherlock Holmes, continually performing magical feats of thought. Even elementary perception—for instance, watching a football game or a ballet—involves elaborate cognitive processes. People must sort through distorted, constantly shifting perceptual inputs and deduce what they see out there in the real world. Imagine, then, the complexity of thought required to read a book, fix an automobile, or balance a checkbook. Of course, all this is not to say that human thought processes are flawless or unequaled. You probably own a $10 calculator that can run circles around you when it comes to computing square roots. As we'll see, some of the most interesting research in this chapter focuses on ways in which people's thinking can be limited, simplistic, or outright illogical.

In any event, as we have noted before, **cognition refers to the mental processes involved in acquiring knowledge.** In other words, cognition involves thinking. When psychology first emerged as an independent science in the 19th century, it focused on the mind. Mental processes were explored through *introspection*—analysis of one's own conscious experience (see Chapter 1). Unfortunately, early psychologists' study of mental processes ran aground, as the method of introspection yielded unreliable results. Psychology's empirical approach depends on observation, and private mental events proved difficult to observe. Furthermore, during the first half of the 20th century, the study of cognition was actively discouraged by the theoretical dominance of behaviorism. Herbert Simon, a pioneer of

cognitive psychology, recalls that "you couldn't use a word like *mind* in a psychology journal—you'd get your mouth washed out with soap" (Holden, 1986).

Although it wasn't fully recognized until much later, the 1950s brought a "cognitive revolution" in psychology (Baars, 1986). Renegade theorists, such as Herbert Simon, began to argue that behaviorists' exclusive focus on overt responses was doomed to yield an incomplete understanding of human functioning. More important, creative new approaches to research on cognitive processes led to exciting progress. For example, in his book on the cognitive revolution, Howard Gardner (1985) notes that three major advances were reported at a watershed 1956 conference—in just one day! First, Herbert Simon and Allen Newell described the first computer program to successfully simulate human problem solving. Second, Noam Chomsky outlined a new model that changed the way psychologists studied language. Third, George Miller delivered the legendary paper that we discussed in Chapter 7, arguing that the capacity of short-term memory is seven (plus or minus two) items. Since then, cognitive science has grown into a robust, interdisciplinary enterprise. Besides memory (which we covered in Chapter 7), cognitive psychologists investigate the topics of language, problem solving, decision making, and reasoning, all of which are covered in this chapter. In the Personal Application we'll analyze biases that can distort decision making and in the Critical Thinking Application that follows we'll discuss how language can be manipulated to influence people's thinking.

Language: Turning Thoughts into Words

Language obviously plays a fundamental role in human behavior. Indeed, if you were to ask people, "What characteristic most distinguishes humans from other living creatures?" a great many would reply, "Language." In this section, we'll discuss the nature, structure, and development of language.

What Is Language?

A *language* consists of symbols that convey meaning, plus rules for combining those symbols, that can be used to generate an infinite variety of messages. Language systems include a number of critical properties (Ratner & Gleason, 1993).

First, language is *symbolic*. People use spoken sounds and written words to represent objects,

actions, events, and ideas. The word *lamp*, for instance, refers to a class of objects that have certain properties. The symbolic nature of language greatly expands what people can communicate about. Symbols allow one to refer to objects that may be in another place and to events that happened at another time (for example, a lamp broken at work yesterday). Language symbols are flexible in that a variety of somewhat different objects may be called by the same name (consider the diversity of lamps, for example).

Second, language is *semantic,* or meaningful. The symbols used in a language are arbitrary in that no built-in relationship exists between the look or sound of words and the objects they stand for. Take, for instance, the writing object that you may have in your hand right now. It's represented by the word *pen* in English, *stylo* in French, and *pluma* in Spanish. Although these words are arbitrary (others could have been chosen), they have *shared meanings* for people who speak English, French, and Spanish.

Third, language is *generative*. A limited number of symbols can be combined in an infinite variety of ways to *generate* an endless array of novel messages. Everyone has some "stock sayings," but every day you create sentences that you have never spoken before. You also comprehend many sentences that you have never encountered before (like this one).

Fourth, language is *structured*. Although people can generate an infinite variety of sentences, these sentences must be structured in a limited number of ways. There are rules that govern the arrangement of words into phrases and sentences. Some arrangements are acceptable and some are not. For example, you might say, "The swimmer jumped into the pool," but you would never recombine the same words to say, "Pool the into the jumped swimmer." The structure of language allows people to be inventive with words and still understand each other. Let's take a closer look at the structural properties of language.

The Structure of Language

Human languages have a hierarchical structure (Ratner & Gleason, 1993). As Figure 8.1 shows, basic sounds are combined into units with meaning, which are combined into words. Words are combined into phrases, which are combined into sentences.

Phonemes

At the base of the language hierarchy are **phonemes, the smallest speech units in a language that can be distinguished perceptually.** Considering that an unabridged English dictionary contains more than 450,000 words, you might imagine that there must be a huge number of phonemes. In fact, linguists estimate that humans are capable of producing only about 100 such basic sounds. Moreover, no one language uses all of these phonemes. Different languages use different groups of about 20 to 80 phonemes.

For all its rich vocabulary, the English language is composed of about 40 phonemes, corresponding roughly to the 26 letters of the alphabet plus several variations. Some representative English phonemes are listed in Table 8.1 on the next page. A letter in the alphabet is represented by more than one phoneme if it has more than one pronunciation. For example, the letter *a* is pronounced differently in the words *father, had, call,* and *take.* Each of these pronunciations is represented by a different phoneme. In addition, some phonemes are represented by combinations of letters, such as *ch* and *th.* From this handful of basic sounds, speakers can generate all the words in the English language—and invent new ones besides.

Morphemes

Morphemes **are the smallest units of meaning in a language.** There are approximately 50,000 English morphemes, which include root words as well as prefixes and suffixes. Many words, such as *fire, guard,*

Figure 8.1

An analysis of a simple English sentence. As this example shows, verbal language has a hierarchical structure. At the base of the hierarchy are the *phonemes,* which are units of vocal sound that do not, in themselves, have meaning. The smallest units of meaning in a language are *morphemes,* which include not only root words but such meaning-carrying units as the past tense suffix *ed* and the plural *s.* Complex rules of syntax govern how the words constructed from morphemes may be combined into phrases, and phrases into meaningful statements, or sentences. (Figure from *Child Development: A Topical Approach,* by A. Clarke-Stewart, S. Friedman & J. Koch, p. 417, 1985. Copyright © 1985 by John Wiley & Sons, Inc. Reprinted by permission of John Wiley & Sons, Inc.)

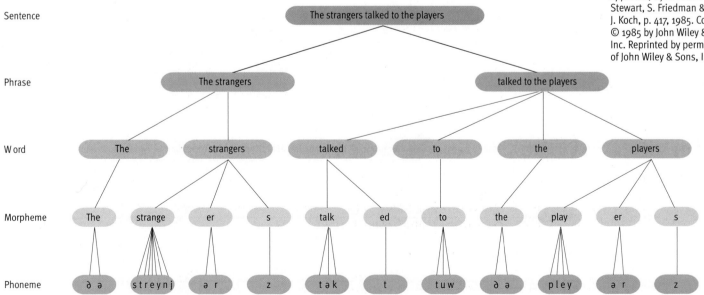

Table **8.1** **Phonemic Symbols for the Sounds of American English**

Consonants

/p/	pill	/t/	toe	/g/	gill
/b/	bill	/d/	doe	/ŋ/	ring
/m/	mill	/n/	no	/h/	hot
/f/	fine	/s/	sink	/?/	uh-oh
/v/	vine	/z/	zinc	/l/	low
/θ/	thigh	/c/	choke	/r/	row
/ð/	thy	/j/	joke	/j/	you
/s/	shoe	/k/	kill	/w/	win
/z/	treasure				

Vowels

/i/	beet	/ɪ/	bit
/e/	bait	/∈/	bet
/u/	boot	/u/	foot
/o/	boat	/ɔ/	caught
/æ/	bat	/a/	pot
/ʌ/	but	/ə/	sofa
/aɪ/	bite	/au/	out
/ɔɪ/	boy		

From *Language Development*, by E. Hoff-Ginsberg © 1997.

and *friend,* consist of a single morpheme. Many others represent combinations of morphemes. For example, the word *unfriendly* consists of three morphemes: the root word *friend,* the prefix *un,* and the suffix *ly.* Each of the morphemes contributes to the meaning of the entire word.

Syntax

Of course, most utterances consist of more than a single word. As we've already noted, people don't combine words randomly. **Syntax is a system of rules that specify how words can be arranged into phrases and sentences.** A simple rule of syntax is that declarative sentences (sentences that make a statement) must have both a *noun phrase* and a *verb phrase.* Thus, "The sound of cars is annoying" is a sentence. However, "The sound of cars" is not a sentence, because it lacks a predicate.

Rules of syntax underlie all language use, even though you may not be aware of them. Thus, although they may not be able to verbalize the rule, virtually all English speakers know that an *article* (such as *the*) comes before the word it modifies. For example, you would never say *swimmer the* instead of *the swimmer.* How children learn the complicated rules of syntax is one of the major puzzles investigated by psychologists interested in language. Like other aspects of language development, children's acquisition of syntax seems to progress at an amazingly rapid pace. Let's look at how this remarkable development unfolds.

Milestones in Language Development

Learning to use language requires learning a number of skills that become important at different points in a child's development (Siegler, 1998). We'll examine this developmental sequence by looking first at how children learn to pronounce words, then at their use of single words, and finally at their ability to combine words to form sentences (see Table 8.2).

Table **8.2** **Overview of Typical Language Development**

Age	General Characteristics
Months	
1–5	*Reflexive communication:* Vocalizes randomly, coos, laughs, cries, engages in vocal play, discriminates language from nonlanguage sounds
6–18	*Babbling:* Verbalizes in response to speech of others; responses increasingly approximate human speech patterns
10–13	*First words:* Uses words typically to refer to objects
12–18	*One-word sentence stage:* Vocabulary grows slowly; uses nouns primarily; overextensions begin
18–24	*Vocabulary spurt:* Fast-mapping facilitates rapid acquisition of new words
Years	
2	*Two-word sentence stage:* Uses telegraphic speech; uses more pronouns and verbs
2–5	*Three-word sentence stage:* Modifies speech to take listener into account; overregularizations begin
3	Uses complete simple active sentence structure; uses sentences to tell stories that are understood by others; uses plurals
3–5	*Expanded grammatical forms:* Expresses concepts with words; uses four-word sentences
4	Uses imaginary speech; uses five-word sentences
5	*Well-developed and complex syntax:* Uses more complex syntax. Uses more complex forms to tell stories
6	Displays metalinguistic awareness

Note: Children often show individual differences in the exact ages at which they display the various developmental achievements outlined here.

Moving Toward Producing Words

Three-month-old infants display a surprising language-related talent: They can distinguish phonemes from all the world's languages, including phonemes that they do not hear in their environment. In contrast, adults cannot readily discriminate phonemes that are not used in their native language. Actually, neither can 1-year-old children, as this curious ability gradually disappears between 4 months and 12 months of age (Werker & Desjardins, 1995). The exact mechanisms responsible for this transition are not understood, but it is clear that long before infants utter their first words, they are making remarkable progess in learning the sound structure of their native language.

During the first six months of life, a baby's vocalizations are dominated by crying, cooing, and laughter, which have limited value as a means of communication. Soon, infants are *babbling*, producing a wide variety of sounds that correspond to phonemes and, eventually, many consonant-vowel combinations. Babbling becomes more complex and increasingly resembles the language spoken by parents and others in the child's environment (De Boysson-Bardies & Vihman, 1991). These trends probably reflect ongoing neural development and the maturation of the infant's vocal apparatus (Sachs, 1985). Babbling lasts until around 18 months, continuing even after children utter their first words.

At around 10 to 13 months of age, most children begin to utter sounds that correspond to words. Most infants' first words are similar in phonetic form and meaning—even in different languages (Gleason & Ratner, 1993). The initial words resemble the syllables that infants most often babble spontaneously. For example, words such as *dada, mama,* and *papa* are names for parents in many languages because they consist of sounds that are easy to produce.

Using Words

After children utter their first words, their vocabulary grows slowly for the next few months (Barrett, 1995). Toddlers typically can say between 3 and 50 words by 18 months. However, their *receptive vocabulary* is larger than their *productive vocabulary*. That is, they can comprehend more words spoken by others than they can actually produce to express themselves (Pease, Gleason, & Pan, 1993). Thus, toddlers can *understand* 50 words months before they can *say* 50 words. Toddlers' early words tend to refer most often to *objects* and secondarily to familiar *actions* (Menyuk, Liebergott, & Schultz, 1995). Children generally acquire nouns before verbs because the

Humans seem uniquely well-suited for learning language. The most amazing aspect of children's language development is how rapidly it proceeds. By the age of 30 months, most children have acquired a decent mastery of their native tongue.

Author's collection

meanings of nouns, which often refer to distinct, concrete objects, tend to be easier to encode than the meanings of verbs, which often refer to more abstract relationships (Gentner & Rattermann, 1991).

Youngsters' vocabularies soon begin to grow at a dizzying pace, as a *vocabulary spurt* often begins at around 18–24 months (Bates & Carnevale, 1993). By the first grade, the average child has a vocabulary of approximately 10,000 words, which builds to an astonishing 40,000 words by the fifth grade (Anglin, 1993; see Figure 8.2). In building these impressive vocabularies, some 2-year-olds learn as many as 20 new words every week. *Fast mapping* appears to be one factor underlying this rapid growth of vocabulary (Mervis & Bertrand, 1994). **Fast mapping is the process by which children map a word onto an underlying concept after only one exposure.** Thus, children often add words like *tank, board,* and *tape* to their vocabularies after

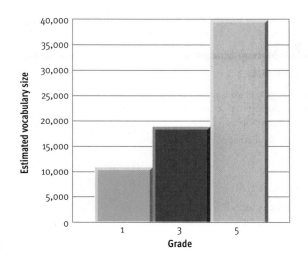

Figure 8.2

The growth of school children's vocabulary.
Vocabulary growth is rapid during the early years of grade school. Youngsters' estimated vocabulary doubles about every two years between first grade and fifth grade. (From "Vocabulary Development: A Morphological Analysis," by J. M. Anglin, 1993, *Child Development, 58,* Serial 238. Copyright © 1993 The Society for Research in Child Development, Inc. Reprinted by permission.)

their first encounter with objects that illustrate these concepts. The vocabulary spurt may be attributable to children's improved articulation skills, improved understanding of syntax, underlying cognitive development, or some combination of these factors (MacWhinney, 1998).

Of course, these efforts to learn new words are not flawless. Toddlers often make errors, such as overextensions and underextensions (G. Miller, 1991). **An *overextension* occurs when a child incorrectly uses a word to describe a wider set of objects or actions than it is meant to.** For example, a child might use the word *ball* for anything round—oranges, apples, even the moon. Overextensions usually appear in children's speech between ages 1 and 2½. Specific overextensions typically last up to several months (Clark, 1983). Toddlers also tend to be guilty of **underextensions, which occur when a child incorrectly uses a word to describe a narrower set of objects or actions than it is meant to.** For example, a child might use the word *doll* to refer only to a single, favorite doll. Overextensions and underextensions show that toddlers are actively trying to learn the rules of language—albeit with mixed success.

Combining Words

Children typically begin to combine words into sentences near the end of their second year. Early sentences are characterized as "telegraphic" because they resemble telegrams (Hoff-Ginsberg, 1997). *Telegraphic speech* **consists mainly of content words; articles, prepositions, and other less critical words are omitted.** Thus, a child might say, "Give doll" rather than "Please give me the doll." Although not unique to the English language, telegraphic speech is not cross-culturally universal, as was once thought (de Villiers & de Villiers, 1992).

CONCEPT **CHECK 8.1**

Tracking Language Development

Check your understanding of how language skills progress in youngsters. Number the utterances below to indicate the developmental sequence in which they would probably occur. The answers can be found in Appendix A.

_____ **1.** "Doggie," while pointing to a cow.

_____ **2.** "The dogs runned away."

_____ **3.** "Doggie run."

_____ **4.** "The dogs ran away."

_____ **5.** "Doggie," while pointing to a dog.

_____ **6.** "Tommy thinks like his head is full of mashed potatoes."

Researchers sometimes track language development by keeping tabs on subjects' *mean length of utterance (MLU)*—**the average length of youngsters' spoken statements (measured in morphemes).** After children begin to combine words, their vocal expressions gradually become longer (Riley, 1987).

By the end of their third year, most children can express complex ideas such as the plural or the past tense. However, their efforts to learn the rules of language continue to generate revealing mistakes. *Overregularization* **occurs when grammatical rules are incorrectly generalized to irregular cases where they do not apply.** For example, children will say things like "The girl goed home" or "I hitted the ball." Cross-cultural research suggests that these overregularizations occur in all languages (Slobin, 1985). Most theorists believe that overregularizations demonstrate that children are working actively to master the *rules* of language (Marcus, 1996). Children don't learn the fine points of grammar and usage in a single leap but gradually acquire them in small steps.

Refining Language Skills

Youngsters make their largest strides in language development in their first 4 to 5 years. However, they continue to refine their language skills during their school-age years. They generate longer and more complicated sentences as they receive formal training in written language.

As their language skills develop, school-age children begin to appreciate ambiguities in language. They can, for instance, recognize two possible meanings in sentences such as "Visiting relatives can be bothersome." This interest in ambiguities indicates that they're developing *metalinguistic awareness*—**the ability to reflect on the use of language.** As metalinguistic awareness grows, children begin to "play" with language, coming up with puns and jokes. They begin to make more frequent and sophisticated use of metaphors, such as "We were packed in the room like sardines" (Gentner, 1988). They also learn to recognize hidden meanings often found in everyday discourse, such as sarcastic comments (Capelli, Nakagawa, & Madden, 1990).

Learning More Than One Language: Bilingualism

Given the complexities involved in acquiring one language, you may be wondering about the ramifications of being asked to learn *two* languages. *Bilingualism* is the acquisition of two languages that use different speech sounds, vocabulary, and grammatical rules. Although nearly half of the world's population grows up bilingual (Snow, 1993), bilingualism has sparked considerable controversy in the United States, as a host of new laws and court rulings have reduced the availability of bilingual educational programs in many school systems (Hakuta, 1999). These laws are based on the implicit assumption that bilingualism hampers language development and has a negative impact on youngsters' educational progress. But does the empirical evidence support this assumption? Let's take a look at the research.

Does Learning Two Languages in Childhood Slow Down Language Development?

If youngsters are learning two languages simultaneously, does one language interfere with the other so that the acquisition of both is impeded? Some studies *have* found that bilingual children have smaller vocabularies in each of their languages than monolingual children have in their one language (Umbel et al., 1992). But when their two overlapping vocabularies are added, their total vocabulary is similar to that of children learning a single language (Pearson, Fernandez, & Oller, 1993). Taken as a whole, the available evidence suggests that bilingual and monolingual children are largely similar in the course and rate of their language development (de Houwer, 1995; Nicoladis & Genesee, 1997) Thus, although more research is needed, so far, there is little empirical support for the assumption that bilingualism has a negative effect on language development.

Does Bilingualism Affect Cognitive Processes and Skills?

Does knowing two languages make thinking more difficult, or could bilingualism enhance thought processes? The evidence is mixed, depending on the variables measured and the exact nature of the subject populations that are compared. When middle-class bilingual subjects who are fluent in both languages are studied, they tend to score somewhat *higher* than monolingual subjects on measures of cognitive flexibility, analytical reasoning, selective attention, and metalinguistic awareness (Bialystok, 1999; Campbell & Sais, 1995; Lambert, 1990). However, on some types of tasks, bilinguals may have a slight disadvantage in terms of raw language-processing *speed* (Taylor & Taylor, 1990). Nonetheless, when researchers control for the effects of social class, they do not find significant cognitive deficits in bilingual people.

What Factors Influence the Acquistion of a Second Language?

A great many bilingual individuals do not learn their two languages simultaneously. Rather, they learn their native language first and then learn a second language later. Do any key considerations govern the learning of a second language? Yes, the evidence clearly indicates that *age* is a crucial determinant of how effectively people can acquire a second language—and younger is better. For example, Figure 8.3, from a study by Johnson and Newport (1989), maps out the relationship between immigrants' age of arrival in the U.S. and their subsequent mastery of English grammar. As you can see, people who started learning English at an early age achieved greater mastery than those who began later. For reasons that are not well understood, language learning unfolds more effectively when initiated prior to age 7, and younger continues to be better up through age 15. Older children and adults can certainly become proficient in a second language, but they generally do not become as proficient as native speakers (Hoff-Ginsberg, 1997). As you will see momentarily, the relative ease with which young children learn language looms large in the long-running debate about the processes underlying language acquisition.

Theories of Language Acquisition

Since the 1950s, a great debate has raged about the key processes involved in language acquisition. As with arguments in other areas of psychology that we have seen previously, this one centers on the *nature versus nurture* issue. The debate was stimulated by the influential behaviorist B. F. Skinner (1957), who argued that environmental factors govern language development. His provocative analysis brought a rejoinder from Noam Chomsky (1959),

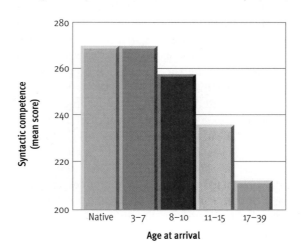

Figure **8.3**

Age and second language learning. In a study of how well immigrants to the United States master English as a second language, Johnson and Newport (1989) examined the relationship between the subjects' age of arrival and their mastery of syntax. As you can see, it was advantageous to start learning English at an earlier age, up through about age 15. After that, age of arrival did not make a difference. For example, those who started at 20 were no better off than those who started at 30. (Adapted from "Critical Period Effects in Second Learning," by J. Johnson and E. Newport, 1989, *Cognitive Psychology, 21,* 60–99. Academic Press.)

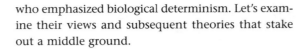
who emphasized biological determinism. Let's examine their views and subsequent theories that stake out a middle ground.

Behaviorist Theories

The behaviorist approach to language was first outlined by Skinner in his book *Verbal Behavior* (1957). He argued that children learn language the same way they learn everything else: through imitation, reinforcement, and other established principles of conditioning. According to Skinner, vocalizations that are not reinforced gradually decline in frequency. The remaining vocalizations are shaped with reinforcers until they are correct. Behaviorists assert that by controlling reinforcement, parents encourage their children to learn the correct meaning and pronunciation of words (Staats & Staats, 1963). For example, as children grow older, parents may insist on closer and closer approximations of the word *water* before supplying the requested drink.

Behavioral theorists also use the principles of imitation and reinforcement to explain how children learn syntax. According to the behaviorists' view, children learn how to construct sentences by imitating the sentences of adults and older children. If children's imitative statements are understood, parents are able to answer their questions or respond to their requests, thus reinforcing their verbal behavior. Learning theory asserts that parents shape children's syntax by translating understandable but ungrammatical statements into correct grammatical form.

Nativist Theories

Skinner's explanation of language acquisition soon inspired a critique and rival explanation from Noam Chomsky (1959, 1965). Chomsky pointed out that there are an infinite number of sentences in a language. It's therefore unreasonable to expect that children learn language by imitation. For example, in English, we add *ed* to the end of a verb to construct past tense. Children routinely overregularize this rule, producing incorrect verbs such as *goed, eated,* and *thinked.* Mistakes such as these are inconsistent with Skinner's emphasis on imitation, because most adult speakers don't use ungrammatical words like *goed.* Children can't imitate things they don't hear. According to Chomsky, children learn the *rules of language,* not specific verbal responses, as Skinner proposed. Chomsky asserts that youngsters' misapplication of rules explains many of their early errors in language.

Critics have also challenged the behaviorist position that children learn to construct correct

"Even at low levels of intelligence, at pathological levels, we find a command of language that is totally unattainable by an ape."
NOAM CHOMSKY

MIT photo by Donna Coveney/MIT News Office

sentences through reinforcement. An influential study by Brown and Hanlon (1970) indicated that parents typically respond to meaning and factual accuracy in their youngsters' speech rather than to grammar. Thus, a mother curling her daughter's hair probably won't correct the ungrammatical statement "Her curl my hair," because it is factually accurate. In other words, parents may not engage in much of the language shaping that is critical to the behavioral explanation of language development (Maratsos, 1983; Pinker, 1990).

An alternative theory favored by Chomsky and others is that humans have an inborn or "native" propensity to develop language (Chomsky, 1975, 1986; Crain, 1991; McNeill, 1970). In this sense, *native* is a variation on the word *nature* as it's used in the nature versus nurture debate. *Nativist theory* proposes that humans are equipped with a **language acquisition device (LAD)—an innate mechanism or process that facilitates the learning of language.** According to this view, humans learn language for the same reason that birds learn to fly—because they're biologically equipped for it. The exact nature of the LAD has not been spelled out in nativist theories. It presumably consists of brain structures and neural wiring that leave humans well prepared to discriminate among phonemes, to fast-map morphemes, to acquire rules of syntax, and so on.

Why does Chomsky believe that children have an innate capacity for learning language? One reason is that children seem to acquire language quickly and effortlessly. How could they develop so complex a skill in such a short time unless they have a built-in capacity for it? Another reason is that language development tends to unfold at roughly the same pace for most children, even though children obviously are reared in diverse home environments. This finding suggests that language development is determined by biological maturation more than personal experience. The nativists also cite evidence that the early course of language development is similar across very different cultures (Slobin, 1985, 1992). They interpret this to mean that children all over the world are guided by the same innate capabilities.

Interactionist Theories

Like Skinner, Chomsky has his critics. His nativist theory has been attacked on a number of grounds. Some critics assert that Chomsky's "language acquisition device" isn't much of an explanation. They ask: What exactly is a language acquisition device? How does the LAD work? What are the neural mechanisms involved? They argue that the LAD concept is terribly vague.

Other critics question whether the rapidity of early language development is as exceptional as nativists assume. They assert that it isn't fair to compare the rapid progress of toddlers, who are immersed in their native language, against the struggles of students, who may devote only 10–15 hours per week to their foreign language course. It is more appropriate to compare youngsters and adults who are learning the same second language after having moved to a new country. Although some studies find that children have an advantage over adults in this situation (Johnson & Newport, 1989), many others suggest that adults can learn a second language about as readily as young children (Snow, 1993). Nativist theories have also been undermined by recent evidence that parents do provide their children with subtle corrective feedback about grammar (Bohannon, MacWhinney, & Snow, 1990; Bohannon & Stanowicz, 1988).

The problems apparent in Skinner's and Chomsky's explanations of language development have led some psychologists to outline *interactionist theories* of language acquisition (Bohannon & Warren-Leubecker, 1989; Farrar, 1990; Meltzoff & Gopnik, 1989). These theories emphasize the importance of both biology and experience. Like the nativists, interactionists believe that the human organism is biologically well equipped for learning language. They also agree that much of this learning involves the acquisition of rules. However, they stress that these realities do not mean that language development is automatic or that environment is irrelevant. Like the behaviorists, they believe that social exchanges with parents and others play a critical role in molding language skills. Thus, interactionist theories maintain that an innate predisposition and a supportive environment both contribute to language development (see Figure 8.4).

Language in Evolutionary Context

Another controversial issue related to language is its evolutionary significance. According to Steven Pinker (1994), humans have a special talent for language, which is a species-specific trait that is the product of natural selection. Pinker argues that language is a valuable means of communication that has enormous adaptive value. As Pinker and Bloom (1992) point out, "There is an obvious advantage in being able to acquire information about the world secondhand . . . one can avoid having to duplicate the possibly time-consuming and dangerous

trial-and-error process that won that knowledge" (p. 460). It does not take much imagination to envision how more effective communication among our ancient ancestors could have aided hunting, gathering, fighting, mating, and the avoidance of poisons, predators, and other dangers.

Although the adaptive value of language seems obvious, some scholars take issue with the assertion that human language is the product of evolution. For example, David Premack (1985) has expressed skepticism that small differences in language skill would influence reproductive fitness in primitive societies where all one had to communicate about was the location of the closest mastadon herd. In an effort to refute this argument, Pinker and Bloom (1992) point out that very small adaptive disparities are sufficient to fuel evolutionary change. For example, they cite an estimate that a 1% difference in mortality rates among overlapping Neanderthal and human populations could have led to the extinction of Neanderthals in just 30 generations. They also note that a trait variation that produces on average just 1% more offspring than its alternative genetic expression would increase in prevalence from 0.1% to 99.9% of the population in 4000 generations. Four thousand generations may seem like an eternity, but in the context of evolution, it is a modest amount of time.

Culture, Language, and Thought

Yet another source of debate in the study of language concerns the relations among culture, language, and thought. Obviously, people from different cultures generally speak different languages. But does your training in English lead you to think about certain things differently than someone who was raised to

MIT photo by Donna Coveney, courtesy of Steven Pinker

If human language is unique in the modern animal kingdom, as it appears to be, the implications for a Darwinian account of its evolution would be as follows: none. A language instinct unique to modern humans poses no more of a paradox than a trunk unique to modern elephants.
STEVEN PINKER

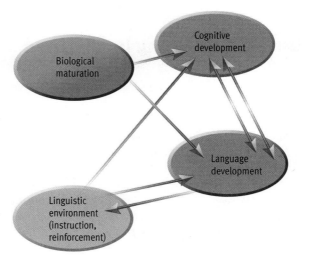

Figure 8.4

Interactionist theories of language acquisition. The interactionist view is that nature and nurture are both important to language acquisition. Maturation is thought to drive language development directly and to influence it indirectly by fostering cognitive development. Meanwhile, verbal exchanges between parents and others are also thought to play a critical role in molding language skills. The complex interrelations depicted here shed some light on why there is room for extensive debate about the crucial factors in language acquisition.

Mia & Klaus Matthes/Superstock

Does the language you speak determine how you think? Yes, said Benjamin Lee Whorf, who argued that the Eskimo language, which has numerous words for snow, leads Eskimos to perceive snow differently than English speakers. However, the overall evidence provides little support for the strong version of Whorf's hypothesis.

speak Chinese or French? In other words, does a cultural group's language determine their thought? Or does thought determine language?

Benjamin Lee Whorf (1956) has been the most prominent advocate of **linguistic relativity, the hypothesis that one's language determines the nature of one's thought.** Whorf speculated that different languages lead people to view the world differently. His classic example compared English and Eskimo views of snow. He asserted that the English language has just one word for snow, whereas the Eskimo language has many words that distinguish among falling snow, wet snow, and so on. Because of this language gap, Whorf argued that Eskimos perceive snow differently than English-speaking people do. However, Whorf's conclusion about these perceptual differences was based on casual observation rather than systematic cross-cultural comparisons of perceptual processes. Moreover, critics subsequently noted that advocates of the linguistic relativity hypothesis had carelessly

overestimated the number of Eskimo words for snow, while conveniently ignoring the variety of English words that refer to snow, such as *slush* and *blizzard* (Martin, 1986; Pullum, 1991).

Nonetheless, Whorf's hypothesis has been the subject of spirited debate. In one of the better-designed experimental tests of this hypothesis, Eleanor Rosch (1973) compared the color perceptions of English-speaking people with those of the Dani, an agricultural people who live in New Guinea. The Dani were chosen because their language includes relatively few *basic color terms* (widely used words for widely agreed upon colors). In fact, the Dani have terms for only two basic colors (bright and dark). In contrast, the English language includes eleven basic color terms. Previous research had shown that English speakers learn arbitrary, nonsense names for these eleven basic colors more easily than for nonbasic colors. If language determines thought, this advantage in learning new names for the eleven basic colors should not be seen among the Dani, since they don't think in terms of these colors. However, the Dani also found it easier to learn nonsense names for the eleven basic colors. Thus, Rosch concluded that the Dani think about color pretty much the same as English speakers do, even though their language treats color differently. Rosch's findings clearly contradict Whorf's hypothesis.

So, what is the status of the linguistic relativity hypothesis? The preponderance of evidence provides little support for the original, strong version of the hypothesis—that a given language makes certain ways of thinking obligatory or impossible (Berry et al., 1992; Eysenck, 1984). However, a weaker version of the linguistic relativity hypothesis—that a given language makes certain ways of thinking easier or more difficult—may still be tenable.

Problem Solving: In Search of Solutions

Look at the two problems below. Can you solve them?

In the Thompson family there are five brothers, and each brother has one sister. If you count Mrs. Thompson, how many females are there in the Thompson family?

Fifteen percent of the people in Topeka have unlisted telephone numbers. You select 200 names at random from the Topeka phone book. How many of these people can be expected to have unlisted phone numbers?

These problems, borrowed from Sternberg (1986, p. 214), are exceptionally simple, but many people fail to solve them. The answer to the first problem is two. The only females in the family are Mrs. Thompson and her one daughter, who is a sister to each of her brothers. The answer to the second problem is none. You won't find any people with unlisted phone numbers in the phone book.

Why do many people fail to solve these simple problems? You'll learn why in a moment, when we discuss barriers to effective problem solving. But first, let's examine a scheme for classifying problems into a few basic types.

Types of Problems

 SIM6, 6d

***Problem solving* refers to active efforts to discover what must be done to achieve a goal that is not readily attainable.** Obviously, if a goal is readily attainable, there isn't a problem. But in problem-solving situations, one must go beyond the information given to overcome obstacles and reach a goal. Jim Greeno (1978) has proposed that problems can be categorized into three basic classes:

1. *Problems of inducing structure.* The person must discover the relations among the parts of the problem. The series completion problems and the *analogy problems* in Figure 8.5 are examples of problems of inducing structure.

2. *Problems of arrangement.* The person must arrange the parts in a way that satisfies some criterion. The parts can usually be arranged in many ways, but only one or a few of the arrangements form a solution. The *string problem* and the *anagrams*

Figure 8.5

Six standard problems used in studies of problem solving. Try solving the problems and identifying which class each belongs to before reading further. The problems can be classified as follows. The *analogy problems* and *series completion problems* are problems of inducing structure. The solutions for the analogy problems are *Buy* and *Patient*. The solutions for the series completion problems are 4 and E. The *string problem* and the *anagram problems* are problems of arrangement. To solve the string problem, attach the screwdriver to one string and set it swinging as a pendulum. Hold the other string and catch the swinging screwdriver. Then you need only untie the screwdriver and tie the strings together. The solutions for the anagram problems are *WATER* and *JOKER*. The *hobbits* and *orcs problem* and the *water jar problem* are problems of transformation. The solutions for these problems are outlined in Figures 8.6 and 8.7.

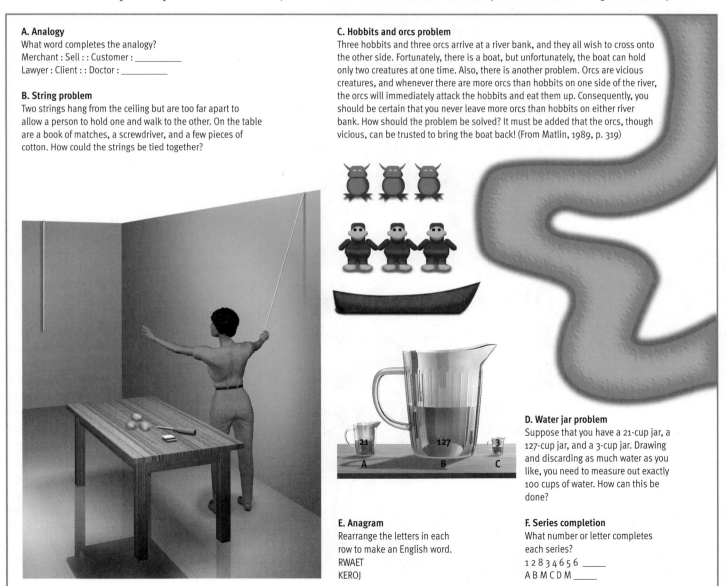

A. Analogy
What word completes the analogy?
Merchant : Sell : : Customer : _____
Lawyer : Client : : Doctor : _____

B. String problem
Two strings hang from the ceiling but are too far apart to allow a person to hold one and walk to the other. On the table are a book of matches, a screwdriver, and a few pieces of cotton. How could the strings be tied together?

C. Hobbits and orcs problem
Three hobbits and three orcs arrive at a river bank, and they all wish to cross onto the other side. Fortunately, there is a boat, but unfortunately, the boat can hold only two creatures at one time. Also, there is another problem. Orcs are vicious creatures, and whenever there are more orcs than hobbits on one side of the river, the orcs will immediately attack the hobbits and eat them up. Consequently, you should be certain that you never leave more orcs than hobbits on either river bank. How should the problem be solved? It must be added that the orcs, though vicious, can be trusted to bring the boat back! (From Matlin, 1989, p. 319)

D. Water jar problem
Suppose that you have a 21-cup jar, a 127-cup jar, and a 3-cup jar. Drawing and discarding as much water as you like, you need to measure out exactly 100 cups of water. How can this be done?

E. Anagram
Rearrange the letters in each row to make an English word.
RWAET
KEROJ

F. Series completion
What number or letter completes each series?
1 2 8 3 4 6 5 6 _____
A B M C D M _____

in Figure 8.5 fit in this category. Arrangement problems are often solved with a burst of insight. **Insight is the sudden discovery of the correct solution following incorrect attempts based primarily on trial and error.**

3. *Problems of transformation.* The person must carry out a sequence of transformations in order to reach a specific goal. The *hobbits* and *orcs problem* and the *water jar problem* in Figure 8.5 are examples of transformation problems. Transformation problems can be challenging. Even though you know exactly what the goal is, it's often not obvious how the goal can be achieved.

Figure 8.6

Solution to the hobbits and orcs problem. This problem is difficult because it is necessary to temporarily work "away" from the goal.

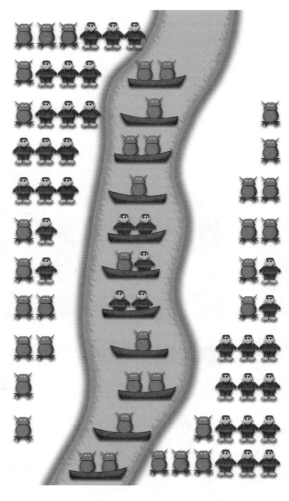

Figure 8.7

The method for solving the water jar problem.
The formula is B – A – 2C.

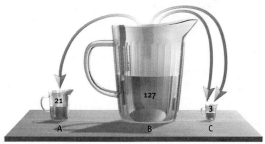

Greeno's list is not an exhaustive scheme for classifying problems, but it provides a useful system for understanding some of the variety seen in everyday problems.

Barriers to Effective Problem Solving

On the basis of their studies of problem solving, psychologists have identified a number of barriers that frequently impede participants' efforts to arrive at solutions. Common obstacles to effective problem solving include a focus on irrelevant information, functional fixedness, mental set, and imposition of unnecessary constraints.

Irrelevant Information

We began our discussion of problem solving with two simple problems that people routinely fail to solve. The catch is that these problems contain *irrelevant information* that leads people astray. In the first problem, the number of brothers is irrelevant in determining the number of females in the Thompson family. In the second problem, participants tend to focus on the figures of 15% and 200 names. But this numerical information is irrelevant, since all the names came out of the phone book.

Sternberg (1986) points out that people often incorrectly assume that all the numerical information in a problem is necessary to solve it. They therefore try to figure out how to use quantitative information before they even consider whether the information is really relevant. Effective problem solving requires that you attempt to figure out what information is relevant and what is irrelevant before proceeding.

Functional Fixedness

Another common barrier to successful problem solving is *functional fixedness*—**the tendency to perceive an item only in terms of its most common use.** Functional fixedness has been seen in the difficulties that people have with the string problem (Maier, 1931). Solving this problem requires finding a novel use for one of the objects: the screwdriver. Participants tend to think of the screwdriver in terms of its usual functions—turning screws and perhaps prying things open. They have a hard time viewing the screwdriver as a weight. Their rigid way of thinking about the screwdriver illustrates functional fixedness (Dominowski & Bourne, 1994).

Mental Set

Rigid thinking is also at work when a mental set interferes with effective problem solving. **A *mental*** *set* exists when people persist in using problem-solving strategies that have worked in the past. The effects of mental set were seen in a classic study by Abraham Luchins (1942). Luchins asked subjects to work a series of water jar problems, like the one introduced earlier. Six such problems are outlined in Figure 8.8, which shows the capacities of the three jars and the amounts of water to be measured out. Try solving these problems.

Were you able to develop a formula for solving these problems? The first four all require the same strategy, which is described in Figure 8.7. You have to fill jar B, draw off the amount that jar A holds once, and draw off the amount that jar C holds twice. Thus, the formula for your solution is B – A – 2C. Although there is an obvious and much simpler solution (A – C) for the fifth problem (see Figure 8.12 on page 247), Luchins found that most participants stuck with the more cumbersome strategy that they had used in problems 1–4. Moreover, most subjects couldn't solve the sixth problem in the allotted time, because they kept trying to use their proven strategy, which does not work for this problem. The participants' reliance on their "tried and true" strategy is an illustration of mental set in problem solving.

Unnecessary Constraints

 6d

Effective problem solving requires specifying all the constraints governing a problem *without assuming any constraints that don't exist.* An example of a problem in which people place an unnecessary constraint on the solution is shown in Figure 8.9 (Adams, 1980). Without lifting your pencil from the paper, try to draw four straight lines that will

Figure 8.8

Additional water jar problems. Using jars A, B, and C, with the capacities indicated in each row, figure out how to measure out the desired amount of water specified on the far right. The solutions are shown in Figure 8.12. (Based on "Mechanization in Problem Solving," by A. S. Luchins, 1942, *Psychological Monographs*, 54 (Whole No. 248).)

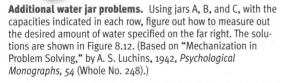

	Capacity of empty jars			Desired amount of water
Problem	A	B	C	
1	14	163	25	99
2	18	43	10	5
3	9	42	6	21
4	20	59	4	31
5	23	49	3	20
6	28	76	3	25

Figure 8.9

The nine-dot problem. Without lifting your pencil from the paper, draw no more than four lines that will cross through all nine dots. For possible solutions, see Figure 8.13. (Adapted from *Conceptional Blockbusting: A Guide to Better Ideas*, by James L. Adams, pp. 17–18. Copyright © 1980 by James L. Adams. Reprinted by permisison of W. H. Freeman & Co., Publishers.)

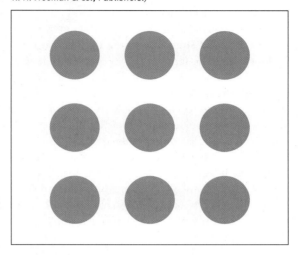

cross through all nine dots. Most people will not draw lines outside the imaginary boundary that surrounds the dots. Notice that this constraint is not part of the problem statement. It's imposed only by the problem solver. Correct solutions, two of which are shown in Figure 8.13 on page 247, extend outside the imaginary boundary. People often make assumptions that impose unnecessary constraints on problem-solving efforts.

Approaches to Problem Solving

People use a variety of strategies in attempting to solve problems. In this section, we'll examine some general strategies.

Trial and Error and Heuristics

Trial and error is a common, albeit primitive, approach to solving problems. **Trial and error involves trying possible solutions sequentially and discarding those that are in error until one works.** Trial and error can be effective when there are relatively few possible solutions to be tried out. However, this method becomes impractical when the number of possible maneuvers is large. Consider, for instance, the problem shown in Figure 8.10. The challenge is to move just two matches to create a pattern containing four equal squares. Sure, you could use a trial-and-error approach in moving pairs of matches about. But you'd better allocate plenty of time to this effort, as there are over 60,000 possible

Figure 8.10

The matchstick problem. Move two matches to form four equal squares. A solution can be found in Figure 8.14. (From *Basic Psychology 3rd Edition*, by Howard H. Kendler, 1974, pp. 403, 404. Copyright © 1974 The Benjamin-Cummings Publishing Co. Adapted by permission of Howard H. Kendler.)

rearrangements to check out (see Figure 8.14 for the solution).

Because trial and error is inefficient, people often use shortcuts called *heuristics* in problem solving. **A heuristic is a guiding principle or "rule of thumb" used in solving problems or making decisions.** Heuristics are often useful, but they don't guarantee success. Helpful heuristics in problem solving include forming subgoals, searching for analogies, and changing the representation of the problem.

Forming Subgoals

It is often useful to tackle problems by formulating *subgoals,* intermediate steps toward a solution. When you reach a subgoal, you've solved part of the problem. Some problems have fairly obvious subgoals, and research has shown that people take advantage of them. For instance, in analogy problems, the first subgoal usually is to figure out the possible relations between the first two parts of the analogy.

The wisdom of formulating subgoals can be seen in the *tower of Hanoi problem,* depicted in Figure 8.11. The terminal goal for this problem is to move all three rings on peg A to peg C, while abiding by two restrictions: only the top ring on a peg can be moved and a ring must never be placed above a smaller ring. See whether you can solve the problem before continuing.

Dividing this problem into subgoals facilitates a solution (Kotovsky, Hayes, & Simon, 1985). If you think in terms of subgoals, your first task is to get ring 3 to the bottom of peg C. Breaking this task into sub-subgoals, subjects can figure out that they should move ring 1 to peg C, ring 2 to peg B, and ring 1 from peg C to peg B. These maneuvers allow you to place ring 3 at the bottom of peg C, thus meeting your first subgoal. Your next subgoal—getting ring 2 over to peg C—can be accomplished in just two steps: move ring 1 to peg A and ring 2 to peg C. It should then be obvious how to achieve your final subgoal—getting ring 1 over to peg C.

Searching for Analogies

Searching for analogies is another major strategy for solving problems (Holyoak & Thagard, 1997). If you can spot an analogy between problems, you may be able to use the solution to a previous problem to solve a current one. Of course, using this strategy depends on recognizing the similarity between two problems, which may itself be a challenging problem. People often are unable to recognize that two problems are similar, but once informed of the similarity, they do reasonably well in making use of the analogous solution (Gick & Holyoak, 1980). Try applying this strategy to the following two problems:

A teacher had 23 pupils in his class. All but 7 of them went on a museum trip and thus were away for the day. How many students remained in class that day?

Susan gets in her car in Boston and drives toward New York City, averaging 50 miles per hour. Twenty minutes later, Ellen gets in her car in New York City and starts driving toward Boston, averaging 60 miles per hour. Both women take the same route, which extends a total of 220 miles between the two cities. Which car is nearer to Boston when they meet?

These problems, taken from Sternberg (1986, pp. 213 and 215), resemble the ones that opened our discussion of problem solving. Each has an obvious solution that's hidden in irrelevant quantitative information. If you recognized this similarity, you probably solved the problems easily. If not, take another look now that you know what the analogy is. Neither problem requires any calculation whatsoever. The answer to the first problem is 7. As for the second problem, when the two cars meet they're in the same place. Obviously, they have to be the same distance from Boston.

Changing the Representation of the Problem

Whether you solve a problem often hinges on how you envision it—your *representation of the problem.* Many problems can be represented in a variety of ways, such as verbally, mathematically, or spatially. You might represent a problem with a list, a table, an equation, a graph, a matrix of facts or numbers, a hierarchical tree diagram, or a sequential flowchart (Halpern, 1996). When you fail to make progress with your initial representation of a problem, changing your representation is often a good strategy. As an illustration, see whether you can solve the *Buddhist monk problem:*

At sunrise, a Buddhist monk sets out to climb a tall mountain. He follows a narrow path that winds around

Figure 8.11

The tower of Hanoi problem. Your mission is to move the rings from peg A to peg C. You can move only the top ring on a peg and can't place a larger ring above a smaller one. The solution is explained in the text.

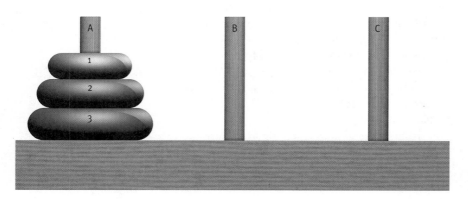

Figure 8.12

Solutions to the additional water jar problems.
The solution for problems 1–4 is the same
(B – A – 2C) as the solution shown in Figure 8.7.
This method will work for problem 5, but there
also is a simpler solution (A – C), which is the
only solution for problem 6. Many subjects
exhibit a mental set on these problems, as they
fail to notice the simpler solution for problem 5.
(Based on "Mechanization in Problem Solving,"
by A. S. Luchins, 1942, *Psychological Monographs*,
54 (Whole No. 248).)

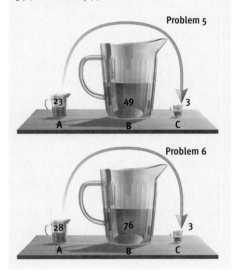

Figure 8.13

Two solutions to the nine-dot problem. The
key to solving the problem is to recognize that
nothing in the problem statement forbids going
outside the imaginary boundary surrounding the
dots. (Adapted from *Conceptional Blockbusting:
A Guide to Better Ideas,* by James L. Adams,
pp. 17–18. Copyright © 1980 by James L. Adams.
Reprinted by permission of W. H. Freeman & Co.,
Publishers).

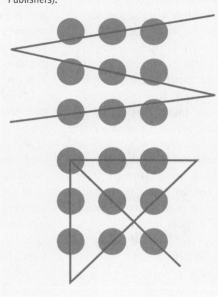

Figure 8.14

Solution to the matchstick problem. T
this problem is to "open up" the figure, s
subjects are reluctant to do because the
sary constraints on the problem. (From *E
Edition,* by Howard H. Kendler, 1974, pp. 403, 404. Copyright
© 1974 The Benjamin-Cummings Publishing Co. Adapted by
permission of Howard H. Kendler.)

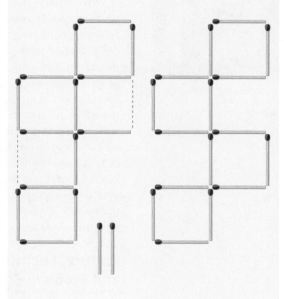

CONCEPT **CHECK 8.2**

Thinking About Problem Solving

Check your understanding of problem solving by answering some questions about the following problem. Begin
by trying to solve the problem.

The candle problem. Using the objects shown—candles, a
box of matches, string, and some tacks—figure out how
you could mount a candle on a wall so that it could be
used as a light.

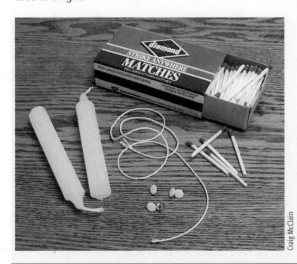

Craig McClain

Work on the problem for a while, then turn to page 248
to see the solution. After you've seen the solution, respond
to the following questions. The answers are in Appendix A.

1. If it didn't occur to you that the matchbox could
be converted from a container to a platform, this
illustrates _____ _____ .

2. While working on the problem, if you thought to
yourself, "How can I create a platform attached to
the wall?" you used the heuristic of
_____ _____ .

3. If it occurred to you suddenly that the matchbox
could be used as a platform, this realization would
be an example of _____ .

4. If you had a hunch that there might be some similarity between this problem and the string problem
in Figure 8.5 (the similarity is the novel use of an
object), your hunch would illustrate the heuristic of
_____ _____ _____ .

5. In terms of Greeno's three types of problems,
the candle problem is a(n) _____
problem.

The solution to the candle problem in Concept Check 8.2.

Craig McClain

the mountain and up to a temple. He stops frequently to rest and climbs at varying speeds, arriving around sunset. After staying a few days, he begins his return journey. As before, he starts at sunrise, rests often, walks at varying speeds, and arrives around sunset. Prove that there must be a spot along the path that the monk will pass on both trips at precisely the same time of day.

Why should there be such a spot? The monk's walking speed varies. Shouldn't it all be a matter of coincidence if he reaches a spot at the same time each day? Moreover, if there is such a spot, how would you prove it? Participants who represent this problem in terms of verbal, mathematical, or spatial information struggle. Subjects who work with a graphic representation fare much better. The best way to represent the problem is to envision the monk (or two different monks) ascending and descending the mountain at the same time. The two monks must meet at some point. If you construct a graph (see Figure 8.15) you can vary the speed of the monks' descent in endless ways, but you can see that there's always a place where they meet.

Culture, Cognitive Style, and Problem Solving

Do the varied experiences of people from different cultures lead to cross-cultural variations in problem solving? Yes, researchers have found cultural differences in the cognitive style that people exhibit in solving problems.

Back in the 1940s, Herman Witkin was intrigued by the observation that some airplane pilots would fly into a cloud bank upright but exit it upside down without realizing that they had turned over. Witkin's efforts to explain this aviation problem led to the discovery of an interesting dimension of cognitive style (Witkin, 1950; Witkin et al., 1962).

Field dependence-independence **refers to individuals' tendency to rely primarily on external versus internal frames of reference when orienting themselves in space.** People who are *field dependent* rely on external frames of reference and tend to accept the physical environment as a given instead of trying to analyze or restructure it. People who are *field independent* rely on internal frames of reference and tend to analyze and try to restructure the physical environment rather than accepting it as is. A person's field dependence-independence can be measured with the Embedded Figures Test, which requires respondents to identify simple designs from within more complex ones.

Research has shown that field dependence-independence is related to diverse aspects of cognitive, emotional, and social functioning (Witkin & Goodenough, 1981). Each style has its strengths and weaknesses, but in many types of problem solving, field independence seems more advantageous. For example, studies have shown that field-independent subjects outperform field-dependent subjects on a variety of classic laboratory problems, including the string problem, matchstick problem, candle problem, and water jar problem (Witkin et al., 1962).

Cultural factors appear to influence whether people become field-dependent or field-independent. For example, because of their demanding environment, the Tuareg nomads of the central sahara are likely to be more field-independent.

© Penny Tweedie/CORBIS

Figure 8.15

Solution to the Buddhist monk problem. If you represent this problem graphically and think in terms of two monks, it is readily apparent that the monk does pass a single spot at the same time each day.

Top 2000 / 1500 / Altitude / 1000 / 500 / Bottom 0

6:00 A.M. Sunrise — 9:00 A.M. — 12:00 NOON — 3:00 P.M. — 6:00 P.M. Sunset

Time

An extensive body of research suggests that some cultures encourage a field-dependent cognitive style, whereas others foster a field-independent style (Berry, 1990; Witkin & Berry, 1975). The educational practices in modern Western societies seem to nourish field independence. A field-independent style is also more likely to be predominant in nomadic societies that depend on hunting and gathering for subsistence and in societies with lenient child-rearing practices that encourage personal autonomy. In contrast, a field-dependent style is found more in sedentary agricultural societies and in societies that stress strict child-rearing practices and conformity. According to John Berry (1976), the predominant cognitive style in a society depends in large part on the culture's ecological demands—that is, the types of skills that are necessary to survive or flourish in the culture. For example, in cultures that depend on hunting and gathering for subsistence, the need to extract information from the surrounding field to locate game and food makes a field-independent style more adaptive. Consistent with this analysis, the Eskimo hunters of the Arctic wastelands and the Aboriginal hunters of the desert wastelands in Australia, who both need to extract information from particularly difficult environments, are among the most field-independent peoples of the world (Goodenough, 1986).

Problems are not the only kind of cognitive challenge that people grapple with on a regular basis. Life also seems to constantly demand decisions. As you might expect, cognitive psychologists have shown great interest in the process of decision making, which is our next subject.

Web Link 8.3

The Critical Thinking Community
The many resources at *The Critical Thinking Community*, maintained at Sonoma State University, are directed primarily toward teachers at every level to help them develop their students' critical thinking skills.

Decision Making: Choices and Chances

Decisions, decisions. Life is full of them. You decided to read this book today. Earlier today you decided when to get up, whether to eat breakfast, and if so, what to eat. Usually you make routine decisions like these with little effort. But on occasion you need to make important decisions that require more thought. Big decisions—such as selecting a car, a home, or a job—tend to be difficult. The alternatives usually have a number of facets that need to be weighed. For instance, in choosing among several cars, you may want to compare their costs, roominess, fuel economy, handling, acceleration, stylishness, reliability, safety features, and warranties.

Decision making involves evaluating alternatives and making choices among them. Most people try to be systematic and rational in their decision making. However, the work that earned Herbert Simon the 1978 Nobel prize in economics showed that people don't always live up to these goals. Before Simon's work, most traditional theories in economics assumed that people made rational choices to maximize their economic gains. Simon (1957) noted that people have a limited ability to process and evaluate information on numerous facets of possible alternatives. He demonstrated that people tend to use simple strategies in decision making that focus on only a few facets of the available options. According to Simon's theory of *bounded rationality*, people use sensible decision strategies, given their cognitive limitations, but these limitations often result in "irrational" decisions that are less than optimal.

Spurred by Simon's analysis, psychologists have devoted several decades to the study of how cognitive biases distort people's decision making. The results of this research have sometimes been disturbing, leading some theorists to conclude that people "do a singularly bad job at the business of reasoning, even when they are calm, clearheaded, and under no pressure to perform quickly" (Stich, 1990, pp. 173–174). Let's look at this research—and recent criticism that it has inspired.

Making Choices: Selecting an Alternative

Many decisions involve choices about *preferences,* which can be made using a variety of strategies (Hogarth, 1987). For instance, imagine that Boris has found two reasonably attractive apartments and is trying to decide between them. How should he go about selecting between his alternatives? Let's look at some strategies Boris might use in trying to make his decision.

If Boris wanted to use an *additive strategy,* he would list the attributes that influence his decision. Then he would rate the desirability of each apartment on each attribute. For example, let's say that Boris wants to consider four attributes: rent, noise level, distance to campus, and cleanliness. He might

People often have to decide between alternative products, such as computers, cars, refrigerators, and so forth, that are not all that different. In making these decisions about preferences, people use a variety of strategies. When many complex factors must be weighed, people tend to shift to simpler decision strategies.

© Don Mason/The Stock Market

Web Link 8.4

Judgment and Decision Making Experiments
Michael Birnbaum (California State University, Fullerton) presents a range of continuing and completed experiments conducted online that illustrate how people make decisions.

make ratings from –3 to +3, like those shown in Table 8.3, add up the ratings for each alternative, and select the one with the largest total. Given the ratings in Table 8.3, Boris should select apartment B.

To make an additive strategy more useful, you can *weight* attributes differently, based on their importance (Goldstein, 1990). For example, if Boris considers distance to campus to be twice as important as the other considerations, he could multiply his ratings of this attribute by 2. The distance rating would then be +6 for apartment A and –2 for apartment B, and apartment A would become the preferred choice.

People also make choices by gradually eliminating less attractive alternatives (Slovic, 1990; Tversky, 1972). This strategy is called *elimination by aspects* because it assumes that alternatives are eliminated by evaluating them on each attribute or aspect in turn. Whenever any alternative fails to satisfy some minimum criterion for an attribute, it is eliminated from further consideration.

To illustrate, suppose Juanita is looking for a new car. She may begin by eliminating all cars that cost over $19,000. Then she may eliminate cars that don't average at least 20 miles per gallon of gas. By continuing to reject choices that don't satisfy some minimum criterion on selected attributes, she can gradually eliminate alternatives until only a single car remains.

The final choice in elimination by aspects depends on the order in which attributes are evaluated. For example, if cost was the last attribute Juanita evaluated, she could have previously eliminated all cars that cost under $19,000! If she has only $19,000 to spend, her decision-making strategy would not have brought her very far. Thus, when using elimination by aspects, it's best to evaluate attributes in the order of their importance.

Both the additive and the elimination-by-aspects strategies have advantages, but which strategy do people actually tend to use? Research by John Payne (1976) suggests that when decisions involve relatively few options that need to be evaluated on only a few attributes, people tend to use additive strategies. However, as more options and factors are added to a decision task, people tend to shift to elimination by aspects. Thus, people adapt their approach to the demands of the task. When their choices become very complex, they shift toward simpler decision strategies (Payne, Bettman, & Johnson, 1992).

Table  **8.3   Application of the Additive Model to Choosing an Apartment**

Attribute	Apartment	
	A	B
Rent	+1	+2
Noise level	–2	+3
Distance to campus	+3	–1
Cleanliness	+2	+2
Total	**+4**	**+6**

Taking Chances: Factors Weighed in Risky Decisions

Suppose you have the chance to play a dice game in which you might win some money. You must decide whether it would be to your advantage to play. You're going to roll a fair die. If the number 6 appears, you win $5. If one of the other five numbers appears, you win nothing. It costs you $1 every time you play. Should you participate?

This problem calls for a type of decision making that is somewhat different from making choices about preferences. In selecting alternatives that reflect preferences, people generally weigh known outcomes (apartment A will require a long commute to campus, car B will get 30 miles per gallon, and so forth). In contrast, **risky decision making involves making choices under conditions of uncertainty.** Uncertainty exists when people don't know what will happen. At best, they know, or can estimate, the probability that a particular event will occur.

One way to decide whether to play the dice game would be to figure out the *expected value* of participation in the game. To do so, you would need to calculate the average amount of money you could expect to win or lose each time you play. The value of a win is $4 ($5 minus the $1 entry fee). The value of a loss is –$1. To calculate expected value, you also need to know the probability of a win or loss. Since a die has six faces, the probability of a win is 1 out of 6, and the probability of a loss is 5 out of 6. Thus, on five out of every six trials, you lose $1. On one out of six, you win $4. The game is beginning to sound unattractive, isn't it? We can figure out the precise expected value as follows:

$$\text{Expected value} = (\tfrac{1}{6} \times 4) + (\tfrac{5}{6} \times -1)$$
$$= \tfrac{4}{6} + (-\tfrac{5}{6}) = -\tfrac{1}{6}$$

The expected value of this game is $-\tfrac{1}{6}$ of a dollar, which means that you lose an average of about 17 cents per turn. Now that you know the expected value, surely you won't agree to play. Or will you?

If we want to understand why people make the decisions they do, the concept of expected value is not enough. People frequently behave in ways that are inconsistent with expected value (Slovic, Lichtenstein, & Fischoff, 1988). Any time the expected value is negative, a gambler should expect to lose money. Yet a great many people gamble at racetracks and casinos and buy lottery tickets. Although they realize that the odds are against them, they continue to gamble. Even people who don't gamble buy homeowner's insurance, which

has a negative expected value. After all, when you buy insurance, your expectation (and hope!) is that you will lose money on the deal.

To explain decisions that violate expected value, some theories replace the objective value of an outcome with its subjective utility (Fischoff, 1988). Subjective utility represents what an outcome is personally worth to an individual. For example, buying a few lottery tickets may allow you to dream about becoming wealthy. Buying insurance may give you a sense of security. Subjective utilities like these vary from one person to another. If we know an individual's subjective utilities, we can better understand that person's risky decision making.

Heuristics in Judging Probabilities

- What are your chances of passing your next psychology test if you study only 3 hours?
- How likely is a major downturn in the stock market during the upcoming year?
- What are the odds of your getting into graduate school in the field of your choice?

These questions ask you to make probability estimates. Amos Tversky and Daniel Kahneman (1982) have conducted extensive research on the *heuristics,* or mental shortcuts, that people use in grappling with probabilities. Sometimes these heuristics yield reasonable estimates, but often they do not.

Availability is one such heuristic. **The *availability heuristic* involves basing the estimated probability of an event on the ease with which relevant instances come to mind.** For example, you may estimate the divorce rate by recalling the number of divorces among your friends' parents. Recalling specific instances of an event is a reasonable strategy to use in estimating the event's probability. However, if instances occur frequently but you have difficulty retrieving them from memory, your estimate will be biased. For instance, it's easier to think of words that begin with a certain letter than words that contain that letter at some other position. Hence, people should tend to respond that there are more words starting with the letter *K* than words having a *K* in the third position. To test this hypothesis, Tversky and Kahneman (1973) selected five consonants (*K, L, N, R, V*) that occur more frequently in the third position of a word than in the first. Subjects were asked whether each of the letters appears more often in the first or third position. Most of the subjects erroneously believed that all five letters were much more frequent in the first than in the third position, confirming the hypothesis.

"People treat their own cases as if they were unique, rather than part of a huge lottery. You hear this silly argument that 'The odds don't apply to me.' Why should God, or whoever runs this lottery, give you special treatment?"
AMOS TVERSKY

"The human mind suppresses uncertainty. We're not only convinced that we know more about our politics, our businesses, and our spouses than we really do, but also that what we don't know must be unimportant."
DANIEL KAHNEMAN

Recognizing Heuristics in Decision Making

Check your understanding of heuristics in decision making by trying to identify the heuristics used in the following example. Each numbered element in the anecdote below illustrates a problem-solving heuristic. Write the relevant heuristic in the space on the left. You can find the answers in Appendix A.

_____ **1.** Marsha can't decide on a college major. She evaluates all the majors available at her college on the attributes of how much she would enjoy them (likability), how challenging they are (difficulty), and how good the job opportunities are in the field (employability). She drops from consideration any major that she regards as "poor" on any of these three attributes.

_____ **2.** When she considers history as a major, she thinks to herself, "Gee, I know four history graduates who are still looking for work," and concludes that the probability of getting a job using a history degree is very low.

_____ **3.** She finds that every major gets a "poor" rating on at least one attribute, so she eliminates everything. Because this is unacceptable, she decides she has to switch to another strategy. Marsha finally focuses her consideration on five majors that received just one "poor" rating. She uses a 4-point scale to rate each of these majors on each of the three attributes she values. She totals the ratings and selects the major with the largest sum as her leading candidate.

Web Link 8.5

Strategy and Conflict: An Introductory Sketch of Game Theory
Economist Roger McCain of Drexel University offers visitors a broad introduction to the field of rational decision making called "Game Theory," which flowed from the work of mathematical genius John von Neumann and others.

Representativeness is another guide in estimating probabilities identified by Kahneman and Tversky (1982). **The *representativeness heuristic* involves basing the estimated probability of an event on how similar it is to the typical prototype of that event.** To illustrate, imagine that you flip a coin six times and keep track of how often the result is heads (H) or tails (T). Which of the following sequences is more likely?

1. T T T T T T
2. H T T H T H

People generally believe that the second sequence is more likely. After all, coin tossing is a random affair, and the second sequence looks much more representative of a random process than the first. In reality, the probability of each exact sequence is precisely the same ($\frac{1}{2} \times \frac{1}{2} \times \frac{1}{2} \times \frac{1}{2} \times \frac{1}{2} \times \frac{1}{2} = \frac{1}{64}$). Let's look at another phenomenon in which the representativeness heuristic plays a key role.

The Tendency to Ignore Base Rates

Steve is very shy and withdrawn, invariably helpful, but with little interest in people or in the world of reality. A meek and tidy soul, he has a need for order and structure and a passion for detail. Do you think Steve is a salesperson or a librarian? (Adapted from Tversky & Kahneman, 1974, p. 1124)

Using the *representativeness heuristic*, participants tend to guess that Steve is a librarian because he resembles their prototype of a librarian (Tversky & Kahneman, 1982). In reality, this is not a very wise guess, because it *ignores the base rates* of librarians and salespeople in the population. Virtually everyone knows that salespeople outnumber librarians by a wide margin (roughly 75 to 1 in the United States). This fact makes it much more likely that Steve is in sales. But in estimating probabilities, people often ignore information on base rates.

Although people do not *always* neglect base rate information, it is a persistent phenomenon (Case, Fantino, & Goodie, 1999; Koehler, 1996). Moreover, people are particularly bad about applying base rates to themselves. For instance, Weinstein (1984; Weinstein & Klein, 1995) has found that people underestimate the risks of their own health-impairing habits while viewing others' risks much more accurately. Thus, smokers are realistic in estimating the degree to which smoking increases someone else's risk of heart attack but underestimate the risk for themselves. Similarly, people starting new companies ignore the high failure rate for new businesses, and burglars underestimate the likelihood that they will end up in jail. Thus, in risky decision making, people often think that they can beat the odds. As Amos Tversky puts it, "People treat their own cases as if they were unique, rather than part of a huge lottery. You hear this silly argument that 'The odds don't apply to me.' Why should God, or whoever runs this lottery, give you special treatment?" (McKean, 1985, p. 27).

The Conjunction Fallacy

Imagine that you're going to meet a man who is an articulate, ambitious, power-hungry wheeler-dealer. Do you think it's more likely that he's a college teacher or a college teacher who's also a politician?

People tend to guess that the man is a "college teacher who's a politician" because the description fits with the typical prototype of politicians. But stop and think for a moment. The broader category of college teachers completely includes the smaller subcategory of college teachers who are politicians (see Figure 8.16). The probability of being in the subcategory cannot be higher than the probability of being in the broader category. It's a logical impossibility!

Tversky and Kahneman (1983) call this error the *conjunction fallacy*. **The *conjunction fallacy* occurs when people estimate that the odds of two uncertain events happening together are greater than the odds of either event happening alone.** The conjunction fallacy has been observed in a number of studies and has generally been attributed to the powerful influence of the representativeness heuristic (Epstein, Donovan, & Denes-Raj, 1999).

Evolutionary Analyses of Flaws in Human Decision Making

A central conclusion of the last 25 years of research on decision making has been that human decision-making strategies are riddled with errors and biases that yield surprisingly irrational results (Goldstein & Hogarth, 1997). Theorists have discovered that people have "mental limitations" and concluded that people are not as bright and rational as they think they are. Conversely, over the same period of time, researchers studying the behavior of animals in their natural environments have been increasingly impressed by how the animals tend to make sound choices that approximate optimal decision making (see Chapter 6) consistent with elaborate mathematical models of optimality (Real, 1991; Shettleworth, 1998). So, we have quite a paradox: How can humans appear so dumb, when animals appear so bright? This paradox has led some evolutionary psychologists to reconsider the work on human decision making, and their take on the matter is quite interesting. They argue that humans only seem irrational because cognitive psychologists have been asking the wrong questions and formulating problems in the wrong ways—ways that have nothing to do with the adaptive problems that the human mind has evolved to solve (Brase, Cosmides, & Tooby, 1998; Cosmides & Tooby, 1996).

According to Leda Cosmides and John Tooby (1994, 1996), the human mind consists of a large number of specialized cognitive mechanisms that have emerged over the course of evolution to solve specific adaptive problems, such as finding food, shelter, and mates, and dealing with allies and enemies (Cosmides & Tooby, 1994). Thus, human decision and problem solving strategies have been tailored to handle real-world adaptive problems. Hence, Cosmides and Tooby assert that *subjects perform poorly in cognitive research because it confronts them with contrived, artificial problems that do not involve natural categories and have no adaptive significance.*

For example, Gigerenzer (1997) argues that the human mind is wired to think in terms of *raw frequencies* rather than *base rates and probabilities*. Asking about the probability of a single event is routine in today's world, where we are inundated with statistical data ranging from batting averages to weather predictions. But our ancient ancestors had access to little data other than their own observations, which were accumulating counts of natural frequencies, such as "we had a good hunt three out of the last five times we went to the north plains." Evolutionary theorists also argue that the human mind is wired to count the frequency of *whole* objects, actions, and events rather than *parts* (Brase et al., 1998). They maintain that our ancestors did not break the world into half-bananas or quarter-tigers and that parsing the world into whole objects remains more natural for humans

Figure 8.16

The conjunction fallacy. People routinely fall victim to the conjunction fallacy, but as this diagram makes obvious, the probability of being in a subcategory (college teachers who are politicians) cannot be higher than the probability of being in the broader category (college teachers). As this case illustrates, it often helps to represent a problem in a diagram.

today. Thus, evolutionary theorists assert that many errors in human reasoning, such as neglect of base rates and the conjunction fallacy, should vanish if classic laboratory problems are reformulated in terms of raw frequencies rather than probabilities and base rates and in terms of whole objects rather than proportions.

For example, consider the following problem originally studied by Bar-Hillel and Falk (1982):

Three cards are in a hat. One is red on both sides (the red-red card). One is white on both sides (the white-white card). One is red on one side and white on the other (the red-white card). A single card is drawn randomly and tossed into the air. What is the probability that the red-red card was drawn, assuming that the drawn card lands with a red side up?

What do you think the answer is? If you are like most people, you probably answered ½. You may have reasoned that if you can see a red side, it's not the white-white card, so it is one out of the other two cards. If so, your reasoning is wrong. But don't feel bad. Only 6%–9% of subjects get this problem right (Bar-Hillel, 1989; Bar-Hillel & Falk, 1982). The answer is ⅔. The trick lies in the fact that the red-white card and the red-red card are not equally likely to land with the red side up. To solve this problem, Brase et al. (1998) point out that you need to think in terms of sides of cards instead of *whole* cards. As they put it: "We know that the card in question landed with a red side up; the red-red card has two red sides, whereas the red-white card has only one red side. That means there are three red sides total, two of which are from the red-red card. Therefore, the answer is 2/3" (p. 9).

According to Brase et al. (1998), this problem is "twice cursed" in that it is not formatted in terms of frequencies and it requires thinking in terms of parts (sides) instead of wholes. However, when they reworded the problem in a frequency format, their subjects' solution rate jumped from 7% to 28%, and when they created a similar problem in both a frequency format and a whole object format, the solution rate jumped to 45%. Based on this and similar evidence from other studies, evolutionary psychologists conclude that many errors and biases in human reasoning are greatly reduced when problems are presented in ways that resemble the type of input humans would have processed in ancestral times (Cosmides & Tooby, 1996; Gigerenzer & Hoffrage, 1995, 1999). Although there is plenty of room for debate, this evidence and a couple of other lines of research are gradually reducing cognitive psychologists' tendency to characterize human reasoning as "irrational."

Putting It in Perspective

Four of our unifying themes have been especially prominent in this chapter. The first concerns the role of heredity and environment in jointly shaping behavior. The controversy about how children acquire language skills replays the nature versus nurture debate. The debate is far from settled, but the accumulating evidence suggests that language development depends on both nature and nurture, as more recent interactionist theories of language acquisition have proposed.

The second pertinent theme is the empirical nature of psychology. For many decades, psychologists paid little attention to cognitive processes, because most of them assumed that thinking is too private to be studied scientifically. During the 1950s and 1960s, however, psychologists began to devise creative new ways to measure mental processes. These innovations fueled the cognitive revolution that put the *psyche* (the mind) back in psychology. Thus, once again, we see how empirical methods are the lifeblood of the scientific enterprise.

Third, the study of cognitive processes shows how there are both similarities and differences across cultures in behavior. On the one hand, we saw that thought processes are largely invariant in spite of sharp differences in cultures' linguistic heritage. On the other hand, we learned that there are cultural variations in cognitive style that reflect the ecological demands of one's environment. And, although the evidence does not support the strong version of the linguistic relativity hypothesis, we saw that a culture's language may make certain ways of thinking easier or more difficult. Thus, cognitive processes are moderated—albeit to a limited degree—by cultural factors.

The fourth theme is the subjective nature of human experience. We have seen that decision making is a highly subjective process. This subjectivity will continue to be prominent in the upcoming Personal Application, which discusses common pitfalls in decision making.

Understanding Pitfalls in Reasoning About Decision Making

Consider the following scenario:

Laura is in a casino watching people play roulette. The 38 slots in the roulette wheel include 18 black numbers, 18 red numbers, and 2 green numbers. Hence, on any one spin, the probability of red or black is slightly less than 50-50 (.474 to be exact). Although Laura hasn't been betting, she has been following the pattern of results in the game very carefully. The ball has landed in red seven times in a row. Laura concludes that black is long overdue and she jumps into the game, betting heavily on black.

Has Laura made a good bet? Do you agree with Laura's reasoning? Or do you think that Laura misunderstands the laws of probability? You'll find out momentarily, as we discuss how people reason their way to decisions—and how their reasoning can go awry.

The pioneering work of Amos Tversky and Daniel Kahneman (1974, 1982) led to an explosion of research on risky decision making. In their efforts to identify the heuristics that people use in decision making, investigators stumbled onto quite a few misconceptions, oversights, and biases. It turns out that people deviate in predictable ways from optimal decision strategies—with surprising regularity. As explained in the chapter, recent evolutionary research on decision making has offered a new explanation for *why* our decision making appears to be muddled. And evolutionary theorists argue that our decision strategies actually are rational—when viewed as evolved mechanisms designed to solve the adaptive problems faced in ancestral times.

But, while the evolutionary explanations for our foibles in reasoning may be on target, the fact remains that *we do not live in ancestral times*. We live in the information age and we have to deal with base rates, probabilities, and percentages on a routine basis. In our modern world, reproductive fitness surely depends more on SAT scores than on counting berries. So, mainstream cognitive research on flaws in human reasoning about decisions remains relevant. Fortunately, there is evidence that increased awareness of common shortcomings in reasoning about decisions can lead to improved decision making (Agnoli & Krantz, 1989; Fischhoff, 1982; Keren, 1990). With this goal in mind, let's look at some common pitfalls in decision making.

The Gambler's Fallacy

As you may have guessed by now, Laura's reasoning in our opening scenario is flawed. A great many people tend to believe that Laura has made a good bet (Rogers, 1998; Tversky & Kahneman, 1982). However, they're wrong. Laura's behavior illustrates the *gambler's fallacy*—**the belief that the odds of a chance event increase if the event hasn't occurred recently.** People believe that the laws of probability should yield fair results and that a random process must be self-correcting. These aren't bad assumptions in the long run. However, they don't apply to individual, independent events.

The roulette wheel does not remember its recent results and make adjustments for them. Each spin of the wheel is an independent event. The probability of black on each spin remains at .474, even if red comes up 100 times in a row! The gambler's fallacy reflects the pervasive influence of the *representativeness heuristic*. In betting on black, Laura is predicting that future results will be more representative of a random process. This logic can be used to estimate the probability of black across a *string of spins*. But it doesn't apply to a *specific spin* of the roulette wheel.

The Law of Small Numbers

Envision a small urn filled with a mixture of red and green beads. You know that two-thirds of the beads are one color and one-third are the other color. However, you don't know whether red or green predominates. A blindfolded person reaches into the urn and comes up with 3 red beads and 1 green bead. These beads are put back in the urn and a second person scoops up 14 red beads and 10 green beads. Both samplings suggest that red beads outnumber green beads in the urn. But which sample provides better evidence? (Adapted from McKean, 1985, p. 25)

Many subjects report that the first sampling is more convincing, because of the greater preponderance of red over green. What are the actual odds that each sampling accurately reflects the dominant color in the urn? The odds for the first sampling are 4 to 1. These aren't bad odds, but the odds that the second sampling is accurate are much higher—16 to 1. Why? Because the second sample is substantially larger than the first. The likelihood of misleading results is much greater in a small sample than a large one. For example, in flipping a fair coin, the odds of getting all heads in a sample of 5 coin flips dwarfs the odds of getting all heads in a sample of 100 coin flips.

Most people appreciate the value of a large sample as an abstract principle, but they don't fully understand that results based on small samples are more variable and more likely to be a fluke (Well, Pollatsek, & Boyce, 1990). Hence, they frequently assume that results based on small samples are representative of the population. Tversky and Kahneman (1971) call this the *belief in the law of small numbers*. This misplaced faith in small numbers explains why people are often willing to draw general conclusions based on a few individual cases.

Overestimating the Improbable

Various causes of death are paired up below. In each pairing, which is the more likely cause of death?

> *Asthma or tornadoes?*
> *Syphilis or botulism (food poisoning)?*
> *Tuberculosis or floods?*
> *Suicide or murder?*

Table 8.4 shows the actual mortality rates for each of the causes of death just listed. As you can see, the first choice in each pair is the more common cause of death. If you guessed wrong for several pairings, don't feel bad. Like many other people, you may be a victim of the tendency to *overestimate the improbable*. People tend to greatly overestimate the likelihood of dramatic, vivid—but infrequent—events that receive heavy media coverage. Thus, the number of fatalities due to tornadoes, floods, food poisonings, and murders is usually overestimated (Slovic, Fischoff, & Lichtenstein, 1982). Fatalities due to asthma and other common diseases, which receive less media coverage, tend to be underestimated. This tendency to exaggerate the improbable reflects the operation of the *availability heuristic*. Instances of floods, tornadoes, and such are readily available in memory because people are exposed to a great deal of publicity about such events.

Confirmation Bias and Belief Perseverance

Imagine a young physician examining a sick patient. The patient is complaining of a high fever and a sore throat. The physician must decide on a diagnosis from among myriad possible diseases. The physician thinks that it may be the flu. She asks the patient if he feels "achy all over." The answer is "yes." The physician asks if the symptoms began a few days ago. Again, the response is "yes." The physician concludes that the patient has the flu. (Adapted from Halpern, 1984, pp. 215–216)

Do you see any flaws in the physician's reasoning? Has she probed into the causes of the patient's malady effectively? No, she has asked about symptoms that would be

Table 8.4	Actual Mortality Rates for Selected Causes of Death		
Cause of Death	**Rate**	**Cause of Death**	**Rate**
Asthma	920	Tornadoes	44
Syphilis	200	Botulism	1
Tuberculosis	1,800	Floods	100
Suicide	12,000	Homicide	9,200

Note: Mortality rates are per 1 million people and are based on U.S. statistics.
Source: Halpern (1996)

consistent with her preliminary diagnosis, but she has not inquired about symptoms that could rule it out. Her questioning of the patient illustrates *confirmation bias*—**the tendency to seek information that supports one's decisions and beliefs while ignoring disconfirming information.** This bias is common in medical diagnosis and other forms of decision making (Nickerson, 1998). There's nothing wrong with searching for supportive evidence. However, people should also seek disconfirming evidence—which they often neglect to do.

Confirmation bias contributes to another, related problem called *belief perseverance*—**the tendency to hang onto beliefs in the face of contradictory evidence.** It is difficult to dislodge an idea after having embraced it. To investigate this phenomenon, researchers have given subjects evidence to establish a belief (example: high risk takers make better firefighters) and later exposed the subjects to information discrediting the idea. These studies have shown that the disconfirming evidence tends to fall on deaf ears (Ross & Anderson, 1982). Thus,

The availability heuristic can be dramatized by juxtaposing the unrelated phenomena of floods and tornadoes versus diseases such as tuberculosis and asthma. Many people are killed by floods and tornadoes, but far more die from TB and asthma. However, since the news media report flood and tornado fatalities with frequency and rarely focus on deaths from TB or asthma, people's probability estimates are distorted by the availability heuristic.

once people arrive at a decision, they are prone to accept supportive evidence at face value while subjecting contradictory evidence to tough, skeptical scrutiny.

The Overconfidence Effect

Make high and low estimates of the total U.S. Defense Department budget for the year 2000. Choose estimates far enough apart to be 98% confident that the actual figure lies between them. In other words, you should feel that there is only a 2% chance that the correct figure is lower than your low estimate or higher than your high estimate. Write your estimates in the spaces provided, before reading further.

High estimate: _____
Low estimate: _____

When working on problems like this one, people reason their way to their best estimate and then create a confidence interval around it. For instance, let's say that you arrived at $200 billion as your best estimate of the defense budget. You would then expand a range around that estimate—say $150 billion to $250 billion—that you're sure will contain the correct figure. The answer in this case is $290 billion. If the answer falls outside your estimated range, you are not unusual. In making this type of estimate, people consistently tend to make their confidence intervals too narrow (Lichtenstein, Fischoff, & Phillips, 1982). For example, subjects' 98% confidence intervals should include the correct answer 98% of the time, but they actually do so only about 60% of the time.

The crux of the problem is that people tend to put too much faith in their estimates, beliefs, and decisions, a principle called the *overconfidence effect* (Gigerenzer, Hoffrage, & Kleinbölting, 1991). The overconfidence effect has been seen in perceptual judgments, predictions of sports results, and economic forecasts, among other things (West & Stanovich, 1997). The overconfidence effect is seen even when people make probability predictions about themselves. For instance, in one study (Vallone et al., 1990), college students were asked to make predictions about personal matters for the upcoming fall quarter and the entire academic year. Their predictions concerned such things as whether they would drop any courses, whether they would vote in an upcoming election, or whether they would break up with their boyfriend or girlfriend. The subjects were also asked to rate their confidence in each of their predictions, from 50% confidence to 100% confidence (the predictions were either/or propositions, making 50% a chance level of accuracy and the lowest possible level of confidence). The accuracy of the subjects' predictions was assessed at the end of the year. The analyses of thousands of predictions revealed that the students were more confident than accurate. Moreover, the more confident subjects were about their predictions, the more likely it was that they were overconfident (see Figure 8.17).

The overconfidence effect is also seen among experts in many walks of life (Fischoff, 1988). Studies have shown that physicians, weather forecasters, military leaders, gamblers, investors, and scientists tend to be overconfident about their predictions. As Daniel Kahneman puts it, "The human mind suppresses uncertainty. We're not only convinced that we know more about our politics, our businesses, and our spouses than we really do, but also that what we don't know must be unimportant" (McKean, 1985, p. 27). Thus, in making major decisions, it usually pays to gather as much information as possible and to move forward cautiously.

Figure 8.17

Results of the Vallone et al. (1990) study. The subjects in this study (sample 1) made 3776 predictions about personal matters. Their mean confidence level for all these predictions was 82.3%, but their mean accuracy was only 68.2%. When the predictions were divided into low-, medium-, and high-confidence predictions, an interesting pattern emerged. As subjects' confidence level went up, the gap between their confidence and their accuracy increased. This finding suggests that the more confident you are about a personal prediction, the more likely it is that you are overconfident.

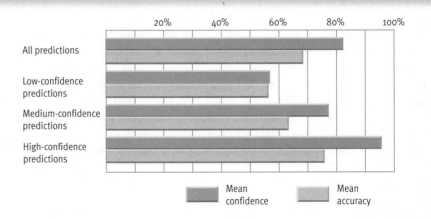

CRITICAL THINKING APPLICATION

Shaping Thought with Language: "Only A Naive Moron Would Believe That"

As explained in the chapter, the strong version of the *linguistic relativity hypothesis*—the idea that people's language determines how they think about things—has not been supported by research (Hunt & Agnoli, 1991). But research does show that carefully chosen words can exert subtle influence on people's thoughts about various issues (Calvert, 1997; Johnson & Dowling-Guyer, 1996; Weatherall, 1992). In everyday life, many people clearly recognize that language can tilt thought along certain lines. This possibility is the basis for some of the concerns that have been expressed about sexist language. Women who object to being called "girls," "chicks," and "babes" believe that these terms influence the way people think about and interact with women. In a similar vein, used car dealers that sell "preowned cars" and airlines that outline precautions for "water landings" are manipulating language to influence thought. Indeed, bureaucrats, politicians, advertisers, and big business have refined the art of shaping thought by tinkering with language, and to a lesser degree the same techniques are used by many people in everyday interactions. Let's look at two of these techniques: semantic slanting and name calling.

Semantic Slanting

Semantic slanting refers to deliberately choosing words to create specific emotional responses. For example, consider the crafty word choices made in the incendiary debate about abortion (Halpern, 1996). The anti-abortion movement recognized that it is better to be *for* something than to be *against* something and then decided to characterize its stance as "pro-life" rather than "anti-choice." Likewise, the faction that favored abortion did not like the conotation of an "anti-life" campaign, so they characterized their position as "pro-choice."

Semantic slanting, which consists of carefully choosing words to create specific emotional reactions, has been used extensively by both sides in the debate about abortion.

The position advocated is exactly the same either way, but the label clearly influences how people respond. Thinking along similar lines, some "pro-life" advocates have asserted that the best way to win the debate about abortion is to frequently use the words *kill* and *baby* in the same sentence (Kahane, 1992). Obviously, these are words that push people's buttons and trigger powerful emotional responses.

In his fascinating book, *Doublespeak*, William Lutz (1989) describes an endless series of examples of how government, business, and advertisers manipulate language to bias people's thoughts and feelings. For example, in the language of the military, an invasion is a "preemptive counterattack," bombing the enemy is providing "air support," civilians accidentally killed or wounded by military strikes are "collateral damage," and troops killed by their own troops are "friendly casualties." In the world of business, layoffs and firings become "headcount reductions," or "workforce adjustments," whereas bad debts become "nonperforming assets." And in the language of bureaucrats, hospital deaths become "negative patient care outcomes" and tax increases become "revenue enhancement initiatives," leading Lutz to quip that "Nothing in life is certain except negative patient care outcome and revenue enhancement." You can't really appreciate how absurd this process can become until you go shopping for "genuine imitation leather" or "real counterfeit diamonds."

Of course, you don't have to be a bureaucrat or military spokesperson to use semantic slanting. For example, if a friend of yours is annoyed at her 60-year-old professor for giving a tough exam and describes him as an "old geezer," she would be using semantic slanting. She would have communicated that the professor's age is a negative factor—one that is associated with a host of unflattering stereotypes about older people.

And she would have implied that he gave an inappropriate exam because of his antiquated expectations or senile incompetence—all with a couple of well-chosen words. We are all the recipients of many such messages containing emotionally laden words and content. An important skill of critical thinking is to recognize when semantic slanting is being used to influence how you think so you can resist this subtle technique.

In becoming sensitive to semantic slanting, notice how the people around you and those whom you see on television and read about in the newspapers refer to people from other racial and ethnic groups. You can probably determine a politician's attitudes toward immigration, for example, by considering the words he or she uses when speaking about people from other countries. Are the students on your campus who come from other countries referred to as "international students" or "foreign students"? The term "international student" seems to convey a more positive image, with associations of being cosmopolitan and worldly. On the other hand, the term "foreign" suggests someone who is strange. Clearly, it pays to be careful when selecting the words you use in your own communication.

Name Calling

Another way that word choice influences thinking is in the way people tend to label and categorize others through the strategy of *name calling*. People often attempt to neutralize or combat views they don't like by attributing such views to "radical feminists," "knee-jerk liberals," "right-wingers," "religious zealots," or "extremists." In everyday interactions, someone who inspires our wrath may be labeled as a "bitch," a "moron," or a "cheapskate." In these examples, the name calling is not subtle and is easy to recognize. But name calling can also be used with more cunning and finesse. Sometimes, there is an *implied threat* that if you make an unpopular decision or arrive at a conclusion that is not favored, a nega-

Briefings on the status of miliary actions are renowned for their creative but unintelligible manipulation of language, which is often necessary to obscure the unpleasant realities of war.

tive label will apply to you. For example, someone might say, "Only a naive moron would believe that" to influence your attitude on an issue. This strategy of *anticipatory name calling* makes it difficult for you to declare that you favor the negatively valued belief because it means that you make yourself look like a "naive moron." Anticipatory name calling can also invoke positive group memberships, such as asserting that "all good Americans will agree . . ." or "people in the know think that . . ." Anticipatory name calling is a shrewd tactic that can be effective in shaping people's thinking.

Regardless of your position on these issues, how would you respond to someone who says, "Only a knee-jerk liberal would support racial quotas or affirmative action programs that give unfair advantages to minorities." Or "Only a stupid bigot would oppose affirmative action programs that rectify the unfair discrimination that minorities face." Can you identify the anticipatory name calling and the attempts at semantic slanting in each of these examples? More important, can you resist attempts like these to influence how you think about a host of complicated social issues?

Table 8.5	Critical Thinking Skills Discussed in This Application
Skill	**Description**
Understanding the way language can influence thought	The critical thinker appreciates that when you want to influence how people think, you should choose your words carefully.
Recognizing semantic slanting	The critical thinker is vigilant about how people deliberately choose certain words to elicit specific emotional responses.
Recognizing name calling and anticipatory name calling	The critical thinker is on the lookout for name calling and the implied threats used in anticipatory name calling.

REVIEW

Key Ideas

Language: Turning Thoughts into Words

● Languages are symbolic, semantic, generative, and structured. Human languages are structured hierarchically. At the bottom of the hierarchy are the basic sound units, called phonemes. At the next level are morphemes, the smallest units of meaning.

● Children typically utter their first words around their first birthday. Vocabulary growth is slow at first, but a vocabulary spurt often begins at around 18–24 months. Children begin to combine words by the end of their second year. Their early sentences are telegraphic, in that they omit many nonessential words. Over the next several years, children gradually learn the complexities of syntax.

● Research does not support the assumption that bilingualism has a negative effect on language development or on cognitive development. The learning of a second language is facilitated by starting at a younger age.

● According to Skinner and other behaviorists, children acquire a language through imitation and reinforcement. Nativist theories assert that humans have an innate capacity to learn language rules. Today, theorists are moving toward interactionist perspectives, which emphasize the role of both biology and experience.

● Many theorists believe that humans' special talent for language is the product of natural selection. To date, the balance of evidence suggests that thought determines language more than vice versa and that cognitive processes are largely invariant across cultures.

Problem Solving: In Search of Solutions

● Psychologists have differentiated among several types of problems, including problems of inducing structure, problems of transformation, and problems of arangement. Common barriers to problem solving include functional fixedness, mental set, getting bogged down in irrelevant information, and placing unnecessary constraints on one's solutions.

● Besides trial and error, a variety of heuristics are used for solving problems, including forming subgoals, searching for analogies, and changing the representation of a problem.

● Because of varied ecological demands, some cultures encourage a field-dependent cognitive style, whereas others foster more field independence. People who are field independent tend to analyze and restructure problems more than those who are field dependent.

Decision Making: Choices and Chances

● Simon's theory of bounded rationality suggests that human decision strategies are simplistic and often yield irrational results. An additive decision model is used when people make decisions by rating the attributes of each alternative and selecting the alternative that has the highest sum of ratings.

● When elimination by aspects is used, people gradually eliminate alternatives if their attributes fail to satisfy some minimum criterion. Models of how people make risky decisions focus on the expected value or subjective utility of various outcomes.

● People use the representativeness and availability heuristics in estimating probabilities. These heuristics can lead people to ignore base rates and to fall for the conjunction fallacy.

● Evolutionary psychologists maintain that many errors and biases in human reasoning are greatly reduced when problems are presented in ways that resemble the type of input humans would have processed in ancestral times

Putting It in Perspective

● Four of our unifying themes surfaced in the chapter. Our discussion of language acquisition revealed once again that all aspects of behavior are shaped by both nature and nurture. The recent progress in the study of cognitive processes showed how science depends on empirical methods. Research on decision making illustrated the importance of subjective perceptions. We also saw that cognitive processes are moderated—to a limited degree—by cultural factors.

Personal Application ● Understanding Pitfalls in Reasoning About Decision Making

● The heuristics that people use in decision making lead to various flaws in reasoning. For instance, the use of the representativeness heuristic contributes to the gambler's fallacy

and faith in small numbers. The availability heuristic underlies the tendency to overestimate the improbable.

● People tend to cling to their beliefs in spite of contradictory evidence, in part because they exhibit confirmation bias—the tendency to only seek information that supports one's view. People generally fail to appreciate these shortcomings, which leads to the overconfidence effect.

Critical Thinking Application ● Shaping Thought with Language: "Only a Naive Moron Would Believe That"

● Language can exert subtle influence over how people feel about various issues. Semantic slanting refers to the deliberate choice of words to create specific emotional responses, as has been apparent in the debate about abortion. In anticipatory name calling, there is an implied threat that a negative label will apply to you if you express certain views.

Key Terms

Availability heuristic
Belief perseverance
Bilingualism
Cognition
Confirmation bias
Conjunction fallacy
Decision making
Fast mapping
Field dependence-
   independence
Functional fixedness
Gambler's fallacy
Heuristic
Insight
Language
Language acquisition
   device (LAD)
Linguistic relativity
Mean length of
   utterance (MLU)
Mental set
Metalinguistic
   awareness
Morphemes
Overextension
Overregularization
Phonemes
Problem solving
Representativeness
   heuristic
Risky decision making
Syntax
Telegraphic speech
Trial and error
Underextensions

Key People

Noam Chomsky
Daniel Kahneman
Herbert Simon
B. F. Skinner
Amos Tversky

PRACTICE TEST

1. Which of the following is *not* a characteristic of language?
   A. It is generative.
   B. It is nomothetic.
   C. It is symbolic.
   D. It has structure.

2. Which of the following is the smallest unit of meaning in a language?
   A. genome
   B. morpheme
   C. phoneme
   D. phonogram

3. The 2-year-old child who refers to every four-legged animal as "doggie" is making which of the following errors?
   A. underextension
   B. overextension
   C. overregularization
   D. underregularization

4. Research suggests that bilingualism has a negative effect on:
   A. language development.
   B. cognitive development.
   C. metalinguistic awareness.
   D. none of the above.

5. Chomsky proposed that children learn a language:
   A. because they possess an innate language acquisition device.
   B. through imitation, reinforcement, and shaping.
   C. as the quality of their thought improves with age.
   D. because they need to in order to get their increasingly complex needs met.

6. The linguistic relativity hypothesis is the notion that:
   A. one's language determines the nature of one's thought.
   B. one's thought determines the nature of one's language.
   C. language and thought are separate and independent processes.
   D. language and thought interact, with each influencing the other.

7. Arrangement problems are often solved _____.
   A. suddenly
   B. without heuristics
   C. gradually
   D. through mental set

8. Problems that require a common object to be used in an unusual way may be difficult to solve because of:
   A. mental set.
   B. irrelevant information.
   C. unnecessary constraints.
   D. functional fixedness.

9. A heuristic is:
   A. a flash of insight.
   B. a guiding principle or "rule of thumb" used in problem solving.
   C. a methodical procedure for trying all possible solutions to a problem.
   D. a way of making a compensatory decision.

10. The field-independent style is predominant in:
    A. Western societies.
    B. sedentary agricultural societies.
    C. societies that stress strict child-rearing practices.
    D. all of the above.

11. The work of Herbert Simon on decision making showed that:
    A. people generally make rational choices that maximize their gains.
    B. people can evaluate an unlimited number of alternatives effectively.
    C. people tend to focus on only a few aspects of their available options and often make "irrational" decisions as a result
    D. the more options people consider, the better their decisions tend to be.

12. When you estimate the probability of an event by judging the ease with which relevant instances come to mind, you are relying on:
    A. an additive decision-making model.
    B. the representativeness heuristic.
    C. the availability heuristic.
    D. a noncompensatory model.

13. The belief that the probability of heads is higher after a long string of tails:
    A. is rational and accurate.
    B. is an example of the "gambler's fallacy."
    C. reflects the influence of the representativeness heuristic.
    D. b and c.

14. The more confident you are about your predictions of upcoming events in your life:
    A. the more likely it is that your predictions are accurate.
    B. the less likely it is that your predictions are overconfident.
    C. the more likely it is that your predictions are overconfident.
    D. a and b.

15. If someone says "Only a congenital pinhead would make that choice," this use of language would represent:
    A. semantic indicting.
    B. syntactic slanting.
    C. anticipatory name calling.
    D. telegraphic speech.

Answers

1	B	pages 234–235	6	A	page 242	11	C	page 249
2	B	page 235	7	A	page 244	12	C	page 251
3	B	page 238	8	D	page 244	13	D	page 255
4	D	page 239	9	B	page 246	14	C	page 257
5	A	page 240	10	A	page 249	15	C	page 259

INFOTRAC
COLLEGE EDITION

Go to the Wadsworth Psychology Study Center for quiz questions, research updates, interactive exercises, and suggested readings in INFOTRAC related to this chapter:
http://psychology.wadsworth.com/product/0534593100s

CHAPTER 9

© Hal Lee Miller Photography

Intelligence and Psychological Testing

© Hal Lee Miller Photography

Have you ever thought about the role that psychological testing has played in your life? In all likelihood, your years in grade school and high school were punctuated with a variety of intelligence tests, achievement tests, creativity tests, aptitude tests, and occupational interest tests. In the lower grades, you were probably given standardized achievement tests once or twice a year. For instance, you may have taken the Iowa Tests of Basic Skills, which measured your progress in reading, language, vocabulary, mathematics, and study skills. Perhaps you still have vivid memories of the serious atmosphere in the classroom, the very formal instructions ("Do not break the seal on this test until your examiner tells you to do so"), and the heavy pressure to work fast (I can still see Sister Dominic marching back and forth with her intense gaze riveted on her stopwatch). Where you're sitting at this very moment may have been influenced by your performance on standardized tests. That is, the college you chose to attend may have hinged on your SAT or ACT scores.

The vast enterprise of modern testing evolved from psychologists' pioneering efforts to measure *general intelligence*. The first useful intelligence tests, which were created soon after the turn of the century, left a great many "descendants." Today, there are over 2600 published psychological tests that measure a diverse array of mental abilities and other behavioral traits.

Clearly, American society has embraced psychological testing (Hanson, 1993). Each year in the United States alone, people take *hundreds of millions* of intelligence and achievement tests. Scholarships, degrees, jobs, and self-concepts are on the line as Americans attempt to hurdle a seemingly endless succession of tests. It's apparent that your life is affected by how you perform on psychological tests. Hence, it pays to be aware of their strengths and limitations.

We'll begin our coverage by introducing some basic concepts in psychological testing. Then we'll explore the history of intelligence tests, because they provided the model for subsequent psychological tests. Next we'll address practical questions about how intelligence tests work. After examining the nature versus nurture debate as it relates to intelligence, we'll explore some new directions in the study of intelligence. In the Personal Application, we'll discuss efforts to measure and understand another type of mental ability: creativity. In the Critical Thinking Application, we will critique some of the reasoning used in the vigorous debate about the roots of intelligence.

Key Concepts in Psychological Testing

A *psychological* test is a standardized measure of a sample of a person's behavior. Psychological tests are measurement instruments. They're used to measure the *individual differences* that exist among people in abilities, aptitudes, interests, and aspects of personality.

Your responses to a psychological test represent a sample of your behavior. The word sample should alert you to one of the key limitations of psychological tests: A particular behavior sample may not be representative of your characteristic behavior. Everyone has bad days. A stomachache, a fight with a friend, a problem with your car—all might affect your responses to a particular test on a particular day. Because of the limitations of the sampling process, test scores should always be interpreted *cautiously*. Many psychological tests are precise measurement devices. However, because of the ever-present sampling problem, test results should not be viewed as the final word on one's personality and abilities.

Principal Types of Tests

Psychological tests are used extensively in research, but most were developed to serve a practical purpose outside of the laboratory. Most tests can be placed in one of two broad categories: mental ability tests and personality tests.

Mental Ability Tests

Psychological testing originated with efforts to measure general mental ability. Today, tests of mental abilities remain the most common kind of psychological test. This broad class of tests includes three principal subcategories: intelligence tests, aptitude tests, and achievement tests.

Intelligence tests measure general mental ability. They're intended to assess intellectual potential rather than previous learning or accumulated knowledge. *Aptitude tests* are also designed to measure potential more than knowledge, but they break mental ability into separate components. Thus, *aptitude tests assess talent for specific kinds of learning.* In other words, aptitude tests measure particular types of mental ability, such as numerical ability, clerical speed and accuracy, mechanical reasoning, and spatial reasoning. Like aptitude tests, *achievement tests* have a specific focus, but they're supposed to measure previous learning instead of potential. Thus, *achievement tests gauge a person's mastery and knowledge of various subjects* (such as reading, English, or history).

Personality Tests

If you had to describe yourself in a few words, what words would you use? Are you introverted? Independent? Ambitious? Conventional? Assertive? Words such as these refer to personality traits. These traits can be assessed systematically with over 500 personality tests. *Personality tests measure various aspects of personality, including motives, interests, values, and attitudes.* Many psychologists prefer to call these tests personality *scales* because, unlike tests of mental abilities, the questions do not have right and wrong answers. We'll look at the different types of personality scales in our upcoming chapter on personality (Chapter 12).

Standardization and Norms

Both personality scales and tests of mental abilities are *standardized* measures of behavior. *Standardization* refers to the uniform procedures used in administrating and scoring a test. All respondents get the same instructions, the same questions, and the same time limits, so that their scores can be compared meaningfully. This means, for instance, that a person taking the Differential Aptitude Tests (DAT) in 1986 in San Diego, another taking the DAT in 1995 in Atlanta, and another taking it in 2001 in Peoria all confront exactly the same test-taking task.

The standardization of a test's scoring system includes the development of test norms. *Test norms provide information about where a score on a psychological test ranks in relation to other scores on that test.* Why are test norms needed? Because in psychological testing, everything is relative. Psychological tests tell you how you score *relative to other people*. They tell you, for instance, that you are average in creativity or slightly above average in clerical ability. These interpretations are derived from the test norms that help you understand what your test score means.

Usually, test norms allow you to convert your "raw score" on a test into a *percentile*. *A percentile score indicates the percentage of people who score at or below the score one has obtained.* For example, imagine that you are tested on a 40-item assertiveness scale and obtain a raw score of 26. In other words, you indicate a preference for the assertive option on 26 of the questions. Your score of 26 has little meaning until you consult the test norms

Web Link 9.1

ERIC/AE Test Locator
Educational Testing Service (ETS) has made available online the ETS Test Collection database listing more than 10,000 tests and research instruments. Users can search the database to discover basic information about each test and its availability.

and find out that it places you at the 82nd percentile. This normative information would indicate that you appear to be as assertive as or more assertive than 82% of the sample of people who provided the basis for the test norms.

The sample of people that the norms are based on is called a test's *standardization group*. Ideally, test norms are based on a large sample of people who were carefully selected to be representative of the broader population. For example, the norms for most intelligence tests are based on samples of 2000–6000 people whose demographic characteristics closely match the overall demographics of the United States (Woodcock, 1994). Although intelligence tests have been standardized pretty carefully, the representativeness of standardization groups for other types of tests varies considerably from one test to another.

Reliability SIM 7, 7b

Any kind of measuring device, whether it's a tire gauge, a stopwatch, or a psychological test, should be reasonably consistent. That is, repeated measurements should yield reasonably similar results. Psychologists call this quality *reliability*. To better appreciate the importance of reliability, think about how you would react if a tire pressure gauge were to give you several very different readings for the same tire. You would probably conclude that the gauge is broken and toss it into the trash. Consistency in measurement is obviously essential to accuracy in measurement.

Reliability refers to the measurement consistency of a test (or of other kinds of measurement techniques). A reliable test is one that yields similar results on repetition of the test (see Figure 9.1). Like most other types of measuring devices, psychological tests are not perfectly reliable. That is, they usually don't yield exactly the same scores when repeated. A certain amount of inconsistency is unavoidable, because human behavior is variable. For example, if you take the Beck Depression Inventory twice, you're not likely to respond to all 21 items in the same way both times.

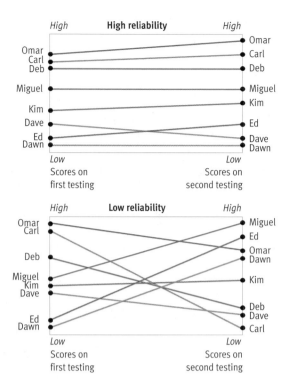

Although a test's reliability can be estimated in several ways, the most widely used approach is to check test-retest reliability. *Test-retest* reliability is estimated by comparing respondents' scores on two administrations of a test. If we wanted to check the test-retest reliability of a newly developed test of assertiveness, we would ask a group of subjects to take the test on two occasions, probably a few weeks apart. The underlying assumption is that assertiveness is a fairly stable aspect of personality that won't change in a matter of a few weeks. Thus, changes in participants' scores across the two administrations of the test would presumably reflect inconsistency in measurement.

Reliability estimates require the computation of correlation coefficients, which we introduced in Chapter 2. Correlation plays a critical role in research on testing, so let's reexamine the concept briefly (see Figure 9.2). A *correlation coefficient* is a numerical index of the degree of relationship between two variables. A *positive* correlation indicates that two

Figure 9.1

Test-retest reliability.
Individuals' scores on the first administration of an assertiveness test are represented on the left, and their scores on a second administration of the same test a few weeks later are shown on the right. If participants obtain similar scores on both administrations, as in the top graph, the test measures assertiveness consistently and has high reliability. If they get very different scores on the second administration, as in the bottom graph, the test has low reliability.

Figure 9.2

Correlation and reliability.
As you may recall from Chapter 2, a positive correlation means that two variables covary in the *same* direction; a negative correlation means that the variables covary in the *opposite* direction. The closer the correlation coefficient gets to either −1.00 or +1.00, the stronger the relationship. At a minimum, reliability estimates for psychological tests must be moderately high positive correlations. Most reliability coefficients fall between .70 and .95.

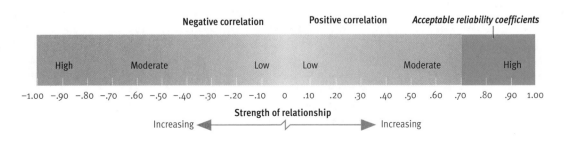

variables covary in the same direction. Thus, high scores on variable *X* are associated with high scores on variable *Y*, and low scores on *X* tend to go with low scores on *Y*. A negative correlation indicates an inverse relationship between two variables. Hence, high scores on variable *X* are associated with low scores on variable *Y*, and high scores on *Y* go with low scores on *X*. The actual coefficient of correlation can vary between 0 and +1.00. The closer a correlation comes to either –1.00 or +1.00 (that is, the farther it is from 0), the stronger the association between the two variables.

In estimating test-retest reliability, the two variables that must be correlated are the two sets of scores from the two administrations of the test. If people get fairly similar scores on the two administrations of our hypothetical assertiveness test, this consistency yields a substantial positive correlation. The magnitude of the correlation gives us a precise indication of the test's consistency over time. The closer the correlation comes to +1.00, the more reliable the test is.

There are no absolute guidelines about acceptable levels of reliability. What's acceptable depends to some extent on the nature and purpose of the test (Reynolds, 1994). The reliability estimates for most psychological tests are above .70. Many exceed .90. The higher the reliability coefficient, the more consistent the test is. As reliability goes down, concern about measurement error increases.

Validity

Even if a test is quite reliable, we still need to be concerned about its validity. ***Validity* refers to the ability of a test to measure what it was designed to measure.** If we develop a new test of assertiveness, we have to provide some evidence that it really measures assertiveness. Validity can be estimated in several ways, depending on the nature of the test (Golden, Sawicki, & Franzen, 1990).

Content Validity

Achievement tests and educational tests such as classroom exams should have adequate content validity. ***Content validity* refers to the degree to which the content of a test is representative of the domain it's supposed to cover.** Imagine a physics exam that includes questions on material that was not covered in class or in assigned reading. The professor has compromised the content validity of the exam. Content validity is evaluated with logic more than with statistics.

Criterion-Related Validity

Psychological tests are often used to make predictions about specific aspects of individuals' behavior. They are used to predict performance in college, job capability, and suitability for training programs, as just a few examples. Criterion-related validity is a central concern in such cases. ***Criterion-related validity* is estimated by correlating subjects' scores on a test with their scores on an independent criterion (another measure) of the trait assessed by the test** (see Figure 9.3).

For example, let's say you developed a test to measure aptitude for becoming an airplane pilot. You could check its validity by correlating participants' scores on your aptitude test with subsequent ratings of their performance in their pilot training program. The performance ratings would be the independent criterion of pilot aptitude. If your test has reasonable validity, people who score high on the test should tend to earn high performance ratings during training, and low scorers should tend to get low ratings. In other words, there ought to be a reasonably strong positive correlation between the test and the criterion measure. Such a correlation would help validate your test's predictive ability.

Construct Validity

Many psychological tests attempt to measure abstract personal qualities, such as creativity, intel-

Figure 9.3

Criterion-related validity. To evaluate the criterion-related validity of a pilot aptitude test, a psychologist would correlate participants' test scores with a criterion measure of their aptitude, such as ratings of their performance in a pilot training program. Test validity is high if scores on the two measures are highly correlated. If little or no relationship exists between the two sets of scores, validity is low, which means that the aptitude test does not measure what it is supposed to measure.

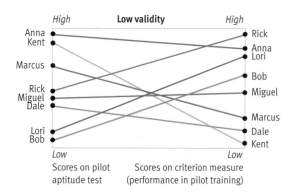

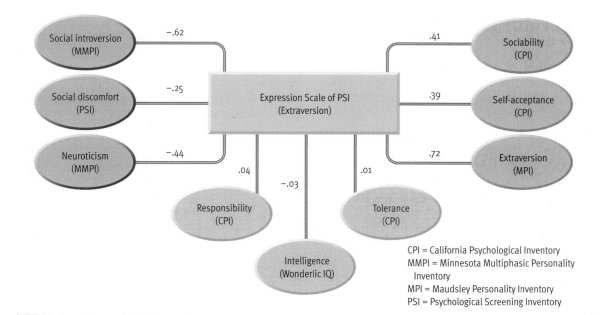

Figure 9.4

Construct validity.
Psychologists evaluate a scale's construct validity by studying how scores on the scale correlate with a variety of variables. For example, some of the evidence on the construct validity of the Expression Scale from the Psychological Screening Inventory is summarized here. This scale is supposed to measure the personality trait of *extraversion*. As you can see on the left side of this network of correlations, the scale correlates negatively with measures of social introversion, social discomfort, and neuroticism, just as one would expect if the scale is really tapping extraversion. On the right, you can see that the scale is correlated positively with measures of sociability and self-acceptance and another index of extraversion, as one would anticipate. At the bottom, you can see that the scale does not correlate with several traits that should be unrelated to extraversion. Thus, the network of correlations depicted here supports the idea that the Expression Scale measures extraversion.

ligence, or independence. There are no obvious criterion measures for these abstract qualities, which are called *hypothetical constructs*. In measuring abstract qualities, psychologists are concerned about **construct validity—the extent to which there is evidence that a test measures a particular hypothetical construct.**

The process of demonstrating construct validity can be complicated. It usually requires a series of studies that examine the correlations between the test and various measures *related* to the trait in question. A thorough demonstration of construct validity requires looking at the correlations between a test and many related measures. For example, some of the evidence on the construct validity of a measure of extraversion (the Expression scale from the

Psychological Screening Inventory) is summarized in Figure 9.4. This network of correlation coefficients shows that the Expression scale correlates negatively, positively, or not at all with various measures, much as one would expect if the scale is really assessing extraversion. Ultimately, it's the overall pattern of correlations that provides convincing (or unconvincing) evidence of a test's construct validity.

The complexities involved in demonstrating construct validity will be apparent in our upcoming discussion of intelligence testing. The ongoing debate about the construct validity of intelligence tests is one of the oldest debates in psychology. Let's look first at the origins of intelligence tests. This historical review will help you appreciate the current controversies about intelligence testing.

CONCEPT CHECK 9.1

Recognizing Basic Concepts in Testing

Check your understanding of basic concepts in psychological testing by answering the questions below. Select your responses from the following concepts:

Test norms   ~~Content validity~~   Construct validity   ~~Test-retest reliability~~   ~~Criterion-related validity~~

1. At the request of the HiTechnoLand computer store chain, Professor Charlz develops a test to measure aptitude for selling computers. Two hundred applicants for sales jobs at HiTechnoLand stores are asked to take the test on two occasions, a few weeks apart. A correlation of +.82 is found between applicants' scores on the two administrations of the test. Thus, the test appears to possess reasonable *Test-retest reliability*

2. All 200 of these applicants are hired and put to work selling computers. After six months Professor Charlz correlates the new workers' aptitude test scores with the dollar value of the computers that each sold during the first 6 months on the job. This correlation turns out to be –21. This finding suggests that the test may lack *Criterion-related validity*

3. Back at the university, Professor Charlz is teaching a course in theories of personality. He decides to use the same midterm exam that he gave last year, even though the exam includes questions about theorists that he did not cover or assign reading on this year. There are reasons to doubt the *Content validity* of Professor Charlz's midterm exam.

Psychological tests play a prominent role in our society, but this wasn't always so. The first psychological tests were invented a little over a hundred years ago. Since then, the reliance on psychological tests has grown gradually. In this section, we discuss the pioneers who launched psychological testing with their efforts to measure general intelligence.

Galton's Studies of Hereditary Genius

It all began with the work of a British scholar, Sir Francis Galton, in the late 19th century. Galton studied family trees and found that success and eminence appeared consistently in some families over generations. For the most part, these families were much like Galton's: well-bred, upper-class families with access to superior schooling and social connections that pave the way to success. Yet Galton discounted the advantages of such an upbringing. In his book *Hereditary Genius,* Galton (1869) concluded that success runs in families because great intelligence is passed from generation to generation through genetic inheritance.

To better demonstrate that intelligence is governed by heredity, Galton needed an objective measure of intelligence. His approach to this problem was guided by the theoretical views of his day. Thus, he assumed that the contents of the mind are built out of elementary *sensations,* and he hypothesized that exceptionally bright people should exhibit exceptional sensory acuity. Working from this premise, he tried to assess innate mental ability by measuring simple sensory processes. Among other things, he measured sensitivity to high-pitched sounds, color perception, and reaction time (the speed of one's response to a stimulus). His efforts met with little success. Research eventually showed that the sensory processes that he measured were largely unrelated to other criteria of mental ability that he was trying to predict (such as success in school or professional life). Although Galton's mental tests were a failure, his work created an interest in the measurement of mental ability, setting the stage for a subsequent breakthrough by Alfred Binet, a prominent French psychologist.

Binet's Breakthrough

In 1904 a commission on education in France asked Alfred Binet to devise a test to identify mentally subnormal children. The commission was motivated by admirable goals. It wanted to single out youngsters in need of special training. It also wanted to avoid complete reliance on teachers' evaluations, which might often be subjective and biased.

In response to this need, Binet and a colleague, Theodore Simon, published the first useful test of general mental ability in 1905. They had the insight to load it with items that required abstract reasoning skills, rather than the sensory skills Galton had measured. Their scale was a success because it was inexpensive, easy to administer, objective, and capable of predicting children's performance in school fairly well (Siegler, 1992). Thanks to these qualities, its use spread across Europe and America.

The Binet-Simon scale expressed a child's score in terms of "mental level" or "mental age." A child's **mental age indicated that he or she displayed the mental ability typical of a child of that chronological (actual) age.** Thus, a child with a mental age of 6 performed like the average 6-year-old on the test. Binet realized that his scale was a somewhat crude initial effort at measuring mental ability. He revised it in 1908 and again in 1911. Unfortunately, his revising came to an abrupt end with his death in 1911. However, other psychologists continued to build on Binet's work.

Terman and the Stanford-Binet

In America, Lewis Terman and his colleagues at Stanford University soon went to work on a major expansion and revision of Binet's test. Their work led to the 1916 publication of the Stanford-Binet Intelligence Scale (Terman, 1916). Although this revision was quite loyal to Binet's original conceptions, it incorporated a new scoring scheme based on the "intelligence quotient" suggested by William Stern (1914). **An *intelligence quotient* (IQ) is a child's mental age divided by chronological age, multiplied by 100.** IQ scores originally involved actual quotients, calculated as follows:

$$IQ = \frac{\text{Mental age}}{\text{Chronological age}} \times 100$$

The ratio of mental age to chronological age made it possible to compare children of different ages. In Binet's system, such comparisons were awkward. The IQ ratio placed all children (regardless of age) on the same scale, which was centered at 100 if their mental age corresponded to their chronological age (see Table 9.1 for examples of IQ calculations).

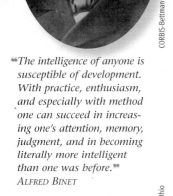

"The intelligence of anyone is susceptible of development. With practice, enthusiasm, and especially with method one can succeed in increasing one's attention, memory, judgment, and in becoming literally more intelligent than one was before."
ALFRED BINET

"It is the method of tests that has brought psychology down from the clouds and made it useful to men; that has transformed the 'science of trivialities' into the 'science of human engineering."
LEWIS TERMAN

CORBIS-Bettman

Archieves of the History of American Psychology, University of Akron, Akron, Ohio

Table **9.1**   **Calculating the Intelligence Quotient**

Measure	Child 1	Child 2	Child 3	Child 4
Mental age (MA)	6 years	6 years	9 years	12 years
Chronological age (CA)	6 years	9 years	12 years	9 years
$IQ = \dfrac{MA}{CA} \times 100$	$\dfrac{6}{6} \times 100 = 100$	$\dfrac{6}{9} \times 100 = 67$	$\dfrac{9}{12} \times 100 = 75$	$\dfrac{12}{9} \times 100 = 133$

Terman's technical and theoretical contributions to psychological testing were modest, but he made an articulate case for the potential educational benefits of testing and became the key force behind American schools' widespread adoption of IQ tests (Chapman, 1988). As a result of his efforts, the Stanford-Binet quickly became the world's foremost intelligence test and the standard of comparison for virtually all intelligence tests that followed (Gregory, 1996). Although many other IQ tests geared to specific populations, age groups, and purposes have been developed, the apparent variety is somewhat misleading. Most of the tests remain loyal to the conception of intelligence originally formulated by Binet and Terman. Since its publication in 1916, the Stanford-Binet has been updated periodically (in 1937, 1960, 1973, and 1986), and it remains one of the world's most widely used psychological tests.

Wechsler's Innovations

As chief psychologist at New York's massive Bellevue Hospital, David Wechsler was charged with overseeing the psychological assessment of thousands of adult patients. He found the Stanford-Binet somewhat unsatisfactory for this purpose. Thus, Wechsler set out to improve on the measurement of intelligence *in adults*. In 1939 he published the first high-quality IQ test designed specifically for adults, which came to be known as the Wechsler Adult Intelligence Scale (WAIS) (Wechsler, 1955, 1981). Ironically, Wechsler (1949, 1967, 1991) eventually devised downward extensions of his scale for children.

The Wechsler scales were characterized by at least two major innovations (Prifitera, 1994). First, Wechsler made his scales less dependent on subjects' verbal ability than the Stanford-Binet. He included many items that required nonverbal reasoning. To highlight the distinction between verbal and nonverbal ability, he formalized the computation of separate scores for verbal IQ, performance (nonverbal) IQ, and full-scale (total) IQ. Examples of test items similar to those on the Wechsler scales are presented in Figure 9.5 on the next page.

Second, Wechsler discarded the intelligence quotient in favor of a new scoring scheme based on the *normal distribution*. This scoring system has since been adopted by most other IQ tests, including the Stanford-Binet. Although the term *intelligence quotient* lingers on in our vocabulary, scores on intelligence tests are no longer based on an actual quotient. We'll take a close look at the modern scoring system for IQ tests a little later.

Intelligence Testing Today

Today, psychologists and educators have many IQ tests available for their use. Basically, these tests fall into two categories: *individual tests* and *group tests*. Individual IQ tests are administered only by psychologists who have special training for this purpose. A psychologist works face to face with a single

The subtests [of the WAIS] are different measures of intelligence, not measures of different kinds of intelligence.
DAVID WECHSLER

CONCEPT **CHECK 9.2**

Recognizing the Ideas of Pioneers in Intelligence Testing

Check your understanding of some of the key ideas of pioneers in intelligence testing by identifying the authors of each of the following quotations. Choose from among (a) Francis Galton, (b) Alfred Binet, (c) Lewis Terman, and (d) David Wechsler.

A **1.** "I propose to show in this book that man's natural abilities are derived from inheritance, under exactly the same limitations as are the form and physical features of the whole organic world."

D **2.** "The grouping of the subtests into Verbal (1–6) and Performance (7–11), while intending to emphasize a dichotomy as regards possible types of ability called for by the individual tests, does not imply that these are the only abilities involved in the tests. Nor does it presume that there are different kinds of intelligence, e.g., verbal, manipulative, etc. It merely implies that these are different ways in which intelligence may manifest itself."

B **3.** "We here present the first rough sketch of a work which was directly inspired by the desire to serve the interesting cause of the education of subnormals. . . . [T]he Minister of Public Instruction named a commission which was charged with the study of measures to be taken for insuring the benefits of instruction to defective children. . . ."

C **4.** "The mental age of a subject is meaningless if considered apart from chronological age. It is only the ratio of retardation or acceleration to chronological age (that is, the IQ) which has significance."

Figure 9.5

Subtests on the Wechsler Adult Intelligence Scale (WAIS). The WAIS is subdivided into a series of tests that yield separate verbal and performance (nonverbal) IQ scores. Examples of test items that resemble those on the WAIS are shown here.

Wechsler Adult Intelligence Scale (WAIS)		
Test	Description	Example
Verbal scale		
Information	Taps general range of information	On what continent is France?
Comprehension	Tests understanding of social conventions and ability to evaluate past experience	Why are children required to go to school?
Arithmetic	Tests arithmetic reasoning through verbal problems	How many hours will it take to drive 150 miles at 50 miles per hour?
Similarities	Asks in what way certain objects or concepts are similar; measures abstract thinking	How are a calculator and a typewriter alike?
Digit span	Tests attention and rote memory by orally presenting series of digits to be repeated forward or backward	Repeat the following numbers backward: 2 4 3 5 1 8 6
Vocabulary	Tests ability to define increasingly difficult words	What does audacity mean?
Performance scale		
Digit symbol	Tests speed of learning through timed coding tasks in which numbers must be associated with marks of various shapes	Shown: Fill in:
Picture completion	Tests visual alertness and visual memory through presentation of an incompletely drawn figure; the missing part must be discovered and named	Tell me what is missing:
Block design	Tests ability to perceive and analyze patterns by presenting designs that must be copied with blocks	Assemble blocks to match this design:
Picture arrangement	Tests understanding of social situations through a series of comic-strip-type pictures that must be arranged in the right sequence to tell a story	Put the pictures in the right order:
Object assembly	Tests ability to deal with part/whole relationships by presenting puzzle pieces that must be assembled to form a complete object	Assemble the pieces into a complete object:

Web Link 9.2

ERIC Clearinghouse on Assessment and Evaluation
This site assembles the most comprehensive set of links regarding psychological testing and assessment on the Web. A recent addition is the full-text library of more than 250 scholarly and professional books and articles regarding assessment.

examinee at a time. The Stanford-Binet and the Wechsler scales are both individual IQ tests.

The problem with individual IQ tests is that they're expensive and time-consuming to administer. Therefore, researchers have developed a number of IQ tests that can be administered to large groups of people at once. Because they're much more cost-effective, group tests such as the Otis-Lennon School Ability Test and the Lorge-Thorndike Intelligence Test enjoy wide usage at all educational levels (Vane & Motta, 1990). Indeed, if you've taken an IQ test, chances are that it was a group test.

Most IQ testing is conducted by school districts, which are largely free to formulate their own unique testing programs. There is little federal or state policy regarding ideal patterns of testing. Some districts administer group intelligence tests to all students at regular intervals. Others only administer individual intelligence tests on an occasional basis, as needed. Schools use intelligence tests to screen for mental retardation, to group students according to their academic ability ("tracking"), to identify gifted children, and to evaluate educational programs.

Basic Questions About Intelligence Testing

Misconceptions abound when it comes to intelligence tests. In this section we'll use a question-and-answer format to explain the basic principles underlying intelligence testing.

What Kinds of Questions Are on Intelligence Tests?

The nature of the questions found on IQ tests varies somewhat from test to test. These variations depend on whether the test is intended for children or adults (or both) and whether the test is designed for individuals or groups. Overall, the questions are fairly diverse in format. The Wechsler scales, with their numerous subtests, provide a representative example of the kinds of items that appear on most IQ tests. As you can see in Figure 9.5, the items in the Wechsler subtests require respondents to furnish information, recognize vocabulary, and demonstrate basic memory. Generally speaking, examinees are required to manipulate words, numbers, and images through abstract reasoning.

What Do Modern IQ Scores Mean?

7c

As we discussed, scores on intelligence tests once represented a ratio of mental age to chronological age. However, this system has given way to one based on the normal distribution and the *standard deviation,* a statistical index of variability in a data distribution, which is explained in Appendix B. **The *normal distribution* is a symmetrical, bell-shaped curve that represents the pattern in which many characteristics are dispersed in the population.** When a trait is normally distributed, most cases fall near the center of the distribution, and the number of cases gradually declines as one moves away from the center in either direction. The normal distribution provides a precise way to measure how people stack up in comparison to each other. The scores under the normal curve are dispersed in a fixed pattern, with the standard deviation serving as the unit of measurement, as shown in Figure 9.6. About 68% of the scores in the distribution fall within one

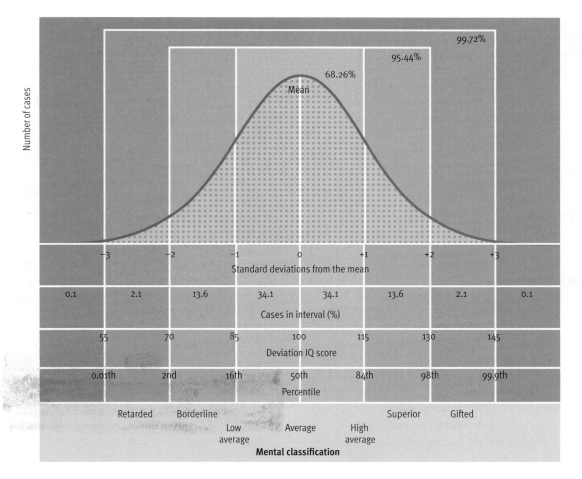

Figure 9.6

The normal distribution and deviation IQ scores. Many characteristics are distributed in a pattern represented by this bell-shaped curve. The horizontal axis shows how far above or below the mean a score is (measured in plus or minus standard deviations). The vertical axis is used to graph the number of cases obtaining each score. In a normal distribution, the cases are distributed in a fixed pattern. For instance, 68.26% of the cases fall between +1 and −1 standard deviation of the mean. Modern IQ scores indicate where a person's measured intelligence falls in the normal distribution. On most IQ tests, the mean is set at an IQ of 100 and the standard deviation at 15. Thus, an IQ of 130 means that a person scored 2 standard deviations above the mean. Any deviation IQ score can be converted into a percentile score, which indicates the percentage of cases obtaining a lower score. The mental classifications at the bottom of the figure are descriptive labels that roughly correspond to ranges of IQ scores.

standard deviation of the mean, whereas 95% of the scores fall within two standard deviations of the mean. Given this fixed pattern, if you know the mean and standard deviation of a normally distributed trait, you can tell where any score falls in the distribution for the trait.

The normal distribution was first discovered by 18th-century astronomers. They found that their measurement errors were distributed in a predictable way that resembled a bell-shaped curve. Since then, research has shown that many human traits, ranging from height to running speed to spatial ability, also follow a normal distribution. Psychologists eventually recognized that intelligence scores also fall into a normal distribution. This insight permitted David Wechsler to devise a more sophisticated scoring system for his tests that has been adopted by virtually all subsequent IQ tests. In this system, raw scores are translated into *deviation IQ scores* that locate respondents precisely within the normal distribution.

For most IQ tests, the mean of the distribution is set at 100 and the standard deviation (SD) is set at 15. These choices were made to provide continuity with the original IQ ratio (mental age to chronological age) that was centered at 100. In this system, which is depicted in Figure 9.6, a score of 115 means that a person scored exactly one SD (15 points) above the mean. A score of 85 means that a person scored one SD below the mean. A score of 100 means that a person showed average performance. *The key point is that modern IQ scores indicate exactly where you fall in the normal distribution of intelligence.* Thus, a score of 120 does not indicate that you answered 120 questions correctly. Nor does it mean that you have 120 "units" of intelligence. A deviation IQ score places you at a specific point in the normal distribution of intelligence (based on the norms for your age group). Deviation IQ scores can be converted into percentile scores, as shown in Figure 9.6.

Do Intelligence Tests Have Adequate Reliability?

Do IQ tests produce consistent results when people are retested? Yes. Most IQ tests report commendable reliability estimates. The correlations often range into the .90s. In comparison to most other types of psychological tests, IQ tests are exceptionally reliable. However, like other tests, they *sample* behavior, and a specific testing may yield an unrepresentative score.

Variations in examinees' motivation to take an IQ test or in their anxiety about the test can sometimes produce misleading scores (Spielberger & Sydeman, 1994; Zimmerman & Woo-Sam, 1984). The most common problem is that low motivation or high anxiety may drag a person's score down on a particular occasion. For instance, a fourth-grader who is made to feel that the test is terribly important may get jittery and be unable to concentrate. The same child might score much higher on a subsequent testing by another examiner who creates a more comfortable atmosphere. Although the reliability of IQ tests is excellent, caution is always in order in interpreting test scores. IQ scores should be viewed as estimates that are accurate within plus or minus 5 points about two-thirds of the time.

Do Intelligence Tests Have Adequate Validity?

Do intelligence tests measure what they're supposed to measure? Yes, but this answer has to be qualified very carefully. IQ tests are valid measures of the kind of intelligence that's necessary to do well in academic work. But if the purpose is to assess intelligence in a broader sense, the validity of IQ tests is questionable.

As you may recall, intelligence tests were originally designed with a relatively limited purpose in mind: to predict school performance. This has continued to be the principal purpose of IQ testing. Efforts to document the validity of IQ tests have usually concentrated on their relationship to grades in school. Typically, positive correlations in the .50s are found between IQ scores and school grades (Kline, 1991). Even higher correlations (between .60 and .80) are found between IQ scores and the number of years of school that people complete (Ceci, 1991).

These correlations are about as high as one could expect, given that many factors besides a person's intelligence are likely to affect grades and school progress. For example, school grades may be influenced by a student's motivation, diligence, or personality, not to mention teachers' subjective biases. Thus, IQ tests are reasonably valid indexes of school-related intellectual ability, or academic intelligence.

However, over the years people have mistakenly come to believe that IQ tests measure mental ability in a truly general sense. In reality, IQ tests have always focused on the abstract reasoning and verbal fluency that are essential to academic success. The tests do not tap social competence, practical problem solving, creativity, mechanical ingenuity, or artistic talent.

When Robert Sternberg and his colleagues (1981) asked people to list examples of intelligent

Web Link 9.3

Educational Psychology Interactive: Intelligence
This site, maintained by Bill Huitt of Valdosta State University, offers a helpful review of psychological approaches to intelligence and is an excellent resource for other topics in educational psychology.

behavior, they found that the examples fell into three categories: (1) *verbal intelligence,* (2) *practical intelligence,* and (3) *social intelligence* (see Figure 9.7). Thus, people generally recognize three basic types of intelligence. For the most part, IQ tests assess only the first of these three types. Although IQ tests are billed as measures of *general* mental ability, they actually focus somewhat narrowly on a specific type of intelligence: academic/verbal intelligence (Sternberg, 1998). Hence, IQ tests are not valid indicators of intelligence in a truly general sense.

Do Intelligence Tests Predict Vocational Success?

Vocational success is a vague, value-laden concept that's difficult to quantify. Nonetheless, researchers have tackled this question by examining correlations between IQ scores and specific indicators of vocational success, such as the prestige of individuals' occupations or ratings of their job performance. On the positive side of the ledger, it's clear that IQ is related to occupational attainment. People who score high on IQ tests are more likely than those who score low to end up in high-status jobs (Austin & Hanisch, 1990; Herrnstein & Murray, 1994; Ree & Earles, 1992). Because IQ tests measure school ability fairly well and because school performance is important in reaching certain occupations, this link between IQ scores and job status makes sense. Of course, the correlations between IQ and occupational attainment are moderate, and there are plenty of exceptions to the general trend. Some people plow through the educational system with bulldog determination and hard work, in spite of limited ability as measured by IQ tests. Such people may go on to prestigious jobs, while people who are brighter (according to their test results), but less motivated, settle for lower-status jobs.

Verbal intelligence	Practical intelligence	Social intelligence
Speaks clearly and articulately	Sees all aspects of a problem	Accepts others for what they are
Is verbally fluent	Sizes up situations well	Has social conscience
Is knowledgeable about a particular field	Makes good decisions	Thinks before speaking and doing
Reads with high comprehension	Poses problems in an optimal way	Is sensitive to other people's needs and desires

On the negative side of the ledger, there is considerable debate about whether IQ scores are effective predictors of performance *within* a particular occupation (Barrett & Depinet, 1991; Ghiselli, 1973; Hunter & Schmidt, 1996; McClelland, 1993; Sternberg & Wagner, 1993; Wagner, 1997). For example, in summarizing data for 446 occupations, Jensen (1993a) reported an unimpressive median correlation of .27 between general intelligence and job performance. On the other hand, in another summary of research involving 515 jobs, Schmidt and Hunter (1998) calculated a much more respectable mean correlation of .51 between measures of general mental ability and job performance. Doubts about the ability of IQ tests to predict job performance and concerns about possible cultural bias in the tests have led to controversy over the use of IQ tests in employee selection. In fact, the use of intelligence testing in making employment decisions has been challenged on legal grounds. Because of these challenges, the practice has declined (Gatewood & Perloff, 1990).

Figure 9.7

Layperson's conceptions of intelligence. Robert Sternberg and his colleagues (1981) asked subjects to list examples of behaviors characteristic of intelligence. The examples tended to sort into three groups that represent the three types of intelligence recognized by the average person: verbal intelligence, practical intelligence, and social intelligence. (Adapted from "People's Conceptions of Intelligence," by R. J. Sternberg, B. E. Conway, J. L. Keton & M. Bernstein, 1981, *Journal of Personality and Social Psychology, 41* (1), p.45. Copyright © 1981 by the American Psychological Association. Adapted by permission of the author.)

These accomplished individuals exemplify the three basic types of intelligence recognized by most people (based on research by Sternberg, et al., 1981). Authors Amy Tan and Stephen King (left photo) exhibit remarkable verbal intelligence. Economist Alan Greenspan (middle photo) has been applauded for his practical intelligence. Television chef Emeril Lagasse (right photo) has brought great social intelligence to his widely viewed cooking shows.

All photos: AP/Wide World Photos

Essentially, court rulings and laws now require that tests used in employment selection measure specific abilities that are clearly related to job performance (Schmidt, Ones, & Hunter, 1992). Companies are increasingly turning to personality tests to select employees who are conscientious, calm under pressure, persistent, reliable, and so forth (Hogan, Hogan, & Roberts, 1996). Psychologists are also trying to develop tests of practical intelligence to aid employers in their hiring decisions (Sternberg et al., 1995). Thus, psychological tests that measure abilities relevant to specific jobs continue to be valuable tools in selecting employees (Landy, Shankster, & Kohler, 1994).

Are IQ Tests Widely Used in Other Cultures?

In other Western cultures with European roots the answer is yes. In most non-Western cultures, the answer is only very little. IQ testing has a long history and continues to be a major enterprise in many Western countries, such as Britain, France, Norway, Canada, and Australia (Irvine & Berry, 1988). However, efforts to export IQ tests to non-Western societies have met with mixed results. The tests have been well received in some non-Western cultures, such as Japan, where the Binet-Simon scales were introduced as early as 1908 (Iwawaki & Vernon, 1988), but they have been met with indifference or resistance in other cultures, such as China and India (Chan & Vernon, 1988; Sinha, 1983).

The bottom line is that Western IQ tests do not translate well into the language and cognitive frameworks of many non-Western cultures (Berry, 1994). Using an intelligence test with a cultural group other than the one for which it was originally designed can be problematic. The entire process of test administration, with its emphasis on rapid information processing, decisive responding, and the notion that ability can be quantified, is foreign to some cultures. Moreover, different cultures have different conceptions of what intelligence is and value different mental skills (Das, 1994; Sternberg & Kaufman, 1998). Even when a non-Western culture is largely in agreement with Western views about the ingredients of intelligent behavior, it can be difficult to construct equivalent tests that measure these ingredients with equal reliability and validity in both cultural contexts (Greenfield, 1997).

Heredity and Environment as Determinants of Intelligence

Most early pioneers of intelligence testing, such as Sir Francis Galton and Lewis Terman maintained that intelligence is inherited (Cravens, 1992). Small wonder, then, that this view lingers on in our society. Gradually, however, it has become clear that both heredity and environment influence intelligence (Locurto, 1991; Plomin & Petrill, 1997; Scarr, 1997). Does this mean that the nature versus nurture debate has been settled with respect to intelligence? Absolutely not. Theorists and researchers continue to argue vigorously about which is more important, in part because the issue has such far-reaching sociopolitical implications.

Theorists who believe that intelligence is largely inherited downplay the value of special educational programs for underprivileged groups (Herrnstein & Murray, 1994; Jensen, 1980). They assert that a child's intelligence cannot be increased noticeably, because a child's genetic destiny cannot be altered. Theorists who believe that intelligence is shaped by experience are highly critical of this view (Angoff, 1988; Wahlstein, 1997). The people in this camp maintain that even more funds should be allocated for remedial education programs, improved schooling in lower-class neighborhoods, and college financial aid for the underprivileged. Because the debate over the role of heredity in intelligence has direct relevance to important social issues and political decisions, we'll take a detailed look at this complex controversy.

Evidence for Hereditary Influence

Galton's observation that intelligence runs in families was quite accurate. However, *family studies* can determine only whether genetic influence on a trait is *plausible*, not whether it is certain. Family members share not just genes, but similar environments. If high intelligence (or low intelligence) appears in a family over several generations, this consistency could reflect the influence of either shared genes or shared environment. Because of this problem, researchers must turn to *twin studies* and *adoption studies* to obtain more definitive evidence on whether heredity affects intelligence.

Twin Studies

The best evidence regarding the role of genetic factors in intelligence comes from studies that compare identical and fraternal twins. The rationale for twin studies is that both identical and fraternal twins normally develop under similar environmental conditions. However, identical twins share more genetic kinship than fraternal twins. Hence, if pairs of identical twins are more similar in intelligence than pairs of fraternal twins, it's presumably because of their greater genetic similarity. (See Chapter 3 for a more detailed explanation of the logic underlying twin studies.)

What are the findings of twin studies regarding intelligence? McGue and colleagues (1993) reviewed the results of over 100 studies of intellectual similarity for various kinds of kinship relations and child-rearing arrangements. The key findings from their review are highlighted in Figure 9.8. This figure plots the average correlation observed for various types of relationships. As you can see, the average correlation reported for identical twins (.86) is very high, indicating that identical twins tend to be quite similar in intelligence. The average correlation for fraternal twins (.60) is significantly lower. This correlation indicates that fraternal twins

also tend to be similar in intelligence, but noticeably less similar than identical twins. These results support the notion that intelligence is inherited to a considerable degree.

Of course, critics have tried to poke holes in this line of reasoning. They argue that identical twins are more alike in IQ because parents and others treat them more similarly than they treat fraternal twins. This environmental explanation of the findings has some merit. After all, identical twins are always the same sex, and gender influences how a child is raised. However, this explanation seems unlikely in light of the evidence on identical twins reared apart as a result of family breakups or adoption (Bouchard, 1997; Bouchard et al., 1990). *Although reared in different environments,* these identical twins still display greater similarity in IQ (average correlation: .72) than fraternal twins reared together (average correlation: .60).

Adoption Studies

Research comparing adopted children to their biological parents also provides evidence about the effects of heredity (and of environment, as we shall see). If adopted children resemble their biological parents in intelligence even though they were not

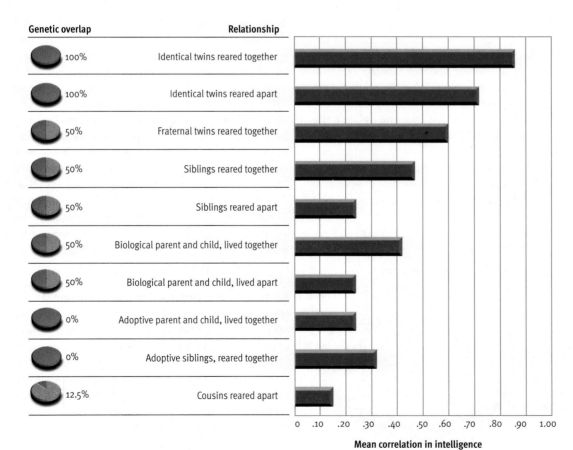

Figure 9.8

Studies of IQ similarity. The graph shows the mean correlations of IQ scores for people of various types of relationships, as obtained in studies of IQ similarity. Higher correlations indicate greater similarity. The results show that greater genetic similarity is associated with greater similarity in IQ, suggesting that intelligence is partly inherited (compare, for example, the correlations for identical and fraternal twins). However, the results also show that living together is associated with greater IQ similarity, suggesting that intelligence is partly governed by environment (compare, for example, the scores of siblings reared together and reared apart). (Based on McGue, et al., 1993.)

reared by these parents, this finding supports the genetic hypothesis. The relevant studies indicate that there is indeed more than chance similarity between adopted children and their biological parents (Turkheimer, 1991) (refer again to Figure 9.8).

Heritability Estimates

Various experts have sifted through mountains of correlational evidence to estimate the *heritability* of intelligence. **A *heritability ratio* is an estimate of the proportion of trait variability in a population that is determined by variations in genetic inheritance.** Heritability can be estimated for any trait. For example, the heritability of height is estimated to be around 90% (Plomin, 1994). Heritability can be estimated in a variety of ways that appear logically and mathematically defensible (Loehlin, 1994; Schonemann, 1994). Given the variety of methods available and the strong views that experts bring to the IQ debate, it should come as no surprise that heritability estimates for intelligence vary considerably (see Figure 9.9).

At the high end, a few theorists, such as Arthur Jensen (1980, 1998), maintain that the heritability of IQ is about 80%. That is, they believe that only about 20% of the variation in intelligence is attributable to environmental factors. Many researchers in this area assert that the 80% figure is higher than the data really support. Most studies suggest that the heritability of IQ is between 50% and 70% (Bouchard et al., 1990; Loehlin, 1989). The consensus estimate of experts hovers around 60% (Snyderman & Rothman, 1987).

Even the estimates at the low end suggest that heredity has a substantial impact on intelligence. However, it's important to understand that heritability estimates have certain limitations (Ceci et al., 1997; Rutter, Silberg, & Simonoff, 1993; Waldman, 1997). First, a heritability estimate is a *group statistic* based on studies of trait variability within a specific group. A heritability estimate cannot be applied meaningfully to *individuals*. In other words, even if the heritability of intelligence truly is 70%, this does not mean that each individual's intelligence is 70% inherited. Second, the heritability of a specific trait may vary from one group to another depending on a variety of factors. For instance, in a group with a given gene pool, heritability will increase if there's a shift toward rearing group members in more similar circumstances. Why? Because the extent of environmental differences will be reduced. To date, heritability estimates for intelligence have been based largely on research with white, middle-class subjects. Hence, they should be applied only to such groups.

Evidence for Environmental Influence

Heredity unquestionably influences intelligence, but a great deal of evidence indicates that upbringing also affects mental ability. We'll examine three lines of research—concerning adoption, environmental deprivation or enrichment, and generational changes in IQ—that show how life experiences shape intelligence.

Adoption Studies

Research with adopted children provides useful evidence about the impact of experience as well as heredity (Locurto, 1990; Loehlin, Horn, & Willerman, 1997). Many of the correlations in Figure 9.8 reflect the influence of the environment. For example, adopted children show some resemblance to their foster parents in IQ. This similarity is usually attributed to the fact that their foster parents shape their environment. Adoption studies also indicate that siblings reared together are more similar in IQ than siblings reared apart. This is true even for identical twins. Moreover, entirely unrelated children who are raised in the same home also show a significant resemblance in IQ. All of these findings indicate that environment influences intelligence.

Environmental Deprivation and Enrichment

If environment affects intelligence, then children who are raised in substandard circumstances should experience a gradual decline in IQ as they grow older (since other children will be progressing more rapidly). This *cumulative deprivation hypothesis* was tested decades ago. Researchers studied children consigned to understaffed orphanages and children raised in the poverty and isolation of the back hills of Appalachia (Sherman & Key, 1932; Stoddard,

Figure 9.9

The concept of heritability. A heritability ratio is an estimate of the portion of variation in a trait determined by hereditary variations—with the remainder presumably determined by environment—as these pie charts illustrate. Typical heritability estimates for intelligence range between a high of 70% and a low of 50%, although some estimates (such as Jensen's) have fallen outside this range. Bear in mind that heritability ratios are *estimates* and have certain limitations that are discussed in the text.

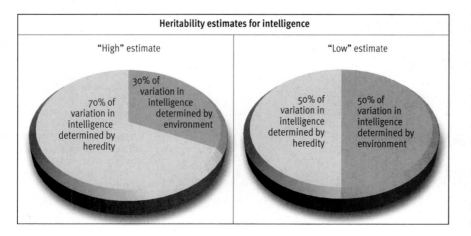

Heritability estimates for intelligence

"High" estimate

30% of variation in intelligence determined by environment

70% of variation in intelligence determined by heredity

"Low" estimate

50% of variation in intelligence determined by heredity

50% of variation in intelligence determined by environment

1943). Generally, investigators *did* find that environmental deprivation led to the predicted erosion in IQ scores.

Conversely, children who are removed from a deprived environment and placed in circumstances more conducive to learning should benefit from their environmental enrichment. Their IQ scores should gradually increase. This hypothesis has been tested by studying children who have been moved from understaffed orphanages or disadvantaged homes into high-quality, middle-class adoptive homes (Scarr & Weinberg, 1977, 1983; Schiff & Lewontin, 1986). Although there are limits on the improvements seen, the IQs of these children tend to increase noticeably (typically 10–12 points). These findings also show that environment influences IQ.

Generational Changes: The Flynn Effect

The most interesting, albeit perplexing, evidence showcasing the importance of the environment is the finding that performance on IQ tests has steadily increased over generations. This trend was not widely appreciated until recently because the tests are renormed periodically with new standardization groups, so that the mean IQ always remains at 100. However, in a study of the IQ tests used by the U.S. military, James Flynn noticed that the level of performance required to earn a score of 100 jumped upward every time the tests were renormed. Curious about this unexpected finding, he eventually gathered extensive data from 20 nations and demonstrated that IQ performance has been rising steadily all over the industrialized world since the 1930s (Flynn, 1987, 1994, 1998, 1999). Thus, the performance that would earn you an average score of 100 today, would have earned you an IQ score of about 120 back in the 1930s (see Figure 9.10). Researchers who study intelligence are now scrambling to explain this trend, which has been dubbed the "Flynn effect." About the only thing they mostly agree on is that the Flynn effect has to be attributed to environmental factors, as the modern world's gene pool could not have changed overnight (in evolutionary terms, 70 years is more like a fraction a second) (Neisser, 1998).

At this point, the proposed explanations for the Flynn effect are extremely conjectural, but it is worth reviewing some of them, as they highlight the diversity of environmental factors that may shape IQ performance. Some theorists attribute generational gains in IQ test performance to reductions in the prevalence of severe malnutrition among children (Lynn, 1998; Sigman & Whaley, 1998). Patricia Greenfield (1998) argues that advances

CONCEPT **CHECK 9.3**

Understanding Correlational Evidence on the Heredity-Environment Question

Check your understanding of how correlational findings relate to the nature versus nurture issue by indicating how you would interpret the meaning of each "piece" of evidence described below. The figures inside the parentheses are the median IQ correlations observed for the relationships described (based on McGue et al., 1993), which are shown in Figure 9.8.

In the spaces on the left, enter the letter H if the findings suggest that intelligence is shaped by heredity, enter the letter E if the findings suggest that intelligence is shaped by the environment, and enter the letter B if the findings suggest that intelligence is shaped by both (or either) heredity and environment. The answers can be found in Appendix A.

H 1. Identical twins reared apart are more similar (.72) than fraternal twins reared together (.60).

E 2. Identical twins reared together are more similar (.86) than identical twins reared apart (.72).

E 3. Siblings reared together are more similar (.47) than siblings reared apart (.24).

B 4. Biological parents and the children they rear are more similar (.42) than unrelated persons who are reared apart (no correlation if sampled randomly).

B 5. Adopted children show similarity to their biological parents (.24) and to their adoptive parents (.24).

in technology, including much maligned media such as television and video games, have enhanced visuospatial skills and other specific cognitive skills that contribute to performance on IQ tests. Wendy Williams (1998) discusses the importance of a constellation of factors, including improved schools, smaller families, better-educated parents, and higher-quality parenting. All of these speculations have some plausibility but are open to rebuttals as well. Thus, the causes of the Flynn effect remain obscure.

Figure 9.10

Generational increases in measured IQ. IQ tests are renormed periodically so that the mean score remains at 100. However, research by James Flynn has demonstrated that performance on IQ tests around the world has been increasing throughout most of the century. This graph traces the estimated increases in the United States. The level of performance that earned a score of 100 in 1995, would have only netted a score of 75 back in 1918. Or, looking at the trend from another angle, if 1918 norms were used in 1995, the average person would score 125. The causes of the "Flynn effect" are unknown, but they have to involve environmental factors. (From J. R. Flynn, 1998. originally from a figure by Dimitry Schidlovsky on p. 14 in "Get Smart, Take a Test," by J. Horgan, *Scientific American 273* (5). Copyright 1995 by Scientific American. Adapted with permission of the artist.)

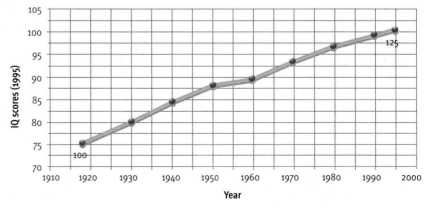

❝My research has been aimed at asking in what kind of environments genetic differences shine through and when do they remain hidden.❞
SANDRA SCARR

The Interaction of Heredity and Environment

 7d

Clearly, heredity and environment both influence intelligence to a significant degree. Indeed, many theorists now assert that the question of which is more important ought to take a backseat to the question of *how they interact* to govern IQ.

The current thinking is that heredity may set certain limits on intelligence and that environmental factors determine where individuals fall within these limits (Bouchard, 1997; Weinberg, 1989). According to Sandra Scarr, a prominent advocate of this position, genetic makeup places an upper limit on a person's IQ that can't be exceeded even when environment is ideal. Heredity is also thought to place a lower limit on an individual's IQ, although extreme circumstances (for example, being locked in an attic until age 20) could drag a person's IQ beneath this boundary. Theorists use the term ***reaction range* to refer to these genetically determined limits on IQ (or other traits).**

According to the reaction-range model, children reared in high-quality environments that promote the development of intelligence should score near the top of their potential IQ range. Children reared under less ideal circumstances should score lower in their reaction range. The reaction range for most people is *estimated* to be around 20–25 points on the IQ scale (Weinberg, 1989). The concept of a reaction range can explain why high-IQ children sometimes come from poor environments. It can also explain why low-IQ children sometimes come from very good environments (see Figure 9.11). Moreover, it can explain these apparent paradoxes without discounting the role that environment undeniably plays.

Cultural Differences in IQ Scores

Although the full range of IQ scores is seen in all ethnic groups, the average IQ for many of the larger minority groups in the United States (such as blacks, Native Americans, and Hispanics) is somewhat lower than the average for whites. The disparity ranges from 3 to 15 points, depending on the group tested and the IQ scale used (Coleman et al., 1966; Perlman & Kaufman, 1990; Suzuki & Vraniak, 1994). There is little argument about the existence of these group differences, variously referred to as racial, ethnic, or cultural differences in intelligence. The controversy concerns *why* the differences are found. A vigorous debate continues as to whether cultural differences in intelligence are due to the influence of heredity or of environment.

Jensen's Heritability Explanation

In 1969 Arthur Jensen sparked a heated war of words by arguing that cultural differences in IQ are largely due to heredity. The cornerstone for Jensen's argument was his analysis suggesting that the heritability of intelligence is about 80%. Essentially, he asserted that (1) intelligence is largely genetic in origin, and (2) therefore, genetic factors are "strongly implicated" as the cause of ethnic differences in intelligence. Jensen's article triggered a huge controversy, a flurry of highly critical rebuttals, and a good deal of additional research on the determinants of intelligence.

Twenty-five years later, Richard Herrnstein and Charles Murray (1994) reignited the same controversy with the publication of their widely discussed book *The Bell Curve.* Their main thesis is that in recent decades intellectual ability, which they believe

<hr />

Figure 9.11

Reaction range. The concept of reaction range posits that heredity sets limits on one's intellectual potential (represented by the horizontal bars), while the quality of one's environment influences where one scores within this range (represented by the dots on the bars). People raised in enriched environments should score near the top of their reaction range, whereas people raised in poor-quality environments should score near the bottom of their range. Genetic limits on IQ can be inferred only indirectly, so theorists aren't sure whether reaction ranges are narrow (like Ted's) or wide (like Chris's). The concept of reaction range can explain how two people with similar genetic potential can be quite different in intelligence (compare Tom and Jack) and how two people reared in environments of similar quality can score quite differently (compare Alice and Jack).

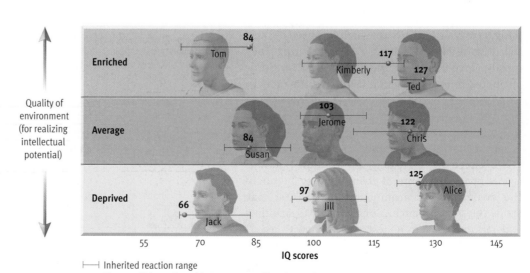

Quality of environment (for realizing intellectual potential)

├──┤ Inherited reaction range
● Measured IQ, as shaped by interaction of heredity and environment

is largely inherited, has become the primary determinant of individuals' success in life. They go on to argue that ethnic and cultural differences in average intelligence are substantial and not easily reduced and that these differences have profound and disturbing implications. Perhaps having learned from the bitter criticism received by Arthur Jensen, they try to tiptoe around the incendiary issue of whether ethnic differences in average IQ are due to heredity. But their discussions of "dysgenic pressures" in ethnic groups clearly imply that these disparities are at least partly genetic in origin. Moreover, the implicit message throughout the book is that disadvantaged groups cannot avoid their fate because it is their genetic destiny.

The central idea of *The Bell Curve,* that we are evolving toward a meritocracy based on intellect, may have merit. Nonetheless, it is curious that neither of the authors has ever published a single scientific article on intelligence (Dorfman, 1995). By choosing to present their data exclusively in a popular book intended for the general reader, Herrnstein and Murray avoided having their data analyses subjected to the critical scrutiny that scientific data must withstand. It is not unusual for scientists to describe their work in a popular book, but this normally occurs after the scientists have published many technical articles on a topic, which they then attempt to summarize for the layperson. Herrnstein and Murray did not have any work of their own on intelligence to summarize.

In any event, heritability explanations for ethnic differences in IQ have a variety of flaws and weaknesses (Dorfman, 1995; Myerson et al., 1998; Resnick & Fienberg, 1997; Sternberg, 1995). For example, a heritability estimate applies only to the specific group on which the estimate is based. Heritability estimates for intelligence have been based on studies dominated by white subjects (Brody, 1992). Hence, there is doubt about the validity of applying this estimate to other cultural groups.

Moreover, even if one accepts the assumption that the heritability of IQ is very high, it does not follow logically that differences in group averages must be due largely to heredity. Leon Kamin has presented a compelling analogy that highlights the logical fallacy in this reasoning (see Figure 9.12):

We fill a white sack and a black sack with a mixture of different genetic varieties of corn seed. We make certain that the proportions of each variety of seed are identical in each sack. We then plant the seed from the white sack in fertile Field A, while that from the black sack is planted in barren Field B. We will observe that

within Field A, as within Field B, there is considerable variation in the height of individual corn plants. This variation will be due largely to genetic factors (seed differences). We will also observe, however, that the average height of plants in Field A is greater than that in Field B. That difference will be entirely due to environmental factors (the soil). The same is true of IQs: differences in the average IQ of various human populations could be entirely due to environmental differences, even if within each population all variation were due to genetic differences! (Eysenck & Kamin, 1981, p. 97)

Kamin's analogy shows that even if the heritability of intelligence is high, group differences in average IQ *could* still be caused entirely (or in part)

Web Link 9.4

Upstream Issues:
The Bell Curve
The editors of *Upstream*, champions of "politically incorrect" conversation, have assembled perhaps the broadest collection of commentaries on the Web regarding Herrnstein & Murray's (1994) *The Bell Curve.* In spite of the marked political conservatism of this site, a full range of opinion and analyses of the book is assembled here.

Between-group differences (cause: the soils in which the plants were grown)

Barren field
Within-group differences (cause: genetic variations in the seeds)

Fertile field
Within-group differences (cause: genetic variations in the seeds)

Figure 9.12

Genetics and between-group differences on a trait.
Kamin's analogy (see text) shows how between-group differences on a trait (the height of corn plants) could be due to environment, even if the trait is largely inherited. The same reasoning presumably applies to the trait of human intelligence.

"Despite more than half a century of repeated efforts by psychologists to improve the intelligence of children, particularly those in the lower quarter of the IQ distribution relative to those in the upper half of the distribution, strong evidence is still lacking as to whether or not it can be done."
ARTHUR JENSEN

by environmental factors, a reality acknowledged by Arthur Jensen (1994b) and the authors of *The Bell Curve*.

Socioeconomic Disadvantage as an Explanation

Many social scientists argue that minority students' IQ scores are depressed because these children tend to grow up in deprived environments that create a disadvantage—both in school and on IQ tests. There is no question that, on the average, whites and minorities tend to be raised in very different circumstances. Most minority groups have endured a long history of economic discrimination and are greatly overrepresented in the lower social classes. A lower-class upbringing tends to carry a number of disadvantages that work against the development of a youngster's full intellectual potential (Blau, 1981; McLoyd, 1998). In comparison to the middle and upper classes, lower-class children tend to be exposed to fewer books, to have fewer learning supplies, to have less privacy for concentrated study, and to get less parental assistance in learning. Typically, they also have poorer role models for language development, experience less pressure to work hard on intellectual pursuits, and attend poorer-quality schools (Wolf, 1965).

In light of these disadvantages, it's not surprising that children from higher classes tend to get higher IQ scores (Bouchard & Segal, 1985; Williams & Ceci, 1997). The average IQ in the lowest social classes runs about 20–30 points lower than the average IQ in the highest social classes (Locurto, 1991). This is true even if race is factored out of the picture by studying whites exclusively. Given the overrepresentation of minorities in the lower classes, many researchers argue that ethnic differences in intelligence are really social class differences in disguise.

Cultural Bias on IQ Tests as an Explanation

Some critics of IQ tests have argued that cultural differences in IQ scores are partly the result of a cultural bias built into IQ tests. They argue that because IQ tests are constructed by white, middle-class psychologists, they naturally draw on experience and knowledge typical of white, middle-class lifestyles and use language and vocabulary that reflect the white, middle-class origins of their developers (Helms, 1992).

Several lines of research provide modest support for the notion that IQ tests are slanted in favor of white middle-class students, at the expense of lower-class ethnic minorities (Bernal, 1984; Cole, 1981; Hilliard, 1984; Williams et al., 1980). However, the balance of evidence suggests that the cultural slant

on IQ tests is less problematic than critics expected. Cultural bias appears to produce only weak negative effects on the IQ scores of minority examinees (R. Kaplan, 1985; Oakland & Parmelee, 1985; Reynolds, 1995).

Nonetheless, taken together, the various rebuttals of Jensen's views provide serious challenges to his theory. Genetic explanations for ethnic differences in IQ appear weak at best—and suspiciously racist at worst. In fairness to Jensen, his writings focus squarely on empirical data and theoretical issues. He studiously avoids racist rhetoric. But Block and Dworkin (1976) note that others have cited his conclusions while advocating social programs with racist overtones.

Unfortunately, since the earliest days of IQ testing, some people have used IQ tests to further elitist goals. The current controversy about ethnic differences in IQ is just another replay of a record that has been heard before. For instance, beginning in 1913, Henry Goddard tested a great many immigrants to the United States at Ellis Island in New York. Goddard reported that 79% of the Italian immigrants, 80% of the Hungarian immigrants, and 83% of the Jewish immigrants tested out as *feeble-minded*. As you can see, claims about ethnic deficits in intelligence are nothing new. Only the victims have changed.

There is, however, one new twist to the debate about cultural differences in intelligence. A handful of recent studies have suggested that some ethnic minority groups—those of Asian American descent—score slightly *above average* on IQ tests (Lynn, 1987, 1991, 1995; Vernon, 1982). Admittedly, the comparative data on Asian Americans' IQ performance are still sparse, and a great deal of additional research is needed (Suzuki & Gutkin, 1994). But the IQ data are consistent with the much more extensive data available on Asian Americans' school performance. These data clearly show that most Asian American groups tend to earn higher grade point averages and to have higher graduation rates (see Figure 9.13) than those of other ethnic groups, including whites (Sue & Okazaki, 1990).

The outstanding intellectual and educational attainments of Asian Americans constitute a perplexing phenomenon in search of an explanation. The tentative explanations proposed thus far focus primarily on how Asian cultural values may encourage and nurture educational achievement. Investigators theorize that in comparison to most other groups, Asian families place greater emphasis on the value of education, put their children under more pressure to succeed in school, instill more respect for elders

Courtesy, Arthur R. Jensen

such as teachers, and exert more control over their children's study habits. Sue and Okazaki (1990) also speculate that Asian Americans have come to view education as their most realistic route to upward mobility, as racial discrimination has limited their opportunities for advancement through noneducational routes (such as entertainment, politics, and sports).

The debate about cultural differences in intelligence illustrates how IQ tests have often become entangled in thorny social conflicts. This is unfortunate, because it brings politics to the testing enterprise. Intelligence testing has many legitimate and valuable uses. However, the controversy associated with intelligence tests has undermined their value, leading to some of the new trends that we discuss in the next section.

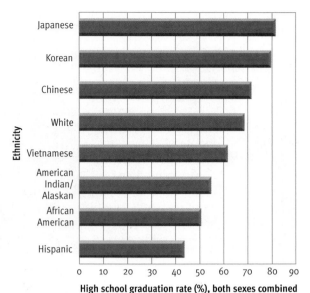

Figure 9.13

Asian Americans' academic success. On various measures of educational success, such as the high school graduation rates shown here, the performance of Asian American students tends to exceed that of other ethnic groups in the United States. More research is needed on the matter, but most theorists believe that cultural factors are responsible for Asian Americans' academic prowess. (Based on data in "Asian-American Educational Achievements: A Phenomenon in Search of an Explanation," by S. Sue and S. Okazaki, 1990, *American Psychologist*, 42, 37–45. American Psychological Association.)

New Directions in the Assessment and Study of Intelligence

Intelligence testing has been through a period of turmoil, and changes are on the horizon. In fact, many changes have occurred already. Let's discuss some of the major new trends and projections for the future.

Reducing Reliance on IQ Tests

In recent decades, many experts in testing and education have recommended a reduced emphasis on standardized tests in the United States. Today, such a reduction is clearly under way. Many school districts are shifting from IQ tests to achievement and aptitude tests. The problem is not so much that IQ tests are flawed—experts generally agree that they are reasonably sound measurement instruments (Snyderman & Rothman, 1987). However, these experts also agree that intelligence tests are terribly misunderstood by the general public. IQ scores are typically viewed as "magical" numbers that capture the essence of individuals' ability (Weinberg, 1989). Far too many people believe that IQ tests measure an innate, fixed mental capacity that is truly general in scope and of the utmost significance for success in life. Some authorities have argued that the concept of IQ is so bound up in myth that it has outlived its usefulness. They suggest that the term "IQ" should be done away with and that intelligence scales should be relabeled as tests of scholastic ability or academic aptitude. Movement in this direction is apparent, as most group intelligence

tests have deleted the word *intelligence* from their names (Fremer, 1994).

Exploring Biological Indexes of Intelligence

Recent years have also seen an increased interest in biological indexes of intelligence. Arthur Jensen (1987, 1993b, 1998), Hans Eysenck (1988, 1989), and other researchers have attempted to find raw physiological indicators of general intelligence. Their search for a "culture-free" measure of intelligence has led them to focus on sensory processes, much as Sir Francis Galton did over a hundred years ago. Armed with much more sophisticated equipment, they hope to succeed where Galton failed.

Jensen's (1982, 1987, 1992) studies of mental speed are representative of this line of inquiry. In his studies, Jensen measures *reaction time* (RT), using a panel of paired buttons and lights. On each trial, the subject rests a hand on a "home button." When one of the lights is activated, the participant is supposed to push the button for that light as quickly as possible. The time between the onset of the stimulus light and the release of the home button is the participant's reaction time. RT is typically averaged over a number of trials involving varied numbers of lights. Modest correlations (.20s to .30s) have been found between faster RTs and higher scores on conventional IQ tests.

Figure 9.14

Research on inspection time as a biological index of intelligence. **(Left)** In studies of inspection time, participants are shown stimuli for very brief durations and are asked to make accurate judgments about them (such as whether the longer line is on the right or the left). **(Right)** Each participant's accuracy in making these perceptual discriminations is graphed as a function of exposure duration. A subject's inspection time for a particular task is the exposure duration required to achieve a certain level of accuracy. In this case, 85% accuracy is the criterion and the subject's inspection time for the task is 14 milliseconds. (Graph adapted from "Nonstationarity and the Measurement of Psychophysical Response in a Visual Inspection Time Task," by I. J. Deary, P. G. Caryl & G. J. Gibson, 1993, *Perception, 22* p. 1250. Copyright © 1993 by Pion Ltd. Adapted by permission.)

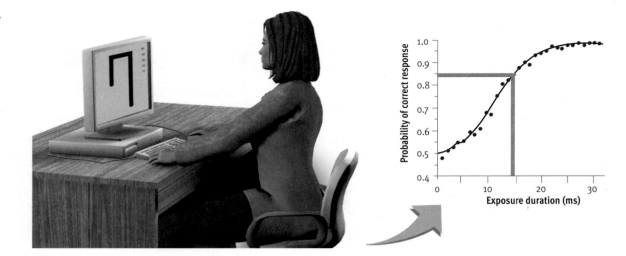

Michael Marsland/Yale University

"To understand intelligent behavior, we need to move beyond the fairly restrictive tasks that have been used both in experimental laboratories and in psychometric tests of intelligence."
ROBERT STERNBERG

Jensen's findings suggest an association between raw mental speed and intelligence, as Galton originally suggested. This correlation is theoretically interesting and, in retrospect, not all that surprising. Many conventional IQ tests have imposed demanding time limits on examinees, working under the assumption that "fast is smart." That said, the correlation between RT and IQ appears to be too weak to give RT any practical value as an index of intelligence.

However, another approach to measuring mental speed may have more practical potential. Measures of *inspection time* assess how long it takes participants to make simple perceptual discriminations that meet a certain criterion of accuracy (Deary & Stough, 1996). For example, in a series of trials, participants may be asked repeatedly to indicate which of two lines is shorter. The pairs of lines are presented for very brief exposures and participants are told to concentrate on making *accurate* judgments. A person's inspection time is the exposure duration required for that person to achieve a specific level of accuracy, such as 85% correct judgments (see Figure 9.14). Correlations in the vicinity of .50 have been found between participants' inspection time scores and their IQ scores (Deary & Stough, 1996). These correlations are high enough to have practical value, although a great deal of work remains to be done to standardize inspection time measures and to figure out why they are associated with intelligence (Deary, 1995).

Investigating Cognitive Processes in Intelligent Behavior

As noted in Chapters 1 and 8, psychologists are increasingly taking a cognitive perspective in their efforts to study many topics. For over a century, the investigation of intelligence has been approached

primarily from a *testing perspective*. This perspective emphasizes measuring the *amount* of intelligence people have and figuring out why some have more than others. In contrast, the *cognitive perspective* focuses on how people *use* their intelligence. The interest is in process rather than amount. In particular, cognitive psychologists focus on the information-processing strategies that underlie intelligence.

The application of the cognitive perspective to intelligence has been spearheaded by Robert Sternberg (1988b, 1991, 1997). His *triarchic theory of human intelligence* consists of three parts: the contextual, experiential, and componential subtheories. In his *contextual subtheory*, Sternberg argues that intelligence is a culturally defined concept. He asserts that different manifestations of intelligent behavior are valued in different contexts. For example, the verbal skills emphasized in North American culture may take a back seat to hunting skills in another culture.

In his *experiential subtheory*, Sternberg explores the relationships between experience and intelligence. He emphasizes two factors as the hallmarks of intelligent behavior. The first is the ability to deal effectively with novelty—new tasks, demands, and situations. The second factor is the ability to learn how to handle familiar tasks automatically and effortlessly. Sternberg's *componential subtheory* describes the specific types of mental processes that intelligent thought depends on (see Figure 9.15).

Investigations of cognitive processes in intelligent behavior have interesting implications for intelligence testing. Cognitive research has shown that more-intelligent subjects spend more time figuring out how to best represent problems and planning how to solve them than less-intelligent subjects do. Because planning takes time, Sternberg (1985) argues that traditional IQ tests place too much emphasis on speed. He also argues that IQ tests are too narrow in terms of what they attempt to measure, which is a theme echoed by others.

Expanding the Concept of Intelligence

In recent years, many theorists have concluded that traditional IQ tests are too narrow in focus (Ceci, 1990; Greenspan & Driscoll, 1997). These theorists argue that to assess intelligence in a truly general sense, tests should sample from a broader range of tasks. This view has been articulated particularly well by Howard Gardner (1983, 1993, 1998).

According to Gardner, IQ tests have generally emphasized verbal and mathematical skills, to the exclusion of other important skills. He suggests the existence of a number of relatively autonomous *human intelligences,* which are listed in Table 9.2. To build his list of separate intelligences, Gardner reviewed the evidence on cognitive capacities in normal individuals, people suffering from brain damage, and special populations, such as prodigies and idiot savants. He concluded that humans exhibit eight intelligences: logical-mathematical, linguistic, musical, spatial, bodily-kinesthetic, interpersonal, intrapersonal, and naturalist. These intelligences obviously include a variety of talents that are not assessed by conventional IQ tests.

Gardner is currently investigating whether these intelligences are largely independent, as his theory

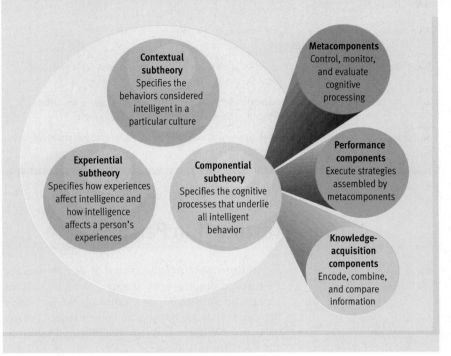

Figure 9.15

Sternberg's triarchic theory of intelligence. Sternberg's model of intelligence consists of three parts: the contextual subtheory, the experiential subtheory, and the componential subtheory. Much of Sternberg's research has been devoted to the componential subtheory, as he has attempted to identify the cognitive processes that contribute to intelligence. He believes that these processes fall into three groups: metacomponents, performance components, and knowledge-acquisition components. (Adapted from *Beyond IQ: A Triarchic Theory of Human Intelligence*, by Robert J. Sternberg, 1985. Copyright © 1985 Cambridge University Press. Adapted by permission.)

Table 9.3   Gardner's Eight Intelligences

Intelligence	End-States	Core Components
Logical-mathematical	Scientist Mathematician	Sensitivity to, and capacity to discern, logical or numerical patterns; ability to handle long chains of reasoning
Linguistic	Poet Journalist	Sensitivity to the sounds, rhythms, and meanings of words; sensitivity to the different functions of language
Musical	Composer Violinist	Abilities to produce and appreciate rhythm, pitch, and timbre; appreciation of the forms of musical expressiveness
Spatial	Navigator Sculptor	Capacities to perceive the visual-spatial world accurately and to perform transformations on one's initial perceptions
Bodily-kinesthetic	Dancer Athlete	Abilities to control one's body movements and to handle objects skillfully
Interpersonal	Therapist Salesperson	Capacities to discern and respond appropriately to the moods, temperaments, motivations, and desires of other people
Intrapersonal	Person with detailed, accurate self-knowledge	Access to one's own feelings and the ability to discriminate among them and draw upon them to guide behavior; knowledge of one's own strengths, weaknesses, desires, and intelligences
Naturalist	Biologist Naturalist	Abilities to recognize and categorize objects and processes in nature

Courtesy of Howard Gardner, photo © Jay Gardner

"*It is high time that the view of intelligence be widened to incorporate a range of human computational capacities. . . . But where is it written that intelligence needs to be determined on the basis of tests?*"
HOWARD GARDNER

(Based on "Multiple Intelligences Go to School: Educational Implications of the Theory of Multiple Intelligences," by H. Gardner and T. Hatch, 1989, *Educational Researcher, 18* (8), 4–10. American Educational Research Association. Additional information from Gardner, 1998)

Recognizing Theories of Intelligence

Check your understanding of various theories on the nature of intelligence by matching the names of their originators with the brief descriptions of the theories' main themes that appear below. Choose from the following theorists: (a) Sir Francis Galton, (b) Howard Gardner, (c) Arthur Jensen, (d) Sandra Scarr, and (e) Robert Sternberg. The answers are in Appendix A.

_B_ **1.** This theorist posited eight human intelligences.

_A_ **2.** On the basis of a study of eminence and success in families, this theorist concluded that intelligence is inherited.

_C_ **3.** This theorist stated that the heritability of intelligence is about 80% and that IQ differences between ethnic groups are mainly due to genetics.

_D_ **4.** This theorist stated that heredity sets certain limits on intelligence and that environmental factors determine where one falls within those limits.

_E_ **5.** This person's theory of intelligence is divided into three parts: the contextual, experiential, and componential subtheories.

asserts. He has devised scales to measure each form of intelligence to examine interrelations among them. Subjects who score more than one standard deviation above the mean on a scale are said to have a "strength" in that area. Participants who score more than one standard deviation below the mean on a scale are said to have a "weakness" in that area. If subjects were to show strength in most areas or weakness in most areas, this result would undermine Gardner's argument that there are a number of basic mental abilites that are largely independent of one another. For the most part, however, Gardner has found that people tend to display a mixture of strong, intermediate, and weak abilities. A great deal of additional research is needed to evaluate Gardner's ambitious and refreshing theory of intelligence. However, demands for broader assessments of intelligence appear likely to continue for the foreseeable future.

Putting It in Perspective

As you probably noticed, three of our integrative themes dominated this chapter. Our discussions repeatedly illustrated that cultural factors shape behavior, that heredity and environment jointly influence behavior, and that psychology evolves in a sociohistorical context.

Pervasive psychological testing is largely a Western phenomenon. Most non-Western cultures depend far less than we do on standardized tests. Indeed, the entire enterprise of testing is downright foreign to many cultures. The concept of general intelligence also has a special, Western flavor to it. Many non-Western cultures have very different ideas about the nature of intelligence. Within Western societies, the observed ethnic differences in average intelligence also illustrate the importance of culture, as these disparities appear to be due in large part to environmental factors associated with culture. Thus, we see once again that if we hope to achieve a sound understanding of behavior, we need to appreciate the cultural contexts in which behavior unfolds.

Human intelligence is shaped by a complex interaction of hereditary and environmental factors. We've drawn a similar conclusion before in other chapters where we examined other topics. However, this chapter should have enhanced your appreciation of this idea by illustrating in detail how scientists arrive at this conclusion. Thus, you saw how psychologists have conducted family stud-

ies, twin studies, adoption studies, environmental enrichment studies, and environmental deprivation studies, in their efforts to document the joint influence of genetics and experience.

Finally, we saw more evidence that psychology evolves in a sociohistorical context. Prevailing social attitudes have always exerted some influence on testing practices and the interpretation of test results. In the first half of the 20th century, a strong current of racial and class prejudice was apparent in the United States and Britain. This prejudice supported the idea that IQ tests measured innate ability and that "undesirable" groups scored poorly because of their genetic inferiority. Although these beliefs did not go unchallenged within psychology, their widespread acceptance in the field reflected the social values of the time. Today, the continuing, ferocious debate about the roots of cultural differences in intelligence shows that issues in psychology often have far-reaching social and political implications.

It's ironic that IQ tests have sometimes been associated with social prejudice. When used properly, intelligence tests provide relatively objective measures of mental ability that are probably less prone to bias than the subjective judgments of teachers or employers. Today, psychological tests serve many diverse purposes. In the upcoming Personal Application, we focus on creativity tests and on the nature of creative thinking and creative people.

PERSONAL APPLICATION

Measuring and Understanding Creativity

Answer the following "true" or "false":

_____ 1 Creative ideas often come out of nowhere.

_____ 2 Creativity usually occurs in a burst of insight.

_____ 3 Creativity depends on inspiration far more than on perspiration.

_____ 4 Creativity and intelligence are unrelated.

Intelligence is not the only type of mental ability that psychologists have studied. They have devised tests to explore a variety of mental abilities. Among these, creativity is certainly one of the most interesting. People tend to view creativity as an essential trait for artists, musicians, and writers, but it is important in *many* walks of life. In this Application, we'll discuss psychologists' efforts to measure and understand creativity. As we progress, you'll learn that all the statements above are false.

The Nature of Creativity

What makes thought creative? *Creativity* **involves the generation of ideas that are original, novel, and useful.** Creative thinking is fresh, innovative, and inventive. But novelty by itself is not enough. In addition to being unusual, creative thinking must be adaptive. It must be appropriate to the situation and problem.

Does Creativity Occur in a Burst of Insight?

It is widely believed that creativity usually involves sudden flashes of insight and great leaps of imagination. Robert Weisberg (1986) calls this belief the "Aha! myth." Undeniably, creative bursts of insight do occur (Feldman, 1988). However, the evidence suggests that major creative achievements generally are logical extensions of existing ideas, involving long, hard work and many small, faltering steps forward

(Weisberg, 1993). Creative ideas do not come out of nowhere. They come from a deep well of experience and training in a specific area, whether it's music, painting, business, or science (Weisberg, 1999). As Snow (1986) puts it, "Creativity is not a light bulb in the mind, as most cartoons depict it. It is an accomplishment born of intensive study, long reflection, persistence, and interest" (p. 1033).

Does Creativity Depend on Divergent Thinking?

According to many theorists, the key to creativity lies in *divergent thinking*—thinking "that goes off in different directions," as J. P. Guilford (1959) put it. Guilford distinguished between convergent thinking and divergent thinking. **In *convergent thinking* one tries to narrow down a list of alternatives to converge on a single correct answer.** For example, when you take a multiple-choice exam, you try to eliminate incorrect options until you hit on the correct response. Most training in school encourages convergent thinking. **In *divergent thinking* one tries to expand the range of alternatives by generating many possible solutions.** Imagine that you work for an advertising agency. To come up with as many slogans as possible for a client's product, you must use divergent thinking. Some of your slogans may be clear losers, and eventually you will have to engage in convergent thinking to pick the best, but coming up with the range of new possibilities depends on divergent thinking.

Thirty years of research on divergent thinking has yielded mixed results. As a whole, the evidence suggests that divergent thinking contributes to creativity, but it clearly does not represent the essence of creativity, as originally proposed (Brown, 1989; Plucker & Renzulli, 1999). In retrospect, it was probably unrealistic to expect creativity to depend on a single cognitive

skill. According to Sternberg (1988a), the cognitive processes that underlie creativity are multifaceted.

Measuring Creativity

Although its nature may be elusive, creativity clearly is important in today's world. Creative masterpieces in the arts and literature enrich human existence. Creative insights in the sciences illuminate people's understanding of the world. Creative inventions fuel our technological progress. Thus, it is understandable that psychologists have been interested in measuring creativity with psychological tests.

How Do Psychological Tests Measure Creativity?

A diverse array of psychological tests have been devised to measure individuals' creativity (Cooper, 1991). Usually, the items on creativity tests give respondents a specific starting point and then require them to generate as many possibilities as they can in a short period of time. Typical items on a creativity test might include the following: (1) List as many uses as you can for a newspaper. (2) Think of as many fluids that burn as you can. (3) Imagine that people no longer need sleep and think of as many consequences as you can. Participants' scores on these tests depend on the *number* of alternatives they generate and on the *originality* and *usefulness* of the alternatives.

Over the years, one of the more widely used creativity tests has been the Remote Associates Test (RAT) developed by Sarnoff and Martha Mednick (1967). This test is based on the assumption that creative people see unusual relationships and make nonobvious connections between ideas. Items on the test require respondents to figure out the obscure links (the remote associations) among three words by coming up with a fourth word that is related to the three stimulus words. Examples of items similar to those found on the RAT are shown in Figure 9.16.

How Well Do Tests Predict Creative Productivity?

In general, studies indicate that creativity tests are mediocre predictors of creative achievement in the real world (Hocevar & Bachelor, 1989; Plucker & Renzulli, 1999). Why? One reason is that these tests measure creativity in the abstract, as a *general trait*. However, the accumulation of evidence suggests that *creativity is specific to particular domains* (Amabile, 1990, 1996; Baer, 1994). Despite some rare exceptions, creative people usually excel in a single field, in which they typically have considerable training and expertise (Policastro & Gardner, 1999). An innovative physicist might have no potential to be a creative poet or an inventive advertising executive. Measuring this person's creativity outside of physics may be meaningless. Thus, creativity tests may have limited value because they measure creativity out of context.

Even if better tests of creativity were devised, predicting creative achievement would probably still prove difficult. Why? Because creative achievement depends on many factors besides creativity. Creative productivity over the course of an individual's career will depend on his or her motivation, personality, and intelligence, as well as on situational factors, including training, mentoring, and good fortune (Amabile, 1983; Feldman, 1999).

Correlates of Creativity

What are creative people like? Are they brighter, or more open minded, or less well adjusted than average? A great deal of research has been conducted on the correlates of creativity.

Is There a Creative Personality?

Creative people exhibit the full range of personality traits, but investigators have found modest correlations between certain personality characteristics and creativity

Instructions: For each set of three words, try to think of a fourth word that is related to all three words. For example, the words ROUGH, RESISTANCE, and BEER suggest the word DRAFT because of the phrases ROUGH DRAFT, DRAFT RESISTANCE, and DRAFT BEER.

1. CHARMING	STUDENT	VALIANT
2. FOOD	CATCHER	HOT
3. HEARTED	FEET	BITTER
4. DARK	SHOT	SUN
5. CANADIAN	GOLF	SANDWICH
6. TUG	GRAVY	SHOW
7. ATTORNEY	SELF	SPENDING
8. MAGIC	PITCH	POWER
9. ARM	COAL	PEACH
10. TYPE	GHOST	STORY

Figure 9.16

Remote associates as an index of creativity. One of the more interesting creativity tests is the Remote Associates Test (RAT) developed by Sarnoff and Martha Mednick (1967). The items shown here (from Matlin, 1989) are similar to those on the RAT. See whether you can identify the remote associations between the three stimulus words by coming up with a fourth word that is related to all three. The answers can be found in Figure 9.17.

(Ochse, 1990). Based on an analysis of over 80 studies, Feist (1998) concludes that highly creative people "are more autonomous, introverted, open to new experiences, norm-doubting, self-confident, self-accepting, driven, ambitious, dominant, hostile, and impulsive" (p. 299). At the core of this set of personality characteristics are the related traits of independence and nonconformity. Creative people tend to think for themselves and are less easily influenced by the opinions of others than the average person is. Sternberg and Lubart (1992) also suggest that creative people are willing to grow and change, willing to take risks, and willing to work at overcoming obstacles.

Are Creativity and Intelligence Related?

Are creative people exceptionally smart? Conceptually, creativity and intelligence represent different types of mental ability. Thus, it's not surprising that measures of creativity and measures of intelligence are only weakly related (Sternberg & O'Hara, 1999). They're not entirely unrelated, however, as creativity in most fields requires a minimum level of intelligence. Hence, most highly creative people are probably above average in intelligence (Ochse, 1990).

Is There a Connection Between Creativity and Mental Illness?

There may be a connection between truly exceptional creativity and mental illness. The list of creative geniuses who suffered from psychological disorders is endless (Prentky, 1989). Kafka, Hemingway, Rembrandt, Van Gogh, Chopin, Tchaikovsky, Descartes, and Newton are but a few examples (see Figure 9.18). Of course, a statistical association cannot be demonstrated by citing a handful of examples.

In this case, however, some statistical data are available. And these data *do* suggest a correlation between creative genius and maladjustment—in particular, mood disorders such as depression. When Andreasen (1987) studied 30 accomplished writers who had been invited as visiting faculty to the prestigious Iowa Writers Workshop, she

Figure 9.17

Answers to the remote associates items.

1. PRINCE	6. BOAT
2. DOG	7. DEFENSE
3. COLD	8. BLACK
4. GLASSES	9. PIT
5. CLUB	10. WRITER

found that 80% of her sample had suffered a mood disorder at some point in their lives. In a similar study of 59 female writers from another writers' conference, Ludwig (1994) found that 56% had experienced depression. These figures are far above the base rate (roughly 8%) for mood disorders in the general population. Other studies have also found an association between creativity and mood disorders, as well as other kinds of psychological disorders (Frantom & Sherman, 1999; Jamison, 1988; Ludwig, 1998; Post, 1996; Schildkraut, Hirshfeld, & Murphy, 1994). Perhaps the most ambitious examination of the issue has been Arnold Ludwig's (1995) analyses of the biographies of 1004 people who achieved eminence in 18 fields. He found greatly elevated rates of depression and other disorders among eminent writers, artists, and composers (see Figure 9.19).

Thus, accumulating empirical data tentatively suggest that there may be a correlation between major creative achievement and vulnerability to mood disorders. According to Andreasen (1996), creativity and maladjustment probably are *not* causally related. Instead, she speculates that certain cognitive styles may both foster creativity and predispose people to psychological disorders. Another, more mundane possibility is that creative individuals' elevated pathology may simply reflect all the difficulty and frustration they experience as they struggle to get their ideas or works accepted in artistic fields that enjoy relatively little public support (Csikszentmihalyi, 1994, 1999).

Figure 9.18

Examples of people who achieved creative eminence and suffered from psychological disorders. As these brief lists show, it is easy to compile rosters of great artists, scientists, composers, and writers who struggled with mental illness. However, while interesting, anecdotal evidence such as this cannot demonstrate that an association exists between creative eminence and mental disorder. (Based on Prentky, 1980 and Rothenberg, 1990)

Artists	Scientists	Composers	Writers
Bosch	Copernicus	Beethoven	Blake
Durer	Descartes	Berlioz	Coleridge
Goya	Kepler	Chopin	Dostoyevsky
Kandinsky	Linnaeus	Handel	Hemingway
Raphael	Mendel	Saint-Saens	Kafka
Rembrandt	Newton	Schubert	Poe
Van Gogh	Pascal	Tchaikovsky	Plath

Rembrandt
Rembrandt, Harmensz, van Rijn, Self-Portrait with Beard. Museu de Arte, Sao Paulo, Brazil. Giraudon/Art Resource, NY.

Chopin
Delacroix, Eugene, Portrait of Chopin, Louvre, Paris: Giraudon/Art Resource, NY.

Copernicus
Pomerian, 16th cent. Portrait of Nicolas Copernicus. Museum, torun, Poland. Erich Lessing/Art Resource, NY.

Figure 9.19

Estimated prevalence of psychological disorders among people who achieved creative eminence. Ludwig (1995) studied biographies of 1004 people who had clearly achieved eminence in one of 18 fields and tried to determine whether each person suffered from any specific mental disorders in their lifetimes. The data summarized here show the prevalence rates for depression and for a mental disorder of any kind for four fields where creativity is often the key to achieving eminence. As you can see, the estimated prevalence of mental illness was extremely elevated among eminent writers, artists, and composers (but not natural scientists) in comparison to the general population, with depression accounting for much of this elevation.

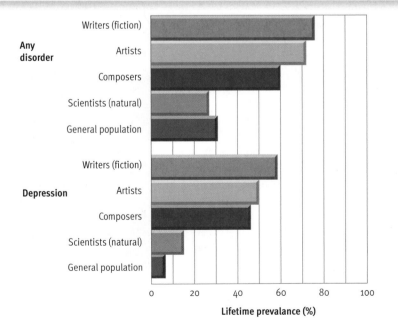

The Intelligence Debate, Appeals to Ignorance, and Reification

A *fallacy* is a mistake or error in the process of reasoning. Cognitive scientists who study how people think have long lists of common errors that people make in their reasoning processes. One of these fallacies has a curious name, which is the *appeal to ignorance*. It involves misusing the general lack of knowledge or information on an issue (a lack of knowledge is a kind of ignorance) to support an argument. This fallacy often surfaces in the debate about the relative influence of heredity and environment on intelligence. Before we tackle the more difficult issue of how this fallacy shows up in the debate about intelligence, let's start with a simpler example.

Appeal to Ignorance

Do ghosts exist? This is probably not the kind of question you expected to find in your psychology textbook, but it can clarify the appeal to ignorance. Those who assert that ghosts *do* exist will often support their conclusion by arguing that no one can prove that ghosts do *not* exist; therefore ghosts must exist. The lack of evidence or inability to show that ghosts do not exist is used to conclude the opposite. Conversely, those who assert that ghosts *do not* exist often rely on the same logic. They argue that no one can prove that ghosts exist; therefore, they must not exist. Can you see what is wrong with these appeals to ignorance? The lack of information on an issue cannot be used to support any conclusion—other than the conclusion that we are too ignorant to draw a conclusion.

One interesting aspect of the appeal to ignorance is that the same appeal can be used to support two conclusions that are diametrically opposed to each other. This paradox is a telltale clue that appeals to ignorance involve flawed reasoning. It is easy to see what is wrong with appeals to ignorance when the opposite arguments

(ghosts exist—ghosts do not exist) are presented together and the lack of evidence on the issue under discussion is obvious. However, when the same fallacy surfaces in more complex debates and the appeal to ignorance is not as blatant, the strategy can be more difficult to recognize. Let's look at how the appeal to ignorance has been used in the debate about intelligence.

As you saw in the main body of the chapter, the debate about the relative contributions of nature and nurture to intelligence is one of psychology's longest-running controversies. This complex and multifaceted debate is exceptionally bitter and acrimonious because it has far-reaching sociopolitical repercussions. In this debate, one argument that has frequently been made is that we have little or no evidence that intelligence can be increased by environmental (educational) interventions; therefore, intelligence must be mostly inherited. In other words, the argument runs: no one has demonstrated that intelligence is largely shaped by environment, so it must be largely inherited. This argument was part of Jensen's (1969) landmark treatise that greatly intensified the debate about intelligence, and it

was one of the arguments made by by Herrnstein and Murray (1994) in their controversial book, *The Bell Curve*. What the argument refers to is the evidence that educational enrichment programs such as Head Start, which have been designed to enhance the intellectual development of underprivileged children, generally have not produced substantial, long-term gains in IQ (Bentler & Woodward, 1978; Neisser et al., 1996). These findings may have some important implications for government policy in the educational arena, but the way in which they have been applied to the nature-nurture debate regarding intelligence has resulted in an appeal to ignorance. In its simplest form, the absence of evidence showing that environmental changes can increase intelligence is used to support the conclusion that intelligence is mostly determined by genetic inheritance. But the absence of evidence (ignorance) cannot be used to argue for or against a position.

By the way, if you have assimilated some of the critical thinking skills discussed in earlier chapters you may be thinking, "Wait a minute. Aren't there alternative explanations for the failure of educational enrichment

For the most part, educational enrichment programs for underprivileged children, such as Head Start, have not produced durable increases in participants' IQ scores. However, as the text explains, this finding does not provide logically sound support for the notion that intelligence is largely inherited.

programs to increase IQ scores?" Yes, one could argue that the programs failed to yield the expected increments in IQ scores because they were poorly planned, poorly executed, too brief, or underfunded (Ramey, 1999; Zigler & Styfco, 1994). The inability of the enrichment programs to produce enduring increases in IQ does not necessarily imply that intelligence is unchangeable because it is largely a product of heredity. You may also be wondering, "Aren't there contradictory data?" Once again, the answer is yes. Some lesser-known educational enrichment programs attempted with smaller groups of children *have* yielded durable gains in IQ scores (Barnett, 1995; Ramey & Ramey, 1998). Moreover, completely different approaches to gauging the impact of environmental enrichment—such as studies of children adopted from underprivileged homes into middle-class homes—have demonstrated that an improved environment can lead to meaningful increases in IQ (Scarr & Weinberg, 1983).

Reification

The dialogue on intelligence has also been marred by the tendency to engage in reification. *Reification* **occurs when a hypothetical, abstract concept is given a name and then treated as though it were a concrete, tangible object.** Some hypothetical constructs just become so familiar and so taken for granted that we begin to think about them as if they were real. People often fall into this trap with the Freudian personality concepts of id, ego, and superego (see Chapter 12). They begin to think of the *ego,* for instance, as a genuine entity that can be strengthened or controlled, when the ego is really nothing more than a hypothetical abstraction. The concept of intelligence has also been reified in many quarters. Like the ego, intelligence is nothing more than a useful abstraction—a hypothetical construct that is estimated, rather arbitrarily, by a collection of paper-and-pencil measures

called IQ tests. Yet people routinely act as if intelligence is a tangible commodity, fighting vitriolic battles over whether it can be measured precisely, whether it can be changed, and whether it can ensure job success. This reification clearly contributes to the tendency for people to attribute excessive importance to the concept of intelligence. It would be wise to remember that intelligence is no more real than the concept of "environment" or "cyberspace" or "the American dream."

Reification has also occurred in the debate about the degree to which intelligence is inherited. Arguments about the heritability coefficient for intelligence often imply that there is a single, true number lurking somewhere "out there" waiting to be discovered. In reality, heritability is a hypothetical construct that can be legitimately estimated in several ways that can lead to somewhat different results. Moreover, heritability ratios will vary from one population to the next, depending on the amount of genetic variability and the extent of environmental variability in the populations. No exactly accurate number that corresponds to "true heritability" awaits discovery. Thus, it is important to understand that hypothetical constructs have great heuristic value in the study of complex phenomena such as human thought and behavior, but they do not actually exist in the world—at least not in the same way that a table or a person exists.

Reification occurs when we think of hypothetical constructs as if they were real. Like intelligence, the concept of cyberspace has been subject to reification. The fact that cyberspace is merely an abstraction becomes readily apparent when artists are asked to "draw" cyberspace for conference posters or book covers. (Cover of Naked in Cyberspace *by Carole A. Lane. Reproduced by courtesy and permission of Information Today, Inc., Medford, NJ.)*

Table 9.3	Critical Thinking Skills Discussed in This Application
Skill	**Description**
Recognizing and avoiding appeals to ignorance	The critical thinker understands that the lack of information on an issue cannot be used to support an argument.
Recognizing and avoiding reification	The critical thinker is vigilant about the tendency to treat hypothetical constructs as if thery were concrete things.
Looking for alternative explanations for findings and events	In evaluating explanations, the critical thinker explores whether there are other explanations that could also account for the findings or events under scrutiny.
Looking for contradictory evidence	In evaluating the evidence presented on an issue, the critical thinker attempts to look for contradictory evidence that may have been left out of the debate.

REVIEW

Key Ideas

Key Concepts in Psychological Testing

● Psychological tests are standardized measures of behavior—usually mental abilities or aspects of personality. Test scores are interpreted by consulting test norms to find out what represents a high or low score. As measuring devices, psychological tests should produce consistent results, a quality called reliability.

● Validity refers to the degree to which there is evidence that a test measures what it was designed to measure. Content validity is crucial on classroom tests. Criterion-related validity is critical when tests are used to predict performance. Construct validity is critical when a test is designed to measure a hypothetical construct.

The Evolution of Intelligence Testing

● The first crude efforts to devise intelligence tests were made by Sir Francis Galton, who wanted to show that intelligence is inherited. Modern intelligence testing began with the work of Alfred Binet, who devised a scale to measure a child's mental age.

● Lewis Terman revised the original Binet scale to produce the Stanford-Binet, which became the standard of comparison for subsequent intelligence tests. David Wechsler devised an improved measure of intelligence for adults and a new scoring system based on the normal distribution. Today, there are many individual and group intelligence tests.

Basic Questions About Intelligence Testing

● Intelligence tests contain a diverse mixture of questions. In the modern scoring system, deviation IQ scores indicate where people fall in the normal distribution of intelligence for their age group. IQ tests are exceptionally reliable. They are reasonably valid measures of academic intelligence, but they do not tap social or practical intelligence.

● IQ scores are correlated with occupational attainment, but doubts have been raised about how well they predict performance within an occupation. IQ tests are not widely used in most non-Western cultures.

Heredity and Environment as Determinants of Intelligence

● Twin studies show that identical twins are more similar in IQ than fraternal twins, suggesting that intelligence is inherited, at least in part. Estimates of the heritability of intelligence range from 50% to 70%, but heritability ratios have certain limitations.

● Many lines of evidence indicate that environment is also an important determinant of intelligence. Of particular interest is the recent discovery of generational increases in measured IQ. The concept of reaction range posits that heredity places limits on one's intellectual potential and the environment determines where one falls within these limits.

● Genetic explanations for cultural differences in IQ have been challenged on a variety of grounds. Even if the heritability of IQ is great, group differences in intelligence may not be due to heredity. Moreover, ethnicity varies with social class, so socioeconomic disadvantage may account for low IQ scores among minority students. Asian American students' comparative success in the educational arena appears to be due to cultural factors.

New Directions in the Assessment and Study of Intelligence

● In the future, schools and society may place less emphasis on intelligence tests because of widespread misconceptions about them. Although biological indexes of intelligence are being explored, far more research is using a cognitive perspective that advocates an expanded concept of intelligence.

● Robert Sternberg's triarchic theory of human intelligence asserts that the hallmarks of intelligence are the abilities to deal effectively with novelty and to handle familiar tasks automatically. Howard Gardner argues that there are eight largely independent types of human intelligence.

Putting It in Perspective

● Three of our integrative themes stood out in the chapter. Our discussions of intelligence showed how heredity and environment interact to shape behavior, how psychology evolves in a sociohistorical context, and how one has to consider cultural contexts to fully understand behavior.

Personal Application • Measuring and Understanding Creativity

● Creativity involves the generation of original, novel, and useful ideas. Creativity does not usually involve sudden insight. Divergent thinking can foster creativity, but it does not represent the essence of creativity.

● Psychologists have developed some clever and useful measures of creativity, but these tests are mediocre predictors of creative productivity in the real world. Creativity is only weakly related to intelligence. Recent evidence suggests that creative geniuses may exhibit heightened vulnerability to mood disorders.

Critical Thinking Application • The Intelligence Debate, Appeals to Ignorance, and Reification

● The appeal to ignorance involves misusing the lack of knowledge or information on an issue to support an argument. This fallacy has surfaced in the debate about intelligence, wherein it has been argued that we have little or no evidence that intelligence can be increased by environmental interventions, therefore intelligence must be mostly inherited.

● Reification occurs when a hypothetical construct is treated as though it were a tangible object. The concepts of intelligence and heritability have both been subject to reification.

Key Terms

Achievement tests
Aptitude tests
Construct validity
Content validity
Convergent thinking
Correlation coefficient
Creativity
Criterion-related validity
Deviation IQ scores
Divergent thinking
Heritability ratio
Intelligence quotient (IQ)
Intelligence tests
Mental age
Normal distribution
Percentile score
Personality tests
Psychological test
Reaction range
Reification
Reliability
Standardization
Test norms
Test-retest reliability
Validity

Key People

Alfred Binet
Sir Francis Galton
Howard Gardner
Arthur Jensen
Sandra Scarr
Robert Sternberg
Lewis Terman
David Wechsler

PRACTICE TEST

1. Which of the following does not belong with the others?
   A. aptitude tests
   B. personality tests
   C. intelligence tests
   D. achievement tests

2. If you score at the 75th percentile on a standardized test, this means that:
   A. 75% of those who took the test scored better than you did.
   B. 25% of those who took the test scored the same or less than you did.
   C. 75% of those who took the test scored the same or less than you did.
   D. you answered 75% of the questions correctly.

3. If a test has good test-retest reliability:
   A. there is a strong correlation between items on the test.
   B. it accurately measures what it says it measures.
   C. it can be used to predict future performance.
   D. the test yields similar scores if taken at two different times.

4. Which of the following is a true statement regarding Sir Francis Galton?
   A. He took the position that intelligence is more a matter of heredity than environment.
   B. He advocated the development of special programs to tap the intellectual potential of the culturally disadvantaged.
   C. He developed tests that identified those children who were unable to profit from a normal education.
   D. He took the position that intelligence is more a matter of environment than heredity.

5. On most modern IQ tests, a score of 115 would be:
   A. about average.
   B. about 15% higher than the average of one's agemates.
   C. an indication of genius.
   D. one standard deviation above the mean.

6. IQ tests have proven to be good predictors of:
   A. social intelligence.
   B. practical problem-solving intelligence.
   C. school performance.
   D. all of the above.

7. The correlation between IQ and occupational attainment appears to be:
   A. positive and moderate.
   B. positive but extremely low.
   C. nonexistent.
   D. negative or inverse.

8. Evidence suggests that IQ scores are a _____ predictor of success within specific occupations.
   A. very strong
   B. strong
   C. weak/moderate
   D. worthless

9. Saying that the heritability of intelligence is 60% would mean that:
   A. 60% of a person's intelligence is due to heredity.
   B. 60% of the variability in intelligence scores in a group is estimated to be due to genetic variations.
   C. intelligence is 40% inherited.
   D. heredity affects intelligence in 60% of the members of the group.

10. In which of the following cases would you expect to find the greatest similarity in IQ?
    A. between fraternal twins
    B. between identical twins
    C. between nontwin siblings
    D. between parent and child

11. Evidence indicating that upbringing affects one's mental ability is provided by which of the following findings?
    A. Identical twins are more similar in IQ than fraternal twins.
    B. There is more than a chance similarity between adopted children and their biological parents.
    C. Siblings reared together are more similar in IQ than siblings reared apart.
    D. Identical twins reared apart are more similar in IQ than siblings reared together.

12. According to theories that use the concept of reaction range, the upper limits of an individual's intellectual potential are:
    A. determined during the first year of life.
    B. largely set by heredity.
    C. determined by a person's unique experiences.
    D. determined by one's heritability quotient.

13. Which of the following is a current trend in the assessment and study of intelligence?
    A. more dependence on the classic intelligence quotient instead of deviation IQ scores
    B. more reliance on IQ tests in schools and the world of work
    C. more emphasis on reducing the convergent heritability of deviation IQ scores
    D. more cognitive research on how people use their intelligence

14. When you try to narrow down a list of alternatives to arrive at a single correct answer, you engage in:
    A. convergent thinking.
    B. divergent thinking.
    C. creativity.
    D. insight.

15. Nora has a blind date with Nick, who, she's been told, is considered a true genius by the faculty in the art department. Now she's having second thoughts, because she's always heard that geniuses are a little off their rocker. Does she have reason to be concerned?
    A. Yes. It's been well documented that the stress of creative achievement often leads to schizophrenic symptoms.
    B. No. Extensive research on creativity and psychological disorders shows no evidence for any connection.
    C. Perhaps. There is evidence of a correlation between major creative achievement and vulnerability to mood disorders.
    D. Of course not. The stereotype of the genius who's mentally ill is purely a product of the jealousy of untalented people.

Answers

1	B	page 264	6	C	pages 272–273	11	C	pages 275–276
2	C	pages 264–265	7	A	page 273	12	B	page 278
3	D	pages 265–266	8	C	page 273	13	D	pages 281–283
4	A	page 268	9	B	page 276	14	A	page 285
5	D	pages 271–272	10	B	pages 275–276	15	C	pages 286–287

INFOTRAC COLLEGE EDITION

Go to the Wadsworth Psychology Study Center for quiz questions, research updates, interactive exercises, and suggested readings in INFOTRAC related to this chapter:
http://psychology.wadsworth.com/product/0534593100s

CHAPTER 10

© Kwame Zikomo/ Superstock

Motivation and Emotion

In September 1983, for the first time in 132 years the United States lost the America's Cup, the foremost trophy in the sport of sailing. An Australian team with a superior new boat design won the Cup. The Australians were understandably ecstatic. In contrast, the U.S. team was devastated by its abrupt and unexpected defeat. Dennis Conner, the team's skipper, wept openly in despair after the last race. Within months, however, Conner had begun a relentless campaign to recapture the America's Cup in the next race in 1987. Working 365 days a year, he secured an unprecedented $15 million in

financial backing. He investigated hundreds of new boat designs, supervised the building of four boats, assembled and trained a crackerjack crew, and sailed in hundreds of races to prepare. Describing his frantic pace, Conner's wife said, "He never relaxes, and we never go on vacations. Hell to Dennis would be a day on the beach." Conner's crew would certainly agree with his wife. Working 12 to 15 hours a day, six or seven days a week, they were pushed through a grueling training regimen for 17 months. Training thousands of miles from their homes, most of them saw their wives or girlfriends only once during this time.

In 1987 the long hours of hard work and sacrifice paid off. Conner and his crew trounced their opponents and recaptured the America's Cup. The jubilation of victory was readily apparent when Conner accepted the trophy. So, did Connor finally relax after the vindication of his 1987 victory? No, he continued his frenetic work pace in the hopes of successfully defending the America's Cup. In 1992 and 1995, however, he once again experienced the bitter taste of defeat.

The saga of Dennis Conner and his crew is packed with motivational riddles. What motivated these men to dedicate their lives to the pursuit of a yachting trophy? Money? No, the well-educated crew members were paid a mere $75 per week during their brutal, monastic months of training. Fame? For Conner perhaps, but the other crew members knew that their names wouldn't become household words. A deep-rooted love of sailing? Maybe for some of them, but Conner noted, "I don't like to sail. I like to compete." That was the key theme for most of the crew. More than anything else, they seemed to be propelled by the excitement of competition and the thrill of victory. As Conner put it, "The bottom line is, people like to win."

Conner's story is also filled with strong emotions. When he lost the America's Cup in 1983, he experienced tremendous dejection and disappointment. When he won the Cup back in 1987, he experienced enormous joy and happiness. His tale illustrates the intimate relation between motivation and emotion—the topics we'll examine in this chapter.

The saga of Dennis Conner and his crew is packed with motivational riddles and intense emotions.

Figure 10.1

The diversity of human motives. People are motivated by a wide range of needs, which can be divided into two broad classes: biological motives and social motives. The list on the left (adapted from Madsen, 1973) shows some important biological needs in humans. The list on the right (adapted from Murray, 1938) provides examples of prominent social needs in humans.

Why did many of Dennis Conner's crew members give up good jobs to join his quest for the America's Cup? Why did the renowned artist Vincent Van Gogh cut off his ear? Why did Greta Garbo suddenly retire from making movies at the peak of her highly acclaimed movie career? Why did you decide to attend college? Why did you start reading this chapter today? In asking these questions, we're looking for the motives underlying the actions. *Motives* are the needs, wants, interests, and desires that propel people in certain directions. In short, ***motivation involves goal-directed behavior.***

Humans display an enormous diversity of motives. Most theories of motivation distinguish between *biological motives* that originate in bodily needs, such as hunger, and *social motives* that originate in social experiences, such as the need for achievement.

People have a limited number of biological needs. According to K. B. Madsen (1968, 1973), most theories identify 10 to 15 such needs, some of which are listed on the left side of Figure 10.1. As you can see, most biological motives reflect needs that are essential to survival, such as the needs for food, water, and maintenance of body temperature within an acceptable range.

People all share the same biological needs, but their social needs vary depending on their experiences. For example, some people acquire a need for orderliness, and some don't. Although people have a limited number of biological needs, they can acquire an unlimited number of social needs through learning and socialization. Some examples of social motives—from an influential list compiled by Henry Murray (1938)—are shown on the right side of Figure 10.1. He theorized that most people have needs for achievement, autonomy, affiliation, dominance, exhibition, and order, among other things. Of course, the strength of these needs varies from person to person, depending on individual history.

Given the range and diversity of human motives, we can only examine a handful in depth. To a large degree, our choices reflect the motives psychologists have studied the most: hunger, sex, and achievement. After our discussion of these motivational systems, we will explore the elements of emotional experience and discuss various theories of emotion.

Examples of Biological Needs in Humans	Examples of Social Needs in Humans
Hunger motive	Achievement motive (need to excel)
Thirst motive	Affiliation motive (need for social bonds)
Sex motive	Autonomy motive (need for independence)
Temperature motive (need for appropriate body temperature)	Nurturance motive (need to nourish and protect others)
Excretory motive (need to eliminate bodily wastes)	Dominance motive (need to influence or control others)
Sleep and rest motive	Exhibition motive (need to make an impression on others)
Activity motive (need for optimal level of stimulation and arousal)	Order motive (need for orderliness, tidiness, organization)
Aggression motive	Play motive (need for fun, relaxation, amusement)

The Motivation of Hunger and Eating

Why do people eat? Because they're hungry. What makes them hungry? A lack of food. Any grade-school child can explain these basic facts. So hunger is a simple motivational system, right? Wrong! Hunger is deceptive. It only looks simple. Actually, it's a puzzling and complex motivational system. Despite extensive studies of hunger, scientists are still struggling to understand the factors that regulate eating behavior. Let's examine a few of these factors.

Biological Factors in the Regulation of Hunger

 2e, 8a

You have probably had embarrassing occasions when your stomach growled loudly at an inopportune moment. Someone may have commented,

"You must be starving!" Most people equate a rumbling stomach with hunger, and, in fact, the first scientific theories of hunger were based on this simple equation. In an elaborate 1912 study, Walter Cannon and A. L. Washburn verified what most people have noticed based on casual observation: There is an association between stomach contractions and the experience of hunger.

Based on this correlation, Cannon theorized that stomach contractions *cause* hunger. However, as we've seen before, correlation is no assurance of causation, and his theory was eventually discredited. Stomach contractions often accompany hunger, but they don't cause it. How do we know? Because later research showed that people continue to experience hunger even after their stomachs have been removed out of medical necessity (Wangensteen &

Carlson, 1931). If hunger can occur without a stomach, then stomach contractions can't be the cause of hunger. This realization led to more elaborate theories of hunger that focus on (1) the role of the brain, (2) blood sugar level, and (3) hormones.

Brain Regulation

Research with laboratory animals eventually suggested that the experience of hunger is controlled in the brain—specifically, in two centers located in the hypothalamus. As we have noted before, the *hypothalamus* is a tiny structure involved in the regulation of a variety of biological needs related to survival (see Figure 10.2). Investigators found that when they lesioned animals' *lateral hypothalamus (LH)*, the animals showed little or no interest in eating, as if their hunger center had been destroyed (Anand & Brobeck, 1951). In contrast, when researchers lesioned animals' *ventromedial nucleus of the hypothalamus (VMH),* the animals ate excessively and gained weight rapidly, as if their ability to recognize satiety (fullness) had been destroyed (Brobeck, Tepperman, & Long, 1943). Given these results, investigators concluded that the LH and VMH were the brain's on-off switches for the control of hunger (Stellar, 1954). However, over the course of several decades, a host of empirical findings complicated this simple picture and undermined the dual-centers model of hunger (Valenstein, 1973; Winn, 1995). The current thinking is that the lateral and ventromedial areas of the hypothalamus are elements in the neural circuitry that regulates hunger, but not the key elements, and not simple on-off centers.

Today, scientists believe that a third area of the hypothalamus—the *paraventricular nucleus (PVN)*—plays a larger role in the modulation of hunger (see Figure 10.2). Research has shown that the infusion of various neurotransmitters into the PVN can influence eating (Leibowitz, 1992). For example, the injection of norepinephrine, GABA, or neuropeptide Y increases the consumption of carbohydrates, whereas serotonin inhibits carbohydrate consumption. The evidence suggests that neuropeptide Y is especially important to the experience of hunger (Leibowitz, 1991; Stanley & Gillard, 1994).

Thus, contemporary theories of hunger focus more on *neural circuits,* rather than on *anatomical centers,* in the brain. Accumulating evidence suggests that the hypothalamus contains a confluence of interacting systems that regulate eating by monitoring a diverse array of physiological processes. Let's look at some other physiological processes that appear to provide input to these systems.

Glucose and Digestive Regulation

Much of the food taken into the body is converted into *glucose,* which circulates in the blood. *Glucose is a simple sugar that is an important source of energy.* Manipulations that decrease blood glucose level can increase hunger. Manipulations that increase glucose level can make people feel satiated. Based on these findings, Jean Mayer (1955, 1968) proposed that hunger is regulated by the rise and fall of blood glucose levels. *Glucostatic theory* proposed that fluctuations in blood glucose level are monitored in the brain by *glucostats*—neurons sensitive to glucose in the surrounding fluid.

Like the dual-centers theory, the glucostatic theory of hunger gradually ran into a host of complications, not the least of which was that glucose levels in the blood really don't fluctuate all that much (LeMagnen, 1981). Still, it appears likely that

Figure 10.2

The hypothalamus. This small structure at the base of the forebrain plays a role in regulating a variety of human biological needs, including hunger. The detailed blowup shows that the hypothalamus is made up of a variety of discrete areas. Scientists used to believe that the lateral and ventromedial areas were the brain's start and stop centers for eating. However, more recent research suggests that the paraventricular nucleus is more crucial to the regulation of hunger.

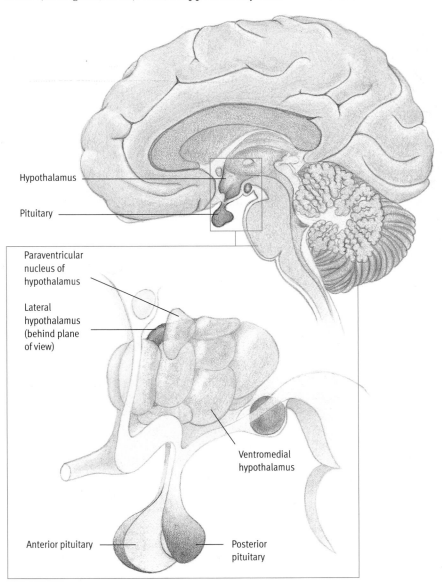

Hypothalamus

Pituitary

Paraventricular nucleus of hypothalamus

Lateral hypothalamus (behind plane of view)

Ventromedial hypothalamus

Anterior pituitary

Posterior pituitary

hunger is regulated, in part, through glucostatic mechanisms (Smith & Campfield, 1993). Some of this regulation may be accomplished through the liver, which is the first stop for nutrients after they are absorbed by the intestine. It appears that glucostats in the liver send signals to the hypothalamus by way of the vagus nerve (Novin et al., 1983).

The digestive system also includes other mechanisms that influence hunger. It turns out that Walter Cannon was not entirely wrong in hypothesizing that the stomach regulates hunger. After you have consumed food, the stomach can send two types of signals to the brain that inhibit further eating (Deutsch, 1990). The vagus nerve carries information about the stretching of the stomach walls that indicates when the stomach is full. Other nerves carry satiety messages that depend on how rich in nutrients the contents of the stomach are.

Hormonal Regulation

A variety of hormones circulating in the bloodstream also appear to contribute to the regulation of hunger. *Insulin* is a hormone secreted by the pancreas. It must be present for cells to extract glucose from the blood. Indeed, an inadequate supply of insulin is what causes diabetes. Many diabetics are unable to use the glucose in their blood unless they are given insulin injections. In nondiabetic individuals, insulin injections stimulate hunger. Normal secretion of insulin by the pancreas is also associated with increased hunger. And, in landmark research, Judith Rodin (1985) demonstrated that the mere sight and smell of enticing food can stimulate the secretion of insulin. Moreover, insulin levels appear to be sensitive to fluctuations in the body's fat stores (Seeley et al., 1996). These findings suggest that insulin secretions play a role in the modulation of hunger.

Finally, the recent discovery of a previously undetected hormone, since christened *leptin,* has shed new light on the hormonal regulation of hunger (Halaas et al., 1995). Leptin is produced by fat cells throughout the body and released into the bloodstream. Higher levels of fat generate higher levels of leptin (Schwartz et al., 1996). Leptin circulates through the bloodstream and ultimately provides the hypothalamus with information about the body's fat stores (Campfield et al., 1995). When leptin levels are high, the propensity to feel hungry diminishes. Leptin apparently activates receptors in the brain that inhibit the release of neuropeptide Y, which leads to activity in the paraventricular nucleus of the hypothalamus, which in turn inhibits eating (Stephens et al., 1995).

If all this sounds confusing, it is, and I haven't even mentioned *all* the physiological processes involved in the regulation of hunger and eating. Figure 10.3 provides an overview of the hunger system that attempts to summarize and integrate the processes that we have discussed. But, frankly, researchers are still struggling to figure out exactly how all these processes work together, as hunger depends on complex interactions between neural circuits, neurotransmitter systems, digestive processes, and hormonal fluctuations.

Environmental Factors in the Regulation of Hunger

Hunger clearly is a biological need, but eating is not regulated by biological factors alone. Studies show that social and environmental factors govern eating to a considerable extent. Three key environmental factors are (1) learned preferences and habits, (2) food-related cues, and (3) stress.

Learned Preferences and Habits

Are you fond of eating calves' brains? How about eels or snakes? Could I interest you in a grasshopper or some dog meat? Probably not, but these are delicacies in some regions of the world. Arctic Eskimos like to eat maggots! You probably prefer chicken, apples, eggs, lettuce, potato chips, pizza, cornflakes, or ice cream. These preferences are acquired through learning. People from different cultures display very different patterns of food consumption (Kittler & Sucher, 1998). If you doubt this fact, just visit a grocery store in an ethnic neighborhood (not your own, of course).

Humans do have some innate taste preferences of a general sort. For example, our preference for high-fat foods appears to be at least partly genetic in origin (Schiffman et al., 1998). Nonetheless, learning wields a great deal of influence over *what* people prefer to eat (Booth, 1991, 1994). Taste preferences are partly a function of learned associations formed through classical conditioning. For example, youngsters can be conditioned to prefer flavors paired with high caloric intake or pleasant social interactions (Logue, 1991). Of course, as we learned in Chapter 6, taste aversions can also be acquired through conditioning when foods are followed by nausea (Bernstein & Meachum, 1990).

Eating habits are also shaped by observational learning (see Chapter 6). To a large degree, food preferences are a matter of exposure (Rozin, 1990). People generally prefer familiar foods. But geographical, cultural, religious, and ethnic factors limit people's

"People's metabolic machinery is constituted in such a way that the fatter they are, the fatter they are primed to become."
JUDITH RODIN

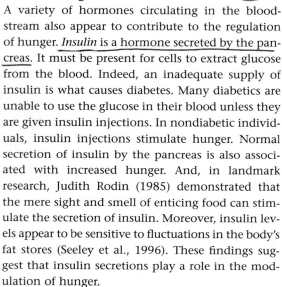

Web Link 10.1

Eating Disorders Shared Awareness (EDSA)
When rhythms of hunger and eating no longer function normally, a person may begin to experience an eating disorder that can become life threatening. EDSA and its closely related sites provide a vast range of information about anorexia, bulimia, and other forms of eating disorders.

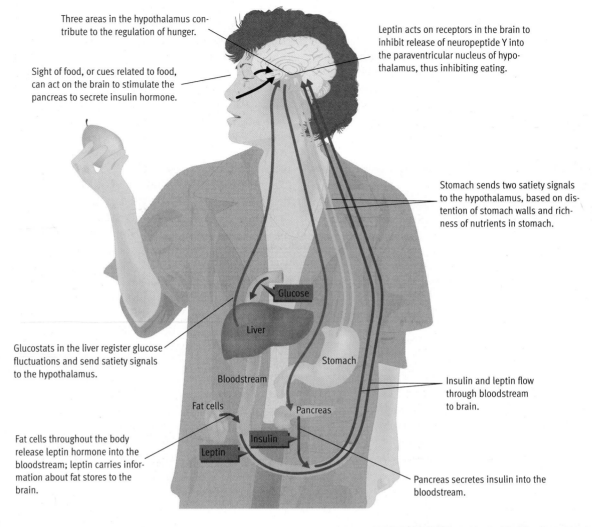

Figure 10.3

Overview of biological factors involved in the regulation of hunger. This diagram pulls together information on the various physiological processes implicated in the modulation of hunger. As you can see, hunger provides another illustration of how behavior often involves complicated, multifactorial causation. Although the hypothalamus clearly lies at the hub of this complex system, the details of how the various processes interact are still being worked out.

Three areas in the hypothalamus contribute to the regulation of hunger.

Sight of food, or cues related to food, can act on the brain to stimulate the pancreas to secrete insulin hormone.

Leptin acts on receptors in the brain to inhibit release of neuropeptide Y into the paraventricular nucleus of hypothalamus, thus inhibiting eating.

Stomach sends two satiety signals to the hypothalamus, based on distention of stomach walls and richness of nutrients in stomach.

Glucose

Liver

Glucostats in the liver register glucose fluctuations and send satiety signals to the hypothalamus.

Stomach

Bloodstream

Insulin and leptin flow through bloodstream to brain.

Fat cells

Pancreas

Insulin

Leptin

Fat cells throughout the body release leptin hormone into the bloodstream; leptin carries information about fat stores to the brain.

Pancreas secretes insulin into the bloodstream.

exposure to various foods. Young children are more likely to taste an unfamiliar food if an adult tries it first. Repeated exposures to a new food usually lead to increased liking. However, as many parents have learned the hard way, forcing a child to eat a specific food can backfire; coercion tends to have a negative effect on a youngster's preference for the mandated food (Birch, 1990). Individuals' reactions to foods are also shaped by the reactions of others around them, such as parents, siblings, and peers. For instance, if you're trying squid for the first time, you're more likely to have a favorable reaction if a companion savors a bite with delight, as opposed to spitting it out in disgust. Learned habits and social considerations also influence *when* and *how much* people eat. For example, a key determinant of when we eat is our memory of how much time has passed since we ate our last meal and what we consumed (Rozin et al., 1998). These expectations about how often and how much we should eat are the product of years of learning.

The fact that culture influences food preferences is evident in these photos, in which you can see delicacies such as grasshoppers (left) and Mopane worms (right).

Food-Related Cues

Hunger can also be influenced by exposure to environmental cues that have been associated with eating (Birch et al., 1989). You have no doubt had your hunger aroused by television commercials for delicious-looking food or by seductive odors coming from the kitchen. These experiences illustrate how food-related cues can trigger hunger. Stanley

Schachter (1971) conducted numerous studies on how external cues affect hunger. He manipulated cues such as how tasty and appealing food appeared, how obvious its availability was, and how much effort was required to eat it. All of these external cues were found to influence eating behavior to some extent (Schachter & Rodin, 1974). Thus, it's clear that hunger and eating are governed in part by a variety of food-related cues.

CONCEPT CHECK 10.1
Understanding Factors in the Regulation of Hunger

Check your understanding of the effects of the various factors that influence hunger by indicating whether hunger would tend to increase or decrease in each of the situations described below. Indicate your choice by marking an *I* (increase), a *D* (decrease), or a *?* (can't be determined without more information) next to each situation. You'll find the answers in Appendix A at the back of the book.

_I._ **1.** The ventromedial nucleus of a rat's brain is destroyed by lesioning.

_I._ **2.** The glucose level in Marlene's bloodstream decreases.

_I._ **3.** Norman, who is not diabetic, receives an injection of insulin.

_D._ **4.** You're offered an exotic food from another culture and are told that everyone in that culture loves it.

_?_ **5.** Your watch has broken, but the clock on the wall says it's an hour past your usual dinnertime.

_I._ **6.** Elton has been going crazy all day. It seems like everything's happening at once and he feels totally stressed out. Finally he's been able to break away for a few minutes so he can catch a bite to eat.

Stress, Arousal, and Eating

When I have an exceptionally stressful day, I often head for the refrigerator, a grocery store, or a restaurant—usually in pursuit of something chocolate. My response is not particularly unusual. Studies have shown that stress leads to increased eating in a substantial percentage of people (Greeno & Wing, 1994). Some studies suggest that stress-induced eating may be more common in women than men (Grunberg & Straub, 1992) and more likely among chronic dieters (Heatherton, Striepe, & Wittenberg, 1998). Actually, it appears to be stress-induced *arousal* rather than stress itself that stimulates eating. Stressful events often lead to physiological arousal, and several lines of evidence suggest a link between heightened arousal and overeating (Striegel-Moore & Rodin, 1986). Thus, stress is another environmental factor that can influence hunger, although it's not clear whether the effects are direct or indirect.

Sexual Motivation and Behavior

How does sex resemble food? Sometimes it seems that people are obsessed with both. People joke and gossip about sex constantly. Magazines, novels, movies, and television shows are saturated with sexual activity and innuendo. The advertising industry uses sex to sell everything from mouthwash to designer jeans to automobiles. This intense interest in sex reflects the importance of sexual motivation. In this portion of the chapter, we will examine the physiology of the human sexual response, review evolutionary analyses of human sexual motivation, and discuss the roots of sexual orientation.

The Human Sexual Response

Assuming people are motivated to engage in sexual activity, exactly what happens to them physically? This may sound like a simple question. But scientists really knew very little about the physiology of the human sexual response before William Masters

and Virginia Johnson did groundbreaking research in the 1960s. Masters and Johnson used physiological recording devices to monitor the bodily changes of volunteers engaging in sexual activities. Their observations and interviews with their subjects yielded a detailed description of the human sexual response and won them widespread acclaim.

Masters and Johnson (1966, 1970) divide the sexual response cycle into four stages: excitement, plateau, orgasm, and resolution. Figure 10.4 shows how the intensity of sexual arousal changes as women and men progress through these stages. Let's take a closer look at these phases in the human sexual response.

Excitement Phase

During the initial phase of excitement, the level of physical arousal usually escalates rapidly. In both sexes, muscle tension, respiration rate, heart rate, and blood pressure increase quickly. *Vasocongestion—*

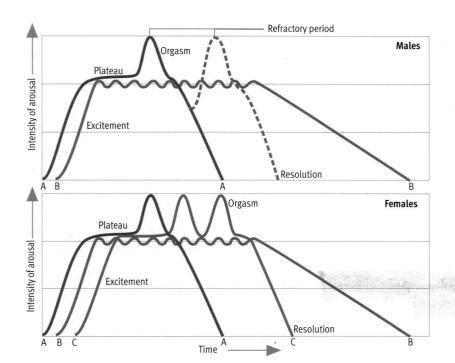

Figure 10.4

The human sexual response cycle. There are similarities and differences between men and women in patterns of sexual arousal. Pattern A, which culminates in orgasm and resolution, is the ideal sequence for both sexes, but not something one can count on (see Figure 10.5). Pattern B, which involves sexual arousal without orgasm followed by a slow resolution, is seen in both sexes but is more common among women. Pattern C, which involves multiple orgasms, is seen almost exclusively in women, as men go through a refractory period before they are capable of another orgasm. (Based on *Human Sexual Response*, by W.H. Masters and V.E. Johnson, 1966. Little, Brown and Company.)

COREIS-UPI/Bettmann Newsphotos

COREIS-UPI/Bettmann Newsphotos

❝*The conviction has grown that the most effective treatment of sexual incompatibility involves the technique of working with both members of the family unit.*❞
WILLIAM MASTERS AND VIRGINIA JOHNSON

engorgement of blood vessels—produces penile erection and swollen testes in males. In females, vasocongestion leads to a swelling and hardening of the clitoris, expansion of the vaginal lips, and vaginal lubrication.

Plateau Phase

During the plateau phase, physiological arousal usually continues to build, but at a much slower pace. In women, further vasocongestion produces a tightening of the vaginal entrance, as the clitoris withdraws under the clitoral hood. Many men secrete a bit of fluid at the tip of the penis. This is not ejaculate, but it may contain sperm. When foreplay is lengthy, it's normal for arousal to fluctuate in both sexes. This fluctuation is more apparent in men; erections may increase and decrease noticeably. In women, this fluctuation may be reflected in changes in vaginal lubrication.

Orgasm Phase

Orgasm occurs when sexual arousal reaches its peak intensity and is discharged in a series of muscular contractions that pulsate through the pelvic area. Heart rate, respiration rate, and blood pressure increase sharply during this exceedingly pleasant spasmodic response. In males, orgasm is accompanied by ejaculation of the seminal fluid. The subjective experience of orgasm is very similar for men and women. When people provide written descriptions of what their orgasms feel like (without

using specific words for genitals), judges can't tell which came from women and which came from men (Wiest, 1977; Weist et al., 1995).

However, there *are* some interesting gender differences in the orgasm phase of the sexual response cycle. On the one hand, women are more likely than men to be *multiorgasmic*. A woman is said to be multiorgasmic if she experiences more than one climax in a very brief time period (pattern C in Figure 10.4). On the other hand, women are more likely than men to engage in intercourse without experiencing an orgasm (see Figure 10.5; Laumann et al., 1994). Whether these differences reflect attitudes and sexual practices versus physiological

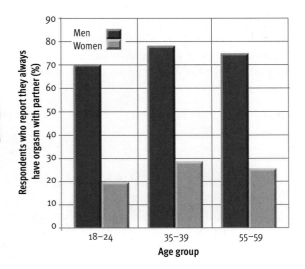

Figure 10.5

The gender gap in orgasm consistency. In their sexual interactions, men seem to reach orgasm more reliably than women. The data shown here, from Laumann et al. (1994), suggest that the gender gap in orgasmic consistency is pretty sizable. Both biological and sociocultural factors may contribute to this gender gap.

processes is open to debate. On the one hand, it is easy to argue that males' greater orgasmic consistency must be a product of evolution, as it would have obvious adaptive significance for men's reproductive fitness. On the other hand, over the years theorists have come up with a variety of plausible environmental explanations for this disparity, such as gender differences in the socialization of guilt feelings about sex, and sexual scripts and practices that are unfavorable to women (Lott, 1987).

Resolution Phase

During the resolution phase, the physiological changes produced by sexual arousal subside. If orgasm has not occurred, the reduction in sexual tension may be relatively slow. After orgasm, men experience a *refractory period,* a time following orgasm during which males are largely unresponsive to further stimulation. The length of the refractory period varies from a few minutes to a few hours and increases with age.

Masters and Johnson's exploration of the human sexual response led to major insights into the nature and causes of sexual problems. Ironically, although Masters and Johnson broke new ground in studying the *physiology* of sexual arousal, their research demonstrated that sexual problems are typically caused by *psychological factors*. Their conclusion shows that, like hunger and eating, sexual behavior involves a fascinating blend of biological and social processes.

Evolutionary Analyses of Human Sexual Motivation

As you have already seen in previous chapters, the relatively new evolutionary perspective in psychology has generated intriguing hypotheses related to a host of topics, including perception, learning, language, and problem solving. However, evolutionary theorists' analyses of sexual behavior have drawn the most attention. Obviously, the task of explaining sexual behavior is crucial to the evolutionary

perspective, given its fundamental thesis that natural selection is fueled by variations in reproductive success. The thinking in this area has been guided by Robert Trivers's (1972) *parental investment theory,* which we introduced in Chapter 3. To quickly recapitulate, Trivers maintains that a species' mating patterns depend on what each sex has to invest, in the way of time, energy, and survival risk, to produce and nurture offspring. According to Trivers, *the sex that makes the smaller investment will compete for mating opportunities with the sex that makes the larger investment, and the sex with the larger investment will tend to be more discriminating in selecting its partners.* Let's look at how this analysis applies to humans.

Like many mammalian species, human males are *required* to invest little in the production of offspring beyond the act of copulation, so their reproductive potential is maximized by mating with as many females as possible. The situation for females is quite different. Females have to invest nine months in pregnancy, and our female ancestors typically had to devote at least several additional years to nourishing offspring through breast feeding. These realities place a ceiling on the number of offspring women can produce, regardless of how many males they mate with. Hence, females have little or no incentive for mating with many males. Instead, females can optimize their reproductive potential by being selective in mating. Thus, in humans, males are thought to compete with other males for the relatively scarce and valuable "commodity" of reproductive opportunities. Parental investment theory predicts that in comparison to women, men will show more interest in sexual activity, more desire for variety in sexual partners, and more willingness to engage in uncommited sex (see Figure 10.6). In contrast, females are thought to be the conservative, discriminating sex that is highly selective in choosing partners. This selectivity supposedly entails seeking partners who have the greatest ability to contribute toward feeding and caring for offspring. Why? Because in the world of our ancient ancestors, males' greater strength and agility would have been crucial assets in

Web Link 10.2

Human Behavior and Evolution Society
This interdisciplinary organization is devoted to the exploration of human behavior from the perspective of evolutionary theory. This site provides a particularly rich set of links to published and online materials and organizations dealing with the evolutionary perspective on behavior.

Figure 10.6

Parental investment theory and mating preferences.
Parental investment theory suggests that basic differences between males and females in parental investment have great adaptive significance and lead to gender differences in mating propensities and preferences, as outlined here.

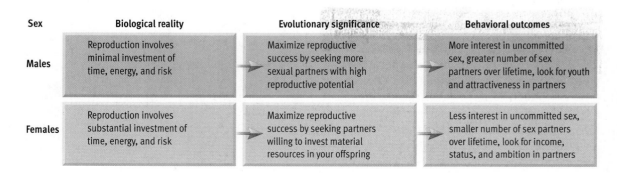

Sex	Biological reality	Evolutionary significance	Behavioral outcomes
Males	Reproduction involves minimal investment of time, energy, and risk	Maximize reproductive success by seeking more sexual partners with high reproductive potential	More interest in uncommitted sex, greater number of sex partners over lifetime, look for youth and attractiveness in partners
Females	Reproduction involves substantial investment of time, energy, and risk	Maximize reproductive success by seeking partners willing to invest material resources in your offspring	Less interest in uncommitted sex, smaller number of sex partners over lifetime, look for income, status, and ambition in partners

the never-ending struggle to find food and shelter and defend one's territory. A female who chose a mate who was lazy or unreliable or who had no hunting, fighting, building, farming, or other useful economic skills would have suffered a substantial disadvantage in her efforts to raise her children and pass on her genes.

Gender Differences in Patterns of Sexual Activity

Consistent with evolutionary theory, males generally show a greater interest in sex than females do. Men think about sex more often than women (see Figure 10.7), they initiate sex more frequently (Morokoff et al., 1997), and they are more interested in sex for its own sake (Whitley, 1988). Some theorists also argue that men's greater liking of pornography reflects the influence of evolutionary forces that have made males more interested in sex (Malamuth, 1996).

Men also are more motivated than women to pursue sex with a variety of partners. Buss and Schmitt (1993) found that college men indicate that they would ideally like to have 18 sex partners across their lives, whereas college women report that they would prefer only 5 partners (see Figure 10.8). Surveys inquiring about adults' actual sexual histories also indicate that men engage in sex with a larger number of partners than women do, on the average (Janus & Janus, 1993).

Clear gender disparities are also seen in regard to people's willingness to engage in casual or uncommitted sex. For example, Buss and Schmitt (1993) asked undergraduates about the likelihood that they would consent to sex with someone they found desirable whom they had known for one hour, one day, one week, one month, or longer periods. Men were much more likely than women to have sex with someone they had known for only a brief period. And, although precise data are hard to come by, it is clear that men are enormously more likely than women to pursue casual sex with prostitutes (Symons, 1979).

Gender Differences in Mate Preferences

According to evolutionary theorists, if males were left to their own devices over the course of history, they probably would have shown little interest in long-term mating commitments, but females have generally demanded long-term commitments from males before consenting to sex (Buss, 1994a). Hence, long-term mating commitments are a normal part of the social landscape in human societies. However, parental investment theory suggests that there

should be some glaring disparities between men and women in what they look for in a long-term mate (see Figure 10.6).

The adaptive problem for our male ancestors was to find a female with good reproductive potential who would be sexually faithful and effective in nurturing children. Given these needs, evolutionary theory predicts that men should place more emphasis than women on partner characteristics such as youthfulness (which allows for more reproductive years) and attractiveness (which is assumed to be correlated with health and fertility). In contrast, the adaptive problem for our female ancestors was to find a male who could provide material resources and protect his family and who was dependable and

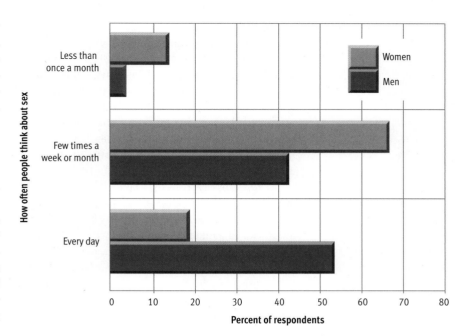

Figure 10.7

The gender gap in how much people think about sex. This graph summarizes data on how often males and females think about sex, based on a large-scale survey by Laumann et al., (1994). As evolutionary theorists would predict, based on parental investment theory, males seem to manifest more interest in sexual activity than their female counterparts.

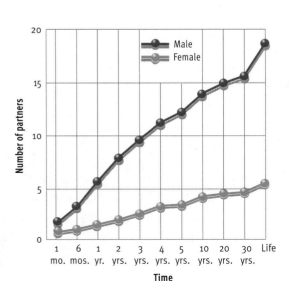

Figure 10.8

The gender gap in desire for a variety of sexual partners. Buss and Schmitt (1993) asked college students about how many sexual partners they ideally would like to have for various time intervals ranging up to one's entire lifetime. As evolutionary theorists would predict, males are interested in having considerably more partners than females. (From "Sexual Strategies Theory: An Evolutionary Perspective on Human Mating," by D. M. Buss and D. P. Schmitt, 1993, *Psychological Review*, 100, 204–232. Copyright © 1993 by the American Psychological Association. Reprinted by permission of the author.)

willing to invest his resources in his family. Given these needs, evolutionary theory predicts that women should place more emphasis than men on partner characteristics such as intelligence, ambition, education, income, and social status (which are associated with the ability to provide more material resources). If these evolutionary analyses of sexual motivation are on the mark, gender differences in mating preferences should be virtually universal and thus transcend culture.

To test this hypothesis, David Buss (1989) and 50 scientists from around the world surveyed more than 10,000 people from 37 cultures about what they looked for in a mate. As predicted by parental investment theory, they found that women placed a higher value than men on potential partners' status, ambition, and financial prospects. These priorities were not limited to industrialized or capitalist countries; they were apparent in third-world cultures, socialist countries, and all varieties of economic systems. In contrast, men around the world consistently showed more interest than women in potential partners' youthfulness and physical attractiveness.

Subsequent studies have provided additional support for the existence of gender disparities in mating preferences. For example, Sprecher, Sullivan, and Hatfield (1994) examined a large, representative sample of adults in the United States and replicated the findings that men look for youth and attractiveness in partners, whereas women are more concerned about potential partners' education and income potential. In a study of personal ads placed in newspapers and magazines, Wiederman (1993) found that female advertisers explicitly sought financial resources in potential partners eleven times as often as male advertisers. In another study of personal ads, Kenrick and Keefe (1992) found that as male advertisers got older, they expressed a preference for increasingly younger women. This finding supports the notion that men are not interested in youth per se as much as they are interested in potential partners' reproductive potential.

Courtesy of David M. Buss

"Evolutionary psychologists develop hypotheses about the psychological mechanisms that have evolved in humans to solve particular adaptive problems that humans have faced under ancestral conditions."
DAVID BUSS

Gender Differences in Relationship Jealousy

In their analyses of human sexual behavior, evolutionary psychologists have also come up with some interesting hypotheses about gender differences in the events that most readily activate jealousy (Bailey et al., 1994; Buss, 1996). Males of many species have to worry about *paternity uncertainty*—that is, whether their children are really theirs. The males of some species solve this adaptive problem by literally guarding their mate around the clock to prevent other males from obtaining sexual access to the partner. Although some possessive men seem to mimic this approach, mate guarding is not a particularly realistic strategy among humans. In any event, the issue of paternity uncertainty means that *sexual infidelity* by one's partner ought to be particularly threatening to the reproductive success of men. In contrast, females are always certain that their offspring are theirs, but they supposedly have to worry more about losing a male partner's material resouces, which depend on his emotional commitment. Hence, males' *emotional infidelity* ought to be particularly threatening to the reproductive success of females (see Figure 10.9). In a test of these hypotheses, Buss and his colleagues (1992) found that sexual infidelity elicited the greatest jealousy in men, whereas emotional infidelity triggered the greatest jealousy in women (see Figure 10.10). Another study replicated these results in the United States, Germany, and the Netherlands (Buunk et al., 1996).

Criticism and Alternative Explanations

So, the findings on gender differences in sexual motivation mesh very nicely with predictions derived from evolutionary theory. But, in the world of science, everyone is a critic—so you may be wondering: What types of criticism has this line of research generated? One set of concerns centers on the fact that the findings do not paint a very flattering picture of human nature. Men end up looking like sordid sexual predators; women come across as cynical, greedy materialists; and evolutionary theory appears

Figure 10.9

Evolutionary hypotheses about gender differences in relationship jealousy. Evolutionary theory suggests that the issue of paternity uncertainty creates basic differences between males and females in the types of infidelity that will elicit the strongest feelings of jealousy, as outlined here.

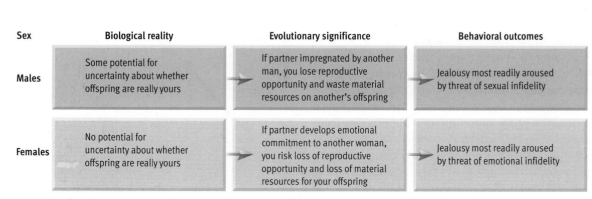

Sex	Biological reality	Evolutionary significance	Behavioral outcomes
Males	Some potential for uncertainty about whether offspring are really yours	If partner impregnated by another man, you lose reproductive opportunity and waste material resources on another's offspring	Jealousy most readily aroused by threat of sexual infidelity
Females	No potential for uncertainty about whether offspring are really yours	If partner develops emotional commitment to another woman, you risk loss of reproductive opportunity and loss of material resources for your offspring	Jealousy most readily aroused by threat of emotional infidelity

Figure 10.10

The gender gap in jealousy. Buss et al. (1992) asked subjects to vividly imagine scenarios involving either sexual or emotional infidelity by their partner. Subjects' distress while imagining these scenarios was assessed by monitoring various indexes of emotional and physiological arousal. As these results show, sexual infidelity generated the most distress in males, whereas emotional infidelity elicited the most distress in females.

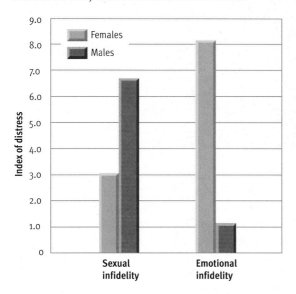

to endorse these realities as the inevitable outcome of natural selection. As Buss (1998) acknowledges, "Much of what I discovered about human mating is not nice" (p. 408). This controversy demonstrates once again that psychological theories can have far-reaching social and political ramifications, but the sociopolitical fallout has no bearing on evolutionary theory's scientific validity or utility.

However, some critics *have* expressed doubts about the validity of evolutionary explanations of gender differences in sexual motivation. They note that one can posit alternative explanations for the findings. For example, women's emphasis on males' material resources could be a by-product of cultural and economic forces rather than the result of biological imperatives (Wallen, 1989). Women may have learned to value males' economic clout because their own economic potential has been severely limited in virtually all cultures by a long history of discrimination (Hrdy, 1997; Kasser & Sharma, 1999). And men's sexual habits and proclivities could simply be a product of gender-role socialization processes. Evolutionary theorists counter these arguments by pointing out that the social and economic roles of men and women may themselves be products of evolution. At present, evolutionary theory appears to provide a more complete account for gender disparities in sexual behavior than the

alternative explanations (Archer, 1996). But more research is needed—and given the controversial nature of the findings, you can rest assured more research will be conducted.

The Mystery of Sexual Orientation

Sex must be a contentious topic, as the controversy swirling around evolutionary explanations of gender differences in sexuality is easily equalled by the controversy surrounding the determinants of *sexual orientation*. **Sexual orientation refers to a person's preference for emotional and sexual relationships with individuals of the same sex, the other sex, or either sex. *Heterosexuals* seek emotional-sexual relationships with members of the other sex, *bisexuals* with members of either sex, and *homosexuals* with members of the same sex.** In recent years, the terms *gay* and *straight* have become widely used to refer to homosexuals and heterosexuals, respectively. Although *gay* can refer to homosexuals of either sex, most homosexual women prefer to call themselves *lesbians*.

People tend to view heterosexuality and homosexuality as an all-or-none distinction. However, in a large-scale survey of sexual behavior, Alfred Kinsey and his colleagues (1948, 1953) discovered that many people who define themselves as heterosexuals have had homosexual experiences—and vice versa. Thus, Kinsey and others have concluded that it is more accurate to view heterosexuality and homosexuality

Web Link 10.3

Go Ask Alice!
One of the longest-standing and most popular sources of frank information on the Net has been Alice! from Columbia University's Health Education Program. Geared especially to the needs of undergraduate students, Alice! visitors will find direct answers to questions about relationships, sexuality and sexual health, alcohol and drug consumption, emotional health, and general health.

In spite of fascinating, groundbreaking research in recent years, the determinants of sexual orientation remain obscure. Like so many other issues in psychology, the debate about the roots of homosexuality centers around the relative importance of nature versus nurture.

Figure **10.11**

Homosexuality and hetero-sexuality as endpoints on a continuum. Sex researchers view heterosexuality and homosexuality as falling on a continuum rather than make an all-or-none distinction. Kinsey and his associates (1948, 1953) created this seven-point scale (from 0 to 6) to describe people's sexual orientation. They used the term *ambisexual* to describe those who fall in the middle of the scale, but such people are commonly called *bisexual* today.

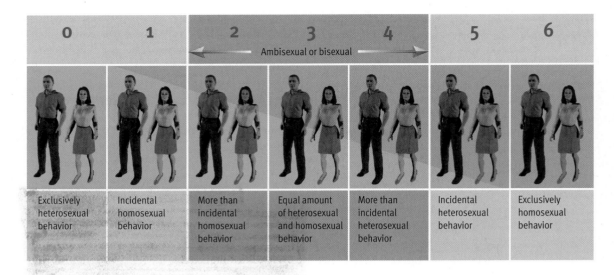

0	1	2	3	4	5	6
		←	Ambisexual or bisexual	→		
Exclusively heterosexual behavior	Incidental homosexual behavior	More than incidental homosexual behavior	Equal amount of heterosexual and homosexual behavior	More than incidental heterosexual behavior	Incidental heterosexual behavior	Exclusively homosexual behavior

as end points on a continuum (Haslam, 1997). Indeed, Kinsey devised a seven-point scale, shown in Figure 10.11, that can be used to characterize individuals' sexual orientation.

How common is homosexuality? No one knows for sure. Part of the problem is that this question is vastly more complex than it appears at first glance (LeVay, 1996). Given that sexual orientation is best represented as a continuum, where do you draw the lines between heterosexuality, bisexuality, and homosexuality? And how do you handle the distinction between overt behavior and desire? Where, for instance, do you put a person who is married and has never engaged in homosexual behavior but who reports homosexual fantasies and acknowledges being strongly drawn to members of the same sex? The other part of the problem is that many people have extremely prejudicial attitudes about homosexuality, which makes gays cautious and reluctant to give candid information about their sexuality (Herek, 1996). Small wonder then that estimates of the portion of the population that is homosexual vary pretty widely (Gonsiorek & Weinrich, 1991). A frequently cited estimate of the number of people who are gay is 10%, but recent surveys suggest that this percentage may be an overestimate. Michaels (1996) has combined data from two of the better large-scale surveys in recent years to arrive at the estimates seen in Figure 10.12. As you can see, the numbers are open to varying interpretations, but as a whole they suggest that about 5%–8% of the population could reasonably be characterized as homosexual.

Environmental Theories

Over the years many environmental theories have been floated to explain the origins of homosexuality, but when tested empirically, these theories have garnered remarkably little support. For example,

Figure **10.12**

How common is homosexuality? The answer to this question is both complex and controversial. Michaels (1996) brought together data from two large-scale surveys to arrive at the estimates shown here. If you look at how many people have actually had a same-sex partner in the last five years, the figures are relatively low, but if you count those who have had a same-sex partner since puberty, the figures more than double. Still another way to look at it is to ask people whether they are attracted to people of the same sex (regardless of their actual behavior). This approach suggests that about 8% of the population could be characterized as homosexual.

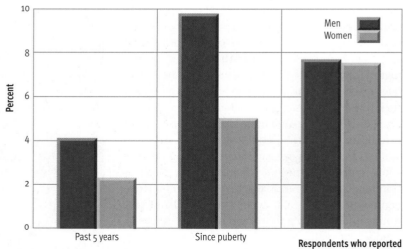

psychoanalytic and behavioral theorists, who usually agree on very little, both proposed environmental explanations for the development of homosexuality. The Freudian theorists argued that a male is likely to become gay when raised by a weak, detached, ineffectual father who is a poor heterosexual role model and by an overprotective, close-binding mother, with whom the boy identifies. Behavioral theorists argued that homosexuality is a learned preference acquired when same-sex stimuli have been paired with sexual arousal, perhaps through chance seductions by adult homosexuals. Extensive research on homosexuals' upbringing and childhood experiences have failed to support either of these theories (Bell, Weinberg, & Hammersmith, 1981).

However, efforts to research homosexuals' personal histories have yielded a number of interesting insights. Extremely feminine behavior in young boys or masculine behavior in young girls does predict the subsequent development of homosexuality (Bailey & Zucker, 1995). For example, 75%–90% of highly feminine young boys eventually turn out to be gay (Blanchard et al., 1995). Consistent with this finding, most gay men and women report that they can trace their homosexual leanings back to their early childhood, even before they understood what sex was really about (Garnets & Kimmel, 1991). Most also report that because of negative parental and societal attitudes about homosexuality, they initially struggled to deny their sexual orientation. Hence, they felt that their homosexuality was not a matter of choice and not something that they could readily change (Breedlove, 1994). These findings obviously suggest that the roots of homosexuality are more biological than environmental.

Biological Theories

Nonetheless, initial efforts to find a biological basis for homosexuality met with little success. Most theorists originally assumed that hormonal differences between heterosexuals and homosexuals must underlie a person's sexual orientation (Doerr et al., 1976; Dorner, 1988). However, studies comparing circulating hormone levels in gays and straights found only small, inconsistent differences that could not be linked to sexual orientation in any convincing way (Garnets & Kimmel, 1991; Gladue, 1988).

Thus, like environmental theorists, biological theorists were stymied for quite a while in their efforts to explain the roots of homosexuality. However, that picture has changed dramatically since the 1990s (Gladue, 1994). For example, in one landmark investigation, Bailey and Pillard (1991) studied gay men who had either a twin brother or

an adopted brother. They found that 52% of the participants' identical twins were gay, that 22% of their fraternal twins were gay, and that 11% of their adoptive brothers were gay. A companion study (Bailey et al., 1993) of lesbians has yielded a similar pattern of results (see Figure 10.13). Given that identical twins share more genetic overlap than fraternal twins, who share more genes than unrelated adoptive siblings, these results suggest that there is a genetic predisposition to homosexuality (see Chapter 3 for an explanation of the logic underlying twin and adoption studies).

In another line of research, LeVay (1991, 1993) has reported anatomical differences between gay and straight men in a region of the brain thought to influence sexual behavior. He focused on a tiny cluster of neurons in the anterior hypothalamus that is known to be larger in men than women. Because the structure is too small to be measured effectively in the living brain, it is studied posthumously. LeVay compared the autopsied brains of 19 homosexual and 16 heterosexual men and found that the targeted structure tended to be about half as large in the gay men. LeVay (1996) stresses that his findings on brain structure should be interpreted with caution, as most of his subjects had died of AIDS, which clearly can wreak havoc in the brain. Although the data on disparities in brain structure are preliminary, they point to a biological basis for sexual orientation.

Many theorists suspect that disparities between heterosexuals and homosexuals in brain structure may reflect the organizing effects of prenatal hormones on neurological development. Several lines of research suggest that hormonal secretions during critical periods of prenatal development may shape sexual development, organize the brain in a lasting manner, and influence subsequent sexual

Figure 10.13

Genetics and sexual orientation. A *concordance rate* indicates the percentage of twin pairs or other pairs of relatives that exhibit the same characteristic. If relatives who share more genetic relatedness show higher concordance rates than relatives who share less genetic overlap, this evidence suggests a genetic predisposition to the characteristic. Recent studies of both gay men and lesbian women have found higher concordance rates among identical twins than fraternal twins, who, in turn, exhibit more concordance than adoptive siblings. These findings are consistent with the hypothesis that genetic factors influence sexual orientation. (Data from Bailey & Pillard, 1991; Bailey et al., 1993)

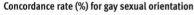

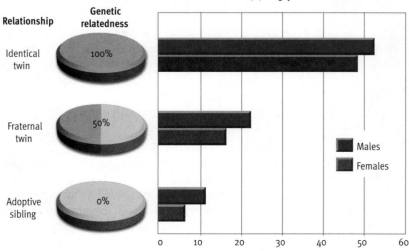

orientation (Berenbaum & Snyder, 1995). For example, researchers have found elevated rates of homosexuality among women exposed prenatally to a synthetic hormone (DES) that was formerly used to reduce the risk of miscarriage (by their mothers) and among women who have an adrenal disorder that results in abnormally high androgen levels during prenatal development (Breedlove, 1994; Meyer-Bahlburg et al., 1995).

Despite the recent breakthroughs, much remains to be learned about the determinants of sexual orientation. The pathways to homosexuality appear to be somewhat different for males as opposed to females (Gladue, 1994). The fact that identical twins of gay subjects turn out to be gay only about half the time suggests that the genetic predisposition to homosexuality is not overpowering. Environmental influences probably contribute to the development of homosexuality (Bem, 1996, 1998), but the nature of these environmental factors remains a matter of speculation.

Web Link 10.4

Queer Resources Directory (QRD)

In its 1994 mission statement, the *Queer Resources Directory* described itself as "an electronic research library specifically dedicated to sexual minorities—groups which have traditionally been labeled as 'queer' and systematically discriminated against." Consisting of more than 22,000 files and still growing, *QRD* offers a rich array of resources.

Sociopolitical Implications

Once again, we can see that the nature versus nurture debate can have far-reaching social and political implications. Homosexuals have long been victims of extensive—and in many instances legal—discrimination. Gays cannot legally formalize their unions in marriage, they are not allowed to openly join the U.S. military, and they are barred from some jobs (for example, many school districts will not hire gay teachers). However, if research were to show that being gay is largely a matter of biological destiny, much like being black or female or short, many of the arguments against equal rights for gays would disintegrate. Why ban gays from teaching, for instance, if their sexual preference cannot "rub off" on their students? Although I would argue that discrimination against gays should be brought to an end either way, many individuals' opinions about gay rights may be swayed by the outcome of the nature-nurture debate on the roots of homosexuality.

Achievement: In Search of Excellence

At the beginning of this chapter, we discussed Dennis Conner's lengthy, laborious, and tenacious pursuit of the America's Cup. He and his crew made great sacrifices and worked countless hours to try to achieve their goal. What motivates people to push themselves so hard? In all likelihood, it's a strong need for achievement. **The *achievement motive* is the need to master difficult challenges, to outperform others, and to meet high standards of excellence.** Above all else, the need for achievement involves the desire to excel—especially in competition with others.

Research on achievement motivation was pioneered by David McClelland and his colleagues (McClelland, 1985; McClelland et al., 1953). McClelland argued that achievement motivation is of the utmost importance. He viewed the need for achievement as the spark that ignites economic growth, scientific progress, inspirational leadership, and masterpieces in the creative arts.

Individual Differences in the Need for Achievement

The need for achievement is a fairly stable aspect of personality. Hence, research in this area has focused mostly on individual differences in achievement motivation. In this research, investigators usually measure participants' need for achievement with some variant of the Thematic Apperception Test (TAT) (Smith, 1992; Spangler, 1992). The TAT is a *projective* test, a test that requires subjects to respond to vague, ambiguous stimuli in ways that may reveal personal motives and traits (see Chapter 12). The stimulus materials for the TAT are pictures of people in ambiguous scenes open to interpretation. Examples include a man working at a desk and a woman seated in a chair staring off into space. Participants are asked to write or tell stories about what's happening in the scenes and what the characters are feeling. The themes of these stories are then scored to measure the strength of various needs. Figure 10.14 shows examples of stories dominated by themes of achievement and as another example, affiliation needs.

The research on individual differences in achievement motivation has yielded interesting findings on the characteristics of people who score high in the need for achievement. They tend to work harder and more persistently on tasks than people low in the need for achievement (Brown, 1974). They also are more likely than others to delay gratification in order to pursue long-term goals (Mischel, 1961; Raynor & Entin, 1982). In terms of careers, they typically go into competitive occupations that provide them with an opportunity to excel (McClelland, 1987).

Courtesy of David C. McClelland

"People with a high need for achievement are not gamblers; they are challenged to win by personal effort, not by luck."
DAVID MCCLELLAND

Affiliation arousal
George is an engineer who is working late. He is *worried that his wife will be annoyed* with him for neglecting her. She has been *objecting* that he cares more about his work than his wife and family. He seems *unable to satisfy* both his boss and his wife, but he *loves her* very much and will do his best to *finish up* fast and get home to her.

Achievement arousal
George is an engineer who *wants to win* a competition in which the man with the *most practicable drawing* will be awarded the contract to build a bridge. He is taking a moment to think *how happy he will be* if he wins. He has been *baffled by how to make such a long span strong*, but he remembers to *specify a new steel alloy* of great strength, submits his entry, but does not win, and is *very unhappy.*

Figure 10.14

Measuring motives with the Thematic Apperception Test (TAT). Subjects taking the TAT tell or write stories about what is happening in a scene, such as this one showing a man at work. The two stories shown here illustrate strong affiliation motivation and strong achievement motivation. The italicized parts of the stories are thematic ideas that would be identified by a TAT scorer. (Descriptions reprinted by permission of Dr. David McClelland.)

Apparently, their persistence and hard work often pay off. High achievement motivation correlates positively with measures of career success and with upward social mobility among lower-class men (Crockett, 1962; McClelland & Boyatzis, 1982).

Do people high in achievement need always tackle the biggest challenges available? Not necessarily. A curious finding has emerged in laboratory studies in which subjects have been asked to choose the difficulty level of a task to work on. Participants high in the need for achievement tend to select tasks of intermediate difficulty (McClelland & Koestner, 1992). For instance, in one study where subjects playing a ring-tossing game were allowed to stand as close to or far away from the target peg as they wanted, high achievers tended to prefer a moderate degree of challenge (Atkinson & Litwin, 1960). Research on the situational determinants of achievement behavior has suggested a reason why.

Situational Determinants of Achievement Behavior 8b

Your achievement drive is not the only determinant of how hard you work. Situational factors can also influence achievement strivings. John Atkinson (1974, 1981, 1992) has elaborated extensively on McClelland's original theory of achievement motivation and has identified some important situational determinants of achievement behavior. Atkinson theorizes that the tendency to pursue achievement in a particular situation depends on the following factors:

• The strength of one's *motivation* to *achieve* success, which is viewed as a stable aspect of personality.
• One's estimate of the *probability of success* for the task at hand. This varies from task to task.

• The *incentive value* of success, which depends on the tangible and intangible rewards for success on the specific task.

The last two variables are situational determinants of achievement behavior (see Figure 10.15). That is, they vary from one situation to another. According to Atkinson, the pursuit of achievement increases as the probability and incentive value of success go up.

Let's apply Atkinson's model to a simple example. According to his theory, your tendency to pursue a good grade in calculus should depend on your general motivation to achieve success, your estimate of the probability of getting a good grade in the class, and the value you place on getting a good grade in calculus. Thus, given a certain motivation to achieve success, you will pursue a good grade in calculus less vigorously if your professor gives impossible exams (thus lowering your expectancy of success) or if a good grade in calculus is not required for your major (lowering the incentive value of success).

Figure 10.15

Determinants of achievement behavior. According to John Atkinson, a person's pursuit of achievement in a particular situation depends on several factors. Some of these factors, such as need for achievement or fear of failure, are relatively stable motives that are part of the person's personality. Many other factors, such as the likelihood and value of success or failure, vary from one situation to another, depending on the circumstances.

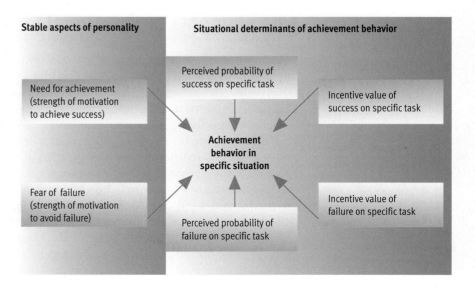

Understanding the Determinants of Achievement Behavior

According to John Atkinson, one's pursuit of achievement in a particular situation depends on several factors. Check your understanding of these factors by identifying each of the following vignettes as an example of one of the following six determinants of achievement behavior: (a) need for achievement; (b) perceived probability of success; (c) incentive value of success; (d) fear of failure; (e) perceived probability of failure; (f) incentive value of failure. The answers can be found in Appendix A.

D 1. Donna has just received a B in biology. Her reaction is typical of the way she responds to many situations involving achievement: "I didn't get an A, it's true, but at least I didn't flunk; that's what I was really worried about."

C. 2. Belinda is nervously awaiting the start of the finals of the 200-meter dash in the last meet of her high school career. "I've gotta win this race! This is the most important race of my life!"

E 3. Corey grins as he considers the easy time he's going to have this semester. "I won't need to study much for this course. This teacher never flunks anyone."

A 4. Diana's gotten the highest grade on every test throughout the semester, yet she's still up all night studying for the final. "I know I've got an A in the bag, but I want to be the best student Dr. McClelland's ever had!"

The joint influence of these situational factors may explain why high achievers prefer tasks of intermediate difficulty. Atkinson notes that the probability of success and the incentive value of success on tasks are interdependent to some degree. As tasks get easier, success becomes less satisfying. As tasks get harder, success becomes more satisfying but becomes less likely. When the probability and incentive value of success are weighed together, moderately challenging tasks seem to offer the best overall value.

Factoring in the Fear of Failure 8b

According to Atkinson, to understand achievement behavior, a person's fear of failure must also be considered (Atkinson & Birch, 1978). He maintains that people vary in their *motivation to avoid failure*. This motive is considered a stable aspect of personality. Together with situational factors such as the probability of failure and the negative value placed on failure, it influences achievement strivings. Figure 10.15 summarizes the factors in Atkinson's model that are thought to govern achievement behavior.

As with the motive to achieve success, the motive to avoid failure can stimulate achievement. For example, you might work very hard and very persistently in calculus primarily because you couldn't tolerate the shame associated with failure. In other words, you might work more to avoid a bad grade than to earn a good grade.

Fear is one of the most fundamental emotions. Thus, the relationship between achievement behavior and fear of failure illustrates how motivation and emotion are often intertwined. On the one hand, *emotion can cause motivation*. For example, *anger* about your work schedule may motivate you to look for a new job. *Jealousy* of an ex-girlfriend may motivate you to ask out her roommate. On the other hand, *motivation can cause emotion*. For example, your motivation to win a photography contest may lead to great *anxiety* during the judging and either *elation* if you win or *gloom* if you don't. Although motivation and emotion are closely related, they're *not* the same thing. We'll analyze the nature of emotion in the next section.

The Elements of Emotional Experience

The most profound and important experiences in life are saturated with emotion. Think of the *joy* that people feel at weddings, the *grief* they feel at funerals, the *ecstasy* they feel when they fall in love. Emotions also color everyday experiences. For instance, you might experience *anger* when a professor treats you rudely, *dismay* when you learn that your car needs expensive repairs, and *happiness* when you see that you aced your economics exam. In some respects, emotions lie at the core of mental health. The two most common complaints that lead people to seek psychotherapy are *depression* and *anxiety*. Clearly, emotions play a pervasive role in people's lives. Reflecting this reality, modern psychologists have increased their research on emotion in recent decades (Cacioppo & Gardner, 1999).

Exactly what is an emotion? Everyone has plenty of personal experience with emotion, but it's an elusive concept to define (LeDoux, 1995). Emotion includes cognitive, physiological, and behavioral components, which are summarized in the following definition: ***Emotion* involves (1) a subjective conscious experience (the cognitive component) accompanied by (2) bodily arousal (the physiological component) and (3) characteristic overt expressions (the behavioral component).** That's a pretty complex definition. Let's take a closer look at each of these three components of emotion.

The Cognitive Component: Subjective Feelings

Over 550 words in the English language refer to emotions (Averill, 1980). Ironically, however, people often have difficulty describing their emotions (Zajonc, 1980). Emotion is a highly personal, experience. In studying the cognitive component of emotions, psychologists generally rely on subjects' verbal reports of what they're experiencing. Their reports indicate that emotions are potentially intense internal feelings that sometimes seem to have a life of their own. People can't switch their emotions on and off like a bedroom light. If it were as simple as that, you could choose to be happy whenever you wanted. As Joseph LeDoux puts it, "Emotions are things that happen to us rather than things we will to occur" (1996, p. 19). Actually, some degree of emotional control is possible (Thayer, 1996), but emotions tend to involve automatic reactions that are difficult to regulate.

People's cognitive appraisals of events in their lives are key determinants of the emotions they experience (Lazarus, 1991, 1995; Parkinson, 1997). A specific event, such as giving a speech, may be highly threatening and thus anxiety arousing for one person but a "ho-hum," routine matter for another. The conscious experience of emotion includes an *evaluative* aspect. People characterize their emotions as pleasant or unpleasant (Lang, 1995; Schlosberg, 1954). Of course, individuals often experience "mixed emotions" that include both pleasant and unpleasant qualities (Cacioppo & Berntson, 1999). For example, an executive just given a promotion with challenging new responsibilities may experience both happiness and anxiety. A young man who has just lost his virginity may experience a mixture of apprehension, guilt, and delight.

The Physiological Component: Diffuse and Multifaceted

Emotional processes are closely tied to physiological processes, but the interconnections are enormously complex. The biological bases of emotions are diffuse and multi-faceted involving many areas in the brain and many neurotransmitter systems, as well as the autonomic nervous system and the endocrine system.

Autonomic Arousal

Imagine your reaction as your car spins out of control on an icy highway. Your fear is accompanied by a variety of physiological changes. Your heart rate and breathing accelerate. Your blood pressure surges, and your pupils dilate. The hairs on your skin stand erect, giving you "goose bumps," and you start to perspire. Although the physical reactions may not always be as obvious as in this scenario, *emotions are accompanied by visceral arousal* (Cacioppo et al., 1993). Surely you've experienced a "knot in your stomach" or a "lump in your throat" thanks to anxiety.

Much of the discernible physiological arousal associated with emotion occurs through the actions of the *autonomic nervous system,* which regulates the activity of glands, smooth muscles, and blood vessels (see Figure 10.16). As you may recall from Chapter 3, the autonomic nervous system is responsible for the highly emotional *fight-or-flight response,* which is largely modulated by the release of adrenal *hormones* that radiate throughout the body. Hormonal changes clearly play a crucial role in emotional responses to stress and may contribute to many other emotions as well (Baum, Grunberg, & Singer, 1992).

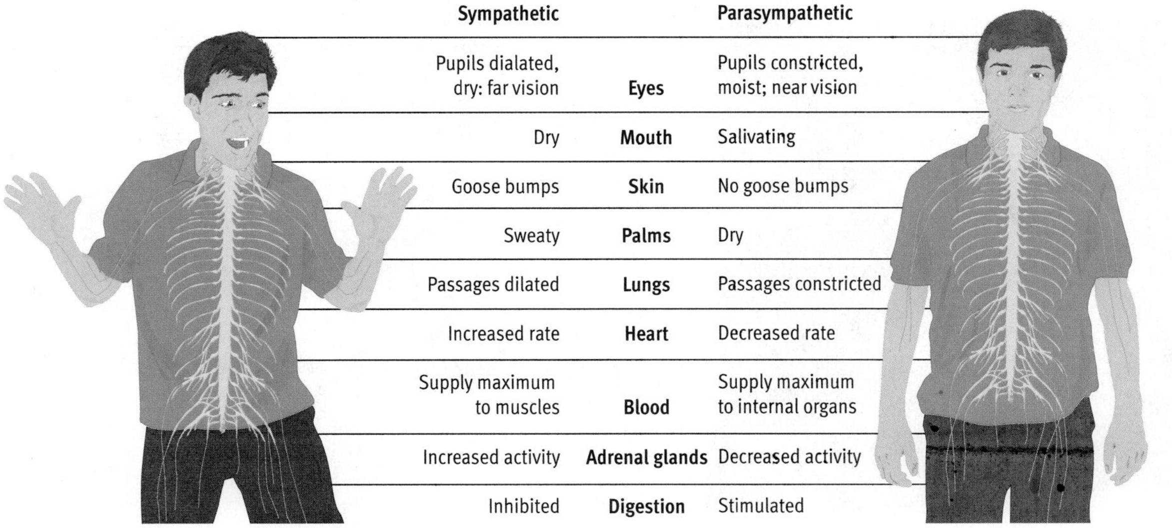

	Sympathetic		Parasympathetic
	Pupils dialated, dry: far vision	**Eyes**	Pupils constricted, moist; near vision
	Dry	**Mouth**	Salivating
	Goose bumps	**Skin**	No goose bumps
	Sweaty	**Palms**	Dry
	Passages dilated	**Lungs**	Passages constricted
	Increased rate	**Heart**	Decreased rate
	Supply maximum to muscles	**Blood**	Supply maximum to internal organs
	Increased activity	**Adrenal glands**	Decreased activity
	Inhibited	**Digestion**	Stimulated

Figure 10.16

Emotion and autonomic arousal. The autonomic nervous system (ANS) is composed of the nerves that connect to the heart, blood vessels, smooth muscles, and glands (consult Figure 3.7 for a more detailed view). The ANS is divided into the *sympathetic division,* which mobilizes bodily resources in response to stress, and the *parasympathetic division,* which conserves bodily resources. Emotions are frequently accompanied by sympathetic ANS activation, which leads to goose bumps, sweaty palms, and the other physical responses listed on the left side of the diagram.

One prominent part of emotional arousal is **the *galvanic skin response (GSR),* an increase in the electrical conductivity of the skin that occurs when sweat glands increase their activity.** GSR is a convenient and sensitive index of autonomic arousal that has been used as a measure of emotion in many laboratory studies.

The connection between emotion and autonomic arousal provides the basis for the *polygraph,* or *lie detector,* a device that records autonomic fluctuations while a subject is questioned.** A polygraph can't actually detect lies. It's really an emotion detector. It monitors key indicators of autonomic arousal, typically heart rate, blood pressure, respiration rate, and GSR. The assumption is that when people lie, they experience emotion (presumably anxiety) that produces noticeable changes in these physiological indicators (see Figure 10.17). The polygraph examiner asks a subject a number of nonthreatening questions to establish the person's baseline on these autonomic indicators. Then the examiner asks the critical questions (for example, "Where were you on the night of the burglary?") and observes whether the subject's autonomic arousal changes.

The polygraph is a potentially useful tool that can help police check out leads and alibis. However, its capacity to assess truthfulness is *far* from perfect (Lykken, 1981; Saxe, 1994). Part of the problem is that people who are telling the truth may experience emotional arousal when they respond to incriminating questions. Thus, polygraph tests often lead to accusations against people who are actually innocent. Another problem is that some people can lie without experiencing anxiety or autonomic arousal. The crux of the problem, as Leonard Saxe (1994) notes, is that "there is no evidence of a unique physiological reaction to deceit" (p. 71). As a general rule, polygraph examiners do a better job of identifying guilty suspects than ruling out innocent ones (Honts & Perry, 1992). Because of their high error rates, polygraph results cannot be submitted as evidence in most types of courtrooms.

Neural Circuits

The autonomic responses that accompany emotions are ultimately controlled in the brain. The hypothalamus, amygdala, and adjacent structures in the *limbic system* have long been viewed as the seat of emotions in the brain (Izard & Saxton, 1988; MacLean, 1993). Recent evidence suggests that the *amygdala* plays a particularly central role in the modulation of emotion. Joseph LeDoux (1986, 1993, 1996) and his colleagues have conducted extensive research on the classical conditioning of fear responses in animals. They have demonstrated that if an animal's amygdala is destroyed, the animal is unable to learn conditioned fear responses. Moreover, brain-imaging studies with human participants indicate that the amygdala is activated when subjects are shown emotion-arousing stimuli, such as pictures of mutilated bodies (Irwin et al., 1996) and when subjects are shown pictures depicting facial expressions of fear (Morris et al., 1996).

According to LeDoux (1996), the amygdala lies at the core of a complex set of neural circuits that process emotion. He believes that sensory inputs capable of eliciting emotions arrive in the thalamus, which simultaneously routes the information along two separate pathways: to the nearby amygdala and to areas in the cortex. The amygdala processes the information quickly, and if it detects a threat it almost instantly triggers activity in the hypothalamus that leads to the autonomic arousal and endocrine (hormonal) responses associated

Figure 10.17

Emotion and the polygraph.
A lie detector measures the autonomic arousal that most people experience when they tell a lie. After using non-threatening questions to establish a baseline, a poly-graph examiner looks for signs of arousal (such as the sharp change in GSR shown here) on incriminating questions. Unfortunately, the polygraph is not a very dependable index of whether people are lying.

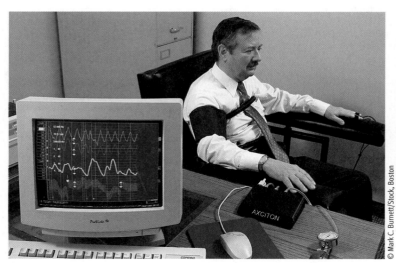

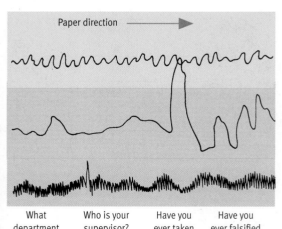

Paper direction

Respiration

GSR

Blood pressure

| What department do you work in? | Who is your supervisor? | Have you ever taken money from the bank? | Have you ever falsified bank records? |

with emotion. The processing in this pathway is extremely fast, so that emotions may be triggered even before the brain has had a chance to really "think" about the input. Meanwhile, the information shuttled along the other pathway is subjected to a more "leisurely" cognitive appraisal in the cortex. LeDoux believes that the rapid-response pathway evolved because it is a highly adaptive warning system that can "be the difference between life and death." Although the amygdala has been widely characterized as a brain center for emotion in general, the research thus far has mainly focused on the single emotion of fear.

The Behavioral Component: Nonverbal Expressiveness

At the behavioral level, people reveal their emotions through characteristic overt expressions such as smiles, frowns, furrowed brows, clenched fists, and slumped shoulders. In other words, *emotions are expressed in "body language," or nonverbal behavior.*

Facial expressions reveal a variety of basic emotions. In an extensive research project, Paul Ekman and Wallace Friesen have asked participants to identify what emotion a person was experiencing on the basis of facial cues in photographs. They have found that subjects are generally successful in identifying six fundamental emotions: happiness, sadness, anger, fear, surprise, and disgust (Ekman & Friesen, 1975, 1984). These studies have been criticized on the grounds that they have used a rather small set of artificial, highly posed photographs that don't do justice to the variety of facial expressions that can accompany specific emotions (Carroll & Russell, 1997). Still, the overall evidence indicates that people are reasonably skilled at deciphering emotions from others' facial expressions (Galati, Scherer, & Ricci-Bitti, 1997).

Some theorists believe that muscular feedback from one's own facial expressions contributes to one's conscious experience of emotions (Izard, 1990; Tomkins, 1991). Proponents of the *facial-feedback hypothesis* assert that facial muscles send signals to the brain and that these signals help the brain recognize the emotion that one is experiencing (see Figure 10.18). According to this view, smiles, frowns, and furrowed brows help create the experience of various emotions. Consistent with this idea, studies show that if subjects are instructed to contract their facial muscles to mimic facial expressions associated with certain emotions, they tend to report that they actually experience these emotions to some degree (Kleinke, Peterson, & Rutledge, 1998; Levenson, 1992).

The facial expressions that go with various emotions may be largely innate (Eibl-Ebesfeldt, 1975). For the most part, people who have been blind since birth smile and frown much like everyone else, even though they've never seen a smile or frown (Galati et al., 1997). The idea that facial expressions of emotion might be biologically built in has led to extensive cross-cultural research on the dynamics of emotion. Let's look at what investigators have learned about culture and the elements of emotional experience.

Culture and the Elements of Emotion

Are emotions innate reactions that are universal across cultures? Or are they socially learned reactions that are culturally variable? The voluminous research on this lingering question has not yielded a simple answer. Investigators have found both remarkable similarities and dramatic differences among cultures in the experience of emotion.

Courtesy of Joseph LeDoux, New York University

"In situations of danger, it is very useful to be able to respond quickly. The time saved by the amygdala in acting on the thalamic information, rather than waiting for the cortical input, may be the difference between life and death."
JOSEPH LEDOUX

Figure 10.18

The facial feedback hypothesis. According to the facial feedback hypothesis, inputs to subcortical centers automatically evoke facial expressions associated with certain emotions and the facial muscles then feed signals to the cortex that help it to recognize the emotion that one is experiencing. According to this view, facial expressions help create the subjective experience of various emotions.

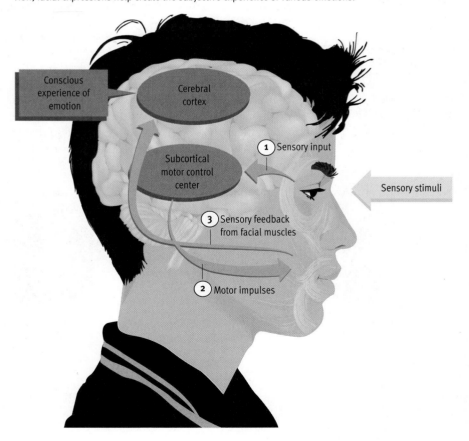

UCSC Perceptual Science Laboratory
Perceptions of other people, especially speech perception and facial expression, serve as a primary focus for research at the Perceptual Science Laboratory at the University of California, Santa Cruz. The site offers a broad set of resources, including a comprehensive guide to nonverbal facial analysis research being conducted in laboratories worldwide.

Figure 10.19

Cross-cultural comparisons of people's ability to recognize emotions from facial expressions. Ekman and Friesen (1975) found that people in highly disparate cultures showed fair agreement on the emotions portrayed in these photos. This consensus across cultures suggests that facial expressions of emotions may have a biological basis. (From *Unmasking the Face*, © 1975 by Paul Ekman, photographs courtesy of Paul Ekman.)

Cross-Cultural Similarities in Emotional Experience

After demonstrating that Western subjects could discern specific emotions from facial expressions, Ekman and Friesen (1975) took their facial-cue photographs on the road to other societies to see whether nonverbal expressions of emotion transcend cultural boundaries. Testing participants in Argentina, Spain, Japan, and other countries, they found considerable cross-cultural agreement in the identification of happiness, sadness, anger, fear, surprise, and disgust based on facial expressions (see Figure 10.19). Still, Ekman and Friesen wondered whether this agreement might be the result of learning rather than biology, given that people in different cultures often share considerable exposure to Western mass media (magazines, newspapers, television, and so forth), which provide many visual depictions of people's emotional reactions. To rule out this possibility, they took their photos to a remote area in New Guinea and showed them to a group of natives (the Fore) who had had virtually no contact with Western culture. Even the people from this preliterate culture did a fair job of identifying the emotions portrayed in the pictures (see Figure 10.19). Subsequent comparisons of many other societies have also shown considerable cross-cultural congruence in the judgment of facial expressions (Biehl et al., 1997; Ekman, 1992, 1993; Izard, 1994).

Cross-cultural similarities have also been found in the cognitive and physiological elements of emotional experience (Scherer & Wallbott, 1994). For example, in making cognitive appraisals of events that might elicit emotional reactions, people from different cultures generally think along the same lines (Mauro, Sato, & Tucker, 1992; Mesquita & Frijda, 1992). Understandably, then, the types of events that trigger specific emotions are fairly similar across cultures (Frijda, 1999; Scherer, 1997). And as one might expect, the physiological arousal that accompanies emotion also appears to be largely invariant across cultures (Wallbott & Scherer, 1988). Thus, researchers have found a great deal of cross-cultural continuity and uniformity in the cognitive, physiological, and behavioral (expressive) elements of emotional experience.

Cross-Cultural Differences in Emotional Experience

The cross-cultural similarities in emotional experience are impressive, but researchers have also found many cultural disparities in how people think about and express their emotions. Foremost among these disparities are the fascinating variations in how cultures categorize emotions. Some basic categories of emotion that are universally understood in Western cultures appear to go unrecognized—or at least unnamed—in some non-Western cultures. James Russell (1991) has compiled numerous examples of English words for emotions that have no equivalent in other languages. For example, Tahitians have no word that corresponds to *sadness*. Many non-Western groups, including the Yoruba of Nigeria, the Kaluli of New Guinea, and the Chinese, lack a word for *depression*. The concept of *anxiety* seems to go unrecognized among Eskimos and the Yoruba, and the Quichua of Ecuador lack a word for *remorse*. After reviewing the extensive evidence on the issue, Russell (1991) concludes that "people of different cultures and speaking different languages categorize the emotions somewhat differently" (p. 444).

A similar conclusion can be drawn about nonverbal expressions of emotion. Although the natural facial expressions associated with basic emotions appear to be pancultural, people can and do learn to control and modify these expressions. *Display rules are norms that regulate the appropriate expression of emotions.* They prescribe when, how, and to whom people can show various emotions. These norms vary from one culture to another (Ekman, 1992), as do attitudes about specific emotions (Wierzbicka, 1994). The Ifaluk, for instance, severely restrict expressions of happiness because they believe that this emotion often leads people to neglect their duties (Lutz, 1987). Japanese culture emphasizes the suppression of negative emotions in public. More so than in other cultures, the Japanese are socialized to mask emotions such as anger, sadness, and disgust with stoic facial expressions or polite smiling. Thus, nonverbal expressions of emotions vary somewhat across cultures because of culture-specific attitudes and display rules.

	Fear	Disgust	Happiness	Anger
	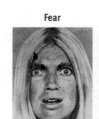			
Country	Agreement in judging photos (%)			
United States	85	92	97	67
Brazil	67	97	95	90
Chile	68	92	95	94
Argentina	54	92	98	90
Japan	66	90	100	90
New Guinea	54	44	82	50

Theories of Emotion

How do psychologists explain the experience of emotion? A variety of theories and conflicting models exist. Some have been vigorously debated for over a century. As we describe these theories, you'll recognize a familiar bone of contention. Like theories of motivation, theories of emotion differ in their emphasis on the innate biological basis of emotion versus the social, environmental basis.

James-Lange Theory

As we noted in Chapter 1, <u>William James</u> was an early theorist who urged psychologists to explore the functions of consciousness. James (1884) developed a theory of emotion over 100 years ago that remains influential today. At about the same time, he and <u>Carl Lange</u> (1885) independently proposed that the *conscious experience of emotion results from one's perception of autonomic arousal.* Their theory stood common sense on its head. Everyday logic suggests that when you stumble onto a rattlesnake in the woods, the conscious experience of fear leads to visceral arousal (the fight-or-flight response). The James-Lange theory of emotion asserts the opposite: that the perception of visceral arousal leads to the conscious experience of fear (see Figure 10.20). In other words, while you might assume that your pulse is racing because you're fearful, James and Lange argue that you're fearful because your pulse is racing.

The James-Lange theory emphasizes the physiological determinants of emotion. According to this view, *different patterns of autonomic activation lead to the experience of different emotions.* Hence, people supposedly distinguish emotions such as fear, joy, and anger on the basis of the exact configuration of physical reactions they experience.

Cannon-Bard Theory

Walter Cannon (1927) found the James-Lange theory unconvincing. Cannon, who developed the concept of the fight-or-flight response, pointed out that physiological arousal may occur without the experience of emotion (if one exercises vigorously, for instance). He also argued that visceral changes are too slow to precede the conscious experience of emotion. Finally, he argued that people experiencing very different emotions, such as fear, joy, and anger, exhibit almost identical patterns of autonomic arousal.

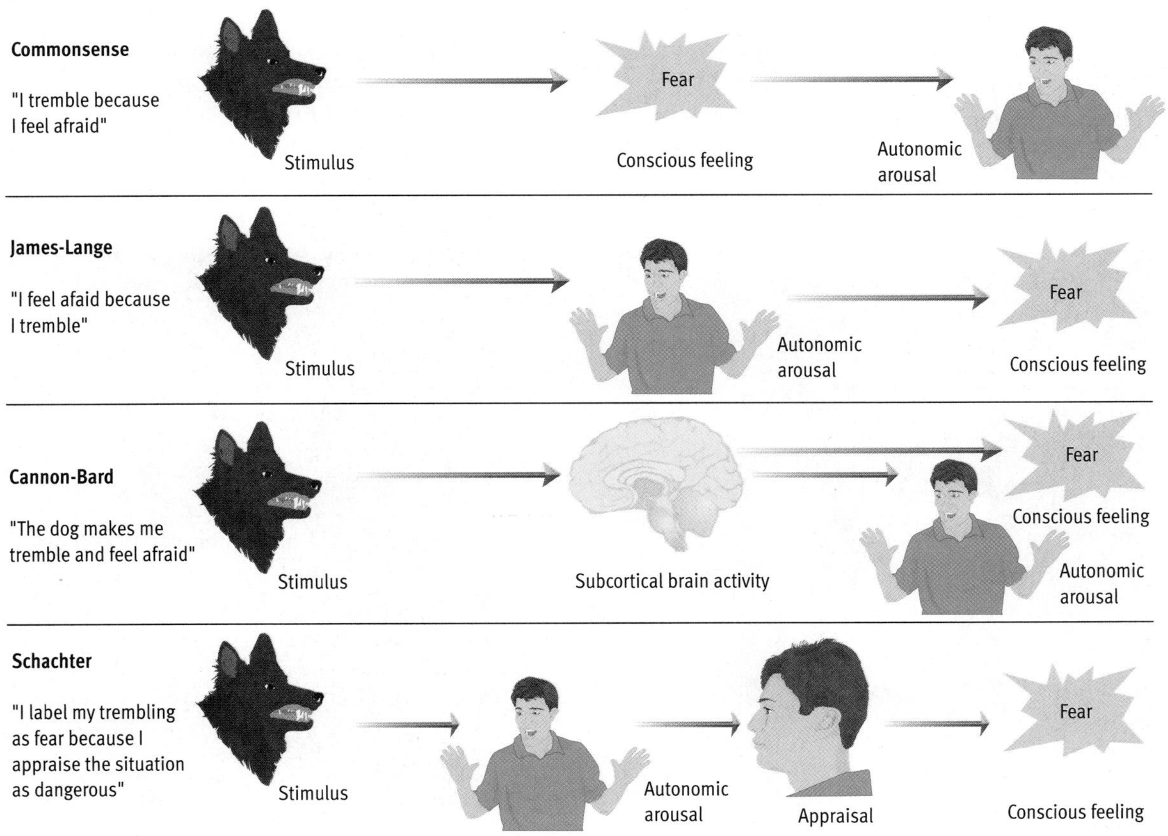

Commonsense

"I tremble because I feel afraid"

Stimulus → Fear (Conscious feeling) → Autonomic arousal

James-Lange

"I feel afaid because I tremble"

Stimulus → Autonomic arousal → Fear (Conscious feeling)

Cannon-Bard

"The dog makes me tremble and feel afraid"

Stimulus → Subcortical brain activity → Fear (Conscious feeling) / Autonomic arousal

Schachter

"I label my trembling as fear because I appraise the situation as dangerous"

Stimulus → Autonomic arousal → Appraisal → Fear (Conscious feeling)

Figure 10.20

Theories of emotion. Three influential theories of emotion are contrasted with one another and with the commonsense view. The James-Lange theory was the first to suggest that feelings of arousal cause emotion, rather than vice versa. Schachter built on this idea by adding a second factor—interpretation (appraisal and labeling) of arousal.

Thus, Cannon espoused a different explanation of emotion. Later, Philip Bard (1934) elaborated on it. The resulting Cannon-Bard theory argues that emotion occurs when the *thalamus* sends signals *simultaneously* to the cortex (creating the conscious experience of emotion) and to the autonomic nervous system (creating visceral arousal). The Cannon-Bard model is compared to the James-Lange model in Figure 10.20. Cannon and Bard were off the mark a bit in pinpointing the thalamus as the neural center for emotion. However, many modern theorists agree with the Cannon-Bard view that emotions originate in subcortical brain structures (LeDoux, 1996; Panksepp, 1991; Rolls, 1990) and with the assertion that people do not discern their emotions from different patterns of autonomic activation (Frijda, 1999; Wagner, 1989).

Schachter's Two-Factor Theory 8d

In another influential analysis, Stanley Schachter asserted that people look at situational cues to differentiate between alternative emotions. According to Schachter (1964; Schachter & Singer, 1962, 1979), the experience of emotion depends on two factors: (1) autonomic arousal and (2) cognitive interpretation of that arousal. Schachter proposed that when you experience visceral arousal, you search your environment for an explanation (see Figure 10.20 again). If you're stuck in a traffic jam, you'll probably label your arousal as anger. If you're taking an important exam, you'll probably label it as anxiety. If you're celebrating your birthday, you'll probably label it as happiness.

Schachter agrees with the James-Lange view that emotion is inferred from arousal. However, he also agrees with the Cannon-Bard position that different emotions yield indistinguishable patterns of arousal. He reconciles these views by arguing that people look to external rather than internal cues to differentiate and label their specific emotions. In essence, Schachter suggests that people think along the following lines: "If I'm aroused and you're obnoxious, I must be angry."

The two-factor theory of emotion has been tested in numerous studies that have produced mixed results. Some aspects of the model have been supported and some have not (Reisenzein, 1983). A naturalistic study of interpersonal attraction by Dutton and Aron (1974) provides a particularly clever example of research that supported the two-factor theory. They arranged for young men crossing a footbridge in a park to encounter a young woman who asked them to stop briefly to fill out a questionnaire. The woman offered to explain the research at some future time and gave the men her phone number. Autonomic arousal was manipulated by enacting this scenario on two very different bridges. One was a long suspension bridge that swayed precariously 230 feet above a river (see the photo below). The other bridge was a solid, safe structure a mere 10 feet above a small stream. The experimenters reasoned that the men crossing the shaky, frightening bridge would be experiencing emotional arousal and that some of them might attribute that arousal to the woman rather than to the bridge. If so, they might mislabel their emotion as lust rather than fear and infer that they were

"Cognitive factors play a major role in determining how a subject interprets his bodily feelings."
STANLEY SCHACHTER

In their naturalistic study of the two-factor theory of emotion, Dutton and Aron (1974) manipulated emotional arousal by arranging for males to encounter a female confederate on this precarious-looking bridge.

attracted to the woman. The dependent variable was how many of the men later called the woman to pursue a date. As predicted, more of the men who met the woman on the precarious bridge called her for a date than did those who met her on the safe bridge.

The Dutton and Aron study supports the hypothesis that people often infer emotion from their physiological arousal and label that emotion in accordance with their cognitive explanation for it. The fact that the explanation may be inaccurate sheds light on why people often seem confused about their own emotions.

Evolutionary Theories of Emotion

In recent years, some theorists interested in emotion have returned to ideas espoused by Charles Darwin over a century ago. Darwin (1872) believed that emotions developed because of their adaptive value. Fear, for instance, would help an organism avoid danger and thus would aid in survival. Hence, Darwin viewed human emotions as a product of evolution. This premise serves as the foundation for several modern theories of emotion developed independently by S. S. Tomkins (1980, 1991), Carroll Izard (1984, 1991), and Robert Plutchik (1984, 1993).

These *evolutionary theories* consider emotions to be largely innate reactions to certain stimuli. As such, emotions should be immediately recognizable under most conditions without much thought. After all, primitive animals that are incapable of complex thought seem to have little difficulty in recognizing their emotions. Evolutionary theorists believe that emotion evolved before thought. They assert that thought plays a relatively small role in emotion, although they admit that learning and cognition may have some influence on human emotions. Evolutionary theories generally assume that emotions originate in subcortical brain structures (such as the hypothalamus and most of the limbic system) that evolved before the higher brain areas (in the cortex) associated with complex thought.

Evolutionary theories also assume that evolution has equipped humans with a small number of innate emotions with proven adaptive value. Thus, the principal question that evolutionary theories of emotion wrestle with is, *What are the fundamental emotions?* Evolutionary theorists attempt to identify these primary emotions by searching for universals—emotions that are expressed and recognized in the

Silvan Tomkins	Carroll Izard	Robert Plutchik
Fear	Fear	Fear
Anger	Anger	Anger
Enjoyment	Joy	Joy
Disgust	Disgust	Disgust
Interest	Interest	Anticipation
Surprise	Surprise	Surprise
Contempt	Contempt	
Shame	Shame	
	Sadness	Sadness
Distress		
	Guilt	
		Acceptance

same way in widely disparate cultures. Figure 10.21 summarizes the conclusions of the leading theorists in this area. As you can see, Tomkins, Izard, and Plutchik have not come up with identical lists, but they show considerable agreement. All three conclude that people exhibit eight to ten primary emotions. Moreover, six of these emotions appear on all three lists: fear, anger, joy, disgust, interest, and surprise.

Of course, people experience more than just eight to ten emotions. How do evolutionary theories account for this variety? They propose that the many emotions that people experience are produced by (1) blends of primary emotions and (2) variations in intensity. For example, Robert Plutchik (1980, 1993) has devised an elegant model of how primary emotions such as fear and surprise may blend into secondary emotions such as awe. Plutchik's model also posits that various emotions, such as apprehension, fear, and terror, involve one primary emotion experienced at different levels of intensity (see Figure 10.22).

Figure 10.21

Primary emotions.
Evolutionary theories of emotion attempt to identify primary emotions. Three leading theorists—Silvan Tomkins, Carroll Izard, and Robert Plutchik—have compiled different lists of primary emotions, but this chart shows great overlap among the basic emotions identified by these theorists. (Based on Mandler, 1984)

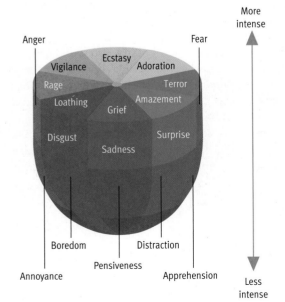

Figure 10.22

Emotional intensity in Plutchik's model. According to Plutchik, diversity in human emotion is a product of variations in emotional intensity, as well as a blending of primary emotions. Each vertical slice in the diagram is a primary emotion that can be subdivided into emotional expressions of varied intensity, ranging from most intense (top) to least intense (bottom). (Based on art in "A Language for Emotions," by R. Plutchik, 1980, *Psychology Today, 13* (9), 68–78. Reprinted with permission from *Psychology Today* magazine. Copyright © 1980, Sussex Publishers, Inc.)

Understanding Theories of Emotion

Check your understanding of theories of emotion by matching the theories we discussed with the statements below. Let's borrow William James's classic example: Assume that you just stumbled onto a bear in the woods. The first statement expresses the commonsense explanation of your fear. Each of the remaining statements expresses the essence of a different theory; indicate which theory in the spaces provided. The answers are provided in Appendix A.

1. You tremble because you're afraid.

Common Sense

2. You're afraid because you're trembling.

James- Lange theory

3. You're afraid because situational cues (the bear) suggest that's why you're trembling.

Schachter's two-factor theory

4. You're afraid because the bear has elicited an innate primary emotion.

Evolutionary theories

Putting It in Perspective

Five of our organizing themes were particularly prominent in this chapter: the influence of cultural contexts, the dense connections between psychology and society at large, psychology's theoretical diversity, the interplay of heredity and environment, and the multiple causes of behavior.

Our discussion of motivation and emotion demonstrated once again that there are both similarities and differences across cultures in behavior. The neural, biochemical, genetic, and hormonal processes underlying hunger and eating, for instance, are universal. But cultural factors influence what people prefer to eat and how much they eat. In a similar vein, researchers have found a great deal of cross-cultural congruence in the cognitive, physiological, and expressive elements of emotional experience, but they have also found cultural variations in how people think about and express their emotions. Thus, as we have seen in previous chapters, psychological processes are characterized by both cultural variance and invariance.

Our discussion of the controversies surrounding evolutionary theory and the determinants of sexual orientation show once again that psychology is not an ivory tower enterprise. It evolves in a sociohistorical context that helps to shape the debates in the field, and these debates often have far-reaching social and political ramifications for society at large. We ended the chapter with a discussion of various theories of emotion, which showed once again that psychology is characterized by great theoretical diversity.

Finally, we repeatedly saw that biological and environmental factors jointly govern behavior. For example, we learned that eating behavior, sexual desire, and the experience of emotion all depend on complicated interactions between biological and environmental determinants. Indeed, complicated interactions permeated the entire chapter, demonstrating that if we want to fully understand behavior, we have to take multiple causes into account. We will see more of this complexity in the upcoming Personal Application, where we will continue our discussion of emotion, looking at recent research on the correlates of happiness. In the Critical Thinking Application that follows, we discuss how to carefully analyze the types of arguments that permeated this chapter.

Exploring the Ingredients of Happiness

Answer the following "true" or "false."

_____ 1 The empirical evidence indicates that most people are relatively unhappy.

_____ 2 Although wealth doesn't *guarantee* happiness, wealthy people are much more likely to be happy than the rest of the population.

_____ 3 People who have children are happier than people without children.

_____ 4 Good health is an essential requirement for happiness.

The answer to all these questions is "false." These assertions are all reasonable and widely believed hypotheses about the correlates of happiness, but they have *not* been supported by empirical research. Recent years have brought a surge of interest in the correlates of *subjective well-being—individuals' personal perceptions of their overall happiness and life satisfaction.* The findings of this research are quite interesting. As you have already seen from our true-false questions, many commonsense notions about happiness appear to be inaccurate.

How Happy Are People?

One of these inaccuracies is the apparently widespread assumption that most people are relatively unhappy. Writers, social scientists, and the general public seem to believe that people around the world are predominantly dissatisfied and unhappy, yet empirical surveys consistently find that the vast majority of respondents—even those who are poor or disabled—characterize themselves as fairly happy (Diener & Diener, 1996; Myers & Diener, 1995). When people are asked to rate their happiness, only a small minority place themselves below the neutral point on the various scales used (see Figure 10.23). When the average subjective well-being of entire nations is computed, based on almost 1000 surveys, the means cluster toward the positive end of the scale

(Veenhoven, 1993). That's not to say that everyone is equally happy. Researchers find substantial and thought-provoking disparities among people in subjective well-being, which we will analyze momentarily, but the overall picture seems rosier than anticipated.

Factors That Do Not Predict Happiness

Let us begin our discussion of individual differences in happiness by highlighting those things that turn out to be relatively unimportant determinants of subjective well-being. Quite a number of factors that you might expect to be influential appear to bear little or no relationship to general happiness.

Money. There *is* a positive correlation between income and subjective feelings of happiness, but in modern, affluent cultures the association is surprisingly weak (Myers & Diener, 1995). For example, one study found a correlation of just .12 between income and happiness in the United States (Diener et al., 1993). On the average, even

wealthy people are only marginally happier than those in the middle classes. The problem with money is that in this era of voracious consumption, most people find a way to spend it all and come out short no matter how much they make.

Age. Age and happiness are consistently found to be unrelated. Age accounts for less than 1 % of the variation in people's happiness (Inglehart, 1990; Myers & Diener, 1997). The key factors influencing subjective well-being may shift some as people grow older—work becomes less important, health more so—but people's average level of happiness tends to remain remarkably stable over the life span.

Parenthood. Children can be a tremendous source of joy and fulfillment, but they can also be a tremendous source of headaches and hassles. Compared to childless couples, parents worry more and experience more marital problems (Argyle, 1987). Apparently, the good and bad aspects of parenthood balance each other out,

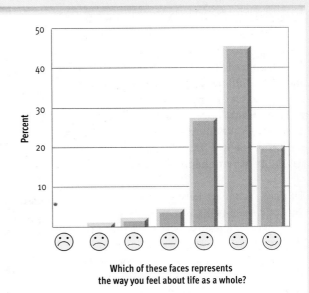

Figure 10.23

Measuring happiness with a nonverbal scale.
Researchers have used a variety of methods to estimate the distribution of happiness. For example, in one study in the United States, respondents were asked to examine the seven facial expressions shown and select the one that "comes closest to expressing how you feel about your life as a whole." As you can see, the vast majority of participants chose happy faces. (Data adapted from Myers, 1992)

Which of these faces represents the way you feel about life as a whole?

because the evidence indicates that people who have children are neither more nor less happy than people without children.

Intelligence and attractiveness.   Intelligence and physical attractiveness are highly valued traits in modern society, but researchers have not found an association between either characteristic and happiness (Diener, 1984; Diener, Wolsic, & Fujita, 1995).

Moderately Good Predictors of Happiness

Research has identified some facets of life that appear to have a *moderate* association with subjective well-being: health, social activity, and religious belief.

Health.   Good physical health would seem to be an essential requirement for happiness, but people adapt to health problems. Research reveals that individuals who develop serious, disabling health conditions aren't as unhappy as one might guess (Myers, 1992). Furthermore, Freedman (1978) argues that good health does not, by itself, produce happiness, because people tend to take good health for granted. Considerations such as these may help to explain why researchers find only a moderate positive correlation (average = .32) between health status and subjective well-being (Argyle, 1999).

Social Activity.   Humans are social animals, and interpersonal relations do appear to contribute to people's happiness. Those who are satisfied with their social support and friendship networks and those who are socially active report above-average levels of happiness (Cooper, Okamura, & Gurka, 1992; Myers, 1999). At the other end of the spectrum, people troubled by loneliness tend to be very unhappy (Argyle, 1987).

Religion.   The link between religiosity and subjective well-being is modest, but a number of large-scale surveys suggest that people with heartfelt religious convictions are more likely to be happy than people who characterize themselves as nonreligious (Argyle, 1999; Poloma & Pendleton, 1990).

Strong Predictors of Happiness

The list of factors that turn out to have fairly strong associations with happiness is surprisingly short. The key ingredients of happiness appear to involve love, work, and personality.

Love and Marriage.   Romantic relationships can be stressful, but people consistently rate being in love as one of the most critical ingredients of happiness (Myers, 1999). Furthermore, although people complain a lot about their marriages, the evidence indicates that marital status is a key correlate of happiness. Among both men and women, married people are happier than people who are single or divorced (see Figure 10.24; Myers & Diener, 1995). However, the causal relations underlying this correlation are unclear. It may be that happiness causes marital satisfaction more than marital satisfaction promotes happiness.

Work.   Given the way people often complain about their jobs, one might not expect work to be a key source of happiness, but it is. Although less critical than love and marriage, job satisfaction has a substantial association with general happiness (Warr, 1999). Studies also show that unemployment has strong negative effects on subjective well-being (Argyle, 1999). It is difficult to sort out whether job satisfaction causes happiness or vice versa, but evidence suggests that causation flows both ways (Argyle, 1987).

Personality.   The best predictor of individuals' future happiness is their past happiness (Diener & Lucas, 1999). Some people seem destined to be happy and others unhappy, regardless of their triumphs or setbacks. Evidence suggests that happiness does not depend on external circumstances—buying a nice house, getting promoted—as much as internal factors, such as one's outlook on life (Lykken & Tellegen, 1996). With this fact in mind, researchers have begun to look for links between personality and subjective well-being, and they have found some relatively strong correlations. Personality correlates of happiness include extraversion, self-esteem and optimism (Lucas, Diener, & Suh, 1996).

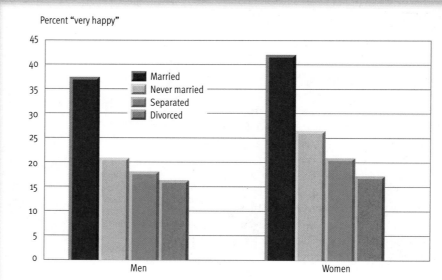

Figure 10.24

Happiness and marital status. This graph shows the percentage of adults characterizing themselves as "Very happy" as a function of marital status. Among both women and men, happiness shows up more in those who are married, as opposed to those who are separated, who are divorced, or who have never married. These data and many others suggest that marital satisfaction is a key ingredient of happiness. (Data from Myers, 1999, in *Well-Being*, by Kahneman, Diener and Schwarz, Eds. Copyright © 1999. Reprinted by permission of Russell Sage Foundation.)

Conclusions About Subjective Well-Being

We must be cautious in drawing inferences about the causes of happiness, because the available data are correlational (see Figure 10.25). Nonetheless, the empirical findings suggest a number of worthwhile insights about the roots of happiness.

First, research on happiness demonstrates that the determinants of subjective well-being are precisely that: subjective. *Objective realities are not as important as subjective feelings.* In other words, your health, your wealth, your job, and your age are not as influential as how you *feel* about your health, wealth, job, and age (Schwarz & Strack, 1999). Second, *when it comes to happiness, everything is relative* (Argyle, 1999). In other words, you evaluate what you have relative to what the people around you have and relative to what you expected to have. Generally, we compare ourselves with others who are similar to us. Thus, people who are wealthy assess what they have by comparing themselves with their wealthy friends and neighbors. This is one reason that there is little correlation between wealth and happiness.

Third, *research on subjective well-being indicates that people often adapt to their circumstances.* This adaptation effect is one reason that increases in income don't necessarily bring increases in happiness. Thus, *hedonic*

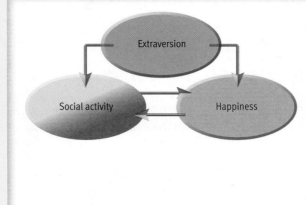

Figure 10.25

Possible causal relations among the correlates of happiness. Although we have considerable data on the correlates of happiness, it is difficult to untangle the possible causal relationships. For example, we know that there is a moderate positive correlation between social activity and happiness, but we can't say for sure whether high social activity causes happiness or whether happiness causes people to be more socially active. Moreover, in light of the research showing that a third variable—extraversion—correlates with both variables, we have to consider the possibility that extraversion causes both greater social activity and greater happiness.

adaptation occurs when the mental scale that people use to judge the pleasantness-unpleasantness of their experiences shifts so that their neutral point, or baseline for comparison, changes. Unfortunately, when people's experiences improve, hedonic adaptation may *sometimes* put them on a *hedonic treadmill*—their neutral point moves upward, so that the improvements yield no real benefits (Kahneman, 1999). However, when people have to grapple with major setbacks, hedonic adaptation probably helps protect their mental and physical health. For example, people who are sent to prison and people who develop debilitating diseases are not as unhappy as one might assume, because they adapt to their changed situations and evaluate events from a new perspective (Frederick & Loewenstein, 1999). This effect is probably related to the fourth conclusion we can draw about subjective well-being: *research shows that the quest for happiness is never hopeless* (Freedman, 1978; Myers, 1992). Although there are no simple recipes for happiness, the evidence indicates that some people find happiness in spite of seemingly insurmountable problems. There is nothing, short of terminal illness—no setback, shortcoming, difficulty, or inadequacy—that makes happiness impossible.

Factors that do not predict happiness-
Money
Age
Parenthood
Intelligence & attractiveness

Moderately Good predictors of happiness-
Health
social activity
religion

Strong predictors of Happiness-
Love & Marriage
Work
personality

Analyzing Arguments:
Making Sense Out of Controversy

Consider the following argument. "Dieting is harmful to your health because the tendency to be obese is largely inherited." What is your reaction to this reasoning? Do you find it convincing? We hope not, as this argument is seriously flawed. Can you see what's wrong? There is no relationship between the conclusion that "dieting is harmful to your health" and the reason given that "the tendency to be obese is largely inherited." The argument is initially seductive because most people know that obesity *is* largely inherited, so the reason provided represents a true statement. But the reason is unrelated to the conclusion advocated. This scenario may strike you as odd, but if you start listening carefully to discussions about controversial issues, you will probably notice that people often cite irrelevant considerations in support of their favored conclusions.

This chapter was loaded with controversial issues that sincere, well-meaning people could argue about for weeks. Are gender differences in mating preferences a product of evolution or of modern economic realities? Is there a biological basis for homosexuality? Unfortunately, arguments about issues such as these typically are unproductive in terms of moving toward resolution

or agreement because most people know little about the rules of argumentation. In this application, we will explore what makes arguments sound or unsound in the hope of improving your ability to analyze and think critically about arguments.

The Anatomy of an Argument

In everyday usage, the word *argument* is used to refer to a dispute or disagreement between two or more people, but in the technical language of rhetoric, **an *argument* consists of one or more premises that are used to provide support for a conclusion.** *Premises* **are the reasons that are presented to persuade someone that a conclusion is true or probably true.** *Assumptions* **are premises for which no proof or evidence is offered.** Assumptions are often left unstated. For example, suppose that your doctor tells you that you should exercise regularly because regular exercise is good for your heart. In this simple argument, the conclusion is "You should exercise regularly." The premise that leads to this conclusion is the idea that "exercise is good for your heart." An unstated assumption is that everyone wants a healthy heart.

In the language of argument analysis, premises are said to support (or not support) conclusions. A conclusion may be supported by one reason or by many reasons. One way to visualize these possibilities is to draw an analogy between the reasons that support a conclusion and the legs that support a table (Halpern, 1996). As shown in Figure 10.26, a table top (conclusion) could be supported by one strong leg (a single strong reason) or many thin legs (lots of weaker reasons). Of course, the reasons provided for a conclusion may fail to support the conclusion. Returning to our table analogy, the table top might not be supported because the legs are too thin (very weak reasons) or because the legs are not attached (irrelevant reasons).

Arguments can get pretty complicated, as they usually have more parts than just reasons and conclusions. In addition, there often are *counterarguments,* which are reasons that take support away from a conclusion. And sometimes the most important part of an argument is something that is not there—reasons that have been omitted, either deliberately or not, that would lead to a different conclusion if they were supplied. Given all the complex variations that are possible in arguments, it is impossible to give you

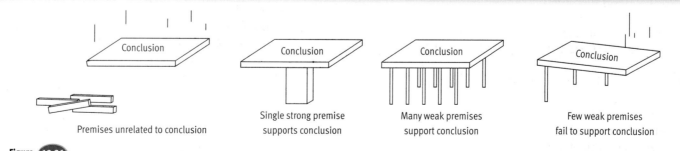

Figure 10.26

An analogy for understanding the strength of arguments. Halpern (1996) draws an analogy between the reasons that support a conclusion and the legs that support a table. She points out that a conclusion may be supported effectively by one strong premise or many weak premises. Of course, the reasons provided for a conclusion may also *fail* to provide adequate support. (From *Thought & Knowledge: An Introduction to Critical Thinking,* by D. F. Halpern, 1996, p. 181, Figure 5.1. Copyright © 1996 Lawrence Erlbaum Associates. Reprinted by permission of Lawrence Erlbaum Associates.)

simple rules for judging arguments, but we can highlight some common fallacies and then provide some criteria you can apply in thinking critically about arguments.

Common Fallacies

As noted previously, cognitive scientists have compiled lenghty lists of fallacies that people frequently display in their arguments. This section describes five common fallacies. To illustrate each one, we will assume the role of someone arguing that pornographic material on the Internet (cyberporn) should be banned or heavily regulated.

Irrelevant Reasons. Reasons cannot provide support for an argument unless they are relevant to the conclusion. Arguments that depend on irrelevant reasons—either intentionally or inadvertently—are quite common. You already saw one example at the beginning of this application. The Latin term for this fallacy is *non sequitur,* which literally translates to "it doesn't follow." In other words, the conclusion does not follow from the premise. For example, in the debate about Internet pornography, you might hear the following *non sequitur:* "We need to regulate cyberporn because research has shown that most date rapes go unreported."

Circular Reasoning. In *circular reasoning* the premise and conclusion are simply restatements of each other. People vary their wording a little so it isn't obvious, but when you look closely, the conclusion is the premise. For example, in arguments about Internet pornography you might hear someone assert, "We need to control cyberporn because it currently is unregulated."

Slippery Slope. The concept of *slippery slope* argumentation takes its name from the notion that if you are on a slippery slope and you don't dig your heels in, you will slide and slide until you reach bottom. A slippery slope argument typically asserts that if you allow X to happen, things will spin out of control and far worse events will follow. The trick is that no inherent connection exists between X and the events that are predicted to follow. For example, in the debate about medical marijuana, opponents have argued, "If you legalize medical marijuana, the next thing you know cocaine and heroin will be legal." In the debate about cyberporn, a slippery slope argument might go, "If we don't ban cyberporn, the next thing you know, grade school children will be watching smut all day long in their school libraries."

Weak Analogies. An *analogy* asserts that two concepts or events are similar in some way. Hence, you can draw conclusions about event B because of its similarity to event A. Analogies are useful in thinking about complex issues, but some analogies are weak or inappropriate because the similarity between A and B is superficial, minimal, or irrelevant to the issue at hand. For example, in the debate about Internet erotica, someone might argue, "Cyberporn is morally offensive, just like child molestation. We wouldn't tolerate child molestation, so we shouldn't permit cyberporn."

False Dichotomy. A *false dichotomy* creates an either-or choice between two outcomes: the outcome advocated and some obviously horrible outcome that any sensible person would want to avoid. These outcomes are presented as the only possible ones, when in reality many other outcomes are possible, including some that lie between the extremes depicted in the false dichotomy. In the debate about Internet pornography, someone might argue, "We can ban cyberporn, or we can hasten the moral decay of modern society."

Evaluating the Strength of Arguments

In everyday life, you frequently need to assess the strength of arguments made by friends, family, coworkers, politicians, media pundits, and so forth. You may also want to evaluate your own arguments when you write papers or speeches for school or prepare presentations for your work. The following questions can help you to make systematic evaluations of arguments (adapted from Halpern, 1996):

- What is the conclusion?
- What are the premises provided to support the conclusion? Are the premises valid?
- Does the conclusion follow from the premises? Are there any fallacies in the chain of reasoning?
- What assumptions have been made? Are they valid assumptions? Should they be stated explicitly?
- What are the counterarguments? Do they weaken the argument?
- Is there anything that has been omitted from the argument?

Table 10.1 Critical Thinking Skills Discussed in This Application

Skill	Description
Understanding the elements of an argument	The critical thinker understands that an argument consists of premises and assumptions that are used to support a conclusion.
Recognizing and avoiding common fallacies, such as irrelevant reasons, circular reasoning, slippery slope reasoning, weak analogies, and false dichotomies	The critical thinker is vigilant about conclusions based on unrelated premises, conclusions that are rewordings of premises, unwarranted predictions that things will spin out of control, superficial analogies, and contrived dichotomies.
Evaluating arguments systematically	The critical thinker carefully assesses the validity of the premises, assumptions, and conclusions in an argument, and considers counterarguments and missing elements.

REVIEW

Key Ideas

The Motivation of Hunger and Eating

● Eating is regulated by a complex interaction of biological and environmental factors. In the brain, the lateral, ventromedial, and paraventricular areas of the hypothalamus appear to be involved in the control of hunger, but their exact role is unclear.

● Fluctuations in blood glucose also seem to play a role in hunger. The stomach can send two types of satiety signals to the brain. Hormonal regulation of hunger depends primarily on insulin and leptin secretions.

● Learning processes, such as classical conditioning and observational learning, influence what people eat. Cultural traditions also shape food preferences. Food-related cues in the environment and stress-induced arousal can stimulate eating.

Sexual Motivation and Behavior

● The human sexual response cycle can be divided into four stages: excitement, plateau, orgasm, and resolution.Consistent with evolutionary theory, males tend to think about and initiate sex more than females and to have more sexual partners and more interest in casual sex than females.

● Gender differences in mating preferences largely transcend cultural boundaries. Males emphasize potential partners' youthfulness and attractiveness, whereas females emphasize potential partners' financial prospects. Researchers have also found gender differences in jealousy that are consistent with evolutionary theory.

● The determinants of sexual orientation are not well understood. Recent studies suggest that there may be a genetic predisposition to homosexuality and that idiosyncrasies in prenatal hormonal secretions may contribute, but much remains to be learned.

Achievement: In Search of Excellence

● McClelland pioneered the use of the TAT to measure achievement motivation. People who are relatively high in the need for achievement work harder and more persistently than others, although they often choose to tackle challenges of intermediate difficulty. The pursuit of achievement tends to increase when the probability of success and the incentive value of success are high.

The Elements of Emotional Experience

● Emotion is made up of cognitive, physiological, and behavioral components. The cognitive component involves subjective feelings that have an evaluative aspect. In the peripheral nervous system, the physiological component is dominated by autonomic arousal. In the brain, the amygdala seems to be the hub of the neural circuits that process emotion. At the behavioral level, emotions are expressed through body language, with facial expressions being particularly prominent.

● Ekman and Friesen have found considerable cross-cultural agreement in the identification of emotions based on facial expressions. Cross-cultural similarities have also been found in the cognitive and physiological components of emotion. However, there are some striking cultural variations in how people categorize and display their emotions.

Theories of Emotion

● The James-Lange theory asserts that emotion results from one's perception of autonomic arousal. The Cannon-Bard theory counters with the proposal that emotions originate in subcortical areas of the brain.

● According to Schachter's two-factor theory, people infer emotion from arousal and then label it in accordance with their cognitive explanation for the arousal. Evolutionary theories of emotion maintain that emotions are innate reactions that require little cognitive interpretation.

Putting It in Perspective

● Our look at motivation and emotion showed once again that psychology is characterized by theoretical diversity, that biology and environment shape behavior interactively, that behavior is governed by multiple causes, that psychological processes are characterized by both cultural variance and invariance, and that psychology evolves in a sociohistorical context.

Personal Application ● Exploring the Ingredients of Happiness

● Factors such as income, age, parenthood, intelligence, and attractiveness are largely uncorrelated with subjective well-being. Physical health, good social relationships, and religious faith appear to have a modest impact on feelings of happiness. Strong predictors of happiness include love and marriage, work satisfaction, and personality.

● Research on happiness indicates that objective realities are not that important, that happiness is relative, that people adapt to their circumstances, and that the quest for happiness is almost never hopeless.

Critical Thinking Application ● Analyzing Arguments: Making Sense out of Controversy

● An argument consists of one or more premises used to provide support for a conclusion. Arguments are often marred by fallacies in reasoning, such as irrelevant reasons, circular reasoning, slippery slope scenarios, weak analogies, and false dichotomies. Arguments can be evaluated more effectively by applying systematic criteria.

Key Terms

Achievement motive
Argument
Assumptions
Bisexuals
Display rules
Emotion
Galvanic skin
  response (GSR)
Glucose
Glucostats
Hedonic adaptation
Heterosexuals
Homosexuals
Lie detector
Motivation
Orgasm
Polygraph
Premises
Refractory period
Sexual orientation
Subjective well-being
Vasocongestion

Key People

David Buss
Walter Cannon
Paul Ekman and
  Wallace Friesen
William James
William Masters and
  Virginia Johnson
David McClelland
Henry Murray
Stanley Schachter

PRACTICE TEST

1. Results of the early studies of hypothalamic manipulations in animals implied that the lateral hypothalamus may be a _____ center, and the ventromedial nucleus of the hypothalamus may be a _____ center.
   - A. "start sleeping"; "stop sleeping"
   - B. "start eating"; "stop eating"
   - C. "stop eating"; "start eating"
   - D. "start copulating"; "stop copulating"

2. Which of the following statements is false?
   - A. Insulin is a hormone secreted by the pancreas.
   - B. Insulin must be present for cells to utilize glucose.
   - C. Increased insulin secretion causes increased hunger.
   - D. Diabetics have too much insulin.

3. Which of the following has *not* been found in research on gender differences in sexual interest?
   - A. Men think about sex more than women.
   - B. Men initiate sex more frequently than women.
   - C. Women are more interested in having many partners than men are.
   - D. Women are less interested in uncommitted sex.

4. Which of the following behaviors on the part of their partner is likely to elicit the greatest jealousy in men, according to evolutionary theory?
   - A. Sexual infidelity
   - B. Emotional infidelity
   - C. Territorial infidelity
   - D. Perimarital infidelity

5. Kinsey maintained that sexual orientation:
   - A. depends on early classical conditioning experiences.
   - B. should be viewed as a continuum.
   - C. depends on normalities and abnormalities in the amygdala.
   - D. should be viewed as an either-or distinction.

6. Which of the following approaches to explaining the origins of homosexuality has received the most empirical support?
   - A. Behavioral
   - B. Biological
   - C. Psychoanalytic
   - D. All of these approaches equally

7. One's need for achievement is usually assessed using the:
   - A. McClelland Achievement Inventory.
   - B. MMPI.
   - C. Thematic Apperception Test.
   - D. Atkinson Manifest Needs Scale.

8. Which of the following determinants of achievement behavior is (are) situational?
   - A. The strength of one's motivation to achieve success
   - B. One's estimate of the probability of success on the task at hand
   - C. The incentive value of success on the task at hand
   - D. Both b and c

9. A polygraph (lie detector) works by:
   - A. monitoring physiological indices of autonomic arousal.
   - B. directly assessing the truthfulness of a person's statements.
   - C. monitoring the person's facial expressions.
   - D. all of the above.

10. Which of the following statements about cross-cultural comparisons of emotional experience is not true?
    - A. The types of events that trigger specific emotions are fairly similar across cultures.
    - B. The physiological reactions that accompany emotions tend to be similar across cultures.
    - C. People of different cultures tend to categorize the emotions in very similar ways.
    - D. People of different cultures learn to control and modify their emotional expressions in different ways.

11. According to the James-Lange theory of emotion:
    - A. the experience of emotion depends on autonomic arousal and on one's cognitive interpretation of that arousal.
    - B. different patterns of autonomic activation lead to the experience of different emotions.
    - C. emotion occurs when the thalamus sends signals simultaneously to the cortex and to the autonomic nervous system.
    - D. emotions develop because of their adaptive value.

12. Which theory of emotion implies that people can change their emotions simply by changing the way they label their arousal?
    - A. The James-Lange theory
    - B. The Cannon-Bard theory
    - C. Schachter's two-factor theory
    - D. Opponent process theory

13. The fact that eating behavior, sexual behavior, and the experience of emotion all depend on interactions between biological and environmental determinants lends evidence to which of your text's organizing themes?
    - A. Psychology's theoretical diversity
    - B. Psychology's empiricism
    - C. People's experience of the world is subjective
    - D. The joint influence of biology and environment

14. Which of the following statements is (are) true?
    - A. For the most part, people are pretty happy.
    - B. Age is largely unrelated to happiness.
    - C. Income is largely unrelated to happiness.
    - D. All of the above.

15. The sales pitch "We're the best dealership in town because the other dealerships just don't stack up against us" is an example of:
    - A. a false dichotomy.
    - B. semantic slanting.
    - C. circular reasoning.
    - D. slippery slope.

Answers

1	B	page 295	6	B	pages 305–306	11	B	page 313
2	D	page 296	7	C	page 306	12	C	pages 313–315
3	C	pages 300–301	8	D	pages 307–308	13	D	page 316
4	A	page 302	9	A	page 310	14	D	page 317
5	B	pages 303–304	10	C	pages 311–312	15	C	page 321

INFOTRAC COLLEGE EDITION

Go to the Wadsworth Psychology Study Center for quiz questions, research updates, interactive exercises, and suggested readings in INFOTRAC related to this chapter: http://psychology.wadsworth.com/product/0534593100s

CHAPTER 11

Stone/Ed Honowitz

Human Development Across the Life Span

Archie Leach grew up in a lower-middle-class British home saturated with frustration and unhappiness. Archie's mother was obsessed with money and felt that her husband never earned enough. When Archie wanted anything, she constantly harped on the fact that money didn't "grow on trees." As a youngster, Archie was a frail, sad-eyed boy. He was often sullen and wrapped up in himself. His parents were miserable with each other, and his mother suffered from depression. When Archie was 10, his father had his mother committed to a mental hospital. Archie was bewildered by his mother's

disappearance. His father gave him only a vague explanation, saying that she had gone away for a "rest." Archie, who didn't learn the truth for more than 20 years, thought that his mother had abandoned him. Understandably, he was deeply hurt and felt betrayed.

As a young man, Archie tried to break into theater in New York. However, at the age of 25, "Archie Leach possessed a low opinion of himself as an actor" (Harris, 1987, p. 42). He was a shy, moody young man who was especially awkward with the opposite sex. One acquaintance remarked, "He was literally tongue-tied around women."

In spite of these humble beginnings, Archie Leach eventually enjoyed great success in the world of entertainment. Blessed with classic good looks, he began to cultivate the image of an elegant man-about-town. "He looked graceless at first, but he knew that to succeed he had to become someone else, and he was not to be put off" (Wansell, 1983, p. 50).

Archie moved to Los Angeles and started working in films. He made remarkable progress in his effort to transform himself into a sophisticated ladies' man.

He earned leading roles in better and better films and went on to star in 72 movies spanning four decades, using the stage name Cary Grant. He became a matinee idol, involved in romances with some of the world's most beautiful and desirable women. As one of his biographers put it, by the end of his career Cary Grant had come to personify such adjectives as "dapper, debonair, charming, jaunty, ageless, dashing, blithe, witty, [and] stylish" (Harris, 1987, p. 4).

Archie Leach's transformation into Cary Grant was a stunning triumph, but many remnants of Archie's past were apparent beneath the surface of Cary Grant's public persona. Having felt betrayed by his mother when she mysteriously disappeared, he had lifelong difficulties trusting women. This lack of trust and the moody self-absorption that he had shown as a child contributed greatly to his four failed marriages. Although he could be glib and charming, he continued to feel strained in social encounters, and he spent much of his time in seclusion. In spite of his acclaimed brilliance as a movie star, he remained terribly insecure. He was never able to shake his mother's obsessive concern about

Archie Leach's evolution into Cary Grant is a developmental story marked by both continuity and transition.

money. Indeed, his miserliness was legendary. He amassed a fortune estimated to be worth $40 million, but he "saved the string from parcels and the tinsel from the Christmas tree, cut the buttons off the shirts he was about to discard in order to save them for future use, [and] marked the wine bottle to make sure that none was drunk while he was not there" (Wansell, 1983, p. 233).

What does Cary Grant have to do with developmental psychology? His story provides an interesting illustration of the two themes that permeate the study of human development: *transition* and *continuity*. In investigating human development, psychologists try to shed light on how people arrive at their various destinations in life. They focus on how people evolve through transitions over time. In looking at these transitions, developmental psychologists inevitably find continuity with the past. This continuity may be the most fascinating element in the story of Cary Grant's personal development. The metamorphosis of shy, awkward little Archie Leach into urbane, debonair Cary Grant was a more radical transformation than most people go through. Nonetheless, the threads of continuity connecting Archie's childhood to the development of Cary Grant's adult personality were quite obvious.

Development is the sequence of age-related changes that occur as a person progresses from conception to death. It is a reasonably orderly, cumulative process that includes both the biological and the behavioral changes that take place as people grow older. An infant's newfound ability to grasp objects, a child's gradual mastery of grammar, an adolescent's spurt in physical growth, a young adult's increasing commitment to a vocation, and an adult's transition into the role of grandparent all represent development. These transitions are predictable changes that are related to age.

Traditionally, psychologists have been most interested in development during childhood. Our coverage reflects this emphasis. However, as Cary Grant's story illustrates, development is a lifelong process. We'll divide the life span into four broad periods: (1) the prenatal period, (2) childhood, (3) adolescence, and (4) adulthood. We'll examine aspects of development that are especially dynamic during each period. Let's begin by looking at prenatal development.

Progress Before Birth: Prenatal Development

Development begins with conception. Conception occurs when fertilization creates a *zygote*, a one-celled organism formed by the union of a sperm and an egg. All of the other cells in your body developed from this single cell. Each of your cells contains enduring messages from your parents carried on the *chromosomes* that lie within its nucleus. Each chromosome houses many *genes*, the functional units in hereditary transmission. Genes carry the details of your hereditary blueprints, which are revealed gradually throughout life (see Chapter 3 for more information on genetic transmission).

The *prenatal* period extends from conception to birth, usually encompassing nine months of pregnancy. A great deal of important development occurs before birth. In fact, development during the prenatal period is remarkably rapid. If you were an average-sized newborn and your physical growth had continued during the first year of your life at a prenatal pace, by your first birthday you would have weighed 200 pounds! Fortunately, you didn't grow at that rate—and no human does—because in the final weeks before birth the frenzied pace of prenatal development tapers off dramatically.

In this section, we'll examine the usual course of prenatal development and discuss how environmental events can leave their mark on development even before birth exposes the newborn to the outside world.

The Course of Prenatal Development

The prenatal period is divided into three phases: (1) the germinal stage (the first two weeks), (2) the embryonic stage (two weeks to two months), and (3) the fetal stage (two months to birth). Some key developments in these phases are outlined here.

Germinal Stage

The *germinal stage* is the first phase of prenatal development, encompassing the first two weeks after conception. This brief stage begins when a zygote is created through fertilization. Within 36 hours, rapid cell division begins, and the zygote becomes a microscopic mass of multiplying cells. This mass slowly migrates along the mother's fallopian tube to the uterine cavity. On about the seventh day, the cell mass begins to implant itself in the uterine wall. This process takes about a week and is far from automatic. Many zygotes are rejected at this point. Research suggests that as many as one in five pregnancies end with the woman never being aware that conception has occurred (Wilcox et al., 1988).

During the implantation process, the placenta begins to form. **The *placenta* is a structure that allows oxygen and nutrients to pass into the fetus from the mother's bloodstream and bodily wastes to pass out to the mother.** This critical exchange takes place across thin membranes that block the passage of blood cells, keeping the fetal and maternal bloodstreams separate.

Embryonic Stage

The *embryonic stage* is the second stage of prenatal development, lasting from two weeks until the end of the second month. During this stage, most of the vital organs and bodily systems begin to form in the developing organism, which is now called an *embryo*. Structures such as the heart, spine, and brain emerge gradually as cell division becomes more specialized. Although the embryo is typically only about an inch long at the end of this stage, it's already beginning to look human. Arms, legs, hands, feet, fingers, toes, eyes, and ears are already discernible.

The embryonic stage is a period of great vulnerability because virtually all the basic physiological structures are being formed. If anything interferes with normal development during the embryonic phase, the effects can be devastating. Most miscarriages occur during this period (Simpson, 1991). Most major structural birth defects are also due to

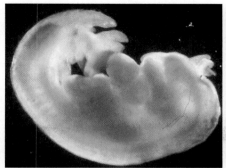

© Petit Format/Science Source/Photo Researchers, Inc..

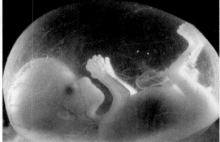

© Petit Format/Guigoz/ Science Source/Photo Researchers, Inc.

© Petit Format/Nestle/Science Source/Photo Researchers, Inc.

problems that occur during the embryonic stage (Mortensen, Sever, & Oakley, 1991).

Fetal Stage

The *fetal stage* is the third stage of prenatal development, lasting from two months through birth. Some highlights of fetal development are summarized in Figure 11.1. The first two months of the fetal stage bring rapid bodily growth, as muscles and bones begin to form (Moore & Persaud, 1993). The developing organism, now called a *fetus*, becomes capable of physical movements as skeletal structures harden. Organs formed in the embryonic stage continue to grow and gradually begin to function. Sex organs start to develop during the third month.

Prenatal development is remarkably rapid. (Top left) This 30-day-old embryo is just 6 millimeters in length. (Bottom left) At 14 weeks, the fetus is approximately 2 inches long. Note the well-developed fingers. The fetus can already move its legs, feet, hands, and head and displays a variety of basic reflexes. (Right) After 4 months of prenatal development, facial features are beginning to emerge.

Figure 11.1

Overview of fetal development. This chart outlines some of the highlights of development during the fetal stage.

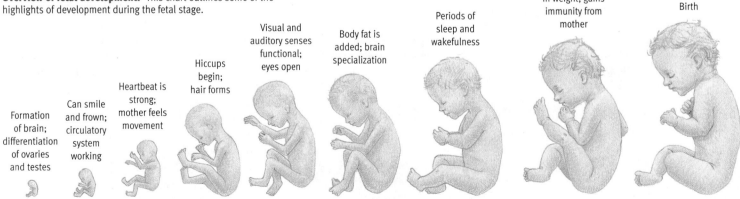

Formation of brain; differentiation of ovaries and testes

Can smile and frown; circulatory system working

Heartbeat is strong; mother feels movement

Hiccups begin; hair forms

Visual and auditory senses functional; eyes open

Body fat is added; brain specialization

Periods of sleep and wakefulness

Rapid increase in weight; gains immunity from mother

Birth

| 9 | 12 | 16 | 20 | 24 | 28 | 32 | 36 | 38 |

Weeks since conception

Full term

During the final three months of the prenatal period, brain cells multiply at a brisk pace. A layer of fat is deposited under the skin to provide insulation, and the respiratory and digestive systems mature. All of these changes ready the fetus for life outside the cozy, supportive environment of its mother's womb. Sometime between 22 weeks and 26 weeks the fetus reaches the *age of viability*—the age at which a baby can survive in the event of a premature birth. The probability of survival is still pretty slim at 22 or 23 weeks, but it climbs steadily over the next month to an 85% survival rate at 26 to 28 weeks (Hack & Fanaroff, 1999; Main & Main, 1991).

Environmental Factors and Prenatal Development

Although the fetus develops in the protective buffer of the womb, events in the external environment can affect it indirectly through the mother because the developing organism and its mother are linked via the placenta. Figure 11.2 shows the periods of prenatal development during which various structures are most vulnerable to damage.

Figure 11.2

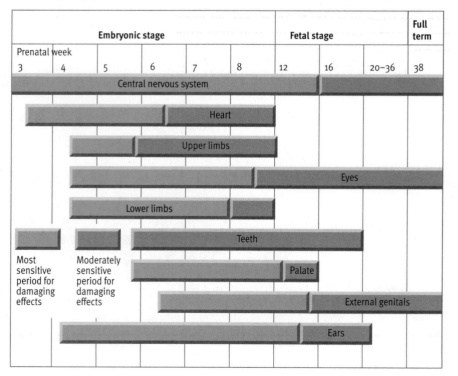

Periods of vulnerability in prenatal development. Generally, structures are most susceptible to damage when they are undergoing rapid development. The red regions of the bars indicate the most sensitive periods for various organs and structures, while the purple regions indicate periods of continued, but lessened, vulnerability. (Figure adapted from Moore, K.L., *The Developing Human: Clinically Oriented Embryology*, 4th ed. Philadelphia, W.B. Saunders Co., 1988. Reprinted by permission.)

Maternal nutrition is very important, as the developing fetus needs a variety of essential nutrients. Severe maternal malnutrition increases the risk of birth complications and neurological deficits for the newborn (Rosenblith, 1992). The impact of moderate malnutrition is more difficult to gauge. However, some studies have found a correlation between moderate maternal dietary deficits during the prenatal period and subsequent poor motor skills, apathy, and irritability during infancy (Chandra, 1991; Zeskind & Ramey, 1981).

Another major source of concern is the mother's consumption of drugs. Unfortunately, most drugs consumed by a pregnant woman can slip through the membranes of the placenta. Virtually all "recreational" drugs can be harmful, with sedatives, narcotics, and cocaine being particularly dangerous (Brockington, 1996; Finnegan & Kandall, 1997). Problems can even be caused by drugs prescribed for legitimate medical reasons and by some over-the-counter drugs (Niebyl, 1991). Tobacco use during pregnancy is also problematic, as pregnant women who smoke have an increased risk for miscarriage, stillbirth, and other birth complications (Chavkin, 1995). Maternal smoking may also increase a child's risk for sudden infant death syndrome (Haglund & Cnattinguis, 1990).

Alcohol consumption during pregnancy also carries serious risks. It has long been clear that *heavy* drinking by a mother can be hazardous to a fetus. *Fetal alcohol syndrome* is a collection of congenital (inborn) problems associated with excessive alcohol use during pregnancy. Typical problems include microcephaly (a small head), heart defects, irritability, hyperactivity, and retarded mental and motor development (Finnegan & Kandall, 1997). Previously, the available evidence suggested that it was safe for women to drink in moderation during pregnancy. However, an ongoing series of studies suggest that normal social drinking during pregnancy can have enduring negative effects on children, including deficits in IQ, reaction time, motor skills, attention span, and math skills, and increased impulsive, antisocial, and delinquent behavior (Hunt et al., 1995; Streissguth et al., 1989; Streissguth et al., 1999).

The placenta is able to screen out quite a number of infectious agents, but not all. Thus, many maternal illnesses can interfere with prenatal development. Diseases such as rubella (German measles), syphilis, cholera, smallpox, mumps, and even severe cases of the flu can be hazardous to the fetus (Isada & Grossman, 1991). Genital herpes and AIDS are two severe diseases that pregnant women can transmit to their offspring. Both are typically transmitted during the birth process itself (Eldred & Chaisson, 1996; Gosden, Nicolaides, & Whitting, 1994). About 30% of pregnant women who carry the virus for AIDS pass the disease on to their babies (Valleroy, Harris, & Way, 1990). AIDS tends to progress rapidly in infants, and few survive for more than a year.

Science has a long way to go before it uncovers all the factors that shape development before birth. For example, the effects of fluctuations in maternal emotions are not well understood. Nonetheless, it's clear that critical developments unfold quickly during the prenatal period. In the next section, you'll learn that development continues at a fast pace during the early years of childhood.

The Wondrous Years of Childhood

There's a certain magic associated with childhood. Young children have an extraordinary ability to captivate adults' attention, especially their parents'. Legions of parents apologize repeatedly to friends and strangers alike as they talk on and on about the cute things their kids do. Most wondrous of all are the rapid and momentous developmental changes of the childhood years. Helpless infants become curious toddlers almost overnight. Before parents can catch their breath, these toddlers are schoolchildren engaged in spirited play with young friends. Then, suddenly, they're insecure adolescents, worrying about dates, part-time jobs, cars, and college. The whirlwind transitions of childhood often seem miraculous.

Of course, the transformations that occur in childhood only *seem* magical. In reality, they reflect an orderly, predictable, gradual progression. In this section you'll see what psychologists have learned about this progression. We'll examine various aspects of development that are especially dynamic during childhood. Language development, which is very rapid during early childhood, is omitted from this section because we covered it in the chapter on language and thought (see Chapter 8). Let's begin by looking at motor development.

Exploring the World: Motor Development

Motor development refers to the progression of muscular coordination required for physical activities. Basic motor skills include grasping and reaching for objects, manipulating objects, sitting up, crawling, walking, running, and so forth.

Basic Principles

A number of principles are apparent in motor development. One is the *cephalocaudal trend— the head-to-foot direction of motor development.* Children tend to gain control over the upper part of their bodies before the lower part. You've seen this trend in action if you've seen an infant learn to crawl. Infants gradually shift from using their arms for propelling themselves to using their legs. The *proximodistal trend is the center-outward direction of motor development.* Children gain control over their torso before their extremities. Thus, infants initially reach for things by twisting their entire body, but gradually they learn to extend just their arms.

Early progress in motor skills has traditionally been attributed almost entirely to the process of maturation. *Maturation is development that reflects the gradual unfolding of one's genetic blueprint.* It is a product of genetically programmed physical changes that come with age—as opposed to experience and learning. However, recent research that has taken a closer look at the *process* of motor development suggests that infants are active agents rather than passive organisms waiting for their brain and limbs to mature (Thelen, 1995). According to the new view, the driving force behind motor development is infants' ongoing exploration of their world and their need to master specific tasks (such as

Web Link 11.1

PBS: The Whole Child
Coordinated to the videotape series of the same name, this Public Broadcasting System site assembles a broad collection of information for parents, caregivers, and others about the developing child from birth through age 5. Presented in English and Spanish, the resources here include an interactive timeline of developmental milestones, reading lists, and a guide to other sites dealing with child development.

grasping a larger toy or looking out a window). Progress in motor development is attributed to infants' experimentation and their learning and remembering the consequences of their activities. Although modern researchers acknowledge that maturation facilitates motor development, they argue that its contribution has been overestimated (Bertenthal & Clifton, 1998).

Understanding Developmental Norms

Parents often pay close attention to early motor development, comparing their child's progress with developmental norms. *Developmental norms indicate the average (median) age at which individuals display various behaviors and abilities.* Developmental norms are useful benchmarks as long as parents don't expect their children to progress exactly at the pace specified in the norms. Some parents get unnecessarily alarmed when their children fall behind developmental norms. What these parents overlook is that developmental norms are group *averages*. Variations from the average are entirely normal. This normal variation stands out in Figure 11.3, which indicates the age at which 25%, 50%, and 90% of youngsters can demonstrate various motor skills. As Figure 11.3 shows, a substantial portion of

children often don't achieve a particular milestone until long after the average time cited in norms.

Cultural Variations and Their Significance

Cross-cultural research has highlighted the dynamic interplay between experience and maturation in motor development. Relatively rapid motor development has been observed in some cultures that provide special practice in basic motor skills. For example, soon after birth the Kipsigis people of Kenya begin active efforts to train their infants to sit up, stand, and walk. Thanks to this training, Kipsigis children achieve these developmental milestones (but not others) about a month earlier than babies in the United States (Super, 1976). In contrast, relatively slow motor development has been found in some cultures that discourage motor exploration. For example, among the Ache, a nomadic people living in the rain forests of Paraguay, safety concerns dictate that children under age 3 rarely venture more than 3 feet from their mothers, who carry them virtually everywhere. As a result of these constraints, Ache children are delayed in acquiring a variety of motor skills and typically begin walking about a year later than other children (Kaplan & Dove, 1987).

Figure 11.3

Landmarks in motor development. The left edge, interior mark, and right edge of each bar indicate the age at which 25%, 50%, and 90% of infants have mastered each motor skill shown. Developmental norms typically report only the median age of mastery (the interior mark), which can be misleading in light of the variability in age of mastery that is apparent in this chart.

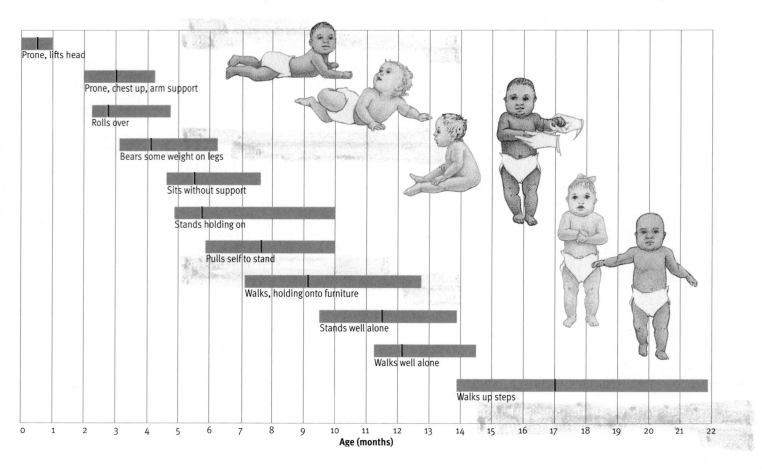

Cultural variations in the emergence of basic motor skills demonstrate that environmental factors can accelerate or slow *early* motor development. Nonetheless, the similarities across cultures in the sequence and timing of early motor development outweigh the differences, and this fact suggests that early motor development depends to a considerable extent on maturation. *Later* motor development is another matter, however. As children in any culture grow older, they acquire more specialized motor skills, some of which may be unique to their culture. Maturation becomes less influential and experience becomes more critical. Obviously, maturation by itself will never lead to the development of ballet or football skills, for example, without exposure to appropriate training.

Easy and Difficult Babies: Differences in Temperament

Infants show considerable variability in temperament. **Temperament refers to characteristic mood, activity level, and emotional reactivity.** From the very beginning, some babies seem animated and cheerful while others seem sluggish and ornery. Infants show consistent differences in emotional tone, tempo of activity, and sensitivity to environmental stimuli very early in life (Rothbart & Bates, 1998).

Alexander Thomas and Stella Chess have conducted a major *longitudinal* study of the development of temperament (Thomas & Chess, 1977, 1989; Thomas, Chess, & Birch, 1970). **In a *longitudinal* study investigators observe one group of participants repeatedly over a period of time.** This approach to the study of development is often contrasted with the cross-sectional approach (the logic of both approaches is diagrammed in Figure 11.4). **In a *cross-sectional study* investigators compare groups of participants of differing age at a single point in time.** For example, in a cross-sectional study an investigator tracing the growth of children's vocabulary might compare 50 six-year-olds, 50 eight-year-olds, and 50 ten-year-olds. In contrast, an investigator using the longitudinal method would assemble one group of 50 six-year-olds and measure their vocabulary at age six, again at age eight, and once more at age ten.

Each method has its advantages. Cross-sectional studies can be completed more quickly, easily, and cheaply than longitudinal studies, which often extend over many years. But longitudinal studies tend to be more sensitive to developmental changes (Magnusson & Stattin, 1998).

To some extent, the choice between the longitudinal approach and the cross-sectional approach depends on what the investigators want to learn

Web Link 11.2

Early Childhood Care and Development
This site's subtitle, International Resources for Early Childhood Development, emphasizes the focus of resources provided here: the worldwide (not just North American) challenge of caring for children from birth through age 6 and the needs of their families.

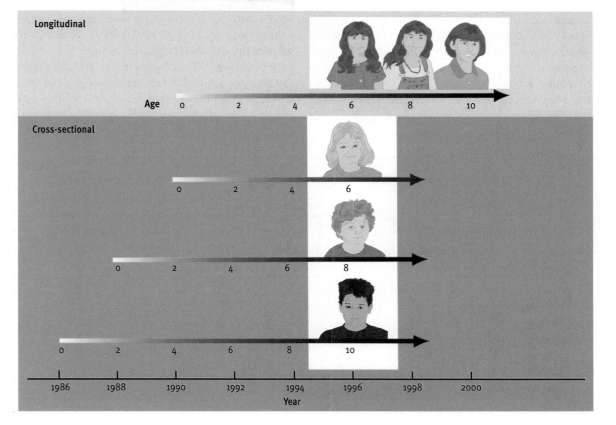

Figure 11.4

Longitudinal versus cross-sectional research. In a longitudinal study of development between ages 6 and 10, the same children would be observed at 6, again at 8, and again at 10. In a cross-sectional study of the same age span, a group of 6-year-olds, a group of 8-year-olds, and a group of 10-year-olds would be compared simultaneously. Note that data collection could be completed immediately in the cross-sectional study, whereas the longitudinal study would require four years to complete.

Web Link 11.3

Child Development Abstracts & Bibliography (CDAB) Online Edition

The CDAB database is sponsored by the Society for Research in Child Development. Now student researchers can access this database online to find abstracts for resources about the growth and development of children published in CDAB since 1990.

about development. Thomas and Chess wanted to learn about the long-term stability of children's temperaments. Given this goal, they needed to follow the same children in a longitudinal study to assess their temperamental stability over time. They began their study in 1956 with a group of 141 middle-class children. In 1961 they added a second group of 95 children of working-class parents. They have tracked the development of most of these subjects into adolescence and adulthood.

Thomas and Chess found that "temperamental individuality is well established by the time the infant is two to three months old" (Thomas & Chess, 1977, p. 153). They identified three basic styles of temperament that were apparent in most of the children. About 40% of the youngsters were *easy children* who tended to be happy, regular in sleep and eating, adaptable, and not readily upset. Another 15% were *slow-to-warm-up children* who tended to be less cheery, less regular in their sleep and eating, and slower in adapting to change. These children were wary of new experiences, and their emotional reactivity was moderate. *Difficult children* constituted 10% of the group. They tended to be glum, erratic in sleep and eating, resistant to change, and relatively irritable. The remaining 35% of the children showed mixtures of these three temperaments.

A child's temperament at 3 months was a fair predictor of the child's temperament at age 10. Infants categorized as "difficult" developed more emotional problems requiring counseling than other children. Although basic changes in temperament were seen in some children, temperament was generally stable over time (Chess & Thomas, 1996). This conclusion has been echoed by other investigators who assert that temperament has a strong biological basis (Gest, 1997; Kagan & Snidman, 1991).

Early Emotional Development: Attachment

Attachment refers to the close, emotional bonds of affection that develop between infants and their caregivers. Researchers have shown a keen interest in how infant-mother attachments are formed early in life. Children eventually form attachments to many people, including their fathers, siblings, grandparents, and others (Cassidy, 1990). However, a child's first important attachment usually occurs with his or her mother because she is typically the principal caregiver in the early months of life (Lamb et al., 1999).

Patterns of Attachment

Contrary to popular belief, infants' attachment to their mothers is *not* instantaneous. Initially, babies show little in the way of a special preference for their mothers. They can be handed over to strangers such as babysitters with relatively little difficulty. This typically changes at around 6 to 8 months of age, when infants begin to show a preference for their mother's company and often protest when separated from her (Lamb, Ketterlinus, & Fracasso, 1992). This is the first manifestation of *separation anxiety—emotional distress seen in many infants when they are separated from people with whom they have formed an attachment.* Separation anxiety, which may occur with other familiar caregivers as well as the mother, typically peaks at around 14 to 18 months and then begins to decline.

Research by Mary Ainsworth and her colleagues (1978) suggests that attachment emerges out of a complex interplay between infant and mother (see Figure 11.5). Studies reveal that mothers who are sensitive and responsive to their children's needs

Figure 11.5

Overview of the attachment process. The unfolding of attachment depends on the interaction between a mother (or other caregiver) and an infant. Research by Mary Ainsworth and others suggests that attachment relations fall into three categories—secure, avoidant, and anxious-ambivalent—which depend on how sensitive and responsive caregivers are to their children's needs. The feedback loops shown in the diagram reflect the fact that babies are not passive bystanders in the attachment drama; their temperament can affect the caregivers' behavior. (Adapted from "Attachment," by P. R. Shaver and C. Hazan. In A. Weber and J. H. Harvey (Eds.), *Perspectives on Close Relationships.* Copyright © 1994 by Allyn and Bacon. Reprinted by permission.)

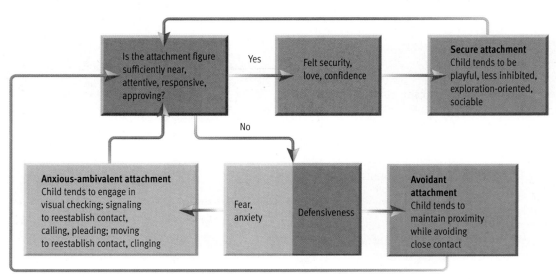

tend to evoke stronger attachments than mothers who are relatively insensitive or inconsistent in their responding (Isabella, 1995; van den Boom, 1994). However, infants are not passive bystanders as this process unfolds. They are active participants who influence the process with their crying, smiling, fussing, and babbling. Difficult infants who spit up most of their food, make bathing a major battle, refuse to go to sleep, and rarely smile may sometimes slow the process of attachment in the mother by undermining her responsiveness (Mangelsdorf et al., 1990). Thus, the type of attachment that emerges between an infant and mother may depend on the nature of the infant's temperament as much as the mother's sensitivity (Seifer et al., 1996; Vaughn & Bost, 1999).

Infant-mother attachments vary in quality. Ainsworth and her colleagues (1978) found that these attachments fall into three categories, which are shown in Figure 11.5. Fortunately, most infants develop a *secure attachment*. However, some become very anxious when separated from their mother, a pattern called *anxious-ambivalent attachment*. Children in the third category seek little contact with their mothers, a condition labeled *avoidant attachment*.

Evidence suggests that the quality of the attachment relationship can have important consequences for children's subsequent development. Infants with a relatively secure attachment tend to become resilient, competent toddlers with high self-esteem (Goldsmith & Harman, 1994). In their preschool years, they display more persistence, curiosity, self-reliance, and leadership and have better peer relations (Weinfeld et al., 1999). Recent studies have also found a relationship between secure attachment and more advanced cognitive development during childhood and adolescence (Jacobsen, Edelstein, & Hofmann, 1994), as well as healthier intimate relations during adulthood (Feeney, 1999; Kirkpatrick, 1999).

Day Care and Attachment

The impact of day care on attachment is the subject of heated debate. The crucial question is whether daily infant-mother separations might disrupt the attachment process. The issue is an important one, given that about two-thirds of the children under age 5 in the United States receive some nonmaternal care (Scarr, 1998; see Figure 11.6). Research by Jay Belsky (1988, 1992) suggests that babies who receive nonmaternal care for more than 20 hours per week have an increased risk of developing insecure attachments to their mothers. Belsky's findings have raised many eyebrows, but they need to be put in perspective.

First, the data suggest that the proportion of day-care infants who exhibit insecure attachments is only slightly higher than the norm in American society and even lower than the norm in some other societies (Lamb, Sternberg, & Prodromidis, 1992). Second, the preponderance of evidence suggests that day care is *not* harmful to children's attachment relationships (Lamb, 1998), including the evidence from a recent ten-site study in the United States funded by the National Institute of Child Health and Human Development (NICHD) that has been characterized as the "most rigorous, and most systematic evaluation of day care ever undertaken" (Rutter & O'Connor, 1999, p. 828). Third, given the deprived child-rearing conditions found in many homes, there is evidence that day care can have *beneficial effects* on some youngsters' social development (Andersson, 1992; Egeland & Hiester, 1995).

Culture and Attachment

Separation anxiety emerges in children at about 6–8 months and peaks at about 14–18 months in cultures around the world (Grossman & Grossman, 1990). This finding suggests that attachment is a universal feature of human development. However, studies have found some interesting cultural variations in the proportion of infants who fall into the three attachment categories described by Ainsworth. Working with white, middle-class subjects in the United States, Ainsworth and colleagues (1978) found that 67% of infants displayed a secure attachment, 21% an anxious-ambivalent attachment, and 12% an avoidant attachment. As Table 11.1 (on the next page) shows, studies in Germany and Japan have yielded very different figures (Cole, 1999). Avoidant attachments were far more common in

Erik Hesse

"Where familial security is lacking, the individual is handicapped by the lack of what might be called a secure base from which to work."
MARY SALTER AINSWORTH

Child-care arrangements

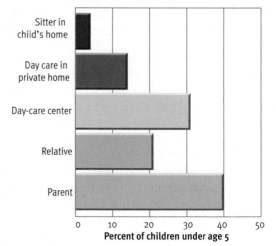

Percent of children under age 5

Figure 11.6

Day care in the United States. This graph shows the distribution of child care arrangements in 1995 for children under age 5 who were not enrolled in school. The percentages add up to more than 100% because some children experienced more than one type of care. As you can see, about two-thirds of children receive some type of day care. (Data from Scarr, 1998)

Table 11.1 Patterns of Attachment (%) From Three Different Cultures			
Country (Study)	Avoidant	Secure	Anxious-Ambivalent
USA (Ainsworth et al., 1978)	21	67	12
Germany (Grossmann et al., 1981)	52	35	13
Japan (Takahashi, 1986)	0	68	32

SOURCE: Adapted from Cole (1999)

Web Link 11.4

Attachment: Theory & Research @ Stony Brook
The pioneering work on early infant and child attachment by Mary S. Ainsworth and others has been followed by exciting work in many research labs, including SUNY at Stony Brook's. This site has posted many papers of its researchers as well as explanations of attachment theory more generally.

the German sample but were nonexistent in the Japanese sample, which yielded more anxious-ambivalent attachments than the U.S. sample.

Researchers have attributed these disparities in attachment patterns to cultural variations in child-rearing practices (Greenfield & Suzuki, 1998). More so than American parents, German parents intentionally try to encourage independence rather than clinging dependence at an early age, thus producing more avoidant attachments (Grossman et al., 1985). In contrast, Japanese parents do not attempt to foster a similar kind of early independence, and infants are rarely away from their mothers during the first year, so avoidant attachments are rare (Takahashi, 1990). Clearly, cultural differences in child-rearing attitudes and practices can influence patterns of attachment.

Evolutionary Perspectives on Attachment

Contemporary evolutionary theorists analyze attachment relations in terms of how they contribute to parents' and children's *reproductive fitness* (Belsky, Steinberg, & Draper, 1991; Chisholm, 1996; Simpson, 1999). For example, these theorists point out that if parents expect to pass their genes on to future generations, they need to raise their offspring to reproductive age *and help them to develop the social maturity required for successful mating.* Hence, they have posited some interesting hypotheses about the evolutionary significance of the specific patterns of attachment seen in children. Jay Belsky (1999b) asserts that *the nature of children's early attachment experiences depends on the character of their environments and that these experiences chart the course of children's social development in ways that are adaptive for their environmental circumstances.* Belsky has outlined hypotheses for all three types of attachment, but we will limit our discussion to the simpler and more fully described comparison between secure and insecure attachments.

According to Belsky, over the course of evolutionary history, if parents had the time and energy to be sensitive and responsive to infants' needs, the local environment was probably relatively safe and rich in resources. Sensitive care presumably

promoted secure attachments and conveyed to infants that the world is safe, others can be trusted, and relationships are enduring. When securely attached children reached adulthood, this mindset supposedly fostered a reproductive strategy that emphasized *quality* in mating relationships, resulting in relatively few sexual partners, more stable, durable romantic bonds, and more parental investment in offspring. In contrast, Belsky theorizes that, historically, when parents were insensitive and unresponsive to infants' needs, the local environment was probably relatively unsafe and resources depleted. Unresponsive care presumably promoted insecure attachments and conveyed to infants that the world is harsh, others cannot be trusted, and relationships are fleeting. When children with insecure attachments reached adulthood, this mindset supposedly fostered an opportunistic reproductive strategy that emphasized *quantity* in mating relationships, resulting in relatively more sexual partners, less stable romantic bonds, and less parental investment in offspring.

Belsky's (1999b) key point is that each reproductive strategy was adaptive for the environment in which it tended to occur. In other words, individuals' reproductive potential was probably maximized by being sexually opportunistic in harsh, depleted environments, where long-term survival was precarious, and by emphasizing enduring relationships and high parental investment in benign, abundant environments, where long-term survival appeared more promising.

Becoming Unique: Personality Development

How do individuals develop their unique constellations of personality traits over time? Many theories have addressed this question. The first major theory of personality development was put together by Sigmund Freud back around the turn of the century. As we'll discuss in Chapter 12, he claimed that the basic foundation of an individual's personality is firmly laid down by age 5. Half a century later, Erik Erikson (1963) proposed a sweeping revision of Freud's theory that has proven influential. Like Freud, Erikson concluded that events in early childhood leave a permanent stamp on adult personality. However, unlike Freud, Erikson theorized that personality continues to evolve over the entire life span.

Building on Freud's earlier work, Erikson devised a stage theory of personality development. As you'll see in reading this chapter, many theories describe development in terms of stages. A *stage* is a developmental period during which characteristic patterns of behavior are exhibited and certain capacities become established. Stage theories assume that (1) individuals must progress through specified stages in a particular order because each stage builds on the previous stage, (2) progress through these stages is strongly related to age, and (3) development is marked by major discontinuities that usher in dramatic transitions in behavior (see Figure 11.7).

Erikson's Stage Theory

Erikson partitioned the life span into eight stages, each characterized by a *psychosocial crisis* involving transitions in important social relationships. According to Erikson, personality is shaped by how individuals deal with these psychosocial crises. Each crisis is a potential turning point that can yield different outcomes. Erikson described the stages in terms of these alternative outcomes, which represent personality traits that people display over the remainder of their lives. All eight stages in Erikson's theory are charted in Figure 11.8. We describe the first four childhood stages here and discuss the remaining stages in the upcoming sections on adolescence and adulthood.

Trust Versus Mistrust Erikson's first stage encompasses the first year of life, when an infant has to depend completely on adults to take care of its basic needs for such necessities as food, a warm blanket, and changed diapers. If an infant's basic biological needs are adequately met by its care-

givers and sound attachments are formed, the child should develop an optimistic, trusting attitude toward the world. However, if the infant's basic needs are taken care of poorly, a more distrusting, insecure personality may result.

Autonomy Versus Shame and Doubt Erikson's second stage unfolds during the second and third years of life, when parents begin toilet training and other efforts to regulate the child. The child must begin to take some personal responsibility for feeding, dressing, and bathing. If all goes well, he or she acquires a sense of self-sufficiency. But if parents are never satisfied with the child's efforts and if parent-child conflicts are constant, the child may develop a sense of personal shame and self-doubt.

Initiative Versus Guilt In Erikson's third stage, roughly from ages 3 to 6, the challenge facing children is to function socially within their families. If children think only of their own needs and desires, family members may begin to instill feelings of guilt, and self-esteem may suffer. But if children

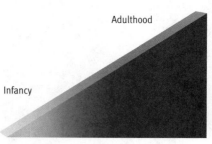
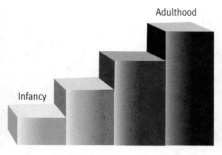

(a) Continuous development

(b) Discontinuous development

Figure 11.7

Stage theories of development. Some theories view development as a relatively continuous process, albeit not as smooth and perfectly linear as depicted on the left. In contrast, stage theories assume that development is marked by major discontinuities (as shown on the right) that bring fundamental, qualitative changes in capabilities or characteristic behavior.

Figure 11.8

Erikson's stage theory. Erikson's theory of personality development posits that people evolve through eight stages over the life span. Each stage is marked by a *psychosocial crisis* that involves confronting a fundamental question, such as "Who am I and where am I going?" The stages are described in terms of alternative traits that are potential outcomes from the crises. Development is enhanced when a crisis is resolved in favor of the healthier alternative (which is listed first for each stage).

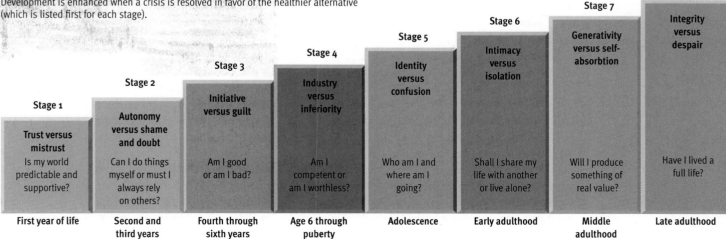

Stage 1	Stage 2	Stage 3	Stage 4	Stage 5	Stage 6	Stage 7	Stage 8
Trust versus mistrust	Autonomy versus shame and doubt	Initiative versus guilt	Industry versus inferiority	Identity versus confusion	Intimacy versus isolation	Generativity versus self-absorbtion	Integrity versus despair
Is my world predictable and supportive?	Can I do things myself or must I always rely on others?	Am I good or am I bad?	Am I competent or am I worthless?	Who am I and where am I going?	Shall I share my life with another or live alone?	Will I produce something of real value?	Have I lived a full life?
First year of life	Second and third years	Fourth through sixth years	Age 6 through puberty	Adolescence	Early adulthood	Middle adulthood	Late adulthood

O'Brien Productions/CORBIS

According to Erik Erikson, school-age children face the challenge of learning how to function in social situations outside of their family, especially with peers and at school. If they succeed, they will develop a sense of competence; if they fail, they may feel inferior.

AP/Wide World Photos

"*Human personality in principle develops according to steps predetermined in the growing person's readiness to be driven toward, to be aware of, and to interact with a widening social radius.*"
ERIK ERIKSON

learn to get along well with siblings and parents, a sense of self-confidence should begin to grow.

Industry Versus Inferiority In the fourth stage (age 6 through puberty), the challenge of learning to function socially is extended beyond the family to the broader social realm of the neighborhood and school. Children who are able to function effectively in this less nurturant social sphere where productivity is highly valued should develop a sense of competence.

Evaluating Erikson's Theory

The strength of Erikson's theory is that it accounts for both continuity and transition in personality development. It accounts for transition by showing how new challenges in social relations stimulate personality development throughout life. It accounts for continuity by drawing connections between early childhood experiences and aspects of adult personality. One measure of a theory's value is how much research it generates, and Erikson's theory continues to guide a fair amount of research (Thomas, 2000).

On the negative side of the ledger, Erikson's theory provides an "idealized" description of "typical" developmental patterns. Thus, it's not well suited for explaining the enormous personality differences that exist among people. Inadequate explanation of individual differences is a common problem with stage theories of development. This shortcoming surfaces again in the next section, where we'll examine Jean Piaget's stage theory of cognitive development.

The Growth of Thought: Cognitive Development

Cognitive development **refers to transitions in youngsters' patterns of thinking, including reasoning, remembering, and problem solving.** The investigation of cognitive development has been dominated in recent decades by the theory of Jean Piaget (Kessen, 1996). Much of our discussion of cognitive development is devoted to Piaget's theory and the research it generated, although we'll also delve into other approaches to cognitive development.

Overview of Piaget's Stage Theory

Jean Piaget (1929, 1952, 1983) was a Swiss scholar whose own cognitive development was exceptionally rapid. In his early 20s, after he had earned a doctorate in natural science and published a novel, Piaget turned to psychology. He met Theodore Simon, who had collaborated with Alfred Binet in devising the first useful intelligence tests. Working in Simon's Paris laboratory, Piaget administered intelligence tests to many children to develop better test norms. In doing this testing, Piaget was intrigued by the reasoning underlying the children's *wrong* answers. He decided that measuring children's intelligence was less interesting than studying how children *use* their intelligence. In 1921 he moved to Geneva, where he spent the remainder of his life studying cognitive development. Many of his ideas were based on insights gleaned from careful observations of his own three children during their infancy.

Noting that children actively explore the world around them, Piaget asserted that interaction with the environment and maturation gradually alter the way children think. Like Erikson's theory, Piaget's model is a *stage theory* of development. Piaget proposed that children's thought processes go through a series of four major stages: (1) the *sensorimotor period* (birth to age 2), (2) the *preoperational period* (ages 2 to 7), (3) the *concrete operational period* (ages 7 to 11), and (4) the *formal operational period* (age 11 onward). Figure 11.9 provides an overview of each of these periods. Piaget regarded his age norms as approximations and acknowledged that transitional ages may vary from one child to another.

Sensorimotor Period

One of Piaget's foremost contributions was to greatly enhance our understanding of mental development in the earliest months of life. The first stage in his theory is the *sensorimotor period,* which lasts from birth to about age 2. Piaget called this stage *sensorimotor* because infants are developing the ability to coordinate their sensory input with their motor actions.

The major development during the sensorimotor stage is the gradual appearance of symbolic thought. At the beginning of this stage, a child's behavior is dominated by innate reflexes. But by the end of the stage, the child can use mental symbols to represent objects (for example, a mental image of a favorite toy). The key to this transition is the acquisition of the concept of object permanence.

Object permanence develops when a child recognizes that objects continue to exist even when they are no longer visible. Although you surely take the permanence of objects for granted, infants aren't aware of this permanence at first. If you show a 4-month-old child an eye-catching toy and then cover the toy with a pillow, the child will not attempt to search for the toy. Piaget inferred from this observation that the child does not understand that the toy continues to exist under the pillow. The notion of object permanence does not dawn on children overnight. The first signs of this insight usually appear between 4 and 8 months of age, when children will often pursue an object that is *partially* covered in their presence. Progress is gradual, and Piaget believed that children typically don't master the concept of object permanence until they're about 18 months old.

Preoperational Period

During the *preoperational period,* which extends roughly from age 2 to age 7, children gradually improve in their use of mental images. Although progress in symbolic thought continues, Piaget emphasized the *shortcomings* in preoperational thought.

Consider a simple problem that Piaget presented to youngsters. He would take two identical beakers and fill each with the same amount of water. After a child had agreed that the two beakers contained the same amount of water, he would pour the water from one of the beakers into a much taller and thinner beaker (see Figure 11.10). He would then ask the child whether the two differently shaped beakers still contained the same amount of water. Confronted with a problem like this, children in the preoperational period generally said "no." They typically focused on the higher water line in the taller beaker and insisted that there was more water in the slender beaker. They had not yet mastered the principle of conservation. **Conservation is Piaget's term for the awareness that physical quantities**

remain constant in spite of changes in their shape or appearance.

Why are preoperational children unable to solve conservation problems? According to Piaget, their inability to understand conservation is the result of some basic flaws in preoperational thinking. These flaws include centration, irreversibility, and egocentrism.

Centration is the tendency to focus on just one feature of a problem, neglecting other important aspects. When working on the conservation problem with water, preoperational children tend to concentrate on the height of the water while ignoring the width. They have difficulty focusing on several aspects of a problem at once.

Stage 1	Stage 2	Stage 3	Stage 4
Sensorimotor period	**Preoperational period**	**Concrete operational period**	**Formal operational period**
Coordination of sensory input and motor responses; development of object permanence	Development of symbolic thought marked by irreversibility, centration, and egocentrism	Mental operations applied to concrete events; mastery of conservation, hierarchical classification	Mental operations applied to abstract ideas, logical, systematic thinking
Birth to 2 years	**2 to 7 years**	**7 to 11 years**	**Age 11 through adulthood**

Figure 11.9

Piaget's stage theory. Piaget's theory of cognitive development identifies four stages marked by fundamentally different modes of thinking through which youngsters evolve. The approximate age norms and some key characteristics of thought at each stage are summarized here.

Figure 11.10

Piaget's conservation task. After watching the transformation shown, a preoperational child will usually answer that the taller beaker contains more water. In contrast, the child in the concrete operations period tends to respond correctly, recognizing that the amount of water in beaker C remains the same as the amount in beaker A.

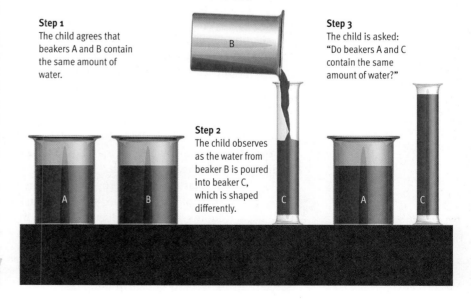

Step 1
The child agrees that beakers A and B contain the same amount of water.

Step 2
The child observes as the water from beaker B is poured into beaker C, which is shaped differently.

Step 3
The child is asked: "Do beakers A and C contain the same amount of water?"

"It is virtually impossible to draw a clear line between innate and acquired behavior patterns."
JEAN PIAGET

Irreversibility is the inability to envision reversing an action. Preoperational children can't mentally "undo" something. For instance, in grappling with the conservation of water, they don't think about what would happen if the water were poured back from the tall beaker into the original beaker.

Egocentrism in thinking is characterized by a limited ability to share another person's viewpoint. Indeed, Piaget felt that preoperational children fail to appreciate that there are points of view other than their own. For instance, if you ask a preoperational girl whether her sister has a sister, she'll probably say no if they are the only two girls in the family. She's unable to view sisterhood from her sister's perspective (this example also shows irreversibility).

A notable feature of egocentrism is **animism—the belief that all things are living,** just like oneself. Thus, youngsters attribute lifelike, human qualities to inanimate objects, asking questions such as, "When does the ocean stop to rest?" or "Why does the wind get so mad?"

As you can see, Piaget emphasized the weaknesses apparent in *pre*operational thought. Indeed, that is why he called this stage preoperational. The ability to perform *operations*—internal transformations, manipulations, and reorganizations of mental structures—emerges in the next stage.

Concrete Operational Period

 9c

The development of mental operations marks the beginning of the *concrete operational period,* which usually lasts from about age 7 to age 11. Piaget called this stage *concrete* operations because children can perform operations only on images of tangible objects and actual events.

Among the operations that children master during this stage are reversibility and decentration. *Reversibility* permits a child to mentally undo an action. *Decentration* allows the child to focus on more than one feature of a problem simultaneously. The newfound ability to coordinate several aspects of a problem helps the child appreciate that there are several ways to look at things. This ability in turn leads to a *decline in egocentrism and gradual mastery of conservation* as it applies to liquid, mass, number, volume, area, and length.

As children master concrete operations, they develop a variety of new problem-solving capacities. Let's examine another problem studied by Piaget. Give a preoperational child seven carnations and three daisies. Tell the child the names for the two types of flowers and ask the child to sort them into carnations and daisies. That should be no

problem. Now ask the child whether there are more carnations or more daisies. Most children will correctly respond that there are more carnations. Now ask the child whether there are more carnations or more flowers. At this point, most preoperational children will stumble and respond incorrectly that there are more carnations than flowers. Generally, preoperational children can't handle *hierarchical classification* problems that require them to focus simultaneously on two levels of classification. However, the child who has advanced to the concrete operational stage is not as limited by centration and can work successfully with hierarchical classification problems.

Formal Operational Period

 9c

The final stage in Piaget's theory is the *formal operational period,* which typically begins at around 11 years of age. In this stage, children begin to apply their operations to *abstract* concepts in addition to concrete objects. Indeed, during this stage, youngsters come to *enjoy* the heady contemplation of abstract concepts. Many adolescents spend hours mulling over hypothetical possibilities related to abstractions such as justice, love, and free will.

According to Piaget, youngsters graduate to relatively adult modes of thinking in the formal operations stage. He did *not* mean to suggest that no further cognitive development occurs once children reach this stage. However, he believed that after children achieve formal operations, further developments in thinking are changes in *degree* rather than fundamental changes in the *nature* of thinking.

Adolescents in the formal operational period become more *systematic* in their problem-solving efforts. Children in earlier developmental stages tend to attack problems quickly, with a trial-and-error approach. In contrast, children who have achieved formal operations are more likely to think things through. They envision possible courses of action and try to use logic to reason out the likely consequences of each possible solution before they act. Thus, thought processes in the formal operational period can be characterized as abstract, systematic, logical, and reflective.

Evaluating Piaget's Theory

Jean Piaget made a landmark contribution to psychology's understanding of children in general and their cognitive development in particular (Beilin, 1992). He founded the field of cognitive development and fostered a new view of children that saw them as active agents constructing their own worlds (Fischer & Hencke, 1996). Above all else, he sought answers to new questions. As he acknowledged in a 1970 interview, "It's just that no adult ever had the idea of asking children about conservation. It was so obvious that if you change the shape of an object, the quantity will be conserved. Why ask a child? The novelty lay in asking the question" (Hall, 1987, p. 56). Piaget's theory guided an enormous volume of productive research that continues through today (Brainerd, 1996). This research has supported many of Piaget's central propositions (Flavell, 1996). In such a far-reaching theory, however, there are bound to be some weak spots. Let's briefly examine some criticisms of Piaget's theory:

1. In many areas, Piaget appears to have underestimated young children's cognitive development (Lutz & Sternberg, 1999). For example, researchers have found evidence that children begin to develop object permanence much earlier than Piaget thought, perhaps as early as 3 to 4 months of age (Baillargeon, 1987, 1994). Others have marshaled evidence that preoperational children exhibit less egocentrism and animism than Piaget believed (Newcombe & Huttenlocher, 1992).

2. Piaget's model suffers from problems that plague most stage theories. Like Erikson, Piaget had little to say about individual differences in development (Siegler, 1994). Also, people often simultaneously display patterns of thinking that are characteristic of several stages. This "mixing" of stages calls into question the value of organizing development in terms of stages (Flavell, 1992; Siegler & Ellis, 1996).

3. Piaget believed that his theory described universal processes that should lead children everywhere to progress through uniform stages of thinking at roughly the same ages. Subsequent research has shown that the *sequence* of stages is largely invariant, but the *timetable* that children follow in passing through these stages varies considerably across cultures (Dasen, 1994; Rogoff, 1990). Thus, Piaget underestimated the influence of cultural factors on cognitive development.

As with any theory, Piaget's is not flawless. However, without Piaget's theory to guide research, many crucial questions about children's development might not have been confronted until decades later (if at all). By some measures, the influence of Piaget is declining (Bjorklund, 1997), but ironically, even many of the new directions in the study of cognitive development grew out of efforts to test, revise, or discredit Piaget's theory (Flavell, 1996). Let's look at some of this newer research.

CONCEPT **CHECK 11.2**

Recognizing Piaget's Stages

Check your understanding of Piaget's theory by indicating the stage of cognitive development illustrated by each of the examples below. For each scenario, fill in the letter for the appropriate stage in the space on the left. The answers are in Appendix A.

a. Sensorimotor period **c.** Concrete operational period
b. Preoperational period **d.** Formal operational period

 1. Upon seeing a glass lying on its side, Sammy says, "Look, the glass is tired. It's taking a nap."

 2. Maria is told that a farmer has nine cows and six horses. The teacher asks, "Does the farmer have more cows or more animals?" Maria answers, "More animals."

_A._ **3.** Alice is playing in the living room with a small red ball. The ball rolls under the sofa. She stares for a moment at the place where the ball vanished and then turns her attention to a toy truck sitting in front of her.

Are Some Cognitive Abilities Innate?

The frequent finding that Piaget underestimated infants' cognitive abilities has led to a rash of research suggesting that infants have a surprising grasp of many complex concepts. The new findings have been made possible by some innovative research methods that permit investigators to draw inferences about the abilities of very young children. Many studies have made use of the *habituation-dishabituation paradigm*. **Habituation** is a gradual reduction in the strength of a response when a stimulus event is presented repeatedly. If you show infants the same event over and over (such as an object dropping onto a platform), they habituate to it—their heart and respiration rates decline and they spend less time looking at the stimulus. *Dishabituation* occurs if a new stimulus elicits an increase in the strength of an habituated response. Patterns of dishabituation can give researchers insights into what types of events infants can tell apart, which events surprise or interest them, and which events violate their expectations.

Working mostly with the habituation-dishabituation paradigm, researchers have discovered that infants understand basic properties of objects and some of the rules that govern them. At 3 to 4 months of age, infants understand that objects are distinct entities with boundaries, that objects move in continuous paths, that one solid object cannot pass through another, that an object cannot pass through an opening that is smaller than the object, and that objects on slopes roll down rather than up (Kim & Spelke, 1992; Spelke & Newport, 1998).

Figure **11.11**

The procedure used to test infants' understanding of number. To see if 5-month-old infants have some appreciation of addition and subtraction, Wynn (1992, 1996) showed them sequences of events like those depicted here. If children express surprise (primarily assessed by time spent looking) when the screen drops and they see only one object, this result suggests that they understand that 1 + 1 = 2. Wynn and others have found that infants seem to have some primitive grasp of simple addition and subtraction. (From "Addition and Subtraction by Human Infants," by K. Wynn, 1992, *Nature, 358,* 749–750. Copyright © 1992 Macmillan Magazines, Ltd. Reprinted with permission from *Nature.*)

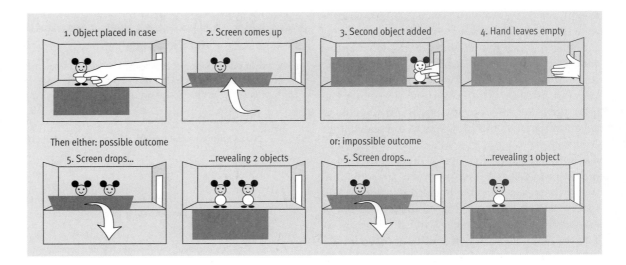

In this line of research, perhaps the most stunning discovery has been the finding that *infants seem to be able to add and subtract small numbers.* If 5-month-old infants are shown a sequence of events in which one object is added to another behind a screen, they expect to see two objects when the screen is removed, and they exhibit surprise when their expectation is violated (see Figure 11.11). This expectation suggests that they understand that 1 + 1 = 2 (Wynn, 1992, 1996). Similar manipulations suggest that infants also understand that 2 – 1 = 1, that 2 + 1 = 3, and that 3 – 1 = 2 (Hauser & Carey, 1998; Wynn, 1998).

Again and again in recent years, research has shown that infants appear to understand surprisingly complex concepts that they have had virtually no opportunity to learn about. These findings have led some theorists to conclude that certain basic cognitive abilities are biologically built into humans' neural architecture. The theorists who have reached this conclusion tend to fall into two camps: nativists and evolutionary theorists. The *nativists* simply assert that humans are prewired to readily understand certain concepts without making any assumptions about *why* humans are prewired in these ways (Spelke, 1994; Spelke & Newport, 1998).Their principal interest is to sort out the complex matter of what is prewired and what isn't.

Evolutionary theorists agree with the nativists that humans are prewired for certain cognitive abilities, but they are keenly interested in *why.* As you might anticipate, they maintain that this wiring is a product of natural selection, and they strive to understand its adaptive significance (Hauser & Carey, 1998; Wynn, 1998). For example, evolutionary theorists are interested in how basic addition-subtraction abilities may have enhanced our hominid ancestors' success in hunting, foraging, and social bargaining.

I hasten to add that the question about whether some cognitive abilities are hardwired is much more complicated than it may appear at first glance. Critics assert that infants' dishabituation responses to various events can be interpreted and explained in a variety of ways without assuming that infants possess innate knowledge of objects, categories, and number (Fischer & Bidell, 1991; Haith & Benson, 1998). For example, infants may spend more time looking at novel events simply because these events require more time for perceptual processing and memory encoding (Bogartz & Shinskey, 1998). Thus, the newly emerging debate about whether infants have some innate knowledge of the world around them promises to be very interesting.

The Development of Moral Reasoning

In Europe, a woman was near death from cancer. One drug might save her, a form of radium that a druggist in the same town had recently discovered. The druggist was charging $2,000, ten times what the drug cost him to make. The sick woman's husband, Heinz, went to everyone he knew to borrow the money, but he could only get together about half of what it cost. He told the druggist that his wife was dying and asked him to sell it cheaper or let him pay later. But the druggist said, "No." The husband got desperate and broke into the man's store to steal the drug for his wife. Should the husband have done that? Why? (Kohlberg, 1969, p. 379)

What's your answer to Heinz's dilemma? Would you have answered the same way 3 years ago? Can you guess what you might have said at age 6?

By presenting similar dilemmas to participants and studying their responses, Lawrence Kohlberg (1976, 1984; Colby & Kohlberg, 1987) developed a model of *moral development*. What is morality? That's a complicated question that philosophers have debated for centuries. For our purposes, it will suffice to say that *morality* involves the ability to discern right from wrong and to behave accordingly.

Kohlberg's Stage Theory

Kohlberg's model is the most influential of a number of competing theories that attempt to explain how youngsters develop a sense of right and wrong. His work was derived from much earlier work by Piaget (1932). Piaget theorized that moral development is determined by cognitive development. By this he meant that the way individuals think out moral issues depends on their level of cognitive development. This assumption provided the springboard for Kohlberg's research.

Kohlberg's theory focuses on moral *reasoning* rather than overt *behavior*. This point is best illustrated by describing Kohlberg's method of investigation. He presented his participants with thorny moral questions such as Heinz's dilemma, then asked the subjects what the actor in the dilemma should do, and more important, why. It was the *why* that interested Kohlberg. He examined the nature and progression of subjects' moral reasoning.

The result of this work is the stage theory of moral reasoning outlined in Figure 11.12. Kohlberg found that individuals progress through a series of three levels of moral development, each of which can be broken into two sublevels, yielding a total of six stages. Each stage represents a different approach to thinking about right and wrong.

Younger children at the *preconventional level* think in terms of external authority. Acts are wrong because they are punished, or right because they

CONCEPT **CHECK 11.3**

Analyzing Moral Reasoning

Check your understanding of Kohlberg's theory of moral development by analyzing hypothetical responses to the following moral dilemma.

A midwest biologist has conducted numerous studies demonstrating that simple organisms such as worms and paramecia can learn through conditioning. It occurs to her that perhaps she could condition fertilized human ova, to provide a dramatic demonstration that abortions destroy adaptable, living human organisms. This possibility appeals to her, as she is ardently opposed to abortion. However, there is no way to conduct the necessary research on human ova without sacrificing the lives of potential human beings. She desperately wants to conduct the research, but obviously, the sacrifice of human ova is fundamentally incompatible with her belief in the sanctity of human life. What should she do? Why? [Submitted by a student (age 13) to Professor Barbara Banas at Monroe Community College]

In the spaces on the left of each numbered response, indicate the level of moral reasoning shown, choosing from the following: (a) preconventional level, (b) conventional level, or (c) postconventional level. The answers are in Appendix A.

C. **1.** She should do the research. Although it's wrong to kill, there's a greater good that can be realized through the research.

B. **2.** She shouldn't do the research because people will think that she's a hypocrite and condemn her.

A. **3.** She should do the research because she may become rich and famous as a result.

lead to positive consequences. Older children who have reached the *conventional level* of moral reasoning see rules as necessary for maintaining social order. They therefore accept these rules as their own. They "internalize" these rules not to avoid punishment but to be virtuous and win approval from others. Moral thinking at this stage is relatively inflexible. Rules are viewed as absolute guidelines that should be enforced rigidly.

During adolescence, some youngsters move on to the *postconventional level*, which involves working out a personal code of ethics. Acceptance of rules is less rigid, and moral thinking shows some flexibility. Subjects at the postconventional level

Courtesy of Harvard University News Office

"*Children are almost as likely to reject moral reasoning beneath their level as to fail to assimilate reasoning too far above their level.*"
LAWRENCE KOHLBERG

Figure **11.12**

Kohlberg's stage theory. Kohlberg's model posits three levels of moral reasoning, each of which can be divided into two stages. This chart summarizes how individuals think about right and wrong at each stage.

Stage 1	Stage 2	Stage 3	Stage 4	Stage 5	Stage 6
Punishment orientation	**Naive reward orientation**	**Good boy/good girl orientation**	**Authority orientation**	**Social contract orientation**	**Individual principles and conscience orientation**
Right and wrong is determined by what is punished.	Right and wrong is determined by what is rewarded.	Right and wrong is determined by close others' approval or disapproval.	Right and wrong is determined by society's rules and laws, which should be obeyed rigidly.	Right and wrong is determined by society's rules which are viewed as fallible rather than absolute.	Right and wrong is determined by abstract ethical principles that emphasize equity and justice.
Preconventional level		**Conventional level**		**Postconventional level**	

Figure 11.13

Age and moral reasoning.
The percentages of different types of moral judgments made by subjects at various ages are graphed here (based on Kohlberg, 1963, 1969). As predicted, preconventional reasoning declines as children mature, conventional reasoning increases during middle childhood, and postconventional reasoning begins to emerge during adolescence; but at each age, children display a mixture of various levels of moral reasoning. (Adapted from "The Development of Children's Orientations Toward a Moral Order: I: Sequence in the Development of Moral Thought," by L. Kohlberg, 1963, *Vita Humana, 6,* 11–33. Copyright © 1963 by S. Karger AG, Basel. Reprinted by permission.)

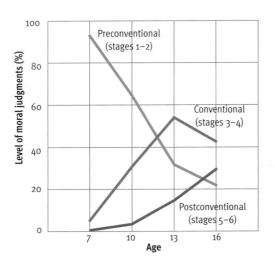

allow for the possibility that someone might not comply with some of society's rules if they conflict with personal ethics. For example, participants at this level might applaud a newspaper reporter who goes to jail rather than reveal a source of information who was promised anonymity.

Evaluating Kohlberg's Theory

How has Kohlberg's theory fared in research? The central ideas have received reasonable support. Progress in moral reasoning is indeed closely tied to

cognitive development (Walker, 1988). Studies also show that youngsters generally do progress through Kohlberg's stages of moral reasoning in the order that he proposed (Walker, 1989). Furthermore, relations between age and level of moral reasoning are in the predicted directions (Rest, 1986). Representative age trends are shown in Figure 11.13. As children get older, stage 1 and stage 2 reasoning declines, while stage 3 and stage 4 reasoning increases. However, there is great variation in the age at which people reach specific stages. Furthermore, only a small percentage of people ever reach stage 6.

Like all influential theorists, Kohlberg has his critics. They have raised the following issues:

1. It's not unusual to find that a person shows signs of several adjacent levels of moral reasoning at a particular point in development (Walker & Taylor, 1991). As we noted in the critique of Piaget, this mixing of stages is a problem for virtually all stage theories.

2. Evidence is mounting that Kohlberg's dilemmas may not be valid indicators of moral development in some cultures (Eckensberger & Zimba, 1997). Some critics believe that the value judgments built into Kohlberg's theory reflect a liberal, individualistic ideology characteristic of modern Western nations that is much more culture-specific than Kohlberg appreciated (Shweder, Mahapatra, & Miller, 1990; Walker & Moran, 1991).

The Transition of Adolescence

Adolescence is a bridge between childhood and adulthood. During this time, individuals continue to make significant progress in cognitive, moral, and social development. However, the most dynamic areas of development during adolescence are physical changes and related transitions in emotional and personality development.

Puberty and the Growth Spurt

Recall for a moment your junior high school days. Didn't it seem that your body grew so fast about this time that your clothes just couldn't "keep up"? This phase of rapid growth in height and weight is called the *adolescent growth spurt*. Brought on by hormonal changes, it typically starts at about 11 years of age in girls and about age 13 in boys (Malina, 1990). Technically, this spurt should be called the *preadolescent growth spurt* because it

actually occurs *prior* to puberty, which is generally recognized as the beginning of adolescence.

The term *pubescence* is used to describe the two-year span preceding puberty during which the changes leading to physical and sexual maturity take place. In addition to growing taller and heavier during pubescence, children begin to develop the physical features that characterize adults of their respective sexes. These features are termed *secondary sex characteristics—physical features that distinguish one sex from the other but that are not essential for reproduction.* For example, males go through a voice change, develop facial hair, and experience greater skeletal and muscle growth in the upper torso, leading to broader shoulders (see Figure 11.14). Females experience breast growth and a widening of the pelvic bones plus increased fat deposits in this area, resulting in wider hips (Litt & Vaughan, 1992).

Note, however, that the capacity to reproduce is not attained in pubescence. This comes later. **Puberty is the stage during which sexual functions reach maturity, which marks the beginning of adolescence.** It is during puberty that the **primary sex characteristics—the structures necessary for reproduction**—develop fully. In the male, these include the testes, penis, and related internal structures. Primary sex characteristics in the female include the ovaries, vagina, uterus, and other internal structures.

In females, the onset of puberty is typically signaled by **menarche—the first occurrence of menstruation.** American girls typically reach menarche at about age 12½, with further sexual maturation continuing until approximately age 16. Most American boys begin to produce sperm by age 14, with complete sexual maturation occurring around age 18 (Brooks-Gunn & Reiter, 1990; Tanner, 1978). Interestingly, *generational* changes have occured in the timing of puberty. Today's adolescents begin puberty at a younger age, and complete it more rapidly, than did their counterparts in earlier generations. This trend apparently reflects improvements in nutrition and medical care (Brooks-Gunn, 1991).

The timing of puberty varies from one adolescent to the next over a range of about 5 years (10–15 for girls, 11–16 for boys). Much of this variability is governed by hereditary differences (Kaprio et al., 1995). Generally, adolescents who mature unusually early or unusually late tend to feel uneasy about it. In particular, *girls who mature early and boys who mature late seem to have a greater risk for psychological problems and social difficulties* (Graber et al., 1997). Early maturation can enhance an adolescent's popularity with peers, but mature appearance can also bring pressures and temptations that a youngster may not be ready for (Ge, Conger, & Elder, 1996). In both males and females, early maturation is associated with greater use of alcohol and drugs and more trouble with the law (Duncan et al., 1985; Stattin & Magnusson, 1990). Among females, early maturation is also correlated with poorer school performance, earlier experience of intercourse, more unwanted pregnancies, and greater risk for eating problems and disorders (Graber et al., 1994; Stattin & Magnusson, 1990). Thus, we might speculate that early maturation often thrusts both sexes (but especially females) toward the adult world too soon.

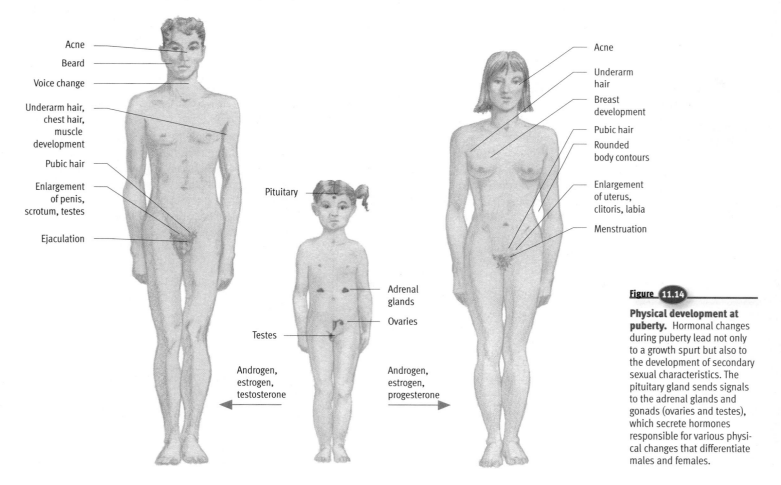

Figure 11.14

Physical development at puberty. Hormonal changes during puberty lead not only to a growth spurt but also to the development of secondary sexual characteristics. The pituitary gland sends signals to the adrenal glands and gonads (ovaries and testes), which secrete hormones responsible for various physical changes that differentiate males and females.

Time of Turmoil?

Back around the turn of the century, G. Stanley Hall (1904), one of psychology's great pioneers, proposed that the adolescent years are characterized by convulsive instability and disturbing turmoil. Hall attributed this turmoil to adolescents' erratic physical changes and resultant confusion about self-image. Over the decades, a host of theorists have agreed with Hall's characterization of adolescence as a stormy period.

Statistics on *adolescent suicide* would seem to support the idea that adolescence is a time marked by turmoil, but the figures can be interpreted in various ways. On the one hand, suicide rates among adolescents have risen alarmingly in recent decades (see Figure 11.15a). On the other hand, even with this steep increase, suicide rates for adolescents are lower than those for older age groups (see Figure 11.15b).

Actually, the suicide crisis among teenagers involves *attempted suicide* more than *completed* suicide. It's estimated that when all age groups are lumped together, suicide attempts outnumber actual suicidal deaths by a ratio of about 8 to 1 (Cross & Hirschfeld, 1986). However, this ratio of attempted to completed suicides is much higher for adolescents than for any other age group. Studies suggest that the ratio among adolescents may be anywhere from 50:1 to 200:1 (Garland & Zigler, 1993).

Returning to our original question, does the weight of evidence support the idea that adolescence is usually a period of turmoil and turbulence? Overall, the recent consensus of the experts has been that adolescence is not an exceptionally difficult period (Petersen et al., 1993; Steinberg & Levine, 1997). However, in a recent reanalysis of the evidence, Jeffrey Arnett (1999) has argued convincingly that "not all adolescents experience storm and stress, but storm and stress is more likely during adolescence than at other ages" (p. 317). Arnett supports his

intermediate position by summarizing research on adolescents' moods, risky behaviors, and conflicts with their parents. Research shows that adolescents do experience more volatile and more negative emotions than their parents or younger children do (Larson & Richards, 1994). Studies also show that various types of risky behavior, such as substance abuse, careless sexual practices, and dangerous driving peak during late adolescence (Arnett, 1992). Finally, adolescence *does* bring an increase in parent-child conflicts (Laursen, Coy, & Collins, 1998). Arnett is quick to emphasize that turmoil in adolescence is far from universal, but he maintains that, on the average, adolescence is somewhat more stressful than other developmental periods. However, he notes that this conclusion *may* only apply to modern, Western cultures characterized by shifting values and an emphasis on individualism. Adolescence appears to be less stressful in traditional, preindustrial cultures.

Although turbulence and turmoil are not *universal* features of adolescence, challenging adaptations *do* have to be made during this period. In particular, most adolescents struggle to some extent in their effort to achieve a sound sense of identity.

The Search for Identity 9b

Erik Erikson was especially interested in personality development during adolescence, which is the fifth of the eight major life stages he described. The psychosocial crisis during this stage pits *identity* against *confusion* as potential outcomes. According to Erikson (1968), the main challenge of adolescence is the struggle to form a clear sense of identity. This struggle involves working out a stable concept of oneself as a unique individual and embracing an ideology or system of values that provides a sense of direction. In Erikson's view, adolescents grapple with questions such as "Who am I?" and "Where am I going in life?"

Web Link 11.5

Adolescence Directory OnLine
Visitors to this site hosted by the University of Indiana will find guides to resources about adolescence that cover many of the health, mental health, safety, personal, and parenting issues important to this phase of development.

Figure 11.15

Adolescent suicide. (a) The suicide rate for adolescents and young adults (15–24 years old) has increased in recent decades far more than the suicide rate for the population as a whole. (b) Nonetheless, suicide rates for this youthful age group are about the same or lower than those for older age groups. (Source: Centers for Disease Control and Prevention)

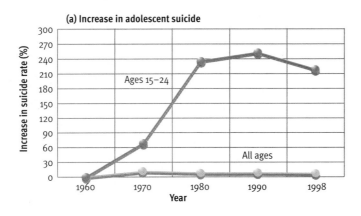

(a) Increase in adolescent suicide

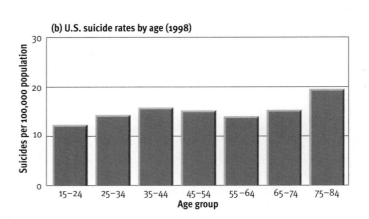

(b) U.S. suicide rates by age (1998)

Although the struggle for a sense of identity is a lifelong process (Waterman & Archer, 1990), it does tend to be especially intense during this period. Adolescents' increased concern about identity probably results from the conjunction of several significant transitions (Lloyd, 1985). First, rapid physical changes stimulate thought about self-image during adolescence. Second, changes in cognitive processes (in Piaget's terminology, the arrival of formal operations) promote personal introspection. Third, decisions about vocational direction require self-contemplation.

Adolescents deal with identity formation in a variety of ways. According to James Marcia (1966, 1980), the presence or absence of *crisis* and *commitment* can combine in various ways to produce four different *identity statuses* (see Figure 11.16). These are not stages that people pass through, but orientations that may occur at a particular time. An individual may get locked into one of these patterns or go through several at various times. Marcia's four identity statuses are as follows:

- *Foreclosure* is a premature commitment to visions, values, and roles prescribed by one's parents. This path allows a person to circumvent much of the "struggle" for an identity. However, it may backfire and cause problems later.
- A *moratorium* involves delaying commitment for a while to experiment with alternative ideologies and careers. Such experimentation can be valuable. Unfortunately, some people

remain indefinitely in what should be a temporary phase.

- *Identity diffusion* is a state of rudderless apathy. Some people simply refuse to confront the challenge of charting a life course and committing to an ideology. Although this stance allows them to evade the struggle, the lack of direction can become problematic.
- *Identity achievement* involves arriving at a sense of self and direction after some consideration of alternative possibilities. Commitments have the strength of some conviction, although they're not absolutely irrevocable.

Erikson, Marcia, and many other theorists believe that adequate identity formation is a cornerstone of sound psychological health. Identity confusion can interfere with important developmental transitions that should happen during the adult years, as you'll see in the next section.

Crisis

		Present	Absent
Commitment	**Present**	*Identity achievement* (successful achievement of a sense of identity)	*Identity foreclosure* (unquestioning adoption of parental or societal values)
	Absent	*Identity moratorium* (active struggling for a sense of identity)	*Identity diffusion* (absence of struggle for identity, with no obvious concern about it)

Figure 11.16

Marcia's four identity statuses. According to Marcia (1980), the occurrence of an identity crisis and the development of personal commitments can combine into four possible identity statuses, as shown in this diagram. (Adapted from "Identity in Adolescence," by J.E. Marcia, 1980. In J. Adelson (Ed.), *Handbook of Adolescent Psychology*, pp. 159–210. Copyright © 1980 by John Wiley & Sons, Inc. Adapted by permission of John Wiley & Sons, Inc.)

The Expanse of Adulthood

The concept of development was once associated almost exclusively with childhood and adolescence, but today it is widely recognized that development is a life-long journey. Moreover, in recent years, psychologists have increasingly recognized that the historical context people live in can have a profound impact on their developmental trajectories. As Stewart and Ostrove (1998) put it, "It makes sense that generations raised with different expectations and in different historical circumstances may age differently" (p. 1185). Events such as the Great Depression, the Vietnam war, the women's movement, the AIDS epidemic, the emergence of television, and the rise of the Internet can leave a lasting mark on the people exposed to them. Complicating the picture further, developmental patterns are becoming increasingly diverse. The boundaries between young, middle, and late adult-

hood are becoming blurred as more and more people have children later than one is "supposed" to, retire earlier than one is "supposed" to, and so forth. In the upcoming pages we will look at some of the major developmental transitions in adult life, but you should bear in mind that in adulthood (even more so than childhood or adolescence) there are many divergent pathways and timetables.

Personality Development

Recent research on adult personality development has been dominated by one key question: How stable is personality over the life span? We'll look at this issue, the question of the midlife crisis, and Erikson's view of adulthood in our discussion of personality development in the adult years.

The Question of Stability

At midlife, Jerry Rubin went from being an outraged, radical political activist to being a subdued, conventional Wall Street businessman. His transformation illustrates that major personality changes sometimes occur during adulthood. But how common are such changes? Is a grouchy 20-year-old going to be a grouchy 40-year-old and a grouchy 65-year-old? Or can the grouchy young adult become a mellow senior citizen?

After tracking subjects through adulthood, many researchers have been impressed by the amount of change observed. Roger Gould (1975) studied two samples of men and women and concluded that "the evolution of a personality continues through the fifth decade of life." In a study following women from their college years through their 40s, Helson and Moane (1987) found that "personality does change from youth to middle age in consistent and often predictable ways." After tracking development between the ages of 20 and 42, Whitbourne and her colleagues (1992) found "consistent patterns of personality change."

In contrast, many other researchers have been struck by the stability and durability they have found in personality. The general conclusion that emerged from several longitudinal studies using objective assessments of personality traits was that personality tends to be quite stable over periods of 20 to 40 years (Block, 1981; Caspi & Herbener, 1990; Costa & McCrae, 1994, 1997). Moreover, a recent review of 150 relevant studies, involving almost 50,000 participants, concluded that personality in early adulthood was a good predictor of personality in late adulthood and that the stability of personality increases with age up to about age 50 (Caspi & Roberts, 1999).

In sum, researchers assessing the stability of personality in adulthood have reached very different conclusions (Kogan, 1990). How can these contradictory conclusions be reconciled? This appears to be one of those debates in which researchers are eyeing the same findings—but from different perspectives. Hence, some conclude that the glass is half full, whereas others conclude that it's half empty. In his discussion of this controversy, Lawrence Pervin (1994) concludes that personality is characterized by *both* stability and change. It appears that some personality traits tend to remain stable, while others tend to change systematically as people grow older.

The Question of the Midlife Crisis

There has also been a spirited debate about whether most people go through a *midlife crisis*—a difficult, turbulent period of doubts and reappraisal of one's life. The two most influential studies of adult development in the 1970s (Gould, 1978; Levinson et al., 1978) both concluded that a midlife crisis is a normal transition experienced by a majority of people. However, since these landmark studies, a host of subsequent studies have failed to detect an increase in emotional turbulence at midlife (Baruch, 1984; Eisler & Ragsdale, 1992; Roberts & Newton, 1987).

How can we explain this discrepancy? Levinson and Gould both studied samples that were less than ideal. Levinson's was unusually small, and Gould's was not very representative. Moreover, both researchers depended primarily on interview and case study methods to gather their data. As we noted in Chapter 2, when knitting together impressionistic case studies, it is easy for investigators to see what they expect to see. Given that the midlife crisis has long been part of developmental folklore, Levinson and Gould may have been prone to interpret their case study data in this light (McCrae & Costa, 1984). In any case, investigators relying on more objective measures of emotional stability have found signs of midlife crises in only a tiny minority (2%–5%) of participants (Chiriboga, 1989; McCrae & Costa, 1990). Midlife may bring a period of increased reflection as people contemplate the remainder of their lives, but it's clear that the fabled midlife *crisis* is not typical (Lemme, 1999).

Erikson's View of Adulthood

Insofar as personality changes during the adult years, Erik Erikson's (1963) theory offers some clues about the kinds of changes people can expect. In his eight-stage model of development over the life span, Erikson divided adulthood into three stages (see again Figure 11.8):

Major transitions in adulthood do occur, as illustrated by the life of one-time radical Jerry Rubin.

Intimacy Versus Isolation   In early adulthood, the key concern is whether one can develop the capacity to share intimacy with others. Successful resolution of the challenges in this stage should promote empathy and openness, rather than shrewdness and manipulativeness.

Generativity Versus Self-Absorption   In middle adulthood, the key challenge is to acquire a genuine concern for the welfare of future generations, which results in providing unselfish guidance to younger people. Self-absorption is characterized by self-indulgent concerns with meeting one's own needs and desires.

Integrity Versus Despair   During the retirement years, the challenge is to avoid the tendency to dwell on the mistakes of the past and on one's imminent death. People need to find meaning and satisfaction in their lives, rather than wallow in bitterness and resentment.

Transitions in Family Life

Many of the important transitions in adulthood involve changes in family responsibilities and relationships. Everyone emerges from a family, and most people go on to form their own families. However, the transitional period during which young adults are "between families" until they form a new family is being prolonged by more and more people. The percentage of young adults who are postponing marriage until their late twenties or early thirties has risen dramatically. This trend is probably the result of a number of factors. Chief

among them are the availability of new career options for women, increased educational requirements in the world of work, and increased emphasis on personal autonomy. Remaining single is a much more acceptable option today than it was a few decades ago. The classic stereotype of single people, which depicted them as lonely, frustrated, and unchosen, is gradually evaporating (Stein, 1989). Nonetheless, over 90% of adults eventually marry.

Adjusting to Marriage

The newly married couple usually settle into their roles as husband and wife gradually. Difficulties with this transition are more likely when spouses come into a marriage with different expectations about marital roles (Kitson & Sussman, 1982; Lye & Biblarz, 1993). Unfortunately, substantial differences in role expectations seem particularly likely in this era of transition in gender roles.

In general, however, the first few years of married life tend to be characterized by great happiness—the proverbial "marital bliss." Numerous studies have measured spouses' overall satisfaction in different stages of the family life cycle and found a U-shaped relationship like that shown in Figure 11.17 (Glenn, 1990; Orbuch et al., 1996). This U shape reflects the fact that satisfaction tends to be greatest at the beginning and end of the family life cycle, with a noticeable decline in the middle. The conventional explanation for this pattern is that the burdens of child rearing, and resulting reduction in time spent together, undermine couples' satisfaction, which gradually climbs back up again as children grow up and these burdens ease. However, marital satisfaction tends to decline in

Figure 11.17

Marital satisfaction across the family life cycle. This graph depicts the percentage of husbands and wives who said their marriage was going well "all the time" at various stages of the family life cycle. The U-shaped relationship shown here has been found in other studies as well. Generally, marital satisfaction tends to be greatest at the beginning and at the end of the family life cycle. (Adapted from "Marital Satisfaction Over the Family Cycle," by Boyd C. Rollins and Harold Feldman, *Journal of Marriage and Family*, 32 (February 1970), p. 25. Copyright © 1975 by the National Council on Family Relations, 3989 Central Ave., N.E., Suite 550, Minneapolis, MN 55421. Reprinted by permission.)

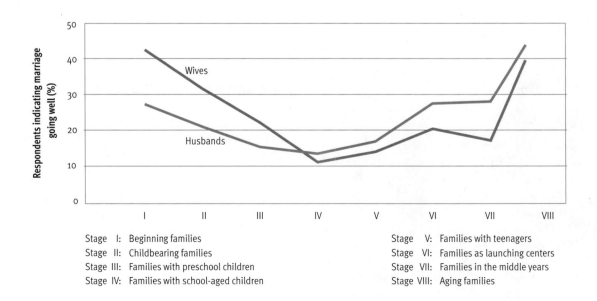

Stage I: Beginning families
Stage II: Childbearing families
Stage III: Families with preschool children
Stage IV: Families with school-aged children

Stage V: Families with teenagers
Stage VI: Families as launching centers
Stage VII: Families in the middle years
Stage VIII: Aging families

the early years of marriage even when there are no children, so other factors and processes may also contribute to this U-shaped pattern (Bradbury, 1998; Glenn, 1998).

Adjusting to Parenthood

Although an increasing number of people are choosing to not have children, the vast majority of married couples continue to plan on becoming parents (Roosa, 1988). Despite the challenges involved in rearing children, most parents report no regret about their choice and rate parenthood as a very positive experience (Demo, 1992). Nonetheless, the arrival of the first child represents a *major* transition, and the disruption of old routines can be extremely stressful (Lavee, Sharlin, & Katz, 1996). The new mother, already physically exhausted by the birth process, is particularly prone to postpartum stress (Hock et al., 1995). Women are especially vulnerable when they have to shoulder the major burden of infant care (Kalmuss, Davidson, & Cushman, 1992).

Crisis during the transition to first parenthood is far from universal, however. Satisfaction with parenting tends to be higher when marital quality is higher (Erel & Burnham, 1995; Rogers & White, 1998). The key to making this transition less stressful may be to have *realistic expectations* about parental responsibilities (Kalmuss et al., 1992). Studies find that stress is greatest in new parents who have overestimated the benefits and underestimated the costs of their new role.

As children grow up, parental influence over them tends to decline, and the early years of parenting—that once seemed so difficult—are often recalled with fondness. When youngsters reach

adolescence and seek to establish their own identities, gradual realignments occur in parent-child relationships. Parent-adolescent relations generally are not as bitter or contentious as widely assumed, but conflicts are common (Silverberg, Tennenbaum, & Jacob, 1992). The conflicts tend to involve everyday matters (chores and appearance) more than substantive issues (sex and drugs) (Barber, 1994). When conflict does occur, mothers often are more adversely affected by it than fathers (Steinberg & Silverberg, 1987). This may be because women's self-esteem tends to be more closely tied to the quality of their family relationships. Ironically, although studies have shown that adolescence is not as turbulent or difficult for youngsters as once believed, their parents *are* stressed out. Parents overwhelmingly rate adolescence as the most difficult stage of child rearing (Gecas & Seff, 1990).

Adjusting to the Empty Nest

When parents have launched all their children into the adult world, they find themselves faced with an "empty nest." This period of transition was formerly thought to be a difficult one for many parents, especially mothers familiar only with the maternal role. Today, however, more women have experience with other roles outside the home, and most look forward to their "liberation" from child-rearing responsibilities (Reinke et al., 1985). Hence, the empty nest transition appears to have little lasting negative impact (Birchler, 1992).

The postparental period often provides couples with new freedom to devote attention to each other. Many couples take advantage of this opportunity by traveling or developing new leisure interests. Thus, as offspring strike out on their own, most couples' marital satisfaction starts climbing to higher levels once again (Brubaker, 1990). It tends to remain fairly high until one of the spouses (usually the husband) dies.

Aging and Physical Changes

People obviously experience many physical changes as they progress through adulthood. In both sexes, hair tends to thin out and become gray, and many males confront receding hairlines and baldness. To the dismay of many, the proportion of body fat tends to increase with age. Overall, weight tends to increase in most adults through the mid-50s, when a gradual decline may begin. These changes have little functional significance, but in our youth-oriented society, they often lead people to view themselves as less attractive.

Web Link 11.6

National Parent Information Network (NPIN)
Parents are faced with all sorts of questions about development; the NPIN site describes many guides to online and other resources to answer those questions.

Although children can be unparalleled sources of joy and satisfaction, the transition to parenthood can be extremely stressful, especially for mothers.

Stone/Jon Gray

The number of active neurons in the brain declines during adulthood. The rate of neuronal loss is hard to measure and appears to vary in different parts of the brain (Duara, London, & Rapoport, 1985). Although this gradual loss of brain cells sounds alarming, it is a normal part of the aging process. Its functional significance is the subject of some debate, but it doesn't appear to contribute to any of the age-related dementias. **A *dementia* is an abnormal condition marked by multiple cognitive deficits that include memory impairment.** Dementia can be caused by quite a variety of diseases, such as Alzheimer's disease, Parkinson's disease, and AIDS, to name just a few. Because some of these diseases are more prevalent in older adults, dementia is seen in about 15% of people over age 65 (Elias, Elias, & Elias, 1990). However, it is important to emphasize that dementia and "senility" are not part of the normal aging process. As Cavanaugh (1993) notes, "The term *senility* has no valid medical or psychological meaning, and its continued use simply perpetuates the myth that drastic mental decline is a product of normal aging" (p. 85).

In the sensory domain, the key developmental changes occur in vision and hearing. The proportion of people with 20/20 visual acuity declines with age. Farsightedness, difficulty adapting to darkness, and poor recovery from glare are common among older people (Fozard, 1990; Kline & Schieber, 1985). Hearing sensitivity begins declining gradually in early adulthood. Noticeable hearing losses requiring corrective treatment are apparent in about three-quarters of people over the age of 75 (Olsho, Harkins, & Lenhardt, 1985). These sensory losses could be problematic, but in modern society they can usually be compensated for with glasses and hearing aids.

Age-related changes also occur in hormonal functioning during adulthood. Among women, these changes lead to *menopause*. This ending of menstrual periods, accompanied by a loss of fertility, typically occurs in the early 50s. Not long ago, menopause was thought to be almost universally accompanied by severe emotional strain. However, it is now clear that women's reactions to menopause vary greatly, depending on their expectations (Matthews, 1992). Most women experience little psychological distress (Dennerstein, 1996). Although people sometimes talk about "male menopause," men don't really go through an equivalent experience. Middle-aged males experience hormonal changes, but they're very gradual.

Aging and Cognitive Changes

The evidence indicates that general intelligence is fairly stable throughout most of adulthood, with a small decline in *average* test scores often seen after age 60 (Schaie, 1990, 1994, 1996). However, this seemingly simple assertion masks many complexities and needs to be qualified carefully. First, group averages can be deceptive in that mean scores can be dragged down by a small minority of people who show a decline. For example, when Schaie (1990) calculated the percentage of people who maintain stable performance on various abilities (see Figure 11.18), he found that about 80% showed no decline by age 60 and that about two-thirds were still stable through age 81. Second, even when age-related decreases in intellectual performance are found, they tend to be small in all but a few individuals (Salthouse, 1991).

Figure 11.18

Age and the stability of primary mental abilities. In his longitudinal study of cognitive performance begun in 1956, Schaie (1983, 1993) has repeatedly assessed the five basic mental abilites listed along the bottom of this chart. The data graphed here show the percentage of subjects who maintained stable levels of performance on each ability through various ages up to age 81. As you can see, even through the age of 81, the majority of subjects show no significant decline on most abilities. (From "Intellectual Development in Adulthood," by K. W. Schaie, 1990. In J.E. Birren and K. W. Schaie (Eds.), *Handbook of the Psychology of Aging,* 3rd ed. pp. 291–309. Reprinted by permission of Academic Press, Inc.)

Contrary to widespread stereotypes, many people remain active and productive in their 70s, 80s, and even beyond.

© Doug Menuez/PhotoDisc, Inc.

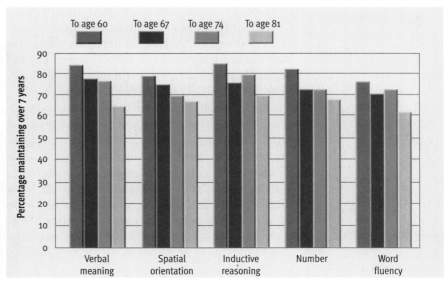

What about memory? Numerous studies report decreases in older adults' memory capabilities (Baltes & Kliegl, 1992; Hultsch & Dixon, 1990). However, most of these studies have asked subjects to memorize simple lists of words or paired associations. Older participants often find these artificial laboratory tasks meaningless and uninteresting. Investigators have only recently begun to study age-related changes in memory for more realistic content. There *do* seem to be some modest decreases in memory for prose, television shows, conversations, past activities, and personal plans (Kausler, 1985), but the memory losses associated with aging are moderate and are not universal (Shimamura et al., 1995). According to Salthouse (1994), an age-related decline in the capacity of *working memory* (see Chapter 7) underlies older adults' poorer performance on memory tasks. He attributes most of the decline in working memory to age-related decreases in the raw speed of mental processing.

In the cognitive domain, aging does seem to take its toll on *speed* first. Many studies indicate that speed in learning, solving problems, and processing information tends to decline with age (Salthouse & Babcock, 1991). The evidence suggests that the erosion of processing speed may be a gradual, lengthy trend beginning in middle adulthood (Verhaeghen & Salthouse, 1997). The general nature of this trend (across differing tasks) suggests that it may be the result of age-related changes in neurological functioning (Cerella & Hale, 1994; Myerson et al., 1990), but doubts about this conclusion have been raised (Bashore, Ridderinkhof, & van der Molen, 1997). Although mental speed declines with age, problem-solving ability remains largely unimpaired if older people are given adequate time to compensate for their reduced speed.

It should be emphasized that many people remain capable of great intellectual accomplishments well into their later years (Simonton, 1990). This reality was verified in a study of scholarly, scientific, and artistic productivity that examined lifelong patterns of work among 738 men who lived at least through the age of 79. Dennis (1966) found that the 40s decade was the most productive in most professions. However, productivity was remarkably stable through the 60s decade and even the 70s in many areas.

Putting It in Perspective

Five of our seven integrative themes surfaced to some degree in our coverage of human development. We saw theoretical diversity in our discussions of cognitive development and personality development. We saw that psychology evolves in a sociohistorical context, investigating complex, real-world issues—such as the controversies surrounding day care and adolescent suicide—that emerge as our society changes. We encountered multifactorial causation of behavior in the development of temperament and attachment, among other things. We saw cultural invariance and cultural diversity in our examination of attachment, motor development, cognitive development, and moral development.

But above all else, we saw how heredity and environment jointly mold behavior. We've encountered the dual influence of heredity and environment before, but this theme is rich in complexity, and each chapter draws out different aspects and implications. Our discussion of development amplified the point that genetics and experience work *interactively* to shape behavior. What does it mean to say that heredity and environment interact? In the language of science, an interaction means that the effects of one variable depend on the effects of another. In other words, heredity and environment do not operate independently. Children with "difficult" temperaments will elicit different reactions from different parents, depending on the parents' personalities and expectations. Likewise, a particular pair of parents will affect different children in different ways, depending on the inborn characteristics of the children. An interplay, or feedback loop, exists between biological and environmental factors.

All aspects of development are shaped jointly by heredity and experience. We often estimate their relative weight or influence, as if we could cleanly divide behavior into genetic and environmental components. Although we can't really carve up behavior that neatly, such comparisons can be of great theoretical interest, as you'll see in our upcoming Personal Application, which discusses the nature and origins of gender differences in behavior.

PERSONAL APPLICATION

Understanding Gender Differences

Answer the following "true" or "false."

_____ 1 Females are more socially oriented than males.

_____ 2 Males outperform females on most spatial tasks.

_____ 3 Females are more irrational than males.

_____ 4 Males are less sensitive to nonverbal cues than females.

_____ 5 Females are more emotional than males.

Are there genuine behavioral differences between the sexes similar to those mentioned above? If so, why do these differences exist? How do they develop? These are the complex and controversial questions that we'll explore in this Personal Application.

Before proceeding further, we need to clarify how some key terms are used, as terminology in this area of research has been evolving and remains a source of confusion (Deaux, 1993; Unger & Crawford, 1993). *Sex* refers to the biologically based categories of female and male. In contrast, *gender* refers to culturally constructed distinctions between femininity and masculinity. Individuals are born female or male. However, they become feminine or masculine through complex developmental processes that take years to unfold.

The statements at the beginning of this Application reflect popular gender stereotypes in our society. *Gender stereotypes* are widely held beliefs about females' and males' abilities, personality traits, and social behavior. Table 11.2 lists some characteristics that are part of the masculine and feminine stereotypes in North American society. The table shows something you may have already noticed on your own. The male stereotype is much more flattering, suggesting that men have virtually cornered the market on competence and rationality. After all, everyone knows that females are more dependent, emotional, irrational, submissive, and talkative than males. Right? Or is that not the case? Let's look at the research.

How Do the Sexes Differ in Behavior?

Gender differences are actual disparities between the sexes in typical behavior or average ability. Mountains of research, literally thousands of studies, exist on gender differences. It's difficult to sort through this huge body of research, but fortunately, many *review articles* on gender differences have been published in recent years. As noted in Chapter 2, review articles summarize and reconcile the findings of a large number of studies on a specific issue.

What does this research show? Are the stereotypes of males and females accurate? Well, the findings are a mixed bag. The research indicates that genuine behavioral differences *do* exist between the sexes and that people's stereotypes are not entirely inaccurate (Eagly, 1995; Swim, 1994). But the differences are fewer in number, smaller in size, and far more complex than stereotypes suggest. As you'll see, only two of the differences mentioned in our opening true-false questions (the even-numbered items) have been largely supported by the research.

Cognitive Abilities

In the cognitive domain, it appears that there are three genuine—albeit very small—gender differences. First, on the average, females tend to exhibit slightly better *verbal skills* than males (Halpern, 1992). In particular, females seem stronger on tasks that require rapid access to semantic and other information in long-term memory (Halpern, 1997). Second, starting during high school, males show a slight advantage on tests of *mathematical ability*. When all students are

Table 11.2	Elements of Traditional Gender Sterotypes
Masculine	**Feminine**
Active	Aware of other's feelings
Adventurous	Considerate
Aggressive	Creative
Ambitious	Cries easily
Competitive	Devotes self to others
Dominant	Emotional
Independent	Enjoys art and music
Leadership qualities	Excitable in a crisis
Likes math and science	Expresses tender feelings
Makes decisions easily	Feelings hurt
Mechanical aptitude	Gentle
Not easily influenced	Home oriented
Outspoken	Kind
Persistent	Likes children
Self-confident	Neat
Skilled in business	Needs approval
Stands up under pressure	Tactful
Takes a stand	Understanding

(Adapted from "Sex Stereotypes: Issues of Change in the 70s", by T. L. Ruble, 1983, *Sex Roles, 9*, 397–402. Copyright © 1983 Kluwer Academic/Plenum Publishing Group. Adapted by permission.)

As more women enter traditionally male professions, what was once a novelty—female football players, contruction workers, and corporate officers—is now much more common-place. The debate is over how such changes in roles are affecting man-woman relationships.

© AP/Wide World Photos

compared, males' advantage is quite small (Hyde, Fennema, & Lamon, 1990). However, at the high end of the ability distribution, the gender gap is larger, as far more males than females are found to be mathematically precocious (Stumpf & Stanley, 1996). Third, starting in the grade-school years, males tend to score higher than females on most measures of *visual-spatial ability* (Voyer, Voyer, & Bryden, 1995). The size of these gender differences varies from moderate to small depending on the exact nature of the spatial task. Males appear to be strongest on tasks that require visual transformations in working memory (Halpern, 1997).

Social Behavior

In regard to social behavior, research findings support the existence of some additional gender differences. First, studies indicate that males tend to be more *aggressive* than females, both verbally and physically (Hyde, 1986; Knight, Fabes, & Higgins, 1996). This disparity shows up early in childhood. Its continuation into adulthood is supported by the fact that men account for a grossly disproportionate number of the violent crimes in our society (Kenrick, 1987). Second, there are gender differences in *nonverbal communication*. The evidence indicates that females are more sensitive than males to subtle nonverbal cues (Hall, 1990). Females also smile and gaze at others more than males do (Hall & Halberstadt, 1986). Third, males are more sexually active than females in a variety of ways, and they have more permissive attitudes about casual, premarital, and extramarital sex (Oliver & Hyde, 1993). In regard to personality, males score a little higher on measures of assertiveness and global self-esteem, whereas females score higher on measures of anxiety, trust, and tender-mindedness (empathy and nurturance) (Feingold, 1994; Kling et al., 1999).

Some Qualifications

Although research has identified some genuine gender differences in behavior, bear in mind that these are group differences that indicate nothing about individuals. Essentially, research results compare the "average man" with the "average woman." However, you are—and every individual is—unique. The average female and male are ultimately figments of our imagination. Furthermore, the genuine group differences noted are relatively small. Figure 11.19 shows how scores on a trait, perhaps verbal ability, might be distributed for men and women. Although the group averages are detectably different, you can see the great variability within each group (sex) and the huge overlap between the two group distributions.

Thus, the behavioral differences between males and females are fewer and smaller than popular stereotypes suggest. Many supposed gender differences have turned out to be more mythical than real (Tavris, 1992). Nonetheless, the gender differences that do exist require explanation, which is the matter we'll attend to next.

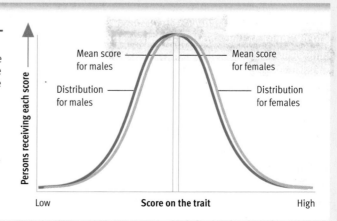

Figure 11.19

The nature of gender differences. Gender differences are group differences that indicate little about individuals because of the great overlap between the groups. For a given trait, one sex may score higher on the average, but far more variation occurs within each sex than between the sexes.

Persons receiving each score

Mean score for males

Distribution for males

Mean score for females

Distribution for females

Low   Score on the trait   High

Biological Origins of Gender Differences

What accounts for the development of documented gender differences? To what degree are they the product of learning or of biology? This question is yet another manifestation of the nature versus nurture issue. Investigations of the biological origins of gender differences have centered on the evolutionary bases of behavior, hormones, and brain organization.

Evolutionary Explanations

Evolutionary psychologists argue that gender differences in behavior reflect different natural selection pressures operating on the sexes over the course of human history (Archer, 1996). Evolutionary analyses usually begin by arguing that gender differences in behavior transcend culture because cultural invariance suggests that biological factors are at work (Kenrick & Trost, 1993). Although research has turned up some fascinating exceptions, the better-documented gender differences in cognitive abilities, aggression, and sexual behavior do appear to be pancultural (Beller & Gafni, 1996; Halpern, 1997).

According to evolutionary psychologists, these differences are found around the world because males and females have confronted different adaptive demands (Buss & Kenrick, 1998). For example, as we discussed in Chapter 10, males supposedly are more sexually active and permissive because they invest less than females in the process of procreation and can maximize their reproductive success by seeking many sexual partners (Buss, 1996). The gender gap in aggression is also explained in terms of reproductive fitness. Because females are more selective about mating than males, males have to engage in more competition for sexual partners than females do. Greater aggressiveness is thought to be adaptive for males in this competition for sexual access because it should foster social dominance over other males and facilitate the acquisition of the material resources emphasized by females when they evaluate potential partners (Geary, 1998, 1999; Kenrick & Trost, 1993). Evolutionary theorists assert that gender differences in spatial ability reflect the division of labor in ancestral hunting and gathering societies in which males typically handled the hunting and females the gathering. Males' superiority on most spatial tasks has been attributed to the adaptive demands of hunting (Silverman & Phillips, 1998; see Chapter 1).

Evolutionary analyses of gender differences are interesting, but controversial. On the one hand, it seems eminently plausible that evolutionary forces could have led to some divergence between males and females in typical behavior. On the other hand, evolutionary hypotheses are highly speculative and difficult to test empirically (Eagly & Wood, 1999; Halpern, 1997). The crux of the problem for some critics is that evolutionary analyses are so "flexible" they can be used to explain almost anything. For example, if the situation regarding spatial ability were reversed—if females scored higher than males—evolutionary theorists might attribute females' superiority to the adaptive demands of gathering food, weaving baskets, and making clothes—and it would be difficult to prove otherwise (Cornell, 1997).

The Role of Hormones

Hormones play a key role in sexual differentiation during prenatal development. The high level of androgens (the principal class of male hormones) in males and the low level of androgens in females lead to the differentiation of male and female genital organs. The critical role of prenatal hormones becomes apparent when something interferes with normal prenatal hormonal secretions. About a half-dozen endocrine disorders can cause overproduction or underproduction of specific gonadal hormones during prenatal development. Scientists have also studied children born to mothers who were given an androgenlike drug to prevent miscarriage. The general trend in this research is that females exposed prenatally to abnormally high levels of androgens exhibit more male-typical behavior than other females do and that males exposed prenatally to abnormally low levels of androgens exhibit more female-typical behavior than other males (Collaer & Hines, 1995). For example, girls with *congenital adrenal hyperplasia* tend to show "tomboyish" interests in vigorous outdoor activities and in "male" toys and have elevated scores on measures of aggressiveness and spatial ability.

These findings suggest that prenatal hormones contribute to the shaping of gender differences in humans. But there are a few problems with this evidence (Basow, 1992; Fausto-Sterling, 1992). First, the evidence is much stronger for females than for males. Second, it's always dangerous to draw conclusions about the general population based on small samples of people who have abnormal conditions. Third, most of the endocrine disorders studied have multiple effects (besides altering hormone levels) that create a variety of sometimes worrisome confounds in the research. Looking at the evidence as a whole, it does seems likely that hormones contribute to gender differences in behavior. However, the findings in this line of research have been equivocal and inconsistent, and a great deal remains to be learned.

Differences in Brain Organization

Interpretive problems have also cropped up in efforts to link gender differences to specialization of the cerebral hemispheres in the brain (see Figure 11.20 on the next page). As you may recall from Chapter 3, in most people the left hemisphere is more actively involved in verbal processing, whereas the right hemisphere is more active in visual-spatial processing (Sperry, 1982; Springer & Deutsch, 1998). After these findings surfaced, theorists began to wonder whether this division of labor in the brain might be related to gender differences in verbal and spatial skills. Consequently, they began looking for sex-related disparities in brain organization.

Some thought-provoking findings *have* been reported. For instance, some studies have found that *males tend to exhibit more cerebral specialization than females* (Bryden, 1988; Hines, 1990). In other words, there's a trend for males to depend more heavily than females do on the left hemisphere in verbal processing and more heavily on the right in spatial processing. Differences between males and females have also been found in the size of the corpus callosum, the band of fibers that connects the two

Figure **11.20**

The cerebral hemispheres and the corpus callosum. As explained in Chapter 3, the cerebral cortex is divided into left and right halves, called the cerebral hemispheres, which are specialized (to some extent) to handle different cognitive functions. In this drawing the cerebral hemispheres have been "pulled apart" to reveal the corpus callosum. This band of fibers is the communication bridge between the right and left halves of the human brain. Some theorists have related gender differences in cognitive abilities to sexual disparities in hemispheric specialization and the size of the corpus callosum.

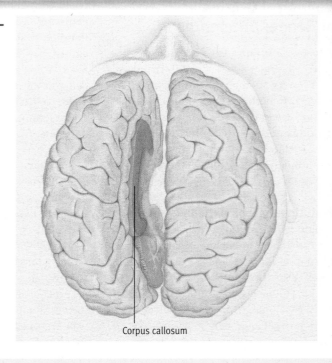

Corpus callosum

hemispheres of the brain (Steinmetz et al., 1995). Some studies suggest that *females tend to have a larger corpus callosum,* which might allow for better interhemispheric transfer of information, which, in turn, might underlie the more bilateral organization of females' brains (Innocenti, 1994). Thus, some theorists have concluded that differences between the sexes in brain organization are responsible for gender differences in verbal and spatial ability (Geschwind & Galaburda, 1987; Kimura & Hampson, 1993).

This idea is intriguing, but psychologists have a long way to go before they can explain gender differences in terms of right brain/left brain specialization. Studies have not been consistent in finding that males have more specialized brain organization than females (Halpern, 1992; Kinsbourne, 1980), and the finding of a larger corpus callosum in females has proven controversial (Bleier, 1988; Byne & Parsons, 1993). Moreover, even if these findings were replicated consistently, no one is really sure just how they would account for the observed gender differences in cognitive abilities.

In summary, researchers have made relatively modest progress in their efforts to document the biological roots of gender differences in behavior. The idea that "anatomy is destiny" has proven difficult to demonstrate. Theorists remain convinced that biological factors contribute to gender differences. However, the overall evidence suggests that biology merely creates predispositions that are shaped by experience. Let's look at some of the experiential factors that contribute to this process.

Environmental Origins of Gender Differences

All societies make efforts to train children about gender roles. *Gender roles* are expectations about what is appropriate behavior for each sex. Although gender roles are in a period of transition in modern Western society, there are still many disparities in how males and females are brought up. Investigators have identified three key processes involved in the development of gender roles: operant conditioning, observational learning, and self-socialization. First we'll examine these processes. Then we'll look at the principal sources of gender-role socialization: families, schools, and the media.

Operant Conditioning

In part, gender roles are shaped by the power of reward and punishment—the key processes in *operant conditioning* (see Chapter 6). Parents, teachers, peers, and others often reinforce (usually with tacit approval) "gender-appropriate" behavior and respond negatively to "gender-inappropriate" behavior (Fagot, Leinbach, & O'Boyle, 1992). If you're a man, you might recall getting hurt as a young boy and being told that "big boys don't cry." If you succeeded in inhibiting your crying, you may have earned an approving smile or even something tangible like an ice cream cone. The reinforcement probably strengthened your tendency to "act like a man" and suppress emotional displays. If you're a woman, chances are your crying wasn't discouraged as gender-inappropriate. Studies suggest that fathers encourage and reward gender-appropriate behavior in their youngsters more than mothers do and that boys experience more pressure to behave in gender-appropriate ways than girls do (Levy, Taylor, & Gelman, 1995).

Observational Learning

Observational learning (see Chapter 6) by children can lead to the imitation of adults' sex-appropriate behavior. Children imitate both males and females, but most children tend to imitate same-sex role models more than opposite-sex role models (Bussey & Bandura, 1984; Frey & Ruble, 1992). Thus, imitation often leads young girls to play with dolls, dollhouses, and toy stoves. Young boys are more likely to tinker with toy trucks, miniature gas stations, or tool kits.

Self-Socialization

Children themselves are active agents in their own gender-role socialization. Several *cognitive theories* of gender-role development emphasize self-socialization (Bem, 1985; Cross & Markus, 1993; Martin & Halverson, 1987). Self-socialization entails three steps. First, children learn to classify themselves as male or female and to recognize their sex as a permanent quality (around ages 5 to 7). Second, this self-categorization motivates them to value those characteristics and behaviors associated with their sex. Third, they strive to bring their behavior in line with what is considered gender-appropriate in their culture. In other words, children get involved in their own socialization, working diligently to discover the rules that are supposed to govern their behavior.

Sources of Gender-Role Socialization

There are three main sources of influence in gender-role socialization: families, schools, and the media. Of course, we are now in an era of transition in gender roles, so the generalizations that follow may say more about how you were socialized than about how children will be socialized in the future.

Families   A great deal of gender-role socialization takes place in the home (Lott & Maluso, 1993; Turner & Gervai, 1995). Fathers engage in more "rough-housing" play with their sons than with their daughters, even in infancy (McBride-Chang & Jacklin, 1993). As children grow, boys and girls are encouraged to play with different types of toys (Etaugh & Liss, 1992). Generally, boys have less leeway to play with "feminine" toys than girls do with "masculine" toys. When children are old enough to help with household chores, the assignments tend to depend on sex (McHale et al., 1990). For example, girls wash dishes and boys mow the lawn.

Schools   Schools and teachers clearly contribute to the socialization of gender roles. The books that children use in learning to read can influence their ideas about what is suitable behavior for males and females (Oskamp, Kaufman, & Wolterbeek, 1996). Traditionally, males have been more likely to be portrayed as clever, heroic, and adventurous in these books, while females have been more likely to be shown doing domestic chores. The depiction of stereotypical gender roles in textbooks has declined considerably since the 1970s, but researchers still find subtle differences in how males and females tend to be portrayed (Kortenhaus & Demarest, 1993; Noddings, 1992; Turner-Bowker, 1996). Preschool and grade-school teachers frequently reward sex-appropriate behavior in their pupils (Fagot et al., 1985; Ruble & Martin, 1998). Interestingly, teachers tend to pay greater attention to males, helping them, praising them, and scolding them more than females (Sadker & Sadker, 1994). As youngsters progress through the school system, they are often channeled in career directions considered appropriate for their sex (Read, 1991).

Media   Television is another source of gender-role socialization (Luecke-Aleksa et al., 1995). There has been some improvement in recent years, but television shows have traditionally depicted men and women in highly stereotypic ways (Signorielli & Bacue, 1999; Zillman, Bryant, & Huston, 1994). Women are often portrayed as submissive, passive, and emotional. Men are more likely to be portrayed as independent, assertive, and competent. Even commercials contribute to the socialization of gender roles (Bretl & Cantor, 1988; Signorielli, McLeod, & Healy, 1994). Women are routinely shown worrying about trivial matters such as the whiteness of their laundry or the shine of their dishes. Music videos frequently portray women as sex objects, and these portrayals appear to influence viewers' attitudes about sexual conduct (Hansen & Hansen, 1988; Signorielli, 1993).

Are Fathers Essential to Children's Well-Being?

Are fathers essential for children to experience normal, healthy development? This question is currently the subject of heated debate. In recent years, a number of social scientists have mounted a thought-provoking argument that father absence is the chief factor underlying a host of modern social ills. For example, David Blankenhorn (1995) argues that "fatherlessness is the most harmful demographic trend of this generation. It is the leading cause of declining child well-being in our society" (p. 1). Expressing a similar view, David Popenoe (1996) maintains that "today's fatherlessness has led to social turmoil-damaged children, unhappy children, aimless children, children who strike back with pathological behavior and violence" (p.192).

The Basic Argument

What is the evidence for the proposition that fathers are essential to healthy development? Over the last 40 years, the proportion of children growing up without a father in the home has more than doubled (see Figure 11.21). During the same time, we have seen dramatic increases in teenage pregnancy, juvenile delinquency, violent crime, drug abuse, eating disorders, teen suicide, and family dysfunction. Moreover, mountains of studies have demonstrated an association between father absence and an elevated risk for these problems. Summarizing this evidence, Popenoe (1996) asserts that "fatherless children have a risk factor two to three times that of fathered children for a wide range of negative outcomes, including dropping out of high school, giving birth as a teenager, and becoming a juvenile delinquent" (p. 192), which leads him to infer that "fathers have a unique and irreplaceable role to play in child development" (p. 197). Working from this premise, Popenoe concludes, "If present trends continue, our society could be

Are fathers crucial to children's well-being? This seemingly simple question has sparked heated debate.

© PhotoDisc, Inc.

on the verge of committing social suicide" (p. 192). Echoing this dire conclusion, Blankenhorn (1995) comments that "to tolerate the trend of fatherlessness is to accept the inevitability of continued societal recession" (p. 222).

You might be thinking, "What's all the fuss about?" Surely, proclaiming the importance of fatherhood ought to be no more controversial than advocacy for motherhood or apple pie. But the assertion that a father is essential to a child's well-being has some interesting sociopolitical implications. It suggests that heterosexual marriage is the only appropriate context in which to raise children and that other family configurations are fundamentally deficient. Based on this line of reasoning, some people have argued for new laws that would make it more difficult to obtain a divorce and other policies and programs that would favor traditional families over families headed by single mothers, cohabiting parents, and gay and lesbian parents (Silverstein & Auerbach, 1999). Thus, the question about the importance of fathers is creating a great deal of controversy, because it is really a question about alternatives to traditional family structure.

Evaluating the Argument

In light of the far-reaching implications of the view that fathers are essential to normal development, it makes sense to subject this view to critical scrutiny. How could you use critical thinking skills to evaluate this argument? At least three previously discussed ideas seem germane.

First, it is important to recognize that the position that fathers are essential for healthy development rests on a foundation of correlational evidence, and as we have seen repeatedly, *correlation is no assurance of causation.* Yes, there has been an increase in fatherlessness that has been paralleled by increases in teenage pregnancy, drug abuse, eating disorders, and other disturbing social problems. But think of all the other changes that have occurred in American culture over the last 40 years, such as the decline of organized religion, the growth of mass media, dramatic shifts in sexual mores, and

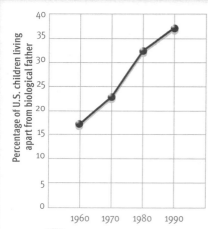

Figure 11.21

Increasing father absence in the United States. Since 1960 the percentage of U.S. children who live in a home without their biological father has risen steadily and probably exceeds 40% today. (Data from Hernandez, 1993)

so forth. Increased fatherlessness has covaried with a host of other cultural trends. Hence, it is highly speculative to infer that father absence is the chief cause of most modern social maladies.

Second, it always pays to think about whether there are *alternative explanations* for findings that you might have doubts about. What other factors might account for the association between father absence and children's maladjustment? Think for a moment: What is the most frequent cause of father absence? Obviously, it is divorce. Divorces tend to be highly stressful events that disrupt children's entire lives. Although the evidence suggests that a majority of children seem to survive divorce without lasting, detrimental effects, it is clear that divorce elevates youngsters' risk for a wide range of negative developmental outcomes (Amato & Keith, 1991; Hetherington, Bridges, & Insabella, 1998). Given that father absence and divorce are inextricably intertwined, it is possible that the negative effects of divorce account for much of the association between father absence and social problems.

Are there any other alternative explanations for the correlation between fatherlessness and social maladies? Yes, critics point out that the prevalence of father absence covaries with socioeconomic status. Father absence is much more common in low-income families. Thus, the effects of father absence are entangled to some extent with the many powerful, malignant effects of poverty, which might account for much of the correlation between fatherlessness and negative outcomes (McLoyd, 1998).

A third possible strategy in thinking critically about the effects of father absence would be to look for some of the *fallacies in reasoning* introduced in Chapter 10 (irrelevant reasons, circular reasoning, slippery slope, weak analogies, and false dichotomy). A couple of the quotes from Popenoe and Blankenhorn were chosen to give you an opportunity to detect two of these fallacies in a new context. Take a look at the quotes once again and see whether you can spot the fallacies.

Popenoe's assertion that "if present trends continue, our society could be on the verge of social suicide" is an example of

slippery slope argumentation, which involves predictions that if one allows X to happen, things will spin out of control and catastrophic events will follow. "Social suicide" is a little vague, but it sounds as if Popenoe is predicting that father absence will lead to the destruction of modern American culture. The other fallacy that you might have spotted was the *false dichotomy* apparent in Blankenhorn's assertion that "to tolerate the trend of fatherlessness is to accept the inevitability of continued societal recession." A false dichotomy creates an either-or choice between the position one wants to advocate (in this case, new social policies to reduce father absence) and some obviously horrible outcome that any sensible person would want to avoid (social decay), while ignoring other possible outcomes that might lie between these extremes.

In summary, we can find a number of flaws and weaknesses in the argument that fathers are *essential* to normal development. However, our critical evaluation of this argument *does not mean that fathers are unimportant.* Many types of evidence suggest that fathers generally make significant contributions to their children's development (Phares, 1996). We could argue with merit that fathers typically provide a substantial advantage for children that fatherless children do not have. But there is a crucial distinction between arguing that fathers *promote* normal, healthy development and

arguing that fathers are *necessary* for normal, healthy development. If fathers are *necessary,* children who grow up without them could not achieve the same level of well-being as those who have fathers, yet it is clear that a great many children from single-parent homes turn out just fine.

Fathers surely are important, and it seems likely that father absence *contributes* to a variety of social maladies. So, why do Blankenhorn (1995) and Popenoe (1996) argue for the much stronger conclusion—that fathers are *essential?* They appear to prefer the stronger conclusion because it raises much more serious questions about the viability of nontraditional family forms. Thus, they seem to want to advance a *political agenda* that champions traditional family values. They are certainly entitled to do so, but when research findings are used to advance a political agenda—whether conservative or liberal—a special caution alert should go off in your head. When a political agenda is at stake, it pays to scrutinize arguments with extra care, because research findings are more likely to be presented in a slanted fashion. The field of psychology deals with a host of complex questions that have profound implications for a wide range of social issues. The skills and habits of critical thinking can help you find your way through the maze of reasons and evidence that hold up the many sides of these complicated issues.

Table 11.3	Critical Thinking Skills Discussed in This Application
Skill	**Description**
Understanding the limitations of correlational evidence	The critical thinker understands that a correlation between two variables does not demonstrate that there is a causal link between the variables.
Looking for alternative explanations for findings and events	In evaluating explanations, the critical thinker explores whether there are other explanations that could also account for the findings or events under scrutiny.
Recognizing and avoiding common fallacies, such as irrelevant reasons, circular reasoning, slippery slope reasoning, weak analogies, and false dichotomies	The critical thinker is vigilant about conclusions based on unrelated premises, conclusions that are rewordings of premises, unwarranted predictions that things will spin out of control, superficial analogies, and contrived dichotomies.

REVIEW

Key Ideas

Progress Before Birth: Prenatal Development

● Prenatal development proceeds through the germinal, embryonic, and fetal stages as the zygote is differentiated into a human organism. During this period, development may be affected by maternal drug use, maternal malnutrition, and some maternal illnesses.

The Wondrous Years of Childhood

● Motor development follows cephalocaudal (head-to-foot) and proximodistal (center-outward) trends. Developmental norms for motor skills and other types of development are only group averages. Cross-cultural research on the pacing of motor development shows that maturation and experience both are important.

● Cross-sectional and longitudinal studies are both well suited to developmental research. Temperamental differences among children are apparent during the first few months of life. Thomas and Chess found that temperament is fairly stable over time.

● Separation anxiety usually appears at around 6 to 8 months of age. Research shows that attachment emerges out of an interplay between infant and mother. Infant-mother attachments fall into three categories: secure, anxious-ambivalent, and avoidant. The effects of day care on attachment are a source of concern, but the evidence is hotly debated.

● Cultural variations in child rearing can affect the patterns of attachment seen in a society. Belsky theorizes that children have been programmed by evolution to respond to sensitive or insensitive care with different attachment patterns that eventually cultivate reproductive strategies that would have been adaptive in the environments that have historically fostered sensitive or insensitive care.

● Erik Erikson's theory of personality development proposes that individuals evolve through eight stages over the life span. Successful progress through the four childhood stages should yield a trustful, autonomous person with a sense of initiative and industry.

● According to Piaget's theory of cognitive development, the key advance during the sensorimotor period is the child's gradual recognition of the permanence of objects. The preoperational period is marked by centration, irreversibility, and egocentrism. During the concrete operations period, children develop the ability to perform operations on mental representations. Formal operations ushers in more abstract, systematic, and logical thought.

● Recent research has shown that infants appear to understand surprisingly complex concepts that they have had virtually no opportunity to learn about, leading some theorists to conclude that basic cognitive abilities are innate.

● According to Kohlberg, moral reasoning progresses through three levels that are related to age and determined by cognitive development. Age-related progress in moral reasoning *has* been found in research, although there is a great deal of overlap between adjacent stages.

The Transition of Adolescence

● The growth spurt at puberty is a prominent event involving the development of reproductive maturity and secondary sexual characteristics. Recent years have brought a surge in attempted suicide by adolescents. Evidence suggests that adolescence may be slightly more stressful than other periods of life. According to Erikson, the key challenge of adolescence is to make some progress toward a sense of identity.

The Expanse of Adulthood

● During adulthood, personality is marked by both stability and change. Doubts have surfaced about whether a midlife crisis is a normal developmental transition. Many landmarks in adult development involve transitions in family relationships, including adjusting to marriage, parenthood, and the empty nest.

● During adulthood, age-related physical transitions include changes in appearance, neuron losses, sensory losses (especially in vision and hearing), and hormonal changes. Menopause is not as problematic as widely suggested. In the cognitive domain, mental speed declines first.

Putting It in Perspective

● Five of our seven integrative themes stood out in this chapter, including the value of theoretical diversity, the influence of cultural factors, the importance of sociohistorical contexts, and the inevitability of multifactorial causation. But above all else, our discussion of development showed how heredity and environment interactively shape behavior.

Personal Application ● Understanding Gender Differences

● Gender differences in behavior are fewer in number and smaller in magnitude than gender stereotypes suggest. Research reviews suggest that there are genuine gender differences in verbal ability, mathematical ability, spatial ability, aggression, nonverbal communication, sexual behavior, and some personality traits.

● Evolutionary explanations of gender differences assert that the adaptive pressures faced by males and females have fostered behavioral disparities. There is research linking gender differences in humans to hormones and brain organization, but the research is marred by interpretive problems. Operant conditioning, observational learning, and self-socialization contribute to the development of gender differences. Families, schools, and the media are among the main sources of gender-role socialization.

Critical Thinking Application ● Are Fathers Essential to Children's Well-Being?

● Some social scientists have argued that father absence is the chief cause of a host of social problems and that fathers are essential for normal, healthy development. Critics have argued that there are alternative explanations for the association between father absence and negative developmental outcomes. Slippery slope argumentation and false dichotomies have also been seen in the debate about the significance of father absence.

Key Terms

Age of viability
Animism
Attachment
Centration
Cephalocaudal trend
Cognitive development
Conservation
Cross-sectional study
Dementia
Development
Developmental norms
Dishabituation
Egocentrism
Embryonic stage
Fetal alcohol syndrome
Fetal stage
Gender
Gender differences
Gender roles
Gender stereotypes
Germinal stage
Habituation
Irreversibility
Longitudinal study
Maturation
Menarche
Midlife crisis
Motor development
Object permanence
Placenta
Prenatal period
Primary sex characteristics
Proximodistal trend
Puberty
Pubescence
Secondary sex characteristics
Separation anxiety
Sex
Stage
Temperament
Zygote

Key People

Mary Ainsworth
Erik Erikson
Lawrence Kohlberg
Jean Piaget
Alexander Thomas and Stella Chess

PRACTICE TEST

1. The stage of prenatal development during which the developing organism is most vulnerable to injury is the:
   - A. zygotic stage.
   - B. germinal stage.
   - C. fetal stage.
   - D. embryonic stage.

2. The cephalocaudal trend in the motor development of children can be described simply as a:
   - A. head-to-foot direction.
   - B. center-outward direction.
   - C. foot-to-head direction.
   - D. body-appendages direction.

3. Developmental norms:
   - A. can be used to make extremely precise predictions about the age at which an individual child will reach various developmental milestones.
   - B. indicate the maximum age at which a child can reach a particular developmental milestone and still be considered "normal."
   - C. indicate the average age at which individuals reach various developmental milestones.
   - D. involve both a and b.

4. When the development of the same subjects is studied over a period of time, the study is called a:
   - A. cross-sectional study.
   - B. life history study.
   - C. longitudinal study.
   - D. sequential study.

5. The formation of an attachment between infant and caregiver seems to be:
   - A. exclusively a function of the infant's temperament.
   - B. exclusively a function of the caregiver's sensitivity.
   - C. largely a matter of how well the child's nutritional needs are met.
   - D. a function of the combined effect of the infant's temperament and the caregiver's sensitivity.

6. During the second year of life, toddlers begin to take some personal responsibility for feeding, dressing, and bathing themselves in an attempt to establish what Erikson calls a sense of:
   - A. superiority.
   - B. industry.
   - C. generativity.
   - D. autonomy.

7. Five-year-old David watches as you pour water from a short, wide glass into a tall, narrow one. He says there is now more water than before. This response demonstrates that:
   - A. David understands the concept of conservation.
   - B. David does not understand the concept of conservation.
   - C. David's cognitive development is "behind" for his age.
   - D. both b and c are happening.

8. Which of the following is *not* one of the criticisms of Piaget's theory of cognitive development?
   - A. Piaget may have underestimated the cognitive skills of children in some areas.
   - B. Piaget may have underestimated the influence of cultural factors on cognitive development.
   - C. The theory does not clearly address the issue of individual differences in development.
   - D. Evidence for the theory is based on children's answers to questions.

9. If a child's primary reason for not drawing pictures on the living room wall with crayons is to avoid the punishment that would inevitably follow this behavior, she would be said to be at which level of moral development?
   - A. Conventional
   - B. Postconventional
   - C. Preconventional
   - D. Unconventional

10. The assumption of a preoperational child that a car is moving because she is in it is an example of:
    - A. egocentrism.
    - B. centration.
    - C. conservation.
    - D. preconventional reasoning.

11. Girls who mature _____ and boys who mature _____ feel especially uneasy about puberty and self-conscious about their looks.
    - A. early; early
    - B. early; late
    - C. late; early
    - D. late; late

12. Sixteen-year-old Foster wants to spend a few years experimenting with different lifestyles and careers before he settles on who and what he wants to be. Foster is in the adolescent phase called:
    - A. moratorium.
    - B. foreclosure.
    - C. identity achievement.
    - D. identity diffusion.

13. The recent evidence suggests that a midlife crisis:
    - A. is universal around the world.
    - B. occurs in the vast majority of people.
    - C. occurs in the vast majority of men, but only a handful of women.
    - D. is seen in only a small minority of people.

14. Two cognitive areas that may decline at around 60 years of age are:
    - A. verbal and math test scores.
    - B. cognitive speed and working memory.
    - C. vocabulary scores and abstract reasoning.
    - D. none of the above.

15. Males have been found to differ slightly from females in three well-documented areas of mental abilities. Which of the following is *not* one of these?
    - A. Verbal ability
    - B. Mathematical ability
    - C. Intelligence
    - D. Visual-spatial abilities

Answers

1	D	pages 327–328	6	D	page 335	11	B	page 343
2	A	page 329	7	B	page 337	12	A	page 345
3	C	page 330	8	D	page 339	13	D	page 346
4	C	page 331	9	C	pages 341–342	14	B	page 350
5	D	pages 332–333	10	A	page 338	15	C	pages 351–352

INFOTRAC
COLLEGE EDITION

Go to the Wadsworth Psychology Study Center for quiz questions, research updates, interactive exercises, and suggested readings in INFOTRAC related to this chapter:
http://psychology.wadsworth.com/product/0534593100s

CHAPTER 12

Stone/Marty Loken

Personality: Theory, Research, and Assessment

Stone/Marty Loken

I have a close friend who has to be one of the world's great optimists. A few years ago, he was driving an all-terrain vehicle in a California desert and flipped it into the air. The vehicle landed on him, shattering one of his legs. Two days later, he called me long-distance (from the hospital) to tell me about the accident. Still in great pain from extensive surgery, and facing more operations, not to mention a year or two on crutches, he was joking about it. He was in his usual cheerful, lighthearted mood. Most of us, of course, would have been rather dejected and gloomy under such circumstances. Consider another example. A number of years ago, I went with the same friend to see the Chicago Cubs play a doubleheader. For most Cubs fans such as ourselves, the baseball that day was boring and depressing. In the first game, the Cubs were shut out, losing 1 to 0. In game two, after eight innings, they still hadn't scored a run and were getting trounced,

9 to 0, when I said, "Let's get out of here. This is disgusting." He turned to me in genuine surprise, saying, "What? Leave? We're gonna rally!"

My friend's optimism is a key facet of his *personality*. In this chapter, we'll explore the mystery of personality. What exactly is personality? How does personality develop over time? For instance, how does someone like my friend get to be so upbeat and optimistic? Is personality largely biological in origin, or is experience critical? What makes for a healthy personality?

Traditionally, the study of personality has been dominated by "grand theories," broad in scope, attempting to explain a great many facets of behavior. Our discussion will reflect this emphasis, as we'll devote most of our time to the sweeping theories of Freud, Jung, Skinner, Rogers, and several others. In the Personal Application, we'll discuss how psychological tests are used to measure various aspects of personality. In the Critical Thinking Application, you'll see how hindsight bias can taint analyses of personality.

The Nature of Personality

Personality is a complex hypothetical construct that has been defined in a variety of ways. Let's take a closer look at the concepts of personality and personality traits.

Defining Personality: Consistency and Distinctiveness

What does it mean to say that my friend has an optimistic personality? This assertion indicates that he has a fairly *consistent tendency* to behave in a cheerful, hopeful, enthusiastic way, looking at the bright side of things, across a wide variety of situations. Although no one is entirely consistent in behavior, this quality of *consistency across situations* lies at the core of the concept of personality.

Distinctiveness is also central to the concept of personality. Personality is used to explain why people do not act the same in similar situations. If you were stuck in an elevator with three people, each might react differently. One might crack jokes to relieve tension. Another might make ominous predictions that "we'll never get out of here." The third person might calmly think about how to escape. These varied reactions to the same situation occur because each person has a different personality. Each person has traits that are seen in other people, but each individual has his or her own distinctive *set* of personality traits.

In summary, the concept of personality is used to explain (1) the stability in a person's behavior over time and across situations (consistency) and (2) the behavioral differences among people reacting to the same situation (distinctiveness). We can combine these ideas into the following definition: **Personality refers to an individual's unique constellation of consistent behavioral traits.** Let's explore the concept of *traits* in more detail.

Personality Traits: Dispositions and Dimensions

Everyone makes remarks like "Jan is very *conscientious*." Or you might assert that "Bill is too *timid* to succeed in that job." These descriptive statements refer to personality traits. **A *personality trait* is a durable disposition to behave in a particular way in a variety of situations.** Adjectives such as *honest, dependable, moody, impulsive, suspicious, anxious, excitable, domineering,* and *friendly* describe dispositions that represent personality traits. People

use an enormous number of these trait terms to describe one another's personality. One prominent personality theorist, Gordon Allport (1937, 1961), went through an unabridged dictionary and identified over 4500 personality traits!

Most approaches to personality assume that some traits are more basic than others. According to this notion, a small number of fundamental traits determine other, more superficial traits. For example, a person's tendency to be impulsive, restless, irritable, boisterous, and impatient might all be derived from a more basic tendency to be excitable.

A number of psychologists have taken on the challenge of identifying the basic traits that form the core of personality. For example, Raymond Cattell (1950, 1966, 1990) has used complex statistical procedures to reduce Allport's list of traits to just 16 basic dimensions of personality. Cattell believes that psychologists can thoroughly describe an individual's personality by measuring these 16 traits. In the Personal Application, we'll discuss a personality test he designed to assess these traits.

The Five-Factor Model of Personality Traits

Robert McCrae and Paul Costa (1987, 1997, 1999) have arrived at an even simpler, *five-factor model of personality.* McCrae and Costa maintain that most aspects of personality are derived from the "Big Five" traits: neuroticism, extraversion, openness to experience, agreeableness, and conscientiousness (see Table 12.1).

Like Cattell, McCrae and Costa maintain that personality can be described adequately by measuring the basic traits that they've identified. Their bold claim has been supported in many studies by other researchers, and the Big Five model has

Table 12.1 McCrae and Costa's Big Five Model of Personality

Factor	Description
Neuroticism	Anxious, insecure, guilt-prone, self-conscious
Extraversion	Talkative, sociable, fun-loving, affectionate
Openness to experience	Daring, nonconforming, showing unusually broad interests, imaginative
Agreeableness	Sympathetic, warm, trusting, cooperative
Conscientiousness	Ethical, dependable, productive, purposeful

(From "Validation of the Five-Factor Model of Personality Across Instruments and Observers," by R. R. McCrae and P. T. Costa, 1987, *Journal of Personality and Social Psychology, 52* (1), 81–90. Data in public domain.)

become the dominant conception of personality structure in contemporary psychology (John & Srivastava, 1999; Ozer & Reise, 1994; Wiggins & Trapnell, 1997). However, some theorists have been critical of the model. For example, Jack Block (1995) has questioned the generality of the model. He points out that the higher-order traits that emerge in statistical analyses depend to some extent on the exact mix of the much larger set of specific traits that are measured in the first place. Thus, he asserts that the five-factor model is more arbitrary than widely appreciated. Other critics of the five-factor model maintain that more than five traits are necessary to account for most of the vari-

ation seen in human personality (Benet & Waller, 1995; Paunonen, 1998; Wiggins, 1992).

The debate about how many dimensions are necessary to describe personality is likely to continue for many years to come. As you'll see throughout the chapter, the study of personality is an area in psychology that has a long history of "dueling theories." We'll divide these diverse personality theories into four broad groups that share certain assumptions, emphases, and interests: (1) psychodynamic perspectives, (2) behavioral perspectives, (3) humanistic perspectives, and (4) biological perspectives. We'll begin our discussion of personality theories by examining the life and work of Sigmund Freud.

Psychodynamic Perspectives

Psychodynamic theories **include all the diverse theories descended from the work of Sigmund Freud that focus on unconscious mental forces.** Freud inspired many brilliant scholars who followed in his intellectual footsteps. Some of these followers simply refined and updated Freud's theory. Others veered off in new directions and established independent, albeit related, schools of thought. Today, the psychodynamic umbrella covers a large collection of loosely related theories that we can only sample from in this text. In this section, we'll examine the ideas of Sigmund Freud in some detail. Then we'll take a briefer look at the psychodynamic theories of Carl Jung and Alfred Adler.

Freud's Psychoanalytic Theory

Born in 1856, Sigmund Freud grew up in a middle-class Jewish home in Vienna, Austria. He showed an early interest in intellectual pursuits and became an intense, hardworking young man, driven to achieve fame. Freud lived in the Victorian era, which was marked by sexual repression. His life was also affected by World War I, which devastated Europe, and by the growing anti-Semitism of the times. We'll see that the sexual repression and aggressive hostilities that Freud witnessed left their mark on his view of human nature.

Freud was a physician specializing in neurology when he began his medical practice in Vienna toward the end of the 19th century. Like other neurologists in his era, he often treated people troubled by nervous problems such as irrational fears, obsessions, and anxieties. Eventually he devoted himself to the treatment of mental disorders using

an innovative procedure he had developed, called psychoanalysis, that required lengthy verbal interactions with patients during which Freud probed deeply into their lives.

Freud's (1901, 1924, 1940) *psychoanalytic theory* grew out of his decades of interactions with his clients in psychoanalysis. Psychoanalytic theory attempts to explain personality, motivation, and psychological disorders by focusing on the influence of early childhood experiences, on unconscious motives and conflicts, and on the methods people use to cope with their sexual and aggressive urges.

Most of Freud's contemporaries were uncomfortable with his theory for at least three reasons. First, in arguing that people's behavior is governed by unconscious factors of which they are unaware, Freud made the disconcerting suggestion that individuals are not masters of their own minds. Second, in claiming that our adult personalities are shaped by childhood experiences and other factors beyond our control, he suggested that people are not masters of their own destinies. Third, by emphasizing the great importance of how people cope with their sexual urges, he offended those who held the conservative, Victorian values of his time. Thus, Freud endured a great deal of criticism, condemnation, and outright ridicule, even after his work began to attract favorable attention. Let's examine the ideas that generated so much controversy.

Structure of Personality

Freud divided personality structure into three components: the id, the ego, and the superego. He saw a person's behavior as the outcome of interactions among these three components.

Web Link 12.1

The Victorian Web
How psychoanalysis initially developed within a late-19th-century context is comprehensively portrayed in George Landow's (Brown University) important hypertext archive.

National Library of Medicine

"No one who, like me, conjures up the most evil of those half-tamed demons that inhabit the human beast, and seeks to wrestle with them, can expect to come through the struggle unscathed."
SIGMUND FREUD

Web Link 12.2

Sigmund Freud Museum, Vienna, Austria

This online museum, in English and German versions, offers both a detailed chronology of Freud's life and an explanation of the most important concepts of psychoanalysis. The highlights of the site are the rich audiovisual resources, including photos, amateur movie clips, and voice recordings of Freud.

Freud's psychoanalytic theory was based on decades of clinical work. He treated a great many patients in the consulting room pictured here. The room contains numerous artifacts from other cultures—and the original psychoanalytic couch.

The *id* **is the primitive, instinctive component of personality that operates according to the pleasure principle.** Freud referred to the id as the reservoir of psychic energy. By this he meant that the id houses the raw biological urges (to eat, sleep, defecate, copulate, and so on) that energize human behavior. The id operates according to **the *pleasure principle,* which demands immediate gratification of its urges.** The id engages in *primary-process thinking,* which is primitive, illogical, irrational, and fantasy oriented.

The *ego* **is the decision-making component of personality that operates according to the reality principle.** The ego mediates between the id, with its forceful desires for immediate satisfaction, and the external social world, with its expectations and norms regarding suitable behavior. The ego considers social realities—society's norms, etiquette, rules, and customs—in deciding how to behave. The ego is guided by **the *reality principle,* which seeks to delay gratification of the id's urges until appropriate outlets and situations can be found.** In short, to stay out of trouble, the ego often works to tame the unbridled desires of the id.

In the long run, the ego wants to maximize gratification, just as the id does. However, the ego engages in *secondary-process thinking,* which is relatively rational, realistic, and oriented toward problem solving. Thus, the ego strives to avoid negative consequences from society and its representatives (for example, punishment by parents or teachers) by behaving "properly." It also attempts to achieve long-range goals that sometimes require putting off gratification.

While the ego concerns itself with practical realities, **the *superego* is the moral component of personality that incorporates social standards about what represents right and wrong.** Throughout their lives, but especially during childhood, people receive training about what constitutes good and bad behavior. Many social norms regarding morality are eventually internalized. The superego emerges out of the ego at around 3 to 5 years of age. In some people, the superego can become irrationally demanding in its striving for moral perfection. Such people are plagued by excessive feelings of guilt.

According to Freud, the id, ego, and superego are distributed differently across three levels of awareness, which we'll describe next.

Levels of Awareness

Perhaps Freud's most enduring insight was his recognition of how unconscious forces can influence behavior. He inferred the existence of the unconscious from a variety of observations that he made with his patients. For example, he noticed that "slips of the tongue" often revealed a person's true feelings. He also realized that his patients' dreams often expressed hidden desires. Most important, through psychoanalysis he often helped patients discover feelings and conflicts they had previously been unaware of.

Freud contrasted the unconscious with the conscious and preconscious, creating three levels of awareness. **The *conscious* consists of whatever one is aware of at a particular point in time.** For example, at this moment your conscious may include the train of thought in this text and a dim awareness in the back of your mind that your eyes are getting tired and you're beginning to get hungry. **The *preconscious* contains material just beneath the surface of awareness that can easily be retrieved.** Examples might include your middle name, what you had for supper last night, or an argument you had with a friend yesterday. **The *unconscious* contains thoughts, memories, and desires that are well below the surface of conscious awareness but that nonetheless exert great influence on behavior.** Examples of material that might be found in your unconscious include a forgotten trauma from childhood, hidden feelings of hostility toward a parent, and repressed sexual desires.

Freud's conception of the mind is often compared to an iceberg that has most of its mass hidden beneath the water's surface (see Figure 12.1). He believed that the unconscious (the mass below the surface) is much larger than the conscious or preconscious. As you can see in Figure 12.1, he proposed that the ego and superego operate at all three levels of awareness. In contrast, the id is entirely unconscious, expressing its urges at a conscious level through the ego. Of course, the id's desires for immediate satisfaction often trigger internal conflicts with the ego and superego. These conflicts play a key role in Freud's theory.

Conflict and the Tyranny of Sex and Aggression

Freud assumed that behavior is the outcome of an ongoing series of internal conflicts. He saw internal battles between the id, ego, and superego as routine. Why? Because the id wants to gratify its urges immediately, but the norms of civilized society frequently dictate otherwise. For example, your id might feel an urge to clobber a co-worker who constantly irritates you. However, society frowns on such behavior, so your ego would try to hold this urge in check. Hence, you would find yourself in conflict. You may be experiencing conflict at this very moment. In Freudian terms, your id may be secretly urging you to abandon reading this chapter so that you can fix a snack and watch some television. Your ego may be weighing this appealing option against your society-induced need to excel in school.

Freud believed that people's lives are dominated by conflict. He asserted that individuals career from one conflict to another. The following scenario provides a concrete illustration of how the three components of personality interact to create constant conflicts:

Imagine lurching across your bed to shut off your alarm clock as it rings obnoxiously. It's 7 A.M. and time to get up for your history class. However, your id (operating according to the pleasure principle) urges you to return to the immediate gratification of additional sleep. Your ego (operating according to the reality principle) points out that you really must go to class since you haven't been able to decipher the textbook on your own. Your id (in its typical unrealistic fashion) smugly assures you that you will get the A grade that you need and suggests lying back to dream about how impressed your roommates will be. Just as you're relaxing, your superego jumps into the fray. It tries to make you feel guilty about all the money your parents paid in tuition for the class that you're about to skip. You haven't even gotten out of bed yet, but there's already a pitched battle in your psyche.

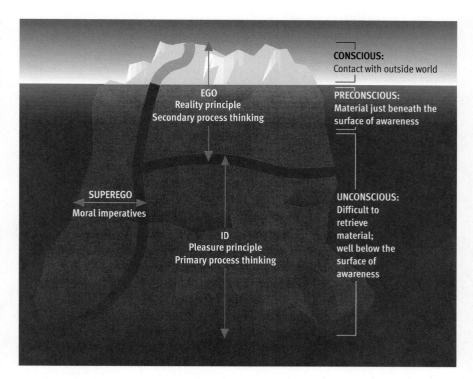

Let's say your ego wins the battle. You pull yourself out of bed and head for class. On the way, you pass a donut shop and your id clamors for cinnamon rolls. Your ego reminds you that you're getting overweight and that you're supposed to be on a diet. Your id wins this time. After you've attended your history lecture, your ego reminds you that you need to do some library research for a paper in philosophy. However, your id insists on returning to your apartment to watch some sitcom reruns. As you reenter your apartment, you're overwhelmed by how messy it is. It's your roommates' mess, and your id suggests that you tell them off. As you're about to lash out, however, your ego convinces you that diplomacy will be more effective. It's only midday—and already you've been through a series of internal conflicts.

Freud believed that conflicts centering on sexual and aggressive impulses are especially likely to have far-reaching consequences. Why did he emphasize sex and aggression? Two reasons were prominent in his thinking. First, he thought that sex and aggression are subject to more complex and ambiguous social controls than other basic motives. The norms governing sexual and aggressive behavior are subtle, and people often get inconsistent messages about what's appropriate. Thus, Freud believed that these two drives are the source of much confusion. Second, he noted that the aggressive and sexual drives are thwarted more regularly than other basic, biological urges. Think about it: If you get hungry or thirsty, you can simply head for a nearby vending

Figure 12.1

Freud's model of personality structure. Freud theorized that people have three levels of awareness: the conscious, the preconscious, and the unconscious. The enormous size of the unconscious is often dramatized by comparing it to the portion of an iceberg that lies beneath the water's surface. Freud also divided personality structure into three components—id, ego, and superego—that operate according to different principles and exhibit different modes of thinking. In Freud's model, the id is entirely unconscious, but the ego and superego operate at all three levels of awareness.

machine or a drinking fountain. But if a department store clerk infuriates you, you aren't likely to reach across the counter and slug him or her. Likewise, when you see an attractive person who inspires lustful urges, you don't normally walk up and propose a tryst in a nearby broom closet. There's nothing comparable to vending machines or drinking fountains for the satisfaction of sexual and aggressive urges. Freud ascribed great importance to these needs because social norms dictate that they're routinely frustrated.

Anxiety and Defense Mechanisms

Most internal conflicts are trivial and are quickly resolved. Occasionally, however, a conflict will linger for days, months, or even years, creating internal tension. More often than not, such prolonged and troublesome conflicts involve sexual and aggressive impulses that society wants to tame. These conflicts are often played out entirely in the unconscious. Although you may not be aware of these unconscious battles, they can produce *anxiety* that slips to the surface of conscious awareness. The anxiety can be attributed to your ego worrying about (1) the id getting out of control and doing something terrible that leads to severe negative consequences or (2) the superego getting out of control and making you feel guilty about a real or imagined transgression.

The arousal of anxiety is a crucial event in Freud's theory of personality functioning (see Figure 12.2). Anxiety is distressing, so people try to rid themselves of this unpleasant emotion any way they can. This effort to ward off anxiety often involves the use of defense mechanisms. **Defense mechanisms are largely unconscious reactions that protect a person from unpleasant emotions such as anxiety and guilt.** Typically, they're mental maneuvers that work through self-deception (see Table 12.2). Consider *rationalization,* **which is creating false but plausible excuses to justify unacceptable behavior.** For example, after cheating someone in a business transaction, you might reduce your guilt by rationalizing that "everyone does it."

According to Freud, the most basic and widely used defense mechanism is repression. *Repression* **is keeping distressing thoughts and feelings buried in the unconscious.** People tend to repress desires that make them feel guilty, conflicts that make them anxious, and memories that are painful. As pointed out in Chapter 7, repression has been called "motivated forgetting." If you forget a dental appointment or the name of someone you don't like, repression may be at work.

Self-deception can also be seen in projection and displacement. *Projection* **is attributing one's own thoughts, feelings, or motives to another.** Usually, the thoughts one projects onto others are those that would make one feel guilty. For example, if lusting for a co-worker makes you feel guilty, you might attribute any latent sexual tension between the two of you to the *other person's* desire to seduce you. *Displacement* **is diverting emotional feelings (usually anger) from their original source to a substitute target.** If your boss gives you a hard time at work and you come home and slam the door, kick the dog, and scream at your spouse, you're displacing your anger onto irrelevant targets. Unfortunately, social constraints often force people to hold back their anger, and they end up lashing out at the people they love the most.

Other prominent defense mechanisms include reaction formation, regression, and identification. *Reaction formation* **is behaving in a way that's exactly the opposite of one's true feelings.** Guilt about sexual desires often leads to reaction formation. Freud theorized that many homophobic males who ridicule homosexuals are defending against their own latent homosexual impulses. The telltale sign of reaction formation is the exaggerated quality of the opposite behavior. *Regression* **is a reversion to immature patterns of behavior.** When anxious about their self-worth, some adults respond with childish boasting and bragging (as opposed to subtle efforts to impress others). For example, a fired executive having difficulty finding a new job might start making ridiculous statements about his incomparable talents and achievements. Such bragging is regressive when it's marked by massive exaggerations that virtually anyone can see through. *Identification* **is bolstering self-esteem by forming an imaginary or real alliance with some person or group.** Youngsters often shore up precarious feelings of self-worth by identifying with rock stars, movie stars, or famous athletes. Adults may join exclusive country clubs or civic organizations as a means of boosting their self-esteem via identification.

Recent years have brought a revival of interest in research on defense mechanisms. For example, a

Figure 12.2

Freud's model of personality dynamics. According to Freud, unconscious conflicts between the id, ego, and superego sometimes create anxiety. This discomfort may lead to the use of defense mechanisms, which may temporarily relieve anxiety.

Intrapsychic conflict (between id, ego, and superego) → Anxiety → Reliance on defense mechanisms

Table 12.2   Defense Mechanisms, with Examples

Defense Mechanism	Definition	Example
Repression	Keeping distressing thoughts and feelings buried in the unconscious	A traumatized soldier has no recollection of the details of a close brush with death.
Projection	Attributing one's own thoughts, feelings, or motives to another	A woman who dislikes her boss thinks she likes her boss but feels that the boss doesn't like her.
Displacement	Diverting emotional feelings (usually anger) from their original source to a substitute target	After parental scolding, a young girl takes her anger out on her little brother.
Reaction formation	Behaving in a way that is exactly the opposite of one's true feelings	A parent who unconsciously resents a child spoils the child with outlandish gifts.
Regression	A reversion to immature patterns of behavior	An adult has a temper tantrum when he doesn't get his way.
Rationalization	Creating false but plausible excuses to justify unacceptable behavior	A student watches TV instead of studying, saying that "additional study wouldn't do any good anyway."
Identification	Bolstering self-esteem by forming an imaginary or real alliance with some person or group	An insecure young man joins a fraternity to boost his self-esteem.

NOTE: See Table 13.2 for additional examples of defense mechanisms.

series of studies have identified a *repressive coping style* and shown that "repressors" have an impoverished memory for emotional events and negative feedback and that they habitually avoid unpleasant emotions by distracting themselves with pleasant thoughts and memories (Boden & Baumeister, 1997; Weinberger & Davidson, 1994). In another line of research, Newman, Duff, and Baumeister (1997) have shed new light on the cognitive dynamics of *projection*. Newman et al. showed that people actively work to suppress thoughts about the possibility that they might have an undesirable trait (say, dishonesty), but this ongoing effort makes thoughts about the unwanted trait highly accessible, so they chronically use this trait concept to explain others' behavior and end up routinely attributing the trait to others. Another very interesting study provided support for the Freudian hypothesis that reaction formation underlies homophobia in males. Adams, Wright, and Lohr (1996) found that when homophobic men are shown an erotic videotape depicting homosexual activity, they exhibit sexual arousal not seen in nonhomophobic subjects.

CONCEPT CHECK 12.1

Identifying Defense Mechanisms

Check your understanding of defense mechanisms by identifying specific defenses in the story below. Each example of a defense mechanism is underlined, with a number beneath it. Write in the defense at work in each case in the numbered spaces after the story. The answers are in Appendix A.

My boyfriend recently broke up with me after we had dated seriously for several years. At first, I cried a great deal and locked myself in my room, where I pouted endlessly. I was sure that my former boyfriend felt as miserable as I did. I told several friends that he was probably lonely and depressed. Later, I decided that I hated him. I was happy about the breakup and talked about how much I was going to enjoy my newfound freedom. I went to parties and socialized a great deal and just forgot about him. It's funny—at one point I couldn't even remember his phone number! Then I started pining for him again. But eventually I began to look at the situation more objectively. I realized that he had many faults and that we were bound to break up sooner or later, so I was better off without him.

1. _____   4. _____

2. _____   5. _____

3. _____

According to Freudian theory, early childhood experiences such as toilet training (a parent's attempt to regulate a child's biological urges) can influence an individual's personality, with the consequences lasting throughout adulthood.

Development: Psychosexual Stages 10a

Freud made the rather startling assertion that the basic foundation of an individual's personality has been laid down by the tender age of 5. To shed light on these crucial early years, Freud formulated a stage theory of development. He emphasized how young children deal with their immature but powerful sexual urges (he used the term *sexual* in a general way to refer to many urges for physical pleasure). According to Freud, these sexual urges shift in focus as children progress from one stage of development to another. Indeed, the names for the stages (oral, anal, genital, and so on) are based on where children are focusing their erotic energy during that period. Thus, *psychosexual stages are developmental periods with a characteristic sexual focus that leave their mark on adult personality.*

Freud theorized that each psychosexual stage has its own unique developmental challenges or tasks (see Table 12.3). The way these challenges are handled supposedly shapes personality. The notion of *fixation* plays an important role in this process. *Fixation involves a failure to move forward from one stage to another as expected.* Essentially, the child's development stalls for a while. Fixation can be caused by excessive *gratification* of needs at a particular stage or by excessive *frustration* of those needs. Either way, fixations left over from childhood affect adult personality. Generally, fixation leads to an overemphasis on the psychosexual needs prominent during the fixated stage. Freud described a series of five psychosexual stages. Let's examine some of the highlights in this sequence and how fixation might occur.

Oral Stage The oral stage encompasses the first year of life. During this period, the main source of erotic stimulation is the mouth (in biting, sucking, chewing, and so on). In Freud's view, the handling of the child's feeding experiences is crucial to subsequent development. He attributed considerable importance to the manner in which the child is weaned from the breast or the bottle. According to Freud, fixation at the oral stage could form the basis for obsessive eating or smoking later in life (among many other things).

Anal Stage In their second year, children get their erotic pleasure from their bowel movements, through either the expulsion or retention of feces. The crucial event at this time is toilet training, which represents society's first systematic effort to regulate the child's biological urges. Severely punitive toilet training leads to a variety of possible outcomes. For example, excessive punishment might produce a latent feeling of hostility toward the "trainer," usually the mother. This hostility might generalize to women as a class. Another possibility is that heavy reliance on punitive measures could lead to an association between genital concerns and the anxiety that the punishment arouses. This genital anxiety derived from severe toilet training could evolve into anxiety about sexual activities later in life.

Phallic Stage In the third through fifth years, the genitals become the focus for the child's erotic energy, largely through self-stimulation. During this pivotal stage, the *Oedipal complex* emerges. That is, little boys develop an erotically tinged preference for their mother. They also feel hostility toward their father, whom they view as a competitor for mom's affection. Similarly, little girls develop a special attachment to their father. Around the same time, they learn that little boys have very different genitals, and supposedly they develop *penis envy*. According to Freud, young girls feel hostile toward their mother because they blame her for their

Table 12.3 Freud's Stages of Psychosexual Development

Stage	Approximate Ages	Erotic Focus	Key Tasks and Experiences
Oral	0–1	Mouth (sucking, biting)	Weaning (from breast or bottle)
Anal	2–3	Anus (expelling or retaining feces)	Toilet training
Phallic	4–5	Genitals (masturbating)	Identifying with adult role models; coping with Oedipal crisis
Latency	6–12	None (sexually repressed)	Expanding social contacts
Genital	Puberty onward	Genitals (being sexually intimate)	Establishing intimate relationships; contributing to society through working

anatomical "deficiency." To summarize, in the *Oedipal complex* **children manifest erotically tinged desires for their opposite-sex parent, accompanied by feelings of hostility toward their same-sex parent.** The name for this syndrome was taken from the Greek myth in which Oedipus, not knowing the identity of his real parents, inadvertently killed his father and married his mother.

According to Freud, the way parents and children deal with the sexual and aggressive conflicts inherent in the Oedipal complex is of paramount importance. The child has to resolve the Oedipal dilemma by purging the sexual longings for the opposite-sex parent and by crushing the hostility felt toward the same-sex parent. In Freud's view, healthy psychosexual development hinges on the resolution of the Oedipal conflict. Why? Because continued hostility toward the same-sex parent may prevent the child from identifying adequately with that parent. Freudian theory predicts that without such identification, many aspects of the child's development won't progress as they should.

Latency and Genital Stages From around age five through puberty, the child's sexuality is largely suppressed—it becomes *latent.* Important events during this *latency stage* center on expanding social contacts beyond the immediate family. With the advent of puberty, the child progresses into the *genital stage.* Sexual urges reappear and focus on the genitals once again. At this point, sexual energy is normally channeled toward peers of the other sex, rather than toward oneself as in the phallic stage.

In arguing that the early years shape personality, Freud did not mean that personality development comes to an abrupt halt in middle childhood. However, he did believe that the foundation for adult personality is solidly entrenched by this time. He maintained that future developments are rooted in early, formative experiences and that significant conflicts in later years are replays of crises from childhood.

In fact, Freud believed that unconscious sexual conflicts rooted in childhood experiences cause most personality disturbances. His steadfast belief in the psychosexual origins of psychological disorders eventually led to bitter theoretical disputes with two of his most brilliant colleagues: Carl Jung and Alfred Adler. Jung and Adler both argued that Freud overemphasized sexuality. Freud summarily rejected their ideas, and the other two theorists felt compelled to go their own way, developing their own psychodynamic theories of personality.

Jung's Analytical Psychology

Carl Jung was born to middle-class Swiss parents in 1875. The son of a Protestant pastor, he was a deeply introverted, lonely child, but an excellent student. Jung had earned his medical degree and was an established young psychiatrist in Zurich when he began to write to Freud in 1906. When the two men had their first meeting, they were so taken by each other's insights, they talked nonstop for 13 hours! They exchanged 359 letters before their friendship and theoretical alliance were torn apart in 1913.

Jung called his new approach *analytical psychology* to differentiate it from Freud's psychoanalytic theory. Unlike Freud, Jung encouraged his followers to develop their own theoretical views. Perhaps because of his bitter conflict with Freud, he deplored the way schools of thought often become dogmatic, discouraging creative, new ideas. Although many theorists came to characterize themselves as "Jungians," Jung himself often remarked, "I am not a Jungian" and said, "I do not want anybody to be a Jungian. I want people above all to be themselves" (van der Post, 1975).

Like Freud, Jung (1921, 1933) emphasized the unconscious determinants of personality. However, he proposed that the unconscious consists of two layers. The first layer, called the *personal unconscious,* is essentially the same as Freud's version of the unconscious. The personal unconscious houses material that is not within one's conscious awareness, because it has been repressed or forgotten. In addition, Jung theorized the existence of a deeper layer he called the collective unconscious. **The *collective unconscious* is a storehouse of latent memory traces inherited from people's ancestral past.** According to Jung, each person shares the collective unconscious with the entire human race (see Figure 12.3). It contains the "whole spiritual heritage of mankind's evolution, born anew in the brain structure of every individual" (Jung, quoted in Campbell, 1971, p. 45).

Jung called these ancestral memories *archetypes.* They are not memories of actual, personal experiences. Instead, ***archetypes* are emotionally charged images and thought forms that have universal meaning.** These archetypal images and ideas show up frequently in dreams and are often manifested in a culture's use of symbols in art, literature, and religion. According to Jung, symbols from very different cultures often show striking similarities because they emerge from archetypes that are shared by the entire human race. For instance, Jung found numerous cultures in which the *mandala,* or

Culver Pictures, Inc.

"I am not a Jungian . . . I do not want anybody to be a Jungian. I want people above all to be themselves."
CARL JUNG

Web Link 12.3

C. G. Jung, Analytical Psychology, & Culture
Synchronicity, archetypes, collective unconscious, introversion, extraversion—these and many other important concepts arising from analytical psychology and Jung's tremendously influential theorizing are examined at this comprehensive site.

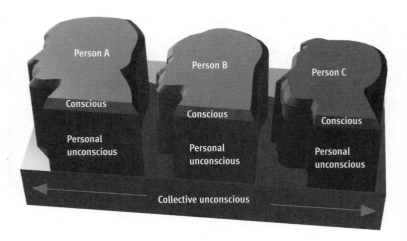

Figure 12.3

Jung's vision of the collective unconscious. Much like Freud, Jung theorized that each person has conscious and unconscious levels of awareness. However, he also proposed that the entire human race shares a collective unconscious, which exists in the deepest reaches of everyone's awareness. He saw the collective unconscious as a storehouse of hidden ancestral memories, called archetypes.

"The goal of the human soul is conquest, perfection, security, superiority."
ALFRED ADLER

"magic circle," has served as a symbol of the unified wholeness of the self (see Figure 12.3). Jung felt that an understanding of archetypal symbols helped him make sense of his patients' dreams. This was of great concern to him, as he thought that dreams contain important messages from the unconscious. Like Freud, he depended extensively on dream analysis in his treatment of patients.

Jung's unusual ideas about the collective unconscious had little impact on the mainstream of thinking in psychology. Their influence was felt more in other fields, such as anthropology, philosophy, art, and religious studies. However, many of Jung's other ideas *have* been incorporated into the mainstream of psychology. For instance, Jung was the first to describe the introverted (inner-directed) and extraverted (outer-directed) personality types. **Introverts tend to be preoccupied with the internal world of their own thoughts, feelings, and experiences.** Like Jung himself, they generally are contemplative and aloof. In contrast, **extraverts tend to be interested in the external world of people and things.** They're more likely to be outgoing, talkative, and friendly, instead of reclusive.

Adler's Individual Psychology

Like Freud, Alfred Adler grew up in Vienna in a middle-class Jewish home. He was a sickly child who struggled to overcome rickets and an almost fatal case of pneumonia. At home, he was overshadowed by an exceptionally bright and successful older brother. Nonetheless, he went on to earn his medical degree, and he practiced ophthalmology and general medicine before his interest turned to psychiatry. He was a charter member of Freud's inner circle—the Vienna Psychoanalytic Society. However, he soon began to develop his own approach to personality, which he christened *individual psychology.*

Like Jung, Adler (1917, 1927) argued that Freud had gone overboard in centering his theory on sexual conflicts. According to Adler, the foremost source of human motivation is a striving for superiority. In his view, this striving does not necessarily translate into the pursuit of dominance or high status. Adler saw *striving for superiority* **as a universal drive to adapt, improve oneself, and master life's challenges.** He noted that young children understandably feel weak and helpless in comparison with more competent older children and adults. These early inferiority feelings supposedly motivate them to acquire new skills and develop new talents. Thus, Adler maintained that striving for superiority is the prime goal of life, rather than physical gratification (as suggested by Freud).

Adler asserted that everyone has to work to overcome some feelings of inferiority—a process he called compensation. *Compensation* **involves efforts to overcome imagined or real inferiorities by developing one's abilities.** Adler believed that compensation is entirely normal. However, in some people inferiority feelings can become excessive, resulting in what is widely known today as an *inferiority complex*—exaggerated feelings of weakness and inadequacy. Adler thought that either parental pampering or parental neglect could cause an inferiority complex. Thus, he agreed with Freud on the importance of early childhood experiences, although he focused on different aspects of parent-child relations.

Adler explained personality disturbances by noting that excessive inferiority feelings can pervert the normal process of striving for superiority. He asserted that some people engage in *overcompensation* to conceal, even from themselves, their feelings of inferiority. Instead of working to master life's challenges, people with an inferiority complex work to achieve status, gain power over others, and acquire the trappings of success (fancy clothes, impressive cars, or whatever looks important to them). They tend to flaunt their success in an effort to cover up their underlying inferiority complex.

Evaluating Psychodynamic Perspectives

The psychodynamic approach has provided a number of far-reaching, truly "grand" theories of personality. These theories yielded some bold new insights when they were first presented. Although one might argue about exact details of interpretation, psychodynamic theory and research have demonstrated (1) that unconscious forces can influence behavior, (2) that internal conflict often plays a key role in generating psychological distress, (3) that early childhood experiences can influence adult personality, and (4) that people do use defense mechanisms to reduce their experience of unpleasant emotions (Westen, 1998; Westen & Gabbard, 1999).

In addition to being praised, psychodynamic formulations have also been criticized on several grounds (Eysenck, 1996; Fine, 1990; Fisher & Greenberg, 1996; Torrey, 1992). Among other things, critics argue that (1) psychodynamic theories have often been too vague to permit a clear scientific test, (2) empirical studies have provided only modest support for central psychodynamic hypotheses, and (3) the psychodynamic approach has generally provided a rather male-centered point of view resulting in a sexist bias against women. Critics also maintain that psychodynamic theories depend too heavily on clinical case studies in which it's much too easy for clinicians to see what they expect to see. Indeed, recent reexaminations of Freud's own clinical work suggest that he frequently distorted his patients' case histories to make them mesh with his theory (Esterson, 1993; Powell & Boer, 1995).

It's easy to ridicule Freud for concepts such as penis envy, and it's easy to point to Freudian ideas that have turned out to be wrong. However, you have to remember that Freud, Jung, and Adler began to fashion their theories about a century ago. It's not entirely fair to compare these theories to other models that are only a decade or two old. That's like asking the Wright brothers to race the Concorde. Freud and his colleagues deserve great credit for breaking new ground with their speculations about psychodynamics. Standing at a distance a century later, we have to be impressed by the extraordinary impact that psychodynamic theory has had on modern intellectual thought. In psychology as a whole, no other school has been so influential—with the exception of behaviorism, which we turn to next.

© Bettmann/CORBIS

Adler's theory has been used to analyze the tragic life of the legendary actress Marilyn Monroe (Ansbacher, 1970). During her childhood, Monroe suffered from parental neglect that left her with acute feelings of inferiority. Her inferiority feelings led her to overcompensate by flaunting her beauty, marrying celebrities (Joe DiMaggio and Arthur Miller), keeping film crews waiting for hours, and seeking the adoration of her fans.

CONCEPT CHECK 12.2

Comparing Psychodynamic Theorists

As followers of Freud, Jung and Adler shared some ideas with their mentor. However, both eventually broke with Freud and established their own theoretical systems because of disagreements on some issues. Below are terms for seven concepts about which Freud, Jung, and Adler agreed or disagreed. Check your understanding of the theorists and their ideas by placing checkmarks in the appropriate spaces to indicate which theorists emphasized which concepts. Then check your answers in Appendix A.

	Freud	Jung	Adler
1. archetypes	_____	_____	_____
2. physical gratification	_____	_____	_____
3. striving for superiority	_____	_____	_____
4. collective unconscious	_____	_____	_____
5. early childhood experiences	_____	_____	_____
6. dream analysis	_____	_____	_____
7. unconscious determinants	_____	_____	_____

Behavioral Perspectives

Behaviorism **is a theoretical orientation based on the premise that scientific psychology should study only observable behavior.** As we saw in Chapter 1, behaviorism has been a major school of thought in psychology since 1913, when John B. Watson began campaigning for the behavioral point of view. Research in the behavioral tradition has focused largely on learning. For many decades behaviorists devoted relatively little attention to the study of personality. However, their interest in personality began to pick up after John Dollard and

Neal Miller (1950) attempted to translate selected Freudian ideas into behavioral terminology. Dollard and Miller showed that behavioral concepts could provide enlightening insights about the complicated subject of personality.

In this section, we'll examine three behavioral views of personality, as we discuss the ideas of B. F. Skinner, Albert Bandura, and Walter Mischel. For the most part, you'll see that behaviorists explain personality the same way they explain everything else—in terms of learning.

Skinner's Ideas Applied to Personality

As we noted in Chapters 1 and 6, modern behaviorism's most prominent theorist has been B. F. Skinner, an American psychologist who lived from 1904 to 1990. After earning his doctorate in 1931, Skinner spent most of his career at Harvard University. There he achieved renown for his research on learning in lower organisms, mostly rats and pigeons. Skinner's (1953, 1957) principles of *operant conditioning* were never meant to be a theory of personality. However, his ideas have affected thinking in all areas of psychology and have been applied to the explanation of personality. Here we'll examine Skinner's views as they relate to personality structure and development.

Personality Structure: A View from the Outside

Skinner made no provision for internal personality structures similar to Freud's id, ego, and superego because such structures can't be observed. Following in the tradition of Watson, Skinner showed little interest in what goes on "inside" people. He argued that it's useless to speculate about private, unobservable cognitive processes. Instead, he focused on how the external environment molds overt behavior. Indeed, he argued for a strong brand of *determinism,* asserting that behavior is fully determined by environmental stimuli.

How can Skinner's theory explain the consistency that can be seen in individuals' behavior? According to his view, people show some consistent patterns of behavior because they have some stable *response tendencies* that they have acquired through

Courtesy, B.F. Skinner

"The practice of looking inside the organism for an explanation of behavior has tended to obscure the variables which are immediately available for a scientific analysis. The objection to inner states is not that they do not exist, but that they are not relevant."
B.F. SKINNER

Figure 12.4

A behavioral view of personality. Staunch behaviorists devote little attention to the structure of personality because it is unobservable, but they implicitly view personality as an individual's collection of response tendencies. A possible hierarchy of response tendencies for a specific stimulus situation is shown here.

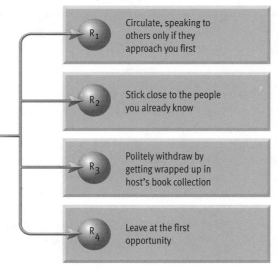

Operant response tendencies

Stimulus situation

Large party where you know relatively few people

R₁ — Circulate, speaking to others only if they approach you first

R₂ — Stick close to the people you already know

R₃ — Politely withdraw by getting wrapped up in host's book collection

R₄ — Leave at the first opportunity

experience. These response tendencies may change in the future, as a result of new experience, but they're enduring enough to create a certain degree of consistency in a person's behavior. Implicitly, then, Skinner viewed an individual's personality as a *collection of response tendencies that are tied to various stimulus situations.* A specific situation may be associated with a number of response tendencies that vary in strength, depending on past conditioning (see Figure 12.4).

Personality Development as a Product of Conditioning

Skinner's theory accounts for personality development by explaining how various response tendencies are acquired through learning. He believed that most human responses are shaped by the type of conditioning that he described: operant conditioning. As we discussed in Chapter 6, Skinner maintained that environmental consequences—reinforcement, punishment, and extinction—determine people's patterns of responding. On the one hand, when responses are followed by favorable consequences (reinforcement), they are strengthened. For example, if your joking at a party pays off with favorable attention, your tendency to joke at parties will increase (see Figure 12.5). On the other hand, when responses lead to negative consequences (punishment), they are weakened. Thus, if your impulsive decisions always backfire, your tendency to be impulsive will decline.

Because response tendencies are constantly being strengthened or weakened by new experiences, Skinner's theory views personality development as a continuous, lifelong journey. Unlike Freud and many other theorists, Skinner saw no reason to break the developmental process into stages. Nor did he attribute special importance to early childhood experiences.

Bandura's Social Learning Theory

Albert Bandura is a modern theorist who has helped reshape the theoretical landscape of behaviorism. He has spent his entire academic career at Stanford University, where he has conducted influential research on behavior therapy and the determinants of aggression.

Bandura is one of several behaviorists who have added a cognitive flavor to behaviorism since the 1960s. Bandura (1977), Walter Mischel (1973), and Julian Rotter (1982) take issue with Skinner's "pure" behaviorism. They point out that humans obviously are conscious, thinking, feeling beings. Moreover,

© Mark Antman/The Image Works

Figure 12.5

Personality development and operant conditioning.
According to Skinner, people's characteristic response tendencies are shaped by reinforcers and other consequences that follow behavior. Thus, if your joking at a party leads to attention and compliments, your tendency to be witty and humorous will be strengthened.

Stimulus context

Party

Telling jokes	Followed by	Attention, compliments

Response   **Reinforcer**

these theorists argue that in neglecting cognitive processes, Skinner ignored the most distinctive and important feature of human behavior. Bandura and like-minded theorists call their modified brand of behaviorism *social learning theory.*

Bandura (1982, 1986, 1999) agrees with the fundamental thrust of behaviorism in that he believes that personality is largely shaped through learning. However, he contends that conditioning is not a mechanical process in which people are passive participants. Instead, he maintains that people actively seek out and process information about their environment to maximize favorable outcomes. In focusing on information processing, he brings unobservable cognitive events into the picture.

Observational Learning

Bandura's foremost theoretical contribution has been his description of observational learning, which we introduced in Chapter 6. *Observational learning occurs when an organism's responding is influenced by the observation of others.* According to Bandura, both classical and operant conditioning can occur vicariously when one person observes another's conditioning. For example, watching your sister get burned by a bounced check upon selling her old stereo could strengthen your tendency to be suspicious of others. Although your sister would be the one actually experiencing the negative consequences, they might also influence you—through observational learning. Bandura maintains that people's characteristic patterns of behavior are shaped by the *models* that they're exposed to. In observational learning, **a *model* is a person whose behavior is observed by another.** At one time or another, everyone serves as a model for others. Bandura's

key point is that many response tendencies are the product of imitation.

As social learning theory has been refined, it has become apparent that some models are more influential than others (Bandura, 1986). Both children and adults tend to imitate people they like or respect more than people they don't. People are also especially prone to imitate the behavior of those whom they consider attractive or powerful (such as rock stars or athletes). In addition, imitation is more likely when people see similarity between models and themselves. Thus, children tend to imitate same-sex role models somewhat more than opposite-sex models. Finally, people are more likely to copy a model if they observe that the model's behavior leads to positive outcomes. According to social learning theory, models have a great impact on personality development. Children learn to be assertive, conscientious, self-sufficient, dependable, easygoing, and so forth by observing parents, teachers, relatives, siblings, and peers behaving in these ways.

Self-Efficacy

Bandura discusses how a variety of personal factors (aspects of personality) govern behavior. In recent years, the factor he has emphasized the most is self-efficacy (Bandura, 1990, 1993, 1995). *Self-efficacy refers to one's belief about one's ability to perform behaviors that should lead to expected outcomes.* When self-efficacy is high, individuals feel confident that they can execute the responses necessary to earn reinforcers. When self-efficacy is low, individuals worry that the necessary responses may be beyond their abilities. Perceptions of self-efficacy are subjective and specific to certain kinds of tasks. For instance, you might feel extremely

Courtesy of Professor Albert Bandura

"Most human behavior is learned by observation through modeling."
ALBERT BANDURA

Web Link 12.4

Television and Violence— Media and Communications Studies Site
Albert Bandura's early studies on the effect of television watching on the development of aggression spawned a wide spectrum of research about media influences on personality and behavior. This subpage at Daniel Chandler's well-known site gathers important research and reflections on the issue.

confident about your ability to handle difficult social situations but doubtful about your ability to handle academic challenges.

Perceptions of self-efficacy can influence which challenges people tackle and how well they perform. Studies have found that feelings of greater self-efficacy are associated with greater success in giving up smoking (Boudreaux et al., 1998); greater adherence to an exercise regimen (Schwarzer & Fuchs, 1995); more success in coping with pain (Lin, 1998); greater persistence and effort in academic pursuits (Zimmerman, 1995); higher levels of academic performance (Pajares, 1996); enhanced performance in athletic competition (Kane et al., 1996); greater receptiveness to technological training (Christoph, Schoenfeld, & Tansky, 1998); and higher work-related performance (Stajkovic & Luthans, 1998), among many other things.

Mischel and the Person-Situation Controversy

Walter Mischel was born in Vienna, not far from Freud's home. His family immigrated to the United States in 1939, when he was 9. After earning his doctorate in psychology, he spent many years on the faculty at Stanford, as a colleague of Bandura's. He has since moved to Columbia University.

Like Bandura, Mischel (1973, 1984) is an advocate of social learning theory. Mischel's chief contribution to personality theory has been to focus attention on the extent to which situational factors govern behavior. This contribution has embroiled him in a fundamental controversy about the consistency of human behavior across varying situations.

According to social learning theory, people make responses that they think will lead to reinforcement in the situation at hand. They try to gauge the reinforcement contingencies and adjust their behavior to the circumstances. Thus, if you believe that hard work in your job will pay off by leading to raises and promotions, you'll probably be diligent and industrious. But if you think that hard work in your job is unlikely to be rewarded, you may behave in a lazy and irresponsible manner.

Social learning theory predicts that people will often behave differently in different situations. Mischel (1968, 1973) reviewed decades of research and concluded that, indeed, people exhibit far less consistency across situations than had been widely assumed. For example, studies show that a person who is honest in one situation may be dishonest in another. Someone who wouldn't dream of being dishonest in a business deal might engage in wholesale

cheating in filling out tax returns. Similarly, some people are quite shy in one situation and outgoing in another. In light of these realities, Mischel maintains that behavior is characterized more by *situational specificity* than by consistency.

Mischel's position strikes at the heart of the concept of personality itself. As we discussed at the beginning of the chapter, the concept of personality is used to explain consistency in people's behavior over time and situations. If there isn't much consistency, then there isn't much need for the concept of personality. Thus, Mischel's provocative ideas have sparked a robust debate about the relative importance of the *person* as opposed to the *situation* in determining behavior.

This debate has led to a growing recognition that both the person and the situation are important determinants of behavior. The concept of personality doesn't require anything approaching *complete* consistency in behavior. There clearly is enough cross-situational consistency in humans' behavior to warrant interest in person variables, or personality. In fact, Mischel has never advocated that the personality concept be discarded. Mischel (1990) merely asserts that more attention should be paid to the situational determinants of behavior and how they interact with personality variables. His arguments and the ensuing debate have led many psychologists to do just that (Kenrick & Funder, 1988).

Evaluating Behavioral Perspectives

Behavioral theories are firmly rooted in extensive empirical research. Skinner's ideas have shed light on how environmental consequences and conditioning mold people's characteristic behavior. Bandura's social learning theory has expanded the horizons of behaviorism and increased its relevance to the study of personality. Mischel deserves credit for increasing psychology's awareness of how situational factors shape behavior.

Of course, each theoretical approach has its shortcomings, and the behavioral approach is no exception. Critics argue (1) that behaviorists have depended too much on animal research and have indiscriminately generalized from animal behavior to human behavior, (2) that they have made little effort to integrate biological factors into their theories, and (3) that in carving personality into stimulus-response bonds, behaviorists have provided a fragmented view of personality (Liebert & Liebert, 1998; Maddi, 1989). Humanistic theorists, whom we shall cover next, have been particularly vocal in criticizing this piecemeal analysis of personality.

University photographer Joe Pineiro, Columbia University

It seems remarkable how each of us generally manages to reconcile his seemingly diverse behavior into one self-consistent whole.
WALTER MISCHEL

Humanistic Perspectives

Humanistic theory emerged in the 1950s as something of a backlash against the behavioral and psychodynamic theories that we have just discussed. The principal charge hurled at these two models was that they are dehumanizing (DeCarvalho, 1991). Freudian theory was criticized for its belief that behavior is dominated by primitive, animalistic drives. Behaviorism was criticized for its preoccupation with animal research and for its mechanistic, fragmented view of personality. Critics argued that both schools of thought are too deterministic and that both fail to recognize the unique qualities of human behavior.

Many of these critics blended into a loose alliance that came to be known as humanism, because of its exclusive focus on human behavior. *Humanism is a theoretical orientation that emphasizes the unique qualities of humans, especially their freedom and their potential for personal growth.* In contrast to most psychodynamic and behavioral theorists, humanistic theorists, such as Carl Rogers and Abraham Maslow, take an optimistic view of human nature. They assume (1) that people can rise above their primitive animal heritage and control their biological urges and (2) that people are largely conscious and rational beings who are not dominated by unconscious, irrational needs and conflicts. Humanistic theorists also maintain that a person's subjective view of the world is more important than objective reality. According to this notion, if you think that you're homely or bright or sociable, then this belief will influence your behavior more than the realities of how homely, bright, or sociable you actually are.

Rogers's Person-Centered Theory

Carl Rogers (1951, 1961, 1980) was one of the fathers of the human potential movement. This movement emphasizes self-realization through sensitivity training, encounter groups, and other exercises intended to foster personal growth. Like Freud, Rogers based his personality theory on his extensive therapeutic interactions with many clients. Because of its emphasis on a person's subjective point of view, Rogers called his approach a *person-centered theory.*

The Self

Rogers viewed personality structure in terms of just one construct. He called this construct the *self,*

although it's more widely known today as the *self-concept.* **A *self-concept* is a collection of beliefs about one's own nature, unique qualities, and typical behavior.** Your self-concept is your own mental picture of yourself. It's a collection of self-perceptions. For example, a self-concept might include beliefs such as "I'm easygoing" or "I'm sly and crafty" or "I'm pretty" or "I'm hardworking." According to Rogers, individuals are aware of their self-concept. It's not buried in their unconscious.

Rogers stressed the subjective nature of the self-concept. Your self-concept may not be entirely consistent with your experiences. Most people tend to distort their experiences to some extent to promote a relatively favorable self-concept. For example, you may believe that you're quite bright, but your grade transcript might suggest otherwise. Rogers called the gap between self-concept and reality "incongruence". *Incongruence* is the degree of disparity between one's self-concept and one's actual experience. In contrast, if a person's self-concept is reasonably accurate, it's said to be *congruent* with reality (see Figure 12.6). Everyone experiences a certain amount of incongruence. The crucial issue is how much. As we'll see, Rogers maintained that too much incongruence undermines one's psychological well-being.

Development of the Self

In terms of personality development, Rogers was concerned with how childhood experiences promote congruence or incongruence between one's self-concept and one's experience. According to Rogers, people have a strong need for affection, love, and acceptance from others. Early in life, parents provide most of this affection. Rogers maintained that some parents make their affection *conditional.*

"I have little sympathy with the rather prevalent concept that man is basically irrational, and that his impulses, if not controlled, will lead to destruction of others and self. Man's behavior is exquisitely rational, moving with subtle and ordered complexity toward the goals his organism is endeavoring to achieve."
CARL ROGERS

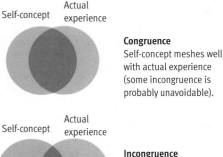

Self-concept / Actual experience

Congruence
Self-concept meshes well with actual experience (some incongruence is probably unavoidable).

Self-concept / Actual experience

Incongruence
Self-concept does not mesh well with actual experience.

Figure 12.6

Rogers's view of personality structure. In Rogers's model, the self-concept is the only important structural component. However, Rogers acknowledged that one's self-concept may not be consistent with the realities of one's actual experience—a condition called incongruence.

That is, it depends on the child's behaving well and living up to expectations. When parental love seems conditional, children often block out of their self-concept those experiences that make them feel unworthy of love. They do so because they're worried about parental acceptance, which appears precarious. At the other end of the spectrum, some parents make their affection *unconditional.* Their children have less need to block out unworthy experiences because they've been assured that they're worthy of affection, no matter what they do.

Rogers believed that unconditional love from parents fosters congruence and that conditional love fosters incongruence. He further theorized that if individuals grow up believing that affection from others is highly conditional, they will go on to distort more and more of their experiences in order to feel worthy of acceptance from a wider and wider array of people.

A person's self-concept evolves throughout childhood and adolescence. As the individual's self-concept gradually stabilizes, he or she begins to feel comfortable with it and is usually loyal to it. This loyalty produces two effects. First, the self-concept becomes a "self-fulfilling prophecy" in that the person tends to behave in ways that are consistent with it. Second, the person becomes resistant to information that contradicts that self-concept.

Anxiety and Defense

According to Rogers, experiences that threaten people's personal views of themselves are the principal cause of troublesome anxiety. The more inaccurate your self-concept is, the more likely you are to have experiences that clash with your self-perceptions. Thus, people with highly incongruent self-concepts are especially likely to be plagued by recurrent anxiety (see Figure 12.7).

To ward off this anxiety, individuals often behave defensively in an effort to reinterpret their experience so that it appears consistent with their self-concept. Thus, they ignore, deny, and twist reality to protect and perpetuate their self-concept. Consider a young lady who, like most people, considers herself a "nice person." Let's suppose that in reality she is rather conceited and selfish. She gets feedback from both boyfriends and girlfriends that she is a "self-centered, snotty brat." How might she react in order to protect her self-concept? She might ignore or block out those occasions when she behaves selfishly. She might attribute her girlfriends' negative comments to their jealousy of her good looks. Perhaps she would blame her boyfriends' negative remarks on their disappointment because she won't get more serious with them. As you can see, people will sometimes go to great lengths to defend their self-concept.

Maslow's Theory of Self-Actualization

Abraham Maslow, who grew up in Brooklyn, described his childhood as "unhappy, lonely, [and] isolated." To follow through on his interest in psychology, he had to resist parental pressures to go into law. Maslow spent much of his career at Brandeis University, where he created an influential theory of motivation and provided crucial leadership for the fledgling humanistic movement. Like Rogers, Maslow (1968, 1970) argued that psychology should take an optimistic view of human nature instead of dwelling on the causes of disorders. "To oversimplify the matter somewhat," he said, "it's as if Freud supplied to us the sick half of psychology and we must now fill it out with the healthy half" (1968, p. 5). Maslow's key contributions to personality theory were his analysis of how motives are organized hierarchically and his description of the healthy personality.

Hierarchy of Needs

Maslow proposed that human motives are organized into a *hierarchy of needs*—a systematic arrangement of needs, according to priority, in which basic needs must be met before less basic needs are aroused. This hierarchical arrangement is usually portrayed as a pyramid (see Figure 12.8). The needs toward the bottom of the pyramid, such as physiological or security needs, are the most

Figure 12.7

Rogers's view of personality development and dynamics. Rogers's theory of development posits that conditional love leads to a need to distort experiences, which fosters an incongruent self-concept. Incongruence makes one prone to recurrent anxiety, which triggers defensive behavior, which fuels more incongruence.

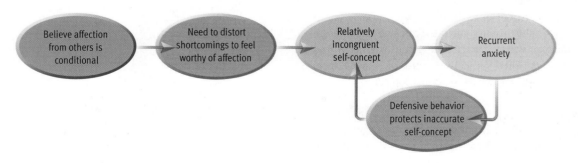

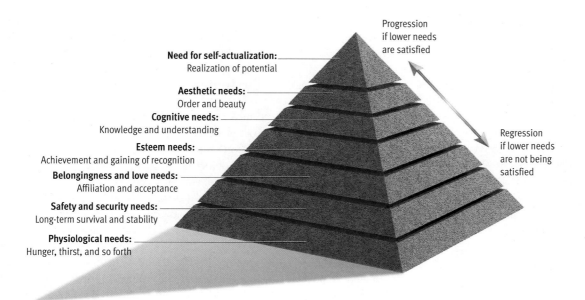

Progression
if lower needs
are satisfied

Need for self-actualization:
Realization of potential

Aesthetic needs:
Order and beauty

Cognitive needs:
Knowledge and understanding

Esteem needs:
Achievement and gaining of recognition

Belongingness and love needs:
Affiliation and acceptance

Safety and security needs:
Long-term survival and stability

Physiological needs:
Hunger, thirst, and so forth

Regression
if lower needs
are not being
satisfied

Figure 12.8

Maslow's hierarchy of needs. According to Maslow, human needs are arranged in a hierarchy, and people must satisfy their basic needs before they can satisfy higher needs. In the diagram, higher levels in the pyramid represent progressively less basic needs. Individuals progress upward in the hierarchy when lower needs are satisfied reasonably well, but they may regress back to lower levels if basic needs are no longer satisfied.

basic. Higher levels in the pyramid consist of progressively less basic needs. When a person manages to satisfy a level of needs reasonably well (complete satisfaction is not necessary), *this satisfaction activates needs at the next level.*

Like Rogers, Maslow argued that humans have an innate drive toward personal growth—that is, evolution toward a higher state of being. Thus, he described the needs in the uppermost reaches of his hierarchy as *growth needs.* These include the needs for knowledge, understanding, order, and aesthetic beauty. Foremost among them is the ***need for self-actualization, which is the need to fulfill one's potential.*** It is the highest need in Maslow's motivational hierarchy. Maslow summarized this concept with a simple statement: "What a man *can* be, he *must* be." According to Maslow, people will be frustrated if they are unable to fully utilize their talents or pursue their true interests. For example, if you have great musical talent but must work as an accountant, or if you have scholarly interests but must work as a sales clerk, your need for self-actualization will be thwarted.

The Healthy Personality 10C

Because of his interest in self-actualization, Maslow set out to discover the nature of the healthy personality. He tried to identify people of exceptional mental health so that he could investigate their characteristics. In one case, he used psychological tests and interviews to sort out the healthiest 1% of a sizable population of college students. He also studied admired historical figures (such as Thomas Jefferson and William James) and personal acquaintances characterized by superior adjustment. Over a period of years, he accumulated his case histories and gradually sketched, in broad strokes, a picture of ideal psychological health.

According to Maslow, ***self-actualizing persons are people with exceptionally healthy personalities, marked by continued personal growth.*** Maslow identified various traits characteristic of self-actualizing people. Many of these traits are listed in Figure 12.9. In brief, Maslow found that self-actualizers are accurately tuned in to reality and that they're at peace with themselves. He found that they're open and spontaneous and that they retain a fresh appreciation of the world around them. Socially, they're sensitive to others' needs and enjoy

"It is as if Freud supplied to us the sick half of psychology and we must now fill it out with the healthy half."
ABRAHAM MASLOW

Characteristics of self-actualizing people	
• Clear, efficient perception of reality and comfortable relations with it	• Mystical and peak experiences
• Spontaneity, simplicity, and naturalness	• Feelings of kinship and identification with the human race
• Problem centering (having something outside themselves they "must" do as a mission)	• Strong friendships, but limited in number
	• Democratic character structure
• Detachment and need for privacy	• Ethical discrimination between good and evil
• Autonomy, independence of culture and environment	• Philosophical, unhostile sense of humor
• Continued freshness of appreciation	• Balance between polarities in personality

Figure 12.9

Maslow's view of the healthy personality. Humanistic theorists emphasize psychological health instead of maladjustment. Maslow's description of characteristics of self-actualizing people evokes a picture of the healthy personality.

rewarding interpersonal relations. However, they're not dependent on others for approval or uncomfortable with solitude. They thrive on their work, and they enjoy their sense of humor. Maslow also noted that they have "peak experiences" (profound emotional highs) more often than others. Finally, he found that they strike a nice balance between many

CONCEPT **CHECK 12.3**

Recognizing Key Concepts in Personality Theories

Check your understanding of psychodynamic, behavioral, and humanistic personality theories by identifying key concepts from these theories in the scenarios below. The answers can be found in Appendix A.

1. Thirteen-year-old Sarah watches a TV show in which the leading female character manipulates her boyfriend by acting helpless and purposely losing a tennis match against him. The female lead repeatedly expresses her slogan, "Never let them [men] know you can take care of yourself." Sarah becomes more passive and less competitive around boys her own age.

   Concept: _____

2. Yolanda has a secure, enjoyable, reasonably well-paid job as a tenured English professor at a state university. Her friends are dumbfounded when she announces that she's going to resign and give it all up to try writing a novel. She tries to explain, "I need a new challenge, a new mountain to climb. I've had this lid on my writing talents for years, and I've got to break free. It's something I have to try. I won't be happy until I do."

   Concept: _____

3. Vladimir, who is 4, seems to be emotionally distant from and inattentive to his father. He complains whenever he's left with his dad. In contrast, he cuddles up in bed with his mother frequently and tries very hard to please her by behaving properly.

   Concept: _____

polarities in personality. For instance, they can be both childlike and mature, both rational and intuitive, both conforming and rebellious.

Evaluating Humanistic Perspectives

The humanists added a refreshing new perspective to the study of personality. Their argument that a person's subjective views may be more important than objective reality has proven compelling. As we noted earlier, even behavioral theorists have begun to take into account subjective personal factors such as beliefs and expectations. The humanistic approach also deserves credit for making the self-concept an important construct in psychology. Today, theorists of many persuasions use the self-concept in their analyses of personality. Finally, the humanists have often been applauded for focusing attention on the issue of what constitutes a healthy personality.

Of course, the balance sheet has a negative side as well (Burger, 1997; Geller, 1982). Critics argue that (1) many aspects of humanistic theory are difficult to put to a scientific test, (2) humanists have been unrealistically optimistic in their assumptions about human nature and their descriptions of the healthy personality, and (3) more experimental research is needed to catch up with the theorizing in the humanistic camp. The latter complaint is precisely the opposite of what we'll encounter in the next section, on biological perspectives, where more theorizing is needed to catch up with the research.

Biological Perspectives

Like many identical twins reared apart, Jim Lewis and Jim Springer found they had been leading eerily similar lives. Separated four weeks after birth in 1940, the Jim twins grew up 45 miles apart in Ohio and were reunited in 1979. Eventually, they discovered that both drove the same model blue Chevrolet, chain-smoked Salems, chewed their fingernails, and owned dogs named Toy. Each had spent a good deal of time vacationing at the same three-block strip of beach in Florida. More important, when tested for such personality traits as flexibility, self-control, and sociability, the twins responded almost exactly alike. (Leo, 1987, p. 63)

So began a *Time* magazine summary of a major twin study conducted at the University of Minnesota Center for Twin and Adoption Research. Since 1979 the investigators at this center have been studying

the personality resemblance of identical twins reared apart. Not all the twin pairs have been as similar as Jim Lewis and Jim Springer, but many of the parallels have been uncanny (Lykken et al., 1992). Identical twins Oskar Stohr and Jack Yufe were separated soon after birth. Oskar was sent to a Nazi-run school in Czechoslovakia while Jack was raised in a Jewish home on a Caribbean island. When they were reunited for the first time during middle age, they showed up wearing similar mustaches, haircuts, shirts, and wire-rimmed glasses! A pair of previously separated female twins both arrived at the Minneapolis airport wearing seven rings on their fingers. One had a son named Richard Andrew and the other had a son named Andrew Richard!

Could personality be largely inherited? These anecdotal reports of striking resemblances between identical twins reared apart certainly raise this possibility. In this section we'll discuss Hans Eysenck's theory, which emphasizes the influence of heredity, look at recent behavioral genetics research on the heritability of personality, and outline evolutionary views on personality.

Eysenck's Theory

Hans Eysenck was born in Germany but fled to London during the era of Nazi rule. He went on to become one of Britain's most prominent psychologists. Eysenck (1967, 1982, 1990a) views personality structure as a hierarchy of traits, in which many superficial traits are derived from a smaller number of more basic traits, which are derived from a handful of fundamental higher-order traits, as shown in Figure 12.10.

According to Eysenck, "Personality is determined to a large extent by a person's genes" (1967, p. 20). How is heredity linked to personality in Eysenck's model? In part, through conditioning concepts borrowed from behavioral theory. Eysenck theorizes that some people can be conditioned more readily than others because of differences in their physiological functioning. These variations in "conditionability" are assumed to influence the personality traits that people acquire through conditioning processes.

Eysenck has shown a special interest in explaining variations in *extraversion-introversion,* the trait dimension first described years earlier by Carl Jung. He has proposed that introverts tend to have high levels of physiological arousal, which make them more easily conditioned than extraverts. According to Eysenck, people who condition easily acquire more conditioned inhibitions than others. These inhibitions make them more bashful, tentative, and uneasy in social situations. This social discomfort leads them to turn inward. Hence, they become introverted.

Behavioral Genetics and Personality

Recent research in behavioral genetics has provided impressive support for the idea that personality is largely inherited (Plomin & Caspi, 1999; Rowe, 1997). For instance, in twin studies of the Big Five personality traits, identical twins have been found to be much more similar than fraternal twins on all five traits (Loehlin, 1992). These findings strongly suggest that genetic factors exert considerable influence over personality.

Some skeptics wonder whether identical twins might exhibit more trait similarity than fraternal twins because they're treated more alike. In other words, they wonder whether environmental factors (rather than heredity) could be responsible for identical twins' greater personality resemblance. This nagging question can be answered only by studying identical twins reared apart, which is why the twin study at the University of Minnesota is so important. The Minnesota study (Tellegen et al., 1988) was the first to administer the same personality test to identical and fraternal twins reared apart, as well as together. Most of the twins reared apart were separated quite early in life (median age of 2.5 months) and remained separated for a long time (median period of almost 34 years).

The results revealed that identical twins reared together were more similar on all three major traits examined in the study (positive emotionality, negative emotionality, and constraint) than fraternal twins reared together. More telling, though, were the results for the identical twins reared apart. On all three traits, identical twins reared apart were still substantially more similar to each other than were fraternal twins reared together. The *heritability estimates* (see Chapter 9) for the three traits ranged from 40% to 58%. A noticeable effect for family environment was found only for the positive emotionality trait.

66Personality is determined to a large extent by a person's genes.99
Hans Eysenck

Mark Gerson, FPIPP, London, courtesy of Hans Eysenck

Web Link 12.6

Great Ideas in Personality
At this great site, Northwestern University personality psychologist G. Scott Acton demonstrates that scientific research programs in personality generate broad and compelling ideas about what it is to be a human being. He charts the contours of 12 research perspectives, including behaviorism, behavioral genetics, and sociobiology, supported by extensive links to published and online resources associated with each perspective.

Figure 12.10

Eysenck's model of personality structure. Eysenck described personality structure as a hierarchy of traits. In this scheme, a few higher-order traits, such as extraversion, determine a host of lower-order traits, which determine a person's habitual responses. (From H. J. Eysenck, *The Biological Basis of Personality*, p. 36, 1976. Courtesy of Charles C. Thomas, Publisher, Springfield, Illinois. Reprinted by permission.)

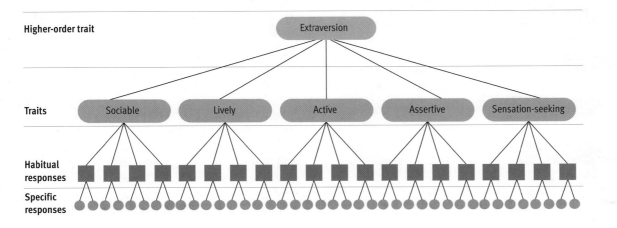

Higher-order trait	Extraversion				
Traits	Sociable	Lively	Active	Assertive	Sensation-seeking
Habitual responses					
Specific responses					

Courtesy of David M. Buss

"In sum, the five factors of personality, in this account, represent important dimensions of the social terrain that humans were selected to attend to and act upon."
DAVID BUSS

The investigators maintain that their results support the hypothesis that genetic blueprints shape the contours of personality.

Another large-scale twin study of the Big Five traits conducted in Germany and Poland yielded similar conclusions (Riemann, Angleitner, & Strelau, 1997). The heritability estimates based on the data from this study are in the same range as the estimates from the Minnesota study (see Figure 12.11). Moreover, a unique feature of this study was that it obtained peer ratings of subjects' personality traits, as well as the usual measures based on participants' responses to personality tests, and these independent ratings yielded roughly similar estimates of heritability. Thus, recent behavioral genetics research suggests that personality is shaped to a considerable degree by hereditary factors.

Research on the heritability of personality has inadvertently turned up an interesting finding that was apparent in the Riemann et al. (1997) study. As you can see in Figure 12.11, shared family environment appears to have remarkably little impact on personality. This unexpected finding has been observed quite consistently in behavioral genetics research (Beer, Arnold, & Loehlin, 1998; Halverson

& Wampler, 1997). It is surprising in that social scientists have long assumed that the family environment shared by children growing up together led to some personality resemblance among them. Recent research has seriously undermined this widespread belief. The perplexing findings have led researchers to ask, "Why are children in the same family so different from one another?" Thus far, the evidence suggests that children in the same family experience home environments that are not nearly as homogeneous as previously assumed (Hetherington, Reiss, & Plomin, 1994). Children in the same home may be treated quite differently, because gender and birth order can influence parents' approaches to child rearing. Temperamental differences between children may also evoke differences in parenting. Focusing on how environmental factors vary *within* families represents a promising new way to explore the determinants of personality.

The Evolutionary Approach to Personality

In the realm of biological perspectives on personality, the most recent development has been the emergence of evolutionary theory. Evolutionary theorists assert that personality has a biological basis because natural selection has favored certain traits over the course of human history. Thus, evolutionary analyses focus on how various personality traits—and the ability to recognize these traits in others—may have contributed to reproductive fitness in ancestral human populations.

For example, David Buss (1991, 1995, 1997) has argued that the Big Five personality traits stand out as important dimensions of personality across a variety of cultures because those traits have had significant adaptive implications. Buss points out that humans historically have depended heavily on groups, which afford protection from predators or enemies, opportunities for sharing food, and a diverse array of other benefits. In the context of these group interactions, people have had to make difficult but crucial judgments about the characteristics of others, asking such questions as: Who will make a good member of my coalition? Who can I depend on when in need? Who will share their resources? Thus, Buss (1995) argues, "those individuals able to accurately discern and act upon these individual differences likely enjoyed a considerable reproductive advantage" (p. 22). According to Buss, the Big Five emerge as fundamental dimensions of personality because humans have evolved special sensitivity to

Figure 12.11

Heritability and environmental variance for the Big Five traits. Based on the twin study data of Riemann et al. (1997), Plomin and Caspi (1999) estimated the heritability of each of the Big Five traits. The data also allowed them to estimate the amount of variance on each trait attributable to shared environment and nonshared environment. As you can see, the heritability estimates hovered in the vicinity of 40%, with two exceeding 50%. As in other studies, the influence of shared environment was modest. (Based on "Behavioral genetics and personality," by R. Plomin and A. Caspi, 1999. In L. A. Pervin, & O. P. John (Eds.), *Handbook of Personality: Theory and Research*. The Guilford Press).

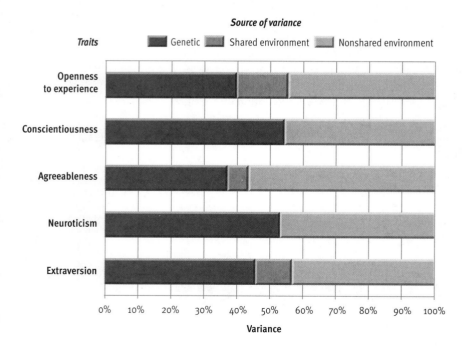

variations in the ability to bond with others (extraversion), the willingness to cooperate and collaborate (agreeableness), the tendency to be reliable and ethical (conscientiousness), the capacity to be an innovative problem solver (openness to experience), and the ability to handle stress (low neuroticism).

In a nutshell, the Big Five supposedly reflect the most salient features of ancestral humans' adaptive landscape. MacDonald (1998) takes this line of thinking one step further, asserting that the traits themselves (as opposed to the ability to recognize them) are products of evolution that were adaptive in ancestral environments.

Evaluating Biological Perspectives

Researchers have compiled convincing evidence that biological factors help shape personality, and findings on the meager effects of shared family environment have launched intriguing new approaches to the investigation of personality development. Nonetheless, we must take note of some weaknesses in biological approaches to personality. Critics assert that (1) heritability ratios should be regarded as ballpark estimates that will vary depending on sampling procedures (McGuire & Haviland, 1985), and (2) there's no comprehensive biological theory of personality, so additional theoretical work is needed to catch up with recent empirical findings.

CONCEPT CHECK 12.4

Understanding the Implications of Major Theories: Who Said This?

Check your understanding of the implications of the personality theories we've discussed by indicating which theorist is likely to have made the statements below. The answers are in Appendix A.

Choose from the following theorists: Alfred Adler   Albert Bandura   Hans Eysenck
Sigmund Freud   Abraham Maslow   Walter Mischel

Quotes

_____ 1. "If you deliberately plan to be less than you are capable of being, then I warn you that you'll be deeply unhappy for the rest of your life."

_____ 2. "I feel that the major, most fundamental dimensions of personality are likely to be those on which [there is] strong genetic determination of individual differences."

_____ 3. "People are in general not candid over sexual matters . . . they wear a heavy overcoat woven of a tissue of lies, as though the weather were bad in the world of sexuality."

Culture and Personality

Are there connections between culture and personality? The investigation of this question dates back to the 1940s and 1950s, when researchers set out to describe various cultures' *modal personality* (Kardiner & Linton, 1945) or *national character* (Kluckhohn & Murray, 1948). These investigations, which were largely guided by Freud's psychoanalytic theory, met with relatively little success (Bruner, 1974). Studies of the links between culture and personality dwindled after the disappointments of the 1940s and 1950s. However, in recent years, psychology's new interest in cultural factors has led to a renaissance of culture-personality research. Like cross-cultural research in other areas of psychology, this research has found evidence of both continuity and variability across cultures.

For the most part, continuity has been apparent in cross-cultural comparisons of the *trait structure* of personality. When English language personality scales have been translated and administered in other cultures, the predicted dimensions of personality have emerged from the statistical analyses. For example, when scales that tap the Big Five personality traits have been administered and subjected to statistical analysis in other cultures, the usual five traits have typically emerged (Katigbak, Church, & Akamine, 1996; McCrae et al., 1998).

The cross-cultural similarities observed thus far seem impressive, but skepticism has been voiced in some quarters. Critics argue that the strategy of "exporting" Western tests to other cultures is slanted

Culture can shape personality. Children in Asiatic cultures, for example, grow up with a value system that allows them to view themselves as interconnected parts of larger social units. Hence, they tend to avoid positioning themselves so that they stand out from others.

© Fujimoro/The Image Works

Four Views of Personality

Theorist and orientation	Source of data and observations	Key motivational forces

A psychodynamic view

Sigmund Freud

Case studies from clinical practice of psychoanalysis

© Peter Aprahamian/CORBIS

Sex and aggression; need to reduce tension resulting from internal conflicts

A behavioral view

B. F. Skinner

Laboratory experiments, primarily with animals

© Richard Wood/The Picture Cube/Index Stock

Pursuit of primary (unlearned) and secondary (learned) reinforcers; priorities depend on personal history

A humanistic view

Carl Rogers

Case studies from clinical practice of client-centered therapy

© Dratch/The Image Works

Actualizing tendency (motive to develop capacities, and experience personal growth) and self-actualizing tendency (motive to maintain self-concept and behave in ways that are consistent with self-concept)

A biological view

Hans Eysenck

Twin, family, and adoption studies of heritability; factor analysis studies of personality structure

© Barbara Penoyar/PhotoDisc

No specific motivational forces singled out

Model of personality structure	**View of personality development**	**Roots of disorders**

Three interacting components (id, ego, superego) operating at three levels of consciousness

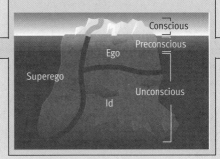

Emphasis on fixation or progress through psychosexual stages; experiences in early childhood (such as toilet training) can leave lasting mark on adult personality

Unconscious fixations and unresolved conflicts from childhood, usually centering on sex and aggression

---

Collections of response tendencies tied to specific stimulus situations

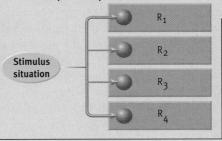

Personality evolves gradually over the life span (not in stages); responses (such as extraverted joking) followed by reinforcement (such as appreciative laughter) become more frequent

Maladaptive behavior due to faulty learning; the "symptom" is the problem, not a sign of underlying disease

---

Self-concept, which may or may not mesh well with actual experience

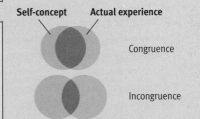

Children who receive unconditional love have less need to be defensive; they develop more accurate, congruent self-concept; conditional love fosters incongruence

Incongruence between self and actual experience (inaccurate self-concept); overdependence on others for approval and sense of worth

---

Hierarchy of traits, with specific traits derived from more fundamental, general traits

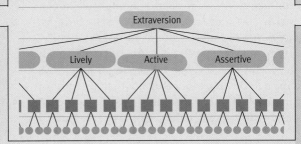

Emphasis on unfolding of genetic blueprint with maturation; inherited predispositions interact with learning experiences

Genetic vulnerability activated in part by environmental factors

Photo and Campus Services, University of Michigan

Courtesy of Shinobu Kitayama

"*Most of what psychologists currently know about human nature is based on one particular view—the so-called Western view of the individual as an independent, self-contained, autonomous entity.*"

HAZEL MARKUS AND
SHINOBU KITAYAMA

in favor of finding cross-cultural compatibility and is unlikely to uncover culture-specific traits (Church & Lonner, 1998). Furthermore, even though the five-factor model has been replicated in many cultures, this finding does not demonstrate that the traits have the same predictive meaning in those cultures (Markus & Kitayama, 1998). In other words, the correlates of a high neuroticism score in China may be different from the correlates that have been observed in Western cultures. In sum, preliminary research tentatively suggests that the basic dimensions of personality trait structure may be pancultural, but a great deal of additional research is needed.

In contrast, when researchers have compared cultural groups on specific aspects of personality, some intriguing disparities have surfaced. Perhaps the most interesting work has been that of Hazel Markus and Shinobu Kitayama (1991, 1994) comparing American and Asian conceptions of the self. According to Markus and Kitayama, American parents teach their children to be self-reliant, to feel good about themselves, and to view themselves as special individuals. Children are encouraged to excel in competitive endeavors and to strive to stand out from the crowd. They are told that "the squeaky wheel gets the grease" and that "you have to stand up for yourself." Thus, Markus and Kitayama argue that *American culture fosters an independent view of the self.* American youngsters learn to define themselves in terms of their personal attributes, abilities, accomplishments, and possessions. Their unique strengths and achievements become the basis for their sense of self-worth.

Most of us take this individualistic mentality for granted. Indeed, Markus and Kitayama maintain that "most of what psychologists currently know about human nature is based on one particular view—the so-called Western view of the individual as an independent, self-contained, autonomous entity" (1991, p. 224). However, they marshal convincing evidence that this view is *not* universal. They argue that in Asian cultures such as Japan and China, socialization practices foster a more *interdependent view of the self,* which emphasizes the fundamental connectedness of people to each other (see Figure 12.12). In these cultures, parents teach their children that they can rely on family and friends, that they should be modest about their personal accomplishments so they don't diminish others' achievements, and that they should view themselves as part of a larger social matrix. Children are encouraged to fit in with others and to avoid standing out from the crowd. A popular adage in Japan reminds children that "the nail that stands out gets pounded down." Hence, Markus and Kitayama assert that Asian youngsters typically learn to define themselves in terms of the groups they belong to. Their harmonious relations with others and their pride in group achievements become the basis for their sense of self-worth.

The ramifications of these discrepant views of self are many. For example, these differing self-construals lead to cultural disparities in self-enhancement. *Self-enhancement* involves focusing on positive feedback from others, exaggerating one's strengths, and seeing oneself as above average. These tendencies are pervasive in Western cultures, but quite rare in Asian cultures, where the norm is to be more sensitive to negative feedback, to reflect on one's shortcomings, and to look for avenues of improvement (Cross & Markus, 1999). In the hopes of fitting in better and contributing more to the group, people with interdependent self-concepts seem to be more interested in *self-criticism* than self-enhancement. Does all this self-criticism lead to lower self-esteem, on the average, in some cultures? Preliminary research suggests that the answer may be yes (Kitayama et al., 1997). But, ironically, low self-esteem may not have the same significance in cultures that encourage interdependent self-concepts. In Japan, for instance, self-esteem does not correlate with subjective well-being the way it does in Western cultures (Diener & Diener, 1995). This finding demonstrates once again that we cannot assume that Western models of psychological processes will apply equally well in other cultures.

Figure 12.12

Culture and conceptions of self. According to Markus and Kitayama (1991), Western cultures foster an independent view of the self as a unique individual who is separate from others, as diagrammed on the left. In contrast, Asian cultures encourage an interdependent view of the self as part of an interconnected social matrix, as diagrammed on the right. The interdependent view leads people to define themselves in terms of their social relationships (for instance, as someone's daughter, employee, colleague, or neighbor). (Adapted from "Culture and the Self: Implications for Cognition, Emotion, and Motivation," by H.R. Markus and S. Kitayama, 1991, *Psychological Review, 98,* 224–253. Copyright © 1991 by the American Psychological Association. Adapted by permission of the author.)

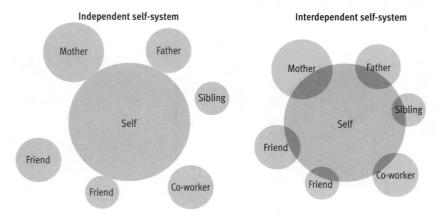

Putting It in Perspective

The preceding discussion of culture and personality obviously highlighted the text's theme that our behavior is influenced by our cultural heritage. This chapter has also been ideally suited for embellishing on two other unifying themes: psychology's theoretical diversity and the idea that psychology evolves in a sociohistorical context.

No other area of psychology is characterized by as much theoretical diversity as the study of personality, where there are literally dozens of insightful theories. Some of this diversity exists because different theories attempt to explain different facets of behavior. Of course, much of this diversity reflects genuine disagreements on basic questions about personality. These disagreements should be apparent on pages 382–383, where you'll find an illustrated comparative overview of the ideas of Freud, Skinner, Rogers, and Eysenck, as representatives of the psychodynamic, behavioral, humanistic, and biological approaches to personality.

The study of personality also highlights the sociohistorical context in which psychology evolves. Personality theories have left many marks on modern culture. The theories of Freud, Adler, and Skinner have had an enormous impact on child-rearing practices. The ideas of Freud and Jung have found their way into literature (influencing the portrayal of fictional characters) and the visual arts. For example, Freud's theory helped inspire surrealism's interest in the world of dreams. Maslow's hierarchy of needs and Skinner's affirmation of the value of positive reinforcement have given rise to new approaches to management in the world of business and industry.

Sociohistorical forces also leave their imprint on psychology. This chapter provided many examples of how personal experiences, prevailing attitudes, and historical events have contributed to the evolution of ideas in psychology. For example, Freud's pessimistic view of human nature and his emphasis on the dark forces of aggression were shaped to some extent by his exposure to the hostilities of World War I and prevailing anti-Semitic sentiments. Freud's emphasis on sexuality was surely influenced by the Victorian climate of sexual repression that existed in his youth. Adler's views also reflected the social context in which he grew up. His interest in inferiority feelings and compensation appears to have sprung from his own sickly childhood and the difficulties he had to overcome. Likewise, it's reasonable to speculate that Jung's childhood loneliness and introversion may have sparked his interest in the introversion-extraversion dimension of personality.

Progress in the study of personality has also been influenced by developments in other areas of psychology. For instance, the enterprise of psychological testing originally emerged out of efforts to measure general intelligence. Eventually, however, the principles of psychological testing were applied to the challenge of measuring personality. In the upcoming Personal Application we discuss the logic and limitations of personality tests.

Understanding Personality Assessment

Answer the following "true" or "false."

_____ 1 Responses to personality tests are subject to unconscious distortion.
_____ 2 The results of personality tests are often misunderstood.
_____ 3 Personality test scores should be interpreted with caution.
_____ 4 Personality tests serve many important functions.

If you answered "true" to all four questions, you earned a perfect score. Yes, personality tests are subject to distortion. Admittedly, test results are often misunderstood, and they should be interpreted cautiously. In spite of these problems, however, psychological tests can be quite useful.

Everyone engages in efforts to size up his or her own personality as well as that of others. When you think to yourself that "Mary Ann is shrewd and poised," or when you remark to a friend that "Howard is timid and submissive," you're making personality assessments. In a sense, then, personality assessment is an ongoing part of daily life. Given the popular interest in personality assessment, it's not surprising that psychologists have devised formal measures of personality.

The Uses of Personality Scales

When and why are psychological tests used to measure personality? They have a variety of purposes. Benjamin Kleinmuntz (1985) lists four principal uses of personality tests:

1. Personality tests are used extensively by mental health professionals in the *clinical diagnosis* of psychological disorders. Although diagnoses are not made on the basis of test results alone, personality scales can be helpful in arriving at diagnostic decisions.

2. Personality measurement may be done for the purpose of *counseling* individuals about a variety of normal, everyday problems. Counselors often use personality scales to help people chart career plans and make vocational decisions.

3. Formal personality assessment often plays a key role in *personnel selection* in business, industry, government, and the military services. This use of personality testing has become controversial in recent years. Nonetheless, many organizations continue to use personality scales to assess applicants' suitability for various jobs.

4. Personality scales are frequently used in *psychological research*. Empirical studies on a great variety of issues require precise measurement of some aspect of personality. For instance, let's say you want to investigate whether introversion is related to a certain style of child rearing. Your task is simplified greatly if you have a personality test that measures introversion.

Personality tests can be divided into two broad categories: *self-report inventories* and *projective tests*. In this Personal Application, we'll discuss some representative tests from both categories and discuss their strengths and weaknesses.

Self-Report Inventories

Self-report inventories **are personality tests that ask individuals to answer a series of questions about their characteristic behavior.** The logic underlying this approach is very simple: Who knows you better? Who has known you longer? Who has more access to your private feelings? We'll look at three examples of self-report scales, the MMPI, the 16PF, and the NEO Personality Inventory.

The MMPI

The most widely used self-report inventory is the Minnesota Multiphasic Personality Inventory (MMPI). This test was originally developed in the 1940s (Hathaway & McKinley, 1943) and thoroughly revised and modernizerd in the late 1980s. The authors of MMPI-2 set out to maintain the original character of the scale while replacing obsolete items, eliminating sexist language, and updating the test norms (Graham, 1990).

The MMPI was originally designed to aid clinicians in the diagnosis of psychological disorders. Consequently, it measures mostly aspects of personality that, when manifested to an extreme degree, are thought to be symptoms of disorders. Examples include traits such as paranoia, depression, and hysteria.

The MMPI is a rather lengthy test. The revised version consists of 567 statements to which the subject answers "true," "false," or "cannot say." The MMPI yields scores on the 14 subscales described in Table 12.4 on the next page. Four of the subscales are *validity* scales that provide indications about whether a respondent has been careless or deceptive in taking the test. The remaining 10 are *clinical scales* that measure various aspects of personality.

Are the MMPI clinical scales valid? That is, do they measure what they were designed to measure? The validity of the MMPI has been investigated in hundreds of studies (Butcher & Keller, 1984). Originally, it was assumed that the 10 clinical subscales would provide direct indexes of specific types of disorders. In other words, a high score on the depression scale would be indicative of depression, a high score on the paranoia scale would be indicative of a paranoid disorder, and so forth. However, research revealed that the relations between MMPI scores and various types of pathology are much more complex than originally anticipated. People with most types of disorders show elevated scores on *several* MMPI subscales. This means that certain score *profiles* are indicative of specific disorders (see Figure 12.13). Thus, the

Table 12.4 Personality Characteristics Associated with High MMPI Scores

Scale	Characteristics Associated with Higher Scores
Validity scale	
Cannot say (?)	May increase evasiveness.
Lie scale (*L*)	Indicates a tendency to present oneself in an overly favorable or highly virtuous light.
Infrequency scale (*F*)	Items on this scale are endorsed very infrequently by most people. Suggests carelessness, confusion, or "faking illness."
Subtle defensiveness (*K*)	Measures defensiveness of a subtle nature.
Clinical scale	
Hypochondriasis (*Hs*)	Indicates person is preoccupied with self, complaining, hostile, and presenting numerous physical problems that tend to be chronic.
Depression (*D*)	Indicates person is moody, shy, despondent, pessimistic, and distressed; one of the most frequently elevated scales in clinical patients.
Hysteria (*Hy*)	Indicates person tends to rely on neurotic defenses such as denial and repression to deal with stress and tends to be dependent, naive, outgoing, infantile, and narcissistic.
Psychopathic deviation (*Pd*)	May indicate rebelliousness, impulsiveness, hedonism, antisocial behavior, difficulty in marital or family relationships, and trouble with the law or authority in general.
Masculinity/femininity (*MF*)	Indicates departure from traditional gender roles. High-scoring men are described as sensitive, aesthetic, passive, or feminine. They may show conflicts over sexual identity and low heterosexual drive. Because the direction of scoring is reversed, high-scoring women are seen as masculine, rough, aggressive, self-confident, unemotional, and insensitive.
Paranoia (*Pa*)	Often indicates person is suspicious, aloof, shrewd, guarded, worrisome, and overly sensitive and likely to project or externalize blame.
Psychasthenia (*Pt*)	Indicates person is tense, anxious, ruminative, preoccupied, obsessional, phobic, rigid, and frequently self-condemning and feeling inferior and inadequate.
Schizophrenia (*Sc*)	Often indicates person is withdrawn, shy, unusual, or strange and has peculiar thoughts or ideas, poor reality contact, and perhaps delusions and hallucinations.
Hypomania (*Ma*)	Indicates person is social, outgoing, impulsive, overly energetic, optimistic, and in some cases amoral, flighty, grandiose, and impulsive.
Social introversion (*Sie*)	Indicates person is introverted, shy, withdrawn, socially reserved, submissive, overcontrolled, lethargic, conventional, tense, inflexible, and guilt-prone.

(Adapted and reprinted with permission from L.S. Keller, J.N. Butcher and W.S. Slutske, "Objective Personality Assessment," 1990. In G. Goldstein and M. Hersen (Eds.), *Handbook of Psychological Assessment,* pp 345-386. Copyright © 1990 Pergamon Press, Ltd.)

Figure 12.13

MMPI profiles. Scores on the 10 clinical scales of the MMPI are often plotted as shown here to create a profile for a client. The normal range for scores on each subscale is 50 to 65. People with disorders frequently exhibit elevated scores on several clinical scales rather than just one.

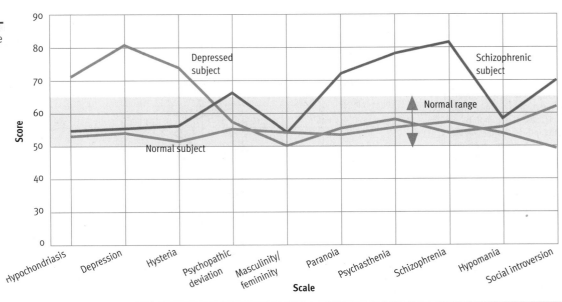

interpretation of the MMPI is quite complicated and critics have expressed concerns about various flaws in the test that were not addressed by the revision (Helmes & Reddon, 1993; Kline, 1992). Nonetheless, the MMPI can be a helpful diagnostic tool for the clinician. The fact that the inventory has been translated into more than 115 languages is a testimonial to its usefulness (Butcher, 1990).

The 16PF and NEO Personality Inventory

Raymond Cattell (1957, 1965) set out to identify and measure the *basic dimensions* of the *normal* personality. He started with a previously compiled list of 4504 personality traits. This massive list was reduced to 171 traits by weeding out terms that were virtually synonymous. Cattell then used a statistical procedure to identify clusters of closely related traits and the factors underlying them. Eventually, he reduced the list of 171 traits to 16 *source traits*. The Sixteen Personality Factor (16PF) Questionnaire is a 187–item scale that assesses these 16 basic dimensions of personality (Cattell, Eber, & Tatsuoka, 1970), which are listed in Figure 12.14.

As we noted in the main body of the chapter, some theorists believe that only five trait dimensions are required to provide a full description of personality. This view has led to the creation of a relatively new test—the NEO Personality Inventory. Developed by Paul Costa and Robert McCrae (1985, 1992), the NEO Inventory is designed to measure the Big Five traits: neuroticism, extraversion, openness to experience, agreeableness, and conscientiousness. In spite of its short life span, the NEO is already widely used in research and clinical work.

Strengths and Weaknesses of Self-Report Inventories

To appreciate the strengths of self-report inventories, consider how else you might inquire about an individual's personality. For instance, if you want to know how assertive someone is, why not just ask the person? Why administer an elaborate 50–item personality inventory that measures assertiveness? The advantage of the personality inventory is that it can provide a more objective and more precise estimate of the person's assertiveness.

Of course, self-report inventories are only as accurate as the information that respondents provide. They are susceptible to several sources of error (Kline, 1995; Paulhus, 1991; Shedler, Mayman, & Manis, 1993), including the following:

1. *Deliberate deception.* Some self-report inventories include many questions whose purpose is easy to figure out. This problem makes it possible for some respondents to intentionally fake particular personality traits.

2. *Social desirability bias.* Without realizing it, some people consistently respond to questions in ways that make them look good. The social desirability bias isn't a matter of deception so much as wishful thinking.

3. *Response sets.* A response set is a systematic tendency to respond to test items in a particular way that is unrelated to the content of the items. For instance, some people, called "yea-sayers," tend to agree with virtually every statement on a test. Other people, called "nay-sayers," tend to disagree with nearly every statement.

Figure 12.14

The Sixteen Personality Factor Questionnaire (16PF). Unlike the MMPI, Cattell's 16PF is designed to assess normal aspects of personality. The pairs of traits listed across from each other in the figure define the 16 factors measured by this self-report inventory. The profile shown is the average profile seen among a group of airline pilots who took the test. (From R. B. Cattell in *Psychology Today* (July) 1973, 40-46. Reprinted by permission from Psychology Today Magazine. Copyright © 1973. Sussex Publishers, Inc.).

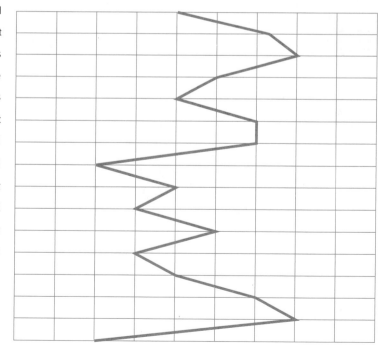

Reserved	Outgoing
Less intelligent	More intelligent
Affected by feelings	Emotionally stable
Submissive	Dominant
Serious	Happy-go-lucky
Expedient	Conscientious
Timid	Venturesome
Tough-minded	Sensitive
Trusting	Suspicious
Practical	Imaginative
Forthright	Shrewd
Self-assured	Apprehensive
Conservative	Experimenting
Group-dependent	Self-sufficient
Uncontrolled	Controlled
Relaxed	Tense

When individuals are given the Rorschach Test, they are shown a series of 10 inkblots and are asked to describe the forms that they see in these ambiguous stimuli. Evidence on the reliability and validity of the Rorschach is not particularly impressive, but the test is still used by many clinicians.

Test developers have devised a number of strategies to reduce the impact of deliberate deception, social desirability bias, and response sets (Berry, Wetter, & Baer, 1995; Lanyon & Goodstein, 1997). For instance, it's possible to insert a "lie scale" into a test to assess the likelihood that a respondent is engaging in deception. The best way to reduce the impact of social desirability bias is to identify items that are sensitive to this bias and drop them from the test. Problems with response sets can be reduced by systematically varying the way in which test items are worded.

Projective Tests

Projective tests, which all take a rather indirect approach to the assessment of personality, are used extensively in clinical work. *Projective tests* **ask participants to respond to vague, ambiguous stimuli in ways that may reveal the subjects' needs, feelings, and personality traits.** The Rorschach test, for instance, consists of a series of ten inkblots. Respondents are asked to describe what they see in the blots (see the photo above). In the Thematic Apperception Test

(TAT), a series of pictures of simple scenes is presented to individuals who are asked to tell stories about what is happening in the scenes and what the characters are feeling. For instance, one TAT card shows a young boy contemplating a violin resting on a table in front of him (see Figure 12.15 for another example).

The Projective Hypothesis

The "projective hypothesis" is that ambiguous materials can serve as a blank screen onto which people project their characteristic concerns, conflicts, and desires (Frank, 1939). Thus, a competitive person who is shown the TAT card of the boy at the table with the violin might concoct a story about how the boy is contemplating an upcoming musical competition at which he hopes to excel. The same card shown to a person high in impulsiveness might elicit a story about how the boy is planning to sneak out the door to go dirt-bike riding with friends.

The scoring and interpretation of projective tests is very complicated. Rorschach responses may be analyzed in terms of content, originality, the feature of the inkblot that determined the response, and the amount of the inkblot used, among other criteria. In fact, five different systems exist

for scoring the Rorschach (Edberg, 1990). TAT stories are examined in terms of heroes, needs, themes, and outcomes.

Strengths and Weaknesses of Projective Tests

Proponents of projective tests assert that the tests have two unique strengths. First, they are not transparent to respondents. That is, the subject doesn't know how the test provides information to the tester. Hence, it's difficult for people to engage in intentional deception (Groth-Marnat, 1997). Second, the indirect approach used in these tests may make them especially sensitive to unconscious, latent features of personality.

Unfortunately, there is inadequate evidence for the reliability (consistency) and validity of projective measures (Lanyon & Goodstein, 1997). In particular, doubts have been raised about the research evidence on the Rorschach test (Garb, Florio, & Grove, 1998; Wood, Nezworski, & Stejskal, 1996). In spite of these problems, projective tests continue to be widely used by clinicians. Although the subjectivity of the tests is a very real problem, their continued popularity suggests that they are effective in eliciting information that is valuable to many clinicians (Groth-Marnat, 1997).

Figure 12.15

The Thematic Apperception Test (TAT).
In taking the TAT, respondents are asked to tell stories about scenes such as this one. The themes apparent in each story can be scored to provide insight about the respondent's personality. (Reprinted by permission of the publishers from Henry A. Murray, *Thematic Apperception Test*, Cambridge, Mass.: Harvard University Press, Copyright © 1943 by The President and Fellows of Harvard College, © 1971 by Henry A. Murray.)

Hindsight in Everyday Analyses of Personality

Consider the case of two close sisters who grew up together: Lorena and Christina. Lorena grew into a frugal adult who is careful about spending her money, only shops when there are sales, and saves every penny she can. In contrast, Christina became an extravagant spender who lives to shop and never saves any money. How do the sisters explain their striking personality differences? Lorena attributes her thrifty habits to the fact that her family was so poor when she was a child that she learned the value of being careful with money. Christina attributes her extravagant spending to the fact that her family was so poor that she learned to really enjoy any money that she might have. Now, it *is* possible that two sisters could react to essentially the same circumstances quite differently, but the more likely explanation is that both sisters have been influenced by the **hindsight bias**—the tendency to mold one's interpretation of the past to fit how events actually turned out. We saw how hindsight can distort memory in Chapter 7. Here, we will see how hindsight tends to make people feel as if they are personality experts and how it creates interpretive problems even for scientific theories of personality.

The Prevalence of Hindsight Bias

The hindsight bias is *ubiquitous,* which means that it occurs in many settings, with all sorts of people. Most of the time, people are not aware of the way their explanations are skewed by the fact that the outcome is already known. The experimental literature on hindsight bias offers a rich array of findings on how the knowledge of an outcome biases the way people think about its causes (Hawkins & Hastie, 1990). For example, when college students were told the results of a hypothetical experiment, each group of students could "explain" why the studies

turned out the way they did, even though different groups were given opposite results to explain (Slovic & Fischhoff, 1977). The students believed that the results of the studies were obvious when they were told what the experimenter found, but when they were given only the information that was available before the outcome was known, it was not obvious at all. This bias is also called the "I knew it all along" effect because that is the typical refrain of people when they have the luxury of hindsight. Indeed, after the fact, people often act as if events that would have been difficult to predict had in fact been virtually *inevitable*. Looking back at the disintegration of the Soviet Union and the end of the Cold War, for instance, many people today act as though these events were bound to happen, but in reality these landmark events were predicted by almost no one.

The hindsight bias shows up in many contexts. For example, when a couple announces that they are splitting up, many people in their social circle will typically claim they "saw it coming." When a football

team loses in a huge upset, you will hear many fans claim, "I knew they were overrated and vulnerable." When public officials make a difficult decision that leads to a disastrous outcome—such as the FBI's 1993 attack on the Branch Davidian compound in Waco, Texas—many of the pundits in the press are quick to criticize, often asserting that only incompetent fools could have failed to foresee the catastrophe. Interestingly, people are not much kinder to themselves when they make ill-fated decisions. When individuals make tough calls that lead to negative results—such as buying a car that turns out to be a lemon, or investing in a stock that plummets— they often say things like, "Why did I ignore the obvious warning signs?" or "How could I be such an idiot?"

Hindsight and Personality

Hindsight bias appears to be pervasive in everyday analyses of personality. Think about it: If you attempt to explain why you are so suspicious, why your mother is so

AP/Wide World Photos

When a public official makes tough decision that backfires, critics are often quick to argue that the person should have foreseen the consequences of his or her decision (which may have been much more difficult than the critics suggest). For example, after Al Gore lost his campaign for the U.S. presidency, the political pundits manifested a great deal of hindsight bias in second-guessing Gore's campaign strategies and decisions.

domineering, or why your best friend is so insecure, the starting point in each case will be the personality outcome. It would probably be impossible to reconstruct the past without being swayed by your knowledge of these outcomes. Thus, hindsight makes everybody an expert on personality, as we can all come up with plausible explanations for the personality traits of people we know well. Perhaps this is why Judith Harris (1998) ignited a firestorm of protest when she wrote a book arguing that parents have relatively little effect on their children's personalities beyond the genetic material that they supply.

In her book *The Nurture Assumption,* Harris summarizes behavioral genetics research (which we discussed in the main body of the chapter) and other evidence suggesting that family environment has surprisingly little impact on children's personality. There is room for debate on this complex issue (Kagan, 1998; Tavris, 1998), but our chief interest here is that Harris made a cogent, compelling argument that attracted extensive coverage in the press, which generated an avalanche of commentary from angry parents who argued that *parents do matter.* For example, *Newsweek* magazine received 350 letters, mostly from parents who provided examples of how they thought they influenced their children's personalities. However, parents' retrospective analyses of their children's personality development have to be treated with great skepticism, as they are likely to be distorted by hindsight bias (not to mention the selective recall frequently seen in anecdotal reports).

Unfortunately, hindsight bias is so prevalent, it also presents a problem for scientific theories of personality. For example, the spectre of hindsight bias has been raised in many critiques of psychoanalytic theory (Torrey, 1992). Freudian theory was originally built mainly on a foundation of case studies of patients in therapy. Obviously, Freudian therapists who knew what their patients' adult personalities were like probably went looking for the types of childhood experiences hypothesized by Freud (oral fixations, punitive toilet training, Oedipal conflicts, and so forth) in their efforts to explain their patients' personalities.

Another problem with hindsight bias is that once researchers know an outcome, more often than not they can fashion some plausible explanation for it. For instance, Torrey (1992) describes a study inspired by Freudian theory that examined breast-size preferences among men. The original hypothesis was that men who scored higher in dependence—thought to be a sign of oral fixation—would manifest a stronger preference for women with large breasts. When the actual results of the study showed just the opposite—that dependence was associated with a preference for smaller breasts—the finding was attributed to reaction formation on the part of the men. Instead of failing to support Freudian theory, the unexpected findings were simply reinterpreted in a way that was consistent with Freudian theory.

The hindsight bias also presents thorny problems for evolutionary theorists, who generally work backward from known outcomes to reason out how adaptive pressures in humans' ancestral past may have led to those outcomes (Cornell, 1997). Consider, for instance, evolutionary theorists' assertion that the Big Five traits are found to be fundamental dimensions of personality around the world because those specific traits have had major adaptive implications over the course of human history (Buss, 1995; MacDonald, 1998). Their explanation makes sense, but what would have happened if some *other traits* had shown up in the Big Five? Would the evolutionary view have been weakened if dominance, or paranoia, or high sensation seeking had turned up in the Big Five? Probably not. With the luxury of hindsight, evolutionary theorists surely could have constructed plausible explanations for how these traits promoted reproductive success in the distant past. Thus, the hindsight bias is a fundamental feature of human cognition and

the scientific enterprise is not immune to this problem.

Other Implications of "20-20 Hindsight"

Our discussion of hindsight has focused on its implications for thinking about personality, but there is ample evidence that hindsight can bias thinking in all sorts of domains. For example, consider the practice of obtaining second opinions on medical diagnoses. The doctor providing the second opinion usually is aware of the first physician's diagnosis, which creates a hindsight bias (Arkes et al., 1981). Second opinions would probably be more valuable if the doctors rendering them were not aware of previous diagnoses. Hindsight also has the potential to distort legal decisions in cases involving allegations of negligence. Jurors' natural tendency to think "How could they have failed to foresee this problem?" may exaggerate the appearance of negligence (LaBine & LaBine, 1996).

The hindsight bias is powerful. The next time you hear of an unfortunate outcome to a decision made by a public official, carefully examine the way news reporters describe the decision. You will probably find that they believe that the disastrous outcome should have been obvious, because they can clearly see what went wrong after the fact. Similarly, if you find yourself thinking, "Only a fool would have failed to anticipate this disaster" or "I would have forseen this problem," take a deep breath and try to review the decision *using only information that was known at the time the decision was being made.* Sometimes good decisions, based on the best available information, can have terrible outcomes. Unfortunately, the clarity of "20-20 hindsight" makes it difficult for people to learn from their own and others' mistakes.

Table 12.5	Critical Thinking Skill Discussed in This Application
Skill	**Description**
Recognizing the bias in hindsight analysis	The critical thinker understands that knowing the outcome of events biases our recall and interpretation of the events.

REVIEW

Key Ideas

The Nature of Personality

⬤ The concept of personality explains the consistency in people's behavior over time and situations while also explaining their distinctiveness. Personality traits are dispositions to behave in certain ways.

⬤ There is considerable debate as to how many trait dimensions are necessary to fully describe personality. Nonetheless, the five-factor model has become the dominant conception of personality structure.

Psychodynamic Perspectives

⬤ Freud's psychoanalytic theory emphasizes the importance of the unconscious. Freud described personality structure in terms of three components—the id, ego, and super-ego—which are routinely involved in an ongoing series of internal conflicts.

⬤ Freud theorized that conflicts centering on sex and aggression are especially likely to lead to significant anxiety. According to Freud, anxiety and other unpleasant emotions such as guilt are often warded off with defense mechanisms, which work primarily through self-deception.

⬤ Freud believed that the first five years of life are extremely influential in shaping adult personality. He described a series of five psychosexual stages of development. Certain experiences during these stages can have lasting effects on adult personality.

⬤ Jung's most innovative and controversial concept was the collective unconscious. Adler's individual psychology emphasizes how people strive for superiority to compensate for their feelings of inferiority. Psychodynamic theories have been criticized for their poor testability, their inadequate base of empirical evidence, their male-centered views, and their over-dependence on case studies.

Behavioral Perspectives

⬤ Behavioral theories explain how personality is shaped through learning. Behaviorists see personality as a collection of response tendencies tied to specific stimulus situations. Skinner assumed that personality development is a life-long process in which response tendencies are shaped by learning.

⬤ Social learning theory focuses on how cognitive factors regulate learned behavior. Bandura's concept of observational learning accounts for the acquisition of responses from models. The behaviorists have been criticized for their overdependence on animal research, their neglect of biological factors, and their fragmented analysis of personality.

Humanistic Perspectives

⬤ Humanistic theories take an optimistic view of people's conscious, rational ability to chart their own courses of action. Rogers focused on the self-concept as the critical aspect of personality. He maintained that anxiety is attributable to incongruence between one's self-concept and reality.

⬤ Maslow theorized that needs are organized hierarchically and that psychological health depends on meeting one's need for self-actualization, which is the need to fulfill one's human potential. Humanistic theories lack a firm base of research, are difficult to put to an empirical test, and may be overly optimistic about human nature.

Biological Perspectives

⬤ Eysenck suggests that heredity influences individual differences in physiological functioning that affect how easily people acquire conditioned responses. Twin and adoption studies provide impressive evidence that genetic factors shape personality.

⬤ Evolutionary analyses of personality have emphasized how the "Big Five" personality traits may have had significant adaptive value. The biological approach has been criticized because of methodological problems with heritability ratios and because it offers no systematic model of how physiology governs personality.

Culture and Personality

⬤ Some studies suggest that the basic trait structure of personality may be much the same across cultures. However, notable differences have been found when researchers have compared cultural groups on specific personality traits, such as their conceptions of self.

Putting It in Perspective

⬤ The study of personality illustrates how psychology is characterized by great theoretical diversity. The study of personality also demonstrates how ideas in psychology are shaped by sociohistorical forces and how cultural factors influence psychological processes.

Personal Application • Understanding Personality Assessment

⬤ Self-report inventories, such as the MMPI, 16PF, and NEO Personality Inventory, ask subjects to describe themselves. Self-report inventories are vulnerable to certain sources of error, including deception, the social desirability bias, and response sets.

⬤ Projective tests, such as the Rorschach and TAT, assume that subjects' responses to ambiguous stimuli reveal something about their personality. While the projective hypothesis seems plausible, projective tests' reliability and validity are disturbingly low.

Critical Thinking Application • Hindsight in Everyday Analyses of Personality

⬤ The hindsight bias often leads people to assert that "I knew it all along" in discussing outcomes that they did not actually predict. Thanks to hindsight, people can almost always come up with plausible-sounding explanations for known personality traits. Problems with hindsight bias have been raised in critiques of Freudian theory and evolutionary theory.

Key Terms

Archetypes
Behaviorism
Collective
  unconscious
Compensation
Conscious
Defense mechanisms
Displacement
Ego
Extraverts
Fixation
Hierarchy of needs
Hindsight bias
Humanism
Id
Identification
Incongruence
Introverts
Model
Need for
  self-actualization
Observational
  learning
Oedipal complex
Personality
Personality trait
Pleasure principle
Preconscious
Projection
Projective tests
Psychodynamic
  theories
Psychosexual stages
Rationalization
Reaction formation
Reality principle
Regression
Repression
Self-actualizing
  persons
Self-concept
Self-efficacy
Self-report inventories
Striving for superiority
Superego
Unconscious

Key People

Alfred Adler
Albert Bandura
Hans Eysenck
Sigmund Freud
Carl Jung
Abraham Maslow
Walter Mischel
Carl Rogers
B. F. Skinner

PRACTICE TEST

1. Harvey Hedonist has devoted his life to the search for physical pleasure and immediate need gratification. Freud would say that Harvey is dominated by:
   A. his ego.
   B. his superego.
   C. his id.
   D. Bacchus.

2. Furious at her boss for what she considers to be unjust criticism, Clara turns around and takes out her anger on her subordinates. Clara may be using the defense mechanism of:
   A. displacement.
   B. reaction formation.
   C. identification.
   D. replacement.

3. Freud believed that most personality disturbances are due to:
   A. the failure of parents to reinforce healthy behavior.
   B. a poor self-concept resulting from excessive parental demands.
   C. unconscious and unresolved sexual conflicts rooted in childhood experiences.
   D. the exposure of children to unhealthy role models.

4. According to Alfred Adler, the prime motivating force in a person's life is:
   A. physical gratification.
   B. existential anxiety.
   C. striving for superiority.
   D. the need for power.

5. Which of the following learning mechanisms does B. F. Skinner see as being the major means by which behavior is learned?
   A. Classical conditioning
   B. Operant conditioning
   C. Observational learning
   D. Insight learning

6. Always having been a good student, Irving is confident that he will do well in his psychology course. According to Bandura's social learning theory, Irving would be said to have:
   A. strong feelings of self-efficacy.
   B. a sense of superiority.
   C. strong feelings of narcissism.
   D. strong defense mechanisms.

7. Which of the following is not a criticism of the behavioral approach to personality?
   A. Overdependence on animal research
   B. Neglect of biological factors
   C. Use of extensive empirical research
   D. Providing a fragmented view of personality

8. Which of the following approaches to personality is least deterministic?
   A. The humanistic approach
   B. The psychoanalytic approach
   C. The social learning approach
   D. The behavioral approach

9. Which of the following did Carl Rogers believe fosters a congruent self-concept?
   A. Conditional love
   B. Appropriate role models
   C. Immediate need gratification
   D. Unconditional love

10. What need was Abraham Maslow expressing when he said, "What a man can be, he must be"?
    A. The need for superiority
    B. The need for unconditional love
    C. The need for self-actualization
    D. The need to achieve

11. The strongest support for the theory that personality is heavily influenced by genetics is provided by strong personality similarity between:
    A. identical twins reared together.
    B. identical twins reared apart.
    C. fraternal twins reared together.
    D. nontwins reared together.

12. In which of the following cultures is an independent view of the self most likely to be the norm?
    A. China
    B. Japan
    C. Korea
    D. United States

13. Which of the following is not a shortcoming of self-report personality inventories?
    A. The accuracy of the results is a function of the honesty of the respondent.
    B. Respondents may attempt to answer in a way that makes them look good.
    C. There is sometimes a problem with "yea-sayers" or "nay-sayers."
    D. They are objective measures.

14. Which of the following is a projective test?
    A. The Rorschach Inkblot Test
    B. The Minnesota Multiphasic Personality Inventory
    C. Cattell's 16 Personality Factor Questionnaire
    D. The NEO Personality Inventory

15. In The Nurture Assumption, Judith Harris argues that the evidence indicates that family environment has _____ on children's personalities.
    A. largely positive effects
    B. largely negative effects
    C. surprisingly little effect
    D. a powerful effect

Answers

1	C	page 364	6	A	pages 373–374	11	B	pages 379–380
2	A	pages 366–367	7	C	page 374	12	D	page 384
3	C	page 369	8	A	page 375	13	D	page 388
4	C	page 370	9	D	pages 375–376	14	A	pages 388–389
5	B	page 372	10	C	page 377	15	C	page 391

INFOTRAC COLLEGE EDITION

Go to the Wadsworth Psychology Study Center for quiz questions, research updates, interactive exercises, and suggested readings in INFOTRAC related to this chapter:
http://psychology.wadsworth.com/product/0534593100s

CHAPTER 13

© 2001 Corbis

Stress, Coping, and Health

© 2001 Corbis

You're in your car headed home from school with a classmate. Traffic is barely moving. A radio report indicates that the traffic jam is only going to get worse. You groan audibly as you fiddle impatiently with the radio dial. Another motorist nearly takes your fender off trying to cut into your lane. Your pulse quickens as you shout insults at the unknown driver, who can't even hear you. You think about the term paper that you have to work on tonight. Your stomach knots up as you recall all the crumpled drafts you tossed into the wastebasket last night. If you don't finish that paper soon, you

won't be able to find any time to study for your math test, not to mention your biology quiz. Suddenly, you remember that you promised the person you're dating that the two of you would get together tonight. There's no way. Another fight looms on the horizon. Your classmate asks how you feel about the tuition increase that the college announced yesterday. You've been trying not to think about it. You're already in debt up to your ears. Your parents are bugging you about changing schools, but you don't want to leave your friends. Your heartbeat quickens as you contemplate the debate you're sure to have with your parents. You feel wired with tension as you realize that the stress in your life never seems to let up.

Many circumstances can create stress. It comes in all sorts of packages: big and small, pretty and ugly, simple and complex. All too often, the package comes as a surprise. In this chapter we'll try to sort out these packages. We'll discuss the nature of stress, how people cope with stress, and the potential effects of stress.

Our examination of the relationship between stress and physical illness will lead us into a broader discussion of the psychology of health. The way people in health professions think about physical illness has changed considerably in the past 10 to 20 years. The traditional view of physical illness as a purely biological phenomenon has given way to a biopsychosocial model of illness. The *biopsychosocial model* holds that physical illness is caused by a complex interaction of biological, psychological, and sociocultural factors. This model does not suggest that biological factors are unimportant. It simply asserts that these factors operate in a psychosocial context that is also influential.

What has led to this shift in thinking? In part, it's a result of changing patterns of illness. Prior to the 20th century, the principal threats to health were *contagious diseases* caused by infectious agents—diseases such as smallpox, typhoid fever, diphtheria, yellow fever, malaria, cholera, tuberculosis, and polio. Today, none of these diseases is among the leading killers in the United States. They were tamed

Figure 13.1

Changing patterns of illness.
Trends in the death rates for various diseases during the 20th century reveal that contagious diseases (shown in blue) have declined as a threat to health. However, the death rates for stress-related chronic diseases (shown in red) have remained quite high. The pie chart (*inset*) shows the results of these trends: three chronic diseases (heart disease, cancer, and stroke) account for 62.4% of all deaths.

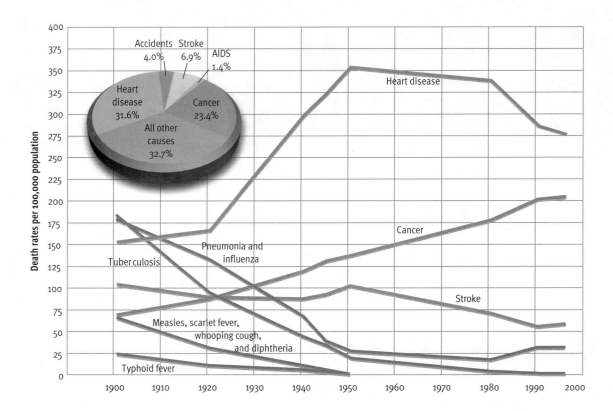

by improvements in nutrition, public hygiene, sanitation, and medical treatment (Grob, 1983). Unfortunately, the void left by contagious diseases has been filled all too quickly by *chronic diseases* that develop gradually, such as heart disease, cancer, and stroke (see Figure 13.1). Psychosocial factors, such as stress and lifestyle, play a large role in the development of these chronic diseases.

The growing recognition that psychological factors influence physical health led to the emergence of a new specialty in psychology. **Health psychology is concerned with how psychosocial factors relate to the promotion and maintenance of health and with the causation, prevention, and treatment of illness.** In the second half of this chapter, we'll explore this domain of psychology. In the Personal Application, we'll focus on strategies for enhancing stress management, and in the Critical Thinking Application we'll discuss strategies for improving health-related decision making.

The Nature of Stress

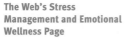

Web Link 13.1

The Web's Stress Management and Emotional Wellness Page
Ernesto Randolfi (Montana State University) has gathered a comprehensive set of resources dealing with stress management. Important topics covered here include cognitive restructuring, relaxation techniques, and stress in the workplace and in college life.

The term *stress* has been used in different ways by different theorists. We'll define *stress* as any circumstances that threaten or are perceived to threaten one's well-being and that thereby tax one's coping abilities. The threat may be to immediate physical safety, long-range security, self-esteem, reputation, peace of mind, or many other things that one values. This is a complex concept, so let's explore it a little further.

Stress as an Everyday Event

The word *stress* tends to spark images of overwhelming, traumatic crises. People may think of hijackings, hurricanes, military combat, and nuclear accidents. Undeniably, major disasters of this sort are extremely stressful events (Rubonis & Bickman, 1991; Weisaeth, 1993). However, these unusual events are only a small part of what stress is. Many everyday events such as waiting in line, having car trouble, shopping for Christmas presents, misplacing your checkbook, and staring at bills you can't pay are also stressful. Of course, major and minor stressors are not entirely independent. A major stressful event, such as going through a divorce, can trigger a cascade of minor stressors, such as looking for an attorney, moving, taking on new household responsibilities, and so forth (Pillow, Zautra, & Sandler, 1996). You might guess that minor stresses would produce minor effects, but that isn't necessarily true. Research indicates that routine hassles may have significant harmful effects on mental and physical health (Delongis, Folkman, & Lazarus, 1988; Johnson & Sherman, 1997).

Appraisal: Stress Lies in the Eye of the Beholder

The experience of feeling stressed depends on what events one notices and how one appraises them. Events that are stressful for one person may be routine for another. For example, many people find flying in an airplane somewhat stressful, but frequent fliers may not be bothered at all. Some people enjoy the excitement of going out on a date with someone new; others find the uncertainty terrifying.

Often, people aren't very objective in their appraisals of potentially stressful events. A study of hospitalized patients awaiting surgery showed only a slight correlation between the objective seriousness of a person's upcoming surgery and the amount of fear experienced by the patient (Janis, 1958). Clearly, some people are more prone than others to feel threatened by life's difficulties. A number of studies have shown that anxious, neurotic people report more stress than others (Watson, David, & Suls, 1999), as do people who are relatively unhappy (Seidlitz & Diener, 1993). Thus, stress lies in the eye (actually, the mind) of the beholder. People's appraisals of stressful events are highly subjective.

Major Types of Stress

An enormous variety of events can be stressful for one person or another. Although they're not entirely independent, the four principal types of stress are (1) frustration, (2) conflict, (3) change, and (4) pressure. As you read about each of these, you'll surely recognize four very familiar adversaries.

Frustration

As psychologists use the term, *frustration* is experienced whenever the pursuit of some goal is thwarted. In essence, you experience frustration when you want something and you can't have it. Everyone has to deal with frustration virtually every day. Traffic jams, for instance, are a routine source of frustration that can affect mood and blood pressure (Novaco, Stokols, & Milanesi, 1990). Fortunately, most frustrations are brief and insignificant. You may be quite upset when you go to a repair shop to pick up your ailing stereo and find that it hasn't been fixed as promised. However, a week later you'll probably have your stereo back, and the frustration will be forgotten. Of course, some frustrations—such as failing to get a promotion at work or losing a boyfriend or girlfriend—can be sources of significant stress.

Conflict

Like frustration, conflict is an unavoidable feature of everyday life. The perplexing question "Should I or shouldn't I?" comes up countless times in one's life. *Conflict* occurs when two or more incompatible motivations or behavioral impulses compete for expression. As we discussed in Chapter 12, Sigmund Freud proposed a century ago that internal conflicts generate considerable psychological distress. This link between conflict and distress was measured with new precision in studies by Laura King and Robert Emmons (1990, 1991). They used an elaborate questionnaire to assess the overall amount of internal conflict experienced by subjects. They found that higher levels of conflict were associated with higher levels of anxiety, depression, and physical symptoms.

Conflicts come in three types, which were originally described by Kurt Lewin (1935) and investigated extensively by Neal Miller (1944, 1959). These three basic types of conflict—approach-approach, avoidance-avoidance, and approach-avoidance—are diagrammed in Figure 13.2.

In an *approach-approach conflict* a choice must be made between two attractive goals. The problem, of course, is that you can choose just one of the two goals. For example: You have a free after-

"We developed the Hassle Scale because we think scales that measure major events miss the point. The constant, minor irritants may be much more important than the large, landmark changes."
RICHARD LAZARUS

Figure 13.2

Types of conflict.
Psychologists have identified three basic types of conflict. In approach-approach and avoidance-avoidance conflicts, a person is torn between two goals. In an approach-avoidance conflict, only one goal is under consideration, but it has both positive and negative aspects.

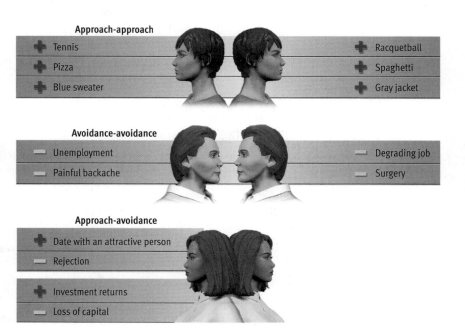

Approach-approach
- Tennis
- Pizza
- Blue sweater
- Racquetball
- Spaghetti
- Gray jacket

Avoidance-avoidance
- Unemployment
- Painful backache
- Degrading job
- Surgery

Approach-avoidance
- Date with an attractive person
- Rejection
- Investment returns
- Loss of capital

noon—should you play tennis or racquetball? You can't afford both the blue sweater and the gray jacket—which should you buy? Among the three kinds of conflict, the approach-approach type tends to be the least stressful. Nonetheless, approach-approach conflicts over important issues may sometimes be troublesome. If you're torn between two appealing college majors or two attractive boyfriends, for example, you may find the decision-making process quite stressful.

In an *avoidance-avoidance conflict* a choice must be made between two unattractive goals. Forced to choose between two repellent alternatives, you are, as they say, "caught between a rock and a hard place." For example, should you continue to collect unemployment checks, or should you take that degrading job at the car wash? Or suppose you have painful backaches. Should you submit to surgery that you dread, or should you continue to live with the pain? Obviously, avoidance-avoidance conflicts are most unpleasant and highly stressful.

In an *approach-avoidance conflict* a choice must be made about whether to pursue a single goal that has both attractive and unattractive aspects. For instance, imagine that you're offered a promotion that will mean a large increase in pay, but you'll have to move to a city that you hate. Approach-avoidance conflicts are common and can be quite stressful. Any time you have to take a risk to pursue some desirable outcome, you're likely to find yourself in an approach-avoidance conflict. Should you risk rejection by approaching that attractive person in class? Should you risk your savings by investing in a new business that could fail? Approach-avoidance conflicts often produce *vacillation* (Miller, 1944). That is, you go back and forth, beset by indecision. You decide to go ahead,

then you decide not to, and then you decide to go ahead again.

Change

Thomas Holmes and Richard Rahe have led the way in exploring the idea that life changes—including positive events, such as getting married or getting a promotion—represent a key type of stress. *Life changes* are any noticeable alterations in one's living circumstances that require readjustment. Based on their theory, Holmes and Rahe (1967) developed the Social Readjustment Rating Scale (SRRS) to measure life change as a form of stress. The scale assigns numerical values to 43 major life events. These values are supposed to reflect the magnitude of the readjustment required by each change (see Table 13.1). In using the scale, respondents are asked to indicate how often they experienced any of these 43 events during a certain time period (typically, the past year). The numbers associated with each event checked are then added. This total is an index of the amount of change-related stress the person has recently experienced.

The SRRS and similar scales based on it have been used in thousands of studies by researchers all over the world. Overall, these studies have shown that people with higher scores on the SRRS tend to be more vulnerable to many kinds of physical illness and to many types of psychological problems as well (Creed, 1993; Derogatis & Coons, 1993; Gruen, 1993). These results have attracted a great deal of attention, and the SRRS has been reprinted in many popular newspapers and magazines. The attendant publicity has led to the widespread conclusion that life change is inherently stressful.

However, experts have criticized this research, citing problems with the methods used (Rabkin, 1993; Raphael, Cloitre, & Dohrenwend, 1991) and

CONCEPT CHECK 13.1

Identifying Types of Conflict

Check your understanding of the three basic types of conflict by identifying the type experienced in each of the following examples. The answers are in Appendix A.

Examples

B. **1.** John can't decide whether to take a demeaning job in a car wash or to go on welfare.

C. **2.** Desiree wants to apply to a highly selective law school, but she hates to risk the possibility of rejection.

A. **3.** Vanessa has been shopping for a new car and is torn between a nifty little sports car and a classy sedan, both of which she really likes.

Types of conflict

a. approach-approach

b. avoidance-avoidance

c. approach-avoidance

problems in interpreting the findings (Critelli & Ee, 1996; Watson & Pennebaker, 1989). At this point, it's a key interpretive issue that concerns us. A variety of critics have collected evidence showing that the SRRS does not measure *change* exclusively (McLean & Link, 1994; Turner & Wheaton, 1995). In reality, it assesses a wide range of different kinds of stressful experiences. Thus, we have little reason

Table 13.1 Social Readjustment Rating Scale

Life Event	Mean Value
Death of a spouse	100
Divorce	73
Marital separation	65
Jail term	63
Death of a close family member	63
Personal injury or illness	53
Marriage	50
Fired at work	47
Marital reconciliation	45
Retirement	45
Change in health of family member	44
Pregnancy	40
Sex difficulties	39
Gain of a new family member	39
Business readjustment	39
Change in financial state	38
Death of a close friend	37
Change to a different line of work	36
Change in number of arguments with spouse	35
Mortgage or loan for major purchase (home, etc.)	31
Foreclosure of mortgage or loan	30
Change in responsibilities at work	29
Son or daughter leaving home	29
Trouble with in-laws	29
Outstanding personal achievement	28
Wife begins or stops work	26
Begin or end school	26
Change in living conditions	25
Revision of personal habits	24
Trouble with boss	23
Change in work hours or conditions	20
Change in residence	20
Change in school	20
Change in recreation	19
Change in church activities	19
Change in social activities	18
Mortgage or loan for lesser purchase (car, TV, etc.)	17
Change in sleeping habits	16
Change in number of family get-togethers	15
Change in eating habits	15
Vacation	13
Christmas	12
Minor violations of the law	11

(Adapted by permission from "The Social Readjustment Rating Scale," by T. H. Holmes and R. H. Rahe, 1967, *Journal of Psychosomatic Research*, *11*, 213–218. Copyright © 1967 by Elsevier Science, Inc.)

to believe that change is *inherently* or *inevitably* stressful. Undoubtedly, some life changes may be quite challenging, but others may be quite benign.

Pressure

At one time or another, most people have remarked that they're "under pressure." What does this mean? ***Pressure* involves expectations or demands that one behave in a certain way.** You are under pressure to *perform* when you're expected to execute tasks and responsibilities quickly, efficiently, and successfully. For example, salespeople are usually under pressure to move merchandise. Professors at research institutions are often under pressure to publish in prestigious journals. Stand-up comedians are under intense pressure to make people laugh. Pressures to *conform* to others' expectations are also common in our lives. Businessmen are expected to wear suits and ties. Suburban homeowners are expected to keep their lawns well manicured. Teenagers are expected to adhere to their parents' values and rules.

Although widely discussed by the general public, the concept of pressure has received scant attention from researchers. However, Weiten (1988b, 1998) has devised a scale to measure pressure as a form of life stress. It assesses self-imposed pressure, pressure from work and school, and pressure from family relations, peer relations, and intimate relations. In research with this scale, a strong relationship has been found between pressure and a variety of psychological symptoms and problems. In fact, pressure has turned out to be more strongly related to measures of mental health than the SRRS and other established measures of stress.

CONCEPT CHECK 13.2

Recognizing Sources of Stress

Check your understanding of the major sources of stress by indicating which type or types of stress are at work in each of the examples below. Bear in mind that the four basic types of stress are not mutually exclusive. There's some potential for overlap, so that a specific experience might include both change and pressure, for instance. The answers are in Appendix A.

Examples

___A___ **1.** Marie is late for an appointment but is stuck in line at the bank.

___D.___ **2.** Tamika decides that she won't be satisfied unless she gets straight A's this year.

___C___ **3.** Jose has just graduated from business school and has taken an exciting new job.

___A,C,D___ **4.** Morris has just been fired from his job and needs to find another.

Types of stress

a. frustration

b. conflict

c. change

d. pressure

The human response to stress is complex and multidimensional. Stress affects the individual at several levels. Consider again the chapter's opening scenario, in which you're driving home in heavy traffic and thinking about overdue papers, tuition increases, and parental pressures. Let's look at some of the reactions that were mentioned. When you groan audibly in reaction to the traffic report, you're experiencing an *emotional response* to stress, in this case annoyance and anger. When your pulse quickens and your stomach knots up, you're exhibiting *physiological responses* to stress. When you shout insults at another driver, your verbal aggression is a *behavioral response* to the stress at hand. Thus, we can analyze a person's reactions to stress at three levels: (1) emotional responses, (2) physiological responses, and (3) behavioral responses. Figure 13.3 provides an overview of this stress process.

Emotional Responses

When people are under stress, they often react emotionally. More often than not, stress elicits unpleasant emotions rather than pleasurable ones (Lazarus, 1993; van Eck, Nicolson, & Berkhof, 1998).

Emotions Commonly Elicited

There are no simple one-to-one connections between certain types of stressful events and particular emotions, but researchers *have* begun to uncover some strong links between specific *cognitive reactions to stress (appraisals)* and specific emotions (Smith & Lazarus, 1993). For example, self-blame tends to lead to guilt, helplessness to sadness, and so forth. Although many emotions can be evoked by stressful events, some are certainly more likely than others. Common emotional responses to stress include the following (Lazarus, 1993; Woolfolk & Richardson, 1978):

1. *Annoyance, anger, and rage.* Stress frequently produces feelings of anger ranging from mild annoyance to uncontrollable rage. Frustration is particularly likely to generate anger.

2. *Apprehension, anxiety, and fear.* Stress probably evokes anxiety and fear more frequently than any other emotions. As we saw in Chapter 12, Freudian theory has long recognized the link between conflict and anxiety. However, anxiety can also be elicited by the pressure to perform, the threat of impending frustration, or the uncertainty associated with change.

3. *Dejection, sadness, and grief.* Sometimes stress—especially frustration—simply brings you down. Routine setbacks, such as traffic tickets and poor grades, often produce feelings of dejection. More profound setbacks, such as deaths and divorces, typically leave one grief-stricken.

Effects of Emotional Arousal

Emotional reponses are a natural and normal part of life. Even unpleasant emotions serve important purposes. Like physical pain, painful emotions can serve as warnings that one needs to take action. However, strong emotional arousal can also interfere with efforts to cope with stress. For example,

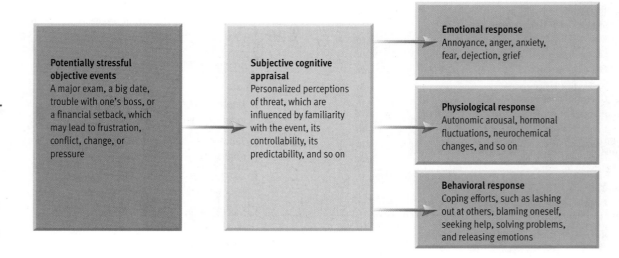

Figure 13.3

Overview of the stress process. A potentially stressful event, such as a major exam, elicits a subjective appraisal of how threatening the event is. If the event is viewed with alarm, the stress may trigger emotional, physiological, and behavioral reactions, as people's response to stress is multidimensional.

Potentially stressful objective events
A major exam, a big date, trouble with one's boss, or a financial setback, which may lead to frustration, conflict, change, or pressure

Subjective cognitive appraisal
Personalized perceptions of threat, which are influenced by familiarity with the event, its controllability, its predictability, and so on

Emotional response
Annoyance, anger, anxiety, fear, dejection, grief

Physiological response
Autonomic arousal, hormonal fluctuations, neurochemical changes, and so on

Behavioral response
Coping efforts, such as lashing out at others, blaming oneself, seeking help, solving problems, and releasing emotions

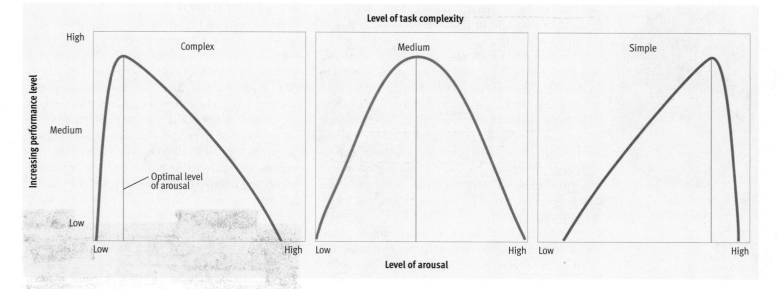

there's evidence that high emotional arousal can interfere with attention and memory retrieval and can impair judgment and decision making (Janis, 1993; Mandler, 1993).

Although emotional arousal may hurt coping efforts, this isn't *necessarily* the case. The *inverted-U hypothesis* predicts that task performance should improve with increased emotional arousal—up to a point, after which further increases in arousal become disruptive and performance deteriorates (Anderson, 1990; Mandler, 1993). This idea is referred to as the inverted-U hypothesis because when performance is plotted as a function of arousal, the resulting graphs approximate an upside-down U (see Figure 13.4). In these graphs, the level of arousal at which performance peaks is characterized as the *optimal level of arousal* for a task.

This optimal level of arousal appears to depend in part on the complexity of the task at hand. The conventional wisdom is that *as a task becomes more complex, the optimal level of arousal (for peak performance) tends to decrease.* This relationship is depicted in Figure 13.4. As you can see, a fairly high level of arousal should be optimal on simple tasks (such as driving 8 hours to help a friend in a crisis). However, performance should peak at a lower level of arousal on complex tasks (such as making a major decision in which you have to weigh many factors).

The research evidence on the inverted-U hypothesis is inconsistent and subject to varied interpretations (Neiss, 1988, 1990). Nonetheless, the inverted-U hypothesis provides a plausible model of how emotional arousal could have either beneficial or disruptive effects on coping, depending on the nature of the stressful demands one encounters.

Physiological Responses

As we just discussed, stress frequently elicits strong emotional responses. Now we'll look at the important physiological changes that often accompany these responses.

The General Adaptation Syndrome

Concern about the physical effects of stress was first voiced by Hans Selye (1936, 1956, 1982), a Canadian scientist who launched stress research decades ago. Selye was born in Vienna but spent his entire professional career at McGill University in Montreal. Beginning in the 1930s, Selye exposed laboratory animals to a diverse array of both physical and psychological stressors (heat, cold, pain, mild shock, restraint, and so on). The patterns of physiological arousal seen in the animals were largely the same, regardless of the type of stress. Thus, Selye concluded that stress reactions are *nonspecific*. In other words, he maintained that the reactions do not vary according to the specific type of stress encountered. Initially, Selye wasn't sure what to call this nonspecific response to a variety of noxious agents. In the 1940s he decided to call it *stress,* and the word has been part of our vocabulary ever since.

Selye (1956, 1974) explained stress reactions in terms of the general adaptation syndrome. **The general adaptation syndrome is a model of the body's stress response, consisting of three stages: alarm, resistance, and exhaustion.** In the first stage, an *alarm reaction* occurs when an organism first recognizes the existence of a threat: physiological arousal occurs as the body musters its resources

Figure 13.4

Arousal and performance. According to the inverted-U hypothesis, graphs of the relationship between emotional arousal and task performance tend to resemble an inverted U, as increased arousal is associated with improved performance up to a point, after which higher arousal leads to poorer performance. The optimal level of arousal for a task depends on the complexity of the task. On complex tasks, a relatively low level of arousal tends to be optimal. On simple tasks, however, performance may peak at a much higher level of arousal.

"There are two main types of human beings: 'racehorses,' who thrive on stress and are only happy with a vigorous, fast-paced lifestyle; and 'turtles,' who in order to be happy require peace, quiet, and a generally tranquil environment."
HANS SELYE

to combat the challenge. Selye's alarm reaction is essentially the fight-or-flight response described in Chapters 3 and 10.

However, Selye took his investigation of stress a few steps further by exposing laboratory animals to *prolonged stress,* similar to the chronic stress often endured by humans. As stress continues, the organism may progress to the second phase of the general adaptation syndrome, the *stage of resistance.* During this phase, physiological changes stabilize as coping efforts get under way. Typically, physiological arousal continues to be higher than normal, although it may level off somewhat as the organism becomes accustomed to the threat.

If the stress continues over a substantial period of time, the organism may enter the third stage, the *stage of exhaustion.* According to Selye, the body's resources for fighting stress are limited. If the stress can't be overcome, the body's resources may be depleted, and physiological arousal will decrease. Eventually, the organism may collapse from exhaustion. During this phase, the organism's resistance declines. This reduced resistance may lead to what Selye called "diseases of adaptation."

Brain-Body Pathways

Even in cases of moderate stress, you may notice that your heart has started beating faster, you've begun to breathe harder, and you're perspiring more than usual. How does all this (and much more) happen? It appears that there are two major pathways along which the brain sends signals to the endocrine system (Felker & Hubbard, 1998; Koranyi, 1989). As we noted in Chapter 3, the *endocrine system* consists of glands located at various sites in the body that secrete chemicals called hormones. The hypothalamus is the part of the brain that appears to initiate action along these two pathways.

The first pathway (see Figure 13.5) is routed through the autonomic nervous system. Your hypothalamus activates the sympathetic division of the ANS. A key part of this activation involves stimulating the central part of the adrenal glands (the adrenal medulla) to release large amounts of *catecholamines* into the bloodstream. These hormones radiate throughout your body, producing the host of physiological changes seen in the fight-or-flight response. The net result of catecholamine elevation is that your body is mobilized for action.

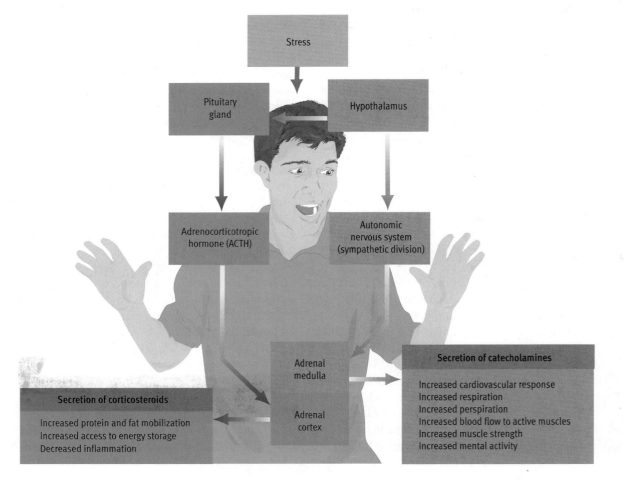

Figure 13.5

Brain-body pathways in stress. In times of stress, the brain sends signals along two pathways. The pathway through the autonomic nervous system controls the release of catecholamine hormones that help mobilize the body for action. The pathway through the pituitary gland and the endocrine system controls the release of corticosteroid hormones that increase energy and ward off tissue inflammation.

The second pathway involves more direct communication between the brain and the endocrine system (see Figure 13.5). The hypothalamus sends signals to the so-called master gland of the endocrine system, the pituitary gland. In turn, the pituitary secretes a hormone (ACTH) that stimulates the outer part of the adrenal glands (the adrenal cortex) to release another important set of hormones—*corticosteroids*. These hormones stimulate the release of more fats and proteins into circulation, thus helping to increase your energy. They also mobilize chemicals that help inhibit tissue inflammation in case of injury.

Thus, it's becoming clear that physiological responses to stress extend into all parts of the body. As you'll see, these physiological reactions can affect both mental and physical health.

Behavioral Responses

Although people respond to stress at several levels, it's clear that behavior is the crucial dimension of their reactions. Most behavioral responses to stress involve coping. *Coping refers to active efforts to master, reduce, or tolerate the demands created by stress.* Notice that this definition is neutral as to whether coping efforts are healthful or maladaptive. The popular use of the term often implies that coping is inherently healthful. When people say that someone "coped with her problems," the implication is that she handled them effectively.

In reality, however, coping responses may be adaptive or maladaptive (Moos & Schaefer, 1993). For example, if you were flunking a history course at midterm, you might cope with this stress by (1) increasing your study efforts, (2) seeking help from a tutor, (3) blaming your professor, or (4) giving up on the class without really trying. Clearly, the first two of these coping responses would be more adaptive than the last two.

People cope with stress in many ways, but most individuals exhibit certain styles of coping that are fairly consistent across situations (Carver & Scheier, 1994; Heszen-Niejodek, 1997). Given the immense variety in coping strategies, we can only highlight some of the more common patterns of coping. In this section we'll focus most of our attention on styles of coping that tend to be less than ideal. We'll discuss more healthful coping strategies in the Personal Application on stress management.

Striking Out at Others

People often respond to stressful events by striking out at others with aggressive behavior. *Aggression is any behavior that is intended to hurt someone,* either physically or verbally. Many years ago, a team of psychologists (Dollard et al., 1939) proposed the *frustration-aggression hypothesis,* which held that aggression is always caused by frustration. Decades of research have supported this idea of a causal link between frustration and aggression (Berkowitz, 1989). However, this research has also shown that there isn't an inevitable, one-to-one correspondence between the two.

In discussing qualifications to the frustration-aggression hypothesis, Berkowitz (1989) has concluded that (1) frustration does not *necessarily* lead to aggression, (2) many situational factors influence whether frustration will lead to aggression, (3) the likelihood of aggression increases with the amount of negative emotions aroused, and (4) frustration may produce responses other than aggression (for example, apathy). Although these are important qualifications, it's clear that frustration does often lead to aggression.

Indulging Oneself

Stress sometimes leads to self-indulgence. When troubled by stress, many people engage in excessive consummatory behavior—unwise patterns of eating, drinking, smoking, using drugs, spending money, and so forth. As I mentioned in Chapter 10, when I have an exceptionally stressful day, I often head for the refrigerator, the grocery store, or a restaurant in pursuit of something chocolate. I have a friend who copes with stress by making a beeline for the nearest shopping mall to indulge in a spending spree.

CONCEPT CHECK 13.3

Tracing Brain-Body Pathways in Stress

Check your understanding of the two major pathways along which the brain sends signals to the endocrine system in the event of stress by separating the eight terms below into two sets of four and arranging each set in the appropriate sequence. You'll find the answers in Appendix A.

ACTH	corticosteriods
adrenal cortex	hypothalamus
adrenal medulla	pituitary
catecholamines	sympathetic division of the ANS

Pathway 1

_____

_____

_____

Pathway 2

_____

_____

_____

It appears that my friend and I are not unusual in our excessive consummatory behavior. It makes sense that when things are going poorly in one area of their lives, people may try to compensate by pursuing substitute forms of satisfaction. When this happens, consummatory responses probably rank high among the substitutes. They're relatively easy to execute, and they tend to be pleasurable. Thus, it's not surprising that studies have linked stress to increases in eating (Grunberg & Straub, 1992), smoking (Cohen & Lichtenstein, 1990), and the consumption of alcohol and drugs (Peyser, 1993).

A new manifestation of this coping strategy that has attracted much attention recently is the tendency to immerse oneself in the online world of the Internet. Kimberly Young (1996, 1998) has described a syndrome called *Internet addiction*, which consists of spending an inordinate amount of time on the Internet and inability to control online use. People who exhibit this syndrome often use the online world as an escape from their problems in the real world. Their Internet use is so excessive, it begins to interfere with their functioning at work, at school, or at home, which leads victims to start concealing the extent of their dependence on the Internet. There are no data yet on how prevalent this new form of self-indulgence is, but Young (1996) had little difficulty recruiting a sample of 396 Internet addicts, so the syndrome does not appear to be rare. The findings from her sample suggest that Internet addiction is not limited to shy, male computer whizzes, as one might expect. Although there is active debate about the wisdom of characterizing exorbitant Internet use as an *addiction,* it is clear that surfing the net is a new coping strategy that is likely to become increasingly common.

Experts disagree about whether excessive Internet use should be characterized as an addiction, but the inability to control online activity appears to be an increasingly common syndrome that illustrates the coping strategy of indulging oneself.

© Bill Aron/PhotoEdit

Defensive Coping 10a

Defensive coping is a common response to stress. We noted in the previous chapter that Sigmund Freud originally developed the concept of the defense mechanism. Though rooted in the psychoanalytic tradition, this concept has gained widespread acceptance from psychologists of most persuasions. Building on Freud's initial insights, modern psychologists have broadened the scope of the concept and added to Freud's list of defense mechanisms.

Defense mechanisms are largely unconscious reactions that protect a person from unpleasant emotions such as anxiety and guilt. Many specific defense mechanisms have been identified. For example, Laughlin (1979) lists 49 different defenses. We described 7 common defense mechanisms in our discussion of Freud's theory in the previous chapter. Table 13.2 introduces another 5 defenses that people use with some regularity: denial, fantasy, intellectualization, undoing, and overcompensation. Although widely discussed in the popular press, defense mechanisms are often misunderstood. To clear up some of the misconceptions, we'll use a question/answer format to elaborate on the nature of defense mechanisms.

What exactly do defense mechanisms defend against? Above all else, defense mechanisms shield the individual from the emotional discomfort so often elicited by stress. Their main purpose is to ward off or reduce the intensity of unwelcome emotions such as anxiety, anger, guilt, and dejection.

How do they work? They work through *self-deception.* Defense mechanisms accomplish their goals by distorting reality so that it doesn't appear so threatening. For example, suppose you're not doing well in school and you're in danger of flunking out. You might use *denial* to block awareness of the possibility that you could flunk, temporarily fending off feelings of anxiety.

Are they conscious or unconscious? Both. Freud originally assumed that defenses operate entirely at an unconscious level. However, the concept of the defense mechanism has been broadened by other theorists to include maneuvers that people may be aware of. Thus, defense mechanisms may operate at varying levels of awareness, although they're largely unconscious.

Table 13.2   Common Defense Mechanisms

Mechanism	Description	Example
Denial of reality	Protecting oneself from unpleasant reality by refusing to perceive or face it	A smoker concludes that the evidence linking cigarette use to health problems is scientifically worthless.
Fantasy	Gratifying frustrated desires by imaginary achievements	A socially inept and inhibited young man imagines himself chosen by a group of women to provide them with sexual satisfaction.
Intellectualization (isolation)	Cutting off emotion from hurtful situations or separating incompatible attitudes so that they appear unrelated	A prisoner on death row awaiting execution resists appeals on his behalf and coldly insists that the letter of the law be followed.
Undoing	Atoning for or trying to magically dispel unacceptable desires or acts	A teenager who feels guilty about masturbation ritually touches door knobs a prescribed number of times following each occurrence of the act.
Overcompensation	Covering up felt weakness by emphasizing some desirable characteristics, or making up for frustration in one area by overgratification in another	A dangerously overweight woman goes on eating binges when she feels neglected by her husband.

NOTE: See Table 12.1 for another list of defense mechanisms. (Adapted form *Abnormal Psychology and Modern Life*, 8th Ed., by R. C. Carson, J. N. Butcher & J. C. Coleman, pp 64–65, 1988. Copyright © 1988 by Scott, Foresman and Company. Adapted by permission of the publisher.)

Are they normal? Definitely. Everyone uses defense mechanisms on a fairly regular basis. They're entirely normal patterns of coping. The notion that only neurotic people use defense mechanisms is inaccurate.

Are they healthy? This is a much more complicated question. More often than not, the answer is "no." Generally, defensive coping is less than optimal for several reasons. First, defensive coping is an avoidance strategy, and avoidance rarely provides a genuine solution to problems (Holahan & Moos, 1985, 1990). Second, a repressive coping style has been related to poor health, in part because repression often leads people to delay facing up to their problems (Weinberger, 1990). For example, if you were to block out obvious warning signs of cancer or diabetes and fail to obtain needed medical care, your defensive behavior could be fatal. Third, defenses such as denial and fantasy represent wishful thinking, which appears to have little adaptive value (Bolger, 1990).

Although defensive behavior tends to be relatively unhealthful, Shelley Taylor and Jonathon Brown (1988, 1994) have reviewed several lines of evidence suggesting that "positive illusions" may be adaptive for mental health and well-being. First, they note that "normal" people tend to have overly favorable self-images. In contrast, depressed subjects exhibit less favorable—but more realistic—self-concepts. Second, normal subjects overestimate the degree to which they control chance events. In comparison, depressed subjects are less prone to this illusion of control. Third, normal individuals are more likely than depressed subjects to display unrealistic optimism in making projections about the future.

Colvin and Block (1994) have expressed considerable skepticism about the idea that illusions are adaptive. They make an eloquent case for the traditional view that accuracy and realism are healthy. Part of the problem in sorting out the evidence on this complex issue is that both ends of the correlational equation are difficult to measure (Asendorpf & Ostendorf, 1998). What exactly is an illusion? It is not easy to precisely determine whether a subject's self-concept is overly favorable. In a similar vein, mental health and well-being are difficult to quantify.

Thus, it is hard to make sweeping generalizations about the adaptive value of self-deception. Some of the personal illusions that people create through defensive coping may help them deal with life's difficulties. Roy Baumeister (1989) theorizes that it's all a matter of degree and that there is an "optimal margin of illusion." According to Baumeister, extreme distortions of reality are maladaptive, but small illusions are often beneficial.

Constructive Coping

Our discussion thus far has focused on coping strategies that usually are less than ideal. Of course, people also exhibit many healthful strategies for dealing with stress. We'll use the term *constructive coping* to refer to relatively healthful efforts that people make to deal with stressful events. No strategy of coping can *guarantee* a successful outcome. Even the healthiest coping responses may turn out to be ineffective in some circumstances. Thus, the concept of constructive coping is simply meant to connote a healthful, positive approach, without promising success.

What makes certain coping strategies constructive? Frankly, it's a gray area in which psychologists' opinions vary to some extent. Nonetheless, a consensus about the nature of constructive coping

Courtesy of Shelley Taylor

"*Rather than perceiving themselves, the world, and the future accurately, most people regard themselves, their circumstances, and the future as considerably more positive than is objectively likely. . . . These illusions are not merely characteristic of human thought; they appear actually to be adaptive, promoting rather than undermining good mental health.*"
SHELLEY TAYLOR

has emerged from the sizable literature on stress management. Key themes in this literature include the following:

1. Constructive coping involves confronting problems directly. It is task relevant and action oriented. It entails a conscious effort to rationally evaluate your options so that you can try to solve your problems.

2. Constructive coping is based on reasonably realistic appraisals of your stress and coping resources. A little self-deception may sometimes be adaptive, but excessive self-deception and highly unrealistic negative thinking are not.

3. Constructive coping involves learning to recognize, and in some cases inhibit, potentially disruptive emotional reactions to stress.

4. Constructive coping includes making efforts to ensure that your body is not especially vulnerable to the possibly damaging effects of stress.

The principles just described provide a rather general and abstract picture of constructive coping. We'll look at patterns of constructive coping in more detail in the Personal Application, which discusses various stress management strategies that people can use. We turn next to some of the possible outcomes of struggles with stress.

The Effects of Stress on Physical Health

People struggle with many stresses every day. Most stresses come and go without leaving any enduring imprint. However, when stress is severe or when many stressful demands pile up, one's mental or physical health may be affected. In Chapter 14 you'll learn that chronic stress contributes to many types of psychological disorders, including depression, schizophrenia, and anxiety disorders. In this section, we'll discuss the link between stress and physical illness.

Prior to the 1970s, it was thought that stress contributed to the development of only a few physical diseases, such as high blood pressure, ulcers, and asthma, which were called *psychosomatic diseases.* However, in the 1970s, research began to uncover new links between stress and a great variety of diseases previously believed to be purely physiological in origin (Elliott, 1989; Hubbard & Workman, 1998). Let's look at some of this research.

People who are classified as being a Type A personality tend to be workaholics. They try to do several things at the same time, and they put themselves under constant time pressure. The extra stress that such people experience may be associated with a higher risk of heart attack.

Type A Behavior and Heart Disease

Heart disease accounts for nearly 40% of the deaths in the United States every year. *Coronary* heart disease involves a reduction in blood flow in the coronary arteries, which supply the heart with blood. This type of heart disease is responsible for about 90% of heart-related deaths.

In the 1960s and 1970s a pair of cardiologists, Meyer Friedman and Ray Rosenman (1974), were investigating the causes of coronary heart disease. Originally, Friedman and Rosenman were interested in the usual factors thought to produce a high risk of heart attack: smoking, obesity, physical inactivity, and so forth. Although they found that these factors were relevant, they eventually recognized that a piece of the puzzle was missing. Many people who smoked constantly, got little exercise, and were severely overweight avoided the ravages of heart disease. At the same time, other people who seemed to be in much better shape in regard to these risk factors experienced the misfortune of a heart attack.

Gradually, Friedman and Rosenman unraveled the riddle. What was their explanation for these perplexing findings? Stress! Specifically, they found a connection between coronary risk and a syndrome they called *Type A behavior,* which involves self-imposed stress and intense reactions to stress.

Elements of Type A Behavior

Friedman and Rosenman divided people into two basic types—Type A and Type B—who exhibit differing characteristics (Friedman, 1996; Rosenman, 1993). **The *Type A personality* includes three** elements: (1) a strong competitive orientation, (2) impatience and time urgency, and (3) anger and hostility. Type A's are ambitious, hard-driving perfectionists who are exceedingly time conscious. They routinely try to do several things at once. Thus, a Type A person may watch TV, talk on the phone, work on a report, and eat dinner all at the same time. Type A's are so impatient that they frequently finish others' sentences for them! They fidget frantically over the briefest delays. Often they are highly competitive, achievement-oriented workaholics who drive themselves with many deadlines. They speak rapidly and emphatically. They are cynical about life and hostile toward others. They are easily irritated and are quick to anger. In contrast, the *Type B personality* is marked by relatively relaxed, patient, easygoing, amicable behavior. Type B's are less hurried, less competitive, and less easily angered than Type A's. The strength of one's Type A tendencies can be measured with either structured interviews or questionnaires. Figure 13.6 lists some questions that are representative of those used in measurements of Type A behavior.

Which aspects of Type A behavior are most strongly related to increased coronary risk? Are competitiveness, time urgency, and hostility equally important? Quite a number of studies suggest that hostility may be more important for coronary risk than other elements of the Type A personality (Burg, 1995; Miller et al., 1996).

How strong is the link between Type A personality and coronary risk? Research on the association between Type A personality and coronary disease has yielded mixed findings (Miller et al., 1991). Taken as a whole, the data suggest that the increased coronary risk for Type A's is perhaps double that for Type B's (Lyness, 1993; Weaver & Rodnick, 1986). The modest nature of this relationship probably means that Type A behavior increases coronary risk for only a portion of the population.

Explaining the Connection

Why is Type A behavior associated with coronary risk? Research on the Type A syndrome has uncovered a number of possible explanations (see Figure 13.7 on the next page).

First, Type A individuals appear to exhibit greater physiological reactivity than Type B's (Lyness, 1993; Smith & Brown, 1991). The frequent ups and downs in heart rate and blood pressure may create wear and tear in their cardiovascular systems.

Second, Type A's probably create more stress for themselves than others do. For example, Smith and

Figure 13.6

The Type A personality. The ten questions shown here highlight some of the behavioral traits associated with the Type A personality.

Measuring Type A behavior

You can use the checklist below to *estimate* the likelihood of your being a Type A personality. However, the checklist should be regarded as providing only a rough estimate, because Friedman and Rosenman (1974) emphasize that how you answer certain questions in their interview is often more significant than the answers themselves. Nonetheless, if you answer "yes" to a majority of the items below, you may want to consider reading their book, *Type A Behavior and Your Heart.*

_____ 1. Do you find it difficult to restrain yourself from hurrying others' speech (finishing their sentences for them)?

_____ 2. Do you often try to do more than one thing at a time (such as eat and read simultaneously)?

_____ 3. Do you often feel guilty if you use extra time to relax?

_____ 4. Do you tend to get involved in a great number of projects at once?

_____ 5. Do you find yourself racing through yellow lights when you drive?

_____ 6. Do you need to win in order to derive enjoyment from games and sports?

_____ 7. Do you generally move, walk, and eat rapidly?

_____ 8. Do you agree to take on too many responsibilities?

_____ 9. Do you detest waiting in lines?

_____ 10. Do you have an intense desire to better your position in life and impress others?

colleagues (1988) found that subjects high in hostility reported more hassles, more negative life events, more marital conflict, and more work-related stress than subjects who were lower in hostility.

Third, thanks to their antagonistic ways of relating to others, Type A personalities tend to have less social support than other people do (Smith & Christensen, 1992). As we'll discuss shortly, research suggests that social support is an important coping resource that promotes health and buffers the effects of stress.

Fourth, perhaps because of their cynicism and their tendency to push themselves to work hard, Type A's tend to exhibit health habits that may contribute to the development of cardiovascular disease. For example, in comparison to others, they drink more alcohol, get less exercise, and ignore symptoms of fatigue more often (Houston & Vavak, 1991; Leiker & Hailey, 1988).

In sum, there are a variety of plausible explanations for the connection between the Type A syndrome and heart disease. With all these mechanisms at work, it's not surprising that Type A behavior is associated with increased coronary risk. What's surprising is that the association isn't even stronger.

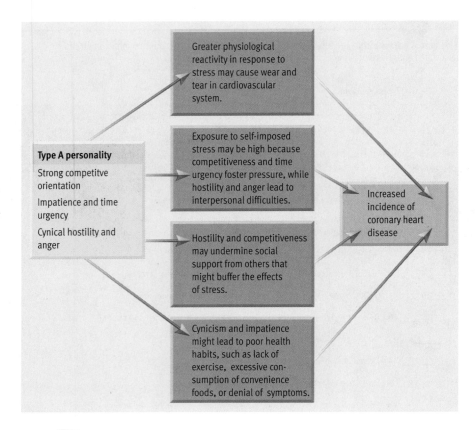

Type A personality

Strong competitve orientation

Impatience and time urgency

Cynical hostility and anger

Greater physiological reactivity in response to stress may cause wear and tear in cardiovascular system.

Exposure to self-imposed stress may be high because competitiveness and time urgency foster pressure, while hostility and anger lead to interpersonal difficulties.

Hostility and competitiveness may undermine social support from others that might buffer the effects of stress.

Cynicism and impatience might lead to poor health habits, such as lack of exercise, excessive consumption of convenience foods, or denial of symptoms.

Increased incidence of coronary heart disease

Figure 13.7

Mechanisms that may link Type A personality to heart disease. Explanations for the apparent link between Type A behavior and heart disease are many and varied. Four widely discussed possibilities are summarized in the middle column of this diagram.

Emotional Reactions, Depression, and Heart Disease

Although the Type A personality syndrome has dominated research on how psychological functioning contributes to heart disease, recent studies suggest that emotional reactions may also be critical. One line of research has supported the hypothesis that transient mental stress and the resulting emotions can tax the heart. Based on anecdotal evidence, cardiologists and laypersons have long voiced suspicions that strong emotional reactions might trigger heart attacks in individuals with coronary disease, but it was difficult to document this connection. However, advances in cardiac monitoring have facilitated investigation of the issue. As suspected, laboratory experiments with cardiology patients have shown that brief periods of mental stress can trigger acute symptoms of heart disease, such as myocardial ischemia (inadequate blood flow to the heart) and chest pain (Gottdiener et al., 1994). Researchers have also examined this issue by having patients keep a diary of their emotions while their cardiac functioning is monitored continuously for 48 hours as they go about their business. The investigators found that the likelihood of myocardial ischemia increased two- or three-fold when people reported negative emotions, such as

tension, frustration, and sadness (Gullette et al., 1997). Consistent with this evidence, another study of cardiology patients showed that stress management training can reduce the likelihood of a second heart attack (Blumenthal et al., 1997). Taken together, these studies suggest that emotional reactions to stressful events may precipitate heart attacks in people with coronary disease and that learning to manage one's emotions better may reduce one's coronary risk.

Another line of research has recently implicated depression as a major risk factor for heart disease. Depressive disorders, which are characterized by persistent feelings of sadness and despair, are a fairly common form of mental illness (see Chapter 14). Elevated rates of depression have been found among patients suffering from heart disease in many studies, but most theorists have explained this correlation by asserting that being diagnosed with heart disease makes people depressed. Recent evidence, however, suggests that the causal relations may be just the opposite—that the emotional dysfunction of depression may cause heart disease. For example, Pratt, and colleagues (1996) examined a large sample of people 13 years after they were screened for depression. The researchers found that participants who were depressed at the time of the original study were four times more likely than others to experience a heart attack during the intervening 13 years. Because the participants' depressive disorders preceded their heart attacks, one cannot argue that their heart disease caused their depression.

Given that there is a correlation between depression and smoking (Breslau, Kilbey, & Andreski, 1993), one might argue that increased smoking is responsible for the elevated incidence of heart disease among people suffering from depression. However, several studies have shown that the predictive link between depression and heart disease remains even after controlling for the effects of smoking (Glassman & Shapiro, 1998). Although the physiological mechanisms that underlie this connection remain obscure (Appels, 1997), it appears that depression may make people more vulnerable to heart disease.

Stress, Other Diseases, and Immune Functioning

The development of questionnaires to measure life stress has allowed researchers to look for correlations between stress and a variety of diseases. These researchers have uncovered many connections between stress and illness. For example, Thomason and colleagues (1992) found an association between life stress and the course of rheumatoid arthritis. Working with a sample of female students, Williams and Deffenbacher (1983) found that life stress was correlated with the number of vaginal (yeast) infections the women reported in the previous year. Other studies have connected stress to the development of genital herpes (VanderPlate, Aral, & Magder, 1988) and periodontal disease (Green et al., 1986). Researchers have also found an association between high stress and flareups of inflammatory bowel disease (Olden, 1998).

These are just a handful of representative examples of studies relating stress to physical diseases. Table 13.3 provides a longer list of health problems that have been linked to stress. Many of these stress-illness connections are based on tentative or inconsistent findings, but the sheer length and diversity of the list is remarkable. Why should stress increase the risk for so many kinds of illness? A partial answer may lie in the body's immune functioning.

The *immune response* is the body's defensive reaction to invasion by bacteria, viral agents, or other foreign substances. The immune response works to protect people from many forms of disease. Immune reactions are multifaceted, but they depend heavily on actions initiated by specialized white blood cells called *lymphocytes*. A wealth of studies indicate that experimentally induced stress can impair immune functioning *in animals* (Ader & Cohen, 1984, 1993; Moynihan & Ader, 1996). Stressors such as crowding, shock, and restraint reduce various aspects of lymphocyte reactivity in laboratory animals.

Some studies have also related stress to suppressed immune activity *in humans* (Kiecolt-Glaser & Glaser, 1995). In one study, medical students provided researchers with blood samples so that their immune response could be assessed (Kiecolt-Glaser et al., 1984). They provided a baseline sample a month before final exams and contributed a high-stress sample on the first day of their finals. The subjects also responded to the SRRS to measure recent stress. Reduced levels of immune activity were found during the extremely stressful finals week. Reduced immune activity was also correlated with higher scores on the SRRS. In another study, investigators exposed quarantined volunteers to respiratory viruses that cause the common cold and found that those under high stress were more likely to be infected by the viruses (Cohen, Tyrell, & Smith, 1993). Thus, scientists are beginning to assemble some impressive evidence that stress can

Table 13.3   Health Problems that May be Linked to Stress

Health Problem	Representative Evidence
Common cold	Stone et al. (1992)
Ulcers	Ellard et al. (1990)
Asthma	Sriram & Silverman (1998)
Headaches	Ghaemi, Irizarry, & Joseph (1998)
Menstrual discomfort	Siegel, Johnson, & Sarason (1979)
Vaginal infections	Williams & Deffenbacher (1983)
Genital herpes	VanderPlate, Aral, & Magder (1988)
Skin disorders	Fava et al. (1989)
Rheumatoid arthritis	Thomason et al. (1992)
Chronic back pain	Craufurd, Creed, & Jayson (1990)
Female reproductive problems	Seibel & McCarthy (1993)
Diabetes	Gonder-Frederick et al. (1990)
Complications of pregnancy	Pagel et al. (1990)
Hernias	Rahe & Holmes (1965)
Glaucoma	Cohen & Hajioff (1972)
Hyperthyroidism	Weiner (1978)
Hemophilia	Buxton et al. (1981)
Tuberculosis	Wolf & Goodell (1969)
Leukemia	Greene & Swisher (1969)
Stroke	Harmsen et al. (1990)
Appendicitis	Creed (1989)
Multiple sclerosis	Grant et al. (1989)
Periodontal disease	Marcenes & Sheiham (1992)
Hypertension	Pickering et al. (1996)
Cancer	Holland and Lewis (1993)
Coronary heart disease	Rosengren, Tibblin, & Wilhelmsen (1991)
AIDS	Ironson et al. (1994)
Inflammatory bowel disease	Olden (1998)
Epileptic seizures	Aird (1998)

temporarily suppress immune functioning (Glaser et al., 1999). This immunosuppression may be the key to many of the links between stress and illness.

Sizing Up the Link Between Stress and Illness

A wealth of evidence shows that stress is related to physical health, and converging lines of evidence suggest that stress contributes to the *causation* of illness. But we have to put this intriguing finding in perspective. Virtually all of the relevant research is correlational, so it can't demonstrate *conclusively* that stress causes illness (see Figure 13.8 on the next page). Subjects' elevated levels of stress and illness

Figure 13.8

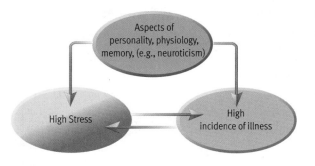

could both be due to a third variable, perhaps some aspect of personality. For instance, some evidence suggests that *neuroticism* may make people overly prone to interpret a variety of events as stressful and overly prone to interpret unpleasant sensations as symptoms of illness, thus inflating the correlation between stress and illness (Brett et al., 1990; Watson & Pennebaker, 1989).

In spite of methodological problems favoring inflated correlations, the research in this area consistently indicates that the *strength* of the relationship between stress and illness is modest. The correlations typically fall in the .20s and .30s. Clearly, stress is not an irresistible force that produces inevitable effects on health. Actually, this fact should come as no surprise, as stress is but one factor operating in a complex network of biopsychosocial determinants of health. Other key factors include one's genetic endowment, exposure to infectious agents and environmental toxins, nutrition, exercise, alcohol and drug use, smoking, use of medical care, and cooperation with medical advice. Furthermore, some people handle stress better than others, which is the matter we turn to next.

Factors Moderating the Impact of Stress

Some people seem to be able to withstand the ravages of stress better than others (Holohan & Moos, 1994). Why? Because a number of moderator variables can lessen the impact of stress on physical and mental health. We'll look at three key *moderator variables*—social support, optimism, and conscientiousness—to shed light on individual differences in how well people tolerate stress.

Social Support

Friends may be good for your health! This startling conclusion emerges from studies on social support as a moderator of stress. **Social support refers to various types of aid and succor provided by members of one's social networks.** In one study, Jemmott and Magloire (1988) examined the effect of social support on immune functioning in a group of students going through the stress of final exams. They found that students who reported stronger social support had higher levels of an antibody that plays a key role in warding off respiratory infections. Positive correlations between high social support and greater immune functioning have also been found in other studies (Uchino, Uno, & Holt-Lunstad, 1999).

Many other studies have found evidence that social support is favorably related to physical health (Uchino, Cacioppo, & Kiecolt-Glaser, 1996; Vogt et al., 1992). Social support seems to be good medicine for the mind as well as the body, as most studies find a positive association between social support and mental health (Davis, Morris, & Kraus, 1998). The mechanisms underlying the connection between social support and wellness are the subject of considerable debate and speculation (Hobfoll & Vaux, 1993). It appears that social support serves as a protective buffer during times of high stress, reducing the negative impact of stressful events. Furthermore, social support has its own positive effects on health, which may be apparent even when people aren't under great stress (Peirce et al., 1996).

Optimism

Defining **optimism as a general tendency to expect good outcomes**, Michael Scheier and Charles Carver (1985) found a correlation between optimism and relatively good physical health in a sample of college students. Another study found optimism to be associated with more effective immune functioning (Segerstrom et al., 1998). Research suggests that optimists cope with stress in more adaptive ways than pessimists (Carver & Scheier, 1999; Chang, 1996, 1998). Optimists are more likely to engage in action-oriented, problem-focused coping. They are more willing than pessimists to seek social support, and they are more likely to emphasize the positive in their appraisals of stressful events. In comparison, pessimists are more likely to deal with stress by giving up or engaging in denial.

In a related line of research, Christopher Peterson and Martin Seligman have studied how people explain bad events (personal setbacks, mishaps, disappointments, and such). They identified a *pessimistic explanatory style* in which some people tend to blame setbacks on their personal shortcomings. In a retrospective study of men who graduated from Harvard back in the 1940s, they found an association between this pessimistic explanatory style and relatively poor health (Peterson, Seligman, & Vaillant, 1988). In their attempt to explain this association, they speculate that pessimism leads to passive coping efforts and poor health care practices. A subsequent study also found an association between pessimism and suppressed immune function (Kamen-Siegel et al., 1991).

Conscientiousness

Optimism versus pessimism is not the only dimension of personality that has been examined as a possible moderator of physical health. Howard Friedman and his colleagues have found evidence that *conscientiousness,* one of the Big Five personality traits discussed in Chapter 12, may have an impact on physical health. Friedman et al. (1993) related personality measures to longevity in a sample of gifted children who have been followed closely by

researchers since 1921. Data were available on six personality traits, which were first measured when the subjects were children. The one trait that predicted greater longevity was conscientiousness. Friedman and his colleagues reasoned, logically enough, that conscientiousness may simply have fostered better health habits, but a follow-up study (Friedman et al., 1995) found little evidence that this was the case. Hence, the investigators have now turned their attention to how conscientiousness may have affected subjects' coping or stress tolerance.

Individual differences among people in social support, optimism, and conscientiousness explain why stress doesn't have the same impact on everyone. Differences in lifestyle may play an even larger role in determining health. We'll examine some critical aspects of lifestyle in the next section.

Courtesy of Martin E. P. Seligman

"The concept of explanatory style brings hope into the laboratory, where scientists can dissect it in order to understand how it works."
MARTIN SELIGMAN

Health-Imparing Behavior

Some people seem determined to dig an early grave for themselves. They do precisely those things that are bad for their health. For example, some people drink heavily even though they know that they're damaging their liver. Others eat all the wrong foods even though they know that they're increasing their risk of a second heart attack. Behavior that's downright *self-destructive* is surprisingly common. In this section we'll discuss how health is affected by smoking, poor nutrition, and lack of exercise, and we'll look at behavioral factors in AIDS. (The health risks of alcohol and drug use are discussed in Chapter 5.)

Smoking

The smoking of tobacco is widespread in our culture. Current consumption in the United States is around 2500 cigarettes a year per adult. Smokers face a much greater risk of premature death than nonsmokers (Schmitz, Jarvik & Schneider, 1997). For example, a 25-year-old male who smokes two packs a day has an estimated life expectancy *8.3 years shorter* than that of a similar nonsmoker (Schlaadt & Shannon, 1994). The increased health risks from smoking are positively correlated with the number of cigarettes smoked and their tar and nicotine content. Jarvik and Schneider (1992) put the health costs of smoking in perspective by noting that smoking accounts for roughly 60 times as many deaths per year as cocaine and heroin use combined.

Why are mortality rates higher for smokers? Smoking increases the likelihood of developing a surprisingly large range of diseases. Lung cancer and heart disease are the two types of illness that kill the largest number of smokers. However, smokers also have an elevated risk for oral, bladder, and kidney cancer, as well as cancers of the larynx, esophagus, and pancreas (Newcomb & Carbone, 1992); arteriosclerosis, hypertension, stroke, and other cardiovascular diseases (McBride, 1992); and bronchitis, emphysema, and other pulmonary diseases (Sherman, 1992). Most smokers know about the risks associated with tobacco use, but they tend to underestimate the actual risks as applied to themselves (Ayanian & Cleary, 1999).

Studies show that if people can give up smoking, their health risks decline reasonably quickly (Samet, 1992). Five to seven years after people stop smoking, their health risk is already noticeably lower than that of people who have continued to smoke (see Figure 13.9 on the next page). The health risks of people who give up tobacco continue to decline until they reach a normal level after about 15 years.

Unfortunately, it's very difficult to give up cigarettes. People who enroll in formal smoking cessation programs aren't any more successful than people who try to quit on their own (Cohen et al., 1989). Long-term success rates are in the vicinity of only 25%, and some studies report even lower figures. Nonetheless, the fact that there are nearly 40 million ex-smokers in the United States indicates

Web Link 13.3

healthfinder
Through the Department of Health and Human Services, the government has opened an ambitious online gateway to consumer-oriented information about health in all its aspects. Annotated descriptions are available for all resources identified in no-cost searches of this database.

Figure 13.9

Quitting smoking and cancer risk. Research indicates that various types of health risks associated with smoking decline gradually after people give up tobacco. The data shown here, from the U.S. Surgeon General's 1990 report on smoking, illustrate the overall effects on mortality rates. (Adapted from *The Health Benefits of Smoking Cessation: A Report of the Surgeon General 1990*, pp. V–VII. U.S. Department of Health and Human Services, Washington, D.C.)

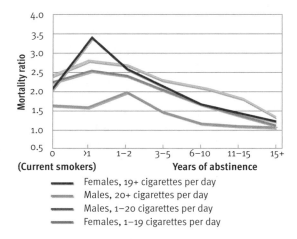

Females, 19+ cigarettes per day
Males, 20+ cigarettes per day
Males, 1–20 cigarettes per day
Females, 1–19 cigarettes per day

Web Link 13.4

Exercise and Sport Psychology For anyone wondering about how psychological science deals with sports and athletics generally, this site, maintained by Division 47 of the American Psychological Association, is an excellent starting point.

Knowing that their personal habits adversely affect their well-being, many people nonetheless persist in doing things that are self-destructive.

that it is possible to quit smoking successfully. Interestingly, many people fail several times before they eventually succeed. Evidence suggests that the readiness to give up smoking builds gradually as people cycle through periods of abstinence and relapse (Herzog et al., 1999; Prochaska, 1994).

Poor Nutritional Habits

Evidence is accumulating that patterns of nutrition influence susceptibility to a variety of diseases and health problems. Possible connections between eating patterns and diseases include the following:

1. Many factors influence the development of obesity, but chronic overeating often plays a prominent role. Overweight people have an increased risk of heart disease, hypertension, stroke, respiratory ailments, arthritis, diabetes, and back problems (Bray, 1990).

2. Heavy consumption of foods that elevate serum cholesterol level (eggs, cheeses, butter, shellfish, sausage, and the like) appears to increase the risk of heart disease (Muldoon, Manuck, & Matthews, 1990). Vulnerability to cardiovascular diseases may also be influenced by other dietary factors. For example, low-fiber diets may increase the likelihood of coronary disease (Ludwig et al., 1999; Wolk et al., 1999), and low consumption of fruit and vegetables may be associated with vulnerability to stroke (Joshipura et al., 1999).

3. High salt intake has long been thought to be a contributing factor to the development of high blood pressure (Kaplan, 1986), although there's still some debate about its role.

4. Diets high in fats and low in fiber have been implicated as possible contributors to some forms of cancer, especially cancers of the colon, prostate, and breast (S. Levy, 1985).

5. Vulnerability to osteoporosis, an abnormal loss of bone mass observed most commonly in postmenopausal women, appears to be elevated by a life-long pattern of inadequate calcium intake (Fahey & Gallagher-Allred, 1990).

Of course, nutritional habits interact with other factors to determine whether one develops a particular disease. Nonetheless, the examples just described indicate that eating habits are relevant to physical health.

Lack of Exercise

There is considerable evidence linking lack of exercise to poor health. Research indicates that regular exercise is associated with increased longevity (Lee, Hsieh, & Paffenbarger, 1995). Why would exercise help people live longer? Because physical fitness promotes a diverse array of specific benefits. For one thing, an appropriate exercise program can enhance cardiovascular fitness and thereby reduce susceptibility to deadly cardiovascular problems (Wei et al., 1999). Second, fitness may indirectly reduce one's risk for a variety of obesity-related health problems, such as diabetes and respiratory difficulties (Epstein et al., 1995). Third, recent studies suggest that physical fitness is also associated with a decreased risk for colon cancer in men and for breast and reproductive

© Bob Daemmrich/The Image Works

cancer in women (Marcus, Bock, & Pinto, 1997). The apparent link between exercise and reduced cancer risk has been a pleasant surprise for scientists, who are now scrambling to figure out the physiological mechanisms underlying this association.

Behavior and AIDS

At present, some of the most problematic links between behavior and health may be those related to AIDS. AIDS stands for *acquired immune deficiency syndrome,* **a disorder in which the immune system is gradually weakened and eventually disabled by the human immunodeficiency virus (HIV).** Being infected with the HIV virus is *not* equivalent to having AIDS. AIDS is the final stage of the HIV infection process, typically manifested about ten years after the original infection (Bartlett, 1993; Brettle & Leen, 1991). With the onset of AIDS, one is left virtually defenseless against a host of opportunistic infectious agents. AIDS inflicts its harm indirectly by opening the door to other diseases. The symptoms of AIDS vary widely depending on the specific constellation of diseases that one develops. Ultimately, AIDS usually is a fatal disorder. Unfortunately, the worldwide prevalence of this deadly disease continues to increase at an alarming rate (Mann & Tarantola, 1998).

Until recently, the average length of survival for people after the onset of the AIDS syndrome was about 18 to 24 months (Libman, 1992). Encouraging new advances in the treatment of AIDS with drugs called protease inhibitors hold out promise for substantially longer survival, but these drugs have been rushed into service and their long-term efficacy remains unknown (Bartlett & Moore, 1998; Kelly et al., 1998). Medical experts are concerned that the general public has gotten the impression that these treatments have transformed AIDS from a fatal disease to a manageable one, which is not the case (Mitka, 1999). Spurred by findings linking stress to immune function, researchers have sought to determine whether stress might speed up the progression of AIDS. Some studies have found a modest association between stress and the course of AIDS, but others have not. Taken as a whole, current evidence suggests that stress is not a key factor modulating how rapidly AIDS progresses (Glaser et al., 1999; Kalichman, 1995).

Transmission

The HIV virus is transmitted through person-to-person contact involving the exchange of bodily fluids, primarily semen and blood. The two principal modes of transmission in the United States have been sexual contact and the sharing of needles by intravenous (IV) drug users. In the United States, sexual transmission has occurred primarily among gay and bisexual men, but heterosexual transmission has increased in recent years (Rosenberg & Biggar, 1998). In the world as a whole, infection through heterosexual relations has been much more common from the beginning (see Figure 13.10). In heterosexual relations, male-to-female transmission is more prevalent than female-to-male transmission (Ickovics & Rodin, 1992). The HIV virus can be found in the tears and saliva of infected individuals, but the concentrations are low and there is no evidence that the infection can be spread through casual contact. Even most forms of noncasual contact, including kissing, hugging, and sharing food with infected individuals, appear safe (Kalichman, 1995).

Misconceptions

Misconceptions about AIDS are widespread. Ironically, the people who hold these misconceptions fall into two polarized camps. On the one hand, a great many people have unrealistic fears that AIDS can be readily transmitted through casual contact with infected individuals. These people worry unnecessarily about contracting AIDS from a handshake, a sneeze, or an eating utensil. They tend to be paranoid about interacting with homosexuals, thus fueling discrimination against gays in regard to housing, employment, and so forth. Some people also believe that it is dangerous to donate blood, when in fact blood *donors* are at no risk whatsoever.

On the other hand, many young heterosexuals who are sexually active with a variety of partners foolishly downplay their risk for HIV, naively

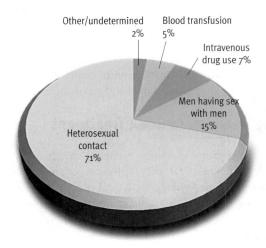

Other/undetermined 2%

Blood transfusion 5%

Intravenous drug use 7%

Men having sex with men 15%

Heterosexual contact 71%

Figure 13.10

HIV transmission worldwide. In the United States, about 80% of HIV transmission thus far has occurred among gay men or intravenous drug users, perhaps leading to misconceptions about the ease of transmission via heterosexual relations. However, in the world as a whole, heterosexual relations are the predominant mode of transmission, as these data show. (Data from *A Global Report: AIDS in the World*, by J. Mann, D. J. M. Tarantola, & T. W. Netter, 1992. Oxford University Press.)

Figure 13.11

A quiz on knowledge of AIDS. Because misconceptions about AIDS abound, it may be wise to take this brief quiz to test your knowledge of AIDS. (Adapted from *Understanding AIDS: A Guide for Mental Health Professionals*, by S. C. Kalichman, 1995. American Psychological Association. Reprinted by permission of the author.)

AIDS Risk Knowledge Test

Answer the following "true" or "false."

T   F   **1.** The AIDS virus cannot be spread through kissing.
T   F   **2.** A person can get the AIDS virus by sharing kitchens and bathrooms with someone who has AIDS.
T   F   **3.** Men can give the AIDS virus to women.
T   F   **4.** The AIDS virus attacks the body's ability to fight off diseases.
T   F   **5.** You can get the AIDS virus by someone sneezing, like a cold or the flu.
T   F   **6.** You can get AIDS by touching a person with AIDS.
T   F   **7.** Women can give the AIDS virus to men.
T   F   **8.** A person who got the AIDS virus from shooting up drugs cannot give the virus to someone by having sex.
T   F   **9.** A pregnant woman can give the AIDS virus to her unborn baby.
T   F   **10.** Most types of birth control also protect against getting the AIDS virus.
T   F   **11.** Condoms make intercourse completely safe.
T   F   **12.** Oral sex is safe if partners "do not swallow."
T   F   **13.** A person must have many different sexual partners to be at risk for AIDS.
T   F   **14.** It is more important to take precautions against AIDS in large cities than in small cities.
T   F   **15.** A positive result on the AIDS virus antibody test often occurs for people who do not even have the virus.
T   F   **16.** Only receptive (passive) anal intercourse transmits the AIDS virus.
T   F   **17.** Donating blood carries no AIDS risk for the donor.
T   F   **18.** Most people who have the AIDS virus look quite ill.

Answers: 1. T   2. F   3. T   4. T   5. F   6. F   7. T   8. F   9. T   10. F   11. F   12. F   13. F   14. F   15. F   16. F   17. T   18. F

assuming that they are safe as long as they avoid IV drug use and sexual relations with gay or bisexual men (Friedman & Goodman, 1992). They greatly underestimate the probability that their sexual partners previously may have used IV drugs or had unprotected sex with an infected individual. Also, many young people believe that prospective sexual partners who carry the HIV virus will exhibit telltale signs of illness. However, as we have already noted, having AIDS and being infected with HIV are not the same thing, and HIV carriers often remain healthy and symptom-free for many years after they are infected. In sum, many myths about AIDS persist, in spite of extensive efforts to educate the public about this complex and controversial disease. Figure 13.11 contains a short quiz to test your knowledge of the facts about AIDS.

Prevention

The behavioral changes that minimize the risk of developing AIDS are fairly straightforward, although making the changes is often much easier said than done (Coates & Collins, 1998). In all groups, the more sexual partners a person has, the higher the risk that one will be exposed to the HIV virus. Thus, people can reduce their risk by having sexual contacts with fewer partners and by using condoms to control the exchange of semen. It is also important to curtail certain sexual practices (in particular, anal sex) that increase the probability of semen/blood mixing. Intravenous drug users could greatly reduce their risk by abandoning their drug use, but their doing so is unlikely, since most are physically dependent on the drugs. Alternatively, they need to improve the sterilization of their needles and avoid sharing syringes with other users.

So far, we've seen that physical health may be affected by stress and by aspects of lifestyle. Next, we'll look at the importance of how people react to physical symptoms, health problems, and health care efforts.

Reactions to Illness

Some people respond to physical symptoms and illnesses by ignoring warning signs of developing diseases, while others actively seek to conquer their diseases. Let's examine the decision to seek medical treatment, communication with health providers, and factors that affect adherence to medical advice.

The Decision to Seek Treatment

Have you ever experienced nausea, diarrhea, stiffness, headaches, cramps, chest pains, or sinus problems? Of course you have; we all experience some of these problems periodically. However, whether we view these sensations as *symptoms* is a matter of individual interpretation. When two persons experience the same unpleasant sensations, one may shrug them off as a nuisance while the other may rush to a physician. Studies suggest that people who are relatively high in anxiety and neuroticism tend to report more symptoms of illness than others do (Feldman et al., 1999; Leventhal et al., 1996). Those who are extremely attentive to bodily sensations and health concerns also report more symptoms than the average person (Barsky, 1988).

Variations in the perceived seriousness and disruptiveness of symptoms help explain the differences among people in their readiness to seek medical treatment (Cameron, Leventhal, & Leventhal, 1993). The biggest problem in regard to treatment seeking is the tendency of many people to delay the pursuit of needed professional consultation. Delays can be critical because early diagnosis and quick intervention may facilitate more effective treatment of many health problems. Unfortunately, procrastination is the norm even when people are faced with a medical emergency, such as a heart attack. Why do people dawdle in the midst of a crisis? Robin DiMatteo (1991), a leading expert on patient behavior, mentions a number of reasons, noting that people delay because they often (a) misinterpret and downplay the significance of their symptoms, (b) fret about looking silly if the problem turns out to be nothing, (c) worry about "bothering" their physician, (d) are reluctant to disrupt their plans (to go out to dinner, see a movie, and so forth), and (e) waste time on trivial matters (such as taking a shower, gathering personal items, or packing clothes) before going to a hospital emergency room.

Communicating with Health Providers

About half of medical patients depart their doctors' offices not understanding what they have been told and what they are supposed to do (DiMatteo, 1991). This reality is most unfortunate because good communication is a crucial requirement for sound medical decisions, informed choices about treatment, and appropriate follow-through by patients (Gambone, Reiter, & DiMatteo, 1994).

There are many barriers to effective provider-patient communication (Beisecker, 1990; DiMatteo, 1997). Economic realities dictate that medical visits are generally quite brief, allowing little time for discussion. Many providers use too much medical jargon and overestimate their patients' understanding of technical terms. Patients who are upset and worried about their illness may simply forget to report some symptoms or to ask questions they meant to ask. Other patients are evasive about their real concerns because they fear a serious diagnosis. Many patients are reluctant to challenge doctors' authority and are too passive in their interactions with providers.

What can you do to improve your communication with health care providers? The key is to not be a passive consumer of medical services (Ferguson, 1993; Kane, 1991). Arrive at a medical visit on time, with your questions and concerns prepared in advance. Try to be accurate and candid in replying to your doctor's questions. If you don't understand something the doctor says, don't be embarrassed about asking for clarification. If you have doubts about the suitability or feasibility of your doctor's recommendations, don't be afraid to voice them.

Adherence to Medical Advice

Many patients fail to adhere to the instructions they receive from physicians and other health care professionals. Such nonadherence is a major problem in our medical care system. The evidence suggests that noncompliance with medical advice may occur 30% to 60% of the time (DiMatteo, 1994).

This point is not intended to suggest that you should passively accept all professional advice from medical personnel. However, when you have doubts about a prescribed treatment, you should speak up and ask questions. Passive resistance can backfire. For instance, if a physician sees no improvement in a patient who falsely insists that he has been taking his medicine, the physician may abandon an accurate diagnosis in favor of an inaccurate one. The inaccurate diagnosis could lead to inappropriate treatments that might be harmful to the patient.

Why don't people comply with the advice that they've sought out from highly regarded health care professionals? Physicians tend to attribute noncompliance to patients' personality traits, but research indicates that other factors are more important. Three considerations are especially prominent (DiMatteo & Friedman, 1982; Evans & Haynes, 1990; Ley, 1997):

Steve Walag, University of California, Riverside

"A person will not carry out a health behavior if significant barriers stand in the way, or if the steps interfere with favorite or necessary activities."
ROBIN DiMATTEO

Many patients do not comply with the directions they receive from their physicians. Research suggests that improvements in doctor-patient communication can increase medical compliance.

Stone/Steven Peters

1. Frequently, nonadherence occurs because the patient doesn't understand the instructions as given. Highly trained professionals often forget that what seems obvious and simple to them may be obscure and complicated to many of their patients.

2. Another key factor is how aversive or difficult the instructions are. If the prescribed regimen is unpleasant, adherence will tend to decrease. And the more that following instructions interferes with routine behavior, the less probable it is that the patient will cooperate successfully.

3. If a patient has a negative attitude toward a physician, the probability of noncompliance will increase. When patients are unhappy with their interactions with the doctor, they're more likely to ignore the medical advice provided, no matter how important it may be.

In response to the noncompliance problem, some health psychologists are exploring ways to increase patients' adherence to medical advice. They've found that the communication process between the practitioner and the patient is of critical importance. Courtesy, encouragement, reassurance, taking time to answer questions, and decreased reliance on medical jargon can improve compliance (DiNicola & DiMatteo, 1984; Hall, Roter, & Katz, 1988). Thus, there's a new emphasis in medicine on enhancing health care professionals' communication skills.

Putting It in Perspective

Which of our themes were prominent in this chapter? As you probably noticed, our discussion of stress and health illustrated multifactorial causation and the subjectivity of experience.

Our discussion of the psychology of health provided a particularly complex illustration of multifactorial causation. As we noted in Chapter 1, people are likely to think simplistically, in terms of single causes. In recent years, the highly publicized research linking stress to health has led many people to point automatically to stress as an explanation for illness. In reality, stress has only a modest impact on physical health. Stress can increase the risk for illness, but health is governed by a dense network of factors. Important factors include inherited vulnerabilities, exposure to infectious agents, health-impairing habits, reactions to symptoms, treatment-seeking behavior, compliance with medical advice, optimism, and social support. In other words, stress is but one actor on a crowded stage. This should be apparent in Figure 13.12, which shows the multitude of biopsychosocial factors that jointly influence physical health. It illustrates multifactorial causation in all its complexity.

The subjectivity of experience was demonstrated by the frequently repeated point that stress lies in the eye of the beholder. The same job promotion may be stressful for one person and invigorating for another. One person's pressure is another's challenge. When it comes to stress, objective reality is not nearly as important as subjective perceptions. More than anything else, the impact of stressful events seems to depend on how people view them. The critical importance of stress appraisals will continue to be apparent in our Personal Application on stress management. Many stress-management strategies depend on altering one's appraisals of events.

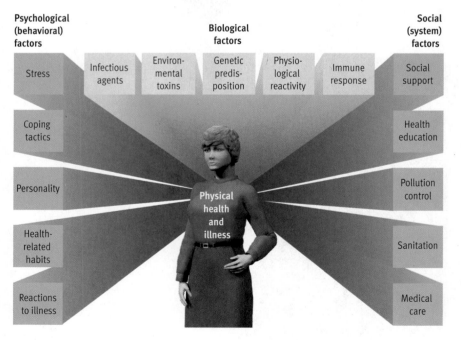

Psychological (behavioral) factors

Biological factors

Social (system) factors

Stress · Coping tactics · Personality · Health-related habits · Reactions to illness

Infectious agents · Environmental toxins · Genetic predisposition · Physiological reactivity · Immune response

Physical health and illness

Social support · Health education · Pollution control · Sanitation · Medical care

Figure 13.12

Biopsychosocial factors in health. Physical health can be influenced by a remarkably diverse set of variables, including biological, psychological, and social factors. The host of factors that affect health provide an excellent example of multifactorial causation.

Improving Coping and Stress Management

Answer the following "true" or "false."

_____ **1** The key to managing stress is to avoid or circumvent it.

_____ **2** It's best to suppress emotional reactions to stress.

_____ **3** Laughing at one's problems is immature.

_____ **4** Exercise has little or no impact on stress resistance.

Courses and books on stress management have multiplied at a furious pace in the last decade. They summarize experts' advice on how to cope with stress more effectively. How do these experts feel about the four statements above? As you'll see in this Personal Application, most would agree that all four are false.

The key to managing stress does not lie in avoiding it. Stress is an inevitable element in the fabric of modern life. As Hans Selye (1973) noted, "contrary to public opinion, we must not—and indeed can't—avoid stress" (p. 693). Thus, most stress-management programs train people to use more effective coping strategies. In this Application, we'll examine a variety of constructive coping tactics, beginning with Albert Ellis's ideas about changing one's appraisals of stressful events.

Reappraisal: Ellis's Rational Thinking

Albert Ellis (1977, 1985, 1996) is a prominent theorist who believes that people can short-circuit their emotional reactions to stress by altering their appraisals of stressful events. Ellis's insights about stress appraisal are the foundation for a widely used system of therapy that he devised. **Rational-emotive therapy is a treatment approach that focuses on altering clients' patterns of irrational thinking to reduce maladaptive emotions and behavior.** Ellis maintains that *you feel the way you think.* He

argues that problematic emotional reactions are caused by negative self-talk, which he calls catastrophic thinking. **Catastrophic thinking involves unrealistically pessimistic appraisals of stress that exaggerate the magnitude of one's problems.** Ellis uses a simple A-B-C sequence to explain his ideas (see Figure 13.13):

A: *Activating event.* The A in Ellis's system stands for the activating event that produces the stress. The activating event may be any potentially stressful transaction. Examples might include an automobile accident, the cancellation of a date, a delay while waiting in line at the bank, or a failure to get a promotion you were expecting.

B: *Belief system.* B stands for your belief about the event, or your appraisal of the stress. According to Ellis, people often view minor setbacks as disasters. Thus, they

engage in catastrophic thinking: "How awful this is. I can't stand it! Things never turn out fair for me. I'll never get promoted."

C: *Consequence.* C stands for the consequences of your negative thinking. When your appraisals of stressful events are highly negative, the consequence tends to be emotional distress. Thus, people feel angry, outraged, anxious, panic stricken, disgusted, or dejected.

Ellis asserts that most people don't understand the importance of phase B in this three-stage sequence. We unwittingly believe that the activating event (A) causes the consequent emotional turmoil (C). However, Ellis maintains that A does *not* cause C. It only appears to do so. Instead, Ellis asserts, B causes C. One's emotional distress is actually caused by one's catastrophic thinking in appraising stressful events.

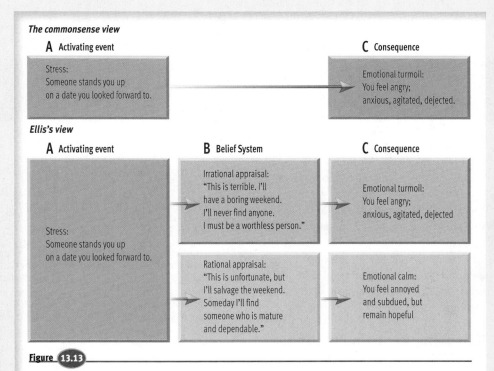

Figure 13.13

Albert Ellis's A-B-C model of emotional reactions. Although most people are prone to attribute their negative emotional reactions directly to events, Ellis argues that people *feel* the way they *think.*

Ellis theorizes that unrealistic appraisals of stress are derived from irrational assumptions that people hold. He maintains that if you scrutinize your catastrophic thinking, you'll find that your reasoning is based on a logically indefensible premise, such as "I must have approval from everyone" or "I must perform well in all endeavors." These faulty assumptions, which people often hold unconsciously, generate catastrophic thinking and emotional turmoil.

How can you reduce your unrealistic appraisals of stress? Ellis asserts that you must learn (1) how to detect catastrophic thinking and (2) how to dispute the irrational assumptions that cause it.

Humor as a Stress Reducer

A number of years ago, the Chicago suburbs experienced their worst flooding in about a century. Thousands of people saw their homes wrecked when two rivers spilled over their banks. As the waters receded, the flood victims returning to their homes were subjected to the inevitable TV interviews. A remarkable number of victims, surrounded by the ruins of their homes, joked about their misfortune. When the going gets tough, it may pay to laugh about it. In a study of coping styles, McCrae (1984) found that 40% of his subjects used humor to deal with stress.

While some psychologists have long suspected that humor might be a worthwhile coping response, evidence to that effect has emerged only in recent years (Abel, 1998; Lefcourt et al., 1995; Martin, 1996). In analyzing the stress-reducing effects of humor, Dixon (1980) noted that finding a humorous aspect in a stressful situation redefines the situation in a less threatening way. Dixon also pointed out that laughter can serve to discharge pent-up emotions. These dual functions of humor may make joking about life's difficulties a particularly useful coping strategy.

Releasing Pent-Up Emotions

Try as you might to redefine situations as less stressful, you no doubt still go through times when you feel wired with stress-induced tension. When this happens, there's merit in the commonsense notion that you should try to release the emotions welling up inside. Why? Because the physiological arousal that accompanies emotions can become problematic. For example, research suggests that people who inhibit the expression of anger and other emotions are somewhat more likely than other people to have elevated blood pressure (Jorgensen et al., 1996). Moreover, research suggests that efforts to actively suppress emotions result in increased autonomic arousal (Gross, 1998; Gross & Levenson, 1997) and decreased immune function (Petrie, Booth, & Pennebaker, 1998).

Although there's no guarantee of it, you can sometimes reduce your physiological arousal by expressing your emotions. Evidence is accumulating that writing or talking about life's difficulites can be valuable in dealing with stress (Clark, 1993; Smyth & Pennebaker, 1999). For example, in one study of college students, half of the subjects were asked to write three essays about their difficulties in adjusting to college. The other half wrote three essays about superficial topics. The subjects who wrote about their personal problems enjoyed better health in the following months than the other subjects did (Pennebaker, Colder, & Sharp, 1990). Subsequent similar studies have replicated this finding (Francis & Pennebaker, 1992; Greenberg, Wortman, & Stone, 1996) and shown that emotional disclosure is associated with better immune functioning (Esterling et al., 1994). So, if you can find a good listener, you may be able to discharge problematic emotions by letting your secret fears, misgivings, and suspicions spill out in a candid conversation.

Learning to Relax

Relaxation is a valuable stress-management technique that can soothe emotional turmoil and suppress problematic physiological arousal (Lehrer & Woolfolk, 1984, 1993). One study even suggests that relaxation training may improve the effectiveness of the immune response (Kiecolt-Glaser et al., 1985).

The value of relaxation became apparent to Herbert Benson (1975; Benson & Klipper, 1988) as a result of his research on

1 Sit quietly in a comfortable position.

2 Close your eyes.

3 Deeply relax all your muscles, beginning at your feet and progressing up to your face. Keep them relaxed.

4 Breathe through your nose. Become aware of your breathing. As you breathe out, say the word "one" silently to yourself. For example, breath in . . . out, "one"; in . . . out, "one"; and so forth. Breathe easily and naturally.

5 Continue for 10 to 20 minutes. You may open your eyes to check the time, but do not use an alarm. When you finish, sit quietly for several minutes, at first with your eyes closed and later with your eyes opened. Do not stand up for a few minutes.

6 Do not worry about whether you are successful in achieving a deep level of relaxation. Maintain a passive attitude and permit relaxation to occur at its own pace. When distracting thoughts occur, try to ignore them by not dwelling on them, and return to repeating "one." With practice, the response should come with little effort. Practice the technique once or twice daily but not within two hours after any meal, since digestive processes seem to interfere with the elicitation of the relaxation response.

Figure 13.14

Benson's relaxation procedure. To benefit from the procedure, you should practice it daily. (From *The Relaxation Response*, by Herbert Benson, M.D. and Miriam Z. Klipper. Copyright © 1975 by William Morrow & Company, Inc. By permission of HarperCollins Publishers, Inc.)

meditation. Benson, a Harvard Medical School cardiologist, believes that relaxation is the key to the beneficial effects of meditation. According to Benson, the elaborate religious rituals and beliefs associated with meditation are irrelevant to its effects. After "demystifying" meditation, Benson set out to devise a simple, nonreligious procedure that could provide similar benefits. He calls his procedure the *relaxation response*. From his study of a variety of relaxation techniques, Benson concluded that four factors promote effective relaxation: (1) a quiet, distraction-free environment, (2) a mental device to focus on (such as a sound or word recited repetitively), (3) a passive attitude, and (4) a comfortable position that isn't conducive to sleep. Benson's simple relaxation procedure is described in Figure 13.14. For full benefit, it should be practiced daily.

Minimizing Physiological Vulnerability

Your body is intimately involved in your response to stress, and the wear and tear of stress can be injurious to your health. To combat this potential problem, it helps to keep your body in relatively sound shape. The potential benefits of regular exercise are substantial. Regular exercise is associated with increased longevity (Paffenbarger, Hyde, & Wing, 1986). Moreover, research has shown that you don't have to be a dedicated athlete to benefit from exercise (Blair et al., 1989). Even a moderate amount of exercise reduces your risk of disease (see Figure 13.15). Successful participation in an exercise program can also lead to improvements in your mood, self-concept, and work efficiency (King, Taylor, & Haskell, 1993).

Embarking on an exercise program is difficult for many people. Exercise is time-consuming, and if you're out of shape, your initial attempts may be painful and discouraging. To avoid these problems, it's wise to (1) select an activity that you find enjoyable, (2) increase your participation gradually, (3) exercise regularly without overdoing it, and (4) reinforce yourself for your efforts (Greenberg, 1990). If you choose a competitive sport (such as basketball or tennis), try to avoid falling into the competition trap. If you become obsessed with winning, you'll put yourself under pressure and *add* to the stress in your life.

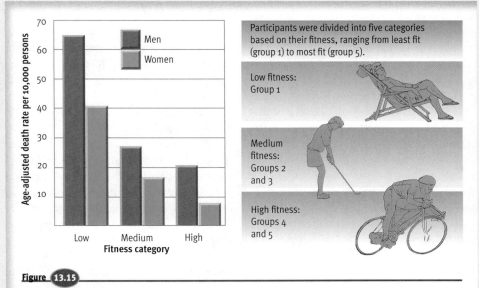

Figure 13.15

Physical fitness and mortality. Blair et al. (1989) studied death rates among men and women who exhibited low, medium, or high fitness. As you can see, fitness was associated with lower mortality rates in both sexes. (Based on data from "Physical Fitness and All-Cause Mortality," by S. N. Blair, W. H. Kohl, R. S. Paffenbarger, D. G. Clark, K. H. Cooper & L. W. Gibbons, 1989, *Journal of the American Medical Association, 262,* 2395–2401. Copyright © 1989 American Medical Association. Reprinted by permission.)

CRITICAL THINKING APPLICATION

Thinking Rationally about Health Statistics and Decisions

With so many conflicting claims about the best ways to prevent or treat diseases, how can anyone ever decide what to do? It seems that every day a report in the media claims that yesterday's health news was wrong. The inconsistency of health news is only part of the problem. We are also overwhelmed by health-related statistics. As mathematics pundit John Allen Paulos (1995, p. 133) puts it, "Health statistics may be bad for our mental health. Inundated by too many of them, we tend to ignore them completely, to accept them blithely, to disbelieve them closemindedly, or simply to misinterpret their significance."

Personal decisions about health-related issues can be extremely important, even a matter of life and death. It may not be easy, but it is particularly important to try to think rationally and systematically about health issues. In this Application, we will discuss a few insights that can help you to think critically about statistics on health risks, then we'll briefly outline a systematic approach to thinking through health decisions.

Evaluating Statistics on Health Risks

News reports seem to suggest that there are links between virtually everything people do, touch, and consume and some type of physical illness. For example, media have reported that coffee consumption is related to hypertension, that sleep loss is related to mortality, and that a high-fat diet is related to heart disease. It's enough to send even the most subdued person into a panic. Fortunately, your evaluation of data on health risks can become more sophisticated by considering the following.

Correlation Is No Assurance of Causation. It is not easy to conduct experiments on health risks, so the vast majority of studies linking lifestyle and demographic factors to diseases are correlational studies. Hence, it pays to remember that there may not be a causal link between two variables that happen to be correlated. Thus, when you hear that a factor is related to some disease, try to dig a little deeper and find out *why* scientists think this factor is associated with the disease. The suspected causal factor may be something vey different from what was measured.

Statistical Significance is Not Equivalent to Practical Significance. Reports on health statistics often emphasize that the investigators uncovered "statistically significant" findings. Statistically significant findings are results that are not likely to be due to chance fluctuations. Statistical significance is a useful concept, but it can sometimes be misleading (Matthey, 1998). Medical studies are often based on rather large samples, because they tend to yield more reliable conclusions than small samples. However, when a large sample is used, weak relationships and small differences between groups can turn out to be statistically significant, and these small differences may not have much practical importance. For example, in one study of sodium (salt) intake and cardiovascular disease, which used a sample of over 14,000 participants, He et al. (1999) found a statistically significant association between high sodium intake and the prevalence of hypertension among normal-weight subjects. However, this statistically significant difference was not particularly large. The prevalence of hypertension among subjects with the lowest sodium intake was 19.1% compared to 21.8% for subjects with the highest sodium intake—not exactly a difference worthy of panic.

Base Rates Should Be Considered in Evaluating Probabilities. In evaluating whether a possible risk factor is associated with some disease, people often fail to consider the base rates of these events and draw far-reaching conclusions based on what may be a matter of sheer coincidence. For example, Paulos (1995) discusses how a handful of cases in which cellular phone users developed brain cancer led to unfounded allegations that cell phones cause brain cancer. Although brain cancer is a rare disease, striking only about 6 out of 100,000 Americans per year, Paulos points out that with 10 million Americans using cell phones (at that time), one would expect to find 600 new cases of brain cancer annually among cell phone users. Given the paucity of reported cases, he playfully concludes that cellular phones must prevent brain cancer.

It is also useful to consider base rates in evaluating percentage increases in diseases. If the base rate of a disease is relatively low, a small increase can sound quite large if it is reported as a percentage. For example, in the He et al. (1999) study, the prevalence of diabetes among subjects with the lowest sodium intake was 2.1% compared to 3.8% for subjects with the highest sodium intake. Based on this small but statistically significant difference, one could say (the investigators did not) that high sodium intake was associated with a 81% increase ($[3.8 - 2.1] \div 2.1$) in the prevalence of diabetes.

Thinking Systematically About Health Decisions

Health decisions are oriented toward the future, which means that there are always uncertainties. And they usually involve weighing potential risks and benefits. None of these variables is unique to health decisions—uncertainty, risks, and benefits play prominent roles in economic and political decisions as well as in personal decisions. Let's apply some basic principles of quantitative reasoning to a treatment decision involving whether to prescribe Ritalin for a boy who has been diagnosed with attention deficit disorder (ADD). Keep in mind that the general principles applied in this example can be used for a wide variety of decisions.

Seek Information to Reduce Uncertainty. Gather information and check it carefully for accuracy, completeness, and the presence or absence of conflicting information. For example, is the diagnosis of ADD correct? Look for conflicting information that does not fit with this diagnosis. For example, if the child can sit and read for a long period of time, maybe the problem is an undetected hearing loss that makes him appear to be hyperactive in some situations.

As you consider the additional information, begin quantifying the degree of uncertainty or its "flip side," your degree of confidence that the diagnosis is correct. A specific value is usually not possible, but a general approximation along a dimension ranging from "highly confident" to "not at all confident" is useful in helping you think about the next step. If you decide that you are not confident about the diagnosis, you may be trying to solve the wrong problem.

Make Risk-Benefit Assessments. What are the risks and benefits of Ritalin? How likely is this child to benefit from Ritalin, and just how much improvement can be expected? If the child is 8 years old and unable to read and is miserable in school and at home, any treatment that could reduce his problems deserves serious consideration. As in the first step, the quantification is at an approximate level. A child who is two years behind at school and has no friends is, in a roughly quantifiable sense, worse off than one who is only 6 months behind in school and has at least one or two friends.

List Alternative Courses of Action. What are the alternatives to Ritalin? How well do they work? What are the risks associated with the alternatives, including the risk of falling further behind in school? Consider the pros and cons of each alternative. A special diet that sometimes works might be a good first step along with the decision to start drug therapy if the child does not show improvement over some time period. What are the relative success rates for different types of treatment for children like the one being considered? In order to answer these questions, you will need to use probability estimates in your decision making.

As you can see from this example, many parts of the problem have been quantified (confidence in the diagnosis, likelihood of improvement, probability of negative outcomes, and so forth). Precise probability values were not used because often the actual numbers are not known. Some of the quantified values reflect value judgments, others reflect likelihoods, and others assess the degree of uncertainty. The decision will have a different outcome depending on the particular child in question, the expected degree of success for alternative modes of treatment, and the associated risks for each treatment. It is important to avoid the (understandable) tendency to give up and do nothing or to just do what the experts say to do, because every course of action has associated risks. It is also important to remember that doing nothing is also a decision, and it may not be the best one.

The decision-making process is not complete even after a decision is made. New decisions are needed as the future unfolds. When new information and new alternatives become available, the decision needs to be reviewed. Decision makers need to adopt deliberate strategies that help them to look for information that conflicts with any decision that was previously made and to avoid the tendency to notice and act only on information that confirms what they already believe to be true.

If you are thinking that the quantification of many unknowns in decision making is a lot of work, you are right. But, it is work worth doing. Whenever there are important decisions to be made about health, the ability to think with numbers will help you reach a better decision. And yes, that assertion is a virtual certainty.

Table 13.4   Critical Thinking Skills Discussed in This Application

Skill	Description
Understanding the limitations of correlational evidence	The critical thinker understands that a correlation between two variables does not demonstrate that there is a causal link between the variables.
Understanding the limitations of statistical significance	The critical thinker understands that weak relationships can be statistically significant when large samples are used in research.
Utilizing base rates in making predictions and evaluating probabilities	The critical thinker appreciates that the initial proportion of some group or event needs to be considered in weighing probabilities.
Seeking information to reduce uncertainty	The critical thinker understands that gathering more information can often decrease uncertainty, and reduced uncertainty can facilitate better decisions.
Making risk-benefit assessments	The critical thinker is aware that most decisions have risks and benefits that need to be weighed carefully.
Generating and evaluating alternative courses of action	In problem solving and decision making, the critical thinker knows the value of generating as many alternatives as possible and assessing their advantages and disadvantages.

REVIEW

Key Ideas

The Nature of Stress

● Stress involves circumstances and experiences that are perceived as threatening. Stress is a common, everyday event, and even seemingly minor stressors or hassles can be problematic. Whether one feels stressed by events depends on how one appraises them.

● Major types of stress include frustration, conflict, change, and pressure. Frustration occurs when an obstacle prevents one from attaining some goal. There are three principal types of conflict: approach-approach, avoidance-avoidance, and approach-avoidance. The third type is especially stressful. Vacillation is a common response to conflict.

● A large number of studies with the SRRS suggest that change is stressful. Although this may be true, it is now clear that the SRRS is a measure of general stress rather than just change-related stress. Two kinds of pressure (to perform and conform) also appear to be stressful.

Responding to Stress

● Emotional reactions to stress typically include anger, fear, and sadness. Emotional arousal may interfere with coping. According to the inverted-U hypothesis, the optimal level of arousal on a task depends on the complexity of the task.

● Selye's general adaptation syndrome describes three stages in physiological reactions to stress: alarm, resistance, and exhaustion. There are two major pathways along which the brain sends signals to the endocrine system in response to stress.

● The behavioral response to stress takes the form of coping. Some coping responses are less than optimal. Two of these are striking out at others with acts of aggression and indulging oneself. Defense mechanisms protect against emotional distress through self-deception. Defensive illusions may sometimes be adaptive. Relatively healthy coping tactics are called constructive coping.

The Effects of Stress on Physical Health

● Stress appears to play a role in many types of illnesses, not just psychosomatic diseases. Type A behavior has been implicated as a contributing cause of coronary heart disease. Hostility may be the most toxic element of the Type A syndrome. Transient emotional reactions and depression have also been identified as cardiovascular risk factors.

● Researchers have found associations between stress and the onset of a great variety of specific diseases. Stress may play a role in a host of diseases because it can temporarily suppress the effectiveness of the immune system.

● While there's little doubt that stress can contribute to the development of physical illness, the link between stress and illness is modest in strength. Stress is only one factor in a complex network of biopsychosocial variables that shape health.

● There are individual differences in how much stress people can tolerate. Social support appears to buffer the effects of stress. Optimism and conscientiousness are personality traits that seem to moderate the relationship between stress and illness.

Health-Impairing Behavior

● People frequently display health-impairing lifestyles. Smokers have much higher mortality rates than nonsmokers because they are more vulnerable to a host of diseases. Poor nutritional habits have been linked to a variety of health problems. Lack of exercise elevates one's risk for cardiovascular diseases and perhaps for certain types of cancer.

● Aspects of behavior also influence one's risk of AIDS, which is transmitted through person-to-person contact involving the exchange of bodily fluids, primarily semen and blood. Misconceptions about AIDS are common, and the people who hold these misconceptions tend to fall into polarized camps, either overestimating or underestimating the risk of infection.

Reactions to Illness

● Ignoring physical symptoms may result in the delay of needed medical treatment. There are many barriers to effective communication between patients and health care providers.

● Nonadherence to medical advice is a major problem. The likelihood of noncompliance is greater when instructions are difficult to understand, when recommendations are difficult to follow, and when patients are unhappy with their doctor.

Putting It in Perspective

● Two of our integrative themes were prominent in this chapter. First, we saw that behavior and health are influenced by multiple causes. Second, we saw that experience is highly subjective, as stress lies in the eye of the beholder.

Personal Application • Improving Coping and Stress Management

● People use a variety of coping strategies, and some are healthier than others. Ellis emphasizes the importance of reappraising stressful events to detect and dispute catastrophic thinking. Humor may be useful in efforts to redefine stressful situations.

● In some cases, it may pay to release pent-up emotions by expressing them. Talking it out may help. Relaxation techniques, such as Benson's relaxation response, can reduce the wear and tear of stress. Physical vulnerability may also be reduced through regular exercise.

Critical Thinking Application • Thinking Rationally About Health Statistics and Decisions

● Evaluations of statistics on health risks can be enhanced by remembering that correlation is no assurance of causation, statistical significance is not equivalent to practical significance, and base rates need to be considered in assessing probabilities.

● In trying to think systematically about health decisions, one should seek information to reduce uncertainty, make risk-benefit assessments, and consider alternative courses of action.

Key Terms

Acquired immune
  deficiency syndrome
  (AIDS)
Aggression
Approach-approach
  conflict
Approach-avoidance
  conflict
Avoidance-avoidance
  conflict
Biopsychosocial
  model
Catastrophic thinking
Conflict
Constructive coping
Coping
Defense mechanisms
Frustration
General adaptation
  syndrome
Health psychology

Immune response
Internet addiction
Life changes
Optimism
Pressure
Rational-emotive
  therapy
Social support
Stress
Type A personality
Type B personality

Key People

Robin DiMatteo
Albert Ellis
Meyer Friedman and
  Ray Rosenman
Thomas Holmes and
  Richard Rahe
Richard Lazarus
Hans Selye
Shelley Taylor

PRACTICE TEST

1. The notion that health is governed by a complex interaction of biological, psychological, and sociocultural factors is referred to as the:
   A. medical model.
   B. multifactoral model.
   C. biopsychosocial model.
   D. interactive model.

2. The four principal sources of stress are:
   A. frustration, conflict, pressure, and anxiety.
   B. frustration, anger, pressure, and change.
   C. anger, anxiety, depression, and annoyance.
   D. frustration, conflict, pressure, and change.

3. When your boss tells you that a complicated report that you have not yet begun to write must be on her desk by this afternoon, you may experience:
   A. burnout.
   B. pressure.
   C. a double bind.
   D. catharsis.

4. You want very badly to ask someone for a date, but you are afraid to risk rejection. You are experiencing:
   A. an approach-avoidance conflict.
   B. an avoidance-avoidance conflict.
   C. optimized arousal.
   D. conformity pressure.

5. Research suggests that a high level of arousal may be most optimal for the performance of a task when:
   A. the task is complex.
   B. the task is simple.
   C. the rewards are high.
   D. an audience is present.

6. The alarm stage of Hans Selye's general adaptation syndrome is essentially the same as:
   A. the fight-or-flight response.
   B. constructive coping.
   C. approach-avoidance conflict.
   D. secondary appraisal.

7. The brain structure responsible for initiating action along the two major pathways through which the brain sends signals to the endocrine system is the:
   A. hypothalamus.
   B. thalamus.
   C. corpus callosum.
   D. medulla.

8. You have been doing poorly in your psychology class and are in danger of flunking. Which of the following qualifies as a defense mechanism in response to this situation?
   A. You seek the aid of a tutor.
   B. You decide to withdraw from the class and take it another time.
   C. You deny the reality that you are hopelessly behind in the class, convinced that you will somehow ace the final without seeking help.
   D. You consult with the instructor to see what you can do to pass the class.

9. Which of the following is least accurate in regard to defense mechanisms?
   A. They are normal in that everyone uses them.
   B. They are always unhealthy.
   C. They work through self-deception.
   D. They are used to ward off unpleasant emotions.

10. Which element of the Type A personality seems to be most strongly related to increased coronary risk?
    A. Time consciousness
    B. Perfectionism
    C. Ambitiousness
    D. Hostility

11. Possible explanations for the association of Type A behavior with coronary risk include:
    A. the greater physiological reactivity of Type A individuals compared to Type B's.
    B. Type A individuals' tendency to create more stress for themselves than others.
    C. the fact that Type A individuals tend to have less social support than others.
    D. all of the above.

12. Research has found that optimists are more likely than pessimists to:
    A. take their time in confronting problems.
    B. identify the negatives before they identify the positives.
    C. engage in action-oriented, problem-solving coping.
    D. seek social support only after they have exhausted all individual efforts to deal with the problem.

13. Which of the following has not been found to be a mode of transmission for the HIV virus?
    A. Sexual contact among homosexual men
    B. The sharing of needles by intravenous drug users
    C. Heterosexual contact
    D. Sharing food

14. The fact that health is governed by a dense network of factors is an illustration of the theme of:
    A. psychology in a sociohistorical context.
    B. the phenomenology of experience.
    C. multifactorial causation.
    D. empiricism.

15. The three phases in Albert Ellis's explanation of emotional reactions are:
    A. alarm, resistance, exhaustion.
    B. id, ego, superego.
    C. activating event, belief system, consequence.
    D. antecedent conditions, behavior, consequence.

Answers

1	C	page 395	**6**	A	pages 401–402	**11**	D	pages 407–408
2	D	pages 397–399	**7**	A	pages 402–403	**12**	C	page 410
3	B	page 399	**8**	C	pages 404–405	**13**	D	page 413
4	A	pages 397-398	**9**	B	pages 404–405	**14**	C	page 416
5	B	page 401	**10**	D	page 407	**15**	C	page 417

INFOTRAC COLLEGE EDITION

Go to the Wadsworth Psychology Study Center for quiz questions, research updates, interactive exercises, and suggested readings in INFOTRAC related to this chapter:
http://psychology.wadsworth.com/product/0534593100s

CHAPTER 14

© by Diana Ong/Superstock

Psychological Disorders

"**T**he government of the United States was overthrown more than a year ago! I'm the president of the United States of America and Bob Dylan is vice president!" So said Ed, the author of a prominent book on journalism, who was speaking to a college journalism class, as a guest lecturer. Ed also informed the class that he had killed both John and Robert Kennedy, as well as Charles de Gaulle, the former president of France. He went on to tell the class that all rock music songs were written about him, that he was the greatest karate expert in the universe, and that he had been fighting "space wars" for 2000 years. The students in the class were mystified by Ed's bizarre, disjointed "lecture," but they assumed that he was putting on a show that would eventually lead to

a sensible conclusion. However, their perplexed but expectant calm was shattered when Ed pulled a hatchet from the props he had brought with him and hurled the hatchet at the class! Fortunately, he didn't hit anyone, as the hatchet sailed over the students' heads. At that point, the professor for the class realized that Ed's irrational behavior was not a pretense. The professor evacuated the class quickly while Ed continued to rant and rave about his presidential administration, space wars, vampires, his romances with female rock stars, and his personal harem of 38 "chicks." (Adapted from Pearce, 1974)

Clearly Ed's behavior was abnormal. Even he recognized that when he agreed later to be admitted to a mental hospital, signing himself in as the "President of the United States of America." What causes such abnormal behavior? Does Ed have a mental illness, or does he just behave strangely? What is the basis for judging behavior as normal versus abnormal? How common are psychological disorders? These are just a few of the questions that we will address in this chapter as we discuss psychological disorders and their complex causes.

Abnormal Behavior: Myths and Realities

Misconceptions about abnormal behavior are common. Hence, we need to clear up some preliminary issues before we describe the various types of disorders. In this section, we will discuss (1) the medical model of abnormal behavior, (2) the criteria of abnormal behavior, and (3) the classification of psychological disorders.

The Medical Model Applied to Abnormal Behavior

In Ed's case, there's no question that his behavior was abnormal. But does it make sense to view his unusual and irrational behavior as an illness? This is a controversial question. **The *medical model* proposes that it is useful to think of abnormal behavior as a disease.** This point of view is the basis for many of the terms used to refer to abnormal behavior, including mental *illness,* psychological *disorder,* and *psychopathology (pathology* refers to manifestations of disease). The medical model gradually became the dominant way of thinking about abnormal behavior during the 18th and 19th centuries, and its influence remains strong today.

The medical model clearly represented progress over earlier models of abnormal behavior. Prior to the 18th century, most conceptions of abnormal behavior were based on superstition. People who behaved strangely were thought to be possessed by demons, to be witches in league with the devil, or to be victims of God's punishment. Their disorders were "treated" with chants, rituals, exorcisms, and such. If the people's behavior was seen as threatening, they were candidates for chains, dungeons, torture, and death (see Figure 14.1).

The rise of the medical model brought improvements in the treatment of those who exhibited abnormal behavior. As victims of an illness, they were viewed with more sympathy and less hatred and fear. Although living conditions in early asylums were often deplorable, gradual progress was made toward more humane care of the mentally ill. It took time, but ineffectual approaches to treatment eventually gave way to scientific investigation of the causes and cures of psychological disorders.

However, in recent decades, some critics have suggested that the medical model may have outlived its usefulness. A particularly vocal critic has been Thomas Szasz (1974, 1990). He asserts that "strictly speaking, disease or illness can affect only the body; hence there can be no mental illness. . . . Minds can be 'sick' only in the sense that jokes are 'sick' or economies are 'sick'" (1974, p. 267). He further argues that abnormal behavior usually involves a deviation from social norms rather than an illness. He contends that such deviations are "problems in living" rather than medical problems. According to Szasz, the medical model's disease analogy converts moral and social questions about what is acceptable behavior into medical questions.

Web Link 14.1

Mental Health Net
This is arguably the premier site on the Net to explore all aspects of mental health, including psychological disorders and treatment, professional issues, and information for consumers. It is a great starting point, with links to more than 8000 resources.

Figure 14.1

Historical conceptions of mental illness. In the Middle Ages people who behaved strangely were sometimes thought to be in league with the devil. The drawing on the right depicts some of the cruel methods used to extract confessions from suspected witches and warlocks. Some psychological disorders were also thought to be caused by demonic possession. The painting below is a detail from Di Benvenuto's *St. Catherine Exorcising Possessed Woman.* (Right: Culver Pictures, Inc.; below: *St. Catherine of Siena Exorcising a Possessed Woman,* c. 1500–1510. Girolamo Di Benvenuto. Denver Art Museum Collection, Gift of Samuel H. Kress Foundation Collection, 1967.171 © Denver Art Museum 2001.)

Although the criticism of Szasz has some merit, we'll take the position that the disease analogy continues to be useful, although one should remember that it is *only* an analogy. Medical concepts such as *diagnosis, etiology,* and *prognosis* have proven valuable in the treatment and study of abnormality. *Diagnosis* **involves distinguishing one illness from another.** *Etiology* **refers to the apparent causation and developmental history of an illness. A** *prognosis* **is a forecast about the probable course of an illness.** These medically based concepts have widely shared meanings that permit clinicians, researchers, and the public to communicate more effectively in their discussions of abnormal behavior.

Criteria of Abnormal Behavior

If your next-door neighbor scrubs his front porch twice every day and spends virtually all his time cleaning and recleaning his house, is he normal? If your sister-in-law goes to one physician after another seeking treatment for ailments that appear imaginary, is she psychologically healthy? How are we to judge what's normal and what's abnormal? More important, who's to do the judging?

These are complex questions. In a sense, *all* people make judgments about normality in that they all express opinions about others' (and perhaps their own) mental health. Of course, formal diagnoses of psychological disorders are made by mental health professionals. In making these diagnoses, clinicians rely on a variety of criteria, the foremost of which are the following:

1. *Deviance.* As Szasz has pointed out, people are often said to have a disorder because their behavior deviates from what their society considers acceptable. What constitutes normality varies somewhat from one culture to another, but all cultures have such norms. When people violate these standards and expectations, they may be labeled mentally ill. For example, *transvestic fetishism* is a sexual disorder in which a man achieves sexual arousal by dressing in women's clothing. This behavior is regarded as disordered because a man who wears a dress, brassiere, and nylons is deviating from our culture's norms. This example illustrates the arbitrary nature of cultural standards regarding normality, as the same overt behavior (cross-sex dressing) is acceptable for women and deviant for men.

2. *Maladaptive behavior.* In many cases, people are judged to have a psychological disorder because their everyday adaptive behavior is impaired. This is the key criterion in the diagnosis of substance use (drug) disorders. In and of itself, alcohol and drug use is not terribly unusual or deviant. However, when the use of cocaine, for instance, begins to interfere with a person's social or occupational functioning, a substance use disorder exists. In such cases, it is the maladaptive quality of the behavior that makes it disordered.

3. *Personal distress.* Frequently, the diagnosis of a psychological disorder is based on an individual's report of great personal distress. This is usually the criterion met by people who are troubled by depression or anxiety disorders. Depressed people, for instance, may or may not exhibit deviant or maladaptive behavior. Such people are usually labeled as having a disorder when they describe their subjective pain and suffering to friends, relatives, and mental health professionals.

Although two or three criteria may apply in a particular case, people are often viewed as disordered when only one criterion is met. As you may have already noticed, diagnoses of psychological disorders involve *value judgments* about what represents normal or abnormal behavior. The criteria of mental illness are not nearly as value-free as the criteria of physical illness. In evaluating physical diseases, people can usually agree that a weak heart or a malfunctioning kidney is pathological, regardless of their personal values. However, judgments about mental illness reflect prevailing cultural values, social trends, and political forces, as well as scientific knowledge (Kirk & Kutchins, 1992; Kutchins & Kirk, 1997).

In an effort to make the criteria of mental illness less value-laden, evolutionary psychologists have proposed that mental disorders ought to be viewed as harmful *evolutionary dysfunction*s (Cosmides & Tooby, 1999; Wakefield, 1999). According to this view, a dysfunction occurs when an evolved psychological mechanism does not perform its naturally selected function adequately or effectively. For example, the emotion of anxiety probably evolved because it enhanced organisms' vigilance for various sources of threat (Stevens & Price, 1996). But when someone becomes chronically anxious about everything, in the absence of real threats, the evolved mechanism is not operating effectively. The premise for the evolutionary argument is that once an evolved psychological mechanism has been described and its function identified, value-free critiera should be available to determine what represents a dysfunction. According to Wakefield (1992), these objective criteria would protect "against arbitrary labeling of socially disvalued conditions as disorders." Evolutionary theorists have provided a fresh perspective on an old and intractable problem, but

"Minds can be 'sick' only in the sense that jokes are 'sick' or economies are 'sick.'"
THOMAS SZASZ

Applying the Criteria of Abnormal Behavior

Check your understanding of the criteria of abnormal behavior by identifying the criteria met by each of the examples below and checking them off in the table provided. Remember, a specific behavior may meet more than one criterion. The answers are in Appendix A.

Behavioral examples

1. Alan's performance at work has suffered because he has been drinking alcohol to excess. Several co-workers have suggested that he seek help for his problem, but he thinks that they're getting alarmed over nothing. "I just enjoy a good time once in a while," he says.

2. Monica has gone away to college and feels lonely, sad, and dejected. Her grades are fine, and she gets along okay with the other students in the dormitory, but inside she's choked with gloom, hopelessness, and despair.

3. Boris believes that he's Napoleon reborn. He believes that he is destined to lead the U.S. military forces into a great battle to recover California from space aliens.

4. Natasha panics with anxiety whenever she leaves her home. Her problem escalated gradually until she was absent from work so often that she was fired. She hasn't been out of her house in nine months and is deeply troubled by her problem.

Criteria met by each example

	Maladaptive behavior	Deviance	Personal distress
1. Alan	✓		
2. Monica			✓
3. Boris	✓	✓	✓
4. Natasha	✓	✓	✓

critics have expressed a wide range of doubts about whether this approach can really yield objective critieria of psychological disorders (Fulford, 1999; Lilienfeld & Marino, 1999). One key problem is that there is often room for debate about exactly what the functions of various evolved mechanisms are (Spitzer, 1999).

Antonyms such as *normal* versus *abnormal* and *mental health* versus *mental illness* imply that people can be divided neatly into two distinct groups: those who are normal and those who are not. In reality, it is often difficult to draw a line that clearly separates normality from abnormality. On occasion, everybody acts in deviant ways, everyone displays some maladaptive behavior, and everyone experiences personal distress. People are judged to have psychological disorders only when their behavior becomes *extremely* deviant, maladaptive, or distressing. Thus, normality and abnormality exist on a continuum. It's a matter of degree, not an either-or proposition.

Psychodiagnosis: The Classification of Disorders

Obviously, we cannot lump all psychological disorders together without giving up all hope of understanding them better. A sound taxonomy of mental disorders can facilitate empirical research and enhance communication among scientists and clinicians (Williams, 1999). Thus, a great deal of effort has been invested in devising an elaborate system for classifying psychological disorders.

Guidelines for psychodiagnosis were extremely vague and informal prior to 1952 when the American Psychiatric Association unveiled its *Diagnostic and Statistical Manual of Mental Disorders* (Grob, 1991). This classification scheme described about 100 disorders. Revisions intended to improve the system were incorporated into the second edition (DSM-II) published in 1968, but the diagnostic guidelines were still pretty sketchy. However, the third edition (DSM-III) published in 1980, represented a major advance, as the diagnostic criteria were made much more explicit, concrete, and detailed to facilitate more consistent diagnoses across clinicians (Blacker & Tsuang, 1999). The current, fourth edition (DSM-IV), which was released in 1994, made use of intervening research to refine the critieria introduced in DSM-III. Each revision of the DSM system has expanded the list of disorders covered. The current version describes about three times as many types of psychological disorders as DSM-I.

The publication of DSM-III in 1980 introduced a new multiaxial system of classification, which asks for judgments about individuals on five separate dimensions, or "axes." Figure 14.2 provides an overview of the entire system and the five axes. The diagnoses of disorders are made on Axes I and II. Clinicians record most types of disorders on Axis I. They use Axis II to list long-running personality disorders or mental retardation. People may receive diagnoses on both Axes I and II.

The remaining axes are used to record supplemental information. A patient's physical disorders are listed on Axis III (General Medical Conditions). On Axis IV (Psychosocial and Environmental Problems), the clinician makes notations regarding the types of stress experienced by the individual in the past year. On Axis V (Global Assessment of Functioning), estimates are made of the individual's current level of adaptive functioning (in social and occupational behavior, viewed as a whole) and of the individual's highest level of functioning in the past year. Most theorists agree that the multiaxial system is a step in the right direction because it recognizes the importance of information besides a traditional diagnostic label.

We are now ready to start examining the specific types of psychological disorders. Obviously, we cannot cover all 200 or so disorders listed in DSM-IV. However, we will introduce most of the major categories of disorders to give you an overview of the many forms abnormal behavior takes. In discussing each set of disorders, we will begin with brief descriptions of the specific syndromes or subtypes that fall in the category. Then we'll focus on the *etiology* of the disorders in that category. Although many paths can lead to specific disorders, some are more common than others. We'll highlight some of the common paths to enhance your understanding of the roots of abnormal behavior.

Figure 14.2

Overview of the DSM diagnostic system. Published by the American Psychiatric Association, the *Diagnostic and Statistical Manual of Mental Disorders* is the formal classification system used in the diagnosis of psychological disorders. It is a *multi-axial* system, which means that information is recorded on the five axes described here. (Reprinted with permission from the *Diagnostic and Statistical Manual of Mental Disorders*, DSM-IV 1994. Copyright © 1994 American Psychiatric Association.)

Axis I
Clinical Syndromes

1. **Disorders usually first diagnosed in infancy, childhood, or adolescence**
   This category includes disorders that arise before adolescence, such as attention deficit disorders, autism, enuresis, and stuttering.

2. **Organic mental disorders**
   These disorders are temporary or permanent dysfunctions of brain tissue caused by diseases or chemicals. Examples are delirium, dementia, and amnesia.

3. **Substance-related disorders**
   This category refers to the maladaptive use of drugs and alcohol. This category requires an abnormal pattern of use, as with alcohol abuse and cocaine dependence.

4. **Schizophrenia and other psychotic disorders**
   The schizophrenias are characterized by psychotic symptoms (for example, grossly disorganized behavior, delusions, and hallucinations) and by over six months of behavioral deterioration. This category also includes delusional disorder and schizoaffective disorder.

5. **Mood disorders**
   The cardinal feature is emotional disturbance. These disorders include major depression, bipolar disorder, dysthymic disorder, and cyclothymic disorder.

6. **Anxiety disorders**
   These disorders are characterized by physiological signs of anxiety (for example, palpitations) and subjective feelings of tension, apprehension, or fear. Anxiety may be acute and focused (panic disorder) or continual and diffuse (generalized anxiety disorder).

7. **Somatoform disorders**
   These disorders are dominated by somatic symptoms that resemble physical illnesses. These symptoms cannot be fully accounted for by organic damage. This category includes somatization and conversion disorders and hypochondriasis.

8. **Dissociative disorders**
   These disorders all feature a sudden, temporary alteration or dysfunction of memory, consciousness, and identity, as in dissociative amnesia and dissociative identity disorder.

9. **Sexual and gender-identity disorders**
   There are three basic types of disorders in this category: gender identity disorders (discomfort with identity as male or female), paraphilias (preference for unusual acts to achieve sexual arousal), and sexual dysfunctions (impairments in sexual functioning).

10. **Eating Disorders**
    Eating disorders are severe disturbances in eating behavior characterized by preoccupation with weight concerns and unhealthy efforts to control weight. Examples include anorexia nervosa and bulimia nervosa.

Axis II
Personality Disorders or Mental Retardation

Personality disorders are longstanding patterns of extreme, inflexible personality traits that are deviant or maladaptive and lead to impaired functioning or subjective distress. *Mental retardation* refers to subnormal general mental ability accompanied by deficiencies in adaptive skills, originating before age 18.

Axis III
General Medical Conditions

Physical disorders or conditions are recorded on this axis. Examples include diabetes, arthritis, and hemophilia.

Axis IV
Psychosocial and Environmental Problems

Axis IV is for reporting psychosocial and environmental problems that may affect the diagnosis, treatment, and prognosis of mental disorders (Axis I and II). A psychosocial or environmental problem may be a negative life event, an environmental difficulty or deficiency, a familial or other interpersonal stress, an inadequacy of social support or personal resources, or another problem that describes the context in which a person's difficulties have developed.

Axis V
Global Assessment of Functioning (GAF) Scale

Code	Symptoms
100	Superior functioning in a wide range of activities
90	Absent or minimal symptoms, good functioning in all areas
80	Symptoms transient and expectable reactions to psychosocial stressors
70	Some mild symptoms or some difficulty in social, occupational, or school functioning, but generally functioning pretty well
60	Moderate symptoms or difficulty in social, occupational, or school functioning
50	Serious symptoms or impairment in social, occupational, or school functioning
40	Some impairment in reality testing or communication or major impairment in family relations, judgment, thinking, or mood
30	Behavior considerably influenced by delusions or hallucinations, serious impairment in communication or judgment, or inability to function in almost all areas
20	Some danger of hurting self or others, occasional failure to maintain minimal personal hygiene, or gross impairment in communication
10	Persistent danger of severely hurting self or others
1	

Anxiety Disorders

Everyone experiences anxiety from time to time. It is a natural and common reaction to many of life's difficulties. For some people, however, anxiety becomes a chronic problem. These people experience high levels of anxiety with disturbing regularity. *Anxiety disorders* are a class of disorders marked by feelings of excessive apprehension and anxiety. There are four principal types of anxiety disorders: generalized anxiety disorder, phobic disorder, panic disorder, and obsessive-compulsive disorder. Studies suggest that anxiety disorders are quite common, occurring in roughly 17% of the population (Robins & Regier, 1991).

Generalized Anxiety Disorder

The *generalized anxiety disorder* is marked by a chronic, high level of anxiety that is not tied to any specific threat. This anxiety is sometimes called "free-floating anxiety" because it is nonspecific. People with this disorder worry constantly about yesterday's mistakes and tomorrow's problems. In particular, they worry about minor matters related to family, finances, work, and personal illness (Sanderson & Barlow, 1990). They often dread decisions and brood over them endlessly. Their anxiety is frequently accompanied by physical symptoms, such as trembling, muscle tension, diarrhea, dizziness, faintness, sweating, and heart palpitations.

Phobic Disorder

In a phobic disorder, an individual's troublesome anxiety has a specific focus. A *phobic disorder* is marked by a persistent and irrational fear of an object or situation that presents no realistic danger. The following case provides an example of a phobic disorder:

Hilda is 32 years of age and has a rather unusual fear. She is terrified of snow. She cannot go outside in the snow. She cannot even stand to see snow or hear about it on the weather report. Her phobia severely constricts her day-to-day behavior. Probing in therapy revealed that her phobia was caused by a traumatic experience at age 11. Playing at a ski lodge, she was buried briefly by a small avalanche of snow. She had no recollection of this experience until it was recovered in therapy. (Adapted from Laughlin, 1967, p. 227)

As Hilda's unusual snow phobia illustrates, people can develop phobic responses to virtually anything.

Nonetheless, certain types of phobias are relatively common, including acrophobia (fear of heights), claustrophobia (fear of small, enclosed places), brontophobia (fear of storms), hydrophobia (fear of water), and various animal and insect phobias (Eaton, Dryman, & Weissman, 1991). Many people troubled by phobias realize that their fears are irrational but still are unable to calm themselves when confronted by a phobic object.

Panic Disorder and Agoraphobia

A *panic disorder* is characterized by recurrent attacks of overwhelming anxiety that usually occur suddenly and unexpectedly. These paralyzing attacks are accompanied by physical symptoms of anxiety. After a number of anxiety attacks, victims often become apprehensive, wondering when their next panic will occur. Their concern about exhibiting panic in public may escalate to the point where they are afraid to leave home. This fear creates a condition called agoraphobia, which is a common complication of panic disorders.

Agoraphobia is a fear of going out to public places (its literal meaning is "fear of the marketplace or open places"). Because of this fear, some people become prisoners confined to their homes, although many will venture out if accompanied by a trusted companion (Hollander, Simeon, & Gorman, 1999). As its name suggests, agoraphobia has traditionally been viewed as a phobic disorder. However, recent evidence suggests that agoraphobia shares more kinship with panic disorders than phobic disorders. Nonetheless, agoraphobia can occur independently of panic disorder, and some theorists question the wisdom of lumping panic and agoraphobia together in the DSM classification system (Noyes, 1988). The vast majority of people who suffer from panic disorder or agoraphobia are female (Rapee & Barlow, 1993).

Obsessive-Compulsive Disorder

Obsessions are *thoughts* that repeatedly intrude on one's consciousness in a distressing way. Compulsions are *actions* that one feels forced to carry out. Thus, an *obsessive-compulsive disorder (OCD)* is marked by persistent, uncontrollable intrusions of unwanted thoughts (obsessions) and urges to engage in senseless rituals (compulsions). To illustrate, let's examine the bizarre behavior of a man once reputed to be the wealthiest person in the world.

The famous industrialist Howard Hughes was obsessed with the possibility of being contaminated by germs. This led him to devise extraordinary rituals to minimize the possibility of such contamination. He would spend hours methodically cleaning a single telephone. He once wrote a three-page memo instructing assistants on exactly how to open cans of fruit for him. The following is just a small portion of the instructions that Hughes provided for a driver who delivered films to his bunga-low. "Get out of the car on the traffic side. Do not at any time be on the side of the car between the car and the curb. . . . Carry only one can of film at a time. Step over the gutter opposite the place where the sidewalk dead-ends into the curb from a point as far out into the center of the road as possible. Do not ever walk on the grass at all, also do not step into the gutter at all. Walk to the bungalow keeping as near to the center of the sidewalk as possible." (Adapted from Barlett & Steele, 1979, pp. 227–237)

The typical age of onset for OCD is early adult-hood (Sturgis, 1993). Obsessions often center on inflicting harm on others, personal failures, suicide, or sexual acts. People troubled by obsessions may feel that they have lost control of their mind. Compulsions usually involve stereotyped rituals that temporarily relieve anxiety. Common exam-ples include constant handwashing, repetitive cleaning of things that are already clean, and end-less rechecking of locks, faucets, and such (Foa & Kozak, 1995). Unusual rituals intended to bring good luck are also a common form of compulsive behavior. Although many of us can be compulsive at times, full-fledged obsessive-compulsive disor-ders occur in roughly 2.5% of the population (Hollander et al., 1999). The frequency of OCD seems to be increasing, but this trend may simply mean that clinicians have become more sensitive to the syndrome (Stoll, Tohen, & Baldessarini, 1992). Most victims of OCD exhibit both obsessions and compulsions, but some experience only one or the other (Foa & Kozak, 1995).

Etiology of Anxiety Disorders

Like most psychological disorders, anxiety disorders develop out of complicated interactions among a variety of factors. Classical conditioning, observa-tional learning, and cognitive and personality fac-tors appear especially important, but biological factors may also contribute to anxiety disorders.

CORBIS-Bettmann

AP/Wide World Photos

As a young man (shown in the photo), Howard Hughes was a handsome, dashing daredevil pilot and movie producer who appeared to be reasonably well adjusted. However, as the years went by, his behavior gradually became more and more mal-adaptive, as obsessions and compulsions came to domi-nate his life. In his later years (shown in the drawing), he spent most of his time in darkened rooms, naked, un-kempt, and dirty, following bizarre rituals to alleviate his anxieties. The drawing was done by an NBC artist and was based on descriptions from men who had seen Hughes.

Biological Factors

In studies that assess the impact of heredity on psy-chological disorders, investigators look at *concordance rates*. A *concordance rate* indicates the percentage of twin pairs or other pairs of relatives that exhibit the same disorder. If relatives who share more genetic similarity show higher concordance rates than relatives who share less genetic overlap, this finding supports the genetic hypothesis. *Twin studies*, which compare identical and fraternal twins (see Chapter 3), suggest that there may be a genetic predisposition to anxiety disorders (Kendler et al., 1992; Pauls et al., 1995). As you can see in Figure 14.3, concordance rates for identical twins are more than twice as high as for fraternal twins.

Figure 14.3

Twin studies of anxiety dis-orders. The concordance rate for anxiety disorders in identi-cal twins is higher than that for fraternal twins, who share less genetic overlap. These results suggest that there is a genetic predisposition to anxi-ety disorders. (Data based on Noyes et al., 1987; Slater & Shields, 1969; Torgersen, 1979, 1983)

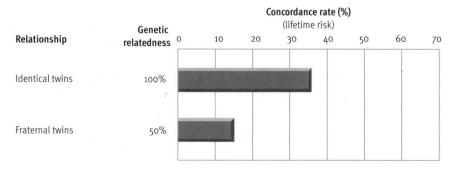

Relationship	Genetic relatedness	Concordance rate (%) (lifetime risk)
Identical twins	100%	~37
Fraternal twins	50%	~15

Another line of research suggests that *anxiety sensitivity* may make people vulnerable to anxiety disorders (Reiss, 1991; Schmidt, Lerew, & Jackson, 1999). According to this notion, some people are very sensitive to the internal physiological symptoms of anxiety and are prone to overreact with fear when they experience these symptoms. Anxiety sensitivity may fuel an inflationary spiral in which anxiety breeds more anxiety, which eventually spins out of control in the form of an anxiety disorder.

Recent evidence suggests that a link may exist between anxiety disorders and neurochemical activity in the brain. As you learned in Chapter 3, *neurotransmitters* are chemicals that carry signals from one neuron to another. Therapeutic drugs (such as Valium) that reduce excessive anxiety appear to alter neurotransmitter activity at GABA synapses. This finding and other lines of evidence suggest that disturbances in the neural circuits using GABA may play a role in some types of anxiety disorders (Longo, 1998). Abnormalities in other neural circuits using serotonin have recently been implicated in panic and obsessive-compulsive disorders (Deakin, 1998). Thus, scientists are beginning to unravel the neurochemical bases for anxiety disorders.

Conditioning and Learning

Many anxiety responses may be *acquired through classical conditioning* and *maintained through operant conditioning* (see Chapter 6). According to Mowrer (1947), an originally neutral stimulus (the snow in Hilda's case, for instance) may be paired with a frightening event (the avalanche) so that it becomes a conditioned stimulus eliciting anxiety (see Figure 14.4). Once a fear is acquired through

classical conditioning, the person may start avoiding the anxiety-producing stimulus. The avoidance response is negatively reinforced because it is followed by a reduction in anxiety. This process involves operant conditioning (see Figure 14.4). Thus, separate conditioning processes may create and then sustain specific anxiety responses (Levis, 1989). Consistent with this view, one study of people suffering from two types of social phobia found that 44% of the subjects could identify a traumatic conditioning experience that contributed to their disorder (Stemberger et al., 1995).

The tendency to develop phobias of certain types of objects and situations may be explained by Martin Seligman's (1971) concept of *preparedness*. Like many theorists, Seligman believes that classical conditioning creates most phobic responses. *However, he suggests that people are biologically prepared by their evolutionary history to acquire some fears much more easily than others.* His theory would explain why people develop phobias of ancient sources of threat (such as snakes and spiders) much more readily than modern sources of threat (such as electrical outlets or hot irons). Some laboratory studies of conditioned fears have yielded evidence consistent with Seligman's theory. For example, Cook and Mineka (1989) found that monkeys acquired conditioned fears of stimuli that they should be prepared to fear, such as snakes, with relative ease in comparison to other stimuli, such as flowers.

Cognitive Factors

Cognitive theorists maintain that certain styles of thinking make some people particularly vulnerable to anxiety disorders. According to these theorists, some people are more likely to suffer from anxiety problems than others because they tend to (a) misinterpret harmless situations as threatening, (b) focus excessive attention on perceived threats, and (c) selectively recall information that seems threatening (Beck, 1997; McNally, 1994, 1996). In one intriguing test of the cognitive view, anxious and nonanxious subjects were asked to read 32 sentences that could be interpreted in either a threatening or a nonthreatening manner (Eysenck et al., 1991). For instance, one such sentence was "The doctor examined little Emma's growth," which could mean that the doctor checked her height or the growth of a tumor. As Figure 14.5 shows, the anxious participants interpreted the sentences in a threatening way more often than the nonanxious participants did. Thus, consistent with our theme that human

Figure 14.4

Conditioning as an explanation for phobias.
(a) Many phobias appear to be acquired through classical conditioning, as a neutral stimulus becomes paired with an anxiety-arousing stimulus. **(b)** Once acquired, a phobia may be maintained through operant conditioning: avoidance of the phobic stimulus reduces anxiety, resulting in negative reinforcement (see Chapter 6 for more discussion of how conditioning may contribute to phobias).

(a) Classical conditioning: Acquisition of phobic fear

(b) Operant conditioning: Maintaining of phobic fear
(negative reinforcement)

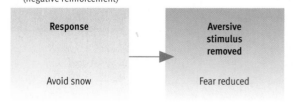

experience is highly subjective, the cognitive view holds that some people are prone to anxiety disorders because they see threat in every corner of their lives (Williams et al., 1997).

Personality

Certain personality traits appear to be related to the likelihood of developing anxiety disorders. Foremost among them is *neuroticism,* one of the Big Five traits described in Chapter 12. People who score high in neuroticism tend to be self-conscious, nervous, jittery, insecure, guilt-prone, and gloomy. Neuroticism is correlated with an elevated prevalance of anxiety disorders and a poorer prognosis for recovery (Clark, Watson, & Mineka, 1994). The mechanisms underlying this association are the subject of debate. One possibility is that the correlation between neuroticism and anxiety disorders may reflect the operation of a third variable—a genetic predisposition to both (Carey & DiLalla, 1994). This explanation appears plausible given the evidence for a genetic component in both neuroticism and anxiety disorders, but more research is needed to rule out other explanations.

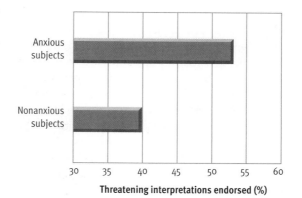

Stress

Finally, studies have supported the long-held suspicion that anxiety disorders are stress related. For instance, Faravelli and Pallanti (1989) found that patients with panic disorder had experienced a dramatic increase in stress in the month prior to the onset of their disorder. In another study, Brown and colleagues (1998) found an association between stress and the development of social phobia. Thus, there is reason to believe that high stress often helps precipitate the onset of anxiety disorders.

Figure 14.5

Cognitive factors in anxiety disorders. Eysenck and his colleagues (1991) compared how subjects with anxiety problems and nonanxious subjects tended to interpret sentences that could be viewed as threatening or non-threatening. Consistent with cognitive models of anxiety disorders, anxious subjects were more likely to interpret the sentences in a threatening light. (From "Bias in Interpretation of Ambiguous Sentences Related to Threat in Anxiety," by M. W. Eysenck, K. Mogg, J. May, A. Richards & A. Mathews, 1991, *Journal of Abnormal Psychology, 100,* 144–150. Copyright © 1991 by the American Psychological Association. Reprinted by permission of the author.)

Somatoform Disorders

Chances are, you have met people who always seem to be complaining about aches, pains, and physical maladies of doubtful authenticity. You may have thought to yourself, "It's all in his head," and concluded that the person exhibited a "psychosomatic" condition. However, the term *psychosomatic* is widely misused. **Psychosomatic diseases are genuine physical ailments caused in part by psychological factors, especially emotional distress.** These diseases, which include maladies such as ulcers, asthma, and high blood pressure, have a genuine organic basis and are not imagined ailments. They are recorded on the DSM axis for physical problems (Axis III). When physical illness appears *largely* psychological in origin, we are dealing with somatoform disorders, which are recorded on Axis I. **Somatoform disorders are physical ailments that cannot be fully explained by organic conditions and are largely due to psychological factors.** Although their symptoms are more imaginary than real, victims of somatoform disorders are *not* simply faking illness. Deliberate feigning of illness for personal gain is another matter altogether, called *malingering.*

People with somatoform disorders typically seek treatment from physicians practicing neurology,

internal medicine, or family medicine, instead of from psychologists or psychiatrists. Making accurate diagnoses of somatoform disorders can be difficult, because the causes of physical ailments are sometimes hard to identify. In some cases, somatoform disorders are misdiagnosed when a genuine organic cause for a person's physical symptoms goes undetected in spite of extensive medical examinations and tests (Martin & Yutzy, 1999).

We will discuss three specific types of somatoform disorders: somatization disorder, conversion disorder, and hypochondriasis. Diagnostic difficulties make it hard to obtain sound data on the prevalence of somatoform disorders. Hypochondriasis seems to be fairly common, but somatization and conversion disorder appear to be relatively infrequent (Barsky, 1989).

Somatization Disorder

Individuals with somatization disorder are often said to "cling to ill health." **A *somatization disorder* is marked by a history of diverse physical complaints that appear to be psychological in origin.** Somatization disorder occurs mostly in

Web Link 14.3

Mental Health: A Report of the Surgeon General
In late 1999, the Surgeon General issued the first comprehensive survey of the state of mental health in the United States. This report will provide a crucial foundation of statistics and other information for understanding the needs for mental health care in the first decade of the 21st century.

Psychological Disorders   **433**

women (Martin & Yutzy, 1999) and often coexists with depression and anxiety disorders (Fink, 1995). Victims report an endless succession of minor physical ailments that seem to wax and wane in response to the stress in their lives (Servan-Schreiber, Kolb, & Tabas, 1999). They usually have a long and complicated history of medical treatment from many doctors. The distinguishing feature of this disorder is the diversity of the victims' physical complaints. Over the years, they report a mixed bag of cardiovascular, gastrointestinal, pulmonary, neurological, and genitourinary symptoms. The unlikely nature of such a smorgasbord of symptoms occurring together often alerts a physician to the possible psychological basis for the patient's problems.

Conversion Disorder

Conversion disorder is characterized by a significant loss of physical function (with no apparent organic basis), usually in a single organ system. Common symptoms include partial or complete loss of vision, partial or complete loss of hearing, partial paralysis, severe laryngitis or mutism, and loss of feeling or function in limbs, such as that seen in the following case:

Mildred was a rancher's daughter who lost the use of both of her legs during adolescence. Mildred was at home alone one afternoon when a male relative attempted to assault her. She screamed for help, and her legs gave way as she slipped to the floor. She was found on the floor a few minutes later when her mother returned home. She could not get up, so she was carried to her bed. Her legs buckled when she made subsequent attempts to walk on her own. Due to her illness, she was waited on hand and foot by her family and friends. Neighbors brought her homemade things to eat or to wear. She became the center of attention in the household. (Adapted from Cameron, 1963, pp. 312–313)

People with conversion disorder are usually troubled by more severe ailments than people with somatization disorder. In some cases of conversion disorder, there are telltale clues about the psychological origins of the illness because the patient's symptoms are not consistent with medical knowledge about their apparent disease. For instance, the loss of feeling in one hand that is seen in "glove anesthesia" is inconsistent with the known facts of neurological organization (see Figure 14.6).

Hypochondriasis

Hypochondriacs constantly monitor their physical condition, looking for signs of illness. Any tiny alteration from their physical norm leads them to conclude that they have contracted a disease. **Hypochondriasis (more widely known as hypochondria) is characterized by excessive preoccupation with one's health and incessant worry about developing physical illnesses.** When hypochondriacs are assured by their physician that they do not have any real illness, they often are skeptical and disbelieving. They frequently assume that the physician must be incompetent, and they go shopping for another doctor. Hypochondriacs don't subjectively suffer from physical distress as much as they *overinterpret* every conceivable sign of illness. Hypochondria often appears alongside other psychological disorders, especially anxiety disorders and depression (Simon & VonKorff, 1991). For example, Howard Hughes's obsessive-compulsive disorder was coupled with profound hypochondria.

Etiology of Somatoform Disorders

Inherited aspects of physiological functioning may predispose people to somatoform disorders (Weiner, 1992). However, available evidence suggests that these disorders are largely a function of personality and learning. Let's look at personality factors first.

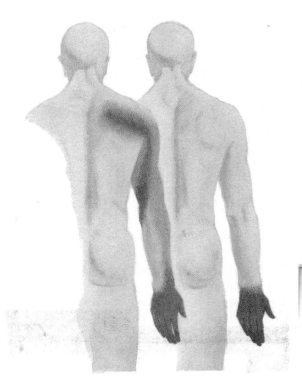

Figure 14.6

Glove anesthesia.
In conversion disorders, the physical complaints are sometimes inconsistent with the known facts of physiology. For instance, given the patterns of nerve distribution in the arm shown in (a), it is impossible that a loss of feeling in the hand exclusively, as shown in (b), has a physical cause, indicating that the patient's problem is psychological in origin.

Personality Factors

People with certain types of personality traits seem to be particularly prone to develop somatoform disorders. The prime candidates are people with *histrionic* personality characteristics (Nemiah, 1985; Slavney, 1990). The histrionic personality tends to be self-centered, suggestible, excitable, highly emotional, and overly dramatic. Such people thrive on the attention that they get when they become ill.

Cognitive Factors

In recent years, theorists have devoted increased attention to how cognitive peculiarities might contribute to somatoform disorders. For example, Barsky, Wyshak, and Klerman (1990) assert that some people focus excessive attention on their internal physiological processes and amplify normal bodily sensations into symptoms of distress, which lead them to pursue unnecessary medical treatment. Recent evidence suggests that people with somatoform disorder tend to draw catastrophic conclusions about minor bodily complaints (Rief, Hiller, & Margraf, 1998). They also seem to apply a faulty standard of good health, equating health with a complete absence of symptoms and discomfort, which is unrealistic (Barsky et al., 1993).

The Sick Role

Perplexing though it may seem, some people grow fond of the role associated with being sick (Lubkin, 1990). Their complaints of physical symptoms may be reinforced by indirect benefits derived from their illness. What are the benefits commonly associated with physical illness? One payoff is that becoming ill is a superb way to avoid having to confront life's challenges. Many people with somatoform disorders are avoiding facing up to marital problems, career frustrations, family responsibilities, and the

CONCEPT **CHECK 14.2**

Distinguishing Anxiety and Somatoform Disorders

Check your understanding of the nature of anxiety and somatoform disorders by making preliminary diagnoses for the cases described below. Read each case summary and write your tentative diagnosis in the space provided. The answers are in Appendix A.

1. Malcolm religiously follows an exact schedule every day. His showering and grooming ritual takes 2 hours. He follows the same path in walking to his classes every day, and he always sits in the same seat in each class. He can't study until his apartment is arranged perfectly. Although he tries not to, he thinks constantly about flunking out of school. Both his grades and his social life are suffering from his rigid routines.

Preliminary diagnosis: *Obsessive - Compulsive*

2. Jane has been unemployed for the last eight years because of poor health. She has suffered through a bizarre series of illnesses of mysterious origin. Troubles with devastating headaches were followed by months of chronic back pain. Then she developed respiratory problems, frequently gasping for breath. Her current problem is stomach pain. Physicians have been unable to find any physical basis for her maladies.

Preliminary diagnosis: *Somatoform*

3. Nathan owns a small restaurant that's in deep financial trouble. He dreads facing the possibility that his restaurant will fail. One day, he suddenly loses all feeling in his right arm and the ability to control the arm. He's hospitalized for his condition, but physicians can't find any organic cause for his arm trouble.

Preliminary diagnosis: *Conversion*

like. After all, when you're sick, others cannot place great demands on you.

Attention from others is another payoff that may reinforce complaints of physical illness. When people become ill, they command the attention of family, friends, co-workers, neighbors, and doctors. The sympathy that illness often brings may strengthen the person's tendency to feel ill. This clearly occurred in Mildred's case of conversion disorder. Her illness paid handsome dividends in terms of attention, consolation, and kindhearted assistance from others.

Dissociative Disorders

Dissociative disorders are among the more unusual syndromes that we will discuss. **Dissociative disorders are a class of disorders in which people lose contact with portions of their consciousness or memory, resulting in disruptions in their sense of identity.** We'll describe three dissociative syndromes—dissociative amnesia, dissociative fugue, and dissociative identity disorder—all of them relatively uncommon.

Dissociative Amnesia and Fugue

Dissociative amnesia and fugue are overlapping disorders characterized by serious memory deficits. **Dissociative amnesia is a sudden loss of memory for important personal information that is too extensive to be due to normal forgetting.** Memory losses may occur for a single traumatic event (such as an automobile accident or home fire) or for an extended period of time surrounding the event. Cases of amnesia have been observed after people have experienced disasters, accidents, combat stress, physical abuse, and rape, or after they have witnessed the violent death of a parent, among other things (Arrigo & Pezdek, 1997; Loewenstein, 1996). **In *dissociative fugue*, people lose their memory for their entire lives along with their sense of personal identity.** These people forget their name, their family, where they live, and where they work! In spite of this wholesale forgetting, they remember matters unrelated to their identity, such as how to drive a car and how to do math.

Dissociative Identity Disorder

Dissociative identity disorder (DID) involves the coexistence in one person of two or more largely complete, and usually very different, personalities. The name for this disorder used to be *multiple personality disorder,* which still enjoys informal usage. In dissociative identity disorder, the divergences in behavior go far beyond those that people normally display in adapting to different roles in life. People with "multiple personalities" feel that they have more than one identity. Each personality has his or her own name, memories, traits, and physical mannerisms. Although rare, this "Dr. Jekyll and Mr. Hyde" syndrome is frequently portrayed in novels, movies, and television shows. In popular media portrayals, the syndrome is often mistakenly called *schizophrenia*. As you will see later, schizophrenic disorders are entirely different.

In dissociative identity disorder, the various personalities are often unaware of each other (Eich et al., 1997). In other words, the experiences of a specific personality are only recalled by that personality and not the others. The alternate personalities commonly display traits that are quite foreign to the original personality. For instance, a shy, inhibited person might develop a flamboyant, extraverted alternate personality. Transitions between identities often occur suddenly. The disparities between identities can be bizarre, as different personalities may assert that they are different in age, race, gender, and sexual orientation (Kluft, 1996).

The 1980s saw a dramatic increase in the diagnosis of multiple-personality disorder. Some theorists believe that these disorders used to be underdiagnosed—that is, they often went undetected (Saxe et al., 1993; Spiegel & Maldonado, 1999). However, other theorists argue that a handful of clinicians have begun overdiagnosing the condition and that some clinicians even contribute to the emergence of DID (McHugh, 1995; Powell & Gee, 1999). Consistent with this view, a survey of all the psychiatrists in Switzerland found that 90% of them had never seen a case of dissociative identity disorder, whereas three of the psychiatrists had each seen more than 20 patients with dissociative identity disorder (Modestin, 1992). The data from this study suggest that 6 psychiatrists (out of 655 surveyed) accounted for two-thirds of the dissociative identity disorder diagnoses in Switzerland.

Etiology of Dissociative Disorders

Psychogenic amnesia and fugue are usually attributed to excessive stress. However, relatively little is known about why this extreme reaction to stress occurs in a tiny minority of people but not in the vast majority who are subjected to similar stress.

The causes of dissociative identity disorder are particularly obscure. Some skeptical theorists, such as Nicholas Spanos (1994, 1996) and others (Lilienfeld et al., 1999) believe that people with multiple personalities are engaging in intentional role playing to use mental illness as a face-saving excuse for their personal failings. Spanos also argues that a small minority of therapists help create DID in their patients by subtly encouraging the emergence of alternate personalities. According to Spanos, dissociative identity disorder is a creation of modern North American culture, much as demonic possession was a creation of early Christianity. To bolster his argument, he discusses how DID patients' symptom presentations seem to have been influenced by popular media. For example, the typical multiple-personality patient used to report having two or three personalities, but since the publication of *Sybil* (Schreiber, 1973) and other books describing patients with many personalities, the average number of alternate personalities has climbed to about 15. In a similar vein, there has been a dramatic upsurge in the number of DID patients reporting that they were victims of ritual satanic abuse during childhood that dates back to the publication of *Michelle Remembers* (Smith & Pazder, 1980), a book about a DID patient who purportedly was tortured by a satanic cult.

In spite of these troubling concerns, many clinicians are convinced that multiple-personality disorder is an authentic disorder (Gleaves, 1996; Kihlstrom, Tataryn, & Hoyt, 1993). They argue that there is no incentive for either patients or therapists to manufacture cases of DID, which are often greeted with skepticism and outright hostility. They maintain that most cases of DID are rooted in severe emotional trauma that occurred during childhood (Draijer & Langeland, 1999). A substantial majority of people with multiple personalities report a history of disturbed home life, beatings and rejection from parents, and sexual abuse (Lewis et al., 1997; Scroppo et al., 1998). In the final analysis, however, very little is known about the causes of dissociative identity disorder, which remains a controversial diagnosis.

Mood Disorders

What did Abraham Lincoln, Marilyn Monroe, Ernest Hemingway, Winston Churchill, Janis Joplin, and Leo Tolstoy have in common? Yes, they all achieved great prominence, albeit in different ways at different times. But, more pertinent to our interest, they all suffered from severe mood disorders. Although mood disorders can be terribly debilitating, people with mood disorders may still achieve greatness, because such disorders tend to be *episodic*. In other words, mood disturbances often come and go, interspersed among periods of normality. These episodes of disturbance can vary greatly in length, but they typically last 5-6 months.

Mood disorders **are a class of disorders marked by emotional disturbances of varied kinds that may spill over to disrupt physical, perceptual, social, and thought processes.** There are two basic types of mood disorders: unipolar and bipolar (see Figure 14.7). People with *unipolar disorder* experience emotional extremes at just one end of the mood continuum, as they are troubled only by *depression*. People with *bipolar disorder* experience emotional extremes at both ends of the mood continuum, going through periods of both *depression and mania* (excitement and elation). The mood swings in bipolar disorder can be patterned in many ways.

Major Depressive Disorder

Everyone gets depressed once in a while. Thus, the line between normal and abnormal depression can be difficult to draw (Kendler & Gardner, 1998). Ultimately, a subjective judgment is required. Crucial considerations in this judgment include the duration of the depression and its disruptive effects. When a depression significantly impairs everyday adaptive behavior for more than a few weeks, there is reason for concern.

In *major depressive disorder* **people show persistent feelings of sadness and despair and a loss of interest in previous sources of pleasure.** Negative emotions form the heart of the depressive syndrome, but many other symptoms may also appear. The most common symptoms of depression

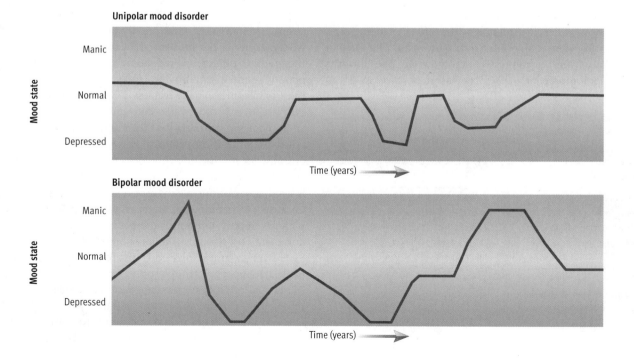

Figure 14.7

Episodic patterns in mood disorders. Time-limited episodes of emotional disturbance come and go unpredictably in mood disorders. People with unipolar disorders suffer from bouts of depression only, whereas people with bipolar disorders experience both manic and depressive episodes. The time between episodes of disturbance varies greatly with the individual and the type of disorder.

Tipper Gore and Ted Turner are two well-known figures who have struggled with mood disorders.

of people who suffer from depression experience more than one episode over the course of their lifetime (Dubovsky & Buzan, 1999).

How common are depressive disorders? Very common. Research suggests that about 7% of Americans endure a depressive disorder at some time (Weissman et al., 1991). However, a large-scale study using more probing interview techniques estimated that the lifetime prevalence of depression may be as high as 17% (Blazer et al., 1994). Moreover, evidence suggests that the prevalence of depression is increasing, as it is higher in more recent age cohorts (Lewinsohn et al., 1993). The factors underlying this rise in depression are not readily apparent, and researchers are scrambling to collect data that might shed light on this unanticipated trend. Researchers also find that the prevalence of depression is about twice as high in women as it is in men (Culbertson, 1997). The many possible explanations for this gender gap are the subject of considerable debate (Nolen-Hoeksema & Girgus, 1994).

Bipolar Disorder

Bipolar disorder (formerly known as manic-depressive disorder) is marked by the experience of both depressed and manic periods. The symptoms seen in manic periods generally are the opposite of those seen in depression (see Table 14.1 for a comparison). In a manic episode, a person's mood becomes elevated to the point of euphoria. Self-esteem skyrockets as the person bubbles over with optimism, energy, and extravagant plans. He or she becomes hyperactive and may go for days without sleep. The individual talks rapidly and shifts topics wildly, as his or her mind races at breakneck speed. Judgment is often impaired. Some people in manic periods gamble impulsively, spend money frantically, or become sexually reckless. Like depressive disorder, bipolar disorder varies considerably in severity.

You may be thinking that the euphoria in manic episodes sounds appealing. If so, you are not entirely wrong. In their milder forms, manic states can seem attractive. The increases in energy, self-esteem, and optimism can be deceptively seductive. Because of the increase in energy, many bipolar patients report temporary surges of productivity and creativity (Goodwin & Jamison, 1990).

However, bipolar mood disorder ultimately proves to be very troublesome for most victims. Manic periods often carry a paradoxical negative undercurrent of uneasiness and irritability (Dilsaver et al., 1999). Moreover, mild manic episodes usually escalate to higher levels that become scary and

are summarized and compared with the symptoms of mania in Table 14.1. Depressed people often give up activities that they used to find enjoyable. For example, a depressed person might quit going bowling or might give up a favorite hobby like photography. Reduced appetite and insomnia are common. People with depression often lack energy. They tend to move sluggishly and talk slowly. Anxiety, irritability, and brooding are commonly observed. Self-esteem tends to sink as the depressed person begins to feel worthless. Depression plunges people into feelings of hopelessness, dejection, and boundless guilt. The severity of abnormal depression varies considerably. The onset of depression can occur at any point in the life span. The median duration of depressive episodes is five months (Solomon et al., 1997). The vast majority (75%–95%)

Table 14.1 Comparisons of Common Symptoms in Manic and Depressive Episodes

Characteristics	Manic Episode	Depressive Episode
Emotional	Elated, euphoric, very sociable, impatient at any hindrance	Gloomy, hopeless, socially withdrawn, irritable
Cognitive	Characterized by racing thoughts, flight of ideas, desire for action, and impulsive behavior; talkative, self-confident; experiencing delusions of grandeur	Characterized by slowness of thought processes, obsessive worrying, inability to make decisions, negative self-image, self-blame, and delusions of guilt and disease
Motor	Hyperactive, tireless, requiring less sleep than usual, showing increased sex drive and fluctuating appetite	Less active, tired, experiencing difficulty in sleeping, showing decreased sex drive and decreased appetite

From *Abnormal Psychology: The Problem of Maladaptive Behavior*, 5/E, by I. G. Sarason & B. G. Sarason © 1987, p. 283. Reprinted by permission of Prentice-Hall, Inc., Englewood Cliffs, NJ.

disturbing. Impaired judgment leads many victims to do things that they greatly regret later, as you'll see in the following case history:

Robert, a dentist, awoke one morning with the idea that he was the most gifted dental surgeon in his tri-state area. He decided that he should try to provide services to as many people as possible, so that more people could benefit from his talents. Thus, he decided to remodel his two-chair dental office, installing 20 booths so that he could simultaneously attend to 20 patients. That same day he drew up plans for this arrangement, telephoned a number of remodelers, and invited bids for the work. Later that day, impatient to get rolling on his remodeling, he rolled up his sleeves, got himself a sledgehammer, and began to knock down the walls in his office. Annoyed when that didn't go so well, he smashed his dental tools, washbasins and X-ray equipment. Later, Robert's wife became concerned about his behavior and summoned two of her adult daughters for assistance. The daughters responded quickly, arriving at the family home with their husbands. In the ensuing discussion, Robert—after bragging about his sexual prowess—made advances toward his daughters. He had to be subdued by their husbands. (Adapted from Kleinmuntz, 1980, p. 309)

Although not rare, bipolar disorder is much less common than unipolar disorder. Bipolar disorder affects a little over 1% of the population (Wittchen, Knauper, & Kessler, 1994). Unlike depressive disorder, bipolar disorder is seen equally often in males and females (Tohen & Goodwin, 1995). As Figure 14.8 shows, the onset of bipolar disorder is age related, with the peak of vulnerability occurring between the ages of 20 and 29 (Goodwin & Jamison, 1990).

Etiology of Mood Disorders

Quite a bit is known about the etiology of mood disorders, although the puzzle hasn't been assembled completely. There appear to be a number of routes into these disorders, involving intricate interactions between psychological and biological factors.

Genetic Vulnerability

The evidence strongly suggests that genetic factors influence the likelihood of developing major depression or bipolar disorder (Dubovsky & Buzan, 1999). *Twin studies* have found a huge disparity between identical and fraternal twins in concordance rates for mood disorders. The concordance rate for identical twins is much higher (see Figure 14.9). This evidence suggests that heredity can create a *predisposition* to

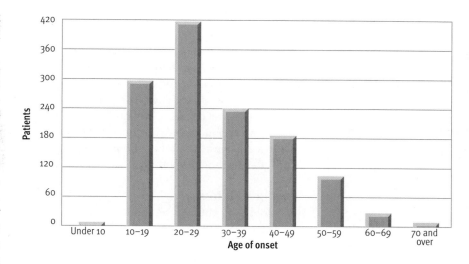

mood disorders. Environmental factors probably determine whether this predisposition is converted into an actual disorder. A recent study found that genetic vulnerability may play a larger role in women's depression than in men's (Bierut et al., 1999). The influence of genetic factors also appears to be stronger for bipolar disorder than for unipolar disorder (Knowles, Kaufmann, & Rieder, 1999).

Neurochemical Factors

Heredity may influence susceptibility to mood disorders by creating a predisposition toward certain types of neurochemical abnormalities in the brain. Correlations have been found between mood disorders and the activity of two neurotransmitters in the brain: norepinephrine and serotonin (Nemeroff, 1998; Zaleman, 1995). Originally, abnormalities at norepinephrine (NE) synapses were believed to be

Figure 14.8

Age of onset for bipolar mood disorder. The onset of bipolar disorder typically occurs in adolescence or early adulthood. The data graphed here, which were combined from ten studies, show the distribution of age of onset for 1304 bipolar patients. As you can see, bipolar disorder emerges most frequently during the 20s decade. (Figure 6-1, "Age of Onset for Bipolar Mood Disorder," from *Manic-Depressive Illness*, by Frederick K. Goodwin and Kay R. Jamison [p. 132]. Copyright © 1990 by Oxford University Press, Inc. Used by permission of Oxford University Press.)

Figure 14.9

Twin studies of mood disorders. The concordance rate for mood disorders in identical twins is much higher than that for fraternal twins, who share less genetic overlap. These results suggest that there must be a genetic predisposition to mood disorders. The disparity in concordance between the two types of twins is greater for mood disorders than for either anxiety disorders (see Figure 14.3) or schizophrenic disorders (see Figure 14.13), which suggests that genetic factors may be particularly important in mood disorders. (Data from Gershon, Berrettini & Goldin, 1989)

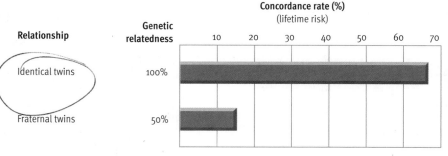

most critical (see Figure 14.10). Depression was thought to be due to decreased secretion of NE and mania to increased release of NE. Further research eventually demonstrated that this picture was much too simple (Schildkraut, Green, & Mooney, 1985). Although researchers still think that disturbances in neural circuits using norepinephrine contribute to mood disorders, the preponderance of evidence suggests that aberrations in serotonin circuits may be more important (Delgado et al., 1992).

Cognitive Factors

 11b

A variety of theories emphasize how cognitive factors contribute to depressive disorders. We will discuss Aaron Beck's (1976, 1987) influential cognitive theory of depression in Chapter 15, where his approach to therapy is described. In this section, we'll examine Martin Seligman's *learned helplessness model* of depression and its most recent descendant, *hopelessness theory*. Based largely on animal research, Seligman (1974) proposed that depression is caused by *learned helplessness*—passive "giving up" behavior produced by exposure to unavoidable aversive events (such as uncontrollable shock in the laboratory). He originally considered learned helplessness to be a product of conditioning but eventually revised his theory, giving it a cognitive slant. The reformulated theory of learned helplessness postulated that the roots of depression lie in how people explain the setbacks and other negative events that they experience (Abramson, Seligman, & Teasdale, 1978). According to Seligman (1990), people who exhibit a *pessimistic explanatory style* are especially vulnerable to depression. These people tend to attribute their setbacks to their personal flaws instead of situational factors, and they tend to draw global, far-reaching conclusions about their personal inadequacies based on these setbacks.

Hopelessness theory builds on these insights by postulating a sense of hopelessness as the "final pathway" leading to depression and by incorporating additional factors that may interact with explanatory style to foster this sense of hopelessness (Abramson, Alloy, & Metalsky, 1995). According to hopelessness theory, a pessimistic explanatory style is just one of several or more factors—along with high stress, low self-esteem, and so forth—that may contribute to hopelessness, and thus depression. Although hopelessness theory casts a wider net than the learned helplessness model, it continues to emphasize the importance of people's *cognitive reactions* to the events in their lives.

In accord with this line of thinking, Susan Nolen-Hoeksema (1991) has found that depressed people who *ruminate* about their depression remain depressed longer than those who try to distract themselves (Just & Alloy, 1997). People who respond to depression with rumination repetitively focus their attention on their depressing feelings, thinking constantly about how sad, lethargic, and unmotivated they are. According to Nolen-Hoeksema (1995), excessive rumination tends to extend and amplify individuals' episodes of depression. She believes that women are more likely to ruminate than men and that this disparity may be the primary reason why depression is more prevalent in women.

Figure 14.10

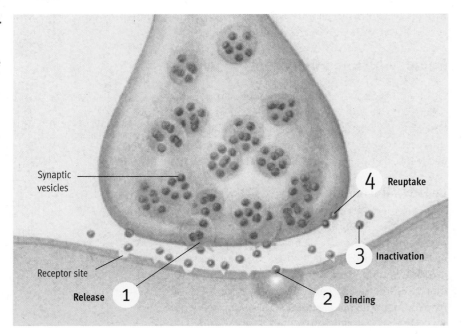

Hypotheses about the neurochemical bases for depression.
Neurochemical models of depression originally posited that depression is associated with lowered levels of activation at norepinephrine (NE) synapses. At first it was assumed that the reduction in NE activity was due to decreased release of NE (1), but studies eventually suggested that reduced sensitivity of NE receptors (2) also played a role. The hypothesis linking low NE levels to depression is supported by evidence that two major classes of antidepressant drugs increase NE levels. Tricyclic antidepressants appear to inhibit reuptake (3), leaving more NE in the synapse, while MAO inhibitors seem to slow the inactivation of NE (4). The picture is complicated greatly by the fact that newer and more effective antidepressants (such as Prozac) inhibit reuptake (4) at *serotonin* synapses. Thus, the current thinking is that complex imbalances in *several* neurotransmitter systems may contribute to depression.

Synaptic vesicles

Receptor site

Release **1**

2 Binding

3 Inactivation

4 Reuptake

In sum, cognitive models of depression maintain that negative thinking is what leads to depression in many people. The principal problem with cognitive theories is their difficulty in separating cause from effect (Barnett & Gotlib, 1988). Does negative thinking cause depression? Or does depression cause negative thinking (see Figure 14.11)? A *clear* demonstration of a causal link between negative thinking and depression is not possible because it would require manipulating people's explanatory style (which is not easy to change) in sufficient degree to produce full-fledged depressive disorders (which would not be ethical). However, recent research has provided impressive evidence consistent with a causal link between negative thinking and vulnerability to depression. Lauren Alloy and her colleagues (1999) assessed the explanatory style of a sample of first-year college students who were not depressed at the outset of the study. The students were characterized as being at high risk or low risk for depression based on whether they exhibited a negative cognitive style. The follow-up data over the next 2.5 years on students who had no prior history of depression showed dramatic differences between the two groups in vulnerability to depression. During this relatively brief period, a major depressive disorder emerged in 17% of the high-risk students in comparison to only 1% of the low-risk students. These high-risk subjects also displayed a much greater incidence of minor depressive episodes (39% versus 6%). These findings and other data from the study suggest that negative thinking makes people more vulnerable to depression.

Interpersonal Roots

Behavioral approaches to understanding depression emphasize how inadequate social skills put people on the road to depressive disorders (Lewinsohn & Gotlib, 1995; Segrin & Abramson, 1994). According to this notion, depression-prone people lack the social finesse needed to acquire many important kinds of reinforcers, such as good friends, top jobs, and desirable spouses (see Figure 14.12). This paucity of reinforcers could understandably lead to negative emotions and depression. Consistent with this theory, researchers have found correlations between poor social skills and depression (Dykman et al., 1991). For example, Joiner (1997) found that shyness was a risk factor for depression among people who had relatively little social support.

Another interpersonal factor is that depressed people tend to be depressing (Joiner, 1994). Individuals suffering from depression often are irritable and pessimistic. They complain a lot and

aren't particularly enjoyable companions. As a consequence, depressed people tend to court rejection from those around them (Joiner & Metalsky, 1995). Depressed people thus have fewer sources of social support than nondepressed people. Social rejection and lack of support may in turn aggravate and deepen a person's depression (Potthoff, Holahan, & Joiner, 1995).

Precipitating Stress

Mood disorders sometimes appear mysteriously in people who are leading benign, nonstressful lives. For this reason, experts used to believe that stress has little influence on mood disorders. However, advances in the measurement of personal stress have altered this picture. The evidence available today suggests the existence of a moderately strong link between stress and the onset of mood disorders (Kendler, Karkowski, & Prescott, 1999; Kessler, 1997). Stress also appears to affect how people with mood disorders respond to treatment and whether they experience a relapse of their disorder (Monroe et al., 1996).

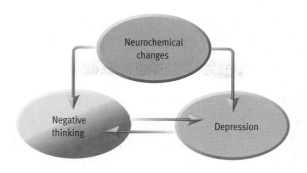

Figure 14.11

Interpreting the correlation between negative thinking and depression. Cognitive theories of depression assert that consistent patterns of negative thinking cause depression. Although these theories are highly plausible, depression could cause negative thoughts, or both could be caused by a third factor, such as neurochemical changes in the brain.

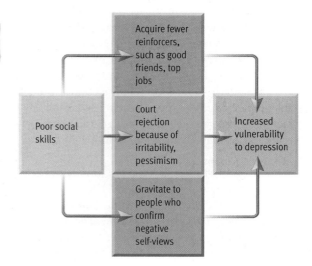

Figure 14.12

Interpersonal factors in depression. Behavioral theories about the etiology of depression emphasize how inadequate social skills may contribute to the development of the disorder.

Schizophrenic Disorders

Literally, *schizophrenia* means "split mind." However, when Eugen Bleuler coined the term in 1911 he was referring to the fragmentation of thought processes seen in the disorder—not to a "split personality." Unfortunately, writers in the popular media often assume that the split-mind notion, and thus schizophrenia, refers to the rare syndrome in which a person manifests two or more personalities. As you have already learned, this syndrome is actually called *multiple-personality disorder* or *dissociative identity disorder.* Schizophrenia is a much more common, and altogether different, type of disorder.

Schizophrenic disorders **are a class of disorders marked by delusions, hallucinations, disorganized speech, and deterioration of adaptive behavior.** How common is schizophrenia? Prevalence estimates suggest that about 1%–1.5% of the population may suffer from schizophrenic disorders (Tsuang, Faraone, & Green, 1999). That may not sound like much, but it means that in the United States alone there may be 3–4 million people troubled by schizophrenic disturbances.

General Symptoms

There are a number of distinct schizophrenic syndromes, but they share some general characteristics that we will examine before looking at the subtypes. Many of these characteristics are apparent in the following case history, adapted from Sheehan (1982).

Sylvia was first diagnosed as schizophrenic at age 15. She has been in and out of many types of psychiatric facilities since then. She has never been able to hold a job for any length of time. During severe flare-ups of her disorder, her personal hygiene deteriorates. She rarely washes, wears clothes that neither fit nor match, smears makeup on heavily but randomly, and slops food all over herself. Sylvia occasionally hears voices talking to her. Sylvia tends to be argumentative, aggressive, and emotionally volatile. Over the years, she has been involved in innumerable fights with fellow patients, psychiatric staff members, and strangers. Her thoughts can be highly irrational, as is apparent from the following quote.

"Mick Jagger wants to marry me. If I have Mick Jagger, I don't have to covet Geraldo Rivera. Mick Jagger is St. Nicholas and the Maharishi is Santa Claus. I want to form a gospel rock group called the Thorn Oil, but Geraldo wants me to be the music critic on Eyewitness News, so what can I do? Got to listen to my boyfriend.

Teddy Kennedy cured me of my ugliness. I'm pregnant with the son of God. I'm going to marry David Berkowitz and get it over with. Creedmoor is the headquarters of the American Nazi Party. They're eating the patients here. Archie Bunker wants me to play his niece on his TV show. I work for Epic Records. I'm Joan of Arc. I'm Florence Nightingale. The door between the ward and the porch is the dividing line between New York and California. Divorce isn't a piece of paper, it's a feeling. Forget about Zip Codes. I need shock treatments. The body is run by electricity. My wiring is all faulty. A fly is a teenage wasp. I'm marrying an accountant. I'm in the Pentecostal Church, but I'm considering switching my loyalty to the Charismatic Church." (Adapted from Sheehan, 1982; quotation from pp. 104–105)

Sylvia's case clearly shows that schizophrenic thinking can be bizarre and that schizophrenia can be a severe and debilitating disorder. Although no single symptom is inevitably present, the following symptoms are commonly seen in schizophrenia (Black & Andreasen, 1999; Grebb & Cancro, 1989).

Irrational Thought

Disturbed, irrational thought processes are the central feature of schizophrenic disorders. Various kinds of delusions are common. **Delusions** **are false beliefs that are maintained even though they clearly are out of touch with reality.** For example, one patient's delusion that he is a tiger (with a deformed body) has persisted for 15 years (Kulick, Pope, & Keck, 1990). More typically, affected persons believe that their private thoughts are being broadcast to other people (Maher & Spitzer, 1993). They may also believe that thoughts are being injected into their mind against their will. In *delusions of grandeur,* people maintain that they are famous or important. Sylvia expressed an endless array of grandiose delusions, such as thinking that Mick Jagger wanted to marry her, that she had dictated the hobbit stories to J. R. R. Tolkien, and that she was going to win the Nobel prize for medicine.

In addition to delusions, the schizophrenic person's train of thought deteriorates. Thinking becomes chaotic rather than logical and linear. A "loosening of associations" occurs, as the person shifts topics in disjointed ways. The quotation from Sylvia illustrates this symptom dramatically. The entire quote involves a wild flight of ideas, but at one point (beginning with the sentence "Creedmoor is the headquarters . . .") she rattles off

Web Link 14.4

Doctor's Guide to the Internet: Schizophrenia
Produced by a communications and medical education consulting company, the free Doctor's Guide site is updated frequently to provide a current overview of the state of research on schizophrenic disorders. A more detailed set of resources for physicians parallels this site, which is intended primarily for patients and their families.

ten consecutive sentences that have no apparent connection to each other.

Deterioration of Adaptive Behavior

Schizophrenia usually involves a noticeable deterioration in the quality of the person's routine functioning in work, social relations, and personal care. Friends will often make remarks such as "Hal just isn't himself anymore." This deterioration is readily apparent in Sylvia's inability to get along with others or to function in the work world. It's also apparent in her neglect of personal hygiene.

Distorted Perception

A variety of perceptual distortions may occur with schizophrenia, the most common being auditory hallucinations. *Hallucinations* are sensory perceptions that occur in the absence of a real, external stimulus or are gross distortions of perceptual input. Schizophrenics frequently report that they hear voices of nonexistent or absent people talking to them. Sylvia, for instance, said she heard messages from former Beatle Paul McCartney. These voices often provide an insulting, running commentary on the person's behavior ("You're an idiot for shaking his hand"). They may be argumentative ("You don't need a bath"), and they may issue commands ("Prepare your home for visitors from outer space").

Disturbed Emotion

Normal emotional tone can be disrupted in schizophrenia in a variety of ways. Some victims show a flattening of emotions. In other words, they show little emotional responsiveness. Others show inappropriate emotional responses that don't jell with the situation or with what they are saying. People with schizophrenia may also become emotionally volatile. This pattern was displayed by Sylvia, who often overreacted emotionally in erratic, unpredictable ways.

Subtypes

Four subtypes of schizophrenic disorders are recognized, including a category for people who don't fit neatly into any of the first three categories. The major symptoms of each subtype are as follows (Black & Andreasen, 1994).

Paranoid Type

As its name implies, *paranoid schizophrenia* is dominated by delusions of persecution, along with delusions of grandeur. In this common form of schizophrenia, people come to believe that they have many enemies who want to harass and oppress them. They may become suspicious of friends and relatives, or they may attribute the persecution to mysterious, unknown persons. They are convinced that they are being watched and manipulated in malicious ways. To make sense of this persecution, they often develop delusions of grandeur. They believe that they must be enormously important people, frequently seeing themselves as great inventors or as great religious or political leaders. For example, in the case described at the beginning of the chapter, Ed's belief that he was president of the United States was a delusion of grandeur.

Catatonic Type

Catatonic schizophrenia is marked by striking motor disturbances, ranging from muscular rigidity to random motor activity. Some patients go into an extreme form of withdrawal known as a catatonic stupor. They may remain virtually motionless and seem oblivious to the environment around them for long periods of time. Others go into a state of catatonic excitement. They become hyperactive and incoherent. Some alternate between these dramatic extremes. The catatonic subtype is not particularly common, and its prevalence seems to be declining.

Disorganized Type

In *disorganized schizophrenia,* a particularly severe deterioration of adaptive behavior is seen. Prominent symptoms include emotional indifference, frequent incoherence, and virtually complete social withdrawal. Aimless babbling and giggling are common. Delusions often center on bodily functions ("My brain is melting out my ears").

Undifferentiated Type

People who are clearly schizophrenic but who cannot be placed into any of the three previous categories are said to have *undifferentiated schizophrenia,* which is marked by idiosyncratic mixtures of schizophrenic symptoms. The undifferentiated subtype is fairly common.

Positive Versus Negative Symptoms

Many theorists have raised doubts about the value of dividing schizophrenic disorders into the four subtypes just described (Nicholson & Neufeld, 1993). Critics note that the catatonic subtype is disappearing and that undifferentiated cases aren't so much a subtype as a hodgepodge of "leftovers." Critics also point out that the subtypes lack meaningful differences in etiology, prognosis, and response to treatment. The absence of such differences casts doubt on the value of the current classification scheme.

Courtesy of Nancy Andreasen

"Schizophrenia disfigures the emotional and cognitive faculties of its victims, and sometimes nearly destroys them."
NANCY ANDREASEN

Because of such problems, Nancy Andreasen (1990) and others (Carpenter, 1992; McGlashan & Fenton, 1992) have proposed an alternative approach to subtyping. This new scheme divides schizophrenic disorders into just two categories based on the predominance of negative versus positive symptoms. *Negative symptoms* involve behavioral deficits, such as flattened emotions, social withdrawal, apathy, impaired attention, and poverty of speech. *Positive symptoms* involve behavioral excesses or peculiarities, such as hallucinations, delusions, bizarre behavior, and wild flights of ideas.

Theorists advocating this scheme hoped to find consistent differences between the two subtypes in etiology, prognosis, and response to treatment, and some progress along these lines *has* been made. For example, a predominance of positive symptoms is associated with better adjustment prior to the onset of schizophrenia and greater responsiveness to treatment (Cuesta, Peralta, & DeLeon, 1994; Fenton & McGlashan, 1994). However, the assumption that patients can be placed into discrete categories based on this scheme now seems untenable. Most patients exhibit both types of symptoms and vary only in the degree to which positive or negative

symptoms dominate (Black & Andreasen, 1999). Although it seems fair to say that the distinction between positive and negative symptoms is enhancing our understanding of schizophrenia, it has not yielded a classification scheme that can replace the traditional subtypes of schizophrenia.

Etiology of Schizophrenia 11c

You can probably identify, at least to some extent, with people who suffer from mood disorders, somatoform disorders, and anxiety disorders. You can probably imagine events that could unfold that might leave you struggling with depression, grappling with anxiety, or worrying about your physical health. But what could possibly have led Ed to believe that he had been fighting space wars and vampires? What could account for Sylvia's thinking that she was Joan of Arc or that she had dictated the hobbit novels to Tolkien? As mystifying as these delusions may seem, you'll see that the etiology of schizophrenic disorders is not all that different from the etiology of other psychological disorders. We'll begin our discussion by examining the matter of genetic vulnerability.

Genetic Vulnerability 11c

Evidence is plentiful that hereditary factors play a role in the development of schizophrenia (Byerley & Coon, 1995). For instance, in twin studies, concordance rates average around 48% for identical twins, in comparison to about 17% for fraternal twins (Gottesman, 1991). Studies also indicate that a child born to two schizophrenic parents has about a 46% probability of developing schizophrenia (as compared to the probability in the general population of about 1%–1.5%). These and other findings that demonstrate the genetic roots of schizophrenia are summarized in Figure 14.13. Overall, the picture is similar to that seen for mood disorders. Several converging lines of evidence indicate that people inherit a genetically transmitted *vulnerability* to schizophrenia (Fowles, 1992).

Neurochemical Factors 11c

Like mood disorders, schizophrenic disorders appear to be accompanied by changes in the activity of one or more neurotransmitters in the brain (Knable, Kleinman, & Weinberger, 1995). Excess *dopamine* activity has been implicated as a possible cause of schizophrenia because most of the drugs that are useful in the treatment of schizophrenia are known to dampen dopamine activity in the brain (Abi-Dargham et al., 1998). However, the evidence

CONCEPT **CHECK 14.3**

Distinguishing Schizophrenic and Mood Disorders

Check your understanding of the nature of schizophrenic and mood disorders by making preliminary diagnoses for the cases described below. Read each case summary and write your tentative diagnosis in the space provided. The answers are in Appendix A.

1. Max hasn't slept in four days. He's determined to write the "great American novel" before his class reunion, which is a few months away. He expounds eloquently on his novel to anyone who will listen, talking at such a rapid pace that no one can get a word in edgewise. He feels like he's wired with energy and is supremely confident about the novel, even though he's only written 10 to 20 pages. Last week, he charged $8000 worth of new computer equipment, which is supposed to help him write his book.

Preliminary diagnosis: *Bipolar, manic depressive*

2. Eduardo maintains that he invented the atomic bomb, even though he was born after its invention. He says he invented it to punish homosexuals, Nazis, and short people. It's short people that he's really afraid of. He's sure that all the short people on TV are talking about him. He thinks that short people are conspiring to make him look like a Republican. Eduardo frequently gets in arguments with people and is emotionally volatile. His grooming is poor, but he says it's okay because he's the Secretary of State.

Preliminary diagnosis: *Paranoid schizophrenia*

3. Margaret has hardly gotten out of bed for weeks, although she's troubled by insomnia. She doesn't feel like eating and has absolutely no energy. She feels dejected, discouraged, spiritless, and apathetic. Friends stop by to try to cheer her up, but she tells them not to waste their time on "pond scum."

Preliminary diagnosis: *Major depression*

linking schizophrenia to high dopamine levels is riddled with inconsistencies, complexities, and interpretive problems (Carson & Sanislow, 1993). Researchers are currently exploring how interactions between the dopamine and serotonin neurotransmitter systems may contribute to schizophrenia (Kapur & Remington, 1996). Thus, investigators are gradually making progress in their search for the neurochemical bases of schizophrenia.

Structural Abnormalities in the Brain 11C

Various studies have suggested that schizophrenic individuals have difficulty in focusing their attention (Dawson et al., 1993; Smith et al., 1998). Some theorists believe that many bizarre aspects of schizophrenic behavior may be due mainly to an inability to filter out unimportant stimuli (Judd et al., 1992). This lack of selectivity supposedly leaves victims of the disorder flooded with overwhelming, confusing sensory input.

These problems with attention suggest that schizophrenic disorders may be caused by neurological defects (Perry & Braff, 1994). Until recently, this theory was based more on speculation than on actual research. However, advances in brain imaging technology are beginning to yield some intriguing data. The findings suggest that there is an association between enlarged brain ventricles (see Figure 14.14) and chronic schizophrenic disturbance (Nopoulous, Flaum, & Andreasen, 1997; Raz, 1993). The significance of enlarged ventricles in the brain is hotly debated, however. Enlarged ventricles are not unique to schizophrenia—they are a sign of many kinds of brain pathology. The consensus seems to be that this brain abnormality probably is an *effect* rather than a *cause* of schizophrenia (Flaum et al., 1995).

The Neurodevelopmental Hypothesis

In recent years, several new lines of evidence have led to the emergence of the *neurodevelopmental hypothesis* of schizophrenia, which posits that schizophrenia is caused in part by various disruptions in the normal maturational processes of the brain before or at birth (Brown, 1999). According to this hypothesis, insults to the brain during sensitive phases of prenatal development or during birth can cause subtle neuorological damage that elevates individuals' vulnerability to schizophrenia years later in adolescence and early adulthood (see Figure 14.15 on the next page). What are the sources of these early insults to the brain? Thus far, research has focused on viral infections or malnutrition during prenatal development and obstetrical complications during the birth process.

The evidence on viral infections has been building since Sarnoff Mednick and his colleagues (1988) discovered an elevated incidence of schizophrenia among individuals who were in their second trimester of prenatal development during a 1957 influenza epidemic in Finland. Several subsequent studies in other locations have also found a link between exposure to influenza during the second trimester and increased prevalence of schizophrenia (Torrey et al., 1994). Another study, which investigated the possible impact of prenatal malnutrition, found an elevated incidence of schizophrenia in a cohort of people who were prenatally exposed to a severe famine in 1944–45 due to a Nazi blockade of food deliveries in the Netherlands during World War II (Susser et al., 1996). Other research has shown that schizophrenic patients are more likely than control subjects to have a history

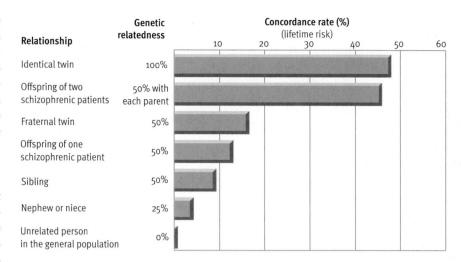

Figure 14.13

Genetic vulnerability to schizophrenic disorders. Relatives of schizophrenic patients have an elevated risk for schizophrenia. This risk is greater among closer relatives. Although environment also plays a role in the etiology of schizophrenia, the concordance rates shown here suggest that there must be a genetic vulnerability to the disorder. These concordance estimates are based on pooled data from 40 studies conducted between 1920 and 1987. (Data from Gottesman, 1991.)

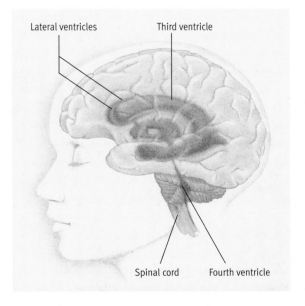

Figure 14.14

Schizophrenia and the ventricles of the brain. Cerebrospinal fluid (CSF) circulates around the brain and spinal cord. The hollow cavities in the brain filled with CSF are called ventricles. The four ventricles in the human brain are depicted here. Recent studies with brain imaging techniques, such as CT scans and MRI scans, suggest that there is an association between enlarged ventricles in the brain and the occurrence of schizophrenic disturbance.

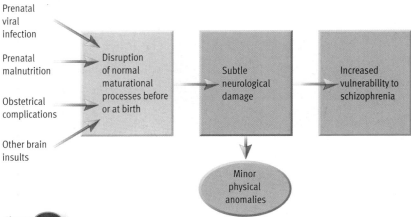

Expressed Emotion

Studies of expressed emotion have primarily focused on how this element of family dynamics influences the *course* of schizophrenic illness, after the onset of the disorder (Leff & Vaughn, 1985). *Expressed emotion* is the degree to which a relative of a schizophrenic patient displays highly critical or emotionally over-involved attitudes toward the patient. Audiotaped interviews of relatives' communication are carefully evaluated for critical comments, resentment toward the patient, and excessive emotional involvement (overprotective, overconcerned attitudes).

Studies show that a family's expressed emotion is a good predictor of the course of a schizophrenic patient's illness (Kavanaugh, 1992). After release from a hospital, schizophrenic patients who return to a family high in expressed emotion show relapse rates three or four times that of patients who return to a family low in expressed emotion (Leff & Vaughn, 1981; Parker & Hadzi-Pavlovic, 1990; see Figure 14.16). Part of the problem for patients returning to homes high in expressed emotion is that their families probably are sources of stress rather than of social support. And like virtually all mental disorders, schizophrenia is influenced to some extent by life stress.

Precipitating Stress

Most theories of schizophrenia assume that stress plays a key role in triggering schizophrenic disorders (Fowles, 1992; Zubin, 1986). According to this notion, various biological and psychological factors influence individuals' *vulnerability* to schizophrenia. High stress may then serve to precipitate a schizophrenic disorder in someone who is vulnerable. Research also indicates that high stress can trigger relapses in schizophrenic patients who have made progress toward recovery (Ventura et al., 1989).

Figure 14.15

The neurodevelopmental hypothesis of schizophrenia. Recent findings have suggested that insults to the brain sustained during prenatal development or at birth may disrupt crucial maturational processes in the brain, resulting in subtle neurological damage that gradually becomes apparent as youngsters develop. This neurological damage is believed to increase both vulnerability to schizophrenia and the incidence of minor physical anomalies.

of obstetrical complications (Geddes & Lawrie, 1995). Finally, research suggests that minor physical anomalies (slight anatomical defects of the head, hands, feet, and face) that would be consistent with prenatal neurological damage are more common among people with schizophrenia than among others (Green, Satz, & Christensen, 1994).

Collectively, these diverse studies argue for a relationship between early neurological trauma and a predisposition to schizophrenia. Much remains to be learned about the neurodevelopmental bases of schizophrenia, but this new line of inquiry should increase our understanding of the etiology of schizophrenic disorders.

CONCEPT CHECK 14.4

Identifying Etiological Factors in Psychological Disorders

The abundance of theories concerning the etiology of psychological disorders exemplifies our theme that behavior is determined by multiple causes. Check your understanding of the etiological factors that appear to play a role in the three categories of disorders shown below by placing check marks in the appropriate spaces in the chart. The column on the left lists the categories of etiological factors. The top row lists three categories of disorders. You'll find the answers in Appendix A.

	Anxiety disorders	Mood disorders	Schizophrenic disorders
Brain structure abnormalities	___	___	✓
Cognitive factors	✓	✓	___
Prenatal neurodevelopmental disruptions	___	___	✓
Conditioning	✓		
Genetic predisposition	✓	✓	✓
Interpersonal factors		✓	
Neurochemical factors	✓	✓	✓
Personality	✓		
Stress	✓	✓	✓

Figure 14.16

Expressed emotion and relapse rates in schizophrenia. Schizophrenic patients who return to a home that is high in expressed emotion have higher relapse rates than those who return to a home low in expressed emotion. (Data adapted from Leff and Vaughn, 1981.)

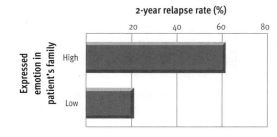

Psychological Disorders and the Law

Societies use the law to enforce their norms of conformity. Given this function, the law has something to say about many issues related to abnormal behavior. In this section we briefly examine the legal issues of insanity and involuntary commitment.

Insanity

Insanity is *not* a diagnosis; it's purely a legal concept. **Insanity is a legal status indicating that a person cannot be held responsible for his or her actions because of mental illness.** Why is this an issue in the courtroom? Because criminal acts must be intentional. The law reasons that people who are "out of their mind" may not be able to appreciate the significance of what they're doing. The insanity defense is used in criminal trials by defendants who admit that they committed the crime but claim that they lacked intent.

No simple relationship exists between specific diagnoses of mental disorders and court findings of insanity. Most people with diagnosed psychological disorders would *not* qualify as insane. The people most likely to qualify are those troubled by severe psychotic disturbances. The courts apply several rules in making judgments about a defendant's sanity, depending on the jurisdiction. According to the most widely used rule, called the M'naghten rule, *insanity exists when a mental disorder makes a person unable to distinguish right from wrong.* As you can imagine, evaluating insanity as defined in the M'naghten rule can be difficult for judges and jurors, not to mention the psychologists and psychiatrists who are called into court as expert witnesses. Although highly publicized and controversial, the insanity defense is actually used less frequently and less successfully than widely believed (Phillips, Wolf, & Coons, 1988). One study found that the general public estimates that the insanity defense is used in 37% of felony cases, when in fact it is used in less than 1% (Silver, Cirincione, & Steadman, 1994). Another study of over 60,000 indictments in Baltimore found that only 190 defendants (0.31%) pleaded insanity, and of these, only 8 were successful (Janofsky et al., 1996).

Involuntary Commitment

The issue of insanity surfaces only in *criminal* proceedings. Far more people are affected by civil proceedings relating to involuntary commitment. **In *involuntary commitment* people are hospitalized in psychiatric facilities against their will.** What are the grounds for such a dramatic action? They vary some from state to state. Generally, people are subject to involuntary commitment when mental health professionals and legal authorities believe that a mental disorder makes them (1) dangerous to themselves (usually suicidal), (2) dangerous to others (potentially violent), or (3) in need of treatment (applied in cases of severe disorientation). In emergency situations psychologists and psychiatrists can authorize *temporary* commitment, usually for 24 to 72 hours. Orders for long-term involuntary commitment are usually set up for renewable six-month periods and can be issued by a court only after a formal hearing. Mental health professionals provide extensive input in these hearings, but the courts make the final decisions (Simon, 1999).

After his attempt to assassinate President Ronald Reagan, John Hinckley, Jr., was found not guilty by reason of insanity. The Hinckley verdict aroused controversy about the concept of insanity, which is a legal status and not a psychodiagnostic category.

Web Link 14.5

David Willshire's Forensic Psychology and Psychiatry Links
This site's webmaster, a senior psychologist at Australia's Victorian Institute of Forensic Mental Health, has brought together a large set of annotated links on all aspects of forensic psychological matters—that is, how the law and criminal justice system interact with psychology and psychiatry.

Culture and Pathology

The legal rules governing insanity and involuntary commitment obviously are culture-specific. And we noted earlier, judgments of normality and abnormality are influenced by cultural norms and values. In light of these realities, would it be reasonable to infer that psychological disorders are culturally variable phenomena? Many social scientists have concluded that the answer to this question is yes. Embracing a *relativistic view* of psychological disorders, they have argued that the criteria of mental illness vary greatly across cultures and that there are no universal standards of normality and abnormality (Lewis-Fernandez & Kleinman, 1994; Marsella, 1979). According to the relativists, the DSM diagnostic system reflects an ethnocentric, Western, white, urban, middle- and upper-class cultural orientation that has limited relevance in other cultural contexts.

Not everyone agrees with this conclusion, however. Many social scientists subscribe to a *pancultural view* of psychological disorders, arguing that the criteria of mental illness are much the same around the world and that basic standards of normality and

Overview of Three Categories of Psychological Disorders

Axis I category	Subtypes	Prevalence/well-known victim

Anxiety disorders

Munch, Edward: *The Scream*. National Gallery, Oslo, Norway/Art Resource/NY)

Edward Munch's *The Scream* expresses overwhelming feelings of anxiety.

Generalized anxiety disorder: Chronic, high level of anxiety not tied to any specific threat

Phobic disorder: Persistent, irrational fear of object or situation that presents no real danger

Panic disorder: Recurrent attacks of overwhelming anxiety that occur suddenly and unexpectedly

Obsessive-compulsive disorder: Persistent, uncontrollable intrusions of unwanted thoughts and urges to engage in senseless rituals

17%
Prevalence

CORBIS-Bettmann

The famous industrialist Howard Hughes suffered from obsessive-compulsive disorder.

Mood disorders

van Gogh, Vincent: *Portrait of Dr. Gachet*. Musee d'Orsay, Paris. Erich Lessing/Art Resource, NY

Vincent van Gogh's *Portrait of Dr. Gachet* captures the profound dejection experienced in depressive disorders.

Major depressive disorder: Two or more major depressive episodes marked by feelings of sadness, worthlessness, despair

Bipolar disorder: One or more manic episodes marked by inflated self-esteem, grandiosity, and elevated mood and energy, usually accompanied by major depressive episodes

7.8%
Prevalence

Tipper Gore has suffered from depression.

© Matt Mendelsohn/Gamma Liaison

Schizophrenic disorders

Derek Bayes, *Life Magazine*, © Time, Inc.

The perceptual distortions seen in schizophrenia probably contributed to the bizarre imagery apparent in this portrait of a cat painted by Louis Wain.

Paranoid schizophrenia: Delusions of persecution and delusions of grandeur; frequent auditory hallucinations

Catatonic schizophrenia: Motor disturbances ranging from immobility to excessive, purposeless activity

Disorganized schizophrenia: Flat or inappropriate emotions; disorganized speech and adaptive behavior

Undifferentiated schizophrenia: Idiosyncratic mixtures of schizophrenic symptoms that cannot be placed into above three categories

1.3%
Prevalence

© Trippett/Sipa Press

John Hinckley, Jr., who attempted to assassinate President Reagan, suffers from schizophrenia.

Etiology: Biological factors

Genetic vulnerability: Twin studies and other evidence suggest a mild genetic predisposition to anxiety disorders.

Anxiety sensitivity: Oversensitivity to physical symptoms of anxiety may lead to overreactions to feelings of anxiety, so anxiety breeds more anxiety.

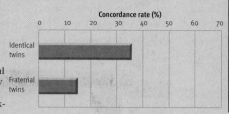

Concordance rate (%)

Neurochemical bases: Disturbances in neural circuits releasing GABA may contribute to some disorders; abnormalities at serotonin synapses have been implicated in panic and obsessive-compulsive disorders.

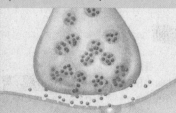

Genetic vulnerability: Twin studies and other evidence suggest a genetic predisposition to mood disorders.

Sleep disturbances: Disruption of biological rhythms and sleep patterns may lead to neurochemical changes that contribute to mood disorders.

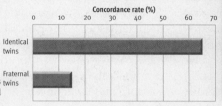

Concordance rate (%)

Neurochemical bases: Disturbances in neural circuits releasing norepinephrine may contribute to some mood disorders; abnormalties at serotonin synapses have also been implicated as a factor in depression.

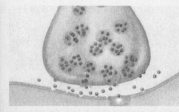

Genetic vulnerability: Twin studies and other evidence suggest a genetic predisposition to schizophrenic disorders.

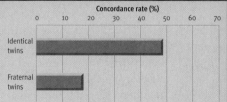

Concordance rate (%)

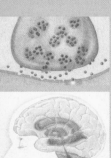

Neurochemical bases: Overactivity in neural circuits releasing dopamine is associated with schizophrenia; this overactivity may be modulated by abnormalties in serotonin circuits.

Structural abnormalities in brain: Enlarged brain ventricles are associated with schizophrenia, but they may be an effect rather than a cause of the disorder.

Etiology: Psychological factors

Learning: Many anxiety responses may be acquired through classical conditioning or observational learning; phobic responses may be maintained by operant reinforcement.

CS
Snow

UCS
Buried in avalanche

CR
Fear
UCR

Personality: Neuroticism is correlated with an elevated prevalence of anxiety disorders.

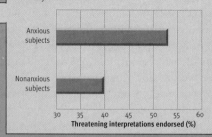

Threatening interpretations endorsed (%)

Stress: High stress may help to precipitate the onset of anxiety disorders.

Cognition: People who misinterpret harmless situations as threatening and who focus excessive attention on perceived threats are more vulnerable to anxiety disorders.

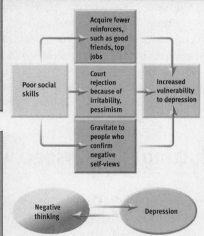

Interpersonal roots: Behavioral theories emphasize how inadequate social skills can result in a paucity of reinforcers and other effects that make people vulnerable to depression.

Stress: High stress can act as precipitating factor that triggers depression or bipolar disorder.

Cognition: Negative thinking can contribute to the development of depression; rumination may extend and amplify depression.

Expressed emotion: A family's expressed emotion is a good predictor of the course of a schizophrenic patient's illness.

Stress: High stress can precipitate schizophrenic disorder in people who are vulnerable to schizophrenia.

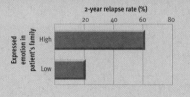

2-year relapse rate (%)

The neurodevelopmental hypothesis: Insults to the brain sustained during prenatal development or at birth may disrupt maturational processes in the brain resulting in elevated vulnerability to schizophrenia.

abnormality are universal across cultures (Frances et al., 1991; Murphy, 1976). Theorists who accept the pancultural view of psychopathology typically maintain that Western diagnostic concepts have validity and utility in other cultural contexts. The debate about culture and pathology basically boils down to this question: Are the psychological disorders seen in Western societies found throughout the world? Let's briefly examine the evidence on this issue.

Most investigators agree that the principal categories of serious psychological disturbance—schizophrenia, depression, and bipolar illness—are identifiable in all cultures (Butcher, Narikiyo, & Vitousek, 1993). Most behaviors that are regarded as clearly abnormal in Western culture are also viewed as abnormal in other cultures. People who are delusional, hallucinatory, disoriented, or incoherent are thought to be disturbed in all societies, although there are cultural disparities in exactly what is considered delusional or hallucinatory.

Cultural variations are more apparent in the recognition of less severe forms of psychological disturbance (Tseng et al., 1986). Additional research is needed, but relatively mild types of pathology that do not disrupt behavior in obvious ways appear to go unrecognized in many societies. Thus, syndromes such as generalized anxiety disorder, hypochondriasis, and somatization disorder, which are firmly established as important diagnostic categories in the DSM, are viewed in some cultures as "run-of-the-mill" difficulties and peculiarities rather than as full-fledged disorders.

Finally, researchers have discovered a small number of *culture-bound disorders* that further illustrate the diversity of abnormal behavior around the world (Guarnaccia & Rogler, 1999; Simons & Hughes, 1993). **Culture-bound disorders are abnormal syndromes found only in a few cultural groups.** For example, *koro,* an obsessive fear that one's penis will withdraw into one's abdomen, is seen only among Chinese males in Malaya and several other regions of southern Asia. *Windigo,* which involves an intense craving for human flesh and fear that one will turn into a cannibal, is seen only among Algonquin Indian cultures. And until recently, *anorexia nervosa,* which involves an intense fear of becoming fat, a loss of appetite, and refusal to eat adequately, was seen almost exclusively in affluent Western cultures (see the Personal Application).

So, what can we conclude about the validity of the relativistic versus pancultural views of psychological disorders? Both views appear to have some merit. As we have seen in other areas of research, psychopathology is characterized by both cultural variance and invariance.

Putting It in Perspective

Our examination of abnormal behavior and its roots has highlighted four of our organizing themes: multifactorial causation, the interplay of heredity and environment, the sociohistorical context in which psychology evolves, and the influence of culture on psychological phenomena.

We can safely assert that every disorder described in this chapter has multiple causes. The development of mental disorders involves an interplay among a variety of psychological, biological, and social factors. We also saw that most psychological disorders depend on an interaction of genetics and experience. This interaction shows up most clearly in the *stress-vulnerability models* for mood disorders and schizophrenic disorders. *Vulnerability* to these disorders seems to depend primarily on heredity, although experience contributes. Stress is largely a function of environment, although physiological factors may influence people's stress reactions. According to stress-vulnerability theories, disorders emerge when high vulnerability intersects with high stress. Thus, the impact of heredity depends on the environment, and the effect of environment depends on heredity.

This chapter also demonstrated that psychology evolves in a sociohistorical context. We saw that modern conceptions of normality and abnormality are largely shaped by empirical research, but social trends, prevailing values, and political realities also play a role. Finally, our discussion of psychological disorders showed once again that psychological phenomena are shaped to some degree by cultural parameters. Although some standards of normality and abnormality transcend cultural boundaries, cultural norms influence some aspects of psychopathology. Indeed, the influence of culture will be apparent in our upcoming Personal Application on eating disorders. These disorders are largely a creation of modern, affluent, Western culture.

PERSONAL APPLICATION

Understanding Eating Disorders

Answer the following "true" or "false."

_____ 1 Although they have only attracted attention in recent years, eating disorders have a long history and have always been fairly common.

_____ 2 People with anorexia nervosa are much more likely to recognize that their eating behavior is pathological than people suffering from bulimia nervosa are.

_____ 3 The prevalence of eating disorders is twice as high in women as it is in men.

_____ 4 The binge-and-purge syndrome seen in bulimia nervosa is not common in anorexia nervosa.

All of the above statements are false, as you will see in this Application. The psychological disorders that we discussed in the main body of the chapter have largely been recognized for centuries and are generally found in one form or another in all cultures and societies. Eating disorders present a sharp contrast to this picture; they have only been recognized in recent decades and they have largely been confined to affluent, Westernized cultures (Russell, 1995; Szmukler & Patton, 1995). In spite of these fascinating differences, eating disorders have much in common with traditional forms of pathology.

Description

Eating disorders are severe disturbances in eating behavior characterized by preoccupation with weight concerns and unhealthy efforts to control weight. The vast majority of cases consist of two sometimes overlapping syndromes: *anorexia nervosa* and *bulimia nervosa*. **Anorexia nervosa** involves intense fear of gaining weight, disturbed body image, refusal to maintain normal weight, and dangerous measures to lose weight. Two subtypes have been observed (Garfinkel, 1995). In *restricting type anorexia nervosa*, people drastically reduce their intake of food, sometimes literally starving themselves. In *binge-eating/purging type anorexia nervosa*, individuals attempt to lose weight by forcing themselves to vomit after meals, by misusing laxatives and diuretics, and by engaging in excessive exercise.

Both types suffer from disturbed body image. No matter how frail and emaciated they become, they insist that they are too fat. Their morbid fear of obesity means that they are never satisfied with their weight. If they gain a pound or two, they panic. The only thing that makes them happy is to lose more weight. The frequent result is a relentless decline in body weight; people entering treatment for anorexia nervosa are typically 25%–30% below their normal weight (Hsu, 1990). Because of their disturbed body image, people suffering from anorexia generally do *not* appreciate the maladaptive quality of their behavior and rarely seek treatment on their own. They are typically coaxed or coerced into treatment by friends or family members who are alarmed by their appearance.

Anorexia nervosa eventually leads to a cascade of medical problems, including *amenorrhea* (a loss of menstrual cycles in women), gastrointestinal problems, low blood pressure, *osteoporosis* (a loss of bone density), and metabolic disturbances that can lead to cardiac arrest or circulatory collapse (Herzog & Becker, 1999). Anorexia is a debilitating illness that leads to death in 2%–10% of patients (Treasure & Szmukler, 1995).

Bulimia nervosa involves habitually engaging in out-of-control overeating followed by unhealthy compensatory efforts, such as self-induced vomiting, fasting, abuse of laxatives and diuretics, and excessive exercise. The eating binges are usually carried out in secret and are followed by intense guilt and concern about gaining weight. These feelings motivate ill-advised strategies to undo the effects of the overeating. However, vomiting prevents the absorption of only about half of recently consumed food, and laxatives and diuretics have negligible impact on caloric intake, so people suffering from bulimia nervosa typically maintain a reasonably normal weight (Beumont, 1995; Kaye et al., 1993). Medical problems associated with bulimia nervosa include cardiac arrythmias, dental problems, metabolic deficiencies, and gastrointestinal problems (Halmi, 1999).

Obviously, bulimia nervosa shares many features with anorexia nervosa, such as a morbid fear of becoming obese, preoccupation with food, and rigid, maladaptive

Eating disorders have become distressingly common. One contributing factor is that the models and actresses who dominate the media, such as Calista Flockhart, who is pictured here, tend to be remarkably slender. Thus, young girls are socialized to believe that they must be thin to be attractive.

AP/Wide World Photos

approaches to controlling weight that are grounded in naive all-or-none thinking. However, the syndromes also differ in crucial ways. First and foremost, bulimia is a much less life-threatening condition. Second, although their appearance is usually more "normal" than that seen in anorexia, people with bulimia are much more likely to recognize that their eating behavior is pathological and are more likely to cooperate with treatment (Striegel-Moore, Silberstein, & Rodin, 1993).

History and Prevalence

Historians have been able to track down descriptions of anorexia nervosa that date back centuries, so the disorder is *not* entirely new, but anorexia nervosa did not become a common affliction until the middle of the 20th century (Russell, 1995). Although binging and purging have a long history in some cultures, they were not part of pathological efforts to control weight, and bulimia nervosa appears to be an entirely new syndrome that emerged gradually in the middle of the 20th century and was first recognized in the 1970s (Parry-Jones & Parry-Jones, 1995; Russell, 1997).

Both disorders are a product of modern, affluent, Western culture, in which food is generally plentiful and the desirability of being thin is widely endorsed. Until recently, these disorders were not seen in developing nations where access to adequate food was often precarious (Hoek, 1995). However, in recent years, advances in communication have exported Western culture to far-flung corners of the globe, and eating disorders have started showing up in developing nations (Wilfley & Rodin, 1995).

There is a huge gender gap in the likelihood of developing eating disorders. About 90%–95% of individuals with anorexia nervosa and bulimia nervosa are female (Hoek, 1995). This staggering discrepancy appears to be a result of cultural pressures rather than biological factors (Striegel-Moore, 1995). Western standards of attractiveness emphasize slenderness more for females than for males, and women generally experience greater pressure to be physically attractive than men do (Sobal, 1995).

Eating disorders mostly afflict *young* women. The typical age of onset for anorexia is 14 to 18; for bulimia it is 15 to 21 (see Figure 14.17).

How common are eating disorders in Western societies? The prevalence of these disorders has increased dramatically in recent decades, although this escalation may be leveling off. Studies of young women suggest that about 1%–1.5% develop anorexia nervosa (Walters & Kendler, 1995) and about 2%–3% develop bulimia nervosa (Hoek et al., 1995). These figures may seem small, but they mean that millions of young women wrestle with serious eating problems.

Etiology of Eating Disorders

Like other types of psychological disorders, eating disorders are caused by multiple determinants that work interactively. Let's take a brief look at some of the factors that contribute to the development of anorexia nervosa and bulimia nervosa.

Genetic Vulnerability

The evidence is not nearly as strong or complete as it is for many other types of psychopathology (such as anxiety, mood, and schizophrenic disorders), but some people may inherit a genetic vulnerability to eating disorders. Studies show that relatives of patients with eating disorders have elevated rates of anorexia nervosa and bulimia nervosa (Strober, 1995). And twin studies suggest that a genetic predisposition may be at work (Walters & Kendler, 1995).

Personality Factors

Strober (1995) has suggested that genetic factors may exert their influence indirectly by fostering certain personality traits that make people more vulnerable to eating disorders. There are innumerable exceptions, but victims of anorexia nervosa tend to be obsessive, rigid, neurotic, and emotionally restrained, whereas victims of bulimia nervosa tend to be impulsive, overly sensitive, and low in self-esteem (Wonderlich, 1995). Most of these personality traits are influenced by genetics, making Strober's hypothesis plausible. Nonetheless, personality-based explanations of eating disorders remain pretty speculative.

Cultural Values

The contribution of cultural values to the increased prevalence of eating disorders can

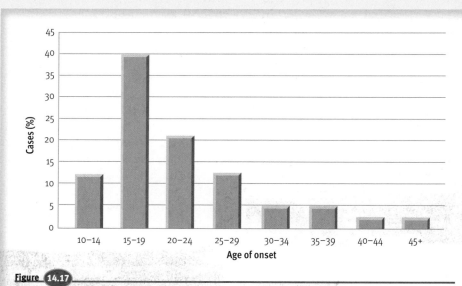

Figure 14.17

Age of onset for anorexia nervosa. Eating disorders mostly emerge during adolescence, as these data for anorexia nervosa show. This graph shows how age of onset was distributed in a sample of 166 female patients from Minnesota. As you can see, over half the patients experienced the onset of their illness before the age of 20, with vulnerability clearly peaking between the ages of 15 and 19. (Data adapted from Lucas, et al., 1991.)

hardly be overestimated (Abramson & Valene, 1991; Striegel-Moore, 1995). In Western society, young women are socialized to believe that they must be attractive, and to be attractive they must be as thin as the actresses and fashion models that dominate the media (Lavine, Sweeney, & Wagner, 1999). As Figure 14.18 shows, the increased premium on being thin is reflected in statistics on Miss America contestants and *Playboy* centerfolds, whose average weight declined gradually between 1959 and 1988 (Garner et al., 1980; Wiseman et al., 1992). Thanks to this cultural milieu, many young women are dissatisfied with their weight and feel that they need to diet (Fredrickson et al., 1998). Unfortunately, in a small portion of these women, the pressure to be thin, in combination with genetic vulnerability, family

pathology, and other factors, leads to unhealthy efforts to control weight.

The Role of the Family

Quite a number of theorists emphasize how family dynamics can contribute to the development of anorexia nervosa and bulimia nervosa in young women (Eisler, 1995). Some theorists suggest that parents who are overly involved in their children's lives turn the normal adolescent push for independence into an unhealthy struggle (Minuchin, Rosman, & Baker, 1978). Needing to assert their autonomy, some adolescent girls seek extreme control over their body, leading to pathological patterns of eating (Bruch, 1978). Other theorists maintain that some mothers contribute to eating disorders simply by endorsing society's message that "you can never be too

thin" and by modeling unhealthy dieting behaviors of their own (Pike & Rodin, 1991).

Cognitive Factors

Cognitive theorists emphasize the role of disturbed thinking in the etiology of eating disorders (Butow, Beumont, & Touyz, 1993; de Silva, 1995). For example, anorexic patients' typical belief that they are fat when they are really wasting away is a dramatic illustration of how thinking goes awry. Patients with eating disorders display rigid, all-or-none thinking and many maladaptive beliefs, such as "I must be thin to be accepted," "If I am not in complete control, I will lose all control," "If I gain one pound, I'll go on to gain enormous weight." Additional research is needed to determine whether distorted thinking is a cause or merely a *symptom* of eating disorders.

Figure 14.18

Weight trends among *Playboy* centerfolds and Miss America contestants. This graph charts how the average weight of *Playboy* centerfolds and Miss America contestants changed over the course of 30 years (from 1959 to 1989). To control for age and height, each woman's weight was compared to the average weight for a woman of that age and height and expressed as a percentage of the expected weight. Given the small samples, the figures are a little erratic, but overall, the data show a clear downward trend. (Data from Garner et al., 1980; Wiseman et al., 1992; graphic from Barlow & Durand, 1999.)

Working with Probabilities in Thinking About Mental Illness

As you read about the various types of psychological disorders, did you think to yourself that you or someone you know was being described? On the one hand, there is no reason to be alarmed. The tendency to see yourself and your friends in descriptions of pathology is a common one, sometimes called the *medical students' disease* because beginning medical students often erroneously believe that they or their friends have whatever diseases they are currently learning about. On the other hand, realistically speaking, it is quite likely that you know *many* people with psychological disorders given that the data from a huge, multisite investigation of the prevalence of mental disorders (Robins & Regier, 1991) suggest that the likelihood of ever having at least one DSM disorder is about one in three (32% to be exact; see Figure 14.19).

This one-third risk estimate strikes most people as surprisingly high. Why is this so? One reason is that when people think about psychological disorders they tend to think of severe disorders, such as bipolar disorder or schizophrenia, which are relatively infrequent, rather than "run of the mill" disturbances, such as anxiety and depressive disorders, which are much more common. In other words, their *prototypes* or "best examples" of mental illness consist of severe disorders that are relatively infrequent, so they underestimate the prevalence of mental disorders. This distortion illustrates the influence of the ***representativeness heuristic*, which is basing the estimated probability of an event on how similar it is to the typical prototype of that event** (see Chapter 8).

Do you still find it hard to believe that the overall prevalence of psychological disorders is about 32%? Another reason this number seems surprisingly high is that many people do not understand that the probability of having *at least one* disorder is much higher than the probability of having the most prevalent disorder by itself. For example, the probability of having an anxiety disorder, the single most common type of disorder, is approximately 17%, but the probability of having an anxiety disorder or a substance-related disorder or a mood disorder or a schizophrenic disorder jumps to 32%. These "or" relationships represent *cumulative probabilities*. Yet another consideration that makes the prevalence figures seem high is that many people confuse different types of *prevalence rates*. The one-third value is for *lifetime prevalence,* which means it is the probability of having *any* disorder *at least once* at any time in one's lifetime. The lifetime prevalence rate is another example of "or" relationships. It is a value that takes into account the probability of having a psychological disorder in childhood *or* adolescence *or* adulthood *or* old age. *Point prevalence rates,* which estimate the percentage of people manifesting various disorders *at a particular point in time,* are much lower because many psychological disorders last only a few months to a few years.

What about "and" relationships—that is, relationships in which we want to know the probability of someone having condition A *and* condition B? For example, given the estimated prevalence figures for each type of disorder shown in the parentheses (based on Robins & Regier, 1991), what is the probability of someone having an anxiety disorder (17% prevalence) *and* a substance use disorder (16.7%) *and* a mood disorder (7.8%) *and* a schizophrenic disorder (1.3%) during his or her lifetime? Such "and" relationships represent *conjunctive probabilities*. Stop and think: What must be true about the probability of having all four types of disorders? Will this probability be less than 17%, between 17% and 32%, or over 32%? You may be surprised to learn that this figure is probably well under 1%. You can't have all four disorders unless you have the least frequent disorder (schizophrenia), which has an estimated prevalence of 1.3%, so the answer *must* be 1.3% or less. Moreover, of all of the people with schizophrenia, only a small subset of them are likely to have all three of the other disorders, so the answer is probably well under

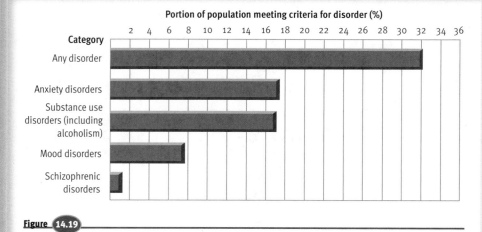

Portion of population meeting criteria for disorder (%)

Figure 14.19

Prevalence of common psychological disorders in the United States. The estimated percentage of people who have, at any time in their life, suffered from one of four types of psychological disorders or from a disorder of any kind (top bar) is shown here. (Based on combined data from several chapters in Robins & Regier, 1991.)

1% (see Figure 14.20). If this type of question strikes you as contrived, think again. Epidemiologists have devoted an enormous amount of research to the estimation of *comorbidity*—the coexistence of two or more disorders—because it greatly complicates treatment issues.

These are two examples of using statistical probabilities as a critical thinking tool. Let's apply this type of thinking to another problem dealing with physical health. Here is a problem used in a study by Tversky and Kahneman (1983, p. 308) that many physicians got wrong:

A health survey was conducted in a sample of adult males in British Columbia, of all ages and occupations. Please give your best estimate of the following values:

What percentage of the men surveyed have had one or more heart attacks? _____

What percentage of the men surveyed both are over 55 years old and have had one or more heart attacks? _____

Fill in the blanks above with your best guesses. Of course, you probably have only a very general idea about the prevalence of heart attacks, but go ahead and fill in the blanks anyway.

The actual values are not as important in this example as the relative values are. Over 65% of the physicians who participated in the experiment by Tversky and Kahneman gave a higher percentage value for the second question than for the first. What is wrong with their answers? The second question is asking about the conjunctive probability of two events. Hopefully, you see why this figure *must* be less than the probability of either one of these events occurring alone. Of all of the men in the survey who had had a heart attack, only some of them are also over 55, so the second number must be smaller than the first. As we saw in Chapter 8, this common error in thinking is called the *conjunction fallacy*. **The *conjunction fallacy* occurs when people estimate that the odds of two uncertain events happening together are greater than the odds of either event happening alone.**

Why did so many physicians get this problem wrong? They were vulnerable to the conjunction fallacy because they were influenced by the *representativeness heuristic*, or the power of prototypes. When physicians think "heart attack," they tend to envision a man over the age of 55. Hence, the second scenario fit so well with their prototype of a heart attack victim, they carelessly overestimated its probability.

Let's consider some additional examples of erroneous reasoning about probabilities involving how people think about psychological disorders. Many people tend to stereotypically assume that mentally ill people are likely to be violent. Near the end of the chapter, we noted that people tend to wildly overestimate (37-fold in one study) how often the insanity defense is used in criminal trials. These beliefs reflect the influence of the *availability heuristic,* **which is basing the estimated probability of an event on the ease with which relevant instances come to mind.** Because of the availability heuristic, people tend to overestimate the probability of dramatic events that receive heavy media coverage, even when these events are rare, because examples of the events are easy to retrieve from memory. Violent acts by former psychiatric patients tend to get lots of attention in the press. And because of the *hindsight bias,* journalists tend to question why authorities couldn't foresee and prevent the violence (see the Critical Thinking Application for Chapter 12), so the mental illness angle tends to be emphasized. In a similar vein, press coverage is usually intense when a defendant in a murder trial mounts an insanity defense.

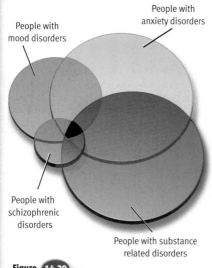

People with mood disorders

People with anxiety disorders

People with schizophrenic disorders

People with substance related disorders

Figure 14.20

Conjunctive probabilities. The probability of someone having all four disorders depicted here cannot be greater than the probability of the least common condition by itself, which is 1.3% for schizophrenia. The intersection of all four disorders (shown in black) has to be a subset of schizophrenic disorders and is probably well under 1%. Efforts to think about probabilities can sometimes be facilitated by creating diagrams that show the relationships and overlap among various events.

In sum, the various types of statistics that come up in thinking about psychological disorders demonstrate that we are constantly working with probabilities, even though we may not realize it. Critical thinking requires a good understanding of the laws of probability because there are very few certainties in life.

Table 14.2   Critical Thinking Skills Discussed in This Application

Skill	Description
Understanding the limitations of the representativeness heuristic	The critical thinker understands that focusing on prototypes can lead to inaccurate probability estimates.
Understanding cumulative probabilities	The critical thinker understands that the probability of at least one of several events occurring is additive and increases with time and the number of events.
Understanding conjunctive probabilities	The critical thinker appreciates that the probability of two uncertain events happening together is less than the probability of either event happening alone.
Understanding the limitations of the availability heuristic	The critical thinker understands that the ease with which examples come to mind may not be an accurate guide to the probability of an event.

REVIEW

Key Ideas

Abnormal Behavior: Myths and Realities

● The medical model assumes that it is useful to view abnormal behavior as a disease. This view has been criticized on the grounds that it turns ethical questions about deviance into medical questions. Although there are serious problems with the medical model, the concept is useful if one remembers that it is only an analogy.

● Three criteria are used in deciding whether people suffer from psychological disorders: deviance, personal distress, and maladaptive behavior. Often, it is difficult to clearly draw a line between normality and abnormality.

● DSM-IV is the official psychodiagnostic classification system in the United States. This system asks for information about patients on five axes or dimensions.

Anxiety Disorders

● The anxiety disorders include generalized anxiety disorder, phobic disorder, panic disorder, and obsessive-compulsive disorder. These disorders may have a genetic component and may be more likely in people who are especially sensitive to physiological symptoms of anxiety. Abnormalities in neurotransmitter activity may also play a role.

● Many anxiety responses, especially phobias, may be caused by classical conditioning and maintained by operant conditioning. Cognitive theorists maintain that a tendency to overinterpret harmless situations as threatening makes some people vulnerable to anxiety disorders. Neuroticism and stress may also contribute to the development of anxiety disorders.

Somatoform Disorders

● Somatoform disorders include somatization disorder, conversion disorder, and hypochondriasis. These disorders often emerge in people with highly suggestible, histrionic personalities. Somatoform disorders may be a learned avoidance strategy reinforced by attention and sympathy.

Dissociative Disorders

● Dissociative disorders include dissociative amnesia, fugue, and dissociative identity disorder. Dissociative identity disorder may be rooted in emotional trauma that occurred during childhood, although some theorists argue that the disorder typically involves intentional role playing.

Mood Disorders

● The principal mood disorders are unipolar depression and bipolar disorder. Mood disorders are episodic. Unipolar depression is more common than bipolar disorder.

● Evidence indicates that people vary in their genetic vulnerability to the severe mood disorders. These disorders are accompanied by changes in neurochemical activity in the brain. Cognitive models posit that negative thinking contributes to depression. Depression is often rooted in interpersonal inadequacies and setbacks and sometimes is stress related.

Schizophrenic Disorders

● Schizophrenic disorders are characterized by deterioration of adaptive behavior, irrational thought, distorted perception, and disturbed mood. Schizophrenic disorders are classified as paranoid, catatonic, disorganized, or undifferentiated. A new classification scheme based on the predominance of positive versus negative symptoms is under study.

● Research has linked schizophrenia to genetic vulnerability, changes in neurotransmitter activity, structural abnormalities in the brain, and disruptions in the normal maturational processes of the brain before or at birth. Precipitating stress and unhealthy family dynamics (high expressed emotion) may also contribute to the development of schizophrenia.

Psychological Disorders and the Law

● Insanity is a legal concept applied to people who cannot be held responsible for their actions because of mental illness. When people appear to be dangerous to themselves or others, courts may rule that they are subject to involuntary commitment in a hospital.

Culture and Pathology

● The principal categories of psychological disturbance are identifiable in all cultures. However, milder disorders may go unrecognized in some societies, and culture-bound disorders further illustrate the diversity of abnormal behavior around the world.

Putting It in Perspective

● This chapter highlighted four of our unifying themes, showing that psychological disorders are governed by multiple causes, that heredity and environment jointly influence mental disorders, that psychology evolves in a sociohistorical context, and that pathology is characterized by both cultural variance and invariance.

Personal Application • Understanding Eating Disorders

● The principal eating disorders consist of anorexia nervosa and bulimia nervosa. Both appear to be largely a product of modern, affluent, Westernized culture. Females account for 90%–95% of eating disorders.

● There appears to be a genetic vulnerability to eating disorders, which may be mediated by heritable personality traits. Cultural pressures on young women to be thin clearly help to foster eating disorders. Unhealthy family dynamics and disturbed thinking can also contribute.

Critical Thinking Application • Working with Probabilities in Thinking About Mental Illness

● Probability estimates can be distorted by the representativeness heuristic, which involves basing the estimated probability of an event on how similar it is to the typical prototype of that event. Cumulative probabilities are additive, whereas conjunctive probabilities are always less than the likelihood of any one of the events happening alone. Probabilty estimates can be biased by the availability heuristic, which involves basing the estimated probability of an event on the ease with which relevant instances come to mind.

Key Terms

Agoraphobia
Anorexia nervosa
Anxiety disorders
Availability heuristic
Bipolar disorder
Bulimia nervosa
Catatonic
  schizophrenia
Comorbidity
Concordance rate
Conjunction fallacy
Conversion disorder
Culture-bound
  disorders
Delusions
Diagnosis
Disorganized
  schizophrenia
Dissociative amnesia
Dissociative disorders
Dissociative fugue
Dissociative identity
  disorder (DID)
Eating disorders
Etiology
Generalized anxiety
  disorder
Hallucinations
Hypochondriasis
Insanity
Involuntary
  commitment

Major depressive
  disorder
Medical model
Mood disorders
Multiple-personality
  disorder
Negative symptoms
Obsessive-compulsive
  disorder (OCD)
Panic disorder
Paranoid
  schizophrenia
Phobic disorder
Positive symptoms
Prognosis
Psychosomatic
  diseases
Representativeness
  heuristic
Schizophrenic
  disorders
Somatization disorder
Somatoform disorders
Undifferentiated
  schizophrenia

Key People

Nancy Andreasen
Martin Seligman
Thomas Szasz

PRACTICE TEST

1. According to Thomas Szasz, abnormal behavior usually involves:
   A. behavior that is statistically unusual.
   B. behavior that deviates from social norms.
   C. a disease of the mind.
   D. biological imbalance.

2. Although Sue always feels a high level of dread, worry, and anxiety, she still manages to meet her daily responsibilities. Sue's behavior:
   A. should not be considered abnormal, since her adaptive functioning is not impaired.
   B. should not be considered abnormal, since everyone sometimes experiences worry and anxiety.
   C. can still be considered abnormal, since she feels great personal distress.
   D. both a and b.

3. The fact that people acquire phobias of ancient sources of threat (such as snakes) much more readily than modern sources of threat (such as electrical outlets) can best be explained by:
   A. classical conditioning.
   B. operant conditioning.
   C. observational learning.
   D. preparedness.

4. Which of the following statements about dissociative identity disorder is true?
   A. The original personality is always aware of the alternate personalities.
   B. The alternate personalities are always unaware of the original personality.
   C. The personalities are typically all quite similar to one another.
   D. During the 1980s, there was a dramatic increase in the diagnosis of dissociative identity disorder.

5. People with unipolar disorder experience _____; people with bipolar disorder experience _____.
   A. alternating periods of depression and mania; mania only
   B. depression only; alternating periods of depression and mania
   C. mania only; alternating periods of depression and mania
   D. alternating periods of depression and mania; depression and mania simultaneously

6. A concordance rate indicates:
   A. the percentage of twin pairs or other close relatives who exhibit the same disorder.
   B. the percentage of people with a given disorder who are currently receiving treatment.
   C. the prevalence of a given disorder in the general population.
   D. the rate of cure for a given disorder.

7. People who consistently come up with _____ explanations for negative events are more prone to depression.
   A. overly optimistic
   B. pessimistic
   C. delusional
   D. dysthymic

8. Mary believes that while she sleeps at night, space creatures are attacking her and invading her uterus, where they will multiply until they are ready to take over the world. Mary was chosen for this task, she believes, because she is the only one with the power to help the space creatures succeed. Mary would most likely be diagnosed as _____ schizophrenic.
   A. paranoid
   B. catatonic
   C. disorganized
   D. undifferentiated

9. As an alternative to the current classification scheme, it has been proposed that schizophrenic disorders be divided into just two categories based on:
   A. whether the prognosis is favorable or unfavorable.
   B. whether the disorder is mild or severe.
   C. the predominance of thought disturbances versus emotional disturbances.
   D. the predominance of negative versus positive symptoms.

10. Most of the drugs that are useful in the treatment of schizophrenia are known to dampen _____ activity in the brain, suggesting that disruptions in the activity of this neurotransmitter may contribute to the development of the disorder.
    A. norepinephrine
    B. serotonin
    C. acetylcholine
    D. dopamine

11. Bipolar disorder occurs in _____ of the population.
    A. about 1%
    B. about 10%
    C. nearly one-third
    D. about 20%

12. Research suggests that there is an association between schizophrenia and:
    A. atrophied brain ventricles.
    B. enlarged brain ventricles.
    C. hippocampal degeneration.
    D. abnormalities in the cerebellum.

13. Involuntary commitment to a psychiatric facility:
    A. can occur only after a mentally ill individual has been convicted of a violent crime.
    B. usually occurs because people appear to be a danger to themselves or others.
    C. no longer occurs under modern civil law.
    D. will be a lifelong commitment, even if the individual is no longer mentally ill.

14. Those who embrace a relativistic view of psychological disorders would assert that:
    A. the criteria of mental illness vary greatly across cultures.
    B. there are universal standards of normality and abnormality.
    C. Western diagnostic concepts have validity and utility in other cultural contexts.
    D. b and c.

15. About _____ of patients with eating disorders are female.
    A. 40%
    B. 50%–60%
    C. 75%
    D. 90%–95%

Answers

1	B	page 426	6	A	page 431	11	A	page 439
2	C	page 427	7	B	pages 440–441	12	B	page 445
3	D	page 432	8	A	page 443	13	B	page 447
4	D	page 436	9	D	pages 443–444	14	A	page 447
5	B	pages 437–438	10	D	page 444	15	D	page 452

INFOTRAC
COLLEGE EDITION

Go to the Wadsworth Psychology Study Center for quiz questions, research updates, interactive exercises, and suggested readings in INFOTRAC related to this chapter:
http://psychology.wadsworth.com/product/0534593100s

CHAPTER 15

© Michael Agilolo/International Stock

Treatment of Psychological Disorders

© Michael Agliolo/International Stock

What do you picture when you hear the term *psychotherapy?* If you're like most people, you probably envision a troubled patient lying on a couch in a book-lined office, with the therapist asking penetrating questions and providing sage advice. Typically, people believe that psychotherapy is only for those who are "sick" and that therapists have special powers that allow them to "see through" their clients. It is also widely believed that successful therapy requires years of deep probing into a client's innermost secrets. Many people further assume that therapists routinely tell their patients how to lead their lives. Like most stereotypes, this picture of psychotherapy is a mixture of fact and fiction, as you'll see in the upcoming pages. In this chapter, we'll take a down-to-earth look at psychotherapy, using the term in its broadest sense, to refer to all the diverse approaches

used in the treatment of mental disorders and psychological problems. We'll start by discussing some general questions about the provision of treatment, including:

- Who seeks treatment?
- What kinds of professionals provide treatment?
- What are the differences between psychiatrists and psychologists?
- How many different approaches to therapy are there?

After we've considered these general issues, we'll examine some of the more widely used approaches to treating psychological problems, analyzing their goals, techniques, and effectiveness. In the Personal Application, we focus on practical issues involved in finding and choosing a therapist, in case you ever have to advise someone about seeking psychotherapy. And in the Critical Thinking Application we address problems involved in determining whether therapy actually helps.

Sigmund Freud is widely credited with launching modern psychotherapy. Ironically, the landmark case that inspired Freud was actually treated by one of his colleagues, Josef Breuer. Around 1880, Breuer began to treat a young woman named Anna O (a pseudonym). Anna exhibited a variety of physical maladies, including headaches, coughing, and a loss of feeling and movement in her right arm. Much to his surprise, Breuer discovered that Anna's physical symptoms cleared up when he encouraged her to talk about emotionally charged experiences from her past.

When Breuer and Freud discussed the case, they speculated that talking things through had enabled Anna to drain off bottled up emotions that had caused her symptoms. Breuer found the intense emotional exchange in this treatment not to his liking, so he didn't follow through on his discovery. However, Freud applied Breuer's insight to other patients, and his successes led him to develop a systematic treatment procedure, which he called *psychoanalysis*. Anna O called her treatment "the talking cure." However, as you'll see, psychotherapy isn't always curative, and many modern therapies place little emphasis on talking.

Freud's breakthrough ushered in a century of progress for psychotherapy. Psychoanalysis spawned many offspring as Freud's followers developed their own systems of treatment. Since then, approaches to psychotherapy have steadily grown more numerous, more diverse, and more effective. Today, people can choose from a bewildering array of therapies.

Treatments: How Many Types Are There?

In their efforts to help people, psychotherapists use many treatment methods. One expert (Kazdin, 1994) estimates that there may be over 400 different approaches to treatment! Fortunately, we can impose some order on this chaos. As varied as therapists' procedures are, approaches to treatment can be classified into three major categories:

1. *Insight therapies*. Insight therapy is "talk therapy" in the tradition of Freud's psychoanalysis. In insight therapies, clients engage in complex, often lengthy verbal interactions with their therapists. The goal in these discussions is to pursue increased insight regarding the nature of the client's difficulties and to sort through possible solutions.

2. *Behavior therapies*. Behavior therapies are based on the principles of learning, which were introduced in Chapter 6. Instead of emphasizing personal insights, behavior therapists make direct efforts to alter problematic responses (phobias, for instance) and maladaptive habits (drug use, for instance). Most of their procedures involve classical conditioning, operant conditioning, or observational learning.

3. *Biomedical therapies*. Biomedical approaches to therapy involve interventions into a person's biological functioning. The most widely used procedures are drug therapy and electroconvulsive (shock) therapy. As the name *biomedical* therapies suggests, these treaments have traditionally been provided only by physicians with a medical degree. This situation may change, however, as psychologists have begun to campaign for prescription privileges (DeLeon & Wiggins, 1996; Pachman, 1996). They have made some progress toward this goal, even though many psychologists have argued against pursuing the right to prescribe medication (DeNelsky, 1996; Hayes & Heiby, 1996).

Clients: Who Seeks Therapy?

In the therapeutic triad (therapists, treatments, clients), the greatest diversity of all is seen among the clients. According to the 1999 U.S. Surgeon General's report on mental health (U.S. Department of Health and Human Services, 1999) about 15% of the U.S. population use mental health services in a given year. These people bring to therapy the full range of human problems: anxiety, depression, unsatisfactory interpersonal relations, troublesome habits, poor self-control, low self-esteem, marital conflicts, self-doubt, a sense of emptiness, and feelings of personal stagnation. The two most common presenting problems are excessive anxiety and depression (Narrow et al., 1993). Interestingly, people often delay for many years before finally seeking treatment for their psychological problems (Kessler, Olfson, & Berglund, 1998).

A client in treatment does *not* necessarily have an identifiable psychological disorder. Some people seek professional help for everyday problems (career decisions, for instance) or vague feelings of discontent (Strupp, 1996). One surprising finding in the Surgeon General's report was that almost half of the people who use mental health services in a given year do not have a specific disorder.

The case of Anna O., whose real name was Bertha Pappenheim, provided the inspiration for Sigmund Freud's invention of psychoanalysis.

Mary Evans/Sigmund Freud Copyrights

Web Link 15.1

Online Dictionary of Mental Health
This thematically arranged "dictionary" assembled at the University of Sheffield (UK) Medical School contains diverse links involving many forms of psychotherapy, the treatment of psychological disorders, and general issues of mental health.

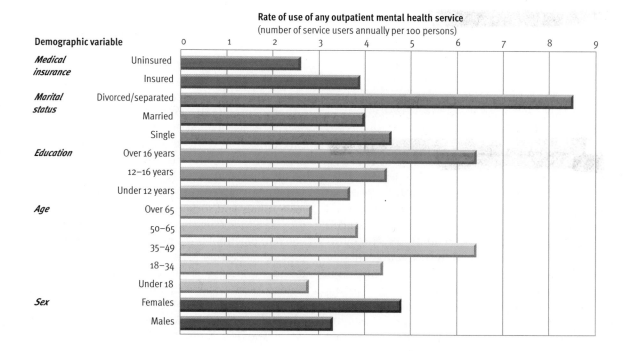

Rate of use of any outpatient mental health service
(number of service users annually per 100 persons)

Demographic variable		0	1	2	3	4	5	6	7	8	9

Medical insurance — Uninsured, Insured
Marital status — Divorced/separated, Married, Single
Education — Over 16 years, 12–16 years, Under 12 years
Age — Over 65, 50–65, 35–49, 18–34, Under 18
Sex — Females, Males

Figure 15.1

Therapy utilization rates.
Olfson and Pincus (1996) gathered data on the use of non-hospital outpatient mental health services in the United States in relation to various demographic variables. As you can see, people are more likely to enter therapy if they have medical insurance than if they do not. In regard to marital status, utilization rates are particularly high among those who are divorced or separated. The use of therapy is greater among those who have more education and, in terms of age, utilization peaks in the 35–49 age bracket. Finally, females are more like to pursue therapy than males.

People vary considerably in their willingness to seek psychotherapy. As you can see in Figure 15.1, women are more likely than men to receive therapy. Treatment is also more likely when people have medical insurance and when they have more education (Olfson & Pincus, 1996). *Unfortunately, it appears that many people who need therapy don't receive it* (Kessler et al., 1999). As Figure 15.2 shows, only a portion of the people who need treatment get it. People who could benefit from therapy do not seek it for a variety of reasons. Lack of health insurance and cost concerns appear to be major barriers to obtaining needed care for many people (Druss & Rosenheck, 1998). According to the Surgeon General's report, the biggest roadblock is the "stigma surrounding the receipt of mental health treatment." Unfortunately, many people equate seeking therapy with admitting personal weakness.

Therapists: Who Provides Professional Treatment?

Friends and relatives may provide you with excellent advice about your personal problems, but their assistance does not qualify as therapy. Psychotherapy refers to *professional* treatment by someone with special training. However, a common source of confusion about psychotherapy is the variety of "helping professions" involved (Murstein & Fontaine, 1993). Psychology and psychiatry are the principal professions involved in the provision of psychotherapy, delivering the lion's share of mental

health care. However, treatment is also provided by other types of therapists. Let's look at these mental health professions.

Psychologists

Two types of psychologists may provide therapy, although the distinction between them is more theoretical than real. *Clinical psychologists* and *counseling psychologists* specialize in the diagnosis and treatment of psychological disorders and

Figure 15.2

Psychological disorders and professional treatment. Not everyone who has a psychological disorder receives professional treatment, and not everyone who seeks treatment has a clear disorder. This graph, from the Surgeon General's report on mental health, shows that 15% of the U.S. adult population receive mental health treatment each year. Almost half of these people (7%) do not receive a psychiatric diagnosis, although some of them probably have milder disorders that are not assessed in epidemiological research. This graph also shows that over two-thirds of the people who do have disorders do *not* receive professional treatment. (Adapted from *Mental Health: A Report of the Surgeon General*, U.S. Department of Health and Human Services, 1999)

Percent of population (28%) with disorder (in one year)

Percent of population (15%) receiving mental health services (in one year)

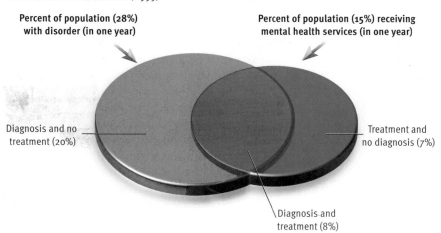

Diagnosis and no treatment (20%)

Treatment and no diagnosis (7%)

Diagnosis and treatment (8%)

everyday behavioral problems. In theory, clinical psychologists' training emphasizes the treatment of full-fledged disorders. In contrast, counseling psychologists' training is supposed to be slanted toward the treatment of everyday adjustment problems in normal people. In practice, however, clinical and counseling psychologists overlap greatly in training, skills, and the clientele they serve.

Both types of psychologists must earn a doctoral degree (Ph.D., Psy.D., or Ed.D.). A doctorate in psychology requires about five to seven years of training beyond a bachelor's degree. The process of gaining admission to a Ph.D. program in clinical psychology is highly competitive (about as difficult as getting into medical school). Psychologists receive most of their training in universities or independent professional schools. They then serve a one-year internship in a clinical setting, such as a hospital, usually followed by one or two years of postdoctoral fellowship training. In providing therapy, psychologists use either insight or behavioral approaches. Clinical and counseling psychologists do psychological testing as well as psychotherapy, and many also conduct research.

Psychiatrists

Psychiatrists are physicians who specialize in the diagnosis and treatment of psychological disorders. Many psychiatrists also treat everyday behavioral problems. However, in comparison to psychologists, psychiatrists devote more time to relatively severe disorders (schizophrenia, mood disorders) and less time to everyday marital, family, job, and school problems. Psychiatrists have an M.D. degree. Their graduate training requires four years of coursework in medical school and a four-year apprenticeship in a residency at a hospital. Their psychotherapy training occurs during their residency. In their provision of therapy, psychiatrists tend to emphasize biomedical treatments and psychoanalytic approaches to insight therapy.

Other Mental Health Professionals

Several other mental health professions provide psychotherapy services. *Psychiatric social workers* and *psychiatric nurses* often work as part of a treatment team with a psychologist or psychiatrist. Although social workers have traditionally worked in hospitals and social service agencies, many also provide a wide range of therapeutic services as independent practitioners. Many kinds of *counselors* also provide therapeutic services. Counselors are usually found working in schools, colleges, and assorted human service agencies. They often specialize in particular types of problems, such as vocational counseling, marital counseling, rehabilitation counseling, and drug counseling.

Although there are clear differences among the helping professions in education, training, and their approach to therapy, their roles in the treatment process overlap considerably. In this chapter, we will refer to psychologists or psychiatrists as needed, but otherwise we'll use the terms *clinician, therapist,* and *mental health professional* to refer to psychotherapists of all kinds, regardless of their professional degree.

Now that we have discussed the basic elements in psychotherapy, we can examine specific approaches to treatment in terms of their goals, procedures, and effectiveness. We'll begin with a few, representative insight therapies.

Insight Therapies

Many schools of thought offer ideas about how to do insight therapy. Therapists with various theoretical orientations use different methods to pursue different kinds of insights. However, what these varied approaches have in common is that *insight therapies* involve verbal interactions intended to enhance clients' self-knowledge and thus promote healthful changes in personality and behavior.

There probably are around 200 different insight therapies, but the leading eight or ten approaches appear to account for the lion's share of treatment. In this section, we'll delve into psychoanalysis, client-centered therapy, and cognitive therapy. We'll also discuss how insight therapy can be done with groups of clients as well as individuals.

Psychoanalysis

After the case of Anna O, Sigmund Freud worked as a psychotherapist for almost 50 years in Vienna. Through a painstaking process of trial and error, he developed innovative techniques for the treatment of psychological disorders and distress. His system of *psychoanalysis* came to dominate psychiatry for many decades. Although the dominance of psychoanalysis has eroded in recent years, a diverse collection of psychoanalytic approaches to therapy continue to evolve and to remain influential today (Eagle & Wolitzky, 1992; Ursano & Silberman, 1999).

Psychoanalysis **is an insight therapy that emphasizes the recovery of unconscious conflicts, motives, and defenses through techniques such as free association and transference.** To appreciate the logic of psychoanalysis, we have to look at Freud's thinking about the roots of mental disorders. Freud mostly treated anxiety-dominated disturbances, such as phobic, panic, obsessive-compulsive, and conversion disorders, which were then called *neuroses*.

Freud believed that neurotic problems are caused by unconscious conflicts left over from early childhood. As explained in Chapter 12, he thought that these inner conflicts involved battles among the id, ego, and superego, usually over sexual and aggressive impulses. He theorized that people depend on defense mechanisms to avoid confronting these conflicts, which remain hidden in the depths of the unconscious (see Figure 15.3). However, he noted that defensive maneuvers often lead to self-defeating behavior. Furthermore, he asserted that defenses tend to be only partially successful in alleviating anxiety, guilt, and other distressing emotions. With this model in mind, let's take a look at the therapeutic procedures used in psychoanalysis.

Probing the Unconscious

Given Freud's assumptions, we can see that the logic of psychoanalysis is quite simple. The analyst attempts to probe the murky depths of the unconscious to discover the unresolved conflicts causing the client's neurotic behavior. In this effort to explore the unconscious, the therapist relies on two techniques: free association and dream analysis.

In *free association* **clients spontaneously express their thoughts and feelings exactly as they occur, with as little censorship as possible.** Clients lie on a couch so they will be better able to let their mind drift freely. In free associating, clients expound on anything that comes to mind, regardless of how trivial, silly, or embarrassing it might be. Gradually, most clients begin to let everything pour out without conscious censorship. The analyst studies these free associations for clues about what is going on in the unconscious.

In *dream analysis* **the therapist interprets the symbolic meaning of the client's dreams.** For Freud, dreams were the "royal road to the unconscious," the most direct means of access to patients' innermost conflicts, wishes, and impulses. Psychoanalytic clients are encouraged and trained to remember their dreams, which they describe in therapy. The therapist then analyzes the symbolism in these dreams to interpret their meaning.

To better illustrate these matters, let's look at an actual case treated through psychoanalysis (adapted from Greenson, 1967, pp. 40–41). Mr. N was troubled by an unsatisfactory marriage. He claimed to love his wife, but he preferred sexual relations with prostitutes. Mr. N reported that his parents also endured lifelong marital difficulties. His childhood conflicts about their relationship appeared to be related to his problems. Both dream analysis and free association can be seen in the following description of a session in Mr. N's treatment:

Mr. N reported a fragment of a dream. All that he could remember is that he was waiting for a red traffic light to change when he felt that someone had bumped into him from behind. . . . The associations led to Mr. N's love of cars, especially sports cars. He loved the sensation, in particular, of whizzing by those fat, old expensive cars. . . . His father always hinted that he had been a great athlete, but he never substantiated it. . . . Mr. N doubted whether his father could really perform. His father would flirt with a waitress in a cafe or make sexual remarks about women passing by, but he seemed to be showing off. If he were really sexual, he wouldn't resort to that.

As is characteristic of free association, Mr. N's train of thought meandered about with little direction. Nonetheless, clues about his unconscious conflicts were apparent. What did Mr. N's therapist extract from this session? The therapist saw sexual overtones in the dream fragment, where Mr. N was bumped from behind. The therapist also inferred that Mr. N had a competitive orientation toward his father, based on the free association about whizzing by fat, old expensive cars. As you can see, analysts must *interpret* their clients' dreams and free associations. This is a critical process throughout psychoanalysis.

Interpretation

Interpretation **refers to the therapist's attempts to explain the inner significance of the client's thoughts, feelings, memories, and behaviors.** Contrary to popular belief, analysts do not interpret

"*The news that reaches your consciousness is incomplete and often not to be relied on.*"
SIGMUND FREUD

Figure 15.3

Freud's view of the roots of disorders. According to Freud, unconscious conflicts between the id, ego, and superego sometimes lead to anxiety. This discomfort may lead to the use of defense mechanisms, which may temporarily relieve anxiety.

Intrapsychic conflict (between id, ego, and superego) → Anxiety → Reliance on defense mechanisms

The original psychoanalytic couch—from Freud's office—is shown here. Today, only a minority of psychoanalytic therapists require their patients to lie on a couch.

everything, and they generally don't try to dazzle clients with startling revelations. Instead, analysts move forward inch by inch, offering interpretations that should be just out of the client's own reach. Mr. N's therapist eventually offered the following interpretations to his client:

I said to Mr. N near the end of the hour that I felt he was struggling with his feelings about his father's sexual life. He seemed to be saying that his father was sexually not a very potent man. . . . He also recalls that he once found a packet of condoms under his father's pillow when he was an adolescent and he thought, "My father must be going to prostitutes." I then intervened and pointed out that the condoms under his father's pillow seemed to indicate more obviously that his father used the condoms with his mother, who slept in the same bed. However, Mr. N wanted to believe his wish-fulfilling fantasy: mother doesn't want sex with father and father is not very potent. The patient was silent and the hour ended.

As you may have already guessed, the therapist concluded that Mr. N's difficulties were rooted in an *Oedipal complex* (see Chapter 12). He had unresolved sexual feelings toward his mother and hostile feelings about his father. These unconscious conflicts, rooted in Mr. N's childhood, were distorting his intimate relations as an adult.

Resistance

How would you expect Mr. N to respond to the therapist's suggestion that he was in competition with his father for the sexual attention of his mother? Obviously, most clients would have great difficulty accepting such an interpretation. Freud fully expected clients to display some resistance to therapeutic efforts. *Resistance* **refers to largely unconscious defensive maneuvers intended to hinder the progress of therapy.** Why would clients try to resist the helping process? Because they don't want to face up to the painful, disturbing conflicts that they have buried in their unconscious. Although they have sought help, they are reluctant to confront their real problems.

Resistance can take many forms. Clients may show up late for their sessions, may merely pretend to engage in free association, or may express hostility toward their therapist. For instance, Mr. N's therapist noted that after the session just described, "The next day he [Mr. N] began by telling me that he was furious with me. . . ." Analysts use a variety of strategies to deal with clients' resistance. Often, a key consideration is the handling of transference, which we consider next.

Transference

Transference **occurs when clients start relating to their therapists in ways that mimic critical relationships in their lives.** Thus, a client might start relating to a therapist as if the therapist were an overprotective mother, a rejecting brother, or a passive spouse. In a sense, the client *transfers* conflicting feelings about important people onto the therapist. For instance, in his treatment, Mr. N transferred some of the competitive hostility he felt toward his father onto his analyst.

Psychoanalysts often encourage transference so that clients can reenact relations with crucial people in the context of therapy. These reenactments can help bring repressed feelings and conflicts to the surface, allowing the client to work through them. The therapist's handling of transference is complicated and difficult, because transference may arouse confusing, highly charged emotions in the client.

Undergoing psychoanalysis is not easy. It can be a slow, painful process of self-examination that routinely requires three to five years of hard work. Ultimately, if resistance and transference can be handled effectively, the therapist's interpretations should lead the client to profound insights. For instance, Mr. N eventually admitted, "The old boy is probably right, it does tickle me to imagine that my mother preferred me and I could beat out my father. Later, I wondered whether this had something to do with my own screwed-up sex life with my wife." According to Freud, once clients recognize the unconscious sources of conflicts, they can resolve these conflicts and discard their neurotic defenses.

Modern Psychodynamic Treatment

Though still available, classical psychoanalysis as done by Freud is not widely practiced anymore. Freud's psychoanalytic method was geared to a particular kind of clientele that he was seeing in Vienna many years ago. As his followers fanned out across Europe and America, many found it necessary to adapt psychoanalysis to different cultures, changing times, and new kinds of patients. Thus, many variations on Freud's original approach to psychoanalysis have developed over the years. These descendants of psychoanalysis are collectively known as *psychodynamic approaches* to therapy.

Some of these adaptations, such as those by Carl Jung (1917) and Alfred Adler (1927), were sweeping revisions based on fundamental differences in theory. Other variations, such as those devised by Melanie Klein (1948) and Heinz Kohut (1971), involved more subtle changes in theory. Still other

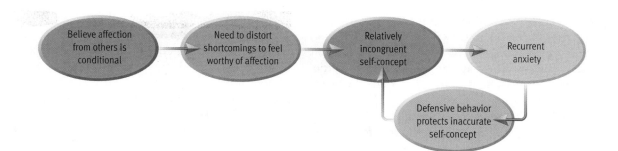

Figure 15.4

Rogers's view of the roots of disorders. Rogers's theory posits that anxiety and self-defeating behavior are rooted in an incongruent self-concept that makes one prone to recurrent anxiety, which triggers defensive behavior, which fuels more incongruence.

revisions (Alexander, 1954; Stekel, 1950) simply involved efforts to modernize and streamline psychoanalytic techniques. Hence, today we have a rich diversity of psychodynamic approaches to therapy.

Client-Centered Therapy

You may have heard of people going into therapy to "find themselves," or to "get in touch with their real feelings." These now-popular phrases emerged out of the human potential movement, which was stimulated in part by the work of Carl Rogers (1951, 1986). Using a humanistic perspective, Rogers devised client-centered therapy (also known as person-centered therapy) in the 1940s and 1950s.

Client-centered therapy is an insight therapy that emphasizes providing a supportive emotional climate for clients, who play a major role in determining the pace and direction of their therapy. Rogers's theory about the principal causes of neurotic anxieties is quite different from the Freudian explanation. As discussed in Chapter 12, Rogers maintains that most personal distress is due to inconsistency, or "incongruence," between a person's self-concept and reality (see Figure 15.4). According to his theory, incongruence makes people feel threatened by realistic feedback about themselves from others. For example, if you inaccurately viewed yourself as a hard-working, dependable person, you would feel threatened by contradictory feedback from friends or co-workers. According to Rogers, anxiety about such feedback often leads to reliance on defense mechanisms, to distortions of reality, and to stifled personal growth. Excessive incongruence is thought to be rooted in clients' overdependence on others for approval and acceptance.

Given Rogers's theory, client-centered therapists stalk insights that are quite different from the repressed conflicts that psychoanalysts go after. Client-centered therapists help clients realize that they do not have to worry constantly about pleasing others and winning acceptance. They encourage clients to respect their own feelings and values.

They help people restructure their self-concept to correspond better to reality. Ultimately, they try to foster self-acceptance and personal growth.

Therapeutic Climate

According to Rogers, the *process* of therapy is not as important as the emotional *climate* in which the therapy takes place. He believes that it is critical for the therapist to provide a warm, supportive, accepting climate. This creates a safe environment in which clients can confront their shortcomings without feeling threatened. The lack of threat should reduce clients' defensive tendencies and thus help them open up. To create this atmosphere of emotional support, client-centered therapists must provide three conditions:

1. *Genuineness.* The therapist must be genuine with the client, communicating honestly and spontaneously. The therapist should not be phony or defensive.

2. *Unconditional positive regard.* The therapist must also show complete, nonjudgmental acceptance of the client as a person. The therapist should

"To my mind, empathy is in itself a healing agent."
CARL ROGERS

Client-centered therapists emphasize the importance of a supportive emotional climate in therapy. They also work to clarify, rather than interpret, the feelings expressed by their patients.

provide warmth and caring for the client, with no strings attached. This does not mean that the therapist must approve of everything that the client says or does. A therapist can disapprove of a particular behavior while continuing to value the client as a human being.

3. *Empathy.* Finally, the therapist must provide accurate empathy for the client. This means that the therapist must understand the client's world from the client's point of view. Furthermore, the therapist must be articulate enough to communicate this understanding to the client.

Rogers firmly believed that a supportive emotional climate is the critical force promoting healthy changes in therapy. In recent years, however, some client-centered therapists have begun to place more emphasis on the therapeutic process (Rice & Greenberg, 1992).

Therapeutic Process 11d

In client-centered therapy, the client and therapist work together as equals. The therapist provides relatively little guidance and keeps interpretation and advice to a minimum. So, just what does the client-centered therapist do, besides creating a supportive climate? Primarily, the therapist provides feedback to help clients sort out their feelings. The therapist's key task is *clarification.* Client-centered therapists try to function like a human mirror, reflecting statements back to their clients, but with enhanced clarity. They help clients become more aware of their true feelings by highlighting themes that may be obscure in the clients' rambling discourse.

By working with clients to clarify their feelings, client-centered therapists hope to gradually build toward more far-reaching insights. In particular, they try to help clients better understand their interpersonal relationships and become more comfortable with their genuine selves. Obviously, these are ambitious goals. Client-centered therapy resembles psychoanalysis in that both seek to achieve a major reconstruction of a client's personality. We'll see more limited and specific goals in cognitive therapy, which we consider next.

Cognitive Therapy

In Chapter 14, we learned that cognitive factors play a key role in the development of many anxiety and mood disorders. Citing the importance of findings such as these, Aaron Beck devised a treatment that focuses on clients' cognitive processes. (1976, 1987). **Cognitive therapy is an insight therapy that emphasizes recognizing and changing negative thoughts and maladaptive beliefs.**

In recent years cognitive therapy has been applied fruitfully to a wide range of disorders (Beck, 1991; Hollon & Beck, 1994), but it was originally devised as a treatment for depression. According to cognitive therapists, depression is caused by "errors" in thinking (see Figure 15.5). They assert that depression-prone people tend to (1) blame their setbacks on personal inadequacies without considering circumstantial explanations, (2) focus selectively on negative events while ignoring positive events, (3) make unduly pessimistic projections about the future, and (4) draw negative conclusions about their worth as a person based on insignificant events. For instance, imagine that you got a low grade on a minor quiz in a class. If you made the kinds of errors in thinking just described, you might blame the grade on your woeful stupidity, dismiss comments from a classmate that it was an unfair test, gloomily predict that you will surely flunk the course, and conclude that you are not genuine college material.

The goal of cognitive therapy is to change the way clients think. To begin, clients are taught to detect their automatic negative thoughts. These are self-defeating statements that people are prone to make when analyzing problems. Examples might include "I'm just not smart enough," "No one really likes me," or "It's all my fault." Clients are then trained to subject these automatic thoughts to reality testing. The therapist helps them to see how unrealistically negative the thoughts are.

The therapist's goal is not to promote unwarranted optimism but rather to help the client use more reasonable standards of evaluation. For example, a cognitive therapist might point out that a client's failure to get a desired promotion at work may be attributable to many factors and that this setback doesn't

Web Link 15.2

The Counseling Web
Counseling psychologists and counselors address both the problems of daily life and psychological distress. Gail Hackett of Arizona State University has constructed a comprehensive set of resource links about counseling in all its aspects.

Web Link 15.3

Basics of Cognitive Therapy
This site provides a good overview of cognitive therapy, addressing topics such as the nature of cognitive therapy, the research background supporting cognitive therapy, the way cognitive therapy is conducted, and ways one can learn more about this popular approach to treatment.

"*Most people are barely aware of the automatic thoughts which precede unpleasant feelings or automatic inhibitions.*"
AARON BECK

Figure 15.5

Beck's view of the roots of disorders. Beck's theory initially focused on the causes of depression, although it was gradually broadened to explain other disorders. According to Beck, depression is caused by the types of negative thinking shown here.

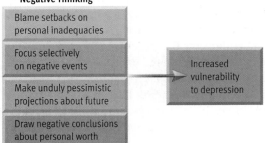

Negative Thinking

Blame setbacks on personal inadequacies

Focus selectively on negative events

Make unduly pessimistic projections about future

Draw negative conclusions about personal worth

→ Increased vulnerability to depression

mean that the client is incompetent. Gradually, the therapist digs deeper, looking for the unrealistic assumptions that underlie clients' constant negative thinking. These, too, have to be changed.

Unlike client-centered therapists, cognitive therapists are actively involved in determining the pace and direction of treatment. They usually talk extensively in the therapy sessions. They may argue openly with clients as they try to persuade them to alter their patterns of thinking.

Cognitive therapy was originally designed as a treatment for individuals. However, it has been adapted for use with groups (Rose, 1999). Most insight therapies can be conducted on either an individual or group basis (Kaplan & Sadock, 1993), so let's take a look at the dynamics of group therapy.

Group Therapy

Although it dates back to the early part of the 20th century, group therapy came of age during World War II and its aftermath in the 1950s (Rosenbaum, Lakin, & Roback, 1992). During this period, the expanding demand for therapeutic services forced clinicians to use group techniques (Scheidlinger, 1993). **Group therapy is the simultaneous treatment of several clients in a group.** Although group therapy can be conducted in a variety of ways, we can provide a general overview of the process as it usually unfolds (see Vinogradov, Cox, & Yalom, 1994; Yalom, 1995).

A therapy group typically consists of 4 to 15 people, with 8 participants regarded as ideal. The therapist usually screens the participants, excluding persons who seem likely to be disruptive. Some theorists maintain that judicious selection of participants is crucial to effective group treatment (Salvendy, 1993). There is some debate about whether or not it is best to have a homogeneous group, made up of people who are similar in age, sex, and psychological problem. Practical necessities usually dictate that groups are at least somewhat diversified.

In group therapy, participants essentially function as therapists for one another. Group members describe their problems, trade viewpoints, share experiences, and discuss coping strategies. Most important, they provide acceptance and emotional support for each other. In this atmosphere, group members work at peeling away the social masks that cover their insecurities. Once their problems are exposed, members work at correcting them. As members come to value one another's opinions, they work hard to display healthy changes to win the group's approval.

CONCEPT **CHECK 15.1**

Understanding Therapists' Conceptions of Disorders

Check your understanding of the three approaches to insight therapy covered in the text by matching each approach with the appropriate explanation of the typical origins of clients' psychological disorders. The answers are in Appendix A.

Theorized causes of disorders

__C.__ **1.** Problems rooted in pervasive negative thoughts about self and errors in thinking

__a.__ **2.** Problems rooted in unconscious conflicts left over from childhood

__b.__ **3.** Problems rooted in inaccurate self-concept and excessive concern about pleasing others

Therapy

a. Psychoanalysis

b. Client-centered therapy

c. Cognitive therapy

In group treatment, the therapist's responsibilities include selecting participants, setting goals for the group, initiating and maintaining the therapeutic process, and protecting clients from harm (Weiner, 1993). The therapist often plays a relatively subtle role in group therapy, staying in the background and focusing mainly on promoting group cohesiveness. The therapist models supportive behaviors for the participants and tries to promote a healthy climate. He or she always retains a special status, but the therapist and clients are on much more equal footing in group therapy than in individual therapy.

Group therapies obviously save time and money, which can be critical in understaffed mental hospitals and other institutional settings. Therapists in private practice usually charge less for group than

Group treatments have proven particularly helpful when members share similar problems, such as alcoholism, overeating, or having been sexually abused as a child. Many approaches to insight therapy that were originally designed for individuals—such as cognitive therapy—have been adapted for treatment of groups.

© Bob Daemmrich/The Image Works

individual therapy, making therapy affordable for more people. However, group therapy is *not* just a less costly substitute for individual therapy. Group therapy has unique strengths of its own, and certain kinds of problems are especially well suited to group treatment (Piper, 1993; Yalom, 1995).

Whether insight therapies are conducted on a group or an individual basis, clients usually invest considerable time, effort, and money. Are these therapies worth the investment? Let's examine the evidence on their effectiveness.

Evaluating Insight Therapies

Evaluating the effectiveness of any approach to psychotherapy is a complex matter (Howard et al., 1996; Roth & Fonagy, 1996). For one thing, psychological disorders sometimes clear up on their own, a phenomenon called *spontaneous remission*. If a client experiences a recovery after treatment, one cannot automatically assume that the recovery was attributable to the treatment (see the Critical Thinking Application). Evaluations of insight therapies are especially complicated given that various schools of thought pursue entirely different goals. Judgments of therapeutic outcome in insight therapy tend to be subjective, with little consensus about the best way to assess therapeutic progress (Lambert & Hill, 1994). Moreover, people enter therapy with diverse problems of varied severity, so the efficacy of treatment can only be evaluated meaningfully for specific clinical problems (Elliott, Stiles, & Shapiro, 1993).

In spite of these difficulties, hundreds of therapy outcome studies have been conducted. These studies have examined a broad range of specific clinical problems and have used diverse methods to assess therapeutic outcomes, including scores on psychological tests and ratings by family members, as well as therapists' and clients' ratings. These studies consistently indicate that insight therapy is superior to no treatment or to placebo treatment and that the effects of therapy are reasonably durable (Barlow, 1996; Kopta et al., 1999; Lambert & Bergin, 1994). In one widely discussed study that focused on patients' self-reports, the vast majority of the respondents subjectively felt that they had derived considerable benefit from their therapy (Seligman, 1995).

Web Link 15.4

The Effectiveness of Psychotherapy: The *Consumer Reports* Study
In 1995, *Consumer Reports* concluded that psychotherapy is effective in the treatment of psychological problems and disorders. Martin Seligman, an important psychotherapy researcher, reviews the study's methods and compares it to other ways of judging psychotherapy's effects.

Behavior Therapies

Behavior therapy is different from insight therapy in that behavior therapists make no attempt to help clients achieve grand insights about themselves. Why not? Because behavior therapists believe that such insights aren't necessary to produce constructive change. For example, consider a client troubled by compulsive gambling. The behavior therapist doesn't care whether this behavior is rooted in unconscious conflicts or parental rejection. What the client needs is to get rid of the maladaptive behavior. Consequently, the therapist simply designs a program to eliminate the compulsive gambling.

The crux of the difference between insight therapy and behavior therapy is this: Insight therapists treat pathological symptoms as signs of an underlying problem, whereas behavior therapists think that the symptoms *are* the problem. Thus, **behavior therapies involve the application of the principles of learning to direct efforts to change clients' maladaptive behaviors.**

Behaviorism has been an influential school of thought in psychology since the 1920s. Nevertheless, behaviorists devoted little attention to clinical issues until the 1950s, when behavior therapy emerged out of three independent lines of research fostered by B. F. Skinner and his colleagues (Skinner, Solomon, & Lindsley, 1953) in the United States, Hans Eysenck (1959) and his colleagues in Britain, and Joseph Wolpe (1958) and his colleagues in South Africa (Glass & Arnkoff, 1992). Since then, there has been an explosion of interest in behavioral approaches to psychotherapy.

General Principles

Behavior therapies are based on certain assumptions (Agras & Berkowitz, 1999). *First, it is assumed that behavior is a product of learning.* No matter how self-defeating or pathological a client's behavior might be, the behaviorist believes that it is the result of past conditioning. *Second, it is assumed that what has been learned can be unlearned.* The same learning principles that explain how the maladaptive behavior was acquired can be used to get rid of it. Thus, behavior therapists attempt to change clients' behavior by applying the principles of classical conditioning, operant conditioning, and observational learning.

Behavior therapies are close cousins of the self-modification procedures described in the Chapter 6

Personal Application. Both use the same principles of learning to alter behavior directly. In discussing *self-modification,* we examined some relatively simple procedures that people can apply to themselves to improve everyday self-control. In our discussion of *behavior therapy,* we will examine more complex procedures used by mental health professionals in the treatment of more severe problems. Like self-modification, behavior therapy involves designing specific procedures for specific types of problems, as you'll see in our discussion of systematic desensitization.

Systematic Desensitization

Devised by Joseph Wolpe (1958), systematic desensitization revolutionized psychotherapy by giving therapists their first useful alternative to traditional "talk therapy" (Fishman & Franks, 1992). *Systematic desensitization* **is a behavior therapy used to reduce clients' anxiety responses through counterconditioning.** The treatment assumes that most anxiety responses are acquired through classical conditioning (as we discussed in Chapter 14). According to this model, a harmless stimulus (for instance, a bridge) may be paired with a fear-arousing event (lightning striking it), so that it becomes a conditioned stimulus eliciting anxiety. The goal of systematic desensitization is to weaken the association between the conditioned stimulus (the bridge) and the conditioned response of anxiety (see Figure 15.6). Systematic desensitization involves three steps.

First, the therapist helps the client build an anxiety hierarchy. The hierarchy is a list of anxiety-arousing stimuli related to the specific source of anxiety, such as flying, academic tests, or snakes. The client ranks the stimuli from the least anxiety arousing to the most anxiety arousing. This ordered list of stimuli is the *anxiety hierarchy.* An example of an anxiety hierarchy for one woman's fear of heights is shown in Figure 15.7.

The second step involves training the client in deep muscle relaxation. This second phase may begin during early sessions while the therapist and client are still constructing the anxiety hierarchy. Various therapists use different relaxation training procedures. Whatever procedures are used, the client must learn to engage in deep, thorough relaxation on command from the therapist.

In the third step, the client tries to work through the hierarchy, learning to remain relaxed while imagining each stimulus. Starting with the least anxiety-arousing stimulus, the client imagines the situation as vividly as possible while relaxing. If the client experiences

Figure 15.6

The logic underlying systematic desensitization. Behaviorists argue that many phobic responses are acquired through classical conditioning, as in the example diagrammed here. Systematic desensitization targets the conditioned associations between phobic stimuli and fear responses.

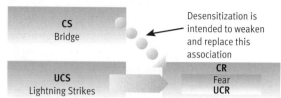

strong anxiety, he or she drops the imaginary scene and concentrates on relaxation. The client keeps repeating this process until he or she can imagine a scene with little or no anxiety. Once a particular scene is conquered, the client moves on to the next stimulus situation in the anxiety hierarchy. Gradually, over a number of therapy sessions, the client progresses through the hierarchy, unlearning troublesome anxiety responses.

As clients conquer *imagined* phobic stimuli, they may be encouraged to confront the *real* stimuli. Desensitization to imagined stimuli can be effective by itself, but many behavior therapists advocate

"Neurotic anxiety is nothing but a conditioned response."
JOSEPH WOLPE

Figure 15.7

Example of an anxiety hierarchy. Systematic desensitization requires the construction of an anxiety hierarchy like the one shown here, which was developed for a woman who had a fear of heights but wanted to go hiking in the mountains. (From *Methods of Self-Change: An ABC Primer,* by K.E. Rudestam, pp.42-43, 1980. Copyright © 1980 by Wadsworth, Inc. Reprinted by permission of the author.)

An Anxiety Hierarchy for Systematic Desensitization

Degree of fear	
5	I'm standing on the balcony of the top floor of an apartment tower.
10	I'm standing on a stepladder in the kitchen to change a light bulb.
15	I'm walking on a ridge. The edge is hidden by shrubs and treetops.
20	I'm sitting on the slope of a mountain, looking out over the horizon.
25	I'm crossing a bridge 6 feet above a creek. The bridge consists of an 18-inch-wide board with a handrail on one side.
30	I'm riding a ski lift 8 feet above the ground.
35	I'm crossing a shallow, wide creek on an 18-inch-wide board, 3 feet above water level.
40	I'm climbing a ladder outside the house to reach a second-story window.
45	I'm pulling myself up a 30-degree wet, slippery slope on a steel cable.
50	I'm scrambling up a rock, 8 feet high.
55	I'm walking 10 feet on a resilient, 18-inch-wide board, which spans an 8-foot-deep gulch.
60	I'm walking on a wide plateau, 2 feet from the edge of a cliff.
65	I'm skiing an intermediate hill. The snow is packed.
70	I'm walking over a railway trestle.
75	I'm walking on the side of an embankment. The path slopes to the outside.
80	I'm riding a chair lift 15 feet above the ground.
85	I'm walking up a long, steep slope.
90	I'm walking up (or down) a 15-degree slope on a 3-foot-wide trail. On one side of the trail the terrain drops down sharply; on the other side is a steep upward slope.
95	I'm walking on a 3-foot-wide ridge. The slopes on both sides are long and more than 25 degrees steep.
100	I'm walking on a 3-foot-wide ridge. The trail slopes on one side. The drop on either side of the trail is more than 25 degrees.

Systematic desensitization is a behavioral treatment for phobias. Early studies of the procedure's efficacy often used people who had snake phobias as research subjects because people with snake phobias were relatively easy to find. This research showed that systematic desensitization is generally an effective treatment.

following it up with direct exposures to the real anxiety-arousing stimuli (Emmelkamp & Scholing, 1990). The desensitization process should reduce anxiety enough so that clients will be able to confront situations they used to avoid. Usually, these real-life confrontations prove harmless, and the person's anxiety response declines further. Although it seems deceptively simple, systematic desensitization can be effective in eliminating specific anxieties (Spiegler & Guevremont, 1998).

Aversion Therapy

Aversion therapy **is a behavior therapy in which an aversive stimulus is paired with a stimulus that elicits an undesirable response.** For example, alcoholics may be given an *emetic drug* (one that causes nausea and vomiting) in conjunction with their favorite drinks during therapy sessions (Landabaso et al., 1999). By pairing the drug with alcohol, the therapist hopes to create a conditioned aversion to alcohol.

Aversion therapy takes advantage of the automatic nature of responses produced through classical conditioning. Admittedly, alcoholics treated with aversion therapy know that they won't be given an emetic outside of their therapy sessions. However, their reflex response to the stimulus of alcohol may be changed so they respond to it with nausea and distaste (see Figure 15.8). Obviously, this response should make it much easier to resist the urge to drink.

Aversion therapy is not a widely used technique, and when it is used it is usually only one element in a larger treatment program. Troublesome behaviors treated successfully with aversion therapy have included drug and alcohol abuse, sexual deviance, gambling, shoplifting, stuttering, cigarette smoking, and overeating (Emmelkamp, 1994; Sandler, 1975; Smith, Frawley, & Polissar, 1997; Wolpe, 1990).

CONCEPT **CHECK 15.2**

Understanding the Types of Behavior Therapy

Check your understanding of the varieties of behavior therapy discussed in your text by matching each therapy with the appropriate description. Choose from the following: (a) systematic desensitization, (b) social skills training, and (c) aversion therapy. The answers are in Appendix A.

_a._ **1.** Anxiety is reduced by conditioning the client to respond positively to stimuli that previously aroused anxiety.

_c._ **2.** Unwanted behaviors are eliminated by conditioning the client to have an unpleasant response to stimuli that previously triggered the behavior.

_b._ **3.** Behavioral techniques are used to teach the client new behaviors aimed at enhancing the quality of their interactions with others.

Figure 15.8

Aversion therapy. Aversion therapy uses classical conditioning to create an aversion to a stimulus that has elicited problematic behavior. For example, in the treatment of drinking problems, alcohol may be paired with a nausea-inducing drug to create an aversion to drinking.

Social Skills Training

Many psychological problems grow out of interpersonal difficulties. Behavior therapists point out that people are not born with social finesse—they acquire social skills through learning. Unfortunately, some people have not learned how to be friendly, how to make conversation, how to express anger appropriately, and so forth. Social ineptitude can contribute to anxiety, feelings of inferiority, and various kinds of disorders. In light of these findings, therapists are increasingly using social skills training in efforts to improve clients' social abilities. This approach to therapy has yielded promising results in the treatment of social anxiety (Shear & Beidel, 1998), autism (Gonzalez-Lopez & Kamps, 1997), and schizophrenia (Wallace, 1998).

Social skills training **is a behavior therapy designed to improve interpersonal skills that emphasizes modeling, behavioral rehearsal, and shaping.** This type of behavior therapy can be conducted with individual clients or in groups. *Modeling* is used by encouraging clients to watch socially skilled friends and colleagues, so that they can acquire appropriate responses (eye contact, active listening, and so on) through observation. In *behavioral rehearsal,* the client tries to practice social techniques in structured role-playing exercises. The therapist provides corrective feedback and uses approval to reinforce progress. Eventually, of course, clients try their newly acquired skills in real-world interactions. Usually, they are given specific homework assignments. *Shaping* is used in that clients are gradually asked to handle more complicated and delicate social situations. For example, a nonassertive client may begin by working on making requests of friends. Only much later will he be asked to tackle standing up to his boss at work.

Evaluating Behavior Therapies

How does the effectiveness of behavior therapy compare with that of insight therapy? In direct comparisons, the differences are usually small. However, these modest differences tend to favor behavioral approaches for certain types of disorders (Lambert & Bergin, 1992). Of course, behavior therapies are not well suited to the treatment of some types of problems (vague feelings of discontent, for instance). Furthermore, it's misleading to make global statements about the effectiveness of behavior therapies, because they include many procedures designed for different purposes. For example, the value of systematic desensitization for phobias has no bearing on the value of aversion therapy for sexual deviance.

For our purposes, it is sufficient to note that there is favorable evidence on the efficacy of most of the widely used behavioral interventions. Behavior therapies can make important contributions to the treatment of phobias, obsessive-compulsive disorders, sexual dysfunction, schizophrenia, drug-related problems, eating disorders, psychosomatic disorders,

CONCEPT CHECK 15.3

Understanding Therapists' Goals

Check your understanding of therapists' goals by matching various therapies with the appropriate description. The answers are in Appendix A.

Principal therapeutic goals

_d._ **1.** Elimination of maladaptive behaviors or symptoms

_b._ **2.** Acceptance of genuine self, personal growth

_a._ **3.** Recovery of unconscious conflicts, character reconstruction

_c._ **4.** Detection and reduction of negative thinking

Therapy

a. Psychoanalysis

b. Client-centered therapy

c. Cognitive therapy

d. Behavior therapy

hyperactivity, autism, and mental retardation (Agras & Berkowitz, 1999; Emmelkamp, 1994).

Many of these problems would not be amenable to treatment with the biomedical therapies, which we consider next. To some extent, the three major approaches to treatment have different strengths. Let's see where the strengths of the biomedical therapies lie.

Biomedical Therapies

Biomedical therapies **are physiological interventions intended to reduce symptoms associated with psychological disorders.** These therapies assume that psychological disorders are caused, at least in part, by biological malfunctions. As we discussed in the previous chapter, this assumption clearly has merit for many disorders, especially the more severe ones. For example, Figure 15.9 outlines how abnormalities in neurotransmitter activity may underlie shcizophrenic disorders. We will discuss two biomedical approaches to psychotherapy: drug therapy and electroconvulsive (shock) therapy.

Treatment with Drugs 11e

Psychopharmacotherapy **is the treatment of mental disorders with medication,** which we will refer to more simply as *drug therapy*. Therapeutic drugs fall into three major groups (with one notable "leftover" that doesn't fit neatly into any of the basic categories): antianxiety drugs, antipsychotic drugs, and antidepressant drugs. The leftover is lithium, which is used in the treatment of bipolar disorder. Of these drugs, the antianxiety agents are the most widely prescribed.

Figure 15.9

The dopamine hypothesis as an explanation for schizophrenia. Overactivity at dopamine synapses has been implicated as a key cause of schizophrenic disorders. The finding that antipsychotic drugs dampen dopamine activity supports this view. However, the exact mechanisms underlying this DA overactivity are still the subject of considerable debate. Similar aberrations in neurotransmitter activity at other types of synapses may underlie severe anxiety and mood disorders (see Chapter 14).

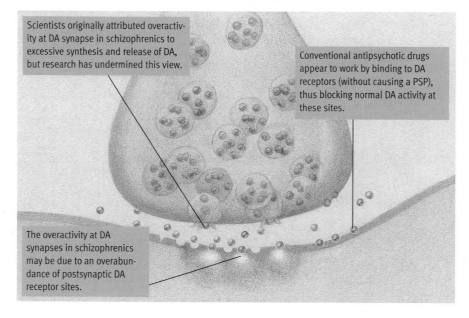

Scientists originally attributed overactivity at DA synapse in schizophrenics to excessive synthesis and release of DA, but research has undermined this view.

Conventional antipsychotic drugs appear to work by binding to DA receptors (without causing a PSP), thus blocking normal DA activity at these sites.

The overactivity at DA synapses in schizophrenics may be due to an overabundance of postsynaptic DA receptor sites.

**Dr. Bob's
Psychopharmacology Tips**
Physician and pharmacology
specialist Robert Hsiang
(University of Chicago), provides
both broad and specific references about the interface of
drugs and the human mind,
including a searchable archive
of professional information.

Antianxiety Drugs

Most of us know someone who pops pills to relieve anxiety. *Antianxiety drugs,* **which reduce tension, apprehension, and nervousness,** are the drugs used in this common coping strategy. The most popular of these drugs are Valium and Xanax (trade names for the generic drugs diazepam and alprazolam, respectively).

Valium, Xanax, and other drugs in the *benzodiazepine* family are often called *tranquilizers.* These drugs exert their effects almost immediately, and they can be fairly effective in alleviating feelings of anxiety (Ballenger, 1995). However, their effects are measured in hours, so their impact is relatively short-lived. Antianxiety drugs are routinely prescribed for people with anxiety disorders, but they are also given to millions of people who simply suffer from chronic nervous tension. In the mid-1970s, pharmacists in the United States were filling nearly 100 million prescriptions each year for Valium and similar antianxiety drugs. Many critics characterized this level of use as excessive (Lickey & Gordon, 1991).

All the drugs used to treat psychological disorders have potentially troublesome side effects that show up in some patients, but not others. The antianxiety drugs are no exception. The most common side effects of Valium and Xanax are listed in Table 15.1. Some of these side effects—such as drowsiness, nausea, and confusion—present serious problems for certain patients. These drugs also have

Table 15.1 Side Effects of Xanax and Valium

Side Effects	Patients Experiencing Side Effects (%)	
	Xanax	Valium
Drowsiness	36.0	49.4
Lightheadedness	18.6	24.0
Dry mouth	14.9	13.0
Depression	11.9	17.0
Nausea, vomiting	9.3	10.0
Constipation	9.3	11.3
Insomnia	9.0	6.7
Confusion	9.3	14.1
Diarrhea	8.5	10.5
Tachycardia, palpitations	8.1	7.2
Nasal congestion	8.1	7.2
Blurred vision	7.0	9.1

(From "New Drug Evaluations: Alprazolam," by R. L. Evans, 1981. *Drug Intelligence and Clinical Pharmacy, 15,* 633–637. Copyright © 1981 by Harvey Whitney Books Company. Reprinted by permission.)

some potential for abuse, drug dependence, and overdoses (Taylor, 1995). Another drawback is that patients who have been on antianxiety drugs for a while often experience withdrawal symptoms when their drug treatment is stopped (Danton & Antonuccio, 1997). Although some psychiatrists argue that the problems associated with the benzodiazepine drugs have been exaggerated, physicians have reduced their prescription of these drugs since the 1970s (Silberman, 1998).

Antipsychotic Drugs

Antipsychotic drugs are used primarily in the treatment of schizophrenia. They are also given to people with severe mood disorders who become delusional. The trade names (and generic names) of some prominent drugs in this category are Thorazine (chlorpromazine), Mellaril (thioridazine), and Haldol (haloperidol). *Antipsychotic drugs* **are used to gradually reduce psychotic symptoms, including hyperactivity, mental confusion, hallucinations, and delusions.** These drugs appear to decrease activity at dopamine synapses, although the exact relationship between their neurochemical effects and their clinical effects remains obscure (Marder & Van Putten, 1995).

Studies suggest that about 70%–90% of psychotic patients respond favorably (albeit in varied degrees) to antipsychotic medication (Buckley & Meltzer, 1995). When antipsychotic drugs are effective, they work their magic gradually, as shown in Figure 15.10. Patients usually begin to respond within two days to a week. Further improvement may occur for several months. Many schizophrenic patients are placed on antipsychotics indefinitely because these drugs can reduce the likelihood of a relapse into an active schizophrenic episode.

Antipsychotic drugs undeniably make a major contribution to the treatment of severe mental disorders, but they are not without problems. They have many unpleasant side effects (Cohen, 1997). Drowsiness, constipation, and cottonmouth are common. Tremors, muscular rigidity, and impaired coordination may also occur. After being released from a hospital, many patients who have been placed on antipsychotics discontinue their drug regimen because of the side effects. Unfortunately, relapse into another schizophrenic episode often occurs within three to nine months after a patient stops taking antipsychotic medication (Marder & Van Putten, 1995). In addition to minor side effects, antipsychotics may cause a more severe and lasting problem called *tardive dyskinesia.* **Tardive dyskinesia is a neurological disorder marked by involuntary**

writing and ticlike movements of the mouth, tongue, face, hands, or feet. Once this debilitating syndrome is established, there is no cure, although spontaneous remission is possible (Gardos et al., 1994).

Psychiatrists are currently enthusiastic about a new class of antipsychotic agents called *atypical antipsychotic drugs.* Although these drugs (such as clozapine, olanzapine, and quetiapine) are not risk-free (Afshar & Rubin, 1999), they seem to produce fewer side effects than traditional antipsychotics (Apter, 1996). Moreover, they appear to help a significant portion of the patients who do not respond to conventional antipsychotic medications (Wahlbeck et al., 1999), and they may carry less risk for tardive dyskinesia (Tollefson et al., 1997). In comparison to traditional antipsychotics, the atypical antipsychotics yield lower relapse rates if patients maintain their drug regimen (Conley et al., 1999) but much higher relapse rates when patients discontinue the regimen (Seeman & Tallerico, 1999).

Antidepressant Drugs

As their name suggests, *antidepressant drugs gradually elevate mood and help bring people out of a depression.* Prior to 1987, there were two principal classes of antidepressants: *tricyclics* (such as Elavil) and *MAO inhibitors* (such as Nardil). These two sets of drugs affect neurochemical activity in different ways and tend to work with different patients. Overall, they are beneficial for about 80% of depressed patients (Potter, Manji, & Rudorfer, 1995). The tricyclics have fewer problematic side effects than the MAO inhibitors (Charney et al., 1995). Like antipsychotic drugs, antidepressants exert their effects gradually over a period of weeks.

Today, psychiatrists are more likely to prescribe a newer class of antidepressants, called *selective serotonin reuptake inhibitors (SSRIs),* which slow the reuptake process at serotonin synapses. The drugs in this class, which include Prozac (fluoxetine), Paxil (paroxetine), and Zoloft (sertraline), seem to yield rapid therapeutic gains in the treatment of depression while producing fewer unpleasant or dangerous side effects (Marangell, Silver, Yudofsky, & 1999). However, Prozac and the other SSRIs are not "miracle drugs," as suggested by some popular magazines. Like all drugs for psychological disorders, the SSRIs have side effects and risks that must be carefully weighed against their benefits (Tollefson, 1995). For example, SSRIs have negative effects on sexual functioning, and patients experience withdrawal symptoms if treatment is terminated abruptly (Balon, 1997; D'Mello, Fernandes, & Colenda, 1997).

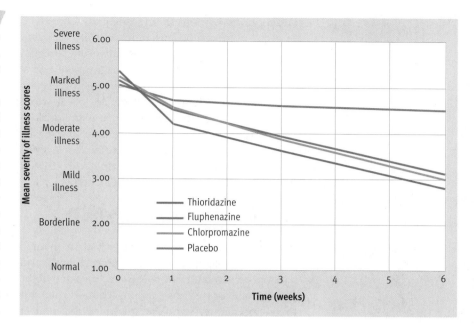

Lithium

Lithium **is a chemical used to control mood swings in patients with bipolar mood disorders.** It can help to prevent *future* episodes of both mania and depression in patients with bipolar illness (Maj et al., 1998; Tondo et al., 1998). Lithium can also be used in efforts to bring patients with bipolar illness out of *current* manic or depressed episodes. However, antipsychotics and antidepressants are more frequently used for these purposes. On the negative side of the ledger, lithium has some dangerous side effects if its use isn't managed skillfully (Lenox & Manji, 1995). Lithium levels in the patient's blood must be monitored carefully, because high concentrations can be toxic and even fatal.

Evaluating Drug Therapies

Drug therapies can produce clear therapeutic gains for many kinds of patients. What's especially impressive is that they can be effective with severe disorders that otherwise defy therapeutic endeavors. Nonetheless, drug therapies are controversial. First, some critics argue that drug therapies are not as effective as advertised and that they often produce superficial, short-lived curative effects (Greenberg & Fisher, 1997). For example, Valium does not really solve problems with anxiety; it merely provides temporary relief from an unpleasant symptom. Moreover, relapse rates are substantial when drug regimens are discontinued. Second, critics charge that many drugs are overprescribed and many patients overmedicated. According to these critics, a number of physicians routinely hand out

Figure 15.10

The time course of antipsychotic drug effects. Antipsychotic drugs reduce psychotic symptoms gradually, over a span of weeks, as graphed here. In contrast, patients given placebo pills show little improvement. (From data in NIMH-PSC Collaborative Study I and reported in "Drugs in the Treatment of Psychosis," by J.O. Cole, S.C. Goldberg & J.M. Davis, 1966, 1985. In P. Solomon, Ed., *Psychiatric Drugs*, Grune & Stratton. Reprinted by permission of J.M. Davis.)

prescriptions without giving adequate consideration to more complicated and difficult interventions. Third, some critics, especially Peter Breggin (1990, 1991), charge that the damaging side effects of therapeutic drugs are underestimated by psychiatrists and that these side effects are often worse than the illnesses that the drugs are supposed to cure. Citing problems such as tardive dyskinesia, lithium toxicity, addiction to antianxiety agents, and so forth, these critics argue that the risks of therapeutic drugs aren't worth the benefits.

Electroconvulsive Therapy (ECT)

In the 1930s, a Hungarian psychiatrist named Ladislas von Meduna speculated that epilepsy and schizophrenia could not coexist in the same body. On the basis of this observation, which turned out to be inaccurate, von Meduna theorized that it might be useful to induce epileptic-like seizures in schizophrenic patients. Initially, a drug was used to trigger these seizures. However, by 1938 a pair of Italian psychiatrists (Cerletti & Bini, 1938) demonstrated that it was safer to elicit the seizures with electric shock. Thus, modern electroconvulsive therapy was born.

Electroconvulsive therapy (ECT) **is a biomedical treatment in which electric shock is used to produce a cortical seizure accompanied by convulsions.** In ECT, electrodes are attached to the skull over the temporal lobes of the brain (see the adjacent photo). A light anesthesia is induced, and the patient is given a variety of drugs to minimize the likelihood of complications, such as spinal fractures. An electric current is then applied for about a second. The current triggers a brief (5–20 seconds)

This patient is being prepared for electroconvulsive therapy (ECT). In ECT an electric shock is used to elicit a brief cortical seizure. The shock is delivered through electrodes attached to the patient's skull.

© W & D McIntyre/Photo Researchers, Inc.

convulsive seizure, during which the patient usually loses consciousness. The patient normally awakens in an hour or two. People typically receive between 6 and 20 treatments as inpatients at a hospital (Fink, 1992).

The clinical use of ECT peaked in the 1940s and 1950s, before effective drug therapies were widely available. ECT has long been controversial, and its use did decline in the 1960s and 1970s. Nonetheless, there has been a recent resurgence in the use of ECT, and it is not a rare form of therapy. Although only about 8% of psychiatrists administer ECT (Hermann et al., 1998), it is estimated that about 100,000 people receive ECT treatments yearly in the United States (Hermann et al., 1995). Some critics argue that ECT is overused because it is a lucrative procedure that boosts psychiatrists' income while consuming relatively little of their time in comparison to insight therapy (Frank, 1990). Conversely, some ECT advocates argue that ECT is underutilized because the public harbors many misconceptions about its risks and side effects (Farah, 1997).

Effectiveness of ECT

Proponents of ECT maintain that it is a remarkably effective treatment (Fink, 1992; Prudic & Sackeim, 1999; Swartz, 1993). However, opponents argue that the available evidence is inconclusive and that ECT is probably no more effective than a placebo (Breggin, 1991; Friedberg, 1983). In light of this debate, conclusions about the value of ECT must be tentative. Overall, there does seem to be enough favorable evidence to justify *conservative* use of ECT in treating severe mood disorders in patients who have not responded to medication (Metzger, 1999; Rudorfer & Goodwin, 1993). However, the possible benefits of ECT need to be weighed against the potential risks.

Risks Associated with ECT

Even ECT proponents acknowledge that memory losses, impaired attention, and other cognitive deficits are common short-term side effects of electroconvulsive therapy (Sobin et al., 1995). However, ECT proponents assert that these deficits are mild and usually disappear within six months (Calev et al., 1993). In contrast, ECT critics maintain that these cognitive losses are significant and often permanent (Breggin, 1991; Frank, 1990), although their evidence seems to be largely anecdotal. The physiological bases of these reported cognitive deficits are not well understood, but the evidence indicates that ECT does not cause any structural damage in the brain (Devanand et al., 1994).

CONCEPT **CHECK 15.4**

Understanding Biomedical Therapies

Check your understanding of biomedical therapies by matching each treatment with its chief use.
The answers are in Appendix A.

Treatment

_C_ **1.** Antianxiety drugs

_a._ **2.** Antipsychotic drugs

_b._ **3.** Antidepressant drugs

_d._ **4.** Lithium

_b._ **5.** Electroconvulsive therapy (ECT)

Chief purpose

a. To reduce psychotic symptoms

b. To bring a major depression to an end

c. To suppress tension, nervousness, and apprehension

d. To prevent future episodes of mania or depression in bipolar disorders

Current Trends and Issues in Treatment

The controversy about ECT is only one of many contentious issues and shifting trends in the world of mental health care. In this section, we will discuss the impact of managed care on psychotherapy, the vigorous debate about empirical validation of specific treatments, the continuing trend toward blending different approaches to therapy, and efforts to respond more effectively to increasing cultural diversity in Western societies.

Grappling with the Constraints of Managed Care

The 1990s brought a dramatic shift in how people in the United States pay for their health care. Alarmed by skyrocketing health care costs, huge numbers of employers and individuals moved from traditional fee-for-service arrangements to managed care health plans. In the *fee-for-service* system, hospitals, physicians, psychologists, and other providers charged fees for whatever health care services were needed, and most of these fees were reimbursed by private insurance or the government (through medicaid, medicare, and other programs). In *managed care systems* people enroll in prepaid plans with small copayments for services, typically run by health maintenance organizations (HMOs), which agree to provide ongoing health care for a specific sum of money. Managed care usually involves a tradeoff: Consumers pay lower prices for their care, but they give up much of their freedom to choose their providers and to obtain whatever treatments they believe necessary. If an HMO's treatment expenses become excessive, it won't turn a profit, so HMOs

have powerful financial incentives to hold treatment costs down. The HMOs originally promised individuals and employers that they would be able to hold costs down without having a negative impact on the quality of care by negotiating lower fees from providers, reducing inefficiency, and cracking down on medically unnecessary services. However, critics charge that managed care systems have squeezed all the savings they can out of the "fat" that existed in the old system and that they have responded to continued inflation in their costs by rationing care and limiting access to medically *necessary* services (Duckworth & Borus, 1999; Giles & Marafiote, 1998; Karon, 1995).

The possibility that managed care is having a negative effect on the quality of treatment is a source of concern throughout the health care professions (Berwick, 1996), but the issue is especially sensitive in the domain of mental health care. Critics maintain that mental health care has suffered particularly severe cuts in services because the question of what is "medically necessary" can be more subjective than in other treatment specialties (such as internal medicine or ophthalmology) and because patients who are denied psychotherapy services are relatively unlikely to complain (Duckworth & Borus, 1999). For example, a business executive who is trying to hide his depression or cocaine addiction from his employer will be reluctant to complain to his employer if therapeutic services are denied.

According to critics, the restriction of mental health services sometimes involves outright denial of treatment, but it often takes more subtle forms, such as underdiagnosing conditions, failing to make needed referrals to mental health specialists, and arbitrarily limiting the length of treatment (Miller, 1996). Long-term therapy is becoming a thing of the past unless patients can pay for it out of pocket, and the goal of treatment has been reduced to reestablishing a reasonable level of functioning (Zatzick, 1999). Many managed care systems hold down costs by erecting *barriers to access,* such as requiring referrals from primary care physicians who don't have appointments available for weeks or months, or authorizing only a few sessions of therapy at a time. Another cost-cutting strategy is the rerouting of patients from highly trained providers, such as psychiatrists and doctoral-level psychologists, to less-well-trained providers, such as masters-level counselors, who may not be adequately prepared to handle serious psychological disorders (Seligman & Levant, 1998). Cost containment is also achieved by requiring physicians to prescribe older antidepressant and antipsychotic drugs instead of the newer and much more expensive SSRIs and atypical antipsychotics (Docherty, 1999).

The extensive utilization review procedures required by managed care have also raised concerns about providers' autonomy and clients' confidentiality (Plante, 1999). Clinicians who have to "sell" their treatment plans to managed care bureaucrats who may know little about mental health care feel that they have lost control over their professional practice. They also worry that the need to divulge the details of clients' problems to justify treatment may breach the confidentiality of the therapist-client relationship.

Unfortunately, there are no simple solutions to these problems on the horizon. Restraining the burgeoning cost of health care without compromising the quality of care, consumers' freedom of choice, and providers' autonomy is an enormously complex and daunting challenge. At this juncture, it is difficult to predict what the future holds. However, it is clear that economic realities have ushered in an era of transition for the treatment of psychological disorders and problems.

Identifying Empirically Validated Treatments

One potentially positive outgrowth of grappling with the constraints of managed care systems—which often demand evidence that treatments are cost effective—has been for clinicians to increase their efforts to demonstrate the efficacy of their interventions. Psychologists have organized a process for identifying *empirically validated treatments* that have solid research support regarding their effectiveness. To qualify as empirically validated, procedures generally must have been found to be superior to placebo or no treatment, for a specific type of problem or disorder, in several or more carefully controlled experiments conducted by at least two or more independent research teams (Chambless & Hollon, 1998). To ensure that a specific *treatment* is tested, the therapists in these studies have to administer a "pure" version of the therapy (no mixing in strategies from other approaches), and they must adhere to detailed treatment manuals that spell out exactly how the therapy should unfold. Working with these standards, quite a variety of empirically validated treatments have been identified (Chambless et al., 1996). The new emphasis on documenting the efficacy of treatments for specific problems seems to be a step in the right direction that promises to make therapeutic interventions more scientific and more reliable (Barlow, 1996; Wilson, 1996).

Blending Approaches to Treatment

In this chapter we have reviewed many approaches to treatment. However, there is no rule that a client must be treated with just one approach. Often, a clinician will use several techniques in working with a client. For example, a depressed person might receive cognitive therapy (an insight therapy), social skills training (a behavior therapy), and antidepressant medication (a biomedical therapy). Multiple approaches are particularly likely when a treatment *team* provides therapy. Studies suggest that there is merit in combining approaches to treatment (Klerman et al., 1994).

The value of multiple approaches may explain why a significant trend seems to have crept into the field of psychotherapy: a movement away from strong loyalty to individual schools of thought and a corresponding move toward integrating various approaches to therapy (Norcross & Goldfried, 1992; Smith, 1999). Most clinicians used to depend exclusively on one system of therapy while rejecting the utility of all others. This era of fragmentation may be drawing to a close. In recent surveys of psychologists' theoretical orientations, researchers have been surprised to find that the greatest proportion of respondents described themselves as eclectic in approach (Garfield & Bergin, 1994). *Eclecticism* in the practice of therapy involves drawing ideas from two or more systems of therapy, instead of committing to just one system.

Increasing Multicultural Sensitivity in Treatment

Modern psychotherapy emerged during the second half of the 19th century in Europe and America, spawned in part by a cultural milieu that viewed the person as an independent, reflective, rational being, capable of self-improvement (Cushman, 1992). Psychological disorders were assumed to have natural causes like physical diseases do and to be amenable to medical treatments derived from scientific research. But the individualized, medicalized institution of modern psychotherapy reflects Western cultural values that are far from universal (Dana, 1993). In many nonindustrialized societies, psychological disorders are attributed to supernatural forces (possession, withcraft, angry gods, and so forth), and victims seek help from priests, shamans, and folk healers, rather than doctors (Wittkower & Warnes, 1984). Thus, efforts to export Western psychotherapies to non-Western cultures have met with mixed success. Indeed, the highly culture-bound origins of modern therapies have raised questions about their applicability to ethnic minorities *within* Western culture.

Research on how cultural factors influence the process and outcome of psychotherapy has burgeoned in recent years, motivated in part by the need to improve mental health services for ethnic minority groups in American society. The data are ambiguous for a couple of ethnic groups, but studies suggest that American minority groups generally underutilize therapeutic services (Mays & Albee, 1992; Vega et al., 1999). Why? A variety of barriers appear to contribute to this problem, including the following (Cheung, 1991; Mays & Albee, 1992; Sue, Zane, & Young, 1994; U.S. Department of Health and Human Services, 1999):

1. *Cultural barriers.* In times of psychological distress, some cultural groups are reluctant to seek professional assistance. Given their socialization, they prefer to rely on informal assistance from family members, the clergy, respected elders, herbalists, acupuncturists, and so forth, who share their cultural heritage. Many members of minority groups have a history of frustrating interactions with American bureaucracies and are distrustful of large, intimidating, foreign institutions, such as hospitals and community mental health centers (Pierce, 1992).

2. *Language barriers.* Effective communication is crucial to the provision of psychotherapy. But most hospitals and mental health agencies are not adequately staffed with therapists who speak the languages used by minority groups in their service areas. The resulting communication problems make it difficult for many minority group members to explain their problems and obtain the help they need.

3. *Institutional barriers.* Stanley Sue and Nolan Zane (1987) argue that the "single most important explanation for the problems in service delivery involves the inability of therapists to provide culturally responsive forms of treatment" (p. 37). The vast majority of therapists have been trained almost exclusively in the treatment of white middle-class Americans and are not familiar with the cultural backgrounds and unique characteristics of various ethnic groups. This culture gap often leads to misunderstandings and ill-advised treatment strategies (Hughes, 1993). Unfortunately, there is a grievous shortage of ethnic therapists to meet the needs of various ethnic groups (Mays & Albee, 1992).

What can be done to improve mental health services for American minority groups? Researchers in this area have offered a variety of suggestions (Homma-True et al., 1993; Pedersen, 1994; Sue & Zane, 1987; Yamamoto et al., 1993). Discussions of possible solutions usually begin with the need to recruit and train more ethnic minority therapists. Studies show that individuals are more likely to go to mental health facilities staffed by a higher proportion of people who share their ethnic background (Snowden & Hu, 1996; Sue et al., 1994). Furthermore, clients' satisfaction with therapy tends to be greater when they are treated by therapists from their own culture. Therapists can also be given special training to work more effectively with people from different cultural backgrounds. For example, Wade and Bernstein (1991) found that a cultural sensitivity training program for white therapists working with an African American clientele resulted in improved client satisfaction. Finally, most authorities urge further investigation of how traditional approaches to therapy can be modified and tailored to be more compatible with specific cultural groups' attitudes, values, norms, and traditions.

Cultural barriers have emerged in the psychotherapy process. A number of minority groups in the United States shy away from using professional services in this field. Those who do try it also tend to quickly terminate treatment more often than white Americans.

Overview of Five Major Approaches to Treatment

Therapy/founder

Roots of disorders

Psychoanalysis

Developed by Sigmund Freud in Vienna, from the 1890s through the 1930s

National Library of Medicine

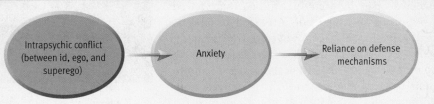

Intrapsychic conflict (between id, ego, and superego) → Anxiety → Reliance on defense mechanisms

Unconscious conflicts resulting from fixations in earlier development cause anxiety, which leads to defensive behavior. The repressed conflicts typically center on sex and aggression.

Client-centered therapy

Created by Carl Rogers at the University of Chicago during the 1940s and 1950s

Courtesy of Center for Studies of the Person

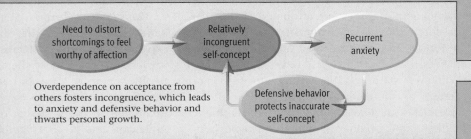

Need to distort shortcomings to feel worthy of affection → Relatively incongruent self-concept → Recurrent anxiety

Defensive behavior protects inaccurate self-concept

Overdependence on acceptance from others fosters incongruence, which leads to anxiety and defensive behavior and thwarts personal growth.

Cognitive therapy

Devised by Aaron Beck at the University of Pennsylvania in the 1960s and 1970s

Courtesy of Aaron T. Beck

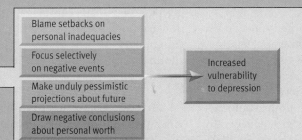

Blame setbacks on personal inadequacies

Focus selectively on negative events

Make unduly pessimistic projections about future

Draw negative conclusions about personal worth

→ Increased vulnerability to depression

Pervasive negative thinking about events related to self fosters anxiety and depression.

Behavior therapy

Launched primarily by South African Joseph Wolpe's description of systematic desensitization in 1958

Courtesy of Dr. Joseph Wolpe

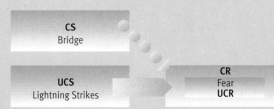

CS
Bridge

UCS
Lightning Strikes

CR
Fear
UCR

Maladaptive patterns of behavior are acquired through learning. For example, many phobias are thought to be created through classical conditioning and maintained by operant conditioning.

Biomedical therapy

Many researchers contributed; key breakthroughs in drug treatment made around 1950 by John Cade in Australia, Henri Laborit in France, and Jean Delay and Pierre Deniker, also in France

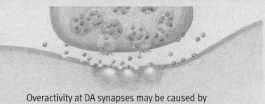

Overactivity at DA synapses may be caused by excessive release of DA or overabundance of DA receptor sites.

Most disorders are attributed to genetic predisposition and physiological malfunctions, such as abnormal neurotransmitter activity. For example, schizophrenia appears to be associated with overactivity at dopamine synapses.

Therapeutic Goals

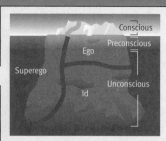

Insights regarding unconscious conflicts and motives; resolution of conflicts; personality reconstruction

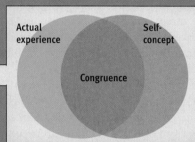

Increased congruence between self-concept and experience; acceptance of genuine self; self-determination and personal growth

Reduction of negative thinking; substitution of more realistic thinking

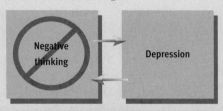

Elimination of maladaptive symptoms; acquisition of more adaptive responses

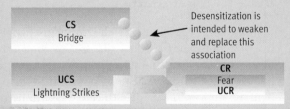

Desensitization is intended to weaken and replace this association

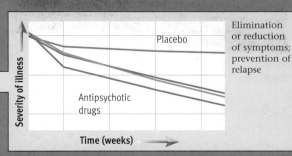

Elimination or reduction of symptoms; prevention of relapse

Therapeutic Techniques

© Peter Aparhamian/CORBIS

Free association, dream analysis, interpretation, transference.

© Vision/Photo Researchers, Inc.

Genuineness, empathy, unconditional positive regard, clarification, reflecting back to client

© Bob Daemmrich/The Image Works

Thought stopping, recording of automatic thoughts, refuting of negative thinking, homework assignments

© Steve McCarroll

Classical and operant conditioning, systematic desensitization, aversive conditioning, social skills training, reinforcement, shaping, punishment, extinction, biofeedback

© W & D McIntyre/ Photo Researchers, Inc.

PhotoDisc, Inc.

Antianxiety, antidepressant, and anti-psychotic drugs; lithium; electroconculsive therapy

Traditionally, much of the treatment of mental illness has been carried out in institutional settings, primarily in mental hospitals. **A *mental hospital* is a medical institution specializing in providing inpatient care for psychological disorders.** In the United States, a national network of state-funded mental hospitals started to emerge in the 1840s through the efforts of Dorothea Dix and other reformers (see Figure 15.11). Prior to these reforms, the mentally ill who were poor were housed in jails and poorhouses or were left to wander the country-side. Today, mental hospitals continue to play an important role in the delivery of mental health services. However, since World War II, institutional care for mental illness has undergone a series of major transitions—and the dust hasn't settled yet. Let's look at how institutional care has evolved in recent decades.

Disenchantment with Mental Hospitals

By the 1950s, it had become apparent that public mental hospitals were not fulfilling their goals very well (Mechanic, 1980). Experts began to realize that hospitalization often *contributed* to the development of pathology instead of curing it.

What were the causes of these unexpected negative effects? Part of the problem was that the facilities were usually underfunded (Bloom, 1984). The lack of adequate funding meant that the facilities were overcrowded and understaffed. Hospital personnel were undertrained and overworked, making them hard-pressed to deliver minimal custodial care. Despite gallant efforts at treatment, the demoralizing conditions made most public mental hospitals decidedly nontherapeutic (Scull, 1990). These problems were aggravated by the fact that state mental hospitals served large geographic regions but were rarely placed near major population centers. Hence, most patients were uprooted from their community and isolated from their social support networks.

Disenchantment with the public mental hospital system inspired the *community mental health movement* that emerged in the 1960s (Duckworth & Borus, 1999). The community mental health movement emphasizes (1) local, community-based care, (2) reduced dependence on hospitalization, and (3) the prevention of psychological disorders. This movement jumped into prominence in 1963 when President John F. Kennedy outlined an ambitious plan to build a national network of community mental health centers. Thus, in the 1960s much of the responsibility for the treatment of psychological disorders was turned over to community mental health centers, which supplement mental hospitals with decentralized and more accessible services.

Deinstitutionalization

Mental hospitals continue to care for many people troubled by chronic mental illness, but their role in patient care has diminished. Since the 1960s, a policy of deinstitutionalization has been followed by the American mental health care establishment. ***Deinstitutionalization* refers to transferring the treatment of mental illness from inpatient institutions to community-based facilities that emphasize outpatient care.** This shift in responsibility was made possible by two developments: (1) the emergence of effective drug therapies for severe disorders and (2) the deployment of community mental health centers to coordinate local care (Goff & Gudeman, 1999).

The exodus of patients from mental hospitals has been dramatic. The average inpatient population in state and county mental hospitals has dropped

Figure 15.11

Dorothea Dix and the advent of mental hospitals in America. During the 19th century, Dorothea Dix campaigned tirelessly to obtain funds for building mental hospitals. Many of these hospitals, such as the New York State Lunatic Asylum shown here, were extremely large facilities. Although public mental hospitals improved the care of the mentally ill, they had a variety of short-comings, which eventually prompted the deinstitutionalization movement.

Detail of painting in Harrisburg State Hospital, photo by Ken Smith/LLR Collection

Culver Pictures, Inc.

from a peak of nearly 550,000 in the mid-1950s to around 80,000 in the late 1990s, as shown in Figure 15.12. This trend does not mean that hospitalization for mental illness has become a thing of the past. A great many people are still hospitalized, but the shift has been toward placing them in local general hospitals for brief periods instead of distant psychiatric hospitals for long periods (Kiesler, 1992). In keeping with the philosophy of deinstitutionalization, these local facilities try to get patients stabilized and back into the community as swiftly as possible.

How has deinstitutionalization worked out? It gets mixed reviews. On the positive side, many people have benefited by avoiding disruptive and unnecessary hospitalization. Ample evidence suggests that alternatives to hospitalization can be as effective as and less costly than inpatient care (Honkonen, Saarinen, & Salokangas, 1999; McGrew et al., 1999). Moreover, follow-up studies of discharged patients reveal that a substantial majority prefer the greater freedom provided by community-based treatment (Leff, Trieman, & Gooch, 1996; Okin et al., 1995).

Nonetheless, some unanticipated problems have arisen (Grob, 1994; A. Johnson, 1990; Scull, 1990). Many patients suffering from chronic psychological disorders had nowhere to go when they were released. They had no families, friends, or homes to return to. Many had no work skills and were poorly prepared to live on their own. These people were supposed to be absorbed by "halfway houses," sheltered workshops, and other types of intermediate care facilities. Unfortunately, many communities were never able to fund and build the planned facilities (H. Lamb, 1998).

Thus, deinstitutionalization left two major problems in its wake: a "revolving door" population of people who flow in and out of psychiatric facilities, and a sizable population of homeless mentally ill people.

Mental Illness, the Revolving Door, and Homelessness

Although the proportion of hospital days attributable to mental illness has dwindled, admission rates for psychiatric hospitalization have actually climbed. What has happened? Deinstitutionalization and drug therapy have created a revolving door through which many mentally ill people pass again and again (Geller, 1992).

Most of the people caught in the mental health system's revolving door suffer from chronic, severe

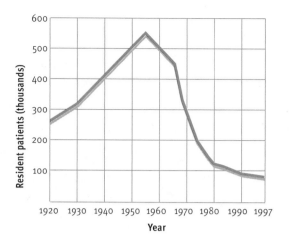

Figure 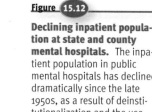 **15.12**

Declining inpatient population at state and county mental hospitals. The inpatient population in public mental hospitals has declined dramatically since the late 1950s, as a result of deinstitutionalization and the use of drug therapy. (Data from the National Institute of Mental Health)

disorders (usually schizophrenia) that frequently require hospitalization (Haywood et al., 1995). However, they respond well to drug therapies in the hospital. Once they're stabilized through drug therapy, they no longer qualify for expensive hospital treatment according to the new standards created by deinstitutionalization. Thus, they're sent back out the door, into communities that often aren't prepared to provide adequate outpatient care. Because they lack appropriate care and support, their condition deteriorates and they soon require readmission to a hospital, where the cycle begins once again. Over two-thirds of all psychiatric inpatient admissions involve rehospitalizing a former patient, as Figure 15.13 shows.

Deinstitutionalization has also been blamed for the growing population of homeless people. Studies have consistently found elevated rates of mental illness among the homeless. Taken as a whole, the evidence suggests that roughly one-third of the homeless suffer from severe mental illness (schizophrenic and mood disorders), that another one-third or so are struggling with alcohol and drug problems, and that many qualify for multiple diagnoses (Bassuk et al., 1998; Haugland et al., 1997; Vazquez, Munoz, & Sanz, 1997).

Figure 15.13

Percentage of psychiatric inpatient admissions that are readmissions. The extent of the revolving door problem is apparent from these figures on the percentage of inpatient admissions that are readmissions at various types of facilities. (Data from the National Institute of Mental Health)

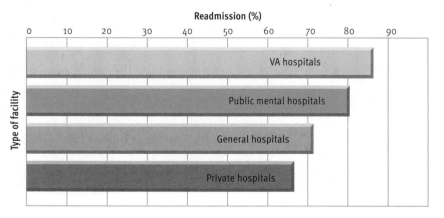

The popular media routinely equate homelessness with mental illness, and it is widely assumed that deinstitutionalization is largely responsible for the rapid growth of homelessness in America. Although deinstitutionalization probably has *contributed* to the growth of homelessness, many experts in this area maintain that it is misleading to blame the problem of homelessness chiefly on deinstitutionalization (Kiesler, 1991; Main, 1998). They note, for instance, that although mental illness is common among the homeless, studies suggest that only about 5%–7% of the homeless population require psychiatric hospitalization (Dennis et al., 1991). Those who criticize the tendency to equate homelessness with mental illness worry that this equation diverts attention from the real causes of the homelessness crisis (Kiesler, 1991). They maintain that homelessness is primarily an economic problem and that it requires economic solutions (Cohen & Thompson, 1992; McCarty et al., 1991; Rossi, 1990).

The issue is a complex one, however, and other theorists disagree. For example, although Baum and Burnes (1993) acknowledge that economic and social trends have contributed to increased homelessness, they assert that today's homeless are a deeply troubled population, beset by high rates of mental illness, substance dependence, and disabling physical conditions. They maintain that that it would be foolish to chart our governmental policy on homelessness working under the assumption that this population merely needs economic assistance.

In light of the revolving door problem and homelessness among the mentally ill, what can we conclude about deinstitutionalization? It appears to be a worthwhile idea that has been poorly executed (H. Lamb, 1998). Overall, the policy has probably been a benefit to countless people with milder disorders but a cruel trick on many others with severe, chronic disorders. Ultimately, it's clear that our society is not providing adequate care for a sizable segment of the mentally ill population (Isaac & Armat, 1990; Torrey, 1996). That's not a new development. Inadequate care for mental illness has always been the norm. Societies always struggle with the problem of what to do with the mentally ill and how to pay for their care (Duckworth & Borus, 1999).

Putting It in Perspective

In our discussion of psychotherapy, one of our unifying themes—the value of theoretical diversity—was particularly prominent, and one other theme—the importance of culture—surfaced briefly. Let's discuss the latter theme first. The approaches to psychotherapy described in this chapter are products of modern, white, middle-class, Western culture. Some of these therapies have proven useful in some other cultures, but many have turned out to be irrelevant or counterproductive when used with different cultural groups. Thus, we have seen once again that Western psychology cannot assume that its theories and practices have universal applicability.

As for theoretical diversity, its value can be illustrated with a rhetorical question: Can you imagine what the state of modern psychotherapy would be if everyone in psychology and psychiatry had simply accepted Freud's theories about the nature and treatment of psychological disorders? If not for theoretical diversity, mental health treatment might still be in the dark ages. Psychoanalysis can be a useful method of therapy, but we would have a tragic state of affairs if it were the *only* treatment available to people experiencing psychological distress. Multitudes of people have benefited from alternative approaches to treatment that emerged out of tension between psychoanalytic theory and various other theoretical perspectives.

Given that people have diverse problems, rooted in varied origins, it is fortunate that they can choose from a diverse array of approaches to treatment. The graphic overview on pages 478–479 summarizes and compares the approaches that we've discussed in this chapter. This overview shows that the major approaches to therapy each have their own vision of the nature of human discontent and the ideal remedy.

Of course, diversity can be confusing. The range and variety of available treatments in modern psychotherapy leaves many people puzzled about their options. Thus, in our Personal Application we'll sort through the practical issues involved in selecting a therapist.

Looking for a Therapist

Answer the following "true" or "false."

_____ **1** Psychotherapy is an art as well as a science.

_____ **2** Psychotherapy can be harmful or damaging to a client.

_____ **3** Mental health treatment does not have to be expensive.

_____ **4** The type of professional degree that a therapist holds is relatively unimportant.

All of these statements are true. Do any of them surprise you? If so, you're in good company. Many people know relatively little about the practicalities of selecting a therapist.

The task of finding an appropriate therapist is no less complex than shopping for any other major service. Should you see a psychologist or a psychiatrist? Should you opt for individual therapy or group therapy? Should you see a client-centered therapist or a behavior therapist? The unfortunate part of this complexity is that people seeking psychotherapy often feel overwhelmed by personal problems. The last thing they need is to be confronted by yet another complex problem.

Nonetheless, the importance of finding a good therapist cannot be overestimated. Therapy can sometimes have harmful rather than helpful effects. We have already discussed how drug therapies and ECT can sometimes be damaging, but problems are not limited to biological interventions. Talking about your problems with a therapist may sound pretty harmless, but studies indicate that insight therapies can also backfire (Lambert & Bergin, 1994; Singer & Lalich, 1996). Although a great many talented therapists are available, psychotherapy, like any other profession, has incompetent practitioners as well. Therefore, you should shop for a skilled therapist, just as you would for a good attorney or a good mechanic.

In this Application, we'll go over some information that should be helpful if you ever have to look for a therapist for yourself or for a friend or family member (based on Amada, 1985; Bruckner-Gordon, Gangi, & Wallman, 1988; Ehrenberg & Ehrenberg, 1986; Pittman, 1994).

Where Do You Find Therapeutic Services?

Psychotherapy can be found in a variety of settings. Contrary to general belief, most therapists are not in private practice. Many work in institutional settings such as community mental health centers, hospitals, and human service agencies. The principal sources of therapeutic services are described in Table 15.2. The exact configuration of therapeutic services available will vary from one community to another. To find out what your community has to offer, it is a good idea to consult your friends, your local phone book, or your local community mental health center.

Is the Therapist's Profession or Sex Important?

Psychotherapists may be trained in psychology, psychiatry, social work, counseling, psychiatric nursing, or marriage and family therapy. Researchers have *not* found any reliable associations between therapists' professional background and therapeutic efficacy (Beutler, Machado, & Neufeldt, 1994), probably because many talented therapists can be found in all of these professions. Thus, the type of degree that a therapist holds doesn't need to be a crucial consideration in your selection process. At the present time, it *is* true that only a psychiatrist can prescribe

Table 15.2	Principal Sources of Therapeutic Services
Source	**Comments**
Private practitioners	Self-employed therapists are listed in the Yellow Pages under their professional category, such as psychologists or psychiatrists. Private practitioners tend to be relatively expensive, but they also tend to be highly experienced therapists.
Community mental health centers	Community mental health centers have salaried psychologists, psychiatrists, and social workers on staff. The centers provide a variety of services and often have staff available on weekends and at night to deal with emergencies.
Hospitals	Several kinds of hospitals provide therapeutic services. There are both public and private mental hospitals that specialize in the care of people with psychological disorders. Many general hospitals have a psychiatric ward, and those that do not usually have psychiatrists and psychologists on staff and on call. Although hospitals tend to concentrate on inpatient treatment, many provide outpatient therapy as well.
Human service agencies	Various social service agencies employ therapists to provide short-term counseling. Depending on your community, you may find agencies that deal with family problems, juvenile problems, drug problems, and so forth.
Schools and workplaces	Most high schools and colleges have counseling centers where students can get help with personal problems. Similarly, some large businesses offer in-house counseling to their employees.

Finding the right therapist is no easy task. You need to take into account the therapist's training and orientation, fees charged, and personality. An initial visit should give you a good idea of what a particular therapist is like.

drugs for disorders that merit drug therapy. However, critics argue that many psychiatrists are too quick to use drugs to solve problems (Breggin, 1991). In any case, other types of therapists can refer you to a psychiatrist if they think that drug therapy would be helpful. If you have a health insurance policy that covers psychotherapy, you may want to check to see whether it carries any restrictions about the therapist's profession.

Whether a therapist's sex is important depends on your attitude. If *you* feel that the therapist's sex is important, then for you it is. The therapeutic relationship must be characterized by trust and rapport. Feeling uncomfortable with a therapist of one sex or the other could inhibit the therapeutic process. Hence, you should feel free to look for a male or female therapist if you prefer to do so. This point is probably most relevant to female clients whose troubles may be related to the extensive sexism in our society (A. Kaplan, 1985). It is entirely reasonable for women to seek a therapist with a feminist perspective if that would make them feel more comfortable.

Speaking of sex, you should be aware that sexual exploitation is an occasional problem in the context of therapy. Studies indicate that a small minority of therapists take advantage of their clients sexually (Pope, Keith-Spiegel, & Tabachnick, 1986). These incidents almost always involve a male therapist making advances to a female client. The available evidence indicates that these sexual liaisons are usually harmful to clients (Williams, 1992). There are absolutely no situations in which therapist-client sexual relations are an ethical therapeutic practice. If a therapist makes sexual advances, a client should terminate treatment.

Is Treatment Always Expensive?

Psychotherapy does not have to be prohibitively expensive. Private practitioners tend to be the most expensive, charging between $75 and $140 per (50-minute) hour. These fees may seem high, but they are in line with those of similar professionals, such as dentists and attorneys. Community mental health centers and social service agencies are usually supported by tax dollars. Hence, they can charge lower fees than most therapists in private practice. Many of these organizations use a sliding scale, so that clients are charged according to how much they can afford to pay. Thus, most communities have inexpensive opportunities for treatment. Moreover, many health insurance plans provide at least partial reimbursement for the cost of psychotherapy.

Is the Therapist's Theoretical Approach Important?

Logically, you might expect that the diverse approaches to therapy vary in effectiveness. For the most part, that is *not* what researchers find, however. After reviewing many studies of therapeutic efficacy, Jerome Frank (1961) and Lester Luborsky and his colleagues (1975) both quote the dodo bird who has just judged a race in *Alice in Wonderland:* "Everybody has won, and *all* must have prizes." Improvement rates for various theoretical orientations usually come out pretty close in most studies (Lambert & Bergin, 1994; Wampold et al., 1997). In their landmark review of outcome studies, Smith and Glass (1977) estimated the effectiveness of many major approaches to therapy. As Figure 15.14 shows, the estimates cluster together closely.

However, these findings are a little misleading, as these estimates of overall effectiveness have been averaged across many types of patients and many types of problems. Most experts seem to think that *for certain types of problems, some approaches to therapy are more effective than others* (Crits-Christoph, 1997; Norcross, 1995). For example, Martin Seligman (1995) asserts that panic disorders respond best to cognitive therapy, that specific phobias are most amenable to treatment with systematic desensitization, and that obsessive-compulsive disorders are best treated with behavior therapy or medication. Thus, for a specific type of problem, a therapist's theoretical approach may make a difference.

It is also important to point out that the finding that different approaches to therapy are roughly equal in overall efficacy does not mean that all *therapists* are created equal. Some therapists unquestionably are more effective than others. However, these variations in effectiveness appear to depend on individual therapists' personal skills rather than on their theoretical orientation (Beutler et al., 1994). Good, bad, and mediocre therapists are found within each school of thought.

The key point is that effective therapy requires skill and creativity. Arnold Lazarus, who devised multimodal therapy, an eclectic approach, emphasizes that therapists "straddle the fence between science and art." Therapy is scientific in that interventions are based on extensive theory and empirical research (Forsyth & Strong, 1986). Ultimately, though, each client is a unique human being, and the therapist has to creatively fashion a treatment program that will help that individual.

What Should You Look For in a Prospective Therapist?

Some clients are timid about asking prospective therapists questions about their training, approach, fees, and so forth. However, these are reasonable questions, and the vast majority of therapists will be most accommodating in providing answers. What should you look for in a therapist? First, you should look for personal warmth and sincere concern. Try to judge whether you will be able to talk to this person in a candid, nondefensive way. Second, look for empathy and understanding. Is the person capable of appreciating your point of view? Third, look for self-confidence. Self-assured therapists will communicate a sense of competence without trying to intimidate you with jargon or boasting needlessly about what they can do for you. When all is said and done, you should *like* your therapist. Otherwise, it will be difficult to establish the needed rapport.

What Is Therapy Like?

It is important to have realistic expectations about therapy, or you may be unnecessarily disappointed. Some people expect miracles. They expect to turn their life around quickly with little effort. Others expect their therapist to run their lives for them. These are unrealistic expectations.

Therapy usually is a slow process. Your problems are not likely to melt away quickly. Moreover, therapy is hard work, and your therapist is only a facilitator. Ultimately, you have to confront the challenge of changing your behavior, your feelings, or your personality. This process may not be pleasant. You may have to face up to some painful truths about yourself. As Ehrenberg and Ehrenberg (1986) point out, "Psychotherapy takes time, effort, and courage."

Figure 15.14

Estimates of the effectiveness of various approaches to psychotherapy. Smith and Glass (1977) reviewed nearly 400 studies in which clients who were treated with a specific type of therapy were compared with a control group made up of individuals with similar problems who went untreated. The bars indicate the percentile rank (on outcome measures) attained by the average client treated with each type of therapy when compared to control subjects. The higher the percentile, the more effective the therapy was. As you can see, the different approaches were fairly similar in their apparent effectiveness. (Adapted from "Meta-analysis of Psychotherapy Outcome Series," by M. L. Smith and G. V. Glass, 1977, *American Psychologist, 32,* 752–760. Copyright © 1977 by the American Psychological Association. Adapted by permission of the author.)

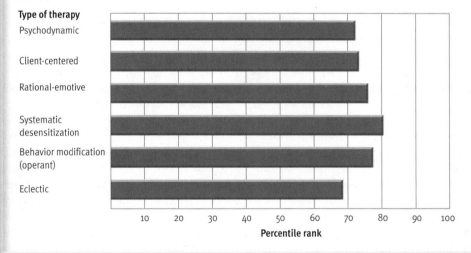

CRITICAL THINKING APPLICATION

From Crisis to Wellness— But Was It the Therapy?

It often happens this way. Problems seem to go from bad to worse—the trigger could be severe pressures at work, an acrimonious fight with your spouse, or a child's unruly behavior spiraling out of control. At some point, you recognize that it might be prudent to seek professional assistance from a therapist, but where do you turn? If you are like most people, you will probably hesitate before actively seeking professional help. People hesitate because therapy carries a stigma, because the task of finding a therapist is daunting, and because they hope that their psychological problems will clear up on their own—which *does* happen with some regularity. When people finally decide to pursue mental health care, it is often because they feel like they have reached rock bottom in terms of their functioning and they have no choice. Motivated by their crisis, they enter into treatment, looking for a ray of hope. Will therapy help them to feel better?

It may surprise you to learn that the answer *generally* would be "yes," even if professional treatment itself were utterly worthless and totally ineffectual. People entering therapy are likely to get better, regardless of whether their treatment is effective, for two major reasons: placebo effects and regression toward the mean. *Placebo effects* occur when people's expectations lead them to experience some change even though they receive a fake treatment (such as getting a sugar pill instead of a real drug). Clients generally enter therapy with expectations that it will have positive effects, and as we have emphasized throughout this text, *people have a remarkable tendency to see what they expect to see*. Because of this factor, studies of the efficacy of medical drugs always include a placebo condition in which subjects are given fake medication (see Chapter 2). Researchers are often quite surprised by just how much the placebo subjects improve (Fisher & Greenberg, 1997).

Placebo effects can be powerful and should be taken into consideration whenever efforts are made to evaluate the efficacy of some approach to treatment.

The other factor at work is the main focus in this Application. It is an interesting statistical phenomenon that we have not discussed previously. *Regression toward the mean* occurs when people who score extremely high or low on some trait are measured a second time and their new scores fall closer to the mean (average). Regression effects work in both directions: On the second measurement high scorers tend to fall back toward the mean and low scorers tend to creep upward toward the mean. For example, let's say we wanted to evaluate the effectiveness of a one-day coaching program intended to improve performance on the SAT test. We reason that coaching is most likely to help students who have performed poorly on the test, so we recruit a sample of high school students who have previously scored in the bottom 20% on the SAT. Thanks to regression toward the mean, most of these students will score higher if they take the SAT a second time, so our coaching program may *look* effective even if it has no value. By the way, if we set out to see whether our coaching program could increase the performance of high scorers, regression effects would be working *against* us. The processes underlying regression toward the mean are complex matters of probability, but they can be approximated by a simple principle: If you are near the bottom, you have almost nowhere to go but up, and if you are near the top, you have almost nowhere to go but down.

What does all of this have to do with the effects of professional treatment for psychological problems and disorders? Well, recall that most people enter psychotherapy during a time of severe crisis, when they are at a really low point in their lives. If you measure the mental health of a group of people entering therapy, most will get relatively low scores. If you measure their mental health again a few months later, chances are that most of them will score higher—with or without therapy—because of regression toward the mean. This is not a matter of idle speculation. Studies of *untreated subjects* demonstrate that poor scores on measures of mental health regress toward the mean when participants are assessed a second time (Flett, Vredenburg, & Krames, 1995; Hsu, 1995).

Does the fact that most people will get better even without therapy mean that there is no sound evidence that psychotherapy works? No, regression effects, along with placebo effects, do create major headaches for researchers evaluating the efficacy of various therapies, but these problems *can* be circumvented. Control groups, random assignment, placebo conditions, and statistical adjustments can be used to control for regression and placebo effects, as well as for other threats to validity. As discussed in the main body of the chapter, researchers have accumulated rigorous evidence that most approaches to therapy have demonstrated efficacy. However, our discussion of placebo and regression effects shows you some of the complexities that make this type of research far more complicated than might be anticipated.

Recognizing how regression toward the mean can occur in a variety of contexts is an important critical thinking skill, so let's look at some additonal examples. Think about an outstanding young pro baseball player who has a fabulous first season and is named "Rookie of the Year." What sort of performance would you predict for this athlete the next year? Statistically speaking, our Rookie of the Year is likely to perform well above average the next year, but not as well as he did in his first year. If you are a sports fan, you may recognize this pattern as the "sophomore slump." Many sports columnists have written about the sopho-more slump, which they typically blame on the athlete's personality or motivation ("He got lazy,'" "He got cocky," "The money and fame went to his head," and so forth). A simple appeal to regression toward the mean could explain this sort of outcome, with no need to denigrate the personality or motivation of the athlete. Of course, sometimes the Rookie of the Year performs even better during his second year. Thus, our baseball example can be used to emphasize an important point. Regression toward the mean is not an inevitability. It is a statistical tendency that predicts what will happen far more often than not, but it is merely a matter of probability—which means it is a much more reliable principle when applied to groups (say, the top ten rookies in a specific year) rather than to individuals.

People who do not understand regression toward the mean can make some interesting mistakes in their efforts to improve task performance. For instance, Kahneman and Tversky (1973) worked with Israeli flight instructors who, logically enough, would praise students when they handled a difficult maneuver exceptionally well and criticize students when they exhibited particularly poor performance. Because of regression toward the mean, the students' performance tended to decline after they earned praise for extremely good work and to improve after they earned criticism for extremely bad work. Taking note of this trend, the flight instructors erroneously concluded that praise led to poorer performance and criticism led to improved performance—until the concept of regression toward the mean was explained to them. Many parents and coaches working to train children have probably made the same mistake and naively inferred that praise has a negative effect on subsequent performance, when what they were really witnessing was regression toward the mean.

Let's return to the world of therapy for one last thought about the significance of both regression and placebo effects. Over the years, a host of quacks, charlatans, con artists, herbalists, and faith healers have marketed and sold an endless array of worthless treatments for both psychological problems and physical maladies. In many instances, people who have been treated with these phony therapies have expressed satisfaction or even praise and gratitude. For instance, you may have heard someone sincerely rave about some herbal remedy or psychic advice that you were pretty sure was really worthless. If so, you were probably puzzled by their glowing testimonials. Well, you now have two highly plausible explanations for why people can honestly believe that they have derived great benefit from harebrained, bogus treatments: placebo effects and regression effects. The people who provide testimonials for worthless treatments may have experienced *genuine* improvements in their conditions, but those improvements were probably the results of placebo effects and regression toward the mean. Placebo and regression effects add to the many reasons that you

Placebo and regression effects can help explain why ineffective interventions can have sincere supporters.

should always be skeptical about anecdotal evidence. And they help explain why charlatans can be so successful and why unsound, ineffective treatments can have sincere proponents.

Table 15.3	Critical Thinking Skills Discussed in This Application	
Skill	**Description**
Recognizing situations in which placebo effects might occur	The critical thinker understands that if people have expectations that a treatment will produce a certain effect, they may experience that effect even if the treatment was fake or ineffectual.
Recognizing situations in which regression toward the mean may occur	The critical thinker understands that when people are selected for their extremely high or low scores on some trait, their subsequent scores will probably fall closer to the mean.
Recognizing the limitations of anecdotal evidence	The critical thinker is wary of anecdotal evidence, which consists of personal stories used to support one's assertions. Anecdotal evidence tends to be unrepresentative, inaccurate, and unreliable.

REVIEW

Key Ideas

The Elements of the Treatment Process
● Approaches to psychotherapy are diverse, but they can be grouped into three categories: insight therapies, behavior therapies, and biomedical therapies.

● Therapists come from a variety of professional backgrounds. Each of these professions shows different preferences for approaches to treatment. Psychologists typically practice insight or behavior therapy. Psychiatrists tend to depend on psychoanalytic approaches to insight therapy and on biomedical therapies.

Insight Therapies
● Insight therapies involve verbal interactions intended to enhance self-knowledge. In psychoanalysis free association and dream analysis are used to explore the unconscious.

● When an analyst's probing hits sensitive areas, resistance can be expected. The transference relationship may be used to overcome this resistance so the client can handle interpretations that lead to insight. Classical psychoanalysis is not widely practiced anymore, but Freud's legacy lives on in a rich diversity of modern psychodynamic therapies.

● Rogers's client-centered therapy assumes that neurotic anxieties are derived from incongruence between a person's self-concept and reality. Accordingly, the client-centered therapist tries to provide a supportive climate in which clients can restructure their self-concept.

● Beck's cognitive therapy concentrates on changing the way clients think about events in their lives. Most theoretical approaches to insight therapy have been adapted for use with groups. Group therapists usually play a subtle role, staying in the background and working to promote group cohesiveness.

● Evaluating the effectiveness of any approach to therapy is complex and difficult. Nonetheless, the weight of the evidence suggests that insight therapies can be effective.

Behavior Therapies
● Behavior therapies use the principles of learning in direct efforts to change specific aspects of behavior. Wolpe's systematic desensitization, a treatment for phobias, involves the construction of an anxiety hierarchy, relaxation training, and step-by-step movement through the hierarchy, pairing relaxation with each phobic stimulus.

● In aversion therapy, a stimulus associated with an unwanted response is paired with an unpleasant stimulus in an effort to eliminate the maladaptive response. Social skills training can improve clients' interpersonal skills through shaping, modeling, and behavioral rehearsal. There is ample evidence that behavior therapies are effective.

Biomedical Therapies
● Biomedical therapies are physiological interventions for psychological problems. The principal types of therapeutic drugs are antianxiety drugs, antipsychotic drugs, antidepressant drugs, and lithium. Drug therapies can be quite effective, but they have their drawbacks, such as problematic side effects.

● Electroconvulsive therapy (ECT) is used to trigger a cortical seizure that is believed to have therapeutic value for mood disorders, especially depression. There is heated debate about the effectiveness of ECT and about possible risks associated with its use.

Current Trends and Issues in Treatment
● Many clinicians and their clients believe that managed care has restriced access to mental health care and undermined its quality. One response to the demands of managed care has been to increase research efforts to validate the efficacy of specific treatments for specific problems.

● Combinations of insight, behavioral, and biomedical therapies are often used fruitfully. Many modern therapists are eclectic, using ideas and strategies gleaned from a number of theoretical approaches.

● The highly culture-bound origins of Western therapies have raised doubts about their applicability to other cultures and even to ethnic groups in Western society. Because of cultural, language, and access barriers, therapeutic services are underutilized by ethnic minorities in America.

Institutional Treatment in Transition
● Disenchantment with the negative effects of mental hospitals led to the advent of more localized community mental health centers and a policy of deinstitutionalization. Unfortunately, deinstitutionalization has left some unanticipated problems in its wake, including the revolving door problem and increased homelessness.

Putting It in Perspective
● Our discussion of psychotherapy highlighted the value of theoretical diversity. Our coverage of therapy also showed once again that cultural factors shape psychological processes.

Personal Application ● Looking for a Therapist
● Therapeutic services are available in many settings, and such services do not have to be expensive. Therapists' personal skills are more important than their professional degree or their theoretical orientation.

● In selecting a therapist, warmth, empathy, confidence, and likability are desirable traits, and it is reasonable to insist on a therapist of one sex or the other. Therapy requires time, hard work, and the courage to confront your problems.

Critical Thinking Application ● From Crisis to Wellness—But Was It the Therapy?
● People entering therapy are likely to get better even if their treatment is ineffective, because of placebo effects and regression toward the mean. Regression toward the mean occurs when people selected for their extremely high or low scores on some trait are measured a second time and their new scores fall closer to the mean. Regression and placebo effects may help explain why people can often be enthusiastic about phony, ineffectual treatments.

Key Terms

Antianxiety drugs
Antidepressant drugs
Antipsychotic drugs
Aversion therapy
Behavior therapies
Biomedical therapies
Client-centered
  therapy
Clinical psychologists
Cognitive therapy
Counseling
  psychologists
Deinstitutionalization
Dream analysis
Electroconvulsive
  therapy (ECT)
Free association
Group therapy
Insight therapies
Interpretation
Lithium
Mental hospital
Placebo effects
Psychiatrists
Psychoanalysis
Psychopharmaco-
  therapy
Regression toward
  the mean
Resistance
Social skills training
Systematic
  desensitization
Tardive dyskinesia
Transference

Key People

Aaron Beck
Sigmund Freud
Carl Rogers
Joseph Wolpe

PRACTICE TEST

1. After undergoing psychoanalysis for several months, Karen has suddenly started "forgetting" to attend her therapy sessions. Karen's behavior is most likely a form of:
   A. resistance.
   B. transference.
   C. insight.
   D. catharsis.

2. Because Suzanne has an unconscious sexual attraction to her father, she behaves seductively toward her therapist. Suzanne's behavior is most likely a form of:
   A. resistance.
   B. transference.
   C. misinterpretation.
   D. an unconscious defense mechanism.

3. The key task of the client-centered therapist is:
   A. interpretation of the client's thoughts, feelings, memories, and behaviors.
   B. clarification of the client's feelings.
   C. confrontation of the client's irrational thoughts.
   D. modification of the client's problematic behaviors.

4. A therapist openly challenges a client's statement that she is a failure as a woman because her boyfriend left her, insisting that she justify it with evidence. Which type of therapy is probably being used?
   A. Psychodynamic therapy
   B. Client-centered therapy
   C. Behavior therapy
   D. Cognitive therapy

5. Therapists who view symptoms as the crux of the problem rather than as signs of an underlying problem are:
   A. behavior therapists.
   B. cognitive therapists.
   C. psychoanalytic therapists.
   D. client-centered therapists.

6. The goal of behavior therapy is to:
   A. identify the early childhood unconscious conflicts that are the source of the client's symptoms.
   B. change the client's thought patterns so that negative emotions can be controlled.
   C. change client's behavior by using conditioning techniques.
   D. alter the client's brain chemistry by prescribing specific drugs..

7. Systematic desensitization is particularly effective for the treatment of _____ disorders.
   A. generalized anxiety
   B. panic
   C. obsessive-compulsive
   D. phobic

8. Linda's therapist has her practice active listening skills in structured role-playing exercises. Later, Linda is gradually asked to practice these skills with family members, friends, and finally, her boss. Linda is undergoing:
   A. systematic desensitization.
   B. cognitive restructuring.
   C. a token economy.
   D. social skills training.

9. After being released from a hospital, many schizophrenic patients stop taking their antipsychotic medication because:
   A. their mental impairment causes them to forget.
   B. of the unpleasant side effects.
   C. most schizophrenics don't believe they are ill.
   D. all of the above.

10. Selective serotonin reuptake inhibitors (SSRIs) appear to have value for the treatment of _____ disorders.
    A. depressive
    B. schizophrenic
    C. dissociative
    D. alcoholic

11. Modern psychotherapy:
    A. was spawned by a cultural milieu that viewed the self as an independent, rational being.
    B. embraces universal cultural values.
    C. has been successfully exported to many non-Western cultures.
    D. both b and c.

12. The community mental health movement emphasizes:
    A. segregation of the mentally ill from the general population.
    B. increased dependence on long-term inpatient care.
    C. the prevention of psychological disorders.
    D. all of the above.

13. Many people repeatedly go in and out of mental hospitals. Typically, such people are released because _____; they are eventually readmitted because _____.
    A. they have been stabilized through drug therapy; their condition deteriorates once again because of inadequate outpatient care
    B. they run out of funds to pay for hospitalization; they once again can afford it
    C. they have been cured of their disorder; they develop another disorder
    D. they no longer want to be hospitalized; they voluntarily recommit themselves

14. The type of professional training a therapist has:
    A. is the most important indicator of his or her competence.
    B. should be the major consideration in choosing a therapist.
    C. is not all that important, since talented therapists can be found in all of the mental health professions.
    D. a and b.

15. Which of the following could be explained by regression toward the mean?
    A. You get an average bowling score in one game and a superb score in the next game.
    B. You get an average bowling score in one game and a very low score in the next game.
    C. You get an average bowling score in one game and another average score in the next game.
    D. You get a terrible bowling score in one game and an average score in the next game.

Answers

1	A	page 464	6	C	page 468	11	A	page 477
2	B	page 464	7	D	pages 469–470	12	C	page 480
3	B	page 466	8	D	page 470	13	A	page 481
4	D	pages 466–467	9	B	page 472	14	C	page 483
5	A	page 468	10	A	page 473	15	D	pages 486–487

INFOTRAC COLLEGE EDITION

Go to the Wadsworth Psychology Study Center for quiz questions, research updates, interactive exercises, and suggested readings in INFOTRAC related to this chapter:
http://psychology.wadsworth.com/product/0534593100s

© Lisette Le Bon/Superstock

CHAPTER 16

Social Behavior

When Muffy, "the quintessential yuppie," met Jake, "the ultimate working-class stiff," her friends got very nervous.

Muffy is a 28-year-old stockbroker and a self-described "snob" with a group of about ten close women friends. Snobs all. They're graduates of fancy business schools. All consultants, investment bankers, and CPAs. All "cute, bright, fun to be with, and really intelligent," according to Muffy. They're all committed to their high-powered careers, but they all expect to marry someday, too.

Unfortunately, most of them don't date much. In fact, they spend a good deal of time "lamenting the dearth of 'good men.'" You know who the "good men" are. Those are the ones who are "committed to their work, open to the idea of marriage and family, and possessed of a good sense of humor."

Well, lucky Muffy actually met one of those "good men." Jake is a salesman. He comes from a working-class neighborhood. His clothes come from Sears.

He wasn't like the usual men Muffy dated. He treats Muffy the way she's always dreamed of being treated. He listens; he cares; he remembers. "He makes me feel safe and more cherished than any man I've ever known," she says.

So she decided to bring him to a little party of about 30 of her closest friends. . . .

Perhaps it was only Jake's nerves that caused him to commit some truly unforgivable faux pas that night. His sins were legion. Where do we start? First of all, he asked for a beer when everyone else was drinking white wine. He wore a worn turtleneck while everyone else had just removed the Polo tags from their clothing. He smoked. . . .

"The next day at least half of the people who had been at the party called to give me their impressions. They all said that they felt they just had to let me know that they thought Jake 'lacked polish' or 'seemed loud' or 'might not be a suitable match,'" Muffy says.

Now, you may think that Muffy's friends are simply very sensitive, demanding people. A group of princes and princesses who can detect a pea under the fluffiest stack of mattresses. But you'd be wrong. Actually, they've been quite accepting of some of the other men that Muffy has brought to their little parties. Or should we call them inquisitions? Winston, for example, was a great favorite.

"He got drunk, ignored me, and asked for other women's phone numbers right in front of me. But he was six-foot-four, the classic preppie, with blond hair, horn-rimmed glasses, and Ralph Lauren clothes."

And most important of all, he didn't ask for a Pabst Blue Ribbon. So now Muffy is confused. "Jake is the first guy I've been out with in a long time that I've really liked. I was excited about him and my friends knew that. I was surprised by their reaction. I'll admit there's some validity to all their comments, but it's hard to

(Excerpt from: *Tales from the Front* by Cheryl Lavin and Laura Kavesh. Copyright © 1988 by Cheryl Lavin and Laura Kavesh. Used by permission of Doubleday, a division of Random House, Inc.)

express how violent it was. It made me think about what these women really want in a man. Whatever they say, what they really want is someone they can take to a business dinner. They want someone who comes with a tux. Like a Ken doll."

Muffy may have come to a crossroads in her young life. It's clear that there's no way she can bring Jake among her friends for a while.

"I don't want their reaction to muddy my feelings until I get them sorted out," she says.

It just may be time for Muffy to choose between her man and her friends.

The preceding account is a real story, taken from a book about intimate relationships titled *Tales from the Front* (Kavesh & Lavin, 1988, pp. 118–121). Muffy is on the horns of a difficult dilemma. Romantic relationships are important to most people, but so are friendships, and Muffy may have to choose between the two. Muffy's story illustrates the significance of social relations in people's lives. It also foreshadows each of the topics that we'll cover in this chapter, as we look at behavior in its social context.

Social psychology **is the branch of psychology concerned with the way individuals' thoughts, feelings, and behaviors are influenced by others.** Our coverage of social psychology will focus on six broad topics. Let's return to Muffy's story to get a glimpse of the various facets of social behavior that we'll examine in the coming pages:

- *Person perception.* The crux of Muffy's problem is that Jake didn't make a very good impression on her friends. To what extent do people's expectations and stereotypes color their impressions of others?
- *Attribution processes.* Muffy is struggling to understand her friends' rejection of Jake. When she

implies that Jake's rejection is due to their snotty elitism, she's engaging in attribution, making an inference about the causes of her friends' behavior. How do people use attributions to explain social behavior?
- *Interpersonal attraction.* Jake and Muffy are different in many important ways—is it true that opposites attract? Does similarity foster liking?
- *Attitudes.* Muffy's girlfriends have negative attitudes about working-class men. How are attitudes formed? What leads to attitude change?
- *Conformity and obedience.* Muffy's friends discourage her from dating Jake, putting her under pressure to conform to their values. What factors influence conformity? Can people be coaxed into doing things that contradict their values?
- *Behavior in groups.* Muffy belongs to a tight-knit group of friends who think along similar lines. Is people's behavior in groups similar to their behavior when alone? Why do people in groups often think alike?

Social psychologists study how people are affected by the actual, imagined, or implied presence of others. Their interest is not limited to individuals' *interactions* with others, as people can engage in social behavior even when they're alone. For instance, if you were driving by yourself on a deserted highway and tossed your trash out your car window, your littering would be a social action. It would defy social norms, reflect your socialization and attitudes, and have repercussions (albeit, small) for other people in your society. Thus, social psychologists often study *individual* behavior in a social context. This interest in understanding individual behavior should be readily apparent in our first section, on person perception.

Person Perception: Forming Impressions of Others

Can you remember the first meeting of your introductory psychology class? What kind of impression did your professor make on you that day? Did your instructor appear to be confident? Easygoing? Pompous? Open-minded? Cynical? Friendly? Were your first impressions supported or undermined by subsequent observations? When you interact with people, you're constantly engaged in **person perception, the process of forming impressions of others.** In this section we consider some of the factors that influence, and often distort, our perceptions of others.

Effects of Physical Appearance

"You shouldn't judge a book by its cover." "Beauty is only skin deep." People know better than to let physical attractiveness determine their perceptions of others' personal qualities. Or do they? Studies have shown that judgments of others' personality are often swayed by their appearance, especially their physical attractiveness. People tend to ascribe desirable personality characteristics to those who are good looking, seeing them as more sociable, friendly, poised, warm, and well adjusted than those who are less attractive (Eagly et al., 1991; Wheeler & Kim, 1997). In reality, research findings suggest that there is little correlation between attractiveness and personality traits (Feingold, 1992). Why do we inaccurately assume that a connection exists between good looks and personality? One reason is that extremely attractive people are vastly overrepresented in the entertainment media, where they are mostly portrayed in a highly favorable light (Smith, McIntosh, & Bazzini, 1999).

Physical attractiveness influences perceptions of competence less than perceptions of personality, but people nevertheless tend to view good-looking individuals as more intelligent and competent than their less attractive counterparts (Eagly et al., 1991). This bias literally pays off for good-looking people, as they tend to secure better jobs and earn higher salaries than less attractive individuals (Collins & Zebrowitz, 1995; Frieze, Olson, & Russell, 1991). Good looks seem to have relatively little impact on perceptions of honesty and integrity (Eagly et al., 1991). However, there is a tendency to view people with *baby-faced features*—such as large eyes, smooth skin, and a rounded chin—as more honest and trustworthy (Zebrowitz, Voinescu, & Collins, 1996). Baby-faced individuals are also seen as relatively warm, submissive, helpless, and naive (Zebrowitz, 1996), although evidence suggests that there is no association between baby-faced features and these traits (Zebrowitz, Collins, & Dutta, 1998).

Cognitive Schemas

Even though every individual is unique, people tend to categorize one another. For instance, in our opening story, Muffy is characterized as "the quintessential yuppie," and Jake as a "working-class stiff." Such labels reflect the use of cognitive schemas in person perception. As we discussed in the chapter on memory (Chapter 7), *schemas* are cognitive structures that guide information processing. Individuals use schemas to organize the world around them—including their social world. *Social schemas* are organized clusters of ideas about categories of social events and people. People have social schemas for events such as dates, picnics, committee meetings, and family reunions, as well as for certain categories of people, such as "dumb jocks," "social climbers," "frat rats," and "wimps" (see Figure 16.1). Individuals depend on social schemas because the schemas help them to efficiently process and store the wealth of information that they take in about others in their interactions.

In general, people have a bias toward viewing good-looking men and women as bright, competent, and talented. However, people sometimes downplay the talent of successful women who happen to be attractive, attributing their success to their good looks instead of to their competence.

When a schema is activated, it's likely to influence one's perceptions of a person (Fiske & Taylor, 1991).

Stereotypes

Some of the schemas that individuals apply to people are unique products of their personal experiences, while other schemas may be part of their shared cultural background. *Stereotypes* are special types of schemas that fall into the latter category. *Stereotypes* are widely held beliefs that people have certain characteristics because of their membership in a particular group.

The most common stereotypes in our society are those based on gender and on membership in ethnic or occupational groups. People who subscribe to traditional *gender stereotypes* tend to assume that

Figure 16.1

Examples of social schemas. Everyone has social schemas for various "types" of people, such as sophisticated professionals or working-class stiffs. Social schemas are clusters of beliefs that guide information processing.

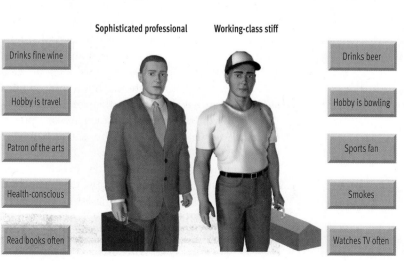

Sophisticated professional | Working-class stiff

Drinks fine wine · Hobby is travel · Patron of the arts · Health-conscious · Read books often

Drinks beer · Hobby is bowling · Sports fan · Smokes · Watches TV often

women are emotional, submissive, illogical, and passive, while men are unemotional, dominant, logical, and aggressive. Preconceived notions that Jews are mercenary, blacks have rhythm, Germans are methodical, and Italians are passionate are examples of common *ethnic stereotypes. Occupational stereotypes* suggest that lawyers are manipulative, programmers are nerdy, accountants are conforming, artists are moody, and so forth.

Stereotyping is a normal cognitive process that is frequently automatic and that saves on the time and effort required to get a handle on people individually (Devine & Monteith, 1999). Stereotypes save energy by simplifying our social world. However, this conservation of energy often comes at some cost in terms of accuracy. Stereotypes frequently are broad overgeneralizations that ignore the diversity within social groups and foster inaccurate perceptions of people (Hilton & von Hippel, 1996). Obviously, not all males, Jews, and lawyers behave alike. Most people who subscribe to stereotypes realize that not all members of a group are identical. For instance, they may admit that some men aren't competitive, some Jews aren't mercenary, and some lawyers aren't manipulative. However, people may still tend to assume that males, Jews, and lawyers are *more likely* than others to have these characteristics. Even if stereotypes mean only that people think in terms of slanted *probabilities,* their expectations may lead them to misperceive individuals with whom they interact. As we've noted in previous chapters, perception is subjective, and people often see what they expect to see.

Subjectivity in Person Perception

Stereotypes and other schemas create biases in person perception that frequently lead to confirmation of people's expectations about others. If there's any ambiguity in someone's behavior, people are likely to interpret what they see in a way that's consistent with their expectations (Olson, Roese, & Zanna, 1996). Thus, after dealing with a pushy female customer, a salesman who holds traditional gender stereotypes might characterize the woman as "emotional." In contrast, he might characterize a pushy male who exhibits exactly the same behavior as "aggressive."

People not only see what they expect to see, they also tend to overestimate how often they see it (Johnson & Mullen, 1994; Shavitt et al., 1999). *Illusory correlation* occurs when people estimate that they have encountered more confirmations of an association between social traits than they have actually seen. People also tend to underestimate the number of disconfirmations they have encountered, as illustrated by statements like "I've never met an honest lawyer."

Memory processes can contribute to confirmatory biases in person perception in a variety of ways. Often, individuals selectively recall facts that fit with their schemas and stereotypes (Fiske, 1998). Evidence for such a tendency was found in a study by Cohen (1981). In this experiment, subjects watched a videotape of a woman, described as either a waitress or a librarian, who engaged in a variety of activities, including listening to classical music, drinking beer, and watching TV. When asked to recall what the woman did during the filmed sequence, participants tended to remember activities consistent with their stereotypes of waitresses and librarians. For instance, participants who thought the woman was a waitress tended to recall her beer drinking, whereas subjects who thought she was a librarian tended to recall her listening to classical music.

An Evolutionary Perspective on Bias in Person Perception

Why is the process of person perception riddled with bias? Evolutionary psychologists argue that many of the biases seen in social perception were adaptive in humans' ancestral environment (Krebs & Denton, 1997). For example, they argue that person perception is swayed by physical attractiveness because attractiveness was associated with reproductive potential in women and with health, vigor, and the accumulation of material resources in men. What about baby-faced features? Evolutionary theorists assert that the tendency to view babies as helpless creatures requiring nurture would be highly adaptive and has probably been preprogammed in humans by natural selection (Springer & Berry, 1997). The tendency to view baby-faced adults as naive, submissive, and honest may simply be a spillover effect from humans' evolutionary heritage.

Evolutionary theorists attribute the human tendency to automatically categorize others to our distant ancestors' need to quickly separate friend from foe. They assert that humans are programmed by evolution to immediately classify people as members of an *ingroup*—a group that one belongs to and identifies with, or as members of an *outgroup*—a group that one does not belong to or identify with. This crucial categorization is thought to structure subsequent perceptions. As Krebs and

Web Link 16.2

Y? The National Forum on People's Differences Home Page
Did you ever want to ask a sensitive question of someone who was different from you—another race or religion or sexual orientation—but were too embarrassed or shy? In a cyberforum with clear rules for courteous and respectful dialogue, newspaper writer and editor Philip J. Milano allows participants to share differences openly and frankly and to learn about what is so frequently kept quiet.

Denton (1997) put it, "It is as though the act of classifying others as ingroup or outgroup members activates two quite different brain circuits" (p. 27). Ingroup members tend to be viewed in a favorable light, whereas outgroup members tend to be viewed in terms of various negative stereotypes. According to Krebs and Denton, these negative stereotypes ("They are inferior; they are all alike; they will exploit us") move outgroups out of our domain of empathy, so we feel justified in not liking them or in discriminating against them. Thus, evolutionary psychologists ascribe much of the bias in person perception to cognitive mechanisms that have been shaped by natural selection. Their speculation is thought provoking, but empirical work is needed to test their hypotheses.

Attribution Processes: Explaining Behavior

It's Friday evening and you're sitting around at home feeling bored. You call a few friends to see whether they'd like to go out. They all say that they'd love to go, but they have other commitments and they can't. Their commitments sound vague, and you feel that their reasons for not going out with you are rather flimsy. How do you explain these rejections? Do your friends really have commitments? Are they worn out by school and work? Are they just lazy and apathetic about going out? These questions illustrate a process that people engage in routinely: the explanation of behavior. *Attributions* play a key role in these explanatory efforts, and they have significant effects on social relations.

What are attributions? **Attributions are inferences that people draw about the causes of events, others' behavior, and their own behavior.** If you conclude that a friend turned down your invitation because she's overworked, you've made an attribution about the cause of her behavior (and, implicitly, rejected other possible explanations). If you conclude that you're stuck at home with nothing to do because you failed to plan ahead, you've made an attribution about the cause of an event (being stuck at home). If you conclude that you failed to plan ahead because you're a procrastinator, you've made an attribution about the cause of your own behavior. *Why do people make attributions?* Individuals make attributions because they have a strong need to understand their experiences. They want to make sense out of their own behavior, others' actions, and the events in their lives.

Internal Versus External Attributions

Fritz Heider (1958) was the first to describe how people make attributions. He asserted that people tend to locate the cause of behavior either *within a person,* attributing it to personal factors, or *outside a person,* attributing it to environmental factors.

Elaborating on Heider's insight, various theorists have agreed that explanations of behavior and events can be categorized as internal or external attributions (Jones & Davis, 1965; Kelley, 1967; Weiner, 1974). **Internal attributions ascribe the causes of behavior to personal dispositions, traits, abilities, and feelings.** *External attributions* **ascribe the causes of behavior to situational demands and environmental constraints.** For example, if a friend's business fails, you might attribute it to your friend's lack of business acumen (an internal, personal factor) or to negative trends in the nation's economic climate (an external, situational explanation). Parents who find out that their teenage son has just banged up the car may blame it on his carelessness (a personal disposition) or on slippery road conditions (a situational factor).

Internal and external attributions can have a tremendous impact on everyday interpersonal interactions. Blaming a friend's business failure on poor business acumen as opposed to a poor economy will have a great impact on how you view your friend—not to mention on whether you'll lend him or her money in the future. Likewise, if parents attribute their son's automobile accident to slippery road conditions, they're likely to deal with the event very differently than if they attribute it to his carelessness.

Attributions for Success and Failure

Some psychologists have sought to discover additional dimensions of attributional thinking besides the internal-external dimension. After studying the attributions that people make in explaining success and failure, Bernard Weiner (1980, 1986, 1994) concluded that people often focus on the *stability* of the causes underlying behavior. According to Weiner, the stable-unstable dimension in attribution cuts across the internal-external dimension,

University of Kansas

Often the momentary situation which, at least in part, determines the behavior of a person is disregarded and the behavior is taken as a manifestation of personal characteristics.
FRITZ HEIDER

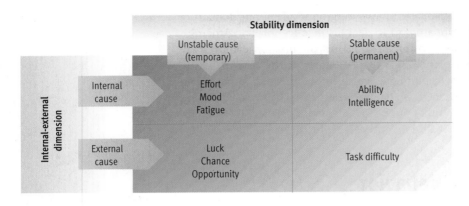

Bias in Attribution

Attributions are only inferences. Your attributions may not be the correct explanations for events. Paradoxical as it may seem, people often arrive at inaccurate explanations even when they contemplate the causes of *their own behavior.* Attributions ultimately represent guesswork about the causes of events, and these guesses tend to be slanted in certain directions. Let's look at the principal biases seen in attribution.

Actor-Observer Bias

Your view of your own behavior can be quite different from the view of someone else observing you. When an actor and an observer draw inferences about the causes of the actor's behavior, they often make different attributions. **The *fundamental attribution error* refers to observers' bias in favor of internal attributions in explaining others' behavior.** Of course, in many instances, an internal attribution may not be an "error." However, observers have a curious tendency to overestimate the likelihood that an actor's behavior reflects personal qualities rather than situational factors. Why? One reason is that attributing others' behavior to their dispositions is a relatively simple, effortless process that borders on automatic (Trope & Liberman, 1993). In contrast, explaining people's behavior in terms of situational factors is a more complex process that requires more thought and effort (Krull & Erickson, 1995; see Figure 16.3).

To illustrate the gap that often exists between actors' and observers' attributions, imagine that you're visiting your bank and you fly into a rage over a mistake made on your account. Observers who witness your rage are likely to make an internal attribution and infer that you are surly, temperamental, and quarrelsome. They may be right, but if asked, you'd probably attribute your rage to the frustrating situation. Perhaps you're normally a calm, easygoing person, but today you've been in line for 20 minutes, you just straightened out a similar error by the same bank last week, and you're being treated rudely by the teller. Observers often are unaware of situational considerations such as these, so they tend to make internal attributions for another's behavior (White & Younger, 1988).

In contrast, the circumstances that have influenced an actor's behavior tend to be more salient to the actor. Hence, actors are more likely than observers to locate the cause of their behavior in the situation. In general, then, *actors favor external attributions for their behavior, while observers are more likely to explain*

Figure 16.2

Weiner's model of attributions for success and failure. Weiner's model assumes that people's explanations for success and failure emphasize internal versus external causes and stable versus unstable causes. Examples of causal factors that fit into each of the four cells in Weiner's model are shown in the diagram. (From E. E. Jones, D. E. Kanouse, H. H. Kelley, R. E. Nisbett, S. Valins & B. Weiner [Eds.] *Perceiving the Causes of Behavior,* 1972. General Learning Press. Used by permission of Dr. Bernard Weiner.)

creating four types of attributions for success and failure, as shown in Figure 16.2.

Let's apply Weiner's model to a concrete event. Imagine that you're contemplating why you failed to get a job that you wanted. You might attribute your setback to internal factors that are stable (lack of ability) or unstable (inadequate effort to put together an eye-catching résumé). Or you might attribute your setback to external factors that are stable (too much outstanding competition) or unstable (bad luck). If you got the job, the explanations you might offer for your success would fall into the same four categories: internal-stable (your excellent ability), internal-unstable (your hard work to assemble a superb résumé), external-stable (lack of topflight competition), and external-unstable (good luck).

CONCEPT CHECK 16.1

Analyzing Attributions

Check your understanding of attribution processes by analyzing possible explanations for an athletic team's success. Imagine that the women's track team at your school has just won a regional championship that qualifies it for the national tournament. Around the campus, you hear people attribute the team's success to a variety of factors. Examine the attributions shown below and place each of them in one of the cells of Weiner's model of attribution (just record the letter inside the cell). The answers are in Appendix A.

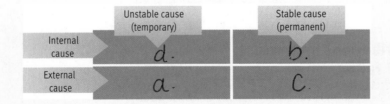

a. "They won only because the best two athletes on Central State's team were out with injuries—talk about good fortune!"
b. "They won because they have some of the best talent in the country."
c. "Anybody could win this region; the competition is far below average in comparison to the rest of the country."
d. "They won because they put in a great deal of last-minute effort and practice, and they were incredibly fired up for the regional tourney after last year's near miss."

Traditional model of attribution

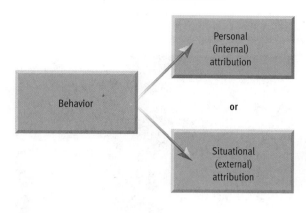

Figure 16.3

An alternative view of the fundamental attribution error. According to Gilbert (1989) and others, the nature of attribution processes favors the *fundamental attribution error*. Traditional models of attribution assume that internal and external attributions are an either-or proposition requiring equal amounts of effort. In contrast, Gilbert posits that people tend to automatically make internal attributions with little effort and then *may* expend additional effort to adjust for the influence of situational factors, which can lead to an external attribution. Thus, external attributions for others' behavior require more thought and effort, which makes them less frequent than personal attributions.

Alternative two-step model of attribution

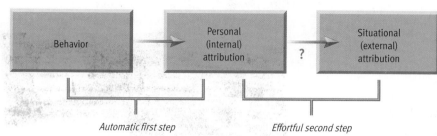

the same behavior with internal attributions (Jones & Nisbett, 1971; Krueger, Ham, & Linford, 1996).

Self-Serving Bias

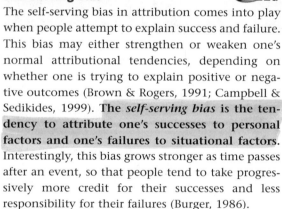 12a

The self-serving bias in attribution comes into play when people attempt to explain success and failure. This bias may either strengthen or weaken one's normal attributional tendencies, depending on whether one is trying to explain positive or negative outcomes (Brown & Rogers, 1991; Campbell & Sedikides, 1999). **The *self-serving bias* is the tendency to attribute one's successes to personal factors and one's failures to situational factors.** Interestingly, this bias grows stronger as time passes after an event, so that people tend to take progressively more credit for their successes and less responsibility for their failures (Burger, 1986).

In explaining *failure,* the usual actor-observer biases are apparent. Actors tend to make external attributions, blaming their failures on unfavorable situational factors, while observers attribute the same failures to the actors' personal shortcomings. In explaining *success,* the usual actor-observer differences are reversed to some degree. Thus, if you get a high exam score, you'll probably make an internal attribution and point to your ability or your hard work (Forsyth & McMillan, 1981). In contrast, an observer may be more likely to infer that the test was easy or that you were lucky (external attributions). In other words, actors like to take credit for their success, while observers lean toward situational explanations for others' triumphs.

CONCEPT **CHECK 16.2**

Recognizing Bias in Social Cognition

Check your understanding of bias in social cognition by identifying various types of errors that are common in person perception and attribution. Imagine that you're a nonvoting student member of a college committee at Southwest State University that is hiring a new political science professor. As you listen to the committee's discussion, you hear examples of (a) the illusory correlation effect, (b) stereotyping, and (c) the fundamental attribution error. Indicate which of these is at work in the excerpts from committee members' deliberations below. The answers are in Appendix A.

_C_ **1.** "I absolutely won't consider the fellow who arrived 30 minutes late for his interview. Anybody who can't make a job interview on time is either irresponsible or hopelessly disorganized. I don't care what he says about the airline messing up his reservations."

_a_ **2.** "You know, I was very, very impressed with the young female applicant, and I would love to hire her, but every time we add a young woman to the faculty in liberal arts, she gets pregnant within the first year." The committee chairperson, who has heard this line from this professor before replies, "You always say that, so I finally did a systematic check of what's happened in the past. Of the last 14 women hired in liberal arts, only one has become pregnant within a year."

_b_ **3.** "The first one I want to rule out is the guy who's been practicing law for the last ten years. Although he has an excellent background in political science, I just don't trust lawyers. They're all ambitious, power hungry, manipulative cutthroats. He'll be a divisive force in the department."

Culture and Attributional Tendencies

Do the patterns of attribution observed in subjects from Western societies transcend culture? More research is needed, but the preliminary evidence suggests not. Some interesting cultural disparities have emerged in research on attribution processes.

According to Harry Triandis (1989, 1994), cultural differences in *individualism* versus *collectivism* influence attributional tendencies as well as other aspects of social behavior. *Individualism* involves putting personal goals ahead of group goals and defining one's identity in terms of personal attributes rather than group memberships. In contrast, *collectivism* involves putting group goals ahead of personal goals and defining one's identity in terms of the groups one belongs to (such as one's family, tribe, work group, social class, caste, and so on). In comparison to individualistic cultures, collectivist cultures place a higher priority on shared values and resources, cooperation, mutual interdependence, and concern for how one's actions will affect other group members. Child-rearing patterns in collectivist cultures emphasize the importance of obedience, reliability, and proper behavior, whereas individualistic cultures emphasize the development of independence, self-esteem, and self-reliance.

A variety of factors influence whether societies cherish individualism as opposed to collectivism. Among other things, increases in a culture's affluence, education, urbanization, and social mobility tend to foster more individualism (Triandis, 1994). Many contemporary societies are in transition, but generally speaking, North American and Western European cultures tend to be individualistic, whereas

The winning Olympic diving champions from mainland China, a collectivist society, probably possess a far different attributional bias about their success than that which would be held by their Western colleagues, who are influenced by a culture centered on individualism.

© Doug Pensinger/Allsport

Asian, African, and Latin American cultures tend to be higher in collectivism (Hofstede, 1980, 1983) (see Figure 16.4).

How does individualism versus collectivism relate to patterns of attribution? The evidence suggests that collectivist cultures may promote different attributional biases than individualistic cultures. For example, people from collectivist societies appear to be less prone to the *fundamental attribution error* than those from individualistic societies (Choi, Nisbett, & Norenzayan, 1999). Westerners are predisposed to explain behavior in terms of people's personality traits and unique abilities. In contrast, collectivists, who value interdependence and obedience, are more likely to assume that one's behavior reflects adherence to group norms. Although the *self-serving bias* has been documented in a variety of cultures (Fletcher & Ward, 1988), it may be particularly prevalent in individualistic, Western societies, where an emphasis on competition and high self-esteem motivates people to try to impress others, as well as themselves. In contrast, Japanese individuals exhibit a *self-effacing bias* in explaining success (Akimoto & Sanbonmatsu, 1999). That is, they tend to attribute their successes to help they receive from others or to the ease of the task, while downplaying the importance of their ability; they attribute their failures mainly to lack of effort. Additional research is needed before any broad conclusions can be drawn, but collectivism may put a different spin on attributional bias.

Figure 16.4

Individualism versus collectivism around the world. Hofstede (1980, 1983) used survey data from over 100,000 employees of a large, multinational corporation to estimate the emphasis on individualism versus collectivism in 50 nations and 3 "regions," for which he combined data for adjacent countries. Data were not available for much of what used to be the Communist bloc or for much of Africa, but his large, diverse international sample remains unequaled to date. As you can see, Hofstede's estimates suggest that most North American and Western European nations tend to be relatively individualistic, whereas more collectivism is found in Asian, African, and Latin American countries.

Hofstede's (1983) rankings of national cultures' individualism

Individualistic cultures	Intermediate cultures	Collectivist cultures
1. United States	19. Israel	37. Hong Kong
2. Australia	20. Spain	38. Chile
3. Great Britain	21. India	40. Singapore
4. Canada	22. Argentina	40. Thailand
4. Netherlands	22. Japan	40. West Africa region
6. New Zealand	24. Iran	42. El Salvador
7. Italy	25. Jamaica	43. Taiwan
8. Belgium	26. Arab region	44. South Korea
9. Denmark	26. Brazil	45. Peru
10. France	28. Turkey	46. Costa Rica
11. Sweden	29. Uruguay	47. Indonesia
12. Ireland	30. Greece	47. Pakistan
13. Norway	31. Philippines	49. Columbia
14. Switzerland	32. Mexico	50. Venezuela
15. West Germany	34. East Africa region	51. Panama
16. South Africa	34. Portugal	52. Ecuador
17. Finland	34. Yugoslavia	53. Guatemala
18. Austria	36. Malaysia	

Interpersonal Attraction: Liking and Loving

"I just don't know what she sees in him. She could do so much better for herself. I suppose he's a nice guy, but they're just not right for each other." Can't you imagine Muffy's friends making these comments in discussing her relationship with Jake? You've probably heard similar remarks on many occasions. These comments illustrate people's interest in analyzing the dynamics of attraction. *Interpersonal attraction* refers to positive feelings toward another. Social psychologists use this term broadly to encompass a variety of experiences, including liking, friendship, admiration, lust, and love.

Key Factors in Attraction

Many factors influence who is attracted to whom. Here we'll discuss factors that promote the development of liking, friendship, and love. Although these are different types of attraction, the interpersonal dynamics at work in each are surprisingly similar. Each is influenced by physical attractiveness, similarity, and reciprocity.

Physical Attractiveness

Although people often say that "beauty is only skin deep," the empirical evidence suggests that most people don't really believe that homily. The importance of physical attractiveness was demonstrated in a recent study of college students in which unacquainted men and women were sent off on a "get-acquainted" date (Sprecher & Duck, 1994). The investigators were mainly interested in how communication might affect the process of attraction, but to put this factor in context they also measured participants' perceptions of their date's physical attractiveness and similarity to themselves. They found that the quality of communication during the date did have some effect on females' interest in friendship, but the key determinant of romantic attraction for both sexes was the physical attractiveness of the other person.

Many other studies have demonstrated the singular prominence of physical attractiveness in the initial stage of dating and have shown that it continues to influence the course of commitment as dating relationships evolve (Hendrick & Hendrick, 1992). In the realm of romance, being physically attractive appears to be more important for females than males (Feingold, 1990). For example, in a study of college students (Speed & Gangestad, 1997), the correlation between romantic popularity (assessed by peer ratings) and physical attractiveness was higher for females (.76) than for males (.47).

Although people prefer physically attractive partners in romantic relationships, they may consider their own level of attractiveness in pursuing dates. What people want in a partner may be different from what they are willing to settle for (Regan, 1998). The *matching hypothesis* proposes that males and females of approximately equal physical attractiveness are likely to select each other as partners. The matching hypothesis is supported by evidence that married couples tend to be very similar in level of physical attractiveness (Feingold, 1988b). Interestingly, people expect that individuals who are similar in attractiveness will be more satisfied as couples and less likely to break up (Garcia & Khersonsky, 1996).

Similarity Effects

Is it true that "birds of a feather flock together," or do "opposites attract"? Research provides far more support for the former than the latter. Married and dating couples tend to be similar in age, race, religion, social class, personality, education, intelligence, physical attractiveness, and attitudes (Kalmijn, 1998; Knox, Zusman, & Nieves, 1997). In married couples, personality similarity appears to be associated with greater marital happiness (Caspi & Herbener, 1990). Similarity is also seen among friends. For instance, adult friends tend to be relatively similar in terms of income, education, occupational status, ethnicity, and religion (Blieszner & Adams, 1992).

The most obvious explanation for these correlations is that similarity causes attraction. Laboratory experiments on *attitude similarity*, conducted by Donn Byrne and his colleagues, suggest that similarity *does* cause liking (Byrne, 1997; Byrne, Clore, & Smeaton, 1986). However, Berscheid and Reis (1998) point out that similarity effects in romantic relationships may simply reflect the fact that for most people, the field of available and eligible potential partners tends to be "overwhelmingly composed of similar persons."

Reciprocity Effects

In his book *How to Win Friends and Influence People,* Dale Carnegie (1936) suggested that people can gain others' liking by showering them with praise and flattery. However, we've all heard that "flattery will get you nowhere." Which advice is right? The

Web Link 16.3

Living in a Social World
This is the homepage of Richard Sherman's (Miami University, Ohio) advanced social psychology course. Many of the projects and postings demonstrate how well an excellent teacher and committed students can use the Internet to research major issues in social psychology.

Courtesy of Ellen Berscheid

❝*The emotion of romantic love seems to be distressingly fragile. As a 16th-century sage poignantly observed, 'the history of a love affair is the drama of its fight against time.*❞
ELLEN BERSCHEID

Figure 16.5

Sternberg's view of love over time. In his theory of love, Robert Sternberg (1988b) hypothesizes that the various elements of love progress in different ways over the course of time. According to Sternberg, passion peaks early in a relationship, whereas intimacy and commitment continue to build gradually.

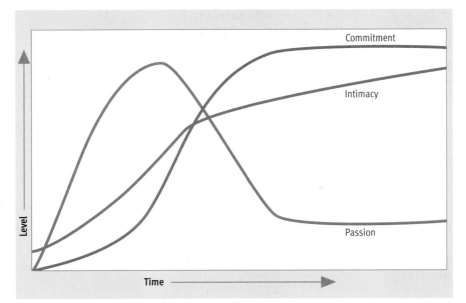

evidence suggests that flattery will get you somewhere, with some people, some of the time.

In interpersonal attraction, *reciprocity* involves **liking those who show that they like you.** In general, research indicates that we tend to like those who show that they like us and that we tend to see others as liking us more if we like them. Thus, it appears that liking breeds liking and loving promotes loving (Sprecher, 1998).

One interesting line of research suggests that in romantic relationships this reciprocity effect even extends to partners "idealizing" each other. Murray, Holmes, and Griffin (1996a) asked 180 married or dating couples to rate themselves, their partner, and their ideal partner on a variety of traits and to rate their satisfaction with their relationship. Common sense would suggest that an accurate view of one's partner would be the best foundation for a stable, satisfying intimate relationship, but this is not what the investigators found. Instead, they discovered that most people viewed their partners more favorably than the partners viewed themselves. Individuals' perceptions of their romantic partners seemed to reflect their ideals for a partner more than reality. Moreover, the data showed that people were happier in their relationship when they idealized their partners and when their partners idealized them. A follow-up study found that individuals who are satisfied with their romantic relationships tend to focus on their partners' virtues and to minimize and rationalize their partners' faults (Murray & Holmes, 1999). This research suggests that positive illusions about one's partner may foster happier and more resilient romantic relationships (Murray & Holmes, 1997).

Perspectives on the Mystery of Love 12b

People have always been interested in love and romance, but love has proven to be an elusive subject for scientific study. It's difficult to define, difficult to measure, and frequently difficult to understand. Nonetheless, psychologists have begun to make some progress in their study of love. Let's look at their theories and research.

Passionate and Companionate Love 12b

Two early pioneers in research on love were Elaine Hatfield and Ellen Berscheid (Berscheid, 1988; Hatfield & Rapson, 1993). They have proposed that romantic relationships are characterized by two kinds of love: passionate love and companionate love. *Passionate love* is a complete absorption in another that includes tender sexual feelings and the agony and ecstasy of intense emotion. *Companionate love* is warm, trusting, tolerant affection for another whose life is deeply intertwined with one's own. Passionate and companionate love *may* coexist, but they don't necessarily go hand in hand.

The distinction between passionate and companionate love has been further refined by Robert Sternberg (1988b), who suggests that love has three facets rather than just two. He subdivides companionate love into intimacy and commitment. *Intimacy* refers to warmth, closeness, and sharing in a relationship. *Commitment* is an intent to maintain a relationship in spite of the difficulties and costs that may arise. Sternberg has mapped out the probable relations between the passage of time and the three components of love, as shown in Figure 16.5. He argues that passion reaches its zenith in the early phases of love and then erodes. He believes that intimacy and commitment increase with time, although at different rates.

Research suggests that commitment is a crucial facet of love that is predictive of relationship stability. For example, declining commitment is associated with an increased likelihood of infidelity in dating relationships (Drigotas, Safstrom, & Gentilia, 1999). In a study of dating couples who were followed for four years, Sprecher (1999) found that participants' feelings of commitment were more predictive of whether they broke up than were their ratings of their overall love. Interestingly, the participants who broke up indicated that their love had remained reasonably stable, but their commitment and satisfaction had declined.

Love as Attachment

Cindy Hazan and Phillip Shaver (1987) have looked not at the types of love but at similarities between adult love and attachment relationships in infancy. We noted in Chapter 11 that infant-caretaker bonding, or *attachment,* emerges in the first year of life. Early attachments vary in quality, and infants tend to fall into three groups (Ainsworth et al., 1978). Most infants develop a *secure attachment.* However, some are very anxious when separated from their caretaker, a syndrome called *anxious-ambivalent attachment.* A third group of infants, characterized by *avoidant attachment,* never bond very well with their caretaker.

According to Hazan and Shaver, romantic love is an attachment process, and people's intimate relationships in adulthood follow the same form as their attachments in infancy. According to their theory, a person who had an anxious-ambivalent attachment in infancy will tend to have romantic relations marked by anxiety and ambivalence in adulthood. In other words, people relive their early bonding with their parents in their adult relationships (see Figure 16.6).

Hazan and Shaver's (1987) initial survey study provided striking support for their theory. They found that adults' love relationships could be sorted into groups that paralleled the three patterns of attachment seen in infants. *Secure adults* found it relatively easy to get close to others and described their love relations as trusting. *Anxious-ambivalent adults* reported a preoccupation with love accompanied by expectations of rejection and described their love relations as volatile and marked by jealousy. *Avoidant adults* found it difficult to get close to others and described their love relations as lacking intimacy. Consistent with their theory, Hazan and Shaver (1987) found that the percentage of adults falling into each category was roughly the same as the percentage of infants in each comparable category—a finding that was subsequently replicated with a nationally representative sample of American adults (Mickelson, Kessler, & Shaver, 1997). Also, subjects' recollections of their childhood relations with their parents were consistent with the idea that people relive their infant attachment experiences in adulthood.

Understandably, Hazan and Shaver's theory has attracted considerable interest and has generated a number of studies within a relatively short period of time. For example, research has shown that securely attached individuals have more committed, satisfying, interdependent, well-adjusted, and longer-lasting relationships compared to people with either anxious-ambivalent or avoidant attachment styles (Feeney, 1999). Moreover, studies have shown that people with different attachment styles are predisposed to think, feel, and behave

> "Passionate love is like any other form of excitement. By its very nature, excitement involves a continuous interplay between elation and despair, thrills and terror."
> ELAINE HATFIELD

Parents' caregiving style	Infant attachment	Adult attachment style
Warm/responsive She/he was generally warm and responsive; she/he was good at knowing when to be supportive and when to let me operate on my own; our relationship was almost always comfortable, and I have no major reservations or complaints about it.	**Secure attachment** An infant-caregiver bond in which the child welcomes contact with a close companion and uses this person as a secure base from which to explore the environment.	**Secure** I find it relatively easy to get close to others and am comfortable depending on them and having them depend on me. I don't often worry about being abandoned or about someone getting too close to me.
Cold/rejecting She/he was fairly cold and distant, or rejecting, not very responsive; I wasn't her/his highest priority, her/his concerns were often elsewhere; it's possible that she/he would just as soon not have had me.	**Avoidant attachment** An insecure infant-caregiver bond, characterized by little separation protest and a tendency of the child to avoid or ignore the caregiver.	**Avoidant** I am somewhat uncomfortable being close to others; I find it difficult to trust them, difficult to allow myself to depend on them. I am nervous when anyone gets too close, and often love partners want me to be more intimate than I feel comfortable being.
Ambivalent/inconsistent She/he was noticeably inconsistent in her/his reactions to me, sometimes warm and sometimes not; she/he had her/his own agenda, which sometimes got in the way of her/his receptiveness and responsiveness to my needs; she/he definitely loved me but didn't always show it in the best way.	**Anxious/ambivalent attachment** An insecure infant-caregiver bond, characterized by strong separation protest and a tendency of the child to resist contact initiated by the caregiver, particularly after a separation.	**Anxious/ambivalent** I find that others are reluctant to get as close as I would like. I often worry that my partner doesn't really love me or won't want to stay with me. I want to merge completely with another person, and this desire sometimes scares people away.

Figure 16.6

Infant attachment and romantic relationships. According to Hazan and Shaver (1987), people's romantic relationships in adulthood are similar in form to their attachment patterns in infancy, which are determined in part by parental caregiving styles. The theorized relations between parental styles, attachment patterns, and intimate relations are outlined here. (Data for parental caregiving styles and adult attachment styles based on Hazan and Shaver, 1986, 1987; infant attachment patterns adapted from Shaffer, 1985)

differently in their relationships (Collins, 1996). For example, anxious-ambivalent people tend to report more intense emotional highs and lows in their romantic relationships. They also find conflicts with a partner more stressful than conflicts with others and feel more negative about their relationship after dealing with a conflict (Simpson, Rholes, & Phillips, 1996). Avoidant individuals tend to engage in more casual sex than others because this strategy allows them to get physically close without incurring the vulnerability of genuine intimacy (Brennan & Shaver, 1995). How do people with various attachment styles tend to pair up? More data are needed to answer this interesting question, but preliminary evidence suggests that avoidant and anxious-ambivalent people are not drawn to their mirror images. In an analysis of 240 couples, Kirkpatrick and Davis (1994) did not find *any* pairings between two avoidant people or two anxious-ambivalent people.

Culture and Close Relationships

Relatively little cross-cultural research has been conducted on the dynamics of interpersonal attraction. The limited evidence suggests that there are both similarities and differences between cultures in romantic relationships. For the most part, similarities have been seen when research has focused on what people look for in prospective mates. As discussed in Chapter 10, David Buss (1989, 1994b) has collected data on mate preferences in 37 divergent cultures and found that people all over the world value mutual attraction, kindness, intelligence, emotional stability, dependability, and good health.

Cultures vary, however, in their emphasis on love—especially passionate love—as a prerequisite for marriage. Love as the basis for marriage is an 18th-century invention of Western culture (Stone, 1977). As Hatfield and Rapson (1993) note, "Marriage-for-love represents an ultimate expression of individualism" (p. 2). In contrast, marriages arranged by families and other go-betweens remain common in cultures high in collectivism, including India (Gupta, 1992), Japan (Iwao, 1993), and China (Xiaghe & Whyte, 1990). This practice is declining in some societies as a result of Westernization, but in collectivist societies people contemplating marriage still tend to think in terms of "What will my parents and other people say?" rather than "What does my heart say?" (Triandis, 1994). Studies show that attitudes about love in collectivist societies reflect these cultural priorities. For example, in

comparison to Western participants, subjects from Eastern countries (such as India, Pakistan, and Thailand) report that romantic love is less important for marriage (Levine et al., 1995).

An Evolutionary Perspective on Attraction

Evolutionary psychologists have a great deal to say about heterosexual attraction. For example, they assert that physical appearance is an influential determinant of attraction because certain aspects of good looks can be indicators of sound health, good genes, and high fertility, all of which can contribute to reproductive potential (Miller, 1998). Consistent with this analysis, recent research has found that some standards of attractiveness are more consistent across cultures than previously believed (Cunningham, Druen, & Barbee, 1997). For example, *facial symmetry* seems to be a key element of attractiveness in highly diverse cultures (Cunningham et al., 1995). Facial symmetry is thought to be valued because a host of environmental insults and developmental abnormalities are associated with physical asymmetries, which may serve as markers of relatively poor genes or health (Gangestad, Thornhill, & Yeo, 1994). Another facet of appearance that may transcend culture is women's *waist-to-hip ratio.* Around the world, men seem to prefer women with a waist-to-hip ratio around .70–.80, which appears to be a meaningful correlate of females' reproductive potential (Singh, 1993).

The most thoroughly documented findings on the evolutionary bases of heterosexual attraction are the findings on gender differences in humans' mating preferences. Consistent with the notion that humans are programmed by evolution to behave in ways that enhance their reproductive fitness, evidence indicates that men generally are more interested than women in seeking youthfulness and physical attractiveness in their mates because these traits should be associated with greater reproductive potential (see Chapter 10). On the other hand, research shows that women place a greater premium on prospective mates' ambition, social status, and financial potential because these traits should be associated with the ability to invest material resources in children (Buss & Kenrick, 1998).

Does the gender gap in mating priorities influence the tactics people actually use in pursuing romantic relationships? Yes, evidence indicates that during courtship men tend to emphasize their material resources whereas women are more likely to work at enhancing their appearance (Buss,

1988). Interestingly, the tactics used by both sexes may include efforts at deception. A recent study found that many men and women would be willing to lie about their personality, income, past relationships, career skills, and intelligence to impress a prospective date who was attractive (Rowatt, Cunningham, & Druen, 1999). Another study found that females anticipate more deception from prospective dates than males do (Keenan et al., 1997). Perhaps this is the reason women tend to underestimate the strength of men's relationship commitment (Haselton & Buss, 2000). Men do not appear to show a similar bias, but they do show a tendency to overestimate women's sexual interest. These cognitive biases seem to have been designed to reduce the probability that ancestral women would consent to sex and then be abandoned and to minimize the likelihood that ancestral men would overlook sexual opportunities. Thus, evolutionary psychologists analyze romantic relationships in terms of the adaptive problems they have presented over the course of human history.

Attitudes: Making Social Judgments

In our chapter-opening story, Muffy's friends exhibited decidedly negative attitudes about working-class men. Their example reveals a basic feature of attitudes: they're evaluative. Social psychology's interest in attitudes has a much longer history than its interest in attraction. Indeed, in its early days social psychology was defined as the study of attitudes. In this section we'll discuss the nature of attitudes, efforts to change attitudes through persuasion, and theories of attitude change.

What are attitudes? **Attitudes are positive or negative evaluations of objects of thought.** "Objects of thought" may include social issues (capital punishment or gun control, for example), groups (liberals, farmers), institutions (the Lutheran church, the Supreme Court), consumer products (yogurt, computers), and people (the president, your next-door neighbor).

Components and Dimensions of Attitudes

Social psychologists have traditionally viewed attitudes as being made up of three components: a cognitive component, an affective component, and a behavioral component. However, in recent years it has become apparent that many attitudes do not include all three components (Olson & Zanna, 1993), so it is more accurate to say that *attitudes may include up to three different types of components*. The *cognitive component* of an attitude is made up of the beliefs that people hold about the object of an attitude. The *affective component* of an attitude consists of the *emotional feelings* stimulated by an object of thought. The *behavioral component* of an attitude consists of *predispositions to act* in certain ways toward an attitude object. Figure 16.7 provides concrete

Figure 16.7

The components of attitudes. Attitudes can be broken into cognitive, affective, and behavioral components, as illustrated here for a hypothetical person's attitude about gun control.

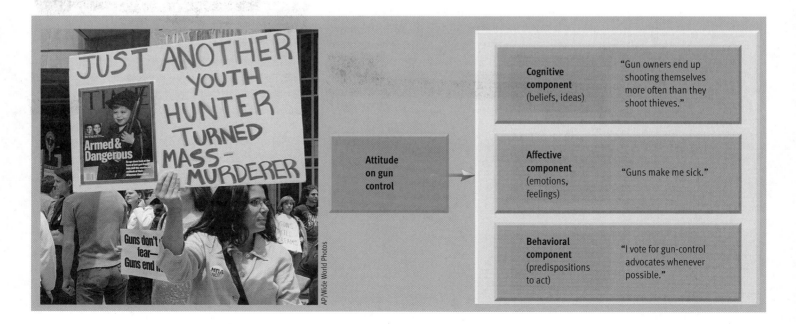

Attitude on gun control

Cognitive component (beliefs, ideas)
"Gun owners end up shooting themselves more often than they shoot thieves."

Affective component (emotions, feelings)
"Guns make me sick."

Behavioral component (predispositions to act)
"I vote for gun-control advocates whenever possible."

AP/Wide World Photos

examples of how someone's attitude about gun control might be divided into its components.

Attitudes vary along several crucial dimensions, including their *strength, accessibility,* and *ambivalence* (Olson & Zanna, 1993). Definitions of *attitude strength* differ, but they generally suggest that strong attitudes as those that are firmly held (durable) and that have a powerful impact on behavior (Krosnick & Petty, 1995). The *accessibility* of an attitude refers to how often one thinks about it and how quickly it comes to mind. Highly accessible attitudes are quickly and readily available (Fazio, 1995). Attitude accessibility is correlated with attitude strength, as highly accessible attitudes *tend* to be strong, but the concepts are distinct and there is no one-to-one correspondence. *Ambivalent attitudes* are conflicted evaluations that include both positive and negative feelings about an object of thought (Thompson, Zanna, & Griffin, 1995). Generally speaking, ambivalence increases as the ratio of positive to negative evaluations gets closer to being equal.

Recent years have brought a great deal of research on the determinants and correlates of attitude strength. One determinant is *importance*—the subjective sense of caring and significance that a person attaches to an attitude. Attitudes that are important to people tend to be relatively strong (Boninger et al., 1995). Another factor is whether a person has a *vested interest* in an attitude. A vested interest exists when an attitude relates to an issue that can affect an individual's personal outcomes. For example, college students tend to have a vested interest in how localities regulate the legal age for drinking alcohol and physicians have a vested interest in whether managed care systems continue to become more influential in the practice of medicine. A vested interest in an attitude tends to make it stronger (Crano, 1995). Yet another consideration is one's knowledge of an attitude object. The more *knowledge and information* one has about an object of thought, the stronger one's attitude about it tends to be (Wood, Rhodes, & Biek, 1995). Perhaps

this is true because thinking carefully about an attitude object can increase attitude strength (Petty, Haugtvedt, & Smith, 1995).

Trying to Change Attitudes: Factors in Persuasion

Every day you're bombarded by efforts to alter your attitudes. In light of this reality, let's examine some of the factors that determine whether persuasion works.

The process of persuasion includes four basic elements: source, receiver, message, and channel (see Figure 16.8). **The *source* is the person who sends a communication, and the *receiver* is the person to whom the message is sent.** Thus, if you watch a presidential news conference on TV, the president is the source, and you and millions of other viewers are the receivers. **The *message* is the information transmitted by the source, and the *channel* is the medium through which the message is sent.** Although the research on communication channels is interesting, we'll confine our discussion to source, message, and receiver variables.

Source Factors

Persuasion tends to be more successful when the source has high *credibility* (O'Keefe, 1990). What gives a person credibility? Either expertise or trustworthiness. *Expertise* tends to be more influential when arguments are ambiguous (Chaiken & Maheswaran, 1994). People try to convey their *expertise* by mentioning their degrees, their training, and their experience or by showing an impressive grasp of the issue at hand. Expertise is a plus, but *trustworthiness* can be even more important. Many people tend to accept messages from trustworthy sources with little scrutiny (Priester & Petty, 1995). Trustworthiness is undermined when a source appears to have something to gain. In contrast, trustworthiness is enhanced when people appear to argue against their own best interests (Hunt, Smith, & Kernan, 1985). *Likability* also

Figure 16.8

Overview of the persuasion process. The process of persuasion essentially boils down to *who* (the source) communicates *what* (the message) *by what means* (the channel) *to whom* (the receiver). Thus, four sets of variables influence the process of persuasion: source, message, channel, and receiver factors. The diagram lists some of the more important factors in each category (including some that are not discussed in the text because of space limitations). (Adapted from Lippa, 1994)

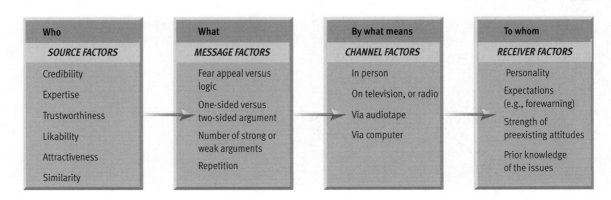

Who	What	By what means	To whom
SOURCE FACTORS	**MESSAGE FACTORS**	**CHANNEL FACTORS**	**RECEIVER FACTORS**
Credibility	Fear appeal versus logic	In person	Personality
Expertise	One-sided versus two-sided argument	On television, or radio	Expectations (e.g., forewarning)
Trustworthiness	Number of strong or weak arguments	Via audiotape	Strength of preexisting attitudes
Likability	Repetition	Via computer	Prior knowledge of the issues
Attractiveness			
Similarity			

increases the effectiveness of a persuasive source (Roskos-Ewoldsen & Fazio, 1992).

The importance of source variables can be seen in advertising. Many companies spend a fortune to obtain an ideal spokesperson, such as Jerry Seinfeld, Michael Jordan, Bill Cosby, or Candace Bergen, who combine trustworthiness and likability. Companies quickly abandon spokespersons when their likability declines.

Message Factors

If you were going to give a speech to a local community group advocating a reduction in state taxes on corporations, you'd probably wrestle with a number of questions about how to structure your message. Should you look at both sides of the issue, or should you just present your side? Should you deliver a low-key, logical speech? Or should you try to strike fear into the hearts of your listeners? These questions are concerned with message factors in persuasion.

In general, two-sided arguments seem to be more effective than one-sided presentations (Petty & Wegener, 1998). Just mentioning that an issue has two sides can increase your credibility with an audience. Fear appeals appear to work—if they are successful in arousing fear. Research reveals that many messages intended to induce fear fail to do so. However, studies involving a wide range of issues (nuclear policy, auto safety, dental hygiene, and so on) have shown that messages that are effective in arousing fear tend to increase persuasion (Block & Keller, 1997; Kimura, 1997). Fear appeals are most likely to work when your listeners view the dire consequences that you describe as exceedingly unpleasant, fairly probable if they don't take your advice, and avoidable if they do (Rogers, 1983; Witte et al., 1998).

Receiver Factors

What about the receiver of the persuasive message? Are some people easier to persuade than others? Undoubtedly, but transient factors such as the forewarning a receiver gets about a persuasive effort and the receiver's initial position on an issue seem to be more influential than the receiver's personality. Consider, for instance, the old adage that "to be forewarned is to be forearmed." The value of *forewarning* does apply to targets of persuasive efforts (Johnson, 1994). When you shop for a new TV, you *expect* salespeople to work at persuading you, and to some extent this forewarning reduces the impact of their arguments.

A receiver's resistance to persuasion also depends on the nature of the attitude or belief that the source is trying to change. Obviously, resistance is greater when you have to advocate a position that is incompatible with the receiver's existing attitudes or beliefs. In general, arguments that are in conflict with one's prior attitudes are scrutinized longer and subjected to more skeptical analysis than arguments that are consistent with one's prior beliefs (Edwards & Smith, 1996).

Furthermore, studies show that *stronger attitudes are more resistant to change* (Eagly & Chaiken, 1995). Strong attitudes may be tougher to alter because they tend to be anchored in networks of beliefs and values that might also require change (Erber, Hodges, & Wilson, 1995). Strong attitudes may also generate more biased and selective processing of persuasive arguments.

Our review of source, message, and receiver variables has shown that attempting to change attitudes through persuasion involves a complex interplay of factors—and we haven't even looked beneath the surface yet. How do people acquire attitudes in the first place? What dynamic processes within people produce attitude change? We turn to these theoretical issues next.

Theories of Attitude Formation and Change

Many theories have been proposed to explain the mechanisms at work in attitude change, whether or not it occurs in response to persuasion. We'll look at three theoretical perspectives: learning theory, dissonance theory, and the elaboration likelihood model.

Learning Theory

We've seen repeatedly that *learning theory* can help explain a wide range of phenomena, from conditioned fears to the acquisition of sex roles to the development of personality traits. Now we can add attitude formation and change to our list.

The affective, or emotional, component in an attitude can be created through *classical conditioning*, just as other emotional responses can (Chaiken, Wood, & Eagly, 1996). As we discussed in the Chapter 6 Critical Thinking Application, advertisers routinely try to take advantage of classical conditioning by pairing their products with stimuli that elicit pleasant emotional responses, such as extremely attractive models, highly likable spokespersons, and cherished events, such as the Olympics (Grossman & Till, 1998). This conditioning process is diagrammed in Figure 16.9 on the next page.

Operant conditioning may come into play when you openly express an attitude, such as "I believe

Web Link 16.4

Influence at Work: The Psychology of Persuasion Social psychologist Kelton Rhodes (in collaboration with Robert Cialdini) has assembled an introduction to the scientific study of social influence processes. This site serves as an adjunct to their professional consulting and publishing activities.

Figure 16.9

Classical conditioning of attitudes in advertising. Advertisers routinely pair their products with likable celebrities in the hope that their products will come to elicit pleasant emotional responses. See the Critical Thinking Application in Chapter 6 for a more in-depth discussion of this practice.

© Katz/Liaison Agency

AP/Wide World Photos

CS Products (e.g., autos, foods)	
UCS Likable celebrity	**CR** Pleasant emotional response **UCR**

that husbands should do more housework." Some people may endorse your view, while others may jump down your throat. Agreement from other people generally functions as a reinforcer, strengthening your tendency to express a specific attitude (Blanchard, Lilly, & Vaughn, 1991). Disagreement often functions as a form of punishment, which may gradually weaken your commitment to your viewpoint.

Another person's attitudes may rub off on you through *observational learning* (Oskamp, 1991). If you hear your uncle say, "Republicans are nothing but puppets of big business," and your mother heartily agrees, your exposure to your uncle's attitude and your mother's reinforcement of your uncle may influence your attitude toward the Republican party. Studies show that parents and their children tend to have similar political attitudes (Sears, 1975). Observational learning presumably accounts for much of this similarity. The opinions of teachers, coaches, co-workers, talk-show hosts, rock stars, and so forth are also likely to sway people's attitudes through observational learning.

Dissonance Theory 12C

Leon Festinger's *dissonance theory* assumes that inconsistency among attitudes propels people in the direction of attitude change. Dissonance theory burst into prominence in 1959 when Festinger and J. Merrill Carlsmith published a famous study of *counterattitudinal behavior*. Let's look at their findings and at how dissonance theory explains them.

CONCEPT **CHECK 16.3**

Understanding Attitudes and Persuasion

Check your understanding of the components of attitudes and the elements of persuasion by analyzing hypothetical political strategies. Imagine you're working on a political campaign and you're invited to join the candidate's inner circle in strategy sessions, as staff members prepare the candidate for upcoming campaign stops. During the meetings, you hear various strategies discussed. For each strategy below, indicate which component of voters' attitudes (cognitive, affective, or behavioral) is being targeted for change, and indicate which element in persuasion (source, message, or receiver factors) is being manipulated. The answers are in Appendix A.

1. "You need to convince this crowd that your program for regulating nursing homes is sound. Whatever you do, don't acknowledge the two weaknesses in the program that we've been playing down. I don't care if you're asked point blank. Just slide by the question and keep harping on the program's advantages."

Cognitive component of attitudes

2. "You haven't been smiling enough lately, especially when the TV cameras are rolling. Remember, you can have the best ideas in the world, but if you don't seem likable, you're not gonna get elected. By the way, I think I've lined up some photo opportunities that should help us create an image of sincerity and compassion."

Affective component of attitudes

3. "This crowd is already behind you. You don't have to alter their opinions on any issue. Get right to work convincing them to contribute to the campaign. I want them lining up to give money."

Behavioral component of attitudes

Festinger and Carlsmith (1959) had male college students come to a laboratory and work on excruciatingly dull tasks, such as turning pegs repeatedly. When a subject's hour was over, the experimenter confided that some participants' motivation was being manipulated by telling them that the task was interesting and enjoyable before they started it. Then, after a moment's hesitation, the experimenter asked if the subject could help him out of a jam. His usual helper was delayed and he needed someone to testify to the next "subject" (really an accomplice) that the experimental task was interesting. He offered to pay the person if he would tell the person in the adjoining waiting room that the task was enjoyable and involving.

This entire scenario was enacted to coax participants into doing something that was inconsistent with their true feelings—that is, to engage in *counterattitudinal behavior.* Some subjects received a token payment of $1 for their effort, while others received a more substantial payment of $20 (an amount equivalent to about $120 today, in light of inflation). Later, a second experimenter inquired about the participants' true feelings regarding the dull experimental task. Figure 16.10 summarizes the design of the Festinger and Carlsmith study.

Who do you think rated the task more favorably—the subjects who were paid $1 or those who were paid $20? Both common sense and learning theory would predict that the subjects who received the greater reward ($20) should come to like the task more. In reality, however, the participants who were paid $1 exhibited more favorable attitude change—just as Festinger and Carlsmith had predicted. Why? Dissonance theory provides an explanation.

According to Festinger (1957), *cognitive dissonance* exists when related cognitions are inconsistent—that is, when they contradict each other. Festinger's model assumes that dissonance is possible only when cognitions are relevant to each other, since unrelated cognitions ("I am hardworking" and "Fire engines are red") can't contradict each other. However, when cognitions are related, they may be consonant ("I am hardworking" and "I'm staying overtime to get an important job done") or dissonant ("I am hardworking" and "I'm playing hooky from work"). When aroused, cognitive dissonance is supposed to create an unpleasant state of tension that motivates people to reduce their dissonance—usually by altering their cognitions.

In the study by Festinger and Carlsmith (1959), the subjects' contradictory cognitions were "The task is boring" and "I told someone the task was enjoyable." The participants who were paid $20 for lying

had an obvious reason for behaving inconsistently with their true attitudes, so these subjects experienced little dissonance. In contrast, the participants paid $1 had no readily apparent justification for their lie and experienced high dissonance. To reduce it, they tended to persuade themselves that the task was more enjoyable than they had originally thought. Thus, dissonance theory sheds light on why people sometimes come to believe their own lies.

Cognitive dissonance is also at work when people turn attitudinal somersaults to justify efforts that haven't panned out, a syndrome called *effort justification.* Aronson and Mills (1959) studied effort justification by putting college women through a "severe initiation" before they could qualify to participate in what promised to be an interesting discussion of sexuality. In the initiation, the women had to read obscene passages out loud to a male experimenter. After all that, the highly touted discussion of sexuality turned out to be a boring, taped

Photo by Karen Zabulon, © 1982, courtesy of New School for Social Research, by permission of Trudy Festinger

"Cognitive dissonance is a motivating state of affairs. Just as hunger impels a person to eat, so does dissonance impel a person to change his opinions or his behavior."
LEON FESTINGER

Figure 16.10

Design of the Festinger and Carlsmith (1959) study. The sequence of events in this landmark study of counterattitudinal behavior and attitude change is outlined here. The diagram omits a third condition (no dissonance), in which subjects were not induced to lie. The results in the nondissonance condition were similar to those found in the low-dissonance condition.

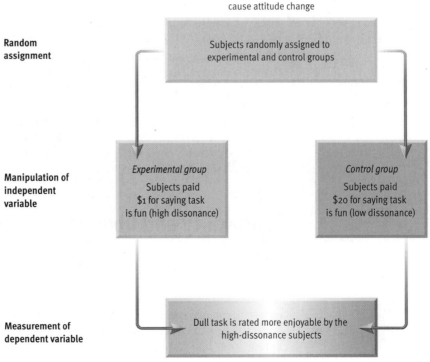

Hypothesis:
High dissonance about counterattitudinal behavior will cause attitude change

Random assignment
Subjects randomly assigned to experimental and control groups

Manipulation of independent variable

Experimental group
Subjects paid $1 for saying task is fun (high dissonance)

Control group
Subjects paid $20 for saying task is fun (low dissonance)

Measurement of dependent variable
Dull task is rated more enjoyable by the high-dissonance subjects

Conclusion:
Dissonance about counterattitudinal behavior does cause attitude change

Figure 16.11

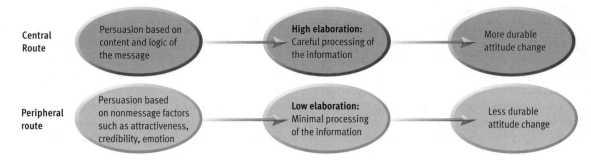

lecture on reproduction in lower animals. Subjects in the severe initiation condition experienced highly dissonant cognitions ("I went through a lot to get here" and "This discussion is terrible"). How did they reduce their dissonance? Apparently by changing their attitude about the discussion, since they rated it more favorably than participants in two control conditions.

Effort justification may be at work in many facets of everyday life. For example, people who wait for hours to be seated at an exclusive restaurant often praise the restaurant afterward even if they have been served a poorly prepared meal. Rock fans who pay hundreds of dollars for scalped concert tickets will tend to view the concert favorably, even if the artists show up in a stupor and play out of tune.

Dissonance theory has been tested in hundreds of studies with mixed, but largely favorable, results. The dynamics of dissonance appear to underlie many important types of attitude changes (Draycott & Dabbs, 1998; Hosseini, 1997; Keller & Block, 1999). Research has supported Festinger's claim that dissonance involves genuine psychological discomfort and even physiological arousal (Croyle & Cooper, 1983; Devine et al., 1999). However, dissonance effects are not among the most reliable phenomena in social psychology, perhaps because people vary in the need for cognitive consistency (Cialdini, Trost, & Newsom, 1995).

Elaboration Likelihood Model

A more recent theory of attitude change proposed by Richard Petty and John Cacioppo (1986) asserts that there are two basic "routes" to persuasion (Petty & Wegener, 1999). The *central route* is taken when people carefully ponder the content and logic of persuasive messages. The *peripheral route* is taken when persuasion depends on nonmessage factors, such as the attractiveness and credibility of the source, or on conditioned emotional responses (see Figure 16.11). For example, a politician who campaigns by delivering carefully researched speeches that thoughtfully analyze complex issues is following the central route to persuasion. In contrast, a politician who depends on marching bands, flag waving, celebrity endorsements, and emotional slogans is following the peripheral route.

Both routes can lead to persuasion. However, according to the elaboration likelihood model, the durability of attitude change depends on the extent to which people elaborate on (think about) the contents of persuasive communications. Studies suggest that the central route to persuasion leads to more enduring attitude change than the peripheral route (Petty & Wegener, 1998). Research also suggests that attitudes changed through central processes predict behavior better than attitudes changed through peripheral processes (Petty, Wegener, & Fabrigar, 1997).

Conformity and Obedience: Yielding to Others

A number of years ago, the area that I lived in experienced a severe spring flood that required the mobilization of the National Guard and a host of other emergency services. At the height of the crisis, a young man arrived at the scene of the flood, announced that he was from an obscure state agency that no one had ever heard of, and proceeded to take control of the emergency. City work crews, the fire department, local police, municipal officials, and the National Guard followed his orders with dispatch for several days, evacuating entire neighborhoods—until an official thought to check and found out that the man was just someone who had walked in off the street. The imposter, who had had small armies at his beck and call for several days, had no training in emergency services, just a history of unemployment and psychological problems.

After news of the hoax spread, people criticized red-faced local officials for their compliance with the imposter's orders. However, many of the critics probably would have cooperated in much the same way if they had been in the officials' shoes. For most people, willingness to obey someone in authority is the rule, not the exception. In this section, we'll analyze the dynamics of social influence at work in conformity and obedience.

Conformity

If you keep a well-manicured lawn and extoll the talents of singer/songwriter Jewel, are you exhibiting conformity? According to social psychologists, it depends on whether your behavior is the result of group pressure. **Conformity occurs when people yield to real or imagined social pressure.** For example, if you maintain a well-groomed lawn only to avoid complaints from your neighbors, you're yielding to social pressure. If you like Jewel because you genuinely enjoy her music, that's *not* conformity. However, if you like Jewel because it's "hip" and your friends would question your taste if you didn't, then you're conforming.

In the 1950s, Solomon Asch (1951, 1955, 1956) devised a clever procedure that minimized ambiguity about whether subjects were conforming, allowing him to investigate the variables that govern conformity. Let's re-create one of Asch's (1955) classic experiments. The participants are male undergraduates recruited for a study of visual perception. A group of seven subjects are shown a large card with a vertical line on it and then are asked to indicate which of three lines on a second card matches the original "standard line" in length (see Figure 16.12). All seven participants are given a turn at the task, and they announce their choice to the group. The subject in the sixth chair doesn't know it, but everyone else in the group is an accomplice of the experimenter, and they're about to make him wonder whether he has taken leave of his senses.

The accomplices give accurate responses on the first two trials. On the third trial, line number 2 clearly is the correct response, but the first five "subjects" all say that line number 3 matches the standard line. The genuine subject is bewildered and can't believe his ears. Over the course of the next 15 trials, the accomplices all give the same incorrect response on 11 of them. How does the real subject respond? The line judgments are easy and unambiguous. So, if the participant consistently agrees with the accomplices, he isn't making honest mistakes—he's conforming.

Averaging across all 50 subjects, Asch (1955) found that the young men conformed on 37% of the trials. The participants varied considerably in their tendency to conform, however. Of the 50 subjects, 13 never caved in to the group, while 14 conformed on more than half the trials. One could argue that the results show that people confronting a unanimous majority generally tend to *resist* the pressure to conform, but given how clear and easy the line judgments were, most social scientists viewed the findings as a dramatic demonstration of humans' propensity to conform (Levine, 1999).

In subsequent studies, *group size* and *group unanimity* turned out to be key determinants of conformity (Asch, 1956). To examine the impact of group size, Asch repeated his procedure with groups that included from 1 to 15 accomplices. Little conformity was seen when a subject was pitted against just one person, but conformity increased rapidly as group size went from 2 to 4, peaked at a group size of 7, and then leveled off (see Figure 16.13). Thus, Asch reasoned that as groups grow larger, conformity increases—up to a point—a conclusion that has been echoed by other researchers (Cialdini & Trost, 1998).

However, group size made little difference if just one accomplice "broke" with the others, wrecking their unanimous agreement. The presence of another dissenter lowered conformity to about one-quarter of its peak, even when the dissenter made *inaccurate* judgments that happened to conflict with the majority view. Apparently, the participants just needed to hear someone else question the accuracy of the group's perplexing responses. The importance of unanimity in fostering conformity has been replicated in subsequent research (Nemeth & Chiles, 1988).

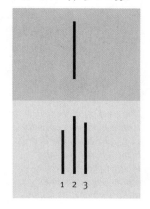

Figure 16.12

Stimuli used in Asch's conformity studies. Subjects were asked to match a standard line (top) with one of three other lines displayed on another card (bottom). The task was easy—until experimental accomplices started responding with obviously incorrect answers. (Figures 16.12 and 16.13 adapted from "Opinion and Social Pressure," by Solomon Asch, *Scientific American*, November 1955, from illustrations by Sara Love on pp. 32 and 35.)

Figure 16.13

Conformity and group size. This graph shows the percentage of trials on which subjects conformed as a function of group size in Asch's research. Asch found that conformity became more frequent as group size increased up to about seven, and then conformity leveled off.

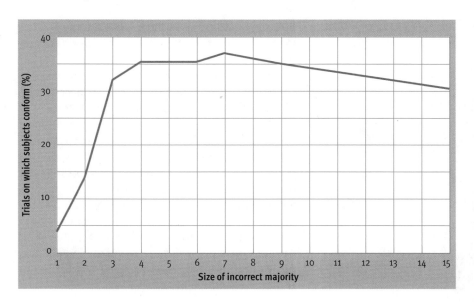

Obedience

Obedience is a form of compliance that occurs when people follow direct commands, usually from someone in a position of authority. To a surprising extent, when an authority figure says, "Jump!" many people simply ask, "How high?"

Milgram's Studies

Stanley Milgram wanted to study this tendency to obey authority figures. Like many other people after World War II, he was troubled by how readily the citizens of Germany followed the orders of dictator Adolf Hitler, even when the orders required morally repugnant actions, such as the slaughter of millions of Jews. Milgram, who had worked with Solomon Asch, set out to design a standard laboratory procedure for the study of obedience, much like Asch's procedure for studying conformity. The clever experiment that Milgram devised became one of the most famous and controversial studies in the annals of psychology.

Milgram's (1963) participants were a diverse collection of 40 men from the local community. They were told that they would be participating in a study concerned with the effects of punishment on learning. When they arrived at the lab, they drew slips of paper from a hat to get their assignments. The drawing was rigged so that the subject always became the "teacher" and an experimental accomplice (a likable 47-year-old accountant) became the "learner."

The learner was strapped into an electrified chair through which a shock could be delivered whenever he made a mistake on the task (see Figure 16.14). The subject was then taken to an adjoining room that housed the shock generator that he would control in his role as the teacher. Although the apparatus looked and sounded realistic, it was a fake and the learner was never shocked.

As the "learning experiment" proceeded, the accomplice made many mistakes that necessitated shocks. The teacher was instructed to increase the shock level after each wrong answer. At 300 volts, the learner began to pound on the wall between the two rooms in protest and soon stopped responding to the teacher's questions. From this point forward, participants frequently turned to the experimenter for guidance. Whenever they did so, the experimenter firmly indicated that the teacher should continue to give stronger and stronger shocks to the now-silent learner. The dependent variable was the maximum shock the participant was willing to administer before refusing to go on.

As Figure 16.14 shows, 26 of the 40 subjects (65%) administered all 30 levels of shock. Although they tended to obey the experimenter, many subjects voiced and displayed considerable distress about harming the learner. The horrified participants groaned, bit their lips, stuttered, trembled, and broke into a sweat, but continued administering the shocks. Based on these results, Milgram concluded that obedience to authority was even more common than he or others anticipated. Before the study was conducted, Milgram had described it to 40 psychiatrists and had asked them to predict how much shock subjects would be willing to administer to their innocent victims. Most of the psychiatrists had predicted that fewer than 1% of the subjects would continue to the end of the series of shocks!

In interpreting his results, Milgram argued that strong pressure from an authority figure can make decent people do indecent things to others. Applying this insight to Nazi war crimes and other travesties, Milgram asserted that some sinister actions may not be due to actors' evil character so much as to situational pressures that can lead normal people to engage in acts of treachery and violence. Thus, he arrived at the disturbing conclusion that given the right circumstances, any of us might obey orders to inflict harm on innocent strangers.

After his initial demonstration, Milgram (1974) tried about 20 variations on his experimental procedure, looking for factors that influenced subjects' obedience. As a whole, Milgram was surprised at how stable participants' obedience remained as he changed various aspects of his experiment.

The Ensuing Controversy

Milgram's study evoked a controversy that continues through today. Some critics argued that Milgram's results wouldn't generalize to the real world (Baumrind, 1964; Orne & Holland, 1968). They maintained that subjects who agree to participate in a scientific study *expect to obey* orders from an experimenter. Milgram (1964, 1968) replied by pointing out that so do soldiers and bureaucrats in the real world who are accused of villainous acts performed in obedience to authority. "I reject Baumrind's argument that the observed obedience doesn't count because it occurred where it is appropriate," said Milgram (1964). "That is precisely why it *does* count." Overall, the weight of evidence supports the generalizability of Milgram's results. They were consistently replicated for many years, in diverse settings, with a variety of subjects and procedural variations (Blass, 1999; Miller, 1986).

© 1981 Eric Kroll, courtesy of Alexandra Milgram

"The essence of obedience is that a person comes to view himself as the instrument for carrying out another person's wishes, and he therefore no longer regards himself as responsible for his actions."
STANLEY MILGRAM

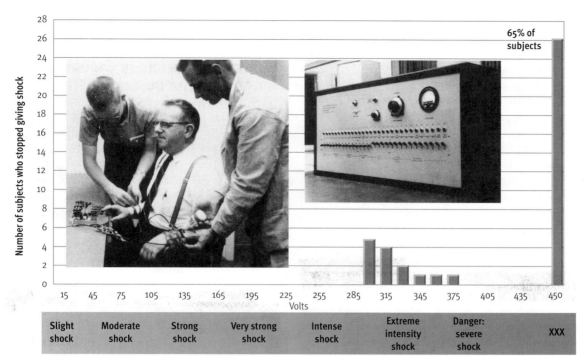

Figure 6.14

Milgram's experiment on obedience. The photo on the left shows the "learner" being connected to the shock generator during one of Milgram's experimental sessions. The photo on the right shows the fake shock generator used in the study. The surprising results of the Milgram (1963) study are summarized in the bar graph. Although subjects frequently protested, the vast majority (65%) delivered the entire series of shocks to the learner. (Photos from the film *Obedience* copyright 1965 by Stanley Milgram and distributed by Pennsylvania State University Media Sales. Permission of Alexandra Milgram.)

Critics also questioned the ethics of Milgram's experimental procedures (Baumrind, 1964; Kelman, 1967). They noted that without prior consent, participants were exposed to extensive deception that could undermine their trust in people and severe stress that could leave emotional scars. Milgram's defenders argued that the brief distress experienced by his subjects was a small price to pay for the insights that emerged from his obedience studies. Looking back, however, many psychologists seem to share the critics' concerns about the ethical implications of Milgram's ground-breaking work. His procedure is questionable by contemporary standards of research ethics, and no replications of his obedience study have been conducted in the United States since the mid-1970s (Blass, 1991)— a bizarre epitaph for what may be psychology's best-known experiment.

Cultural Variations in Conformity and Obedience

Are conformity and obedience unique to American culture? By no means. The Asch and Milgram experiments have been repeated in many different societies, where they have yielded results roughly similar to those seen in the United States. Thus, the phenomena of conformity and obedience seem to transcend culture.

The replications of Milgram's obedience study have largely been limited to industrialized nations similar to the United States. Many of these studies have reported even *higher* obedience rates than those seen in Milgram's American samples (Smith & Bond, 1994). Thus, the surprisingly high level of obedience observed by Milgram does not appear to be peculiar to the United States. The Asch experiment has been repeated in a more diverse range of societies than the Milgram experiment. Various theorists have hypothesized that collectivistic cultures, which emphasize respect for group norms, cooperation, and harmony, have a more positive view of conformity and encourage more conformity than individualistic cultures, with their emphasis on independence (Kim & Markus, 1999; Matsumoto, 1994). Consistent with this analysis, replications of the Asch experiment have tended to find somewhat higher levels of conformity in collectivistic cultures than in individualistic cultures (Bond & Smith, 1996).

Our discussion of conformity and obedience foreshadows our last major topic in this chapter, behavior in groups. Social pressure, for instance, is often at work in group interactions, and being part of a group can have a dramatic impact on an individual's behavior (as it did in the Asch studies). Our review of behavior in groups will begin with a look at the nature of groups.

Social psychologists study groups as well as individuals, but exactly what is a group? Are all the divorced fathers living in Baltimore a group? Are three strangers moving skyward in an elevator a group? What if the elevator gets stuck? How about four students from your psychology class who study together regularly? How about a jury working to render a verdict in a trial? The Boston Celtics? Some of these collections of people are groups and others aren't. Let's examine the concept of a group to find out which of these collections qualify.

In social psychologists' eyes, **a *group* consists of two or more individuals who interact and are interdependent.** The divorced fathers in Baltimore aren't likely to qualify on either count. Strangers sharing an elevator might interact briefly, but they're not interdependent. However, if the elevator gets stuck and they have to deal with an emergency together, they could suddenly become a group. Your psychology classmates who study together qualify as a group, since they interact and depend on each other to achieve shared goals. So do the members of a jury and a sports team such as the Celtics. Historically, most groups have interacted on a face-to-face basis, but advances in telecommunications are rapidly changing that reality. In the era of the Internet, people can interact, become interdependent, and develop a group identity without ever meeting in person (McKenna & Bargh, 1998).

Groups vary in many ways. Obviously, a study group, a basketball team, and a jury are very different in terms of size, purpose, formality, longevity, similarity of members, and diversity of activities. Can anything meaningful be said about groups if they're so diverse? Yes. In spite of their immense variability, groups share certain features that affect their functioning. Among other things, most groups have *roles* that allocate special responsibilities to some members, *norms* about what represents suitable behavior in group interactions, a *communication structure* that reflects who talks to whom, and a *power structure* that determines which members wield the most influence (Forsyth, 1999). For example, a study group and the Celtics may appear to have little in common, but both might have a "harmonizer" whose role is to smooth over conflicts among members, a norm that "everyone pulls his own weight," and an unequal distribution of power among members.

Web Link 16.5

The Psychology of Cyberspace
As the Internet continues to develop into an ever more important reality in our lives, a number of social scientists have begun to examine human behavior in the computer-mediated environment called "cyberspace." Professor John Suler's important site at Rider University presents a major overview of the research being carried out in this new field.

Behavior Alone and in Groups: The Case of the Bystander Effect

Imagine that you have a precarious medical condition and that you must go through life worrying about whether someone will leap forward to provide help if the need ever arises. Wouldn't you feel more secure around larger groups? After all, there's "safety in numbers." Logically, as group size increases, the probability of having a good Samaritan on the scene increases. Or does it? We've seen before that human behavior isn't necessarily logical. When it comes to helping behavior, many studies have uncovered an apparent paradox called the ***bystander effect:* people are less likely to provide needed help when they are in groups than when they are alone.**

Evidence that your probability of getting help *declines* as group size increases was first described by John Darley and Bibb Latané (1968), who were conducting research on the determinants of helping behavior. In the Darley and Latané study, students in individual cubicles connected by an intercom participated in discussion groups of three sizes. Early in the discussion, a student who was an experimental accomplice hesitantly mentioned that he was prone to seizures. Later in the discussion, the same accomplice feigned a severe seizure and cried out for help. Although a majority of participants sought assistance for the student, the tendency to seek help *declined* with increasing group size.

Similar trends have been seen in many other experiments, in which over 6000 subjects have had opportunities to respond to apparent emergencies including fires, asthma attacks, faintings, crashes, and flat tires, as well as less pressing needs to answer a door or to pick up objects dropped by a stranger. Pooling the results of this research, Latané and Nida (1981) estimated that participants who were alone provided help 75% of the time, whereas participants in the presence of others provided help only 53% of the time.

What accounts for the bystander effect? A number of factors may be at work. For instance, the *diffusion of responsibility* that occurs in a group is important. If you're by yourself when you encounter someone in need of help, the responsibility to provide help rests squarely on your shoulders. However, if other people are present, the responsibility is divided among you, and you may all say to yourselves "Someone else will help." A reduced sense of responsibility may contribute to other aspects of behavior in groups, as we'll see in the next section.

Group Productivity and Social Loafing

Have you ever driven through a road construction project—at a snail's pace, of course—and become irritated because so many workers seem to be just standing around? Maybe the irony of the posted sign "Your tax dollars at work" made you imagine that they were all dawdling. And then again, perhaps not. Individuals' productivity often does decline in larger groups (Latané, Williams, & Harkins, 1979).

Two factors appear to contribute to reduced individual productivity in larger groups. One factor is *reduced efficiency* resulting from the *loss of coordination* among workers' efforts. As you put more people on a yearbook staff, for instance, you'll probably create more and more duplication of effort and increase how often group members end up working at cross purposes.

The second factor contributing to low productivity in groups involves *effort* rather than efficiency. **Social loafing is a reduction in effort by individuals when they work in groups as compared to when they work by themselves.** To investigate social loafing, Latané et al. (1979) measured the sound output produced by subjects who were asked to cheer or clap as loudly as they could. So they couldn't see or hear other group members, participants were told that the study concerned the importance of sensory feedback and were asked to don blindfolds and put on headphones through which loud noise was played. This maneuver permitted a simple deception: subjects were led to *believe* that they were working alone or in a group of two or six, when in fact *individual* output was actually measured.

When subjects *thought* that they were working in larger groups, their individual output declined. Because lack of coordination could not affect individual output, the participants' decreased sound production had to be due to reduced effort. Latané and his colleagues also had the same subjects clap and shout in genuine groups of two and six and found an additional decrease in production that was attributed to loss of coordination. Figure 16.15 shows how social loafing and loss of coordination combined to reduce productivity as group size increased.

Social loafing and the bystander effect appear to share a common cause: diffusion of responsibility in groups (Comer, 1995; Latané, 1981). As group size increases, the responsibility for getting a job done is divided among more people, and many group members ease up because their individual contribution is less recognizable. Thus, social loafing occurs in situations where individuals can "hide in the crowd." Consistent with this line of thinking, research shows that social loafing is more likely (a) in larger groups, (b) on tasks where individual output is hard to evaluate, and (c) in situations where group members expect their co-workers to perform well and "carry them" (Karau & Williams, 1993).

Cultural factors may influence the likelihood of social loafing. Studies with subjects from Japan, China, and Taiwan suggest that social loafing may be less prevalent in collectivistic cultures, which place a high priority on meeting group goals and contributing to ones' ingroups (Karau & Williams, 1995; Matsumoto, 1994).

Decision Making in Groups

Productivity is not the only issue that commonly concerns groups. When people join together in groups, they often have to make decisions about what the group will do and how it will use its resources. Whether it's your study group deciding what type of pizza to order, a jury deciding on a verdict, or Congress deciding whether to pass a bill, groups make decisions. Social psychologists have discovered some interesting tendencies in group decision making. We'll take a brief look at *group polarization* and *groupthink*.

Group Polarization

Who leans toward more cautious decisions: individuals or groups? Common sense suggests that groups will work out compromises that cancel out members'

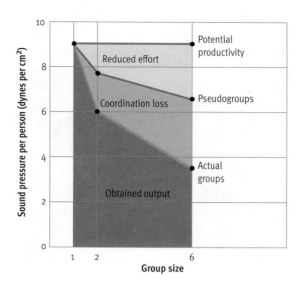

Figure 16.15

The effect of loss of coordination and social loafing on group productivity. The amount of sound produced per person declined noticeably when people worked in actual groups of two or six (orange line). This decrease in productivity reflects both loss of coordination and social loafing. Sound per person also declined when subjects merely thought they were working in groups of two or six (purple line). This decrease in productivity is due to social loafing. (Adapted from "Many Hands Make Light the Work: The Causes and Consequences of Social Loafing," by B. Latane, K. Williams & S. Harkins, 1979, *Journal of Personality and Social Psychology, 37,* 822–832. Copyright © 1979 by the American Psychological Association. Adapted by permission of the author.)

Many types of groups have to arrive at collective decisions. The social dynamics of group decisions are complicated, and a variety of factors can undermine effective decision making.

© Keith Brofsky/PhotoDisc, Inc.

Figure 16.16

Group polarization.
Two examples of group polarization are diagrammed here. In the first example (top), a group starts out mildly opposed to an idea, but after discussion sentiment is stronger against the idea. In the second example (bottom), a group starts out with a favorable disposition toward an idea, and this disposition is strengthened by group discussion.

extreme views. Hence, the collective wisdom of the group should yield relatively conservative choices. Is common sense correct? To investigate this question, Stoner (1961) asked individual participants to give their recommendations on tough decisions and then asked the same subjects to engage in group discussion to arrive at joint recommendations. When Stoner compared individuals' average recommendation against their group decision generated through discussion, he found that groups arrived at *riskier* decisions than individuals did. Stoner's finding was replicated in other studies (Pruitt, 1971), and the phenomenon acquired the name *risky shift*.

However, investigators eventually determined that groups can shift either way, toward risk or caution, depending on which way the group is leaning

to begin with (Myers & Lamm, 1976). A shift toward a more extreme position, an effect called *polarization,* is often the result of group discussion. Thus, **group polarization occurs when group discussion strengthens a group's dominant point of view and produces a shift toward a more extreme decision in that direction** (see Figure 16.16). Group polarization does not involve widening the gap between factions in a group, as its name might suggest. In fact, group polarization can contribute to consensus in a group, as we'll see in our discussion of groupthink.

Groupthink

In contrast to group polarization, which is a normal process in group dynamics, groupthink is more like a "disease" that can infect decision making in groups. **Groupthink occurs when members of a cohesive group emphasize concurrence at the expense of critical thinking in arriving at a decision.** As you might imagine, groupthink doesn't produce very effective decision making. Indeed, groupthink often leads to major blunders that may look incomprehensible after the fact. Irving Janis (1972) first described groupthink in his effort to explain how President John F. Kennedy and his advisers could have miscalculated so badly in deciding to invade Cuba at the Bay of Pigs in 1961. The attempted invasion failed miserably and, in retrospect, seemed remarkably ill-conceived. Applying his many years of research on group dynamics to the Bay of Pigs fiasco, Janis developed a model of groupthink, which is summarized in Figure 16.17.

When groups get caught up in groupthink, members suspend their critical judgment and the group starts censoring dissent as the pressure to conform increases. Soon, everyone begins to think alike. Moreover, "mind guards" try to shield the group from information that contradicts the group's view. If the group's view is challenged from outside, victims of groupthink tend to think in simplistic "us versus them" terms. Members begin to overestimate the ingroup's unanimity, and they begin to view the outgroup as the enemy. Groupthink also promotes incomplete gathering of information. The group's search for information is biased in favor of facts and opinions that support their decision.

Recent research has uncovered another factor that may contribute to groupthink—individual members in groups often fail to share information that is unique to them (Levine & Moreland, 1998). Sound decision making depends on group members combining their information effectively (Winquist & Larson, 1998). However, when groups discuss

Before group discussion	After group discussion
Group average	Group average
Neutral Views held by individual group members	Neutral Views held by individual group members
Group average	Group average
Neutral Views held by individual group members	Neutral Views held by individual group members

issues, they have an interesting tendency to focus mainly on the information that the members already share as opposed to encouraging offers of information unique to individual members (Larson et al., 1996). Additonal research is needed to determine why groups are mediocre at pooling members' information.

What causes groupthink? The key precondition is high group cohesiveness. **Group cohesiveness refers to the strength of the liking relationships linking group members to each other and to the group itself.** Members of cohesive groups are close-knit, are committed, have "team spirit," and are loyal to the group. Cohesiveness itself isn't bad. It can help groups achieve great things. But Janis maintains that the danger of groupthink is greater when groups are highly cohesive. Groupthink is also more likely when a group works in relative isolation, when its power structure is dominated by a strong, directive leader, and when it is under stress to make a major decision (see Figure 16.17). Under these conditions, group discussions can lead to group polarization, strengthening the group's dominant view.

Only a handful of experiments have been conducted to test Janis's theory, because the antecedent conditions thought to foster groupthink—such as high decision stress, strong group cohesiveness, and dominating leadership—are difficult to create effectively in laboratory settings (Aldag & Fuller, 1993). Although one recent experimental study by Turner and her associates (1992) found support for certain aspects of Janis's theory, the evidence on groupthink consists almost entirely of retrospective case studies of major decision-making fiascos. In analyzing these cases Janis and other investigators may have tended to see what they expected to see (Tetlock et

al., 1992). Thus, Janis's model of groupthink should probably be characterized as an innovative, sophisticated, intuitively appealing theory that needs to be subjected to much more empirical study.

Figure 16.17

Overview of Janis's model of groupthink. The antecedent conditions and symptoms of groupthink are outlined here, along with the resultant effects on a group's decision making. (Adapted with permission of The Free Press, a Division of Simon & Schuster, from *Decision Making: A Psychological Analysis of Conflict, Choice and Commitment*, by Irving J. Janis and Leon Mann. Copyright © 1977 by The Free Press.)

Antecedent conditions
1. High cohesiveness
2. Insulation of the group
3. Lack of methodical procedures for search and appraisal
4. Directive leadership
5. High stress with low degree of hope for finding better solution than the one favored by the leader or other influential persons

Concurrence-seeking tendency

Symptoms of groupthink
1. Illusion of invulnerability
2. Collective rationalization
3. Belief in inherent morality of the group
4. Stereotypes of outgroups
5. Direct pressure on dissenters
6. Self-censorship
7. Illusion of unanimity
8. Self-appointed mind guards

Symptoms of defective decision making
1. Incomplete survey of alternatives
2. Incomplete survey of objectives
3. Failure to examine risks of preferred choice
4. Poor information search
5. Selective bias in processing information at hand
6. Failure to reappraise alternatives
7. Failure to work out contingency plans

CONCEPT CHECK 16.4

Scrutinizing Common Sense

Check your understanding of the implications of research in social psychology by indicating whether the common sense assertions listed below have been supported by empirical findings. Do the trends in research summarized in this chapter indicate that the following statements are true or false? The answers are in Appendix A.

___F___ **1.** Generally, in forming their impressions of others, people don't judge a book by its cover.

___T___ **2.** When it comes to attraction, birds of a feather flock together.

___F___ **3.** In the realm of love, opposites attract.

___T___ **4.** If you're the target of persuasion, to be forewarned is to be forearmed.

___F___ **5.** When you need help, there's safety in numbers.

Putting It in Perspective

Our discussion of social psychology has provided a final embellishment on three of our seven unifying themes. One of these is the value of psychology's commitment to empiricism—that is, its reliance on systematic observation through research to arrive at conclusions. The second theme that stands out is the importance of cultural factors in shaping behavior, and the third is the extent to which people's experience of the world is highly subjective. Let's consider the virtues of empiricism first.

It's easy to question the need to do scientific research on social behavior, because studies in social psychology often seem to verify common sense. While most people wouldn't presume to devise their own theory of color vision or question the significance of REM sleep, everyone has beliefs about the nature of love, how to persuade others, and the limits of obedience. Thus, when studies demonstrate that credibility enhances persuasion, or that good looks facilitate attraction, it's tempting to conclude that social psychologists go to great lengths to document the obvious, and some critics say, "Why bother?"

You saw why in this chapter. Research in social psychology has repeatedly shown that the predictions of logic and common sense are often wrong. Consider just a few examples. Even psychiatric experts failed to predict the remarkable obedience to authority uncovered in Milgram's research. The bystander effect in helping behavior violates cold-blooded mathematical logic. Dissonance research has shown that after a severe initiation, the bigger the letdown, the more favorable people's feelings are. These findings defy common sense.

Thus, research on social behavior provides dramatic illustrations of why psychologists put their faith in empiricism. The moral of social psychology's story is this: Although scientific research often supports ideas based on common sense and logic, we can't count on this result. If psychologists want to achieve sound understanding of the principles governing behavior, they have to put their ideas to an empirical test.

Our coverage of social psychology also demonstrated once again that behavior is characterized by both cultural variance and invariance. Although basic social phenomena such as stereotyping, attraction, obedience, and conformity probably occur all over the world, cross-cultural studies of social behavior show that research findings based on American samples may not generalize precisely to other cultures.

Research in social psychology is also uniquely well suited for making the point that people's view of the world is highly personal and subjective. In this chapter we saw how physical appearance can color perception of a person's ability or personality, how social schemas can lead people to see what they expect to see in their interactions with others, how pressure to conform can make people begin to doubt their senses, and how groupthink can lead group members down a perilous path of shared illusions.

The subjectivity of social perception will surface once again in our applications for the chapter. The Personal Application focuses on prejudice, a practical problem that social psychologists have shown great interest in, whereas the Critical Thinking Application examines aspects of social influence.

PERSONAL APPLICATION

Understanding Prejudice

Answer the following "true" or "false."

_____**1** Prejudice and discrimination amount to the same thing.

_____**2** Stereotypes are always negative or unflattering.

_____**3** Ethnic and racial groups are the only widespread targets of prejudice in modern society.

_____**4** People see members of their own ingroup as being more alike than the members of outgroups.

Prejudice is a major social problem. It harms victims' self-concepts, suppresses human potential, creates tension and strife between groups, and even instigates wars. The first step toward reducing prejudice is to understand its roots. Hence, in this Application we'll strive to achieve a better understanding of why prejudice is so common. Along the way, you'll learn the answers to the true-false questions above.

Prejudice and discrimination are closely related concepts, and the terms have become nearly interchangeable in popular use. Social scientists, however, prefer to define their terms precisely, so let's clarify which is which. **Prejudice is a negative attitude held toward members of a group.** Like other attitudes, prejudice can include three components (see Figure 16.18): beliefs ("Indians are mostly alcoholics"), emotions ("I despise Jews"), and behavioral dispositions ("I wouldn't hire a Mexican"). Racial prejudice receives the lion's share of publicity, but prejudice is not limited to ethnic groups. Women, homosexuals, the aged, the disabled, and the mentally ill are also targets of widespread prejudice. Thus, many people hold prejudicial attitudes toward one group or another, and many have been victims of prejudice.

Prejudice may lead to **discrimination, which involves behaving differently, usually unfairly, toward the members of a group.** Prejudice and discrimination tend

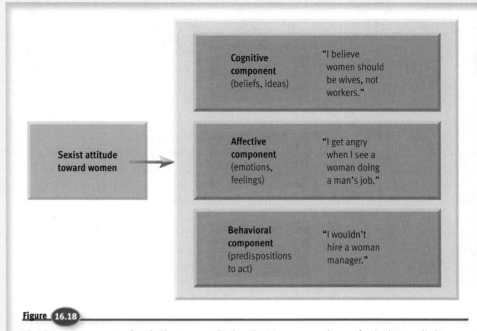

Figure 16.18

The three components of prejudice as an attitude. The tricomponent theory of attitudes, applied to prejudice against women, defines sexism as beliefs about women (cognitive component) that lead to a feeling of dislike (affective component), which in turn leads to a readiness to behave in a discriminatory manner (behavioral component).

to go hand in hand, but attitudes and behavior do not necessarily correspond (see Figure 16.19 on the next page). In our discussion, we'll concentrate primarily on the attitude of prejudice. Let's begin by looking at processes in person perception that promote prejudice.

Stereotyping and Subjectivity in Person Perception 12d

Perhaps no factor plays a larger role in prejudice than *stereotypes*. However, stereotypes are not inevitably negative. Although it's a massive overgeneralization, it's hardly insulting to assert that Americans are ambitious or that the Japanese are industrious. Unfortunately, many people *do* subscribe to derogatory stereotypes of

various ethnic groups. Although studies suggest that negative racial stereotypes have diminished over the last 50 years, they're not a thing of the past (Devine & Elliot, 1995; Gaertner et al., 1999). According to a variety of investigators, modern racism has merely become more subtle (Dovidio & Gaertner, 1999).

Research indicates that stereotypes are so pervasive and insidious they are often activated automatically (Bargh, 1999). According to Devine and Monteith (1999), prejudicial stereotypes are highly accessible cognitive schemas that are readily activated, even in people who truly renounce prejudice. Thus, a heterosexual man who rejects prejudice against homosexuals may still feel uncomfortable sitting next to a gay male on a bus, even though he regards his reaction as inappropriate.

Figure **16.19**

Relationship between prejudice and discrimination. As these examples show, prejudice can exist without discrimination and discrimination without prejudice. In the green cells, there is a disparity between attitude and behavior.

		Prejudice	
		Absent	Present
Discrimination	Absent	No relevant behaviors	A restaurant owner who is bigoted against gays treats them fairly because he needs their business
	Present	An executive with favorable attitudes toward blacks doesn't hire them because he would get in trouble with his boss	A professor who is hostile toward women grades his female students unfairly

Unfortunately, stereotypes are highly resistant to change. When people encounter members of a group that they view with prejudice who happen to deviate from their stereotype of that group, they often discount this evidence by assuming that the "atypical" group members constitute a distinct subtype of that group, such as wealthy African Americans or conservative homosexuals (Kunda & Oleson, 1995, 1997). Consigning deviants to a subtype that is viewed as unrepresentative of the group allows people to preserve their stereotype of the group.

Stereotypes also persist because the *subjectivity* of person perception makes it likely that people will see what they expect to see when they actually come into contact with groups that they view with prejudice (Dunning & Sherman, 1997). For example, Duncan (1976) had white subjects watch and evaluate interaction on a TV monitor that was supposedly live (actually it was a videotape), and varied the race of a person who gets into an argument and gives another person a slight shove. The shove was coded as "violent behavior" by 73% of the participants when the actor was black but by only 13% of the participants when the actor was white. As we've noted before, people's perceptions are highly subjective.

Because of stereotypes, even "violence" may lie in the eye of the beholder.

Memory biases are also tilted in favor of confirming people's prejudices (Fiske, 1998). For example, if a man believes that "women are not cut out for leadership roles," he may dwell with delight on his female supervisor's mistakes and quickly forget about her achievements. Thus, the *illusory correlation effect* can contribute to the maintenance of prejudicial stereotypes (McConnell, Leibold, & Sherman, 1997).

Making Biased Attributions 12d

Attribution processes can also help perpetuate stereotypes and prejudice. Research taking its cue from Weiner's (1980) model of attribution has shown that people often make *biased attributions for success and failure*. For example, men and women don't get equal credit for their successes (Swim & Sanna, 1996). Observers often discount a woman's success by attributing it to good luck, sheer effort, or the ease of the task (except on traditional feminine tasks). In comparison, a man's success is more likely to be attributed to his outstanding ability. Figure 16.20 shows how gender bias tends to affect attributions for success and failure. These biased patterns of attribution help sustain the stereotype that men are more competent than women. Similar patterns of bias have been seen in attributional explanations of ethnic minorities' successes and failures (Jackson, Sullivan, & Hodge, 1993; Kluegel, 1990).

Members of many types of groups are victims of prejudice. Besides racial minorities and the disabled, others that have been stereotyped and discriminated against include gays and lesbians, women, the homeless, and those who are overweight.

© Steven Rubin/The Image Works

Figure 16.20

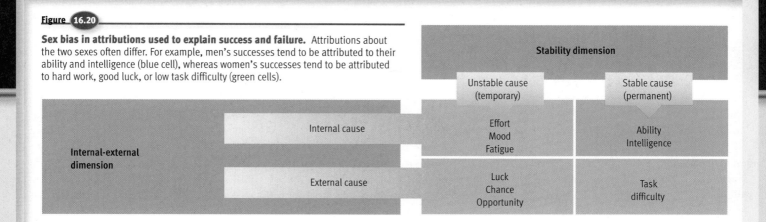

Sex bias in attributions used to explain success and failure. Attributions about the two sexes often differ. For example, men's successes tend to be attributed to their ability and intelligence (blue cell), whereas women's successes tend to be attributed to hard work, good luck, or low task difficulty (green cells).

		Stability dimension	
		Unstable cause (temporary)	Stable cause (permanent)
Internal-external dimension	Internal cause	Effort Mood Fatigue	Ability Intelligence
	External cause	Luck Chance Opportunity	Task difficulty

Recall that the *fundamental attribution error* is a slant toward explaining events by pointing to the personal characteristics of the actors as causes (internal attributions). Research suggests that people are particularly likely to make this error when evaluating targets of prejudice (Hewstone, 1990). Thus, when people take note of ethnic neighborhoods dominated by crime and poverty, they blame the personal qualities of the residents for these problems, while downplaying or ignoring other explanations emphasizing situational factors (job discrimination, poor police service, and so on).

Forming and Preserving Prejudicial Attitudes 12d

If prejudice is an attitude, where does it come from? Many prejudices appear to be handed down as a legacy from parents (Ponterotto & Pedersen, 1993). Prejudicial attitudes can be found in children as young as ages 4 to 7 (Aboud, 1987). This transmission of prejudice across generations presumably depends to some extent on *observational learning*. For example, if a young boy hears his father ridicule homosexuals, his exposure to his father's attitude is likely to affect his attitude about gays. If the young boy then goes to school and makes disparaging

remarks about gays that are reinforced by approval from peers, his prejudice will be strengthened through *operant conditioning*. Consistent with this analysis, one study found that college students' opinions on racial issues were swayed by overhearing others voice racist or antiracist sentiments (Blanchard, Lilly, & Vaughn, 1991).

Dividing the World into Ingroups and Outgroups 12d

As noted in the main body of the chapter, people sometimes divide the social world into "us versus them," or *ingroups versus outgroups*. As you might anticipate, people tend to evaluate outgroup members less favorably than ingroup members (Krueger, 1996). One reason is that derogating an outgroup tends to make people feel superior, and this feeling helps affirm their self-worth (Fein & Spencer, 1997). The more strongly one identifies with an ingroup, the more one tends to note outgroup membership, and the more one tends to be prejudiced toward competing outgroups (Blascovich et al., 1997; Perreault & Bourhis, 1999). People also tend to think simplistically about outgroups. They tend to see diversity among the members of their ingroup but to overestimate the homogeneity of the outgroup (Lorenzi-Cioldi, 1993;

Ostrom & Sedikides, 1992). At a simple, concrete level, the essense of this process is captured by the statement "They all look alike." Indeed, studies have found that blacks and whites do have more difficulty distinguishing among the faces of outgroup members (Anthony, Copper, & Mullen, 1992). The illusion of homogeneity in the outgroup makes it easier to sustain stereotypic beliefs about its members (Ryan, Park, & Judd, 1996). This point disposes of our last unanswered question from the list that opened the Application. Just in case you missed one of the answers, they all were false.

Our discussion has shown that a plethora of processes conspire to create and maintain personal prejudices. Most of the factors at work reflect normal, routine processes in social behavior. Thus, it is understandable that most people probably harbor some prejudicial attitudes. Our analysis of the causes of prejudice may have permitted you to identify prejudices of your own or their sources. Perhaps it's wishful thinking on my part, but an enhanced awareness of your personal prejudices may help you become a little more tolerant of the endless diversity seen in human behavior. If so, that alone would mean that my efforts in writing this book have been amply rewarded.

CRITICAL THINKING APPLICATION

Analyzing Credibility and Social Influence Tactics

You can run, but you cannot hide. This statement aptly sums up the situation that exists when it comes to persuasion and social influence. There is no way to successfully evade the constant, pervasive, omnipresent efforts of others to shape your attitudes and behavior. In this Application we will discuss two topics that can enhance your resistance to manipulation. First, we will outline some ideas that can be useful in evaluating the credibility of a persuasive source. Second, we will describe some widely used social influence strategies that it pays to know about.

Evaluating Credibility

The salesperson at your local health food store swears that a specific herb combination improves memory and helps people stay healthy. A popular singer touts a psychic hotline, where the operators can "really help" with the important questions in life. Speakers at a "historical society" meeting claim that the Holocaust never happened. These are just a few real-life examples of how people attempt to persuade the public to believe something. In these examples, the "something" people are expected to believe runs counter to the conventional or scientific view, but who is to say who is right? After all, people are entitled to their own opinions, aren't they?

Yes, people *are* entitled to their own opinions, but that does not mean that all opinions are equally valid. Some opinions are just plain wrong and others are highly dubious. Every person is not equally believable. In deciding what to believe, it is important to carefully examine the evidence presented and the logic of the argument that supports the conclusion (see the Critical Thinking Application for Chapter 10). In deciding what to believe, you also need to decide *whom* to believe, a task that requires assessing the *credibility* of the source of the information. Let's look at

some questions that can provide guidance in this process.

Does the source have a vested interest in the issue at hand? If the source is likely to benefit in some way from convincing you of something, you need to take a skeptical attitude. In the examples provided here, it is easy to see how the sales clerk and popular singer will benefit if you buy the products they are selling, but what about the so-called historical society? How would members benefit by convincing large numbers of people that the Holocaust never happened? Like the sales clerk and singer, they are also selling something, in this case a particular view of history that they hope will influence future events in certain ways. Of course, the fact that these sources have a vested interest does not necessarily mean that their arguments are invalid. But a source's credibility needs to be evaluated with extra caution when the person or group has something to gain.

What are the source's credentials? Does the person have any special training, an advanced degree, or any other basis for claiming special knowledge about the topic? The usual training for a sales clerk or singer does not include how to assess research results in medical journals or to evaluate claims of psychic powers. The Holocaust deniers are more difficult to evaluate. Some of them have studied history and written books on the topic, but the books are mostly self-published, and few of these "experts" hold positions at reputable universities where scholars are subject to peer evaluation. That's *not* to say that legitimate credentials ensure a source's credibility. A number of popular diets that are widely regarded by nutritional experts as worthless, if not hazardous (Drewnowski, 1995; Dwyer, 1995), were created and marketed by genuine physicians. Of course, these physicians have a *vested interest* in the diets, as they have made millions of dollars from them.

Is the information grossly inconsistent with the conventional view on the issue? Just being different from the mainstream view certainly does *not* make a conclusion wrong. But claims that vary radically from most other information on a subject should raise a red flag that leads to careful scrutiny. Bear in mind that charlatans and hucksters are often successful because they typically try to persuade people to believe things that they want to believe. Wouldn't it be great if we could effortlessly enhance our memory, foretell the future, eat all we want and still lose weight, and earn hundreds of dollars per hour working at home? And wouldn't it be nice if the Holocaust never happened? It pays to be wary of wishful thinking.

What was the method of analysis used in reaching the conclusion? The purveyors of miracle cures and psychic advice inevitably rely on anecdotal evidence. But you have already learned about the perils and unreliability of anecdotal evidence (see the Critical Thinking Application for Chapter 2). One method frequently used by charlatans is to undermine the credibility of conventional information by focusing on trivial inconsistencies. This is one of the many strategies used by the people who argue that the Holocaust never occurred. They question the credibility of thousands of historical documents, photographs, and artifacts, and the testimony of countless people, by highlighting small inconsistencies among historical records relating to trivial matters, such as the number of people transported to a concentration camp in a specific week, or the number of bodies that could be disposed of in a single day (Shermer, 1997). Some inconsistencies are exactly what one should expect based on piecing together multiple accounts from sources working with different portions of incomplete information. But the strategy of focusing on trivial inconsistencies is a standard method for raising doubts about credible information.

For example, this strategy was employed brilliantly by the defense attorneys in the O. J. Simpson murder trial.

Recognizing Social Influence Strategies

It pays to understand social influence strategies because advertisers, salespeople, and fundraisers—not to mention our friends and neighbors—frequently rely on them to manipulate our behavior. Let's look at four basic strategies: the foot-in-the-door technique, misuse of the reciprocity norm, the lowball technique, and feigned scarcity.

Door-to-door salespeople have long recognized the importance of gaining a *little* cooperation from sales targets (getting a "foot in the door") before hitting them with the real sales pitch. **The *foot-in-the-door technique* involves getting people to agree to a small request to increase the chances that they will agree to a larger request later.** This technique is widely used in all walks of life. For example, groups seeking donations often ask people to simply sign a petition first.

In an early study of the foot-in-the-door technique (Freedman & Fraser, 1966), the large request involved asking homemakers whether a team of six men doing consumer research could come into their home to classify *all* their household products. Only 22% of the control subjects agreed to this outlandish request. However, when the same request was made three days after a small request (to answer a few questions about soap preferences), 53% of the participants agreed to the large request. Why does the foot-in-the-door technique work? According to Burger (1999), quite a variety of processes contribute to its effectiveness, including people's tendency to try to behave consistently (with their initial response) and their reluctance to renege on their sense of commitment to the person who made the initial request.

Most of us have been socialized to believe in the *reciprocity norm*—the rule that we should pay back in kind what we receive from others. Robert Cialdini (1993) has written extensively about how the reciprocity norm is used in social influence efforts. For example, groups seeking donations routinely send address labels, key rings, and other small gifts with their pleas. Salespeople using the reciprocity principle distribute free samples to prospective customers. When they return a few days later, most of the customers feel obligated to buy some of their products. The reciprocity rule is meant to promote fair exchanges in social interactions. However, when people manipulate the reciprocity norm, they usually give something of minimal value in the hopes of getting far more in return (Howard, 1995).

The lowball technique is even more deceptive. The name for this technique derives from a common practice in automobile sales, in which a customer is offered

Advertisers often try to artificially create scarcity to make their products seem more desirable.

a terrific bargain on a car. The bargain price gets the customer to commit to buying the car. Soon after this commitment is made, however, the dealer starts revealing some hidden costs. Typically, the customer learns that options assumed to be included in the original price are actually going to cost extra. Once they have committed to buying a car, most customers are unlikely to cancel the deal. Thus, **the *lowball technique* involves getting someone to commit to a seemingly attractive proposition before its hidden costs are revealed.** Car dealers aren't the only ones who use this technique, which is a surprisingly effective strategy (Cialdini & Trost, 1998).

A number of years ago, Jack Brehm (1966) demonstrated that telling people they can't have something only makes them want it more. This phenomenon helps explain why companies often try to create the impression that their products are in scarce supply. Scarcity threatens your freedom to choose a product, thus creating an increased desire for the scarce commodity. Advertisers frequently feign scarcity to drive up the demand for products. Thus, we constantly see ads that scream "limited supply available," "for a limited time only," "while they last," and "time is running out." Like genuine scarcity, feigned scarcity can enhance the desirability of a commodity (Highhouse et al., 1998; Lynn, 1992).

Table 16.1	Critical Thinking Skills Discussed in This Application
Skill	**Description**
Judging the credibility of an information source	The critical thinker understands that credibility and bias are central to determining the quality of information and looks at factors such as vested interests, credentials, and appropriate expertise.
Recognizing social influence strategies	The critical thinker is aware of manipulative tactics such as the foot-in-the-door and lowball techniques, misuse of the reciprocity norm, and feigned scarcity.

REVIEW

Key Ideas

Person Perception: Forming Impressions of Others

● Perceptions of others can be distorted by a variety of factors, including physical appearance. People attribute desirable personality characteristics and competence to those who are good-looking. People use social schemas to categorize others into types.

● Stereotypes may lead people to see what they expect to see and to overestimate how often they see it. Evolutionary psychologists argue that many biases in person perception were adaptive in humans' ancestral past.

Attribution Processes: Explaining Behavior

● Internal attributions ascribe behavior to personal dispositions and traits, whereas external attributions locate the cause of behavior in the environment. Weiner's model proposes that attributions for success and failure should be analyzed in terms of the stability of causes, as well as along the internal-external dimension.

● Observers favor internal attributions to explain another's behavior (the fundamental attribution error), while actors favor external attributions to explain their own behavior. The self-serving bias is the tendency to attribute one's good outcomes to personal factors and one's bad outcomes to situational factors. Cultures vary in their emphasis on individualism as opposed to collectivism, and these differences appear to influence attributional tendencies.

Interpersonal Attraction: Liking and Loving

● People tend to like and love others who are similar, who reciprocate expressions of affection, and who are physically attractive. Some theorists have distinguished between passionate love and companionate love, which can be subdivided into intimacy and commitment. Hazan and Shaver's theory suggests that love relationships in adulthood mimic attachment patterns in infancy.

● The characteristics that people seek in prospective mates appear to transcend culture. However, cultures vary considerably in their emphasis on passionate love as a prerequisite for marriage. According to evolutionary psychologists, certain aspects of good looks influence attraction because they are indicators of reproductive fitness.

Attitudes: Making Social Judgments

● Attitudes may be made up of cognitive, affective, and behavioral components. Attitudes vary in strength, accessibility, and ambivalence. A source of persuasion who is credible, expert, trustworthy, and likable tends to be relatively effective. Two-sided arguments and fear arousal tend to be effective in persuasive efforts.

● Persuasion is more difficult when a receiver is forewarned, when the source advocates a position that is incompatible with the receiver's existing attitudes, or when the source tries to change strong attitudes.

● Attitudes may be shaped through classical conditioning, operant conditioning, and observational learning. Dissonance theory asserts that inconsistent attitudes cause tension and that people alter their attitudes to reduce dissonance. The elaboration likelihood model holds that the central route to persuasion tends to yield longer-lasting attitude change than the peripheral route.

Conformity and Obedience: Yielding to Others

● Asch found that conformity in groups becomes more likely as group size increases, up to a size of seven. In Milgram's landmark study of obedience to authority, adult men drawn from the community showed a remarkable tendency, in spite of their misgivings, to follow orders to shock an innocent stranger. The generalizability of Milgram's findings has stood the test of time, but his work also helped to stimulate stricter ethical standards for research.

Behavior in Groups: Joining with Others

● People who help someone in need when alone are less likely to provide help when a group is present. The bystander effect occurs primarily because a group creates diffusion of responsibility. Productivity often declines in larger groups because of loss of coordination and social loafing.

● Group polarization occurs when the group shifts toward a more extreme decision in the direction it was already leaning. In groupthink, a cohesive group suspends critical judgment in a misguided effort to promote agreement in decision making.

Putting It in Perspective

● Social psychology illustrates the value of empiricism because research in this area often proves that common sense is wrong. Additionally, research in social psychology demonstrates that people's experience of the world is highly subjective and that culture shapes behavior.

Personal Application ● Understanding Prejudice

● Prejudice is a negative attitude toward a group. Prejudice is supported by subjectivity in person perception, stereotyping, and attributional biases.

● Negative attitudes about groups are often acquired through observational learning and supported by operant conditioning. The tendency to see outgroups as homogenous may also serve to strengthen prejudice.

Critical Thinking Application ● Analyzing Credibility and Social Influence Tactics

● Useful criteria in judging credibility include whether a source has vested interests, or appropriate credentials. One should also consider the method of analysis used in reaching conclusions, and why information might not coincide with conventional wisdom.

● To resist manipulative efforts, it helps to be aware of social influence tactics, such as the foot-in-the-door technique, misuse of the reciprocity norm, the lowball technique, and feigned scarcity.

Key Terms

Attitudes
Attributions
Bystander effect
Channel
Cognitive dissonance
Collectivism
Companionate love
Conformity
Discrimination
External attributions
Foot-in-the-door technique
Fundamental attribution error
Group
Group cohesiveness
Group polarization
Groupthink
Illusory correlation
Individualism
Ingroup
Internal attributions
Interpersonal attraction
Lowball technique
Matching hypothesis
Message
Obedience
Outgroup
Passionate love
Person perception
Prejudice
Receiver
Reciprocity
Reciprocity norm
Self-serving bias
Social loafing
Social psychology
Social schemas
Source
Stereotypes

Key People

Solomon Asch
Ellen Berscheid
Leon Festinger
Elaine Hatfield
Fritz Heider
Irving Janis
Stanley Milgram

PRACTICE TEST

1. Stereotypes are:
   A. special types of schemas that are part of people's shared cultural background.
   B. widely held beliefs that people have certain characteristics because of their membership in a particular group.
   C. equivalent to prejudice.
   D. both a and b.

2. You believe that short men have a tendency to be insecure. The concept of *illusory correlation* implies that you will:
   A. overestimate how often short men are insecure.
   B. underestimate how often short men are insecure.
   C. overestimate the frequency of short men in the population.
   D. falsely assume that shortness in men causes insecurity.

3. A father suggests that his son's low marks in school are due to the child's laziness. The father has made _____ attribution.
   A. an external
   B. an internal
   C. a situational
   D. a high consensus

4. Bob explains his failing grade on a term paper by saying that he really didn't work very hard at it. According to Weiner's model, Bob is making an _____ attribution about his failure.
   A. internal-stable
   B. internal-unstable
   C. external-stable
   D. external-unstable

5. The fundamental attribution error refers to the tendency of:
   A. observers to favor external attributions in explaining the behavior of others.
   B. observers to favor internal attributions in explaining the behavior of others.
   C. actors to favor external attributions in explaining the behavior of others.
   D. actors to favor internal attributions in explaining their behavior.

6. Which of the following factors is *not* one that influences interpersonal attraction?
   A. Physical attractiveness
   B. Similarity
   C. Reciprocity
   D. Latitude of acceptance

7. According to Hazan and Shaver (1987):
   A. romantic relationships in adulthood follow the same form as attachment relationships in infancy.
   B. those who had ambivalent attachments in infancy are doomed never to fall in love as adults.
   C. those who had avoidant attachments in infancy often overcompensate by becoming excessively intimate in their adult love relationships.
   D. all of the above.

8. Cross-cultural similarities are most likely to be found in which of the following areas?
   A. What people look for in prospective mates
   B. The tradition of prearranged marriages
   C. Passionate love as a prerequisite for marriage
   D. All of the above

9. Which of the following variables does *not* tend to facilitate persuasion?
   A. Source credibility
   B. Source trustworthiness
   C. Forewarning of the receiver
   D. A two-sided argument

10. Cognitive dissonance theory predicts that after people engage in counterattitudinal behavior, they will:
    A. convince themselves they really didn't perform the behavior.
    B. change their attitude to make it more consistent with their behavior.
    C. change their attitude to make it less consistent with their behavior.
    D. do nothing.

11. The elaboration likelihood model of attitude change suggests that:
    A. the peripheral route results in more enduring attitude change.
    B. the central route results in more enduring attitude change.
    C. only the central route to persuasion can be effective.
    D. only the peripheral route to persuasion can be effective.

12. The results of Milgram's (1963) study imply that:
    A. in the real world, most people will refuse to follow orders to inflict harm on a stranger.
    B. many people will obey an authority figure even if innocent people get hurt.
    C. most people are willing to give obviously wrong answers when ordered to do so.
    D. most people stick to their own judgment, even when group members unanimously disagree.

13. According to Latané (1981), social loafing is due to:
    A. social norms that stress the importance of positive interactions among group members.
    B. duplication of effort among group members.
    C. diffusion of responsibility in groups.
    D. a bias toward making internal attributions about the behavior of others.

14. Groupthink occurs when members of a cohesive group:
    A. are initially unanimous about an issue.
    B. stress the importance of caution in group decision making.
    C. emphasize concurrence at the expense of critical thinking in arriving at a decision.
    D. shift toward a less extreme position after group discussion.

15. The foot-in-the-door technique involves asking people to agree to a _____ request first to increase the likelihood that they will comply with a _____ request later.
    A. large; small
    B. small; large
    C. large; large
    D. large; larger

Answers

1	D	page 493	6	D	pages 499–500	11	B	page 508
2	A	page 494	7	A	page 501	12	B	page 510
3	B	page 495	8	A	page 502	13	C	page 513
4	B	pages 495–496	9	C	pages 504–505	14	C	page 514
5	B	page 496	10	B	page 507	15	B	page 521

INFOTRAC COLLEGE EDITION

Go to the Wadsworth Psychology Study Center for quiz questions, research updates, interactive exercises, and suggested readings in INFOTRAC related to this chapter:
http://psychology.wadsworth.com/product/0534593100s

Appendix A Answers to Concept Checks

Chapter 1

Concept Check 1.1

1. c. John B. Watson (1930, p. 103) dismissing the importance of genetic inheritance while arguing that traits are shaped entirely by experience.

2. a. Wilhelm Wundt (1904 revision of an earlier text, p. v) campaigning for a new, independent science of psychology.

3. b. William James (1890) commenting negatively on the structuralists' efforts to break consciousness into its elements and his view of consciousness as a continuously flowing stream.

Concept Check 1.2

1. b. B. F. Skinner (1971, p. 17) explaining why he believes that freedom is an illusion.

2. a. Sigmund Freud (1905, pp. 77–78) arguing that it is possible to probe into the unconscious depths of the mind.

3. c. Carl Rogers (1961, p. 27) commenting on others' assertion that he had an overly optimistic (Pollyannaish) view of human potential and discussing humans' basic drive toward personal growth.

Concept Check 1.3

1. c. Thomas and Chess's (1977) well-known New York Longitudinal Study is a landmark in developmental psychology.

2. a. Olds and Milner (1954) made this discovery by accident and thereby opened up a fascinating line of inquiry in physiological psychology.

3. e. Zuckerman (1971) pioneered the study of sensation seeking as a personality trait.

Concept Check 1.4

1. d. Industrial and organizational psychologists often strive to improve workers' productivity and morale.

2. c. One of the chief concerns of educational and school psychologists is achievement testing, which is intended to measure students' educational accomplishments.

3. a. Multiple personality disorder is a serious mental illness that is treated by clinical psychologists (and psychiatrists).

4. b. Though the work of counseling psychologists may overlap with that of clinical psychologists, more often their work focuses on the adjustment challenges that people face in everyday life, such as vocational decisions.

Concept Check 1.5

a. 2. Psychology is theoretically diverse.

b. 6. Heredity and environment jointly influence behavior.

c. 4. Behavior is determined by multiple causes.

d. 7. Our experience of the world is highly subjective.

Chapter 2

Concept Check 2.1

1. IV: Film violence (present versus absent).
DV: Heart rate and blood pressure (there are two DVs).

2. IV: Courtesy training (training versus no training).
DV: Number of customer complaints.

3. IV: Stimulus complexity (high versus low) and stimulus contrast (high versus low) (there are two IVs).
DV: Length of time spent staring at the stimuli.

4. IV: Group size (large versus small).
DV: Conformity.

Concept Check 2.2

1. b and e. The other three conclusions all equate correlation with causation.

2. a. Negative. As age increases, more people tend to have visual problems and acuity tends to decrease.

b. Positive. Studies show that highly educated people tend to earn higher incomes and that people with less education tend to earn lower incomes.

c. Negative. As shyness increases, the size of one's friendship network should decrease. However, research suggests that this inverse association may be weaker than widely believed.

Concept Check 2.3

1. d. Survey. You would distribute a survey to obtain information on subjects' social class, education, and attitudes about nuclear disarmament.

2. c. Case study. Using a case study approach, you could interview people with anxiety disorders, interview their parents, and examine their school records to look for similarities in childhood experiences. As a second choice, you might have people with anxiety disorders fill out a survey about their childhood experiences.

3. b. Naturalistic observation. To answer this question properly, you would want to observe baboons in their natural environment, without interference.

4. a. Experiment. To demonstrate a causal relationship, you would have to conduct an experiment. You would manipulate the presence or absence of food-related cues in controlled circumstances where subjects had an opportunity to eat some food, and monitor the amount eaten.

Concept Check 2.4

Methodological flaw	Study 1	Study 2
Sampling bias	✓	✓
Placebo effects	✓	
Confounding of variables	✓	
Distortions in self-report data		✓
Experimenter bias	✓	

Explanations for Study 1. Sensory deprivation is an unusual kind of experience that may intrigue certain potential subjects, who may be more adventurous or more willing to take risks than the population at large. Using the first 80 students who sign up for this study may not yield a sample that is representative of the population. Assigning the first 40 subjects who sign up to the experimental group may confound these extraneous variables with the treatment (students who sign up most quickly may be the most adventurous). In announcing that he will be examining the detrimental effects of sensory deprivation, the experimenter has created expectations in the subjects. These expectations could lead to placebo effects that have not been controlled for with a placebo group. The experimenter has also revealed that he has a bias about the outcome of the study. Since he supervises the treatments, he knows which subjects are in the experimental and control groups, thus aggravating potential problems with experimenter bias. For example, he might unintentionally give the control group subjects better instructions on how to do the pursuit-rotor task and thereby slant the study in favor of finding support for his hypothesis.

Explanations for Study 2. Sampling bias is a problem because the researcher has sampled only subjects from a low-income, inner-city neighborhood. A sample obtained in this way is not likely to be representative of the population at large. People are sensitive about the issue of racial prejudice, so distortions in self-report data are also likely. Many subjects may be swayed by social desirability bias and rate themselves as less prejudiced than they really are.

Chapter 3

Concept Check 3.1

1. d. Dendrite.
2. f. Myelin.
3. b. Neuron.
4. e. Axon.
5. a. Glia.
6. g. Terminal button.
7. h. Synapse.

Concept Check 3.2

1. d. Serotonin.
2. b and d. Norepinephrine and serotonin.
3. e. Endorphins.
4. c. Dopamine.
5. a. Acetylcholine.

Concept Check 3.3

1. Left hemisphere damage, probably to Wernicke's area.
2. Deficit in dopamine synthesis in an area of the midbrain.
3. Deterioration of myelin sheaths surrounding axons.
4. Disturbance in dopamine activity.

Please note that neuropsychological assessment is not as simple as this introductory exercise may suggest. There are many possible causes of most disorders, and we discussed only a handful of leading causes for each.

Concept Check 3.4

1. Closer relatives; more distant relatives.
2. Identical twins; fraternal twins.
3. Biological parents; adoptive parents.
4. Genetic overlap or closeness; trait similarity.

Chapter 4

Concept Check 4.1

Dimension	Rods	Cones
Physical shape	Elongated	Stubby
Number in the retina	125 million	6.4 million
Area of the retina in which they are dominant receptor	Periphery	Center/fovea
Critical to color vision	No	Yes
Critical to peripheral vision	Yes	No
Sensitivity to dim light	Strong	Weak
Speed of dark adaptation	Slow	Rapid

Concept Check 4.2

	Trichromatic	Opponent process
Theory proposed by:	Young, Helmholtz	Hering
Can/can't account for complementary afterimages	can't	can
Explains first/later stage of color processing	first	later
Does/doesn't account for need for four terms to describe colors	doesn't	does

Concept Check 4.3

✓ 1. Interposition. The arches in front cut off part of the corridor behind them.

✓ 2. Height in plane. The back of the corridor is higher on the horizontal plane than the front of the corridor is.

✓ 3. Texture gradient. The more distant portions of the hallway are painted in less detail than the closer portions are.

✓ 4. Relative size. The arches in the distance are smaller than those in the foreground.

✓ 5. Light and shadow. Light shining in from the crossing corridor (it's coming from the left) contrasts with shadow elsewhere.

✓ 6. Linear perspective. The lines of the corridor converge in the distance.

Concept Check 4.4

Dimension	Vision	Hearing
1. Stimulus	Light waves	Sound waves
2. Elements of stimulus and related perceptions	Wavelength/hue Amplitude/ brightness Purity/saturation	Frequency/pitch Amplitude/ loudness Purity/timbre
3. Receptors	Rods and cones	Hair cells
4. Location of receptors	Retina	Basilar membrane
5. Main location of processing in brain	Occipital lobe, visual cortex	Temporal lobe, auditory cortex

Concept Check 4.5

Dimension	Taste	Smell	Touch
Stimulus	Soluble chemicals in saliva	Volatile chemicals in air	Mechanical, thermal, and chemical energy due to external contact
Receptors	Clusters of taste cells	Olfactory cilia (hairlike structures)	Many (at least 6) types
Location of receptors	Taste buds on tongue	Upper area of nasal passages	Skin
Basic elements of perception	Sweet, sour, salty, bitter	No satisfactory classification scheme	Pressure, hot, cold, pain

Chapter 5

Concept Check 5.1

Characteristic	REM sleep	NREM sleep
Type of EEG activity	"Wide awake" brain waves, mostly beta	Varied, lots of delta waves
Eye movements	Rapid, lateral	Slow or absent
Dreaming	Frequent, vivid	Less frequent
Depth (difficulty in awakening)	Difficult to awaken	Varied, generally easier to awaken
Percentage of total sleep (in adults)	About 20%	About 80%
Increases or decreases (as percentage of sleep) during childhood	Percent decreases	Percent increases
Timing in sleep (dominates early or late)	Dominates later in cycle	Dominates early in cycle

Concept Check 5.2

1. Beta. Video games require alert information processing, which is associated with beta waves.

2. Alpha. Meditation involves relaxation, which is associated with alpha waves, and studies show increased alpha in meditators.

3. Theta. In stage 1 sleep, theta waves tend to be prevalent.

4. Beta. Nightmares are dreams, so you're probably in REM sleep, which paradoxically produces "wide awake" beta waves.

5. Beta. If you're a beginner, typing will require alert, focused attention, which should generate beta waves.

Concept Check 5.3

1. c. Stimulants.

2. d. Hallucinogens.

3. b. Sedatives.

4. f. Alcohol.

5. a. Narcotics.

6. e. Cannabis.

Chapter 6

Concept Check 6.1

1. CS: Fire in fireplace
   UCS: Pain from burn   CR/UCR: Fear

2. CS: Brake lights in rain
   UCS: Car accident   CR/UCR: Tensing up

3. CS: Sight of cat
   UCS: Cat dander   CR/UCR: Wheezing

Concept Check 6.2

1. d. Stimulus generalization.

2. a. Acquisition.

3. f. Higher-order conditioning.

4. e. Stimulus discrimination.

5. c. Spontaneous recovery.

6. b. Extinction.

Concept Check 6.3

1. FR. Each sale is a response and every third response earns reinforcement.

2. VI. A varied amount of time elapses before the response of doing yard work can earn reinforcement.

3. VR. Reinforcement occurs after a varied number of unreinforced casts (time is irrelevant; the more casts Martha makes, the more reinforcers she will receive).

4. CR. The designated response (reading a book) is reinforced (with a gold star) each and every time.

5. FI. A fixed time interval (3 years) has to elapse before Skip can earn a salary increase (the reinforcer).

Concept Check 6.4

1. Punishment.

2. Positive reinforcement.

3. Punishment.

4. Negative reinforcement (for Audrey); the dog is positively reinforced for its whining.

5. Negative reinforcement.

6. Extinction. When Sharma's co-workers start to ignore her complaints, they are trying to extinguish the behavior (which had been positively reinforced when it won sympathy).

Concept Check 6.5

1. Classical conditioning. Midori's blue windbreaker is a CS eliciting excitement in her dog.

2. Operant conditioning. Playing new songs leads to negative consequences (punishment), which weaken the tendency to play new songs. Playing old songs leads to positive reinforcement, which gradually strengthens the tendency to play old songs.

3. Classical conditioning. The song was paired with the passion of new love so that it became a CS eliciting emotional, romantic feelings.

4. Both. Ralph's workplace is paired with criticism so that his workplace becomes a CS eliciting anxiety. Calling in sick is operant behavior that is strengthened through negative reinforcement (because it reduces anxiety).

Chapter 7

Concept Check 7.1

Feature	Sensory memory	Short-term memory	Long-term memory
Main encoding format	Copy of input	Largely phonemic	Largely semantic
Storage capacity	Limited	Small (7 ± 2 chunks)	No known limit
Storage duration	about ¼ second	Up to 20 seconds	Minutes to years

Concept Check 7.2

1. Ineffective encoding due to lack of attention.

2. Retrieval failure due to motivated forgetting.

3. Proactive interference (previous learning of Joe Cocker's name interferes with new learning).

4. Retroactive interference (new learning of sociology interferes with older learning of history).

Concept Check 7.3

1. a. Declarative memory.

2. e. Long-term memory.

3. h. Sensory memory.

4. d. Implicit memory.

5. b. Episodic memory.

6. f. Procedural memory.

7. g. Semantic memory.

8. i. Short-term memory.

Chapter 8

Concept Check 8.1

1. 2. One word is overextended to refer to a similar object.

2. 4. Words are combined into a sentence, but the rule for past tense is overgeneralized.

3. 3. Telegraphic sentence.

4. 5. Words are combined into a sentence, and past tense is used correctly.

5. 1. One word is used to refer to an entity.

6. 6. "Longer" sentence with metaphor.

Concept Check 8.2

1. Functional fixedness.

2. Forming subgoals.

3. Insight.

4. Searching for analogies.

5. Arrangement problem.

Concept Check 8.3

1. Elimination by aspects.

2. Availability heuristic.

3. Shift to an additive model.

Chapter 9

Concept Check 9.1

1. Test-retest reliability.

2. Criterion-related validity.

3. Content validity.

Concept Check 9.2

1. a. Galton (1869).

2. d. Wechsler (1958).

3. b. Binet and Simon (1948).

4. c. Terman (1916).

Concept Check 9.3

1. H. Given that the identical twins were reared apart, their greater similarity in comparison to fraternals reared together can only be due to heredity. This comparison is probably the most important piece of evidence supporting the genetic determination of IQ.

2. E. We tend to associate identical twins with evidence supporting heredity, but in this comparison genetic similarity is held constant since both sets of twins are identical. The only logical explanation for the greater similarity in identicals reared together is the effect of their being reared together (environment).

3. E. This comparison is similar to the previous one. Genetic similarity is held constant and a shared environment produces greater similarity than being reared apart.

4. B. This is nothing more than a quantification of Galton's original observation that intelligence runs in families. Since families share both genes and environment, either or both could be responsible for the observed correlation.

5. B. The similarity of adopted children to their biological parents can only be due to shared genes, and the similarity of adopted children to their foster parents can only be due to shared environment, so these correlations show the influence of both heredity and environment.

Concept Check 9.4

1. b. Gardner.

2. a. Galton.

3. c. Jensen.

4. d. Scarr.

5. e. Sternberg.

Chapter 10

Concept Check 10.1

1. I. Early studies indicated that the VMH was a "stop eating" center, since artificially stimulating it curtails eating in rats while lesioning leads to overeating. Subsequent research indicates that the situation is somewhat more complicated; the VMH is not simply a "stop eating" center.

2. I. According to Mayer (1955, 1968), hunger increases when the amount of glucose in the blood decreases. Glucostats in the brain apparently monitor the uptake of glucose by cells in the body.

3. I. Insulin, a hormone produced by the pancreas, must be present for cells to extract glucose from the blood. If insulin is increased, more glucose is extracted, glucostats respond to the increase, and one experiences increased hunger.

4. D. Food preferences are learned; we tend to like what we are accustomed to eating. So no matter how delicious someone from another culture thinks some exotic delicacy is, you're not likely to be eager to eat it.

5. ?. Schachter and Gross (1968) found that obese people tend to snack when external cues indicate that it's dinnertime, while nonobese people tend not to, so they won't spoil their dinner.

6. I. Reasearch suggests that stress leads to increased eating in many people, although it could be stress-induced arousal that leads to eating, rather than stress itself.

Concept Check 10.2

1. d. Fear of failure.

2. c. Incentive value of success.

3. e. Perceived probability of failure.

4. a. Need for achievement.

Concept Check 10.3

2. James-Lange theory.

3. Schachter's two-factor theory.

4. Evolutionary theories.

Chapter 11

Concept Check 11.1

	Event	Stage	Organism	Time span
1.	Uterine implantation	Germinal	Zygote	0–2 weeks
2.	Muscle and bone begin to form	Fetal	Fetus	2 months to birth
3.	Vital organs and body systems begin to form	Embryonic	Embryo	2 weeks to 2 months

Concept Check 11.2

1. b. Animism is characteristic of the preoperational period.

2. c. Mastery of hierarchical classification occurs during the concrete operational period.

3. a. Lack of object permanence is characteristic of the sensorimotor period.

Concept Check 11.3

1. c. Commitment to personal ethics is characteristic of postconventional reasoning.

2. b. Concern about approval of others is characteristic of conventional reasoning.

3. a. Emphasis on positive or negative consequences is characteristic of preconventional reasoning.

Chapter 12

Concept Check 12.1

1. Regression.

2. Projection.

3. Reaction formation.

4. Repression.

5. Rationalization.

Concept Check 12.2

	Freud	Jung	Adler
1. Archetypes		✓	
2. Physical gratification	✓		
3. Striving for superiority			✓
4. Collective unconscious		✓	
5. Early childhood experiences	✓		✓
6. Dream analysis	✓	✓	
7. Unconscious determinants	✓	✓	

Concept Check 12.3

1. Bandura's observational learning. Sarah imitates a role model from television.

2. Maslow's need for self-actualization. Yolanda is striving to realize her fullest potential.

3. Freud's Oedipal complex. Vladimir shows preference for his opposite-sex parent and emotional distance from his same-sex parent.

Concept Check 12.4

1. Maslow (1971, p. 36) commenting on the need for self-actualization.

2. Eysenck (1977, pp. 407–408) commenting on the biological roots of personality.

3. Freud (in Malcolm, 1980) commenting on the repression of sexuality.

Chapter 13

Concept Check 13.1

1. b. A choice between two unattractive options.

2. c. Weighing the positive and negative aspects of a single goal.

3. a. A choice between two attractive options.

Concept Check 13.2

1. a. Frustration due to delay.

2. d. Pressure to perform.

3. c. Change associated with leaving school and taking a new job.

4. a. Frustration due to loss of job.

   c. Change in life circumstances.

   d. Pressure to perform (in quickly obtaining new job).

Concept Check 13.3

Pathway 1: pituitary, ACTH, adrenal cortex, corticosteroids.

Pathway 2: hypothalamus, sympathetic division of the ANS, adrenal medulla, catecholamines.

Chapter 14

Concept Check 14.1

	Deviance	Maladaptive behavior	Personal distress
1. Alan		✓	
2. Monica			✓
3. Boris	✓		
4. Natasha	✓	✓	✓

Concept Check 14.2

1. Obsessive-compulsive disorder (key symptoms: frequent rituals, ruminations about school).

2. Somatization disorder (key symptoms: history of physical complaints involving many different organ systems).

3. Conversion disorder (key symptoms: loss of function in single organ system).

Concept Check 14.3

1. Bipolar disorder, manic episode (key symptoms: extravagant plans, hyperactivity, reckless spending).

2. Paranoid schizophrenia (key symptoms: delusions of persecution and grandeur, along with deterioration of adaptive behavior).

3. Major depression (key symptoms: feelings of despair, low self-esteem, lack of energy).

Concept Check 14.4

	Anxiety disorders	Mood disorders	Schizophrenic disorders
Brain structure abnormalities			✓
Cognitive factors	✓	✓	
Prenatal neuro-developmental disruptions			✓
Conditioning	✓		
Genetic predisposition	✓	✓	✓
Interpersonal factors		✓	
Neurochemical factors	✓	✓	✓
Personality	✓		
Stress	✓	✓	✓

Chapter 15

Concept Check 15.1
1. c. **2.** a. **3.** b.

Concept Check 15.2
1. a. Systematic desensitization.

2. c. Aversion therapy.

3. b. Social skills training.

Concept Check 15.3
1. d. **2.** b. **3.** a. **4.** c.

Concept Check 15.4
1. c. **2.** a. **3.** b. **4.** d. **5.** b.

Chapter 16

Concept Check 16.1

	Unstable	Stable
Internal	d	b
External	a	c

Concept Check 16.2
1. c. Fundamental attribution error (assuming that arriving late reflects personal qualities).

2. a. Illusory correlation effect (overestimating how often one has seen confirmations of the assertion that young, female professors get pregnant soon after being hired).

3. b. Stereotyping (assuming that all lawyers have certain traits).

Concept Check 16.3
1. *Target:* Cognitive component of attitudes (beliefs about program for regulating nursing homes).

Persuasion: Message factor (advice to use one-sided instead of two-sided arguments).

2. *Target:* Affective component of attitudes (feelings about candidate).

Persuasion: Source factor (advice on appearing likable, sincere, and compassionate).

3. *Target:* Behavioral component of attitudes (making contributions).

Persuasion: Receiver factor (considering audience's initial position regarding the candidate).

Concept Check 16.4
1. False. **2.** True. **3.** False.

4. True. **5.** False.

Empiricism depends on observation; precise observation depends on measurement; and measurement requires numbers. Thus, scientists routinely analyze numerical data to arrive at their conclusions. Over 2000 empirical studies are cited in this text, and all but a few of the simplest ones required a statistical analysis. *Statistics* **is the use of mathematics to organize, summarize, and interpret numerical data.** We discussed correlation briefly in Chapter 2, but in this Appendix we look at a variety of statistics.

To illustrate statistics in action, let's assume that we want to test a hypothesis that has generated quite an argument in your psychology class. The hypothesis is that college students who watch a great deal of television aren't as bright as those who watch TV infrequently. For the fun of it, your class decides to conduct a correlational study of itself, collecting survey and psychological test data. Your classmates all agree to respond to a short survey on their TV viewing habits. Because everyone at your school has had to take the Scholastic Aptitude Test (SAT), the class decides to use scores on the SAT verbal subtest as an index of how bright students are. All of them agree to allow the records office at the college to furnish their SAT scores to the professor, who replaces each student's name with a subject number (to protect students' right to privacy). Let's see how we could use statistics to analyze the data collected in our pilot study (a small, preliminary investigation).

Graphing Data

After collecting our data, our next step is to organize the data to get a quick overview of our numerical results. Let's assume that there are 20 students in your class, and when they estimate how many hours they spend per day watching TV, the results are as follows:

3	2	0	3	1
3	4	0	5	1
2	3	4	5	2
4	5	3	4	6

One of the simpler things that we can do to organize data is to create a *frequency distribution*—*an* **orderly arrangement of scores indicating the frequency of each score or group of scores.** Figure B.1(a) shows a frequency distribution for our data on TV viewing. The column on the left lists the possible scores (estimated hours of TV viewing) in order, and the column on the right lists the number of subjects with each score. Graphs can provide an even better overview of the data. One approach is to portray the data in a *histogram,* **which is a bar graph that presents data from a frequency distribution.** Such a histogram, summarizing our TV viewing data, is presented in Figure B.1(b).

Another widely used method of portraying data graphically is the *frequency polygon*—**a line figure used to present data from a frequency distribution.** Figures B.1(c) and B.1(d) show how our TV viewing data can be converted from a histogram to a frequency polygon. In both the bar graph and the line figure, the horizontal axis lists the possible scores and the vertical axis is used to indicate the frequency of each score. This use of the axes is nearly universal for frequency polygons, although sometimes it is reversed in histograms (the vertical axis lists possible scores, so the bars become horizontal).

Figure B.1

Graphing data. (a) Our raw data are tallied into a frequency distribution. **(b)** The same data are portrayed in a bar graph called a histogram. **(c)** A frequency polygon is plotted over the histogram. **(d)** The resultant frequency polygon is shown by itself.

Score	Tallies	Frequency
6	I	1
5	III	3
4	IIII	4
3	THI	5
2	III	3
1	II	2
0	II	2

(a) Frequency distribution

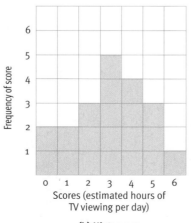

(b) Histogram

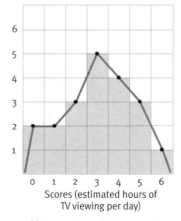

(c) Conversion of histogram into frequency polygon

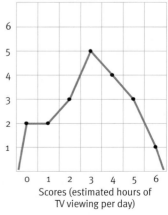

(d) Frequency polygon

Our graphs improve on the jumbled collection of scores that we started with, but *descriptive statistics,* **which are used to organize and summarize data,** provide some additional advantages. Let's see what the three measures of central tendency tell us about our data.

Measuring Central Tendency

In examining a set of data, it's routine to ask "What is a typical score in the distribution?" For instance, in this case we might compare the average amount of TV watching in our sample against national estimates, to determine whether our subjects appear to be representative of the population. The three measures of central tendency, the median, the mean, and the mode, give us indications regarding the typical score in a data set. **The *median* is the score that falls in the center of a distribution, the *mean* is the arithmetic average of the scores,** and **the *mode* is the score that occurs most frequently.**

All three measures of central tendency are calculated for our TV viewing data in Figure B.2. As you can see, in this set of data, the mean, median, and mode all turn out to be the same score, which is 3. The correspondence among the three measures of central tendency seen in our TV viewing data is quite common, but there are situations in which the mean, median, and mode can yield very different estimates of central tendency. To illustrate, imagine that you're interviewing for a sales position at a company. Unbeknownst to you, the company's five salespeople earned the following incomes in the previous year: $20,000, $20,000, $25,000, $35,000, and $200,000. You ask how much the typical salesperson earns in a year. The sales director proudly announces that her five salespeople earned *a mean* income of $60,000 last year. However, before you order that expensive, new sports car, you had better inquire about the *median* and *modal* income for the sales staff. In this case, one extreme score

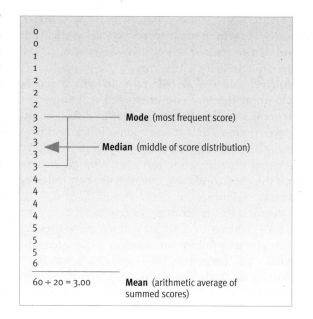

Measures of central tendency. The mean, median, and mode usually converge, as in the case of our TV viewing data.

($200,000) has inflated the mean, making it unrepresentative of the sales staff's earnings. In this instance, the median ($25,000) and the mode ($20,000) both provide better estimates of what you are likely to earn.

In general, the mean is the most useful measure of central tendency because additional statistical manipulations can be performed on it that are not possible with the median or mode. However, the mean is sensitive to extreme scores in a distribution, which can sometimes make the mean misleading. Thus, lack of agreement among the three measures of central tendency usually occurs when a few extreme scores pull the mean away from the center of the distribution, as shown in Figure B.3. The curves plotted in Figure B.3 are simply "smoothed out" frequency polygons based on data from many subjects. They show that when a distribution is symmetric, the measures of central tendency fall together, but this is not true in skewed or unbalanced distributions.

Figure B.3

Measures of central tendency in skewed distributions. In a symmetrical distribution (**a**), the three measures of central tendency converge. However, in a negatively skewed distribution (**b**) or in a positively skewed distribution (**c**), the mean, median, and mode are pulled apart as shown here. Typically, in these situations the median provides the best index of central tendency.

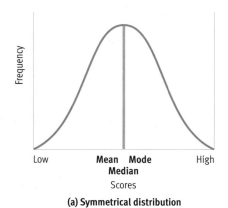

(a) Symmetrical distribution

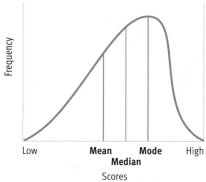

(b) Negatively skewed distribution

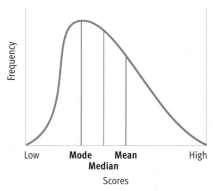

(c) Positively skewed distribution

Figure B.3(b) shows a *negatively skewed distribution,* **in which most scores pile up at the high end of the scale** (the negative skew refers to the direction in which the curve's "tail" points). A *positively skewed distribution,* **in which scores pile up at the low end of the scale**, is shown in Figure B.3(c). In both types of skewed distributions, a few extreme scores at one end pull the mean, and to a lesser degree the median, away from the mode. In these situations, the mean may be misleading and the median usually provides the best index of central tendency.

In any case, the measures of central tendency for our TV viewing data are reassuring, since they all agree and they fall reasonably close to national estimates regarding how much young adults watch TV (Huston & Wright, 1982). Given the small size of our group, this agreement with national norms doesn't *prove* that our sample is representative of the population, but at least there's no obvious reason to believe that they're unrepresentative.

Measuring Variability

Of course, everyone in our sample did not report identical TV viewing habits. Virtually all data sets are characterized by some variability. *Variability* **refers to how much the scores tend to vary or depart from the mean score.** For example, the distribution of golf scores for a mediocre, erratic golfer would be characterized by high variability, while scores for an equally mediocre but more consistent golfer would show less variability.

The *standard deviation* **is an index of the amount of variability in a set of data.** It reflects the dispersion of scores in a distribution. This principle is portrayed graphically in Figure B.4, where the two distributions of golf scores have the same mean but the left one has less variability because the scores are "bunched up" in the center (for the consistent golfer). The distribution in Figure B.4(b) is characterized by more variability, as the erratic golfer's scores are more spread out. This distribution will yield a higher standard deviation than the distribution in Figure B.4(a).

The formula for calculating the standard deviation is shown in Figure B.5, where *d* stands for each score's deviation from the mean and $\sum$ stands for summation. A step-by-step application of this formula to our TV viewing data, shown in Figure B.5, reveals that the standard deviation for our TV viewing data is 1.64. The standard deviation has a variety of uses. One of these uses will surface in the next section, where we discuss the normal distribution.

The Normal Distribution

The hypothesis in our study is that brighter students watch less TV than relatively dull students. To test this hypothesis, we're going to correlate TV viewing with SAT scores. But to make effective use of the SAT data, we need to understand what SAT scores mean, which brings us to the normal distribution.

The *normal distribution* **is a a symmetrical, bell-shaped curve that represents the pattern in which many human characteristics are dispersed in the population.** A great many physical qualities (for example, height, nose length, and running speed) and psychological traits (intelligence, spatial reasoning ability, introversion) are distributed in a manner that closely resembles this bell-shaped curve. When a trait is normally distributed, most scores fall near the center of the distribution (the mean) and the number of scores gradually declines as one moves away from the center in either direction. The normal distribution is *not* a law of nature. It's a mathematical function, or theoretical curve, that approximates the way nature seems to operate.

Figure B.4

The standard deviation and dispersion of data. Although both these distributions of golf scores have the same mean, their standard deviations will be different. In (a) the scores are bunched together and there is less variability than in (b), yielding a lower standard deviation for the data in distribution (a).

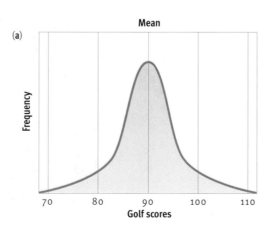

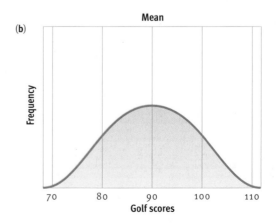

The normal distribution is the bedrock of the scoring system for most psychological tests, including the SAT. As we discuss in Chapter 9, psychological tests are *relative measures;* they assess how people score on a trait in comparison to other people. The normal distribution gives us a precise way to measure how people stack up in comparison to each other. The scores under the normal curve are dispersed in a fixed pattern, with the standard deviation serving as the unit of measurement, as shown in Figure B.6. About 68% of the scores in the distribution fall within plus or minus 1 standard deviation of the mean, while 95% of the scores fall within plus or minus 2 standard deviations of the mean. Given this fixed pattern, if you know the mean and standard deviation of a normally distributed trait, you can tell where any score falls in the distribution for the trait.

Although you may not have realized it, you probably have taken many tests in which the scoring system is based on the normal distribution. On the SAT, for instance, raw scores (the number of items correct on each subtest) are converted into standard scores that indicate where you fall in the normal distribution for the trait measured. In this conversion, the mean is set arbitrarily at 500 and the standard

TV viewing score (X)	Deviation from mean (d)	Deviation squared (d²)
0	−3	9
0	−3	9
1	−2	4
1	−2	4
2	−1	1
2	−1	1
2	−1	1
3	0	0
3	0	0
3	0	0
3	0	0
3	0	0
4	+1	1
4	+1	1
4	+1	1
4	+1	1
5	+2	4
5	+2	4
5	+2	4
6	+3	9

$N = 20$

$$\Sigma X = 60 \qquad \Sigma d^2 = 54$$

$$\text{Mean} = \frac{\Sigma X}{N} = \frac{60}{20} = 3.0$$

$$\text{Standard deviation} = \sqrt{\frac{\Sigma d^2}{N}} = \sqrt{\frac{54}{20}}$$

$$= \sqrt{2.70} = 1.64$$

Steps in calculating the standard deviation.
(1) Add the scores (ΣX) and divide by the number of scores (*N*) to calculate the mean (which comes out to 3.0 in this case). (2) Calculate each score's deviation from the mean by subtracting the mean from each score (the results are shown in the second column). (3) Square these deviations from the mean and total the results to obtain (Σd^2) as shown in the third column. (4) Insert the numbers for N and Σd^2 into the formula for the standard deviation and compute the results.

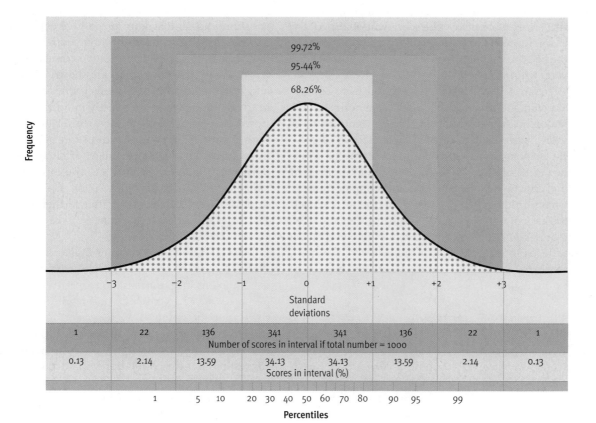

Figure B.6

The normal distribution.
Many characteristics are distributed in a pattern represented by this bell-shaped curve (each dot represents a case). The horizontal axis shows how far above or below the mean a score is (measured in plus or minus standard deviations). The vertical axis shows the number of cases obtaining each score. In a normal distribution, most cases fall near the center of the distribution, so that 68.26% of the cases fall within plus or minus 1 standard deviation of the mean. The number of cases gradually declines as one moves away from the mean in either direction, so that only 13.59% of the cases fall between 1 and 2 standard deviations above or below the mean, and even fewer cases (2.14%) fall between 2 and 3 standard deviations above or below the mean.

The normal distribution and SAT scores. The normal distribution is the basis for the scoring system on many standardized tests. For example, on the Scholastic Aptitude Test (SAT), the mean is set at 500 and the standard deviation at 100. Hence, an SAT score tells you how many standard deviations above or below the mean you scored. For example, a score of 700 means you scored 2 standard deviations above the mean.

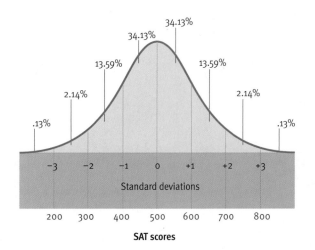

deviation at 100, as shown in Figure B.7. Therefore, a score of 400 on the SAT verbal subtest means that you scored 1 standard deviation below the mean, while an SAT score of 600 indicates that you scored 1 standard deviation above the mean. Thus, SAT scores tell you how many standard deviations above or below the mean your score was. This system also provides the metric for IQ scales and many other types of psychological tests (see Chapter 9).

Test scores that place examinees in the normal distribution can always be converted to percentile scores, which are a little easier to interpret. A *percentile score* indicates the percentage of people who score at or below the score you obtained. For example, if you score at the 60th percentile, 60% of the people who take the test score the same or below you, while the remaining 40% score above you. There are tables available that permit us to convert any standard deviation placement in a normal distribution into a precise percentile score. Figure B.6 gives some percentile conversions for the normal curve.

Of course, not all distributions are normal. As we saw in Figure B.3, some distributions are skewed in one direction or the other. As an example, consider what would happen if a classroom exam were much too easy or much too hard. If the test were too easy, scores would be bunched up at the high end of the scale, as in Figure B.3(b). If the test were too hard, scores would be bunched up at the low end, as in Figure B.3(c).

Measuring Correlation

To determine whether TV viewing is related to SAT scores, we have to compute a *correlation coefficient*—a numerical index of the degree of relationship that exists between two variables. As discussed in Chapter 2, a *positive* correlation

means that the two variables—say X and Y—covary together. This means that high scores on variable X are associated with high scores on variable Y and that low scores on X are associated with low scores on Y. A *negative* correlation indicates that there is an inverse relationship between two variables. This means that people who score high on variable X tend to score low on variable Y, whereas those who score low on X tend to score high on Y. In our study, we hypothesized that as TV viewing increases, SAT scores will decrease, so we should expect a negative correlation between TV viewing and SAT scores.

The *magnitude* of a correlation coefficient indicates the *strength* of the association between two variables. This coefficient can vary between 0 and ± 1.00. The coefficient is usually represented by the letter r (for example, $r = .45$). A coefficient near 0 tells us that there is no relationship between two variables. A coefficient of $+1.00$ or -1.00 indicates that there is a perfect, one-to-one correspondence between two variables. A perfect correlation is found only rarely when working with real data. The closer the coefficient is to either -1.00 or $+1.00$, the stronger the relationship is.

The direction and strength of correlations can be illustrated graphically in scatter diagrams. A *scatter diagram is a graph in which paired X and Y scores for each subject are plotted as single points.* Figure B.8 shows scatter diagrams for positive correlations in the upper half and for negative correlations in the bottom half. A perfect positive correlation and a perfect negative correlation are shown on the far left. When a correlation is perfect, the data points in the scatter diagram fall exactly in a straight line. However, positive and negative correlations yield lines slanted in the opposite direction because the lines map out opposite types of associations. Moving to the right in Figure B.8, you can see what happens when the magnitude of a correlation decreases. The data points scatter farther and farther from the straight line that would represent a perfect relationship.

What about our data relating TV viewing to SAT scores? Figure B.9 shows a scatter diagram of these data. Having just learned about scatter diagrams, perhaps you can estimate the magnitude of the correlation between TV viewing and SAT scores. The scatter diagram of our data looks a lot like the one seen in the bottom right corner of Figure B.8, suggesting that the correlation will be in the vicinity of $-.20$.

The formula for computing the most widely used measure of correlation—the Pearson product-

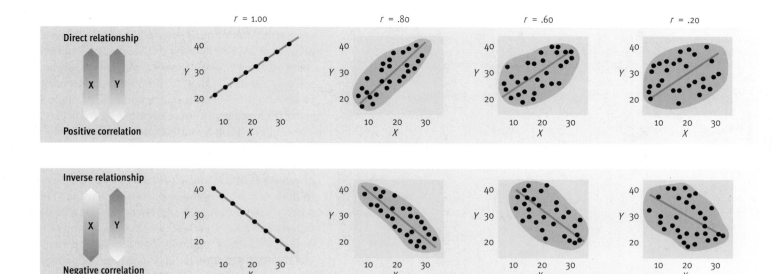

moment correlation—is shown in Figure B.10 on the next page, along with the calculations for our data on TV viewing and SAT scores. The data yield a correlation of $r = -.24$. This coefficient of correlation reveals that we have found a weak inverse association between TV viewing and performance on the SAT. Among our subjects, as TV viewing increases, SAT scores decrease, but the trend isn't very strong. We can get a better idea of how strong this correlation is by examining its predictive power.

Correlation and Prediction

As the magnitude of a correlation increases (gets closer to either −1.00 or +1.00), our ability to predict one variable based on knowledge of the other variable steadily increases. This relationship between the magnitude of a correlation and predictability can be quantified precisely. All we have to do is square the correlation coefficient (multiply it by itself) and this gives us the *coefficient of determination,* **the percentage of variation in one variable that can be predicted based on the other variable.** Thus, a correlation of .70 yields a coefficient of determination of .49 (.70 × .70 = .49), indicating that variable X can account for 49% of the variation in variable Y. Figure B.11 on the next page shows how the coefficient of determination goes up as the magnitude of a correlation increases.

Unfortunately, a correlation of .24 doesn't give us much predictive power. We can account only for a little over 6% of the variation in variable Y. So, if we tried to predict individuals' SAT scores based on how much TV they watched, our predictions

wouldn't be very accurate. Although a low correlation doesn't have much practical, predictive utility, it may still have theoretical value. Just knowing that there is a relationship between two variables can be theoretically interesting. However, we haven't yet addressed the question of whether our observed correlation is strong enough to support our hypothesis that there is a relationship between TV viewing and SAT scores. To make this judgment, we have to turn to inferential statistics and the process of hypothesis testing.

Hypothesis Testing

Inferential statistics go beyond the mere description of data. *Inferential statistics* **are used to interpret data and draw conclusions.** They permit researchers to decide whether their data support their hypotheses.

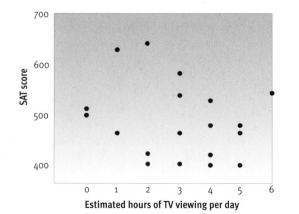

Figure B.8

Scatter diagrams of positive and negative correlations. Scatter diagrams plot paired X and Y scores as single points. Score plots slanted in the opposite direction result from positive (top row) as opposed to negative (bottom row) correlations. Moving across both rows (to the right), you can see that progressively weaker correlations result in more and more scattered plots of data points.

Figure B.9

Scatter diagram of the correlation between TV viewing and SAT scores. Our hypothetical data relating TV viewing to SAT scores are plotted in this scatter diagram. Compare it to the scatter diagrams seen in Figure B.8 and see whether you can estimate the correlation between TV viewing and SAT scores in our data (see the text for the answer).

Computing a correlation coefficient. The calculations required to compute the Pearson product-moment coefficient of correlation are shown here. The formula looks intimidating, but it's just a matter of filling in the figures taken from the sums of the columns shown above the formula.

Subject number	TV viewing score (X)	X^2	SAT score (Y)	Y^2	XY
1	0	0	500	250,000	0
2	0	0	515	265,225	0
3	1	1	450	202,500	450
4	1	1	650	422,500	650
5	2	4	400	160,000	800
6	2	4	675	455,625	1350
7	2	4	425	180,625	850
8	3	9	400	160,000	1200
9	3	9	450	202,500	1350
10	3	9	500	250,000	1500
11	3	9	550	302,500	1650
12	3	9	600	360,000	1800
13	4	16	400	160,000	1600
14	4	16	425	180,625	1700
15	4	16	475	225,625	1900
16	4	16	525	275,625	2100
17	5	25	400	160,000	2000
18	5	25	450	202,500	2250
19	5	25	475	225,625	2375
20	6	36	550	302,500	3300
$N = 20$	$\Sigma X = 60$	$\Sigma X^2 = 234$	$\Sigma Y = 9815$	$\Sigma Y^2 = 4,943,975$	$\Sigma XY = 28,825$

Formula for Pearson product-moment correlation coefficient

$$r = \frac{(N)\,\Sigma XY - (\Sigma X)(\Sigma Y)}{\sqrt{[(N)\,\Sigma X^2 - (\Sigma X)^2][(N)\,\Sigma Y^2 - (\Sigma Y)^2]}}$$

$$= \frac{(20)(28,825) - (60)(9815)}{\sqrt{[(20)(234) - (60)^2][(20)(4,943,975) - (9815)^2]}}$$

$$= \frac{-12,400}{\sqrt{[1080][2,545,275]}}$$

$$= -.237$$

In our study of TV viewing we hypothesized that we would find an inverse relationship between amount of TV watched and SAT scores. Sure enough, that's what we found. However, we have to ask ourselves a critical question: Is this observed correlation large enough to support our hypothesis, or might a correlation of this size have occurred by chance?

We have to ask a similar question nearly every time we conduct a study. Why? Because we are working only with a sample. In research, we observe a limited *sample* (in this case, 20 subjects) to draw conclusions about a much larger *population* (college students in general). There's always a possibility that if we drew a different sample from the population, the results might be different. Perhaps our results are unique to our sample and not generalizable to the larger population. If we were able to collect data on the entire population, we would not have to wrestle with this problem, but our dependence on a sample necessitates the use of inferential statistics to precisely evaluate the likelihood that our results are due to chance factors in sampling. Thus, inferential statistics are the key to making the inferential leap from the sample to the population (see Figure B.12).

Although it may seem backward, in hypothesis testing we formally test the *null* hypothesis. As applied to correlational data, the **null hypothesis is the assumption that there is no true relationship between the variables observed.** In our study, the null hypothesis is that there is no genuine association between TV viewing and SAT scores. We want to determine whether our results will permit us to *reject* the null hypothesis and thus conclude that our *research hypothesis* (that there is a relationship

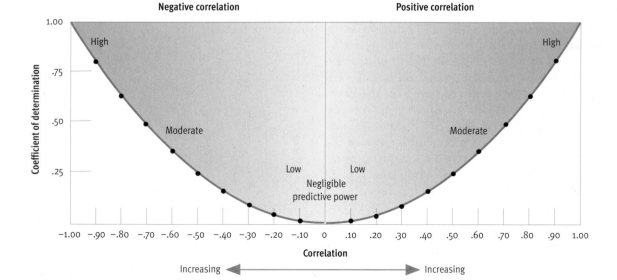

Correlation and the coefficient of determination. The coefficient of determination is an index of a correlation's predictive power. As you can see, whether positive or negative, stronger correlations yield greater predictive power.

between the variables) has been supported. Why do we test the null hypothesis instead of the research hypothesis? Because our probability calculations depend on assumptions tied to the null hypothesis. Specifically, we compute the probability of obtaining the results that we have observed if the null hypthesis is indeed true. The calculation of this probability hinges on a number of factors. A key factor is the amount of variability in the data, which is why the standard deviation is an important statistic.

Statistical Significance

When we reject the null hypothesis, we conclude that we have found *statistically significant* results. **Statistical significance is said to exist when the probability that the observed findings are due to chance is very low, usually less than 5 chances in 100.** This means that if the null hypothesis is correct and we conduct our study 100 times, drawing a new sample from the population each time, we will get results such as those observed only 5 times out of 100. If our calculations allow us to reject the null hypothesis, we conclude that our results support our research hypothesis. Thus, statistically significant results typically are findings that *support* a research hypothesis.

The requirement that there be less than 5 chances in 100 that research results are due to chance is the *minimum* requirement for statistical significance. When this requirement is met, we say the results are significant at the .05 level. If researchers calculate that there is less than 1 chance in 100 that their results are due to chance factors in sampling, the results are significant at the .01 level. If there is less than a 1 in 1000 chance that findings are attributable to sampling error, the results are significant at the .001 level. Thus, there are several *levels* of significance that you may see cited in scientific articles.

Because we are only dealing in matters of probability, there is always the possibility that our decision to accept or reject the null hypothesis is wrong. The various significance levels indicate the probability of erroneously rejecting the null hypothesis (and inaccurately accepting the research hypothesis). At the .05 level of significance, there are 5 chances in 100 that we have made a mistake when we conclude that our results support our hypothesis,

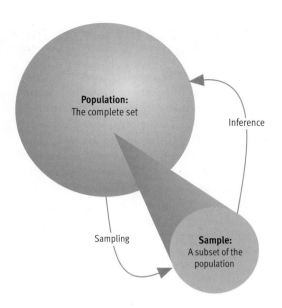

The relationship between the population and the sample. In research, we are usually interested in a broad population, but we can observe only a small sample from the population. After making observations of our sample, we draw inferences about the population, based on the sample. This inferential process works well as long as the sample is reasonably representative of the population.

and at the .01 level of significance the chance of an erroneous conclusion is 1 in 100. Although researchers hold the probability of this type of error quite low, the probability is never zero. This is one of the reasons that competently executed studies of the same question can yield contradictory findings. The differences may be due to chance variations in sampling that can't be prevented.

What do we find when we evaluate our data linking TV viewing to students' SAT scores? The calculations indicate that, given our sample size and the variability in our data, the probability of obtaining a correlation of $-.24$ by chance is greater than 20%. That's not a high probability, but it's not low enough to reject the null hypothesis. Thus, our findings are not strong enough to allow us to conclude that we have supported our hypothesis.

Statistics and Empiricism

In summary, conclusions based on empirical research are a matter of probability, and there's always a possibility that the conclusions are wrong. However, two major strengths of the empirical approach are its precision and its intolerance of error. Scientists can give you precise estimates of the likelihood that their conclusions are wrong, and because they're intolerant of error, they hold this probability extremely low. It's their reliance on statistics that allows them to accomplish these goals.

Appendix C URLs for Recommended Web Links

The recommended Web Links sprinkled throughout the chapters in this text are intended to spark your interest in further exploration of psychological issues on the World Wide Web. We chose to not include the addresses (URLs) in the annotated Web Links because the Web is a fluid, dynamic medium in which change is the only constant. Many of the URLs for suggested sites will change before this book makes it off the printing press.

If you are interested in accessing some of the recommended Web sites, we suggest that you do so through the *Psychology: Themes & Variations* home page at the Wadsworth Psychology Study Center Web site (http://psychology.wadsworth.com). Links to all of the recommended Web sites are maintained there, and the Wadsworth Webmaster periodically updates the URLs.

Nonetheless, recognizing that you may want to go directly to a specific site or to give a suggested URL to a friend, we have compiled a list of the current URLs for all the recommended Web sites in this Appendix. They are organized by chapter and are listed in the order of their appearance in the book.

Web Site	Web Address (URL)
Chapter 1: The Evolution of Psychology	
1.1 HistPsyc: History of Psychology Headlines Index	http://www.unb.ca/web/units/psych/likely/headlines/
1.2 Mind and Body: René Descartes to William James	http://serendip.brynmawr.edu/Mind/Table.html
1.3 History and Philosophy of Psychology Web Resources	http://www.yorku.ca/dept/psych/orgs/resource.htm
1.4 Museum of the History of Psychological Instrumentation	http://www.chss.montclair.edu/psychology/museum/museum.html
1.5 Psychology: Careers for the 21st Century	http://www.apa.org/students/brochure/
1.6 Marky Lloyd's Career Page	http://www.psywww.com/careers/index.htm
1.7 A Student's Guide to Careers in the Helping Professions	http://www.lemoyne.edu/OTRP/otrpresources/helping-online.html
Chapter 2: The Research Enterprise in Psychology	
2.1 PubMed	http://www.ncbi.nlm.nih.gov/PubMed/
2.2 AskERIC	http://ericir.syr.edu/
2.3 Links to Psychological Journals	http://www.wiso.uni-augsburg.de/sozio/hartmann/psycho/journals.html
2.4 HyperStat Online	http://davidmlane.com/hyperstat/index.html
2.5 The Troubling Legacy of the Tuskegee Syphilis Study	http://www.med.virginia.edu/hs-library/historical/apology/index.html
2.6 Animal Welfare Information Center	http://www.nal.usda.gov/awic/
Chapter 3: The Biological Bases of Behavior	
3.1 Neuropsychology Central	http://www.neuropsychologycentral.com/index.html
3.2 Molecular Neurobiology: A Gallery of Animations	http://www.neuroguide.com/cajal_gallery.html
3.3 Neurosciences on the Internet	http://www.neuroguide.com/
3.4 The Visible Human Project	http://www.nlm.nih.gov/research/visible/visible_human.html
3.5 The Whole Brain Atlas	http://www.med.harvard.edu/AANLIB/home.html
3.6 Brain Briefings:The Society for Neuroscience	http://www.sfn.org/briefings/

Web Site	Web Address (URL)
Chapter 4: Sensation and Perception	
4.1 Vision Science: An Internet Resource for Research in Human and Animal Vision	http://www.visionscience.com/
4.2 The Joy of Visual Perception: A Web Book	http://www.yorku.ca/eye/thejoy.htm
4.3 IllusionWorks	http://www.illusionworks.com
4.4 The Moon Illusion Explained	http://facstaff.uww.edu/mccreadd/index.html
4.5 Seeing, Hearing, and Smelling the World	http://www.hhmi.org/senses/start.htm
Chapter 5: Variations in Consciousness	
5.1 NSF Center for Biological Timing	http://www.cbt.virginia.edu/
5.2 The Sleep Well	http://www.stanford.edu/~dement/
5.3 Sleep Medicine Homepage	http://www.users.cloud9.net/~thorpy/
5.4 States of Consciousness	http://www.psywww.com/asc/asc.html
5.5 Web of Addictions	http://www.well.com/user/woa/
5.6 National Institute of Alcohol Abuse and Alcoholism	http://www.niaaa.nih.gov/
Chapter 6: Learning Through Conditioning	
6.1 Behaviour Analysis	http://server.bmod.athabascau.ca/html/aupr/ba.htm
6.2 The B. F. Skinner Foundation	http://www.lafayette.edu/allanr/skinner.html
6.3 Animal Behavior and Welfare Sites	http://www.erols.com/mandtj/
6.4 *Journal of the Experimental Analysis of Behavior* and *Journal of Applied Behavioral Analysis*	http://www.envmed.rochester.edu/wwwrap/behavior/jeabjaba.htm
Chapter 7: Human Memory	
7.1 The Magical Number Seven Plus or Minus Two	http://www.well.com/user/smalin/miller.html
7.2 Mind Tools—Memory Techniques and Mnemonics	http://www.mindtools.com/memory.html
7.3 False Memory Syndrome Foundation (FMSF) Online	http://www.fmsfonline.org/
7.4 False Memory Syndrome Facts	http://www.fmsf.org/
7.5 Alzheimer Page	http://www.biostat.wustl.edu/alzheimer/
Chapter 8: Language and Thought	
8.1 John Lawler's Homepage (Linguistics and Language)	http://www-personal.umich.edu/~jlawler/index.html
8.2 Coglab	http://coglab.psych.purdue.edu/coglab/
8.3 The Critical Thinking Community	http://www.criticalthinking.org/
8.4 Judgment and Decision-Making Experiments	http://psych.fullerton.edu/mbirnbaum/exp.htm
8.5 Strategy and Conflict: An Introductory Sketch of Game Theory	http://www.coba.drexel.edu/economics/mccain/game/game.html

Web Site	Web Address (URL)
Chapter 9: Intelligence and Psychological Testing	
9.1 ERIC/AE Test Locator	http://ericae.net/testcol.htm
9.2 ERIC Clearinghouse on Assessment and Evaluation	http://ericae.net/
9.3 Educational Psychology Interactive: Intelligence	http://www.valdosta.edu/~whuitt/psy702/cogsys/intell.html
9.4 Upstream-Issues: The Bell Curve	http://www.mugu.com/cgi-bin/Upstream/Issues/bell-curve/index.html
Chapter 10: Motivation and Emotion	
10.1 Eating Disorders Shared Awareness (EDSA)	http://www.eating-disorder.com/
10.2 Human Behavior and Evolution Society	http://hbes.homepage.com/
10.3 Go Ask Alice!	http://www.alice.columbia.edu/
10.4 Queer Resources Directory (QRD)	http://www.qrd.org/QRD/
10.5 UCSC Perceptual Science Laboratory	http://mambo.ucsc.edu/
Chapter 11: Human Development Across the Life Span	
11.1 PBS: The Whole Child	http://www.pbs.org/wholechild/
11.2 Early Childhood Care and Development	http://www.ecdgroup.com/
11.3 Child Development Abstracts and Bibliography (CDAB) Online Edition	http://WWW.SRCD.ORG/cdab/default.shtml
11.4 Attachment: Theory and Research	http://www.psychology.sunysb.edu/ewaters/@ Stony Brook
11.5 Adolescence Directory OnLine	http://education.indiana.edu/cas/adol/adol.html
11.6 National Parent Information Network (NPIN)	http://npin.org/
11.7 Administration on Aging: Information on Older Americans	http://www.aoa.gov/
Chapter 12: Personality: Theory, Research, and Assessment	
12.1 The Victorian Web	http://www.stg.brown.edu/projects/hypertext/landow/victorian/victov.html
12.2 Sigmund Freud Museum, Vienna, Austria	http://freud.to.or.at/
12.3 C. G. Jung, Analytical Psychology, and Culture	http://www.cgjungpage.org/
12.4 Television and Violence—Media and Communications Studies Site	http://www.aber.ac.uk/~dgc/tv07.html
12.5 The Personality Project	http://pmc.psych.nwu.edu/personality.html
12.6 Great Ideas in Personality	http://www.personalityresearch.org/
Chapter 13: Stress, Coping, and Health	
13.1 The Web's Stress Management and Emotional Wellness Page	http://imt.net/~randolfi/StressPage.html
13.2 Stress Management and Peak Performance	http://tc.unl.edu/stress/
13.3 healthfinder	http://www.healthfinder.gov/
13.4 Exercise and Sport Psychology	http://www.psyc.unt.edu/apadiv47/

Web Site	Web Address (URL)

Chapter 14: Psychological Disorders

Web Site	Web Address (URL)
14.1 Mental Health Net	http://mentalhelp.net/
14.2 National Alliance for the Mentally Ill (NAMI)	http://www.nami.org/
14.3 Mental Health: A Report of the Surgeon General	http://www.surgeongeneral.gov/library/mentalhealth/index.html
14.4 Doctor's Guide to the Internet: Schizophrenia	http://www.docguide.com/news/content.nsf/PatientResAllCateg/ Schizophrenia?OpenDocument
14.5 David Willshire's Forensic Psychology and Psychiatry Links	http://www.ozemail.com.au/~dwillsh/

Chapter 15: Treatment of Psychological Disorders

Web Site	Web Address (URL)
15.1 Online Dictionary of Mental Health	http://www.shef.ac.uk/~psysc/psychotherapy/index.html
15.2 The Counseling Web	http://seamonkey.ed.asu.edu/~gail/index.htm
15.3 The Albert Ellis Institute	http://www.rebt.org/
15.4 The Effectiveness of Psychotherapy: The *Consumer Reports* Study	http://www.apa.org/journals/seligman.html
15.5 Dr. Bob's Psychopharmacology Tips	http://www.dr-bob.org/tips/

Chapter 16: Social Behavior

Web Site	Web Address (URL)
16.1 Social Psychology Network	http://www.socialpsychology.org/
16.2 Y? The National Forum on People's Differences Home Page	http://www.yforum.com/index.html
16.3 Living in a Social World	http://miavx1.muohio.edu/~shermarc/p324.htmlx
16.4 Influence at Work: The Psychology of Persuasion	http://www.influenceatwork.com/index.html
16.5 The Psychology of Cyberspace	http://www.rider.edu/users/suler/psycyber/psycyber.html

Glossary

A

Absolute refractory period The minimum length of time after an action potential during which another action potential cannot begin.

Achievement motive The need to master difficult challenges, to outperform others, and to meet high standards of excellence.

Achievement tests Tests that gauge a person's mastery and knowledge of various subjects.

Acquired immune deficiency syndrome (AIDS) A disorder in which the immune system is gradually weakened and eventually disabled by the human immunodeficiency virus (HIV).

Acquisition The formation of a new conditioned response tendency.

Action potential A brief change in a neuron's electrical charge.

Adaptation An inherited characteristic that increased in a population (through natural selection) because it helped solve a problem of survival or reproduction during the time it emerged.

Additive color mixing Formation of colors by superimposing lights, putting more light in the mixture than exists in any one light by itself.

Adoption studies Research studies that assess hereditary influence by examining the resemblance between adopted children and both their biological and their adoptive parents.

Afferent nerve fibers Axons that carry information inward to the central nervous system from the periphery of the body.

Afterimage A visual image that persists after a stimulus is removed.

Age of viability The age at which a baby can survive in the event of a premature birth.

Aggression Any behavior that is intended to hurt someone, either physically or verbally.

Agonist A chemical that mimics the action of a neurotransmitter.

Agoraphobia A fear of going out to public places.

Alcohol A variety of beverages containing ethyl alcohol.

Amnesia A significant memory loss that is too extensive to be due to normal forgetting. See also *Anterograde amnesia, Psychogenic amnesia, Retrograde amnesia.*

Anecdotal evidence Personal stories about specific incidents and experiences.

Animism The belief that all things are living.

Anorexia nervosa Eating disorder characterized by intense fear of gaining weight, disturbed body image, refusal to maintain normal weight, and dangerous measures to lose weight.

Antagonist A chemical that opposes the action of a neurotransmitter.

Antecedents In behavior modification, events that typically precede the target response.

Anterograde amnesia Loss of memories for events that occur after a head injury.

Antianxiety drugs Medications that relieve tension, apprehension, and nervousness.

Antidepressant drugs Medications that gradually elevate mood and help bring people out of a depression.

Antipsychotic drugs Medications used to gradually reduce psychotic symptoms, including hyperactivity, mental confusion, hallucinations, and delusions.

Anxiety disorders A class of disorders marked by feelings of excessive apprehension and anxiety.

Applied psychology The branch of psychology concerned with everyday, practical problems.

Approach-approach conflict A conflict situation in which a choice must be made between two attractive goals.

Approach-avoidance conflict A conflict situation in which a choice must be made about whether to pursue a single goal that has both attractive and unattractive aspects.

Aptitude tests Psychological tests used to assess talent for specific types of mental ability.

Archetypes According to Jung, emotionally charged images and thought forms that have universal meaning.

Argument One or more premises used to provide support for a conclusion.

Assumptions Premises for which no proof or evidence is offered.

Attachment A close, emotional bond of affection between infants and their caregivers.

Attention Focusing awareness on a narrowed range of stimuli or events.

Attitudes Orientations that locate objects of thought on dimensions of judgment.

Attributions Inferences that people draw about the causes of events, others' behavior, and their own behavior.

Autonomic nervous system (ANS) The system of nerves that connect to the heart, blood vessels, smooth muscles, and glands.

Availability heuristic Basing the estimated probability of an event on the ease with which relevant instances come to mind.

Aversion therapy A behavior therapy in which an aversive stimulus is paired with a stimulus that elicits an undesirable response.

Avoidance-avoidance conflict A conflict situation in which a choice must be made between two unattractive goals.

Avoidance learning Learning that has occurred when an organism engages in a response that prevents aversive stimulation from occurring.

Axon A long, thin fiber that transmits signals away from the neuron cell body to other neurons, or to muscles or glands.

B

Basilar membrane A structure that runs the length of the cochlea in the inner ear and holds the auditory receptors, called hair cells.

Behavior Any overt (observable) response or activity by an organism.

Behavior modification A systematic approach to changing behavior through the application of the principles of conditioning.

Behavior therapies Application of the principles of learning to direct efforts to change clients' maladaptive behaviors.

Behavioral contract A written agreement outlining a promise to adhere to the contingencies of a behavior modification program.

Behaviorism A theoretical orientation based on the premise that scientific psychology should study only observable behavior.

Belief perseverance The tendency to hang onto beliefs in the face of contradictory evidence.

Bilingualism The acquisition of two languages that use different speech sounds, vocabularies, and grammatical rules.

Binocular depth cues Clues about distance based on the differing views of the two eyes.

Biological rhythms Periodic fluctuations in physiological functioning.

Biomedical therapies Physiological interventions intended to reduce symptoms associated with psychological disorders.

Biopsychosocial model A model of illness that holds that physical illness is caused by a complex interaction of biological, psychological, and sociocultural factors.

Bipolar disorder (formerly known as manic-depressive disorder) Mood disorder marked by the experience of both depressed and manic periods.

Bisexuals Persons who seek emotional-sexual relationships with members of either sex.

Bulimia nervosa Eating disorder characterized by habitually engaging in out-of-control overeating followed by unhealthy compensatory efforts, such as self-induced vomiting, fasting, abuse of laxatives and diuretics, and excessive exercise.

Bystander effect A paradoxical social phenomenon in which people are less likely to provide needed help when they are in groups than when they are alone.

C

Cannabis The hemp plant from which marijuana, hashish, and THC are derived.

Case study An in-depth investigation of an individual subject.

Catastrophic thinking Unrealistically pessimistic appraisals of stress that exaggerate the magnitude of one's problems.

Catatonic schizophrenia A type of schizophrenia marked by striking motor disturbances, ranging from muscular rigidity to random motor activity.

Central nervous system (CNS) The brain and the spinal cord.

Centration The tendency to focus on just one feature of a problem, neglecting other important aspects.

Cephalocaudal trend The head-to-foot direction of motor development.

Cerebral cortex The convoluted outer layer of the cerebrum.

Cerebral hemispheres The right and left halves of the cerebrum.

Channel The medium through which a message is sent.

Chromosomes Threadlike strands of DNA (deoxyribonucleic acid) molecules that carry genetic information.

Chunk A group of familiar stimuli stored as a single unit.

Circadian rhythms The 24-hour biological cycles found in humans and many other species.

Classical conditioning A type of learning in which a neutral stimulus acquires the ability to evoke a response that was originally evoked by another stimulus.

Client-centered therapy An insight therapy that emphasizes providing a supportive emotional climate for clients, who play a major role in determining the pace and direction of their therapy.

Clinical psychologists Psychologists who specialize in the diagnosis and treatment of psychological disorders and everyday behavioral problems.

Clinical psychology The branch of psychology concerned with the diagnosis and treatment of psychological problems and disorders.

Cochlea The fluid-filled, coiled tunnel in the inner ear that contains the receptors for hearing.

Coefficient of determination The percentage of variation in one variable that can be predicted based on the other variable.

Cognition The mental processes involved in acquiring knowledge.

Cognitive development Transitions in youngsters' patterns of thinking, including reasoning, remembering, and problem solving.

Cognitive dissonance A psychological state that exists when related cognitions are inconsistent.

Cognitive therapy An insight therapy that emphasizes recognizing and changing negative thoughts and maladaptive beliefs.

Collective unconscious According to Jung, a storehouse of latent memory traces inherited from people's ancestral past.

Collectivism Putting group goals ahead of personal goals and defining one's identity in terms of the groups one belongs to.

Color blindness Deficiency in the ability to distinguish among colors.

Comorbidity The coexistence of two or more disorders.

Companionate love Warm, trusting, tolerant affection for another whose life is deeply intertwined with one's own.

Comparitors People, objects, events, and other standards that are used as a baseline for comparisons in making judgments.

Compensation According to Adler, efforts to overcome imagined or real inferiorities by developing one's abilities.

Complementary colors Pairs of colors that produce gray tones when added together.

Concordance rate The percentage of twin pairs or other pairs of relatives that exhibit the same disorder.

Concurrent schedules of reinforcement Two or more reinforcement schedules that operate simultaneously and independently, each for a different response.

Conditioned reinforcers. See *Secondary reinforcers*.

Conditioned response (CR) A learned reaction to a conditioned stimulus that occurs because of previous conditioning.

Conditioned stimulus (CS) A previously neutral stimulus that has, through conditioning, acquired the capacity to evoke a conditioned response.

Cones Specialized visual receptors that play a key role in daylight vision and color vision.

Confirmation bias The tendency to seek information that supports one's decisions and beliefs while ignoring disconfirming information.

Conflict A state that occurs when two or more incompatible motivations or behavioral impulses compete for expression.

Conformity The tendency for people to yield to real or imagined social pressure.

Confounding of variables A condition that exists whenever two variables are linked together in a way that makes it difficult to sort out their independent effects.

Conjunction fallacy An error that occurs when people estimate that the odds of two uncertain events happening together are greater than the odds of either event happening alone.

Connectionist models See *Parallel distributed processing (PDP) models*

Conscious Whatever one is aware of at a particular point in time.

Consciousness One's awareness of internal and external stimuli.

Conservation Piaget's term for the awareness that physical quantities remain constant in spite of changes in their shape or appearance.

Consolidation A hypothetical process involving the gradual conversion of information into durable memory codes stored in long-term memory.

Construct validity The extent to which there is evidence that a test measures a particular hypothetical construct.

Constructive coping Relatively healthful efforts that people make to deal with stressful events.

Content validity The degree to which the content of a test is representative of the domain it's supposed to cover.

Continuous reinforcement Reinforcing every instance of a designated response.

Control group Subjects in a study who do not receive the special treatment given to the experimental group.

Convergent thinking Narrowing down a list of alternatives to converge on a single correct answer.

Conversion disorder A somatoform disorder characterized by a significant loss of physical function (with no apparent organic basis), usually in a single organ system.

Coping Active efforts to master, reduce, or tolerate the demands created by stress.

Corpus callosum The structure that connects the two cerebral hemispheres.

Correlation The extent to which two variables are related to each other.

Correlation coefficient A numerical index of the degree of relationship between two variables.

Counseling psychologists Psychologists who specialize in the treatment of everyday adjustment problems.

Creativity The generation of ideas that are original, novel, and useful.

Criterion-related validity Test validity that is estimated by correlating subjects' scores on a test with their scores on an independent criterion (another measure) of the trait assessed by the test.

Critical period A limited time span in the development of an organism when it is optimal for certain capacities to emerge because the organism is especially responsive to certain experiences.

Critical thinking The use of cognitive skills and strategies that increase the probability of a desired outcome.

Cross-sectional study A research design in which investigators compare groups of subjects of differing age who are observed at a single point in time.

Culture The widely shared customs, beliefs, values, norms, institutions, and other products of a community that are transmitted socially across generations.

Culture-bound disorders Abnormal syndromes found only in a few cultural groups.

Cumulative recorder A graphic record of reinforcement and responding in a Skinner box as a function of time.

D

Dark adaptation The process in which the eyes become more sensitive to light in low illumination.

Data collection techniques Procedures for making empirical observations and measurements.

Decay theory The idea that forgetting occurs because memory traces fade with time.

Decision making The process of evaluating alternatives and making choices among them.

Declarative memory system Memory for factual information.

Defense mechanisms Largely unconscious reactions that protect a person from unpleasant emotions such as anxiety and guilt.

Deinstitutionalization Transferring the treatment of mental illness from inpatient institutions to community-based facilities that emphasize outpatient care.

Delusions False beliefs that are maintained even though they are clearly out of touch with reality.

Dementia An abnormal condition marked by multiple cognitive defects that include memory impairment.

Dendrites Branchlike parts of a neuron that are specialized to receive information.

Dependent variable In an experiment, the variable that is thought to be affected by the manipulation of the independent variable.

Depth perception Interpretation of visual cues that indicate how near or far away objects are.

Descriptive statistics Statistics that are used to organize and summarize data.

Development The sequence of age-related changes that occur as a person progresses from conception to death.

Developmental norms The average age at which individuals display various behaviors and abilities.

Deviation IQ scores Scores that locate subjects precisely within the normal distribution, using the standard deviation as the unit of measurement.

Diagnosis Distinguishing one illness from another.

Discrimination Behaving differently, usually unfairly, toward the members of a group.

Discriminative stimuli Cues that influence operant behavior by indicating the probable consequences (reinforcement or nonreinforcement) of a response.

Dishabituation An increase in the strength of a habituated response elicited by a new stimulus.

Disorganized schizophrenia A type of schizophrenia in which particularly severe deterioration of adaptive behavior is seen.

Displacement Diverting emotional feelings (usually anger) from their original source to a substitute target.

Display rules Cultural norms that regulate the appropriate expressions of emotions.

Dissociation A splitting off of mental processes into two separate, simultaneous streams of awareness.

Dissociative amnesia A sudden loss of memory for important personal information that is too extensive to be due to normal forgetting.

Dissociative disorders A class of disorders in which people lose contact with portions of their consciousness or memory, resulting in disruptions in their sense of identity.

Dissociative fugue A disorder in which people lose their memory for their entire lives along with their sense of personal identity.

Dissociative identity disorder A type of dissociative disorder characterized by the coexistence in one person of two or more largely complete, and usually very different, personalities. Also called multiple-personality disorder.

Distal stimuli Stimuli that lie in the distance (that is, in the world outside the body).

Divergent thinking Trying to expand the range of alternatives by generating many possible solutions.

Door-in-the-face technique Making a large request that is likely to be turned down as a way to increase the chances that people will agree to a smaller request later.

Double-blind procedure A research strategy in which neither subjects nor experimenters know which subjects are in the experimental or control groups.

Dream analysis A psychoanalytic technique in which the therapist interprets the symbolic meaning of the client's dreams.

Dual-coding theory Paivio's theory that memory is enhanced by forming semantic and visual codes, since either can lead to recall.

E

Eating disorders Severe disturbances in eating behavior characterized by preoccupation with weight concerns and unhealthy efforts to control weight.

Efferent nerve fibers Axons that carry information outward from the central nervous system to the periphery of the body.

Ego According to Freud, the decision-making component of personality that operates according to the reality principle.

Egocentrism A limited ability to share another person's viewpoint.

Elaboration Linking a stimulus to other information at the time of encoding.

Electrocardiograph (EKG) A device that records the contractions of the heart.

Electroconvulsive therapy (ECT) A biomedical treatment in which electric shock is used to produce a cortical seizure accompanied by convulsions.

Electroencephalograph (EEG) A device that monitors the electrical activity of the brain over time by means of recording electrodes attached to the surface of the scalp.

Electromyograph (EMG) A device that records muscular activity and tension.

Electrooculograph (EOG) A device that records eye movements.

Elicit To draw out or bring forth.

Embryonic stage The second stage of prenatal development, lasting from two weeks until the end of the second month.

Emit To send forth.

Emotion A subjective conscious experience (the cognitive component) accompanied by bodily arousal (the physiological component) and by characteristic overt expressions (the behavioral component).

Empiricism The premise that knowledge should be acquired through observation.

Encoding Forming a memory code.

Encoding specificity principle The idea that the value of a retrieval cue depends on how well it corresponds to the memory code.

Endocrine system A group of glands that secrete chemicals into the bloodstream that help control bodily functioning.

Endorphins The entire family of internally produced chemicals that resemble opiates in structure and effects.

Episodic memory system Chronological, or temporally dated, recollections of personal experiences.

Escape learning A type of learning in which an organism acquires a response that decreases or ends some aversive stimulation.

Etiology The apparent causation and developmental history of an illness.

Evolutionary psychology Theoretical perspective that examines behavioral processes in terms of their adaptive value for a species over the course of many generations.

Experiment A research method in which the investigator manipulates a variable under carefully controlled conditions and observes whether any changes occur in a second variable as a result.

Experimental group The subjects in a study who receive some special treatment in regard to the independent variable.

Experimenter bias A phenomenon that occurs when a researcher's expectations or preferences about the outcome of a study influence the results obtained.

Explicit memory Intentional recollection of previous experiences.

External attributions Ascribing the causes of behavior to situational demands and environmental constraints.

Extinction The gradual weakening and disappearance of a conditioned response tendency.

Extraneous variables Any variables other than the independent variable that seem likely to influence the dependent variable in a specific study.

Extraverts People who tend to be interested in the external world of people and things.

F

Family studies Scientific studies in which researchers assess hereditary influence by examining blood relatives to see how much they resemble each other on a specific trait.

Farsightedness A visual deficiency in which distant objects are seen clearly but close objects appear blurry.

Fast mapping The process by which children map a word onto an underlying concept after only one exposure to the word.

Feature analysis The process of detecting specific elements in visual input and assembling them into a more complex form.

Feature detectors Neurons that respond selectively to very specific features of more complex stimuli.

Fetal alcohol syndrome A collection of congenital (inborn) problems associated with excessive alcohol use during pregnancy.

Fetal stage The third stage of prenatal development, lasting from two months through birth.

Field dependence-independence Individuals' tendency to rely primarily on external versus internal frames of reference when orienting themselves in space.

Fitness The reproductive success (number of descendants) of an individual organism relative to the average reproductive success of the population.

Fixation According to Freud, failure to move forward from one psychosexual stage to another as expected.

Fixed-interval (FI) schedule A reinforcement schedule in which the reinforcer is given for the first response that occurs after a fixed time interval has elapsed.

Fixed-ratio (FR) schedule A reinforcement schedule in which the reinforcer is given after a fixed number of nonreinforced responses.

Flashbulb memories Unusually vivid and detailed recollections of momentous events.

Foot-in-the-door technique Getting people to agree to a small request to increase the chances that they will agree to a larger request later.

Forebrain The largest and most complicated region of the brain, encompassing a variety of structures, including the thalamus, hypothalamus, limbic system, and cerebrum.

Forgetting curve A graph showing retention and forgetting over time.

Fovea A tiny spot in the center of the retina that contains only cones; visual acuity is greatest at this spot.

Free association A psychoanalytic technique in which clients spontaneously express their thoughts and feelings exactly as they occur, with as little censorship as possible.

Frequency distribution An orderly arrangement of scores indicating the frequency of each score or group of scores.

Frequency polygon A line figure used to present data from a frequency distribution.

Frustration The feeling that people experience in any situation in which their pursuit of some goal is thwarted.

Functional fixedness The tendency to perceive an item only in terms of its most common use.

Functionalism A school of psychology based on the belief that psychology should investigate the function or purpose of consciousness, rather than its structure.

Fundamental attribution error Observers' bias in favor of internal attributions in explaining others' behavior.

G

Galvanic skin response (GSR) An increase in the electrical conductivity of the skin that occurs when sweat glands increase their activity.

Gambler's fallacy The belief that the odds of a chance event increase if the event hasn't occurred recently.

Gender Culturally constructed distinctions between masculinity and femininity.

Gender differences Actual disparities between the sexes in typical behavior or average ability.

Gender roles Expectations about what is appropriate behavior for each sex.

Gender stereotypes Widely held beliefs about males' and females' abilities, personality traits, and behavior.

General adaptation syndrome Selye's model of the body's stress response, consisting of three stages: alarm, resistance, and exhaustion.

Generalized anxiety disorder A psychological disorder marked by a chronic, high level of anxiety that is not tied to any specific threat.

Genes DNA segments that serve as the key functional units in hereditary transmission.

Germinal stage The first phase of prenatal development, encompassing the first two weeks after conception.

Glucose A simple sugar that is an important source of energy.

Glucostats Neurons sensitive to glucose in the surrounding fluid.

Group Two or more individuals who interact and are interdependent.

Group cohesiveness The strength of the liking relationships linking group members to each other and to the group itself.

Group polarization A phenomenon that occurs when group discussion strengthens a group's dominant point of view and produces a shift toward a more extreme decision in that direction.

Group therapy The simultaneous treatment of several clients in a group.

Groupthink A process in which members of a cohesive group emphasize concurrence at the expense of critical thinking in arriving at a decision.

Gustatory system The sensory system for taste.

H

Habituation A gradual reduction in the strength of a response when a stimulus event is presented repeatedly.

Hallucinations Sensory perceptions that occur in the absence of a real, external stimulus, or gross distortions of perceptual input.

Hallucinogens A diverse group of drugs that have powerful effects on mental and emotional functioning, marked most prominently by distortions in sensory and perceptual experience.

Health psychology The subfield of psychology concerned with how psychosocial factors relate to the promotion and maintenance of health and with the causation, prevention, and treatment of illness.

Hedonistic adaptation An effect that occurs when the mental scale that people use to judge the pleasantness-unpleasantness of their experiences shifts so that their neutral point, or baseline for comparison, changes.

Heritability ratio An estimate of the proportion of trait variability in a population that is determined by variations in genetic inheritance.

Heterosexuals Persons who seek emotional-sexual relationships with members of the other sex.

Heuristic A strategy, guiding principle, or rule of thumb used in solving problems or making decisions.

Hierarchy of needs Maslow's systematic arrangement of needs according to priority, which assumes that basic needs must be met before less basic needs are aroused.

Higher-order conditioning A type of conditioning in which a conditioned stimulus functions as if it were an unconditioned stimulus.

Hindbrain The part of the brain that includes the cerebellum and two structures found in the lower part of the brainstem: the medulla and the pons.

Hindsight bias The tendency to mold one's interpretation of the past to fit how events actually turned out.

Histogram A bar graph that presents data from a frequency distribution.

Homosexuals Persons who seek emotional-sexual relationships with members of the same sex.

Hormones The chemical substances released by the endocrine glands.

Humanism A theoretical orientation that emphasizes the unique qualities of humans, especially their freedom and their potential for personal growth.

Hypnosis A systematic procedure that typically produces a heightened state of suggestibility.

Hypochondriasis A somatoform disorder characterized by excessive preoccupation with health concerns and incessant worry about developing physical illnesses.

Hypothalamus A structure found near the base of the forebrain that is involved in the regulation of basic biological needs.

Hypothesis A tentative statement about the relationship between two or more variables.

I

Id According to Freud, the primitive, instinctive component of personality that operates according to the pleasure principle.

Identification Bolstering self-esteem by forming an imaginary or real alliance with some person or group.

Illusory correlation A misperception that occurs when people estimate that they have encountered more confirmations of an association between social traits than they have actually seen.

Immune response The body's defensive reaction to invasion by bacteria, viral agents, or other foreign substances.

Implicit memory Type of memory apparent when retention is exhibited on a task that does not require intentional remembering.

Impossible figures Objects that can be represented in two-dimensional pictures but cannot exist in three-dimensional space.

Inclusive fitness The sum of an individual's own reproductive success plus the effects the organism has on the reproductive success of related others.

Incongruence The degree of disparity between one's self-concept and one's actual experience.

Independent variable In an experiment, a condition or event that an experimenter varies in order to see its impact on another variable.

Individualism Putting personal goals ahead of group goals and defining one's identity in terms of personal attributes rather than group memberships.

Inferential statistics Statistics that are used to interpret data and draw conclusions.

Ingroup The group that people belong to and identify with.

Insanity A legal status indicating that a person cannot be held responsible for his or her actions because of mental illness.

Insight In problem solving, the sudden discovery of the correct solution following incorrect attempts based primarily on trial and error.

Insight therapies Psychotherapy methods characterized by verbal interactions intended to enhance clients' self-knowledge and thus promote healthful changes in personality and behavior.

Insomnia Chronic problems in getting adequate sleep.

Intelligence quotient (IQ) A child's mental age divided by chronological age, multiplied by 100.

Intelligence tests Psychological tests that measure general mental ability.

Interference theory The idea that people forget information because of competition from other material.

Intermittent reinforcement A reinforcement schedule in which a designated response is reinforced only some of the time.

Internal attributions Ascribing the causes of behavior to personal dispositions, traits, abilities, and feelings.

Internet addiction Spending an inordinate amount of time on the Internet and being unable to control online use.

Interpersonal attraction Positive feelings toward another.

Interpretation In psychoanalysis, the therapist's attempts to explain the inner significance of the client's thoughts, feelings, memories, and behaviors.

Introspection Careful, systematic observation of one's own conscious experience.

Introverts People who tend to be preoccupied with the internal world of their own thoughts, feelings, and experiences.

Involuntary commitment A civil proceeding in which people are hospitalized in psychiatric facilities against their will.

Irreversibility The inability to envision reversing an action.

J

Journal A periodical that publishes technical and scholarly material, usually in a narrowly defined area of inquiry.

K

Kinesthetic system The sensory system that monitors the positions of the various parts of one's body.

L

Language A set of symbols that convey meaning, and rules for combining those symbols, that can be used to generate an infinite variety of messages.

Language acquisition device (LAD) An innate mechanism or process that facilitates the learning of language.

Latent content According to Freud, the hidden or disguised meaning of the events in a dream.

Learning A relatively durable change in behavior or knowledge that is due to experience.

Lens The transparent eye structure that focuses the light rays falling on the retina.

Levels-of-processing theory The theory holding that deeper levels of mental processing result in longer-lasting memory codes.

Lie detector See *Polygraph*.

Life changes Any noticeable alterations in one's living circumstances that require readjustment.

Light adaptation The process whereby the eyes become less sensitive to light in high illumination.

Limbic system A densely connected network of structures roughly located along the border between the cerebral cortex and deeper subcortical areas.

Linguistic relativity The theory that one's language determines the nature of one's thought.

Link method Forming a mental image of items to be remembered in a way that links them together.

Lithium A chemical used to control mood swings in patients with bipolar mood disorders.

Long-term memory (LTM) An unlimited capacity store that can hold information over lengthy periods of time.

Longitudinal study A research design in which investigators observe one group of subjects repeatedly over a period of time.

Lowball technique Getting someone to commit to an attractive proposition before revealing the hidden costs.

M

Major depressive disorder Mood disorder characterized by persistent feelings of sadness and despair and a loss of interest in previous sources of pleasure.

Manifest content According to Freud, the plot of a dream at a surface level.

Matching hypothesis The idea that males and females of approximately equal physical attractiveness are likely to select each other as partners.

Matching law The fact that, under concurrent schedules of reinforcement, organisms' relative rate of responding to each alternative tends to match each alternative's relative rate of reinforcement.

Maturation Development that reflects the gradual unfolding of one's genetic blueprint.

Mean The arithmetic average of the scores in a distribution.

Mean length of utterance (MLU) The average length of children's spoken statements (measured in phonemes).

Median The score that falls exactly in the center of a distribution of scores.

Medical model The view that it is useful to think of abnormal behavior as a disease.

Meditation A family of mental exercises in which a conscious attempt is made to focus attention in a nonanalytical way.

Menarche The first occurrence of menstruation.

Mental age In intelligence testing, a score that indicates that a child displays the mental ability typical of a child of that chronological (actual) age.

Mental hospital A medical institution specializing in providing inpatient care for psychological disorders.

Mental set Persisting in using problem-solving strategies that have worked in the past.

Message The information transmitted by a source.

Metalinguistic awareness The ability to reflect on the use of language.

Method of loci A mnemonic device that involves taking an imaginary walk along a familiar path where images of items to be remembered are associated with certain locations.

Midbrain The segment of the brain stem that lies between the hindbrain and the forebrain.

Midlife crisis A difficult, turbulent period of doubts and reappraisal of one's life.

Misinformation effect Phenomenon that occurs when participants' recall of an event they witnessed is altered by introducing misleading postevent information.

Mnemonic devices Strategies for enhancing memory.

Mode The score that occurs most frequently in a distribution.

Model A person whose behavior is observed by another.

Monocular depth cues Clues about distance based on the image from either eye alone.

Mood disorders A class of disorders marked by emotional disturbances of varied kinds that may spill over to disrupt physical, perceptual, social, and thought processes.

Morphemes The smallest units of meaning in a language.

Motivated forgetting Purposeful suppression of memories.

Motivation Goal-directed behavior.

Motor development The progression of muscular coordination required for physical activities.

Multiple-personality disorder See *Dissociative identity disorder*.

N

Narcotics (opiates) Drugs derived from opium that are capable of relieving pain.

Natural selection Principle stating that heritable characteristics that provide a survival or reproductive advantage are more likely than alternative characteristics to be passed on to subsequent generations and thus come to be "selected" over time.

Naturalistic observation A descriptive research method in which the researcher engages in careful, usually prolonged, observation of behavior without intervening directly with the subjects.

Nearsightedness A visual deficiency in which close objects are seen clearly but distant objects appear blurry.

Need for self-actualization The need to fulfill one's potential.

Negative reinforcement The strengthening of a response because it is followed by the removal of an aversive (unpleasant) stimulus.

Negative symptoms Schizophrenic symptoms that involve behavioral deficits, such as flattened emotions, social withdrawal, apathy, impaired attention, and poverty of speech.

Negatively skewed distribution A distribution in which most scores pile up at the high end of the scale.

Neurons Individual cells in the nervous system that receive, integrate, and transmit information.

Neurotransmitters Chemicals that transmit information from one neuron to another.

Non-REM (NREM) sleep Sleep stages 1 through 4, which are marked by an absence of rapid eye movements, relatively little dreaming, and varied EEG activity.

Nonsense syllables Consonant-vowel-consonant arrangements that do not correspond to words.

Normal distribution A symmetric, bell-shaped curve that represents the pattern in which many characteristics are dispersed in the population.

Null hypothesis In inferential statistics, the assumption that there is no true relationship between the variables being observed.

O

Obedience A form of compliance that occurs when people follow direct commands, usually from someone in a position of authority.

Object permanence Recognizing that objects continue to exist even when they are no longer visible.

Observational learning A type of learning that occurs when an organism's responding is influenced by the observation of others, who are called models.

Obsessive-compulsive disorder (OCD) A type of anxiety disorder marked by persistent, uncontrollable intrusions of unwanted thoughts (obsessions) and urges to engage in senseless rituals (compulsions).

Oedipal complex According to Freud, children's manifestation of erotically tinged desires for their opposite-sex parent, accompanied by feelings of hostility toward their same-sex parent.

Olfactory system The sensory system for smell.

Operant conditioning A form of learning in which voluntary responses come to be controlled by their consequences.

Operational definition A definition that describes the actions or operations that will be made to measure or control a variable.

Opiates. See *Narcotics*.

Optical illusion An apparently inexplicable discrepancy between the appearance of a visual stimulus and its physical reality.

Optimal foraging theory The idea that the food-seeking behaviors of many animals maximize the nutrition gained in relation to the energy expended to locate, secure, and consume various foods.

Optimism A general tendency to expect good outcomes.

Orgasm The release of sexual tension that occurs when arousal reaches its peak intensity and is discharged in a series of muscular contractions that pulsate through the pelvic area.

Outgroup People who are not part of the ingroup.

Overextension Using a word incorrectly to describe a wider set of objects or actions than it is meant to.

Overlearning Continued rehearsal of material after one first appears to have mastered it.

Overregularization In children, incorrect generalization of grammatical rules to irregular cases where they do not apply.

P

Panic disorder A type of anxiety disorder characterized by recurrent attacks of overwhelming anxiety that usually occur suddenly and unexpectedly.

Parallel distributed processing (PDP) models Models of memory that assume cognitive processes depend on patterns of activation in highly interconnected computational networks that resemble neural networks. Also called connectionist models.

Parallel processing Simultaneously extracting different kinds of information from the same input.

Paranoid schizophrenia A type of schizophrenia that is dominated by delusions of persecution along with delusions of grandeur.

Parental investment What each sex invests—in terms of time, energy, survival risk, and forgone opportunities—to produce and nurture offspring.

Participants See *Subjects*.

Passionate love A complete absorption in another that includes tender sexual feelings and the agony and ecstasy of intense emotion.

Pavlovian conditioning. See *Classical conditioning*.

Percentile score A figure that indicates the percentage of people who score below the score one has obtained.

Perception The selection, organization, and interpretation of sensory input.

Perceptual constancy A tendency to experience a stable perception in the face of continually changing sensory input.

Perceptual hypothesis An inference about which distal stimuli could be responsible for the proximal stimuli sensed.

Perceptual set A readiness to perceive a stimulus in a particular way.

Peripheral nervous system All those nerves that lie outside the brain and spinal cord.

Person perception The process of forming impressions of others.

Personality An individual's unique constellation of consistent behavioral traits.

Personality tests Psychological tests that measure various aspects of personality, including motives, interests, values, and attitudes.

Personality trait A durable disposition to behave in a particular way in a variety of situations.

Phi phenomenon The illusion of movement created by presenting visual stimuli in rapid succession.

Phobias Irrational fears of specific objects or situations.

Phobic disorder A type of anxiety disorder marked by a persistent and irrational fear of an object or situation that presents no realistic danger.

Phonemes The smallest units of sound in a spoken language.

Physical dependence The condition that exists when a person must continue to take a drug to avoid withdrawal illness.

Pictorial depth cues Clues about distance that can be given in a flat picture.

Pituitary gland The "master gland" of the endocrine system; it releases a great variety of hormones that fan out through the body, stimulating actions in the other endocrine glands.

Place theory The idea that perception of pitch corresponds to the vibration of different portions, or places, along the basilar membrane.

Placebo effects The fact that subjects' expectations can lead them to experience some change even though they receive an empty, fake, or ineffectual treatment.

Placenta A structure that allows oxygen and nutrients to pass into the fetus from the mother's bloodstream and bodily wastes to pass out to the mother.

Pleasure principle According to Freud, the principle upon which the id operates, demanding immediate gratification of its urges.

Polygenic traits Characteristics that are influenced by more than one pair of genes.

Polygraph A device that records autonomic fluctuations while a subject is questioned, in an effort to determine whether the subject is telling the truth.

Polygyny A mating system in which each male seeks to mate with multiple females, while each female mates with only one male.

Population The larger collection of animals or people from which a sample is drawn and that researchers want to generalize about.

Positive reinforcement Reinforcement that occurs when a response is strengthened because it is followed by the presentation of a rewarding stimulus.

Positive symptoms Schizophrenic symptoms that involve behavioral excesses or peculiarities, such as hallucinations, delusions, bizarre behavior, and wild flights of ideas.

Positively skewed distribution A distribution in which scores pile up at the low end of the scale.

Postsynaptic potential (PSP) A voltage change at the receptor site on a postsynaptic cell membrane.

Preconscious According to Freud, the level of awareness that contains material just beneath the surface of conscious awareness that can easily be retrieved.

Prejudice A negative attitude held toward members of a group.

Premises The reasons presented to persuade someone that a conclusion is true or probably true.

Prenatal period The period from conception to birth, usually encompassing nine months of pregnancy.

Pressure Expectations or demands that one behave in a certain way.

Primary reinforcers Events that are inherently reinforcing because they satisfy biological needs.

Primary sex characteristics The sexual structures necessary for reproduction.

Proactive interference A memory problem that occurs when previously learned information interferes with the retention of new information.

Problem solving Active efforts to discover what must be done to achieve a goal that is not readily available.

Procedural memory system The repository of memories for actions, skills, and operations.

Prognosis A forecast about the probable course of an illness.

Projection Attributing one's own thoughts, feelings, or motives to another.

Projective tests Psychological tests that ask subjects to respond to vague, ambiguous stimuli in ways that may reveal the subjects' needs, feelings, and personality traits.

Proximal stimuli The stimulus energies that impinge directly on sensory receptors.

Proximodistal trend The center-outward direction of motor development.

Psychiatrists Physicians who specialize in the diagnosis and treatment of psychological disorders.

Psychoactive drugs Chemical substances that modify mental, emotional, or behavioral functioning.

Psychoanalysis An insight therapy that emphasizes the recovery of unconscious conflicts, motives, and defenses through techniques such as free association and transference.

Psychoanalytic theory A theory developed by Freud that attempts to explain personality, motivation, and mental disorders by focusing on unconscious determinants of behavior.

Psychodynamic theories All the diverse theories descended from the work of Sigmund Freud that focus on unconscious mental forces.

Psychogenic amnesia A sudden loss of memory for important personal information that is too extensive to be due to normal forgetting.

Psychological dependence The condition that exists when a person must continue to take a drug in order to satisfy intense mental and emotional craving for the drug.

Psychological test A standardized measure of a sample of a person's behavior.

Psychology The science that studies behavior and the physiological and cognitive processes that underlie it, and the profession that applies the accumulated knowledge of this science to practical problems.

Psychopharmacotherapy The treatment of mental disorders with medication.

Psychosexual stages According to Freud, developmental periods with a characteristic sexual focus that leave their mark on adult personality.

Psychosomatic diseases Physical ailments with a genuine organic basis that are caused in part by psychological factors, especially emotional distress.

Puberty The period of early adolescence marked by rapid physical growth and the development of sexual (reproductive) maturity.

Pubescence The two-year span preceding puberty during which the changes leading to physical and sexual maturity take place.

Punishment An event that follows a response that weakens or suppresses the tendency to make that response.

Pupil The opening in the center of the iris that helps regulate the amount of light passing into the rear chamber of the eye.

R

Random assignment The constitution of groups in a study such that all subjects have an equal chance of being assigned to any group or condition.

Rational-emotive therapy An approach to therapy that focuses on altering clients' patterns of irrational thinking to reduce maladaptive emotions and behavior.

Rationalization Creating false but plausible excuses to justify unacceptable behavior.

Reaction formation Behaving in a way that's exactly the opposite of one's true feelings.

Reaction range Genetically determined limits on IQ or other traits.

Reality principle According to Freud, the principle on which the ego operates, which seeks to delay gratification of the id's urges until appropriate outlets and situations can be found.

Recall A memory test that requires subjects to reproduce information on their own without any cues.

Receiver The person to whom a message is sent.

Receptive field of a visual cell The retinal area that, when stimulated, affects the firing of that cell.

Reciprocity Liking those who show that they like you.

Reciprocity norm The rule that people should pay back in kind what they receive from others.

Recognition A memory test that requires subjects to select previously learned information from an array of options.

Refractory period A time following orgasm during which males are largely unresponsive to further stimulation.

Regression A reversion to immature patterns of behavior.

Regression toward the mean Effect that occurs when people who score extremely high or low on some trait are measured a second time and their new score falls closer to the mean (average).

Rehearsal The process of repetitively verbalizing or thinking about information to be stored in memory.

Reification Giving an abstract concept a name and then treating it as though it were a concrete, tangible object.

Reinforcement An event following a response that strengthens the tendency to make that response.

Reinforcement contingencies The circumstances or rules that determine whether responses lead to the presentation of reinforcers.

Relearning A memory test that requires a subject to memorize information a second time to determine how much time or effort is saved by having learned it before.

Reliability The measurement consistency of a test (or of other kinds of measurement techniques).

REM sleep A deep stage of sleep marked by rapid eye movements, high-frequency brain waves, and dreaming.

Replication The repetition of a study to see whether the earlier results are duplicated.

Representativeness heuristic Basing the estimated probability of an event on how similar it is to the typical prototype of that event.

Repression Keeping distressing thoughts and feelings buried in the unconscious.

Research methods Differing approaches to the manipulation and control of variables in empirical studies.

Resistance Largely unconscious defensive maneuvers a client uses to hinder the progress of therapy.

Resistance to extinction In operant conditioning, the phenomenon that occurs when an organism continues to make a response after delivery of the reinforcer for it has been terminated.

Respondent conditioning. See *Classical conditioning.*

Resting potential The stable, negative charge of a neuron when it is inactive.

Retention The proportion of material retained (remembered).

Retina The neural tissue lining the inside back surface of the eye; it absorbs light, processes images, and sends visual information to the brain.

Retinal disparity A cue to the depth based on the fact that objects within 25 feet project images to slightly different locations on the left and right retinas, so the right and left eyes see slightly different views of the object.

Retrieval Recovering information from memory stores.

Retroactive interference A memory problem that occurs when new information impairs the retention of previously learned information.

Retrograde amnesia Loss of memories for events that occurred prior to a head injury.

Reuptake A process in which neurotransmitters are sponged up from the synaptic cleft by the presynaptic membrane.

Reversible figure A drawing that is compatible with two different interpretations that can shift back and forth.

Risky decision making Making choices under conditions of uncertainty.

Rods Specialized visual receptors that play a key role in night vision and peripheral vision.

S

Sample The collection of subjects selected for observation in an empirical study.

Sampling bias A problem that occurs when a sample is not representative of the population from which it is drawn.

Scatter diagram A graph in which paired X and Y scores for each subject are plotted as single points.

Schedule of reinforcement A specific presentation of reinforcers over time.

Schema An organized cluster of knowledge about a particular object or sequence of events.

Schizophrenic disorders A class of psychological disorders marked by disturbances in thought that spill over to affect perceptual, social, and emotional processes.

Secondary (conditioned) reinforcers Stimulus events that acquire reinforcing qualities by being associated with primary reinforcers.

Secondary sex characteristics Physical features that are associated with gender but that are not directly involved in reproduction.

Sedatives Sleep-inducing drugs that tend to decrease central nervous system activation and behavioral activity.

Self-actualizing persons People with exceptionally healthy personalities, marked by continued personal growth.

Self-concept A collection of beliefs about one's own nature, unique qualities, and typical behavior.

Self-efficacy One's belief about one's ability to perform behaviors that should lead to expected outcomes.

Self-esteem A person's overall assessment of her or his personal adequacy or worth.

Self-monitoring The degree to which people attend to and control the impression they make on others in social interactions.

Self-report inventories Personality tests that ask individuals to answer a series of questions about their characteristic behavior.

Self-serving bias The tendency to attribute one's successes to personal factors and one's failures to situational factors.

Semantic memory system General knowledge that is not tied to the time when the information was learned.

Semantic network Concepts joined together by links that show how the concepts are related.

Sensation The stimulation of sense organs.

Sensory adaptation A gradual decline in sensitivity to prolonged stimulation.

Sensory memory The preservation of information in its original sensory form for a brief time, usually only a fraction of a second.

Separation anxiety Emotional distress seen in many infants when they are separated from people with whom they have formed an attachment.

Serial-position effect In memory tests, the fact that subjects show better recall for items at the beginning and end of a list than for items in the middle.

Sex The biologically based categories of male and female.

Sexual orientation A person's preference for emotional and sexual relationships with individuals of the same sex, the other sex, or either sex.

Shaping The reinforcement of closer and closer approximations of a desired response.

Short-term memory (STM) A limited-capacity store that can maintain unrehearsed information for about 20 to 30 seconds.

Skinner box A small enclosure in which an animal can make a specific response that is systematically recorded while the consequences of the response are controlled.

Slow-wave sleep (SWS) Sleep stages 3 and 4, during which low-frequency delta waves become prominent in EEG recordings.

Social comparison theory The idea that people compare themselves with others to understand and evaluate their own behavior.

Social desirability bias A tendency to give socially approved answers to questions about oneself.

Social loafing A reduction in effort by individuals when they work in groups as compared to when they work by themselves.

Social psychology The branch of psychology concerned with the way individuals' thoughts, feelings, and behaviors are influenced by others.

Social schemas Organized clusters of ideas about categories of social events and people.

Social skills training A behavior therapy designed to improve interpersonal skills that emphasizes shaping, modeling, and behavioral rehearsal.

Social support Various types of aid and succor provided by members of one's social networks.

Socialization The acquisition of the norms, roles, and behaviors expected of people in a particular society.

Soma The cell body of a neuron; it contains the nucleus and much of the chemical machinery common to most cells.

Somatic nervous system The system of nerves that connect to voluntary skeletal muscles and to sensory receptors.

Somatization disorder A type of somatoform disorder marked by a history of diverse physical complaints that appear to be psychological in origin.

Somatoform disorders A class of psychological disorders involving physical ailments with no authentic organic basis that are due to psychological factors.

Source The person who sends a communication.

Source monitoring The process of making attributions about the origins of memories.

Source-monitoring error An error that occurs when a memory derived from one source is misattributed to another source.

Split-brain surgery A procedure in which the bundle of fibers that connects the cerebral hemispheres (the corpus callosum) is cut to reduce the severity of epileptic seizures.

Spontaneous recovery In classical conditioning, the reappearance of an extinguished response after a period of nonexposure to the conditioned stimulus.

SQ3R A study system designed to promote effective reading by means of five steps: survey, question, read, recite, and review.

Stage A developmental period during which characteristic patterns of behavior are exhibited and certain capacities become established.

Standard deviation An index of the amount of variability in a set of data.

Standardization The uniform procedures used in the administration and scoring of a test.

Statistical significance The condition that exists when the probability that the observed findings are due to chance is very low.

Statistics The use of mathematics to organize, summarize, and interpret numerical data. See also *Descriptive statistics, Inferential statistics.*

Stereotypes Widely held beliefs that people have certain characteristics because of their membership in a particular group.

Stimulants Drugs that tend to increase central nervous system activation and behavioral activity.

Stimulus contiguity A temporal association between two events.

Stimulus discrimination The phenomenon that occurs when an organism that has learned a response to a specific stimulus does not respond in the same way to stimuli that are similar to the original stimulus.

Stimulus generalization The phenomenon that occurs when an organism that has learned a response to a specific stimulus responds in the same way to new stimuli that are similar to the original stimulus.

Storage Maintaining encoded information in memory over time.

Stress Any circumstances that threaten or are perceived to threaten one's well-being and that thereby tax one's coping abilities.

Striving for superiority According to Adler, the universal drive to adapt, improve oneself, and master life's challenges.

Structuralism A school of psychology based on the notion that the task of psychology is to analyze consciousness into its basic elements and to investigate how these elements are related.

Subjective well-being Individuals' perceptions of their overall happiness and life satisfaction.

Subliminal perception The registration of sensory input without conscious awareness.

Subtractive color mixing Formation of colors by removing some wavelengths of light, leaving less light than was originally there.

Superego According to Freud, the moral component of personality that incorporates social standards about what represents right and wrong.

Survey A descriptive research method in which researchers use questionnaires or interviews to gather information about specific aspects of subjects' behavior.

Synapse A junction where information is transmitted from one neuron to the next.

Synaptic cleft A microscopic gap between the terminal button of a neuron and the cell membrane of another neuron.

Syntax A system of rules that specify how words can be combined into phrases and sentences.

Systematic desensitization A behavior therapy used to reduce clients' anxiety responses through counterconditioning.

T

Tactile system The sensory system for touch.

Tardive dyskinesia A neurological disorder marked by chronic tremors and involuntary spastic movements.

Telegraphic speech Speech that consists mainly of content words; articles, prepositions, and other less critical words are omitted.

Temperament An individual's characteristic mood, activity level, and emotional reactivity.

Terminal buttons Small knobs at the end of axons that secrete chemicals called neurotransmitters.

Test-retest reliability A type of reliability estimated by comparing subjects' scores on two administrations of a test.

Test norms Standards that provide information about where a score on a psychological test ranks in relation to other scores on that test.

Testwiseness The ability to use the characteristics and format of a cognitive test to maximize one's score.

Thalamus A structure in the forebrain through which all sensory information (except smell) must pass to get to the cerebral cortex.

Theory A system of interrelated ideas that is used to explain a set of observations.

Tip-of-the-tongue phenomenon A temporary inability to remember something accompanied by a feeling that it's just out of reach.

Token economy A system for doling out symbolic reinforcers that are exchanged later for a variety of genuine reinforcers.

Tolerance A progressive decrease in a person's responsiveness to a drug.

Top-down processing In form perception, a progression from the whole to the elements.

Transference In therapy, the phenomenon that occurs when clients start relating to their therapists in ways that mimic critical relationships in their lives.

Trial In classical conditioning, any presentation of a stimulus or pair of stimuli.

Trial and error Trying possible solutions sequentially and discarding those that are in error until one works.

Twin studies A research design in which hereditary influence is assessed by comparing the resemblance of identical twins and fraternal twins with respect to a trait.

Type A personality Personality characterized by (1) a strong competitive orientation, (2) impatience and time urgency, and (3) anger and hostility.

Type B personality Personality characterized by relatively relaxed, patient, easygoing, amicable behavior.

U

Unconditioned response (UCR) An unlearned reaction to an unconditioned stimulus that occurs without previous conditioning.

Unconditioned stimulus (UCS) A stimulus that evokes an unconditioned response without previous conditioning.

Unconscious According to Freud, thoughts, memories, and desires that are well below the surface of conscious awareness but that nonetheless exert great influence on behavior.

Underextensions Errors that occur when a child incorrectly uses a word to describe a narrower set of objects or actions than it is meant to.

Undifferentiated schizophrenia A type of schizophrenia marked by idiosyncratic mixtures of schizophrenic symptoms.

V

Validity The ability of a test to measure what it was designed to measure.

Variability The extent to which the scores in a data set tend to vary from each other and from the mean.

Variable-interval (VI) schedule A reinforcement schedule in which the reinforcer is given for the first response after a variable time interval has elapsed.

Variable-ratio (VR) schedule A reinforcement schedule in which the reinforcer is given after a variable number of nonreinforced responses.

Variables Any measurable conditions, events, characteristics, or behaviors that are controlled or observed in a study.

Vasocongestion Engorgement of blood vessels.

Vestibular system The sensory system that responds to gravity and keeps people informed of their body's location in space.

Z

Zygote A one-celled organism formed by the union of a sperm and an egg.

References

Abel, M. H. (1998). Interaction of humor and gender in moderating relationships between stress and outcomes. *Journal of Psychology, 132,* 267–276.

Abi-Dargham, A., Gil, R., Krystal, J., Baldwin, R. M., Seibyl, J. P., Bowers, M., van Dyck, C. H., Charney, D. S., Innis, R. B., & Laruelle, M. (1998). Increased striatal dopamine transmission in schizophrenia: Confirmation in a second cohort. *American Journal of Psychiatry, 155,* 761–767.

Aboud, F. E. (1987). The development of ethnic self-identification and attitudes. In J. S. Phinney & M. J. Rotheram (Eds.), *Children's ethnic socialization: Pluralism and development.* Newbury Park, CA: Sage.

Abramov, I., & Gordon, J. (1994). Color appearance: On seeing red—or yellow, or green, or blue. *Annual Review of Psychology, 45,* 451–485.

Abramson, E. E., & Valene, P. (1991). Media use, dietary restraint, bulimia and attitudes towards obesity: A preliminary study. *British Review of Bulimia Anorexia Nervosa, 5,* 73–76.

Abramson, L. Y., Alloy, L. B., & Metalsky, J. I. (1995). Hopelessness depression. In J. N. Buchanan, & M. E. P. Seligman (Eds.), *Explanatory style.* Hillsdale, NJ: Erlbaum.

Abramson, L. Y., Seligman, M. E. P., & Teasdale, J. (1978). Learned helplessness in humans: Critique and reformulation. *Journal of Abnormal Psychology, 87,* 32–48.

Adams, H. E., Wright, L. W., Jr., & Lohr, B. A. (1996). Is homophobia associated with homosexual arousal? *Journal of Abnormal Psychology, 105,* 440–445.

Adams, J. L. (1980). *Conceptual blockbusting.* San Francisco: W. H. Freeman.

Adams, R. D., & Victor, M. (1993). *Principles of neurology* (5th ed.). New York: McGraw-Hill.

Ader, R., & Cohen, N. (1981). Conditioned immunopharmacologic responses. In R. Ader (Ed.), *Psychoneuroimmunology.* New York: Academic Press.

Ader, R., & Cohen, N. (1984). Behavior and the immune system. In W. D. Gentry (Ed.), *Handbook of behavioral medicine.* New York: Guilford Press.

Ader, R., & Cohen, N. (1993). Psychoneuroimmunology: Conditioning and stress. *Annual Review of Psychology, 44,* 53–85.

Adler, A. (1917). *Study of organ inferiority and its psychical compensation.* New York: Nervous and Mental Diseases Publishing Co.

Adler, A. (1927). *Practice and theory of individual psychology.* New York: Harcourt, Brace & World.

Adler, A. (1964). *Superiority and social interest: A collection of later writings* (Edited by H. L. Ansbacher & R. Ansbacher). New York: Viking.

Adler, L. L. (Ed.). (1993). *International handbook on gender roles.* Westport, CT: Greenwood.

Afshar, M., & Rubin, E. (1999). Clozapine: Psychiatric/primary care interface. *Primary Psychiatry, 6,* 90–104.

Agnoli, F., & Krantz, D. H. (1989). Suppressing natural heuristics by formal instruction: The case of the conjunction fallacy. *Cognitive Psychology, 21,* 515–550.

Agras, W. S., & Berkowitz, R. I. (1999). Behavior therapies. In R. E. Hales, S. C. Yudofsky, & J. A. Talbott (Eds.), *American Psychiatric Press textbook of psychiatry.* Washington, DC: American Psychiatric Press.

Ainsworth, M. D. S., Blehar, M. C., Waters, E., & Wall, S. (1978). *Patterns of attachment: A psychological study of the strange situation.* Hillsdale, NJ: Erlbaum.

Aird, R. B. (1988). The importance of seizure-inducing factors in youth. *Brain Development, 10,* 73.

Akerstedt, T. (1988). Sleepiness as a consequence of shift work. *Sleep, 11,* 17–34.

Akerstedt, T., Hume, K., Minors, D., & Waterhouse, J. (1997). Good sleep—Its timing and physiological sleep characteristics. *Journal of Sleep Research, 6,* 221–229.

Akimoto, S. A., & Sanbonmatsu, D. M. (1999). Differences in self-effacing behavior between European and Japanese Americans: Effect on competence evaluations. *Journal of Cross-Cultural Psychology, 30,* 159–177.

Alcock, J. (1998). *Animal behavior: An evolutionary approach.* Sunderland, MA: Sinauer Associates.

Aldag, R. J., & Fuller, S. R. (1993). Beyond fiasco: A reappraisal of the groupthink phenomenon and a new model of group decision processes. *Psychological Bulletin, 113,* 533–552.

Alexander, C. N., Chandler, H. M., Langer, E. J., Newman, R. I., & Davies J. L. (1989). Transcendental Meditation, mindfulness, and longevity: An experimental study with the elderly. *Journal of Personality and Social Psychology, 57,* 950–964.

Alexander, C. N., Rainforth, M. V., & Gelderloos, P. (1991). Transcendental Meditation, self actualization, and psychological health: A conceptual overview and statistical meta-analysis. *Journal of Social Behavior and Personality, 6*(5), 189–247.

Alexander, F. (1954). Psychoanalysis and psychotherapy. *Journal of the American Psychoanalytic Association, 2,* 722–733.

Alexander, R. D., Hoogland, J. L., Howard, R. D., Noonan, K. M., & Sherman, P. W. (1979). Sexual dimorphism and breeding systems in pinnipeds, ungulates, primates, and humans. In N. A. Chagnon, & W. Irons (Eds.), *Evolutionary biology and human social behavior.* North Scituate, MA: Duxbury Press.

Allan, R. W. (1998). Operant-respondent interactions. In W. O'Donohue (Ed.), *Learning and behavior therapy.* Boston: Allyn & Bacon.

Alloy, L. B., Abramson, L. Y., Whitehouse, W. G., Hogan, M. E., Tashman, N. A., Steinberg, D. L., Rose, D. T., & Donovan, P. (1999). Depressogenic cognitive styles: Predictive validity, information processing and personality characteristics, and developmental origins. *Behavioral Research and Therapy, 37,* 503–531.

Allport, G. W. (1937). *Personality: A psychological interpretation.* New York: Holt.

Allport, G. W. (1961). *Pattern and growth in personality.* New York: Holt.

Altman, I. (1990). Centripetal and centrifugal trends in psychology. In L. Brickman & H. Ellis (Eds.), *Preparing psychologists for the 21st century: Proceedings of the National Conference on Graduate Education in Psychology.* Hillsdale, NJ: Erlbaum.

Alvarez, P., & Squire, L. (1994). Memory consolidation and the medial temporal lobe: A simple network model. *Proceedings of the National Academy of Sciences, USA, 91,* 7041–7045.

Amabile, T. M. (1983). *The social psychology of creativity.* New York: Springer-Verlag.

Amabile, T. M. (1990). Within you, without you: The social psychology of creativity, and beyond. In M. A. Runco & R. S. Albert (Eds.), *Theories of creativity.* Newbury Park, CA: Sage.

Amabile, T. M. (1996). *Creativity in context.* Boulder, CO: Westview.

Amada, G. (1985). *A guide to psychotherapy.* Lanham, MD: Madison Books.

Amato, P. R., & Keith, B. (1991). Parental divorce and adult well-being: A meta-analysis. *Journal of Marriage and the Family, 53,* 43–58.

American Psychiatric Association. (1952). *Diagnostic and statistical manual of mental disorders.* Washington, DC: Author.

American Psychiatric Association. (1968). *Diagnostic and statistical manual of mental disorders* (2nd ed.). Washington, DC: Author.

American Psychiatric Association. (1980). *Diagnostic and statistical manual of mental disorders* (3rd ed.). Washington, DC: Author.

American Psychiatric Association. (1987). *Diagnostic and statistical manual of mental disorders* (3rd ed., rev.). Washington, DC: Author.

American Psychiatric Association. (1994). *Diagnostic and statistical manual of mental disorders* (4th ed.). Washington, DC: Author.

American Psychological Association. (1984). *Behavioral research with animals.* Washington, DC: Author.

American Psychological Association. (1992). Ethical principles of psychologists and code of conduct. *American Psychologist, 47,* 1597–1611.

American Psychological Association. (1997). *Profile of all APA members: 1997.* Washington, DC: Author.

Anand, B. K., & Brobeck, J. R. (1951). Hypothalamic control of food intake in rats and cats. *Yale Journal of Biology and Medicine, 24,* 123–140.

Anch, A. M., Browman, C. P., Mitler, M. M., & Walsh, J. K. (1988). *Sleep: A scientific perspective.* Englewood Cliffs, NJ: Prentice-Hall.

Anderson, K. J. (1990). Arousal and the inverted-U hypothesis: A critique of Neiss's "reconceptualizing arousal." *Psychological Bulletin, 107,* 96–100.

Anderson, M. C., & Neely, J. H. (1996). Interference and inhibition in memory retrieval. In E. L. Bjork, & R. A. Bjork (Eds.), *Memory.* San Diego: Academic Press.

Anderson, V. L., Levinson, E. M., Barker, W., & Kiewra, K. R. (1999). The effects of meditation on teacher perceived occupational stress, state and trait anxiety and burnout. *School Psychology Quarterly, 14,* 3–25.

Andersson, B. E. (1992). Effects of day-care on cognitive and socioemotional competence of thirteen-year-old Swedish schoolchildren. *Child Development, 63*, 20–36.

Andreasen, N. C. (1987). Creativity and mental illness: Prevalence rates in writers and their first-degree relatives. *American Journal of Psychiatry, 144*, 1288–1292.

Andreasen, N. C. (1988). Brain imaging: Applications in psychology. *Science, 239*, 1381–1388.

Andreasen, N. C. (1990). Positive and negative symptoms: Historical and conceptual aspects. In N. C. Andreasen (Ed.), *Modern problems of pharmacopsychiatry: Positive and negative symptoms and syndromes.* Basel: Karger.

Andreasen, N. C. (1996). Creativity and mental illness: A conceptual and historical overview. In J. J. Schildkraut & A. Otero (Eds.), *Depression and the spiritual in modern art: Homage to Miro.* New York: Wiley.

Anglin, J. M. (1993). Vocabulary development: A morphological analysis. *Monographs of the Society for Research in Child Development, 58.*

Angoff, W. H. (1988). The nature-nurture debate, aptitudes, and group differences. *American Psychologist, 43*(9), 713–720.

Angst, J., & Preizig, M. (1995). Course of a clinical cohort of unipolar, bipolar and schizoaffective patients: Results of a prospective study from 1959–1985. *Schweiz Archives of Neurology and Psychiatry, 146*, 1–16.

Ansbacher, H. (1970, February). Alfred Adler, individual psychology. *Psychology Today*, 42–44, 66.

Anthenelli, R. M., & Schuckit, M. A. (1997). Genetics. In J. H. Lowinson, P. Ruiz, R. B. Millman, & J. G. Langrod (Eds.), *Substance abuse: A comprehensive textbook.* Baltimore: Williams & Wilkins.

Anthony, T., Copper, C., & Mullen, B. (1992). Cross-racial facial identification: A social cognitive integration. *Personality and Social Psychology Bulletin, 18*, 296–301.

Antrobus, J. (1993). Characteristics of dreams. In M. A. Carskadon (Ed.), *Encyclopedia of sleep and dreaming.* New York: Macmillan.

Appels, A. (1997). Depression and coronary heart disease: Observations and questions. *Journal of Psychosomatic Research, 43*, 443–452.

Apter, J. T. (1996). A new generation of antipsychotics emerges: A guide for the practicing physician. *Primary Psychiatry, 3*, 22–23.

Archer, J. (1996). Sex differences in social behavior: Are the social role and evolutionary explanations compatible? *American Psychologist, 51*, 909–917.

Arendt, J. (1994). Clinical perspectives for melatonin and its agonists. *Biological Psychiatry, 35*, 1–2.

Arendt, J. (1996). Melatonin: Claims made in the popular media are mostly nonsense. *British Medical Journal, 312*, 1242–1243.

Argyle, M. (1987). *The psychology of happiness.* London: Metheun.

Argyle, M. (1999). Causes and correlates of happiness. In D. Kahneman, E. Diener, & N. Schwarz (Eds.), *Well-being: The foundations of hedonic psychology.* New York: Russell Sage Foundation.

Arkes, H. R., Wortmann, R. L., Saville, P. D., & Harkness, A. R. (1981). Hindsight bias among physicians weighing the likelihood of diagnoses. *Journal of Applied Psychology, 66*, 252–254.

Arkin, A. M., & Antrobus, J. S. (1991). The effects of external stimuli applied prior to and during sleep on sleep experience. In S. J. Ellman & J. S. Antrobus (Eds.), *The mind in sleep: Psychology and psychophysiology* (2nd ed.). New York: Wiley.

Arnett, J. J. (1992). Reckless behavior in adolescence: A developmental perspective. *Developmental Review, 12*, 339–373.

Arnett, J. J. (1999). Adolescent storm and stress, reconsidered. *American Psychologist, 54*, 317–326.

Aronson, E., Brewer, M., & Carlsmith, J. M., (1985). Experimentation in social psychology. In G. Lindzey & E. Aronson (eds.), *Handbook of social psychology* (3rd ed., Vol. 1). New York: Random House.

Aronson, E., & Mills, J. (1959). The effect of severity of initiation on liking for a group. *Journal of Abnormal and Social Psychology, 59*, 177–181.

Aronson, J., Cohen, G., & Nail, P. R. (1999). Self-affirmation theory: An update and appraisal. In E. Harmon-Jones, & J. Mills (Eds.), *Cognitive dissonance: Progress on a pivotal theory in social psychology.* Washington, DC: American Psychological Association.

Arrigo, J. M., & Pezdek, K. (1997). Lessons from the study of psychogenic amnesia. *Current Directions in Psychological Science, 6*, 148–152.

Asch, S. E. (1951). Effects of group pressure on the modification and distortion of judgments. In H. Guetzkow (Ed.), *Groups, leadership and men.* Pittsburgh: Carnegie Press.

Asch, S. E. (1955). Opinions and social pressures. *Scientific American, 193*(5), 31–35.

Asch, S. E. (1956). Studies of independence and conformity: A minority of one against a unanimous majority. *Psychological Monographs, 70*(9, Whole No. 416).

Asendorpf, J. B., & Ostendorf, F. (1998). Is self-enhancement healthy? Conceptual, psychometric, and empirical analysis. *Journal of Personality and Social Psychology, 74*, 955–966.

Aserinsky, E., & Kleitman, N. (1953). Regularly occurring periods of eye mobility and concomitant phenomena during sleep. *Science, 118*, 273–274.

Ashford, J. W., Mattson, M., & Kumar, V. (1998). Neurobiological systems disrupted by Alzheimer's disease and molecular biological theories of vulnerability. In V. Kumar & C. Eisdorfer (Eds.), *Advances in the diagnosis and treatment of Alzheimer's disease.* New York: Springer Publishing Company.

Aslin, R. N. (1993). Perception of visual direction in human infants. In C. E. Granrud (Ed.), *Visual perception and cognition in infancy.* Hillsdale, NJ: Erlbaum.

Atkinson, J. W. (1974). The mainsprings of achievement-oriented activity. In J. W. Atkinson & J. O. Raynor (Eds.), *Motivation and achievement.* New York: Wiley.

Atkinson, J. W. (1981). Studying personality in the context of an advanced motivational psychology. *American Psychologist, 36*, 117–128.

Atkinson, J. W. (1992). Motivational determinants of thematic apperception. In C. P. Smith (Ed.), *Motivation and personality: Handbook of thematic content analysis.* New York: Cambridge University Press.

Atkinson, J. W., & Birch, D. (1978). *Introduction to motivation.* New York: Van Nostrand.

Atkinson, J. W., & Litwin, G. H. (1960). Achievement motive and test anxiety conceived as motive to approach success and to avoid failure. *Journal of Abnormal and Social Psychology, 60*, 52–63.

Atkinson, R. C., & Shiffrin, R. M. (1968). Human memory: A proposed system and its control processes. In K. W. Spence & J. T. Spence (Eds.), *The psychology of learning and motivation* (Vol. 2). New York: Academic Press.

Atkinson, R. C., & Shiffrin, R. M. (1971). The control of short-term memory. *Scientific American, 225*, 82–90.

Austin, J. T., & Hanisch, K. A. (1990). Occupational attainment as a function of abilities and interests: A longitudinal analysis using Project TALENT data. *Journal of Applied Psychology, 75*, 77–86.

Averill, J. A. (1980). A constructivist view of emotion. In R. Plutchik & H. Kellerman (Eds.), *Emotion: Theory, research, and experience: Vol. 1. Theories of emotion.* New York: Academic Press.

Axel, R. (1995, April). The molecular logic of smell. *Scientific American, 273*, 154–159.

Ayanian, J. Z., & Cleary, P. D. (1999). Perceived risks of heart disease and cancer amoung cigarette smokers. *Journal of the American Medical Association, 281*, 1019–1021.

Ayers, M. S., & Reder, L. M. (1998). A theoretical review of the misinformation effect: Predictions from an activation-based memory model. *Psychonomic Bulletin & Review, 5*, 1–21.

Ayres, J. J. B. (1998). Fear conditioning and avoidance. In W. O'Donohue (Ed.), *Learning and behavior therapy.* Boston: Allyn & Bacon.

Baars, B. J. (1986). *The cognitive revolution in psychology.* New York: Guilford Press.

Baddeley, A. D. (1986). *Working memory.* New York: Oxford University Press.

Baddeley, A. D. (1989). The uses of working memory. In P. R. Soloman, G. R. Goethals, C. M. Kelley, & B. R. Stephens (Eds.), *Memory: Interdisciplinary approaches.* New York: Springer-Verlag.

Baddeley, A. D. (1992). Working memory. *Science, 255*, 556–559.

Baddeley, A. D., & Hitch, G. (1974). Working memory. In G. H. Bower (Ed.), *The psychology of learning and motivation* (Vol. 8). New York: Academic Press.

Badia, P. (1990). Memories in sleep: Old and new. In R. R. Bootzin, J. F. Kihlstrom, & D. L. Schacter (Eds.), *Sleep and cognition.* Washington, DC: American Psychological Association.

Baenninger, M., & Newcombe, N. (1995). Environmental input to the development of sex-related differences in spatial and mathematical ability. *Learning & Individual Differences, 7*, 363–379.

Baer, J. (1994). Divergent thinking is not a general trait: A multi-domain training experiment. *Creativity Research Journal, 7*, 35–36.

Bahrick, H. P., Bahrick, P. C., & Wittlinger, R. P. (1975). Fifty years of memories of names and faces: A cross-sectional approach. *Journal of Experimental Psychology: General, 104*, 54–75.

Bailey, J. M., Gaulin, S., Agyei, Y., & Gladue, B. A. (1994). Effects of gender and sexual orientation on evolutionarily relevant aspects of human mating psychology. *Journal of Personality and Social Psychology, 66*, 1081–1093.

Bailey, J. M., & Pillard, R. C. (1991). A genetic study of male homosexual orientation. *Archives of General Psychology, 48*, 1089–1097.

Bailey, J. M., Pillard, R. C., Neale, M. C. I., & Agyei, Y. (1993). Heritable factors influence sexual orientation in women. *Archives of General Psychiatry, 50*, 217–223.

Bailey, J. M., & Zucker, K. J. (1995). Childhood sex-typed behavior and sexual orientation: A conceptual analysis and quantitative review. *Developmental Psychology, 31*, 43–55.

Baillargeon, R. (1987). Object permanence in 3.5- and 4.5-month-old infants. *Developmental Psychology, 23*, 655–664.

Baillargeon, R. (1994). How do infants learn about the physical world? *Current Directions in Psychological Science, 3*, 133–140.

Bakan, P. (1971, August). The eyes have it. *Psychology Today*, pp. 64–69.

Baker, S. W. (1980). Psychosexual differentiation in the human. *Biology of Reproduction, 22*, 61–72.

Ballenger, J. C. (1995). Benzodiazepines. In A. F. Schatzberg & C. B. Nemeroff (Eds.), *The American Psychiatric Press textbook of psychopharmacology*. Washington, DC: American Psychiatric Press.

Balon, R. (1997). Seratonin reuptake inhibitors and sexual dysfunction. *Primary Psychiatry, 4*, 28–33.

Balsam, P. D. (1988). Selection, representation, and equivalence of controlling stimuli. In R. C. Atkinson, R. J. Herrnstein, G. Lindzey, & R. D. Luce (Eds.), *Stevens' handbook of experimental psychology*. New York: Wiley.

Baltes, P. B., & Kliegl, R. (1992). Further testing of limits of cognitive plasticity: Negative age differences in a mnemonic skill are robust. *Developmental Psychology, 28*, 121–125.

Bandura, A. (1973). *Aggression: A social learning analysis*. Englewood Cliffs, NJ: Prentice-Hall.

Bandura, A. (1977). *Social learning theory*. Englewood Cliffs, NJ: Prentice-Hall.

Bandura, A. (1982). The psychology of chance encounters and life paths. *American Psychologist, 37*, 747–755.

Bandura, A. (1986). *Social foundations of thought and action: A social-cognitive theory*. Englewood Cliffs, NJ: Prentice-Hall.

Bandura, A. (1990). Perceived self-efficacy in the exercise of personal agency. *Journal of Applied Sport Psychology, 2*(2), 128–163.

Bandura, A. (1993). Perceived self-efficacy in cognitive development and functioning. *Educational Psychologist, 28*(2), 117–148.

Bandura, A. (1995). Exercise of personal and collective efficacy in changing societies. In A. Bandura (Ed.), *Self-efficacy in changing societies*. New York: Cambridge University Press.

Bandura, A. (1999). Social cognitive theory of personality. In L. A. Pervin, & O. P. John (Eds.), *Handbook of personality: Theory and research*. New York: Guilford Press.

Banich, M. T., & Heller, W. (1998). Evolving perspectives on lateralization of function. *Current Directions in Psychological Science, 7*, 1.

Banks, W. P., & Krajicek, D. (1991). Perception. *Annual Review of Psychology, 42*, 305–331.

Banyard, V. L., & Williams, L. M. (1999). Memories for child sexual abuse and mental health functioning: Findings on a sample of women and implications for future research. In L. M. Williams & V. L. Banyard (Eds.), *Trauma & memory*. Thousand Oaks, CA: Sage Publications.

Barba, G. D., Parlato, V., Jobert, A., Samson, Y., & Pappata, S. (1998). Cortical networks implicated in semantic and episodic memory: Common or unique. *Cortex, 34*, 547–561.

Barber, B. K. (1994). Cultural, family, and personal contexts of parent-adolescent conflict. *Journal of Marriage and the Family, 56*, 375–386.

Barber, T. X. (1979). Suggested ("hypnotic") behavior: The trance paradigm versus an alternative paradigm. In E. Fromm & R. E. Shor (Eds.), *Hypnosis: Developments in research and new perspectives*. New York: Aldine.

Barber, T. X. (1986). Realities of stage hypnosis. In B. Zilbergeld, M. G. Edelstien, & D. L. Araoz (Eds.), *Hypnosis: Questions and answers*. New York: Norton.

Bard, P. (1934). On emotional experience after decortication with some remarks on theoretical views. *Psychological Review, 41*, 309–329.

Bargh, J. A. (1999). The cognitive monster: The case against the controllability of automatic stereotype effects. In S. Chaiken & Y. Trope (Eds.), *Dual-process theories in social psychology*. New York: Guilford Press.

Bar-Hillel, M. (1989). Discussion: How to solve probability teasers. *Philosophy of Science, 56*, 348–358.

Bar-Hillel, M., & Falk, R. (1982). Some teasers concerning conditional probabilities. *Cognition*, 109–122.

Barlett, D. L., & Steele, J. B. (1979). *Empire: The life, legend and madness of Howard Hughes*. New York: Norton.

Barlow, D. H. (1996). The effectiveness of psychotherapy: Science and policy. *Clinical Psychology: Science & Practice, 3*, 236–240.

Barlow, D. H., & Durand, V. M. (1999). *Abnormal psychology: An investigative approach*. Belmont, CA: Wadsworth.

Barnett, P. A., & Gotlib, I. H. (1988). Psychosocial functioning and depression: Distinguishing among antecedents, concomitants, and consequences. *Psychological Bulletin, 104*, 97–126.

Barnett, W. S. (1995). Long-term effects of early childhood programs on cognitive and school outcomes. *Future of Children, 5*, 25–50.

Barnier, A. J., & McConkey, K. M. (1998). Posthypnotic responding away from the hypnotic setting. *Psychological Science, 9*, 256–262.

Barrett, D. (1988–1989). Dreams of death. *Omega, 19*(2), 95–101.

Barrett, G. V., & Depinet, R. L. (1991). A reconsideration of testing for competence rather than intelligence. *American Psychologist, 46*, 1012–1024.

Barrett, M. (1995). Early lexical development. In P. Fletcher & B. MacWhinney (Eds.), *The handbook of child language*. Cambridge, MA: Blackwell.

Barsky, A. J. (1988). The paradox of health. *New England Journal of Medicine, 318*, 414–418.

Barsky, A. J. (1989). Somatoform disorders. In H. I. Kaplan & B. J. Sadock (Eds.), *Comprehensive textbook of psychiatry/V*. Baltimore: Williams & Wilkins.

Barsky, A. J., Coeytaux, R. R., Sarnie, M. K., & Cleary, P. D. (1993). Hypochondriacal patients' beliefs about good health. *American Journal of Psychiatry, 150*, 1085–1090.

Barsky, A. J., Wyshak, G., & Klerman, G. L. (1990). The Somatosensory Amplification Scale and its relationship to hypochondriasis. *Journal of Psychiatry Research, 24*, 323–334.

Bartlett, J. G. (1993). *The Johns Hopkins Hospital guide to medical care of patients with HIV infection* (3rd ed.). Baltimore: Williams & Wilkins.

Bartlett, J. G., & Moore, R. D. (1998). Improving HIV therapy. *Scientific American, 279* (1), 84–93.

Bartoshuk, L. M. (1988). Taste. In R. C. Atkinson, R. J. Herrnstein, G. Lindzey, & R. D. Luce (Eds.), *Stevens' handbook of experimental psychology: Perception and motivation* (Vol. 1). New York: Wiley.

Bartoshuk, L. M. (1991). Taste, smell and pleasure. In R. C. Bolles (Ed.), *The hedonics of taste*. Hillsdale, NJ: Erlbaum.

Bartoshuk, L. M. (1993a). Genetic and pathological taste variation: What can we learn from animal models and human disease? In D. Chadwick, J. Marsh, & J. Goode (Eds.), *The molecular basis of smell and taste transduction*. New York: Wiley.

Bartoshuk, L. M. (1993b). The biological basis of food perception and acceptance. *Food Quality and Preference, 4*, 21–32.

Bartoshuk, L. M., & Beauchamp, G. K. (1994). Chemical senses. *Annual Review of Psychology, 45*, 419–449.

Bartoshuk, L. M., Duffy, V. B., & Miller, I. J. (1994). PTC/PROP taste: Anatomy, psychophysics, and sex effects. *Physiology & Behavior, 56*, 1165–1171.

Baruch, G. K. (1984). The psychological well-being of women in the middle years. In G. K. Baruch & J. Brooks-Gunn (Eds.), *Women in midlife*. New York: Plenum.

Basbaum, A. I., & Fields, H. L. (1984). Endogenous pain control systems: Brainstem spinal pathways and endorphin circuitry. *Annual Review of Neuroscience, 7*, 309–338.

Bashore, T. R., Ridderinkhof, K. R., & van der Molen, M. W. (1997). The decline of cognitive processing speed in old age. *Current Directions in Psychological Science, 6*, 163–169.

Basow, S. A. (1992). *Gender: Stereotypes and roles*. Pacific Grove, CA: Brooks/Cole.

Bassuk, E. L., Buckner, J. C., Perloff, J. N., & Bassuk, S. S. (1998). Prevalence of mental health and substance use disorders among homeless and low-income housed mothers. *American Journal of Psychiatry, 155*, 1561–1564.

Bates, E., & Carnevale, G. (1993). New directions in research on language development. *Developmental Review, 13*, 436–70.

Bates, M. S., Edwards, W. T., & Anderson, K. O. (1993). Ethnocultural influences on variation in chronic pain perception. *Pain, 52*(1), 101–112.

Baum, A. S., & Burnes, D. W. (1993). *A nation in denial: The truth about homelessness*. Boulder, CO: Westview Press.

Baum, A., Grunberg, N. E., & Singer, J. E. (1992). Biochemical measurements in the study of emotion. *Psychological Science, 3*, 56–60.

Baumeister, R. F. (1989). The optimal margin of illusion. *Journal of Social and Clinical Psychology, 8,* 176–189.

Baumrind, D. (1964). Some thoughts on the ethics of reading Milgram's "Behavioral study of obedience." *American Psychologist, 19,* 421–423.

Baumrind, D. (1985). Research using intentional deception: Ethical issues revisited. *American Psychologist, 40,* 165–174.

Baylis, G. C., & Driver, J. (1995). One-sided edge assignment in vision: 1. Figure-ground segmentation and attention to objects. *Current Directions in Psychological Science, 4,* 140–146.

Beahrs, J. O. (1983). Co-consciousness: A common denominator in hypnosis, multiple personality and normalcy. *American Journal of Clinical Hypnosis, 26*(2), 100–113.

Beck, A. T. (1976). *Cognitive therapy and the emotional disorders.* New York: International Universities Press.

Beck, A. T. (1987). Cognitive therapy. In J. K. Zeig (Ed.), *The evolution of psychotherapy.* New York: Brunner/Mazel.

Beck, A. T. (1991). Cognitive therapy: A 30-year retrospective. *American Psychologist, 46,* 368–375.

Beck, A. T. (1997). Cognitive therapy: Reflections. In J. K. Zeig (Ed.), *The evolution of psychotherapy: The third conference.* New York: Brunner/Mazel.

Beck, J. (1995). *Cognitive therapy: Basics and beyond.* New York: Guilford Press.

Beckham, J. C., Moore, S. D., Feldman, M. E., Hertzberg, M. A., Kirby, A. C., & Fairbank, J. A. (1998). Health status, somatization, and severity of posttraumatic stress disorder in Vietnam combat veterans with posttraumatic stress disorder. *American Journal of Psychiatry, 155,* 1565–1569.

Beeman, M. J., & Chiarello, C. (1998). Complementary right and left hemisphere language comprehension. *Current Directions in Psychological Science, 7,* 2–7.

Beer, J. M., Arnold, R. D., & Loehlin, J. C. (1998). Genetic and environmental influences on MMPI Factor Scales: Joint model fitting to twin and adoption data. *Journal of Personality and Social Psychology, 74,* 818–827.

Beilin, H. (1992). Piaget's enduring contribution to developmental psychology. *Developmental Psychology, 28,* 191–204.

Beisecker, A. E. (1990). Patient power in doctor-patient communication: What do we know? *Health Communication, 2,* 105–122.

Békésy, G. von. (1947). The variation of phase along the basilar membrane with sinusoidal vibrations. *Journal of the Acoustical Society of America, 19,* 452–460.

Bell, A. P., Weinberg, M. S., & Hammersmith, S. K. (1981). *Sexual preference: Its development in men and women.* Bloomington: Indiana University Press.

Beller, M., & Gafni, N. (1996). The 1991 international assessment of educational progress in mathematics and sciences: The gender differences perspective. *Journal of Educational Psychology, 88,* 365–377.

Belli, R. F., Winkielman, P., Read, J. D., Schwarz, N., & Lynn, S. J. (1998). Recalling more childhood events leads to judgments of poorer memory: Implications for the recovered/false memory debate. *Psychonomic Bulletin & Review, 5,* 318–323.

Belsky, J. (1988). The "effects" of infant day care reconsidered. *Early Childhood Research Quarterly, 3,* 235–272.

Belsky, J. (1992). Consequences of child care for children's development: A deconstructionist view. In A. Booth (Ed.), *Child care in the 1990s.* Hillsdale, NJ: Erlbaum.

Belsky, J. (1999a). Interactional and contextual determinants of attachment security. In J. Cassidy & P. R. Shaver (Eds.), *Handbook of attachment: Theory, research and clinical applications.* New York: Guilford Press.

Belsky, J. (1999b). Modern evolutionary theory and patterns of attachment. In J. Cassidy & P. R. Shaver (Eds.), *Handbook of attachment: Theory, research and clinical applications.* New York: Guilford Press.

Belsky, J., Steinberg, L., & Draper, P. (1991). Childhood experience, interpersonal development, and reproductive strategy: An evolutionary theory of socialization. *Child Development, 62,* 647–670.

Bem, D. J. (1996). Exotic becomes erotic: A developmental theory of sexual orientation. *Psychological Review, 103,* 320–335.

Bem, D. J. (1998). Is EBE theory supported by the evidence? Is it androcentric? A reply to Peplau et al. (1998). *Psychological Review, 105,* 395–398.

Bem, S. L. (1985). Androgyny and gender schema theory: A conceptual and empirical integration. In T. B. Sonderegger (Ed.), *Nebraska symposium on motivation, 1984: Psychology and gender* (Vol. 32). Lincoln: University of Nebraska Press.

Benet, V., & Waller, N. G. (1995). The big seven factor model of personality description: Evidence for its cross-cultural generality in a Spanish sample. *Journal of Personality and Social Psychology, 69,* 701–718.

Benjamin, L. T., Jr., Cavell, T. A., & Shallenberger, W. R., III. (1984). Staying with initial answers on objective tests: Is it a myth? *Teaching of Psychology, 11,* 133–141.

Bennett, H. L. (1993). The mind during surgery: The uncertain effects of anesthesia. *Advances, 9*(1), 5–16.

Benson, H. (1975). *The relaxation response.* New York: Morrow.

Benson, H., & Klipper, M. Z. (1988). *The relaxation response.* New York: Avon.

Bentler, P. M., & Woodward, J. A. (1978). A Head Start reevaluation: Positive effects are not yet demonstrable. *Evaluation Quarterly, 2,* 493–510.

Berenbaum, S. A., & Snyder, E. (1995). Early hormonal influences on childhood sex-typed activity and playmate preferences: Implications for the development of sexual orientation. *Developmental Psychology, 31,* 31–42.

Berger, H. (1929). Über das elektrenkephalogramm des menchen. *Archiv für Psychiatric und Nervenkrankheiten, 99,* 555–574.

Berkowitz, L. (1989). Frustration-aggression hypothesis: Examination and reformulation. *Psychological Bulletin, 106,* 59–73.

Berkowitz, L. (1999). Evil is more than banal: Situationism and concept of evil. *Personality and Social Psychology Review, 3,* 246–253.

Berliner, L., & Briere, J. (1999). Trauma, memory, and clinical practice. In L. M. Williams & V. L. Banyard (Eds.), *Trauma & memory.* Thousand Oaks, CA: Sage Publications.

Bernal, E. M. (1984). Bias in mental testing: Evidence for an alternative to the heredity-environment controversy. In C. R. Reynolds & R. T. Brown (Eds.), *Perspectives on bias in mental testing.* New York: Plenum.

Bernhardt, P. C. (1997). Influences of serotonin and testosterone in aggression and dominance: Convergence with social psychology. *Current Directions in Psychological Science, 6,* 44–48.

Bernstein, I. L., & Meachum, C. L. (1990). Food aversion learning: Its impact on appetite. In E. D. Capaldi & T. L. Powley (Eds.), *Taste, experience, and feeding.* Washington, DC: American Psychological Association.

Berry, D. T. R., Wetter, M. W., & Baer, R. A. (1995). Assessment of malingering. In J. N. Butcher (Ed.), *Clinical personality assessment: Practical approaches.* New York: Oxford University Press.

Berry, J. W. (1976). *Human ecology and cognitive style: Comparative studies in cultural and psychological adaptation.* New York: Sage/Halsted.

Berry, J. W. (1990). Cultural variations in cognitive style. In S. P. Wapner (Ed.), *Bio-psycho-social factors in cognitive style.* Hillsdale, NJ: Erlbaum.

Berry, J. W. (1994). Cross-cultural variations in intelligence. In R. J. Sternberg (Ed.), *Encyclopedia of human intelligence.* New York: Macmillan.

Berry, J. W., Poortinga, Y., Segall, M., & Dasen, P. (1992). *Cross-cultural psychology.* New York: Cambridge University Press.

Berscheid, E. (1988). Some comments on love's anatomy: Or, whatever happened to old-fashioned lust. In R. J. Sternberg & M. L. Barnes (Eds.), *The psychology of love.* New Haven: Yale University Press.

Berscheid, E., & Reis, H. T. (1998). Attraction and close relationships. In D. T. Gilbert, S. T. Fiske, & G. Lindzey (Eds.), *The handbook of social psychology.* New York: McGraw-Hill.

Bertenthal, B. I., & Clifton, R. K. (1998). Perception and action. In W. Damon (Ed.), *Handbook of child psychology (Vol. 2): Cognition, perception, and language.* New York: Wiley.

Berwick, D. M. (1996). Quality of health care, part 5: Payment by capitation and the quality of care. *New England Journal of Medicine, 335,* 1227–1231.

Betancourt, H., & Lopez, S. R. (1993). The study of culture, ethnicity, and race in American psychology. *American Psychologist, 48,* 629–637.

Beumont, P. J. V. (1995). The clinical presentation of anorexia and bulimia nervosa. In K. D. Brownell & C. G. Fairburn (Eds.), *Eating disorders and obesity: A comprehensive handbook.* New York: Guilford Press.

Beumont, P. J. V., Garner, D. M., & Touyz, S. W. (1994). Diagnosis of eating or dieting disorders: What may we learn from past mistakes? *International Journal of Eating Disorders, 16,* 349–362.

Beutler, L. E., Machado, P. P. P., & Neufeldt, S. A. (1994). Therapist variables. In A. E. Bergin & S. L. Garfield (Eds.), *Handbook of psychotherapy and behavior change* (4th ed.). New York: Wiley.

Bialystok, E. (1999). Cognitive complexity and attentional control in the bilingual mind. *Child Development, 70,* 636–644.

Biederman, I., Hilton, H. J., & Hummel, J. E. (1991). Pattern goodness and pattern recognition. In G. R. Lockhead & J. R. Pomerantz (Eds.), *The perception of structure.* Washington, DC: American Psychological Association.

Biehl, M., Matsumoto, D., Ekman, P., Hearn, V., Heider, K., Kudoh, T., & Ton, V. (1997). Matsumoto and Ekman's Japanese and Caucasian Facial Expressions of Emotion (JACFEE): Reliability data and cross-national differences. *Journal of Nonverbal Behavior, 21*, 3–21.

Bierut, L. J., Heath, A. C., Bucholz, K. K., Dinwiddie, S. H., Madden, P. A. F., Statham, D. J., Dunne, M. P., & Martin, N. G. (1999). Major depressive disorder in a community-based twin sample. *Archives of General Psychiatry, 56*, 557–563.

Binet, A. (1911). Nouvelle recherches sur la mesure du niveau intellectuel chez les enfants d'école. *L'Année Psychologique, 17*, 145–201.

Binet, A., & Simon, T. (1905/1948). Méthodes nouvelles pour le diagnostic du niveau intellectuel des anormaux. *L'Année Psychologique, 11*, 191–244.

Birch, L. L. (1990). The control of food intake by young children: The role of learning. In E. D. Capaldi & T. L. Powley (Eds.), *Taste, experience, and feeding*. Washington, DC: American Psychological Association.

Birch, L. L., McPhee, L., Sullivan, S., & Johnson, S. (1989). Conditioned meal initiation in young children. *Appetite, 13*, 105–113.

Birchler, G. R. (1992). Marriage. In V. B. Van Hasselt & M. Hersen (Eds.), *Handbook of social development: A lifespan perspective*. New York: Plenum.

Bjork, R. A. (1992). Interference and forgetting. In L. R. Squire (Ed.), *Encyclopedia of learning and memory*. New York: Macmillan.

Bjorklund, D. F. (1997). In search of a metatheory for cognitive development (or, Piaget is dead and I don't feel so good myself). *Child Development, 68*, 144–148.

Black, D. W., & Andreasen, N. C. (1994). Schizophrenia, schizophreniform disorder, and delusional (paranoid) disorder. In R. E. Hales, S. C. Yudofsky, & J. A. Talbott (Eds.), *The American Psychiatric Press textbook of psychiatry* (2nd ed.). Washington, DC: American Psychiatric Press.

Black, D. W., & Andreasen, N. C. (1999). Schizophrenia, schizophreniform disorder, and delusional (paranoid) disorders. In R. E. Hales, S. C. Yudofsky, & J. A. Talbott (Eds.), *American Psychiatric Press textbook of psychiatry*. Washington, DC: American Psychiatric Press.

Blacker, D., & Tsuang, M. T. (1999). Classification and DSM-IV. In A. M. Nicholi (Ed.), *The Harvard guide to psychiatry*. Cambridge, MA: Harvard University Press.

Blair, S. N., Kohl, H. W., Gordon, N. F., & Paffenbarger, R. S. (1992). How much physical activity is good for health? In G. S. Omenn, J. E. Fielding, & L. B. Lave (Eds.), *Annual review of public health* (Vol. 13). Palo Alto, CA: Annual Reviews.

Blair, S. N., Kohl, H. W., Paffenbarger, R. S., Clark, D. G., Cooper, K. H., & Gibbons, L. W. (1989). Physical fitness and all-cause mortality: A prospective study of healthy men and women. *Journal of the American Medical Association, 262*, 2395–2401.

Blakeslee, T. R. (1980). *The right brain*. Garden City, NY: Doubleday/ Anchor.

Blanchard, F. A., Lilly, T., & Vaughn, L. A. (1991). Reducing the expression of racial prejudice. *Psychological Science, 2*, 101–105.

Blanchard, R., Zucker, K. J., Bradley, S. J., & Hume, C. S. (1995). Birth order and siblings sex ratio in homosexual male adolescents and probably prehomosexual feminine boys. *Developmental Psychology, 31*, 22–30.

Blankenhorn, D. (1995). *Fatherless America: Confronting our most urgent social problem*. New York: Basic Books.

Blascovich, J., Wyer, N. A., Swart, L. A., & Kibler, J. L. (1997). Racism and racial categorization. *Journal of Personality and Social Psychology, 72*, 1364–1372.

Blass, T. (1991). Understanding behavior in the Milgram obedience experiment: The role of personality, situations, and their interactions. *Journal of Personality and Social Psychology, 60*, 398–413.

Blass, T. (1999). The Milgram Paradigm after 35 years: Some things we now know about obedience to authority. *Journal of Applied Social Psychology, 29*, 955–978.

Blau, Z. S. (1981). *Black children/ white children: Competence, socialization and social structure*. New York: Free Press.

Blazer, D. G., Hughes, D., George, L. K., Swartz, M., & Boyer, R. (1991). Generalized anxiety disorder. In L. N. Robins & D. A. Regier (Eds.), *Psychiatric disorders in America: The epidemiologic catchment area study*. New York: Free Press.

Blazer, D. G., Kessler, R. C., McGonagle, K. A., & Swartz, M. S. (1994). The prevalence and distribution of major depression in a national community sample: The national comorbidity survey. *American Journal of Psychiatry, 151*, 979–986.

Bleier, R. (1988). A decade of feminist critiques in the natural sciences. *Signs: Journal of Women in Culture and Society, 14*, 186–195.

Bleuler, E. (1911). *Dementia praecox or the group F schizophrenias*. New York: International Universities Press.

Blieszner, R., & Adams, R. G. (1992). *Adult friendship*. Newbury Park, CA: Sage.

Bliwise, D. L. (1994). Normal aging. In M. H. Kryger, T. Roth, & W. C. Dement (Eds.), *Principles and practice of sleep medicine* (2nd ed.). Philadelphia: Saunders.

Block, J. (1981). Some enduring and consequential structures of personality. In A. I. Rabins, J. Aronoff, A. Barclay & R. Zucker (Eds.), *Further explorations in personality*. New York: Wiley.

Block, J. (1995). A contrarian view of the five-factor approach to personality description. *Psychological Bulletin, 117*, 187–215.

Block, J., & Dworkin, G. (1976). Heritability and inequality. In N. J. Block and G. Dworkin (Eds.), *The IQ controversy: Critical readings*. New York: Pantheon.

Block, L. G., & Keller, P. A. (1997). Effects of self-efficacy and vividness on the persuasiveness of health communication. *Journal of Consumer Psychology, 6*, 31–54.

Bloom, B. L. (1984). *Community mental health: A general introduction*. Pacific Grove, CA: Brooks/Cole.

Bloom, F. E. (1995). Cellular mechanisms active in emotion. In M. S. Gazzaniga (Ed), *The cognitive neurosciences*. Cambridge, MA: MIT Press.

Bloomfield, H. H., & Kory, R. B. (1976). *Happiness: The TM program, psychiatry, and enlightenment*. New York: Simon & Schuster.

Blumenthal, J. A., Jiang, W., Babyak, M. A., Krantz, D. S., Frid, D. J., Coleman, R. E., Waugh, R., Hanson, M., Applebaum, M., O'Connor, C., & Morris, J. J. (1997). Stress management and exercise training in cardiac patients with myocardial ischemia: Effects on prognosis and evaluation of mechanisms. *Archives of Internal Medicine, 157*, 2213–2223.

Blundell, J. E., & Halford, J. C. G. (1998). Serotonin and appetite regulation: Implications for the pharmacological treatment of obesity. *CNS Drugs, 9*, 473–495.

Boden, J. M., & Baumeister, R. F. (1997). Repressive coping: Distraction using pleasant thoughts and memories. *Journal of Personality and Social Psychology, 73*, 45–62.

Boehm, L. E. (1994). The validity effect: A search for mediating variables. *Personality and Social Psychology Bulletin, 20*, 285–293.

Bogartz, R. S., & Shinskey, J. L. (1998). On perception of a partially occluded object in 6-month-olds. *Cognitive Development, 13*, 141–163.

Bohannon, J. N., III, MacWhinney, B., & Snow, C. (1990). No negative evidence revisited: Beyond learnability or who has to prove what to whom. *Developmental Psychology, 26*, 221–226.

Bohannon, J. N., III, & Stanowicz, L. (1988). The issue of negative evidence: Adult responses to children's language errors. *Developmental Psychology, 24*, 684–689.

Bohannon, J. N., III, & Warren-Leubecker, A. (1989). Theoretical approaches to language acquisition. In J. Berko Gleason (Ed.), *The development of language*. Columbus, OH: Merrill.

Bohning, D. E., Lorberbaum, J. P., Shastri, A., Nahas, Z., & George, M. S. (1998). Structural brain imaging (CT and MRI) in primary psychiatry. *Primary Psychiatry, 5*, 46–51.

Bolger, N. (1990). Coping as a personality process: A prospective study. *Journal of Personality and Social Psychology, 59*, 525–537.

Bond, A. J., & Cleare, A. J. (1997). Manipulation of serotonergic status related to subjective and behavioral measures of aggression. *Biological Psychiatry, 41*, 1147.

Bond, R., & Smith, P. B. (1996). Culture and conformity: A meta-analysis of studies using Asch's line judgment task. *Psychological Bulletin, 119*, 111–137.

Boninger, D. S., Krosnick, J. A., Berent, M. K., & Fabrigar, L. R. (1995). The causes and consequences of attitude importance. In R. E. Petty & J. A. Krosnick (Eds.), *Attitude strength: Antecedents and consequences*. Mahwah, NJ: Erlbaum.

Bonn, D. (1996). Melatonin's multifarious marvels: Miracle or myth? *Lancet, 347*, 184.

Booth, D. (1991). Learned ingestive motivation and the pleasures of the palate. In R. C. Bolles (Ed), *The hedonics of taste*. Hillsdale, NJ: Erlbaum.

Booth, D. (1994). Palatability and the intake of food and drinks. In M. S. Westerterp-Plantenga, E. W. H. M. Frederix & A. B. Steffens (Eds.), *Food intake and energy expenditure*. Boca Raton, FL: CRC Press.

Bootzin, R. R., Manber, R., Perlis, M. L., Salvio, M. A., & Wyatt, J. K. (1993). Sleep disorders. In P. B. Sutker & H. E. Adams (Eds.), *Comprehensive handbook of psychopathology* (2nd ed.). New York: Plenum.

Borbely, A. A. (1986). *Secrets of sleep*. New York: Basic Books.

Borgida, E., & Nisbett, R. E. (1977). The differential impact of abstract vs. concrete information on decisions. *Journal of Applied Social Psychology, 7*, 258–271.

Boring, E. G. (1966). A note on the origin of the word *psychology*. *Journal of the History of the Behavioral Sciences, 2*, 167.

Bornstein, B. H., & Zickafoose, D. J. (1999). "I know I know it, I know I saw it": The stability of the confidence-accuracy relationship across domains. *Journal of Experimental Psychology: Applied, 5*, 76–88.

Bouchard, T. J., Jr. (1997). IQ similarity in twins reared apart: Findings and responses to critics. In R. J. Sternberg, & E. L. Grigorenko (Eds.), *Intelligence, heredity, and environment*. New York: Cambridge University Press.

Bouchard, T. J., Jr., Lykken, D. T., McGue, M., Segal, N. L., & Tellegen, A. (1990). Sources of human psychological differences: The Minnesota study of twins reared apart. *Science, 250*, 223–228.

Bouchard, T. J., Jr., & Segal, N. L. (1985). Environment and IQ. In B. B. Wolman (Ed.), *Handbook of intelligence: Theories, measurements and applications*. New York: Wiley.

Boudreaux, E., Carmack, C. L., Scarinci, I. C., & Brantley, P. J. (1998). Predicting smoking stage of change among a sample of low socioeconomic status, primary care outpatients: Replication and extension using decisional balance and self-efficacy theories. *International Journal of Behavioral Medicine, 5*, 148–165.

Bourguignon, E. (1972). Dreams and altered states of consciousness in anthropological research. In F. L. K. Hsu (Ed.), *Psychological anthropology* (2nd ed.). Cambridge, MA: Schenkman.

Bouton, M. E. (1994). Context, ambiguity, and classical conditioning. *Current Directions in Psychological Science, 3*, 49–53.

Bower, G. H. (1970). Organizational factors in memory. *Cognitive Psychology, 1*, 18–46.

Bower, G. H., & Clark, M. C. (1969). Narrative stories as mediators of serial learning. *Psychonomic Science, 14*, 181–182.

Bower, G. H., & Springston, F. (1970). Pauses as recoding points in letter series. *Journal of Experimental Psychology, 83*, 421–430.

Bowmaker, J. K., & Dartnall, H. J. A. (1980). Visual pigments of rods and cones in a human retina. *Journal of Physiology, 298*, 501–511.

Boynton, R. M. (1990). Human color perception. In K. N. Leibovic (Ed.), *Science of vision*. New York: Springer-Verlag.

Boynton, R. M., & Gordon, J. (1965). Bezold-Brucke hue shift measured by color naming technique. *Journal of the Optical Society of America, 55*, 78–86.

Braak, H., Braak, E., Yilmazer, D., Schultz, C., de Vos, R. A. I., & Jansen, E. N. H. (1995). Nigral and extranigral pathology in Parkinson's disease. *Journal of Neural Transmission, 46*, 15–31.

Bradbury, T. N. (1998). *The developmental course of marital dysfunction*. New York: Cambridge University Press.

Bradshaw, J. L. (1989). *Hemispheric specialization and psychological function*. New York: Wiley.

Brady, K. T., Myrick, H., & Malcolm, R. (1999). Sedative-hypnotic and anxiolytic agents. In B. S. McCrady & E. E. Epstein (Eds.), *Addictions: A comprehensive guidebook*. New York: Oxford University Press.

Brainerd, C. J. (1996). Piaget: A centennial celebration. *Psychological Science, 7*, 191–195.

Brase, G. L., Cosmides, L., & Tooby, J. (1998). Individuation, counting, and statistical inference: The role of frequency and whole-object representations in judgment under certainty. *Journal of Experimental Psychology: General, 127*, 3–21.

Bray, G. A. (1990). Exercise and obesity. In C. Bouchard et al., *Exercise, fitness, and health: A consensus of current kowledge*. Champaign, IL: Human Kinetics Books.

Breedlove, S. M. (1992). Sexual differentiation of the brain and behavior. In J. B. Becker, S. M. Breedlove, & D. Crews (Eds.), *Behavioral endocrinology*. Cambridge, MA: MIT Press.

Breedlove, S. M. (1994). Sexual differentiation of the human nervous system. *Annual Review of Psychology, 45*, 389–418.

Breggin, P. R. (1990). Brain damage, dementia and persistent cognitive dysfunction associated with neuroleptic drugs: Evidence, etiology, implications. *The Journal of Mind and Behavior, 11*(3/4), 425–464.

Breggin, P. R. (1991). *Toxic psychiatry*. New York: St. Martin's Press.

Brehm, J. W. (1966). *A theory of psychological reactance*. New York: Academic Press.

Breland, K., & Breland, M. (1961). The misbehavior of organisms. *American Psychologist, 16*, 681–684.

Breland, K., & Breland, M. (1966). *Animal behavior*. New York: Macmillan.

Brennan, K. A., & Shaver, P. R. (1995). Dimensions of adult attachment, affect regulation, and romantic relationship functioning. *Personality and Social Psychology Bulletin, 21*, 267–283.

Breslau, N., Kilbey, M. M., & Andreski, P. (1991). Nicotine dependence, major depression, and anxiety in young adults. *Archives of General Psychiatry, 48*, 1069–1074.

Breslau, N., Kilbey, M. M., & Andreski, P. (1993). Nicotine dependence and major depression: New evidence from a prospective investigation. *Archives of General Psychiatry, 50*, 31–35.

Bretl, D. J., & Cantor, J. (1988). The portrayal of men and women in U.S. television commercials: A recent content analysis and trend over 15 years. *Sex Roles, 18*, 595–609.

Brett, J. F., Brief, A. P., Burke, M. J., George, J. M., & Webster, J. (1990). Negative affectivity and the reporting of stressful life events. *Health Psychology, 9*, 57–68.

Brettle, R. P., & Leen, L. S. (1991). The natural history of HIV and AIDS in women. *AIDS, 5*, 1283–1292.

Brewer, C. L. (1991). Perspectives on John B. Watson. In G. A. Kimble, M. Wertheimer, & C. White (Eds.), *Portraits of pioneers in psychology*. Hillsdale, NJ: Erlbaum.

Brewer, W. F., & Treyens, J. C. (1981). Role of schemata in memory for places. *Cognitive Psychology, 13*, 207–230.

Briere, J., & Conte, J. R. (1993). Self-reported amnesia for abuse in adults molested as children. *Journal of Traumatic Stress, 6*(1), 21–31.

Bringmann, W. G., & Balk, M. M. (1992). Another look at Wilhelm Wundt's publication record. *History of Psychology Newsletter, 24*(3/4), 50–66.

Brislin, R. (1993). *Understanding culture's influence on behavior*. Fort Worth: Harcourt Brace College Publishers.

Broadbent, D. E. (1958). *Perception and communication*. New York: Pergamon Press.

Brobeck, J. R., Tepperman, T., & Long, C. N. (1943). Experimental hypothalamic hyperphagia in the albino rat. *Yale Journal of Biology and Medicine, 15*, 831–853.

Brockington, I. (1996). *Motherhood and mental health*. Oxford, England: Oxford University Press.

Brody, N. (1992). *Intelligence*. San Diego: Academic Press.

Brooks-Gunn, J. (1991). Maturational timing variations in adolescent girls, antecedents of. In R. M. Lerner, A. C. Petersen, & J. Brooks-Gunn (Eds.), *Encyclopedia of adolescence*. New York: Garland.

Brooks-Gunn, J., & Reiter, E. O. (1990). The role of pubertal process. In S. S. Feldman & G. R. Elliot (Eds.), *At the threshold: The developing adolescent*. Cambridge, MA: Harvard University Press.

Brown, A. S. (1991). A review of the tip-of-the-tongue experience. *Psychological Bulletin, 109*, 204–223.

Brown, A. S. (1999). New perspectives on the neurodevelopmental hypothesis of schizophrenia. *Psychiatric Annals, 29*, 128–130.

Brown, D., Scheflin, A. W., & Hammond, D. C. (1998). *Memory, trauma treatment, and the law*. New York: Norton.

Brown, E. J., Juster, H. R., Heimberg, R. G., & Winning, C. D. (1998). Stressful life events and personality styles: Relation to impairment and treatment outcome in patients with social phobia. *Journal of Anxiety Disorders, 12*, 233–251.

Brown, H. D., & Kosslyn, S. M. (1993). Cerebral lateralization. *Current Opinion in Neurobiology, 3*, 183–186.

Brown, J. D., & Rogers, R. J. (1991). Self-serving attributions: The role of physiological arousal. *Personality and Social Psychology Bulletin, 17*, 501–506.

Brown, M. (1974). Some determinants of persistence and initiation of achievement-related activities. In J. W. Atkinson & J. O. Raynor (Eds.), *Motivation and achievement*. Washington, DC: Halsted.

Brown, R. T. (1989). Creativity: What are we to measure? In J. A. Glover, R. R. Ronning, & C. R. Reynolds (Eds.), *Handbook of creativity*. New York: Plenum.

Brown, R., & Hanlon, C. (1970). Derivational complexity and order of acquisition. In J. R. Hayes (Ed.), *Cognition and the development of language*. New York: Wiley.

Brown, R., & Kulik, J. (1977). Flashbulb memories. *Cognition, 5*, 73–99.

Brown, R., & McNeill, D. (1966). The "tip-of-the-tongue" phenomenon. *Journal of Verbal Learning and Verbal Behavior, 5*(4), 325–337.

Browne, A., & Finkelhor, D. (1998). The impact of child sexual abuse: A review of the research. In R. A. Baker (Ed.), *Child sexual abuse and false memory syndrome*. Amherst, NY: Prometheus Books.

Brownell, H. H., & Gardner, H. (1981). Hemisphere specialization: Definitions not incantations. *Behavioral and Brain Sciences, 4*, 64–65.

Brubaker, T. (1990). Families in later life: A burgeoning research area. *Journal of Marriage and the Family, 52,* 959–982.

Bruch, H. (1978). *The golden cage: The enigma of anorexia nervosa.* Cambridge, MA: Harvard University Press.

Bruckner-Gordon, F., Gangi, B. K., & Wallman, G. U. (1988). *Making therapy work: Your guide to choosing, using, and ending therapy.* New York: Harper & Row.

Bruer, J. T. (1999). *The myth of the first three years: A new understanding of early brain development and lifelong learning.* New York: Free Press.

Bruner, J. S. (1974). Concluding comments and summary of conference. In J. L. M. Dawson & W. J. Lonner (Eds.), *Readings in cross-cultural psychology.* Hong Kong: University of Hong Kong Press.

Bryden, M. P. (1982). *Laterality: Functional asymmetry in the intact brain.* New York: Academic Press.

Bryden, M. P. (1988). An overview of the dichotic listening procedure and its relation to cerebral organization. In K. Hugdahl (Ed.), *Handbook of dichotic listening.* Chichester, England: Wiley.

Buckley, K. W. (1994). Misbehaviorism: The case of John B. Watson's dismissal from Johns Hopkins University. In J. T. Todd & E. K. Morris (Eds.), *Modern perspectives on John B. Watson and classical behaviorism.* Westport, CT: Greenwood Press.

Buckley, P. F., & Meltzer, H. Y. (1995). Treatment of schizophrenia. In A. F. Schatzberg & C. B. Nemeroff (Eds.), *The American Psychiatric Press textbook of psychopharmacology.* Washington, DC: American Psychiatric Press.

Bühler, C., & Allen, M. (1972). *Introduction to humanistic psychology.* Pacific Grove, CA: Brooks/Cole.

Burg, M. W. (1995). Anger, hostility, and coronary heart disease: A review. *Mind/Body Medicine, 1,* 159–172.

Burger, J. M. (1986). Temporal effects on attributions: Actor and observer differences. *Social Cognition, 4,* 377–387.

Burger, J. M. (1997). *Personality.* Pacific Grove: Brooks/Cole.

Burger, J. M. (1999). The foot-in-the-door compliance procedure: A multiple process analysis review. *Personality and Social Psychology Review, 3,* 303–325.

Burnstein, E., Crandall, C., & Kitayama, S. (1994). Some neo-Darwinian decision rules for altruism: Weighing cues for inclusive fitness as a function of the biological importance of the decision. *Journal of Personality and Social Psychology, 67,* 773–789.

Buss, D. M. (1985). Human mate selection. *American Scientist, 73,* 47–51.

Buss, D. M. (1988). The evolution of human intrasexual competition: Tactics of mate attraction. *Journal of Personality and Social Psychology, 54,* 616–628.

Buss, D. M. (1989). Sex differences in human mate preferences: Evolutionary hypotheses tested in 37 cultures. *Behavioral and Brain Sciences, 12,* 1–49.

Buss, D. M. (1991). Evolutionary personality psychology. *Annual Review of Psychology, 42,* 459–491.

Buss, D. M. (1994a). *The evolution of desire: Strategies of human mating.* New York: Basic Books.

Buss, D. M. (1994b). Mate preferences in 37 cultures. In W. J. Lonner & R. S. Malpass (Eds.), *Psychology and culture.* Boston: Allyn & Bacon.

Buss, D. M. (1995). Evolutionary psychology: A new paradigm for psychological science. *Psychological Inquiry, 6,* 1–30.

Buss, D. M. (1996). The evolutionary psychology of human social strategies. In E. T. Higgins & A. W. Kruglanski (Eds.), *Social psychology: Handbook of basic principles.* New York: Guilford Press.

Buss, D. M. (1997). Evolutionary foundation of personality. In R. Hogan, J. Johnson, & S. Briggs (Eds.), *Handbook of personality psychology.* San Diego: Academic Press.

Buss, D. M. (1998). The psychology of human mate selection: Exploring the complexity of the strategic repertoire. In C. Crawford, & D. L. Krebs (Eds.), *Handbook of evolutionary psychology: Ideas, issues, and applications.* Mahwah, NJ: Erlbaum.

Buss, D. M. (1999). *Evolutionary psychology: The new science of the mind.* Boston: Allyn & Bacon.

Buss, D. M., & Kenrick, D. T. (1998). Evolutionary social psychology. In D. T. Gilbert, S. T. Fiske, & G. Lindzey (Eds.), *The handbook of social psychology.* New York: McGraw-Hill.

Buss, D. M., Larsen, R. J., Westen, D., & Semmelroth, J. (1992). Sex differences in jealousy: Evolution, physiology, and psychology. *Psychological Science, 3,* 251–255.

Buss, D. M., & Schmitt, D. P. (1993). Sexual strategies theory: A contextual evolutionary analysis of human mating. *Psychological Review, 100,* 204–232.

Bussey, K., & Bandura, A. (1984). Influence of gender constancy and social power on sex-linked modeling. *Journal of Personality and Social Psychology, 47,* 1292–1302.

Butcher, J. N. (1990). *The MMPI-2 in psychological treatment.* New York: Oxford University Press.

Butcher, J. N., & Keller, L. S. (1984). Objective personality assessment. In G. Goldstein & M. Hersen (Eds.), *Handbook of psychological assessment.* New York: Pergamon Press.

Butcher, J. N., Narikiyo, T., & Vitousek, K. B. (1993). Understanding abnormal behavior in cultural context. In P. B. Sutker & H. E. Adams (Eds.), *Comprehensive handbook of psychopathology.* New York: Plenum.

Butow, P., Beumont, P., & Touyz, S. (1993). Cognitive processes in dieting disorders. *International Journal of Eating Disorders, 14,* 319–330.

Buunk, B. P., Angleitner, A., Oubaid, V., & Buss, D. M. (1996). Sex differences in jealousy in evolutionary and cultural perspective: Test from the Netherlands, Germany, and the United States. *Psychological Science, 7,* 359–363.

Buxton, C. E. (1985). American functionalism. In C. E. Buxton (Ed.), *Points of view in the modern history of psychology.* Orlando: Academic Press.

Buxton, M. N., Arkey, Y., Lagos, J., Deposito, F., Lowenthal, F., & Simring, S. (1981). Stress and platelet aggregation in hemophiliac children and their family members. *Research Communications in Psychology, Psychiatry and Behavior, 6*(1), 21–48.

Byerley, W., & Coon, H. (1995). Strategies to identify genes for schizophrenia. In J. M. Oldham & M. B. Riba (Eds.), *Review of Psychiatry* (Vol. 14). Washington, DC: American Psychiatric Press.

Byne, W., & Parsons, B. (1993). Human sexual orientation: The biological theories reappraised. *Archives of General Psychiatry, 50,* 228–239.

Byrne, D. (1997). An overview (and underview) of research and theory within the attraction paradigm. *Journal of Social and Personal Relationships, 14,* 417–431.

Byrne, D., Clore, G. L., & Smeaton, G. (1986). The attraction hypothesis: Do similar attitudes affect anything? *Journal of Personality and Social Psychology, 51,* 1167–1170.

Cacioppo, J. T., & Berntson, G. G. (1999). The affect system: Architecture and operating characteristics. *Current Directions in Psychological Science, 8,* 133–137.

Cacioppo, J. T., & Gardner, W. L. (1999). Emotion. *Annual Review of Psychology, 50,* 191–214.

Cacioppo, J. T., Klein, D. J., Berntson, G. G., & Hatfield, E. (1993). The psychophysiology of emotions. In M. Lewis & J. M. Haviland (Eds.), *Handbook of emotions.* New York: Guilford Press.

Cain, W. S. (1988). Olfaction. In R. C. Atkinson, R. J. Herrnstein, G. Lindzey, & R. D. Luce (Eds.), *Stevens' handbook of experimental psychology: Perception and motivation* (Vol. 1). New York: Wiley.

Calev, A., Phil, D., Pass, H. L., Shapira, B., Fink, M., Tubi, N., & Lerer, B. (1993). ECT and memory. In C. E. Coffey (Ed.), *The clinical science of electroconvulsive therapy.* Washington, DC: American Psychiatric Press.

Calof, D. (1998). Facing the truth about false memory. In R. A. Baker (Ed.), *Child sexual abuse and false memory syndrome.* Amherst, NY: Prometheus Books.

Calvert, C. (1997). Hate speech and its harms: A communication theory perspective. *Journal of Communication, 47,* 4–19.

Cameron, L., Leventhal, E. A., & Leventhal, H. (1993). Symptom representations and affect as determinants of care seeking in a community-dwelling, adult sample population. *Health Psychology, 12,* 171–179.

Cameron, N. (1963). *Personality development and psychopathology.* Boston: Houghton Mifflin.

Campbell, J. (1971). *Hero with a thousand faces.* New York: Harcourt Brace Jovanovich.

Campbell, R., & Sais, E. (1995). Accelerated metalinguistic (phonological) awareness in bilingual children. *British Journal of Developmental Psychology, 13,* 61–68.

Campbell, W. K., & Sedikides, C. (1999). Self-threat magnifies the self-serving bias: A meta-analytic integration. *Review of General Psychology, 3,* 23–43.

Campfield, L. A., Smith, F. J., Gulsez, Y., Devos, R., & Burn, P. (1995). Mouse OB proteiin: Evidence for a peripheral signal linking adiposity and central neural networks. *Science, 269,* 546–549.

Cannon, W. B. (1927). The James-Lange theory of emotions: A critical examination and an alternate theory. *American Journal of Psychology, 39,* 106–124.

Cannon, W. B. (1929). *Bodily changes in pain, hunger, fear and rage.* New York: Appleton.

Cannon, W. B. (1932). *The wisdom of the body.* New York: Norton.

Cannon, W. B., & Washburn, A. L. (1912). An explanation of hunger. *American Journal of Physiology, 29,* 444–454.

Capaldi, E. D., & VandenBos, G. R. (1991). Taste, food exposure, and eating behavior. *Hospital and Community Psychiatry, 42*(8), 787–789.

Capelli, C. A., Nakagawa, N., & Madden, C. M. (1990). How children understand sarcasm: The role of context and intonation. *Child Development, 61*, 1824–1841.

Caporael, L. R., & Brewer, M. B. (1995). Hierarchical evolutionary theory: There is an alternative, and it's not creationism. *Psychological Inquiry, 6*, 31–34.

Carey, G., & DiLalla, D. L. (1994). Personality and psychopathology: Genetic perspectives. *Journal of Abnormal Psychology, 103*, 32–43.

Carli, L. L. (1999). Cognitive, reconstruction, hindsight, and reactions to victims and perpetrators. *Personality & Social Psychology Bulletin, 25*, 966–979.

Carnegie, D. (1936). *How to win friends and influence people.* New York: Simon & Schuster.

Carpenter, W. T. (1992). The negative symptom challenge. *Archives of General Psychiatry, 49*, 236–237.

Carrington, P. (1987). Managing meditation in clinical practice. In M. A. West (Ed.), *The psychology of meditation.* Oxford: Clarendon Press.

Carroll, J. M., & Russell, J. A. (1997). Facial expressions in Hollywood's portrayal of emotion. *Journal of Personality and Social Psychology, 72*, 164–176.

Carskadon, M. A., & Dement, W. C. (1994). Normal human sleep: An overview. In M. H. Kryger, T. Roth, & W. C. Dement (Eds.), *Principles and practice of sleep medicine* (2nd ed.). Philadelphia: Saunders.

Carskadon, M. A., & Rechtschaffen, A. (1994). Monitoring and staging human sleep. In M. H. Kryger, T. Roth, & W. C. Dement (Eds.), *Principles and practice of sleep medicine* (2nd ed.). Philadelphia: Saunders.

Carson, R. C., & Sanislow, C. A., III. (1993). The schizophrenias. In P. B. Sutker & H. E. Adams (Eds.), *Comprehensive handbook of psychopathology* (2nd ed.). New York: Plenum.

Cartwright, R. D. (1977). *Night life: Explorations in dreaming.* Englewood Cliffs, NJ: Prentice-Hall.

Cartwright, R. D. (1994). Dreams and their meaning. In M. H. Kryger, T. Roth, & W. C. Dement (Eds.), *Principles and practice of sleep medicine* (2nd ed.). Philadelphia: Saunders.

Cartwright, R. D., & Lamberg, L. (1992). *Crisis dreaming.* New York: HarperCollins.

Carver, C. S., & Scheier, M. F. (1994). Situational coping and coping dispositions in a stressful transaction. *Journal of Personality and Social Psychology, 66*, 184–195.

Carver, C. S., & Scheier, M. F. (1999). Optimism. In C. R. Snyder (Ed.), *Coping: The psychology of what works.* New York: Oxford University Press.

Case, D. A., Fantino, E., & Goodie, A. S. (1999). Base-rate training without case cues reduces base-rate neglect. *Psychonomic Bulletin & Review, 6*, 310–327.

Casey, R., & Rozin, P. (1989). Changing children's food preferences: Parent opinions. *Appetite, 12*, 171–182.

Caspi, A., & Herbener, E. S. (1990). Continuity and change: Assortative marriage and the consistency of personality in adulthood. *Journal of Personality and Social Psychology, 58*(2), 250–258.

Caspi, A., & Roberts, B. W. (1999). Personality continuity and change across the life course. In L.A. Pervin, & O. P. John (Eds.), *Handbook of personality: Theory and research.* New York: Guilford Press.

Cassidy, J. (1999). The nature of the child's ties. In J. Cassidy & P. R. Shaver (Eds.), *Handbook of attachment: Theory, research, and clinical applications.* New York: Guilford Press.

Castelloci, V. F. (1986). The chemical senses: Taste and smell. In E. R. Kandel & J. H. Schwartz (Eds.), *Principles of neural science.* New York: Elsevier.

Catalano, E. M. (1990). *Getting to sleep.* Oakland, CA: New Harbinger.

Catania, A. C. (1992). Reinforcement. In L. R. Squire (Ed.), *Encyclopedia of learning and memory.* New York: Macmillan.

Cattell, J. M. (1890). Mental tests and measurements. *Mind, 15*, 373–381.

Cattell, R. B. (1950). *Personality: A systematic, theoretical and factual study.* New York: McGraw-Hill.

Cattell, R. B. (1957). *Personality and motivation: Structure and measurement.* New York: Harcourt, Brace & World.

Cattell, R. B. (1965). *The scientific analysis of personality.* Baltimore: Penguin.

Cattell, R. B. (1966). *The scientific analysis of personality.* Chicago: Aldine.

Cattell, R. B. (1990). Advances in Cattellian personality theory. In L. A. Pervin (Ed.), *Handbook of personality: Theory and research.* New York: Guilford Press.

Cattell, R. B., Eber, H. W., & Tatsuoka, M. M. (1970). *Handbook of the Sixteen Personality Factor Questionnaire (16PF).* Champaign, IL: Institute for Personality and Ability Testing.

Cavanaugh, J. C. (1993). *Adult development and aging* (2nd ed.). Pacific Grove, CA: Brooks/Cole.

Ceci, S. J., Rosenblum, T., de Bruyn, E., & Lee, D. Y. (1997). A bio-ecological model of intellectual development: Moving beyond h^2. In R. J. Sternberg & E. L. Grigorenko (Eds.), *Intelligence, heredity, and environment.* New York: Cambridge University Press.

Cerella, J., & Hale, S. (1994). The rise and fall in information-processing rates over the life span. *Acta Psychologica, 86*, 109–197.

Cerletti, U., & Bini, L. (1938). Un nuevo metodo di shockterapie "L'elettro-shock". *Boll. Acad. Med. Roma, 64*, 136–138.

Chaiken, S., & Maheswaran, D. (1994). Heuristic processing can bias systematic processing: Effects of source credibility, argument ambiguity, and task importance on attitude judgment. *Journal of Personality and Social Psychology, 66*, 460–473.

Chaiken, S., Wood, W., & Eagly, A. H. (1996). Principles of persuasion. In E. T. Higgins & A. W. Kruglanski (Eds.), *Social psychology: Handbook of basic principles.* New York: Guilford Press.

Chambless, D. L., & Hollon, S. D. (1998). Defining empirically supported therapies. *Journal of Consulting & Clinical Psychology, 66*, 7–18.

Chambless, D. L., Sanderson, W. C., Shoham, V., Johnson, S. B., Pope, K. S., Crits-Christoph, P., Baker, M., Johnson, B., Woody, S. R., Sue, S., Beutler, L., Williams, D., & McCurry, S. (1996). An update on empirically validated therapies. *The Clinical Psychologist, 49*, 5–18.

Chan, J. W. C., & Vernon, P. E. (1988). Individual differences among the peoples of China. In S. H. Irvine & J. W. Berry (Eds.), *Human abilities in cultural context.* New York: Cambridge University Press.

Chandler, C. C., & Fisher, R. P. (1996). Retrieval processes and witness memory. In E. L. Bjork & R. A. Bjork (Eds.), *Memory.* San Diego: Academic Press.

Chandra, R. K. (1991). Interactions between early nutrition and the immune system. In *Ciba Foundation Symposium No. 156.* Chichester, England: Wiley.

Chang, E. C. (1996). Cultural differences in optimism, pessimism, and coping: Predictors of subsequent adjustment in Asian American and Caucasian American college students. *Journal of Counseling Psychology, 43*, 113–123.

Chang, E. C. (1998). Dispositional optimism and primary and secondary appraisal of a stressor: Controlling for confounding influences and relations to coping and psychological and physical adjustment. *Journal of Personality and Social Psychology, 74*, 1109–1120.

Chapman, P. D. (1988). *Schools as sorters: Lewis M. Terman, applied psychology, and the intelligence testing movement.* New York: New York University Press.

Charney, D. S., Miller, H. L., Licinio, J., & Salomon, R. (1995). Treatment of depression. In A. F. Schatzberg & C. B. Nemeroff (Eds.), *The American Psychiatric Press textbook of psychopharmacology.* Washington, DC: American Psychiatric Press.

Chavkin, W. (1995). Substance abuse in pregnancy. In B. P. Sachs, R. Beard, E. Papiernik, & C. Russell (Eds.), *Reproductive health care for women and babies.* New York: Oxford University Press.

Chess, S., & Thomas, A. (1996). *Temperament: Theory and practice.* New York: Brunner/Mazel.

Cheung, F. (1991). The use of mental health services by ethnic minorities. In H. F. Myers, P. Wohlford, L. P. Guzman, & R. Echemendia (Eds.), *Ethnic minority perspectives on clinical training and services in psychology.* Washington, DC: American Psychological Association.

Chiriboga, D. A. (1989). Mental health at the midpoint: Crisis, challenge, or relief? In S. Hunter & M. Sundel (Eds.), *Midlife myths: Issues, findings, and practice implications.* Newbury Park, CA: Sage.

Chisholm, J. S. (1996). The evolutionary ecology of attachment organization. *Human Nature, 7*, 1–38.

Choi, I., Nisbett, R. E., & Norenzayan, A. (1999). Causal attribution across cultures: Variation and universality. *Psychological Bulletin, 125*, 47–63.

Cholewiak, R., & Collins, A. (1991). Sensory and physiological bases of touch. In M. A. Heller & W. Schiff (Eds.), *The psychology of touch.* Hillsdale, NJ: Erlbaum.

Chomsky, N. (1957). *Syntactic structures.* The Hague: Mouton.

Chomsky, N. (1959). A review of B. F. Skinner's "Verbal Behavior." *Language, 35*, 26–58.

Chomsky, N. (1965). *Aspects of theory of syntax.* Cambridge, MA: MIT Press.

Chomsky, N. (1975). *Reflections on language.* New York: Pantheon.

Chomsky, N. (1986). *Knowledge of language: Its nature, origins, and use.* New York: Praeger.

Christensen, L. (1988). Deception in psychological research: When is its use justified? *Personality and Social Psychology Bulletin, 14,* 664–675.

Christoph, R. T., Schoenfeld, G. A., & Tansky, J. W. (1998). Overcoming barriers to training utilizing technology: The influence of self-efficacy factors on multimedia-based training receptiveness. *Human Resource Development Quarterly, 9,* 25–38.

Chu, J. A., Frey, L. M., Ganzel, B. L., & Matthews, J. A. (1999). Memories of childhood abuse: Dissociation, amnesia, and corroboration. *American Journal of Psychiatry, 156,* 749–755.

Chumlea, W. C. (1982). Physical growth in adolescence. In B. B. Wolman (Ed.), *Handbook of developmental psychology.* Englewood Cliffs, NJ: Prentice-Hall.

Church, A. T., & Lonner, W. J. (1998). The cross-cultural perspective in the study of personality: Rationale and current research. *Journal of Cross-Cultural Psychology, 29,* 32–62.

Cialdini, R. B. (1993). *Influence: Science and practice.* Glenview, IL: HarperCollins.

Cialdini, R. B., & Trost, M. R. (1998). Social influence: Social norms, conformity, and compliance. In D. T. Gilbert, S. T. Fiske, & G. Lindzey (Eds.), *The handbook of social psychology.* New York: McGraw-Hill.

Cialdini, R. B., Trost, M. R., & Newsom, J. T. (1995). Preference for consistency: The development of a valid measure and the discovery of surprising behavioral implications. *Journal of Personality and Social Psychology, 69,* 318–328.

Cipolli, C., Baroncini, P., Fagioli, I., & Fumai, A. (1987). The thematic continuity of mental sleep experience in the same night. *Sleep, 10*(5), 473–479.

Clark, E. V. (1983). Meanings and concepts. In J. H. Flavell & E. M. Markman (Eds.), *Handbook of child psychology* (Vol. 3). New York: Wiley.

Clark, E. V. (1995). Later lexical development and word formation. In P. Fletcher, & B. MacWhinney (Eds.), *The handbook of child language.* Cambridge, MA: Blackwell.

Clark, L. A., Watson, D., & Mineka, S. (1994). Temperament, personality, and the mood and anxiety disorders. *Journal of Abnormal Psychology, 103,* 103–116.

Clark, L. F. (1993). Stress and the cognitive-conversational benefits of social interaction. *Journal of Social and Clinical Psychology, 12,* 25–55.

Coates, T. J., & Collins, C. (1998). Preventing HIV infection. *Scientific American, 279* (1), 96–97.

Coenen, A. (1998). Neuronal phenomena associated with vigilance and consciousness: From cellular mechanisms to electroencephalographic patterns. *Consciousness & Cognition: An International Journal, 7,* 42–53.

Cohen, C. E. (1981). Person categories and social perception: Testing some boundaries of the processing effects of prior knowledge. *Journal of Personality and Social Psychology, 40,* 441–452.

Cohen, C. I., & Thompson, K. S. (1992). Homeless mentally ill or mentally ill homeless? *American Journal of Psychiatry, 149,* 816–823.

Cohen, D. (1997). A critique of the use of neuroleptic drugs in psychiatry. In S. Fisher & R. P. Greenberg (Eds.), *From placebo to panacea: Putting psychiatric drugs to the test.* New York: Wiley.

Cohen, N. J., Ryan, J., Hunt, C., Romine, L., Wszalek, T., & Nash, C. (1999). Hippocampal system and declarative (relational) memory: Summarizing the data from functional neuroimaging studies. *Hippocampus, 9,* 83–98.

Cohen, S., & Hajioff, J. (1972). Life events and the onset of acute closed-angle glaucoma. *Journal of Psychosomatic Research, 16,* 335–341.

Cohen, S., & Lichtenstein, E. (1990). Perceived stress, quitting smoking, and smoking relapse. *Health Psychology, 9,* 466–478.

Cohen, S., Lichtenstein, E., Prochaska, J. O., Rossi, J. S., Gritz, E. R., Carr, C. R., Orleans, C. T., Schoenbach, V. J., Biener, L., Abrams, D., DiClemente, C., Curry, S., Marlatt, G. A., Cummings, K. M., Emont, S. L., Giovino, A., & Ossip-Klien, D. (1989). Debunking myths about self-quitting: Evidence from 10 prospective studies of persons who attempt to quit smoking by themselves. *American Psychologist, 44,* 1355–1365.

Cohen, S., Tyrrell, D. A. J., & Smith, A. P. (1993). Negative life events, perceived stress, negative affect, and susceptibility to the common cold. *Journal of Personality and Social Psychology, 64,* 131–140.

Colby, A., & Kohlberg, L. (1984). Invariant sequence and internal consistency in moral judgment stages. In W. M. Kurtines & J. L. Gewirtz (Eds.), *Morality, moral behavior, and moral development.* New York: Wiley.

Colby, A., & Kohlberg, L. (1987). *The measurement of moral judgment* (Vols. 1–2). New York: Cambridge University Press.

Cole, J. O., Goldberg, S. C., & Davis, J. M. (1966). Drugs in the treatment of psychosis. In P. Solomon (Ed.), *Psychiatric drugs.* New York: Grune & Stratton.

Cole, M. (1999). Culture in development. In M. H. Bornstein & M. E. Lamb (Eds.), *Developmental psychology: An advanced textbook* (4th ed.). Hillsdale, NJ: Erlbaum.

Cole, N. S. (1981). Bias in testing. *American Psychologist, 36,* 1067–1077.

Cole, S. W., Kemeny, M. E., Taylor, S. E., & Visscher, B. R. (1996). Elevated physical health risk among gay men who conceal their homosexual identity. *Health Psychology, 15,* 243–251.

Coleman, J. S., Campbell, E. O., Hobson, C. J., McPartland, J., Moody, A. M., Weinfield, F. D., & York, R. L. (1966). *Equality of educational opportunity.* Washington, DC: U.S. Government Printing Office.

Collaer, M. L., & Hines, M. (1995). Human behavioral sex differences: A role for gonadal hormones during early development? *Psychological Bulletin, 118,* 55–107.

Collins, A. M., & Loftus, E. F. (1975). A spreading activation theory of semantic processing. *Psychological Review, 82,* 407–428.

Collins, M. A., & Zebrowitz, L. A. (1995). The contributions of appearance to occupational outcomes in civilian and military settings. *Journal of Applied Social Psychology, 25,* 129–163.

Collins, N. L. (1996). Working models of attachment: Implications for explanation, emotion, and behavior. *Journal of Personality and Social Psychology, 71,* 810–832.

Colquhoun, W. P. (1984). Effects of personality on body temperature and mental efficiency following transmeridian flight. *Aviation, Space & Environmental Medicine, 55*(6), 493–496.

Colvin, S. R., & Block, J. (1994). Do positive illusions foster mental health? An examination of the Taylor and Brown formulation. *Psychological Bulletin, 116,* 3–20.

Colwill, R. M. (1993). An associative analysis of instrumental learning. *Current Directions in Psychological Science, 2*(4), 111–116.

Comer, D. R. (1995). A model of social loafing in real work groups. *Human Relations, 48,* 647–667.

Conley, R. R., Love, R. C., Kelly, D. L., & Bartko, J. J. (1999). Rehospitalization rates of patients recently discharged on a regimen of risperidone or clozapine. *American Journal of Psychiatry, 156,* 863–868.

Conrad, R. (1964). Acoustic confusions in immediate memory. *British Journal of Psychology, 55,* 75–84.

Cook, M., & Mineka, S. (1989). Observational conditioning of fear to fear-relevant versus fear-irrelevant stimuli in rhesus monkeys. *Journal of Abnormal Psychology, 98,* 448–459.

Coon, D. J. (1994). "Not a creature of reason": The alleged impact of Watsonian behaviorism on advertising in the 1920s. In J. T. Todd & E. K. Morris (Eds.), *Modern perspectives on John B. Watson and classical behaviorism.* Westport, CT: Greenwood Press.

Cooper, E. (1991). A critique of six measures for assessing creativity. *Journal of Creative Behavior, 25*(3), 194–204.

Cooper, H., Okamura, L., & Gurka, V. (1992). Social activity and subjective well-being. *Personality and Individual Differences, 13,* 573–583.

Cooper, J. R., Bloom, F. E., & Roth, R. H. (1996). *The biochemical basis of neuropharmacology.* New York: Oxford University Press.

Corballis, M. C. (1991). *The lopsided ape.* New York: Oxford University Press.

Coren, S. (1992). *The left-hander syndrome: The causes and consequences of left-handedness.* New York: Free Press.

Coren, S. (1996). *Sleep thieves: An eye-opening exploration into the science and mysteries of sleep.* New York: Free Press.

Coren, S., & Aks, D. J. (1990). Moon illusion in pictures: A multimechanism approach. *Journal of Experimental Psychology: Human Perception and Performance, 16,* 365–380.

Coren, S., & Girgus, J. S. (1978). *Seeing is deceiving: The psychology of visual illusions.* Hillsdale, NJ: Erlbaum.

Corkin, S. (1984). Lasting consequences of bilateral medial temporal lobectomy: Clinical course and experimental findings in H. M. *Seminars in Neurology, 4,* 249–259.

Cornell, D. G. (1997). Post hoc explanation is not prediction. *American Psychologist, 52,* 1380.

Cornoldi, C., & De Beni, R. (1996). Mnemonics and metacognition. In D. J. Herrmann, C. McEvoy, C. Hertzog, P. Hertel, & M. K. Johnson (Eds.), *Basic and applied memory research: Practical applications.* Mahwah, NJ: Erlbaum.

Cosmides, L. L., & Tooby, J. (1989). Evolutionary psychology and the generation of culture. Part II. Case study: A computational theory of social exchange. *Ethology and Sociobiology, 10,* 51–97.

Cosmides, L., & Tooby, J. (1994). Beyond intuition and instinct blindness: Toward an evolutionarily rigorous cognitive science. *Cognition, 50,* 41–77.

Cosmides, L., & Tooby, J. (1996). Are humans good intuitive statisticians after all? Rethinking some conclusions from the literature on judgment under uncertainty. *Cognition, 58*, 1–73.

Cosmides, L., & Tooby, J. (1999). Toward an evolutionary taxonomy of treatable conditions. *Journal of Abnormal Psychology, 108*, 453–464.

Costa, G. (1996). The impact of shift and night work on health. *Applied Ergonomics, 27*, 9–16.

Costa, P. T., Jr., & McCrae, R. (1985). *NEO Personality Inventory*. Odessa, FL: Psychological Assessment Resources.

Costa, P. T., Jr., & McCrae, R. (1992). *Revised NEO Personality Inventory: NEO PI and NEO Five-Factor Inventory* (Professional Manual). Odessa, FL: Psychological Assessment Resources.

Costa, P. T., Jr., & McCrae, R. R. (1994). Set like plaster? Evidence for the stability of adult personality. In T. F. Heatherton & J. L. Weinberger (Eds.), *Can personality change?* Washington, DC: American Psychological Association.

Costa, P. T., Jr., & McCrae, R. R. (1997). Longitudinal stability of adult personality. In R. Hogan, J. Johnson, & S. Briggs (Eds.), *Handbook of personality psychology*. San Diego: Academic Press.

Coté, L., & Crutcher, M. D. (1991). The basal ganglia. In E. R. Kandel, J. H. Schwartz, & T. M. Jessell (Eds.), *Principles of neural science* (3rd ed.). New York: Elsevier.

Cowan, N. (1988). Evolving conceptions of memory storage, selective attention, and their mutual constraints within the human information-processing system. *Psychological Bulletin, 104*, 163–191.

Cowan, N. (1995). *Attention and memory: An integrated framework*. New York: Oxford University Press.

Cowan, N., Wood, N. L., Nugent, L. D., & Treisman, M. (1997). There are two word-length effects in verbal short-term memory: Opposed effects on duration and complexity. *Psychological Science, 8*, 290–295.

Cowey, A. (1994). Cortical visual areas and the neurobiology of higher visual processes. In M. J. Farah & G. Ratcliff (Eds.), *The neuropsychochology of high-level vision: Collected tutorial essays*. Hillsdale, NJ: Erlbaum.

Craig, J. C., & Rollman, G. B. (1999). Somesthesis. *Annual Review of Psychology, 50*, 305–331.

Craik, F. I. M., Govoni, R., Naveh-Benjamin, M., & Anderson, N. D. (1996). The effects of divided attention on encoding and retrieval processes in human memory. *Journal of Experimental Psychology: General, 125*, 159–180.

Craik. F. I. M., & Lockhart, R. S. (1972). Levels of processing: A framework for memory research. *Journal of Verbal Learning and Verbal Behavior, 11*, 671–684.

Craik, F. I. M., & Tulving, E. (1975). Depth of processing and the retention of words in episodic memory. *Journal of Experimental Psychology: General, 104*, 268–294.

Craik, F. I. M., Moroz, T. M., Moscovitch, M., Stuss, D. T., Winocur, G., Tulving, E., & Kapur, S. (1999). In search of the self: A positron emission tomography study. *Psychological Science, 10*, 26–34.

Crain, S. (1991). Language acquisition in the absence of experience. *Behavioral and Brain Sciences, 14*, 597–650.

Crano, W. D. (1995). Attitude strength and vested interest. In R. E. Petty & J. A. Krosnick (Eds.), *Attitude strength: Antecedents and consequences*. Mahwah, NJ: Erlbaum.

Craufurd, D. I. O., Creed, F., & Jayson, M. D. (1990). Life events and psychological disturbance in patients with low-back pain. *Spine, 15*, 490–494.

Cravens, H. (1992). A scientific project locked in time: The Terman Genetic Studies of Genius, 1920s–1950s. *American Psychologist, 47*, 183–189.

Creed, F. (1989). Appendectomy. In G. W. Brown & T. O. Harris (Eds.), *Life events and illness*. New York: Guilford Press.

Creed, F. (1993). Stress and psychosomatic disorders. In L. Goldberger & S. Breznitz (Eds.), *Handbook of stress: Theoretical and clinical aspects* (2nd ed.). New York: Free Press.

Critelli, J. W., & Ee, J. S. (1996). Stress and physical illness: Development of an integrative model. In T. W. Miller (Ed.), *Theory and assessment of stressful life events*. Madison, CT: International Universities Press.

Crits-Christoph, P. (1997). Limitations of the dodo bird verdict and the role of clinical trials in psychotherapy research: Comment on Wampold et al (1997). *Psychological Bulletin, 122*, 216–220.

Crockett, H. (1962). The achievement motive and differential occupational mobility in the United States. *American Sociological Review, 27*, 191–204.

Cross, C. K., & Hirschfeld, R. M. A. (1986). Epidemiology of disorders in adulthood: Suicide. In G. L. Klerman, M. M. Weissman, P. S. Appelbaum, & L. H. Roth (Eds.), *Psychiatry: Vol. 5. Social, epidemiologic, and legal psychiatry*. New York: Basic Books.

Cross, S. E., & Markus, H. R. (1993). Gender in thought, belief, and action: A cognitive approach. In A. E. Beall & R. J. Sternberg (Eds.), *The psychology of gender*. New York: Guilford Press.

Cross, S. E., & Markus, H. R. (1999). The cultural constitution of personality. In L. A. Pervin & O. P. John (Eds.), *Handbook of personality: Theory and research*. New York: Guilford Press.

Crowder, R. G. (1993). Short-term memory: Where do we stand? *Memory & Cognition, 21*, 142–45.

Crowder, R. G., & Neath, I. (1991). The microscope metaphor in human memory. In W. E. Hockley & S. Lewandowsky (Eds.), *Relating theory and data: Essays on human memory in honor of Bennet B. Murdock*. Hillsdale, NJ: Erlbaum.

Croyle, R. T., & Cooper, J. (1983). Dissonance arousal: Physiological evidence. *Journal of Personality and Social Psychology, 45*, 782–791.

Csikszentmihalyi, M. (1994). Creativity. In R. J. Sternberg (Ed.), *Encyclopedia of human intelligence*. New York: Macmillan.

Csikszentmihalyi, M. (1999). Implications of a systems perspective for the study of creativity. In R. J. Sternberg (Ed.), *Handbook of creativity*. New York: Cambridge University Press.

Cuesta, M. J., Peralta, B., & DeLeon, J. (1994). Schizophrenic syndromes associated with treatment response. *Progress in Neurology, Psychopharmacology, and Biological Psychiatry, 18*, 87–99.

Culbertson, F. M. (1997). Depression and gender: An international review. *American Psychologist, 52*, 25–31.

Cunningham, M. R., Druen, P. B., & Barbee, A. P. (1997). Angels, mentors, and friends: Tradeoffs among evolutionary, social, and individual variables in physical appearance. In J. A. Simpson & D. T. Kenrick (Eds.), *Evolutionary social psychology*. Mahwah, NJ: Erlbaum.

Cunningham, M. R., Roberts, A. R., Barbee, A. P., Druen, P. B., & Wu, C. (1995). "Their ideas of beauty are, on the whole, the same as ours": Consistency and variability in the cross-cultural perception of female physical attractiveness. *Journal of Personality and Social Psychology, 68*, 261–279.

Cushman, P. (1992). Psychotherapy to 1992: A historically situated interpretation. In D. K. Freedheim (Ed.), *History of psychotherapy: A century of change*. Washington, DC: American Psychological Association.

Cutler, B. L., & Penrod, S. D. (1995). *Mistaken identification: The eyewitness, psychology, and the law*. New York: Cambridge University Press.

Czeisler, C. A., Moore-Ede, M. C., & Coleman, R. M. (1982). Rotating work shift schedules that disrupt sleep are improved by applying circadian principles. *Science, 217*, 460–463.

Dallos, P. (1981). Cochlear physiology. *Annual Review of Psychology, 32*, 153–190.

Daly, M., & Wilson, M. (1985). Child abuse and other risks of not living with both parents. *Ethology and Sociobiology, 6*, 197–210.

Daly, M., & Wilson, M. (1988). *Homicide*. Hawthorne, NY: Aldine.

Dana, R. H. (1993). *Multicultural assessment perspectives for professional psychology*. Boston: Allyn & Bacon.

D'Andrade, R. G. (1961). Anthropological studies of dreams. In F. Hsu (Ed.), *Psychological anthropology: Approaches to culture and personality*. Homewood, IL: Dorsey Press.

Danton, W. G., & Antonuccio, D. O. (1997). A focused empirical analysis of treatments for panic and anxiety. In S. Fisher & R. P. Greenberg (Eds.), *From placebo to panacea: Putting psychiatric drugs to the test*. New York: Wiley.

Danziger, K. (1990). *Constructing the subject: Historical origins of psychological research*. Cambridge, England: Cambridge University Press.

Darley, J. M., & Latané, B. (1968). Bystander intervention in emergencies: Diffusion of responsibility. *Journal of Personality and Social Psychology, 8*, 377–383.

Darwin, C. (1859). *On the origin of species*. London: Murray.

Darwin, C. (1871). *Descent of man*. London: Murray.

Darwin, C. (1872). *The expression of emotions in man and animals*. New York: Philosophical Library.

Das, J. P. (1994). Eastern views of intelligence. In R. J. Sternberg (Ed.), *Encyclopedia of human intelligence*. New York: Macmillan.

Dasen, P. R. (1994). Culture and cognitive development from a Piagetian perspective. In W. J. Lonner & R. Malpass (Eds.), *Psychology and culture*. Boston: Allyn & Bacon.

Davidson, J. (1976). Physiology of meditation and mystical states of consciousness. *Perspectives in Biology and Medicine, 19*, 345–380.

Davis, J. M. (1985). Antipsychotic drugs. In H. I. Kaplan & B. J. Sadock (Eds.), *Comprehensive textbook of psychiatry/IV*. Baltimore: Williams & Wilkins.

Davis, M. H., Morris, M. M., & Kraus, L. A. (1998). Relationship-specific and global perceptions of social support: Associations with well-being and attachment. *Journal of Personality and Social Psychology, 74*, 468–481.

Dawson, M. E., Hazlett, E. A., Filion, D. L., Neuchterlein, K. H., & Schell, A. M. (1993). Attention and schizophrenia: Impaired modulation of the startle reflex. *Journal of Abnormal Psychology, 102*, 633–641.

Day, R. H. (1965). Inappropriate constancy explanation of spatial distortions. *Nature, 207*, 891–893.

Deakin, J. F. W. (1998). The role of serotonin in depression and anxiety. *European Psychiatry, 13*, 57s-63s.

Deary, I. J. (1995). Auditory inspection time and intelligence: What is the direction of causation? *Developmental Psychology, 31*, 237–250.

Deary, I. J., Caryl, P. G., & Gibson, G. J. (1993). Nonstationarity and the measurement of psychological response in a visual inspection time task. *Perception, 22*, 1245–1256.

Deary, I. J., & Stough, C. (1997). Intelligence and inspection time: Achievements, prospects, and problems. *American Psychologist, 51*, 599–608.

Deaux, K. (1993). Commentary: Sorry, wrong number—A reply to Gentile's call. *Psychological Science, 4*, 125–126.

De Boysson-Bardies, B., & Vihman, M. (1991). Adaptation to language: Evidence from babbling and early words in four languages. *Language, 61*, 297–319.

DeCarvalho, R. J. (1991). *The founders of humanistic psychology*. New York: Praeger.

Deeks, S. G., Smith, M., Holodniy, M., & Kahn, J. O. (1997). HIV-1 protease inhibitors: A review for clinicians. *Journal of the Amercian Medical Association, 277*, 145–154.

de Houwer, A. (1995). Bilingual language acquisition. In P. Fletcher & B. MacWhinney (Eds.), *The handbook of child language*. Oxford, OH: Basil Blackwell.

DeLeon, P. H., & Wiggins, J. G., Jr. (1996). Prescription privileges for psychologists. *American Psychologist, 51*, 225–229.

Delgado, P. L., Price, L. H., Heninger, G. R., & Charney, D. S. (1992). Neurochemistry. In E. S. Paykel (Ed.), *Handbook of affective disorders* (2nd ed.). New York: Guilford Press.

Delis, D. C., & Lucas, J. A. (1996). Memory. In B. S. Fogel, R. B. Schiffer, & S. M. Rao (Eds.), *Neuropsychiatry*. Baltimore: Williams & Wilkins.

DeLongis, A., Folkman, S., & Lazarus, R. S. (1988). The impact of daily stress on health and mood: Psychological and social resources as mediators. *Journal of Personality and Social Psychology, 54*, 486–495.

Delprato, D. J., & Midgley, B. D. (1992). Some fundamentals of B. F. Skinner's behaviorism. *American Psychologist, 47*, 1507–1520.

DeMaio, T. J. (1984). Social desirability and survey measurement: A review. In C. F. Turner & E. Martin (Eds.), *Surveying subjective phenomena* (Vol. 2). New York: Russell Sage Foundation.

Dement, W. C. (1978). *Some must watch while some must sleep*. New York: Norton.

Dement, W. C. (1994). History of sleep physiology and medicine. In M. H. Kryger, T. Roth, & W. C. Dement (Eds.), *Principles and practice of sleep medicine* (2nd ed.). Philadelphia: Saunders.

Dement, W. C. (1997). The perils of drowsy driving. *New England Journal Medicine, 337*, 783–784.

Dement, W. C., & Vaughan, C. (1999). *The promise of sleep*. New York: Delacorte Press.

Dement, W. C., & Wolpert, E. (1958). The relation of eye movements, bodily motility, and external stimuli to dream content. *Journal of Experimental Psychology, 53*, 543–553.

Demo, D. H. (1992). Parent-child relations: Assessing recent changes. *Journal of Marriage and the Family, 54*, 104–117.

Dempster, F. N. (1996). Distributing and managing the conditions of encoding and practice. In E. L. Bjork & R. A. Bjork (Eds.), *Memory*. San Diego: Academic Press.

DeNelsky, G. Y. (1996). The case against prescription privileges for psychologists. *American Psychologist, 51*, 207–212.

Dennerstein, L. (1996). Well-being, symptoms and the menopausal transition. *Maturitas, 23*, 147–157.

Dennis, D. L., Buckner, J. C., Lipton, F. R., & Levine, I. S. (1991). A decade of research and services for homeless mentally ill persons: Where do we stand? *American Psychologist, 46*, 1129–1138.

Dennis, W. (1966). Age and creative productivity. *Journal of Gerontology, 21*(1), 1–8.

Deregowski, J. B. (1989). Real space and represented space: Cross-cultural perspectives. *Behavioral and Brain Sciences, 12*, 51–119.

Derogatis, L. R., & Coons, H. L. (1993). Self-report measures of stress. In L. Goldberger & S. Breznitz (Eds.), *Handbook of stress: Theoretical and clinical aspects* (2nd ed.). New York: Free Press.

de Silva, P. (1995). Cognitive-behavioral models of eating disorders. In G. Szmukler, C. Dare, & J. Treasure (Eds.), *Handbook of eating disorders: Theory, treatment and research*. New York: Wiley.

Desimone, R. (1991). Face selective cells in the temporal cortex of monkeys. *Journal of Cognitive Neuroscience, 3*, 1–8.

Deutsch, J. A. (1990). Food intake: Gastric factors. In E. M. Stricker (Ed), *Handbook of behavioral neurobiology: Vol 10. Neurobiology of food and fluid intake*. New York: Plenum.

DeValois, R. L., & Jacobs, G. H. (1984). Neural mechanisms of color vision. In I. Darian-Smith (Ed.), *The nervous system* (Vol. 3). Baltimore: Williams & Wilkins.

Devanand, D. P., Dwork, A. J., Hutchinson, E. R., Bolwig, T. G., & Sackeim, H. A. (1994). Does ECT alter brain structure? *American Journal of Psychiatry, 151*, 957–970.

De Villiers, P. (1977). Choice in concurrent schedules and a quantitative formulation of the law of effect. In W. K. Honig & J. E. R. Staddon (Eds.), *Handbook of operant behavior*. Englewood Cliffs, NJ: Prentice-Hall.

De Villiers, P. A. & De Villiers, J. G. (1992). Language development. In M. H. Bornstein & M. E. Lamb (Eds.), *Developmental psychology: An advanced textbook* (3rd ed.). Hillsdale, NJ: Erlbaum.

Devine, P. G., & Baker, S. M. (1991). Measurements of racial stereotypes subtyping. *Personality and Social Psychology Bulletin, 17*, 44–50.

Devine, P. G., & Elliot, A. J. (1995). Are racial stereotypes really fading? The Princeton trilogy revisited. *Personality and Social Psychology Bulletin, 21*, 1139–1150.

Devine, P. G., & Monteith, M. J. (1999). Automaticity and control in stereotyping. In S. Chaiken & Y. Trope (Eds.), *Dual-process theories in social psychology*. New York: Guilford Press.

Devine, P. G., Tauer, J. M., Barron, K. E., Elliot, A. J., & Vance, K. M. (1999). Moving beyond attitude change in the study of dissonance-related processes. In E. Harmon-Jones & J. Mills (Eds.), *Cognitive dissonance: Progress on a pivotal theory in social psychology*. Washington, DC: American Psychological Association.

de Wijk, R. A., Schab, F. R., & Cain, W. S. (1995). Odor identification. In F. R. Schab & R. G. Crowder (Eds.), *Memory for odors*. Mahwah, NJ: Erlbaum.

Diener, E. (1984). Subjective well-being. *Psychological Bulletin, 93*, 542–575.

Diener, E., & Diener, M. (1995). Cross-cultural correlates of life satisfaction and self-esteem. *Journal of Personality and Social Psychology, 68*, 653–663.

Diener, E., Sandvik, E., Seidlitz, L., & Diener, M. (1993). The relationship between income and subjective well-being. Relative or absolute? *Social Indicators Research, 28*, 195–223.

Diener, E., Wolsic, B., & Fujita, F. (1995). Physical attractiveness and subjective well-being. *Journal of Personality and Social Psychology, 69*, 120–129.

Dillbeck, M. C., & Orme-Johnson, D. W. (1987). Physiological differences between transcendental meditation and rest. *American Psychologist, 42*, 879–881.

Dilsaver, S. C., Chen, Y. R., Shoaib, A. M., & Swann, A. C. (1999). Phenomenology of mania: Evidence for distinct depressed, dysphoric, and euphoric presentations. *American Journal of Psychiatry, 156*, 426–430.

DiMatteo, M. R. (1991). *The psychology of health, illness, and medical care: An individual perspective*. Pacific Grove, CA: Brooks/Cole.

DiMatteo, M. R. (1994). Enhancing patient adherence to medical recommendations. *Journal of the American Medical Association, 271*, 79–83.

DiMatteo, M. R. (1997). Health behaviors and care decisions: An overview of professional-patient communication. In D. S. Gochman (Ed.), *Handbook of health behavior research II: Provider determinants*. New York: Plenum.

DiMatteo, M. R., & Friedman, H. S. (1982). *Social psychology and medicine*. Cambridge, MA: Oelgeschlager, Gunn & Hain.

Dinges, D. F. (1989). Napping patterns and effects in human adults. In D. F. Dinges & R. J. Broughton (Eds.), *Sleep and alertness: Chronobiological, behavioral, and medical aspects of napping*. New York: Raven.

Dinges, D. F. (1993). Napping. In M.A. Carskadon (Ed.), *Encyclopedia of sleep and dreaming*. New York: Macmillan.

Dinges, D. F. (1995). Overview of sleepiness and accidents. *Journal of Sleep Research, 4*, 4–14.

DiNicola, D. D., & DiMatteo, M. R. (1984). Practitioners, patients, and compliance with medical regimens: A social psychological perspective. In A. Baum, S. E. Taylor, & J. E. Singer (Eds.), *Handbook of psychology and health: Vol. 4. Social psychological aspects of health.* Hillsdale, NJ: Erlbaum.

Dinsmoor, J. A. (1998). Punishment. In W. O'Donohue (Ed.), *Learning and behavior therapy.* Boston: Allyn & Bacon.

Dixon, M., & Laurence, J. R. (1992). Two hundred years of hypnosis research: Questions resolved? Questions unanswered! In E. Fromm & M. R. Nash (Eds.), *Contemporary hypnosis research.* New York: Guilford Press.

Dixon, N. F. (1980). Humor: A cognitive alternative to stress? In I. G. Sarason & C. D. Spielberger (Eds.), *Stress and anxiety* (Vol. 7). Washington, DC: Hemisphere.

D'Mello, D. A., Fernandes, C. L., & Colenda, C. C. I. (1997). Seratonin reuptake inhibitor antidepressant withdrawal syndromes. *Primary Psychiatry, 4,* 51–56.

Dobzhansky, T. (1937). *Genetics and the origin of species.* New York: Columbia University Press.

Docherty, J. P. (1999). Cost of treating mental illness from a managed care perspective. *Journal of Clinical Psychiatry, 60,* 49–53.

Doerr, P., Pirke, K. M., Kockott, G., & Dittmor, F. (1976). Further studies on sex hormones in male homosexuals. *Archives of General Psychiatry, 33,* 611–614.

Dollard, J., Doob, L. W., Miller, N. E., Mowrer, O. H., & Sears, R. R. (1939). *Frustration and aggression.* New Haven: Yale University Press.

Dollard, J., & Miller, N. E. (1950). *Personality and psychotherapy: An analysis in terms of learning, thinking and culture.* New York: McGraw-Hill.

Dominowski, R. L., & Bourne, L. E. Jr. (1994). History of research on thinking and problem solving. In R. J. Sternberg (Ed.), *Thinking and problem solving.* San Diego: Academic Press.

Domjan, M. (1992). Adult learning and mate choice: Possibilities and experimental evidence. *American Zoologist, 32,* 48–61.

Domjan, M. (1994). Formulation of a behavior system for sexual conditioning. *Psychonomic Bulletin & Review, 1,* 421–428.

Domjan, M. (1998). *The principles of learning and behavior.* Pacific Grove: Brooks/Cole.

Domjan, M., & Purdy, J. E. (1995). Animal research in psychology: More than meets the eye of the general psychology student. *American Psychologist, 50,* 496–503.

Domjan, M., Blesbois, E., & Williams, J. (1998). The adaptive significance of sexual conditioning: Pavlovian control of sperm release. *Psychological Science, 9,* 411–415.

Dorfman, D. D. (1995). Soft science with a neoconservative agenda. *Contemporary Psychology, 40,* 418–421.

Dorner, G. (1988). Neuroendocrine response to estrogen and brain differentiation. *Archives of Sexual Behavior, 17*(1), 57–75.

Doty, R. L. (1991). Olfactory system. In T. V. Getchell, R. L. Doty, L. M. Bartoshuk, & J. B. Snow, Jr. (Eds.), *Smell and taste in health and disease.* New York: Raven.

Dovidio, J. F., & Gaertner, S. L. (1999). Reducing prejudice: Combating intergroup biases. *Current Directions in Psychological Science, 8,* 101–105.

Draijer, N., & Langeland, W. (1999). Childhood trauma and perceived parental dysfunction in the etiology of dissociative symptoms in psychiatric inpatients. *American Journal of Psychiatry, 156,* 379–385.

Draycott, S., & Dabbs, A. (1998). Cognitive dissonance 1: An overview of the literature and its integration into theory and practice of clinical psychology. *British Journal of Clinical Psychology, 37,* 341–353.

Drewnowski, A. (1995). Standards for the treatment of obesity. In K. D. Brownell, & C. G. Fairburn (Eds.), *Eating disorders and obesity: A comprehensive handbook.* New York: Guilford Press.

Drigotas, S. M., Safstrom, C. A., & Gentilia, T. (1999). An investment model prediction of dating infidelity. *Journal of Personality and Social Psychology, 77,* 509–524.

Driskell, J. E., & Mullen, B. (1990). Status, expectations, and behavior: A meta-analytic review and test of the theory. *Personality and Social Psychology Bulletin, 16,* 541–553.

Driskell, J. E., Willis, R. P., & Copper, C. (1992). Effect of overlearning on retention. *Journal of Applied Psychology, 77*(5), 615–622.

Druss, B. G., & Rosenheck, R. A. (1998). Mental disorders and access to medical care in the United States. *American Journal of Psychiatry, 155,* 1775–1777.

Duara, R. London, E. D., & Rapoport, S. I. (1985). Changes in structure and energy metabolism of the aging brain. In C. E. Finch & E. L. Schneider (Eds.), *Handbook of the biology of aging.* (2nd ed.). New York: Van Nostrand Reinhold.

Dubovsky, S. L., & Buzan, R. (1999). Mood disorders. In R. E. Hales, S. C. Yudofsky, & J. A. Talbott (Eds.), *American Psychiatric Press Textbook of Psychiatry.* Washington, DC: American Psychiatric Press.

DuBreuil, S. C., Garry, M., & Loftus, E. F. (1998). Tales from the crib: Age regression and the creation of unlikely memories. In S. J. Lynn & K. M. McConkey (Eds.), *Truth in memory.* New York: Guilford Press.

Duckworth, K., & Borus, J. F. (1999). Population-based psychiatry in the public sector and managed care. In A. M. Nicholi (Ed.), *The Harvard guide to psychiatry.* Cambridge, MA: Harvard University Press.

Duncan, B. L. (1976). Differential social perception and attribution of intergroup violence: Testing the lower limits of stereotyping of blacks. *Journal of Personality and Social Psychology, 34,* 590–598.

Duncan, P. D., Ritter, P. L., Dornbusch, S. M., Gross, R. T., & Carlsmith, J. M. (1985). The effects of pubertal timing on body image, school behavior, and deviance. *Youth and Adolescence, 14,* 227–235.

Dunning, D., & Sherman, D. A. (1997). Stereotypes and tacit inference. *Journal of Personality and Social Psychology, 73,* 459–471.

Dutton, D., & Aron, A. (1974). Some evidence for heightened sexual attraction under conditions of high anxiety. *Journal of Personality and Social Psychology, 30,* 510–517.

Dwyer, J. (1995). Popular diets. In K. D. Brownell & C. G. Fairburn (Eds.), *Eating disorders and obesity.* New York: Guilford Press.

Dykman, B. M., Horowitz, L. M., Abramson, L. Y., & Usher, M. (1991). Schematic and situational determinants of depressed and nondepressed students' interpretation feedback. *Journal of Abnormal Psychology, 100,* 45–55.

Eagle, M. N., & Wolitzky, D. L. (1992). Psychoanalytic theories of psychotherapy. In D. K. Freedheim (Ed.), *History of psychotherapy: A century of change.* Washington, DC: American Psychological Association.

Eagly, A. H. (1992). Uneven progress: Social psychology and the study of attitudes. *Journal of Personality and Social Psychology, 63,* 693–710.

Eagly, A. H., & Chaiken, S. (1995). Attitude strength, attitude structure, and resistance to change. In R. E. Petty & J. A. Krosnick (Eds.), *Attitude strength: Antecedents and consequences.* Mahwah, NJ: Erlbaum.

Eagly, A. H., & Wood, W. (1999). The origins of sex differences in human behavior: Evolved dispositions versus social roles. *American Psychologist, 54,* 408–423.

Eagly, A. H., Ashmore, R. D., Makhijani, M. G., & Longo, L. C. (1991). What is beautiful is good, but . . .: A meta-analytic review of research on the physical attractiveness stereotype. *Psychological Bulletin, 110,* 109–128.

Eaton, W. W., Dryman, A., & Weissman, M. M. (1991). Panic and phobia. In L. N. Robins & D. A. Regier (Eds.), *Psychiatric disorders in America: The epidemiologic catchment area study.* New York: Free Press.

Ebbinghaus, H. (1885/1964). *Memory: A contribution to experimental psychology* (H. A. Ruger & E. R. Bussemius, Trans.). New York: Dover. (Original work published 1885)

Eckensberger, L., & Zimba, R. (1997). The development of moral judgment. In J. W. Berry, P. R. Dasen, & T. S. Saraswathi (Eds.), *Handbook of cross-cultural psychology.* Boston: Allyn & Bacon.

Edberg, P. (1990). Rorschach assessment. In A. Goldstein & M. Hersen (Eds.), *Handbook of psychological assessment.* New York: Pergamon Press.

Edlin, G., & Golanty, E. (1992). *Health and wellness: A holistic approach.* Boston: Jones and Bartlett.

Edwards, B. (1989). *Drawing on the right side of the brain.* Los Angeles: J. P. Tarcher.

Edwards, K., & Smith, E. E. (1996). A disconfirmation bias in the evaluation of arguments. *Journal of Personality an Social Psychology, 71,* 5–24.

Efron, R. (1990). *The decline and fall of hemispheric specialization.* Hillsdale, NJ: Erlbaum.

Egeland, B., & Hiester, M. (1995). The long-term consequences of infant day-care and mother-infant attachment. *Child Development, 66,* 474–485.

Ehlers, D. L., & Kupfer, D. J. (1989). Effects of age on delta and REM sleep parameters. *Electroencephalography & Clinical Neurophysiology, 72*(2), 118–125.

Ehrenberg, O., & Ehrenberg, M. (1986). *The psychotherapy maze.* Northvale, NJ: Aronson.

Eibl-Eibesfeldt, I. (1975). *Ethology: The biology of behavior.* New York: Holt, Rinehart & Winston.

Eich, E. (1990). Learning during sleep. In R. R. Bootzin, J. F. Kihlstrom, & D. L. Schacter (Eds.), *Sleep and cognition.* Washington, DC: American Psychological Association.

Eich, E., Macaulay, D., Loewenstein, R. J., & Dihle, P. H. (1997). Memory, amnesia, and dissociative identity disorder. *Psychological Science, 8*, 417–422.

Eichenbaum, H. (1997). Declarative memory: Insights from cognitive neurobiology. *Annual Review of Psychology, 48*, 547–572.

Eisler, I. (1995). Family models of eating disorders. In G. Szmukler, C. Dare, & J. Treasure (Eds.), *Handbook of eating disorders: Theory, treatment and research.* New York: Wiley.

Eisler, R. M., & Ragsdale, K. (1992). Masculine gender role and midlife transition in men. In V. B. Van Hasselt & M. Hersen (Eds.), *Handbook of social development: A lifespan perspective.* New York: Plenum.

Ekman, P. (1992). Facial expressions of emotion: New findings, new questions. *Psychological Science, 3*, 34–38.

Ekman, P. (1993). Facial expression and emotion. *American Psychologist, 48*, 384–392.

Ekman, P., & Friesen, W. V. (1975). *Unmasking the face.* Englewood Cliffs, NJ: Prentice-Hall.

Ekman, P., & Friesen, W. V. (1984). *Unmasking the face.* Palo Alto: Consulting Psychologists Press.

Eldred, L., & Chaisson, R. (1996). The clinical course of HIV infection in women. In R. R. Faden & N. E. Kass (Eds.), *HIV, AIDS, and childbearing.* New York: Oxford University Press.

Elias, M. F., Elias, J. W., & Elias, P. K. (1990). Biological and health influences on behavior. In J. E. Birren & K. W. Schaie (Eds.), *Handbook of the psychology of aging.* San Diego: Academic Press.

Ellard, K., Beaurepaire, J., Jones, M., Piper, D., & Tennant, C. (1990). Acute chronic stress in duodenal ulcer disease. *Gastroenterology, 99*, 1628–1632.

Elliott, E. (1989). Stress and illness. In S. Cheren (Ed.), *Psychosomatic medicine: Theory, physiology, and practice* (Vol. 1). Madison, CT: International Universities Press.

Elliott, R., Stiles, W. B., & Shapiro, D. A. (1993). Are some therapies more equivalent than others? In T. R. Giles (Ed.), *Handbook of effective psychotherapy.* New York: Plenum.

Ellis, A. (1977). *Reason and emotion in psychotherapy.* Seacaucus, NJ: Lyle Stuart.

Ellis, A. (1985). *How to live with and without anger.* New York: Citadel Press.

Ellis, A. (1996). How I learned to help clients feel better and get better. *Psychotherapy, 33*, 149–151.

Ellman, S. J., Spielman, A. J., Luck, D., Steiner, S. S., & Halperin, R. (1991). REM deprivation: A review. In S. J. Ellman & J. S. Antrobus (Eds.), *The mind in sleep: Psychology and psychophysiology* (2nd ed.). New York: Wiley.

Emmelkamp, P. M. G. (1994). Behavior therapy with adults. In A. E. Bergin & S. L. Garfield (Eds.), *Handbook of psychotherapy and behavior change* (4th ed.). New York: Wiley.

Emmelkamp, P. M. G., & Scholing, A. (1990). Behavioral treatment for simple and social phobias. In R. Noyes, Jr., M. Roth, & G. D. Burrows (Eds.), *Handbook of anxiety: The treatment of anxiety* (Vol. 4). Amsterdam: Elsevier.

Engen, T. (1987). Remembering odors and their names. *American Scientist, 75*, 497–503.

Epley, N., & Huff, C. (1998). Suspicion, affective response, and educational benefit as a result of deception in psychology research. *Personality and Social Psychology Bulletin, 24*, 759–768.

Eppley, K., Abrams, A., & Shear, J. (1989). The differential effects of relaxation techniques on trait anxiety: A meta-analysis. *Journal of Clinical Psychology, 45*(6), 957–974.

Epstein, L. H., Valoski, A. M., Vara, L. S., McCurley, J., Wisniewski, L., Kalarchian, M. A., Klein, K. R., & Shrager, L. R. (1995). Effects of decreasing sedentary behavior and increasing activity on weight change in obese children. *Health Psychology, 14*, 109–115.

Epstein, S. P. (1982). Conflict and stress. In L. Goldberger & S. Breznitz (Eds.), *Handbook of stress: Theoretical and clinical aspects.* New York: Free Press.

Epstein, S., Donovan, S., & Denes-Raj, V. (1999). The missing link in the paradox of the Linda conjunction problem: Beyond knowing and thinking of the conjunction rule, the intrinsic appeal of heuristic processing. *Personality and Social Psychology Bulletin, 25*, 204–214.

Erber, M. W., Hodges, S. D., & Wilson, T. D. (1995). Attitude strength, attitude stability, and the effects of analyzing reasons. In R. E. Petty & J. A. Krosnick (Eds.), *Attitude strength: Antecedents and consequences.* Mahwah, NJ: Erlbaum.

Erel, O., & Burnham, B. (1995). Interrelatedness of marital relations and parent-child relations: A meta-analytic review. *Psychological Bulletin, 118*, 108–132.

Ericsson, K. A., & Polson, P. G. (1988). An experimental analysis of the mechanisms of a memory skill. *Journal of Experimental Psychology: Learning, Memory and Congnition, 14*, 305–316.

Erikson, E. (1963). *Childhood and society.* New York: Norton.

Erikson, E. (1968). *Identity: Youth and crisis.* New York: Norton.

Esterling, B. A., Antoni, M. H., Fletcher, M. A., Margulies, S., & Schniederman, N. (1994). Emotional disclosure through writing or speaking modulates latent Epstein-Barr virus antibody titers. *Journal of Consulting and Clinical Psychology, 62*, 130–140.

Esterson, A. (1993). *Seductive mirage: An exploration of the work of Sigmund Freud.* Chicago: Open Court.

Estes, R. E., Coston, M. L., & Fournet, G. P. (1990). *Rankings of the most notable psychologists by department chairpersons.* Unpublished manuscript.

Estes, W. K. (1999). Models of human memory: A 30-year retrospective. In C. Izawa (Ed.), *On human memory: Evolution, progress, and reflections on the 30th anniversary of the Atkinson-Shiffrin model.* Mahwah, NJ: Erlbaum.

Etaugh, C., & Liss, M. B. (1992). Home, school, and playroom: Training grounds for adult gender roles. *Sex Roles, 26*, 129–147.

Evans, C. E., & Haynes, R. B. (1990). Patient compliance. In R. E. Rakel (Ed.), *Textbook of family practice.* Philadelphia: Saunders.

Evans, F. J. (1990). Behavioral responses during sleep. In R. R. Bootzin, J. F. Kihlstrom, & D. L. Schacter (Eds.), *Sleep and cognition.* Washington, DC: American Psychological Association.

Evans, R. L. (1981). New drug evaluations: Alprazolam. *Drug Intelligence and Clinical Pharmacy, 15*, 633–637.

Eysenck, H. J. (1959). Learning theory and behaviour therapy. *Journal of Mental Science, 195*, 61–75.

Eysenck, H. J. (1967). *The biological basis of personality.* Springfield, IL: Charles C. Thomas.

Eysenck, H. J. (1977). *Crime and personality.* London: Routledge & Kegan Paul.

Eysenck, H. J. (1982). *Personality, genetics and behavior: Selected papers.* New York: Praeger.

Eysenck, H. J. (1988). The concept of "intelligence": Useful or useless? *Intelligence, 12*(1), 1–16.

Eysenck, H. J. (1989). Discrimination reaction time and "g": A reply to Humphreys. *Intelligence, 13*(4), 325–326.

Eysenck, H. J. (1990a). Biological dimensions of personality. In L. A. Pervin (Ed.), *Handbook of personality: Theory and research.* New York: Guilford Press.

Eysenck, H. J. (1990b). *Decline and fall of the Freudian empire.* Washington, DC: Scott-Townsend.

Eysenck, H. J. (1991). Dimensions of personality: 16, 5, or 3?—Criteria for a taxonomic paradigm. *Personality and Individual Differences, 12*, 773–790.

Eysenck, H. J., & Kamin, L. (1981). *The intelligence controversy.* New York: Wiley.

Eysenck, M. W. (1984). *A handbook of cognitive psychology.* Hillsdale, NJ: Erlbaum.

Eysenck, M. W., Mogg, K., May, J., Richards, A., & Mathews, A. (1991). Bias in interpretation of ambiguous sentences related to threat in anxiety. *Journal of Abnormal Psychology, 100*, 144–150.

Fagot, B. I., Hagan, R., Leinbach, M. D., & Kronsberg, S. (1985). Differential reactions to assertive and communicative acts of toddler boys and girls. *Child Development, 56*, 1499–1505.

Fagot, B. I., Leinbach, M. D., & O'Boyle, C. (1992). Gender labeling, gender stereotyping, and parenting behaviors. *Developmental Psychology, 28*, 225–230.

Fahey, P. J., & Gallagher-Allred, C. (1990). Nutrition. In R. E. Rakel (Ed.), *Textbook of family practice* (4th ed.). Philadelphia: Saunders.

Falls, W. A. (1998). Extinction: A review of therapy and the evidence suggesting that memories are not erased with nonreinforcement. In W. O'Donohue (Ed.), *Learning and behavior therapy.* Boston: Allyn & Bacon.

Fancher, R. E. (1979). *Pioneers of psychology.* New York: Norton.

Faraday, A. (1974). *The dream game.* New York: Harper & Row.

Farah, A. (1997). An overview of ECT. *Primary Psychiatry, 4*, 58–62.

Faravelli, C., & Pallanti, S. (1989). Recent life events and panic disorders. *American Journal of Psychiatry, 146*, 622–626.

Farbman, A. I. (1992). *Cell biology of olfaction.* Cambridge: Cambridge University Press.

Farrar, M. J. (1990). Discourse and the acquisition of grammatical morphemes. *Journal of Child Language, 17*, 607–624.

Fausto-Sterling, A. (1992). *Myths of gender.* New York: Basic Books.

Fava, G. A., Perini, G. I., Santonastaso, P., & Fornasa, C. V. (1989). Life events and psychological distress in dermatologic disorders: Psoriasis, chronic urticaria, and fungal infections. In T. W. Miller (Ed.), *Stressful life events.* Madison, CT: International Universities Press.

Fazio, R. H. (1995). Attitudes as object-evaluation associations: Determinants, consequences, and correlates of attitude accessibility. In R. E. Petty & J. A. Krosnick (Eds.), *Attitude strength: Antecedents and consequences*. Mahwah, NJ: Erlbaum.

Feeney, J. A. (1999). Adult romantic attachment and couple relationships. In J. Cassidy & P. R. Shaver (Eds.), *Handbook of attachment: Theory, research, and clinical applications*. New York: Guilford Press.

Fein, S., & Spencer, S. J. (1997). Prejudice as self-image maintenance: Affirming the self through derogating others. *Journal of Personality and Social Psychology, 73*, 31–44.

Feingold, A. (1988a). Cognitive gender differences are disappearing. *American Psychologist, 43*, 95–103.

Feingold, A. (1988b). Matching for attractiveness in romantic partners and same-sex friends: A meta-analysis and theoretical critique. *Psychological Bulletin, 104*, 226–235.

Feingold, A. (1990). Gender differences in effects of physical attractiveness on romantic attraction: A comparison across five research paradigms. *Journal of Personality and Social Psychology, 59*, 981–993.

Feingold, A. (1992). Good-looking people are not what we think. *Psychological Bulletin, 111*, 304–341.

Feingold, A. (1994). Gender differences in personality: A meta-analysis. *Psychological Bulletin, 116*, 429–456.

Feist, G. J. (1998). A meta-analysis of personality in scientific and artistic creativity. *Personality and Social Psychology Review, 2*, 290–309.

Feldman, D. H. (1988). Creativity: Dreams, insights, and transformations. In R. J. Sternberg (Ed.), *The nature of creativity: Contemporary psychological perspectives*. Cambridge: Cambridge University Press.

Feldman, D. H. (1999). The development of creativity. In R. J. Sternberg (Ed.), *Handbook of creativity*. New York: Cambridge University Press.

Feldman, P. J., Cohen, S., Doyle, W. J., Skoner, D. P., & Gwaltney, J. M. Jr. (1999). The impact of personality on the reporting of unfounded symptoms and illness. *Journal of Personality and Social Psychology, 77*, 370–378.

Felker, B., & Hubbard, J. R. (1998). Influence of mental stress on the endocrine system. In J. R. Hubbard & E. A. Workman (Eds.), *Handbook of stress medicine: An organ system approach*. New York: CRC Press.

Fenton, W. S., & McGlashan, T. H. (1994). Antecedents, symptom progression, and long-term outcome of the deficit syndrome in schizophrenia. *American Journal of Psychiatry, 151*, 351–356.

Fenwick, P. (1987). Meditation and the EEG. In M. A. West (Ed.), *The psychology of meditation*. Oxford: Clarendon Press.

Ferguson, T. (1993). Working with your doctor. In D. Goleman & J. Gurin (Eds.), *Mind-body medicine: How to use your mind for better health*. Yonkers, NY: Consumer Reports Books.

Ferster, C. S., & Skinner, B. F. (1957). *Schedules of reinforcement*. New York: Appleton-Century-Crofts.

Festinger, L. (1957). *A theory of cognitive dissonance*. Stanford, CA: Stanford University Press.

Festinger, L., & Carlsmith, J. M. (1959). Cognitive consequences of forced compliance. *Journal of Abnormal and Social Psychology, 58*, 203–210.

Fincham, F. D., & Bradbury, T. N. (1993). Marital satisfaction, depression, and attributions: A longitudinal analysis. *Journal of Personality and Social Psychology, 63*, 442–452.

Fincham, F. D., Bradbury, T. N., Arias, I., Byrne, C. A., & Karney, B. R. (1997). Marital violence, marital distress, and attributions. *Journal of Family Psychology, 11*, 367–372.

Fine, R. (1990). *The history of psychoanalysis*. New York: Continuum.

Finer, B. (1980). Hypnosis and anaesthesia. In G. D. Burrows & L. Dennerstein (Eds.), *Handbook of hypnosis and psychosomatic medicine*. Amsterdam: Elsevier/North Holland Biomedical Press.

Fink, M. (1992). Electroconvulsive therapy. In E. S. Paykel (Ed.), *Handbook of affective disorders* (2nd ed.). New York: Guilford Press.

Fink, P. (1995). Psychiatric illness in patients with persistent somatisation. *British Journal of Psychiatry, 166*, 93–99.

Finnegan, L. P., & Kandal, S. R. (1997). Maternal and neonatal effects of alcohol and drugs. In J. H. Lowinson, P. Ruiz, R. B. Millman, & J. G. Langrod (Eds.), *Substance abuse: A comprehensive textbook*. Baltimore: Williams & Wilkins.

Fischer, K. W., & Bidell, T. (1991). Constraining nativist inferences about cognitive capacities. In S. Carey & R. Gelman (Eds.), *The epigenesis of mind: Essays on biology and cognition*. Hillsdale, NJ: Erlbaum.

Fischer, K. W., & Hencke, R. W. (1996). Infants' construction of actions in context: Piaget's contribution to research on early development. *Psychological Science, 7*, 204–210.

Fischhoff, B. (1982). Debiasing. In D. Kahneman, P. Slovic, & A. Tversky (Eds.), *Judgment under uncertainty: Heuristics and biases*. Cambridge, MA: Cambridge University Press.

Fischhoff, B. (1988). Judgment and decision making. In R. J. Sternberg & E. E. Smith (Eds.), *The psychology of human thought*. Cambridge: Cambridge University Press.

Fisher, C., & Fyrberg, D. (1994). College students weigh the costs and benefits of deceptive research. *American Psychologist, 49*, 417–427.

Fisher, S., & Greenberg, R. P. (1996). *Freud scientifically reappraised: Testing the theories and therapy*. New York: Wiley.

Fisher, S., & Greenberg, R. P. (1997). The curse of the placebo: Fanciful pursuit of a pure biological therapy. In S. Fisher & R. P. Greenberg (Eds.), *From placebo to panacea: Putting psychiatric drugs to the test*. New York: Wiley.

Fishman, D. B., & Franks, C. M. (1992). Evolution and differentiation within behavior therapy: A theoretical epistemological review. In D. K. Freedheim (Ed.), *History of psychotherapy: A century of change*. Washington, DC: American Psychological Association.

Fiske, S. T. (1998). Stereotyping, prejudice, and discrimination. In D. T. Gilbert, S. T. Fiske, & G. Lindzey (Eds.), *The handbook of social psychology*. New York: McGraw-Hill.

Fiske, S. T., & Taylor, S. E. (1991). *Social cognition*. New York: McGraw-Hill.

Flaum, M., Swayze, V. W., O'Leary, D. S., Yuh, W. T. C., Ehrhardt, J. C., Arndt, S. V., & Andreasen, N. C. (1995). Effects of diagnosis, laterality, and gender on brain morphology in schizophrenia. *American Journal of Psychiatry, 152*, 704–714.

Flavell, J. H. (1992). Cognitive development: Past, present, and future. *Developmental Psychology, 28*, 998–1005.

Flavell, J. H. (1996). Piaget's legacy. *Psychological Science, 7*, 200–203.

Fletcher, G. J. O., & Ward, C. (1988). Attribution theory and processes: A cross-cultural perspective. In M. H. Bond (Ed.), *The cross-cultural challenge to social psychology*. Newbury Park, CA: Sage.

Flett, G. L., Vredenburg, K., & Krames, L. (1995). The stability of depressive symptoms in college students: An empirical demonstration of regression to the mean. *Journal of Psychopathology & Behavioral Assessment, 17*, 403–415.

Flynn, J. R. (1987). Massive IQ gains in 14 nations: What IQ tests really measure. *Psychological Bulletin, 101*, 171–191.

Flynn, J. R. (1994). IQ gains over time. In R. J. Sternberg (Ed.), *The encyclopedia of human intelligence*. New York: Macmillan.

Flynn, J. R. (1998). IQ gains over time: Toward finding the causes. In U. Neisser (Ed.), *The rising curve: Long-term gains in IQ and related measures*. Washington, DC: American Psychological Association.

Flynn, J. R. (1999). Searching for justice: The discovery of IQ gains over time. *American Psychologist, 54*, 5–20.

Foa, E. B., & Kozak, M. J. (1995). DSM-IV field trial: Obsessive-compulsive disorder. *American Journal of Psychiatry, 152*, 90–96.

Forsyth, D. R. (1999). *An introduction to group dynamics*. Belmont, CA: Wadsworth.

Forsyth, D. R., & McMillan, J. H. (1981). Attributions, affect, and expectations: A test of Weiner's three-dimensional model. *Journal of Educational Psychology, 73*, 393–403.

Forsyth, D. R., & Strong, S. R. (1986). The scientific study of counseling and psychotherapy: A unificationist view. *American Psychologist, 41*, 113–119.

Foulkes, D. (1985). *Dreaming: A cognitive-psychological analysis*. Hillsdale, NJ: Erlbaum.

Foulkes, D. (1996). Dream research: 1953–1993. *Sleep, 19*, 609–624.

Fowers, B. J., & Richardson, F. C. (1996). Why is multiculturalism good? *American Psychologist, 51*, 609–621.

Fowler, R. D. (1986, May). Howard Hughes: A psychological autopsy. *Psychology Today*, 22–33.

Fowles, D. C. (1992). Schizophrenia: Diathesis-stress revisited. *Annual Review of Psychology, 43*, 303–336.

Fozard, J. L. (1990). Vision and hearing in aging. In J. E. Birren & K.W. Schaie (Eds.), *Handbook of the psychology of aging* (3rd ed.). San Diego: Academic Press.

Frances, A. J., First, M. B., Widiger, T. A., Miele, G. M., Tilly, S. M., Davis, W. W., & Pincus, H. A. (1991). An A to Z guide to DSM-IV conundrums. *Journal of Abnormal Psychology, 100*, 407–412.

Francis, M. E., & Pennebaker, J. W. (1992). Putting stress into words: The impact of writing on psychological, absentee and self-reported emotional well-being measures. *American Journal of Health Promotion, 6*, 280–287.

Frank, J. D. (1961). *Persuasion and healing.* Baltimore: Johns Hopkins University Press.

Frank, L. K. (1939). Projective methods for the study of personality. *Journal of Psychology, 8*, 343–389.

Frank, L. R. (1990). Electroshock: Death, brain damage, memory loss, and brainwashing. *The Journal of Mind and Behavior, 11*(3/4), 489–512.

Frantom, C., & Sherman, M. F. (1999). At what price art? Affective instability within a visual art population. *Creativity Research Journal, 12*, 15–23.

Frederick, S., & Loewenstein, G. (1999). Hedonic adaptation. In D. Kahneman, E. Diener, & N. Schwarz (Eds.), *Well-being: The foundations of hedonic psychology.* New York: Russell Sage Foundation.

Fredrickson, B. L., Roberts, T. A., Noll, S. M., Quinn, D. M., & Twenge, J. M. (1998). That swimsuit becomes you: Sex differences in self-objectification, restrained eating, and math performance. *Journal of Personality and Social Psychology, 75*, 269–284.

Freedman, J. L. (1978). *Happy people.* New York: Harcourt Brace Jovanovich.

Freedman, J. L., & Fraser, S. C. (1966). Compliance without pressure: The foot-in-the-door technique. *Journal of Personality and Social Psychology, 4*, 195–202.

Fremer, J. (1994). Group Tests. In R. J. Sternberg (Ed.), *Encyclopedia of Human Intelligence.* New York: Macmillan.

Freud, S. (1900/1953). *The interpretation of dreams.* In J. Strachey (Ed.), *The standard edition of the complete psychological works of Sigmund Freud* (Vols. 4 and 5). London: Hogarth.

Freud, S. (1901/1960). *The psychopathology of everyday life.* In J. Strachey (Ed.), *The standard edition of the complete psychological works of Sigmund Freud* (Vol. 6). London: Hogarth.

Freud, S. (1905/1953). *Fragment of an analysis of a case of hysteria.* In J. Strachey (Ed.), *The standard edition of the complete psychological works of Sigmund Freud* (Vol. 7). London: Hogarth.

Freud, S. (1924). *A general introduction to psychoanalysis.* New York: Boni & Liveright.

Freud, S. (1933/1964). *New introductory lectures on psychoanalysis.* In J. Strachey (Ed.), *The standard edition of the complete psychological works of Sigmund Freud* (Vol. 22). London: Hogarth.

Freud, S. (1940). An outline of psychoanalysis. *International Journal of Psychoanalysis, 21*, 27–84.

Frey, K. S., & Ruble, D. N. (1992). Gender constancy and the cost of sex-typed behavior: A test of the conflict hypothesis. *Developmental Psychology, 28*, 714–721.

Friedberg, J. M. (1983). Shock treatment II: Resistance in the 1970's. In R. F. Morgan (Ed.), *The iatrogenics handbook: A critical look at research and practice in the helping professions.* Fair Oaks, CA: Morgan Foundation Publishers.

Friedman, H. S., Tucker, J. S., Schwartz, J. E., Martin, L. R., Tomlinson-Keasey, C., Wingard, D. L., & Criqui, M. H. (1995). Childhood conscientiousness and longevity: Health behaviors and cause of death. *Journal of Personality and Social Psychology, 68*, 696–703.

Friedman, H. S., Tucker, J. S., Tomlinson-Keasey, C., Schwartz, J. E., Wingard, D. L., & Criqui, M. H. (1993). Does childhood personality predict longevity? *Journal of Personality and Social Psychology, 65*, 176–185.

Friedman, L. S., & Goodman, E. (1992). Adolescents at risk for HIV infection. *Primary Care, 19*(1), 171–190.

Friedman, M. (1996). *Type A behavior: Its diagnosis and treatment.* New York: Plenum.

Friedman, M., & Rosenman, R. F. (1974). *Type A behavior and your heart.* New York: Knopf.

Frieze, I. H., Olson, J. E., & Russell, J. (1991). Attractiveness and income for men and women in management. *Journal of Applied Social Psychology, 21*, 1039–1057.

Frijda, N. H. (1999). Emotions and hedonic experience. In D. Kahneman, E. Diener, & N. Schwarz (Eds.), *Well-being: The foundations of hedonic psychology.* New York: Russell Sage Foundation.

Fromm, E. (1979). The nature of hypnosis and other altered states of consciousness: An ego-psychological theory. In E. Fromm & R. E. Shor (Eds.), *Hypnosis: Developments in research and new perspectives.* New York: Aldine.

Fromm E. (1992). An ego-psychological theory of hypnosis. In E. Fromm & M. R. Nash (Eds.), *Contemporary hypnosis research.* New York: Guilford Press.

Frumkes, T. E. (1990). Classical and modern psychophysical studies of dark and light adaptation and their relationship to underlying retinal function. In K. N. Leibovic (Ed.), *Science of vision.* New York: Springer-Verlag.

Fulford, K. W. M. (1999). Nine variations and a coda on the theme of an evolutionary definition of dysfunction. *Journal of Abnormal Psychology, 108*, 412–420.

Furnham, A. (1986). Response bias, social desirability, and dissimulation. *Personality and Individual Differences, 7*, 385–400.

Furumoto, L. (1980). Mary Whiton Calkins (1863–1930). *Psychology of Women Quarterly, 5*, 55–68.

Furumoto, L., & Scarborough, E. (1986). Placing women in the history of psychology: The first American women psychologists. *American Psychologist, 41*, 35–42.

Fuster, J. M. (1996). Frontal lobe lesions. In B. S. Fogel, R. B. Schiffer, & S. M. Rao (Eds), *Neuropsychiatry.* Baltimore: Williams & Wilkins.

Gabrieli, J. D. E. (1998). Cognitive neuroscience of human memory. *Annual Review of Psychology, 49*, 87–115.

Gaertner, S. L., Dovidio, J. F., Nier, J. A., Ward, C. M., & Banker, B. S. (1999). Across cultural divides: The value of a superordinate identity. In D. A. Prentice & D. T. Miller (Eds.), *Cultural divides: Understanding and overcoming group conflict.* New York: Russell Sage Foundation.

Galati, D., Scherer, K. R., & Ricci-Bitti, P. E. (1997). Voluntary facial expression of emotion: Comparing congenitally blind with normally sighted encoders. *Journal of Personality and Social Psychology, 73*, 1363–1379.

Galton, F. (1869). *Hereditary genius: An inquiry into its laws and consequences.* New York: Appleton.

Gambone, J. C., Reiter, R. C., & DiMatteo, M. R. (1994). *The PREPARED provider: A guide for improved patient communication.* Beaverton, OR: Mosybl Great Performance.

Gangestad, S. W., Thornhill, R., & Yeo, R. A. (1994). Facial attractiveness, developmental stability, and fluctuating asymmetry. *Ethology and Sociobiology, 15*, 73–85.

Gantt, W. H. (1975, April 25). Unpublished lecture, Ohio State University. Cited in D. Hothersall, (1984), *History of psychology.* New York: Random House.

Garb, H. N., Florio, C. M., & Grove, W. M. (1998). The validity of the Rorschach and the Minnesota Multiphasic Personality Inventory: Results form meta-analysis. *Psychological Science, 9*, 402–404.

Garcia, J. (1989). Food for Tolman: Cognition and cathexis in concert. In T. Archer & L. G. Nilsson (Eds.), *Aversion, avoidance, and anxiety: Perspectives on aversively motivated behavior.* Hillsdale, NJ: Erlbaum.

Garcia, J., Clarke, J. C., & Hankins, W. G. (1973). Natural responses to scheduled rewards. In P. P. G. Bateson & P. Klopfer (Eds.), *Perspectives in ethology.* New York: Plenum.

Garcia, J., & Koelling, R. A. (1966). Learning with prolonged delay of reinforcement. *Psychonomic Science, 5*, 121–122.

Garcia, J., & Rusiniak, K. W. (1980). What the nose learns from the mouth. In D. Muller-Schwarze & R. M. Silverstein (Eds.), *Chemical signals.* New York: Plenum.

Garcia, S. D., & Khersonsky, D. (1996). "They make a lovely couple": Perceptions of couple attractiveness. *Journal of Social Behavior and Personality, 11*, 667–682.

Gardner, E. (1975). *Fundamentals of neurology.* Philadelphia: Saunders.

Gardner, E. L. (1997). Brain reward mechanisms. In J. H. Lowinson, P. Ruiz, R. B. Millman, & J. G. Langrod (Eds.), *Substance abuse: A comprehensive textbook.* Baltimore: Williams & Wilkins.

Gardner, H. (1983). *Frames of mind: The theory of multiple intelligences.* New York: Basic Books.

Gardner, H. (1985). *The mind's new science: A history of the cognitive revolution.* New York: Basic Books.

Gardner, H. (1993). *Multiple intelligences: The theory in practice.* New York: Basic Books.

Gardner, H. (1998). A multiplicity of intelligences. *Scientific American Presents Exploring Intelligence, 9*, 18–23.

Gardner, H.. & Hatch, T. (1989). Multiple intelligences go to school: Educational implications of the theory of multiple intelligences. *Educational Researcher, 18*(8), 4–10.

Gardos, G., Casey, D. E., Cole, J. O., Perenyi, A., Kocsis, E., Arato, M., Samson, J. A., & Conley, C. (1994). Ten-year outcome of tardive dyskinesia. *American Journal of Psychiatry, 151*, 836–841.

Garfield, S. L., & Bergin, A. E. (1994). Introduction and historical overview. In A. E. Bergin & S. L. Garfield (Eds.), *Handbook of psychotherapy and behavior change* (4th ed.). New York: Wiley.

Garfinkel, P. E. (1995). Classification and diagnosis of eating disorders. In K. D. Brownell, & C. G. Fairburn (Eds.), *Eating disorders and obesity: A comprehensive handbook.* New York: Guilford Press.

Garland, A. F., & Zigler, E. (1993). Adolescent suicide prevention: Current research and social policy implications. *American Psychologist, 48*(2), 169–182.

Garner, D. M., Garfindel, P. E., Schwartz, D., & Thompson, M. (1980). Cultural expectations of thinness in women. *Psychological Reports, 47*, 483–491.

Garnets, L., & Kimmel, D. (1991). Lesbian and gay male dimensions in the psychological study of human diversity. In J. D. Goodchilds (Ed.), *Psychological perspectives on human diversity in America*. Washington, DC: American Psychological Association.

Garvey, C. R. (1929). List of American psychology laboratories. *Psychological Bulletin, 26*, 652–660.

Gatewood, R., & Perloff, R. (1990). Testing and industrial application. In G. Goldstein & M. Hersen (Eds.), *Handbook of psychological assessment*. New York: Pergamon Press.

Gazzaniga, M. S. (1970). *The bisected brain*. New York: Appleton-Century-Crofts.

Gazzaniga, M. S., Bogen, J. E., & Sperry, R. W. (1965). Observations on visual perception after disconnection of the cerebral hemispheres in man. *Brain, 88*, 221–236.

Ge, X., Conger, R. D., & Elder, G. H. Jr. (1996). Coming of age too early: Pubertal influences on girls' vulnerability to psychological distress. *Child Development, 67*, 3386–3400.

Geary, D. C. (1998). *Male, female: The evolution of human sex differences*. Washington, DC: American Psychological Association.

Geary, D. C. (1999). Evolution and developmental sex differences. *Current Directions in Psychological Science, 8*, 115–120.

Gecas, V., & Seff, M. A. (1990). Families and adolescents: A review of the 1980s. *Journal of Marriage and the Family, 52*, 941–958.

Geddes, J. R., & Lawrie, S. M. (1995). Obstetrical complications and schizophrenia: A meta-analysis. *British Journal of Psychiatry, 167*, 786–793.

Geiger, M. A. (1997). An examination of the relationship between answer changing, testwiseness and examination performance. *Journal of Experimental Education, 66*, 49–60.

Geldard, F. A. (1962). *Fundamentals of psychology*. New York: Wiley.

Gelderloos, P., Walton, K. G., Orme-Johnson, D. W., & Alexander, C. N. (1991). Effectiveness of the Transcendental Meditation program in preventing and treating substance misuse: A review. *The International Journal of Addictions, 26*(3), 293–325.

Geller, J. L. (1992). A historical perspective on the role of state hospitals viewed from the era of the "revolving door." *American Journal of Psychiatry, 149*, 1526–1533.

Geller, L. (1982). The failure of self-actualization theory: A critique of Carl Rogers and Abraham Maslow. *Journal of Humanistic Psychology, 22*, 56–73.

Gentner, D. (1988). Metaphor as structure mapping: The relational shift. *Child Development, 59*, 47–59.

Gentner, D., & Rattermann, M. J. (1991). Language and the career of similarity. In S. A. Gelman & J. P. Byrnes (Eds.), *Perspectives on language and thought: Interrelations in development*. Cambridge, MA: Cambridge University Press.

George, M. S., Terrence, A. K., Parekh, P. I., Horowitz, B., Herscovitch, P., & Post, R. M. (1995). Brain activity during transient sadness and happiness in healthy women. *American Journal of Psychiatry, 152*, 341–351.

Gerard, M. (Ed.). (1968). *Dali*. Paris: Draeger.

Gergen, K. J., Gulerce, A., Lock, A., & Misra, G. (1996). Psychological science in cultural context. *American Psychologist, 51*, 496–503.

Gershon, E. S., Berrettini, W. H., & Goldin, L. R. (1989). Mood disorders: Genetic aspects. In H. I. Kaplan & B. J. Sadock (Eds.), *Comprehensive textbook of psychiatry/V*. Baltimore: Williams & Wilkins.

Geschwind, N., & Galaburda, A. M. (1987). *Cerebral lateralization: Biological mechanisms, associations, and pathology*. Cambridge, MA: MIT Press.

Gest, S. D. (1997). Behavioral inhibition: Stability and associations with adaptation from childhood to early adulthood. *Journal of Personality and Social Psychology, 72*, 467–475.

Getchell, T. V., & Getchell, M. L. (1991). Physiology of olfactory reception and transduction: General principles. In D. G. Laing, R. L. Doty, & W. Breipohl (Eds.), *The human sense of smell*. Berlin: Springer-Verlag.

Ghaemi, S. N., Irizarry, M. C., & Joseph, A. B. (1998). The effect of psychological stress on neurological disorders. In J. R. Hubbard & E. A. Workman (Eds.), *Handbook of stress medicine: An organ system approach*. New York: CRC Press.

Ghez, C. (1991). The cerebellum. In E. R. Kandel, J. H. Schwartz, & T. M. Jessell (Eds.), *Principles of neural science* (3rd ed.). New York: Elsevier.

Ghiselli, E. E. (1973). The validity of aptitude tests in personnel selection. *Personnel Psychology, 26*, 461–477.

Gibbon, J., & Fairhurst, S. (1994). Ratio versus difference comparators in choice. *Journal of the Experimental Analysis of Behavior, 62*, 409–434.

Gibson, H. B., & Heap, M. (1991). *Hypnosis in therapy*. Hillsdale, NJ: Erlbaum.

Gick, M. L., & Holyoak, K. (1980). Analogical problem solving. *Cognitive Psychology, 12*, 306–355.

Gigerenzer, G. (1997). Ecological intelligence: An adaption for frequencies. *Psychologische Beitraege, 39*, 107–125.

Gigerenzer, G., & Hoffrage, U. (1995). How to improve Bayesian reasoning without instruction: Frequency formats. *Psychological Review, 102*, 684–704.

Gigerenzer, G., & Hoffrage, U. (1999). Overcoming difficulties in Bayesian reasoning: A reply to Lewis and Keren (1999) and Mellers and McGraw (1999). *Psychological Review, 106*, 425–430.

Gigerenzer, G., Hoffrage, U., & Kleinbölting, H. (1991). Probabilistic mental models: A Brunswikian theory of confidence. *Psychological Review, 98*, 506–528.

Gilbert, D. T. (1989). Thinking lightly about others: Automatic components of the social inference process. In J. S. Uleman & J. A. Bargh (Eds.), *Unintended thought: Limits of awareness, intention, and control*. New York: Guilford Press.

Giles, T. R., & Marafiote, R. A. (1998). Managed care and the practitioner: A call for unity. *Clinical Psychology: Science & Practice, 5*, 41–50.

Gilgen, A. R. (1982). *American psychology since World War II: A profile of the discipline*. Westport, CT: Greenwood Press.

Gillberg, M., Kecklund, G., Axelsson, J., & Akerstedt, T. (1996). The effects of a short daytime nap after restricted night sleep. *Sleep, 19*, 570–575.

Gladue, B. A. (1988). Hormones in relationship to homosexual/bisexual/heterosexual gender orientation. In J. M. A. Sitesen (Ed.), *Handbook of sexology: The pharmacology and endocrinology of sexual function* (Vol. 6). Amsterdam: Elsevier.

Gladue, B. A. (1994). The biopsychology of sexual orientation. *Current Directions in Psychological Science, 3*, 150–154.

Glaser, R., Rabin, B., Chesney, M., Cohen, S., & Natelson, B. (1999). Stress-induced immuno-modulation: Implications for infectious diseases? *Journal of the American Medical Association, 281*, 2268–2270.

Glass, C. R., & Arnkoff, D. B. (1992). Behavior therapy. In D. K. Freedheim (Ed.), *History of psychotherapy: A century of change*. Washington, DC: American Psychological Association.

Glassman, A. H., & Shapiro, P. A. (1998). Depression and the course of coronary artery disease. *American Journal of Psychiatry, 155*, 4–11.

Gleason, J. B., & Ratner, N. B. (1993). Language development in children. In J. B. Gleason & N. B. Ratner (Eds.), *Psycholinguistics*. Fort Worth: Harcourt Brace Jovanovich.

Gleaves, D. H. (1994). On "The reality of repressed memories". *American Psychologist, 49*, 440–441.

Gleaves, D. H. (1996). The sociocognitive model of dissociative disorder: A reexamination of the evidence. *Psychological Bulletin, 120*, 42–59.

Glenberg, A. M. (1992). Distributed practice effects. In L. R. Squire (Ed.), *Encyclopedia of learning and memory*. New York: Macmillan.

Glenn, N. D. (1990). Quantitative research on marital quality in the 1980s: A critical review. *Journal of Marriage and the Family, 52*, 818–831.

Glenn, N. D. (1998). The course of marital success and failure in five American 10-year marriage cohorts. *Journal of Marriage and the Family, 60*, 569–576.

Gliksman, L., Newton-Taylor, B., Adlaf, E., & Giesbrecht, N. (1997). Alcohol and other drug use by Ontario university students: The roles of gender, age, year of study, academic grades, place of residence and programme of study. *Drugs: Education, Prevention & Policy, 4*, 117–129.

Gluck, M. A., & Myers, C. E. (1997). Psychobiological models of hippocampal function in learning and memory. *Annual Review of Psychology, 48*, 481–514.

Goddard, H. H. (1917). Mental tests and the immigrant. *Journal of Delinquency, 2*, 243–277.

Goff, D. C., & Gudeman, J. E. (1999). The person with chronic mental illness. In A. M. Nicholi (Ed.), *The Harvard guide to psychiatry*. Cambridge, MA: Harvard University Press.

Gold, M. S. (1997). Cocaine (and crack): Clinical aspects. In J. H. Lowinson, P. Ruiz, R. B. Millman, & J. G. Langrod (Eds.), *Substance abuse: A comprehensive textbook*. Baltimore: Williams & Wilkins.

Gold, M. S., & Miller, N. S. (1997). Cocaine (and crack): Neurobiology. In J. H. Lowinson, P. Ruiz, R. B. Millman, & J. G. Langrod (Eds.), *Substance abuse: A comprehensive textbook*. Baltimore: Williams & Wilkins.

Golden, C. J., Sawicki, R. F., & Franzen, M. D. (1990). Test construction. In G. Goldstein & M. Hersen (Eds.), *Handbook of psychological assessment*. New York: Pergamon Press.

Goldenberg, H. (1983). *Contemporary clinical psychology*. Pacific Grove, CA: Brooks/Cole.

Goldman-Rakic, P. S. (1993). Working memory and the mind. In *Mind and brain: Readings from Scientific American magazine*. New York: W. H. Freeman.

Goldman-Rakic, P. S. (1998). The prefrontal landscape: Implications of functional architecture for understanding human mentation and the central executive. In A. C. Roberts, T. W. Robbins, & L. Weiskrantz (Eds), *The prefrontal cortex: Executive and cognitive functions*. New York: Oxford University Press.

Goldsmith, H. H., & Harman, C. (1994). Temperament and attachment; individuals and relationships. *Current Directions in Psychological Science, 3*, 53–57.

Goldstein, E. B. (1996). *Sensation and perception* (4th ed.). Pacific Grove, CA: Brooks/Cole.

Goldstein, E., & Farmer, K. (Eds.) (1993). *True stories of false memories*. Boca Raton, FL: Sir Publishing.

Goldstein, W. M. (1990). Judgments of relative importance in decision making: Global vs. local interpretations of subjective weight. *Organizational Behavior and Human Decision Processes, 47*, 313–336.

Goldstein, W. M., & Hogarth, R. M. (1997). Judgment and decision research: Some historical context. In W. M. Goldstein, & R. M. Hogarth (Eds.), *Research on judgment and decision making*. New York: Cambridge University Press.

Gonder-Frederick, L. A., Carter, W. R., Cox, D. J., & Clarke, W. L. (1990). Environmental stress and blood glucose change in insulin-dependent diabetes mellitus. *Health Psychology, 9*, 503–515.

Gonsiorek, J. C., & Weinrich, J. D. (1991). The definition and scope of sexual orientation. In J. C. Gonsiorek & J. D. Weinrich (Eds.), *Homosexuality: Research implications for public policy*. Newbury Park, CA: Sage.

Gonzalez-Lopez, A., & Kamps, D. M. (1997). Social skills training to increase social interactions between children with autism and their typical peers. *Focus on Autism & Other Developmental Disabilities, 12*, 2–14.

Goodenough, D. R. (1986). History of the field dependence construct. In M. Bertini, L. Pizzamiglio, & S. Wapner (Eds.), *Field dependence in psychological theory, research, and application*. Hillsdale, NJ: Erlbaum.

Goodenough, D. R. (1991). Dream recall: History and current status of the field. In S. J. Ellman & J. S. Antrobus (Eds.), *The mind in sleep: Psychology and psychophysiology* (2nd ed.). New York: Wiley.

Goodwin, C. J. (1991). Misportraying Pavlov's apparatus. *American Journal of Psychology, 104*(1), 135–141.

Goodwin, D. W., & Gabrielli, W. F. (1997). Alcohol: Clinical aspects. In J. H. Lowinson, P. Ruiz, R. B. Millman, & J. G. Langrod (Eds.), *Substance abuse: A comprehensive textbook*. Baltimore: Williams & Wilkins.

Goodwin, F. K., & Jamison, K. R. (1990). *Manic-depressive illness*. New York: Oxford University Press.

Gopnik, A., Meltzoff, A. N., & Kuhl, P. K. (1999). *The scientist in the crib: Minds, brains, and how children learn*. New York: Morrow.

Gordon, H. W. (1990). The neurobiological basis of hemisphericity. In C. Trevarthen (Ed.), *Brain circuits and functions of the mind. Essays in honor of Roger W. Sperry*. Cambridge, MA: Cambridge University Press.

Gosden, C., Nicolaides, K., & Whitting, V. (1994). *Is my baby all right? A guide for expectant parents*. Oxford, England: Oxford University Press.

Gottdiener, J. S., Krantz, D. S., Howell, R. H., Hecht, G. M., Klein, J., Falconer, J. J., & Rozanski, A. (1994). Induction of silent myocardial ischemia with mental stress testing: Relationship to the triggers of ischemia during daily life activities and to ischemic functional severity. *Journal of the American College of Cardiology, 24*, 1645–1651.

Gottesman, I. I. (1991). *Schizophrenia genesis: The origins of madness*. New York: W. H. Freeman.

Gottesman, I. I. (1993). Origins of schizophrenia: Past as prologue. In R. Plomin & G. E. McClearn (Eds.), *Nature, nurture and psychology*. Washington, DC: American Psychological Association.

Gould, R. L. (1975, February). Adult life stages: Growth toward self-tolerance. *Psychology Today*, pp. 74–78.

Gould, R. L. (1978). *Transformations: Growth and change in adult life*. New York: Simon & Schuster.

Gould, S. J. (1993). The sexual politics of classification. *Natural History*, 20–29.

Gould, S. J., & Eldredge, N. (1977). Punctuated equilibria: The tempo and mode of evolution reconsidered. *Paleobiology, 3*, 115–151.

Gould, S. J., & Eldredge, N. (1993). Punctuated equilibrium comes of age. *Nature, 366*, 223–227.

Gouras, P. (1991). Color vision. In E. R. Kandel, J. H. Schwartz, & T. M. Jessell (Eds.), *Principles of neural science* (3rd ed.). New York: Elsevier.

Graber, J. A., Brooks-Gunn, J., Paikoff, R. L., & Warren, M. P. (1994). Prediction of eating problems: An 8-year study of adolescent girls. *Developmental Psychology, 30*, 823–834.

Graber, J. A., Brooks-Gunn, J., & Warren, M. P. (1995). The antecedents of menarcheal age: Heredity, family environment, and stressful life events. *Child Development, 66*, 346–359.

Graber, J. A., Lewinsohn, P. M., Seeley, J. R., & Brooks-Gunn, J. (1997). Is psychopathology associated with the timing of pubertal development? *Journal of the American Academy of Child & Adolescent Psychiatry, 36*, 1768–1776.

Graf, P., & Gallie, K. A. (1992). A transfer-appropriate processing account for memory and amnesia. In L. R. Squire & N. Butters (Eds.), *Neuropsychology of memory* (2nd ed.). New York: Guilford Press.

Graham, J. R. (1990). *MMPI-2: Assessing personality and psychopathology*. New York: Oxford University Press.

Granberg, G., & Holmberg, S. (1991). Self-reported turnout and voter validation. *American Journal of Political Science, 35*, 448–459.

Grant, I., McDonald, W. I., Patterson, T., & Trimble, M. R. (1989). Multiple sclerosis. In G. W. Brown & T. O. Harris (Eds.), *Life events and illness*. New York: Guilford Press.

Gratton, A. (1996). In vivo analysis of the role of dopamine in stimulant and opiate self-administration. *Journal of Psychiatry & Neuroscience, 21*, 264–279.

Graziano, W. G. (1995). Evolutionary psychology: Old music, but now on CDs? *Psychological Inquiry, 6*, 41–44.

Grebb, J. A., & Cancro, R. (1989). Schizophrenia: Clinical features. In H. I. Kaplan & B. J. Sadock (Eds.), *Comprehensive textbook of psychiatry/V*. Baltimore: Williams & Wilkins.

Green, C. D., & Vervaeke, J. (1997). But what have you done for us lately? Some recent perspectives on linguistic nativism. In D. M. Johnson & C. E. Erneling (Eds.), *The future of the cognitive revolution*. New York: Oxford University Press.

Green, L. W., Tryon W. W., Marks, B., & Huryn, J. (1986). Periodontal disease as a function of life events stress. *Journal of Human Stress, 12*(1), 32–36.

Green, M. F., Satz, P., & Christensen, C. (1994). Minor physical remedies in schizophrenia patients, bipolar patients, and their siblings. *Schizophrenia Bulletin, 20*, 433–440.

Greenberg, J. S. (1990). *Comprehensive stress management*. Dubuque, IA: William C. Brown.

Greenberg, M. A., Wortman, C. B., & Stone, A. A. (1996). Emotional expression and physical health: Revising traumatic memories or fostering self-regulation? *Journal of Personality and Social Psychology, 71*, 588–602.

Greenberg, R. P., & Fisher, S. (1997). Mood-mending medicines: Probing drug, psychotherapy and placebo solutions. In S. Fisher & R. P. Greenberg (Eds.), *From placebo to panacea: Putting psychiatric drugs to the test*. New York: Wiley.

Greene, R. L. (1992a). Repetition and learning. In L. R. Squire (Ed.), *Encyclopedia of learning and memory*. New York: Macmillian.

Greene, R. L. (1992b). *Human memory: Paradigms and paradoxes*. Hillsdale, NJ: Erlbaum.

Greene, W. A., & Swisher, S. N. (1969). Psychological and somatic variables associated with the development and course of monozygotic twins discordant for leukemia. *Annals of the New York Academy of Sciences, 164*, 394–408.

Greenfield, P. M. (1997). You can't take it with you: Why ability assessments don't cross cultures. *American Psychologist, 52*, 1115–1124.

Greenfield, P. M. (1998). The cultural evolution of IQ. In U. Neisser (Ed.), *The rising curve: Long-term gains in IQ and related measures*. Washington, DC: American Psychological Association.

Greenfield, P. M., & Suzuki, L. K. (1998). Culture and human development: Implications for parenting, education, pediatrics, and mental health. In W. Damon (Ed.), *Handbook of child psychology (Vol. 4): Child psychology in practice*. New York: Wiley.

Greeno, C. G., & Wing, R. R. (1994). Stress-induced eating. *Psychological Bulletin, 115*, 444–464.

Greeno, J. G. (1978). Nature of problem-solving abilities. In W. K. Estes (Ed.), *Handbook of learning and cognitive processes* (Vol. 5). Hillsdale, NJ: Erlbaum.

Greenough, W. T. (1975). Experiential modification of the developing brain. *American Scientist, 63*, 37–46.

Greenough, W. T. (1991). The animal rights assertions: A researcher's perspective. *Psychological Science Agenda, 4*(3), 10–12.

Greenough, W. T., & Volkmar, F. R. (1973). Pattern of dendritic branching in occipital cortex of rats reared in complex environments. *Experimental Neurology, 40,* 491–504.

Greenson, R. R. (1967). *The technique and practice of psychoanalysis* (Vol. 1). New York: International Universities Press.

Greenspan, S., & Driscoll, J. (1997). The role of intelligence in a broad model of personal competence. In D. P. Flanagan, J. L. Genshaft, & P. L. Harrison (Eds.), *Contemporary intellectual assessment: Theories, tests, and issues.* New York: Guilford Press.

Gregory, R. J. (1996). *Psychological testing: History, principles, and applications* (2nd ed.). Boston: Allyn & Bacon.

Gregory, R. L. (1973). *Eye and brain.* New York: McGraw-Hill.

Gregory, R. L. (1978). *Eye and brain* (2nd ed.). New York: McGraw-Hill.

Griggs, R. A., Jackson, S. L., & Napolitano, T. J. (1994). Brief introductory psychology textbooks: An objective analysis. *Teaching of Psychology, 21,* 136–140

Grinspoon, L., & Bakalar, J. B. (1997). Marihuana. In J. H. Lowinson, P. Ruiz, R. B. Millman, & J. G. Langrod (Eds.), *Substance abuse: A comprehensive textbook.* Baltimore: Williams & Wilkins.

Grob, G. N. (1983). Disease and environment in American history. In D. Mechanic (Ed.), *Handbook of health, health care, and the health professions.* New York: Free Press.

Grob, G. N. (1991). Origins of DSM-I: A study in appearance and reality. *American Journal of Psychiatry, 148,* 421–431.

Grob, G. N. (1994). *The mad among us: A history of the care of America's mentally ill.* New York: Free Press.

Gross, J. J. (1998). Antecedent and response focused emotion regulation: Divergent consequences for experience, expression, and physiology. *Journal of Personality and Social Psychology, 74,* 224–237.

Gross, J. J., & Levenson, R. W. (1997). Hiding feelings: The acute effects of inhibiting negative and positive emotion. *Journal of Abnormal Psychology, 106,* 95–103.

Grossman, R. P., & Till, B. D. (1998). The persistence of classically conditioned brand attitudes. *Journal of Advertising, 27,* 23–31.

Grossman, S. P., Dacey, D., Halaris, A. E., Collier, T., & Routtenberg, A. (1978). Aphagia and adipsia after preferential destruction of nerve cell bodies in hypothalamus. *Science, 202,* 537–539.

Grossmann, K. E., & Grossmann, K. (1990). The wider concept of attachment in cross-cultural research. *Human Development, 33,* 31–47.

Grossmann, K., Grossmann, K. E., Spangler, S., Suess, G., & Unzner, L. (1985). Maternal sensitivity and newborn orientation responses as related to quality of attachment in northern Germany. In I. Bretherton & E. Waters (Eds.), Growing points of attachment theory. *Monographs of the Society for Research for Child Development, 50,* (1–2, Serial No. 209).

Groth-Marnat, G. (1997). *Handbook of psychological assessment.* New York: Wiley.

Gruen, R. J. (1993). Stress and depression: Toward the development of integrative models. In L. Goldberger & S. Breznitz (Eds.), *Handbook of stress: Theoretical and clinical aspects.* New York: Free Press.

Grunberg, N. E., & Straub, R. O. (1992). The role of gender and taste class in the effects of stress on eating. *Health Psychology, 11,* 97–100.

Grunberg, N. E., Bowen, D. J., & Winders, S. E. (1986). Effects of nicotine on body weight and food consumption in female rats. *Psychopharmacology, 90,* 101–105.

Guarnaccia, P. J., & Rogler, L. H. (1999). Research on culture-bound syndromes: New directions. *American Journal of Psychiatry, 156,* 1322–1327.

Guenther, K. (1988). Mood and memory. In G. M. Davies & D. M. Thomson (Eds.), *Memory in context: Context in memory.* New York: Wiley.

Guilford, J. P. (1959). Three faces of intellect. *American Psychologist, 14,* 469–479.

Gullette, E. C. D., Blumenthal, J. A., Babyak, M., Jiang, W., Waugh, R. A., Frid, D. J., O'Connor, C. M., Morris, J. J., & Krantz, D. S. (1997). Effects of mental stress on myocardial ischema during daily life. *Journal of the American Medical Association, 277,* 1521–1526.

Gupta, G. R. (1992). Love, arranged marriage, and the Indian social structure. In J. J. Macionis & N. V. Benokraitis (Eds.), *Seeing ourselves: Classic, contemporary and cross-cultural reading in sociology.* Englewood Cliffs, NJ: Prentice-Hall.

Guyton, A. C. (1991). *Textbook of medical physiology.* Philadelphia: Saunders.

Hack, M., & Fanaroff, A. A. (1999). Outcomes of children of extremely low birthweight and gestational age in the 1990's. *Early Human Development, 53,* 193–218.

Haglund, B., & Cnattingius, S. (1990). Cigarette smoking as a risk factor for sudden infant death syndrome: A population-based study. *American Journal of Public Health, 80,* 29–32.

Haimov, I., & Lavie, P. (1996). Melatonin: A soporific hormone. *Current Directions in Psychological Science, 5,* 106–111.

Haith, M. M., & Benson, J. B. (1998). Infant cognition. In W. Damon (Ed), *Handbook of child psychology (Vol. 2): Cognition, perception, and language.* New York: Wiley.

Hakuta, K. (1999). The debate on bilingual education. *Journal of Developmental & Behavioral Pediatrics, 20,* 36–37.

Halaas, J. L., Gajiwala, K. S., Maffel, M., Cohen, S. L., Chait, B. T., Rabinowitz, D., Lallone, R. L., Burley, S. K., & Friedman, J. M. (1995). Weight-reducing effects of the plasma protein encoded by the obese gene. *Science, 269,* 543–546.

Hales, D. (1987). *How to sleep like a baby.* New York: Ballantine.

Hall, C. C. I. (1997). Cultural malpractice: The growing obsolescence of psychology with the changing U.S. population. *American Psychologist, 52,* 642–651.

Hall, C. S. (1966). *The meaning of dreams.* New York: McGraw-Hill.

Hall, C. S. (1979). The meaning of dreams. In D. Goleman & R. J. Davidson (Eds.), *Consciousness: Brain, states of awareness, and mysticism.* New York: Harper & Row.

Hall, C. S., & Nordby, V. J. (1972). *The individual and his dreams.* New York: Mentor.

Hall, E. (1987). *Growing and changing: What the experts say.* New York: Random House.

Hall, G. S. (1904). *Adolescence.* New York: Appleton.

Hall, J. A. (1990). *Nonverbal sex differences: Communication accuracy and expressive style* (2nd ed.). Baltimore: Johns Hopkins University Press.

Hall, J. A., & Halbertstadt, A. G. (1986). Smiling and gazing. In J. S. Hyde & M. C. Lynn (Eds.), *The psychology gender: Advances through meta-analysis.* Baltimore: Johns Hopkins University Press.

Hall, J. A., Roter, D. L., & Katz, N. R. (1988). Meta-analysis of correlates of provider behavior in medical encounters. *Medical Care, 26,* 1–19.

Hall, W., Solowij, N., & Lemon, J. (1994). *The health and psychological consequences of cannabis use.* Canberra, Australia: Australian Government Publishing Service.

Halmi, K. A. (1999). Eating disorders: Anorexia nervosa, bulimia nervosa, and obesity. In R. E. Hales, S. C. Yudofsky, & J. A. Talbott (Eds.), *American Psychiatric Press Textbook of Psychiatry.* Washington, DC: American Psychiatric Press.

Halpern, D. F. (1992). *Sex differences in cognitive abilities.* Hillsdale, NJ: Erlbaum.

Halpern, D. F. (1994). A national assessment of critical thinking skills in adults: Taking steps toward the goal. In A. Greenwood (Ed.), *The national assessment of college student learning: Identification of the skills to be taught, learned, and assessed.* Washington, DC: U.S. Department of Education, National Center for Educational Statistics.

Halpern, D. F. (1996). *Thought and knowledge: An introduction to critical thinking.* Mahwah, NJ: Erlbaum.

Halpern, D. F. (1997). Sex differences in intelligence: Implications for education. *American Psychologist, 52,* 1091–1102.

Halpern, D. F. (1998). Teaching critical thinking for transfer across domains: Dispositions, skills, structure training, and metacognitive monitoring. *American Psychologist, 53,* 449–455.

Halverson, C. F. Jr., & Wampler, K. S. (1997). Family influences on personality development. In R. Hogan, J. Johnson, & S. Briggs (Eds.), *Handbook of personality psychology.* San Diego: Academic Press.

Hamill, R., Wilson T. D., & Nisbett, R. E. (1980). Insensitivity to sample bias: Generalizing from atypical cases. *Journal of Personality and Social Psychology, 39,* 578–589.

Hamilton, W. D. (1964). The evolution of social behavior. *Journal of Theoretical Biology, 7,* 1–52.

Hamilton, W. D., & Zuk, M. (1982). Heritable true fitness and bright birds: A role for parasites. *Science, 218 ,* 384–387.

Hansen, C. H., & Hansen, R. D. (1988). How rock music videos can change what is seen when boy meets girl: Priming stereotypic appraisal of social interactions. *Sex Roles, 19,* 287–316.

Hanson, F. A. (1993). *Testing testing: Social consequences of the examined life.* Berkeley: University of California Press.

Hanson, V. L. (1990). Recall of order information by deaf signers: Phonetic coding in temporal order of recall. *Memory & Cognition, 18,* 604–610.

Harmsen, P., Rosengren, A., Tsipogianni, A., & Wilhelmsen, L. (1990). Risk factors for stroke in middle-aged men in Goteborg, Sweden. *Stroke, 21,* 23–29.

Harrington, M. E., Rusak, B., & Mistlberger, R. E. (1994). Anatomy and physiology of the mammalian circadian system. In M. H. Kryger, T. Roth, & W. C. Dement (Eds.), *Principles and practice of sleep medicine* (2nd ed.). Philadelphia: Saunders.

Harris, J. R. (1998). *The nurture assumption: Why children turn out the way they do*. New York: Free Press.

Harris, W. G. (1987). *Cary Grant: A touch of elegance*. New York: Doubleday.

Harrower, M. R. (1936). Some factors determining figure-ground articulation. *British Journal of Psychology, 26*(4), 407–424.

Harte, J. L., Eifert, G. H., & Smith, R. (1995). The effects of running and meditation on beta-endorphin, corticotropin-releasing hormone and cortisol in plasma, and on mood. *Biological Psychology, 40*, 251–265.

Harvey, M. H. (1999). Memory research and clinical practice: A critique of three paradigms and a framework for psychotherapy with trauma survivors. In L. M. Williams & V. L. Banyard (Eds.), *Trauma & memory*. Thousand Oaks, CA: Sage Publications.

Haselton, M. G., & Buss, D. M. (2000). Error management theory: A new perspective on biases in cross-sex mind reading. *Journal of Personality and Social Psychology, 78*, 81–91.

Haslam, N. (1997). Evidence that male sexual orientation is a matter of degree. *Journal of Personality and Social Psychology, 73*, 862–870.

Hastorf, A., & Cantril, H. (1954). They saw a game: A case study. *Journal of Abnormal and Social Psychology, 49*, 129–134.

Hatfield, E., & Rapson, R. L. (1993). *Love, sex, and intimacy: Their psychology, biology, and history*. New York: HarperCollins.

Hathaway, S. R., & McKinley, J. C. (1943). *Manual for the Minnesota Multiphasic Personality Inventory*. New York: Psychological Corporation.

Haugland, G., Siegel, C., Hopper, K., & Alexander, M. J. (1997). Mental illness among homeless individuals in a suburban county. *Psychiatric Services, 48*, 504–509.

Hauser, M., & Carey, S. (1998). Building a cognitive creature from a set of primitives: Evolutionary and developmental insights. In D. D. Cummins & C. Allen (Eds.), *The evolution of mind*. New York: Oxford University Press.

Hawkins, S. A., & Hastie, R. (1990). Hindsight: Biased judgments of past events after the outcomes are known. *Psychological Bulletin, 107*, 311–327.

Hayashi, M., Watanabe, M., & Hori, T. (1999). The effects of a 20-minute nap in the mid-afternoon on mood, performance and EEG activity. *Clinical Neurophysiology, 110*, 272–279.

Hayes, S. C., & Heiby, E. (1996). Psychology's drug problem: Do we need a fix or should we just say no? *American Psychologist, 51*, 198–206.

Haywood, T. W., Kravitz, H. M., Grossman, L. S., Cavanaugh, J. L., Jr., Davis, J. M., & Lewis, D. A. (1995). Predicting the "revolving door" phenomenon among patients with schizophrenic, schizoaffective, and affective disorders. *American Journal of Psychiatry, 152*, 861–956.

Hazan, C., & Shaver, P. (1986). *Parental caregiving style questionnaire*. Unpublished questionnaire.

Hazan, C., & Shaver, P. (1987). Romantic love conceptualized as an attachment process. *Journal of Personality and Social Psychology, 52*, 511–524.

He, J., Ogden, L. G., Vupputuri, S., Bazzano, L. A., Loria, C., & Whelton, P. K. (1999). Dietary sodium intake and subsequent risk of cardiovascular disease in overweight adults. *Journal of the American Medical Association, 282*, 2027–2034.

Healy, A. F. (1992). Serial Organization. In L. R. Squire (Ed.), *Encyclopedia of learning and memory*. New York: Macmillian.

Healy, A. F., & McNamara, D. S. (1996). Verbal learning and memory: Does the modal model still work? *Annual Review of Psychology, 47*, 143–72.

Hearn, W. (1995, Nov. 6). Melatonin caution: Latest magic bullet may not hit target. *American Medical News, 28*, 30.

Hearst, E. (1988). Fundamentals of learning and conditioning. In R. C. Atkinson, R. J. Herrnstein, G. Lindzey, & R. D. Luce (Eds.), *Stevens' handbook of experimental psychology*. New York: Wiley.

Heatherton, T. F., Striepe, M., & Wittenberg, L. (1998). Emotional distress and disinhibited eating: The role of self. *Personality and Social Psychology Bulletin, 24*, 301–313.

Heider, F. (1958). *The psychology of interpersonal relations*. New York: Wiley.

Hellige, J. B. (1990). Hemispheric asymmetry. *Annual Review of Psychology, 41*, 55–80.

Hellige, J. B. (1993). Unity of thought and action: Varieties of interaction between left and right cerebral hemispheres. *Current Directions in Psychological Science, 2*(1), 21–25.

Helmes, E., & Reddon, J. R. (1993). A perspective on developments in assessing psychopathology: A critical review of the MMPI and MMPI-2. *Psychological Bulletin, 113*, 453–471.

Helmholtz, H. von. (1852). On the theory of compound colors. *Philosophical Magazine, 4*, 519–534.

Helmholtz, H. von. (1863). *On the sensations of tone as a physiological basis for the theory of music* (A. J. Ellis, Trans.). New York: Dover.

Helms, J. E. (1992). Why is there no study of cultural equivalence in standard cognitive ability testing? *American Psychologist, 47*, 1083–1101.

Helson, R., & Moane, G. (1987). Personality change in women from college to midlife. *Journal of Personality and Social Psychology, 53*, 176–186.

Hendrick, S. S., & Hendrick, C. (1992). *Liking, loving, and relating* (2nd ed.). Pacific Grove, CA: Brooks/Cole.

Henry, K. R. (1984). Cochlear damage resulting from exposure to four different octave bands of noise at three different ages. *Behavioral Neuroscience, 1*, 107–117.

Herek, G. M. (1996). Heterosexism and homophobia. In R. P. Cabaj & T. S. Stein (Eds.), *Textbook of homosexuality and mental health*. Washington, DC: American Psychiatric Press.

Hering, E. (1878). *Zür lehre vom lichtsinne*. Vienna: Gerold.

Herman, J. L. (1992). *Trauma and recovery*. New York: Basic Books.

Herman, J. L. (1994). Presuming to know the truth. *Nieman Reports, 48*, 43–45.

Hermann, R. C., Dorwart, R. A., Hoover, C. W., & Brody, J. (1995). Variation in ECT use in the United States. *American Journal of Psychiatry, 152*, 869–875.

Hermann, R. C., Ettner, S. L., Dorwart, R. A., Hoover, C. W., & Yeung, E. (1998). Characteristics of psychiatrists who perform ECT. *American Journal of Psychiatry, 155*, 889–894.

Hermans, H. J. M., & Kempen, H. J. G. (1998). Moving cultures: The perilous problems of cultural dichotomies in a globalizing society. *American Psychologist, 53*, 1111–1120.

Hernandez, D. J. (1993). *America's children: Resources from family, government, and the economy*. New York: Russell Sage Foundation.

Herrnstein, R. J., & Murray, C. (1994). *The Bell Curve: Intelligence and class structure in American life*. New York: Free Press.

Herzog, D. B., & Becker, A. E. (1999). Eating disorders. In A. M. Nicholi (Ed.), *The Harvard guide to psychiatry*. Cambridge, MA: Harvard University Press.

Herzog, T. A., Abrams, D. B., Emmons, K. M., Linnan, L. A., & Shadel, W. G. (1999). Do processes of change predict smoking stage movements? A prospective analysis of the transtheoretical model. *Health Psychology, 18*, 369–375.

Heszen-Niejodek, I. (1997). Coping style and its role in coping with stressful encounters. *European Psychologist, 2*, 342–351.

Heth, C. D., & Rescorla, R. A. (1973). Simultaneous and backward fear conditioning in the rat. *Journal of Comparative and Physiological Psychology, 82*, 434–443.

Hetherington, E. M., Bridges, M., & Insabella, G. M. (1998). What matters? What does not? Five perspectives on the association between marital transitions and children's adjustments. *American Psychologist, 53*, 167–184.

Hetherington, E. M., Reiss, D., & Plomin, R. (1994). *Separate social worlds of siblings: The impact of nonshared enviornment on development*. Hillsdale, NJ: Erlbaum.

Hettich, P. I. (1998). *Learning skills for college and career*. Pacific Grove, CA: Brooks/Cole.

Hewstone, M. (1990). The "ultimate attribution error"? A review of the literature on intergroup causal attribution. *European Journal of Social Psychology, 20*, 311–335.

Highhouse, S., Beadle, D., Gallo, A., & Miller, L. (1998). Get 'em while they last! Effects of scarcity information in job advertisements. *Journal of Applied Social Psychology, 28*, 779–795.

Hilgard, E. R. (1965). *Hypnotic susceptibility*. New York: Harcourt, Brace & World.

Hilgard, E. R. (1986). *Divided consciousness: Multiple controls in human thought and action*. New York: Wiley.

Hilgard, E. R. (1987). *Psychology in America: A historical survey*. San Diego: Harcourt Brace Jovanovich.

Hilgard, E. R. (1992). Dissociation and theories of hypnosis. In E. Fromm & M. R. Nash (Eds.), *Contemporary hypnosis research*. New York: Guilford Press.

Hilliard, A. G., III. (1984). IQ testing as the emperor's new clothes: A critique of Jensen's *Bias in Mental Testing*. In C. R. Reynolds & R. T. Brown (Eds.), *Perspectives on bias in mental testing*. New York: Plenum.

Hillner, K. P. (1984). *History and systems of modern psychology: A conceptual approach*. New York: Gardner Press.

Hilton, J. L., & von Hippel, W. (1996). Stereotypes. *Annual Review of Psychology, 47*, 237–271.

Hines, M. (1990). Gonadal hormones and human cognitive development. In J. Balthazart (Ed.), *Hormones, brain and behavior in vertebrates: 1. Sexual differentiation, neuroanatomical aspects, neurotransmitters and neuropeptides*. Basel: Karger.

Hirsh, I. J., & Watson, C. S. (1996). Auditory psychophysics and perception. *Annual Review of Psychology, 47*, 461–484.

Hobfoll, S. E., & Vaux, A. (1993). Social support: Resources and context. In L. Goldberger & S. Breznitz (Eds.), *Handbook of stress: Theoretical and clinical aspects* (2nd ed.). New York: Free Press.

Hobson, J. A. (1988). *The dreaming brain*. New York: Basic Books.

Hobson, J. A. (1989). *Sleep*. New York: Scientific American Library.

Hobson, J. A., & McCarley, R. W. (1977). The brain as a dream state generator: An activation-synthesis hypothesis of the dream process. *American Journal of Psychiatry, 134*, 1335–1348.

Hocevar, D., & Bachelor, P. (1989). A taxonomy and critique of measurements used in the study of creativity. In J. A. Glover, R. R. Ronning, & C. R. Reynolds (Eds.), *Handbook of creativity*. New York: Plenum.

Hochberg, J. (1988). Visual perception. In R. C. Atkinson, R. J. Herrnstein, G. Lindzey, & R. D. Luce (Eds.), *Stevens' handbook of experimental psychology* (2nd ed., Vol. 1). New York: Wiley.

Hock, E., Schirtzinger, M. B., Lutz, W. J., & Widaman, K. (1995). Maternal depressive symptomatology over the transition to parenthood: Assessing the influence of marital satisfaction and marital sex role traditionalism. *Journal of Family Psychology, 9*, 79–88.

Hodgkin, A. L., & Huxley, A. F. (1952). Currents carried by sodium and potassium ions through the membrane of the giant axon of Loligo. *Journal of Physiology, 116*, 449–472.

Hoek, H. W. (1995). The distribution of eating disorders. In K. D. Brownell, & C. G. Fairburn (Eds.), *Eating disorders and obesity: A comprehensive handbook*. New York: Guilford Press.

Hoek, H. W., Bartelds, A. I. M., Bosveld, J. J. F., van der Graaf, Y., Limpens, V. E. L., Maiwald, M., & Spaaij, C. J. K. (1995). Impact of urbanization on detection rates of eating disorders. *American Journal of Psychiatry, 152*, 1272–1278.

Hoff-Ginsberg, E. (1997). *Language development*. Pacific Grove, CA: Brooks/Cole.

Hoffman, E. (1994). *The drive for self: Alfred Adler and the founding of individual psychology*. Reading, MA: Addison-Wesley.

Hofstede, G. (1980). *Culture's consequences: International differences in work-related values*. Beverly Hills, CA: Sage.

Hofstede, G. (1983). Dimensions of national cultures in fifty countries and three regions. In J. Deregowski, S. Dziurawiec, & R. Annis (Eds.), *Explications in cross-cultural psychology*. Lisse: Swets and Zeitlinger.

Hogan, R., Hogan, J., & Roberts, B. W. (1996). Personality measurement and employment decisions. *American Psychologist, 51*, 469–477.

Hogarth, R. M. (1987). *Judgment and choice*. New York: Wiley.

Holahan, C. J., & Moos, R. H. (1985). Life stress and health: Personality, coping, and family support in stress resistance. *Journal of Personality and Social Psychology, 49*, 739–747.

Holahan, C. J., & Moos, R. H. (1990). Life stressors, resistance factors, and improved psychological functioning: An extension of the stress resistance paradigm. *Journal of Personality and Social Psychology, 58*, 909–917.

Holahan, C. J., & Moos, R. H. (1994). Life stressors and mental health: Advances in conceptualizing stress resistance. In W. R. Avison, & J. H. Gotlib (Eds.), *Stress and mental health: Contemporary issues and prospects for the future*. New York: Plenum.

Holden, C. (1986, October). The rational optimist. *Psychology Today*, pp. 55–60.

Hollan, D. (1989). The personal use of dream beliefs in the Toraja Highlands. *Ethos, 17*, 166–186.

Holland, J. C., & Lewis, S. (1993). Emotions and cancer: What do we really know? In D. Goleman & J. Gurin (Eds.), *Mind/body medicine: How to use your mind for better health*. Yonkers, NY: Consumer Reports Books.

Hollander, E., Simeon, D., & Gorman, J. M. (1999). Anxiety disorders. In R. E. Hales, S. C. Yudofsky, & J. A. Talbott (Eds.), *American Psychiatric Press Textbook of Psychiatry*. Washington, DC: American Psychiatric Press.

Hollands, C. (1989). Trivial and questionable research on animals. In G. Langley (Ed.), *Animal experimentation: The consensus changes*. New York: Chapman & Hall.

Hollis, K. L. (1997). Contemporary research on Pavlovian conditioning: A "new" functional analysis. *American Psychologist, 52*, 956–965.

Hollon, S. D., & Beck, A. T. (1994). Cognitive and cognitive-behavioral therapies. In A. E. Bergin & S. L. Garfield (Eds.), *Handbook of psychotherapy and behavior change* (4th ed.). New York: Wiley.

Holmes, D. S. (1987). The influence of meditation versus rest on physiological arousal: A second examination. In M. A. West (Ed.), *The psychology of meditation*. Oxford: Clarendon Press.

Holmes, D. S. (1990). The evidence for repression: An examination of sixty years of research. In J. Singer (Ed.), *Repression and dissociation: Implications for personality, theory, psychopathology, and health*. Chicago: University of Chicago Press.

Holmes, T. H., & Rahe, R. H. (1967). The Social Readjustment Rating Scale. *Journal of Psychosomatic Research, 11*, 213–218.

Holyoak, K. J. (1990). Problem solving. In D. N. Osherson & E. E. Smith (Eds.), *Thinking: An invitation to cognitive science* (Vol. 3). Cambridge, MA: MIT Press.

Holyoak, K. J., & Thagard, P. (1997). The analogical mind. *American Psychologist, 52*, 35–44.

Homma-True, R., Greene, B., Lopez, S. R., & Trimble, J. E. (1993). Ethnocultural diversity in clinical psychology. *The Clinical Psychologist, 46*(2), 50–63.

Honig, W. K., & Alsop, B. (1992). Operant behavior. In L. R. Squire (Ed.), *Encyclopedia of learning and memory*. New York: Macmillan.

Honkonen, T., Saarinen, S., & Salokangas, R. K. R. (1999). Deinstitutionalization and schizophrenia in Finland: II. Discharged patients and their psychosocial functioning. *Schizophrenia Bulletin, 25*, 543–551.

Honts, C. R., & Perry, M. V. (1992). Polygraph admissibility: Changes and challenges. *Law and Human Behavior, 16*, 357–379.

Hooper, J., & Teresi, D. (1986). *The 3-pound universe—The brain*. New York: Laurel.

Horn, J. L. (1979). Trends in the measurement of intelligence. In R. J. Sternberg & D. K. Detterman (Eds.), *Human intelligence: Perspectives on its theory and measurement*. Norwood, NJ: Ablex.

Hornstein, G. A. (1992). The return of the repressed: Psychology's problematic relations with psychoanalysis, 1909–1960. *American Psychologist, 47*, 254–263.

Horowitz, F. D. (1992). John B. Watson's legacy: Learning and environment. *Developmental Psychology, 28*, 360–367.

Hosseini, H. (1997). Cognitive dissonance as a means of explaining economics of irrationality and uncertainty. *Journal of Socio-Economics, 26*, 181–189.

Houston, B. K., & Vavak, C. R. (1991). Hostility: Developmental factors, psychosocial correlates, and health behaviors. *Health Psychology, 10*, 9–17.

Howard, A., Pion, G. M., Gottfredson, G. D., Flattau, P. E., Oskamp, S., Pfafflin, S. M., Bray, D. W., & Burstein, A. G. (1986). The changing face of American psychology: A report from the committee on employment and human resources. *American Psychologist, 41*, 1311–1327.

Howard, D. J. (1995). "Chaining" the use of influence strategies for producing compliance behavior. *Journal of Social Behavior and Personality, 10*, 169–185.

Howard, K. I., Moras, K., Brill, P. L., Martinovich, Z., & Lutz, W. (1996). Evaluation of psychotherapy: Efficacy, effectiveness, and patient progress. *American Psychologist, 51*, 1059–1064.

Hrdy, S. B. (1997). Raising Darwin's consciouness: Female sexuality and the prehominid origins of patriarchy. *Human Nature: An Interdiciplinary Biosocial Perspective, 8*, 1–49.

Hsu, L. K. G. (1990). *Eating disorders*. New York: Guilford Press.

Hsu, L. M. (1995). Regression toward the mean associated with measurement error and the identification of improvement and deterioration in psychotherapy. *Journal of Consulting & Clinical Psychology, 63*, 141–144.

Hubbard, J. R., & Workman, E. A. (1998). *Handbook of stress medicine: An organ system approach*. New York: CRC Press.

Hubel, D. H., & Wiesel, T. N. (1962). Receptive fields, binocular interaction and functional architecture in the cat's visual cortex. *Journal of Physiology, 160*, 106–154.

Hubel, D. H., & Wiesel, T. N. (1963). Receptive fields of cells in striate cortex of very young visually inexperienced kittens. *Journal of Neurophysiology, 26*, 994–1002.

Hubel, D. H., & Wiesel, T. N. (1979). Brain mechanisms of vision. In Scientific American (Eds.), *The brain*. San Franciso: W. H. Freeman.

Hudson, W. (1960). Pictorial depth perception in sub-cultural groups in Africa. *Journal of Social Psychology, 52*, 183–208.

Hudson, W. (1967). The study of the problem of pictorial perception among unacculturated groups. *International Journal of Psychology, 2*, 89–107.

Hughes, C. C. (1993). Culture in clinical psychiatry. In A. C. Gaw (Ed.), *Culture, ethnicity, and mental illness*. Washington, DC: American Psychiatric Press.

Hughes, J., Smith, T. W., Kosterlitz, H. W., Fothergill, L. A., Morgan, B. A., & Morris, H. R. (1975). Identification of two related pentapeptides from the brain with the potent opiate agonist activity. *Nature, 258*, 577–579.

Hultsch, D. F., & Dixon, R. A. (1990). Learning and memory in aging. In J. E. Birren & K. W. Schaie (Eds.), *Handbook of the psychology of aging* (3rd ed.). San Diego: Academic Press.

Hunt, E. (1994). Problem solving. In R. J. Sternberg (Ed.), *Thinking and problem solving*. San Diego: Academic Press.

Hunt, E., & Agnoli, F. (1991). The Whorfian hypothesis: A cognitive psychology perspective. *Psychological Review, 98*, 377–389.

Hunt, E., Streissguth, A. P., Kerr, B., & Olsen, H. C. (1995). Mothers' alcohol consumption during pregnancy: Effects on spatial-visual reasoning in 14-year-old children. *Psychological Science, 6*, 339–342.

Hunt, H. (1989). *The multiplicity of dreams: Memory, imagination and consciousness*. New Haven: Yale University Press.

Hunt, J. M., Smith, M. F., & Kernan, J. B. (1985). The effects of expectancy disconfirmation and argument strength on message processing level: An application to personal selling. In E. C. Hirschman & M. B. Holbrook (Eds.), *Advances in consumer research* (Vol. 12). Provo, UT: Association for Consumer Research.

Hunter, J. E., & Schmidt, F. L. (1996). Intelligence and job performance: Economic and social implications. *Psychology, Public Policy, & Law, 2*, 447–472.

Hurvich, L. M. (1981). *Color vision*. Sunderland, MA: Sinnauer Associates.

Huston, A. C., & Wright, J. C. (1982). Effects of communications media on children. In C. B. Kopp & J. B. Krakow (Eds.), *The child: Development in a social context*. Reading, MA: Addison-Wesley.

Huttenlocher, P. R. (1979). Synaptic density in human frontal cortex: Developmental changes of ageing. *Brain Research, 163*, 195–205.

Hyde, J. S. (1986). Gender differences in aggression. In J. S. Hyde & M. C. Linn (Eds.), *The psychology of gender differences: Advances through meta-analysis*. Baltimore: Johns Hopkins University Press.

Hyde, J. S., Fennema, E., & Lamon, S. J. (1990). Gender differences in mathematics performance: A meta-analysis. *Psychological Bulletin, 107*, 139–155.

Hyman, I. E., & Kleinknecht, E. E. (1999). False childhood memories: Research, theory, and applications. In L. M. Williams, & V. L. Banyard (Eds.), *Trauma & memory*. Thousand Oaks, CA: Sage Publications.

Hyman, I. E., Jr., Husband, T. H., & Billings, J. F. (1995). False memories of childhood experiences. *Applied Cognitive Psychology, 9*, 181–197.

Ickovics, J. R., & Rodin, J. (1992). Women and AIDS in the United States: Epidemiology, natural history, and mediating mechanisms. *Health Psychology, 11*, 1–16.

Inglehart, R. (1990). *Culture shift in advanced industrial society*. Princeton, NJ: Princeton University Press.

Innocenti, G. M. (1994). Some new trends in the study of the corpus callosum. *Behavioral and Brain Research, 64*, 1–8.

Ironson, G., Wynings, C., Schneiderman, N., Baum, A., Rodriguez, M., Greenwood, D., Benight, C., Antoni, M., LaPerriere, A., Huang, H. S., Klimas, N., & Fletcher, M. A. (1997). Post-traumatic stress symptoms, intrusive thoughts, loss, and immune function after Hurricane Andrew. *Psychosomatic Medicine, 59*, 128–141.

Irvine, S. H., & Berry, J. W. (1988). *Human abilities in cultural context*. New York: Cambridge University Press.

Irwin, W., Davidson, R. J., Lowe, M. J., Mock, B. J., Sorenson, J. A., & Turski, P. A. (1996). Human amygdala activation detected with echo-planar functional magnetic resonance imaging. *NeuroReport, 7*, 1765–1769.

Isaac, R. J., & Armat, V. C. (1990). *Madness in the streets: How psychiatry and the law abandoned the mentally ill*. New York: Free Press.

Isabella, R. A. (1995). The origins of infant-mother attachment: Maternal behavior and infant development. In R. Vasta (Ed.), *Annals of child development*. London: Jessica Kingsley.

Isada, N. B., & Grossman, J. H., III. (1991). Perinatal infections. In S. G. Gabbe, J. R. Niebyl, & J. L. Simpson (Eds.), *Obstetrics: Normal and problem pregnancies*. New York: Churchill Livingstone.

Iwao, S. (1993). *The Japanese woman: Traditional image and changing reality*. New York: Free Press.

Iwawaki, S., & Vernon, P. E. (1988). Japanese abilities and achievements. In S. H. Irvine & J. W. Berry (Eds.), *Human abilities in cultural context*. New York: Cambridge University Press.

Izard, C. E. (1984). Emotion-cognition relationships and human development. In C. E. Izard, J. Kagan, & R. B. Zajonc (Eds.), *Emotions, cognition and behavior*. Cambridge, England: Cambridge University Press.

Izard, C. E. (1990). Facial expressions and the regulation of emotions. *Journal of Personality and Social Psychology, 58*, 487–498.

Izard, C. E. (1991). *The psychology of emotions*. New York: Plenum.

Izard, C. E. (1994). Innate and universal facial expressions: Evidence from developmental and cross-cultural research. *Psychological Bulletin, 115*, 288–299.

Izard, C. E., & Saxton, P. M. (1988). Emotions. In R. C. Atkinson, R. J. Herrnstein, G. Lindzey, & R. D. Luce (Eds.), *Stevens' handbook of experimental psychology* (Vol. 1). New York: Wiley.

Jackson, L. A., Sullivan, L. A., & Hodge, C. N. (1993). Stereotype effects on attributions, predictions, and evaluations: No two social judgments are quite alike. *Journal of Personality and Social Psychology, 65*, 69–84.

Jacobsen, T., Edelstein, W., & Hoffman, V. (1994). A longitudinal study of the relations between representation of attachment in childhood and cognitive function in childhood and adolescence. *Developmental Psychology, 30*, 112-124.

James, W. (1884). What is emotion? *Mind, 19*, 188–205.

James, W. (1890). *The principles of psychology*. New York: Holt.

James, W. (1902). *The varieties of religious experience*. New York: Modern Library.

Jamison, K. R. (1988). Manic-depressive illness and accomplishment: Creativity, leadership, and social class. In F. K. Goodwin & K. R. Jamison (Eds.), *Manic-depressive illness*. Oxford, England: Oxford University Press.

Janis, I. L. (1958). *Psychological stress*. New York: Wiley.

Janis, I. L. (1972). *Victims of groupthink*. Boston: Houghton Mifflin.

Janis, I. L. (1993). Decision making under stress. In L. Goldberger & S. Breznitz (Eds.), *Handbook of stress: Theoretical and clinical aspects* (2nd ed.). New York: Free Press.

Janofsky, J. S., Dunn, M. H., Roskes, E. J., Briskin, J. K., & Rudolph, M. S. L. (1996). Insanity defense pleas in Baltimore city: An analysis of outcome. *American Journal of Psychiatry, 153*, 1464–1468.

Janus, S. S., & Janus, C. L. (1993). *The Janus report on sexual behavior*. New York: Wiley.

Jaroff, L. (1993, November 29). Lies of the mind. *Time*, pp. 52–59.

Jarvik, M. E., & Schneider, N. G. (1992). Nicotine. In J. H. Lowinson, P. Ruiz, & R. B. Millman (Eds.), *Substance abuse: A comprehensive textbook* (2nd ed.). Baltimore: Williams & Wilkins.

Jemmott, J. B., III, & Magloire, K. (1988). Academic stress, social support, and secretory immunoglobin A. *Journal of Personality and Social Psychology, 55*, 803–810.

Jensen, A. R. (1969). How much can we boost IQ and scholastic achievement? *Harvard Educational Review, 39*, 1–23.

Jensen, A. R. (1980). *Bias in mental testing*. New York: Free Press.

Jensen, A. R. (1982). Reaction time and psychometric g. In H. J. Eysenck (Ed.), *A model for intelligence*. New York: Springer-Verlag.

Jensen, A. R. (1987). Process differences and individual difference in some cognitive tasks. *Intelligence, 11*, 107–136.

Jensen, A. R. (1992). The importance of intra-individual variation in reaction time. *Personality and Individual Differences, 13*, 869–881.

Jensen, A. R. (1993a). Test validity: g versus "tacit knowledge." *Current Directions in Psychological Science, 2*(1), 9–10.

Jensen, A. R. (1993b). Why is reaction time correlated with psychometric g? *Current Directions in Psychological Science, 2*(2), 53–56.

Jensen, A. R. (1994a). Francis Galton. In R. J. Sternberg (Ed.), *Encyclopedia of human intelligence*. New York: Macmillan.

Jensen, A. R. (1994b). Race and IQ scores. In R. J. Sternberg (Ed.), *Encyclopedia of human intelligence*. New York: Macmillan.

Jensen, A. R. (1998). *The g factor: The science of mental ability*. Westport, CT: Praeger.

Jessell, T. M., & Kelly, D. D. (1991). Pain and analgesia. In E. R. Kandel, J. H. Schwartz, & T. M. Jessell (Eds.), *Principles of neural science* (3rd ed.). New York: Elsevier.

John, O. P., & Srivastava, S. (1999). The big five trait taxonomy: History, measurement, and theoretical perspectives. In L. A. Pervin, & O. P. John (Eds.), *Handbook of personality: Theory and research*. New York: Guilford Press.

Johnson, A. B. (1990). *Out of bedlam: The truth about deinstitutionalization*. New York: Basic Books.

Johnson, B. T. (1994). Effects of outcome-relevant involvement and prior information on persuasion. *Journal of Experimental Social Psychology, 30*, 556–579.

Johnson, C., & Mullen, B. (1994). Evidence for the accessibility of paired distinctiveness in distinctiveness-based illusory correlation in stereotyping. *Personality and Social Psychology Bulletin, 20*, 65–70.

Johnson, D. (1990). Animal rights and human lives: Time for scientists to right the balance. *Psychological Science, 1*, 213–214.

Johnson, J. G., & Sherman, M. F. (1997). Daily hassles mediate the relationship between major life events and psychiatric symptomatology: Longitudinal findings from an adolescent sample. *Journal of Social and Clinical Psychology, 16*, 389–404.

Johnson, J. S., & Newport, E. L. (1989). Critical period effects in second language learning: The influence of maturational state on the acquisition of English as a second language. *Cognitive Psychology, 21*, 60–99.

Johnson, M. E., & Dowling-Guyer, S. (1996). Effects of inclusive vs. exclusive language on evaluations of the counselor. *Sex Roles, 34*, 407–418.

Johnson, M. K. (1996). Fact, fantasy, and public policy. In D. J. Herrmann, C. McEvoy, C. Hertzog, P. Hertel, & M. K. Johnson (Eds.), *Basic and applied memory research: Theory in context* (Vol. 1). Mahwah, NJ: Erlbaum.

Johnson, M. K., Hashtroudi, S., & Lindsay, D. S. (1993). Source monitoring. *Psychological Bulletin, 114*, 3–28.

Johnston, W. A., & Dark, V. J. (1986). Selective attention. *Annual Review of Psychology, 37*, 43–75.

Johnston, W. A., & Heinz, S. P. (1978). Flexibility and capacity demands of attention. *Journal of Experimental Psychology: General, 107*, 420–435.

Joiner, T. E., Jr. (1994). Contagious depression: Existence, specificity to depressed symptoms, and the role of reassurance seeking. *Journal of Personality and Social Psychology, 67*, 287–296.

Joiner, T. E., Jr. (1997). Shyness and low social support as interactive diatheses, with loneliness as mediator: Testing an interpersonal-personality view of vulnerablity to depressive symptoms. *Journal of Abnormal Psychology, 106*, 386–394.

Joiner, T. E., Jr., & Metalsky, G. I. (1995). A prospective test of an integrative interpersonal theory of depression: A naturalistic study of college students. *Journal of Personality and Social Psychology, 69*, 778–788.

Jones, E. E., & Davis, K. E. (1965). From acts to dispositions: The attribution process in person perception. In L. Berkowitz (Ed.), *Advances in experimental social psychology* (Vol. 2). New York: Academic Press.

Jones, E. E., & Nisbett, R. E. (1971). The actor and the observer: Divergent perceptions of the causes of behavior. In E. E. Jones, D. E. Kanouse, H. H. Kelley, R. E. Nisbett, S. Valins, & B. Weiner (Eds.), *Attribution: Perceiving the causes of behavior.* Morristown, NJ: General Learning Press.

Jones, G. V. (1990). Misremembering a common object: When left is not right. *Memory & Cognition, 18*(2), 174–182.

Jordan, B. (1983). *Birth in four cultures.* Quebec, Canada: Eden Press.

Jorgensen, R. S., Johnson, B. T., Kolodziej, M. E., & Schreer, G. E. (1996). Elevated blood pressure and personality: A meta-analytic review. *Psychological Bulletin, 120*, 293–320.

Joseph, R. (1992). *The right brain and the unconscious.* New York: Plenum.

Joseph, R. (1996). *Neuropsychiatry, neuropsychology, and clinical neuroscience. Emotion, evolution, cognition, language, memory, brain damage, and abnormal behavior* (2nd ed.). Baltimore: Williams & Wilkins.

Joshipura, K. J., Ascherio, A., Manson, J. E., Stampfer, M. J., Rimm, E. B., Speizer, F. E., Hennekens, C. H., Speigelman, D., & Willett, W. C. (1999). Fruit and vegetable intake in relation to risk of Ischemic Stroke. *Journal of the American Medical Association, 282*, 1233–1239.

Judd, L. L., McAdams, L. A., Budnick, B., & Braff, D. L. (1992). Sensory gating effects in schizophrenia: New results. *American Journal of Psychiatry, 149*, 488–493.

Julien, R. M. (1998). *A primer of drug action.* New York: W. H. Freeman.

Jung, C. G. (1917/1953). *On the psychology of the unconscious.* In H. Read, M. Fordham, & G. Adler (Eds.), *Collected works of C. G. Jung* (Vol. 7). Princeton, NJ: Princeton University Press.

Jung, C. G. (1921/1960). *Psychological types.* In H. Read, M. Fordham, & G. Adler (Eds.), *Collected works of C. G. Jung* (Vol. 6). Princeton, NJ: Princeton University Press.

Jung, C. G. (1933). *Modern man in search of a soul.* New York: Harcourt, Brace & World.

Just, N., & Alloy, L. B. (1997). The response styles theory of depression: Tests and an extension of the theory. *Journal of Abnormal Psychology, 106*, 221–229.

Kagan, J. (1998). A parent's influence is peerless. *Harvard Education Letter, November/December.*

Kagan, J., & Snidman, N. (1991). Temperamental factors in human development. *American Psychologist, 46*, 856–862.

Kahan, T. L., & LaBerge, S. (1994). Lucid dreaming as metacognition: Implications for cognitive science. *Consciousness and Cognition, 3*, 246–264.

Kahan, T. L., & LaBerge, S. (1996). Cognition and metacognition in dreaming and waking: Comparisons of first- and third-person ratings. *Dreaming, 6*, 235–249.

Kahane, H. (1992). *Logic and contemporary rhetoric: The use of reason in everyday life.* Belmont, CA: Wadsworth.

Kahneman, D. (1999). Objective happiness. In D. Kahneman, E. Diener, & N. Schwarz (Eds.), *Well-being: The foundations of hedonic psychology.* New York: Russell Sage Foundation.

Kahneman, D., & Tversky, A. (1973). On the psychology of prediction. *Psychological Review, 80*, 237–251.

Kahneman, D., & Tversky, A. (1982). Subjective probability: A judgment of representativeness. In D. Kahneman, P. Slovic, & A. Tversky (Eds.), *Judgment under uncertainty: Heuristics and Biases.* Cambridge: Cambridge University Press.

Kahneman, D., & Tversky, A. (1984). Choices, values, and frames. *American Psychologist, 39*, 341–350.

Kalant, H., & Kalant, O. J. (1979). Death in amphetamine users: Causes and Rates. In D. E. Smith (Ed.), *Amphetamine use, misuse and abuse.* Boston: G. K. Hall.

Kalat, J. W. (1993). *Introduction to psychology.* Pacific Grove, CA: Brooks/Cole.

Kalat, J. W. (1996). *Introduction to psychology.* Pacific Grove, CA: Brooks/Cole.

Kales, J. D., Kales, A., Bixler, E. O., Soldatos, C. R., Cadieux, R. J., Kashurba, G. J., & Vela-Bueno, A. (1984). Biopsychobehavioral correlates of insomnia: V. Clinical characteristics and behavioral correlates. *American Journal of Psychiatry, 141*, 1371–1376.

Kalichman, S. C. (1995). *Understanding AIDS: A guide for mental health professionals.* Washington, DC: American Psychological Association.

Kalmijn, M. (1998). Intermarriage and homogamy: Causes, patterns, trends. *Annual Review of Sociology, 24*, 395–421.

Kalmuss, D., Davidson, A., & Cushman, L. (1992). Parenting expectations, experiences, and adjustment to parenthood: A test of the violated expectations framework. *Journal of Marriage and the Family, 52*, 516–526.

Kamen-Siegel, L., Rodin, J., Seligman, M. E. P., & Dwyer, J. (1991). Explanatory style and cell-mediated immunity in elderly men and women. *Health Psychology, 10*, 229–235.

Kamin, L. J. (1965). Temporal and intensity characteristics of the conditioned stimulus. In W. F. Prokasy (Ed.), *Classical conditioning.* New York: Appleton-Century-Crofts.

Kamiya, J. (1969). Operant control of the EEG rhythm and some of its reported effects on consciousness. In C. T. Tart (Ed.), *Altered states of consciousness.* New York: Wiley.

Kandel, E. R., & Jessell, T. M. (1991). Touch. In E. R. Kandel, J. H. Schwartz, & T. M. Jessell (Eds.), *Principles of neural science* (3rd ed.). New York: Elsevier.

Kandel, E. R., & Schwartz, J. H. (1991). Directly gated transmission at central synapses. In E. R. Kandel, J. H. Schwartz, & T. M. Jessell (Eds.), *Principles of neural science* (3rd ed.). New York: Elsevier.

Kane, J. (1991). *Be sick well: A healthy approach to chronic illness.* Oakland, CA: New Harbinger Publications.

Kane, T. D., Marks, M. A., Zaccaro, S. J., & Blair, V. (1996). Self-efficacy, personal goals, and wrestlers' self-regulation. *Journal of Sport & Exercise Psychology, 18*, 36–48.

Kaplan, A. G. (1985). Female or male therapists for women patients: New formulations. *Psychiatry, 48*, 111–121.

Kaplan, H. I., & Sadock, B. J. (Eds.). (1993). *Comprehensive group psychotherapy.* Baltimore: Williams & Wilkins.

Kaplan, H., & Dove, H. (1987). Infant development among the Ache of Eastern Paraguay. *Developmental Psychology, 23*, 190–198.

Kaplan, N. M. (1986). Dietary aspects of the treatment of hypertension. In L. Breslow, J. E. Fielding, & L. B. Lave (Eds.), *Annual review of public health* (Vol. 7). Palo Alto, CA: Annual Reviews.

Kaplan, R. M. (1985). The controversy related to the use of psychological tests. In B. B. Wolman (Ed.), *Handbook of intelligence: Theories, measurements, and applications.* New York: Wiley.

Kaprio, J., Rimpela, A., Winter, T., Viken, R. J., Rimpela, M., & Rose, R. J. (1995). Common genetic influence on BMI and age at menarche. *Human Biology, 67,* 739–753.

Kapur, S., & Remington, G. (1996). Serotonin-dopamine interaction and its relevance to schizophrenia. *American Journal of Psychiatry, 153,* 466–476.

Karau, S. J., & Williams, K. D. (1993). Social loafing: A meta-analytic review and theoretical integration. *Journal of Personality and Social Psychology, 65,* 681–706.

Karau, S. J., & Williams, K. D. (1995). Social loafing: Research findings, implications, and future directions. *Current Directions in Psychological Science, 4,* 134–140.

Kardiner, A., & Linton, R. (1945). *The individual and his society.* New York: Columbia University Press.

Karon, B. P. (1995). Provision of psychotherapy under managed health care: A growing crisis and national nightmare. *Professional Psychology: Research and Practice, 26,* 5–9.

Kasser, T., & Sharma, Y. S. (1999). Reproductive freedom, educational equality, and females' preference for resource-aquisition characteristics in mates. *Psychological Science, 10,* 374–377.

Katigbak, M. S., Church, A. T., & Akamine, T. X. (1996). Cross-cultural generalizability of personality dimensions: Relating indigenous and imported dimensions in two cultures. *Journal of Personality and Social Psychology, 70,* 99–114.

Kaufman, L., & Rock, I. (1962). The moon illusion I. *Science, 136,* 953–961.

Kausler, D. H. (1985). Episodic memory: Memorizing performance. In N. Charness (Ed.), *Aging and human performance.* Chichester, England: Wiley.

Kavanagh, D. J. (1992). Recent developments in expressed emotion in schizophrenia. *British Journal of Psychiatry, 160,* 601–620.

Kavesh, L., & Lavin, C. (1988). *Tales from the front.* New York: Doubleday.

Kaye, W. H., Weltzin, T. E., Hsu, L. K. G., McConaha, C. W., & Bolton, B. (1993). Amount of calories retained after binge eating and vomiting. *American Journal of Psychiatry, 150,* 969–971.

Kazdin, A. E. (1982). History of behavior modification. In A. S. Bellack, M. Hersen, & A. E. Kazdin (Eds.), *International handbook of behavior modification and behavior therapy.* New York: Plenum.

Kazdin, A. E. (1994). Methodology, design, and evaluation in psychotherapy research. In A. E. Bergin & S. L. Garfield (Eds.), *Handbook of psychotherapy and behavior change* (4th ed.). New York: Wiley.

Keenan, J. P., Gallup, G. G. Jr., Goulet, N., & Kulkarni, M. (1997). Attributions of deception in human mating strategies. *Journal of Social Behavior and Personality, 12,* 45–52.

Keesey, R. E., & Powley, T. L. (1975). Hypothalamic regulation of body weight. *American Scientist, 63,* 558–565.

Kehoe, E. J., & Macrae, M. (1998). Classical conditioning. In W. O'Donohue (Ed.), *Learning and behavior therapy.* Boston, Allyn & Bacon.

Keller, L. S., Butcher, J. N., & Slutske, W. S. (1990). Objective personality assessment. In G. Goldstein & M. Hersen (Eds.), *Handbook of psychological assessment.* New York: Pergamon Press.

Keller, P. A., & Block, L. G. (1999). The effect of affect-based dissonance versus cognition-based dissonance on motivated reasoning and health-related persuasion. *Journal of Experimental Psychology: Applied, 5,* 302–313.

Kelley, H. H. (1950). The warm-cold variable in first impressions of persons. *Journal of Personality, 18,* 431–439.

Kelley, H. H. (1967). Attributional theory in social psychology. *Nebraska Symposium on Motivation, 15,* 192–241.

Kelly, J. A., Otto-Salaj, L. L., Sikkema, K. J., Pinkerton, S. D., & Bloom, F. R. (1998). Implications of HIV treatment advances for behavioral research on AIDS: Protease inhibitors and new challenges in HIV secondary prevention. *Health Psychology, 17,* 310–319.

Kelly, J. P. (1991). The sense of balance. In E. R. Kandel, J. H. Schwartz, & T. M. Jessell (Eds.), *Principles of neural science* (3rd ed.). New York: Elsevier.

Kelman, H. C. (1967). Human use of human subjects: The problem of deception in social psychological experiments. *Psychological Bulletin, 67,* 1–11.

Kelman, H. C. (1982). Ethical issues in different social science methods. In T. L. Beauchamp, R. R. Faden, R. J. Wallace, Jr., & L. Walters (Eds.), *Ethical issues in social science research.* Baltimore: Johns Hopkins University Press.

Kendler, K. S., & Gardner, C. O. Jr. (1998). Boundaries of major depression: An evaluation of DSM-IV criteria. *American Journal of Psychiatry, 155,* 172–177.

Kendler, K. S., Karkowski, L. M., & Prescott, C. A. (1999). Causal relationship between stressful life events and the onset of major depression. *American Journal of Psychiatry, 156,* 837–841.

Kendler, K. S., Neale, M. C., Kessler, R. C., Heath, A. C., & Eaves, L. J. (1992). Generalized anxiety disorder in women: A population-based twin study. *Archives of General Psychiatry, 49,* 267–272.

Kennedy, T. E., Hawkins, R. D., & Kandel, E. R. (1992). Molecular interrelationships between short- and long-term memory. In L. R. Squire & N. Butters (Eds.), *Neuropsychology of Memory* (2nd ed.). New York: Wiley.

Kenrick, D. T. (1987). Gender, genes, and the social environment. In P. C. Shaver & C. Hendrick (Eds.), *Review of Personality and Social Psychology* (Vol. 8). Beverly Hills, CA: Sage.

Kenrick, D. T. (1995). Evolutionary theory versus the confederacy of dunces. *Psychological Inquiry, 6,* 56–62.

Kenrick, D. T., & Funder, D. C. (1991). The person-situation debate: Do personality traits really exist? In N. J. Derlega, B. A. Winstead, & W. H. Jones (Eds.), *Personality: Contemporary theory and research.* Chicago: Nelson-Hall.

Kenrick, D. T., & Gutierres, S. E. (1980). Contrast effects and judgments of physical attractiveness: When beauty becomes a social problem. *Journal of Personality and Social Psychology, 38,* 131–140.

Kenrick, D. T., & Keefe, R. C. (1992). Age preferences in mates reflect sex differences in reproductive strategies. *Behavioral and Brain Sciences, 15,* 75–133.

Kenrick, D. T., & Trost, M. R. (1993). The evolutionary perspective. In A. E. Beall, & R. J. Sternberg (Eds.), *The psychology of gender.* New York: Guilford Press.

Keren, G. (1990). Cognitive aids and debiasing methods: Can cognitive pills cure cognitive ills? In J. P. Caverni, J. M. Fabre, & M. Gonzalez (Eds.), *Cognitive biases.* Amsterdam: North-Holland.

Kerfoot, P., Sakoulas, G., & Hyman, S. E. (1996). Cocaine. In L. S. Friedman, N. F. Fleming, D. H. Roberts, & S. E. Hyman (Eds.), *Source book of substance abuse and addiction.* Baltimore: Williams & Wilkins.

Kesner, R. P. (1998). Neural mediation of memory for time: Role of the hippocampus and medial prefrontal cortex. *Pscyhonomic Bulletin & Review, 5,* 585–596.

Kessen, W. (1996). American psychology just before Piaget. *Psychological Science, 7,* 196–199.

Kessler, R. C. (1997). The effects of stressful life events on depression. *Annual Review of Psychology, 48,* 191–214.

Kessler, R. C., Olfson, M., & Berglund, P. A. (1998). Patterns and predictors of treatment contact after first onset of psychiatric disorders. *American Journal of Psychiatry, 155,* 62–69.

Kessler, R. C., Zhao, S., Katz, S. J., Kouzis, A. C., Frank, R. G., Edlund, M., & Leaf, P. (1999). Past-year use of outpatient services for psychiatric problems in the National Comorbidity Survey. *American Journal of Psychiatry, 156,* 115–123.

Kiang, N. Y. S., & Peake, W. T. (1988). Physics and physiology of hearing. In R. C. Atkinson, R. J. Herrnstein, G. Lindzey, & R. D. Luce (Eds.), *Stevens' handbook of experimental psychology* (2nd ed., Vol. 1). New York: Wiley.

Kiecolt-Glaser, J. K., Garner, W., Speicher, C., Penn, G. M., Holliday, J., & Glaser, R. (1984). Psychosocial modifiers of immunocompetence in medical students. *Psychosomatic Medicine, 46*(1), 7–14.

Kiecolt-Glaser, J. K., & Glaser, R. (1995). Measurement of immune response. In S. Cohen, R. C. Kessler, & L. U. Gordon (Eds.), *Measuring stress: A guide for health and social scientists.* New York: Oxford University Press.

Kiecolt-Glaser, J. K., Glaser, R., Williger, D., Stout, J., Messick, G., Sheppard, S., Ricker, D., Romisher, S. C., Briner, W., Bonnell, G., & Donnerberg, R. (1985). Psychosocial enhancement of immunocompetence in a geriatric population. *Health Psychology, 4,* 25–42.

Kiesler, C. A. (1991). Homelessness and public policy priorities. *American Psychologist, 46,* 1245–1252.

Kiesler, C. A. (1992). U.S. mental health policy: Doomed to fail. *American Psychologist, 47,* 1077–1082.

Kihlstrom, J. F. (1998a). Dissociations and dissociation theory in hypnosis: Comment on Kirsch and Lynn (1998). *Psychological Bulletin, 123,* 186–191.

Kihlstrom, J. F. (1998b). Exhumed memory. In S. J. Lynn, & K. M. McConkey (Eds.), *Truth in memory.* New York: Guilford Press.

Kihlstrom, J. F., Tataryn, D. J., & Hoyt, I. P. (1993). Dissociative disorders. In P. B. Sutker & H. E. Adams (Eds.), *Comprehensive handbook of psychopathology* (2nd ed.). New York: Plenum.

Killeen, P. R. (1981). Learning as causal inference. In M. L. Commons & J. A. Nevin (Eds.), *Quantitative analyses of behavior: Vol. 1. Discriminative properties of reinforcement schedules.* Cambridge, MA: Ballinger.

Kim, H., & Markus, H. R. (1999). Deviance or uniqueness, harmony or conformity? A cultural analysis. *Journal of Personality and Social Psychology, 77*, 785–800.

Kim, K., & Spelke, E. S. (1992). Infants' sensitivity to effects of gravity on visible object motion. *Journal of Experimental Psychology: Human Perception and Performance, 18*, 385–393.

Kimberg, D. Y., D'Esposito, M., & Farah, M. J. (1997). Cognitive functions in the prefrontal cortex-Working memory and executive control. *Current Directions in Psychological Science, 6*, 185–192.

Kimura, D. (1973). The asymmetry of the human brain. *Scientific American, 228*, 70–78.

Kimura, D., & Hampson, E. (1993). Neural and hormonal mechanisms mediating sex differences in cognition. In P. A. Vernon (Ed.), *Biological approaches to the study of human intelligence*. Norwood, NJ: Ablex.

Kimura, K. (1997). A review of studies on threat appeals from the viewpoint of protection motivation theory. *Japanese Journal of Experimental Social Psychology, 37*, 85–96.

King, A. C., Oman, R. F., Brassington, G. S., Bliwise, D. L., & Haskell, W. L. (1997). Moderate-intensity exercise and self-rated quality of sleep in older adults: A randomized controlled trial. *Journal of the American Medical Association, 277*, 32–37.

King, A. C., Taylor, C. B., & Haskell, W. L. (1993). Effects of differing intensities and formats of 12 months of exercise training on psychological outcomes in older adults. *Health Psychology, 12*, 292–300.

King, G. R., & Ellinwood, E. H., Jr. (1997). Amphetamines and other stimulants. In J. H. Lowinson, P. Ruiz, R. B. Millman, & J. G. Langrod (Eds), *Substance abuse: A comprehensive textbook*. Baltimore: Williams & Willkins.

King, L. A., & Emmons, R. A. (1990). Conflict over emotional expression: Psychological and physical correlates. *Journal of Personality and Social Psychology, 58*, 864–877.

King, L. A., & Emmons, R. A. (1991). Psychological, physical, and interpersonal correlates of emotional expressiveness, conflict and control. *European Journal of Personality, 5*, 131–150.

Kinsbourne, M. (1980). If sex differences in brain lateralization exist, they have yet to be discovered. *Behavioral and Brain Sciences, 3*, 241–242.

Kinsey, A. C., Pomeroy, W. B., & Martin, C. E. (1948). *Sexual behavior in the human male*. Philadelphia: Saunders.

Kinsey, A. C., Pomeroy, W. B., Martin, C. E., & Gebhard, P. H. (1953). *Sexual behavior in the human female*. Philadelphia: Saunders.

Kirk, S. A., & Kutchins, H. (1992). *The selling of DSM: The rhetoric of science in psychiatry*. New York: Aldine de Gruyter.

Kirkpatrick, L. A. (1999). Attachment and religious representations and behavior. In J. Cassidy & P. R. Shaver (Eds.), *Handbook of attachment: Theory, research and clinical applications*. New York: Guilford Press.

Kirkpatrick, L. A., & Davis, K. E. (1994). Attachment style, gender, and relationship stability: A longitudinal study. *Journal of Personality and Social Psychology, 66*, 502–512.

Kirsch, I. (1997). Response expectancy theory and application: A decennial review. *Applied and Preventive Psychology, 6*, 69–79.

Kirsch, I., & Lynn, S. J. (1998). Dissociation theories of hypnosis. *Psychological Bulletin, 123*, 100–115.

Kitayama, S., Markus, H. R., Matsumoto, H., & Norasakkunkit, V. (1997). Individual and collective processes in the constuction of the self: Self-enhancement in the United States and self-criticism in Japan. *Journal of Personality and Social Psychology, 72*, 1245–1267.

Kitchens, A. (1991). Left brain/right brain theory: Implications for developmental math instruction. *Review of Research in Developmental Education, 8*, 20–23.

Kitson, G. C., & Sussman, M. B. (1982). Marital complaints, demographic characteristics, and symptoms of mental distress in divorce. *Journal of Marriage and the Family, 44*, 87–101.

Kittler, P. G., & Sucher, K. (1989). *Food and culture in America: A nutrition handbook*. New York: Van Nostrand Reinhold.

Kittler, P. G., & Sucher, K. P. (1998). *Food and culture in America: A nutrition handbook*. St. Paul: West.

Klein, M. (1948). *Contributions to psychoanalysis*. London: Hogarth.

Kleinke, C. L., Peterson, T. R., & Rutledge, T. R. (1998). Effects of self-generated facial expressions on mood. *Journal of Personality and Social Psychology, 74*, 272–279.

Kleinmuntz, B. (1980). *Essentials of abnormal psychology*. San Francisco: Harper & Row.

Kleinmuntz, B. (1985). *Personality and psychological assessment*. Malabar, FL: Robert E. Krieger.

Klerman, E. B. (1993). Deprivation, selective: NREM sleep. In M. A. Carskadon (Ed.), *Encyclopedia of sleep and dreaming*. New York: Macmillan.

Klerman, G. L., Weissman, M. M., Markowitz, J. C., Glick, I., Wilner, P. J., Mason, B., & Shear, M. K. (1994). Medication and psychotherapy. In A. E. Bergin & S. L. Garfield (Eds.), *Handbook of psychotherapy and behavior change* (4th ed.). New York: Wiley.

Kline, D. W., & Schieber, F. (1985). Vision and aging. In J. E. Birren & K. W. Schaie (Eds.), *Handbook of the psychology of aging* (2nd ed.). New York: Van Nostrand Reinhold.

Kline, P. (1991). *Intelligence: The psychometric view*. New York: Routledge, Chapman, & Hall.

Kline, P. (1992). *The handbook of psychological testing*. London: Routledge.

Kline, P. (1995). A critical review of the measurement of personality and intelligence. In D. H. Saklofske & M. Zeidner (Eds.), *International handbook of personality and intelligence*. New York: Plenum.

Kling, K. C., Hyde, J. S., Showers, C. J., & Buswell, B. N. (1999). Gender differences in self-esteem: A meta-analysis. *Psychological Bulletin, 125*, 470–500.

Kluckhohn, C., & Murray, H. A. (1948). *Personality in nature, society and culture*. New York: Knopf.

Kluegel, J. R. (1990). Trends in whites' explanations of the black-white gap in socioeconomic status. *American Sociological Review, 55*, 512–525.

Kluft, R. P. (1996). Dissociative identity disorder. In L. K. Michelson, & W. J. Ray (Eds.), *Handbook of dissociation: Theoretical, empirical, and clinical perspectives*. New York: Plenum.

Kluft, R. P. (1999). True lies, false truths, and naturalistic raw data: Applying clinical research findings to the false memory debate. In L. M. Williams, & V. L. Banyard (Eds.), *Trauma & memory*. Thousand Oaks, CA: Sage Publications.

Knable, M. B., Kleinman, J. E., & Weinberger, D. R. (1995). Neurobiology of schizophrenia. In A. F. Schatzberg & C. B. Nemeroff (Eds.), *The American Psychiatric Press textbook of psychopharmacology*. Washington, DC: American Psychiatric Press.

Knight, G. P., Fabes, R. A., & Higgins, D. A. (1996). Concerns about drawing causal inference from meta-analysis: An example in the study of gender differences in aggression. *Psychological Bulletin, 119*, 410–421.

Knowles, J. A., Kaufmann, C. A., & Rieder, R. O. (1999). Genetics. In R. E. Hales, S. C. Yudofsky, & J. A. Talbott (Eds.), *American Psychiatric Press Textbook of Psychiatry*. Washington, DC: American Psychiatric Press.

Knox, D., Zusman, M., & Nieves, W. (1997). College students' homogamous preferences for a date and mate. *College Student Journal, 31*, 445–448.

Koehler, J. J. (1996). The base rate fallacy reconsidered: Descriptive, normative, and methodological challenges. *Behavioral Brain Sciences, 19*, 1–53.

Koester, J. (1991). Voltage-grated ion channels and the generation of the action potential. In E. R. Kandel, J. H. Schwartz, & T. M. Jessell (Eds.), *Principles of neural science* (3rd ed.). New York: Elsevier.

Kogan, N. (1990). Personality and aging. In J. E. Birren & K. W. Schaie (Eds.), *Handbook of the psychology of aging*. San Diego: Academic Press.

Kohlberg, L. (1963). The development of children's orientations toward a moral order: I. Sequence in the development of moral thought. *Vita Humana, 6*, 11–33.

Kohlberg, L. (1969). Stage and sequence: The cognitive-developmental approach to socialization. In D. A. Goslin (Ed.), *Handbook of socialization theory and research*. Chicago: Rand McNally.

Kohlberg, L. (1976). Moral stages and moralization: Cognitive-developmental approach. In T. Lickona (Ed.), *Moral development and behavior: Theory, research and social issues*. New York: Holt, Rinehart & Winston.

Kohut, H. (1971). *Analysis of the self*. New York: International Universities Press.

Kolb, B., & Whishaw, I. Q. (1990). *Fundamentals of human neuropsychology*. New York: W. H. Freeman.

Koob, G. F. (1997). Neurochemical explanations for addiction. *Hospital Practice, April*, 12–14.

Koob, G. F., & Bloom, F. E. (1988). Cellular and molecular mechanisms of drug dependence. *Science, 242*, 715–723.

Kopta, S. M., Lueger, R. J., Saunders, S. M., & Howard, K. I. (1999). Individual psychotherapy outcome and process research: Challenges leading to greater turmoil or a positive transition? *Annual Review of Psychology, 50*, 441–69.

Koranyi, E. K. (1989). Physiology of stress reviewed. In S. Cheren (Ed.), *Psychosomatic medicine: Theory, physiology, and practice* (Vol. 1). Madison, CT: International Universities Press.

Koriat, A., & Melkman, R. (1987). Depth of processing and memory organization. *Psychological Research, 49*, 183–188.

Koriat, A., Lichtenstein, S., & Fischhoff, B. (1980). Reasons for confidence. *Journal of Experimental Psychology, 6*, 107–118.

Korn, J. (1987). Judgments of acceptability of deception in psychological research. *Journal of General Psychology, 114*, 205–216.

Korn, J. H., Davis, R., & Davis, S. F. (1991). Historians' and chairpersons' judgments of eminence among psychologists. *American Psychologist, 46*, 789–792.

Kortenhaus, C. M., & Demarest, J. (1993). Gender role stereotyping in children's literature: An update. *Sex Roles, 3, 219–232.

Kotovsky, K., Hayes, J. R., & Simon, H. A. (1985). Why are some problems hard? Evidence from Tower of Hanoi. *Cognitive Psychology, 17*, 248–294.

Kotulak, R. (1996). *Inside the brain: Revolutionary discoveries of how the mind works.* Kansas City, Mo: Andrews McMeel.

Kracke, W. (1991). Myths in dreams, thought in images: An Amazonian contribution to the psychoanalytic theory of primary process. In B. Tedlock (Ed.), *Dreaming: Anthropological and psychological interpretations.* Santa Fe, NM: School of American Research Press.

Kracke, W. (1992). Languages of dreaming: Anthropological approaches to the study of dreaming in other cultures. In J. Gackenbach & A. Sheik (Eds.), *Dream Images: A Call to Mental Arms.* Amityville, NY: Baywood.

Krakauer, D., & Dallenbach, K. M. (1937). Gustatory adaptation to sweet, sour, and bitter. *American Journal of Psychology, 49*, 469–475.

Kramer, M. (1994). The scientific study of dreaming. In M. H. Kryger, T. Roth, & W. C. Dement (Eds.), *Principles and practice of sleep medicine* (2nd ed.). Philadelphia: Saunders.

Krebs, D. L., & Denton, K. (1997). Social illusions and self-deception: The evolution of biases in person perception. In J. A. Simpson & D. T. Kénrick (Eds.), *Evolutionary social psychology.* Mahwah, NJ: Erlbaum.

Krebs, J. R., & McCleery, R. H. (1984). Optimization in behavioral ecology. In J. R. Krebs, & N. B. Davies (Eds.), *Behavioral ecology* (2nd ed.). Sunderland, MA: Sinauer.

Krishnan, K. R. R., & Hamilton, M. A. (1997). Obesity. *Primary Psychiatry, 5*, 49–53.

Krosnick, J. A. (1999). Survey research. *Annual Review Psychology, 50*, 537–567.

Krosnick, J. A., & Fabrigar, L. R. (1998). *Designing good questionnaires: Insights from psychology.* New York: Oxford University Press.

Krosnick, J. A., & Petty, R. E. (1995). Attitude strength: An overview. In R. E. Petty, & J. A. Krosnick (Eds.), *Attitude strength: Antecedents and consequences.* Mahwah, NJ: Erlbaum.

Krueger, J. (1996). Personal beliefs and cultural stereotypes about racial characteristics. *Journal of Personality and Social Psychology, 71*, 536–548.

Krueger, J., Ham, J. J., & Linford, K. M. (1996). Perceptions of behavioral consistency: Are people aware of the actor-observer effect? *Psychological Science, 7*, 259–264.

Krueger, W. C. F. (1929). The effect of overlearning on retention. *Journal of Experimental Psychology, 12*, 71–78.

Krull, D. S., & Erickson, D. J. (1995). Inferential hopscotch: How people draw social inferences from behavior. *Current Directions in Psychological Science, 4*, 35–38.

Kryger, M. H. (1993). Snoring. In M. A. Carskadon (Ed.), *Encyclopedia of sleep and dreaming.* New York: Macmillan.

Kryger, M. H., Roth, T., & Carskadon, M. (1994). Circadian rhythms in humans: An overview. In M. H. Kryger, T. Roth, & W. C. Dement (Eds.), *Principles and practice of sleep medicine* (2nd ed.). Philadelphia: Saunders.

Kulick, A. R., Pope, H. G., & Keck, P. E. (1990). Lycanthropy and self-identification. *Journal of Nervous & Mental Disease, 178*(2), 134–137.

Kunda, Z., & Oleson, K. C. (1995). Maintaining stereotypes in the face of disconfirmation: Constructing grounds for subtyping deviants. *Journal of Personality and Social Psychology, 68*, 565–579.

Kunda, Z., & Oleson, K. C. (1997). When exceptions prove the rule: How extremity of deviance determines the impact of deviant examples on stereotypes. *Journal of Personality and Social Psychology, 72*, 965–979.

Kupfermann, I. (1991). Hypothalamus and the limbic system: Motivation. In E. R. Kandel, J. H. Schwartz, & T. M. Jessell (Eds.), *Principles of neural science* (3rd ed.). New York: Elsevier.

Kutchins, H., & Kirk, S. A. (1997). *Making us crazy: DSM—The psychiatric Bible and the creation of mental disorders.* New York: Free Press.

LaBine, S. J., & LaBine, G. (1996). Determinations of negligence and the hindsight bias. *Law & Human Behavior, 20*, 501–516.

La Cerra, P., & Kurzban, R. (1995). The structure of scientific revolutions and the nature of the adapted mind. *Psychological Inquiry, 6*, 62–65.

Lachman, S. J. (1996). Processes in perception: Psychological transformations of highly structured stimulus material. *Perceptual and Motor Skills, 83*, 411–418.

Lakein, A. (1996). *How to get control of your time and your life.* New York: New American Library.

Lall, R., & Schandler, S. L. (1991). Michigan Alcohol Screening Test (MAST) scores and academic performance in college students. *College Student Journal, 25*, 245–251.

Lamb, H. R. (1998). Deinstitutionalization at the beginning of the new millenium. *Harvard Review of Psychiatry, 6*, 1–10.

Lamb, M. E., Hwang, C. P., Ketterlinus, R. D., & Fracasso, M. P. (1999). Parent-child relationships: Development in the context of the family. In M. H. Bornstein, & M. E. Lamb (Eds.), *Developmental psychology and advanced textbook.* Mahwah, NJ: Erlbaum.

Lamb, M. E., Ketterlinus, R. D., & Fracasso, M. P. (1992). Parent-child relationships. In M. H. Bornstein & M. E. Lamb (Eds.), *Developmental psychology: An advanced textbook* (3rd ed.). Hillsdale, NJ: Erlbaum.

Lamb, M. E., Sternberg, K. J., & Prodromidis, M. (1992). Nonmaternal care and the security of infant-mother attachment: A reanalysis of the data. *Infant Behavior and Development, 15*, 71–83.

Lambert, M. J., & Bergin, A. E. (1992). Achievements and limitations of psychotherapy research. In D. K. Freedheim (Ed.), *History of psychotherapy: A century of change.* Washington, DC: American Psychological Association.

Lambert, M. J., & Bergin, A. E. (1994). The effectiveness of psychotherapy. In A. E. Bergin & S. L. Garfield (Eds.), *Handbook of psychotherapy and behavior change* (4th ed.). New York: Wiley.

Lambert, M. J., & Hill, C. E. (1994). Assessing psychotherapy outcomes and processes. In A. E. Bergin & S. L. Garfield (Eds.), *Handbook of psychotherapy and behavior change* (4th ed.). New York: Wiley.

Lambert, W. E. (1990). Persistent issues in bilingualism. In B. Harley, P. Allen, J. Cummins, & M. Swain (Eds.), *The development of second language proficiency.* Cambridge, England: Cambridge University Press.

Lampinen, J. M., Neuschatz, J. S., & Payne, D. G. (1999). Source attributions and false memories: A test of the demand characteristics account. *Psychonomic Bulletin & Review, 6*, 130–135.

Landabaso, M. A., Iraurgi, I., Sanz, J., Calle, R., Ruiz de Apodaka, J., Jimenez-Lerma, J. M., & Gutierrez-Fraile, M. (1999). Naltrexone in the treatment of alcoholism. Two-year follow up results. *European Journal of Psychiatry, 13*, 97–105.

Landy, F. J. (1988). The early years of I/O: "Dr. Mayo." *The Industrial and Organizational Psychologist, 25*, 53–55.

Landy, F. J., Shankster, L. J., & Kohler, S. S. (1994). Personnel selection and placement. *Annual Review of Psychology, 45*, 261–296.

Lang, P. J. (1995). The emotion probe: Studies of motivation and attention. *American Psychologist, 50*, 372–385.

Lange, C. (1885). One leuds beveegelser. In K. Dunlap (Ed.), *The emotions.* Baltimore: Williams & Wilkins.

Lanyon, R. I., & Goodstein, L. D. (1997). *Personality assessment.* New York: Wiley.

Larson, J. R. Jr., Christensen, C., Abbott, A. S., & Franz, T. M. (1996). Diagnosing groups: Charting the flow of information in medical decision making teams. *Journal of Personality and Social Psychology, 71*, 315–370.

Larson, R., & Richards, M. H. (1994). *Divergent realities: The emotional lives of mothers, fathers, and adolescents.* New York: Basic Books.

Latané, B. (1981). The psychology of social impact. *American Psychologist, 36*, 343–356.

Latané, B., & Nida, S. A. (1981). Ten years of research on group size and helping. *Psychological Bulletin, 89*, 308–324.

Latané, B., Williams, K., & Harkins, S. (1979). Many hands make light the work: The causes and consequences of social loafing. *Journal of Personality and Social Psychology, 37*, 822–832.

Lattal, K. A. (1992). B. F. Skinner and psychology [Introduction to the Special Issue]. *American Psychologist, 27*, 1269–1272.

Latz, S., Wolf, A. W., & Lozoff, B. (1999). Cosleeping in context: Sleep practices and problems in young children in Japan and United States. *Archives of Pediatrics & Adolescent Medicine, 153*, 339–346.

Laughlin, H. (1967). *The neuroses*. Washington, DC: Butterworth.

Laughlin, H. (1979). *The ego and its defenses*. New York: Aronson.

Laumann, E. O., Gagnon, J. H., Michael, R. T., & Michaels, S. (1994). *The social organization of sexuality: Sexual practices in the United States*. Chicago: University of Chicago Press.

Laursen, B., Coy, K. C., & Collins, W. A. (1998). Reconsidering changes in parent-child conflict across adolescence: A meta-analysis. *Child Development, 69*, 817–832.

Lavee, Y., Sharlin, S., & Katz, R. (1996). The effect of parenting stress on marital quality: An integrated mother-father model. *Journal of Family Issues, 17*, 114–135.

Lavine, H., Sweeney, D., & Wagner, S. H. (1999). Depicting women as sex objects in television advertising: Effects on body dissatisfaction. *Personality and Social Psychology Bulletin, 25*, 1049–1058.

Lazarus, R. S. (1991). *Emotion and adaptation*. New York: Oxford University Press.

Lazarus, R. S. (1993). Why we should think of stress as a subset of emotion. In L. Goldberger & S. Breznitz (Eds.), *Handbook of stress: Theoretical and clinical aspects* (2nd ed.). New York: Free Press.

Lazarus, R. S. (1995). Vexing research problems inherent in cognitive-mediational theories of emotion—and some solutions. *Psychological Inquiry, 6*, 183–196.

Lazarus, R. S. (1999). *Stress and emotion: A new synthesis*. New York: Springer Publishing Company.

Leahey, T. H. (1991). *A history of modern psychology*. Englewood Cliffs, NJ: Prentice-Hall.

Leahey, T. H. (1992). The mythical revolutions of American psychology. *American Psychologist, 47*, 308–318.

Leavitt, F. (1995). *Drugs and behavior* (3rd ed.). Thousand Oaks, CA: Sage.

LeBoeuf, M. (1980, February). Managing time means managing yourself. *Business Horizons*, 41–46.

LeDoux, J. E. (1986). The neurobiology of emotion. In J. E. LeDoux & W. Hirst (Eds.), *Mind and brain: Dialogues in cognitive neuroscience*. Cambridge, England: Cambridge University Press.

LeDoux, J. E. (1993). Emotional networks in the brain. In M. Lewis & J. M. Haviland (Eds.), *Handbook of emotions*. New York: Guilford Press.

LeDoux, J. E. (1995). Emotion: Clues from the brain. *Annual Review of Psychology, 46*, 209–235.

LeDoux, J. E. (1996). *The emotional brain*. New York: Simon & Schuster.

Lee, I. M., Hsieh, C., & Paffenbarger, R. S. Jr. (1995). Exercise intensity and longevity in men. *Journal of the American Medical Association, 273*, 1179–1184.

Leeper, R. W. (1935). A study of a neglected portion of the field of learning: The development of sensory organization. *Journal of Genetic Psychology, 46*, 41–75.

Lefcourt, H. M., Davidson, K., Shepherd, R., Phillips, M., Prkachin, K., & Mills, D. (1995). Perspective-taking humor: Accounting for stress moderation. *Journal of Social and Clinical Psychology, 14*, 373–391.

Leff, J., & Vaughn, C. (1981). The role of maintenance therapy and relatives' expressed emotion in relapse of schizophrenia: A two-year follow-up. *British Journal of Psychiatry, 139*, 102–104.

Leff, J., & Vaughn, C. (1985). *Expressed emotion in families*. New York: Guilford Press.

Leff, J., Trieman, N., & Gooch, C. (1996). Team for the Assessment of Psychiatric Services (TAPS) Project 33: Prospective follow-up study of long-stay patients discharged from two psychiatric hospitals. *American Journal of Psychiatry, 153*, 1318–1324.

Lehrer, P. M., & Woolfolk, R. L. (1984). Are stress reduction techniques interchangeable, or do they have specific effects? A review of the comparative empirical literature. In R. L. Woolfolk & P. M. Lehrer (Eds.), *Principles and practice of stress management*. New York: Guilford Press.

Lehrer, P. M., & Woolfolk, R. L. (1993). Specific effects of stress management techniques. In P. M. Lehrer & R. L. Woolfolk (Eds.), *Principles and practice of stress management* (2nd ed.). New York: Guilford Press.

Leibovic, K. N. (1990). Vertebrate photoreceptors. In K. N. Leibovic (Ed.), *Science of vision*. New York: Springer-Verlag.

Leibowitz, S. F. (1991). Brain neuropeptide Y: An integrator of endocrine, metabolic and behavioral processes. *Brain Research Bulletin, 27*, 333–337.

Leibowitz, S. F. (1992). Neurochemical-neuroendocrine systems in the brain controlling macronutrient intake and metabolism. *Trends in Neuroscience, 15*, 491–497.

Leiker, M., & Hailey, B. J. (1988). A link between hostility and disease: Poor health habits. *Behavioral Medicine, 14*, 129–133.

LeMagnen, J. (1981). The metabolic basis of dual periodicity of feeding in rats. *Behavioral and Brain Sciences, 4*, 561–607.

Lemme, B. H. (1999). *Development in adulthood*. Boston: Allyn & Bacon.

Lenox, R. H., & Manji, H. K. (1995). Lithium. In A. F. Schatzberg & C. B. Nemeroff (Eds.), *The American Psychiatric Press textbook of psychopharmacology*. Washington, DC: American Psychiatric Press.

Leo, J. (1987, January). Exploring the traits of twins. *Time*, p. 63.

Leshner, A. I. (1997). Drug abuse and addiction are biomedical problems. *Hospital Practice, April*, 2–4.

LeVay, S. (1991). A difference in hypothalamic structure between heterosexual and homosexual men. *Science, 253*, 1034–1037.

LeVay, S. (1993). *The sexual brain*. Cambridge, MA: MIT Press.

LeVay, S. (1996). *Queer science: The use and abuse of research into homosexuality*. Cambridge, MA: MIT Press.

Levenson, R. W. (1992). Autonomic nervous system differences among emotions. *Psychological Science, 3*, 23–27.

Leventhal, E. A., Hansell, S., Diefenbach, M., Leventhal, H., & Glass, D. C. (1996). Negative affect and self-report of physical symptoms: Two longitudinal studies of older adults. *Health Psychology, 15*, 193–199.

Levine, J. M. (1999). Solomon Asch's legacy for group research. *Personality and Social Psychology Review, 3*, 358–364.

Levine, J. M., & Moreland, R. L. (1998). Small groups. In D. T. Gilbert, S. T. Fiske, & G. Lindzey (Eds.), *The handbook of social psychology*. New York: McGraw-Hill.

Levine, R., & Norenzayan, A. (1999). The pace of life in 31 countries. *Journal of Cross-Cultural Psychology, 30*, 178–205.

Levine, R., Sata, S., Hashimoto, T., & Verma, J. (1995). Love and marriage in eleven cultures. *Journal of Cross-Cultural Psychology, 26*, 554–571.

Levinson, D. J., with Darrow, C. M., Klein, E. G., Levinson, M. H., & McKee, B. (1978). *The seasons of a man's life*. New York: Knopf.

Levinthal, C. F. (1999). *Drugs, behavior, and modern society*. Boston: Allyn & Bacon.

Levis, D. J. (1989). The case for a return to a two-factor theory of avoidance: The failure of non-fear interpretations. In S. B. Klein & R. R. Bowrer (Eds.), *Contemporary learning theories: Pavlovian conditioning and the status of traditional learning theory*. Hillsdale NJ: Erlbaum.

Levy, G. D., Taylor, M. G., & Gelman, S. A. (1995). Traditional and evaluative aspects of flexibility in gender roles, social conventions, moral rules, and physical laws. *Child Development, 66*, 515–531.

Levy, J. (1985, May). Right brain, left brain: Fact or fiction. *Psychology Today*, 38–44.

Levy, J., Trevarthen, C., & Sperry, R. W. (1972). Perception of bilateral chimeric figures following hemispheric disconnection. *Brain, 95*, 61–78.

Levy, S. M. (1985). *Behavior and cancer*. San Francisco: Jossey-Bass.

Lewin, K. (1935). *A dynamic theory of personality*. New York: McGraw-Hill.

Lewinsohn, P. M., & Gotlib, I. H. (1995). Behavioral theory and treatment of depression. In E. E. Beckham & W. R. Leber (Eds.), *Handbook of depression* (2nd ed.). New York: Guilford Press.

Lewinsohn, P. M., Rohde, P., Seeley, J. R., & Fischer, S. A. (1993). Age-cohort changes in the lifetime occurrence of depression and other mental disorders. *Journal of Abnormal Psychology, 102*, 110–120.

Lewis, D. O., Pincus, J. H., Feldman, M., Jackson, L., & Bard, B. (1986). Psychiatric, neurological, and psychoeducational characteristics of 15 death row inmates in the United States. *American Journal of Psychiatry, 143*, 838–845.

Lewis, D. O., Yeager, C. A., Swica, Y., Pincus, J. H., & Lewis, M. (1997). Objective documentation of child abuse and dissociation in 12 murderers with dissociative identity disorder. *American Journal of Psychiatry, 154*, 1703–1710.

Lewis-Fernandez, R., & Kleinman, A. (1994). Culture, personality, and psychology. *Journal of Abnormal Psychology, 103*, 67–71.

Ley, P. (1997). Compliance among patients. In A. Baum, S. Newman, J. Weiman, R. West, & C. McManus (Eds.), *Cambridge handbook of psychology, health, and medicine*. Cambridge, England: Cambridge University Press.

Liberman, R. P., & Bedell, J. R. (1989). Behavior therapy. In H. I. Kaplan & B. J. Sadock (Eds.), *Comprehensive textbook of psychiatry/ V*. Baltimore: Williams & Wilkins.

Libman, H. (1992). Pathogenesis, natural history, and classification of HIV infection. *Primary Care, 19*(1), 1–17.

Lichtenstein, S., Fischhoff, B., & Phillips, L. (1982). Calibration of probabilities: The state of the art to 1980. In D. Kahneman, P. Slovic, & A. Tversky (Eds.), *Judgment under uncertainty: Heuristics and biases*. Cambridge, England: Cambridge University Press.

Lickey, M. E., & Gordon, B. (1991). *Medicine and mental illness: The use of drugs in psychiatry*. New York: W. H. Freeman.

Lieberman, M. A. (1993). Self-help groups. In H. I. Kaplan & B. J. Sadock (Eds.), *Comprehensive group psychotherapy*. Baltimore: Williams & Wilkins.

Liebert, R. M., & Liebert, L. L. (1998). *Liebert & Spiegler's personality strategies and issues*. Pacific Grove: Brooks/Cole.

Lilienfeld, S. O., Lynn, S. J., Kirsch, I., Chaves, J. F., Sarbin, T. R., Ganaway, G. K., & Powell, R. A. (1999). Dissociative identity disorder and the sociocognitive model: Recalling the lessons of the past. *Psychological Bulletin, 125*, 507–523.

Lilienfeld, S. O., & Marino, L. (1999). Essentialism revisited: Evolutionary theory and the concept of mental disorder. *Journal of Abnormal Psychology, 108*, 400–411.

Lin, C. (1998). Comparison of the effects of perceived self-efficacy on coping with chronic cancer pain and coping with chronic low back pain. *Clinical Journal of Pain, 14*, 303–310.

Lindgren, H. C. (1969). *The psychology of college success: A dynamic approach*. New York: Wiley.

Lindsay, D. S. (1993). Eyewitness suggestibility. *Current Directions in Psychological Science, 2*(3), 86–89.

Lindsay, D. S. (1998). Depolarizing views on recovered memory experiences. In S. J. Lynn & K. M. McConkey (Eds.), *Truth in memory*. New York: Guilford Press.

Lindsay, D. S., & Johnson, M. K. (1991). Recognition memory and source monitoring. *Bulletin of the Psychonomic Society, 29*, 203–205.

Lindsay, D. S., & Poole, D. A. (1995). Remembering childhood sexual abuse in therapy: Psychotherapists' self–reported beliefs, practices, and experiences. *Journal of Psychiatry & Law*, 461–476.

Lindsay, D. S., & Read, J. D. (1994). Psychotherapy and memories of childhood sexual abuse: A cognitive perspective. *Applied Cognitive Psychology, 8*, 281–338.

Lindsay, P. H., & Norman, D. A. (1977). *Human information processing*. New York: Academic Press.

Lippa, R. A. (1994). *Introduction to social psychology*. Pacific Grove, CA: Brooks/Cole.

Lipsey, M. W., & Wilson, D. B. (1993). The efficacy of psychological, educational, and behavioral treatment: Confirmation from meta-analysis. *American Psychologist, 48*, 1181–1209.

Litt, I. F., & Vaughan, V. C., III. (1992). Adolescence. In R. E. Behrman (Ed.), *Nelson textbook of pediatrics*. Philadelphia: Saunders.

Liu, S., Siegel, P. Z., Brewer, R. D., Mokdad, A. H., Sleet, D. A., & Serdula, M. (1997). Prevalence of alcohol-impaired driving: Results from a national self-reported survey of health behaviors. *Journal of the American Medical Association, 277*, 122–125.

Lloyd, G. D., Fletcher, A., & Minchin, M. C. W. (1992). GABA agonists as potential anxiolytics. In G. D. Burrows, S. M. Roth, & R. Noyes Jr. (Eds.), *Handbook of anxiety*. Oxford: Elsevier.

Lloyd, M. A. (1985). *Adolescence*. New York: HarperCollins.

Lockhart, R. S. (1992). Measurement of memory. In L. R. Squire (Ed.), *Encyclopedia of learning and memory*. New York: Macmillan.

Lockhart, R. S., & Craik, F. I. (1990). Levels of processing: A retrospective commentary on a framework for memory research. *Canadian Journal of Psychology, 44*(1), 87–112.

Locurto, C. (1990). The malleability of IQ as judged from adoption studies. *Intelligence, 14*, 275–292.

Locurto, C. (1991). *Sense and nonsense about IQ: The case for uniqueness*. New York: Praeger.

Loehlin, J. C. (1992). *Genes and environment in personality development*. Newbury Park, CA: Sage.

Loehlin, J. C. (1994). Behavior genetics. In R. J. Sternberg (Ed.), *Encyclopedia of human intelligence*. New York: Macmillan.

Loehlin, J. C., Horn, J. M., & Willerman, L. (1997). Heredity, environment, and IQ in the Texas Adoption Project. In R. J. Sternberg, & E. L. Grigorenko (Eds.), *Intelligence, heredity, and environment*. New York: Cambridge University Press.

Loewenstein, R. J. (1996). Dissociative amnesia and dissociative fugue. In L. K. Michelson, & W. J. Ray (Eds.), *Handbook of dissociation: Theoretical, empirical, and clinical perspectives*. New York: Plenum.

Loftus, E. F. (1979). *Eyewitness testimony*. Cambridge, MA: Harvard University Press.

Loftus, E. F. (1992). When a lie becomes memory's truth: Memory distortion after exposure to misinformation. *Current Directions in Psychological Science, 1*, 121–123.

Loftus, E. F. (1993). Psychologist in the eyewitness world. *American Psychologist, 48*, 550–552.

Loftus, E. F. (1993). The reality of repressed memories. *American Psychologist, 48*, 518–537.

Loftus, E. F. (1994). The repressed memory controversy. *American Psychologist, 49*, 443–445.

Loftus, E. F. (1997, September). Creating false memories. *Scientific American*, 71–75.

Loftus, E. F. (1998). Remembering dangerously. In R. A. Baker (Ed.), *Child sexual abuse and false memory syndrome*. Amherst, NY: Prometheus Books.

Loftus, E. F., & Ketcham, K. (1994). *The myth of repressed memory: False memories and allegations of sexual abuse*. New York: St. Martin's Press.

Loftus, E. F., & Palmer, J. C. (1974). Reconstruction of automobile destruction: An example of the interaction between language and memory. *Journal of Verbal Learning and Verbal Behavior, 13*, 585–589.

Logue, A. W. (1991). *The psychology of eating and drinking* (2nd ed.). New York: W. H. Freeman.

Longman, D. G., & Atkinson, R. H. (1996). *College learning and study skills*. Belmont, CA: West/Wadsworth.

Longo, L. P. (1998). Anxiety: Neurobiologic underpinnings. *Psychiatric Annals, 28*, 130–138.

Lorenzi-Cioldi, F. (1993). They all look alike, but so do we. . . sometimes: Perceptions of ingroup and outgroup homogeneity as a function of sex and context. *British Journal of Social Psychology, 32*, 111–124.

Lott, B. (1987). *Women's lives*. Pacific Grove, CA: Brooks/Cole.

Lott, B., & Maluso, D. (1993). The social learning of gender. In A. E. Beall & R. J. Sternberg (Eds.), *The psychology of gender*. New York: Guilford Press.

Lowinson, J. H., Ruiz, P., Millman, R. B., & Langrod, J. G. (Eds.). (1997). *Substance abuse: A comprehensive textbook*. Baltimore: Williams & Wilkins.

Lubkin, I. M. (1990). Illness roles. In I. M. Lubkin (Ed.), *Chronic illness: Impact and interventions* (2nd ed.). Boston: Jones and Bartlett.

Luborsky, L., Singer, B., & Luborsky, L. (1975). Comparative studies of psychotherapies: Is it true that everyone has won and all must have prizes? *Archives of General Psychiatry, 32*, 995–1008.

Lucas, A. R., Beard, C. M., O'Fallon, W. M., & Kurland, L. T. (1991). 50-year trends in the incidence of anorexia nervosa in Rochester, Minn.: A population-based study. *American Journal of Psychiatry, 148*, 917–922.

Lucas, R. E., Diener, E., & Suh, E. (1996). Discriminant validity of well-being measures. *Journal of Personality and Social Psychology, 71*, 616–628.

Luchins, A. S. (1942). Mechanization in problem solving. *Psychological Monographs, 54* (6, Whole No. 248).

Ludwig, A. M. (1994). Mental illness and creative activity in female writers. *American Journal of Psychiatry, 151*, 1650–1656.

Ludwig, A. M. (1995). *The price of greatness: Resolving the creativity and madness controversy*. New York: Guilford Press.

Ludwig, A. M. (1998). Method and madness in the arts and sciences. *Creativity Research Journal, 11*, 93–101.

Ludwig, D. S., Pereira, M. A., Kroenke, C. H., Hilner, J. E., Van Horn, L., Slattery, M. L., & Jacobs, D. R. Jr. (1999). Dietary fiber, weight gain, and cardiovascular disease risk factors in young adults. *Journal of the American Medical Association, 282*, 1539–1546.

Luecke-Aleksa, D., Anderson, D. R., Collins, P. A., & Schmitt, K. L. (1995). Gender constancy and television viewing. *Developmental Psychology, 31*, 773–780.

Lugaresi, E., Cirignotta, F., Montagna, P., & Sforza, E. (1994). Snoring: Pathogenic, clinical, and therapeutic aspects. In M. H. Kryger, T. Roth, & W. C. Dement (Eds.), *Principles and practice of sleep medicine* (2nd ed.). Philadelphia: Saunders.

Luh, C. W. (1922). The conditions of retention. *Psychological Monographs, 31*.

Lutz, C. (1987). Goals, events and understanding in Ifaluk emotion theory. In N. Quinn & D. Holland (Eds.), *Cultural models in language and thought*. Cambridge, England: Cambridge University Press.

Lutz, D. J., & Sternberg, R. J. (1999). Cognitive development. In M. H. Bornstein, & M. E. Lamb (Eds.), *Developmental psychology an advanced textbook*. Mahwah, NJ: Erlbaum.

Lutz, W. (1989). *Doublespeak*. New York: Harper Perennial.

Lye, D. N., & Biblarz, T. J. (1993). The effects of attitudes toward family life and gender roles on marital satisfaction. *Journal of Family Issues, 14*, 157–188.

Lykken, D. T. (1981). *A tremor in the blood: Uses and abuses of the lie detector.* New York: McGraw-Hill.

Lykken, D. T., McGue, M., Tellegen, A., & Bouchard, T. J., Jr. (1992). Emergenesis: Genetic traits that may not run in families. *American Psychologist, 47,* 1565–1577.

Lykken, D., & Tellegen, A. (1996). Happiness is a stochastic phenomenon. *Psychological Science, 7,* 186–189.

Lyness, S. A. (1993). Predictors of differences between Type A and Type B individuals in heart rate and blood pressure reactivity. *Psychological Bulletin, 114,* 266–295.

Lynn, M. (1992). Scarcity's enhancement of desirability: The role of naive economic theories. *Basic & Applied Social Psychology, 13,* 67–78.

Lynn, R. (1987). The intelligence of the Mongoloids: A psychometric, evolutionary and neurological theory. *Personality and Individual Differences, 8,* 813–844.

Lynn, R. (1991). Educational achievements of Asian Americans. *American Psychologist, 46*(8), 875–876.

Lynn, R. (1995). Cross-cultural differences in intelligence and personality. In D. H. Saklofske & M. Zeidner (Eds.), *International handbook of personality and intelligence.* New York: Plenum.

Lynn, R. (1998). In support of the Nutrition Theory. In U. Neisser (Ed.), *The rising curve: Long-term gains in IQ and related measures.* Washington, DC: American Psychological Association.

Lynn, S. J., & Nash, M. (1994). Truth in memory: Ramifications for psychotherapy and hypnotherapy. *Journal of Clinical Hypnosis, 36,* 194–208.

Lynn, S. J., Lock, T. G., Myers, B., & Payne D. G. (1997). Recalling the unrecallable: Should hypnosis be used to recover memories in psychotherapy? *Current Directions in Psychological Science, 6,* 79–83.

Maas, J. B. (1998). *Power sleep.* New York: Harper Perennial.

MacCoun, R. J. (1998). Biases in the interpretation and use of research results. *Annual Review Psychology, 49,* 259–287.

MacDonald, K. (1998). Evolution, culture, and the five-factor model. *Journal of Cross-Cultural Psychology, 29,* 119–149.

Mackie, D. M., Worth, L. T., & Asuncion, A. G. (1990). Processing of persuasive in-group messages. *Journal of Personality and Social Psychology, 58,* 812–822.

MacLean, P. D. (1954). Studies on limbic system ("viosceal brain") and their bearing on psychosomatic problems. In E. D. Wittkower & R. A. Cleghorn (Eds.), *Recent developments in psychosomatic medicine.* Philadelphia: Lippincott.

MacLean, P. D. (1993). Cerebral evolution of emotion. In M. Lewis & J. M. Haviland (Eds.), *Handbook of emotions.* New York: Guilford Press.

MacMillan, H. L., Fleming, J. E., Trocme, N., Boyle, M. H., Wong, M., Racine, Y. A., Beardslee, W. R., & Offord, D. R. (1997). Prevalence of child physical and sexual abuse in the community: Results from the Ontario health supplement. *Journal of the American Medical Association, 278,* 131–135.

Macmillan, M. (1991). *Freud evaluated: The completed arc.* Amsterdam: North-Holland.

MacWhinney, B. (1998). Models of the emergence of language. *Annual Review of Psychology, 49,* 199–227.

Maddi, S. R. (1989). *Personality theories: A comparative analysis.* Chicago, IL: Dorsey Press.

Madsen, K. B. (1968). *Theories of motivation.* Copenhagen: Munksgaard.

Madsen, K. B. (1973). Theories of motivation. In B. B. Wolman (Ed.), *Handbook of general psychology.* Englewood Cliffs, NJ: Prentice-Hall.

Magnusson, D., & Stattin, H. (1998). Person-context interaction theories. In W. Damon (Ed.), *Handbook of child psychology (Vol. 1): Theoretical models of human development.* New York: Wiley.

Maguire, W., Weisstein, N., & Klymenko, V. (1990). From visual structure to perceptual function. In K. N. Leibovic (Ed.), *Science of vision.* New York: Springer-Verlag.

Maher, B. A., & Spitzer, M. (1993). Delusions. In P. B. Sutker & H. E. Adams (Eds.), *Comprehensive handbook of psychopathology* (2nd ed.). New York: Plenum.

Maier, N. R. F. (1931). Reasoning and learning. *Psychological Review, 38,* 332–346.

Main, D. M., & Main, E. K. (1991). Preterm birth. In S. G. Gabbe, J. R. Niebyl, & J. L. Simpson (Eds.), *Obstetrics: Normal and problem pregnancies.* New York: Churchill Livingstone.

Main, T. (1998). How to think about homelessness: Balancing structural and individual causes. *Journal of Social Distress & the Homeless, 7,* 41–54.

Maj, M., Pirozzi, R., Magliano, L., & Bartoli, L. (1998). Long-term outcome of lithium prophylaxis in bipolar disorder: A 5-year prospective study on 402 patients at a lithium clinic. *American Journal of Psychiatry, 155,* 30–35.

Malamuth, N. M. (1996). Sexually explicit media, gender differences, and evolutionary theory. *Journal of Communication, 46,* 8–31.

Malcolm, J. (1980: Pt. 1, Nov. 24; Pt. 2, Dec. 1). The impossible profession. *The New Yorker,* pp. 55–133, 54–152.

Malina, R. M. (1990). *Growth and development: The first twenty years in man.* Minneapolis: Burgess Publishing.

Malle, B. F., & Knobe, J. (1997). Which behaviors do people explain? A basic actor-observer asymmetry. *Journal of Personality and Social Psychology, 72,* 288–304.

Maltzman, I. (1994). Why alcoholism is a disease. *Journal of Psychoactive Drugs, 26,* 13–31.

Mandler, G. (1984). *Mind and body.* New York: Norton.

Mandler, G. (1989). Memory: Conscious and unconscious. In P. R. Soloman, G. R. Goethals, C. M. Kelley, & B. R. Stephens (Eds.), *Memory: Interdisciplinary approaches.* New York: Springer-Verlag.

Mandler, G. (1993). Thought, memory, and learning: Effects of emotional stress. In L. Goldberger & S. Breznitz (Eds.), *Handbook of stress: Theoretical and clinical aspects* (2nd ed.). New York: Free Press.

Mangelsdorf, S., Gunnar, M., Kestenbaum, R., Lang, S., & Andreas, D. (1990). Infant proneness-to-distress temperament, maternal personality, and mother-infant attachment: Associations and goodness of fit. *Child Development, 61,* 830–831.

Mann, J. M., & Tarantola, D. J. M. (1998). HIV 1998: The global picture. *Scientific American, 279* (1), 82–83.

Marangell, L. B., Silver, J. M., & Yudofsky, S. C. (1999). Psychopharmacology and electroconvulsive therapy. In R. E. Hales, S. C. Yudofsky, & J. A. Talbott (Eds.), *American Psychiatric Press textbook of psychiatry.* Washington, DC: American Psychiatric Press.

Maratsos, M. (1983). Some current issues in the study of the acquisition of grammar. In J. H. Flavell & E. M. Markman (Eds.), *Handbook of child psychology* (Vol. 3). New York: Wiley.

Marcenes, W. G., & Sheiham, A. (1992). The relationship between work stress and oral health status. *Social Science and Medicine, 35,* 1511.

Marcia, J. E. (1966). Development and validation of ego identity status. *Journal of Personality and Social Psychology, 3,* 551–558.

Marcia, J. E. (1980). Identity in adolescence. In J. Adelson (Ed.), *Handbook of adolescent psychology.* New York: Wiley.

Marcus, B. H., Bock, B. C., & Pinto, B. M. (1997). Initiation and maintenance of exercise behavior. In D. S. Gochman (Ed.), *Handbook of health behavior research II: Provider determinants.* New York: Plenum.

Marcus, G. F. (1996). Why do children say "breaked"? *Current Directions in Psychological Science, 5,* 81–85.

Marder, S. R., & Van Putten, T. (1995). Antipsychotic medications. In A. F. Schatzberg & C. B. Nemeroff (Eds.), *The American Psychiatric Press textbook of psychopharmacology.* Washington, DC: American Psychiatric Press.

Marks, I. M. (1987). *Fears, phobias, and rituals: Panic, anxiety, and their disorders.* New York: Oxford University Press.

Markus, H. R., & Kitayama, S. (1991). Culture and the self: Implications for cognition, emotion, and motivation. *Psychological Review, 98,* 224–253.

Markus, H. R., & Kitayama, S. (1994). The cultural construction of self and emotion: Implications for social behavior. In S. Kitayama & H. R. Markus (Eds.), *Emotions and culture: Empirical studies of mutual influence.* Washington, DC: American Psychological Association.

Markus, H. R., & Kitayama, S. (1998). The cultural psychology of personality. *Journal of Cross-Cultural Psychology, 29,* 63–87.

Marschark, M. (1992). Coding processes: Imagery. In L. R. Squire (Ed.), *Encyclopedia of learning and memory.* New York: Macmillan.

Marsella, A. J. (1979). Cross-cultural studies of mental disorders. In A. J. Marsella, R. Tharp, & T. Ciborowski (Eds.), *Perspectives in cross-cultural psychology.* New York: Academic Press.

Martin, C. L., & Halverson, C. F., Jr. (1987). The role of cognition in sex role acquisition. In D. B. Carter (Ed.), *Current conceptions of sex roles and sex typing: Theory and research.* New York: Praeger.

Martin, L. (1986). "Eskimo words for snow": A case study in the genesis and decay of an anthropological example. *American Psychologist, 88,* 418–423.

Martin, R. A. (1996). The situational humor response questionnaire (SHRQ) and coping humor scale (CHS): A decade of research findings. *Humor: International Journal of Humor Research, 9,* 251–272.

Martin, R. L., & Yutzy, S. H. (1999). Somatoform disorders. In R. E. Hales, S. C. Yudofsky, & J. A. Talbott (Eds.), *American Psychiatric Press Textbook of Psychiatry.* Washington, DC: American Psychiatric Press.

Maslow, A. H. (1954). *Motivation and personality.* New York: Harper & Row.

Maslow, A. H. (1968). *Toward a psychology of being.* New York: Van Nostrand.

Maslow, A. H. (1970). *Motivation and personality.* New York: Harper & Row.

Massaro, D. W., & Loftus, G. R. (1996). Sensory and perceptual storage: Data and theory. In E. L. Bjork & R. A. Bjork (Eds.), *Memory.* San Diego: Academic Press.

Masters, R. D. (1995). Mechanism and function in evolutionary psychology: Emotion, cognitive neuroscience, and personality. *Psychological Inquiry, 6,* 65–68.

Masters, W. H., & Johnson, V. E. (1966). *Human sexual response.* Boston: Little, Brown.

Masters, W. H., & Johnson, V. E. (1970). *Human sexual inadequacy.* Boston: Little, Brown.

Matlin, M. W. (1989). *Cognition.* New York: Holt, Rinehart & Winston.

Matsumoto, D. (1994). *People: Psychology from a cultural perspective.* Pacific Grove, CA: Brooks/Cole.

Matthews, K. A. (1992). Myths and realities of the menopause. *Psychosomatic Medicine, 54*(1), 1–9.

Matthey, S. (1998). p<.05—But is it clinically *significant?*: Practical examples for clinicians. *Behaviour Change, 15,* 140–146.

Matute, H., & Miller, R. R. (1998). Detecting causal relations. In W. O'Donohue (Ed.), *Learning and behavior therapy.* Boston, Allyn & Bacon.

Mauro, R., Sato, K., & Tucker, J. (1992). The role of appraisal in human emotions: A cross-cultural study. *Journal of Personality and Social Psychology, 62,* 301–317.

Mayer, J. (1955). Regulation of energy intake and the body weight: The glucostatic theory and the lipostatic hypothesis. *Annals of the New York Academy of Science, 63,* 15–43.

Mayer, J. (1968). *Overweight: Causes and control.* Englewood Cliffs, NJ: Prentice-Hall.

Mayes, A. R. (1992). What are the functional deficits that underlie amnesia? In L. R. Squire & N. Butters (Eds.), *Neuropsychology of memory* (2nd ed.). New York: Guilford Press.

Mays, V. M., & Albee, G. W. (1992). Psychotherapy and ethnic minorities. In D. K. Freedheim (Ed.), *History of psychotherapy: A century of change.* Washington, DC: American Psychological Association.

Mays, V. M., Rubin, J., Sabourin, M., & Walker, L. (1996). Moving toward a global psychology: Changing theories and practice to meet the needs of a changing world. *American Psychologist, 51,* 485–487.

McAdams, D. P. (1992). The five-factor model in personality: A critical appraisal. *Journal of Personality, 60,* 329–361.

McAllister, L. E., & Boyle, J. S. (1998). Without money, means, or men: African American women receiving prenatal care in a housing project. *Family & Community Health, 21,* 67–79.

McAllister, W. R., & McAllister, D. E. (1995). Two-factor fear theory: Implications from understanding anxiety-based clinical phenomena. In W. O'Donohue, & L. Krasner (Eds.), *Theories of behavior therapy: Exploring behavior change.* Washington, DC: American Psychological Association.

McBride, P. E. (1992). The health consequences of smoking: Cardiovascular diseases. *Medical Clinics of North America, 76,* 333–353.

McBride-Chang, C., & Jacklin, C. N. (1993). Early play arousal, sex-typed play, and activity level as precursors to later rough-and-tumble play. *Early Education & Development, 4,* 99–108.

McCann, T. S. (1981). Aggression and sexual activity of male southern elephant seals, *Mirounga leonina. Journal of Zoology, 195,* 295–310.

McCarley, R. W. (1994). Dreams and the biology of sleep. In M. H. Kryger, T. Roth, & W. C. Dement (Eds.), *Principles and practice of sleep medicine* (2nd ed.). Philadelphia: Saunders.

McCarty, D., Argeriou, M., Huebner, R. B., & Lubran, B. (1991). Alcoholism, drug abuse, and the homeless. *American Psychologist, 46,* 1139–1148.

McCauley, M. E., Eskes, G., & Moscovitch, M. (1996). The effect of imagery on explicit and implicit tests of memory in young and old people: A double dissociation. *Canadian Journal of Experimental Psychology, 50,* 34–41.

McClelland, D. C. (1985). How motives, skills and values determine what people do. *American Psychologist, 40,* 812–825.

McClelland, D. C. (1987). Characteristics of successful entrepreneurs. *Journal of Creative Behavior, 3,* 219–233.

McClelland, D. C. (1993). Intelligence is not the best predictor of job performance. *Current Directions in Psychological Science, 2*(1), 5–6.

McClelland, D. C., Atkinson, J. W., Clark, R. A., & Lowell, E. L. (1953). *The achievement motive.* New York: Appleton-Century-Crofts.

McClelland, D. C., & Boyatzis, R. E. (1982). The leadership motive pattern and long-term success in management. *Journal of Applied Psychology, 67,* 737–743.

McClelland, D. C., & Koestner, R. (1992). The achievement motive. In C. P. Smith (Ed.), *Motivation and personality: Handbook of thematic content analysis.* New York: Cambridge University Press.

McClelland, J. L. (1992). Parallel-distributed processing models of memory. In L. R. Squire (Ed.), *Encyclopedia of learning and memory.* New York: Macmillan.

McClelland, J. L., & Rumelhart, D. E. (1985). Distributed memory and the representation of general and specific information. *Journal of Experimental Psychology: General, 114,* 159–188.

McCloskey, M. (1992). Special versus ordinary memory mechanisms in the genesis of flashbulb memories. In E. Winograd & U. Neisser (Eds.). *Affect and accuracy in recall: Studies of "flashbulb" memories.* New York: Cambridge University Press.

McConnell, A. R., Leibold, J. M., & Sherman, S. J. (1997). Within-target illusory correlations and the formation of context-dependent attitudes. *Journal of Personality and Social Psychology, 73,* 675–686.

McConnell, J. V. (1962). Memory transfer through cannibalism in planarians. *Journal of Neuropsychiatry, 3*(Suppl. 1), 542–548.

McCrae, R. R. (1984). Situational determinants of coping responses: Loss, threat and challenge. *Journal of Personality and Social Psychology, 46,* 919–928.

McCrae, R. R., & Costa, P. T., Jr. (1984). *Emerging lives, enduring dispositions: Personality in adulthood.* Boston: Little, Brown.

McCrae, R. R., & Costa, P. T., Jr. (1987). Validation of the five-factor model of personality across instruments and observers. *Journal of Personality and Social Psychology, 52,* 81–90.

McCrae, R. R., & Costa, P. T., Jr. (1990). *Personality in adulthood.* New York: Guilford Press.

McCrae, R. R., & Costa, P. T., Jr. (1997). Personality trait structure as a human universal. *American Psychologist, 52,* 509–516.

McCrae, R. R., & Costa, P. T., Jr. (1999). A five-factor theory of personality. In L. A. Pervin, & O. P. John (Eds.), *Handbook of personality: Theory and research.* New York: Guilford Press.

McCrae, R. R., Costa, P. T., Jr., del Pilar, G. H., Rolland, J., & Parker, W. D. (1998). Cross-cultural assessment of the five-factor model: The revised NEO Personality Inventory. *Journal of Cross-Cultural Psychology, 29,* 171–188.

McDaniel, M. A., & Einstein, G. O. (1986). Bizarre imagery as an effective memory aid: The importance of distinctiveness. *Journal of Experimental Psychology: Learning, Memory & Cognition, 12,* 54–65.

McDaniel, M. A., Waddill, P. J., & Shakesby, P. S. (1996). Study strategies, interest, and learning from text: The application of material appropriate processing. In D. J. Herrmann, C. McEvoy, C. Hertzog, P. Hertel, & M. K. Johnson (Eds.), *Basic and applied memory research: Theory in context* (Vol. 1). Mahwah, NJ: Erlbaum.

McGaugh, J. L. (1992). Hormones and memory. In L. R. Squire (Ed.), *Encyclopedia of learning and memory.* New York: Macmillan.

McGaugh, J. L. (1995). Emotional activation, neuromodulatory systems, and memory. In D. L. Schacter, J. T. Coyle, G. D. Fischbach, M. Mesulam, & L. E. Sullivan (Eds.), *Memory distortion.* Cambridge, MA: Harvard University Press.

McGeoch, J. A., & McDonald, W. T. (1931). Meaningful relation and retroactive inhibition. *American Journal of Psychology, 43,* 579–588.

McGinty, D. (1993). Thermoregulation. In M. A. Carskadon (Ed.), *Encyclopedia of sleep and dreaming.* New York: Macmillan.

McGlashan, T. H., & Fenton, W. S. (1992). The positive-negative distinction in schizophrenia: Review of natural history validators. *Archives of General Psychiatry, 49,* 63–72.

McGrew, J. H., Wright, E. R., Pescosolido, B. A., & McDonel, E. C. (1999). The closing of Central State Hospital: Long-term outcomes for persons with severe mental illness. *Journal of Behavioral Health Services & Research, 26,* 246–261.

McGue, M., Bouchard, T. J., Jr., Iacono, W. G., & Lykken, D. T. (1993). Behavioral genetics of cognitive ability: A life-span perspective. In R. Plomin & G. E. McClearn (Eds.), *Nature, nurture and psychology.* Washington, DC: American Psychological Association.

McGuire, T. R., & Haviland, J. M. (1985). Further considerations for behavior-genetic analysis of humans. *Journal of Personality and Social Psychology, 49,* 1434–1436.

McHale, S. M., Bartko, W. T., Crouter, A. C., & Perry-Jenkins, M. (1990). Children's housework and psychosocial functioning: The mediating effects of parents' sex-role behaviors and attitudes. *Child Development, 61,* 1413–1426.

McHugh, P. R. (1995). Dissociative identity disorder as a socially constructed artifact. *Journal of Practical Psychiatry and Behavioral Health, 1,* 158–166.

McKean, K. (1985, June). Decisions, decisions. *Discover,* pp. 22–31.

McKenna, J. J. (1993). Co-sleeping. In M. A. Carskadon (Ed.), *Encyclopedia of sleep and dreaming.* New York: Macmillan.

McKenna, K. Y. A., & Bargh, J. A. (1998). Coming out in the age of the Internet: Identity "demarginalization" through virtual group participation. *Journal of Personality and Social Psychology, 75,* 681–694.

McLean, D. E., & Link, B. G. (1994). Unraveling complexity: Strategies to refine concepts, measures, and research designs in the study of life events and mental health. In W. R. Avison, & I. H. Gotlib (Eds.), *Stress and mental health: Contemporary issues and prospects for the future.* New York: Plenum.

McLoyd, V. C. (1998). Socioeconomic disadvantage and child development. *American Psychologist, 53,* 185–204.

McNally, R. J. (1994). Cognitive bias in panic disorder. *Current Directions in Psychological Science, 3,* 129–132.

McNally, R. J. (1996). *Panic disorder: A critical analysis.* New York: Guilford Press.

McNeill, D. (1970). *The acquisition of language: The study of developmental psycholinguistics.* New York: Harper & Row.

Mechanic, D. (1980). *Mental health and social policy.* Englewood Cliffs, NJ: Prentice-Hall.

Mednick, S. A., & Mednick, M. T. (1967). *Examiner's manual, Remote Associates Test.* Boston: Houghton Mifflin.

Mednick, S. A., Machon, R. A., Huttunen, M. O., & Bonett, D. (1988). Adult schizophrenia following prenatal exposure to an influenza epidemic. *Archives of General Psychiatry, 45,* 189–192.

Mega, M. S., Cummings, J. L., Salloway, S., & Malloy, P. (1997). The limbic system: An anatomic, phylogenetic, and clinical perspective. *Journal of Neuropsychiatry & Clinical Neurosciences, 9,* 315–330.

Meiser, T., & Klauer, K. C. (1999). Working memory and changing-state hypothesis. *Journal of Experimental Psychology: Learning, Memory, & Cognition, 25,* 1272–1299.

Meltzoff, A. N., & Gopnik, A. (1989). On linking nonverbal imitation, representation, and language learning in the first two years of life. In G. E. Speidel & K. E. Nelson (Eds.), *The many faces of imitation in language learning.* New York: Springer-Verlag.

Melzack, R., & Wall, P. D. (1965). Pain mechanisms: A new theory. *Science, 150,* 971–979.

Melzack, R., & Wall, P. D. (1982). *The challenge of pain.* New York: Basic Books.

Mendelson, W. B. (1987). *Human sleep: Research and clinical care.* New York: Plenum.

Mendelson, W. B. (1990). Insomnia: The patient and the pill. In R. R. Bootzin, J. F. Kihlstrom, & D. L. Schacter (Eds.), *Sleep and cognition.* Washington, DC: American Psychological Association.

Mendelson, W. B. (1993). Sleeping pills. In M. A. Carskadon (Ed.), *Encyclopedia of sleep and dreaming.* New York: Macmillan.

Mentzer, R. L. (1982). Response biases in multiple-choice test item files. *Educational and Psychological Measurement, 42,* 437–448.

Menyuk, P., Liebergott, J. W., & Schultz, M. C. (1995). *Early language development in full-term and premature infants.* Hillsdale, NJ: Erlbaum.

Mervis, C. B., & Bertrand, J. (1994). Acquisition of the novel name-nameless category principle. *Child Development, 65,* 1646–1662.

Mesquita, B., & Frijda, N. H. (1992). Cultural variations in emotions: A review. *Psychological Bulletin, 112,* 179–204.

Metzger, E. D. (1999). Electroconvulsive therapy. In A. M. Nicholi (Ed.), *The Harvard guide to psychiatry.* Cambridge, MA: Harvard University Press.

Meyer, D. E., & Schvaneveldt, R. W. (1976). Meaning, memory structure, and mental processes. *Science, 192,* 27–33.

Meyer, R. E. (1996). The disease called addiction: Emerging evidence in a 200-year debate. *The Lancet, 347,* 162–166.

Meyer, R. G. (1992). *Practical clinical hypnosis: Techniques and applications.* New York: Lexington Books.

Meyer-Bahlburg, H. F. L., Ehrhardt, A. A., Rosen, L. R., Gruen, R. S., Veridiano, N. P., Vann, F. H., & Neuwalder, H. F. (1995). Prenatal estrogens and the development of homosexual orientation. *Developmental Psychology, 31,* 12–21.

Michaels, S. (1996). The prevelance of homosexuality in the United States. In R. P. Cabaj, & T. S. Stein (Eds.), *Textbook of homosexuality and mental health.* Washington, DC: American Psychiatric Press.

Mickelson, K. D., Kessler, R. C., & Shaver, P. R. (1997). Adult attachment in a nationally representative sample. *Journal of Personality and Social Psychology, 73,* 1092–1106.

Middlebrooks, J. C., & Knudsen, E. I. (1984). A neural code for auditory space in the cat's superior colliculus. *The Journal of Neuroscience, 4,* 2621–2634.

Milgram, S. (1963). Behavioral study of obedience. *Journal of Abnormal and Social Psychology, 67,* 371–378.

Milgram, S. (1964). Issues in the study of obedience. *American Psychologist, 19,* 848–852.

Milgram, S. (1968). Reply to the critics. *International Journal of Psychiatry, 6,* 294–295.

Milgram, S. (1974). *Obedience to authority.* New York: Harper & Row.

Miller, A. G. (1986). *The obedience experiments: A case study of controversy in social science.* New York: Praeger.

Miller, G. A. (1956). The magical number seven, plus or minus two: Some limits on our capacity for processing information. *Psychological Review, 63,* 81–97.

Miller, G. A. (1991). *The science of words.* New York: Scientific American Library.

Miller, G. F. (1998). How mate choice shaped human nature: A review of sexual selection and human evolution. In C. Crawford & D. L. Krebs (Eds.), *Handbook of evolutionary psychology: Ideas, issues, and applications.* Mahwah, NJ: Erlbaum.

Miller, I. J. (1996). Managed care is harmful to outpatient mental health services: A call for accountability. *Professional Psychology: Research and Practice, 27,* 349–363.

Miller, I. J., & Reedy, F. E. Jr. (1990). Variations in human taste-bud density and taste intensity perception. *Physiological Behavior, 47,* 1213–1219.

Miller, J. G. (1999). Cultural psychology: Implications for basic psychological theory. *Psychological Science, 10,* 85–91.

Miller, N. E. (1941). The frustration-aggression hypothesis. *Psychological Review, 48,* 337–342.

Miller, N. E. (1944). Experimental studies of conflict. In J. M. Hunt (Ed.), *Personality and the behavior disorders* (Vol. 1). New York: Ronald.

Miller, N. E. (1959). Liberalization of basic S-R concepts: Extension to conflict behavior, motivation, and social learning. In S. Koch (Ed.), *Psychology: A study of a science* (Vol. 2). New York: McGraw-Hill.

Miller, N. E. (1985). The value of behavioral research on animals. *American Psychologist, 40,* 423–440.

Miller, R. R., & Barnet, R. C. (1993). The role of time in elementary associations. *Current Directions in Psychological Science, 2*(4), 106–111.

Miller, T. Q., Smith, T. W., Turner, C. W., Guijarro, M. L., & Hallet, A. J. (1996). A meta-analytic review of research on hostility and physical health. *Psychological Bulletin, 119,* 322–348.

Miller, T. Q., Turner, C. W., Tindale, R. S., Posavac, E. J., & Dugoni, B. L. (1991). Reasons for the trend toward null findings in research on Type A behavior. *Psychological Bulletin, 110,* 469–485.

Millman, J., Bishop, C. H., & Ebel, R. (1965). An analysis of test-wiseness. *Educational and Psychological Measurement, 25,* 707–726.

Millstone, E. (1989). Methods and practices of animal experimentation. In G. Langley (Ed.), *Animal experimentation: The consensus changes.* New York: Chapman & Hall.

Minuchin, S., Rosman, B. L., & Baker, L. (1978). *Psychosomatic families: Anorexia nervosa in context.* Cambridge, MA: Harvard University Press.

Mischel, W. (1961). Delay of gratification, need for achievement, and acquiescence in another culture. *Journal of Abnormal and Social Psychology, 62,* 543–552.

Mischel, W. (1968). *Personality and assessment.* New York: Wiley.

Mischel, W. (1973). Toward a cognitive social learning conceptualization of personality. *Psychological Review, 80,* 252–283.

Mischel, W. (1984). Convergences and challenges in the search for consistency. *American Psychologist, 39,* 351–364.

Mischel, W. (1990). Personality dispositions revisited and revised: A view after three decades. In L. A. Pervin (Ed.), *Handbook of personality: Theory and research.* New York: Guilford Press.

Mischel, W., & Shoda, Y. (1999). Integrating dispositions and processing dynamics within a unified theory of personality: The cognitive-affective personality system. In L. A. Pervin & O. P. John (Eds.), *Handbook of personality: Theory and research*. New York: Guilford Press.

Mitka, M. (1999). Slowing decline in AIDS deaths prompts concern. *Journal of the American Medical Association, 282*, 1216–1217.

Mitler, M. M. (1993). Public safety in the workplace. In M. A. Carskadon (Ed.), *Encyclopedia of sleep and dreaming*. New York: Macmillan.

Mitler, M. M., Dinges, D. F., & Dement, W. C. (1994). Sleep medicine, public policy, and public health. In M. H. Kryger, T. Roth, & W. C. Dement (Eds.), *Principles and practice of sleep medicine* (2nd ed.). Philadelphia: Saunders.

Moak, D. H., & Anton, R. F. (1999). Alcohol. In B. S. McCrady & E. E. Epstein (Eds.), *Addictions: A comprehensive guidebook*. New York: Oxford University Press.

Modestin, J. (1992). Multiple personality disorder in Switzerland. *American Journal of Psychiatry, 149*, 88–92.

Moffitt, A. (1995). Dreaming: Functions and meaning. *Impuls, 3*, 18–31.

Moghaddam, F. M., Taylor, D. M., & Wright, S. C. (1993). *Social psychology in cross-cultural perspective*. New York: W. H. Freeman.

Moline, M. L. (1993). Jet lag. In M. A. Carskadon (Ed.), *Encyclopedia of sleep and dreaming*. New York: Macmillan.

Mollon, J. D. (1989). "Tho' she kneel'd in that place where they grew . . .". *Journal of Experimental Biology, 146*, 21–38.

Monk, T. H. (1994). Shift work. In M. H. Kryger, T. Roth, & W. C. Dement (Eds.), *Principles and practice of sleep medicine* (2nd ed.). Philadelphia: Saunders.

Monroe, S. M., Roberts, J. E., Kupfer, D. J., & Frank, E. (1996). Life stress and treatment course of recurrent depression: II. Postrecovery associations with attrition, symptom course, and recurrence over 3 years. *Journal of Abnormal Psychology, 105*, 313–328.

Moore, K. L., & Persaud, T. V. N. (1993). *Before we are born*. Philadelphia: Saunders.

Moore, R. Y. (1990). The circadian system and sleep-wake behavior. In J. Montplaisir & R. Godbout (Eds.), *Sleep and biological rhythms: Basic mechanisms and applications to psychiatry*. New York: Oxford University Press.

Moore, R. Y. (1995). Neural control of the pineal gland. *Behavioral Brain Research, 73*, 125–130.

Moos, R. H., & Schaefer, J. A. (1993). Coping resources and processes: Current concepts and measures. In L. Goldberger & S. Breznitz (Eds.), *Handbook of stress: Theoretical and clinical aspects* (2nd ed.). New York: Free Press.

Mori, E., Ikeda, M., Hirono, N., Kitagaki, H., Imamura, T., & Shimomura, T. (1999). Amygdalar volume and emotional memory in Alzheimer's disease. *American Journal of Psychiatry, 156*, 216–222.

Morokoff, P. J., Quina, K., Harlow, L. L., Whitmire, L., Grimley, D. M., Gibson, P. R., & Burkholder, G. J. (1997). Sexual assertivenes scale (SAS) for women: Development and validation. *Journal of Personality and Social Psychology, 73*, 790–804.

Morris, J. S., Frith, C. D., Perrett, D. I., Rowland, D., Young, A. W., Calder, A. J., & Dolan, R. J. (1996). A differential neural response in the human amygdala to fearful and happy facial expressions. *Nature, 383*, 812–815.

Mortensen, M. E., Sever, L. E., & Oakley, G. P., Jr. (1991). Teratology and the epidemiology of birth defects. In S. G. Gabbe, J. R. Niebyl, & J. L. Simpson (Eds.), *Obstetrics: Normal and problem pregnancies*. New York: Churchill Livingstone.

Moscovitch, M. (1995). Recovered consciousness: A hypothesis concerning modularity and episodic memory. *Journal of Clinical and Experimental Neuropsychology, 17*, 276–290.

Mowrer, O. H. (1947). On the dual nature of learning: A reinterpretation of "conditioning" and "problem-solving." *Harvard Educational Review, 17*, 102–150.

Moynihan, J. A., & Ader, R. (1996). Psychoneuroimmunology: Animal models of disease. *Psychosomatic Medicine, 58*, 546–558.

Mozell, M. M., Smith, B. P., Smith P. E., Sullivan, R. L., & Swender, P. (1969). Nasal chemoreception in flavor identification. *Archives of Otolaryngology, 90*, 367–373.

Mukherjee, S., Sackeim, H. A., & Schnur, D. B. (1994). Electroconvulsive therapy of acute manic episodes: A review of 50 years' experience. *American Journal of Psychiatry, 151*, 169–176.

Muldoon, M. F., Manuck, S. B., & Matthews, K. A. (1990). Effects of cholesterol lowering on mortality: A quantitative review of primary prevention trials. *British Medical Journal, 301*, 309–314.

Mulligan, N. W. (1998). The role of attention during encoding in implicit and explicit memory. *Journal of Experimental Psychology: Learning, Memory, & Cognition, 24*, 27–47.

Murphy, C. (1996, Aug. 20). Researchers urge skepticism on melatonin at NIH-sponsored meeting, scientists say claims for hormone are largely unfounded. *Washington Post,* Z07.

Murphy, J. M. (1976). Psychiatric labeling in cross-cultural perspective. *Science, 191*, 1019–1028.

Murray, H. A. (1938). *Explorations in personality*. New York: Oxford University Press.

Murray, S. L., & Holmes, J. G. (1997). A leap of faith? Positive illusions in romantic relationships. *Personality and Social Psychology Bulletin, 23*, 586–604.

Murray, S. L., & Holmes, J. G. (1999). The (mental) ties that bind: Cognitive structures that predict relationship resilience. *Journal of Personality and Social Psychology, 77*, 1228–1244.

Murray, S. L., Holmes, J. G., & Griffin, D. W. (1996a). The benefits of positive illusions: Idealization and the construction of satisfaction in close relationships. *Journal of Personality and Social Psychology, 70*, 79–98.

Murray, S. L., Holmes, J. G., & Griffin, D. W. (1996b). The self-fulfilling nature of positive illusions in romantic relationships: Love is not blind, but prescient. *Journal of Personality and Social Psychology, 71*, 1155–1180.

Murstein, B. I., & Fontaine, P. A. (1993). The public's knowledge about psychologists and other mental health professionals. *American Psychologist, 48*, 839–845.

Myers, D. G. (1992). *The pursuit of happiness: Who is happy—and why*. New York: Morrow.

Myers, D. G. (1999). Close relationships and quality of life. In D. Kahneman, E. Diener, & N. Schwarz (Eds.), *Well-being: The foundations of hedonic psychology*. New York: Russell Sage Foundation.

Myers, D. G., & Diener, E. (1995). Who is happy? *Psychological Science, 6*, 10–19.

Myers, D. G., & Diener, E. (1997). The pursuit of happiness. *Scientific American Special Issue, 7*, 40–43.

Myers, D. G., & Lamm, H. (1976). The group polarization phenomenon. *Psychological Bulletin, 83*, 602–627.

Myerson, J., Hale, S., Wagstaff, D., Poon, L. W., & Smith, G. A. (1990). The information-loss model: A mathematical theory of age-related cognitive slowing. *Psychological Review, 97*, 475–487.

Myerson, J., Rank, M. R., Raines, F. Q., & Schnitzler, M. A. (1998). Race and general cognitive ability: The myth of diminishing returns to education. *Psychological Science, 9*, 139–142.

Mynatt, C. R., Doherty, M. E., & Tweney, R. D. (1978). Consequences of confirmation and disconfirmation in a simulated research environment. *Quarterly Journal of Experimental Psychology, 30*, 395–406.

Nadel, L., & Jacobs, W. J. (1998). Traumatic memory in special. *Current Directions in Psychological Science, 7 ,* 154–157.

Nahas, Z., George, M. S., Lorberbaum, J. P., Risch, S. C., & Spicer, K. M. (1998). SPECT and PET in neuropsychiatry. *Primary Psychiatry, 5*, 52–59.

Nairne, J. S. (1996). Short-term/ working memory. In E. L. Bjork, & R. A. Bjork (Eds.), *Memory*. San Diego: Academic Press.

Nairne, J. S., Neath, I., & Serra, M. (1997). Proactive interference plays a role in the word-length effect. *Psychonomic Bulletin & Review, 4*, 541–545.

Nakajima, S., & Patterson, R. L. (1997). The involvement of dopamine D2 receptors, but not D3 or D4 receptors, in the rewarding effect of brain stimulation in the rat. *Brain Research, 760*, 74–79.

Narrow, W. E., Regier, D. A., Rae, D. S., Manderscheid, R. W., & Locke, B. Z. (1993). Use of services by persons with mental and addictive disorders: Findings from the National Institute of Mental Health Epidemiologic Catchment Area Program. *Archives of General Psychiatry, 50*, 95–107.

Nash, M. R. (1987). What, if anything, is regressed about hypnotic age regression? *Psychological Bulletin, 102*, 42–52.

Nathan, K. I., Musselman, D. L., Schatzberg A. F., & Nemeroff, C. B. (1995). Biology of mood disorders. In A. F. Schatzberg & C. B. Nemeroff (Eds.), *The American Psychiatric Press textbook of psychopharmacology*. Washington, DC: American Psychiatric Press.

Neath, I. (1998). *Human memory: An introduction to research, data, and theory*. Pacific Grove: Brooks/Cole.

Neiss, R. (1988). Reconceptualizing arousal: Psychobiological states in motor performance. *Psychological Bulletin, 103*, 345–366.

Neiss, R. (1990). Ending arousal's reign of error: A reply to Anderson. *Psychological Bulletin, 107*, 101–105.

Neisser, U. (1967). *Cognitive psychology*. New York: Appleton-Century-Crofts.

Neisser, U. (1998). Introduction: Rising test scores and what they mean. In U. Neisser (Ed.), *The rising curve: Long-term gains in IQ and related measures*. Washington, DC: American Psychological Association.

Neisser, U., & Harsch, N. (1992). Phantom flashbulbs: False recollections of hearing the news about *Challenger*. In E. Winograd & U. Neisser (Eds.), *Affect and accuracy in recall: Studies of "flashbulb" memories*. New York: Cambridge University Press.

Nelson, T. O. (1978). Detecting small amounts of information in memory: Savings for nonrecognized items. *Journal of Experimental Psychology: Human Learning and Memory, 4*, 453–468.

Nemeth, C., & Chiles, C. (1988). Modelling courage: The role of dissent in fostering independence. *European Journal of Social Psychology, 18*, 275–280.

Nemiah, J. C. (1985). Somatoform disorders. In H. I. Kaplan & B. J. Sadock (Eds.), *Comprehensive textbook of psychiatry/IV*. Baltimore: Williams & Wilkins.

Nermeroff, C. B. (1998). The neurobiology of depression. *Scientific American, June*, 42–49.

Neubauer, D. N. (1999). Sleep problems in the elderly. *American Family Physician, 59*, 2551–2558.

Nevin, J. A. (1998). Choice and behavior momentum. In W. O'Donohue (Ed.), *Learning and behavior therapy*. Boston: Allyn & Bacon.

Newcomb, P. A., & Carbone, P. P. (1992). The health consequences of smoking: Cancer. *Medical Clinics of North America, 76*, 305–331.

Newcombe, N., & Huttenlocher, J. (1992). Children's early ability to solve perspective-taking problems. *Developmental Psychology, 28*, 635–643.

Newell, A., Shaw, J. C., & Simon, H. A. (1958). Elements of a theory of human problem solving. *Psychological Review, 65*, 151–166.

Newman, L. S., Duff, K. J., & Baumeister, R. F. (1997). A new look at defensive projection: Thought suppression, accessibility, and biased person perception. *Journal of Personality and Social Psychology, 72*, 980–1001.

Newsom, C., Favell, J. E., & Rincover, A. (1983). Side effects of punishment. In S. Axelrod & J. Apsche (Eds.), *The effects of punishment on human behavior*. New York: Academic Press.

Nicholson, A. N., Pascoe, P. A., Spencer, M. B., Stone, B. M., Roehis, T., & Roth, T. (1986). Sleep after transmeridian flights. *Lancet, 2*, 1205–1208.

Nicholson, I. R., & Neufeld, R. W. J. (1993). Classification of the schizophrenias according to symptomatology: A two-factor model. *Journal of Abnormal Psychology, 102*, 259–270.

Nickerson, R. S. (1998). Confirmation bias: A ubiquitous phenomenon in many guises. *Review of General Psychology, 2*, 175–220.

Nickerson, R. S., & Adams, M. J. (1979). Long-term memory for a common object. *Cognitive Psychology, 11*, 287–307.

Nicoladis, E., & Genesee, F. (1997). Language development in preschool bilingual children. *Journal of Speech-Language Pathology & Audiology, 21*, 258–270.

Niebyl, J. R. (1991). Drugs in pregnancy and lactation. In S. G. Gabbe, J. R. Niebyl, & J. L. Simpson (Eds.), *Obstetrics: Normal and problem pregnancies*. New York: Churchill Livingstone.

Nikelly, A. G. (1994). Alcoholism: Social as well as psycho-medical problem—The missing "big picture". *Journal of Alcohol & Drug Education, 39*, 1–12.

Nisbett, R. E. (Ed.). (1993). *Rules for reasoning*. Hillsdale, NJ: Erlbaum.

Nishino, S., Mignot, E., & Dement, W. C. (1995). Sedative-hypnotics. In A. F. Schatzberg & C. B. Nemeroff (Eds.), *American Psychiatric Press textbook of psychopharmacology*. Washington, D.C.: American Psychiatric Press.

Noddings, N. (1992). Gender and the curriculum. In P. W. Jackson (Ed.), *Handbook of research on curriculum*. New York: Macmillan.

Nolen-Hoeksema, S. (1991). Responses to depression and their effects on the duration of depressive episodes. *Journal of Abnormal Psychology, 100*, 569–582.

Nolen-Hoeksema, S. (1995). Gender differences in coping with depression across the lifespan. *Depression, 3*, 81–90.

Nolen-Hoeksema, S., & Girgus, J. S. (1994). The emergence of gender differences in depression during adolescence. *Psychological Bulletin, 115*, 424–443.

Nopoulos, P., Flaum, M., & Andreasen, N. C. (1997). Sex differences in brain morphology in schizophrenia. *American Journal of Psychiatry, 154*, 1648–1654.

Norcross, J. C. (1995). Dispelling the dodo bird verdict and the exclusivity myth in psychotherapy. *Psychotherapy, 32*, 500–504.

Norcross, J. C., & Goldfried, M. R. (Eds.). (1992). *Handbook of psychotherapy integration*. New York: Basic Books.

Novaco, R. W., Stokols, D., & Milanesi, L. (1990). Objective and subjective dimensions of travel impedance as determinants of commuting stress. *American Journal of Community Psychology, 18*, 231–257.

Novin, D., Robinson, B. A., Culbreth, L. A., & Tordoff, M. G. (1983). Is there a role for the liver in the control of food intake? *American Journal of Clinical Nutrition, 9*, 223–246.

Nowlis, D. P., & Kamiya, J. (1970). The control of electroencephalographic alpha rhythms through auditory feedback and the associated mental activity. *Psychophysiology, 6*, 476–484.

Noyes, R., Jr. (1988). Revision of the DSM-III classification of anxiety disorders. In R. Noyes, Jr., M. Roth, & G. D. Burrows (Eds.)., *Handbook of Anxiety: Classification, etiological factors, and associated disturbances* (Vol. 2). Amsterdam: Elsevier.

Noyes, R., Clarkson, C., Crowe, R. R., Yates, W. R., & McChesney, C. M. (1987). A family study of generalized anxiety disorder. *American Journal of Psychiatry, 144*, 1019–1024.

Oakland, T., & Parmelee, R. (1985). Mental measurement of minority-group children. In B. B. Wolman (Ed.), *Handbook of intelligence: Theories, measurements, and applications*. New York: Wiley.

Ochse, R. (1990). *Before the gates of excellence: The determinants of creative genius*. Cambridge, England: Cambridge University Press.

O'Donohue, W. (1998). Conditioning and third generation behavior therapy. In W. O'Donohue (Ed.), *Learning and behavior therapy*. Boston: Allyn & Bacon.

Ogilvie, R. D., & Wilkinson, R. T. (1988). Behavioral versus EEG-based monitoring of all-night sleep/wake patterns. *Sleep, 11*(2), 139–155.

Ogilvie, R. D., Wilkinson, R. T., & Allison, S. (1989). The detection of sleep onset: Behavioral, physiological, and subjective convergence. *Sleep, 12*(5), 458–474.

Okin, R. L., Borus, J. F., Baer, L., & Jones, A. L. (1995). Long-term outcome of state hospital patients discharged into structured community residential settings. *Psychiatric Services, 46*, 73–78.

O'Keefe, D. J. (1990). *Persuasion: Theory and research*. Newbury Park, CA: Sage.

Olden, K. W. (1998). Stress and the gastro-intestinal tract. In J. R. Hubbard, & E. A. Workman (Eds.), *Handbook of stress medicine: An organ system approach*. New York: CRC Press.

Olds, J. (1956). Pleasure centers in the brain. *Scientific American, 193*, 105–116.

Olds, J., & Milner, P. (1954). Positive reinforcement produced by electrical stimulation of the septal area and other regions of the rat brain. *Journal of Comparative and Physiological Psychology, 47*, 419–427.

Olds, M. E., & Fobes, J. L. (1981). The central basis of motivation: Intracranial self-stimulation studies. *Annual Review of Psychology, 32*, 523–574.

O'Leary, K. D., Kent, R. N., & Kanowitz, J. (1975). Shaping data collection congruent with experimental hypotheses. *Journal of Applied Behavior Analysis, 8*, 43–51.

Olfson, M., & Pincus, H. A. (1994). Outpatient psychotherapy in the United States, I: Volume, costs, and user characteristics. *American Journal of Psychiatry, 151*, 1281–1288.

Olfson, M., & Pincus, H. A. (1996). Outpatient mental health care in nonhospital settings: Distribution of patients across provider groups. *American Journal of Psychiatry, 153*, 1353–1356.

Olio, K. (1994). Truth in memory. *American Psychologist, 49*, 442–443.

Oliver, M. B., & Hyde, J. S. (1993). Gender differences in sexuality: A meta-analysis. *Psychological Bulletin, 114*, 29–51.

Olsho, L. W., Harkins, S. W., & Lenhardt, M. L. (1985). Aging and the auditory system. In J. E. Birren & K. W. Schaie (Eds.), *Handbook of the psychology of aging* (2nd ed.). New York: Van Nostrand Reinhold.

Olson, J. M., Roese, N. J., & Zanna, M. P. (1996). Expectancies. In E. T. Higgins, & A. W. Kruglanski (Eds.), *Social psychology: Handbook of basic principles*. New York: Guilford Press.

Olson, J. M., & Zanna, M. P. (1993). Attitudes and attitude change. *Annual Review of Psychology, 44*, 117–154.

Orbuch, T. L., House, J. S., Mero, R. P., & Webster, P. S. (1996). Marital quality over the life course. *Social Psychology Quarterly, 59*, 162–171.

Orne, M. T. (1951). The mechanisms of hypnotic age regression: An experimental study. *Journal of Abnormal and Social Psychology, 46*, 213–225.

Orne, M. T., & Dinges, D. F. (1989). Hypnosis. In H. I. Kaplan & B. J. Sadock (Eds.), *Comprehensive textbook of psychiatry/V* (Vol. 2). Baltimore: Williams & Wilkins.

Orne, M. T., & Holland, C. C. (1968). On the ecological validity of laboratory deceptions. *International Journal of Psychiatry, 6,* 282–293.

Ornstein, R. E. (1977). *The psychology of consciousness.* New York: Harcourt Brace Jovanovich.

Ornstein, R. E., & Dewan, T. (1991). *The evolution of consciousness: Of Darwin, Freud, and cranial fire—The origins of the way we think.* New York: Prentice-Hall.

Ortmann, A., & Hertwig, R. (1997). Is deception acceptable? *American Psychologist, 52,* 746–747.

Oskamp, S. (1991). *Attitudes and opinions.* Englewood Cliffs, NJ: Prentice-Hall.

Oskamp, S., Kaufman, K., & Wolterbeek, L. A. (1996). Gender role portrayals in preschool picture books. *Journal of Social Behavior and Personality, 11,* 27–39.

Ostrom, T. M., & Sedikides, C. (1992). Outgroup homogeneity effects in natural and minimal groups. *Psychological Bulletin, 112,* 536–552.

Ozer, D. J., & Reise, S. P. (1994). Personality assessment. *Annual Review of Psychology, 45,* 357–388.

Pachman, J. S. (1996). The dawn of a revolution in mental health. *American Psychologist, 51,* 213–215.

Paffenbarger, R. S., Hyde, R. T., & Wing, A. L. (1990). Physical activity and physical fitness as determinants of health and longevity. In C. Bouchard et al. (Eds), *Exercise, fitness, and health: A consensus of current knowledge.* Champaign, IL: Human Kinetics Books.

Pagel, M. D., Smilkstein, G., Regen, H., & Montano, D. (1990). Psychosocial influences on newborn outcomes: A controlled prospective study. *Social Science Medicine, 30,* 597–604.

Paivio, A. (1969). Mental imagery in associative learning and memory. *Psychological Review, 76,* 241–263.

Paivio, A. (1986). *Mental representations: A dual coding approach.* New York: Oxford University Press.

Paivio, A., Smythe, P. E., & Yuille, J. C. (1968). Imagery versus meaningfulness of nouns in paired-associate learning. *Canadian Journal of Psychology, 22,* 427–441.

Pajares, F. (1996). Self-efficacy beliefs and mathematical problem-solving of gifted students. *Contemporary Educational Psychology, 21,* 325–344.

Palladino, J. J., & Carducci, B. J. (1984). Students' knowledge of sleep and dreams. *Teaching of Psychology, 11,* 189–191.

Palmer, L. K., Frantz, C. E., Armsworth, M. W., Swank, P., Copley, J. V., & Bush, G. A. (1999). Neuropsychological sequelae of chronically psychologically traumatized children: Specific findings in memory and higher cognitive functions. In L. M. Williams & V. L. Banyard (Eds.), *Trauma & memory.* Thousand Oaks, CA: Sage Publications.

Palmere, M., Benton, S. L., Glover, J. A., & Ronning, R. (1983). Elaboration and recall of main ideas in prose. *Journal of Educational Psychology, 75,* 898–907.

Panksepp, J. (1991). Affective neuroscience: A conceptual framework for the neurobiological study of emotions. In K. T. Strongman (Ed), *International review of studies on emotion.* Chichester, England: Wiley.

Paradiso, S. P., Robinson, R. G., Andreasen, N. C., Downhill, J. E., Davidson, R. J., Kirchner, P. T., Watkins, G. L., Boles Ponto, L. L., & Hichwa, R. D. (1997). Emotional activation of limbic circuitry in elderly normal subjects in a PET study. *American Journal of Psychiatry, 154,* 384–389.

Parke, R. D., & Slaby, R. G. (1983). The development of aggression. In E. M. Hetherington (Ed.), *Handbook of child psychology: Socialization, personality, and social development* (Vol. 4). New York: Wiley.

Parker, D. E. (1980). The vestibular apparatus. *Scientific American, 243*(5), 118–135.

Parker, G. A., & Smith, J. M. (1990). Optimality theory in evolutionary biology. *Nature, 348,* 27–33.

Parker, G., & Hadzi-Pavlovic, D. (1990). Expressed emotion as a predictor of schizophrenic relapse: An analysis of aggregated data. *Psychological Medicine, 20,* 961–965.

Parkinson, B. (1997). Untangling the appraisal-emotion connection. *Personality and Social Psychology Review, 1,* 62–79.

Parks, T. E. (1984). Illusory figures: A (mostly) atheoretical review. *Psychological Bulletin, 95,* 282–300.

Parry-Jones, B., & Parry-Jones, W. L. (1995). History of bulimia and bulimia nervosa. In K. D. Brownell & C. G. Fairburn (Eds.), *Eating disorders and obesity: A comprehensive handbook.* New York: Guilford Press.

Partinen, M. (1994). Epidemiology of sleep disorders. In M. H. Kryger, T. Roth, & W. C. Dement (Eds.), *Principles and practice of sleep medicine* (2nd ed.). Philadelphia: Saunders.

Pashler, H., & Carrier, M. (1996). Stuctures, processes, and the flow of information. In E. L. Bjork, & R. A. Bjork (Eds.), *Memory.* San Diego: Academic Press.

Patterson, D. R., Adcock, R. J., & Bombardier, C. H. (1997). Factors predicting hypnotic analgesia in clinical burn pain. *International Journal of Clinical & Experimental Hypnosis, 45,* 377–395.

Paulhus, D. L. (1991). Measurement and control of response bias. In J. P. Robinson, P. Shaver, & L. S. Wrightsman (Eds.), *Measures of personality and social psychological attitudes.* San Diego: Academic Press.

Paulos, J. A. (1995). *A mathematician reads the newspaper.* New York: Doubleday.

Pauls, D. L., Alsobrook, J. P. I., Goodman, W., Rasmussen, S., & Leckman, J. F. (1995). A family study of obsessive-compulsive disorder. *American Journal of Psychiatry, 152,* 76–84.

Paunonen, S. V. (1998). Hierarchical organization of personality and prediction of behavior. *Journal of Personality and Social Psychology, 74,* 538–556.

Pavlov, I. P. (1906). The scientific investigation of psychical faculties or processes in the higher animals. *Science, 24,* 613–619.

Pavlov, I. P. (1927). *Conditioned reflexes* (G. V. Anrep, Trans.). London: Oxford University Press.

Payne, D. G., & Blackwell, J. M. (1998). Truth in memory: Caveat emptor. In S. J. Lynn & K. M. McConkey (Eds.), *Truth in memory.* New York: Guilford Press.

Payne, D. G., & Wenger, M. J. (1996). Practice effects in memory: Data, theory, and unanswered questions. In D. J. Herrmann, C. McEvoy, C. Hertzog, P. Hertel, & M. K. Johnson (Eds.), *Basic and applied memory research: Practical applications* (Vol. 2). Mahwah, NJ: Erlbaum.

Payne, J. W. (1976). Task complexity and contingent processing in decision making: An informational search and protocol analysis. *Organizational Behavior and Human Performance, 16,* 366–387.

Payne, J. W., Bettman, J. R., & Johnson, E. J. (1992). Behavioral decision research: A constructive processing perspective. *Annual Review of Psychology, 43,* 87–131.

Pearce, L. (1974). Duck! It's the new journalism. *New Times, 2*(10), 40–41.

Pearlman, C. A. (1982). Sleep structure variation and performance. In W. B. Webb (Ed.), *Biological rhythms, sleep and performance.* New York: Wiley.

Pearson, B. Z., Fernandez, S. C., & Oller, D. K. (1993). Lexical development in bilingual infants and toddler: Comparison to monolingual norms. *Language Learning, 43,* 93–120.

Pease, D. M., Gleason, J. B., & Pan, B. A. (1993). Learning the meaning of words: Semantic development and beyond. In J. B. Gleason (Ed.), *The development of language.* New York: MacMillan.

Pechnick, R. N., & Ungerleider, J. T. (1997). Hallucinogens. In J. H. Lowinson, P. Ruiz, R. B. Millman, & J. G. Langrod (Eds.), *Substance abuse: A comprehensive textbook.* Baltimore: Williams & Wilkins.

Pedersen, P. (1994). A culture-centered approach to counseling. In W. J. Lonner & R. Malpass (Eds.), *Psychology and culture.* Boston: Allyn & Bacon.

Peele, S. (1989). *Diseasing of America: Addiction treatment out of control.* Lexington, MA: Lexington Books.

Peirce, R. S., Frone, M. R., Russell, M., & Cooper, M. L. (1996). Financial stress, social support, and alcohol involvement: A longitudinal test of the buffering hypothesis in a general population survey. *Health Psychology, 15,* 38–47.

Pennebaker, J. W., Colder, M., & Sharp, L. K. (1990). Accelerating the coping process. *Journal of Personality and Social Psychology, 58,* 528–537.

Peplau, L. A., Garnets, L. D., Spalding, L. R., Conley, T. D., & Veniegas, R. C. (1998). A critique of Bem's "Exotic Becomes Erotic" theory of sexual orientation. *Psychological Review, 105,* 387–394.

Perlman, M. D., & Kaufman, A. S. (1990). Assessment of child intelligence. In G. Goldstein & M. Hersen (Eds.), *Handbook of psychological assessment.* New York: Pergamon Press.

Perone, M., Galizio, M., & Baron, A. (1988). The relevance of animal-based principles in the laboratory study of human operant conditioning. In G. Davey & C. Cullen (Eds.), *Human operant conditioning and behavior modification.* New York: Wiley.

Perreault, S., & Bourhis, R. Y. (1999). Ethnocentrism, social identification, and discrimination. *Personality and Social Psychology Bulletin, 25,* 92–103.

Perry, W., & Braff, D. L. (1994). Information-processing deficits and thought disorder in schizophrenia. *American Journal of Psychiatry, 151*, 363–367.

Pert, C. B., & Snyder, S. H. (1973). Opiate receptor: Demonstration in the nervous tissue. *Science, 179*, 1011–1014.

Pervin, L. A. (1994). Personality stability, personality change, and the question of process. In T. F. Heatherton & J. L. Weinberger (Eds.), *Can personality change?* Washington, DC: American Psychological Association.

Petersen, A. C., Compas, B. E., Brooks-Gunn, J., Stemmler, M., Ey, S., & Grant, K. E. (1993). Depression in adolescence. *American Psychologist, 48*, 155–168.

Peterson, C., Seligman, M. E. P., & Vaillant, G. E. (1988). Pessimistic explanatory style is a risk factor for physical illness: A thirty-five-year longitudinal study. *Journal of Personality and Social Psychology, 55*, 23–27.

Peterson, L. R., & Peterson, M. J. (1959). Short-term retention of individual verbal items. *Journal of Experimental Psychology, 58*, 193–198.

Petrie, K. J., Booth, R. J., & Pennebaker, J. W. (1998). The immunological effects of thought suppression. *Journal of Personality and Social Psychology, 75*, 1264–1272.

Petty, R. E., & Cacioppo, J. T. (1986). *Communication and persuasion: Central and peripheral routes to attitude change.* New York: Springer-Verlag.

Petty, R. E., Haugtvedt, C. P., & Smith, S. M. (1995). Elaboration as a determinant of attitude strength: Creating attitudes that are persistent, resistant, and predictive of behavior. In R. E. Petty & J. A. Krosnick (Eds.), *Attitude strength: Antecedents and consequences.* Mahwah, NJ: Erlbaum.

Petty, R. E., & Wegener, D. T. (1998). Attitude change: Multiple roles for persuasion variables. In D. T. Gilbert, S. T. Fiske, & G. Lindzey (Eds.), *The handbook of social psychology.* New York: McGraw-Hill.

Petty, R. E., & Wegener, D. T. (1999). The elaboration likelihood model: Current status and controversies. In S. Chaiken & Y. Trope (Eds.), *Dual-process theories in social psychology.* New York: Guilford Press.

Petty, R. E., Wegener, D. T., & Fabrigar, L. R. (1997). Attitudes and attitude change. *Annual Review of Psychology, 48*, 609–647.

Peyser, H. S. (1993). Stress, ethyl alcohol, and alcoholism. In L. Goldberger & S. Breznitz (Eds.), *Handbook of stress: Theoretical and clinical aspects* (2nd ed.). New York: Free Press.

Pfaffmann, C. (1974). Specificity of the sweet receptors of the squirrel monkey. *Chemical Senses and Flavor, 1*, 61–67.

Pfaffmann, C. (1978). The vertebrate phylogeny, neural code, and integrative process of taste. In C. Carterette & M. P. Friedman (Eds.), *Handbook of Perception* (Vol. 6A). New York: Academic Press.

Pfau, M., Kenski, H. C., Nitz, M., & Sorenson, J. (1990). Efficacy of inoculation strategies in promoting resistance to political attack messages: Application to direct mail. *Communication Monographs, 57*, 25–43.

Phares, V. (1996). *Fathers and developmental psychopathology.* New York: Wiley.

Phillips, M. R., Wolf, A. S., & Coons, D. J. (1988). Psychiatry and the criminal justice system: Testing the myths. *American Journal of Psychiatry, 145*, 605–610.

Phillips, R. G., & LeDoux, J. E. (1992). Differential contribution of amygdala and hippocampus to cued and contextual fear conditioning. *Behavioral Neuroscience, 106*, 274–285.

Piaget, J. (1929). *The child's conception of the world.* New York: Harcourt, Brace.

Piaget, J. (1932). *The moral judgment of the child.* Glencoe, IL: Free Press.

Piaget, J. (1952). *The origins of intelligence in children.* New York: International Universities Press.

Piaget, J. (1954). *The construction of reality in the child.* New York: Basic Books.

Piaget, J. (1983). Piaget's theory. In P. H. Mussen (Ed.), *Handbook of child psychology* (Vol. 1). New York: Wiley.

Pickering, T. G., Devereux, R. B., James, G. D., Gerin, W., Landsbergis, P., Schnall, P. L., & Schwartz, J. E. (1996). Environmental influences on blood pressure and the role of job strain. *Journal of Hypertension, 14*, S179–S185.

Pierce, C. M. (1992). Contemporary psychiatry: Racial perspectives on the past and future. In A. Kales, C.M. Pierce, & M. Greenblatt (Eds.), *The mosaic of contemporary psychiatry in perspective.* New York: Springer-Verlag.

Pike, K. M., & Rodin, J. (1991). Mothers, daughters, and disordered eating. *Journal of Abnormal Psychology, 100*, 198–294.

Pilcher, J. J., Ginter, D. R., & Sadowsky, B. (1997). Sleep quality versus sleep quantity: Relationships between sleep and measures of health, well-being and sleepiness in college students. *Journal of Psychosomatic Research, 42*, 583–596.

Pilcher, J. J., & Huffcutt, A. I. (1996). Effects of sleep deprivation on performance: A meta-analysis. *Sleep, 19*, 318–326.

Pilcher, J. J., & Walters, A. S. (1997). How sleep deprivation affects psychological variables related to college students' cognitive performance. *Journal of American College Health, 46*, 121–126.

Pillow, D. R., Zautra, A. J., & Sandler, I. (1996). Major life events and minor stressors: Identifying mediational links in the stress process. *Journal of Personality and Social Psychology, 70*, 381–394.

Pinker, S. (1990). Language acquisition. In D. N. Osherson & H. Lasnik (Eds.), *Language: An invitation to cognitive science* (Vol. 1). Cambridge, MA: MIT Press.

Pinker, S. (1994). *Language is to us as flying is to geese.* New York: Morrow.

Pinker, S., & Bloom, P. (1992). Natural language and natural selection. In J. H. Barkow, L. Cosmides, & J. Tooby (Eds.), *The adapted mind: Evolutionary psychology and the generation of culture.* New York: Oxford University Press.

Piper, W. E. (1993). Group psychotherapy research. In H. I. Kaplan & B. J. Sadock (Eds.), *Comprehensive group psychotherapy.* Baltimore: Williams & Wilkins.

Pittman, F., III. (1994, January/February). A buyer's guide to psychotherapy. *Psychology Today*, 50–53, 74–81.

Pivik, R. T. (1994). The psychophysiology of dreams. In M. H. Kryger, T. Roth, & W. C. Dement (Eds.), *Principles and practice of sleep medicine* (2nd ed.). Philadelphia: Saunders.

Plante, T. G. (1999). *Contemporary clinical psychology.* New York: Wiley & Sons, Inc.

Plomin, R. (1990). *Nature and nurture: An introduction to human behavioral genetics.* Pacific Grove, CA: Brooks/Cole.

Plomin, R. (1993). Nature and nurture: Perspective and prospective. In R. Plomin & G. E. McClearn (Eds.), *Nature, nurture and psychology.* Washington, DC: American Psychological Association.

Plomin, R. (1994). Nature, nurture, and development. In R. J. Sternberg (Ed.), *Encyclopedia of human intelligence.* New York: Macmillan.

Plomin, R., & Caspi, A. (1999). Behavioral genetics and personality. In L. A. Pervin, & O. P. John (Eds.), *Handbook of personality: Theory and research.* New York: Guilford Press.

Plomin, R., & Petrill, S. A. (1997). Genetics and intelligence: What's new? *Intelligence, 24*, 53–77.

Plomin, R., & Rende, R. (1991). Human behavioral genetics. *Annual Review of Psychology, 42*, 161–190.

Plotkin, H. (1998). *Evolution in mind: An introduction to evolutionary psychology.* Cambridge, MA: Harvard University Press.

Plucker, J. A., & Renzulli, J. S. (1999). Psychometric approaches to the study of human creativity. In R. J. Sternberg (Ed.), *Handbook of creativity.* New York: Cambridge University Press.

Plutchik, R. (1980, February). A language for the emotions. *Psychology Today*, pp. 68–78.

Plutchik, R. (1984). Emotions: A general psycho-evolutionary theory. In K. R. Scherer & P. Ekman (Eds.), *Approaches to emotion.* Hillsdale, NJ: Erlbaum.

Plutchik, R. (1993). Emotions and their vicissitudes: Emotions and psychopathology. In M. Lewis & J. M. Haviland (Eds.), *Handbook of emotions.* New York: Guilford Press.

Policastro, E., & Gardner, H. (1999). From case studies to robust generalizations: An approach to the study of creativity. In R. J. Sternberg (Ed.), *Handbook of creativity.* New York: Cambridge University Press.

Poloma, M., & Pendleton, B. F. (1990). Religious domains and general well-being. *Social Indicators Research, 22*, 255–276.

Ponterotto, J. G., & Pedersen, P. B. (1993). *Preventing prejudice: A guide for counselors and educators.* Newbury Park, CA: Sage.

Pope, H. G., Jr., & Hudson, J. I. (1998). Can memories of childhood sexual abuse be repressed? In R. A. Baker (Ed.), *Child sexual abuse and false memory syndrome.* Amherst, NY: Prometheus Books.

Pope, K. S. (1996). Memory, abuse, and science: Questioning claims about the false memory syndrome epidemic. *American Psychologist, 51*, 957–974.

Pope, K. S., & Brown, L. (1996). *Recovered memories of abuse: Assessment, thereapy, forensics.* Washington, D.C.: American Psychological Association.

Pope, K. S., Keith-Spiegel, P., & Tabachnick, B. G. (1986). Sexual attraction to clients. *American Psychologist, 41*, 147–158.

Popenoe, D. (1996). *Life without father*. New York: Pressler Press.

Posner, M. I., & Raichle, M. E. (1994). *Images of mind*. New York: Scientific American Library.

Post, F. (1996). Verbal creativity, depression and alcoholism: An investigation of one hundred American and British writers. *British Journal of Psychiatry, 168,* 545–555.

Postman, L. (1985). Human learning and memory. In G. A. Kimble & K. Schlesinger (Eds.), *Topics in the history of psychology*. Hillsdale, NJ: Erlbaum.

Potter, W. Z., Manji, H. K., & Rudorfer, M. V. (1995). Tricyclics and tetracyclics. In A. F. Schatzberg & C. B. Nemeroff (Eds.), *The American Psychiatric Press textbook of psychopharmacology*. Washington, DC: American Psychiatric Press.

Potthoff, J. G., Holahan, C. J., & Joiner, T. E. Jr. (1995). Reassurance-seeking, stress generation, and depressive symptoms: An integrative model. *Journal of Personality and Social Psychology, 68,* 664–670.

Powell, R. A., & Boer, D. P. (1995). Did Freud misinterpret reported memories of sexual abuse as fantasies? *Psychological Reports, 77,* 563–570.

Powell, R. A., & Gee, T. L. (1999). The effects of hypnosis on dissociative identity disorder: A reexamination of the evidence. *Canadian Journal of Psychiatry, 44,* 914–916.

Pratkanis, A. R., & Aronson, E. (1992). *Age of propaganda: The everyday use and abuse of persuasion*. New York: W. H. Freeman.

Pratt, L. A., Ford, D. E., Crum, R. M., Armenian, H. K., Gallo, J. J., & Eaton, W. W. (1996). Depression, psychotropic medication, and risk of myocardinal infarction: Prospective data from Baltimore ECA follow-up. *Archives of Internal Medicine, 94,* 3123–3129.

Premack, D. (1985). "Gavagai!" or the future history of the animal language controversy. *Cognition, 19,* 207–296.

Prentky, R. A. (1989). Creativity and psychopathology: Gamboling at the seat of madness. In J. A. Glover, R. R. Ronning, & C. R. Reynolds (Eds.), *Handbook of creativity*. New York: Plenum.

Priester, J. R., & Petty, R. E. (1995). Source attributions and persuasion; Perceived honesty as a determinant of message scrutiny. *Personality and Social Psychology Bulletin, 21,* 637–654.

Prifitera, A. (1994). Wechsler scales of intelligence. In R. J. Sternberg (Ed.), *Encyclopedia of human intelligence*. New York: Macmillan.

Prochaska, J. O. (1994). Strong and weak principles for progressing from precontemplation to action on the basis of twelve problem behaviors. *Health Psychology, 13,* 47–51.

Prudic, J., & Sackeim, H. A. (1999). Electroconvulsive therapy and suicide risk. *Journal of Clinical Psychiatry, 60,* 104–110.

Pruitt, D. G. (1971). Choice shifts in group discussion: An introductory review. *Journal of Personality and Social Psychology, 20,* 339–360.

Pugh, E. N., Jr. (1988). Vision: Physics and retinal physiology. In R. C. Atkinson, R. J. Herrnstein, G. Lindzey, & R. D. Luce (Eds.), *Stevens' handbook of experimental psychology* (Vol. 1). New York: Wiley.

Pullum, G. K. (1991). *The Great Eskimo vocabulary hoax*. Chicago: University of Chicago Press.

Rabkin, J. G. (1993). Stress and psychiatric disorders. In L. Goldberger & S. Breznitz (Eds.), *Handbook of stress: Theoretical and clinical aspects* (2nd ed.). New York: Free Press.

Rachman, S. J. (1992). Behavior therapy. In L. R. Squire (Ed.), *Encyclopedia of learning and memory*. New York: Macmillan.

Rahe, R. H., & Holmes, T. H. (1965). Social, psychologic, and psychophysiologic aspects of inguinal hernia. *Journal of Psychosomatic Research, 8,* 487–491.

Raichle, M. E. (1994). Images of the mind: Studies with modern imaging techniques. *Annual Review of Psychology, 45,* 333–356.

Rakic, P., Bourgeois, J. P., & Goldman-Rakic, P. S. (1994). Synaptic development of the cerebral cortex: Implications for learning, memory, and mental illness. *Progress in brain research*.

Ramey, C. T., & Ramey, S. L. (1998). Prevention of intellectual disabilities: Early interventions to improve cognitive development. *Preventive Medicine: An International Devoted to Practice & Theory, 27,* 224–232.

Ramey, S. L. (1999). Head Start and preschool education: Toward continued improvement. *American Psychologist, 54,* 344–346.

Rapaport, K., & Burkhart, B. R. (1984). Personality and attitudinal characteristics of sexually coercive college males. *Journal of Abnormal Psychology, 93,* 216–221.

Rapee, R. M., & Barlow, D. H. (1993). Generalized anxiety disorder, panic disorder, and the phobias. In P. B. Sutker & H. E. Adams (Eds.), *Comprehensive handbook of psychopathology* (2nd ed.). New York: Plenum.

Raphael, K. G., Cloitre, M., & Dohrenwend, B. P. (1991). Problems of recall and misclassification with checklist methods of measuring stressful life events. *Health Psychology, 10,* 62–74.

Rasmussen, T., & Milner, B. (1977). The role of early left brain injury in determining lateralization of cerebral speech functions. *Annals of the New York Academy of Sciences, 299,* 355–369.

Ratner, N. B., & Gleason, J. B. (1993). An introduction to psycholinguistics: What do language users know? In J. B. Gleason & N. B. Ratner (Eds.), *Psycholinguistics*. Fort Worth: Harcourt Brace Jovanovich.

Rauscher, F. H., Shaw, G. L., & Ky, K. N. (1993). Music and spatial task performance. *Nature, 365,* 611.

Rauscher, F. H., Shaw, G. L., & Ky, K. N. (1995). Listening to Mozart enhances spatial-temporal reasoning: Towards a neurophysiological basis. *Neuroscience Letters, 185,* 44–47.

Ray, O., & Ksir, C. (1996). *Drugs, society & human behavior*. St. Louis: Times Mirror/Mosby.

Raynor, J. O., & Entin, E. E. (1982). Future orientation and achievement motivation. In J. O. Raynor & E. E. Entin (Eds.), *Motivation, career striving, and aging*. New York: Hemisphere.

Raz, S. (1993). Structural cerebral pathology in schizophrenia: Regional or diffuse? *Journal of Abnormal Psychology, 102,* 445–452.

Read, C. R. (1991). Achievement and career choices: Comparisons of males and females. *Roeper Review, 13,* 188–193.

Real, L. (1991). Animal choice behavior and the evolution of cognitive architecture. *Science, 253,* 980–986.

Rechtschaffen, A. (1994). Sleep onset: Conceptual issues. In R. D. Ogilvie & J. R. Harsh (Eds.), *Sleep onset: Normal and abnormal processes*. Washington, DC: American Psychological Association.

Ree, M. J., & Earles, J. A. (1992). Intelligence is the best predictor of job performance. *Current Directions in Psychological Science, 1,* 86–89.

Reed, J. G., & Baxter P. M. (1992). *Library use: A handbook for psychology*. Washington, DC: American Psychological Association.

Regan, P. C. (1998). What if you can't get what you want? Willingness to compromise ideal mate selection standards as a function of sex, mate value, and relationship context. *Personality and Social Psychology Bulletin, 24,* 1294–1303.

Regan, T. (1989). Ill-gotten gains. In G. Langley (Ed.), *Animal experimentation: The consensus changes*. New York: Chapman & Hall.

Regestein, Q. R., & Monk, T. H. (1991). Is the poor sleep of shift workers a disorder? *American Journal of Psychiatry, 148,* 1487–1493.

Reinke, B. J., Ellicott, A. M., Harris, R. L., & Hancock, E. (1985). Timing of psychosocial changes in women's lives. *Human Development, 28,* 259–280.

Reisenzein, R. (1983). The Schachter theory of emotion: Two decades later. *Psychological Bulletin, 94,* 239–264.

Reisner, A. D. (1998). Repressed memories: True and false. In R. A. Baker (Ed.), *Child sexual abuse and false memory syndrome*. Amherst, NY: Prometheus Books.

Reiss, S. (1991). Expectancy model of fear, anxiety and panic. *Clinical Psychology Review, 11,* 141–154.

Rescorla, R. A. (1978). Some implications of a cognitive perspective on Pavlovian conditioning. In S. H. Hulse, H. Fowler, & W. K. Honig (Eds.), *Cognitive processes in animal behavior*. Hillsdale, NJ: Erlbaum.

Rescorla, R. A. (1980). *Pavlovian second-order conditioning*. Hillsdale, NJ: Erlbaum.

Rescorla, R. A., & Wagner, A. R. (1972). A theory of Pavlovian conditioning: Variations in the effectiveness of reinforcement and nonreinforcement. In A. H. Black & W. F. Prokasky (Eds.), *Classical conditioning: II. Current research and theory*. New York: Appleton-Century-Crofts.

Resnick, D. P., & Fienberg, S. E. (1997). Science, public policy, and *The Bell Curve*. In B. Devlin, S. E. Fienberg, D. P. Resnick, & K. Roeder (Eds.), *Intelligence, genes, and success: Scientists respond to The Bell Curve*. New York: Springer-Verlag.

Rest, J. R. (1986). *Moral development: Advances in research and theory*. New York: Praeger.

Reuter-Lorenz, P. A., & Miller, A. C. (1998). The cognitive neuroscience of human laterality: Lessons from the bisected brain. *Current Directions in Psychological Science, 7,* 15–20.

Reynolds, C. R. (1994). Reliability. In R. J. Sternberg (Ed.), *Encyclopedia of human intelligence*. New York: Macmillan.

Reynolds, C. R. (1995). Test bias and the assessment of intelligence and personality. In D. H. Saklofske & M. Zeidner (Eds.), *International handbook of personality and intelligence*. New York: Plenum.

Rice, L. N., & Greenberg, L. S. (1992). Humanistic approaches to psychotherapy. In D. K. Freedheim (Ed.), *History of psychotherapy: A century of change*. Washington, DC: American Psychological Association.

Richardson, G. S. (1993). Circadian rhythms. In M. A. Carskadon (Ed.), *Encyclopedia of sleep and dreaming*. New York: Macmillan.

Richardson, J. T. E., & Zucco, G. M. (1989). Cognition and olfaction: A review. *Psychological Bulletin, 105*, 352–360.

Rieber, R. W. (1998). The assimilation of psychoanalysis in America: From popularization to vulgarization. In R. W. Rieber & K. D. Salzinger (Eds.), *Psychology: Theoretical-historical perspectives*. Washington, DC: American Psychological Association.

Rief, W., Hiller, W., & Margraf, J. (1998). Cognitive aspects of hypochondriasis and the somatization syndrome. *Journal of Abnormal Psychology, 107*, 587–595.

Riemann, R., Angleitner, A., & Strelau, J. (1997). Genetic and environmental influences on personality: A study of twins reared together using the self-and peer report NEO-FFI scales. *Journal of Personality, 65*, 449–476.

Riley, L. R. (1987). *Psychology of language development: A primer*. Toronto: C. J. Hogrefe.

Rilling, M. (1996). The mystery of the vanished citations: James McConnell's forgotten 1960s quest for planarian learning, a biochemical engram, and celebrity. *American Psychologist, 51*, 589–598.

Roberts, P., & Newton, P. M. (1987). Levinsonian studies of women's adult development. *Psychology and Aging, 2*, 154–163.

Robins, L. N., & Regier, D. A. (Eds.). (1991). *Psychiatric disorders in America: The epidemiologic catchment area study*. New York: Free Press.

Robins, R. W., Gosling, S. D., & Craik, K. H. (1999). An empirical analysis of trends in psychology. *American Psychologist, 54*, 117–128.

Robinson, F. P. (1970). *Effective study* (4th ed.). New York: Harper & Row.

Rodgers, J. E. (1982). The malleable memory of eyewitnesses. *Science Digest, 3*, 32–35.

Rodin, J. (1985). Insulin levels, hunger, and food intake: An example of feedback loops in body weight regulation. *Health Psychology, 4*, 1–24.

Roediger, H. L., III. (1980). Memory metaphors in cognitive psychology. *Memory & Cognition, 8*, 231–246.

Roediger, H. L., III. (1990). Implicit memory: Retention without remembering. *American Psychologist, 45*, 1043–1056.

Roediger, H. L., Wheeler, M. A., & Rajaram, S. (1993). Remembering, knowing, and reconstructing the past. In D. L. Medin (Ed.), *The psychology of learning and motivation: Advances in research and theory*. San Diego: Academic Press.

Roehrs, T. A., Merlotti, L., Zorick, F., & Roth, T. (1992). Rebound insomnia in normals and patients with insomnia after abrupt and tapered discontinuation. *Psychopharmacology, 108*(1–2), 67–71.

Roehrs, T. A, Zorick, F., & Roth, T. (1994). Transient and short-term insomnia. In M. H. Kryger, T. Roth, & W. C. Dement (Eds.), *Principles and practice of sleep medicine* (2nd ed.). Philadelphia: Saunders.

Roffwarg, H. P., Muzio, J. N., & Dement, W. C. (1966). Ontogenetic development of the human sleep-dream cycle. *Science, 152*, 604–619.

Rogers, C. R. (1951). *Client-centered therapy: Its current practice, implications, and theory*. Boston: Houghton Mifflin.

Rogers, C. R. (1961). *On becoming a person: A therapist's view of psychotherapy*. Boston: Houghton Mifflin.

Rogers, C. R. (1980). *A way of being*. Boston: Houghton Mifflin.

Rogers, C. R. (1986). Client-centered therapy. In I. L. Kutash & A. Wolf (Eds.), *Psychotherapist's casebook*. San Francisco: Jossey-Bass.

Rogers, P. (1998). The cognitive psychology of lottery gambling: A theoretical review. *Journal of Gambling Studies, 14*, 111–134.

Rogers, R. W. (1983). Cognitive and physiological processes in fear appeals and attitude change: A revised theory of protection motivation. In J. Cacioppo & R. Petty (Eds.), *Social psychophysiology*. New York: Guilford Press.

Rogers, S. J., & White, L. K. (1998). Satisfaction with parenting: The role of marital happiness, family structure, and parents' gender. *Journal of Marriage and the Family, 60*, 293–308.

Rogers, W. T., & Yang, P. (1996). Test-wiseness: Its nature and application. *European Journal of Psychological Assessment, 12*, 247–259.

Rogoff, B. (1990). *Apprenticeship in thinking*. New York: Oxford University Press.

Role, L. W., & Kelly, J. P. (1991). The brain stem: Cranial nerve nuclei and the monoaminergic systems. In E. R. Kandel, J. H. Schwartz, & T. M. Jessell (Eds.), *Principles of neural science* (3rd ed.). New York: Elsevier.

Rollman, G. B. (1992). Cognitive effects in pain and pain judgments. In D. Algom (Ed.), *Psychophysical approaches to cognition*. Amsterdam: North Holland.

Rolls, E. T. (1990). A theory of emotion, and its application to understanding the neural basis of emotion. *Cognitive and Emotion, 4*, 161–190.

Rolls, E. T. (1992). Neurophysiological mechanisms and underlying face processing within and beyond the temporal cortical visual areas. *Transactions of the Royal Society of London, B335*, 11–21.

Rolls, E. T., & Tovee, M. T. (1995). Sparseness of the neuronal representation of stimuli in the primate temporal visual cortex. *Journal of Neurophysiology, 73*, 713–726.

Roosa, M. W. (1988). The effect of age in the transition to parenthood: Are delayed child-bearers a unique group? *Family Relations, 37*, 322–327.

Rosch, E. H. (1973). Natural categories. *Cognitive Psychology, 4*, 328–350.

Rose, R. J. (1995). Genes and human behavior. *Annual Review of Psychology, 46*, 625–654.

Rose, S. D. (1999). Group therapy: A cognitive-behavioral approach. In J. R. Price, & D. R. Hescheles (Ed.), *A guide to starting psychotherapy groups*. San Diego: Academic Press.

Rose, S. P. R. (1992). Protein synthesis in long-term memory in vertebrates. In L. R. Squire (Ed.), *Encyclopedia of learning and memory*. New York: Macmillan.

Rosenbaum, M., Lakin, M., & Roback, H. B. (1992). Psychotherapy in groups. In D. K. Freedheim (Ed.), *History of psychotherapy: A century of change*. Washington, DC: American Psychological Association.

Rosenberg, P. S., & Biggar, R. J. (1998). Trends in HIV incidence among young adults in the United States. *Journal of the American Medical Association, 279*, 1894–1899.

Rosenblith, J. F. (1992). *In the beginning: Development from conception to age two*. Newbury Park, CA: Sage.

Rosengren, A., Tibblin, G., & Wilhelmsen, L. (1991). Self-perceived psychological stress and incidence of coronary artery disease in middle-aged men. *American Journal of Cardiology, 68*, 1171–1175.

Rosenman, R. H. (1993). Relationships of the Type A behavior pattern with coronary heart disease. In L. Goldberger & S. Breznitz (Eds.), *Handbook of stress: Theoretical and clinical aspects* (2nd ed.). New York: Free Press.

Rosenthal, R. (1976). *Experimenter effects in behavioral research*. New York: Halsted.

Rosenthal, R. (1994). Interpersonal expectancy effects: A 30–year perspective. *Current Directions in Psychological Science, 3*, 176–179.

Rosenthal, R., & Fode, K. L. (1963). Three experiments in experimenter bias. *Psychological Reports, 12*, 491–511.

Rosenzweig, M. R. (1996). Aspects of the search for neural mechanisms of memory. *Annual Review of Psychology, 47*, 1–32.

Rosenzweig, M. R., Krech, D., & Bennett, E. L. (1961). Heredity, environment, brain biochemistry, and learning. In *Current trends in psychological theory*. Pittsburgh: University of Pittsburgh Press.

Rosenzweig, M., Krech, D., Bennett, E. L., & Diamond, M. (1962). Effects of environmental complexity and training on brain chemistry and anatomy: A replication and extension. *Journal of Comparative and Physiological Psychology, 55*, 429–437.

Rosenzweig, S. (1985). Freud and experimental psychology: The emergence of idiodynamics. In S. Koch & D. E. Leary (Eds.), *A century of psychology as a science*. New York: McGraw-Hill.

Roskos-Ewoldsen, D. R., & Fazio, R. H. (1992). The accessibility of source likability as a determinant of persuasion. *Personality and Social Psychology Bulletin, 18*, 19–25.

Ross, B. (1991). William James: Spoiled child of American psychology. In G. A. Kimble, M. Wertheimer, & C. White (Eds.), *Portraits of pioneers in psychology*. Hillsdale, NJ: Erlbaum.

Ross, L. D., & Anderson, C. A. (1982). Shortcomings in the attribution process: On the origins and maintenance of erroneous social assessments. In D. Kahneman, P. Slovic, & A. Tversky (Eds.), *Judgment under uncertainty: Heuristics and biases*. Cambridge: Cambridge University Press.

Rossi, P. H. (1990). The old homeless and the new homelessness in historical perspective. *American Psychologist, 45*(8), 954–959.

Roth, A., & Fonagy, P. (1996). *What works for whom? A critical review of psychotherapy*. New York: Guilford Press.

Rothbart, M. K., & Bates, J. E. (1998). Temperament. In W. Damon (Ed.), *Handbook of child psychology (Vol. 3): Social, emotional, and personality development*. New York: Wiley.

Rothenberg, A. (1990). *Creativity and madness*. Baltimore: Johns Hopkins University Press.

Rotter, J. B. (1982). *The development and application of social learning theory*. New York: Praeger.

Rowatt, W. C., Cunningham, M. R., & Druen, P. B. (1999). Lying to get a date: The effect of facial physical attractiveness on the willingness to deceive prospective dating partners. *Journal of Social & Personal Relationships, 16*, 209–223.

Rowe, D. C. (1997). Genetics, temperament, and personality. In R. Hogan, J. Johnson, & S. Briggs (Eds.), *Handbook of personality psychology*. San Diego: Academic Press.

Rozin, P. (1990). The importance of social factors in understanding the acquisition of food habits. In E. D. Capaldi & T. L. Powley (Eds.), *Taste, experience, and feeding*. Washington, DC: American Psychological Association.

Rozin, P. (1996). Towards a psychology of food and eating: From motivation to module to model to marker, morality, meaning, and metaphor. *Current Directions in Psychological Science, 5*, 18–24.

Rozin, P., Dow, S., Moscovitch, M., & Rajaram, S. (1998). What causes humans to begin and end a meal? A role for memory for what has been eaten, as evidenced by a study of multiple meal eating in amnesic patients. *Psychological Science, 9*, 392–396.

Ruble, D. N., & Martin, C. L. (1998). Gender development. In W. Damon (Ed.), *Handbook of child psychology (Vol. 3): Social, emotional, and personality development*. New York: Wiley.

Ruble, T. L. (1983). Sex stereotypes: Issues of change in the 70s. *Sex Roles, 9*, 397–402.

Rubonis, A. V., & Bickman, L. (1991). Psychological impairment in the wake of disaster: The disaster-psychopathology relationship. *Psychological Bulletin, 109*, 384–399.

Rudorfer, M. V., & Goodwin, F. K. (1993). Introduction. In C. E. Coffey (Ed.), *The clinical science of electroconvulsive therapy*. Washington, DC: American Psychiatric Press.

Russell, G. F. M. (1995). Anorexia nervosa through time. In G. Szmukler, C. Dare, & J. Treasure (Eds.), *Handbook of eating disorders: Theory, treatment, and research*. New York: Wiley.

Russell, G. F. M. (1997). The history of bulimia nervosa. In D. M. Garner, & P. E. Garfinkel (Eds.), *Handbook of treatment for eating disorders*. New York: Guilford Press.

Russell, J. A. (1991). Culture and the categorization of emotions. *Psychological Bulletin, 110*, 426–450.

Russo, N. F., & Denmark, F. L. (1987). Contributions of women to psychology. *Annual Review of Psychology, 38*, 279–298.

Rutherford, W. (1886). A new theory of hearing. *Journal of Anatomy and Physiology, 21*, 166–168.

Rutter, M. L. (1997). Nature-nurture integration: The example of antisocial behavior. *American Psychologist, 52*, 390–398.

Rutter, M., & O'Connor, T. G. (1999). Implications of attachment theory for child care policies. In J. Cassidy, & P.R. Shaver (Eds.), *Handbook of attachment: Theory, research and clinical applications*. New York: Guilford Press.

Rutter, M., Silberg, J., & Simonoff, E. (1993). Whither behavioral genetics?—A developmental psychopathological perspective. In R. Plomin & G. E. McClearn (Eds.), *Nature, nurture and psychology*. Washington, DC: American Psychological Association.

Ryan, C. S., Park, B., & Judd, C. M. (1996). Assessing stereotype accuracy: Implications for understanding the stereotyping process. In C. N. Macrae, C. Stangor, & M. Hewstone (Eds.), *Stereotypes and stereotyping*. New York: Guilford Press.

Sachs, J. (1985). Prelinguistic development. In J. B. Gleason (Ed.), *The development of language*. Columbus: Charles E. Merrill.

Sacks, O. (1987). *The man who mistook his wife for a hat*. New York: Harper & Row.

Sadker, M., & Sadker, D. (1994). *Failing at fairness: How America's schools cheat girls*. New York: Scribners.

Salthouse, T. A. (1991). Mediation of adult age differences in cognition by reductions in working memory and speed of processing. *Psychological Science, 2*, 179–183.

Salthouse, T. A. (1994). The nature of the influence of speed on adult age differences in cognition. *Developmental Psychology, 30*, 240–259.

Salthouse, T. A., & Babcock, R. L. (1991). Decomposing adult age differences in working memory. *Developmental Psychology, 27*, 763–776.

Salvendy, J. T. (1993). Selection and preparation of patients and organization of the group. In H. I. Kaplan & B. J. Sadock (Eds.), *Comprehensive group psychotherapy*. Baltimore: Williams & Wilkins.

Samelson, F. (1981). Struggle for scientific authority: The reception of Watson's behaviorism, 1913–1920. *Journal of the History of the Behavioral Sciences, 17*, 399–425.

Samelson, F. (1994). John B. Watson in 1913: Rhetoric and practice. In J. T. Todd, & E. K. Morris (Eds.), *Modern perspectives on John B. Watson and classical behaviorism*. Westport, CT: Greenwood Press.

Samet, J. M. (1992). The health benefits of smoking cessation. *Medical Clinics of North America, 76*, 399–414.

Sanderson, W. C., & Barlow, D. H. (1990). A description of patients diagnosed with DSM-III-R generalized anxiety disorder. *Journal of Nervous and Mental Disease, 178*, 588–591.

Sandler, J. (1975). Aversion methods. In F. H. Kanfer & A. P. Goldstein (Eds.), *Helping people change: A textbook of methods*. New York: Pergamon Press.

Sapolsky, R. M. (1992). Neuroendocrinology and the stress-response. In J. B. Becker, S. M. Breedlove, & D. Crews (Eds.), *Behavioral Endocrinology*. Cambridge, MA: MIT Press.

Sarason, I. G., & Sarason, B. G. (1987). *Abnormal psychology: The problem of maladaptive behavior*. Englewood Cliffs, NJ: Prentice-Hall.

Saxe, G. N., van der Kolk, B. A., Berkowitz, R., Chinman, G., Hall, K., Lieberg, G., & Schwartz, J. (1993). Dissociative disorders in psychiatric inpatients. *American Journal of Psychiatry, 150*, 1037–1042.

Saxe, L. (1994). Detection of deception: Polygraph and integrity tests. *Current Directions in Psychological Science, 3*, 69–73.

Scarr, S. (1997). Behavior-genetic and socialization theories of intelligence: Truce and reconciliation. In R. J. Sternberg, & E. L. Grigorenko (Eds.), *Intelligence, heredity, and environment*. New York: Cambridge University Press.

Scarr, S. (1998). American child care today. *American Psychologist, 53*, 95–108.

Scarr, S., & Weinberg, R. A. (1977). Intellectual similarities within families of both adopted and biological children. *Intelligence, 32*, 170–190.

Scarr, S., & Weinberg, R. A. (1983). The Minnesota adoption studies: Genetic differences and malleability. *Child Development, 54*, 260–267.

Schachter, S. (1959). *The psychology of affiliation*. Stanford, CA: Stanford University Press.

Schachter, S. (1964). The interaction of cognitive and physiological determinants of emotional state. In L. Berkowitz (Ed.), *Advances in experimental social psychology* (Vol. 1). New York: Academic Press.

Schachter, S. (1971). *Emotion, obesity and crime*. New York: Academic Press.

Schachter, S., & Gross, L. (1968). Manipulated time and eating behavior. *Journal of Personality and Social Psychology, 10*, 98–106.

Schachter, S., & Rodin, J. (1974). *Obese humans and rats*. Hillsdale, NJ: Erlbaum.

Schachter, S., & Singer, J. E. (1962). Cognitive, social and physiological determinants of emotional state. *Psychological Review, 69*, 379–399.

Schachter, S., & Singer, J. E. (1979). Comments on the Maslach and Marshall-Zimbardo experiments. *Journal of Personality and Social Psychology, 37*, 989–995.

Schacter, D. L. (1987). Implicit memory: History and current status. *Journal of Experimental Psychology: Learning, Memory and Cognition, 14*, 501–518.

Schacter, D. L. (1989). On the relation between memory and consciousness: Dissociable interactions and conscious experience. In H. L. Roediger, III, & F. I. M. Craik (Eds.), *Varieties of memory and consciousness*. Hillsdale, NJ: Erlbaum.

Schacter, D. L. (1992). Understanding implicit memory: A cognitive neuroscience approach. *American Psychologist, 47*, 559–569.

Schacter, D. L. (1994). Priming and multiple memory systems: Perceptual mechanisms of implicit memory. In D. L. Schacter & E. Tulving (Eds.), *Memory systems*. Cambridge, MA: MIT Press.

Schacter, D. L. (1996). *Searching for memory: The brain, the mind, and the past*. New York: Basic Books.

Schacter, D. L. (1999). The seven sins of memory: Insights from psychology and cognitive neuroscience. *American Psychologist, 54*, 182–203.

Schacter, D. L., Chiu, C. Y. P., & Ochsner, K. N. (1993). Implicit memory: A selective review. *Annual Review of Neuroscience, 16*, 159–182.

Schaie, K. W. (1983). The Seattle longitudinal study: A twenty-one-year exploration of psychometric intelligence in adulthood. In K. W. Schaie (Ed.), *Longitudinal studies of adult psychological development*. New York: Guilford Press.

Schaie, K. W. (1990). Intellectual development in adulthood. In J. E. Birren & K. W. Schaie (Eds.), *Handbook of the psychology of aging* (3rd ed.). San Diego: Academic Press.

Schaie, K. W. (1993). The Seattle longitudinal studies of adult intelligence. *Current Directions, 2,* 171–175.

Schaie, K. W. (1994). The course of adult intellectual development. *American Psychologist, 49,* 304–313.

Schaie, K. W. (1996). *Adult intellectual development: The Seattle longitudinal study.* New York: Cambridge University Press.

Scheidlinger, S. (1993). History of group psychotherapy. In H. I. Kaplan & B. J. Sadock (Eds.), *Comprehensive group psychotherapy.* Baltimore: Williams & Wilkins.

Scheier, M. F., & Carver, C. S. (1985). Optimism, coping and health: Assessment and implications of generalized expectancies. *Health Psychology, 4,* 219–247.

Scherer, K. R. (1997). The role of culture in emotion-antecedent appraisal. *Journal of Personality and Social Psychology, 73,* 902–922.

Scherer, K. R., & Wallbott, H. G. (1994). Evidence for universality and cultural variation of differential emotion response patterning. *Journal of Personality and Social Psychology, 66,* 310–328.

Schiff, M., & Lewontin, R. (1986). *Education and class: The irrelevance of IQ genetic studies.* Oxford: Clarendon Press.

Schiffman, S. S., Graham, B. G., Sattely-Miller, E. A., & Warwick, Z. S. (1998). Orosensory perception of dietary fat. *Current Directions in Psychological Science, 7,* 137–143.

Schildkraut, J. J., Green, A. I., Mooney, J. J. (1985). Affective disorders: Biochemical aspects. In H. I. Kaplan & B. J. Sadock (Eds.), *Comprehensive textbook of psychiatry/IV.* Baltimore: Williams & Wilkins.

Schildkraut, J. J., Hirshfeld, A. J., & Murphy, J. M. (1994). Mind and mood in modern art, II: Depressive disorders, spirituality, and early deaths in the abstract expressionist artists of the New York School. *American Journal of Psychiatry, 151,* 482–488.

Schlaadt, R. G., & Shannon, P. T. (1994). *Drugs: Use, misuse, and abuse* (4th ed.). Englewood Cliffs, NJ: Prentice-Hall.

Schlosberg, H. (1954). Three dimensions of emotion. *Psychological Review, 61,* 81–88.

Schmidt, F. L., & Hunter, J. E. (1998). The validity and utility of selection methods in personnel psychology: Practical and theoretical implications of 85 years of research findings. *Psychological Bulletin, 124,* 262–274.

Schmidt, F. L., Ones, D. S., & Hunter, J. E. (1992). Personnel selection. *Annual Review of Psychology, 43,* 627–670.

Schmidt, N. B., Lerew, D. R., & Jackson, R. J. (1999). Prospective evaluation of anxiety sensitivity in the pathogenesis of panic: Replication and extension. *Journal of Abnormal Psychology, 108,* 532–537.

Schmitz, J. M., Jarvik, M. E., & Schneider, N. G. (1997). Nicotine. In J. H. Lowinson, P. Ruiz, R. B. Millman, & J. G. Langrod (Eds.), *Substance abuse: A comprehensive textbook.* Baltimore: Williams & Wilkins.

Schneer, J. A., & Reitman, F. (1994). The importance of gender in mid-career: A longitudinal study of MBAs. *Journal of Organizational Behavior Management, 15,* 199–207.

Schonemann, P. H. (1994). Heritability. In R. J. Sternberg (Ed.), *Encyclopedia of human intelligence.* New York: Macmillan.

Schooler, J. W. (1999). Seeking the core: The issues and evidence surrounding recovered accounts of sexual trauma. In L. M. Williams, & V. L. Banyard (Eds.), *Trauma & memory.* Thousand Oaks, CA: Sage Publications.

Schooler, J. W., & Fiore, S. M. (1997). Consciousness and the limits of language: You can't always say what you think or think what you say. In J. D. Cohen, & J. W. Schooler (Eds.), *Scientific approaches to consciousness.* Mahwah, NJ: Erlbaum.

Schreiber, F. R. (1973). *Sybil.* New York: Warner.

Schuman, H., & Kalton, G. (1985). Survey methods. In G. Lindzey & E. Aronson (Eds.), *Handbook of social psychology* (3rd ed.). New York: Random House.

Schwartz, B., & Robbins, S. J. (1995). *Psychology of learning and behavior* (4th ed.). New York: Norton.

Schwartz, M. W., Peskind, E., Raskind, M., Nicolson, M., Moore, J., Morawiecki, A., Boyko, E. J., & Porte, D. J. (1996). Cerebrospinal fluid leptin levels: Relationship to plasma levels and to adiposity in humans. *Nature Medicine, 2,* 589–593.

Schwartz, N., & Strack, F. (1999). Reports of subjective well-being: Judgmental processes and their methodological implications. In D. Kahneman, E. Diener, & N. Schwarz (Eds.), *Well-being: The foundations of hedonic psychology.* New York: Russell Sage Foundation.

Schwartz, W. J. (1996). Internal timekeeping. *Science & Medicine, 3,* 44–53.

Schwarz, N. (1999). Self-reports: How the questions shape the answers. *American Psychologist, 54,* 93–105.

Schwarzer, R., & Fuchs, R. (1995). Changing risk behaviors and adopting health behaviors: The role of self-efficacy beliefs. In A. Bandura (Ed.), *Self-efficacy in changing societies.* New York: Cambridge University Press.

Scoville, W. B., & Milner, B. (1957). Loss of recent memory after bilateral hippocampal lesions. *Journal of Neurology, Neurosurgery & Psychiatry, 20,* 11–21.

Scroppo, J. C., Drob, S. L., Weinberger, J. L., & Eagle, P. (1998). Identifying dissociative identity disorder: A self-report and projective study. *Journal of Abnormal Psychology, 107,* 272–284.

Scull, A. (1990). Deinstitutionalization: Cycles of despair. *The Journal of Mind and Behavior, 11*(3/4), 301–312.

Searleman, A. (1996). Personality variables and prospective memory performance. In D. J. Herrmann, C. McEvoy, C. Hertzog, P. Hertel, & M. K. Johnson (Eds.), *Basic and applied memory research: Practical applications* (Vol. 2). Mahwah, NJ: Erlbaum.

Searleman, A., & Herrmann, D. (1994). *Memory from a broader perspective.* New York: McGraw-Hill.

Sears, D. O. (1975). Political socialization. In F. I. Greenstein & N. W. Polsby (Eds.), *Handbook of political science* (Vol. 2). Reading, MA: Addison-Wesley.

Seeley, R. J., Matson, C. A., Chavez, M., Woods, S. C., & Schwartz, M. W. (1996). Behavioral, endocrine and hypothalamic responses to involuntary overfeeding. *American Journal of Physiology, 271,* R819–R823.

Seeman, P., & Tallerico, T. (1999). Rapid release of antipsychotic drugs from dopamine D2 receptors: An explanation for low receptor occupancy and early clinical relapse upon withdrawal of clozapine or quetiapine. *American Journal of Psychiatry, 156,* 876–884.

Segall, M. H., Campbell, D. T., Herskovits, M. J. (1966). *The influence of culture on visual perception.* Indianapolis: Bobbs-Merrill.

Segall, M. H., Dasen, P. R., Berry, J. W., & Poortinga, Y. H. (1990). *Human behavior in global perspective: An introduction to cross-cultural psychology.* New York: Pergamon Press.

Segerstrom, S. C., Taylor, S. E., Kemeny, M. E., & Fahey, J. L. (1998). Optimism is associated with mood, coping and immune change in response to stress. *Journal of Personality and Social Psychology, 74,* 1646–1655.

Segrin, C., & Abramson, L. Y.(1994). Negative reactions to depressive behaviors: A communication theories analysis. *Journal of Abnormal Psychology, 103,* 655–668.

Seibel, M. M., & McCarthy, J. A. (1993). Infertility, pregnancy, and the emotions. In D. Goleman & J. Gurin (Eds.), *Mind/body medicine: How to use your mind for better health.* Yonkers, NY: Consumer Reports Books.

Seidlitz, L., & Diener, E. (1993). Memory for positive versus negative life events: Theories for the differences between happy and unhappy persons. *Journal of Personality and Social Psychology, 64,* 654–664.

Seifer, R., Schiller, M., Sameroff, A. J., Resnick, S., & Riordan, K.(1996). Attachment, maternal sensitivity, and infant temperament during the first year of life. *Developmental Psychology, 32,* 12–25.

Self, D. W. (1997). Neurobiological adaptations to drug use. *Hospital Practice, April,* 5–9.

Seligman, M. E. P. (1971). Phobias and preparedness. *Behavior Therapy, 2,* 307–321.

Seligman, M. E. P. (1974). Depression and learned helplessness. In R. J. Friedman & M. M. Katz (Eds.), *The psychology of depression: Contemporary theory and research.* New York: Wiley.

Seligman, M. E. P. (1990). *Learned optimism.* New York: Pocket Books.

Seligman, M. E. P. (1995). The effectiveness of psychotherapy. *American Psychologist, 50,* 965–974.

Seligman, M. E. P., & Hager, J. L. (1972, August). Biological boundaries of learning (The sauce béarnaise syndrome). *Psychology Today,* 59–61, 84–87.

Seligman, M. E. P., & Levant, R. F. (1998). Managed care policies rely on inadequate science. *Professional Psychology: Research and Practice, 29,* 211–212.

Selye, H. (1936). A syndrome produced by diverse nocuous agents. *Nature, 138,* 32.

Selye, H. (1956). *The stress of life.* New York: McGraw-Hill.

Selye, H. (1973). The evolution of the stress concept. *American Scientist, 61*(6), 672–699.

Selye, H. (1974). *Stress without distress*. New York: Lippincott.

Selye, H. (1982). History and present status of the stress concept. In L. Goldberger & S. Breznitz (Eds.), *Handbook of stress: Theoretical and clinical aspects*. New York: Free Press.

Servan-Schreiber, D., Kolb, R., & Tabas, G. (1999). The somatizing patient. *Primary Care, 26*, 225–242.

Shaffer, D. R. (1985). *Developmental psychology: Theory, research, and applications*. Pacific Grove, CA: Brooks/Cole.

Shapiro, D. H., Jr. (1984). Overview: Clinical and physiological comparison of meditation with other self-control strategies. In D. H. Shapiro, Jr., & R. N. Walsh (Eds.), *Meditation: Classic and contemporary perspectives*. New York: Aldine.

Shapiro, D. H., Jr. (1987). Implications of psychotherapy research for the study of meditation. In M. A. West (Ed.), *The psychology of meditation*. Oxford: Clarendon Press.

Shapley, R. (1995). Parallel neural pathways and visual function. In M. S. Gazzaniga (Ed.), *The cognitive neurosciences*. Cambridge, MA: MIT Press.

Sharpe, D., Adair, J. G., & Roese, N. J. (1992). Twenty years of deception research: A decline in subjects' trust? *Personality and Social Psychology Bulletin, 18*, 585–590.

Shatz, C. J. (1992, September). The developing brain. *Scientific American*, 60–67.

Shaver, P. R., & Hazan, C. (1994). Attachment. In A. L. Weber & J. H. Harvey (Eds.), *Perspectives on close relationships*. Boston: Allyn & Bacon.

Shavitt, S., Sanbonmatsu, D. M., Smittipatana, S., & Posavac, S. S. (1999). Broadening the conditions for illusory correlation formation: Implications for judging minority groups. *Basic & Applied Social Psychology, 21*, 263–279.

Shear, M. K., & Beidel, D. C. (1998). Psychotherapy in the overall management strategy for social anxiety disorder. *Journal of Clinical Psychiatry, 59*, 39–46.

Shedler, J., Mayman, M., & Manis, M. (1993). The illusion of mental health. *American Psychologist, 48*, 1117–1131.

Sheehan, S. (1982). *Is there no place on earth for me?* Boston: Houghton Mifflin.

Shepard, R. N. (1990). *Mind sights*. New York: W. H. Freeman.

Sherman, C. B. (1992). The health consequences of cigarette smoking: Pulmonary diseases. *Medical Clinics of North America, 76*, 355–375.

Sherman, M., & Key, C. B. (1932). The intelligence of isolated mountain children. *Child Development, 3*, 279–290.

Sherman, P. W. (1981). Kinship, demography, and Belding's ground squirrel nepotism. *Behavioral Ecology and Sociobiology, 8*, 251–259.

Shermer, M. (1997). *Why people believe weird things: Pseudoscience, superstition, and other confusions of our time*. New York: W. H. Freeman.

Sherry, D. F. (1992). Evolution and learning. In L. R. Squire (Ed.), *Encyclopedia of learning and memory*. New York: Macmillan.

Shettleworth, S. J. (1998). *Cognition, evolution, and behavior*. New York: Oxford University Press.

Shiffrin, R. M. (1988). Attention. In R. C. Atkinson, R. J. Herrnstein, G. Lindzey, & R. D. Luce (Eds.), *Stevens' handbook of experimental psychology* (Vol. 2). New York: Wiley.

Shimamaura, A. P. (1995). Memory and the prefrontal cortex. In J. Grafman, K. J. Holyoak, & F. Boller (Eds), *Structure and functions of the human prefrontal cortex*. New York: New York Academy of Sciences.

Shimamura, A. P. (1996). Unraveling the mystery of the frontal lobes: Explorations in cognitive neuroscience. *Psychological Science Agenda*, September-October, 8–9.

Shimamura, A. P., Berry, J. M., Mangels, J. A., Rusting, C. L., & Jurica, P. J. (1995). Memory and cognitive abilities in university professors: Evidence for successful aging. *Psychological Science, 6*, 271–277.

Shweder, R. A., & Sullivan, M. A. (1993). Cultural psychology: Who needs it? *Annual Review of Psychology, 44*, 497–523.

Shweder, R. A., Mahapatra, M., & Miller, J. G. (1990). Culture and moral development. In J. W. Stigler, R. A. Shweder, & G. Herdt (Eds.), *Cultural psychology*. New York: Cambridge University Press.

Sicard, G., & Holley, A. (1984). Receptor cell responses to odorants: Similarities and differences among odorants. *Brain Research, 292*, 283–296.

Siebert, A. (1995). *Student success: How to succeed in college and still have time for your friends*. Fort Worth: Harcourt Brace Jovanovich.

Siegel, J. M., Johnson, J. H., & Sarason, I. G. (1979). Life changes and menstrual discomfort. *Journal of Human Stress, 5*, 41–46.

Siegler, R. S. (1992). The other Alfred Binet. *Developmental Psychology, 28*, 179–190.

Siegler, R. S. (1994). Cognitive variability: A key to understanding cognitive development. *Current Directions in Psychological Science, 3*(1), 1–5.

Siegler, R. S. (1998). *Children's thinking*. Upper Saddle River, NJ: Prentice-Hall.

Siegler, R. S., & Ellis, S. (1996). Piaget on childhood. *Psychological Science, 7*, 211–215.

Sigman, M., & Whaley, S. E. (1998). The role of nutrition in the development of intelligence. In U. Neisser (Ed.), *The rising curve: Long-term gains in IQ and related measures*. Washington, DC: American Psychological Association.

Signorielli, N. (1993). Television, the portrayal of women, and children's attitudes. In G. Berry, & J. K. Asamen (Eds.), *Children and television: Images in a changing sociocultural world*. Newbury Park, CA: Sage.

Signorielli, N., & Bacue, A. (1999). Recognition and respect: A content analysis of prime-time television characters across three decades. *Sex Roles, 40*, 527–544.

Signorielli, N., McLeod, D., & Healy, E. (1994). Gender stereotypes in MTV commercials: The beat goes on. *Journal of Broadcasting & Electronic Media, 38*, 91–101.

Siiter, R. J. (1999). *Introduction to animal behavior*. Pacific Grove: Brooks/Cole.

Silberman, E. K. (1998). Psychiatrists' and internists' beliefs. *Primary Psychiatry, 5*, 65–71.

Silver, E., Cirincion, C., & Steadman, H. J. (1994). Demythologizing inaccurate perceptions of the insanity defense. *Law & Human Behavior, 18*, 63–70.

Silverberg, S. B., Tennenbaum, D. L., & Jacob, T. (1992). Adolescence and family interaction. In V. B. Van Hasselt & M. Hersen (Eds.), *Handbook of social development: A lifespan perspective*. New York: Plenum.

Silverman, I., & Eals, M. (1992). Sex differences in spatial ability: Evolutionary theory and data. In J. Barkow, L. Cosmides, & J. Tooby (Eds.), *The adapted mind*. New York: Oxford University Press.

Silverman, I., & Phillips, K. (1998). The evolutionary psychology of spatial sex differences. In C. Crawford, & D. L. Krebs (Eds.), *Handbook of evolutionary psychology: Ideas, issues, and applications*. Mahwah, NJ: Erlbaum.

Silverstein, L. B., & Auerbach, C. F. (1999). Deconstructing the essential father. *American Psychologist, 54*, 397–407.

Simon, E. J. (1992). Opiates: Neurobiology. In J. H. Lowinson, P. Ruiz, & R. B. Millman (Eds.), *Substance abuse: A comprehensive textbook* (2nd ed.). Baltimore: Williams & Wilkins.

Simon, G. E., & VonKorff, M. (1991). Somatization and psychiatric disorder in the NIMH epidemiologic catchment area study. *American Journal of Psychiatry, 148*, 1494–1500.

Simon, G. E., & VonKorff, M. (1997). Prevalence, burden, and treatment of insomnia in primary care. *American Journal Psychiatry, 154*, 1417–1423.

Simon, H. A. (1957). *Models of man*. New York: Wiley.

Simon, H. A. (1974). How big is a chunk? *Science, 183*, 482–488.

Simon, H. A. (1992). Alternative representations for cognition: Search and reasoning. In H. L. Pick, Jr., P. Van Den Broek, & D. C. Knill (Eds.), *Cognition: Conceptual and methodological issues*. Washington, DC: American Psychological Association.

Simon, R. I. (1999). The law and psychiatry. In R. E. Hales, S. C. Yudofsky, & J. A. Talbott (Eds.), *American Psychiatric Press Textbook of Psychiatry*. Washington, DC: American Psychiatric Press.

Simons, R. C., & Hughes, C. C. (1993). Culture-bound syndromes. In A. C. Gaw (Ed.), *Culture, ethnicity, and mental illness*. Washington, DC: American Psychiatric Press.

Simonton, D. K. (1990). Creativity and wisdom in aging. In J. E. Birren & K. W. Schaie (Eds.), *Handbook of the psychology of aging*. San Diego: Academic Press.

Simpson, J. A. (1990). Influence of attachment styles on romantic relationships. *Journal of Personality and Social Psychology, 59*, 971–980.

Simpson, J. A. (1999). Attachment theory in modern evolutionary perspective. In J. Cassidy & P. R. Shaver (Eds.), *Handbook of attachment: Theory, research, and clinical applications*. New York: Guilford Press.

Simpson, J. A., Rholes, W. S., & Phillips, D. (1996). Conflict in close relationships: An attachment perspective. *Journal of Personality and Social Psychology, 71*, 899–914.

Simpson, J. L. (1991). Fetal wastage. In S. G. Gabbe, J. R. Niebyl, & J. L. Simpson (Eds.), *Obstetrics: Normal and problem pregnancies*. New York: Churchill Livingstone.

Sinclair, D. (1981). *Mechanisms of cutaneous stimulation*. Oxford, England: Oxford University Press.

Singer, M. T., & Lalich, J. (1996). *Crazy therapies: What are they? Do they work?* San Francisco: Jossey-Bass.

Singh, D. (1993). Adaptive significance of female physical attractiveness: Role of waist-to-hip ratio. *Journal of Personality and Social Psychology, 65*, 293–307.

Sinha, D. (1983). Human assessment in the Indian context. In S. H. Irvine & J. W. Berry (Eds.), *Human assessment and cultural factors*. New York: Plenum.

Skinner, B. F. (1938). *The behavior of organisms*. New York: Appleton-Century-Crofts.

Skinner, B. F. (1953). *Science and human behavior*. New York: Macmillan.

Skinner, B. F. (1957). *Verbal behavior*. New York: Appleton-Century-Crofts.

Skinner, B. F. (1969). *Contingencies of reinforcement*. New York: Appleton-Century-Crofts.

Skinner, B. F. (1971). *Beyond freedom and dignity*. New York: Knopf.

Skinner, B. F. (1984). Selection by consequences. *Behavioral and Brain Sciences, 7*(4), 477–510.

Skinner, B. F., Solomon, H. C., & Lindsley, O. R. (1953). *Studies in behavior therapy: Status report I*. Waltham, MA: Unpublished report, Metropolitan State Hospital.

Slamecka, N. J. (1985). Ebbinghaus: Some associations. *Journal of Experimental Psychology: Learning, Memory and Cognition, 11*, 414–435.

Slamecka, N. J. (1992). Forgetting. In L. R. Squire (Ed.), *Encyclopedia of learning and memory*. New York: Macmillan.

Slater, E., & Shields, J. (1969). Genetical aspects of anxiety. In M. H. Lader (Ed.), *Studies of anxiety*. Ashford, England: Headley Brothers.

Slaughter, M. (1990). The vertebrate retina. In K. N. Leibovic (Ed.), *Science of vision*. New York: Springer-Verlag.

Slavney, P. R. (1990). *Perspectives on hysteria*. Baltimore: Johns Hopkins University Press.

Slobin, D. I. (1985). *A cross-linguistic study of language acquisition*. Hillsdale, NJ: Erlbaum.

Slobin, D. I. (1992). *The cross-linguistic study of language acquisition*. Hillsdale, NJ: Erlbaum.

Slovic, P. (1990). Choice. In D. N. Osherson & E. E. Smith (Eds.), *Thinking: An invitation to cognitive science* (Vol. 3). Cambridge, MA: MIT Press.

Slovic, P., & Fischhoff, B. (1977). On the psychology of experimental surprises. *Journal of Experimental Psychology: Human Perception and Performance, 3*, 544–551.

Slovic, P., Fischhoff, B., & Lichtenstein, S. (1982). Facts versus fears: Understanding perceived risk. In D. Kahneman, P. Slovic, & A. Tversky (Eds.), *Judgment under uncertainty: Heuristics and biases*. Cambridge, England: Cambridge University Press.

Slovic, P., Lichtenstein, S., & Fischhoff, B. (1988). Decision making. In R. C. Atkinson, R. J. Herrnstein, G. Lindzey, & R. D. Luce (Eds.), *Stevens' handbook of experimental psychology* (Vol. 2). New York: Wiley.

Smail, B. (1983). Spatial visualization skills and technical crafts education. *Educational Research, 25*, 230–231.

Smedley, S. R., & Eisner, T. (1996). Sodium: A male moth's gift to its offspring. *Proceedings of the National Academy of Sciences, 93*, 809–813.

Smilkstein, G. (1990). Psychosocial influences on health. In R. E. Rakel (Ed.), *Textbook of family practice*. Philadelphia: Saunders.

Smith, C. A., & Lazarus, R. S. (1993). Appraisal components, core relational themes, and the emotions. *Cognition and Emotion, 7*, 233–269.

Smith, C. P. (1992). Reliability issues. In C. P. Smith (Ed.), *Motivation and personality: Handbook of thematic content analysis*. New York: Cambridge University Press.

Smith, D. A. (1999). The end of theoretical orientations? *Applied & Preventative Psychology, 8*, 269–280.

Smith, F. J., & Campfield, L. A. (1993). Meal initiation occurs after experimental induction of transient declines in blood glucose. *American Journal of Physiology, 265*, 1423–1429.

Smith, G. L., Large, M. M., Kavanagh, D. J., Karayanidis, F., Barrett, N. A., Michie, P. T., & O'Sullivan, B. T. (1998). Further evidence for a deficit in switching attention in schizophrenia. *Journal of Abnormal Psychology, 197*, 390–398.

Smith, G. N., Flynn, S. W., Kopala, L. C., Bassett, A. S., Lapointe, J. S., Falkai, P., & Honer, W. G. (1997). A comprehensive method of assessing routine CT scans in schizophrenia. *Acta Psychiatrica Scandinavica, 96*, 395–401.

Smith, G. S., Dewey, S. L., Brodie, J. D., Logan, J., Vitkun, S. A., Simkowitz, P., Schloesser, R., Alexoff, D. A., Hurley, A., Cooper, T., & Volkow, N. D. (1997). Serotonergic modulation of dopamine measured with [11C] raclopride and PET in normal human subjects. *American Journal of Psychiatry, 154*, 490–496.

Smith, J. C. (1975). Meditation and psychotherapy: A review of the literature. *Psychological Bulletin, 32*, 553–564.

Smith, J. W., Frawley, P. J., & Polissar, N. L. (1997). Six- and twelve-month abstinence rates in inpatient alcoholics treated with either faradic aversion or chemical aversion compared with matched inpatients from a treatment registry. *Journal of Addictive Diseases, 16* , 5–24.

Smith, M. L., & Glass, G. V. (1977). Meta-analysis of psychotherapy outcome studies. *American Psychologist, 32*, 752–760.

Smith, M., & Pazder, L. (1980). *Michelle remembers*. New York: Pocket Books.

Smith, P. B., & Bond, M. H. (1994). *Social psychology across cultures: Analysis and perspectives*. Boston: Allyn & Bacon.

Smith, S. (1988). Environmental context-dependent memory. In G. M. Davies & D. M. Thomson (Eds.), *Memory in context: Context in memory*. New York: Wiley.

Smith, S. M., McIntosh, W. D., & Bazzini, D. G. (1999). Are the beautiful good in Hollywood? An investigation of the beauty-and-goodness stereotype on film. *Basic & Applied Social Psychology, 21*, 69–80.

Smith, T. W., & Brown, P. C. (1991). Cynical hostility, attempts to exert social control, and cardiovascular reactivity in married couples. *Journal of Behavioral Medicine, 14*(6), 581–592.

Smith, T. W., & Christensen, A. J. (1992). Hostility, health, and social contexts. In H. S. Friedman (Ed.), *Hostility coping and health*. Washington, DC: American Psychological Association.

Smith, T. W., Pope, M. K., Sanders, J. D., Allred, K. D., & O'Keefe, J. L. (1988). Cynical hostility at home and work: Psychosocial vulnerability across domains. *Journal of Research in Personality, 22*, 525–548.

Smolensky, P. (1995). On the proper treatment of connectionism. In C. Madonald, & G. Macdonald (Eds.), *Connectionism: Debates on psychological explanation*. Cambridge, USA: Blackwell.

Smyth, J. M., & Pennebaker, J. W. (1999). Sharing one's story: Translating emotional experiences into words as a coping tool. In C. R. Snyder (Ed.), *Coping: The psychology of what works*. New York: Oxford University Press.

Snow, C. E. (1993). Bilingualism and second language acquisition. In J. B. Gleason & N. B. Ratner (Eds.), *Psycholinguistics*. Fort Worth: Harcourt Brace Jovanovich.

Snow, R. E. (1986). Individual differences in the design of educational programs. *American Psychologist, 41*, 1029–1039.

Snowden, L. R., & Hu, T. W. (1996). Outpatient service use in minority-serving mental health programs. *Administration and Policy in Mental Health, 24*, 149–159.

Snyder, S. H. (1996). *Drugs and the brain*. New York: Scientific American Library.

Snyderman, M., & Rothman, S. (1987). Survey of expert opinion on intelligence and aptitude testing. *American Psychologist, 42*, 137–144.

Sobal, J. (1995). Social influences on body weight. In K. D. Brownell, & C. G. Fairburn (Eds.), *Eating disorders and obesity: A comprehensive handbook*. New York: Guilford Press.

Sobin, C., Sackeim, H. A., Prudic, J., Devanand, D. P., Moody, B. J., & McElhiney, M. C. (1995). Predictors of retrograde amnesia following ECT. *American Journal of Psychiatry, 152*, 995–1001.

Solomon, D. A., Keller, M. B., Leon, A. C., Mueller, T. I., Shea, M. T., Warshaw, M., Maser, J. D., Coryell, W., & Endicott, J. (1997). Recovery from major depression: A 10-year prospective follow-up across multiple episodes. *Archives of General Psychiatry, 54*, 1001–1006.

Solso, R. L. (1994). *Cognition and the visual arts*. Cambridge, MA: MIT Press.

Sotiriou, P. E. (1996). *Integrating college study skills: Reasoning in reading, listening, and writing*. Belmont, CA: Wadsworth.

Spangler, W. D. (1992). Validity of questionnaire and TAT measures of need for achievement: Two meta-analyses. *Psychological Bulletin, 112*, 140–154.

Spanos, N. P. (1986). Hypnotic behavior: A social-psychological interpretation of amnesia, analgesia, and "trance logic." *Behavioral & Brain Sciences, 9*(3), 449–467.

Spanos, N. P. (1994). Multiple identity enactments and multiple personality disorder: A sociocognitive perspective. *Psychological Bulletin, 116*, 143–165.

Spanos, N. P. (1996). *Multiple identities and false memories*. Washington, DC: American Psychological Association.

Spanos, N. P., & Coe, W. C. (1992). A social-psychological approach to hypnosis. In E. Fromm & M. R. Nash (Eds.), *Contemporary hypnosis research*. New York: Guilford Press.

Speed, A., & Gangestad, S. W. (1997). Romantic popularity and mate preferences: A peer-nomination study. *Personality and Social Psychology Bulletin, 23*, 928–936.

Spelke, E. S. (1994). Initial knowledge: Six suggestions. *Cognition, 50*, 431–455.

Spelke, E. S., & Newport, E. L. (1998). Nativism, empiricism, and the development of knowledge. In W. Damon (Ed.), *Handbook of child psychology (Vol. 1): Theoretical models of human development*. New York: Wiley.

Sperling, G. (1960). The information available in brief visual presentations. *Psychological Monographs, 74*(11, Whole No. 498).

Sperry, R. W. (1982). Some effects of disconnecting the cerebral hemispheres. *Science, 217*, 1223–1226, 1250.

Spiegel, D., Cutcomb, S., Ren, C., & Pribram, K. (1985). Hypnotic hallucination alters evoked potentials. *Journal of Abnormal Psychology, 94*, 249–255.

Spiegel, D., & Maldonado, J. R. (1999). Dissociative disorders. In R. E. Hales, S. C. Yudofsky, & J. A. Talbott (Eds.), *American Psychiatric Press Textbook of Psychiatry*. Washington, DC: American Psychiatric Press.

Spiegel, D., & Spiegel, H. (1985). Hypnosis. In H. I. Kaplan & B. J. Sadock (Eds.), *Comprehensive textbook of psychiatry/IV*. Baltimore: Williams & Wilkins.

Spiegler, M. D., & Guevremont, D. C. (1998). *Contemporary behavior therapy*. Pacific Grove, CA: Brooks/Cole.

Spielberger, C. D., & Sydeman, S. J. (1994). Anxiety. In R. J. Sternberg (Ed.), *Encyclopedia of human intelligence*. New York: Macmillan.

Spitzer, R. L. (1999). Harmful dysfunction and the DSM definition of mental disorder. *Journal of Abnormal Psychology, 108*, 430–432.

Spitzer, R. L., Terman, M., Williams, J. B. W., Terman, J. S., Malt, U. F., Singer, F., & Lewy, A. J. (1999). Jet lag: Clinical features, validation of a new syndrome-specific scale, and lack of response to melatonin in a randomized, double-blind trial. *American Journal Psychiatry, 156*, 1392–1396.

Spoont, M. R. (1992). Modulatory role of serotonin in neural information processing: Implications for human psychopathology. *Psychological Bulletin, 112*, 330–350.

Sprecher, S. (1998). Insiders' perspectives on reasons for attraction to a close other. *Social Psychology Quarterly, 61*, 287–300.

Sprecher, S. (1999). "I love you more today than yesterday": Romantic partners' perceptions of changes in love and related affect over time. *Journal of Personality and Social Psychology, 76*, 46–53.

Sprecher, S., & Duck, S. (1994). Sweet talk: The importance of perceived communication for romantic and friendship attraction experienced during a get-acquainted date. *Personality and Social Psychology Bulletin, 20*, 391–400.

Sprecher, S., Sullivan, Q., & Hatfield, E. (1994). Mate selection preferences: Gender differences examined in a national sample. *Journal of Personality and Social Psychology, 66*, 1074–1080.

Springer, K., & Berry, D. S. (1997). Rethinking the role of evolution in the ecological model of social perception. In J. A. Simpson & D. T. Kenrick (Eds.), *Evolutionary psychology*. Mahwah, NJ: Erlbaum.

Springer, S. P., & Deutsch, G. (1998). *Left brain, right brain*. New York: W. H. Freeman.

Squire, L. R. (1994). Declarative and nondeclarative memory: Multiple brain systems supporting learning and memory. In D. L. Schacter & E. Tulving (Eds.), *Memory systems*. Cambridge, MA: MIT Press.

Squire, L. R., Knowlton, B., & Musen, G. (1993). The structure and organization of memory. *Annual Review of Psychology, 44*, 453–495.

Sriram, T. G., & Silverman, J. J. (1998). The effects of stress on the respiratory system. In J. R. Hubbard & E. A. Workman (Eds.), *Handbook of stress medicine: An organ system approach*. New York: CRC Press.

Staats, A. W., & Staats, C. K. (1963). *Complex human behavior*. New York: Holt, Rinehart & Winston.

Stajkovic, A. D., & Luthans, F. (1998). Self-efficacy and work-related performance: A meta-analysis. *Psychological Bulletin, 124*, 240–261.

Stampi, C. (1989). Ultrashort sleep/wake patterns and sustained performance. In D. F. Dinges & R. J. Broughton (Eds.), *Sleep and alertness: Chronobiological, behavioral, and medical aspects of napping*. New York: Raven.

Stanley, B. G., & Gillard, E. R. (1994). Hypothalamic neuropeptide Y and the regulation of eating behavior and body weight. *Current Directions in Psychological Science, 3*, 9–15.

Stattin, H., & Magnusson, D. (1990). *Pubertal maturation in female development*. Hillsdale, NJ: Erlbaum.

Steele, K. M., Bass, K. E., & Crook, M. D. (1999). The mystery of the Mozart Effect: Failure to replicate. *Psychological Science, 10*, 366–369.

Stein, B. E., & Meredith, M. A. (1993). *Vision, touch, and audition: Making sense of it all*. Cambridge, MA: MIT Press.

Stein, P. J. (1989). The diverse world of single adults. In J. M. Henslin (Ed.), *Marriage and family in a changing society* (3rd ed.). New York: Free Press.

Steinberg, L., & Levine, A. (1997). *You and your adolescent: A parents' guide for ages 10 to 20*. New York: Harper Perennial.

Steinberg, L., & Silverberg, S. B. (1987). Influences on marital satisfaction during the middle stages of the family life cycle. *Journal of Marriage and the Family, 49*, 751–760.

Steinmetz, H., Staiger, J. F., Schluag, G., Huang, Y., & Jancke, L. (1995). Corpus callosum and brain volume in women and men. *Neuroreport, 6*, 1002–1004.

Steinmetz, J. E. (1998). The localization of a simple type of learning and memory: The cerebellum and classical eyeblink conditioning. *Current Directions in Psychological Science, 7*, 72–77.

Stekel, W. (1950). *Techniques of analytical psychotherapy*. New York: Liveright.

Stellar, E. (1954). The physiology of motivation. *Psychological Review, 61*, 5–22.

Stemberger, R. T., Turner, S. M., Beidel, D. C., & Calhoun, K. S. (1995). Social phobia: An analysis of possible developmental factors. *Journal of Abnormal Psychology, 104*, 526–531.

Stephens, R. S. (1999). Cannabis and hallucinogens. In B. S. McCrady & E. E. Epstein (Eds.), *Addictions: A comprehensive guidebook*. New York: Oxford University Press.

Stephens, T. W., Basinski, M., Bristow, P. K., Bue-Valleskey, J. M., Burgett, S. G., Craft, L., Hale, J., Hoffman, J., Hsiung, H. M., Kriauciunas, A., MacKellar, W., Rosteck, P. R. Jr., Schoner, B., Smith, D., Tinsley, F. C., Zhang, W. Y., & Heiman, M. (1995). The role of neuropeptide Y in the antiobesity action of the obese gene product. *Nature, 377*, 530–532.

Sternberg, R. J. (1985). *Beyond IQ: A triarchic theory of human intelligence*. New York: Cambridge University Press.

Sternberg, R. J. (1986). *Intelligence applied: Understanding and increasing your intellectual skills*. New York: Harcourt Brace Jovanovich.

Sternberg, R. J. (1988a). A three-facet model of creativity. In R. J. Sternberg (Ed.), *The nature of creativity: Contemporary psychological perspectives*. Cambridge, England: Cambridge University Press.

Sternberg, R. J. (1988b). *The triarchic mind: A new theory of human intelligence*. New York: Viking.

Sternberg, R. J. (1991). Theory-based testing of intellectual abilities: Rationale for the triarchic abilities test. In H. A. H. Rowe (Ed.), *Intelligence: Reconceptualization and measurement*. Hillsdale, NJ: Erlbaum.

Sternberg, R. J. (1997). Educating intelligence: Infusing the triarchic theory into school instruction. In R. J. Sternberg, & E. L. Grigorenko (Eds.), *Intelligence, heredity, and environment*. New York: Cambridge University Press.

Sternberg, R. J. (1998). How intelligent is intelligence testing? *Scientific American Presents Exploring Intelligence, 9*, 12–17.

Sternberg, R. J., & Kaufman, J. C. (1998). Human abilities. *Annual Review of Psychology, 49*, 479–502.

Sternberg, R. J., Conway, B. E., Ketron, J. L., & Bernstein, M. (1981). People's conceptions of intelligence. *Journal of Personality and Social Psychology, 41*, 37–55.

Sternberg, R. J., & Lubart, T. I. (1992). Buy low and sell high: An investment approach to creativity. *Current Directions in Psychological Science, 1*(1), 1–5.

Sternberg, R. J., & O'Hara, L. A. (1999). Creativity and intelligence. In R. J. Sternberg (Ed.), *Handbook of creativity*. New York: Cambridge University Press.

Sternberg, R. J., & Wagner, R. K. (1993). The g-ocentric view of intelligence and job performance is wrong. *Current Directions in Psychological Science, 2*(1), 1–5.

Sternberg, R. J., Wagner, R. K., Williams, W. M., & Horvath, J. A. (1995). Testing common sense. *American Psychologist, 50*, 912–927.

Stevens, A., & Price, J. (1996). *Evolutionary psychiatry: A new beginning*. New York: Routledge.

Stevens, S. S. (1955). The measurement of loudness. *Journal of the Acoustical Society of America, 27*, 815–819.

Stewart, A. J., & Ostrove, J. M. (1998). Women's personality in middle age: Gender, history, and midcourse corrections. *American Psychologist, 53*, 1185–1194.

Stich, S. P. (1990). Rationality. In D. N. Osherson & E. E. Smith (Eds.), *Thinking: An invitation to cognitive science* (Vol. 3). Cambridge, MA: MIT Press.

Stine, S. M., & Kosten, T. R. (1999). Opioids. In B. S. McCrady, & E. E. Epstein (Eds.), *Addictions: A comprehensive guidebook*. New York: Oxford University Press.

Stoddard, G. (1943). *The meaning of intelligence*. New York: Macmillan.

Stoll, A. L., Tohen, M., & Baldessarini, R. J. (1992). Increasing frequency of the diagnosis of obsessive-compulsive disorder. *American Journal of Psychiatry, 149*, 638–640.

Stone, A. A. (1999). Psychiatry and the law. In A. M. Nicholi (Ed.), *The Harvard guide to psychiatry*. Cambridge, MA: Harvard University Press.

Stone, A. A., Bovbjerg, D. H., Neale, J. M., Napoli, A., Valdimarsdottir, H., Cox, D., Hayden, F. G., & Gwaltney, J. M. (1992). Development of the common cold symptoms following experimental rhinovirus infection is related to prior stressful events. *Behavioral Medicine, 18*, 115–120.

Stone, L. (1977). *The family, sex and marriage in England 1500–1800*. New York: Harper & Row.

Stoner, J. A. F. (1961). *A comparison of individual and group decisions involving risk*. Unpublished master's thesis, Massachusetts Institute of Technology.

Stoohs, R. A., Blum, H. C., Haselhorst, M., Duchna, H. W., Guilleminault, C., & Dement, W. C. (1998). Normative data on snoring: A comparison between younger and older adults. *European Respiratory Journal, 11*, 451–457.

Stoolmiller, M. (1999). Implications of the restricted range of family environments for estimates of heritability and nonshared environment in behavior-genetic adoption studies. *Psychological Bulletin, 125*, 392–409.

Streissguth, A. P., Barr, H. M., Bookstein, F. L., Sampson, P. D., & Olson, H. C. (1999). The long-term neurocognitive consequences of prenatal alcohol exposure: A 14-year study. *Psychological Science, 10*, 186–190.

Streissguth, A. P., Barr, H. M., Sampson, P. D., Darby, B. L., & Martin, D. C. (1989). IQ at age 4 in relation to maternal alcohol use and smoking during pregnancy. *Developmental Psychology, 25*, 3–11.

Striegel-Moore, R. H. (1995). A feminist perspective on the etiology of eating disorders. In K. D. Brownell & C. G. Fairburn (Eds), *Eating disorders and obesity: A comprehensive handbook*. New York: Guilford Press.

Striegel-Moore, R., & Rodin, J. (1986). The influence of psychological variables in obesity. In K. D. Brownell & J. P. Foreyt (Eds.), *Handbook of eating disorders: Physiology, psychology, and treatment of obesity, anorexia and bulimia*. New York: Basic Books.

Striegel-Moore, R. H., Silberstein, L. R., & Rodin, J. (1993). The social self in bulimia nervosa: Public self-consciousness, social anxiety, and perceived fraudulence. *Journal of Abnormal Psychology, 102*.

Strober, M. (1995). Family-genetic perspectives on anorexia nervosa and bulimia nervosa. In K. D. Brownell & C. G. Fairburn (Eds.), *Eating disorders and obesity: A comprehensive handbook*. New York: Guilford Press.

Strupp, H. H. (1996). The tripartite model and the *Consumer Reports* study. *American Psychologist, 51*, 1017–1024.

Stuart, E. W., Shimp, T. A., & Engle, R. W. (1987). Classical conditioning of consumer attitudes: Four experiments in an advertising context. *Journal of Consumer Research, 14*, 334–349.

Stumpf, H., & Stanley, J. C. (1996). Gender-related differences on the College Board's Advanced Placement and Achievement Tests, 1982–1992. *Journal of Educational Psychology, 88*, 353–364.

Sturgis, E. T. (1993). Obsessive-comulsive disorders. In P. B. Sutker & H. E. Adams (Eds.), *Comprehensive handbook of psychopathology* (2nd ed.). New York: Plenum.

Subrahmanyam, K., & Greenfield, P. M. (1996). Effect of video game practice on spatial skills in girls and boys. In P. M. Greenfield & R. R. Cocking (Eds.), *Interacting with video*. Norwood, NJ: Ablex Publishing Corp.

Sue, S., & Okazaki, S. (1990). Asian-American educational achievements: A phenomenon in search of an explanation. *American Psychologist, 45*, 913–920.

Sue, S., & Zane, N. (1987). The role of culture and cultural techniques in psychotherapy: A critique and reformulation. *American Psychologist, 42*, 37–45.

Sue, S., Zane, N., & Young, K. (1994). Research on psychotherapy with culturally diverse populations. In A. E. Bergin & S. L. Garfield (Eds.), *Handbook of psychotherapy and behavior change* (4th ed.). New York: Wiley.

Super, C. M. (1976). Environmental effects on motor development: A case of African infant precocity. *Developmental Medicine and Child Neurology, 18*, 561–567.

Susser, E., Neugebauer, R., Hoek, H. W., Brown, A. S., Lin, S., Labovitz, D., & Gorman, J. M. (1996). Schizophrenia after prenatal famine: Further evidence. *Archives of General Psychiatry, 53*, 25–31.

Suzuki, L. A., & Gutkin, T. B. (1994). Asian Americans. In R. J. Sternberg (Ed.), *Encyclopedia of human intelligence*. New York: Macmillan.

Suzuki, L. A., & Vraniak, D. A. (1994). Ethnicity, race, and measured intelligence. In R. J. Sternberg (Ed.), *Encyclopedia of human intelligence*. New York: Macmillan.

Swartz, C. M. (1993). Clinical and laboratory predictors of ECT response. In C. E. Coffey (Ed.), *The clinical science of electroconvulsive therapy*. Washington, DC: American Psychiatric Press.

Swim, J. K. (1994). Perceived versus meta-analytic effect sizes: An assessment of the accuracy of gender stereotypes. *Journal of Personality and Social Psychology, 66*, 21–36.

Swim, J. K., & Sanna, L. J. (1996). He's skilled, she's lucky: A meta-analysis of observers' attributions for women's and men's successes and failures. *Personality and Social Psychology Bulletin, 22*, 507–519.

Symons, D. (1979). *The evolution of human sexuality*. New York: Oxford University Press.

Szasz, T. (1974). *The myth of mental illness*. New York: Harper & Row.

Szasz, T. (1990). Law and psychiatry: The problems that will not go away. *The Journal of Mind and Behavior, 11*(3/4), 557–564.

Szmukler, G. I., & Patton, G. (1995). Sociocultural models of eating disorders. In G. Szmukler, C. Dare, & J. Treasure (Eds.), *Handbook of eating disorders: Theory, treatment, and research*. New York: Wiley.

Takahashi, K. (1990). Are the key assumptions of the "Strange Situation" procedure universal? *Human Development, 33*, 23–30.

Tanner, J. M. (1978). *Fetus into man: Physical growth from conception to maturity*. Cambridge, MA: Harvard University Press.

Tart, C. T. (1988). From spontaneous event to lucidity: A review of attempts to consciously control nocturnal dreaming. In J. Gackenbach & S. LaBerge (Eds.), *Conscious mind, sleeping brain: Perspectives on lucid dreaming*. New York: Plenum.

Taub, S. (1996). The legal treatment of recovered memories of child sexual abuse. *Journal of Legal Medicine, 17*, 183–214.

Tavris, C. (1992). *The mismeasure of woman*. New York: Simon & Schuster.

Tavris, C. (1998, September 13). Peer pressure (Review of *The Nurture Assumption*). *The New York Times Book Review, 103*, p. 14.

Taylor, C. B. (1995). Treatment of anxiety disorders. In A. F. Schatzberg & C. B. Nemeroff (Eds.), *The American Psychiatric Press textbook of psychopharmacology*. Washington, DC: American Psychiatric Press.

Taylor, E. (1999). An intellectual renaissance of humanistic psychology. *Journal of Humanistic Psychology, 39*, 7–25.

Taylor, I., & Taylor, M. M. (1990). *Psycholinguistics: Learning and using language*. Englewood Cliffs, NJ: Prentice-Hall.

Taylor, S. E., & Brown, J. D. (1988). Illusion and well-being: A social psychological perspective on mental health. *Psychological Bulletin, 103*, 193–210.

Taylor, S. E., & Brown, J. D. (1994). Positive illusions and well-being revisited: Separating fact from fiction. *Psychological Bulletin, 116*, 21–27.

Tedlock, B. (1992). Zuni and Quiche dream sharing and interpreting. In B. Tedlock (Ed.), *Dreaming: Anthropological and psychological interpretations*. Santa Fe, NM: School of American Research Press.

Tellegen, A., Lykken, D. T., Bouchard, T. J., Jr., Wilcox, K. J., Segal, N. L., & Rich, S. (1988). Personality similarity in twins reared apart and together. *Journal of Personality and Social Psychology, 54*, 1031–1039.

Tepper, B. J., & Nurse, R. J. (1997). Fat perception is related to PROP taster status. *Physiology & Behavior, 61*, 949–954.

Terman, L. M. (1916). *The measurement of intelligence*. Boston: Houghton Mifflin.

Terr, L. (1994). *Unchained memories*. New York: Basic Books.

Tessier-Lavigne, M. (1991). Photo-transduction and information processing in the retina. In E. R. Kandel, J. H. Schwartz, & T. M. Jessell (Eds.), *Principles of neural science* (3rd ed.). New York: Elsevier.

Testa, K. (1996). Church to pay $1 million in false-memory case. *San Jose Mercury News*, 8A.

Tetlock, P. E., Peterson, R. S., McGuire, C., Chang, S., & Feld, P. (1992). Assessing political group dynamics: A test of the groupthink model. *Journal of Personality and Social Psychology, 63*, 403–425.

Teuber, M. (1974). Sources of ambiguity in the prints of Maurits C. Escher. *Scientific American, 231*, 90–104.

Thayer, R. E. (1996). *The origin of everyday moods.* New York: Oxford University Press.

Thelen, E. (1995). Motor development: A new synthesis. *American Psychologist, 50,* 79–95.

Thomas, A., & Chess, S. (1977). *Temperament and development.* New York: Brunner/Mazel.

Thomas, A., & Chess, S. (1989). Temperament and personality. In G. A. Kohnstamm, J. E. Bates, & M. K. Rothbart (Eds.), *Temperament in childhood.* New York: Wiley.

Thomas, A., Chess, S., & Birch, H. G. (1970). The origin of personality. *Scientific American, 223*(2), 102–109.

Thomas, D. R. (1992). Discrimination and generalization. In L. R. Squire (Ed.), *Encyclopedia of learning and memory.* New York: Macmillan.

Thomas, R. M. (2000). *Comparing theories of child development.* Belmont, CA: Wadsworth.

Thomason, B. T., Brantkey, P. J., Jones, G. N., Dyer, H. R., & Morris, J. L. (1992). The relation between stress and disease activity in rheumatoid arthritis. *Journal of Behavioral Medicine, 15,* 215–220.

Thompson, M. M., Zanna, M. P., & Griffin, D. W. (1995). Let's not be indifferent about (attitudinal) ambivalence. In R. E. Petty & J. A. Krosnick (Eds.), *Attitude Strength: Antecedents and consequences.* Mahwah, NJ: Erlbaum.

Thompson, R. A. (1999). The individual child: Temperament, emotion, self, and personality. In M. H. Bornstein & M. E. Lamb (Eds.), *Developmental psychology: An advanced textbook.* Mahwah, NJ: Erlbaum.

Thompson, R. F. (1989). A model system approach to memory. In P. R. Solomon, G. R. Goethals, C. M. Kelley, & B. R. Stephens (Eds.), *Memory: Interdisciplinary approaches.* New York: Springer-Verlag.

Thompson, R. F. (1992). Memory. *Current Opinion in Neurobiology, 2,* 203–208.

Thorndyke, P. W., & Hayes-Roth, B. (1979). The use of schemata in the acquisition and transfer of knowledge. *Cognitive Psychology, 11,* 83–106.

Thorne, B. M., & Henley, T. B. (1997). *Connections in the history and systems of psychology.* Boston: Houghton Mifflin.

Thornhill, R. (1976). Sexual selection and nuptial feeding behavior in *Bittacus apicalis* (Insecta: Mecoptera). *American Naturalist, 110,* 529–548.

Thornton, B., & Moore, S. (1993). Physical attractiveness contrast effect: Implications for self-esteem and evaluations of the social self. *Personality and Social Psychology Bulletin, 19,* 474–480.

Thrope, S. J., & Salkozskis, P. M. (1995). Phobia beliefs: Do cognitive factors play a role in specific phobias? *Behavioral Research and Therapy, 33,* 805–816.

Todd, J. T., & Morris, E. K. (1992). Case histories in the great power of steady misrepresentation. *American Psychologist, 47,* 1441–1453.

Todes, D. P. (1997). From the machine to the ghost within: Pavlov's transition from digestive physiology to conditional reflexes. *American Psychologist, 52,* 947–955.

Tohen, M., & Goodwin, F. K. (1995). Epidemiology of bipolar disorder. In M. T. Tsuang, M. Tohen, & G. E. P. Zahner (Eds.), *Textbook in psychiatric epidemiology.* New York: Wiley.

Tollefson, G. (1995). Selective serotonin reuptake inhibitors. In A. F. Schatzberg & C. B. Nemeroff (Eds.), *The American Psychiatric Press textbook of psychopharmacology.* Washington, DC: American Psychiatric Press.

Tollefson, G. D., Beasley, C. M. Jr., Tamura, R. N., Tran, P. V., & Potvin, J. H. (1997). Blind, controlled, long-term study of the comparative incidence of treatment-emergent tardive dyskinesia with olanzapine or haloperidol. *American Journal of Psychiatry, 154,* 1248–1254.

Tolman, E. C. (1922). A new formula for behaviorism. *Psychological Review, 29,* 44–53.

Tolman, E. C. (1932). *Purposive behavior in animals and men.* New York: Appleton-Century-Crofts.

Tomkins, S. S. (1980). Affect as amplification: Some modifications in theory. In R. Plutchik & H. Kellerman (Eds.), *Emotion: Theory, research and experience* (Vol. 1). New York: Academic Press.

Tomkins, S. S. (1991). *Affect, imagery, consciousness: 3. Anger and fear.* New York: Springer-Verlag.

Tondo, L., Baldessarini, R. J., Hennen, J., & Floris, G. (1998). Lithium maintenance treatment of depression and mania in bipolar I and bipolar II disorders. *American Journal of Psychiatry, 155,* 638–645.

Tooby, J., & Cosmides, L. (1989). Evolutionary psychology and the generation of culture: Part 1. Theoretical considerations. *Ethology and Sociobiology, 10,* 29–49.

Tooby, J., & Cosmides, L. (1990). On the universality of human nature and the uniqueness of the individual: The role of genetics and adaptation. *Journal of Personality, 58,* 17–68.

Torgersen, S. (1979). The nature and origin of common phobic fears. *British Journal of Psychiatry, 119,* 343–351.

Torgersen, S. (1983). Genetic factors in anxiety disorders. *Archives of General Psychiatry, 40,* 1085–1089.

Torrey, E. F. (1992). *Freudian fraud: The malignant effect of Freud's theory on American thought and culture.* New York: Harper Perennial.

Torrey, E. F. (1996). *Out of the shadows.* New York: Wiley.

Torrey, E. F., Bowler, A. E., Taylor, E. H., & Gottesman, I. I. (1994). *Schizophrenia and manic-depressive disorder.* New York: Basic Books.

Torsvall, L., Akerstedt, T., Gillander, K., & Knutsson, A. (1989). Sleep on the night shift: 24-hour EEG monitoring of spontaneous sleep/walk behavior. *Psychophysiology, 26*(3), 352–358.

Toufexis, A. (1990, December 17). Drowsy America. *Time,* pp. 78–85.

Treasure, J., & Szmukler, G. I. (1995). Medical complications of chronic anorexia nervosa. In G. I. Szmukler, C. Dare, & J. Treasure (Eds.), *Handbook of eating disorders: Theory, treatment and research.* Chichester, England: Wiley.

Triandis, H. C. (1989). Self and social behavior in differing cultural contexts. *Psychological Review, 96,* 269–289.

Triandis, H. C. (1994). *Culture and social behavior.* New York: McGraw-Hill.

Trivers, R. L. (1971). The evolution of reciprocal altruism. *Quarterly Review of Biology, 46,* 35–57.

Trivers, R. L. (1972). Parental investment and sexual selection. In B. Campbell (Ed.), *Sexual selection and the descent of man.* Chicago: Aldine.

Trope, Y., & Liberman, A. (1993). The use of trait conceptions to identify other people's behavior and to draw inferences about their personalities. *Personality and Social Psychology Bulletin, 19,* 553–562.

Tseng, W. S., Di, X., Ebata, K., Hsu, J., & Yuhua, C. (1986). Diagnostic pattern for neuroses in China, Japan, and the United States. *American Journal of Psychiatry, 43,* 1010–1014.

Tsuang, M. T., Faraone, S. V., & Green, A. I. (1999). Schizophrenia and other psychotic disorders. In A. M. Nicholi (Ed.), *The Harvard guide to psychiatry.* Cambridge, MA: Harvard University Press.

Tulving, E. (1986). What kind of a hypothesis is the distinction between episodic and semantic memory? *Journal of Experimental Psychology: Learning, Memory and Cognition, 12,* 307–311.

Tulving, E. (1993). What is episodic memory? *Current Directions in Psychological Science, 2*(3), 67–70.

Tulving, E., & Psotka, J. (1971). Retroactive inhibition in free recall: Inaccessibility of information available in the memory store. *Journal of Experimental Psychology, 87,* 1–8.

Tulving, E., & Schacter, D. L. (1990). Priming and human memory systems. *Science, 247,* 301–306.

Tulving, E., & Thomson, D. M. (1973). Encoding specificity and retrieval processes in episodic memory. *Psychological Review, 80,* 352–373.

Turk, D. C. (1994). Perspectives on chronic pain: The role of psychological factors. *Current Directions in Psychological Science, 3,* 45–48.

Turkheimer, E. (1991). Individual and group differences in adoption studies of IQ. *Psychological Bulletin, 110,* 392–405.

Turkkan, J. S. (1989). Classical conditioning: The new hegemony. *Behavioral and Brain Sciences, 12,* 121–179.

Turner, J. R., & Wheaton, B. (1995). Checklist measurement of stressful life events. In S. Cohen, R. C. Kessler, & L. U. Gordon (Eds.), *Measuring stress: A guide for health and social scientists.* New York: Oxford University Press.

Turner, M. E., Pratkanis, A. R., Probasco, P., & Leve, C. (1992). Threat, cohesion, and group effectiveness: Testing a social identity maintenance perspective on groupthink. *Journal of Personality and Social Psychology, 63,* 781–796.

Turner, P. J., & Gervai, J. (1995). A multidimensional study of gender typing in preschool children and their parents: Personality, attitudes, preferences, behavior, and cultural differences. *Developmental Psychology, 31,* 759–772.

Turner-Bowker, D. M. (1996). Gender stereotyped descriptions in children's picture books: Does "curious Jane" exist in the literature? *Sex Roles, 35,* 461–488.

Tversky, A. (1972). Elimination by aspects: A theory of choice. *Psychological Review, 79,* 281–299.

Tversky, A., & Kahneman, D. (1971). Belief in the law of small numbers. *Psychological Bulletin, 76,* 105–110.

Tversky, A., & Kahneman, D. (1973). Availability: A heuristic for judging frequency and probability. *Cognitive Psychology, 5,* 207–232.

Tversky, A., & Kahneman, D. (1974). Judgments under uncertainty: Heuristics and biases. *Science, 185,* 1124–1131.

Tversky, A., & Kahneman, D. (1982). Judgment under uncertainty: Heuristics and biases. In D. Kahneman, P. Slovic, & A. Tversky (Eds.), *Judgment under uncertainty: Heuristics and biases.* New York: Cambridge University Press.

Tversky, A., & Kahneman, D. (1983). Extensional versus intuitive reasoning: The conjunction fallacy in probability judgment. *Psychological Review, 90,* 283–315.

Uchino, B. N., Cacioppo, J. T., & Kiecolt-Glaser, J. K. (1996). The relationship between social support and physiological processes: A review with emphasis on underlying mechanisms and implications for health. *Psychological Bulletin, 119,* 488–531.

Uchino, B. N., Uno, D., & Holt-Lunstad, J. (1999). Social support, physiological processes, and health. *Current Directions in Psychological Science, 8,* 145–148.

Ulrich, R. E. (1991). Animal rights, animal wrongs and the question of balance. *Psychological Science, 2,* 197–201.

Umbel, V. M., Pearson, B. Z., Fernandez, S. C., & Oller, D. K. (1992). Measuring bilingual children's receptive vocabularies. *Child Development, 63,* 1012–1020.

Underwood, B. J. (1961). Ten years of massed practice on distributed practice. *Psychological Review, 68,* 229–247.

Underwood, B. J. (1970). A breakdown of the total-time law in free-recall learning. *Journal of Verbal Learning and Verbal Behavior, 9,* 573–580.

Unger, R. K., & Crawford, M. (1993). Commentary: Sex and gender—The troubled relationship between terms and concepts. *Psychological Science, 4,* 122–124.

Ungerleider, L. G., & Haxby, J. V. (1994). "What" and "where" in the human brain. *Current Opinion in Neurobiology, 4,* 157–165.

Ursano, R. J., & Silberman, E. K. (1999). Psychoanalysis, psychoanalytic psychotherapy, and supportive psychotherapy. In R. E. Hales, S. C. Yudofsky, & J. A. Talbott (Eds.), *American Psychiatric Press textbook of psychiatry.* Washington, DC: American Psychiatric Press.

U.S. Department of Health and Human Services. (1990). *The health benefits of smoking cessation: A report of the surgeon general.* Washington, DC: U.S. Government Printing Office.

U.S. Department of Health and Human Services. (1999). *Mental health: A report of the Surgeon General.* Washington, DC: U.S. Government Printing Office.

Valenstein, E. S. (1973). *Brain control.* New York: Wiley.

Valleroy, L. A., Harris, J. R., & Way, P. O. (1990). The impact of HIV infection on child survival in the developing world. *AIDS, 4,* 667–672.

Vallone, R. P., Griffin, D. W., Lin, S., & Ross, L. (1990). Overconfident prediction of future actions and outcomes by self and others. *Journal of Personality and Social Psychology, 58,* 582–592.

Van de Castle, R. L. (1994). *Our dreaming mind.* New York: Ballantine Books.

van den Boom, D. C. (1994). The influence of temperament and mothering on attachment and exploration: An experimental manipulation of sensitive responsiveness among lower-class mothers and irritable infants. *Child Development, 65,* 1457–1477.

VanderPlate, C., Aral, S. O., & Magder, L. (1988). The relationship among genital herpes simplex virus, stress, and social support. *Health Psychology, 7,* 159–168.

van der Post, L. (1975). *Jung and the story of our time.* New York: Vintage Books.

van Eck, M., Nicolson, N. A., & Berkhof, J. (1998). Effects of stressful daily events on mood states: Relationship to global perceived stress. *Journal of Personality and Social Psychology, 75,* 1572–1585.

Van Houten, R. (1983). Punishment: From the animal laboratory to the applied setting. In S. Axelrod & J. Apsche (Eds.), *The effects of punishment on human behavior.* New York: Academic Press.

Vane, J. R., & Motta, R. W. (1990). Group intelligence tests. In G. Goldstein & M. Hersen (Eds.), *Handbook of psychological assessment.* New York: Pergamon Press.

Vaughn, B. E., & Bost, K. K. (1999). Attachment and temperament: Redundant, independent, or interacting influences on interpersonal adaptation and personality development? In J. Cassidy & P. R. Shaver (Eds.), *Handbook of attachment: Theory, research, and clinical applications.* New York: Guilford Press.

Vazquez, C., Munoz, M., & Sanz, J. (1997). Lifetime and 12-month prevalence of DSM-III-R mental disorders among the homeless in Madrid: A European study using the CIDI. *Acta Psychiatrica Scandinavica, 95,* 523–530.

Veenhoven, R. (1993). *Happiness in nations.* Rotterdam, Netherlands: Risbo.

Vega, W. A., Kolody, B., Aguilar-Gaxiola, S., & Catalano, R. (1999). Gaps in service utilization by Mexican Americans with mental health problems. *American Journal of Psychiatry, 156,* 928–934.

Ventura, J., Nuechterlein, K. H., Lukoff, D., & Hardesty, J. P. (1989). A prospective study of stressful life events and schizophrenic relapse. *Journal of Abnormal Psychology, 98,* 407–411.

Verhaeghen, P., & Salthouse, T. A. (1997). Meta-analyses of age-cognition relations in adulthood: Estimates of linear and nonlinear age effects and structural models. *Psychological Bulletin, 122,* 231–249.

Vernon, P. E. (1982). *The abilities and achievements of Orientals in North America.* New York: Academic Press.

Vierck, C. (1978). Somatosensory system. In R. B. Masterson (Ed.), *Handbook of sensory neurobiology.* New York: Plenum.

Vinogradov, S., Cox, P. D., & Yalom, I. D. (1999). Group therapy. In R. E. Hales, S. C. Yudofsky, & J. A. Talbott (Eds.), *American Psychiatric Press textbook of psychiatry.* Washington, DC: American Psychiatric Press.

Vinogradov, S., & Yalom, I. D. (1988). Group therapy. In J. A. Talbott, R. E. Hales, & S. C. Yudofsky (Eds.), *The American Psychiatric Press textbook of psychiatry.* Washington, DC: American Psychiatric Press.

Vodelhozer, U., Homyak, M., Thiel, B., Huwig-Poppe, C., Kiemen, A., Konig, A., Backhaus, J., Reimann, D., Berger, M., & Hohagen, R. (1998). Impact of experimentally induced serotonin deficiency by tryphophan depletion on sleep EEG in healthy subjects. *Neuropsychopharmacology, 18,* 112–124.

Vogt, T., Mullooly, J., Ernst, D., Pope, C., & Hollis, J. (1992). Social networks as predictors of ischemic heart disease, cancer, stroke and hypertension: Incidence, survival and mortality. *Journal of Clinical Epidemiology, 45,* 659–666.

Volkow, N. D. (1997). The role of the dopamine system in addiction. *Hospital Practice, April,* 22–26.

Voyer, D., Voyer, S., & Bryden, M. P. (1995). Magnitude of sex differences in spatial abilities: A meta-analysis and consideration of critical variables. *Psychological Bulletin, 117,* 250–270.

Wade, P., & Bernstein, B. (1991). Culture sensitivity training and counselor's race: Effects on Black female client's perceptions and attrition. *Journal of Counseling Psychology, 38,* 9–15.

Wagner, H. (1989). The physiological differentiation of emotions. In H. Wagner & A. Manstead (Eds), *Handbook of social psychophysiology.* New York: Wiley.

Wagner, R. K. (1997). Intelligence, training, and employment. *American Psychologist, 52,* 1059–1069.

Wahlbeck, K., Cheine, M., Essali, A., & Adams, C. (1999). Evidence of clozapine's effectiveness in schizophrenia: A systematic review and meta-analysis of randomized trials. *American Journal of Psychiatry, 156,* 990–999.

Wahlsten, D. (1997). The malleability of intelligence is not constrained by heritability. In B. Devlin, S. E. Fienberg, D. P. Resnick, & K. Roeder (Eds.), *Intelligence, genes, and success: Scientists respond to* The Bell Curve. New York: Springer-Verlag.

Wakefield, J. C. (1992). The concept of mental disorder: On the boundary between biological facts and social values. *American Psychologist, 47,* 373–388.

Wakefield, J. C. (1999). Evolutionary versus prototype analyses of the concept of disorder. *Journal of Abnormal Psychology, 108,* 374–399.

Wald, G. (1964). The receptors of human color vision. *Science, 145,* 1007–1017.

Waldman, I. D. (1997). Unresolved questions and future directions in behavior-genetic studies of intelligence. In R. J. Sternberg, & E. L. Grigorenko (Eds.), *Intelligence, heredity, and environment.* New York: Cambridge University Press.

Walker, I., & Hulme, C. (1999). Concrete words are easier to recall than abstract words: Evidence for a semantic contribution to short-term serial recall. *Journal of Experimental Psychology: Learning, Memory, & Cognition, 25,* 1256–1271.

Walker, L. J. (1988). The development of moral reasoning. In R. Vasta (Ed.), *Annals of child development* (Vol. 5). Greenwich, CT: JAI Press.

Walker, L. J. (1989). A longitudinal study of moral reasoning. *Child Development, 60,* 157–166.

Walker, L. J. (1995). Sexism in Kohlberg's moral psychology? In W. M. Kurtines, & J. L. Gewirtz (Eds.), *Moral development: An introduction.* Boston: Allyn & Bacon.

Walker, L. J., & Moran, T. J. (1991). Moral reasoning in a Communist Chinese society. *Journal of Moral Education, 20,* 139–155.

Walker, L. J., & Taylor, J. H. (1991). Strange transitions in moral reasoning: A longitudinal study of developmental processes. *Developmental Psychology, 27,* 330–337.

Wallace, B., & Fisher, L. E. (1999). *Consciousness and behavior.* Boston: Allyn & Bacon.

Wallace, C. J. (1998). Social skills training in psychiatric rehabilitation: Recent findings. *International Review of Psychiatry, 10,* 9–10.

Wallace, R. K., & Benson, H. (1972). The physiology of meditation. *Scientific American, 226,* 84–90.

Wallbott, H. G., & Scherer, K. R. (1988). How universal and specific is emotional experience? Evidence from 27 countries. In K. R. Scherer (Ed.), *Facets of emotions.* Hillsdale, NJ: Erlbaum.

Wallen, K. (1989). Mate selection: Economics and affection. *Behavioral and Brain Sciences, 12,* 37–38.

Walraven, J., Enroth-Cugell, C., Hood, D. C., MacLeod, D. I. A., & Schnapf, J. L. (1990). The control of visual sensitivity: Receptoral and postreceptoral processes. In L. Spillmann & J. S. Werner (Eds.), *Visual perception: The neurophysiological foundations.* San Diego: Academic Press.

Walters, E. E., & Kendler, K. S. (1995). Anorexia nervosa and anorexic-like syndromes in a population-based female twin sample. *American Journal of Psychiatry, 152,* 64–71.

Waltz, J. A., Knowlton, B. J., Holyoak, K. J., Boone, K. B., Mishkin, F. S., de Menezes Santos, M., Thomas, C. R., & Miller, B. L. (1999). A system for relational reasoning in human prefrontal cortex. *Psychological Science, 10,* 119–125.

Wampold, B. E., Mondin, G. W., Moody, M., Stich, F., Benson, K., & Ahn, H. N. (1997). A meta-analysis of outcome studies comparing bona fide psychotherapies: Empirically, "all must have prizes". *Psychological Bulletin, 122,* 203–215.

Wandell, B. A. (1995). *Foundations of vision.* Sunderland, MA: Sinauer.

Wangensteen, O. H., & Carlson, A. J. (1931). Hunger sensation after total gastrectomy. *Proceedings of the Society for Experimental Biology, 28,* 545–547.

Wansell, G. (1983). *Haunted idol: The story of the real Cary Grant.* New York: Ballantine.

Warr, P. (1999). Well-being and the workplace. In D. Kahneman, E. Diener, & N. Schwarz (Eds.), *Well-being: The foundations of hedonic psychology.* New York: Russell Sage Foundation.

Warrington, E. K., & Weiskrantz, L. (1970). Amnesic syndrome: Consolidation or retrieval? *Nature, 228,* 629–630.

Waterman, A., & Archer, S. (1990). A life-span perspective on identity formation: Development in form, function, and process. In P. B. Baltes, D. L. Featherman, & R. M. Lerner (Eds.), *Life-span development and behavior* (Vol. 10). Hillsdale, NJ: Erlbaum.

Watson, D., David, J. P., & Suls, J. (1999). Personality, affectivity, and coping. In C. R. Snyder (Ed.), *Coping: The psychology of what works.* New York: Oxford University Press.

Watson, D., & Pennebaker, J. W. (1989). Health complaints, stress, and distress: Exploring the central role of negative affectivity. *Psychological Review, 96,* 234–254.

Watson, D. L., & Tharp, R. G. (1997). *Self-directed behavior: Self-modification for personal adjustment* (6th edition). Pacific Grove, CA: Brooks/Cole.

Watson, J. B. (1913). Psychology as the behaviorist views it. *Psychological Review, 20,* 158–177.

Watson, J. B. (1919). *Psychology from the standpoint of a behaviorist.* Philadelphia: Lippincott.

Watson, J. B. (1924). *Behaviorism.* New York: Norton.

Watson, J. B. (1930). *Behaviorism.* New York: Norton.

Watson, J. B., & Rayner, R. (1920). Conditioned emotional reactions. *Journal of Experimental Psychology, 3,* 1–14.

Waugh, N. C., & Norman, D. A. (1965). Primary memory. *Psychological Review, 72,* 89–104.

Weatherall, A. (1992). Gender and languages: Research in progress. *Feminism & Psychology, 2,* 177–181.

Weaver, C. A., III, (1993). Do you need a "flash" to form a flashbulb memory? *Journal of Experimental Psychology: General, 122,* 39–46.

Weaver, M. F., & Schnoll, S. H. (1999). Stimulants: Amphetamines and cocaine. In B. S. McCrady & E. E. Epstein (Eds.), *Addictions: A comprehensive guidebook.* New York: Oxford University Press.

Weaver, R. C., & Rodnick, J. E. (1986). Type-A behavior: Clinical significance, evaluation, and management. *Journal of Family Practice, 23*(3), 255–261.

Webb, W. B. (1992a). Developmental aspects and a behavioral model of human sleep. In C. Stampi (Ed.), *Why we nap: Evolution, chronobiology, and functions of polyphasic and ultrashort sleep.* Boston: Birkhaeuser.

Webb, W. B. (1992b). *Sleep: The gentle tyrant.* Bolton, MA: Anker.

Webb, W. B., & Dinges, D. F. (1989). Cultural perspectives on napping and the siesta. In D. F. Dinges & R. J. Broughton (Eds.), *Sleep and alertness: Chronobiological, behavioral, and medical aspects of napping.* New York: Raven.

Wechsler, D. (1949). *Wechsler intelligence scale for children.* New York: Psychological Corporation.

Wechsler, D. (1955). *Manual, Wechsler adult intelligence scale.* New York: Psychological Corporation.

Wechsler, D. (1967). *Manual for the Wechsler preschool and primary scale of intelligence.* New York: Psychological Corporation.

Wechsler, D. (1981). *Manual for the Wechsler adult intelligence scale—revised.* New York: Psychological Corporation.

Wechsler, D. (1991). *WISC-III manual.* San Antonio: Psychological Corporation.

Wechsler, H., Davenport, A., Dowdall, G., Moeykens, B., & Castillo, S. (1994). Health and behavioral consequences of binge drinking in college. A national survey of students at 140 campuses. *Journal of the American Medical Association,* 1672–1677.

Wegner, D. M. (1997). Why the mind wanders. In J. D. Cohen & J. W. Schooler (Eds.), *Scientific approaches to consciousness.* Mahwah, NJ: Erlbaum.

Wei, M., Kampert, J. B., Barlow, C. E., Nichaman, M. Z., Gibbons, L. W., Paffenbarger, R. S., & Blair, S. N. (1999). Relationship between low cardiorespiratory fitness and mortality in normal weight, overweight, and obese men. *Journal of the American Medical Association, 282,* 1547–1553.

Weinberg, R. A. (1989). Intelligence and IQ: Landmark issues and great debates. *American Psychologist, 44,* 98–104.

Weinberger, D. A. (1990). The construct validity of the repressive coping style. In J. L. Singer (Ed.), *Repression and dissociation.* Chicago: University of Chicago Press.

Weinberger, D. A., & Davidson, M. A. (1994). Styles of inhibiting emotional expression: Distinguishing repressive coping from impression management. *Journal of Personality, 62,* 589–611.

Weiner, B. (Ed.). (1974). *Achievement motivation and attribution theory.* Morristown, NJ: General Learning Press.

Weiner, B. (1980). *Human motivation.* New York: Holt, Rinehart & Winston.

Weiner, B. (1986). *An attributional theory of motivation and emotion.* New York: Springer-Verlag.

Weiner, B. (1994). Integrating social and personal theories of achievement striving. *Review of Educational Research, 64,* 557–573.

Weiner, H. (1978). Emotional factors. In S. C. Werner & S. H. Ingbar (Eds.), *The thyroid.* New York: Harper & Row.

Weiner, H. (1992). *Perturbing the organism: The biology of stressful experience.* Chicago: University of Chicago Press.

Weiner, M. F. (1993). Role of the leader in group psychotherapy. In H. I. Kaplan & B. J. Sadock (Eds.), *Comprehensive group psychotherapy.* Baltimore: Williams & Wilkins.

Weinfield, N. S., Sroufe, L. A., Egeland, B., & Carlson, E. A. (1999). The nature of individual differences in infant-caregiver attachment. In J. Cassidy & P. R. Shaver (Eds.), *Handbook of attachment: Theory, research, and clinical applications.* New York: Guilford Press.

Weinstein, N. D. (1984). Why it won't happen to me: Perceptions of risk factors and susceptibility. *Health Psychology, 3,* 431–458.

Weinstein, N. D., & Klein, W. M. (1995). Resistance of personal risk perceptions to debiasing interventions. *Health Psychology, 14,* 132–140.

Weisaeth, L. (1993). Disasters: Psychological and psychiatric aspects. In L. Goldberger & S. Breznitz (Eds.), *Handbook of stress: Theoretical and clinical aspects* (2nd ed.). New York: Free Press.

Weisberg, R. W. (1986). *Creativity: Genius and other myths.* New York: W. H. Freeman.

Weisberg, R. W. (1993). *Creativity: Beyond the myth of genius.* New York: W. H. Freeman.

Weisberg, R. W. (1999). Creativity and knowledge: A challenge to theories. In R. J. Sternberg (Ed.), *Handbook of creativity.* New York: Cambridge University Press.

Weissman, M. M., Bruce, M. L., Leaf, P. J., Florio, L. P., & Holzer, C., III. (1991). Affective disorders. In L. N. Robins & D. A. Regier (Eds.), *Psychiatric disorders in America: The epidemiologic catchment area study.* New York: Free Press.

Weiten, W. (1984). Violation of selected item-construction principles in educational measurement. *Journal of Experimental Education, 51,* 46–50.

Weiten W. (1988a). Objective features of introductory psychology textbooks as related to professors' impressions. *Teaching of Psychology, 15,* 10–16.

Weiten, W. (1988b). Pressure as a form of stress and its relationship to psychological symptomatology. *Journal of Social and Clinical Psychology, 6*(1), 127–139.

Weiten, W. (1998). Pressure, major life events, and psychological symptoms. *Journal of Social Behavior and Personality, 13,* 51–68.

Weiten, W., & Diamond, S. S. (1979). A critical review of the jury-simulation paradigm: The case of defendant characteristics. *Law and Human Behavior, 3,* 71–93.

Weiten, W. Guadagno, R. E., & Beck, C. A. (1996). Students' perceptions of textbook pedagogical aids. *Teaching of Psychology, 23,* 105–107.

Weiten, W., & Wight, R. D. (1992). Portraits of a discipline: An examination of introductory psychology textbooks in America. In A. E. Puente, J. R. Matthews, & C. L. Brewer (Eds.), *Teaching psychology in America: A history.* Washington, DC: American Psychological Association.

Well, A. D., Pollatsek, A., & Boyce, S. J. (1990). Understanding the effects of sample size on the variability of the mean. *Organizational Behavior and Human Decision Processes, 47,* 289–312.

Wells, G. L., & Bradfield, A. L. (1998). "Good, you identified the suspect": Feedback to eyewitnesses distorts their reports of the witnessing experience. *Journal of Applied Psychology, 83,* 360–376.

Werker, J. F., & Desjardins, R. N. (1995). Listening to speech in the 1st year of life: Experiential influences on phoneme perception. *Current Directions in Psychological Science, 4,* 76–81.

Wertheimer, M. (1912). Experiment-elle studien Über das sehen von bewegung. *Zeitschrift für Psychologie, 60,* 312–378.

Wertz, F. J. (1998). The role of the humanistic movement in the history of psychology. *Journal of Humanistic Psychology, 38,* 42–70.

West, R. F., & Stanovich, K. E. (1997). The domain specificity and generality of overconfidence: Individual differences in performance estimation bias. *Psychonomic Bulletin & Review, 4,* 387–392.

Westen, D. (1998). The scientific legacy of Sigmund Freud: Toward a psychodynamically informed psychological science. *Psychological Bulletin, 124,* 333–371.

Westen, D., & Gabbard, G. O. (1999). Psychoanalytic approaches to personality. In L. A. Pervin & O. P. John (Eds.), *Handbook of personality: Theory and research.* New York: Guilford Press.

Wheeler, L., & Kim, Y. (1997). What is beautiful is culturally good: The physical attractiveness stereotype has different content in collectivistic cultures. *Personality and Social Psychology Bulletin, 23,* 795–800.

Wheeler, M. A., Stuss, D. T., & Tulving, E. (1997). Toward a theory of episodic memory: The frontal lobes and autonoetic consciousness. *Psychological Bulletin, 121,* 331–354.

Whitbourne, S. K., Zuschlag, M. K., Elliot, L. B., & Waterman, A. S. (1992). Psychosocial development in adulthood: A 22-year sequential study. *Journal of Personality and Social Psychology, 63,* 260–271.

White, P. A., & Younger, D. P. (1988). Differences in the ascription of transient internal states to self and other. *Journal of Experimental Psychology, 24,* 292–309.

Whitfield, C. L. (1995). *Memory and abuse: Remembering and healing the effects of trauma.* Deerfield Beach, FL: Health Communications.

Whitley, B. E., Jr. (1988). *College students' reasons for sexual intercourse: A sex role perspective.* Paper presented at the 96th Annual Meeting of the American Psychological Association, Atlanta.

Whorf, B. L. (1956). Science and linguistics. In J. B. Carroll (Ed.), *Language, thought and reality: Selected writings of Benjamin Lee Whorf.* Cambridge, MA: MIT Press.

Wickens, T. D. (1999). Measuring the time course of retention. In C. Izawa (Ed.), *On human memory: Evolution, progress, and reflections on the 30th anniversary of the Atkinson-Shiffrin model.* Mahwah, NJ: Erlbaum.

Wiederman, M. W. (1993). Evolved gender differences in mate preferences: Evidence from personal advertisements. *Ethology and Sociobiology, 14,* 331–352.

Wierzbicka, A. (1994). Emotion, language, and cultural scripts. In S. Kitayama & H. R. Markus (Eds.), *Emotion and culture: Empirical studies of mutual influence.* Washington, DC: American Psycholgoical Association.

Wiest, W. (1977). Semantic differential profiles of orgasm and other experiences among men and women. *Sex Roles, 3,* 399–403.

Wiest, W., Harrison, J., Johanson, C., Laubsch, B., & Whitley, A. (1995, February 25). *Paper presented at the Oregon Academy of Sciences meeting.* Portland, OR: Reed College.

Wiggins, J. S. (1992). Have model, will travel. *Journal of Personality, 60,* 527–532.

Wiggins, J. S., & Trapnell, P. D. (1997). Personality structure: The return of the big five. In R. Hogan, J. Johnson, & S. Briggs (Eds.), *Handbook of personality psychology.* San Diego, CA: Academic Press.

Wiggs, C. L., Weisberg, J., & Martin, A. (1999). Neural correlates of semantic and episodic memory retrieval. *Neuropsychologia, 37,* 103–118.

Wilcox, A. J., Weinberg, C. R., O'Connor, J. F., Baurd, D. D., Schlatterer, J. P., Canfield, R. E., Armstrong, E. G., & Nisula, B. C. (1988). Incidence of early loss of pregnancy. *New England Journal of Medicine, 319,* 189–194.

Wilding, J., & Valentine, E. (1996). Memory expertise. In D. J. Herrmann, C. McEvoy, C. Hertzog, P. Hertel, & M. K. Johnson (Eds.), *Basic and applied memory research: Theory in context* (Vol. 1). Mahwah, NJ: Erlbaum.

Wiley, J. L. (1999). Cannabis: Discrimination of "internal bliss?" *Pharmacology, Biochemistry & Behavior, 64,* 257–260.

Wilfley, D. E., & Rodin, J. (1995). Cultural influences on eating disorders. In K. D. Brownell & C. G. Fairburn (Eds.), *Eating disorders and obesity: A comprehensive handbook.* New York: Guilford Press.

Willett, W. C., & Manson, J. E. (1995). Epidemiologic studies of health risks due to excess weight. In K. D. Brownell & C. G. Fairburn (Eds.), *Eating disorders and obesity: A comprehensive handbook.* New York: Guilford Press.

Williams, B. A. (1988). Reinforcement, choice, and response strength. In R. C. Atkinson, R. J. Herrnstein, G. Lindzey, & R. D. Luce (Eds.), *Stevens' handbook of experimental psychology.* New York: Wiley.

Williams, B. A. (1994). Conditioned reinforcement: Neglected or outmoded explanatory construct? *Psychonomic Bulletin & Review, 1,* 457–475.

Williams, G. C. (1966). *Adaptation and natural selection.* Princeton, NJ: Princeton University Press.

Williams, J. B. W. (1994). Psychiatric classification. In R. E. Hales, S. C. Yudofsky, & J. A. Talbott (Eds.), *The American Psychiatric Press textbook of psychiatry* (2nd ed.). Washington, DC: American Psychiatric Press.

Williams, J. B. W. (1999). Psychiatric classification. In R. E. Hales, S. C. Yudofsky, & J. A. Talbott (Eds.), *American Psychiatric Press textbook of psychiatry.* Washington, DC: American Psychiatry Press.

Williams, J. M. G., Watts, F. N., MacLeod, C., & Mathews, A. (1997). *Cognitive psychology and emotional disorders.* Chichester, England: Wiley.

Williams, M. H. (1992). Exploitation and inference: Mapping the damage from therapist-patient sexual involvement. *American Psychologist, 47,* 412–421.

Williams, N. A., & Deffenbacher, J. L. (1983). Life stress and chronic yeast infections. *Journal of Human Stress, 9*(1), 26–31.

Williams, R. L., Dotson, W., Dow, P., & Williams, W. S. (1980). The war against testing: A current status report. *Journal of Negro Education, 49,* 263–273.

Williams, R. W., & Herrup, K. (1988). The control of neuron number. *Annual Review of Neuroscience, 11,* 423–453.

Williams, W. M. (1998). Are we raising smarter children today? School-and-home-related influences on IQ. In U. Neisser (Ed.), *The rising curve: Long-term gains in IQ and related measures.* Washington, DC: American Psychological Association.

Williams, W. M., & Ceci, S. J. (1997). Are Americans becoming more or less alike?: Trends in race, class, and ability differences in intelligence. *American Psychologist, 52,* 1226–1235.

Willis, W. D. (1985). *The pain system. The neural basis of nociceptive transmission in the mammalian nervous system.* Basel: Karger.

Willoughby, T., Motz, M., & Wood, E. (1997). The impact of interest and strategy use on memory performance for child, adolescent, and adult learners. *Alberta Journal of Educational Research, 43,* 127–141.

Wilson, G. T. (1982). Alcohol and anxiety: Recent evidence on the tension reduction theory of alcohol use and abuse. In K. R. Blankstein & J. Polivy (Eds.), *Self-control and self-modification of emotional behavior.* New York: Plenum.

Wilson, G. T. (1996). Empirically validated treatments: Realities and resistance. *Clinical Psychology: Science & Practice, 3,* 241–244.

Wilson, M. (1993). DSM-III and the transformation of American psychiatry: A history. *American Journal of Psychiatry, 150,* 399–410.

Windholz, G. (1997). Ivan P. Pavlov: An overview of his life and psychological work. *American Psychologist, 52 ,* 941–946.

Winick, C. (1992). Epidemiology of alcohol and drug abuse. In J. H. Lowinson, P. Ruiz, & R. B. Millman (Eds.), *Substance abuse: A comprehensive textbook*. Baltimore: Williams & Wilkins.

Winn, P. (1995). The lateral hypothalmus and motivated behavior: An old syndrome reassessed and a new perspective gained. *Current Directions in Psychological Science, 4*, 182–187.

Winograd, T. (1975). Frame representations and the declarative-procedural controversy. In D. Bobrow & A. Collins (Eds.), *Representation and understanding: Studies in cognitive science*. New York: Academic Press.

Winquist, J. R., & Larson, J. R. Jr. (1998). Information pooling: When it impacts group decision making. *Journal of Personality and Social Psychology, 74*, 371–377.

Winzelberg, A. J., & Luskin, F. M. (1999). The effect of a meditation training in stress levels in secondary school teachers. *Stress Medicine, 15*, 69–77.

Wise, R. (1995). D-sub-1– and D-sub-2–type contributions to psychomotor sensitization and reward: Implications for pharmacological treatment strategies. *Clinical Neuropharmacology, 18*, S74–S83.

Wiseman, C. V., Gray, J. J., Mosimann, J. E., & Ahrens, A. H. (1992). Cultural expectations of thinness in women: An update. *International Journal of Eating Disorders, 11*, 85–89.

Witkin, H. A. (1950). Individual differences in ease of perception of embedded figures. *Journal of Personality, 19*, 1–15.

Witkin, H. A., & Berry, J. W. (1975). Psychological differentiation in cross-cultural perspective. *Journal of Cross-Cultural Psychology, 6*, 4–87.

Witkin, H. A., & Goodenough, D. (1981). *Cognitive styles: Essence and origins*. New York: International Universities Press.

Witkin, H. A., Dyk, R. B., Paterson, H. F., Goodenough, D. R., & Karp, S. (1962). *Psychological differentiation*. New York: Wiley.

Wittchen, H. U., Knauper, B., & Kessler, R. C. (1994). Lifetime risk of depression. *British Journal of Psychiatry, 165*, 116–122.

Witte, K., Berkowitz, J. M., Cameron, K. A., & McKeon, J. K. (1998). Preventing the spread of genital warts: Using fear appeals to promote self-protective behaviors. *Health Education & Behavior, 25*, 571–585.

Wittkower, E. D., & Warnes, H. (1984). Cultural aspects of psychotherapy. In J. E. Mezzich & C. E. Berganza (Eds.), *Culture and psychopathology*. New York: Columbia University Press.

Wolf, R. M. (1965). The measurement of environments. In C. W. Harris (Ed.), *Proceedings of the 1964 invited conference on testing problems*. Princeton, NJ: Educational Testing Service.

Wolf, S., & Goodell, H. (1968). *Stress and disease*. Springfield, IL: Charles C. Thomas.

Wolk, A., Manson, J. E., Stampfer, M. J., Colditz, G. A., Hu, F. B., Speizer, F. E., Hennekens, C. H., & Willett, W. C. (1999). Long-term intake of dietary fiber and decreased risk of coronary heart disease among women. *Journal of the American Medical Association, 281*, 1998–2004.

Wolpe, J. (1958). *Psychotherapy by reciprocal inhibition*. Stanford, CA: Stanford University Press.

Wolpe, J. (1990). *The practice of behavior therapy*. Elmsford, NY: Pergamon Press.

Wonderlich, S. A. (1995). Personality and eating disorders. In K. D. Brownell & C. G. Fairburn (Eds.), *Eating disorders and obesity: A comprehensive handbook*. New York: Guilford Press.

Wood, F., Ebert, V., & Kinsbourne, M. (1982). The episodic-semantic memory distinction in memory and amnesia: Clinical and experimental observations. In L. Cermak (Ed.), *Human memory and amnesia*. Hillsdale, NJ: Erlbaum.

Wood, J. M., Nezworski, M. T., & Stejskal, W. J. (1996). The comprehensive system for the Rorschach: A critical examination. *Psychological Science, 7*, 3–10.

Wood, W., Rhodes, N., & Biek, M. (1995). Working knowledge and attitude strength: An information-processing analysis. In R. E. Petty & J. A. Krosnick (Eds.), *Attitude strength: Antecedents and consequences*. Mahwah, NJ: Erlbaum.

Woodcock, R. W. (1994). Norms. In R. J. Sternberg (Ed.), *Encyclopedia of human intelligence*. New York: Macmillan.

Woolfolk, R. L. (1975). Psycho-physiological correlates of meditation. *Archives of General Psychiatry, 32*, 1326–1333.

Woolfolk, R. L., & Richardson, F. C. (1978). *Stress, sanity and survival*. New York: Sovereign/Monarch.

Woolsey, C. N. (1981). *Cortical sensory organization*. Clifton, NJ: Humana Press.

Wooten, V. (1994). Medical causes of insomnia. In M. H. Kryger, T. Roth, & W. C. Dement (Eds.), *Principles and practice of sleep medicine* (2nd ed.). Philadelphia: Saunders.

Wundt, W. (1874/1904). *Principles of physiological psychology*. Leipzig: Engelmann.

Wylie, M. S. (1998). The shadow of a doubt. In R. A. Baker (Ed.), *Child sexual abuse and false memory syndrome*. Amherst, NY: Prometheus Books.

Wynn, K. (1992). Addition and subtraction by human infants. *Nature, 358*, 749–750.

Wynn, K. (1996). Infants' individuation and enumeration of sequential actions. *Psychological Science, 7*, 164–169.

Wynn, K. (1998). An evolved capacity for number. In D. D. Cummins & C. Allen (Eds.), *The evolution of mind*. New York: Oxford University Press.

Xiaghe, X., & Whyte, M. K. (1990). Love matches and arranged marriages: A Chinese replication. *Journal of Marriage and the Family, 52*, 709–722.

Yalom, I. D. (1995). *The theory and practice of group psychotherapy* (4th ed.). New York: Basic Books.

Yamamoto, J., Silva, J. A., Justice, L. R., Chang, C. Y., & Leong, G. B. (1993). Cross-cultural psychotherapy. In A. C. Gaw (Ed.), *Culture, ethnicity, and mental illness*. Washington, DC: American Psychiatric Press.

Yates, F. A. (1966). *The art of memory*. London: Routledge & Kegan Paul.

Yerkes, R. M., & Morgulis, S. (1909). The method of Pavlov in animal psychology. *Psychological Bulletin, 6*, 257–273.

Young, K. S. (1996, August). Internet addiction: The emergence of a new clinical disorder. Paper presented at the meeting of the American Psychological Association: Toronto, Ontario, Canada.

Young, K. S. (1998). *Caught in the net: How to recognize the signs of Internet addiction—and a winning strategy for recovery*. New York: Wiley.

Zajonc, R. B. (1980). Feeling and thinking: Preferences need no inferences. *American Psychologist, 35*, 151–175.

Zaleman, S. (1995). Neural bias of psychopathology. In S. H. Koslow, D. L. Meinecke, I. I. Lederhendler, H. Khachaturian, R. K. Nakamura, D. Karp, L. Vitkovic, D. L.Glanzman, & S. Zaleman (Eds.), *The neuroscience of mental health II: A report on neuroscience research—Status and potential for mental health and mental illness*. Rockville, MD: National Institute of Mental Health.

Zarcone, V. P., Jr. (1994). Sleep hygiene. In M. H. Kryger, T. Roth, & W. C. Dement (Eds.), *Principles and practice of sleep medicine* (2nd ed.). Philadelphia: Saunders.

Zatzick, D. F. (1999). Managed care and psychiatry. In R. E. Hales, S. C. Yudofsky & J. A. Talbott (Eds.), *American Psychiatric Press textbook of psychiatry*. Washington, DC: American Psychiatric Press.

Zatzick, D. F., & Dimsdale, J. E. (1990). Cultural variations in response to painful stimuli. *Psychosomatic Medicine, 52*(5), 544–557.

Zebrowitz, L. A. (1996). *Reading faces*. Boulder, CO: Westview Press.

Zebrowitz, L. A., Collins, M. A., & Dutta, R. (1998). The relationship between appearance and personality across the life span. *Personality and Social Psychology Bulletin, 24*, 736–749.

Zebrowitz, L. A., Voinescu, L., & Collins, M. A. (1996). "Wide-eyed" and "crooked-face": Determinants of perceived and real honesty across the life span. *Personality and Social Psychology Bulletin, 22*, 1258–1269.

Zechmeister, E. B., & Nyberg, S. E. (1982). *Human memory: An introduction to research and theory*. Pacific Grove, CA: Brooks/Cole.

Zeiler, M. (1977). Schedules of reinforcement: The controlling variables. In W. K. Honig & J. E. R. Staddon (Eds.), *Handbook of operant behavior*. Englewood Cliffs, NJ: Prentice-Hall.

Zenhausen, R. (1978). Imagery, cerebral dominance and style of thinking: A unified field model. *Bulletin of the Psychonomic Society, 12*, 381–384.

Zepelin, H. (1993). Internal alarm clock. In M. A. Carskadon (Ed.), *Encyclopedia of sleep and dreaming*. New York: Macmillan.

Zeskind, P. S., & Ramey, C. T. (1981). Preventing intellectual and interactional sequelae of fetal malnutrition: A longitudinal, transactional and synergistic approach to development. *Child Development, 52*, 213–218.

Zhdanova, I. V., Wurtman, R. J., Lynch, H. J., Ives, J. R., Dollins, A. B., Morabito, C., Matheson, J. K., & Schomer, D. L. (1995). Sleep-inducing effects of low doses of melatonin ingested in the evening. *Clinical Pharmacology and Therapeutics, 57*, 552–558.

Zigler, E., & Styfco, S. J. (1994). Head Start: Criticisms in a constructive context. *American Psychologist, 49*, 127–132.

Zillmann, D., Bryant, J., & Huston, A. C. (1994). *Media, family, and children*. Hillsdale, NJ: Erlbaum.

Zimmerman, B. J. (1995). Self-efficacy and educational development. In A. Bandura (Ed.), *Self-efficacy in changing societies*. New York: Cambridge University Press.

Zimmerman, I. L., & Woo-Sam, J. M. (1984). Intellectual assessment of children. In G. Goldstein & M. Hersen (Eds.), *Handbook of psychological assessment*. New York: Pergamon Press.

Zrenner, E., Abramov, I., Akita, M., Cowey, A., Livingstone, M., & Valberg, A. (1990). Color perception: Retina to cortex. In L. Spillman & J. S. Werner (Eds.), *Visual perception: The neurophysiological foundations*. San Diego: Academic Press.

Zubin, J. (1986). Implications of the vulnerability model for DSM-IV with special reference to schizophrenia. In T. Millon & G. L. Klerman (Eds.), *Contemporary directions in psychopathology: Toward the DSM-IV*. New York: Guilford Press.

Zuckerman, M. (1971). Dimensions of sensation seeking. *Journal of Consulting and Clinical Psychology, 36*, 45–52.

Name Index

Heinz, S. P., 203
Heller, W., 87
Hellige, J. B., 88, 89
Helmes, E., 388
Helmholtz, H. von, 105, 119
Helms, J. E., 280
Helson, R., 346
Hencke, R. W., 338
Hendrick, C., 499
Hendrick, S. S., 499
Henley, T. B., 3
Henry, K. R., 117
Herbener, E. S., 346, 499
Herek, G. M., 304
Hering, E., 106
Herman, J. L., 217
Hermann, R. C., 474
Hermans, H. J. M., 12
Hernandez, D. J., 356
Hernnstein, R. J., 273, 274, 278–279, 288
Herrmann, D., 225
Herrup, K., 66
Herskovits, M. J., 114
Hertwig, R., 49
Herzog, D. B., 451
Herzog, T. A., 412
Heszen-Niejodek, I., 403
Heth, C. D., 171
Hetherington, E. M., 357, 380
Hettich, P. I., 23
Hewstone, M., 519
Hiester, M., 333
Higgins, D. A., 352
Highhouse, S., 521
Hilgard, E. R., 3, 4, 18, 150, 151
Hill, C. E., 468
Hiller, W., 435
Hilliard, A. G., III, 280
Hillner, K. P., 8
Hilton, H. J., 109
Hilton, J. L., 494
Hines, M., 353
Hirschfeld, A. J., 287
Hirschfeld, R. M. A., 344
Hirsh, I. J., 116
Hitch, G., 207
Hobfoil, S. E., 410
Hobson, J. A., 148, 149, 160
Hocevar, D., 286
Hochberg, J., 110, 111
Hock, E., 348
Hodge, C. N., 518
Hodges, S. D., 505
Hodgkin, A. L., 61
Hoek, H. W., 452
Hoff-Ginsberg, E., 238, 239
Hoffrage, U., 254, 257
Hofmann, V., 333
Hofstede, G., 498
Hogan, J., 274
Hogan, R., 274
Hogarth, R. M., 249, 253
Holahan, C. J., 405, 410, 441
Holden, C., 234
Hollan, D., 148
Holland, C. K., 510
Holland, J. C., 409
Hollander, E., 430, 431
Hollands, C., 49
Holley, A., 121
Hollingworth, L. S., 5
Hollis, K. L., 187
Hollon, S. D., 466, 476

Holmberg, S., 47
Holmes, D. S. ., 152, 217
Holmes, J. G., 500
Holmes, T. H., 398, 409
Holt-Lunstad, J., 410
Holyoak, K. J., 246
Homma-True, R., 477
Honkonen, T., 481
Honts, C. R., 310
Hooper, J., 89
Hori, T., 159
Horn, J. N., 276
Hornstein, G. A., 8
Horowitz, F. D., 6
Hosseini, H., 508
Houston, B. K., 407
Howard, A., 14
Howard, D. J., 521
Howard, K. I., 468
Hoyt, I. P., 436
Hrdy, S. B., 303
Hsieh, C., 412
Hsu, L. K. G., 451
Hu, T. W., 477
Hubbard, J. R., 402, 406
Hubel, D. H., 10, 12, 74, 90, 101–102, 108
Hudson, W., 112
Huff, C., 48
Huffcutt, A. I., 144, 145
Hughes, C. C., 450, 477
Hughes, J., 66
Hulme, C., 209
Hultsch, D. F., 350
Hummel, J. E., 109
Hunt, E., 258, 328
Hunt, H., 148
Hunt, J. M., 504
Hunter, J. E., 273, 274
Hurvich, L. M., 107
Hus, L. k. G., 486
Husband, T. H., 218
Huston, A. C., 355, 536
Huttenlocher, J., 339
Huttenlocher, P. R., 91
Huxley, A. F., 61
Hyde, J. S., 352
Hyde, R. T., 419
Hyman, I. E., Jr., 218
Hyman, S. E, 157

I

Ickovics, J. R, 413
Inglehart, R., 317
Innocenti, G. M., 354, 91
Insabella, G. M., 357
Irizarry, M. C., 409
Ironson, G., 409
Irvine, S. H., 274
Isaac, R. J., 482
Isabella, R. A., 333
Isada, N. B., 328
Iwao, S., 502
Iwawaki, S., 274
Izard, C. E., 310, 311, 312, 315

J

Jacklin, C. N., 355
Jackson, L. A., 518
Jackson, R. J., 432
Jacob, T., 348
Jacobs, G. H., 106

Jacobs, W. J., 221
Jacobsen, T., 333
James, W., 313, 4, 9, 136
Jamison, K. R., 287, 438, 439
Janis, I. L, 401, 397, 514, 515
Janofsky, J. S., 447
Janus, C. L., 301
Janus, S. S., 301
Jaroff, L., 218
Jarvik, M. E., 411
Jayson, M. D., 409
Jemmott, J. B., III, 410
Jensen, A. R., 273, 274, 276, 278–279, 280, 281–282, 288
Jessell, T. M., 122, 124
Jey, C. B., 276
John, O. P., 363
Johnson, B. T., 505
Johnson, C., 494
Johnson, D., 49, 481
Johnson, E. J., 250
Johnson, J. G., 397
Johnson, J. H., 409
Johnson, J. S., 239, 241
Johnson, M. E., 258
Johnson, M. K., 212, 213
Johnson, V. E., 298–300
Johnston, W. A., 203
Joiner, T. E., Jr., 441
Jones, E. E., 495, 497
Jones, G. V., 201
Jordan, B., 123
Jorgensen, R. S., 418
Joseph, A. B., 409
Joseph, P., 87
Joshipura, K. J., 412
Judd, C. M., 519
Judd, L. L., 445
Julien, R. M., 153
Jung, C. G., 10, 368–370, 385, 464
Just, N., 440

K

Kagan, J., 332, 391
Kahan, T. L., 136, 147
Kahane, H., 258
Kahneman, D., 251, 252, 253, 255, 257, 319, 455, 487
Kalant, H, 157
Kalant, O. J, 157
Kales, J. D., 160,, 161
Kalichman, S. C, 413, 414
Kalmijn, M., 499
Kalmuss, D., 348
Kalton, G., 47
Kamen-Siegel, L., 411
Kamin, L. J., 171, 279
Kamiya, J., 135
Kamps, D. M., 470
Kandall, S. R., 328
Kandel, E. R., 63, 64, 122, 221
Kane, J., 415
Kane, T. D., 374
Kanowitz, J., 47
Kaplan, A. G., 484
Kaplan, H., 330
Kaplan, H. I., 467
Kaplan, N. M., 412
Kaplan, R. M., 280
Kaprio, J., 343
Kapur, S., 445
Karau, S. J., 513
Kardiner, A., 381

Karkowski, K. M., 441
Karon, B. P., 475
Kasser, T., 303
Katigbak, M. S., 381
Katz, N. R,, 416
Katz, R., 348
Kaufman, J. C., 274
Kaufman, K., 355
Kaufman, L., 114
Kaufmann, C. A., 439
Kausler, D. H., 350
Kavanaugh, D. J., 446
Kavesh, L., 492
Kaye, W. H., 451
Kazdin, A. E., 193
Kazdin, A. E., 480
Keck, P. E., 442
Keefe, R. C., 302
Keenan, J. P., 503
Keesey, R. E., 72
Kehoe, E. J., 171
Keith, C., 357
Keith-Spiegel, P., 484
Keller, L. S., 386
Keller, P. A., 505
Keller, P. A., 508
Kelley, H. H., 20
Kelley, H. H., 495
Kelly, D. D., 124
Kelly, J. A, 413
Kelly, J. P., 72, 124
Kelman, H. C., 49
Kelman, J. S., 511
Kemeny, M. E., 33
Kempen, H. J. G., 12
Ken, P. N., 47
Kendler, K. S, 431, 437, 441, 452
Kenrick, D. T., 13, 131, 302, 352, 353, 374, 502
Keren, G., 255
Kerfoot, P, 157
Kernan, J. B., 504
Kesner, R. P., 74
Kessen, W., 336
Kessler, R. C., 439, 441, 460, 461, 501
Ketcham, K., 217
Ketterlinus, R. D., 332
Khersonsky, D., 499
Kiang, N. Y. S., 118
Kiecolt-Glaser, J. K., 409, 410, 418
Kiesler, C. A., 481, 482
Kihlstrom, J. F., 151, 436
Kilbey, M. M., 41, 408
Killeen, F. R., 189
Kim, H., 511
Kim, K., 339
Kim, O., 493
Kimberg, D. Y., 74
Kimmel, D., 305
Kimura, D., 354, 505, 88
Kinsbourne, M., 224, 354
Kinsey, A., 303, 304
Kirk, S. A., 427
Kirkpatrick, L. A., 333, 502
Kirsch, I., 150, 151
Kitayama, S., 84, 384
Kitchens, A., 87
Kitson, G. C., 347

Kittler, P. G., 121, 296
Klauer, K. C., 209
Klein, M., 464
Klein, W. M., 252
Kleinbölting, H., 257
Kleinke, C. L., 311
Kleinman, A., 447
Kleinman, J. E., 444
Kleinmuntz, B., 386, 439
Kleinnecht, E. E., 218
Kleitman, N., 141
Klerman, E. B., 145
Klerman, G. L., 435, 476
Kliegl, R., 350
Kline, D. W., 349
Kline, P., 272, 388
Kling, K. C., 352
Klipper, M. Z., 418
Kluckhohn, C., 381
Kluegel, J. R., 518
Kluft, R. P., 218, 436
Klymenko, V., 102
Knable, M. B., 444
Knauper, B., 439
Knight, G. P., 352
Knowles, J. A., 439
Knowlton, B., 220
Knox, R., 499
Knudsen, E. I., 72
Koehler, J. J., 252
Koelling, R. A., 187
Koestler, J., 61
Koestner, R., 307
Kogan, N., 346
Kohlberg, L., 340–342
Kohler, S. S., 274
Kohut, H., 464
Kolb, B., 66
Kolb, R., 434
Koob, G. F, 156
Kopta, S. M., 468
Koranyi, E. K., 402
Koriat, A., 204, 229
Korn, J. H., 9
Korn, J., 49
Kortenhaus, C. M., 355
Kory, R. B., 152
Kosslyn, S. M., 88
Kosten, T. R, 156
Kotovsky, K., 246
Kotulak, R., 90
Kozak, M. J, 431
Kracke, W., 147, 148
Krajicek, D., 110
Krakauer, D., 121
Kramer, M., 147
Krames, L., 486
Krantz, D. H., 255
Kraus, L. A., 410
Krebs, D. L., 494–495
Krebs, J. R., 182
Krosnick, J. A., 47, 504
Kruegel, W. C. F., 225
Krueger, J., 497, 519
Krull, D. S., 496
Kryger, M. H., 138, 159
Ksir, C., 146
Kuhl, P. K., 91
Kulick, R. R., 442
Kulik, J., 208
Kumar, V., 220
Kunda, Z., 518
Kupfer, D. J., 142
Kupferman, I., 72
Kurzban, R., 13

Subject Index

Conner, Dennis, 293
conscientiousness, 362, 380, 381, 411
conscious mind, 364, 365
consciousness
  dissociated, 151
  drugs and, 152–158
  evolutionary roots of, 137
  in hypnosis, 151
  James on, 4–5
  nature of, 136–137
  states of, 135, 137
  stream of, 5, 136
  Wundt's study of, 3
conservation, 337–338
consolidation, memory, 220
constancies, perceptual, 113
construct validity, 266–267
constructive coping, 405–406, 417–419
consummatory behavior, 403–404
  self-modification of, 193–195
contagious diseases, 395–396
content validity, 266
context, memory retrieval and, 212
context effects, in perception, 111, 115
contingencies, reinforcement, 176
continuity, as Gestalt principle, 109
contradictory evidence, 27
contrast effects, in persuasion, 130–131
control
  as goal of scientific approach, 32
  illusion of, 405
control group, 37, 38
conventional level, of moral reasoning, 341
convergent thinking, 285
conversion disorder, 434
coping
  constructive, 405–406, 417–419
  defensive, 376, 404–405
  defined, 403
  repressive, 367
  styles of, 403–406
cornea, 97, 98
coronary heart disease, 406–407, 408, 412
corpus callosum, 71, 74, 76, 353–354
correlation, 39, 40, 265
  causation and, 41–42, 356, 420
  measuring, 538–539
  positive vs. negative, 40, 41, 266, 538
  prediction and, 40–41, 539
  reliability and, 265–266
  strength of, 40, 538
correlation coefficient, 39, 40, 41, 265–266, 538–539, 540
corticosteroids, 403
co-sleeping, 142
counseling psychologists, 462
counseling psychology, 16, 386
counselors, 462

counterarguments, 320
counterattitudinal behavior, 506, 507
counterconditioning, 469
courtship behavior, 85
  tactics in, 502–503
crack cocaine, 154, 157
crank cocaine, 154
creativity, 285–287
  correlates of, 286–287
  defined, 285
  intelligence and, 286
  measuring, 285–286
  mental illness and, 286–287
credibility
  evaluating, 520–521
  of information sources, 504, 505
criterion-related validity, 266
critical periods, 90
critical thinking skills, 26–27, 31
cross dressing, 427
cross-sectional studies, 331
cross-situational consistency, 374
CT (computerized tomography) scans, 69
Cubism, 127
cultural bias, in IQ tests, 280
cultural diversity, psychology and, 12–13
cultural values, eating disorders and, 452–453
culture
  attachment and, 333–334
  attributional tendencies and, 498
  child-rearing patterns and, 498
  cognitive style and, 248–249
  conformity and, 511
  defined, 19
  depth perception and, 112–113
  dreaming and, 147–148
  emotions and, 311–312
  gender differences and, 353
  IQ scores and, 278–281
  IQ testing and, 274
  language and, 241–242
  language learning and, 238
  love and, 502
  marriage and, 502
  mate selection and, 302, 502
  moral reasoning and, 342
  motor development and, 330
  pace of life and, 42, 43
  pain perception and, 123
  perception and, 125
  personality and, 381, 384
  problem solving and, 248–249
  psychological disorders and, 447, 450
  psychological testing and, 284
  psychotherapy and, 477
  romantic relationships and, 502
  sleep habits and, 142, 144
  social loafing and, 513
  taste preferences and, 122, 296–297

visual illusions and, 114, 115
culture-bound disorders, 450
cumulative deprivation hypothesis, 276–277
cumulative recorder, 176, 177
curare, 65
cynicism, 407

D

daily cycles, 138
Dali, Salvador, 128, 146
Dani, 242
dark adaptation, 99–100
data
  analyzing, 34
  collecting, 34
  organizing, 534
dating, 500
  attractiveness and, 499
  tactics in, 502–503
day care, attachment and, 333
death row inmates, 43
decay, memory, 209, 215
decentration, 338
deception
  in research, 48–49, 511
  in self-report inventories, 388
decibels, 117
decision making, 249–254
  defined, 249
  evidence-based, 55
  evolutionary view of, 253–354
  flaws in, 253–254
  in groups, 513–515
  about health-related issues, 420–421
  heuristics in, 251–252, 255
  models for, 249–250
  pitfalls in, 255–257
  risky, 251, 255, 514
declarative memory system, 222–223
defense mechanisms, 366–367, 404–405, 463, 465
defensive coping, 376
definitions, power of, 162–163
deinstitutionalization, 480–482
dejection, 400
delta waves, 137, 141
delusions, 442
delusions of grandeur, 442, 443
dementia, 349
dendrites, 60, 61
dendritic trees, 60
denial of reality, 405
dentate gyrus, 73, 220, 221
dependence, drug, 155, 157
dependent variable, 36, 37, 38
depression (depressive disorders), 427, 437–441
  cognitive factors in, 440–441
  cognitive therapy for, 466
  creativity and, 286–287
  culture and, 450
  drug therapy for, 473
  ECT for, 474
  etiology of, 439–441
  gender differences in, 438
  genetic vulnerability to, 439

illusion of control and, 405
interpersonal factors in, 441
neurotransmitters and, 65, 439–440
prevalence of, 438, 448
smoking and, 408
stress and, 441
symptoms of, 437–438
deprivation, environmental, 276–277
depth perception, 111–113
description, as goal of scientific approach, 32
descriptive statistics, 535
descriptive/correlational research, 39–42
determinism, 8, 372
development, 326
  See also specific types of development
developmental norms, 330
developmental psychology, 15
deviance, 427
diabetes, 296
diagnosis, 427
Diagnostic and Statistical Manual of Mental Disorders (DSM), 428–429
dichromatic color blindness, 105
diet
  of pregnant women, 328
  poor, 412
diffusion of responsibility, 512–513
digestive system, 295–296
disciplining, of children, 185–186
disconfirming evidence, 229, 256
discrimination
  in classical conditioning, 174, 179
  in operant conditioning, 179
discrimination (social), 495, 517, 518
discriminative stimuli, 179
diseases
  chronic, 396
  contagious, 395–396
  psychosomatic, 406, 433
  See also illness; specific diseases
dishabituation, 339–340
disinhibition, with hypnosis, 150
disorganized schizophrenia, 443
displacement, 367
display rules, 312
dissociation, in hypnosis, 151
dissociative amnesia, 435–436
dissociative disorders, 429, 435–437
dissociative fugue, 436
dissociative identity disorder (DID), 436–437
dissonance theory, 506–508
distal stimuli, 110, 116
distance perception, 111–113
distinctiveness, of personality, 362
distribution
  frequency, 534

normal, 269, 271–272, 536–538
skewed, 535, 536
divergent thinking, 285
divorce, 357
Dix, Dorothea, 480
dizygotic twins. See fraternal twins
DNA, 79
door-in-the-face technique, 130
dopamine, 444–445, 472, 473, 65, 73, 155–156
double-blind procedure, 48
Doublespeak (Lutz), 258
Doyle, A. Conan, 233
dream analysis, 463
dreams (dreaming), 146–149, 160–161
  content of, 146–147
  culture and, 147–148
  falling in, 161
  interpretation of, 148, 161
  links to waking life in, 147
  recall of, 148, 160–161
  REM sleep and, 141
  theories of, 148–149
  value of, 146
drinking, problem, 154–155
drives, biological, 72
  See also motivation; motives
driving, drunk, 158
drug dependence, 155, 157
drug therapy, 471–474, 481
drug use (abuse), 152, 427
  during pregnancy, 328
  effect on physical health, 157–158
  effect on psychological health, 159
  effect on sleep, 159–160
drugs, 152–158
  effects of, 153, 154, 155
  neurotransmitters and, 65, 73
  See also specific drugs
DSM-IV, 428, 429
dual-coding theory, 205

E

ear, auditory processing in, 117–118
eardrum, 118
eating behavior, 294–298
  brain and, 72
  food-related cues for, 298
  in rats, 84
  neurotransmitters and, 65
eating disorders, 429, 451–455
  etiology of, 452–453
  prevalence of, 452
eating habits
  culture and, 296–297
  poor, 412
eclecticism, in psychotherapy, 476
education programs, for underprivileged, 274
educational enrichment programs, 288, 289
educational/school psychology, 16
efferent nerve fibers, 67
effort justification, 507–508

gonadotropins, 78
gonads, 78, 79, 343
Gore, Tipper, 438
Grant, Cary, 325–326
graphs, 534
grasshoppers, camouflage of, 84
Greenspan, Alan, 273
grief, 400
group cohesiveness, 514, 515
group dynamics, 513–515
group polarization, 513–514
group size, conformity and, 509
group tests, 269–270
group therapy, 467–468
groups, 512–515
  bystander effect and, 512–513
  coordination in, 513
  cultural differences and, 19
  decision making in, 513–515
  defined, 512
  diffusion of responsibility in, 512–513
  productivity in, 513
  social loafing in, 513
  types of, 512
groupthink, 514–515
growth hormone, 138
growth needs, 377
growth spurt, adolescent, 342
guilt
  defense mechanisms and, 366
  depression and, 438
gustatory system, 119, 120–121

H
H. M., 220
habits, health-impairing, 252
habituation, 339–340
hair cells,
  for hearing, 118, 119
  for sense of balance, 124
hallucinations, 443
  in hypnosis, 150
hallucinogens, 153, 154, 155, 157
happiness, 317–319
  in marriage, 347–348
  measurement of, 317
  moderate predictors of, 318
  noncorrelates of, 317–318
  strong predictors of, 319
Harvard School of Public Health, 154–155
hashish, 153, 154
hassles, 397
Head Start, 288
health
  happiness and, 318
  stress and, 406–411
health care, costs of, 475
health-impairing behavior, 411–414
health maintenance organizations (HMOs), 475
health providers, communication with, 415
health psychology, 396
hearing, 116–119
  aging and, 349

theories of, 119
heart attack, 406, 407, 408, 412
heart disease
  emotions and, 408
  smoking and, 411
  Type A behavior and, 406–407
height in plane, 112
helping behavior, 512–513
helplessness, learned, 440
hemispheric specialization, 75–78, 87–89
  gender differences in, 353–354
Hereditary Genius (Galton), 268
heredity
  anxiety disorders and, 431–432
  basic principles of, 79–80
  environment and, 20, 81, 86, 278, 284
  homosexuality and, 305, 306
  intelligence and, 268, 274–276, 278
  mood disorders and, 439
  personality and, 378–380
  schizophrenia and, 444
  study of, 80–81
heritability, 289
  of intelligence, 276, 278–279
  of personality traits, 379–380
heritability ratios, 276
heroin, 66, 153
herpes, genital, 409
hertz (Hz), 116
heterosexuality, 303
heuristics
  in judging probabilities, 251–252, 255, 256, 455
  in problem solving, 245
hierarchical classification, 338
hierarchy of needs, 376–377
higher-order conditioning, 174
highway hypnosis, 151
Hinckley, John, Jr., 447
hindbrain, 70, 71
hindsight bias, 228–229, 390–391, 455
hippocampus, 71, 72, 73, 220
histogram, 534
histrionic personality, 435
Hitler, Adolf, 520
HIV (human immunodeficiency virus), 413
hobbits and orcs problem, 243, 244
Holmes, Sherlock, 233
home environment, personality and, 280
homelessness, mental illness and, 481–482
homosexuality, 303–306
  AIDS and, 413, 414
  biological explanations of, 305–306
  causes of, 304–306
  concealing, 33–34
  environmental explanations of, 304–305
  prevalence of, 304
hopelessness theory, 440

hormones, 78–79
  in adolescence, 343
  aging and, 349
  in fight-or-flight response, 309
  gender differences and, 353
  homosexuality and, 305–306
  hunger and, 296
  memory and, 221
  stress and, 402–403
hospitalization, psychiatric, 480–482
hostility, 407
How to Sleep Like a Baby (Hales), 160
How to Win Friends and Influence People (Carnegie), 499
Hughes, Howard, 431
human nature, 9–10
human potential movement, 465
humanism, 375, 9–10
humanistic perspective
  on personality, 375–378, 382–383
  on psychotherapy, 465
humanistic theories
  evaluation of, 378
  Maslow's, 375–376
  Rogers's, 376–378
humor, as stress reducer, 418
hunger
  biological factors in, 294–296, 297
  environmental factors in, 296–298
  as motive, 294–298
hunger centers, in brain, 72
hunting and gathering culture, 13, 27, 353
hydrophobia, 430
hypertension, 420
hypnosis, 149–151
  as anesthesia, 149, 150
  defined, 150
  memory and, 151, 209
  regression under, 151
  theories of, 150–151
hypnotic induction, 150
hypochondriasis, 434, 450
hypothalamus, 71, 72, 73, 78, 79, 305
  autonomic arousal and, 402, 403
  biological clocks and, 138
  emotions and, 310
  hunger and, 295, 296, 297
hypotheses, 32
  perceptual, 110, 114, 115
  testing of, 539–541
hypothetical constructs, 267, 289

I
"I have a friend who" syndrome, 55
id, 364, 365, 366, 463
idealization, of romantic partners, 500
identical twins, 81
  homosexuality in, 305
  intelligence and, 275
  See also twin studies

identification, 366, 367, 368
identity diffusion, 345
identity formation, 344–345
identity statuses, 345
identity vs. role confusion, 344
Ifaluk, 312
ignorance, appeal to, 288–289
illness
  biopsychosocial model of, 395
  immune functioning and, 408–409
  life changes and, 398–399
  patterns of, 395–396
  reactions to, 414–416
  statistics and, 420–421
  stress and, 406–411
illusions
  optical, 113–115
  positive, 405, 500
illusory correlation, 494, 518
imagery, memory and, 204–205, 227
imitation. *See* modeling
immigrants, testing of, 280
immune functioning
  optimism and, 410
  stress and, 408–409, 411, 418
immune response, 409
immune system, 171
  AIDS and, 413
immunosuppression, 171
impatience, 407
implicit memory, 222, 223
impossible figures, 114, 115, 129
impression formation, 492–495
Impressionism, 126–127
improbable, overestimating, 256
incentive value, 307, 308
inclusive fitness, 84
incongruence, 375, 465
independent variable, 36–37, 38, 39
individual differences
  in achievement motive, 306–307
  testing of, 264
individual psychology, Adler's, 370
individualistic cultures, 498, 502, 511
induced structure, problems of, 243
industrial/organizational psychology, 16
industry vs. inferiority, 336
infants
  attachment patterns in, 332–333
  brain development in, 90
  cognitive development in, 336–337
  emotional development in, 331–334
  innate cognitive abilities of, 339–340
  language development in, 237
  mathematical abilities in, 340

motor development in, 329–331
personality development in, 335
sleep patterns in, 141–142, 143
temperaments in, 331–332
See also children
inferential statistics, 539–540
inferiority complex, 370
infidelity, 302
  in dating, 500
information
  irrelevant, 244
  organization of, 226
information processing, 203
  connectionist model of, 211
  in nervous system, 60
  in retina, 100, 101
  in visual cortex, 101–102, 107
information-processing theory, 205, 206
infrared spectrum, 97
ingroups, 494–495, 519
inhibition
  emotional, 33–34
  conditioned, 379
inhibitory PSPs, 63
initiative vs. guilt, 335–336
inner ear, 118, 124
insanity, 447
insight, 244, 285
insight therapies, 460, 462–468, 478–479
  effectiveness of, 468
insomnia, 145–146, 160
inspection time, 282
instinctive drift, 186
institutionalization, 480
insulin, 296, 297
integrity vs. despair, 347
intellectualization, 405
intelligence
  adoption studies of, 275–276
  aging and, 349
  attractiveness and, 493
  biological indexes of, 281–282
  cognitive perspective on, 282–283
  creativity and, 286
  environmental factors in, 276–277, 278
  ethnic/cultural differences in, 278–281
  expanding the concept of, 283–284
  experience and, 282
  happiness and, 318
  heredity and, 274–276, 278
  heritability estimates for, 276, 278–279
  as hypothetical construct, 289
  interaction of heredity and environment in, 278
  manifestations of, 282
  reification of, 289
  triarchic theory of, 282, 283
  twin studies of, 81, 275
  types of, 273
intelligence quotient (IQ), 268–270

unconditioned stimulus (UCS), 169, 170, 171, 174, 187
unconscious
    defense mechanisms and, 404
    forgetting and, 217
    Freud's view of, 7, 8, 18, 136, 364–365, 366, 369, 463
underextension, 238
understanding, as goal of scientific approach, 32
undifferentiated schizophrenia, 443
undoing, 405
unipolar disorder, 437
University of Leipzig, 3
University of Minnesota twin study, 378, 379
U.S. Surgeon General's Report on mental health, 460, 461
utility, subjective, 251

V
vacillation, 398
validity
    of intelligence tests, 272–273

of psychological tests, 266–267
Valium, 472, 473
van Gogh, Vincent, 113
variability, measures of, 536
variable-interval schedule, 181
variable-ratio schedule, 180, 181, 182
variables, 32, 36
    confounding, 38
    correlations between, 39–40, 41–42, 538–539
    extraneous, 37–38
    multiple, 39
Vasarely, Victor, 128, 129
vasocongestion, 298–299
ventricles, of brain, 445
ventromedial nucleus, of hypothalamus (VMH), 295
Verbal Behavior (Skinner), 240
verbal skills, gender differences in, 351, 353
verifiability, 6
vested interest, 504, 520
vestibular system, 124–125
vision
    aging and, 349

basic processes in, 97–100
brain processing of, 77, 101–103
color, 99, 103–107
constancies in, 113
visual acuity, 99
visual agnosia, 95
visual cortex, 74, 75, 101–102, 103, 106
visual field, 76, 77, 102
visual imagery, memory and, 204–205, 227
visual-spatial ability, gender differences in, 13, 27, 352, 353
visual system, 96–115
visuospatial sketchpad, 208
vocabulary spurt, 237–238
vocalizations, of infants, 237
vulnerability, genetic, 81, 419

W
waist-to-hip ratio, 502
Walker, Alice, 88
walking, development of, 330

water jar problem, 243, 244, 245
wavelength
    of light waves, 96, 97, 103–104, 107
    of sound waves, 116
Wechsler Adult Intelligence Scale (WAIS), 269, 270
weight, obsession with, 451, 452
well-being, subjective, 317–319
Wernicke's area, 75
Whorfian hypothesis, 242
Windigo, 450
wine tasting, 120, 121
wish fulfillment, dreams as, 148
withdrawal illness, 157
    with antianxiety drugs, 472
    with antipsychotic drugs, 473
Woods, Tiger, 506
words, 235
    children's learning of, 237
work, happiness and, 318
work shifts, sleep and, 139

working memory, 208
    aging and, 350
    brain and, 74
World War I, 10
World War II, 10–11
writers, mood disorders and, 286–287

X
Xanax, 472

Y
yeast infections, 409
Yoruba, 312

Z
Zollner illusion, 114
Zoloft, 473
Zulus, 115
zygote, 326, 327

Credits

This page constitutes an extension of the copyright page. We have made every effort to trace the ownership of all copyrighted material and to secure permission from copyright holders. In the event of any question arising as to the use of any material, we will be pleased to make the necessary corrections in future printings. Thanks are due to the following authors, publishers, and agents for permission to use the material indicated.

Photo Credits

Cover
"Untitled" by Victor Vasarely, screenprint. Bridgeman Art Library. Copyright © 2001 by Artists Rights Society (ARS), New York / ADAGP, Paris.

Contents
xxiii: © Bill Ross/CORBIS; xxiv: © Jodi Cobb/NGS Image Collection; xxv: © Airelle-Joubert/Phanie/Stock Connection; xxvi: © Eastcott-Momatiuk/The Image Works xxvii: © Mitchell Funk; xxviii: © Carl Vanderschuit/Index Stock Imagery; xxix: © Goavec Pierre-Yves/The Image Bank; xxx: © William Whitehurst 1997/The Stock Market; xxxi: © Hal Lee Miller Photography; xxxii: © Galen Rowell/CORBIS; xxxiii: Stone/Ed Honowitz; xxxiv: Stone/Marty Loken; xxxvi: © by Diana Ong/Superstock xxxv: © 2001 Corbis xxxvii: © Michael Agliolo/International Stock; xxxviii: © Lisette Le Bon/Superstock

Chapter 1
1: © Bill Ross/CORBIS; 2: © Bill Ross/CORBIS; 2: (left) Susumu Takahaski/Reuters/Archive Photos 2: (right) © Ed Eckstein/CORBIS 5: (all) Archives of the History of American Psychology, University of Akron, Akron, Ohio 8: Courtesy of the Clark University Archives 9: Copyright 1971 *Time* Inc. Reprinted by permission 19: © Bob Daemmrich/Stock Boston 23: © Chuck Pelley/Stock, Boston

Chapter 2
30: Jodi Cobb/NGS Image Collection 31: Jodi Cobb/NGS Image Collection 43: (right) © Peter Turnley/CORBIS 47: Courtesy of Robert Rosenthal 49: (top) Yale University 51: (bottom) Craig McClain 54: (left) © Wally McNamee/CORBIS 54: (right) © Douglas Kirkland/CORBIS

Chapter 3
58: © Airelle-Joubert/Phanie/Stock Connection 59: © Airelle-Joubert/Phanie/Stock Connection 65: (top) © 1991 Analisa Kraft 66: © Dan McCoy/Rainbow 69: (left) © Alvis Upitis/The Image Bank 69: (right) © Dan McCoy/

Rainbow 70: (top) © ISM-Sovereign/PhotoTake 70: (bottom) © Wellcome Dept of Cognitive Neurology/Science Photo Library/Photo Researchers, Inc. 71: (top) © Manfred Kage/Peter Arnold, Inc. 76: Courtesy of Roger Sperry 81: (top) The Pennsylvania State University Center for Development and Health Genetics; 82: CORBIS-Bettmann 83: (bottom) John Dominis , Life Magazine © Time Inc. 84: Courtesy of John Alcock 86: (inset) © C. K. Lorenz/Photo Researchers, Inc. 88: (left) © Renato Rotolo/CORBIS 88: (right) © Owen Franken/CORBIS

Chapter 4
94: © Eastcott-Momatiuk/The Image Works 95: (top) © Eastcott-Momatiuk/The Image Works 95: (center) © Diane Padys/FPG International 99: (right) Craig McClain 101: (right) © Ira Wyman/CORBIS-Sygma 104: (right center) Courtesy BASF 108: (photo) Archives of the History of American Psychology, University of Akron, Akron, Ohio; 112: (center center) © John Elk III/Stock, Boston 112: (top center) © Christopher Talbot Frank 112: (top left) © Peter Turner/The Image Bank 112: (center right) U.S. Department of Energy 112: (top right) © Deborah Davis/Photo Edit 112: (center left) © Deborah Davis/Photo Edit 113: (top) van Gogh, Vincent, *Corridor in the Asylum* (1889), gouche and watercolor, 24-3/8 × 18-1/2 inches (61.5 × 47.cm). Metropolitan Museum of Art. Bequest of Abby Aldrich Rockefeller, 1948. (48.190.2) Photograph © 1998 The Metropolitan Museum of Art. 115: © Peter Menzel/Stock, Boston 117: (inset) Stone/David Barnes 119: (photo) Stock Montage 121: Courtesy of the Yale School of Medicine ; 126: (4.42) Maestro della cattura di Cristo, Cattura di Cristo, parte centrale, Assisi, S. Francisco, Scala/Art Resource, New York 126: (4.43) Brera Predica di S. Marco Pinaocteca, by Gentile and Giovanni Belini in Egitto Scala/Art Resource, New York; 127: (4.44) Georges Seurat, French, 1859–1891, *Sunday Afternoon on the Island of La Grande Jatte,* oil on canvas, 1884–1886, 207.6 × 308 cm, Helen Birch Bartlett Memorial Collection, 1926.224, © 1990 The Art Institute of Chicago, all rights reserved 127: (4.45) Pablo Picasso, *Violin and Grapes, Céret and Sorgues* (spring-early fall 1912), oil on canvas, 20 × 24 inches (50.6 × 61 cm), collection, The Museum of Modern Art, New York, Mrs. David M. Levy Bequest. © The Museum of Modern Art, New York. © 2001 Estate of Pablo Picasso/Artists Rights Society (ARS), New York 128: Salvador Dali, *The Slave Market with the Disappearing Bust of Voltaire,* (1940), Oil on canvas, 18-1/4 × 25-3/8 inches. Collection of The Salvador Dali Museum, St. Petersburg, Fl. Copyright © 2001 The Salvador Dali Museum, Inc. © 2001 Kingdom of Spain, Gala-Salvador Dali Foundation/Artists Rights Society (ARS),

New York. 129: (top left) M.C. Escher's "Waterfall"© Gordon Art BV-Baarn-Holland. All rights reserved. 129: (top) M.C. Escher's "Belvedere" © Gordon Art BV-Baarn-Holland. All rights reserved. 129: (bottom right) Vasarely, Victor. "Tukoer-Ter-Ur," 1989 Private Collection, Monaco. Erich Lessing/Art Resource, NY. Copyright © 2001 Artists Rights Society (ARS),New York/ADAGP, Paris 129: (bottom left) Magritte, Rene, *Les Promenades d'Euclide,* The Minneapolis Institute of Arts, The William Hood Dunwoody Fund. Copyright © 2001 C. Herscovic, Brussels/Artists Rights Society (ARS) New York.

Chapter 5
134: © Mitchell Funk 135: © Mitchell Funk 136: Gene Sladek 140: © Andrew Holmgren/Peter Arnold, Inc. 145: Courtesy of William Dement 145: © Joseph Sohm/ChromoSohm-CORBIS 147: © Christine Caborne/CORBIS 148: National Library of Medicine 148: Rush Presbyterian St. Luke's Medical Center 150: Biomedical Research Foundation 151: AP/Wide World Photos 151: Courtesy of Ernest R. Hilgard 160: © Topham/The Image Works

Chapter 6
166: © Carl Vanderschuit/Index Stock Imagery 167: © Carl Vanderschuit/Index Stock Imagery 168: Sovfoto/Eastfoto 169: CORBIS-Bettmann 171: Craig McClain 173: Archives of the History of American Psychology, University of Akron, Akron, Ohio 174: Archives of the History of American Psychology, University of Akron, Akron, Ohio 175: Courtesy of B. F. Skinner 177: © Richard Wood/The Picture Cube/Index Stock 178: Courtesy of Animal Behavior Enterprises, Inc. 178: © Gerald Davis/Colorific! 181: © David Woods/The Stock Market 181: © Rick Doyle/Uniphoto 181: © Julian Cotton/International Stock 181: © David Falconer/Folio, Inc 183: © Art Wolfe/Photo Researchers, Inc. 183: © Stephen J. Krasemann/DRK Photo 187: Courtesy of John Garcia 188: University of Pennsylvania 189: Courtesy of Albert Bandura 191: CORBIS-Bettmann 191: Archives of the History of American Psychology, University of Akron, Akron, Ohio 191: © Gerald Davis/Colorific! 191: © David Falconer/Folio, Inc. 191: © J. Markham/Bruce Coleman, Inc. 191: Stone/Andy Sacks 192: Stone/Andy Sacks 192: © J. Markham/Bruce Coleman, Inc. 196: © The Purcell Team/CORBIS

Chapter 7
200: © Goavec Pierre-Yves/The Image Bank 201: (top) ©Goavec Pierre-Yves/The Image Bank 206: © Jeffry W. Myers/Stock, Boston 207: Courtesy of George Miller 209: © Peter Turnley/CORBIS 210: Courtesy of W. F. Brewer. Brewer, W. F., and Treyens, J. C.,

"Role of schemata in memory of places," Cognitive Psychology, 1981, 13, 207–230. **211:** Denise Applewhite/Communications Department, Princeton University **212:** University of Washington News and Information Office **213:** Welcome Institute for the History of Medicine, London **219:** AP/Wide World Photos **223:** (top) © Tim Mosenfelder/CORBIS **223:** (right) Courtesy of Endel Tulving **228:** (left & right) CORBIS/Bettmann-UPI **229:** © Bob Daemmrich/The Image Works

Chapter 8
232: © William Whitehurst 1997/The Stock Market **233:** © William Whitehurst 1997/The Stock Market **234:** Carnegie-Mellon University **237:** Author's collection **240:** MIT photo by Donna Coveney/MIT News Office **241:** MIT photo by Donna Coveney, courtesy of Steven Pinker **242:** © Mia & Klaus Matthes/Superstock **247:** Craig McClain **248:** (top) Craig McClain **248:** (right) © Penny Tweedie/CORBIS **250:** © Don Mason/The Stock Market **251:** (top) Stanford University News and Publication Service **251:** (bottom) Courtesy of Daniel Kahneman **256:** Fort Worth Star Telegram/Sipa Press **257:** AP/Wide World Photos **258:** © Les Stone/CORBIS-Sygma **259:** © Reza/CORBIS-Sygma

Chapter 9
262: © Hal Lee Miller Photography **263:** © Hal Lee Miller Photography **268:** (top) CORBIS-Bettmann **268:** (bottom) Archives of the History of American Psychology, University of Akron, Akron, Ohio **269:** Archives of the History of American Psychology, University of Akron, Akron, Ohio **273:** (all-3) AP/Wide World Photos **278:** Courtesy of Sandra Scarr **279:** Cover of *The Bell Curve: Intelligence and Class Structure in American Life,* by R. J. Hernstein and M. Murray, Jacket, Copyright © 1994 by Simon & Schuster, Inc. By permission of The Free Press, a division of Simon & Schuster, Inc. **280:** Courtesy, Arthur R. Jensen **282:** Michael Marsland/Yale University **283:** Courtesy of Howard Gardner, photo © Jay Gardner **287:** (left) Rembrandt, Harmensz, vva Rijn, *Self-Portrait with Beard.* Museu de Arte, Sao Paulo, Brazil. Giraudon/Art Resource, NY **287:** (center) Delacroix, Eugene, *Portrait of Chopin,* Louvre, Paris: Giraudon/Art Resource, NY **287:** (right) Pomerian, 16th cent. *Portrait of Nicolas Copernicus.* Museum, Torun, Poland. Erich Lessing/Art Resource, NY **288:** AP/Wide World Photos **289:** Cover of *Naked in Cyberspace* by Carole A. Lane: Reproduced by courtesy and permission of Information Today, Inc., Medford, NJ

Chapter 10
292: © Kwame Zikomo/ Superstock **293:** (top) © Kwame Zikomo/ Superstock **293:** (center) Corbis-UPI/Bettmann Newsphotos **293:** (bottom) Guy Gurney/Sports Illustrated **296:** Courtesy of Judith Rodin **297:** (right) © Peter Menzel/Stock, Boston **297:** (left) © Peter Menzel/Stock, Boston **299:** (right-2) CORBIS-

UPI/Bettmann Newsphotos **302:** Courtesy of David M. Buss **303:** © Catherine Karnow/CORBIS **306:** Courtesy of David C. McClelland **310:** (left) © Mark C. Burnett/Stock, Boston **311:** Courtesy of Joseph LeDoux, New York University **312:** From *Unmasking the Face,* © 1975 by Paul Ekman, photograph courtesy of Paul Ekman **314:** (bottom) Courtesy of Donald G. Dutton, Department of Psychology, University of British Columbia; **314:** (left) © Bill Apple, courtesy of Stanley Schachter

Chapter 11
324: Stone/Ed Honowitz **325:** (top) Stone/Ed Honowitz **325:** (bottom) The Kobal Collection **327:** (top left) © Petit Format/Science Source/Photo Researchers, Inc. **327:** (center left) © Petit Format/Guigoz/ Science Source/Photo Researchers, Inc. **327:** (right) © Petit Format/Nestle/Science Source/Photo Researchers, Inc. **333:** Erik Hesse **336:** (bottom) AP/Wide World Photos **336:** (top) © O'Brien Productions/CORBIS **338:** (top) © Yves de Braine/Black Star **341:** Courtesy of Harvard University News Office **346:** (left) AP/Wide World Photos **346:** (right) Axel Koester/Los Angeles Times **348:** Stone/Jon Gray **349:** (left) © Doug Menuez/PhotoDisc, Inc. **352:** AP/Wide World Photos **356:** PhotoDisc, Inc.

Chapter 12
360: Stone/Marty Loken **361:** Stone/Marty Loken **363:** National Library of Medicine **364:** © Peter Aprahamian/CORBIS **368:** © Laura Dwight/CORBIS **369:** Culver Pictures, Inc. **370:** Culver Pictures, Inc. **371:** © Bettmann/CORBIS **372:** Courtesy, B.F. Skinner **373:** (top left) © Mark Antman/The Image Works **373:** (right) Courtesy of Professor Albert Bandura **374:** University photographer Joe Pineiro, Columbia University **375:** Courtesy of Center for Studies of the Person **377:** Brooks/Cole Collection **379:** Mark Gerson, FPIPP, London, courtesy of Hans Eysenck **380:** Courtesy of David M. Buss **381:** © Fujimoro/The Image Works **382:** (center above) © Richard Wood/The Picture Cube/Index Stock **382:** (center below) © Dratch/The Image Works **382:** (bottom) © Barbara Penoyar/PhotoDisc **382:** (top) © Peter Aprahamian/CORBIS **383:** (top) © Laura Dwight/CORBIS **383:** (center above) © Mark Antman/The Image Works **383:** (center below) © Syracuse Newspaper/The Image Works **384:** (left center) Courtesy of Shinobu Kitayama **384:** (left top) Photo and Campus Services, University of Michigan **389:** (top) © Laura Dwight/CORBIS **389:** (bottom) Reprinted by permission of the publishers from Henry A. Murray, Thematic Apperception Test, Cambridge, Mass.: Harvard University Press, Copyright © 1943 by The President and Fellows of Harvard College, © 1971 by Henry A. Murray. **390:** AP/Wide World Photos

Chapter 13
394: © 2001 Corbis **395:** © 2001 Corbis **397:** Courtesy of Richard S. Lazarus **402:** © Yousuf Karsh/Woodfin Camp & Associates **404:** © Bill

Aron/Photo Edit **405:** Courtesy Taylor **406:** © Arlene Collins **411:** © Martin E. P. Seligman **412:** © Bob Daemm... The Image Works **415:** (top) Steve Walag, University of California, Riverside **415:** (bottom) Stone/Steven Peters

Chapter 14
424: © by Diana Ong/Superstock **425:** © by Diana Ong/Superstock **426:** (right) Culver Pictures, Inc. **426:** (left) *St. Catherine of Siena Exorcising a Possessed Woman,* c. 1500–1510. Girolamo Di Benvenuto. Denver Art Museum Collection, Gift of Samuel H. Kress Foundation Collection, 1961.171 © Denver Art Museum 2001. **427:** Courtesy of Thomas Szasz **431:** (top) CORBIS-Bettmann **431:** (center) AP/Wide World Photos **438:** (left) © Matt Mendelsohn/Gamma Liaison **438:** (right) © Rick Maiman/CORBIS-Sygma **444:** Courtesy of Nancy Andreasen **447:** © Trippett/Sipa Press **448:** (top left) Munch, Edvard: *The Scream.* National Gallery, Oslo, Norway/Art Resource/NY **448:** (left center) van Gogh, Vincent: *Portrait of Dr. Gachet.* Musee d'Orsay, Paris. Erich Lessing/Art Resource, NY **448:** (bottom left) Derek Bayes, *Life Magazine,* © Time, Inc. **448:** (top right) CORBIS-Bettmann **448:** (right center) © Matt Mendelsohn/Gamma Liaison **448:** (bottom right) © Trippett/Sipa Press **451:** AP/Wide World Photos

Chapter 15
458: © Michael Agliolo/International Stock **459:** © Michael Agliolo/International Stock **460:** Mary Evans/Sigmund Freud Copyrights **463:** National Library of Medicine **464:** © Peter Aprahamian/CORBIS **465:** (right) Courtesy of Center for Studies of the Person **465:** (bottom) © Vision/Photo Researchers, Inc. **466:** Courtesy of Aaron T. Beck **467:** © Bob Daemmrich/The Image Works **469:** Courtesy, Dr. Joseph Wolpe **470:** © Steve McCarroll **474:** © W & D McIntyre/Photo Researchers, Inc. **477:** © Najiah Feanny/Stock, Boston **478:** National Library of Medicine **478:** (top center) Courtesy of Center for Studies of the Person **478:** (bottom center) Courtesy of Aaron T. Beck **478:** (bottom) Courtesy, Dr. Joseph Wolpe **479:** (3rd from top) © Bob Daemmrich/The Image Works **479:** (top) © Peter Aparhamian/CORBIS **479:** (2nd from top) © Vision/Photo Researchers, Inc. **479:** (4th from top) © Steve McCarroll **479:** (bottom left) © W & D McIntyre/Photo Researchers, Inc. **479:** (bottom right) PhotoDisc, Inc. **480:** (inset) Detail of painting in Harrisburg State Hospital, photo by Ken Smith/LLR Collection. **480:** (right) Culver Pictures, Inc. **484:** © Tom McCarthy/SKA **487:** © Tony Freeman/Photo Edit

Chapter 16
490: © Lisette Le Bon/Superstock **491:** © Lisette Le Bon/Superstock **493:** © Andrew Wakeford/PhotoDisc, Inc. **495:** University of Kansas **498:** © Doug Pensinger/Allsport **500:** Courtesy of Ellen Berscheid **501:** Courtesy of

Figure Credits

Chapter 1

9: Fig. 1.3 Adapted from "Historians' and Chairpersons' Judgements of Eminence Among Psychologists," by J. H. Korn, R. Davis & S. F. Davis, 1991, *American Psychologist, 46* (7), 789–792, (with data from "Rankings of the Most Notable Psychologists by Department Chairpersons," by R. E. Estes, M. L. Coston & G. P. Fournet, 1990 ((unpublished manuscript)) and adapted by permission.) Copyright © 1991 by the American Psychological Association. 12: Fig. 1.4 Adapted from "An Empirical Analysis of Trends in Psychology," by R. W. Robins, S. D. Gosling, & K. H. Craik, 1999, *American Psychologist, 54* (2), 117–128. Copyright © 1999 by the American Psychological Association. Reprinted by permission of the author. 14: Fig. 1.5 Adapted from data from the American Psychological Association by permission 22: Fig. 1.10 Adapted from "The Psychology of College Success: A Dynamic Approach" by H.C. Lindgren, 1969. John Wiley & Sons. Copyright © 1969 by Henry Clay Lindgren. Adapted by permission of H.C. Lindgren. 25: Fig. 1.11 Adapted from "Staying With Initial Answers on Objective Tests: Is It a Myth?," by L.T. Benjamin, Jr., T.A. Cavell & W. R. Shallenberger III, 1984, *Teaching of Psychology, 11* (3), 133–141. Copyright © 1984 Lawrence Erlbaum Associates, Inc. Adapted by permission of the author. 25: Fig. 1.12 Adapted from "Staying With Initial Answers on Objective Tests: Is It a Myth?," by L.T. Benjamin, Jr., T.A. Cavell & W. R . Shallenberger III, 1984, Teaching of Psychology, 11 (3), 133–141. Copyright © 1984 Lawrence Erlbaum Associates, Inc. Adapted by permission of the author. 27: Fig. 1.13 *From Form AA, 1962, Identical Blocks,* by R. E. Stafford and H. Gullikson.

Chapter 2

35: Fig. 2.3 Data from "elevated physical health risk among gay men who conceal their homosexual identity," by S. W. Cole, M. E. Taylor, B. R. Visscher, 1996, *Health Psychology, 15,* 243–251. 43: Table 2.2 Adapted from "The Pace of Life in 31 Countries" by R. V. Levine and A. Norenzayan, 1999, *Journal of Cross-Cultural Psychology, 30* (2), 178–205. Copyright © 1999 by Sage Publications, Inc. Reprinted

by permission. [e-book: Copied and delivered electroncially by permission; no further copying permitted without the written permission of of publisher] 44: Table 2.3 Adapted from "Personality and Attitudinal Characteristics of Sexually Coercive College Males, " by D. Rapaport and B.R. Burkhart, 1984. *Journal of Abnomal Psychology, 93,* (2), 216–221. Copyright © 1984 by the American Psychological Association. Adapted by permission of the author. 52: Fig. 2.13 This material is reprinted with permission of the American Psychological Association, publisher of PsycINFO Database (copyright © 1887–2001 APA), and may not be reproduced without prior permission. 53: (Fig. 2.14 This material is reprinted with permission of the American Psychological Association, publisher of PsycINFO Database (copyright © 1887–2001 APA), and may not be reproduced without prior permission.

Chapter 3

81: Fig. 3.20 Based on data from "Behavioral Genetics of Cognitive Ability:A Life-Span Perspective," by M. McGue, T.J. Bouchard, W.G. Iacono & D.T. Lykken, 1993. In R. Plomin & G.E. McClearn (Eds.), *Nature, Nurture and Psychology.* American Psychological Association. Extraversion data based on Genes and Environment in Personality Development, by J. C. Loehlin, 1992, Sage Publications. 85: (Table 3.2 Adapted from *Animal Behavior* by John Alcock, 1998, p. 463. Copyright © 1998 John Alcock. Reprinted by permission of Sinauer Associates and the author. 86: Fig. 3.21 From "Aggression and Sexual Activity of Male Southern Elephant Seals, Mirounga leonina," by T. S. McCann, 1981, Journal of Zoology, 195, 295–310. 87: Fig. 3.22 © Roy Doty 88: Fig. 3.23 Reprinted by permission of Jeremy P. Tarcher, Inc., a division of Penguin Putnam Publishing Group from DRAWING ON THE RIGHT SIDE OF THE BRAIN by Betty Edwards. Copyright © 1989 Betty Edwards. 89: Fig. 3.24 Data from "The Asymmetry of the Human Brain," by D. Kimura, 1973, *Scientific American, 228,* 70–78.

Chapter 4

112: Fig. 4.26 Adapted by permission from an illustration by Ilil Arbel on page 83 of "Pictorial Perception and Culture," by Jan B. Deregowski in *Scientific American, 227* (5) November 1972. Copyright © 1972 by Scientific American, Inc. All rights reserved. 117: Fig. 4.34 Table 5-3, adapted from *Introduction to Psychology, Ninth Edition,* by Rita L. Atkinson, Richard C. Atkinson, Edward F. Smith, and Ernest R. Hilgard, copyright © 1987 by Harcourt Inc., reprinted by permission of the publisher.

Chapter 5

138: Fig. 5.2 (Adapted) from *Wide Awake at 3:00 AM,* by Coleman. Copyright © 1986 by Richard M. Coleman. Used with permission of W. H. Freeman and Company. 139: Fig. 5.3

Data from "Sleep After Transmeridian Flights," by A. N. Nicholson, P.A. Pascoe, M. B. Spencer, B.M. Stone, T. Roehis & T. Roth, 1986, Lancet, 2, 1201–08. 141: Fig. 5.4 Figure from "Current Concepts:The Sleep Disorders," by P. Hauri, 1982, The Upjohn Company, Kalamazoo, Michigan. Reprinted by permission. 143: Fig. 5.6 Figure adapted from an updated revision of a figure in "Ontogenetic Development of Human Sleep Dream Cycle," by H.P. Roffwarg, J.N. Muzio, and W.C. Dement, 1966. *Science, 152,* 604–609. Copyright © 1966 by the American Association for the Advancement of Science. Adapted and revised by permission of the author. 148: Table 5.2 Adapted from "The Personal Use of Dream Beliefs in the Toraja Highlands," by D. Hollan, 1989, *Ethos, 17,* 166–186. Copyright © 1989 by the American Anthropological Association. Reproduced by permission of the American Anthropological Association from Ethos 17:2, June 1989. Not for further reproduction. 152: Fig. 5.9 (Redrawn) from illustration on p. 86 by Lorelle A. Raboni of *Scientific American, 226,* 85–90, Feb. 1972). From "The Physiology of Meditation," by R. K. Wallace and H. Benson. Copyright © 1972 by Scientific American, Inc. 154: Fig. 5.10 Figure 5.15 from *Health and Wellness, Third Edition,* by Edlin and Golanty, p. 294. Copyright © 1992, Jones & Bartlett Publishers, Inc. Reprinted with permission. 159: Fig. 5.13 Adapted from Sleep, the Gentle Tyrant, 2nd Ed. by Wilse B. Webb, 1992. Copyright © 1992 by Anker Publishing Co., Bolton, Ma. Adapted by permission. 160: Fig. 5.14 Adapted from *Power Sleep* by James B. Maas, PhD. Copyright © 1998 by James B. Mass, Ph. D. Reprinted by permission of Villard Books, a division of Random House, Inc. 161: Fig. 5.16 Based on data from Evaluation and Treatment of Insomnia, by A. Kales and J.D. Kales, p. 95, 1984. Copyright © 1984 by Oxford University Press. Reprinted by permission.

Chapter 6

168: Fig. 6.1 Adapted from "The Method of Pavlov in Animal Psychology," by R. M. Yerkes and S. Morgulis, 1909, *Psychological Bulletin, 6,* 257–273. American Psychological Association. 195: Fig. 6.22 Adapted from *Self-Directed Behavior: Self-Modification for Personal Adjustment,* by D. L. Watson and R.G. Tharp, 1989, 1997, p. 271. Copyright ©, 1997, 1989 by Wadsworth, Inc. Adapted by permission .

Chapter 7

201: Fig. 7.1 From "Long-Term Memory for a Common Object," by R. S. Nickerson and M.J. Adams, 1979, *Cognitive Psychology, 11,* 287–307. Copyright © 1979 by Academic Press, Inc. Reprinted by permission. 211: Fig. 7.10 Adapted from "A Spreading Activation Theory of Semantic Processing, " by A.M. Collins and E.F. Loftus, 1975, *Psychological Review, 82,* 407–428. Copyright © 1975 by the American Psychological Association. Adapted by permission. 213: Fig. 7.10 Based on "Reconstruction of Automobile Destruction: An Example of Interaction Between Language and Memory," by E. F. Loftus and J.C. Palmer, 1974, *Journal of Verbal Learning and Verbal Behavior, 13,* 585–589. Academic Press, Inc. Adapted by permission of the author. **218:** Fig. 7.16 Based on data from "Prevalence of Child Physical and Sexual Abuse in the Community," by H. L. MacMillan, J. E. Fleming, N. Trocme, M. H. Boyle, M. Wong, Y. A. Racine, W. R. Beardslee, & D. R. Offord, 1997, *JAMA,* 278 (2), 131–135. **218:** Fig. 7.17 From "Lies of the Mind" *Time,* 11/29/93. Copyright © 1993 Time Inc. Reprinted by permission. **225:** Fig. 7.21 Adapted from "Analysis of Rehearsal Processes in Free Recall," by D. Rundus, 1971, *Journal of Experimental Psychology, 89,* 63–77. Copyright © 1971 by the American Psychological Association. Adapted by permission of the author. **226:** Fig 7.22 Adapted from "A Breakdown of the Total-Time Law in Free-Recall Learning," by B. J. Underwood, 1970, *Journal of Verbal Learning and Verbal Behavior, 9,* 573–580. Copyright © 1970 by Academic Press, Inc. Adapted by permission of the publisher and author. **227:** Fig. 7.23 Adapted from "Narrative Stories as Mediators of Serial Learning," by G.H. Bower and M.C. Clark, 1969, *Psychonomic Science, 14,* 181–182. Copyright © 1969 by the Psychonomic Society. Adapted by permisson of the Psychonomic Society. **227:** Fig. 7.24 From "Analysis of a Mnemonic Device," by G.H. Bower, 1970, *American Scientist, 58,* Sept–Oct., 496–499. Copyright © 1970 by Scientific Research Society. Reprinted by permission.

Chapter 8

235: Fig 8.1 Figure from *Child Development: A Topical Approach,* by A. Clarke-Stewart, S. Friedman & J. Koch, p. 417, 1985. Copyright © 1985 by John Wiley & Sons, Inc. Reprinted by permission of John Wiley & Sons, Inc. **236:** Table 8.1 *From Language Development, 1st edition,* by E. Hoff-Ginsberg © 1997. Reprinted with permission of Wadsworth, a division of Thomson Learning. Fax 800 730-2215. **237:** Fig. 8.2 From "Vocabulary Development: A Morphological Analysis," by J. M. Anglin, 1993, *Child Development, 58,* Serial 238. Copyright © 1993 The Society for Research in Child Development, Inc. Reprinted by permission. **239:** Fig. 8.3 Adapted from "Critical Period Effects in Second Learning," by J. Johnson and E. Newport, 1989, *Cognitive Psychology, 21,* 60–99. Academic Press. **245:** Fig. 8.8 Based on "Mechanization in Problem Solving," by A. S. Luchins, 1942, *Psychological Monographs, 54* (Whole No. 248). **245:** Fig. 8.9 Adapted from *Conceptional Blockbusting: A Guide to Better Ideas,* by James L. Adams, pp. 17–18. Copyright © 1980 by James L. Adams. Reprinted by permission of W. H. Freeman & Co., Publishers. **245:** Fig. 8.10 From *Basic Psychology 3rd Edition,* by Howard H. Kendler, 1974, pp. 403, 404. Copyright © 1974 The Benjamin-Cummings Publishing Co. Adapted by permission of Howard H. Kendler. **247:** Fig.

8.12 Based on "Mechanization in Problem Solving," by A. S. Luchins, 1942, *Psychological Monographs, 54* (Whole No. 248). **247:** Fig. **8.13** Adapted from *Conceptional Blockbusting: A Guide to Better Ideas,* by James L. Adams, pp. 17–18. Copyright © 1980 by James L. Adams. Reprinted by permisison of W. H. Freeman & Co., Publishers. **247:** Fig. 8.14 From *Basic Psychology 3rd Edition,* by Howard H. Kendler, 1974, pp. 403, 404. Copyright © 1974 The Benjamin-Cummings Publishing Co. Adapted by permission of Howard H. Kendler.

Chapter 9

273: Fig. 9.7: Adapted from "People's Conceptions of Intelligence," by R. J. Sternberg, B.E. Conway, J. L. Keton & M. Bernstein, 1981, *Journal of Personality and Social Psychology, 41* (1), p.45. Copyright © 1981 by the American Psychological Association. Adapted by permission of the author. **275:** Fig. 9.8: Based on data from "Behavorial Genetics of Cognitive Ability: A Life-Span Perspective," by M. McGue, T. J. Bouchard, W. Gl Iacono, & D. T. Lykken, 1993. In R. Plomin & G. E. McClearn (Eds.), *Nature, Nurture and Psychology,* American Psychiatric Association. **277:** Fig. 9.10: From "IQ Gains Over Time: Toward Finding the Causes," by J. R. Flynn, 1998. In U. Neisser, (Ed.) *The The Rising Curve: Long-term Gains in IQ and Related Measures,* p. 37, American Psychological Association, adapted from a figure on pg. 14 by Dimitry Schildlovsky "Get Smart, Take a Test," by J. Horgan, *Scientific American 273* (5), Copyright 1995 by Scienfic American. Adapted with permission of the artist. **281:** Fig. 9.13: Based on data in "Asian-American Educational Achievements: A Phenomenon in Search of an Explanation," by S. Sue and S. Okazaki, 1990, *American Psychologist, 42,* 37–45. American Psychological Association . **282:** Fig. 9.14: Graph adapted from "Nonstationarity and the Measurement of Psychophysical Response in a Visual Inspection Time Task," by I. J. Deary, P. G. Caryl & G. J. Gibson, 1993, *Perception, 22* p. 1250. Copyright © 1993 by Pion Ltd. Adapted by permission. **283:** Fig. 9.15: Adapted from *Beyond IQ: A Triarchic Theory of Human Intelligence,* by Robert J. Sternberg, 1985. Copyright © 1985 Cambridge University Press. Adapted by permision. **283:** Table 9.3: Based on "Multiple Intelligences Go to School: Educational Implications of the Theory of Multiple Intelligences," by H. Gardner and T. Hatch, 1989, *Educational Researcher, 18* (8), 4–10. American Educational Research Association. Additional data from Gardner, 1998

Chapter 10

299: Fig. 10.4 Based on *Human Sexual Response,* by W.H. Masters and V.E. Johnson, 1966. Little, Brown and Company. **301:** Fig. 10.8 From "Sexual Strategies Theory: An Evolutionary Perspective on Human Mating," by D. M. Buss and D. P. Schmitt, 1993, *Psychological Review, 100,* 204–232. Copyright © 1993 by the American Psychological Association. Reprinted by permission of the

author. **307:** Fig. 10.14 Descrip[…] by permission of Dr. David McClella[…] Fig. 10.19 From *Unmasking the Face,* © 1[…] by Paul Ekman, photograph courtesy of Paul Ekman 315: Fig. 10.22 Based on art in "A Language for Emotions," by R. Plutchik, 1980, *Psychology Today, 13* (9), 68–78. Reprinted with permission from Psychology Today Magazine. Copyright © 1980 (Sussex Publishers, Inc.). **318:** Fig. 10.24 From *Well-Being,* by Kahneman, Diener and Schwarz, Eds. 1999. Copyright © 1999 . Reprinted by permission of Russell Sage Foundation. **320:** Fig. 10.26 From *Thought & Knowledge: An Introduction to Critical Thinking,* by D. F. Halpern, 1996, p. 181, figure 5.1. Copyright © 1996 Lawrence Erlbaum Associates. Reprinted by permission of Lawrence Erlbaum Associates.

Chapter 11

328: Fig. 11.2 Figure adapted from Moore, K.L.: *The Developing Human: Clincially Oriented Embryology, 4th ed.* Philadelphia, W.B. Saunders Co., 1988. Reprinted by permission. **332:** Fig. 11.5 Adapted from "Attachment," by P.R. Shaver and C. Hazan. In A. Weber and J.H. Harvey (Eds.), *Perspectives on Close Relationships.* Copyright © 1994 by Allyn and Bacon. Reprinted by permission. **340:** Fig. 11.11 From "Addition and Subtraction by Human Infants," by K. Wynn, 1992, *Nature, 358,* 749–750. Copyright © 1992 Macmillan Magazines, Ltd. Reprinted with permission from Nature. **342:** Fig. 11.13: Adapted from "The Development of Children's Orientations Toward a Moral Order: I: Sequence in the Development of Moral Thought," by L. Kohlberg, 1963, *Vita Humana, 6,* 11–33. Copyright © 1963 by S. Karger AG, Basel. Reprinted by permission. **345:** Fig. 11.16: Adapted from "Identity in Adolescence," by J.E. Marcia, 1980. In J. Adelson (Ed.), *Handbook of Adolescent Psychology,* pp. 159–210. Copyright © 1980 by John Wiley & Sons, Inc. Adapted by permission of John Wiley & Sons, Inc. **347:** Fig. 11.17: Adapted from "Marital Satisfaction Over the Family Cycle," by Boyd C. Rollins and Harold Feldman, *Journal of Marriage and Family, 32* (February 1970), p. 25. Copyright © 1975 by the National Council on Family Relations, 3989 Central Ave., N.E., Suite 550, Minneapolis, MN 55421. Reprinted by permission. **349:** Fig. 11.18 From "Intellectural Development in Adulthood," by K. W. Schaie, 1990. In J.E. Birren and K. W. Schaie (Eds.), *Handbook of the Psychology of Aging, 3rd ed.* pp. 291–309. Reprinted by permission of Academic Press, Inc. **351:** Table 11.2: Adapted from "Sex Stereotypes: Issues of Change in the 70s", by T. L. Ruble, 1983, *Sex Roles, 9,* 397–402. Copyright © 1983 Plenum Publishing Group. Adapted by permission of Kluwer Academic/Plenum Publishers.

Chapter 12

362: Table 12. 1 From "Validation of the Five-Factor Model of Personality Across Instruments

...rea and P. T. ...nality and Social ...Data in public ...Adapted from ...arch and Application, by ...len, p. 246. Brooks/Cole ...ny. Copyright © 1986 by C... ...m Allen. Adapted by permission ...or. **379:** Fig. 12.10: From H. J. Eysenck, ... Biological Basis of Personality, 1st Ed., p. 36, 1976. Courtesy of Charles C. Thomas, Publisher, Springfield, Illinois. [Reprinted by permission]. **380:** Fig. 12.11: Based on "Behavioral Genetics and Personality," by R. Plomin and A. Caspi, 1999. In L. A. Pervin, & O. P. John (Eds.), Handbook of Personality: Theory and Research. The Guilford Press. **384:** Fig. 12.12: Adapted from "Culture and the Self: Implications for Cognition, Emotion, and Motivation," by H.R. Markus and S. Kitayama, 1991, Psychological Review, 98, 224–253. Copyright © 1991 by the American Psychological Association. Adapted by permission of the author. **387:** Table 12.4: [Adaptation] Reprinted with permission from L.S. Keller, J.N. Butcher and W.S. Slutske, "Objective Personality Assessment," 1990. In G. Goldstein and M. Hersen (Eds.), Handbook of Psychological Assessment, pp 345–386. Copyright © 1990 Pergamon Press, Ltd. **388:** Fig. 12.14: From R. B. Cattrell in Psychology Today (July) 1973, 40–46. Reprinted by permission from Psychology Today Magazine. Copyright © 1973 (Sussex Publishers,Inc.).

Chapter 13

399: Table 13.1: Adapted by permission from "The Social Readjustment Rating Scale," by T. H. Holmes and R. H. Rahe, 1967, Journal of Psychosomatic Research, 11, 213–218. Copyright © 1967 by Elsevier Science, Inc. **405:** Table 13.2: Adapted from Abnormal Psychology and Modern Life (8th Ed.) by R. C. Carson, J. N. Butcher & J. C. Coleman, pp 64–65, 1988. Copyright © 1988 by Scott, Foresman and Company. Adapted by permission of the publisher. **412:** Fig. 13.9: Adapted from The Health Benefits of Smoking Cessation: A Report of the Surgeon General 1990, pp. V–VII. U. S. Department of Health and Human Services, Washington, D.C. **413:** Fig. 13.10: Data from A Global Report: AIDS in the World, by J. Mann, D. J. M. Tarantola, & T. W. Netter, 1992. Oxford University Press. **414:** Fig. 13.11: Adapted from Understanding AIDS: A Guide for Mental Health Professionals by S. C. Kalichman, 1995. American Psychological Association . Reprinted by permission of the author. **418:** Fig. 13.14: "Relaxation Procedure" from The Relaxation Response, by Herbert Benson, M.D. and Miriam Z. Klipper. Copyright © 1975 by William Morrow & Company, Inc. By permission of HarperCollins Publishers, Inc.; **419:** Fig. 13.15: Based on data from "Physical Fitness and All-Cause Mortality," by S.N. Blair, W.H. Kohl, R.S. Paffenbarger, D.G. Clark, K.H. Cooper & L.W. Gibbons, 1989, Journal of the American Medical Association, 262, 2395–2401.

Copyright © 1989 American Medical Association. Reprinted by permission.

Chapter 14

429: Fig. 14.2: Reprinted with permission from the Diagnostic and Statisical Manual of Mental Disorders, DSM-IV 1994. Copyright © 1994 American Psychiatric Association. **433:** Fig. 14.5: From "Bias in Interpretation of Ambiguous Sentences Related to Threat in Anxiety," by M.W. Eysenck, K. Mogg, J. May, A. Richards & A. Mathews, 1991, Journal of Abnormal Psychology, 100, 144–150. Copyright © 1991 by the American Psychological Association. Reprinted by permission of the author. **438:** Table 14:.1: From Abnormal Psychology: The Problem of Maladaptive Behavior, 5/E, by I. G. Sarason & B. G. Sarason © 1987, p. 283. Reprinted by permission of Prentice-Hall, Inc., Englewood Cliffs, NJ. **439:** Fig. 14.8: Figure 6-1, "Age of Onset for Bipolar Mood Disorder", from Manic-Depressive Illness, by Frederick K. Goodwin and Kay R. Jamison [p. 132]. Copyright © 1990 by Oxford University Press., Inc. Used by permission of Oxford University Press. **439:** Fig. 14.9: Based on data from "Mood Disorders: Genetic Aspects," by E.S. Gershon, W.H Berrettini & L.R. Goldin, 1989. In H.I. Kaplan & B.J. Sadock (Eds.) Comprehensive Textbook of Psychiatry. Williams & Wilkins. **445:** Fig, 14.13: Adapted from "Clues to the Genetics and Neurobiology of Schizophrenia," by S.E. Nicol and I.I. Gottesman, 1983, American Scientist, 71, 398–404. Copyright © 1983 by Sigma Xi. Additional data from Schizophrenia Genesis: The Origins of Madness, by I.I. Gottesman, 1991. Copyright © 1991 by W.H. Freeman. **446:** Fig. 14.16: Data adapted from "The Role of Maintenance Therapy and Relatives' Expression Emotion in Relapse of Schizophrenia: A Two-Year Follow-Up," by J. Leff and C. Vaughn, 1981, British Journal of Psychiatry, 138, 102–104. **452:** Fig. 14.17: Data adapted from "50-Year Trends in the Incidence of Anorexia Nervosa in Rochester, Minn., A Population-based Study," by A. R. Lucas, C. M. Beard, W. M. O'Fallon, & L. T. Kurland, 1991, American Journal of Psychiatry, 148, 917–922. American Psychiatric Association. **453:** Fig. 14.18: Data from "Cultural Expectations of Thinness in Women, by D. M. Garner, P. E. Garfinkel, D. Schwartz, & M. Thompson, 1980, Psychological Reports, 47, 483–491. Copyright © 1980 Psychological Reports, and "Cultural Expections of Thinness in Women: An Update," by C. V. Wiseman, J. J. Gray, J. E. Mosimann, & A. H. Ahrens, 1992, International Journal of Eating Disorders, 11, 85–89. Copyright © 1992 John Wiley & Sons. Graphic adapted from Abnormal Psychology: An Investigative Approach by D. H. Barlow & V. M. Durand, 1999. Copyright © 1999 Wadsworth Publishing Company. **454:** Fig. 14.19: Based on data from several chapters from L.N. Robins and D.A. Regier, (Eds.) in Psychiatric Disorders in America:The Epidemiologic Catchment Area Study, 1991. The Free Press.

Chapter 15

461: Fig. 15.1: Data from "Outpatient mental health care in nonhospital settings: Distribution of patients across provider groups," by M. Oflson and H. A. Pincus, 1996, American Journal of Psychiatry, 153, pp. 1353–1356. **461:** Fig. 15.2: Adapted from Mental Health: A Report of the Surgeon General, U.S. Department of Health and Human Services, 1999) **464:** pg 464: Adapted from The Technique and Pracrtice of Psychoanalysis, Vol. 1, by R. R. Greenson, 1967. International Universities Press. **469:** Fig. 15.7: From Methods of Self-Change: An ABC Primer, by K.E. Rudestam, pp.42–43, 1980. Copyright © 1980 by Wadsworth, Inc. Reprinted by permission of the author. **472:** Table 15.1: From "New Drug Evaluations: Alprazolam," by R. L. Evans, 1981. Drug Intelligence and Clinical Pharmacy, 15, 633–637. Copyright © 1981 by Harvey Whitney Books Company. Reprinted by permission. **473:** Fig. 15.10: From data in NIMH-PSC Collaborative Study I and reported in "Drugs in the Treatment of Psychosis," by J.O. Cole, S.C. Goldberg & J.M. Davis, 1966, 1985. In P. Solomon (Ed.) Psychiatric Drugs, Grune & Stratton. Reprinted by permission of J.M. Davis. **485:** Fig. 15.14: Adapted from "Meta Analysis of Psychotherapy Outcome Series," by M.L. Smith and G.V. Glass, 1977, American Psychologist, 32 (Sept), 752–760. Copyright © 1977 by the American Psychological Association. Adapted by permission of the author.

Chapter 16

491: Excerpt [pg 490–1] from: Tales from the Front by Cheryl Lavin and Laura Kavesh, copyright © 1988 by Cheryl Lavin and Laura Kavesh. Used by permission of Doubleday, a division of Random House, Inc. **496:** Fig. 16.2: Based on "Perceiving the Causes of Success and Failure," by B. Weiner, I. Friese, A. Kukla, L. Reed & R.M. Rosenbaum. In E.E. Jones, D.E. Kanuouse, H.H. Kelley, R.E. Nisbett, S. Valins & B. Weiner (Eds.) Perceiving the Causes of Behavior, 1972. General Learning Press. Used by permission of Dr. Bernard Weiner. **504:** Fig. 16.8: Based on Introduction to Social Psychology, by R.A. Lippa, 1994. Brooks/Cole. Copyright © 1994 by Wadsworth, Inc. **509:** Fig. 16.12 & 16.13 Adapted from "Opinion and Social Pressure," by Solomon Asch, Scientific American, November 1955, from illustrations by Sara Love on pp. 32 and 35. **513:** Fig. 16.15: Adapted from "Many Hands Make Light the Work: The Causes and Consequences of Social Loafing," by B. Latane, K. Williams & S. Harkins, 1979, Journal of Personality and Social Psychology, 37, 822–832. Copyright © 1979 by the American Psychological Association. Adapted by permission of the author. **515:** Fig. 16.17: Adapted with permission of The Free Press, a Division of Simon & Schuster Inc., from Decision Making: A Psychological Analysis of Conflict, Choice and Commitment, by Irving J. Janis and Leon Mann. Copyright © 1977 by The Free Press.